6th
Canadian
Edition

OPERATIONS MANAGEMENT

William J. Stevenson
Rochester Institute of Technology

Mehran Hojati
University of Saskatchewan

James Cao
University of Saskatchewan

Mc
Graw
Hill
Education

OPERATIONS MANAGEMENT, SIXTH CANADIAN EDITION

ISBN-13: 978-1-25-927015-4
ISBN-10: 1-25-927015-7

3 4 5 6 7 TCP 21 20 19

Printed and bound in Canada.

Portfolio Director, Business & Economics, International: *Nicole Meehan*
Portfolio Managers: *Alwynn Pinard and Keara Emmett*
Senior Marketing Manager: *Cathie Lefebvre*
Content Developer: *Brianna McIlwain*
Senior Portfolio Associate: *Stephanie Giles*
Supervising Editors: *Jessica Barnoski and Janie Deneau*
Photo/Permissions Editor: *Karen Hunter*
Copy Editor: *Laurel Sparrow*
Plant Production Coordinator: *Michelle Saddler*
Manufacturing Production Coordinator: *Sheryl MacAdam*
Interior and Cover Design: *Lightbox Visual Communications, Inc.*
Cover Image: © *D-BASE / Getty Images*
Page Layout: *MPS Limited*
Printer: *Transcontinental Printing Group*

About the Authors

William Stevenson
Saunders College of Business
Rochester Institute of Technology

This book is dedicated to you.

Dr. William Stevenson is an associate professor of decision sciences in the Saunders College of Business at Rochester Institute of Technology. He teaches graduate and undergraduate courses in operations management, management science, quality concepts, and quality applications.

He is the author of textbooks/eBooks in management science and statistics, as well as operations management. His articles have appeared in *Management Science, Decision Sciences, Quality Progress*, and other journals.

Dr. Stevenson received a bachelor's degree in industrial engineering, an M.B.A., and a Ph.D. in production/operations management from Syracuse University.

Mehran Hojati
Edwards School of Business
University of Saskatchewan

I dedicate this book to my mother, Mahvash Hojati.

Dr. Hojati is an associate professor of operations management in the Edwards School of Business at the University of Saskatchewan. He teaches operations management, and purchasing and supply management. He has taught and prepared teaching materials for the Purchasing Management Association of Canada (now Supply Chain Management Association). His articles have appeared in *International Journal of Production Economics, Production & Inventory Management Journal*, and others. His research interests are in the applications of operations research techniques in operations.

Dr. Hojati received a bachelor's degree in economics and a master's degree in operational research from London School of Economics, and a Ph.D. in management science from the University of British Columbia. He is certified in Production and Inventory Management (CPIM), awarded by APICS (the Association for Supply Chain Management).

James Cao
Edwards School of Business
University of Saskatchewan

I dedicate this book to my dearest wife, Vivian, whose love and support has given my life both meaning and direction.

Dr. Cao is an assistant professor at the Edwards School of Business, University of Saskatchewan. He received bachelor's degrees in mathematics, economics, and psychology from the University of California at Irvine. He also has a Ph.D. in management, with a specialization in operations management, from the same school. Dr. Cao has taught undergraduate and graduate classes in operations management, statistics, management science, and quality management. His research interests lie in the field of supply chain management, which deals with both matching supply with demand and the coordination of multi-party decision making.

Brief Contents

Chapter Supplements Available on Connect2

Contents

Preface

This textbook/eBook is intended as an introduction to operations management in Canada, and demonstrates its applications to service and manufacturing operations. We've included eight chapter supplements which offer a comprehensive and flexible amount of content that can be selected as appropriate for different courses and formats, including undergraduate, graduate, and executive education. This allows instructors to select the chapters that are most relevant for their purposes. That flexibility also extends to the choice of relative weighting of the qualitative or quantitative aspects of the material and the order in which chapters are covered, because chapters do not depend on sequence. For example, some instructors cover project management early, while others cover quality or JIT/lean early.

The topics covered include both strategic issues and planning/control decisions. Activities such as capacity, designing production process and work methods, inventory management and control, and assuring and improving quality are core issues in organizations. Whether operations is your field of study or not, knowledge of operations management will certainly benefit you and the organization you work for.

The advantages of using a Canadian textbook for your operations management learning are numerous, including:

- Canadian locations and companies are showcased
- Examples of Canadian organizations and their decisions are highlighted
- Issues important for Canadian instructors and reviewers are addressed
- International examples are framed and reflected from a Canadian perspective
- There is a focus on Canadian data for context

What's New in the Sixth Canadian Edition?

The new Canadian edition features 12 new Canadian and four other new chapter openers. There are two new Canadian and one other new Operations Tours. There are 22 new Canadian and 16 new other OM in Actions. There are eight new Canadian and 12 new photos with captions. There are five new mini-cases and over 16 new problems. Also, many new discussion and review questions as well as critical thinking, experiential learning, and Internet exercises have been added. These updates provide students with a realistic understanding of Canadian manufacturing and service organizations and the problems they face today.

The table on the next page notes some important chapter-by-chapter changes.

Features Retained From Previous Edition

Balanced Content. The textbook/eBook strives to achieve a careful balance in the presentation of operations management. Care has been taken to balance definitions and concepts with quantitative, hands-on problems; to balance theoretical material with real-life applications; and to balance classical topics in operations management with new developments that particularly interest students.

Problem-Solving Approach. To further students' hands-on experience of OM, the textbook/ eBook contains examples with solutions throughout. At the end of most chapters is a group of solved problems to illustrate concepts and techniques. Some of the end-of-chapter problems have answers at the end of the book.

Easy to Read. The writing style is clear, concise, and student friendly, while maintaining the technical rigour necessary for the subject matter. From step-by-step problem solving, to theoretical exposition, to in-depth mini-cases and readings, the book is designed to promote student understanding of the role of operations management in successful organizations—which, in turn, promotes student success in class.

Chapter	Title	Important Changes/Additions
1	Introduction to Operations Management	Expanded coverage of business analytics
2	Competitiveness, Strategic Planning, and Productivity	Clarified key purchasing criteria
3	Demand Forecasting	Added the annual average method for forecasting in the presence of seasonality
4	Product Design	Added material selection and service blueprinting sub-sections; added sections on Kano model and failure modes and effects analysis
5	Strategic Capacity Planning	Expanded coverage of overall equipment effectiveness including an example
6	Process Design and Facility Layout	Added business processes, new service blueprinting and swim lane diagram examples
7	Work/Job Design	Added Human Performance System factors, role of information and communication technologies, mental health at work; deleted MOST
8	Location Planning and Analysis	Added microfactory and clustering to factors that affect location decisions
9	Management of Quality	Added Taguchi loss function, ISO 9001 requirements, Canada Awards of Excellence drivers, affinity diagram, 5 Whys
10	Statistical Quality Control	Added run tests
11	Supply Chain Management	Expanded coverage of RFID including more examples; added risk management and resiliency
12	Inventory Management	Replaced the warehouse operations tour
13	Aggregate Operations Planning and Master Scheduling	Added an example for calculating full-time equivalent
14	Material Requirements Planning and Enterprise Resource Planning	Clarified description of regenerative and net change MRPs
15	Just-in-Time and Lean Production	Added section on world class manufacturing
16	Job and Staff Scheduling	Added subsections on sequencing jobs through one work centre/machine in order to minimize number of late jobs and sequencing jobs through three or more work centres/machines in order to minimize make-span
17	Project Management	Added an example for earned value analysis; updated Microsoft Project tutorial
18	Waiting-Line Analysis	Added border crossing mini-case

Pedagogy and Learning Tools

A number of key features in this textbook/eBook have been specifically designed to help introductory students learn, understand, and apply operations concepts and problem-solving techniques. All of these have been carefully developed over six Canadian editions and thirteen U.S. editions and have proven successful.

Learning Objectives. Every chapter lists the learning objectives as a short guide to studying the chapter. These objectives are linked to each section and to the questions and problems at the end of the chapter.

Opening Vignettes. Every chapter has an opening vignette (chapter opener) that illustrates the importance of the topic, usually highlighting a company.

Figures and Photos. The sixth Canadian edition includes extensive photographs and graphic illustrations to support student study and provide interest and motivation for all types of learners.

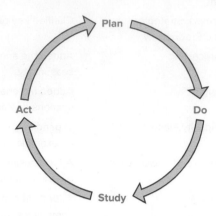

OM in Action. Throughout the new edition are readings about applications of OM. These OM in Action boxes highlight important real-world applications, provide examples of operations issues, and/or offer further elaboration of the content. They also provide a basis for classroom discussion and generate interest in the subject matter.

 OM in Action

British Petroleum

In the evening of April 20, 2010, British Petroleum's Deepwater Horizon offshore oil platform was drilling an exploratory well at a record depth of more than 4,000 metres below the ocean surface in the Gulf of Mexico off of Louisiana. At approximately 9:50 p.m., the protective cement barrier around the well suddenly failed, allowing high-pressure methane gas to rise up onto the oil platform. The escaped gas ignited and began a chain reaction that culminated in a series of catastrophic explosions. Eleven men lost their lives that evening, and an unprecedented amount of oil began to

In addition, they attempted to work faster and more cheaply by cancelling an independent diagnostic test used to test the strength of the cement. The test would have detected the problems with the cement seal at a cost of only $140,000. In sharp contrast to this modest sum, BP ultimately had to pay out more than $46 billion in fines to restore the damaged shoreline and compensate the millions of people who lived and worked in the region. The tragic loss of life and the subsequent pollution of the Gulf of Mexico were the results of poor management decisions, based on a lack of understanding of the costs of quality.

Examples With Solutions. Throughout the new edition, wherever a quantitative technique is introduced, an example is included to illustrate the application of that technique. These are designed to be easy to follow.

Compute 2s control limits for forecast errors when the MSE is 9.0.

EXAMPLE 3-14

SOLUTION

$$s = \sqrt{\text{MSE}} = \sqrt{9} = 3$$
$$\text{UCL} = 0 + 2(3.0) = +6.0$$
$$\text{LCL} = 0 - 2(3.0) = -6.0$$

Service Icons. Where **operations management service** topics are addressed in the new edition, a service icon appears in the corresponding margin to flag the attention of both students and instructors.

  ervice

Web Links. Web addresses of relevant websites are highlighted in the margin with a web icon.

Globe Icons. Where a concept or example has international effect, it is flagged with a globe icon.

End-of-Chapter Resources

For student study and review, the following items are provided at the end of each chapter.

Summary. An overview of the material covered is given in point form.

Key Terms. Key terms are highlighted in the text.

Solved Problems. At the end of most chapters, solved problems illustrate problem solving and the core concepts of the chapter. These have been carefully prepared to enhance student understanding, as well as to provide additional examples of problem solving.

Solved Problems

Problem 1

The tasks shown in the following precedence network are to be assigned to workstations with the intent of minimizing percentage idle time. Management desires an output rate of 275 units per day. Assume 440 minutes are available per day.

a. Determine the appropriate cycle time.

b. What is the minimum number of workstations possible?

c. Assign the tasks using the "Assign the task with the largest positional weight" heuristic rule.

d. Calculate efficiency.

Excel Spreadsheet Solutions. Where applicable, the solved problems include screen shots of a spreadsheet solution. These are taken from the Excel templates, which can be found on *Connect2*.

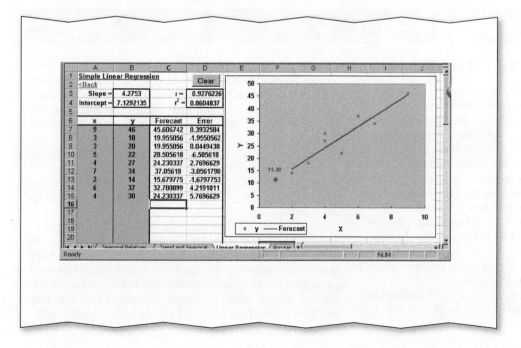

Discussion and Review Questions. These are intended to serve as a student self-review or as class discussion starters.

Taking Stock, Critical Thinking Exercises, Experiential Learning Exercises, and Internet Exercises. These activities encourage analytical thinking and help broaden conceptual understanding.

Critical Thinking Exercises

 1. Think of a new or revised good or service that you would like to see on the market. Discuss the implications of designing and producing that product relative to legal, profitability, competitiveness, design, and production issues.

 2. The speed of product development has continued to increase because of technological advances such as CAD. Do you expect this trend to continue?

 3. In wintry conditions, highway safety is improved by treating road surfaces with substances that will provide traction and/or melt snow and ice. Sand and rock salt are two widely used substances. Recently, a combination of beet juice and rock salt started being used in some parts of the country to treat road surfaces. Suppose you have been asked to provide a list of factors to consider for a switch from rock salt alone to using a combination of beet juice and rock salt. Name the major considerations you would take into account in making a decision in the following categories: cost considerations; environmental considerations, both positive and negative; and other considerations.

Problems. Most chapters have numerous problems, ranging from simple practice problems that apply techniques to more difficult conceptual problems that provide a challenge and require students to integrate concepts (these are marked with an asterisk).

Operations Tours. These readings give students a descriptive look at operations in action at manufacturing or service organizations. These real-life illustrations show direct application to reinforce the importance of the concepts described in the textbook/eBook.

Mini-Cases. Many chapters include short cases, selected to provide a broader, more integrated thinking opportunity for students.

Q MINI-CASE www.harveys.ca

Open Wide and Say "Ultra"

In fourth place behind McDonald's, A&W, and Burger King, Harvey's, the Canadian quick-service hamburger chain with more than 340 restaurants, needed a new idea in the mid-1990s. Harvey's is part of Cara Operations Ltd., the airline food services company that also owns the Swiss Chalet chain of restaurants, approximately 100 Air Terminal Restaurants, and Summit Food Services Distributors. Harvey's had had new ideas before (open grill and fresh vegetables, for one), but these had become old hat by 1995. Gabe Tsampalieros, Cara's new president, who was a major franchisee with 60 Harvey's and Swiss Chalet restaurants, started working on the idea in October 1995, and by the following month the mission was clear: "Create Canada's best-selling hamburger." Tsampalieros and Harvey's vice-president planned the launch of the new burger for May 1996.

Harvey's began polling burger lovers across Canada in January 1996, first by telephone and later in focus groups of 8 to shipped around the country). Bonacini produced 12 "taste profiles"—from the bland to the bizarre—and introduced them to the Harvey's executives at a suburban Harvey's training centre. This would be the first in a long series of tasting exercises. (Bonacini thinks he ate 275 bite-sized burgers in a four-month period.)

Each of Harvey's executives tasted a portion of the 12 unlabelled patties and ranked it for "mouth feel," taste, linger, fill factor, and bite. Exotic offerings (Cajun, Oriental, Falafel, and so forth) were rejected, leaving three simply seasoned burgers on the short list.

McCormick Canada Inc., Harvey's spice supplier, was employed to determine the final proportions of seasonings and secret ingredients to replicate the taste of Bonacini's samples in a way that could survive the fast-food process. "They [the meat packagers] would give us a 500-pound batch—that's 2,000 burgers—and we would taste them a couple of days after they had been mixed. Then we would also taste them at one-, two-,

Superior Learning Solutions and Support

The McGraw-Hill Ryerson team is ready to help you assess and integrate any of our products, technology, and services into your course for optimal teaching and learning performance. Whether it's helping your students improve their grades, or putting your entire course online, the McGraw-Hill Ryerson team is here to help you do it. Contact your Learning Solutions Consultant today to learn how to maximize all of McGraw-Hill Ryerson's resources!

For more information on the latest technology and Learning Solutions offered by McGraw-Hill Ryerson and its partners, please visit us online: **www.mheducation.ca/he/solutions.**

Acknowledgments

We gratefully acknowledge the input of contributors to the sixth Canadian edition, including:

Kent Kostuk
Federated Cooperatives Ltd

Dave Ostertag
PotashCorp

Luke Jamaat, Progressive
Turf Equipment

Bryan McCrea
3Twenty Modular

Keith WilloughbyUniversity
of Saskatchewan

Amanda H. Butler, Director-
Investor Relations, Lincoln
Electric Holdings

Samantha Dearing
ERCO Worldwide

Gwen Miller
Global Institute for Food Security

Shelley Darling, Michael
Garron Hospital (formerly
Toronto East General Hospital)

We would like to thank the McGraw-Hill Ryerson staff, including Portfolio Managers, Alwynn Pinard and Keara Emmett; Content Developer, Brianna McIlwain; Supervising Editors, Janie Deneau and Jessica Barnoski; Permissions Editor, Karen Hunter; and Copy Editor, Laurel Sparrow, for their excellent work.

Mehran Hojati
James Cao

The Complete Course Solution

We listened to educators from around the world, learned about their challenges, and created a whole new way to deliver a course.

Connect2 is a collaborative teaching and learning platform that includes an instructionally designed complete course framework of learning materials that is flexible and open for instructors to easily personalize, add their own content, or integrate with other tools and platforms.

- Save time and resources building and managing a course.
- Gain confidence knowing that each course framework is pedagogically sound.
- Help students master course content.
- Make smarter decisions by using real-time data to guide course design, content changes, and remediation.

MANAGE — Dynamic Curriculum Builder

Quickly and easily launch a complete course framework developed by instructional design experts. Each Connect2 course is a flexible foundation for instructors to build upon by adding their own content or drawing upon the wide repository of additional resources.

- Easily customize Connect2 by personalizing the course scope and sequence.
- Get access to a wide range of McGraw-Hill Education content within one powerful teaching and learning platform.
- Receive expert support and guidance on how best to utilize content to achieve a variety of teaching goals.

MASTER — Student Experience

Improve student performance with instructional alignment and leverage Connect2's carefully curated learning resources. Deliver required reading through Connect2's award-winning adaptive learning system.

- Teach at a higher level in class by helping students retain core concepts.
- Tailor in-class instruction based on student progress and engagement.
- Help focus students on the content they don't know so they can prioritize their study time.

MEASURE — Advanced Analytics

Collect, analyze and act upon class and individual student performance data. Make real-time course updates and teaching decisions backed by data.

- Visually explore class and student performance data.
- Easily identify key relationships between assignments and student performance.
- Maximize in-class time by using data to focus on areas where students need the most help.

Course Map
The flexible and customizable course map provides instructors full control over the pre-designed courses within Connect2. Instructors can easily add, delete, or rearrange content to adjust the course scope and sequence to their personal preferences.

Implementation Guide
Each Connect2 course includes a detailed implementation guide that provides guidance on what the course can do and how best to utilize course content based on individual teaching approaches.

Instructor Resources
A comprehensive collection of instructor resources are available within Connect2. Instructor Support and Seminar Materials provide additional exercises and activities to use for in-class discussion and teamwork.

For more information, please visit www.mheconnect2.com

Chapter 1
Introduction to Operations Management

Courtesy of Case IH Agriculture

World class manufacturing (WCM) is an advanced version of just-in-time/lean manufacturing. Fiat Group started using it in 2005 and brought it to Case New Holland (now CNH Industrial) in 2008 and to Chrysler Group soon after becoming the majority shareholder in 2009.[1] Many other companies have adopted WCM, including Lucerne Foods, Unilever, Magna International, Otis Elevator, Michelin, Celestica, and ArcelorMittal.

CNH Industrial Saskatoon is the only CNH Industrial plant in Canada. It produces planters, headers, air carts, and other equipment for the agriculture division of CNH Industrial, Case IH, and New Holland Agriculture. Over 70 percent of its products are sold in the United States. In order to remain competitive, including with other CNH Industrial plants in the United States, the Saskatoon plant started to implement WCM in 2009. Since then, there has been constant improvement in its WCM score. In five years, its productivity is up approximately 30 percent; it has had no lost-time injury for 3 million hours; warranty claims are down 90 percent; and it hasn't missed a delivery shipment in three years. The Saskatoon plant's score ranks it number seven in the CNH Industrial family, which comprises 54 plants worldwide practising WCM. It recently achieved the Silver status in implementing WCM, the first among the North American CNH Industrial plants.

---

[1] https://www.fcagroup.com/en-US/group/brand_stories/Pages/wcm_global_quality.aspx

LO1 Introduction

operations management
The management of processes (i.e., sequence of activities and resources) that create goods and/or provide services.

process A sequence of activities, usually performed by more than one person, which uses resources and achieves a desired result.

good A tangible item.

service An act or work for someone.

Operations management is the management of processes that create goods and/or provide services. A **process** is a sequence of activities, usually performed by more than one person, which uses resources and achieves a desired result. A **good** is a tangible item, whereas a **service** is an act or work for someone (a customer or client).

Let's use an airline to illustrate the processes involved in its operations. The resources include staff, aircraft, airports, and maintenance facilities. The processes can be classified as core, support, and managerial:

- *Core processes* include taking customer reservations, communicating with customers, checking and boarding, in-flight service, and baggage handling.
- *Support processes* include employee recruitment and training, buying and maintaining aircraft, and buying fuel and spare parts.
- *Managerial processes* include forecasting travel demand, capacity and flight planning, locating maintenance facilities, scheduling planes/pilots/crew and counter staff/baggage handlers, managing inventories, and ensuring that quality standards are met. Most of the managerial processes fall into the realm of operations management.

Now let's consider a bicycle factory:

- *Core processes* include buying raw materials (tubes, etc.) and parts (gears, chains, tires, etc.), fabrication (forming and welding the frame, etc.), and assembly process.
- *Support processes* include recruiting and training workers, and purchasing and maintaining equipment.
- *Managerial processes* include deciding on the style of bicycle (product design), deciding which components to make and which to buy, forecasting demand, scheduling production, and ensuring that quality standards are met.

Obviously, an airline and a bicycle factory are completely different. One is a service provider, the other a producer of goods. Nonetheless, these two companies have many support and managerial processes in common. Both involve buying and managing equipment and supplies, recruiting and training employees, forecasting demand, scheduling activities, and satisfying quality standards.

Cycles Devinci is a Canadian manufacturer of bicycles, founded in Chicoutimi, Quebec, in 1987. In addition to a full line of road, mountain, and hybrid bicycles, Devinci also manufactures the Bixi brand of bicycles used in bike sharing programs in cities such as Montreal and Toronto. See http://www.vitalmtb.com /photos/features/Inside-the -Industry-Devinci-Cycles -Factory-Tour,10452/ Slideshow,0/FredLikesTrikes, 18548 for a tour of the Devinci factory.

Peter Macdiarmid /Getty Staff

Many companies use operations management strategies, tactics, and actions in order to improve their efficiency and effectiveness. **Efficiency** is operating at minimum cost and time. **Effectiveness** is achieving the intended goals (quality and timeliness).

This textbook contains many practical and real-life examples of operations management in the form of chapter openers, photos with captions, readings in the form of OM in Action boxes, mini-cases, problems, and operations tours. For example, the chapter openers are: IKEA's strategy (Chapter 2), Bombardier Business Aircraft forecasting (Chapter 3), 3D printing (Chapter 4), Ford's capacity planning (Chapter 5), Ford's factory changeover (Chapter 6), GE Aviation's participative management (Chapter 7), Feihe's new plant in Kingston (Chapter 8), Lac-Megantic rail disaster (Chapter 9), Trek Bikes quality control (Chapter 10), online-to-store channel (Chapter 11), Federated Cooperatives' inventory management (Chapter 12), Canada Post's holiday planning (Chapter 13), Progressive Turf Equipment's material requirements planning (Chapter 14), lean production in healthcare (Chapter 15), Pier 1 Imports' staff scheduling (Chapter 16), ExxonMobil's project management (Chapter 17), and border crossing waiting line management (Chapter 18).

> **efficiency** Operating at minimum cost and time.
>
> **effectiveness** Achieving quality and timeliness.

Why Study Operations Management?

There are a number of reasons to study operations management. First, because a large percentage of a company's expenses occur in the operations area (e.g., purchasing materials, paying workforce salaries), more efficient operations can result in large increases in profit.

Second, a number of management jobs are in operations management—including jobs in purchasing, quality assurance, production planning and control, scheduling, logistics, inventory management, and many more (see the "**Two Operations Management Job Ads**" OM in Action).

 OM in Action

Two Operations Management Job Ads

Manufacturing Operations Manager

Location: London, Ontario
Salary: Yearly: min. $80,000; max. $100,000 for 40.0 hours per week
Education: Completion of college/CEGEP/vocational or technical training
Experience: 5 years or more
Staff Responsibility: 21–50
Budgetary Responsibility: $500,001–$1,500,000
Type of Industry: Chemical
Specific Skills: Plan, organize, direct, and control daily operations; Evaluate efficiency of production; Determine adequacy of personnel, equipment, and technologies used for operations; Maintain inventory; Prepare work schedules; Schedule and oversee the maintenance of plant equipment; Plan and manage budgets; Direct quality control inspections; Develop production reporting procedures; Oversee the analysis of data and information; Analyze cost and quality data
Additional Skills: Train staff; Arrange training for staff; Conduct performance reviews; Establish and implement safe work practices and procedures

Work Conditions and Physical Capabilities: Fast-paced environment; Work under pressure; Tight deadlines; Attention to detail; Large workload
Other Information: 5+ yrs exp. as Operations Manager for large-scale Silicon products manufacturer.

Inventory Team Lead

Location: Calgary, Alberta
JOB OVERVIEW: As the Inventory Team Lead, you will lead a team of Inventory Analysts while managing and optimizing composition and replenishment of a portion of inventory held at all operating locations using standard SAP based processes and tools.

KEY ACCOUNTABILITIES

- Manage staff and participate in setting Inventory Management function objectives
- Apply advanced SAP knowledge to execute complex tasks in daily work and make professional judgment based on industry standards, internal guidelines, and best practices
- Analyze business plans and utilize inventory forecasting and modelling techniques to set inventory targets and control levels, develop short-term supply plans, and determine the impact of inventory control issues on service levels

(Cont'd)

- Lead the analysis of inventory status reports and develop inventory performance plan and strategies utilizing total cost of ownership analysis including, but not limited to, inventory levels, inventory turns, Critical Spare Parts Management (CSPM), and fill rates
- Assess risk, identify trends and opportunities, and make recommendations to develop contingency plans and improve CSPM processes, policies, and procedures
- Communicate with internal and external stakeholders on day-to-day inventory management and CSPM issues to initiate stock purchase and disposal processes, and to align inventory management strategies with other company initiatives
- Consult with senior specialists on complex issues and resolve or escalate Inventory Management issues
- Proactively recommend ways to improve Inventory Management activities
- Identify issues in standards, methods, and tools for analysis and control of inventory
- Participate in regular Inventory Management, Material Management and Logistics meetings to evaluate business unit requirements and expectations, and evaluate process and performance optimization opportunities

REQUIRED QUALIFICATIONS

Education and Experience:

- 5+ years of experience in Supply Chain Management with increasing levels of responsibility

- Post-secondary business or Supply Chain and Operations Management degree/accreditation
- SAP Inventory Management experience required
- Inventory modelling and forecasting experience required
- Oil & Gas, Mining or Utilities industry experience preferred
- Supervisory experience preferred

Skills and Knowledge:

- Strong analytical skills required
- Ability to be adaptable and build trust and confidence in colleagues and customers preferred
- Solid experience around Inventory Management including Critical Spare Parts Management, Supply/Demand Planning and Inventory Modelling and forecasting is required
- Possess a strong knowledge in ERP (SAP preferred), Spend Analysis, Business Performance Management (KPIs), as well as Critical Spare Parts Management
- Good understanding of SCM Development, Sourcing Strategy, Supplier Integration, Category Management, Total Cost of Ownership (TCO) and Reverse Logistics is preferred

Working Conditions: Office environment and infrequent business travel will be required to operating locations and third parties.

Third, activities in all the other areas of organizations—such as finance, accounting, human resources, management information systems, and marketing—are all interrelated with operations management activities. So, it is essential for people who work in these areas to have a basic understanding of operations management.

Fourth, operations innovations lead to marketplace and strategic benefits. Examples include Toyota Production System, Dell's direct shipping of personal computers, Zara's fast and responsive supply chain, and Walmart's cross-docking (goods received from suppliers at a distribution centre are transferred to outbound trucks to retail stores without being stored).[2] For an example of operational innovation, see the **"Progressive Insurance"** OM in Action.

 OM in Action www.progressive.com

Progressive Insurance

Progressive Insurance (PI) has introduced several operational innovations:

- 1990: Immediate response claims service (serving customers at the accident scene). In 1994, specially marked PI vehicles were used by adjusters to drive to the scene of accidents.

- 1996: Customers could obtain comparison rates online. In 1997, customers could buy auto insurance policies online.
- 2003: Concierge level of claims service (PI takes care of vehicle repair).

Source: https://www.progressive.com/progressive-insurance/history.

---

[2] https://hbr.org/2004/04/deep-change-how-operational-innovation-can-transform-your-company.

Careers in Operations Management

If you are thinking of a career in operations management, you can obtain relevant information from one or more of the following associations:

- Supply Chain Management Association (SCMA)
- Canadian Institute of Traffic and Transportation (CITT)
- Canadian Supply Chain Sector Council (CSCSC)
- American Production and Inventory Control Society (APICS), now known as the Association for Supply Chain Management
- American Society for Quality (ASQ)
- Project Management Institute (PMI)

http://scma.com/en/
http://www.citt.ca
http://www.supplychaincanada.org
http://www.apics.org
http://www.asq.org
http://www.pmi.org

Most of these associations offer certification programs and a job bank.

Functions Within Organizations

Organizations are formed to pursue goals that are achieved more efficiently and effectively by the concerted efforts of a group of people rather than by individuals working alone. Organizations are usually structured into departments or functions. Each department is given resources and managed independently, however, they have to collaborate on multi-functional processes.

Organizations are devoted to producing goods and/or providing services. They may be for-profit (i.e., businesses) or non-profit (e.g., hospitals). Their goals, design, management, and outputs (goods/services) may be similar or quite different. Nonetheless, their functions and their processes are similar.

A typical organization has three basic functions: operations (representing manufacturing/service), finance, and marketing (including sales) (see Figure 1-1).

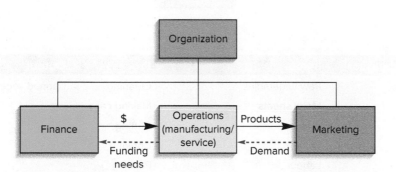

◀ FIGURE 1-1

The three basic functions of an organization and flows between them.

These three functions and other supporting functions (e.g., research and development) perform different but related processes necessary for the organization. The functions must interact to achieve the goals and objectives of the organization, and each makes an important contribution. For instance, unless operations and marketing work together, marketing may promote goods or services that operations cannot profitably deliver, or operations may turn out goods or services for which there is no demand. Similarly, unless finance and operations work closely, funds for materials, building expansion, and new equipment may not be available when needed. Let's take a closer look at these functions.

Operations

The operations function, representing manufacturing/service processes, manages all the activities *directly* related to producing goods or providing services. Hence, it exists both in manufacturing industries which are *goods producing* and in service industries which provide services (see Table 1-1).

Industries	Examples
Goods producing	Farming, mining, construction, manufacturing
Services	Healthcare, transportation, food, warehousing, retailing, wholesaling, banking, film production, broadcasting, phone

The production of goods or services involves *transforming/converting* inputs into finished goods or services. For example, a car body manufacturing process converts sheets of steel into a car body by cutting, forming, and welding operations.

The production process must be an adaptive system. To ensure that the desired outputs are obtained, measurements should be taken at various points (*feedback),* and then compared with previously established standards to determine whether corrective action is needed (*control).* Figure 1-2 shows the conversion process. Table 1-2 provides two examples of inputs, transformation processes, and outputs.

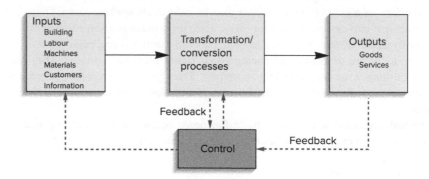

Food Processor	Inputs	Process	Output
	Raw vegetables	Cleaning	Canned vegetables
	Metal sheets	Making cans	
	Water	Cutting	
	Energy	Cooking	
	Labour	Packing	
	Building	Labelling	
	Equipment		
Hospital	**Inputs**	**Process**	**Output**
	Sick patients, doctors, nurses	Examination	Healthy patients
	Building	Surgery	
	Medical supplies and drugs	Monitoring	
	Equipment	Medication	
	Laboratories	Therapy	

It is important to note that goods and services often occur jointly. For example, having the oil changed in your car is a service, but the new oil is a good. Similarly, house painting is a service, but the paint is a good. The goods–service package is a continuum. It can range from primarily goods with little service to primarily service with few goods (see Figure 1-3).

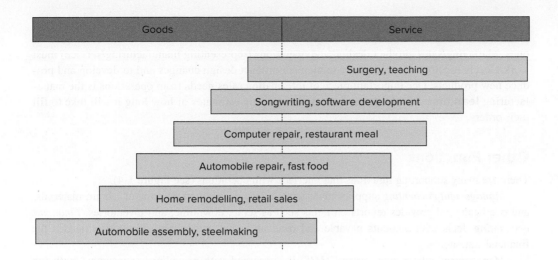

The goods–service continuum.

The essence of the operations function is to *add value* during the transformation process: **Value added** is the term used to describe the difference between the cost of inputs and the value or price of outputs. In non-profit organizations, the value of outputs (e.g., highway construction, police and fire protection) is their value to society; the greater the value added, the greater the efficiency of these operations. In for-profit organizations, the value of outputs is measured by the prices that customers are willing to pay for those goods or services. Companies use the money generated by value added for research and development, investment in new facilities and equipment, workers' salaries, and owners' *profits*. Consequently, the greater the value added, the greater the amount of funds available for these purposes.

value added The difference between the cost of inputs and the value or price of outputs.

One way that organizations attempt to become more productive (i.e., make more output with the same or fewer inputs) is to critically examine whether any of their activities adds value. Those that do not add value are wasteful. Eliminating or improving such wastes decreases the cost of inputs or transformation, thereby increasing the value added. For instance, a company may discover that it is producing an item much earlier than the scheduled delivery date to a customer, thus requiring the storage of the item in a warehouse until delivery. In effect, additional costs are incurred by storing the item without adding to the value of the item. Reducing storage time would reduce the transformation cost and, hence, increase the value added. A similar comment applies for receiving raw material/parts too early. This is the concept called *just-in-time* (more in Chapter 15). Obviously, working with suppliers and customers can lead to increased productivity for all sides. This is called *supply chain management* (more in Chapter 11).

Finance

The finance function secures funds at favourable terms and allocates those funds throughout the organization. Finance and operations management personnel cooperate by exchanging information and expertise in activities such as:

- *Provision of funds.* The necessary funding of operations and the amount and timing of funding can be important and even critical when funds are tight. Careful planning can help avoid cash flow problems. Most businesses obtain the majority of their funds through the revenues generated by sales of their goods and services.
- *Economic analysis of capital investment proposals.* Evaluation of alternative investments in plant and equipment requires inputs from both operations and finance people.

Marketing

Marketing, including sales, is responsible for receiving customer wants/needs and feedback, and for communicating them to operations and to product design (usually engineers). Operations uses forecast demand/sales to purchase materials and schedule production, while product design people use that information to improve the quality of current goods and services, and to design new ones. Marketing/sales, product design, and operations (representing manufacturing/service) must work closely together to successfully implement product design changes and to develop and produce new products. One important piece of information sales needs from operations is the manufacturing **lead time** in order to give customers realistic estimates of how long it will take to fill their orders.

lead time The time between the placement of an order and the shipment of the completed order to the customer.

Other Functions

There are many supporting functions that interface with operations (see Figure 1-4).

Management accounting supplies management with information on costs of labour, materials, and overhead, and provides reports on items such as scrap, downtime, and inventories. *Financial accounting* deals with accounts payable and receivable, and gathers the information needed for financial statements.

Management information systems (MIS) is concerned with providing management with the information it needs to manage effectively. This occurs through computer and communication systems (hardware and software) that capture relevant information and prepare reports.

Purchasing has responsibility for procurement of materials, supplies, equipment, and services. Close contact with operations is necessary to ensure items are ordered when needed. The purchasing staff identifies appropriate suppliers and facilitates close supplier relationships. Purchasing may also be involved in arranging incoming transportation.

The *personnel* or *human resources* department is concerned with recruitment and training of personnel, labour relations, contract negotiations, wage and salary administration, and ensuring the health and safety of employees.

Manufacturing engineering is responsible for the machines and equipment needed in the production process. Also called process engineers, they are mainly trained as mechanical engineers, but other fields such as electrical and chemical engineering may also be needed.

Maintenance and facility management is responsible for the upkeep and repair of equipment, buildings and grounds, heating and air conditioning, removing wastes, parking, and security.

Product design in manufacturing companies is done by design engineers, but in other companies it could be done by people such as architects, scientists, chemists, and chefs. This function is also called research and development. Designers create goods and services from information given to them by marketing people and provide product specifications to operations to make the products.

Logistics involves the transportation of raw material to the plant; storage and warehousing; and transportation of goods to warehouses, retail outlets, or final customers.

Some of these interfaces are elaborated on in later chapters.

FIGURE 1-4 ▼

Operations interfaces with a number of supporting functions.

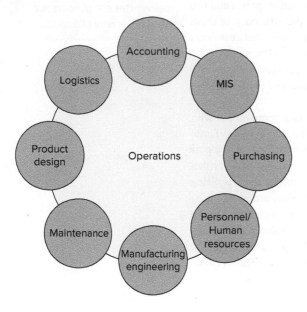

LO3 The Scope of Operations Management

We have already noted that operations management is responsible for the creation of goods and services. This encompasses acquisition of resources and the conversion of raw material into outputs using one or more transformation processes. This involves designing, planning, scheduling, executing, and controlling the activities/operations that make up the processes.

A primary function of operations management is decision making. Certain decisions affect the *design* of the system, and others are *planning/control*. Design decisions are usually strategic and long-term (1–5 years ahead), whereas planning decisions are tactical and medium-term

(1–12 months ahead), and control decisions (including scheduling and execution) are short-term (1–12 weeks ahead).

Design involves product, production process, capacity, facility location, layout (arrangement of departments and equipment within a building), buying equipment, and work/job. Planning/control involves quality, inventory, production, scheduling, and project. Operations management is more involved in day-to-day operating decisions and planning than design. However, it has a vital stake in design because *design determines limitations of operations,* which affects price, timeliness, and quality of products. Even though operations management is not solely responsible for design, it can provide information that will have a bearing on design. Table 1-3 provides additional details on the design and planning/control decisions, and indicates in which chapter each topic is discussed.

Decision Area	Basic Question(s)	Chapter
Forecasting	What will the demand be?	3
Design		
Product design	What do customers want? How can products be designed?	4
Capacity (long term)	How much capacity will be needed? How can the organization best meet capacity requirements?	5
Process design	What production process should the organization use?	6
Layout	What is the best arrangement for departments, machines, and equipment, in terms of work flow?	6
Work/job design	How to improve work methods? How to measure work?	7
Location	What is a satisfactory location for a facility (factory, warehouse, etc.)?	8
Planning/control		
Quality	How is quality defined? How is quality achieved and improved?	9
Quality control	Are processes performing adequately (i.e., are they in control and capable)?	10
Supply chain management	How can supplier–customer pairs collaborate? Which supplier to choose? How to transport goods?	11
Inventory management	How much to order? When to reorder?	12
Aggregate planning	How to plan production in the medium term?	13
Material requirements planning	How many parts and sub-assemblies will be needed, and when?	14
Just-in-time	How to manage production so that it is fast and lean?	15
Scheduling	How can jobs best be scheduled? How can staff be scheduled?	16
Project management	How to plan, schedule, execute, and control a project?	17
Waiting lines	How to model waiting lines? What service capacity is appropriate?	18

◄ TABLE 1-3

Design and planning/control decisions.

Differentiating Production of Goods and Services

Production of *goods* results in a *tangible output*, such as an automobile, a building, or wheat—anything that we can see or touch. Production industries include manufacturing, construction, agriculture, forestry, fisheries, mining, and oil and gas. Among these, manufacturing is the largest, and consists of these categories: food and beverage, textile and clothing, wood products and furniture, paper and printing, petroleum, chemicals, plastics, primary metals and nonmetals, fabricated metals and nonmetals, machinery, computers and electronics, electrical equipment and appliances, and transportation equipment.

Services, on the other hand, imply *acts*. A physician's examination, auto repair, lawn care, and theatre are examples of services. The majority of services fall into these categories: government services (federal, provincial, and municipal), wholesale/retail (clothing, food, appliances, stationery, toys, etc.), finance and insurance (banking, stock brokerage, insurance, etc.), real estate rental and leasing, health care (doctors, dentists, hospitals, etc.), professional and technical services (lawyers, accountants, architects, auto mechanics), personal services (laundry, dry cleaning, hair/beauty, lawn care, etc.), business support services (data processing, ebusiness, advertising, employment agencies, etc.), education (schools, colleges, universities, etc.), hotels and restaurants, information, culture and recreation, transportation and warehousing, and utilities.

Production of goods and performance of services are often similar in many design and planning/control decisions. However, they differ in:

1. Customer contact, use of inventories, and demand variability.
2. Uniformity of inputs.
3. Labour content of jobs.
4. Uniformity of outputs.
5. Measurement of productivity.
6. Quality assurance.

Let us consider each of these differences.

Service

1. Often, by its nature, a service involves a much higher degree of customer contact. The performance of a service often occurs at the point of consumption. For example, repairing a leaky roof must take place where the roof is, and surgery requires the presence of the patient. On the other hand, goods production allows a separation between production and consumption, so that it may occur away from the consumer. This permits a fair degree of latitude in selecting work methods, assigning jobs, scheduling work, and exercising control over operations. In addition, manufacturers can build up inventories of finished goods, enabling them to absorb some of the shocks caused by variability of demand. Services, however, cannot build up inventories and are much more sensitive to demand variability—banks and supermarkets alternate between lines of customers waiting for service and idle tellers or cashiers waiting for customers.

2. Services are subject to greater variability of inputs than typical manufacturers. Each patient, each lawn, and each auto repair presents a specific problem that often must be diagnosed before it can be remedied. Manufacturers often have the ability to carefully control the amount of variability of their inputs.

3. Services often require a higher labour content, whereas goods production typically can be more capital intensive (i.e., mechanized).

4. Because high mechanization generates products with low variability, goods production tends to be smooth and efficient; service activities sometimes appear to be slow and awkward, and output is more variable. Automated services such as ATMs are an exception to this.

5. Measurement of productivity (i.e., ratio of outputs to inputs) is more straightforward in goods production due to the high degree of uniformity of items produced. In services, variations in

requirements from job to job make productivity measurement considerably more difficult. For example, compare the productivity of two doctors. One may have a large number of routine cases while the other deals with complications, so their productivity appears to differ.

6. Quality assurance is more challenging in services because performance and consumption occur at the same time. In goods production, errors can be corrected before the customer receives the product.

Both service and the goods-producing industries are important to the economy. However, services have been growing faster and now account for more than 79 percent of jobs in Canada. See Figure 1-5.

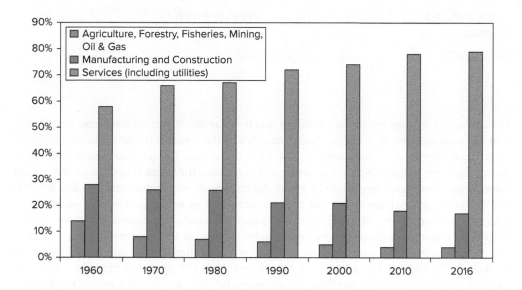

◀ **FIGURE 1-5**

Percentage of total labour force by industry.

Source: Adapted from Statistics Canada CANSIM database, Table 282–0094, various series.

The Operations Manager's Job

LO5

The operations manager has the ultimate responsibility for the creation of goods or performance of services. Note that the person performing this job may have a different title. For example, a fast-food chain's restaurant manager is essentially the restaurant's operations manager. At the district level, the district manager is essentially the operations manager, and at the executive level there is usually a vice-president of operations. In an independent restaurant, the manager also performs finance and marketing activities. Even if a job's title is "operations manager," it may involve other activities such as technical product-specific aspects of production, finance/accounting, project management, engineering, etc.

The kinds of jobs that operations managers oversee vary tremendously from organization to organization, largely because of the different goods or services produced. Thus, managing a bank branch obviously requires a different kind of expertise than managing a steel mill. However, they are both essentially *managerial*. In every case, the operations manager must coordinate the use of resources through the management activities of planning, organizing, directing, and controlling. Note that these activities are defined a little differently than in Table 1-3. Examples of the responsibilities of operations managers according to these classifications are given in Table 1-4.

In a survey of operations managers of 114 Canadian companies,[3] the following characteristics were discovered: 87 percent of companies were manufacturers, 80 percent employed under

---

[3] A.S. Sohal et al., "The Roles and Responsibilities of Production/Operations Managers in SMEs: Evidence From Canada," *Technovation* 21, pp. 437–448.

TABLE 1-4 ▶

Responsibilities of operations managers.

Planning	Organizing
Capacity	Degree of centralization
Location	Departments
Mix of products	Subcontracting
Production process	Suppliers
Layout	Staffing
Controlling	**Directing**
Inventory control	Scheduling
Quality control	Issuance of work orders
Production pace	Job assignments
Motivation	Purchasing
Cost control	Logistics

100 employees, average age of the operations manager was 45, 91 percent were men, and 47 percent had a university/college degree. Approximately one-third were deficient in business management, accounting/finance, and computer skills. Most started their full-time job in another area and had an average of four jobs before transferring into operations. But, when in operations, they stayed (average operations experience was 10 years). Ninety percent of salaries were between $40,000 and $110,000. Approximately half had total authority over planning, quality, and maintenance, whereas the other half provided major inputs into these decisions. Approximately half would have liked more control over planning decisions. Ninety-five percent were responsible for cost reduction and productivity, 90 percent for work and worker organization, and 85 percent for quality and technology. They spent 25 percent of their time on operations, 18 percent on planning, 12 percent on quality, 11 percent on customer liaison, 8 percent on labour relations, and 8 percent on improvements. Most operations managers were given targets for improvement. A list of job content and satisfaction of respondents is given in Figure 1-6. Most enjoy the challenges, whereas more than half are not happy with the heavy hours of work. Further questions revealed that most are happy with their compensation, work variety, work importance, autonomy, benefits, social interaction, feedback from top management, and advancement opportunity. For an example, see the "Seth Beytien" OM in Action.

FIGURE 1-6 ▶

Level of job satisfaction.

Source: Adapted from Table 13 in A. S. Sohal et al., "The Roles and Responsibilities of Production/Operations Managers In SMEs: Evidence From Canada", *Technovation* 21(7), pp. 437–448.

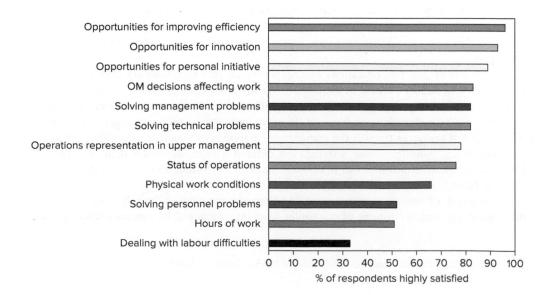

OM in Action

Seth Beytien

Seth is a graduate of Iowa State University who majored in operations and supply chain management. After working for a few companies and a consulting firm in process improvement, he joined CNH Industrial in 2011 and later moved to Saskatoon as the operations manager of the CNH Industrial plant. After two years, Seth was promoted to the plant manager job at the Saskatoon plant.

As the operations manager, Seth was responsible for the manufacturing side of the plant. The three area managers who were responsible for fabrication, welding, and assembly, as well as the maintenance manager, reported to him. Seth (along with the materials manager, the manufacturing engineering manager, and the quality manager) reported to the plant manager, providing updates on employees and production.

A typical day for Seth began with meetings with staff and managers, discussing issues from the previous day, making sure problems wouldn't happen again, and identifying issues (safety, quality, and cost) for the current day. Then, Seth walked through the plant observing and discussing the progress of the projects (25–50) with employees in charge. Later in the day, there was another meeting with managers to discuss achievement of daily targets (KPI).

Seth participated in monthly meetings about the level of workforce needed. Also, there were strategic issues to be

Photo by Kari Thiesen. Courtesy of Seth Beytien

addressed such as the introduction of new products and continuation of existing products in the plant.

Source: Operations Management Students' Association, University of Saskatchewan, www.theomsa.com/events/2013-10/.

Operations Managers and Decision Making

The chief role of an operations manager is that of decision maker. In this capacity, the operations manager exerts considerable influence over the degree to which the goals and objectives of the organization are realized.

Throughout this textbook, you will encounter the broad range of decisions that operations managers must make, and you will be introduced to the tools necessary to handle those decisions. This section describes general approaches to decision making, including the use of models, quantitative techniques, analysis of trade-offs, the systems approach, establishing priorities, and ethics.

Models

A **model** is an abstraction of reality, a simplified representation of something. There are different types of models. For example, a child's toy car is a *physical (iconic)* model of a real automobile. *Mathematical (symbolic)* models represent important characteristics of the object by mathematical symbols and their relationship by mathematical equations and inequalities. *Schematic* models are graphs, charts, and drawings. Common *statistical* models include Normal distribution and regression equations.

Real life involves an overwhelming amount of detail, much of which is irrelevant for any particular problem. Models ignore the unimportant details so that attention can be concentrated on the most important aspects of a problem, thus increasing the opportunity to understand a problem and find its solution.

Because mathematical, schematic, and statistical models play a significant role in operations management decision making, they are heavily integrated into the material of this textbook. For each

model An abstraction of reality; a simplified representation of something.

model, try to learn (1) its purpose, (2) how it is used to generate results, (3) how these results are interpreted and used, and (4) what assumptions and limitations apply.

Quantitative Techniques

Quantitative techniques are methods that focus on objective measurements and analysis of numbers in order to draw conclusions. They include *deterministic* and *statistical* techniques. Examples are:

- *Optimization* (i.e., finding the best solution to a mathematical model of a managerial decision problem). A popular technique is ***linear programming***, which is widely used for optimal allocation of scarce resources.
- *Queuing techniques* for analyzing situations in which waiting lines form.
- *Inventory techniques* to control inventories.
- *Project scheduling technique* PERT (program evaluation and review technique) for planning, coordinating, and controlling large-scale projects.
- *Forecasting techniques* to forecast demand.
- *Statistical techniques* for quality control.

Use of most of these quantitative techniques is time consuming and requires computers. In contrast, a **heuristic** is a quick way to find a good solution. For example, in designing the work of an assembly-line worker, a good heuristic is to choose the longest eligible task that will fit. For many decisions, a heuristic may be the only practical solution.

Analysis of Trade-Offs

A **trade-off** is a balance achieved between two incompatible features—a compromise. For example, (a) in deciding on the amount of inventory to stock, the manager may take into account the trade-off between the increased level of customer service (availability) that the additional inventory would yield and the increased cost of holding that inventory in storage; (b) in selecting a piece of equipment, a manager may evaluate the merits of extra features relative to the cost of those extra features; (c) in the scheduling of overtime to increase output, the manager may weigh the value of the increased output against the higher costs of overtime.

Throughout this textbook you will be presented with solution methods that reflect these kinds of trade-offs. Managers sometimes deal with these decisions by listing the advantages and disadvantages—the *pros* and *cons*—of alternatives to better understand the consequences of the decisions they must make. In some instances, managers can score these outcomes. This can help them "net out" the impact of the trade-offs on their decision. An example of this is the factor-rating approach described in Chapter 8 on location planning and analysis.

The Systems Approach

A **system** is a set of interrelated parts that must work together. The systems approach emphasizes interrelationships among these parts. From a systems viewpoint, the output and objectives of the organization as a whole take precedence over those of any one department. A high-level systems view of a manufacturing organization is displayed in Figure 1-7. In addition to major departments/functions, it shows the customers, the products, and the flows of work. It enables us to see how work actually gets done, which is through processes that cut *across* functional boundaries. It also shows the *internal customer–supplier relationships* through which goods and services are produced.

The systems approach is essential whenever a product is being designed, redesigned, implemented, improved, or otherwise changed. It is important to take into account the impact on all parts of the system. For example, to investigate if the upcoming model of a vehicle will have automatic parking, a designer must take into account how customers will use it, instructions for its use, chances for misuse, the cost of the software (to control steering, acceleration, and braking) and sensors (to detect objects around the vehicle), and procedures for installing and repairing the sensors and the software. In addition, quality standards will have to be established, marketing must be informed of the new feature, and a software developer and a sensor manufacturer must be selected.

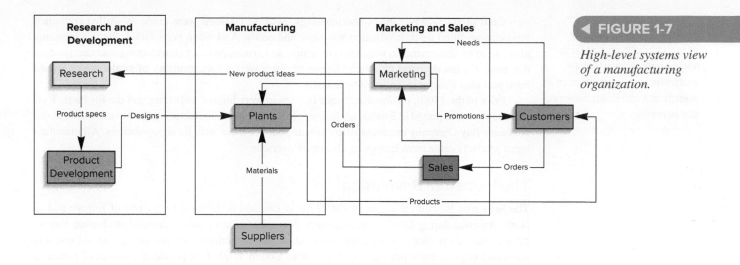

◀ FIGURE 1-7

High-level systems view of a manufacturing organization.

Establishing Priorities

In virtually every situation, managers discover that certain elements are more important than others. Recognizing this fact of life enables the managers to direct their efforts to where they will do the most good and to avoid wasting time and energy on insignificant elements. This is referred to as the **Pareto phenomenon**, which says that some things (a few) will be very important for achieving an objective or solving a problem, and other things (many) will not. This is also known as the *80–20 rule*, which states that approximately 20 percent of factors will impact approximately 80 percent of the results achieved. The implication is that a manager should deal with only important problems, and, for the selected problem, search for the one or two factors that will have the greatest impact. This is one of the most important and pervasive concepts in operations management. In fact, this concept can be applied to all decision making, both professional and personal.

Pareto phenomenon A few factors account for a high percentage of results achieved.

Ethics

Ethics are moral principles that govern a person's behaviour. Operations managers, like all managers, have the responsibility to make ethical decisions. Ethical issues arise in:

ethics Moral principles that govern a person's behaviour.

- Worker safety: providing adequate training, maintaining equipment in good working condition, and maintaining a safe working environment.
- Product safety: providing products that eliminate the risk of injury to the users.
- The environment: not doing things that will harm the environment.
- Closing facilities: taking into account the impact on the community, and honouring commitments that have been made.

In making decisions, managers must consider how their decisions will affect shareholders, employees, customers, suppliers, the community at large, and the environment. Finding solutions that will be in the best interest of all of these stakeholders is not always easy, but it is a goal that all operations managers should strive to achieve.

The Historical Evolution of Operations Management

In the earliest days, goods were produced using **craft production**: highly skilled workers using simple, flexible tools produced goods according to customer specification. Goods were produced in small shops by craftsmen and their apprentices. Under that system, it was common for one person to be responsible for making a product, such as a horse-drawn wagon or a piece of furniture, from start to finish. Only simple tools were available; the machines that we use today had not been invented.

craft production Highly skilled workers using simple, flexible tools to produce small quantities of customized goods.

economies of scale The economic conditions that favour larger plants and machines/equipment by causing minimum average unit cost to decrease as size increases.

Craft production had major shortcomings. Because products were made by skilled craftsmen who custom-fitted parts, production was slow and costly. And when parts failed, the replacements also had to be custom made, which was also slow and costly. Another shortcoming was that production costs did not decrease as volume increased; there were no **economies of scale**, which would have provided a major incentive for expansion.

Prior to the 1700s, business activities in Canada were limited to fishing and the fur trade. Raw materials were exported to Europe for further processing and manufacturing. Companies such as the Hudson's Bay Company imported British-made goods to trade with local populations. All manufactured products came from Europe or elsewhere overseas.

The Industrial Revolution

The Industrial Revolution began in the 1770s in England and spread to the rest of Europe and to North America during the nineteenth century. A number of innovations changed production forever by substituting machine power for human or animal power. Perhaps the most significant of these was the steam engine, made practical by James Watt around 1769. This provided a source of power to operate machines in factories. The spinning jenny (1770) and power loom (1785) revolutionized the textile industry. Machines made of iron replaced simple wooden machines. Two concepts assisted in large-scale production: division of labour and interchangeable parts.

division of labour Breaking up a production process into small tasks so that each worker performs a small portion of the overall job.

Division of labour, which Adam Smith wrote about in *The Wealth of Nations* (1776), means that the production process is divided up into a series of small tasks and individual workers are assigned to each one of these tasks. Unlike craft production, where each worker was responsible for doing many tasks and thus required skills, with division of labour the tasks were so narrow that virtually no skill was required.

interchangeable parts Parts of a product made to such precision that they do not have to be custom fitted.

The **interchangeable parts** concept is attributed to Eli Whitney, an American inventor who applied the concept to assembling muskets in the late 1700s. The basis for interchangeable parts is to standardize parts and make them so precisely that any part in a batch of parts would fit the product without alteration. This meant that parts did not have to be custom fitted, as they were in craft production. The standardized parts could also be used as replacement parts. The result was a tremendous decrease in assembly time and cost.

Soon after their invention in Britain, the iron-making and steam engine technologies were imported into North America. In Canada, a few small mills began operating in the first half of the 1800s. By the second half of the 1800s, canals and railways were built, and timber was being exported.

The discovery of electricity by Thomas Edison in the late 1800s allowed replacement of electricity for steam as a power source, improving the efficiency and working environment of factories.

Despite the major changes that were taking place, management theory and practice had not progressed much from early years. What was needed was a systematic approach to management.

Scientific Management

scientific management Applying science to observe, measure, analyze, and improve work methods, including the use of economic incentives.

Scientific management is applying science to observe, measure, analyze, and improve work methods, including the use of economic incentives. It was spearheaded by American efficiency engineer Frederick Taylor over a century ago. He studied work methods in great detail to identify the best method for doing each job.

Taylor's methods emphasized transferring control from workers to management and maximizing output. The methods were not always popular with workers, who sometimes thought they were used to unfairly increase output without a corresponding increase in compensation. Certainly some companies did abuse workers in their quest for efficiency. Eventually, the public outcry reached the halls of the U.S. Congress, and hearings were held on the matter. Taylor himself was called to testify in 1911, the same year his classic book *The Principles of Scientific Management* was published. The publicity from those hearings actually helped scientific management achieve wide acceptance in industry.

A number of other pioneers also contributed to this movement, including:

- *Frank Gilbreth,* an industrial engineer who is often referred to as the father of time and motion study. He developed the principles of motion economy that could be applied to small portions of a task.

- *Lillian Gilbreth,* a psychologist and the wife of Frank Gilbreth, who worked with her husband, focusing on the human factor in work. (The Gilbreths were the subject of a classic 1950 film, *Cheaper by the Dozen,* which was remade in 2003.) Many of her studies in the 1920s dealt with worker fatigue.

- *Henry Gantt,* who developed a widely used tool for scheduling, called a Gantt chart or a horizontal bar chart.

During the early part of the twentieth century, automobiles were just coming into vogue in North America. Ford's Model T was such a success that the company had trouble keeping up with orders for the cars. In an effort to improve the efficiency of operations, Henry Ford introduced the **moving assembly line**, a type of assembly line in which the car is pulled along the line at a fixed speed while the workers assemble its parts (you can watch the video "Ford and Taylor Scientific Management (Edited)" at https://www.youtube.com/watch?v=8PdmNbqtDdI).

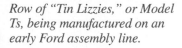

moving assembly line
A type of assembly line in which the product is pulled along the line at a fixed speed while the workers assemble its parts.

An Assembly Line
of the
Ford Motor Company

© Rykoff Collection/Corbis

Row of "Tin Lizzies," or Model Ts, being manufactured on an early Ford assembly line.

Ford's production system is an example of **mass production**, a system of production in which large volumes of standardized goods are produced by low-skilled or semiskilled workers using highly specialized, and often costly, equipment.

mass production System in which lower-skilled workers use specialized machinery to produce high volumes of standardized goods.

The Industrial Revolution and scientific management allowed some industrialization in Canada in the beginning of the twentieth century. These changes allowed for more effective exploitation of Canada's resources, such as minerals and agriculture. Import tariffs encouraged foreign entrepreneurs and companies, mainly Americans, to set up factories and sales offices in Canada; the transfer of technology helped both countries. For example, Massey Ferguson was established and grew as one of the world leaders in agricultural harvesting machinery, and McLaughlin Motor Co. was established in partnership with Buick and later became General Motors of Canada. The United States replaced Britain as Canada's largest trading partner and investor in 1926.

The Human Relations Movement

Whereas scientific management emphasized the technical aspects of work in work design, the human relations movement emphasized the importance of workers in work design. There was much emphasis on motivation. During the 1930s, Elton Mayo conducted studies at the Hawthorne division of Western Electric. His studies revealed that, in addition to the physical and technical aspects of work, giving special attention to workers is critical for improving productivity. During the 1940s, Abraham Maslow developed motivational theories that Frederick Hertzberg refined in the 1950s. Douglas McGregor added to this in the 1960s. In the 1970s, William Ouchi combined the Japanese approach (featuring such things as lifetime employment, employee problem solving, and consensus building) with the traditional Western approach (featuring short-term employment, specialists, and individual decision making and responsibility). In the 1980s, Edward E. Lawler III put forward the concept of high-involvement organization where self-directed teams play a big role (for an example, see the Chapter 7 Opener).

Decision Models and Computers

The factory movement was accompanied by the development of several quantitative models and techniques. In 1913, F.W. Harris developed one of the first models: a mathematical model for economic order quantity in inventory management. In the 1930s, three co-workers at Bell Telephone Labs—H.F. Dodge, H.G. Romig, and W. Shewhart—developed statistical procedures for sampling and quality control.

At first, these quantitative models were not widely used in industry. However, the onset of the Second World War changed that. The war generated tremendous pressures on manufacturing output, and specialists from many disciplines combined efforts to achieve advancements in the military and in manufacturing. This area became known as operations research. After the war, efforts to develop and refine quantitative tools for decision making continued, facilitated by the advent of the mainframe computer in 1951. This resulted in decision models for forecasting, production planning (using the linear programming of Dantzig), project management, and other areas of operations management.

During the 1960s and 1970s, quantitative techniques were highly regarded (these modelling and solutions for business are called *management science*); in the 1980s, they lost some favour. However, the widespread use of personal computers (invented in the late 1970s by Apple Computer) and user-friendly software in the workplace is causing resurgence in the popularity of these techniques. In 1975, Orlicky proposed *material requirements planning (MRP)*, mainly for assembly operations.

The advent of the computer resulted in its use in machine automation starting in the 1960s. In the mid-to-late 1980s, network computing began to increase, with applications such as electronic data interchange (EDI) and the ability to instantaneously receive point-of-sale data. This has led to more cooperation with the suppliers in the form of partnering, and formation of supply chains. In the early 1990s, the Internet and business process re-engineering began to play major roles in operations. In the late 1990s, more and more companies began to use enterprise resources planning (ERP) software to coordinate their sales, materials management, production planning/manufacturing, and accounting/finance activities.

The vast amount of data available now (e.g., customer purchases in a supermarket) has led to the popularity of powerful business analytics software. **Business analytics** comprises software used to build analysis models and simulations to create scenarios, understand realities, and predict future states. Business analytics includes data mining, predictive analytics (forecasting), applied analytics, and statistics.[4] Data mining looks for unusual patterns and relationships in data. For example, Walmart has discovered that just before a storm, sales of granola bars peak in its affected stores. Avis Budget uses customer rental data to forecast frequency of future rentals, which is used to decide its customer contact strategy.[5] Many websites (e.g., Amazon.com) collect a history of your purchases or even look-ups and recommend items to you (including third party ads). Xerox has built a model predicting whether a potential employee for its call centres will quit before having worked six months. Interestingly, experience does not matter. An inquisitive person who uses social networks and lives close by with reliable transportation will make an enduring call centre employee.[6]

business analytics
Software used to build analysis models and simulations to create scenarios, understand realities, and predict future states.

The Influence of Japanese Manufacturers

A number of Japanese manufacturers have developed or refined management practices that have increased the productivity of their operations and the quality of their products. This has made them very competitive, sparking interest in their approaches by companies outside Japan. One of their

---

[4] http://www.gartner.com/it-glossary/business-analytics/

[5] https://www.forbes.com/sites/avidan/2014/03/26/how-avis-budget-group-uses-data-to-drive-its-marketing/#1d8762aa7a7e

[6] J. Walker, "Meet the New Boss: Big Data—Companies Trade-In Hunch-Based Hiring for Computer Modeling," *Wall Street Journal*, Eastern Edition, September 20, 2012, B.1.

approaches, total quality management (TQM), emphasizes quality and continuous improvement, worker empowerment and teams, and achieving customer satisfaction. A related approach is the lean production system and just-in-time (JIT) manufacturing.

Lean production uses significantly fewer resources than mass production systems—less space, less inventory, and fewer workers—to produce a comparable amount of output. Lean production systems use a highly skilled workforce and flexible equipment. In effect, they incorporate advantages of both mass production (high volume, low unit cost) and craft production (high variety and flexibility). And quality is higher than in mass production. Lean production is a broad approach to just-in-time manufacturing. World class manufacturing (WCM) is a combination of TQM and JIT with some worker-initiated maintenance (called autonomous maintenance) and industrial engineering. WCM is recently being used by Fiat Chrysler Automobiles, CNH, and others to improve their productivity.

The skilled workers in lean production are more involved in maintaining and improving the system than their mass production counterparts are. They are taught to stop production if they discover a defect, and to work with other employees to find and correct the cause of the defect so that it won't reoccur. This results in an increasing level of quality over time, and eliminates the need to inspect and rework at the end of the line.

Because lean production systems operate with lower amounts of inventory, additional emphasis is placed on anticipating when problems might occur *before* they arise, and avoiding those problems through careful planning. Even so, problems still occur at times, and quick resolution is important. Workers participate in both the planning and correction stages. Technical experts are still used, but more as consultants rather than substitutes for workers. The focus is on designing a system so that workers will be able to achieve high levels of quality and quantity.

Compared to workers in traditional systems, much more is expected of workers in lean production systems. They must be able to function in teams, playing active roles in operating and improving the system. Individual creativity is much less important than team success. Responsibilities are also much greater, which can lead to pressure and anxiety not present in traditional systems. Moreover, a flatter organizational structure means career paths are not as steep in lean production organizations. Workers tend to become generalists rather than specialists, another contrast to more traditional organizations.

Unions often oppose conversion from a traditional system to a lean system because they view the added responsibility and multiple tasks as an expansion of job requirements without comparable increases in pay. In addition, workers sometimes complain that the company is the primary beneficiary of employee-generated improvements.

Table 1-5 provides a comparison of craft production, mass production, and lean production. Keep in mind that all three of these systems of production are in existence today.

▼ **TABLE 1-5**

A comparison of craft, mass, and lean production.

	Craft Production	Mass Production	Lean Production
Description	High variety, customized output, with one or a few skilled workers responsible for an entire unit of output.	High volume of standardized output, emphasis on volume. Capitalizes on division of labour, specialized equipment, and interchangeable parts.	Moderate to high volume of output, with more variety than mass production. Less inventory. Emphasis on quality. Employee involvement and teamwork are important.
Examples of goods and services produced	Home remodelling and landscaping, tailoring, portrait painting, diagnosis and treatment of injuries, surgery.	Sugar, steel, movie theatres, airlines, hotels, mail sorting, paper.	Automobiles and their components, electronics, industrial equipment.
Advantages	Wide range of choice, output tailored to customer needs.	Low cost per unit, requires mostly low-skilled workers.	Flexibility, variety, high quality of goods.
Disadvantages	Slow, requires skilled workers, few economies of scale, high cost, and low standardization.	Rigid system, difficult to accommodate changes in output volume, product design, or process design. Volume may be emphasized at the expense of quality.	No safety nets to offset any system breakdowns, fewer opportunities for employee advancement, more worker stress, requires higher-skilled workers than mass production.

Table 1-6 provides a chronological summary of some of the key developments in the evolution of operations management.

TABLE 1-6 ▶

Historical summary of operations management.

Year	Contribution/Concept	Originator
1769	Steam engine	James Watt
1776	Division of labour	Adam Smith
1790	Interchangeable parts	Eli Whitney
1911	Principles of scientific management	Frederick W. Taylor
1911	Time and motion study	Frank and Lillian Gilbreth
1912	Chart for scheduling activities	Henry Gantt
1913	Moving assembly line	Henry Ford
1913	Mathematical model for inventory management	F.W. Harris
1930	Hawthorne studies on worker motivation	Elton Mayo
1935	Statistical procedures for sampling and quality control	H.F. Dodge, H.G. Romig, W. Shewhart
1940	Operations research applications in warfare	Operations research groups
1947	Linear programming	George Dantzig
1951	Commercial digital computers	Sperry Univac
1960s	Computer-aided automation	Numerous
1970s	Personal computers	Apple
1975	Material requirements planning	Joseph Orlicky
1980s	Total quality management and lean production/just-in-time	Quality gurus; Toyota, and Taiichi Ohno
1990s	Internet and ecommerce, globalization, supply chains, and outsourcing	Numerous
2000–	Business analytics, world class manufacturing, sustainability	Numerous

LO8 Major Trends

Organizations must constantly monitor major trends affecting their operations and take them into account in their strategies and tactics. Lean, TQM/employee involvement, and business analytics, covered in the previous section, are still trending. It appears that the slowdown in the world economy still lingers. Low oil and gas prices have negatively impacted the Western Canadian economy.

Some other major trends affecting operations, which we have not covered yet, are as follows:

1. *The Internet and ecommerce.* The Internet (the global system of interconnected computer networks) has nurtured ecommerce, which is the use of the Internet to buy and sell goods and services. Ecommerce has resulted in significant operations efficiencies. Social networking sites such as Facebook, Twitter, and LinkedIn are being used by organizations for marketing and recruiting purposes. On the downside, criminals are using the connectivity of the Internet to break into organizations' computer systems and steal private information or spread computer viruses. This has made cybersecurity essential.

2. *Technology.* Technological advances have led to a vast array of new products and processes. Undoubtedly the computer has had—and will continue to have—the greatest impact on organizations. Applications include computer-aided product design, rapid prototyping, computer

numerically controlled machines, enterprise resource planning (ERP) software, and electronic (data) communication.

3. *Globalization.* **Globalization** is worldwide movement toward economic, financial, trade, and operations integration. Increased competition has put downward pressure on product prices, necessitating reduced product life cycles, increased innovation, rapid new product development, and increased outsourcing. China has become the factory of the world, leading to long international supply chains and the importance of managing them.

4. *Supply chains.* A supply chain is the sequence of organizations that are involved in producing and delivering a product. The sequence begins with suppliers of raw materials and extends all the way to the final consumers. Facilities might include warehouses, factories, distribution centres, and retail outlets.

> **globalization** Worldwide movement toward economic, financial, trade, and operations integration.

   Figure 1-8 provides an illustration of the bread supply chain: it begins with wheat growing on a farm and ends with a consumer buying a loaf of bread in a grocery store. Notice that the value of the product increases as it moves down the supply chain. Obviously, if members of a supply chain work together and coordinate their activities, they can all benefit. This is called *supply chain management* (see Chapter 11).

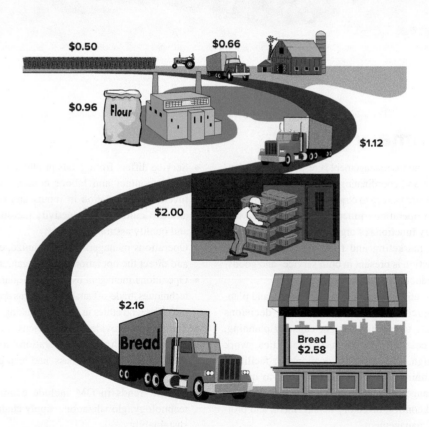

◀ **FIGURE 1-8**

Supply chain for bread.

5. *Sustainability.* **Sustainability** refers to reduced use of resources and harm to the environment so that the future is not threatened. Concerns about global warming and pollution have caused governments to impose stricter environmental regulations to reduce their carbon footprint. Activities that are most affected are product design, purchasing and supply chain management, production process, and disaster preparation and response. Note that purchasing of goods from overseas increases not only transportation costs, but also fuel consumption and carbon released into the atmosphere. Green initiatives include reducing packaging, materials, and water and energy use, and buying locally. Other initiatives include refurbishing used equipment (e.g., printers and copiers) and recycling.

> **sustainability** Reduced use of resources and harm to the environment so that the future is not threatened.

Puma's "Clever Little Bag" changed the concept of the shoe box by wrapping footwear in a cardboard structure with 65 percent less cardboard. It uses a bag made of recycled plastic as the outer layer that holds the inner cardboard structure together. Puma expects to cut carbon dioxide emissions by 10,000 tons per year and water, energy, and diesel use by 60 percent by using fewer materials—8,500 fewer tons of paper to be specific—and the new packaging's lighter weight.

Getty Images/Staff

Summary

- Operations management is responsible for planning and coordinating the use of the organization's resources to convert inputs into outputs.
- The operations function is one of three primary functions of organizations; the other two are marketing and finance. The operations function is present in both service- and goods-producing organizations.
- Operations decisions involve design and planning/control decisions. Design decisions relate to product design, capacity planning, process design, layout of facilities, work design, and selecting locations for facilities. Planning/control decisions relate to quality management, production planning, scheduling and control, inventory management, and project management.

- Service differs from goods production in customer contact and labour content, lack of inventories, variation in inputs and outputs, and difficulties in productivity measurement and quality assurance.
- Operations managers plan, organize, control, and direct the operations of an organization.
- Operations managers use models, quantitative techniques, trade-off analysis, systems approach, priorities, and ethics in decision making.
- The chapter provides a brief discussion of the historical evolution of operations management, including craft, mass, and lean production systems.
- Recent trends in OM include ecommerce, technology, globalization, supply chains, and sustainability.

Key Terms

business analytics	efficiency	interchangeable parts
craft production	ethics	lead time
division of labour	globalization	mass production
economies of scale	good	model
effectiveness	heuristic	moving assembly line

operations management	scientific management	sustainability
Pareto phenomenon	service	system
process	supply chain	trade-off
quantitative techniques	supply chain management	value added

Discussion and Review Questions

Note: An asterisk indicates that a question or problem may be more challenging.

LO1 1. Briefly define the term *operations management*.

LO1 2. Name the titles of three jobs in operations management.

LO1 3. Why is operations management important to any organization?

LO2 4. Identify the three major functional areas of organizations and briefly describe how they interrelate.

LO2 & 5 5. Describe the operations function and the nature of the operations manager's job.

LO3 6. Explain the difference between design and planning/control decisions.

LO4 7. List five important differences between producing goods and performing services.

LO2 & 4 *8. Give an example of a pure service (i.e., one where no goods are exchanged). What do you think is being transformed?

LO5 9. Give three specific activities an operations manager is likely involved in. (*Hint:* Use Figure 1-6.)

LO7 10. Briefly discuss each of these terms related to the historical evolution of operations management:
  a. Industrial Revolution.
  b. Scientific management.
  c. Interchangeable parts.
  d. Division of labour.

LO4 11. Why are services important? Why is manufacturing important? Give two examples of each.

LO6 12. What is a model and why are models important?

LO7 13. Name three people who have contributed to the development of operations management.

LO6 *14. List the trade-offs you would consider for each of these decisions:
  a. Owning a car versus using public transportation.
  b. Buying a computer now versus waiting for an improved model.
  c. Buying a new car versus buying a used car.
  d. Speaking up in class versus waiting to get called on by the instructor.

LO7 15. Describe each of these systems, including their main advantage and disadvantage, and give an example for each: craft production, mass production, and lean production.

LO7 16. Why might some people prefer not to work in a lean production system?

LO8 *17. How have technological changes affected you? Are there any downsides to technological change? Explain.

LO8 18. Identify some of the current trends in operations management and relate them to recent news or to your personal experience.

LO6 19. Give an example of an unethical behaviour you have observed.

LO2 20. Explain the term *value added*.

LO8 *21. What is a supply chain and what is supply chain management?

LO8 22. What is sustainability and why is it important?

LO1 23. Name three process types, and give an example for each.

LO7 24. What is business analytics? Name its various types.

LO6 25. What is meant by *an internal customer–supplier relationship*?

Taking Stock

This item appears at the end of each chapter. It is intended to focus your attention on four key issues for organizations in general, and operations management, in particular. These issues are trade-off analysis, collaboration among various functional areas of the organization, the impact of technology, and ethical issues. You will see four questions relating to these issues.

LO6 1. What is a trade-off? Why is careful consideration of trade-offs important in decision making?

LO2 2. Why is it important for the various functions of an organization to collaborate?

LO8 3. In what ways has technology impacted operations?

LO6 4. Why is employing child labour (10- to 15-year-olds) in developing countries unethical?

Critical Thinking Exercises

This item also will appear in every chapter. It allows you to critically apply information you learned in the chapter to practical situations.

 1. Many organizations offer a combination of goods and services to their customers. As you learned in this chapter, there are some key differences between production of goods and delivery of services. What are the implications of these differences to managing operations?

 2. Some people who work in the knowledge or arts sectors and whose jobs involve creativity argue that their job cannot be defined as a process (i.e., a sequence of predetermined activities). Discuss.

 3. Car sharing is a model of car rental in which people rent cars for short periods of time, often by the hour. The car has to be located close to the customer's residence or workplace, so cars are distributed in the community. The rental process has to be self-service and cars need to be available 24 hours a day. The primary markets are large metropolitan areas, universities, and corporate campuses where there is a relatively high burden of car ownership. The car-share operator pays for maintenance, parking, gas, and insurance of the vehicle. Explain in detail how a car sharing business such as Enterprise CarShare (https://www.enterprisecarshare.ca/ca/en/home.html) operates.

Experiential Learning Exercises

These exercises also appear at the end of each chapter. They are designed to help you see the relevance of operations management firsthand.

 1. Visit a fast-food restaurant and answer these questions:
   a. In what ways is quality, or lack of quality, visible?
   b. What items must be stocked in addition to the food?
   c. How important do you think employee scheduling is? Explain.
   d. How might capacity decisions affect the success or failure of the restaurant?

 2. Does your car insurer provide the innovative services that Progressive Insurance provides? Briefly explain your auto collision claim process.

Internet Exercises

This item will appear at the end of each chapter. It allows you to use the Internet to gain additional knowledge about chapter material. Here are the first exercises.

 1. Visit the web page of one of the associations listed under Careers in Operations Management and briefly list the targeted members and the services that they provide to their members.

 2. Visit https://www.youtube.com/watch?v=lzUygLWhn_Y and watch the video of steel making by Dofasco. What are the (a) inputs, (b) process operations, and (c) outputs?

🔍 MINI-CASE

Sharing Economy

Internet-based services such as Airbnb and Uber have flourished over the last decade or so. They have allowed individual suppliers to provide their goods and services to consumers without a large investment to actually start a business and without government regulations and control. However, the success of these services depends on goodwill and mutual trust of both the goods/service providers and consumers. For example, an Airbnb guest may trash the place or damage or steal valuable furniture/appliances, and an Airbnb host may cancel the reservation at the last minute or have a filthy place despite posting a picture of an attractive, clean location on the Airbnb website.

Questions

1. How do these companies develop mutual trust between their users (suppliers and consumers)? Name two or three ways.

2. Which side is potentially more at risk in the deal?

3. What is the effect of these services on regulated competitors such as hotels and taxi companies?

4. How would review of either side by the other side help with improving the operations?

MINI-CASE

Lynn

Lynn had worked for the same major Canadian company for almost 15 years. Although the company had gone through some tough times, things were starting to turn around. Customer orders were up, and quality and productivity had improved dramatically from what they had been only a few years earlier due to a companywide quality improvement program. So it came as a real shock to Lynn and about 400 of her co-workers when they were suddenly terminated following the new CEO's decision to downsize the company.

After recovering from the initial shock, Lynn tried to find employment elsewhere. Despite her efforts, after eight months of searching she was no closer to finding a job than the day she started. Her funds were being depleted and she was getting more discouraged. There was one bright spot, though: she was able to bring in a little money by mowing lawns for her neighbours. She got involved quite by chance when she heard one neighbour remark that now that his children were on their own, nobody was around to cut the grass. Almost jokingly, Lynn asked him how much he'd be willing to pay. Soon Lynn was mowing the lawns of five neighbours. Other neighbours wanted her to work on their lawns, but she didn't feel that she could spare any more time from her job search.

However, as the rejection letters began to pile up, Lynn knew she had to make an important decision in her life. On a rainy Tuesday morning, she decided to go into business for herself—taking care of neighbourhood lawns. She was relieved to give up the stress of job hunting, and she was excited about the prospect of being her own boss. But she was also fearful of being completely on her own. Nevertheless, Lynn was determined to make a go of it.

At first, business was a little slow, but once people realized Lynn was available, many asked her to take care of their lawns. Some people were simply glad to turn the work over to her; others switched from professional lawn care services. By the end of her first year in business, Lynn knew she could earn a living this way.

She also performed other services such as fertilizing lawns, weeding lawns and gardens, and trimming shrubbery. Business became so good that Lynn hired two part-time workers to assist her and, even then, she believed she could expand further if she wanted to. During winter months (January and February), Lynn takes her vacation in Florida.

Questions

1. Lynn is the operations manager of her business. Among her responsibilities are forecasting, inventory management, scheduling, quality assurance, and maintenance.

   a. What kinds of things would likely require forecasts?

   b. What inventory items does Lynn probably have? Name one inventory decision she has to make periodically.

   c. What scheduling must she do? What situations might arise, disrupting schedules and causing Lynn to reschedule?

   d. How important is quality assurance to Lynn's business? Explain.

   e. What kinds of maintenance must be performed?

2. What are some of the trade-offs that Lynn probably considered relative to:

   a. Working for a company instead of for herself?

   b. Expanding the business?

   c. Launching a website?

3. Lynn decided to offer the students who worked for her a bonus of $25 for ideas on how to improve the business, and they provided several good ideas. One idea that she initially rejected now appears to hold great promise. The student who proposed the idea has left, and is currently working for a competitor. Should Lynn send that student a cheque for the idea?

4. Lynn is thinking of making her operations sustainable. Name one or two ideas she might consider.

 MINI-CASE

Sobeys

Sobeys Inc. is the second largest grocery store chain in Canada (the largest is Loblaw). Sobeys distinguishes itself from Loblaw by offering better quality fresh food and customer service.

Sobeys grew out of Nova Scotia mostly through acquisition of other grocery chains. The integration of the latest acquisition, Safeway Canada (over 200 stores in Western Canada), has been challenging. Sobeys now owns 908 grocery stores and franchises 977 stores throughout Canada. Sobeys has revenues of over $24 billion and employs over 125,000 people. Sobeys is also a wholesaler to over 8,000 retail accounts.

Sobeys has five different store sizes and formats, and uses them in each location based on market size and customer demographics. There is the large full-service format (such as Sobeys, Sobeys extra, IGA extra, Safeway and Thrifty Foods); urban fresh format (such as Sobeys Urban Fresh and IGA in Quebec); small community format (such as Foodland, Marché Bonichoix, and Les Marchés Tradition); discount format (such as FreshCo and Price Chopper); and convenience format (such as Needs Convenience and IGA express). Approximately 350 large full-service stores have in-store pharmacies. Sobeys also has a chain of 78 drugstores (Lawtons Drugs) in Atlantic Canada, over 300 retail gas stations, and 80 liquor stores.

Sam Dao/Alamy Stock Images

In addition to national brands, Sobeys has its own private label brands: Compliments (over 5,000 products) and S!gnal. Sobeys also has its own manufacturer—Big 8 Beverages—for its private label soft drinks and water in Atlantic Canada.

Sobeys is a wholly owned subsidiary of Empire Company Limited, which also has a 41.5 percent equity interest in Crombie REIT, a real estate development and management company. Crombie owns the buildings and shopping plazas that Sobeys stores occupy, as well as other properties.

Sobeys has implemented SAP (an enterprise resource planning software) nationwide and across its brand stores. The stores are organized by region: Atlantic Canada/Ontario, Quebec, and Western Canada.

Most products are bought centrally and distributed to the stores through 34 regional distribution centres (DCs) located throughout the country. The fully automated Vaughan and Terrebonne DCs are state of the art. Sobeys is retrofitting the Rocky View Alberta DC that it bought from Target Canada.

Operations management activities and decisions are split between corporate office and store operations.

The corporate office initiates and manages various programs to increase the number of customers, including constant evaluation of store performance, closing low-profit stores, opening new stores, and modernizing existing stores. It also manages the computer technology, performs data analytics to improve category management, initiates training programs, and performs accounting and finance activities. Directors of operations (i.e., district managers) interact with the store managers in their district to implement improvement programs such as sharing best practices.

A store manager manages all facets of the store and ensures operational excellence in retail merchandising, inventory management, and customer relations. He/she ensures execution of the retail programs by communicating the operational requirements and/or changes and store vision to the employees. This includes occupational health and safety, food safety, and other regulatory requirements and procedures. The store manager also oversees recruitment, orientation, training, and performance management.

Sobeys cares about its employees and their training. It has a careers website, provides on-the-job and web-based training, and even provides scholarships to exemplary employees who are still in high school.

Sobeys also cares about sustainability. It sets targets for greenhouse gas reduction and measures its progress. It has reduced its use of electricity and amount of material sent to landfill.

Questions

1. What are the inputs, process, output, and feedback/control for a grocery store such as Sobeys?

2. What are the operations decisions for running a grocery store such as Sobeys?

Source: http://www.empireco.ca/site/media/Empireco/Empire%20AR%202016 _ENG%20FINAL%20SEDAR.pdf.

Problem-Solving Guide

Here is a procedure that will help you to solve most of the end-of-chapter problems in this textbook and on exams:

1. Identify the question to be answered.

2. Summarize the information given in the problem statement using the appropriate symbols.

3. Determine what type of problem it is so you can select the appropriate problem-solving tools, such as a formula or table. Check your notes from class, chapter examples, and the Solved Problems section of the chapter, and any preceding chapter problems you have already solved for guidance.

4. Solve the problem and indicate your answer.

Example 1

Department A can produce parts at a rate of 50/day. Department B uses those parts at the rate of 10/day. Each day unused parts are added to inventory. At what rate does the inventory of unused parts build up?

Solution

1. The question to be answered: At what rate does inventory of unused parts build up (i.e., increase) per day?

2. The given information: Production rate = 50 parts/day

Usage rate   = 10 parts/day

3. For this simple problem, no formula or table is needed. Inventory buildup is simply the difference between the production and usage rates.

4. Production rate   = 50 parts/day

Usage rate   = 10 parts/day

Inventory buildup = 40 parts/day

Example 2

Companies often use this formula (the economic order quantity) to determine how much of a certain item to order:

$$Q = \sqrt{\frac{2DS}{H}}$$

where

Q = Order quantity

D = Annual demand

S = Ordering cost

H = Annual holding cost per unit

If annual demand is 400 units, ordering cost is $36, and annual holding cost is $2 per unit, what is the order quantity?

Solution

1. The question to be answered: What is the order quantity, Q?

2. The information given in the problem: D = 400 units/year, S = $36, H = $2 per year

3. To solve the problem, substitute the values given in the problem into the formula.

4. Solution: $Q = \sqrt{\frac{2(400 \text{ units/yr.})\$36}{\$2/\text{unit/yr.}}} = 120$ units

Chapter 2
Competitiveness, Strategic Planning, and Productivity

Jackbluee/Dreamstime.com

LEARNING OBJECTIVES

After completing this chapter, you should be able to:

LO1 List and discuss the primary ways that organizations compete.

LO2 Describe a company's strategic planning; mission/vision/values; goals and objectives; strategies, tactics, and action plans; operations strategy and its formulation; and generic operations strategies.

LO3 Define and measure productivity, solve typical problems, explain why measuring the productivity of services is difficult, and describe factors affecting productivity.

A typical furniture store maximizes customization and service but does so at the expense of price. Usually there are a lot of choices of wood, fabric, and styles. After a salesperson takes the order, the customer has to wait a few weeks to receive the furniture from the manufacturer.

In contrast, IKEA serves customers who are happy to trade service for price. It targets young furniture buyers who want style at low cost. IKEA uses no salespeople but has huge stores in suburban locations, which are open until late evening, with clear in-store displays and a lot of inventory. IKEA designs its own modular low-cost furniture which is packaged in the smallest box(es) possible and is easy to assemble. Customers usually do their own in-store pick-up, delivery, and at-home assembly.

IKEA's vision is "to create a better everyday life for the people." Its business idea is "to offer a wide range of well designed, functional home furnishing products at prices so low that as many people as possible will be able to afford them." It achieves quality at affordable prices through optimizing its entire supply chain, by building long-term supplier relationships, investing in highly automated production, and producing large volumes.

IKEA has 20 in-house designers and approximately 200 external designers working on contract. They regularly visit people's homes, observing and taking photos, and produce a quarterly report. The in-person intimate approach to customer understanding enables them to uncover new routines, food habits, and wishes that people develop. IKEA has approximately 9,500 products and, every year, around 2,000 products are renewed and refreshed.

IKEA is the world's largest furniture retailer, with revenue of 35 billion euros in 2016. It has close to 1,000 suppliers in 50 countries, 27 trading service (purchasing) offices in 23 countries, 43 manufacturing plants in 11 countries, and 33 distribution centres (that supply its stores) and 15 customer distribution centres (that ship directly to customers) in 17 countries. It has 328 franchised stores in 28 countries and employs 155,000 people.

Sources: M. E. Porter, "What Is Strategy?" *Harvard Business Review*, Nov–Dec 1996, pp. 61–78; http://www.ikea.com/ca/en/; https://www.forbes.com/sites/deniselyohn/2015/06/10/how-ikea-designs-its-brand-success/#189f1bd86755.

This chapter describes competitiveness, strategic planning, and productivity: three related topics that are vitally important to organizations. **Competitiveness** is the ability and performance of an organization in the market compared to other organizations that offer similar goods or services. **Strategy** is the long-term plans that determine the direction an organization takes to become (or remain) competitive. **Strategic planning** is the managerial process that determines a strategy for the organization and implements it through allocation of resources and action plans. Lastly, **productivity** is a measure of productive use of resources.

Slumping productivity growth in recent years and the impressive successes of foreign competition in the market have caused many North American companies to rethink their strategies and to place increased emphasis on their operations.

Competitiveness

A company must be competitive relative to others to profitably sell its goods and services in the market. Competitiveness is the reason a company prospers, barely gets by, or fails. Competitiveness depends on its capabilities and performance in its market.

Capabilities or competencies are developed over time by focusing on a limited range of goods or services and/or on a technology. Companies use past experience and expertise in design, manufacturing/service, or marketing, and leverage them to introduce new goods and services.[1]

An organization's performance in the market depends on the expectation of its customers for the purchase of goods or services. A customer can be a consumer (i.e., the final or end customer) or another company. The main buying factors that customers use are price, quality, variety, and timeliness; these are called **key purchasing criteria** and are briefly described below.

- *Price* is the amount a customer must pay for the good or service. If all other factors are equal, customers will choose the good or service that has the lowest price.

- *Quality* refers to characteristics of a good or service that are determined by its design, material, workmanship, performance, consistency, etc. (We will explore this further in Chapter 9.) Here, we also include *customer service* (i.e., easy and fast returns, warranty repairs, response to requests, etc.) and *innovation* in products (e.g., iPhone).

- *Variety* is the choice of models and options available to customers. The more variety, the wider the range of potential customers.

- *Timeliness* is the availability of goods or services when they are needed by the customer. This means orders being delivered *on time* (as in just-in-time purchasing) or *quickly*. We also include convenience of location here.

For an example of amazing customer service, see the "Seven Customer Service Lessons From Amazon's CEO Jeff Bezos" OM in Action.

competitiveness Ability and performance of an organization in the market compared to other organizations that offer similar goods or services.

strategy The long-term plans that determine the direction an organization will take to become (or remain) competitive.

strategic planning The managerial process that determines a strategy for the organization, and implements it through allocation of resources and action plans.

productivity A measure of productive use of resources, usually expressed as the ratio of output to input.

key purchasing criteria The major factors influencing a purchase: price, quality, variety, and timeliness.

Courtesy of Apple Inc.

A major key to Apple's continued success is its ability to keep pushing the boundaries of innovation. Apple has demonstrated how to create growth by dreaming up products so new and ingenious that they have upended one market after another.

[1]H. Hayes, et al., *Strategic Operations—Competing Through Capabilities*, New York: The Free Press, 1996.

OM in Action

Seven Customer Service Lessons From Amazon's CEO Jeff Bezos

Amazon.com is the undisputed leader in customer service. Amazon's CEO, Jeff Bezos, has built his company based on the philosophy of serving the customer. Here are seven lessons for customer service from Jeff Bezos:

1. Understand your customers. As part of training each year, Amazon managers attend two days of call-centre training.
2. Serve the needs of the customer. "We're not competitor obsessed, we're customer obsessed."
3. The most important person in the room is the customer. Bezos used to bring an empty chair to his executive meetings to represent the customer.
4. Don't be satisfied until customer satisfaction is 100 percent. In December 2011, Amazon delivered 99.9 percent of packages to its customers before Christmas. Bezos stated: "We're not satisfied until it's 100 percent."
5. Respond to unhappy customers. "If you make customers unhappy in the physical world, they might each tell six friends. If you make customers unhappy on the Internet, they can each tell 6,000."
6. Create a customer-centric company where company interests are aligned with customers' interests. "We don't focus on the optics of the next quarter; we

Uwe Zucchi/AFP/Getty Images

focus on what is going to be good for customers." Amazon is completely data-driven, which is based on its customer experience.

7. Don't be afraid to apologize for mistakes. In 2009, Amazon remotely deleted illegally sold copies of the ebooks *1984* and *Animal Farm* from customers' Kindles. The incident resulted in a big outcry from Internet users. Bezos personally apologized: "We will use the scar tissue from this painful mistake to help make better decisions going forward."

Source: https://www.salesforce.com/blog/2013/06/jeff-bezos-lessons.html.

Customers' purchasing criteria vary based on the product they are buying, its intended use, and the marketing channel. As an example, for online shopping, consumers value the following criteria (in order): low prices, free shipping, flexible return policy, website easy to use, pickup or return at store, and toll-free "live" customer service, as Figure 2-1 shows.

Most customers tend to trade off price against the other purchasing criteria and choose the "best buy" or best "value":

$$\text{Value} = \frac{\text{Quality, timeliness, etc.}}{\text{Price}}$$

order qualifiers Purchasing criteria that customers perceive as minimum standards of acceptability to be considered for purchase.

order winners Purchasing criteria that cause the selling organization to be perceived as better than the competition.

In complex purchases, customers may use two categories of purchasing criteria: order qualifiers and order winners.[2] **Order qualifiers** are the purchasing criteria that customers perceive as minimum standards of acceptability for purchase. However, these may not be sufficient to get a customer to purchase from the selling organization. **Order winners** are the purchasing criteria that cause the selling organization to be perceived as better than the competition.

Purchasing criteria such as price, on-time delivery, fast delivery, and quality can be order qualifiers or order winners. Over time a characteristic that once was an order winner may become an order qualifier, and vice versa. For example, in the past, a certain percentage of defective items was acceptable to most industrial buyers, but not now. This means that excellent quality (close to zero defects) was not an order qualifier before but has become one now.

Obviously, it is important to determine the set of order qualifiers and order winners, and the relative importance of each, for each market so that appropriate attention can be given to them. Marketing

[2] T. Hill, *Manufacturing Strategy: Text and Cases*, 3rd ed. New York: McGraw-Hill, 2000.

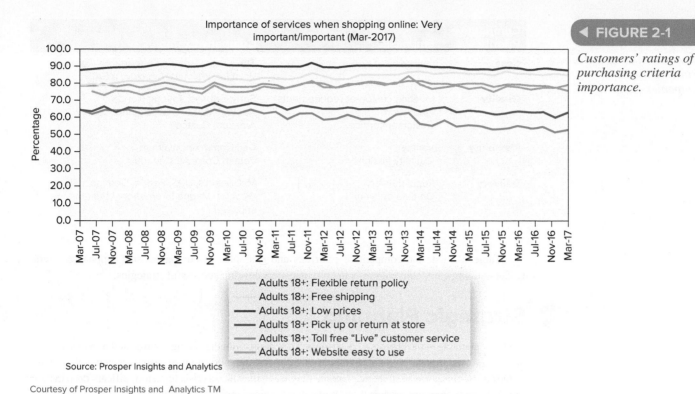

Importance of services when shopping online: Very important/important (Mar-2017)

- Adults 18+: Flexible return policy
- Adults 18+: Free shipping
- Adults 18+: Low prices
- Adults 18+: Pick up or return at store
- Adults 18+: Toll free "Live" customer service
- Adults 18+: Website easy to use

Source: Prosper Insights and Analytics

Courtesy of Prosper Insights and Analytics TM

◀ FIGURE 2-1

Customers' ratings of purchasing criteria importance.

must make that determination and communicate it to operations. For example, for business air travellers, comfort/convenience (quality and customer service) and being on time are most important (i.e., are order qualifiers), whereas for economy air travellers, price is most important (i.e., is the order qualifier). Also, for high-tech products such as an iPhone, innovative features relating to quality are most important, but for mature products, price, quality, and availability/on-time delivery are paramount.

Organizations compete by emphasizing one or more of the key purchasing criteria in their operations. From an organization's point of view, these are called **competitive priorities**:

- *Cost* is the unit production cost of a good or a service to the organization. Organizations that compete based on cost (i.e., price from a customer's perspective) emphasize lowering their operating costs.

- *Quality* from an organization's perspective means determining customers' quality requirements, translating these into specifications for goods or services, and consistently producing goods or services to these specifications. Customer satisfaction and product innovation are included here.

- *Flexibility* is being able to produce a variety of goods or services. This also includes customization, which is modifying goods or services to meet the requirements of individual customers. It may also refer to being able to easily increase or decrease the production quantity of goods or services (*quantity flexibility*). Flexibility is usually achieved by having general-purpose equipment, excess capacity and/or inventory, and multi-skilled workers, resulting in easy changeover between products.

- *Delivery reliability and speed* relate to being able to consistently and promptly meet promised due dates by producing/delivering goods or services on time and quickly. This also includes locating close to customers. Delivery reliability and speed is achieved by using faster and more reliable resources/processes.

If an organization is far from being competitive, it may be able to improve many or all of its competitive priorities simultaneously. However, as the organization becomes more competitive, it tends to reach a point where improving one priority can be achieved only by reducing the emphasis on another priority (i.e., a trade-off is required, perhaps in delivery speed versus cost). The result of this is a focus on only one priority at a time. It has been observed that most companies first emphasize quality, and only after their quality has reached a competitive level do they focus on delivery reliability, then on low-cost operations, and finally on flexibility.

competitive priorities The importance given to operations characteristics: cost, quality, flexibility, and delivery.

TABLE 2-1 ▶

Examples of competitive priorities used by companies.

Competitive Priority	Emphasis	Company Examples
Cost	Low cost	The Great Canadian Superstore (Loblaw), WestJet, Walmart, Amazon, IKEA
Quality	Meeting customer requirements Innovation Customer service	Sony, Sobeys, Toyota, Honda Apple, 3M, IKEA, GE, Boeing, Disney Amazon, Costco
Flexibility	Variety Quantity flexibility	Dell Computer, Walmart Potash Corp, Air Canada
Delivery	Rapid delivery On-time delivery	McDonald's, UPS, FedEx, Domino's Pizza WestJet, Magna International (just-in-time supplier)

Table 2-1 lists the competitive priorities and examples of companies that emphasize them. Understanding competitive issues can help managers develop successful strategies.

L02 Strategic Planning

Strategic planning is the process of determining a strategy—that is, a long-term plan that will set a new direction for an organization—and implementing it through allocation of resources and action plans. Some companies perform strategic planning only when they face a crisis (e.g., a significant drop in their sales). More progressive organizations perform strategic planning on a regular basis, usually annually.

Briefly, strategic planning starts with top management soliciting the performance of current strategy from stakeholders (department managers and employees, shareholders, customers, suppliers, and society) and commissioning a market research study of the industry and where it is headed in the next five years or so. Then, the management team may form/adjust the organization's mission and vision (based on the organization's values), determine a set of goals and objectives, and brainstorm and evaluate alternative ways (strategies) to achieve them. Finally, the chosen strategy is implemented by determining a set of action plans at the department level. A related framework is called the Balanced Scorecard (see Figure 2-2).

FIGURE 2-2 ▶

The Balanced Scorecard.

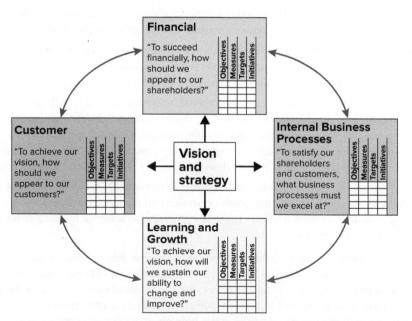

Source: Reprinted with permission of Harvard Business School Press from Robert Kaplan and David Norton, *Balanced Scorecard: Translating Strategy Into Action.* Copyright © 1996 by the Harvard Business School Publishing Corporation. All rights reserved.

The analysis usually concerns the competitiveness of the organization. A well known decision aid is the strengths, weaknesses, opportunities, and threats (SWOT) analysis. The organization will try to identify these and to use/build up its strengths (relative to its competitors) to take advantage of market opportunities, and to avoid/neutralize its weaknesses (relative to its competitors) to defend against the threats.

A more detailed strategic planning process for a business involves answering the following questions:[3]

1. Get started.
   a. What is the scope of business?
   b. Is the current strategy working?
   c. What are the issues/problems?

2. Analyze the industry and source of competitive advantage (i.e., earning above-average profit).
   a. How intense is the competitive rivalry?
   b. How large is the bargaining power of suppliers?
   c. How hard is it for new entrants to enter the industry?
   d. How easily can substitute goods or services be developed?
   e. How large is the bargaining power of customers?
   f. How would trends and changes (demand, technology, regulation, etc.) affect the industry?
   g. How can generic strategies of niche market, low cost, and product differentiation be used in this industry?
   h. How can we gain and sustain competitive advantage?

3. Analyze customers.
   a. What are the market segments?
   b. What are customers' key purchasing criteria?

4. Analyze competitors.
   a. What are the strategies and positions (i.e., relative competitive comparison of products) of winners and losers?
   b. Why do competitors behave as they do? Can we influence them?
   c. How has their strategy been changing through time?

5. Assess our relative position.
   a. What are our products' strengths and weaknesses as customers see them? Profitability?

6. Assess the state of our business.
   a. What are the major issues (in order of importance)?
   b. What should our goals be?
   c. Should we grow, maintain, or sell off part of our business?

7. Develop and evaluate alternative strategies.
   a. Can strategies be found for each major issue?
   b. What investments should we make? What actions should we take?
   c. For each alternative, do financial returns justify it?

8. Choose and refine the recommended strategy.
   a. What strategy should we choose?
   b. What actions and policies are required? Do they fit together? Are they reinforcing?
   c. What resources are required? Timelines? Expected results?

9. Identify major actions and implement them.
   a. How can we coordinate the actions and monitor overall progress?

---

[3] S. Early, "Issues and Alternatives: Key to FMC's Strategic Planning System," *Planning Review* 18(3), May/June 1990, pp. 26–33.

EXAMPLE 2-1

BC Frozen Food Ltd. (BCFF) is a processor of fruits and vegetables located in Mission, British Columbia. Most of BCFF's products are grown locally within 50 kilometres of the plant. The best products are sold fresh to local markets and inferior products are made into jam, but most products are individually quick frozen. Ever since the company was founded in 1989, its owners, the Shah family, have been working very hard to keep BCFF profitable.

Initially, BCFF sold frozen products in bulk to distributors such as Sysco. Throughout the years, however, an increasing number of local processors as well as some large companies (such as Lucerne and General Mills) have opened processing plants nearby in Abbotsford. The response from the Shah

family has been to diversify, both in products and in distribution channels. They expanded the plant to be able to process green beans, and acquired a vacuum pack machine to be able to package the products in small vacuum sealed plastic bags. To be able to convince their partner farmers to grow green beans, BCFF purchased seven large bean harvesting machines.

BCFF house-brand and private-label fruit and vegetable bags are now sold in retail stores such as Federated Co-op stores and Krogers, the largest grocery chain in the United States. Also, cases of one or two kilogram bags of BCFF house brand are sold to foodservice and restaurants such as Dairy Queen. The retail and foodservice industries now provide the majority of BCFF's revenue.

Sources: S. Shah and I. A. Ghazzawi, "BC Frozen Food Limited: Challenges and Change," *Journal of the International Academy for Case Studies*, Volume 18, Number 7, 2012, pp. 1–17; www.bcfrozenfoods.com.

Mission, Vision, and Values

Some organizations determine and use a mission, vision, and values statement during their strategic planning process. This may help build consensus within the organization as well. An organization's **mission** is where the organization is going now, its products, and its markets. **Vision** is where the organization desires to be in the future. Vision has to be realistic. **Values** are the shared beliefs of the organization's stakeholders that should drive everything else such as culture, mission/vision, and strategy.

It is important that an organization have a clear and simple mission/vision/values statement. Table 2-2 provides some sample mission/vision/values statements.

mission Where the organization is going now, its products, and its markets.

vision Where the organization desires to be in the future.

values Shared beliefs of the organization's stakeholders.

Goals and Objectives Mission/vision provides a general direction for an organization and should lead to organizational *goals*, which provide substance to the overall mission/vision. For example, one goal of an organization may be to capture more market share for a product; another goal may be to achieve high profitability. An objective is a specific goal containing numerical values. For example, an objective of a company may be a 5 percent reduction in operating costs.

Strategies, Tactics, and Action Plans A *strategy* comprises the long-term plans that determine the direction an organization will take to become (or remain) competitive. A strategy is determined during the strategic planning process.

An organization usually has an overall *organizational* strategy. In the past, organizational strategies were dominated by long-term financial and marketing plans, but recently long-term operations plans have dominated. Examples of organizational strategy include branding, growth (products, markets, process/vertical integration), niche market (e.g., IKEA), product differentiation (e.g., Porter Airlines), first-to-market, technology innovation, ecommerce, low cost, global selling and operations, partnership, and sustainability.

The long-term functional plans are sometimes called *functional* strategies—for example, financial strategy or marketing strategy or operations strategy. The functional strategies, if different from organizational strategy, should obviously be congruent with it.

tactics Medium-term plans used as components of a strategy.

action plan A medium- or short-term project to accomplish a specific objective, assigned to an individual, with a deadline and the resources needed.

Tactics are medium-term plans used as components of a strategy. They are more specific in nature than a strategy, and they provide guidance for determining policies and carrying out an **action plan** (a medium- or short-term project to accomplish a specific objective, assigned to an individual or a team, with a deadline and the resources needed).

It should be apparent that the overall relationship that exists from the mission/vision down to actual policies and action plans—that is, *policy deployment*—is hierarchical (i.e., top down) in

Sobeys	Mission and values:
	We want to be Canada's destination for better food by delivering on our 7 promises: • The fresher, the better, the tastier. • Save time. Eat well. Everyday. • Choose the healthy life. • We live here too. • We make sustainable attainable. • Good food is not a luxury. It's a right. • Even our guarantee is guaranteed. Source: http://www.sobeys.com/en/mission-and-values/?f=671
WestJet	Our mission:
	To enrich the lives of everyone in WestJet's world by providing safe, friendly, and affordable air travel.
	Our values:
	• Commitment to safety • Positive and passionate in everything we do • Appreciative of our people and guests • Fun, friendly, and caring • Align the interests of WestJetters with the interests of the company. • Honest, open, and keep our commitments Source: http://www.westjet.ca/guest/en/about/index.shtml
Cameco	Our vision:
	Cameco will energize the world as the global leader of fuel supply for clean-air nuclear power.
	Mission:
	Our mission is to bring the multiple benefits of nuclear energy to the world.
	Values:
	Our values guide our decisions and actions. They are: • Safety and environment • People • Integrity • Excellence Source: https://www.cameco.com/about/our-vision

TABLE 2-2

Selected company mission/vision/values statements.

nature. This is illustrated in Figure 2-3. However, a strategy should also reflect the day-to-day experience of employees (bottom up). The action plans should be consistent (i.e., fit together) and be reinforcing. They should not only improve the performance of an organization to meet its customers' needs, but also increase the organization's long-term capabilities. Note that radical changes will face resistance and should be implemented carefully.

A simple example may help put these concepts into perspective.

EXAMPLE 2-2

Lily is a high school student. She would like to live comfortably. A possible scenario for achieving her mission/vision might look something like this:

• Mission/vision: Live a good life.
• Goal: Successful career, good income.
• Strategy: Obtain a college/university degree.

• Tactics: Select a college/university and a major; decide how to finance the education.
• Action plans: Register, buy books, take courses, study, pass exams, graduate.

FIGURE 2-3 ▶

Strategic planning is hierarchical in organizations.

Based on J. H. Sheridan, "America's Best Plants: Wilson Sporting Goods," *Industry Week 241(20)*, October 19, 1992, pp. 59–62.

The following example shows the use of a goal, improvement objectives, and an action plan.

EXAMPLE 2-3 ▶

A few years ago, the management of Wilson Sporting Goods decided to become the leader in the special-order golf ball business (selling golf balls that have personalized logos). This goal was to be accomplished over a five-year period by improving quality and delivery. Specific improvement objectives were determined for each competitive priority, and these objectives were cascaded down the organization to appropriate departmental teams, where action plans were established for each needed activity. The objectives and an example of an action plan are shown in Figure 2-4.[4]

FIGURE 2-4 ▶

An example of objectives and an action plan.

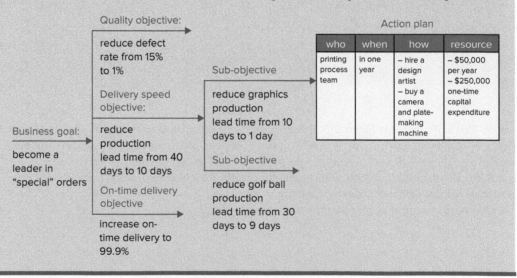

The difficulty of implementing a strategy depends on its scale (size), complexity (the parts of the organization it affects), and uncertainty (how novel it is). Powerful stakeholders should be kept informed and managed. Informal/unwritten practices also play a role. For an example of a product differentiation strategy, see the "Porter Airlines" OM in Action.

---

[4] Based on J.H. Sheridan, "America's Best Plants: Wilson Sporting Goods," *Industry Week* 241 (20), October 19, 1992, pp. 59–62.

OM in Action   www.flyporter.com

Porter Airlines

In 2006, Bob Deluce thought, "Why not use the Billy Bishop Toronto City Airport as the hub, providing a quick and hassle-free alternative for Toronto business travellers?" This small regional airport is within five minutes of downtown Toronto on an island in Lake Ontario (accessible by ferry or a pedestrian tunnel), whereas Pearson International Airport is one hour away on a busy highway.

Deluce bought the small, old airport and spent $50 million to renovate and expand it. He then bought several Bombardier Q400 Dash 8 turboprops (no jets are permitted at the airport). Their range is limited but sufficient to reach major cities around Toronto. Porter Airlines started having 10 to 15 daily scheduled flights between Toronto, Ottawa, and Montreal.

Deluce initially terminated the landing and take-off rights of Jazz, Air Canada's regional subsidiary, thus protecting his competitive advantage, the airport. However, one year later, Air Canada was given a very small number of landing/take-off slots.

To compensate for the disadvantage of turboprop airplanes (relative to jets), Porter offers a lounge with free Wi-Fi and beverages, courteous service, and leather seats with plenty of leg room and free beverages in the planes. More than 2 million travellers use Porter in a year. Now, Porter flies to more than 23 cities, most within 1,000 km of Toronto, including 8 in the United States. It has 28 planes and employs more than 1,400 people. It appears that Porter has found a way to survive in the tough airline business.

Sources: http://business.financialpost.com/news/transportation/dogfight-inside-the-decades-long-battle-over-torontos-billy-bishop-airport; https://www.flyporter.com/en-ca/about-porter/porter-experience#convenience.

Olga Gabai/Dreamstime.com

Operations Strategy

The operations function can play a proactive role in strategic planning by helping shape the operations strategy (as opposed to the reactive role of just fixing operations problems). **Operations strategy** comprises a set of well coordinated policies, objectives, and action plans, directly affecting the operations function, which is aimed at securing a long-term sustainable advantage over the competition.[5]

In order to formulate an operations strategy, the operations function has to cooperate with all of the other functions of the business to collectively monitor the external markets. For example, marketing should be aware of competitors' new product development and customers' expectations in the product markets, and engineering/R&D should be aware of new processing technologies in the technology markets.

> **operations strategy** A set of well coordinated policies, objectives, and action plans, directly affecting the operations function, which is aimed at securing a long-term sustainable advantage over the competition.

[5] C.H. Fine and A.C. Hax, "Manufacturing Strategy: A Methodology and an Illustration," *Interfaces* 15(6), November/December 1985, pp. 28–46.

The role of operations should be identified. Usually, operations' objectives/performance measures are determined in terms of competitive priorities such as cost (e.g., unit cost, labour productivity, inventory turnover), quality (e.g., percentage of products defective, cost of quality), delivery (e.g., percentage of on-time deliveries, lead time), and flexibility (e.g., response to product/quantity changes). As mentioned earlier, trade-offs must be made among these priorities because operations cannot excel in all of them simultaneously. For example, a flexible operation cannot produce the products at minimum cost.

The operations policies, objectives, and action plans can be classified into nine strategic decision categories.

Nine Strategic Decision Categories

1. *Facility.*   The number and location of facilities influence the operations and marketing strengths of the organization. In addition, for a manufacturer, a major decision is how to specialize or focus each facility:

   - *product-focused* (e.g., each plant of Procter & Gamble makes the whole of a group of products), or
   - *process-focused* (e.g., each component plant of GM makes a segment of a car).

   This decision usually depends on the economics and ease of production. A product-focused factory should be assigned similar products in terms of competitive priorities/volume and type of technology/equipment used. If more than one product group is produced in a factory, each should have its own "plant within a plant."[6]

2. *Capacity.*   This decision is related to the facility decision. Long-term capacity decisions relate to size of plants and major equipment (which affect economies of scale and unit production costs). The main issue is whether and how to change the capacity in anticipation of future demand. Capacity under-utilization or shortage affects operating/opportunity costs. Inventory can be held to address medium- and short-term capacity imbalances.

3. *Vertical integration/outsourcing.*   **Vertical integration** is ownership of a major part or the whole of a supply chain. **Outsourcing** is letting a supplier perform some of the production/service function, by buying goods or services instead of producing or providing them in-house (called insourcing). Cost, coordination, and control are the important decision factors. Operations is expected to play an important role in the supply chain.

> **vertical integration**
> Ownership of a major part or the whole of the supply chain.
>
> **outsourcing** Buying goods or services instead of producing or providing them in-house (called insourcing).

Indian operators take calls at Quatro call centre in Gurgaon on the outskirts of New Delhi. Many North American companies have outsourced their customer service and support to call centres in India in order to take advantage of communications and software support there to drive down costs. This industry in India already provides over 1 million jobs.

Terry Vine/Brand X Pictures/Getty Images RF

---

[6] W. Skinner, "The Focused Factory," *Harvard Business Review* 52(3), May/June 1974, pp. 113–121.

4. *Supplier relationship/partnership.*   The two extremes of the supplier relationship are transactional arm's length and cooperative close relationships (i.e., partnership). This decision also determines how the quality of purchased goods will be assured: either work with a supplier to supervise/control its production processes, or inspect the incoming parts. The purchasing agent's knowledge and effective performance are important for operations' strength.

5. *Product mix and new products.*   The challenge of operations management increases as the variety of products and the rate of new product introduction increase. These require flexible production systems. Products designed for easy manufacturing and assembly increase operations' strength.

6. *Production process types and technology.*   There are four generic production process types: job shop, batch flow, assembly line, and continuous flow. The product–process matrix (described in Chapter 6) can be used to relate product characteristics to production process characteristics (and technologies). The matrix also shows the important trade-offs required in production process choice. The production process type determines the appropriate technologies and degree of automation. In-house process-technology knowledge, using new/efficient technologies, and a good facility layout are important for operations' strength.

7. *Human resources.*   With the help of the personnel department, workers/staff are appraised, selected, developed/trained, motivated, promoted, and rewarded to work as a team to achieve the organization's goals. Various types of compensation and incentives can be used. Organizational learning and flexible organizational structure also play important roles in gaining competency.

8. *Quality.*   Product quality is determined during the design and production stages. Conformance to specification during production requires quality planning, control, and improvement. The tools that can be used include statistical process control and continuous improvement/Six Sigma. A major decision is whether to assign the responsibility of quality control to the workers.

9. *Operations infrastructure and systems.*   These decisions include planning and control (including forecasting, material requirements planning, and scheduling), using a software *program* for planning and control, whether to use just-in-time production, operations policies, and the production/inventory strategies used (make-to-stock, make-to-order, etc.).

Most of these nine strategic decision categories are described in detail later in the textbook. The following steps can be used to formulate an operations strategy.

Formulation of an Operations Strategy

1. Link the organizational goals (e.g., becoming a leader in an industry) to the operations strategy: determine operations requirements of the organizational goals.

2. Categorize/segment the customers into types: for example, major customers (with whom a closer relationship is desirable) and others (with whom a transactional arm's length relationship is adequate). For each category, determine which of the four competitive priorities (cost, quality, delivery, and flexibility) should be emphasized.

3. Group product lines into types: for example, classify the product lines into low volume and high volume.

4. Conduct an operations audit to determine the strengths/weaknesses of the current operations strategy in each of the nine strategic decision categories. Also, for each customer category/segment, assess the relative standing of products (relative to desired competitive priorities) against those of the most relevant competitors.

5. For a multi-plant corporation, assess the degree of focus at each plant (a focused plant is more efficient). Use the product–process matrix (described in Chapter 6) to detect the degree of congruence between a product line and its production process. For example, a low volume–high variety product line should be produced using a job shop process.

6. Develop an operations strategy and reallocate product lines to plants if necessary. For each of the nine strategic decision categories, state the objectives, policies, and action plans. Deploy these policies and action plans.

Example 2-4 illustrates the formulation of an operations strategy, and the "Visioneering" OM in Action is another application.

EXAMPLE 2-4

Rohm and Haas (R&H) is a major North American producer of specialty chemicals such as polymer emulsions used in water-based paint.[7]

In the mid-1990s, R&H was being squeezed between suppliers (petrochemical companies) and major customers such as Walmart and Home Depot. Furthermore, competitors were taking market share. R&H's selling price had remained the same for five years whereas costs were going up. In addition, the production and order fulfillment was chaotic and stressful. The 11 plants each made all of the approximately 800 products. All customers, approximately 4,000, received the same service, such as customized certificate of analysis or packaging/labelling. There was no fixed lead time; the due date was negotiated between the customer service representative (CSR) and the schedulers. The production schedule kept changing, with less than a day's notice.

To fix these problems, R&H spent $100 million on an enterprise resource planning (ERP) software, but after three years of implementation, there was no real change to its business processes. Then, it formed a management team consisting of sales, marketing, manufacturing, operations, and logistics managers, and some internal consultants. The team analyzed R&H's customer base, dividing them into four categories/tiers: (1) partners or potential partners, (2) strategically important, (3) important, and (4) others.

It was decided that the approximately 3,200 customers in Tier 4 would be supplied by three exclusive distributors and not by R&H directly. This would save CSRs and schedulers time and save production/transportation costs as larger batches to the distributors would be cheaper per unit.

Sales and marketing people interviewed Tier 1 customers to find out what service they valued most and what R&H's competitors were offering. They categorized the services, estimated their cost, and formed a matrix that related each customer tier with the service categories it would receive. For example, Tier 1 customers would receive special services such as customized packaging/labelling, Tier 2 would receive standard services, and Tier 3 would receive limited services.

Also, the team studied the demand characteristic of the approximately 800 products. The results showed that most high-volume products were ordered regularly, whereas most low-volume products were ordered irregularly. The team mathematically modelled one of the facilities and performed a simulation study to find out the effect of dedicating the chemical reactors in the facility to either high-volume or low-volume products. The results showed that the capacity of the facility would increase by 20 percent and on-time delivery would improve.

The team recommended specializing some of the plants/reactors to make the high-volume products and the others to make the low-volume products. Also, the high-volume products, whose demand can be forecasted accurately, are to be made to stock, with a lead time of two days. On the other hand, it was decided not to carry any stocks of the low-volume products. These are made to order with a lead time of seven days, and a minimum order quantity equal to the production batch size. Tier 1 customers have accepted the increase in lead time for low-volume products because delivery time is certain.

As a result of these changes, R&H saved millions of dollars, increased its production capacity, and improved its on-time delivery rates. Rohm and Haas is now part of Dow Chemical.

Source: A. J. D'Alessandro and A. Baveja, "Divide and Conquer: Rohm and Haas' Response to a Changing Specialty Chemicals Market," *Interfaces* 30(6), November/December 2000, pp. 1–16.

Generic Operations Strategies Generic operations strategies are theme-based operations improvement programs and plans, such as just-in-time production and total quality management or continuous improvement. These are generic because they have been frequently used irrespective of the market conditions and competitive situation. However, if every company in an industry pursues the same generic strategy, every company becomes more efficient and/or more effective without gaining competitive advantage. Therefore, these are, strictly speaking, not strategies, though they are commonly considered so.

[7] A. J. D'Alessandro and A. Baveja, "Divide and Conquer: Rohm and Haas' Response to a Changing Specialty Chemicals Market," *Interfaces* 30(6), November/December 2000, pp. 1–16.

OM in Action   http://viscor.com/PC/index.htm

Visioneering

Visioneering Corp (VC) of Toronto is engaged in the extremely competitive LED and fluorescent lighting business. At one time, the firm manufactured standard 4- and 8-foot fluorescent lights. But the imports of cheap products from China caused a decline in its revenues. VC's management realized that these competitors relied on mass production of standard items, which were shipped in ocean containers and took months to arrive. As a result, VC's strategy was changed to focus on building low-volume nonstandard bulkier products on short notice. VC invested in high-precision, programmable machines that reduced labour cost, shortened changeover times, and improved quality. VC's lead time to its customers has been reduced to a few days.

Courtesy of Visioneering, www.viscor.com

Source: Based on C. Piper, "Reversing the Tide in Canadian Manufacturing," *Ivey Business Journal Online* 72.5 (Sep/Oct 2008).

The popular generic operations strategies have been changing over time. To illustrate, the generic operations strategies some Japanese manufacturing companies have used since the Second World War are:

- *Low labour-cost strategy.* Immediately after the war, they exploited the (then) inexpensive labour pool.

- *Scale-based strategy.* During the 1960s, they used capital-intensive methods to achieve higher labour productivity and lower unit costs.

- *Focused factories strategy.* During the 1970s, they used smaller factories that focused on narrow product lines to take advantage of specialization and achieve higher quality.

- *Flexible factories strategy.* During the 1980s, they reduced the time needed to add new product and process designs. They used flexible equipment that allowed volume and design changes, as well as product variety. They also continued to stress quality.

- *Continuous improvement strategy.* In the 1990s, they introduced new product features and continuous improvement of both products and processes.

Another generic strategy used by some organizations in the 1990s was **business process re-engineering** (BPR). This is a radical process redesign that involves process reorientation, breaking up functional silos, and integrating operations into customer-focused processes. In Canada, Nova Scotia Power was quick to adopt BPR.

Another generic strategy related to BPR occurred just before the year 2000, when many organizations changed their legacy computer systems and installed enterprise resource planning (ERP) software. ERP automates business processes and can reduce cost and data entry errors, but requires data to be entered in a central database as soon as a transaction occurs anywhere in the organization.

We will briefly describe the following two generic operations strategies that are still popular.

A **quality-based strategy** focuses on improving the quality of an organization's goods or services. Quality is a factor in both attracting and retaining customers. Quality-based strategies may be motivated by a variety of factors. They may reflect an effort to overcome an image of poor quality, a desire to catch up with the competition, a desire to maintain an existing image of high quality, or some combination of these and other factors. Interestingly enough, quality-based strategies can be part of another strategy such as cost reduction, productivity improvement, or time reduction, all of which benefit from higher quality.

business process re-engineering Radical process redesign that involves process reorientation, breaking up functional silos, and integrating operations into customer-focused processes.

quality-based strategy Strategy that focuses on quality of an organization's goods and services.

Nova Scotia Power, just after privatization in the early 1990s, was one of the first companies in Canada to implement BPR. One of the changes was combining the jobs of meter reader, meter installer (who replaced broken meters), and bill collector (who disconnected service because of an overdue account). The new customer service field representative (CSFR) required technical training to work with live electricity! Overall BPR initiatives allowed NS Power to reduce its employment by 400 jobs. However, the CSFR job no longer exists. NS Power has now grown into an international power company called Emera.

David Wei/Alamy Stock Images

Sources: J. Helms-Mills, *Making Sense of Organization Change*, Routledge, 2003; L. R. Comeau, "Re-Engineering for a More Competitive Tomorrow," *Canadian Business Review*, 21(4), 1994, pp. 51–52.

Recently, some organizations are using a quality improvement initiative called Six Sigma, which employs more advanced statistical methods than continuous improvement, as well as the BPR approach. Chapter 9 and Chapter 10 cover more details of quality and Six Sigma.

A **time-based strategy** focuses on reducing the time required to accomplish various activities (e.g., develop new products and market them, respond to a change in customer demand). By doing so, organizations seek to gain a competitive advantage over rivals that take more time to accomplish the same tasks. Also, costs are generally less, productivity is higher, and quality tends to be higher. Just-in-time production is a special case.

An example of a Canadian company using a time-based strategy is StandardAero, based in Winnipeg. By redesigning its processes into U-shaped cells, and controlling the activities using a visual system, StandardAero performs repairs/overhauls of small airplane engines in only two weeks, much faster than its competitors. More on just-in-time and lean production appears in Chapter 15.

Minimizing operating costs through becoming more efficient is a common strategy for most organizations. A related topic is productivity, which we discuss in the next section.

> **time-based strategy**
> Strategy that focuses on reduction of time needed to accomplish tasks.

(L03) Productivity

One of the primary responsibilities of an operations manager is to achieve *productive use* of an organization's resources. The term *productivity* is used to describe this. Productivity measures output (goods and services) per unit input (machine, labour, materials, energy) used to produce them. It is usually expressed as the ratio of output to input:

$$\text{Productivity} = \frac{\text{Output}}{\text{Input}} \tag{2-1}$$

A productivity ratio can be computed for a worker, a department, an organization, or an entire country.

A related measure is the rate of *productivity growth*. Productivity growth is the increase in productivity from the previous period to the current period relative to the productivity in the previous period. Thus,

$$\text{Productivity growth} = \frac{\text{Current period productivity} - \text{Previous period productivity}}{\text{Previous period productivity}} \qquad (2\text{-}2)$$

For example, if productivity increased from 80 to 84, the growth rate would be

$$\frac{84 - 80}{80} = 0.05 \text{ or } 5\%$$

Productivity growth is a key factor in a country's standard of living. Productivity increases add value to the economy while keeping price inflation in check.

Measuring Productivity

Productivity measures can be based on a single input (*partial* productivity), on more than one input (*multi-factor* productivity), or on all inputs (*total* productivity). Table 2-3 lists different types of inputs for these productivity measures. The choice of productivity measure depends primarily on the purpose of the measurement. If the purpose is to track improvements in labour productivity, then labour becomes the obvious input.

Partial	$\dfrac{\text{Output}}{\text{Labour}}$	$\dfrac{\text{Output}}{\text{Machine}}$	$\dfrac{\text{Output}}{\text{Material}}$	$\dfrac{\text{Output}}{\text{Energy}}$
Multi-factor	$\dfrac{\text{Output}}{\text{Labour} + \text{Machine}}$		$\dfrac{\text{Output}}{\text{Labour} + \text{Material} + \text{Energy}}$	
Total	$\dfrac{\text{Goods or services produced}}{\text{All inputs used to produce them}}$			

◀ **TABLE 2-3**

Different types of inputs for productivity measures.

Partial measures are often of greatest use in operations management. Table 2-4 provides some examples of partial productivity measures.

Labour productivity	Units of output per labour hour Units of output per shift Value-added per labour hour Dollar value of output per labour hour
Machine productivity	Units of output per machine hour Dollar value of output per machine hour
Material productivity	Units of output per unit material input, for example, kilometres per gallon. *Note*: Litres per 100 km is the inverse of the productivity measure, but it is still used to measure productivity. Dollar value of output per unit material input
Energy productivity	Units of output per kilowatt-hour Dollar value of output per kilowatt-hour

◀ **TABLE 2-4**

Some examples of partial productivity measures.

The unit of output used in a productivity measure depends on the type of job performed. The following are different examples of labour productivity:

$$\frac{\text{Square metres of carpet installed}}{\text{Labour hours}} = \text{Square metres of carpet installed per labour hour}$$

$$\frac{\text{Number of offices cleaned}}{\text{Number of shifts}} = \text{Number of offices cleaned per shift}$$

$$\frac{\text{Board feet of lumber cut}}{\text{Number of weeks}} = \text{Board feet of lumber cut per week (Board foot} = \text{Volume of lumber that covers 1 foot} \times 1 \text{ foot} \times 1 \text{ inch)}$$

Similar examples can be listed for *machine productivity* (e.g., the number of pieces produced by a machine per hour).

EXAMPLE 2-5

Determine the productivity for these cases:

a. Four workers installed 720 square metres of carpet in eight hours.

b. A machine produced 68 usable (i.e., good quality) pieces of a part in two hours.

SOLUTION

a. $\text{Productivity} = \dfrac{\text{Square metres of carpet installed}}{\text{Labour hours worked}}$

$= \dfrac{720 \text{ square metres}}{4 \text{ workers} \times 8 \text{ hours}}$

$= \dfrac{720 \text{ square metres}}{32 \text{ worker hours}}$

$= 22.5 \text{ square metres/worker hour}$

b. $\text{Productivity} = \dfrac{\text{Usable pieces}}{\text{Production time}}$

$= \dfrac{68 \text{ pieces}}{2 \text{ hours}}$

$= 34 \text{ pieces/hour}$

The inputs in a multi-factor productivity measure should have a common unit of measurement, such as dollars. For example:

$$\frac{\text{Quantity of production}}{\text{Labour cost (\$)} + \text{Materials cost (\$)} + \text{Machine overhead (\$)}} \tag{2-3}$$

EXAMPLE 2-6

Determine the multi-factor productivity for the combined inputs of labour, materials, and machine time using the following data:

Output: 7,040 units

Input costs:

Labour (line and support staff, including benefits): $1,000

Materials: $520

Machine overhead: $2,000

SOLUTION

$\dfrac{\text{Multi-factor}}{\text{productivity}} = \dfrac{\text{Output}}{\text{Labour} + \text{Materials} + \text{Machine overhead}}$

$= \dfrac{7,040 \text{ units}}{\$1,000 + \$520 + \$2,000}$

$= 2 \text{ units/dollar input}$

Even though labour cost as a proportion of total cost has been decreasing in manufacturing, labour productivity is still the main measure used to gauge the performance of individuals, processes, and plants. In addition, its use in services has been increasing as services are employing more workers.

We should not confuse productivity with efficiency. Efficiency is a narrower concept that means getting the most out of a *fixed* set of resources; productivity is a broader concept that means better use of overall resources. For example, an efficiency perspective on mowing a lawn, if we have a hand mower, would focus on the best way to use the hand mower (e.g., follow a route that minimizes backtracking); a productivity perspective would include the possibility of using a power mower.

Labour productivity and average operation time for a task are inversely related. For example, if it takes an average of five minutes to produce one unit, this implies a productivity of (60 minutes per hour)/(5 minutes per unit) = 12 units per hour.

Productivity measures are useful on a number of levels. For an individual, process, department, or organization, productivity measures can be used to track performance *over time*. This allows managers to judge performance and to decide where improvements are needed. For example, if a manager finds that productivity has slipped in a certain area, the manager can examine the factors used to compute productivity to determine what has changed and then devise a means of improving productivity in subsequent periods. Labour productivity is sometimes used in labour wage negotiations where wage raises are tied to productivity growth.

Total productivity and profit of a company are directly related: Total productivity = Revenue/Total cost, whereas Profit = Revenue − Total cost.

Productivity measures can also be used to judge the performance of an entire industry or a country as a whole. These productivity measures are *aggregate* measures.

In essence, productivity measurements serve as scorecards of the efficient use of resources. Business leaders are concerned with productivity as it relates to *competitiveness*: If two companies both have the same level of output, but one requires less input because of higher productivity, that one will be able to charge a lower price and consequently increase its share of the market, or it might elect to charge the same price, thereby reaping a greater profit.

Productivity Measurement of Services

Service productivity measurement is more problematic than manufacturing. However, in services where there is also a large goods component, a measure of output is not hard to find. For example, in the transport (hauling) industry, ton-miles is used; in the power industry, kilowatt-hours is used; and in the communication industry, number of phone calls is used. In other situations. it is more difficult to measure output because it is partly intangible (e.g., state of health of a patient), it involves intellectual activities (e.g., learning operations management), or the output has a high degree of variability (e.g., getting legal advice). Because the outcome is usually an improved state for the customer, and customers start off in different states, the inputs can also be variable. Think about medical diagnosis, surgery, consulting, legal services, education, hotels and restaurants, and recreation.

As an illustration, consider the "Examples of Health Care Productivity Measurement" OM in Action, which considers productivity measurement for treating/managing four common diseases.

Sometimes measures of output used in services could result in misleading conclusions about productivity growth. For example, a hospital's aggregate output is usually measured by the number of patient days of care provided. Suppose that the hospital becomes more productive, resulting in faster patient discharge. This reduces the number of patient days, which will reduce the productivity measure of the hospital!

Factors That Affect Productivity

Numerous factors affect productivity. Generally, they are methods and management, equipment and technology, and labour. Consider a student who plans to type a lengthy term paper. The student is an average typist and can turn out about three pages per hour. How could the student increase her productivity

A skilled carpet weaver takes approximately one year to weave a 1.7 m by 3.2 m area carpet (this carpet is valued more than $10,000). The Staubli Alpha 500 carpet weaving machine, with a maximum of 33,000 pile threads, can weave virtually the same 1.7 m by 3.2 m area carpet (with the same intricate pattern) in less than 10 minutes (this carpet is valued at less than $500).

Klam10839/Dreamstime.com

Courtesy of Stäubli International AG

(i.e., turn out more pages per hour)? One way would be to enroll in a short course to improve typing skills (labour). Another way might be to replace her old computer with a more expensive computer and word-processing package (equipment and technology). Still other productivity improvements might be achieved through improving organization and preparation for the actual typing (methods and management). The incentive of receiving a good grade and the pride of doing a good job might also be important. The point is that all these factors are potential sources of productivity, not only for typing papers but also for any kind of work, and it is generally up to the manager to see that they are fully exploited.

OM in Action

Examples of Health Care Productivity Measurement

Diabetes, the imbalance of blood sugar, has no cure. The patient has to monitor his diet and blood sugar, and possibly use insulin to restore it to normal range. Hospital visits are usually confined to outpatient care, but if not in check, diabetes results in serious complications that require inpatient care in hospitals. The output of a health care system can be measured as quality-adjusted life years, (i.e., the expected life years minus complication rates multiplied by their impact). The complication rate depends on clearly identifying serious cases and assisting them intensively. The input cost is measured as cost of staff (doctors, nurses, etc.) at hospitals for both outpatient and inpatient needs (which depend on staffing level and length of stay), plus cost of insulin. Cost of diagnosis (blood test) is not significant; neither is the cost of continuous monitoring of blood sugar (usually self-paid).

Gallstones develop in the gallbladder, and result in abdominal pain. If the case is serious enough, the only treatment is surgery to remove the gallbladder. Then, the patient is cured for life. Because the seriousness of this disease is subjective, the choice of surgery is also subjective. There are two types of surgery: traditional surgery involving opening the stomach, and laparoscopic surgery (which results in only three small incisions). Using laparoscopic surgery will result in a considerably shorter hospital stay, which reduces the input cost (cost of the surgery and hospital stay) significantly. The output, quality-adjusted life years, depends on the timing of the decision to go for surgery.

Breast cancer is the most common type of cancer among women. The only treatment is removing the malignant lump, and likely the whole breast, before the cancer spreads. This requires identifying it first. The screening is done by physical exams and mammography. If the initial test indicates possible cancer, a biopsy is performed. Biopsy and surgery can be performed together in one step, or sequentially in two steps. The two-step procedure is less costly because (a) biopsy can be done on an outpatient basis, and (b) some biopsies indicate no cancer, thus making the second step redundant. Cost of screening and diagnosis can be significantly reduced if only women 50 years of age or older are targeted. Output can be measured in percentage of diagnosed patients who survive at least five years. This depends on how early cancer is detected.

Lung cancer is fatal in approximately 25 percent of the cases. The diagnosis may use expensive CT scanners. If it is treatable, surgery and chemotherapy are used. Chemotherapy is usually done on an outpatient basis. Output can be measured by a five-year survival rate. Input costs include cost of diagnosis, surgery, hospital stay, and chemotherapy.

Source: M. N. Bailey et al., "Health Care Productivity," *Brookings Papers on Economic Activity,* 1997, pp. 143–202.

Courtesy of Hyundai Motor Group

Productivity can be enhanced by the use of robotic equipment. Robots can operate for long periods with consistent precision and high speed.

A commonly held misconception is that workers are the main determinant of productivity. According to that theory, the route to productivity gains involves getting employees to work harder. However, the fact is that many productivity gains in the past have come from *equipment and technological* improvements. Familiar examples include machine automation and computers, text processing, spreadsheets, CAD software, bar codes and scanners, and Internet and email.

Effective management and methods result in better design, planning, and operating decisions, standardizing and improving processes, improving quality, reducing waste (as in just-in-time production), providing better layout, and using technology, equipment, and labour more effectively and efficiently.

Summary

- Competition is the driving force in many companies. They compete by emphasizing one or more competitive priorities: cost, quality, flexibility, and delivery (reliability and speed).
- Customers' purchasing criteria are: price, quality, variety, and timeliness.
- To develop an effective strategy for an organization, it is essential to determine the key purchasing criteria of its customers, and to identify which are order qualifiers and which are order winners.
- Strategies are plans for directing the organization to achieve its mission/vision/goals.
- Mission/vision is what the company wants to achieve, its products and services, and its markets (now and in the future, respectively).
- Organizations generally have overall strategies for the entire organization and functional strategies for each of the functional areas. Functional strategies are narrower in scope and should be linked to overall strategy.
- An operations strategy is a coordinated set of policies, objectives, and action plans for the operations function.
- An operations strategy can be classified into nine strategic decision categories: facility, capacity, vertical integration/outsourcing, supplier relationship/partnership, production process types and technology, product mix and new products, human resources, quality, and operations infrastructure and systems.
- Quality-based and time-based strategies are among the most widely used generic operations strategies.
- Productivity is a measure of productive use of resources. Organizations want higher productivity because it yields higher profits and helps them become more competitive.
- Productivity is measured as output/input.
- The most common productivity measure is labour productivity (e.g., number of units produced per hour by a worker).
- Productivity of services is harder to measure because outputs are usually intangible and variable, and inputs are variable too.
- Factors affecting productivity include methods and management, equipment and technology, and labour.

Key Terms

action plan	order qualifiers	tactics
business process re-engineering	order winners	time-based strategy
competitive priorities	outsourcing	values
competitiveness	productivity	vertical integration
key purchasing criteria	quality-based strategy	vision
mission	strategic planning	
operations strategy	strategy	

Solved Problems

Problem 1

A company that processes fruits and vegetables is able to produce 400 cases of canned peaches in one-half hour with four workers. What is its labour productivity?

Solution

$$\text{Labour productivity} = \frac{\text{Quantity produced}}{\text{Labour hours}}$$

$$= \frac{400 \text{ cases}}{4 \text{ workers} \times 1/2 \text{ hour}}$$

$$= 200 \text{ cases per worker hour}$$

Problem 2

A wrapping paper company produced 2,000 rolls of paper in one day. Labour cost was $160, material cost was $50, and overhead was $320. Determine the multi-factor productivity.

Solution

$$\text{Multi-factor productivity} = \frac{\text{Quantity produced}}{\text{Labour cost} + \text{Material cost} + \text{Overhead}}$$

$$= \frac{2,000 \text{ rolls}}{\$160 + \$50 + \$320}$$

$$= 3.77 \text{ rolls per dollar input}$$

Problem 3

A pottery manufacturer that sells to flower shops and department stores had the following output and costs during the last three weeks. Average labour cost is $10 per hour during regular time (first 40 hours of a week) and $15 per hour during overtime (any hours in excess of 40 hours a week), and pottery clay cost was $2/kg. Calculate the multi-factor productivity for each week and comment on the results.

Week	1	2	3
Units produced	1,000	1,500	1,500
No. of workers	2	2	3
Hours per week per worker	40	60	40
Material (kg)	150	250	300

Solution

Multi-factor productivity = Units produced/(Labour cost + Material cost)

Week	1	2	3
Units produced	1,000	1,500	1,500
Labour cost	2(40)($10) = $800	$800 + 2(20)($15) = $1,400	3(40)($10) = $1,200
Material cost	150($2) = $300	250($2) = $500	300($2) = $600
Total cost	$1,100	$1,900	$1,800
Multi-factor productivity (pots per $ input)	1,000/$1,100 = 0.91	1,500/$1,900 = 0.79	1,500/$1,800 = 0.83

Multi-factor productivity decreased as overtime was used in week 2, but increased as another worker was added in week 3 and no overtime was used. However, material cost increased in week 3 due to mistakes of the new worker.

Problem 4

A health club has two employees who work on lead generation. Each employee works 40 hours a week, and is paid $20 an hour. Each employee identifies an average of 400 possible leads a week from a list of 8,000 names. Approximately 10 percent of the leads become members and pay a one-time fee of $100. Material costs are $130 per week, and overhead costs are $1,000 per week. Calculate the multi-factor productivity for this operation in fees generated per dollar of input.

Solution

$$\text{MFP} = \frac{(\text{Possible leads})(\text{No. of workers})(\text{Fee})(\text{Conversion percentage})}{\text{Labour cost} + \text{Material cost} + \text{Overhead cost}}$$

$$= \frac{(400)(2)(\$100)(0.10)}{2(40)(\$20) + \$130 + \$1,000} = \frac{\$8,000}{\$2,730} = 2.93$$

Discussion and Review Questions

Note: An asterisk indicates that a question or problem may be more challenging.

LO1 **1.** How do you use the four key purchasing criteria personally when buying goods and services? Give an example.

LO1 **2.** Give an example for each of the four competitive priorities.

LO1 **3.** Explain the difference between order qualifiers and order winners. Give an example.

LO1 *4. Explain how a company can gain competitive advantage.

LO2 **5.** What is strategic planning and why is it important?

LO2 **6.** Briefly list the steps used in strategic planning.

LO2 **7.** Describe what an operations strategy is.

LO2 **8.** List the nine strategic decision categories.

LO2 **9.** Describe how an operations strategy is formulated.

LO2 **10.** Give an example of a policy and an action plan.

LO2 **11.** Explain the term *time-based strategy* and give two examples of companies using it.

LO2 *12. A few years ago, Boeing's strategy was focused on its 787 Dreamliner mid-to-large size plane and its ability to fly into smaller, non-hub airports. Rival European Airbus's strategy was focused on its very large A380 plane. What assumption about future demand for air travel was each company making?

LO3 **13.** What is productivity and why is it important?

LO3 **14.** Name some factors that can affect productivity and give an example of each that should improve productivity.

LO3 **15.** A typical Japanese automobile manufacturing plant in North America produces more cars with fewer workers than a typical Big Three North American plant.[8] In other words, total manufacturing labour hours per vehicle (body stamping, engine, transmission, and assembly hours) are lower for Japanese transplants (30 vs. 33 hours). What are some possible explanations for this?

LO3 **16.** A century ago, most people worked in agriculture, but now less than 4 percent of workers work in agriculture in Canada. Yet due to mechanization and automation, the agricultural output is much more now than a century ago. The majority of people now work in other industries. Also, the standard of living is much higher now than a century ago. Discuss the following statement: "If productivity increases, fewer workers will be needed."

LO3 **17.** Explain the difference between productivity and efficiency.

LO3 **18.** Give two reasons that productivity measurement in health care (e.g., treatment of diabetes) is difficult.

LO1 **19.** Who are IKEA's target customers?

LO1 **20.** Give an example of Amazon's customer service.

LO1 **21.** What purchasing criteria (price, quality, variety, and timeliness) are important for online shoppers?

LO2 **22.** Give an example of what Nova Scotia Power did as part of its business process re-engineering.

Taking Stock

LO2 **1.** Who needs to be involved in formulating organizational strategy?

LO1 **2.** Name some of the competitive trade-offs that might arise in a fast-food restaurant.

3. How does technology improve each of these?

LO1 **a.** Competitiveness.

LO3 **b.** Productivity.

LO2 **4.** How can ethics be included in strategic planning? (*Hint:* See http://www.scu.edu/ethics/practicing/focusareas/business/strategic-plan.html.)

Critical Thinking Exercise

LO3 A company has two manufacturing plants: one in Canada, and another overseas. Both produce the same product. However, their labour productivity figures are quite different. The analyst thinks that this is because the Canadian plant uses more automated equipment for production while the overseas plant uses a higher percentage of labour. Explain how that factor can cause labour productivity measures to be misleading. Is there another way to compare the two plants that would be more meaningful?

[8] See, for example, http://www.autonews.com/article/20080605/OEM01/306059997/harbour-report:
-chrysler-toyota-tie-for-2007-efficiency-title

Experiential Learning Exercises

LO1 **1.** Select one store that you shop at regularly. What advantage does this store have over its competitors that causes you to shop there? Try to use a purchasing criterion or competitive priority given in the chapter.

LO2 **2.** Name one of your personal goals. Determine a plan to reach it (this is the strategy).

LO2 **3.** Pick an organization and determine one of its goals and the associated strategy. (*Hint:* Its goal may be discerned from its mission/vision statement. Its strategy may be discerned from its action plans.)

Internet Exercises

LO2 **1.** Find the mission/vision/goals/strategy of a company. Try to relate them to the concepts of this chapter.

LO1 **2.** Visit http://www.timbuk2.com/. What is Timbuk2's competitive priority?

LO1 & 2 **3.** View McDonald's "Made for You" video at http://bevideos .mhhe.com/business/video_library/0072917776/swf /Clip_08.html and answer the following questions:
   a. What competitive priority is McDonald's trying to maintain (according to the video)?
   b. What goal and associated strategy/actions is McDonald's pursuing, according to the video?

LO2 **4.** Visit http://www.jiffylube.ca/about/historyandmission.aspx and answer the following questions:
   a. What market niche does Jiffy Lube fill?
   b. What is its competitive priority?

LO1 & 2 **5.** Visit http://www.canadapost.ca/cpo/mc/assets/pdf/aboutus/5 _en.pdf and answer the following questions:
   a. Why is Canada Post in trouble financially? Give two reasons.
   b. Does Canada Post have a competitive priority? Briefly explain.
   c. What are four action plans aimed at reducing Canada Post's operating costs?

Problems

LO3 **1.** A company produced 300 standard bookcases last week using seven workers, and 240 standard bookcases this week using five workers. In which period was labour productivity higher? Explain.

LO3 **2.** The manager of a crew that installs carpets has tracked the crew's output over the past several weeks, obtaining these figures:

Week	Crew Size	Square Metres Installed
1	4	960
2	3	702
3	4	968
4	2	500
5	3	696
6	2	500

Calculate the labour productivity for each week. On the basis of your calculations, what can you conclude about crew size and productivity?

LO3 **3.** Calculate the multi-factor productivity measure for each week below. What do the productivity figures suggest? Assume 40-hour weeks and an hourly wage rate of $12. Overhead is 1.5 times weekly labour cost. Material cost is $6 per kilogram. Selling price is $140 per unit.

Week	Output (units)	Workers	Material (kg)
1	300	6	45
2	338	7	46
3	322	7	46
4	354	8	48

LO3 **4.** A company that makes shopping carts for supermarkets and other stores recently purchased some new equipment that reduces the labour content of the jobs needed to produce the shopping carts. Prior to buying the new equipment, the company used four workers, who produced an average of 80 carts per hour. Labour cost was $10 per hour and machine cost was $40 per hour. With the new equipment, it was possible to transfer one of the workers to another department. Machine cost increased by $10 per hour while output increased by four carts per hour.
   a. Calculate labour productivity before and after the new equipment. Use carts per worker per hour as the measure of labour productivity.
   b. Calculate the multi-factor productivity before and after the new equipment. Use carts per dollar cost (labour plus machine) as the measure.
   c. Comment on the changes in productivity according to the two measures. Which one do you believe is more pertinent for this situation?

LO3 **5.** An operation has a 10 percent scrap rate. As a result, only 82 good pieces per hour are produced. What is the potential increase in labour productivity that could be achieved by eliminating the scrap?

LO3 **6.** A manager checked production records and found that a worker produced 160 units while working 40 hours. In the previous week, the same worker produced 138 units while working 36 hours. Calculate the labour productivity growth. Explain.

LO3 * **7.** Teradyne Connection Systems (now part of Amphenol) made "backplanes" (large printed circuit-board assemblies) for communication and storage devices. A few years ago, the company converted its production process from batch into assembly line. It also used computers to assist the workers at workstations. As a result, productivity shot up. The site manager, Mark Galvin, said: "Operators made 300 backplanes in seven days using three shifts by the batch process (i.e., seven days, 24 hours a day). Later, they assembled 500 backplanes in five days using just two shifts with the new assembly-line approach (i.e., five days, 16 hours a day)." Assuming that the same number of workers worked during each shift, and before and after the conversion, what was the percentage growth in labour productivity?

LO3 **8.** A land title search office had a staff of three, each working eight hours per day (for a total payroll cost of $480/day), and overhead costs of $300 per day. This office processed an average of seven titles each day. Then, the office purchased a computerized title-search system that allowed the processing of an average of 12 titles per day. Although the staff, work hours, and pay were the same, the overhead costs went up to $600 per day.

    a. Calculate the labour productivity in the old and the new systems. How much (in percentage) did the labour productivity grow?

    b. Calculate the multi-factor productivity in the old and the new systems. How much (in percentage) did the multi-factor productivity grow?

    c. Which productivity measure is more appropriate for the land title search office?

LO3 **9.** When Henry Ford introduced moving assembly lines in his Ford Motor Company plants in 1913, the productivity soared.[9] An example of this is the coil line, an electrical component that makes high voltage for ignition. Before, a skilled worker took approximately 20 minutes to make a coil from start to finish. After an assembly line was set up and the job was divided into 29 different tasks performed by 29 workers, it took only approximately 13 minutes to assemble one coil. (*Note:* Because workers work simultaneously, approximately every 0.5 minute a coil is produced.)

    a. Calculate the labour productivity before and after the conversion into an assembly line.

    b. Calculate the percentage increase in labour productivity due to the assembly line.

LO3 **10.** **(i)** One person using a hammer will take five days to nail new shingles onto the roof of a 300 m^2 house.

    (ii) Two people using one hammer but working together (one holds a shingle, the other swings the hammer) will take two days to do the same job.

    (iii) One person using a nail gun will take one day to do the same job.

    a. Define a labour productivity measure and determine its value for each of the above cases.

    b. Calculate the percentage increase in productivity due to method improvement from (i) to (ii).

    c. Calculate the percentage increase in productivity due to technology from (i) to (iii).

LO3 **11.** Southwest Tube[10] (now called Webco Industries) is a fabricator of specialty tubes used in boilers and other equipment. Southwest buys the tubes in long segments and cuts, bends, cold draws, and welds the pieces to make what is needed for the products. A few years ago, Southwest Tube was facing tough competition. The prices were falling while the costs were rising. To improve productivity, consultants were brought in. They pointed out problems with labour turnover, absenteeism, weak supervision, staffing mismatch, lack of performance goals, and a dislike for the weekly rotating schedule as causes of the problem. One of the solutions tried, in addition to other improvements, was changing the work schedule to four 12-hour days followed by three days off. The productivity seemed to improve gradually. To ascertain this, the following data for two physically demanding work centres were collected starting the year before the change in work schedule.

Question: Has workers' productivity in the two work centres increased? Explain.

	Cold Draw Department			Weld Mill Department	
	Labour	**Output**		**Labour**	**Output**
Year	(1,000 hr)	(1,000 ft)	Year	(1,000 hr)	(1,000 ft)
0	228	18,269	0	132	22,434
1	234	19,576	1	157	34,777
2	183	17,633	2	102	26,715
3	150	18,870	3	77	25,227

LO3 ***12.** The following data (all in billion $) were the sales and profit of Hudson's Bay Company during a three-year period.

HBC	3	2	1
Total sales & revenue	7.1	7.3	7.3
EBIT	0.13	0.17	0.18

EBIT = Earnings before interest and tax
Hint: Inputs = Total cost = Total sales & revenue – EBIT

The following data (all in billion $) were the sales, cost of sales (which equals cost of goods sold), and operating and overhead expenses of Walmart during the same three-year period:

Walmart	3	2	1
Net sales	285	256	230
Cost of sales (COS)	220	199	178
Operating, selling, general & admin costs (OSGA)	51	45	40

Hint: Inputs = Total cost = COS + OSGA

---

[9] J.C. Wood and M.C. Wood, eds., *Henry Ford: Critical Evaluations in Business and Management*, London: Routledge, 2003.

[10] J.M. Shirley and T.M. Box, "Productivity Gains at Southwest Tube," Production and Inventory Management Journal, Fourth Quarter 1987, 28(4), pp. 57–60. Reprinted with permission of the APICS. Also see http://www.webcotube.com/

Calculate an appropriate measure of productivity for each company and compare. Which company was more productive? Explain.

 *13. The following data (all in billions of dollars) were the sales and costs (excluding selling and general and administrative costs) of McDonald's for company-operated restaurants (i.e., excluding franchise restaurants) during a three-year period.

   a. Calculate the labour productivity (in dollars of sales over dollars of payroll and benefits costs) and its growth over time. Interpret your results.

   b. Calculate the multi-factor productivity (in dollars of sales over dollars of all operating costs given) and its growth over time. Interpret your results.

McDonald's	1	2	3
Sales	16.6	16.6	15.5
Operating costs food & paper	5.5	5.9	5.2
Payroll & benefits	4.3	4.3	4.0
Occupancy (lease, etc)	3.9	3.8	3.5

 *14. The following data were the production of potash (KCl), in 1,000 tonne units, and number of active mine-site employees for two mine/mill facilities of the Potash Corp (of Saskatchewan) during a four-year period.

   Calculate the labour productivity (in 1,000 tonnes per employee per year) and its changes over time for each facility, and interpret your results (over time and across the two facilities).

	Lanigan		Rocanville	
Year	Production	Employees	Production	Employees
1	2,025	364	1,833	328
2	2,023	378	2,573	340
3	1,471	402	1,897	343
4	1,907	441	2,647	354

 15. Frank Gilbreth is the "father" of motion study. One of the first operations he studied was bricklaying. He noticed that there was unnecessary stooping, walking, and reaching. Also some bricks were damaged, which required the bricklayer to inspect each brick and find the better side before laying it. Stooping per brick laid was once for the mortar, and another for the brick. Gilbreth designed a non-stooping scaffolding platform that was raised by a lifting jack as work progressed up the wall so that the mortar and bricks were always at easy reach of the bricklayer. The worker could easily pick up a brick in one hand and mortar in the other. Motions per brick were reduced from 18 to 5, and average time went down from 29 seconds per brick laid to 10 seconds per brick laid. Calculate the labour productivity before and after the improvement, and the percentage of increase.

 16. A company offers identity-theft protection. It obtains client leads from banks. Three employees work 40 hours a week on the leads, at a pay rate of $25 per hour per employee. Each employee identifies an average of 3,000 potential leads a week from a list of 5,000. An average of 4 percent actually sign up for the service, paying a one-time fee of $70. Material costs are $1,000 per week, and overhead costs are $9,000 per week. Calculate the multi-factor productivity for this operation in fees generated per dollar of input.

 17. The following are some of the operating performance indicators used by Canadian Pacific Railway (CPR).[11] Determine an appropriate measure of CPR's labour (employee) productivity using some of the following indicators, and calculate it for each year of the 2014–2016 period. Comment on its pattern over time.

Performance Indicator	2014	2015	2016
Gross ton-miles (millions)	272,862	263,344	242,694
Train miles (thousands)	36,252	34,064	30,373
Average train length (feet)	6,682	6,935	7,217
Total employees (average)	14,604	13,858	12,082

 18. A human carpet weaver takes 4,000 hours to weave a 3.6 m by 6 m area carpet, whereas a carpet weaving machine can weave the same carpet in half an hour. Calculate their respective productivity and compare.

[11] http://s21.q4cdn.com/736796105/files/doc_financials/Annual-Report/2016/March-9/CP-Annual-Report-2016.pdf, p. 63.

Q MINI-CASE

Canadian Pacific Railway

Canadian Pacific Railway (CPR) is one of the two major railways in Canada and its history goes as far back as Canada itself does. However, it is second to Canadian National Railway (CN) in terms of size, and was having a hard time competing with CN before 2012. In 2012, a major institutional investor, unhappy with its performance, removed its head and some of its directors through a proxy contest, and brought in Hunter Harrison (the ex-CEO of CN) as the new CEO, despite a legal challenge by CN.

In less than six months, Harrison turned CPR around by accomplishing the following tasks:

a. Closed four of the five hump yards (classification yards using gravity) in Toronto, Winnipeg, Calgary, and Chicago; combined the pair of inter-modal yards in each of Chicago and Toronto into a larger one; converted the Winnipeg yard to a local switching yard; and closed Milwaukee inter-modal yard.

b. Increased train speed by 15 percent and reduced yard dwell time by 12 percent, allowing CPR to reduce the number of its locomotives, rail-cars, and workers, and to offer a fast four-day inter-modal service from Vancouver to Toronto or Chicago, which is faster than CN's.

c. Negotiated five-year collective agreements with major CPR unions.

d. Moved the CPR HQ from downtown to Ogden rail yard in Calgary.

e. Taught 700 managers how to run locomotives and rail yards.

f. Reduced the number of customer service staff from 800 to 200.

g. Lengthened some of its trains from approximately 2 km to 3–4 km.

Courtesy of Canadian Pacific, www.cpr.ca

Questions

1. What was Harrison's most important competitive priority?

2. Relate the above seven actions to the nine strategic decision categories.

Q MINI-CASE   www.loblaw.ca

Competing the Loblaw Way

Loblaw is Canada's largest grocery store chain, with annual revenue of over $46 billion and over 135,000 full-time and part-time employees. Some stores also sell housewares, clothing, health and beauty products, and drugs. Some stores also have a gas station. Loblaw purchased Shoppers Drug Mart, Canada's largest pharmacy chain, for $12 billion in 2014. It offers financial services, including a MasterCard, and loyalty programs PC Plus and Shoppers Optimum.

When Richard J. Currie was appointed president of Loblaw in 1976, Loblaw was only a regional chain (mainly in Ontario), with low profits and cash flow problems. Most store buildings were leased on a long-term basis and the company had no strategic direction. Currie closed some unprofitable stores, including those in the United States, and concentrated on maximizing sales per square foot of the other stores. Loblaw did not open new stores. Although it appeared weak to its competitors, this strategy allowed Loblaw to survive.

Currie believed that Loblaw should own its stores, rather than lease them. The leases were long-term and inflexible, which frequently resulted in the company having to pay for the building well after the store was closed. Also, changing a leased building to accommodate new departments was problematic. So, Loblaw gradually reduced its leases and increased its real estate ownership. Loblaw now owns more than 70 percent of the buildings it uses. In 2013, Loblaw created a separate company, Choice Properties, which owns and manages over 519 properties, mostly Loblaw store buildings.

Currie also believed that controlling the buying activities and labour costs was most important. Given that cost of goods is over 90 percent of the selling price of groceries, there is not much margin for labour and overhead costs. Also, he believed that union workers were much more costly than non-union workers. Given that most stores were already unionized, the way around the low margin was to expand the high-volume large stores.

Another problem in the food retailing business was that competitors competed using periodic sales (promotions), following a "high–low" pricing strategy. Currie believed that selling anything below cost was absurd, but he could not convince his competitors. He believed that customers just needed "quality products, reliably available, and priced competitively." His solution was to introduce the No-Name private label brand in 1978. This way, Loblaw could provide reasonable quality products at reduced prices every day. This was very successful. Later Loblaw continued its private brand (or "control label" products, as it calls them) with President's Choice in 1984, and eight others later, including the Joe Fresh Style line of clothing in 2006, for a total of over 5,000 items (over 1,800 of which are No-Name products). Shoppers' private brand is called Life Brand. Loblaw in-store pharmacies also dispense generic drugs.

Currie also believed in the advantage of an online in-store computerized information system. The use of bar codes and scanners allowed efficient data gathering that was used to identify profitability of items. This allowed Loblaw to control costs back up its supply chain.

Throughout the years, Loblaw has grown immensely through buying smaller regional chains and opening new stores. The owners (the Weston family) believe in investing any free cash in the business. Loblaw uses multi-format stores in different markets. It now owns approximately 565 franchises and approximately 533 grocery stores (approximately 70 million square feet of floor space) under several different banners, including large superstores such as The Real Canadian Superstore in the West and Ontario, Dominion in Newfoundland, and Atlantic Superstore; medium-size food-focused stores (called Market stores) such as Loblaw's and Zehrs (mainly in Ontario), and Provigo (in Quebec); discount food stores such as Extra Foods (in the West), No Frills (franchised), and Maxi and Maxi & Co in Quebec; wholesale stores such as Real Canadian Wholesale Club, Cash & Carry, Fortinos (in Ontario), Presto; and ethnic (Chinese) chain T&T Supermarkets. Shoppers Drug Mart's more than 1,326 stores are franchised (pharmacist-owned).

Valentino Visentini/Dreamstime.com

The different store banners sell basically the same products, with over 25 percent being Loblaw's private brands. However, the general merchandise is sold only through large superstores. Until recently, pricing was not coordinated across different banners and regions. Relations with unions are fairly good. Loblaw has obtained wage cuts from its employees several times.

Loblaw's supply and distribution network is fairly efficient. It has 27 distribution centres throughout Canada, and has the largest fleet of trucks in the country. Administrative activities are now centralized in a huge office (for 2,000 employees) in Brampton, Ontario. This includes the information system (for inventory tracking, store ordering, forecasting, purchasing, and merchandising). Installation of the enterprise software SAP has been completed.

Control label products are continuously being expanded, with the objective that they constitute 30 percent of sales. Over 200 stores were renovated recently. Joe Fresh is now sold online and internationally. Other Loblaw digital initiatives include Click & Collect (online grocery ordering and pick-up at a store), and Shoppers' BeautyBoutique.ca ecommerce site. Loblaw's revenues are growing annually, and its profit margin is approximately 2.25 percent per year, which is high for a grocery chain.

Questions

1. What competitive priority does Loblaw emphasize?

2. Describe and evaluate Loblaw's operations strategy. Use the nine strategic decision categories.

Sources: Loblaw Annual Reports various years. http://www.loblaw.ca; Richard J. Curry, "Loblaw's: Putting the Super in Supermarket," *Business Quarterly*, Summer 1994, pp. 24–30.

 MINI-CASE   www.westjet.ca

WestJet's Strategy

WestJet is a fast-growing Canadian discount airline, headquartered in Calgary. It started in 1996 with three used aircraft targeting short trips in Western Canada (between Calgary, Edmonton, Kelowna, Winnipeg, and Vancouver). Clive Beddoe, one of the founders of WestJet, got the idea for WestJet after having to pay exorbitant fares to Air Canada for his frequent flights between Calgary (his hometown) and Edmonton and Vancouver, where he owned plastic manufacturing plants. According to Beddoe, "The key to expanding the market and luring masses of people who don't travel and those who drive is to charge them bargain-basement fares." He called this market the "visiting friends and relatives" market. In order to be able to offer low prices, WestJet needed to run low-cost operations. WestJet studied successful discount airlines in the United States such as Southwest Airlines, and copied most of their operations principles.

How could WestJet have planned for an operating cost per available seat mile approximately half that of Air Canada? The main principles of WestJet's plan were:

- Short-distance flights.
- Single class of passengers (no first or business class).
- No seat assignment.
- Use only one type of airplane: Boeing 737.
- Fly to smaller cities.
- Recruit young, enthusiastic employees whose salary is slightly lower than the industry average, but who receive profit-sharing bonuses and can participate in an employee share-purchase program.
- Emphasize a "fun and friendly culture" and empower the employees.

- Use equity financing and tight financial controls.
- Use paperless tickets (WestJet was the first airline in North America to do so).
- No connecting flights and no baggage transfers.
- No frequent flyer program.

WestJet gradually and carefully added to its flights. In 2000, WestJet expanded eastward to Hamilton, then to Windsor, Halifax, Montreal, Gander, and St. John's, and, in 2002, to Toronto. Now, WestJet has flights to over 100 Canadian, U.S., Mexican, Caribbean, and European cities. The sun destinations flights (WestJet Vacations) are mainly seasonal, offered in the winter when travel inside Canada dips.

In concert with increasing flights, WestJet has been gradually adding to its fleet of Boeing 737 planes, simultaneously replacing the old 737-200 (with 125 seats) with new next-generation 737s in three sizes: 737-600 (119 seats), 737-700 (136 seats), and 737-800 (166 seats). Now it has over 115 next-generation 737 planes, which are 30 percent more fuel efficient. New planes can be operated close to 12 hours a day, versus 10 hours for the old planes. Clearly, their maintenance cost is lower than the old planes had. The new planes have leather seats and individual live seat-back satellite TV (WestJet Connect) for each passenger. Recently, the legroom in the first three rows of seating (called premium economy) has been expanded.

WestJet is not afraid to spend money on useful technology. An example is the installation of blended winglets on the end of the wings of new planes, which will increase lift and reduce drag, thus increasing fuel economy by 4 percent. The $600,000 investment per plane pays back in four years.

WestJet has entered into 42 interline partnerships with international airlines, 16 of which involve code sharing. It has upgraded its online booking system at the cost of $40 million.

WestJet has started a regional subsidiary called Encore that uses 34 Bombardier Q400 turboprops on over 200 daily flights across Canada. In addition, WestJet now flies internationally from St. John's to Dublin, Ireland, and from Halifax to Glasgow, Scotland. With its four used Boeing 767s, it has daily flights from Calgary and Toronto to London, England. WestJet is planning to expand its long-distance flights—it has ordered 67 new Boeing 767s to be received over the next 10 years.

The expansion strategy has resulted in many changes in its initial operations principles: WestJet is now flying some medium and long distance flights (e.g., to Hawaii and the United Kingdom), assigning seats, using three types of airplanes, flying to big cities, having connecting flights and baggage transfers, and having a frequent flyer reward program and a MasterCard.

WestJet now employs over 10,000 employees (still non-unionized but mostly shareholders) and has approximately 35 percent of the air travel market in Canada. WestJet's revenue-passenger-miles was 24 billion in 2016, whereas Air Canada's was 76 billion (including overseas flights). WestJet has one of the best on-time (within 15 minutes of the scheduled time) arrival and departure performances, and is one of the most profitable airlines in North America. Its load factor (percentage of seats occupied) has been increasing from 70 percent in the late 1990s to 80–83 percent now, and its revenue is over $4.1 billion.

Questions

1. What market segment did WestJet originally compete in?

2. What competitive priority did WestJet originally have?

3. What were the advantages of each of the initial principles used by WestJet in 1996 to reduce its operating costs?

4. How has WestJet kept its operating costs low while growing?

Sources: WestJet's Annual Reports, various years, http://www.westjet.com /guest/en/about/index.shtml.

Courtesy of WestJet, www.westjet.com

Chapter 3
Demand Forecasting

Courtesy of Bombardier Aerospace

Every year, Bombardier Business Aircraft (BBA) produces a 10-year rolling demand forecast for its business jets. Factors such as world GDP growth, stock market returns, positive interest rate spread, and oil prices are all closely monitored inputs to the forecasting process. The worldwide business jet market is partitioned into major regions, including North America, Latin America, Europe, Middle East, Africa, Commonwealth of Independent States, Greater China, South Asia, and Asia Pacific. In each region, previous sales history and predicted economic growth are used to forecast fleet growth. For example, North America is expected to have an annual economic growth rate of 2.2 percent and a fleet growth rate of 2 percent. In 2015, the North American fleet stood at 10,355 units; it is forecasted to grow to 12,895 units in 2025, assuming a compounded annual growth of 2 percent. BBA then estimates total aircraft retirements over the same 10-year duration, and adds this number to obtain the number of deliveries in 10 years. For example, BBA expects 1,390 retirements in the next 10 years, resulting in 12,895 − 10,355 + 1,390 = 3,930 deliveries.

Source: http://ir.bombardier.com/var/data/gallery/document/85/38/92/64/14/Bombardier-Business-Aircraft-2016-2025-Market-Forecast-en.pdf.

(LO1) **Introduction**

Demand forecasts are basic inputs for many kinds of decisions in organizations. Consequently, it is important for *all* managers to be able to understand and use demand forecasts. Although product demand forecasts are typically developed by the sales/marketing function, the operations function (through production planning) will receive and use the demand forecasts. Also, the operations function develops demand/usage forecasts for supplies and spare parts.

Forecasts are a basic input in the decision processes of operations management because they provide information on future demand. The importance of forecasting to operations management cannot be overstated. The primary goal of operations management is to match supply to demand. Having a forecast of demand is essential for determining how much capacity or supply will be needed to meet demand. For instance, operations needs to know what capacity will be needed to make staffing and equipment decisions, budgets must be prepared, purchasing needs information for ordering from suppliers, and supply chain partners need to make their plans.

Planning is an integral part of an operations manager's job. If uncertainties cloud the planning process, operations managers will find it difficult to plan effectively. Demand forecasts help operations managers by reducing some of the uncertainty, thereby enabling them to develop more meaningful plans. A **demand forecast** is the estimate of expected demand during a specified future period.

> **demand forecast** The estimate of expected demand during a specified future period.

People make and use demand forecasts in their everyday life. They might say, for example, "How much food and drink will I need?" when visiting a grocery store, or "How much cash or gas will I need?" when visiting a bank or gas station. To make these forecasts, they take into account two kinds of information: current factors or conditions, and past experience in a similar situation. Sometimes they will rely more on one than the other, depending on which approach seems more relevant at the time. Demand forecasting for business purposes involves similar approaches. Businesses make plans for future operations based on anticipated future demand. Anticipated demand is derived from two possible sources: actual customer orders and forecasts. For businesses where customer orders make up most or all of anticipated demand, planning is straightforward, and little or no forecasting is needed. However, for many businesses, most or all of anticipated demand is derived from forecasts, and more formal methods are used to make demand forecasts and to assess forecast accuracy. Demand forecasting basically involves modelling the past pattern of demand for an item and projecting it into the future while taking new developments into account.

There are three types of uses for demand forecasts in operations: (1) to help managers design the system, (2) to help them plan the medium-term use of the system, and (3) to schedule the short-term use of the system. Designing the system involves long-term plans about which goods and services to offer; which capacities, facilities, and equipment to have; where to locate; and so on. Planning the medium-term use of the system involves tasks such as planning overall inventory and workforce levels, and planning production at the aggregate product family level. Scheduling the short-term use of the system involves scheduling of production, purchasing of parts and raw materials, and staff scheduling. Demand forecasting jobs are in high demand. Visit https://ca.indeed.com /Demand-Forecasting-jobs for forecasting positions throughout Canada.

Business forecasting pertains to more than predicting demand. Financial and economic forecasts are used to predict variables such as profits, revenues, costs, stock prices, and GDP. This chapter will focus on the forecasting of demand (sales of goods/services or usage of spare parts/ supplies). Keep in mind, however, that the concepts and techniques presented in this chapter apply equally well to the other types of business forecasting.

In spite of its use of computers and sophisticated mathematical models, forecasting is not an exact science. Instead, successful forecasting often requires a skillful blending of art and science. Experience, judgment, technical expertise, information, and communication all play a role in developing useful forecasts. Along with these, a certain amount of luck and a dash of humility can be helpful, because the worst forecasters occasionally produce a very good forecast, and even the best forecasters sometimes miss completely.

Two aspects of forecasts are important: (1) the expected level of demand, and (2) the degree of accuracy that can be assigned to a forecast (i.e., the potential size of forecast error). The expected level of demand can be a function of some structural variation, such as a trend or seasonal variation.

Forecast accuracy is a function of the ability of forecasters to correctly model demand, random variation, and sometimes unforeseen events.

Generally speaking, the responsibility for preparing demand forecasts for finished goods or services lies with the marketing or sales departments rather than operations. Nonetheless, because demand forecasts are major inputs for many operations decisions, operations managers must be knowledgeable about the kinds of forecasting techniques available, the assumptions that underlie their use, and their limitations. Also the operations function provides feedback about the feasibility of producing the demand forecasts. In addition, inventory managers (see Chapter 12) make forecasts of usage of supplies and spare parts. See the "Forecasting in Ocean Spray" OM in Action for an application.

 OM in Action   http://www.oceanspray.com

FOTOimage Montreal/Shutterstock.com

Forecasting in Ocean Spray

Ocean Spray is an agricultural cooperative owned by approximately 800 cranberry growers and 100 grapefruit growers in the United States and Canada (British Columbia and Quebec). It produces juices in bottles and cans in different flavour mixes and container sizes. When all of the combinations of products, sizes, and types of containers are taken into account, the number of different products ranges in the hundreds. For example, a case of eight 1.89 litre Cran-Apple juice drink bottles is a product. The company also keeps track of groups of similar products, called categories, and groups of same-size products (e.g., a group of all 1.89 litre cranberry drink bottles). Also, the products and groups in each of the company's four North American manufacturing plants and for the major customers, the retail chains, are tracked separately.

Forecasting is performed by the demand planning group, which is located in the logistics and planning department. It consists of a manager and five demand planners, who are each responsible for a combination of approximately 300 different products and category/size/manufacturing plant/major customer groupings. Forecasts are primarily used for production planning, purchasing, and shipment of the products. The planning process is called sales and operations planning, and is discussed in more detail later, in Chapter 13.

During the first week of every month, the demand planners run software by Manugistics (now part of JDA Software) that uses the past three years' history of shipments and time series models to forecast shipments for the next six months. These forecasts are shared with local sales managers to check and adjust based on local knowledge of customer intentions, inventory, and promotions. During the second week, the adjusted forecasts are further examined and adjusted by regional and divisional marketing managers in a group meeting called the forecast alignment meeting. During the third week, the aligned forecasts are passed to the production/supply planning team for review in the supply alignment meeting. Finally, during the last week of the month, upper managers from sales, marketing, operations, and finance meet with demand planners (in a sales and operations planning meeting) to review and implement the results of the alignment meetings.

Before setting up the above formal process and using Manugistics in 1998, Ocean Spray did not have one unique forecast for each product and grouping. The accuracy of forecasts was low—the mean absolute percentage error (MAPE) was approximately 45 percent at the product level. Now, MAPE is approximately 25 percent.

A challenge for the demand planners is the seasonality of sales of cranberries. Approximately 90 percent of sales occur during the fall, primarily before Thanksgiving and Christmas. Ocean Spray constantly introduces new products, such as a new mix of another fruit with cranberry. If a similar product has been introduced before, this product's sales history will be used as a guide for the new product's demand. Otherwise, the services of the consumer research department will be needed.

Sources: http://www.oceanspray.com; P. Gelly, "Managing Bottom Up and Top Down Approaches: Ocean Spray's Experience," *Journal of Business Forecasting Methods & Systems* 18(4), Winter 1999/2000, pp. 3–5; J. Malehorn, "Forecasting at Ocean Spray Cranberries," *Journal of Business Forecasting Methods & Systems* 20(2), Summer 2001, pp. 6–8; http://www.manugistics.com/documents/collateral/Ocean_Spray_ManuCS.pdf; H. Landi, "Straight From the Bog to the Bottle," *Beverage World* 124(1757) December 15, 2005, pp. 38–42.

Recently, supply chain partners have started to collaborate on the forecasting process. The customer company makes the forecast in consultation with the supplier, allowing for both sides to provide inputs such as the expectation of customers for increased quantities during a promotion, the capacity limitations of the supplier, etc. This is called *collaborative planning, forecasting, and replenishment (CPFR)* (more on this in Chapter 11 on supply chain management). For an example of the consequences of not collaborating in forecasting in a supply chain, see the "Barilla SpA" OM in Action.

 OM in Action

Barilla SpA

Barilla SpA, a pasta manufacturer, was founded in 1875 when Pietro Barilla opened a small shop in Parma, Italy. Competing in an oversaturated field of over 2,000 pasta manufacturers, Barilla was able to differentiate its products and grow the company using highly innovative marketing programs. Within 100 years, the company had become the largest pasta manufacturer in the world.

In the past, Barilla had experienced problems with large amounts of variability in demand, resulting in significant operational inefficiencies and increased manufacturing costs. Management wondered how there could be large fluctuations in demand for a staple food product—as per capita consumption of pasta does not tend to fluctuate much from month to month.

The reasons for the demand fluctuations are varied, but a significant portion of those fluctuations can be traced to the use of sales promotions and lack of collaborative forecasting. Barilla's sales strategy relied heavily on the use of promotions ranging from 1.4 percent all the way up to 10 percent. This would cause a hockey stick effect with low demand in the beginning of each month and high demand at the end of each month as sales representatives pushed harder to clear out inventory. Downstream retailers and distributors were also reluctant to provide proprietary sales data that Barilla needed. With collaborative forecasting, Barilla and its distributors and retailers would work together to forecast demand, which would increase fill rates while reducing inventories.

Source: Janice H. Hammond, "Barilla SpA (A)", *Harvard Business Review*, Case 9-694-046. Rev. March 25, 2008.

Forecasts affect decisions and activities throughout an organization, in accounting, finance, human resources, marketing, and management information systems (MIS), as well as in operations and other areas. Here are some examples of uses of forecasts in business organizations:

Accounting: New product/process cost estimates, profit projections, cash management.

Finance: Equipment/equipment replacement needs, timing and amount of funding/borrowing needs.

Human resources: Hiring activities, including recruitment, interviewing, and training; layoff planning, including outplacement counselling.

Marketing: Pricing and promotion, ebusiness strategies, global competition strategies.

MIS: New/revised information systems, Internet services.

Operations: Schedules, capacity planning, work assignments and workloads, inventory planning, make-or-buy decisions, outsourcing, project management.

Product/service design: Revision of current features, design of new products or services.

Features Common to All Forecasts

A wide variety of forecasting techniques are in use. In many respects, they are quite different from one another, as you shall soon discover. Nonetheless, certain features are common to all techniques and forecasts, and it is important to recognize them.

1. Forecasting techniques generally assume that the same underlying causal system that existed in the past will continue to exist in the future.

2. Forecasts are rarely perfect; actual results usually differ from predicted values. No one can predict *precisely* how related factors will impinge upon the variable in question; this, and the presence of randomness, precludes a perfect forecast. Allowances should be made for inaccuracies.

3. Forecasts for groups of items tend to be more accurate than forecasts for individual items, because forecasting errors among items in a group usually have a cancelling effect. For example, the forecast for total sales of a new T-shirt will be more accurate than the forecast for each size and colour.

4. Forecast accuracy decreases the farther the forecasted time period is into the future. Generally speaking, short-term forecasts must contend with fewer uncertainties than longer-term forecasts, so the former tend to be more accurate. The **forecasting horizon** is the range of time periods we are forecasting for.

> **forecasting horizon** The range of time periods we are forecasting for.

An important consequence of the last point is that flexible business organizations—those that can respond quickly to changes in demand—require a shorter forecasting horizon and, hence, benefit from more accurate short-term forecasts than competitors that are less flexible and must therefore use longer forecasting horizons. Flexibility can be achieved by shortening the lead time required to produce goods/services and to purchase raw materials/parts/supplies, and by using related approaches such as postponement (i.e., waiting until the customer order is received to add differentiating features to standard components or products).

A manager cannot simply delegate forecasting to models or computers and then forget about it, because unplanned or special occurrences can wreak havoc with forecasts. For instance, weather-related events, sales promotions, and changes in features or prices of the company's own and competing goods or services can have a major impact on demand. Consequently, a manager must be alert to such occurrences and be ready to override forecasts.

Elements of a Good Forecast

A forecast should fulfill certain requirements:

1. The forecast should be *timely.* The forecasting horizon must cover the time necessary to implement possible changes so that its results can be used.

2. The forecast should be *accurate*, and the degree of accuracy of the forecast should be stated. This will enable users to plan for possible errors and will provide a basis for comparing alternative forecasts.

3. The forecasting method/software chosen should be *reliable*; it should work consistently.

4. The forecast should be expressed in *meaningful units.* Financial planners need to know demand in *dollars*, whereas demand and production planners need to know demand in *units*. The choice of units depends on user needs.

The Disney Advanced Analytics team forecasts volume and revenue for the theme parks, water parks, and resort hotels, as well as merchandise, food, and beverage revenue by location to ensure services are not interrupted (see https://www .informs.org/Impact/O.R. -Analytics-Success-Stories /Industry-Profiles/Disney for more details).

 ervice

Vlad Ghiea/Dreamstime.com

5. The forecast should be *in writing*. Although this will not guarantee that all concerned are using the same information, it will at least increase the likelihood of it. In addition, a written forecast will permit an objective basis for evaluating the forecast once actual results are in.

6. The forecasting technique should be *simple to understand and use*. Users often lack confidence in forecasts based on sophisticated techniques; they do not understand either the circumstances in which the techniques are appropriate or the limitations of the techniques. Misuse of techniques is an obvious consequence. Not surprisingly, fairly simple forecasting techniques enjoy widespread popularity because users are more comfortable working with them.

7. The forecast should be *cost-effective*. The benefits should outweigh the costs.

Steps in the Forecasting Process

There are six basic steps in the forecasting process (only Steps 4 to 6 are used on a continuing basis):

1. *Determine the purpose of the forecast.* Determine the level of detail required, the amount of resources (personnel, computer time, dollars) that can be justified, and the level of accuracy necessary.

2. *Establish a forecasting horizon.* The forecast must indicate a time interval, keeping in mind that accuracy decreases as the time horizon increases.

3. *Gather and analyze relevant historical data.* Ensure that the data is of past demand rather than sales or shipments, which will be different if there were stock-outs. Identify any assumptions that are made.

4. *Select a forecasting technique.*

5. *Prepare the forecast.*

6. *Monitor the forecast.* If it is not performing in a satisfactory manner, re-examine the parameters of the technique or use a different technique.

Approaches to Forecasting

There are two general approaches to forecasting: judgmental and quantitative. Judgmental methods consist mainly of subjective inputs, which may defy precise numerical description (but may still depend on historical data). Quantitative methods involve either the use of a time series model to extend the historical pattern of data into the future, or the development of associative models that attempt to utilize *causal (explanatory) variables* to make a forecast.

Judgmental techniques permit inclusion of *soft* information (e.g., human factors, personal opinions, hunches) in the forecasting process. Those factors are often omitted or downplayed when quantitative techniques are used because they are difficult to quantify. Quantitative techniques consist mainly of analyzing objective, or *hard*, data. They usually avoid personal biases that sometimes contaminate judgmental methods. In practice, either or both approaches might be used to develop a forecast.

Judgmental methods rely on nonquantitative analysis of historical data and/or analysis of subjective inputs obtained from various sources, such as consumers (surveys), similar products (historical analogies), the sales staff, managers and executives, and panels of experts. Quite frequently, these sources provide insights that are not otherwise available (e.g., for new product development, promotions, etc.). Long-term forecasting typically uses judgmental methods because quantitative techniques may be inaccurate in this case.

Some forecasting techniques simply attempt to project past data into the future. These techniques use historical, or time series, data with the assumption that the future will be like the past.

Time series models identify specific patterns in the data and project or extrapolate those patterns into the future, without trying to identify causes of the patterns.

Associative models use equations that consist of one or more *explanatory* variables that can be used to predict future demand for the variable of interest. For example, demand for a particular paint might be explained by variables such as the price, the amount spent on advertising it, and the season, as well as specific characteristics of the paint (e.g., quality).

"I recommend our 'wild' expectations be downgraded to 'great.'"

judgmental methods Use nonquantitative analysis of historical data and/or analysis of subjective inputs from consumers, sales staff, managers, executives, similar products, and experts to help develop a forecast.

time series models Extend the pattern of data into the future.

associative models Use explanatory variables to predict future demand for the variable of interest.

Overview of Demand Forecasting by Forecasting Horizon

Forecasting *long-term* demand typically involves annual data (for, say, the next five years). It requires knowledge of the specific market and judgment of experts/managers. For new products, either consumer surveys and test markets are undertaken, or demand for an analogous product is used. A common approach is to forecast the demand for the whole market, estimate the market share for the new product, and multiply the two to get the demand forecast. If historical data are available, the trend is estimated and projected into the future (using regression, for example).

Forecasting *medium-term* demand typically involves monthly demand (for the next 12 months, say). A mix of judgmental and quantitative methods is used. *Seasonal* effects are taken into account.

Forecasting *short-term* demand typically involves daily or weekly demand (for, say, the next 12 weeks). Usually there are thousands of products/parts to forecast. Therefore, a simple quantitative method (e.g., an averaging technique) is used. Sales promotions are forecasted separately.

Judgmental Methods

In some situations, forecasters may rely solely on judgment and opinion to make forecasts. When introducing new products, redesigning existing products, and using sales promotions, judgmental forecasting is needed, as well as when analyzing future actions of customers and competitors. In such instances, forecasts may be based on collective executive opinions, opinions of the sales staff, consumer surveys, historical analogies, or opinions of experts.

Executive Opinions

A small group of upper-level managers (e.g., VPs of marketing, operations, and finance) may meet and collectively develop a forecast. This approach is often used as part of long-term strategic planning and new product development. It has the advantage of bringing together the considerable knowledge and talents of various managers. However, there is the risk that the view of one person will prevail, and the possibility that diffusing responsibility for the forecast over the entire group may result in less pressure to produce a good forecast.

Sales Force Opinions

The sales staff or the customer service staff is often a good source of information because of their direct contact with customers. They are often aware of any plans that the customers may be considering for the future, including the current level of customer inventory.

Consumer Surveys

Because it is the potential consumers who ultimately determine sales, it seems natural to solicit input from them. In some instances, every customer or potential customer can be contacted. However, usually there are too many customers or there is no way to identify all potential customers. Therefore, organizations seeking consumer input usually resort to consumer surveys, which enable them to *sample* consumer opinions. This could be in the form of questionnaires conducted by mail or phone to a large sample of potential consumers. It also could be through group meetings with a small number of potential consumers (focus groups).

Historical Analogies

Sometimes the demand for a similar product in the past, after some adjustment, can be used to forecast a new product's demand. For example, the demand for cranberry–apple drink can be used to forecast the demand for cranberry–grape drink.

Expert Opinions

> **Delphi method** Experts complete a series of questionnaires, each developed from the previous one, to achieve a consensus forecast.

The forecaster may solicit opinions from a number of experts. One way of doing this, the **Delphi method**, involves circulating a series of questionnaires among experts. Responses are kept anonymous, which tends to encourage honest responses and reduces the risk that one person's opinion will prevail. Each new questionnaire is developed using the information extracted from the previous one, thus enlarging the scope of information on which participants can base their judgments. The goal is to achieve a consensus forecast.

One application of the Delphi method is for *technological* forecasting—assessing changes in technology and their impact on an organization. Often the goal is to predict *when* a certain event will occur. For instance, the goal of a Delphi forecast might be to predict when video telephones might be installed in at least 50 percent of residential homes, or when a vaccine for a disease might be developed. For the most part, these are long-term, single-time forecasts, which usually have very little hard information to go by.

Time Series Models: Introduction and Averaging

Introduction

> **time series** A time-ordered sequence of observations taken at regular intervals of time.

A **time series** is a time-ordered sequence of observations taken at regular intervals over a period of time (e.g., hourly, daily, weekly, monthly, quarterly, annually). Forecasting techniques based on time series data are made on the assumption that future values of the series can be estimated from their own past values. Although no attempt is made to identify variables that influence the series, these methods are widely used, often with quite satisfactory results.

Analysis of time series data requires the analyst to identify the underlying behaviour of the series. This can often be accomplished by merely *plotting* the data and visually examining the plot. One or more patterns might appear: level (i.e., average), trend, seasonal variation, and cycle. In addition, there can be random and irregular (one-time) variations. These behaviours can be described as follows:

> **level (average)** A horizontal pattern of time series.
>
> **trend** A persistent upward or downward movement in data.

1. **Level (average)**, or constant, refers to a horizontal pattern of time series.
2. **Trend** refers to a persistent upward or downward movement in the data. Population growth, increasing incomes, and cultural changes often account for such movements.

3. **Seasonality** refers to regular repeating wavelike variations generally related to factors such as the calendar, weather, or recurring events. For example, sales of ice cream are higher in the summer. Restaurants, supermarkets, and theatres experience weekly and even daily "seasonal" variations.

4. **Cycles** are wavelike variations lasting more than one year. These are often related to a variety of economic, political, and even agricultural conditions, such as supply of cattle.

5. **Irregular variations** are due to unusual one-time explainable circumstances not reflective of typical behaviour, such as severe weather conditions, strikes, or sales promotions. They do not reflect typical behaviour, and whenever possible should be identified and removed from the data.

6. **Random variations** are residual variations that remain after all other behaviours have been accounted for (also called *noise*). This randomness arises from the combined influence of many—perhaps a great many—relatively unimportant factors, and it cannot be reliably predicted. Time series techniques smooth random variations in the data.

Some of these behaviours are illustrated in Figure 3-1. The small "bumps" in the plots represent random variations. The following sections have descriptions of the various approaches to the analysis of time series data.

> **seasonality** Regular wavelike variations related to the calendar, weather, or recurring events.
>
> **cycles** Wavelike variations lasting more than one year.
>
> **irregular variations** Caused by unusual one-time explainable circumstances not reflective of typical behaviour.
>
> **random variations** Residual variations after all other behaviours are accounted for (also called noise).

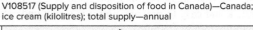
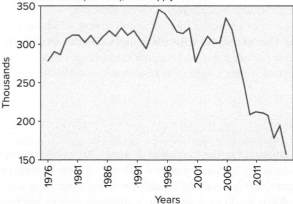

Source: Statistics Canada, CANSIM database, Table 002-0010, Series v108517

◀ FIGURE 3-1

Level, trend, and seasonal variations (from top left to bottom right).

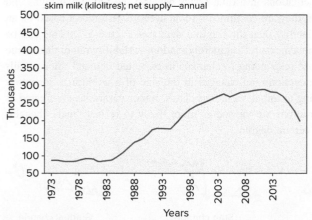

Source: Statistics Canada, CANSIM database, Table 002-0010, Series v108612

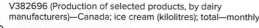
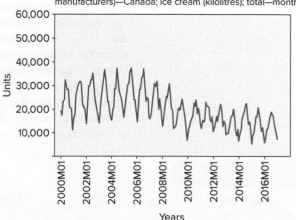

Source: Statistics Canada, CANSIM database; Table 0003-0010, series v382696

Naïve Methods

A simple but widely used approach to forecasting is the naïve method. The naïve method can be used with a stable series (level or average with random variations), with seasonal variations, or with trend. With a stable series, the last data point becomes the **naïve forecast** for the next period. Thus, if the demand for a product last week was 20 cases, the forecast for this week is 20 cases. With seasonal variations, the naïve forecast for this "season" is equal to the value of the series last "season." For example, the forecast for demand for turkeys this Christmas is equal to demand for turkeys last Christmas. For data with trend, the naïve forecast is equal to the last value of the series plus or minus the difference between the last two values of the series. For example, suppose the last two values were 50 and 53:

> **naïve forecast** For a stable series, the next forecast equals the previous period's actual value.

Period	Actual	Change From Previous Value	Naïve Forecast
$t-1$	50		
t	53	+3	
$t+1$			$53 + 3 = 56$

Although at first glance the naïve method may appear *too* simplistic, it is nonetheless a legitimate forecasting tool used by some businesses such as restaurants and retail stores. Consider the advantages: it has virtually no cost, it is quick and easy to prepare, and it is easily understandable. The main objection to this method is its inability to provide highly accurate forecasts.

The accuracy of a naïve forecast can serve as a standard of comparison against which to judge the cost and accuracy of other techniques. One weakness of the naïve method is that the forecast just *traces* the actual data, with a lag of one period; it does not smooth the random variations out at all. But by expanding the number of historical data a forecast is based on, this difficulty can be overcome.

Averaging Methods

Historical data typically contain a certain amount of random variation that tends to obscure systematic movements in the data. This randomness arises from the combined influence of many—perhaps a great many—relatively unimportant factors, and it cannot be reliably predicted. Averaging techniques smooth variations in the data. Ideally, it would be desirable to completely remove any randomness from the data and leave only "real" variations, such as changes in the demand. As a practical matter, however, it is usually impossible to distinguish between these two kinds of variations, so the best one can hope for is that the small variations are random and the large variations are "real."

Averaging techniques smooth fluctuations in a time series because the individual highs and lows in the data offset each other when they are combined into an average. A forecast based on an average thus tends to exhibit less variability than the original data (see Figure 3-2). This can be advantageous because many of these movements reflect merely random variability rather than a true change in the series. Moreover, because responding to changes in expected demand often entails considerable cost (e.g., changes in production rate, changes in the size of a workforce, inventory changes), it is desirable to avoid reacting to minor variations. Thus, minor variations are treated as random variations, whereas larger variations are viewed as more likely to reflect "real" changes, although these, too, are smoothed to a certain degree.

FIGURE 3-2 ▶

Averaging applied various patterns.

Data
Forecast -------

Ideal

Step change
(Forecast lags)

Gradual change
(Forecast lags)

Averaging methods generate forecasts that reflect the recent level (i.e., an average) of a time series. They can handle stable series (i.e., a level series with random variations around it), where there is no trend or seasonality. Three techniques for averaging are described in this section:

1. Moving average.
2. Weighted moving average.
3. Exponential smoothing.

Moving Average The **moving average** technique averages a *number* of recent actual data values and uses the average as the forecast for the current period. The moving average forecast is updated as a new value becomes available. The *n*-period moving average forecast for period *t* is the average of *n* most recent actual values.

$$F_t = \mathrm{MA}_n = \frac{\sum_{i=t-1}^{t-n} A_i}{n} \tag{3-1}$$

> **moving average** Technique that averages a number of recent actual values as forecast for current period. It is updated as new values become available.

where

i = An index that corresponds to age of the period ($i = t - 1$: last period; $i = t - 2$: two periods back, . . .)

n = Number of periods (data points) in the moving average

A_i = Actual value in period i

MA_n = n period moving average

F_t = Forecast for this period (i.e., period t)

◀ **EXAMPLE 3-1**

Calculate a three-period moving average forecast for the demand of a product, given its demand for the last five periods.

Period	Demand
1	42
2	40
3	43 ⎤
4	40 ⎬ the three most recent demands
5	41 ⎦

If actual demand in period 6 turns out to be 39, the moving average forecast for period 7 would be

$$F_7 = \frac{40 + 41 + 39}{3} = 40.00$$

Note that in a moving average, as each new actual value becomes available, the forecast is updated by adding the newest value and dropping the oldest and then calculating the average. Consequently, the forecast "moves" by reflecting only the most recent values.

SOLUTION

$$F_6 = \frac{43 + 40 + 41}{3} = 41.33$$

Figure 3-3 illustrates a three-period moving average forecast plotted against the actual demand during 31 periods. Note how the moving average forecast *lags* behind the actual values and how smooth the forecasted values are compared with the actual values.

The moving average forecast can incorporate as many data points as desired. In selecting the number of periods to include, the decision maker must take into account that the number of data points in the moving average determines its sensitivity to each new data point: the fewer the data points in a moving average, the more sensitive (responsive) to most recent data the moving average tends to be. (See Figure 3-4.) If responsiveness is important, a moving average with relatively few data points should be used. This will permit quick adjustment to a change in the data, but it will also cause the forecast to be somewhat responsive even to random variations. Conversely, moving

A moving average forecast tends to smooth the data but lags behind the data.

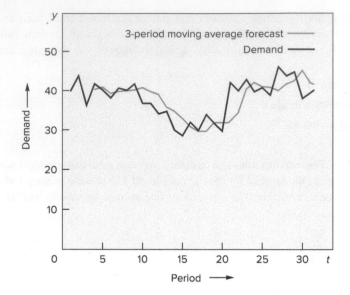

The fewer time periods in a moving average, the greater the responsiveness of the forecast to the most recent data.

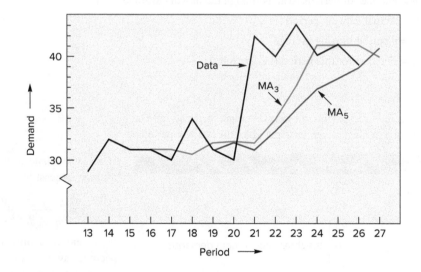

averages based on more data points will be smoother but less responsive to "real" changes. Hence, the decision maker must weigh the cost of responding more slowly to changes in the data against the cost of responding to what might simply be random variations. A review of forecast errors (later in the chapter) can help in this decision.

The advantages of a moving average forecast are that it is easy to calculate and easy to understand. A possible disadvantage is that all values in the moving average forecast are weighted equally. For instance, in a five-period moving average forecast, each value has a weight of 1/5. Hence, the oldest value has the *same weight* as the most recent value.

weighted moving average
A variation of moving average where more recent values in the time series are given larger weight in calculating a forecast.

Weighted Moving Average A **weighted moving average** is similar to a moving average, except that it assigns larger weight to the most recent values in a time series in calculating a forecast. For instance, the most recent value might be assigned a weight of 0.40, the next most recent value a weight of 0.30, the next after that a weight of 0.20, and the next after that a weight of 0.10. Note that the weights sum to 1.00 (because averaging methods assume that there is no trend), and that the heaviest weights are assigned to the most recent values.

Given the following demand data,

a. Calculate a weighted moving average forecast for period 6 using a weight of 0.40 for the most recent period, 0.30 for the next most recent, 0.20 for the next, and 0.10 for the next.

b. If the actual demand for period 6 is 39, forecast the demand for period 7 using the same weights as in part *a*.

Period	Demand
1	42
2	40
3	43
4	40
5	41

SOLUTION

a. $F_6 = 0.40(41) + 0.30(40) + 0.20(43) + 0.10(40) = 41.0$

b. $F_7 = 0.40(39) + 0.30(41) + 0.20(40) + 0.10(43) = 40.2$

Note that if four weights are used, only the *four most recent* demand values should be used to prepare the forecast.

The advantage of a weighted moving average over a simple moving average is that the weighted moving average is more reflective of the most recent observations. However, the choice of weights is somewhat arbitrary and generally involves the use of trial and error to find a suitable weighting scheme.

Exponential Smoothing **Exponential smoothing** is a sophisticated weighted averaging method where a new forecast is based on the previous forecast plus a percentage of the difference between that forecast and the previous actual value. That is:

exponential smoothing
Weighted averaging method based on previous forecast plus a percentage of the difference between that forecast and the previous actual value.

Forecast = Previous forecast + α(Previous actual − Previous forecast)

where (Previous actual − Previous forecast) represents the *forecast error* and α is a proportion less than one. More concisely,

$$F_t = F_{t-1} + \alpha(A_{t-1} - F_{t-1}) \tag{3-2a}$$

where

F_t = Forecast for period t
F_{t-1} = Forecast for period $t - 1$
α = Smoothing constant, $0 < \alpha < 1$
A_{t-1} = Actual demand in period $t - 1$

For example, suppose that the previous forecast was 42 units, previous actual demand was 40 units, and α = 0.10. The new forecast would be computed as follows:

$$F_t = 42 + 0.10(40 - 42) = 41.8$$

Then, if the actual demand turns out to be 43, the next forecast would be:

$$F_t = 41.8 + 0.10(43 - 41.8) = 41.92$$

An alternative form of Formula 3-2a reveals the weighting of the previous forecast and the previous actual demand:

$$F_t = (1 - \alpha)F_{t-1} + \alpha A_{t-1} \tag{3-2b}$$

For example, if α = 0.10, this would be

$$F_t = 0.90F_{t-1} + 0.10A_{t-1}$$

The quickness of adjustment by forecast error is determined by the smoothing constant, α. The closer its value is to zero, the slower the forecast will adjust by forecast error (i.e., the greater the smoothing). Conversely, the closer the value of α is to 1.0, the greater the responsiveness and the less the smoothing. This is illustrated in Example 3-3.

EXAMPLE 3-3 ▶

The following table illustrates two series of exponential smoothing forecasts for a data set, and the resulting (Actual − Forecast) = Error, for each period. One forecast uses α = 0.10 and the other uses α = 0.40. The following figure plots the actual data and both sets of forecasts. It can be observed that the 0.10 forecast plot is smoother and less responsive than the 0.40 forecast plot.

Period (t)	Actual Demand	α = 0.10		α = 0.40	
		Forecast	Error	Forecast	Error
1	42	—	—	—	—
2	40	42	−2	42	−2
3	43	41.8	1.2	41.2	1.8
4	40	41.92	−1.92	41.92	−1.92
5	41	41.73	−0.73	41.15	−0.15
6	39	41.66	−2.66	41.09	−2.09
7	46	41.39	4.61	40.25	5.75
8	44	41.85	2.15	42.55	1.45
9	45	42.07	2.93	43.13	1.87
10	38	42.36	−4.36	43.88	−5.88
11	40	41.92	−1.92	41.53	−1.53
12		41.73		40.92	

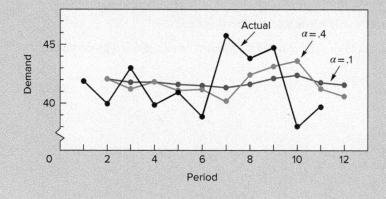

Selecting a smoothing constant is basically a matter of judgment or trial and error (or one can use the forecast errors to guide the decision). The goal is to select a smoothing constant that balances the benefits of smoothing random variations with the benefits of responding to real changes if and when they occur. Commonly used values of α range from 0.05 to 0.50. Low values of α are used when the underlying average tends to be stable; higher values are used when the underlying average is susceptible to change.

Some computer packages include a feature that permits automatic modification of the smoothing constant so that the forecast errors do not become unacceptably large. This method is called **adaptive (or variable response) exponential smoothing**.

Exponential smoothing is one of the most widely used techniques in forecasting, partly because of its ease of computation and partly because of the ease with which the weighting scheme can be altered—simply by changing the value of α.

Note: A number of different approaches can be used to obtain a starting forecast for period 2, such as the average of the first several periods, a subjective estimate, or the first actual value (i.e., the naïve approach). For simplicity, the naïve approach is used in this book. In practice, using an average of, say, the first three values as a forecast for period 4 would provide a better starting forecast because it would be more stable.

adaptive (or variable response) exponential smoothing A version of exponential smoothing where the smoothing constant is automatically modified in order to prevent large forecast errors from occurring.

Techniques for Trend

Analysis of trend involves developing an equation that will suitably describe the trend (assuming that trend is present in the data). The trend component may be linear or it may be nonlinear. Some commonly encountered nonlinear trend types are illustrated in Figure 3-5. A simple plot of the data can often reveal the existence and nature of a trend. We will first focus on *linear* trend because this is fairly common. Linear trend is usually fitted using regression. Microsoft Excel facilitates this, in addition to many types of nonlinear trend.

Linear Trend Equation The **linear trend equation** has the form

$$\hat{y}_t = a + bt \tag{3-3}$$

where

t = Index of time periods, starting from $t = 1$ for the first period
$\hat{y}_t$ = Value of trend line at period t
a = Value of trend line at $t = 0$ (intercept)
b = Slope of the trend line

Forecast for period t: $F_t = a + bt$

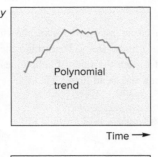

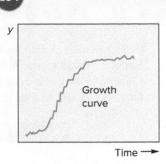

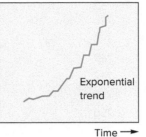

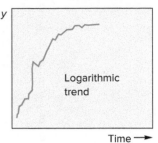

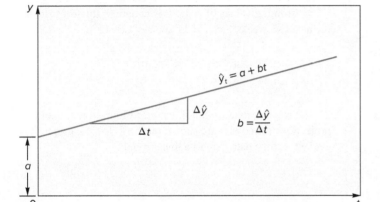

The line intersects the y axis where $\hat{y}_t = a$. The slope of the line = b.

▲ FIGURE 3-5

Graphs of some nonlinear trends.

linear trend equation
$\hat{y}_t = a + bt$, used to develop forecasts when linear trend is present.

For example, consider the trend equation $\hat{y}_t = 45 + 5t$. The intercept (i.e., value of $\hat{y}_t$ when $t = 0$) is 45, and the slope is 5, which means that, on the average, the value of the forecast will increase by five units for each time period. If $t = 10$, the forecast, F_t, is $45 + 5(10) = 95$ units. The equation can be plotted by finding two points on the line. One can be found by substituting some value of t into the equation (e.g., $t = 10$). The other point is $(0, a)$ (i.e., $\hat{y}_t$ at $t = 0$). Plotting those two points and drawing a straight line through them yields the graph of the linear trend line.

The coefficients of the line, a and b, can be computed from data using these two equations:

$$b = \frac{n\sum ty - \sum t \sum y}{n\sum t^2 - (\sum t)^2} \tag{3-4}$$

$$a = \frac{\sum y - b\sum t}{n} \text{ or } \bar{y} - b\bar{t} \tag{3-5}$$

where

n = Total number of periods
y = Value of the demand time series

Note that these equations are identical to those used for computing a linear regression line, except that t replaces x in the equations.

EXAMPLE 3-4

Cellphone sales of a company over the last 10 weeks are shown below. The data appear to have a linear trend. Determine the equation of the linear trend and predict the sales of cellphones for weeks 11 and 12. Plot the data and trend line.

Week	Unit Sales
1	700
2	724
3	720
4	728
5	740
6	742
7	758
8	750
9	770
10	775

Week (t)	y	ty	t^2
5	740	3,700	25
6	742	4,452	36
7	758	5,306	49
8	750	6,000	64
9	770	6,930	81
10	775	7,750	100
55	7,407	41,358	385

Using Formulas 3-4 and 3-5, we can calculate the coefficients of the trend line:

$$b = \frac{10(41,358) - 55(7,407)}{10(385) - 55(55)} = \frac{6,195}{825} = 7.51$$

$$a = \frac{7,407 - 7.51(55)}{10} = 699.40$$

Thus, the trend line is $\hat{y}_t = 699.40 + 7.51t$.

Substituting values of t into this equation, the forecasts for the next two weeks (i.e., $t = 11$ and $t = 12$) are:

$$F_{11} = 699.40 + 7.51(11) = 782.01$$
$$F_{12} = 699.40 + 7.51(12) = 789.52$$

The original data (in blue), the trend line (in red), and five projections (forecasts) are shown on the following graph. It is evident that the data exhibit a linear trend.

SOLUTION

Week (t)	y	ty	t^2
1	700	700	1
2	724	1,448	4
3	720	2,160	9
4	728	2,912	16

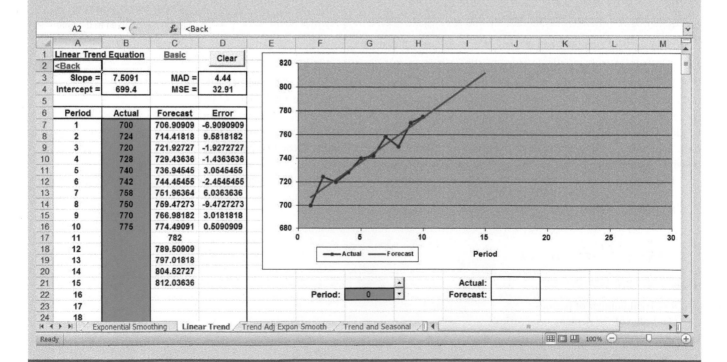

We can use the Excel template from Connect2 to solve this problem. Alternatively, we can set up our own Excel template. In fact, Excel has a feature that makes fitting a trend line very easy. In Excel, click "Insert" on the command bar and then click "Scatter with Straight Lines and Markers." Next, click on a white space on the chart (Option menu will appear on the right). Click on "+" and choose "Trendline." Click the trendline on the graph and right-click to "Format Trendline ...," and tick "Display Equation on chart."

Nonlinear Trend

Although a linear trend is appropriate for some series, it is inadequate for others, such as demand for a new product that has a faster growth or for an old product that has a slower growth. Example 3-5 illustrates an exponential trend.

◀ EXAMPLE 3-5

PHH Fantus Corp. (now part of Deloitte) was involved in facility location and capacity planning consulting work.[1] One project involved a manufacturer of audio products with a production facility in the United Kingdom that needed more production capacity. From this plant, the company was supplying all of Europe. The question was where to locate a second plant and what capacity to build it for. The historical sales for all major European countries were available. From these, Fantus forecasted 1991–1995 sales. The largest sales market was in Germany, and it appeared to have an exponential trend (see the graph). We wish to find out the equation for this trend and extend it one year further.

Year (x)	Projected Sales in Germany (in million units)
1991	11.3
1992	13.4
1993	16.1
1994	19.2
1995	22.9

SOLUTION

After entering the data in Excel and drawing the time series line plot using "Chart," we use the "Trendline" function to fit the best exponential trend to the data. The equation will also be displayed if you select the "Display equation on chart" option.

The exponential trend equation is approximately, $\hat{y}_t = 9.4431e^{0.1772x}$, where $e = 2.7182818$. Note that this exponential trend assumes a constant *percentage* increase in sales from one year to the next. This constant growth rate can be determined as follows: take the coefficient of year index x from regression, raise e to the power of the coefficient, subtract 1, and multiply by 100. For this example, $e^{0.1772} = 1.194$, so the constant percentage yearly increase in sales is 19.4 percent. This can be confirmed by subtracting any year's sales from the following year's sales and dividing by the same year's sales. For example: (Forecast sales 1995 − Forecast sales 1994)/Forecast sales 1994 = (22.9 − 19.2)/19.2 = 0.193, or 19.3 percent (the difference to 19.4 percent is rounding error). The forecast for 1996 is $F_{96} = 9.4431e^{0.1772(6)} = 27.3$ million units.

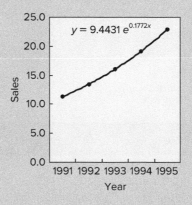

$y = 9.4431 \, e^{0.1772x}$

Trend-Adjusted Exponential Smoothing

A variation of simple exponential smoothing can be used when a time series exhibits trend. It is called **trend-adjusted exponential smoothing** or *double exponential smoothing*. If a series exhibits trend, and exponential smoothing is used on it, the forecasts will all lag behind the trend: if the data are increasing, each forecast will be too low; if the data are decreasing, each forecast will be too high.

> **trend-adjusted exponential smoothing** Variation of exponential smoothing used when a time series exhibits trend.

[1] M.P. Butler, "Facility and Capacity Planning Using Sales Forecasting by Today's Industrial Engineer," *Industrial Engineering* 22(6), June 1990, pp. 52–55.

The trend-adjusted forecast (TAF) for period $t + 1$ is composed of two forecasts:

$$\text{TAF}_{t+1} = S_t + T_t \tag{3-6}$$

where

S_t = Smoothed series at the end of period t
T_t = Smoothed trend at the end of period t

which are in turn estimated by:

$$S_t = \text{TAF}_t + \alpha(A_t - \text{TAF}_t) \tag{3-7}$$
$$T_t = T_{t-1} + \beta(S_t - S_{t-1} - T_{t-1})$$

where α and β are smoothing constants, and A_t = actual value in period t. In order to use this method, one must select values of α and β (usually through trial and error) and make an estimate of starting smoothed series and smoothed trend. We will use the first few data points to estimate the smoothed series and smoothed trend.

EXAMPLE 3-6 ▶

Using the cellphone data from Example 3-4 (where it was concluded that the data exhibited a linear trend), use trend-adjusted exponential smoothing to prepare forecasts for periods 5 through 11, with $\alpha = 0.4$ and $\beta = 0.3$. Use the first four weeks to estimate starting smoothed series and smoothed trend.

SOLUTION

Table 3-1 displays the data again in the Actual column. We will use the average of the first four weeks as the starting smoothed series:

$$S_4 = (700 + 724 + 720 + 728)/4 = 718.$$

The starting smoothed trend can be based on the net change of $728 - 700 = 28$ for the *three* changes from week 1 to week 4, for an average of $T_4 = 28/3 = 9.33$.

The trend-adjusted forecast for week 5 is:

$$\text{TAF}_5 = S_4 + T_4 = 718 + 9.33 = 727.33$$

After observing the actual sales in week 5 (740 units), we can calculate the smoothed series and smoothed trend at the end of week 5:

$$S_5 = \text{TAF}_5 + \alpha(A_5 - \text{TAF}_5)$$
$$= 727.33 + 0.4(740 - 727.33)$$
$$= 732.40$$
$$T_5 = T_4 + \beta(S_5 - S_4 - T_4)$$
$$= 9.33 + 0.3(732.40 - 718 - 9.33)$$
$$= 10.85$$

TABLE 3-1 ▼

Trend-adjusted forecast calculations for Example 3-6.

t (Week)	A_t (Actual)	$\text{TAF}_t + \alpha(A_t - \text{TAF}_t) = S_t$	$T_{t-1} + \beta(S_t - S_{t-1} - T_{t-1}) = T_t$	$\text{TAF}_{t+1} = S_t + T_t$
1	700			
2	724	Starting values:		
3	720	$S_4 = (700 + 724 + 720 + 728)/4 = 718$, $T_4 = (728 - 700)/3 = 9.33$		
4	728	$\text{TAF}_5 = 718 + 9.33 = 727.33$		
5	740	$727.33 + 0.4(740 - 727.33) = 732.40$	$9.33 + 0.3(732.40 - 718 - 9.33) = 10.85$	743.25
6	742	$743.25 + 0.4(742 - 743.25) = 742.75$	$10.85 + 0.3(742.75 - 732.40 - 10.85) = 10.70$	753.45
7	758	$753.45 + 0.4(758 - 753.45) = 755.27$	$10.70 + 0.3(755.27 - 742.75 - 10.70) = 11.25$	766.52
8	750	$766.52 + 0.4(750 - 766.52) = 759.91$	$11.25 + 0.3(759.91 - 755.27 - 11.25) = 9.27$	769.18
9	770	$769.18 + 0.4(770 - 769.18) = 769.51$	$9.27 + 0.3(769.51 - 759.91 - 9.27) = 9.37$	778.88
10	775	$778.88 + 0.4(775 - 778.88) = 777.33$	$9.37 + 0.3(777.33 - 769.51 - 9.37) = 8.90$	786.23

Therefore, the trend-adjusted forecast for week 6 is:

$$\text{TAF}_6 = S_5 + T_5 = 732.40 + 10.85 = 743.25$$

After observing the actual sales in week 6 (742 units), we can calculate the smoothed series at the end of week 6:

$$S_6 = \text{TAF}_6 + \alpha(A_6 - \text{TAF}_6)$$
$$= 743.25 + 0.4(742 - 743.25)$$
$$= 742.75$$

and the smoothed trend at the end of week 6 is:

$$T_6 = T_5 + \beta(S_6 - S_5 - T_5)$$
$$= 10.85 + 0.3(742.75 - 732.40 - 10.85)$$
$$= 10.70.$$

Therefore, the trend-adjusted forecast for week 7 is:

$$\text{TAF}_7 = S_6 + T_6 = 742.75 + 10.70 = 753.45.$$

This process is continued until the trend-adjusted forecast for week 11, $\text{TAF}_{11} = 786.23$, is determined (see Table 3-1).

Although calculations for trend-adjusted exponential smoothing are somewhat more involved than for a linear trend line, trend-adjusted exponential smoothing has the ability to adjust to *changes* in trend. A manager must decide if this benefit justifies the extra calculations. The following figure shows the graph of the actual demand and the trend-adjusted exponential smoothing forecasts. See the "Canadian Vehicle Sales" OM in Action for an example of how forecasts are used.

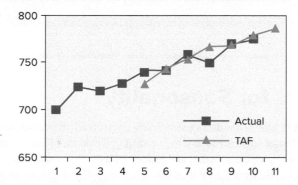

OM in Action

Canadian Vehicle Sales

Canadian automobile sales continue to rise and to break sales records from each of the previous four years, according to DesRosiers, one of the most trusted names in the auto industry. In just 2016 alone, an astounding 1.95 million new vehicles were sold nationally, beating even the most optimistic sales forecasts. Strong and steady performance in the auto sector has helped to prop up an ailing economy, long suffering from precipitous drops in oil and other major commodity prices. Industry experts attribute the record-breaking sales figures to multiple factors including cheap financing rates and longer financing terms.

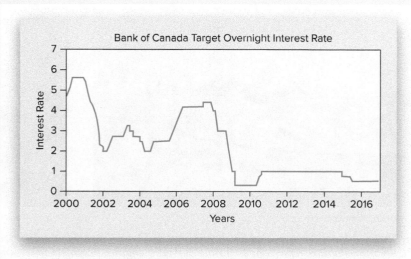

Source: CANSIM database, Table 176-0048, accessed February 12, 2017.

In order to stimulate economic activity, the Bank of Canada has kept the target overnight rate at a historic low of 0.5 percent, giving average Canadians even more access to cheap lines of credit. Cheap money combined with longer loan terms has improved affordability like never before, and achieves the desired result of bringing customers in to car dealerships like never before. Although automobile sales are difficult to forecast because demand is cyclical in nature, industry experts see strong indications that sales will continue to remain strong in the foreseeable future. Forecasts such as these are useful for vehicle manufacturers, parts suppliers, financial institutions, industry associations, and governmental institutions.

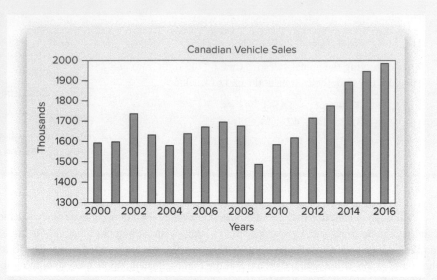

Source: CANSIM database, Series v42169911, accessed February 12, 2017.

Source: http://www.theglobeandmail.com/report-on-business/industry-news/canadian-us-car-sales-hit-record-levels-in-2016/article33502204/; https://www.td.com/document/PDF/economics/special/CanadianAutoSales_2016.pdf

LO5 Techniques for Seasonality

seasonal variations
Regularly repeating wavelike movements in series values that can be tied to recurring events, weather, or a calendar.

Seasonal variations in time series data or seasonality are regularly repeating wavelike movements in series values that can be tied to recurring events, weather, or a calendar. Familiar examples of data with seasonality are retail trade, ice cream sales, and residential natural gas sales. Most seasonal variations repeat annually. However, the term *seasonal variation* is also applied to shorter lengths of repeating patterns. For example, rush-hour traffic occurs twice a day—incoming in the morning and outgoing in the late afternoon. Theatres and restaurants often experience weekly repeating demand patterns, with higher demand on Fridays or weekends. Banks may experience daily repeating "seasonal" variations (heavier traffic during the noon hour and just before closing), weekly repeating variations (heavier toward the end of the week), and monthly repeating variations (heavier around the beginning of the month because of payroll cheques being cashed or deposited). Most products and services have seasonality.

Mark Herreid/Dreamstime.com

Webandblack/Dreamstime.com

Demand for products such as Sea-Doo watercraft and boats, Can-Am roadsters, all-terrain and side-by-side vehicles, Ski-Doo and Lynx snowmobiles, as well as Evinrude outboard engines is subject to seasonal fluctuations. Bombardier Recreational Products offsets these fluctuations by alternating its manufacturing capacity to deliver a diverse product portfolio.

Seasonality in a time series is expressed in terms of the amount that actual value during a season deviates from the *average* value of a series during the length of a repeating pattern (e.g., a year). If trend is present, seasonality is measured relative to the trend value.

There are two different models of seasonality: additive and multiplicative. In the *additive* model, seasonality is expressed as a *quantity* (e.g., 20 units), which is added to or subtracted from the series average (or trend). In the *multiplicative* model, seasonality is expressed as a *proportion* of the average (or trend) amount (e.g., 1.10), which is then multiplied by the average (or trend) of the series. Figure 3-6 illustrates the two models for a linear trend line. In practice, most organizations use the multiplicative model, so we shall focus exclusively on the multiplicative model.

The seasonal proportions in the multiplicative model are referred to as **seasonal relatives** or *seasonal indexes*. Suppose that the seasonal relative for the quantity of toys sold in November at a store is 1.20. This indicates that toy sales for that month are 20 percent above the monthly average (i.e., annual sales/12). A seasonal relative of 0.90 for July indicates that July sales are 90 percent of the monthly average. Figure 3-7 displays a variety of seasonal variations.

Knowledge of seasonal variations is an important factor in retail planning and scheduling. Moreover, seasonality can be an important factor in capacity planning for systems that must be designed to handle peak loads (e.g., public transportation, electric power plants, highways, and bridges).

Knowledge of the extent of seasonality in a time series can enable one to *remove* seasonality from the data (i.e., to seasonally adjust or deseasonalize the data) in order to discern other patterns. Thus, one frequently reads or hears about, for example, the "seasonally adjusted unemployment rate."

The next section briefly describes how seasonal relatives are used, and the following section describes how seasonal relatives are computed.

Using Seasonal Relatives Seasonal relatives are used first to *deseasonalize* the data, and later to *incorporate seasonality* in the forecast of deseasonalized data (i.e., to reseasonalize the data).

To deseasonalize the data is to remove the seasonal component from the data in order to get a clearer picture of the nonseasonal components. Deseasonalizing data is accomplished by *dividing* each data point by its seasonal relative (e.g., divide November demand by the November relative, divide December demand by the December relative, and so on).

Reseasonalizing the forecasts of the deseasonalized demand is accomplished by multiplying each forecast by its seasonal relative.

The complete steps of forecasting seasonal demand, called *time series decomposition*, are as follows:

1. Compute the seasonal relatives.
2. Deseasonalize the demand data.
3. Fit a model to the deseasonalized demand data (e.g., moving average or trend).
4. Forecast using this model (to obtain the deseasonalized forecasts).
5. Reseasonalize the deseasonalized forecasts.

Example 3-7 illustrates Steps 3 and 5 of this approach.

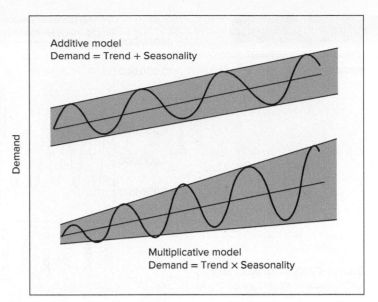

▲ **FIGURE 3-6**

Seasonality: the additive and multiplicative models compared using a linear trend.

seasonal relatives
Proportion of average or trend for a season in the multiplicative model.

FIGURE 3-7 ▶

Examples of seasonal variation.

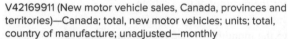

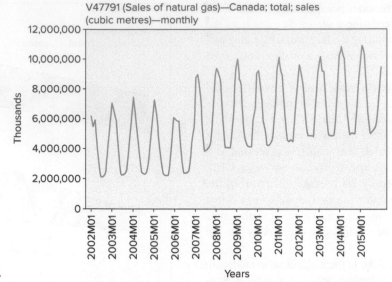

Source: CANSIM database, Series v47791, accessed February 26, 2017.

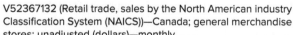

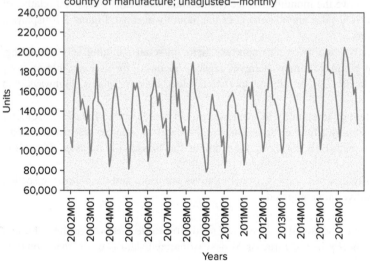

Source: CANSIM database, Series v42169911, accessed February 26, 2017.

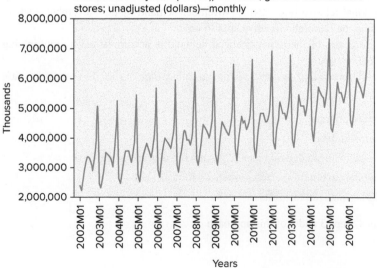

Source: CANSIM database, Series v52367132; accessed February 26, 2017.

A furniture manufacturer wants to predict quarterly demand for a certain love seat for quarters 15 and 16, which happen to be the second and third quarters of a particular year. The series has both trend and seasonality. Quarter relatives are $Q_1 = 1.20$, $Q_2 = 1.10$, $Q_3 = 0.75$, and $Q_4 = 0.95$. The trend portion of deseasonalized demand data is projected using the equation $\hat{y}_t = 124 + 7.5t$, where t is the index of the quarter and $\hat{y}_t$ is the estimate of the trend component of demand in quarter t. Use this information to predict demand for quarters 15 and 16.

Multiplying the trend value by the appropriate quarter relative yields a forecast that includes both trend and seasonality. Given that $t = 15$ is a second quarter and $t = 16$ is a third quarter, the forecasts are:

$$F_{15}: 236.5(1.10) = 260.15$$
$$F_{16}: 244.0(0.75) = 183.00$$

SOLUTION

The trend values at $t = 15$ and $t = 16$ are:

$$\hat{y}_{15} = 124 + 7.5(15) = 236.5$$
$$\hat{y}_{16} = 124 + 7.5(16) = 244.0$$

Computing Seasonal Relatives   We need to first compute the average (or trend) of all periods during the length of a repeating pattern (e.g., a year). A simple method is just to use the average of all periods. However, this ignores any trends. If there is a linear trend, then regression can be used to model it. However, seasonality could influence the slope of the line. A better way is to use **centred moving average (CMA)**. The computations are similar to those for a moving average forecast. However, the values are not projected as in a forecast; instead, they are *positioned in the middle of* the set of periods used to compute the moving average. The implication is that the CMA is most representative of that point in the series. For example, consider the following time series data where the length of a repeating pattern is three periods:

centred moving average (CMA) A moving average positioned at the centre of the data that were used to compute it.

Period	Demand	Three-Period Centred Average	
1	40		
2	46	42.67	Average $= \dfrac{40 + 46 + 42}{3} = 42.67$
3	42		

The three-period average is 42.67. As a centred average, it is positioned at period 2; the average is most representative of the series at that point.

The ratio of demand at period 2 to this centred average at period 2 is an estimate of the seasonal relative at that point. Because the ratio is $46/42.67 = 1.08$, the series is 8 percent above average at that point. However, to achieve a reliable estimate of seasonality for any season, it is necessary to compute seasonal ratios for a number of seasons and then average these ratios. For example, average the ratios of two or three Fridays for the Friday relative, average two or three Saturdays for the Saturday relative, and so on.

The manager of a parking lot has calculated the daily relatives for the number of cars per day in the parking lot. The length of a repeating pattern is a week. The calculations are displayed below (about three weeks are shown for illustration). A seven-period centred moving average is used because there are seven days (seasons) per week.

Day	No. of Cars	Centred MA$_7$	No. of Cars/CMA$_7$
Tues	67		
Wed	75		
Thur	82		
Fri	98	71.86	98/71.86 = 1.36 (Friday)
Sat	90	70.86	90/70.86 = 1.27
Sun	36	70.57	36/70.57 = 0.51
Mon	55	71.00	55/71.00 = 0.77
Tues	60	71.14	60/71.14 = 0.84 (Tuesday)
Wed	73	70.57	73/70.57 = 1.03
Thur	85	71.14	85/71.14 = 1.19
Fri	99	70.71	99/70.71 = 1.40 (Friday)
Sat	86	71.29	86/71.29 = 1.21
Sun	40	71.71	40/71.71 = 0.56
Mon	52	72.00	52/72.00 = 0.72
Tues	64	71.57	64/71.57 = 0.89 (Tuesday)
Wed	76	71.86	76/71.86 = 1.06
Thur	87	72.43	87/72.43 = 1.20
Fri	96	72.14	96/72.14 = 1.33 (Friday)
Sat	88		
Sun	44		
Mon	50		

The estimated Friday relative is $(1.36 + 1.40 + 1.33)/3 = 1.36$. Relatives for other days can be calculated in a similar manner. For example, the estimated Tuesday relative is $(0.84 + 0.89)/2 = 0.87$. The sum of average ratios of the seven days of the week should be seven (because an average day has a seasonal relative of one and there are seven average days in a week). If it is not, the average ratios should be adjusted by re-scaling them.

The number of periods needed in a centred moving average is equal to the number of "seasons" involved. For example, with quarterly data, a four-period centred moving average is needed. When the number of periods is even, one additional step is needed because the middle of an even set of periods falls between two middle periods. The additional step requires taking a centred two-period moving average of the even-numbered centred moving average, which results in averages that "line up" with data points and, hence, permit determination of seasonal ratios. The following example illustrates this case, as well as the other steps of the time series decomposition.

EXAMPLE 3-9 ▶

Below are quarterly data for the amount of ice cream produced in Canada from quarter 1 of 2013 to quarter 4 of 2016.[2]

a. Calculate the quarterly relatives using the centred moving average method.

b. Deseasonalize the data, fit an appropriate model, project it four quarters ahead, and reseasonalize to obtain forecasts for ice cream demand for Q1 to Q4 of 2017.

---
[2] Adapted from CANSIM 2 Series v382696.

SOLUTION

a.

Quarter		Production (Thousand litres)	CMA$_4$	CMA$_2$	Production/CMA$_2$
2013	1	33			
	2	52			
			40.250		
	3	47		41.000	47/41.000 = 1.146
			41.750		
	4	29		42.750	29/42.750 = 0.678
			43.750		
2014	1	39		44.750	0.872
			45.750		
	2	60		46.375	1.294
			47.000		
	3	55		48.375	1.186
			45.750		
	4	34		45.125	0.753
			44.500		
2015	1	34		43.250	0.786
			42.000		
	2	55		41.375	1.329
			40.750		
	3	45		40.750	1.104
			40.750		
	4	29		40.375	0.718
			40.000		
2016	1	34		40.625	0.837
			41.250		
	2	52		41.375	1.257
			41.500		
	3	50			
	4	30			

Year	QUARTER				Total
	1	2	3	4	
2013			1.146	0.678	
2014	0.872	1.294	1.186	0.753	
2015	0.786	1.329	1.104	0.718	
2016	0.837	1.257			
Average	0.832	1.293	1.146	0.717	3.987
Adjusted	0.832(4/3.987) = 0.834	1.293(4/3.987) = 1.297	1.149	0.719	4.000

b.

Quarter		Production (million litres)	Seasonal Relatives	Deseasonalized Production
2013	1	33	0.834	33/0.834 = 39.558
	2	52	1.297	52/1.297 = 40.077
	3	47	1.149	40.896
	4	29	0.719	40.332
2014	1	39	0.834	46.750
	2	60	1.297	46.243
	3	55	1.149	47.857
	4	34	0.719	47.286
2015	1	34	0.834	40.757
	2	55	1.297	42.389
	3	45	1.149	39.156
	4	29	0.719	40.332
2016	1	34	0.834	40.757
	2	52	1.297	40.077
	3	50	1.149	43.506
	4	30	0.719	41.723

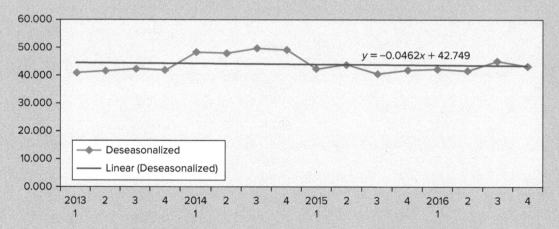

The deseasonalized data has a (decreasing) linear trend. Therefore, a linear trend is fitted to the deseasonalized data using regression, and its equation is displayed at the top of the chart above.

Using the regression equation, the trend forecasts for periods 17 to 20 (Q1 to Q4 of 2017) are:

$$Y_{17} = -0.0462(17) + 42.749 = 41.963$$
$$Y_{18} = -0.0462(18) + 42.749 = 41.917$$

$$Y_{19} = -0.0462(19) + 42.749 = 41.871$$
$$Y_{20} = -0.0462(20) + 42.749 = 41.825$$

The reseasonalized forecasts for Q1 to Q4 of 2017 are:

$$F_{17} = 41.963(0.834) = 35.01$$
$$F_{18} = 41.917(1.297) = 54.39$$
$$F_{19} = 41.871(1.149) = 48.12$$
$$F_{20} = 41.825(0.719) = 30.07$$

annual average method
A simpler method for finding seasonal relatives that involves finding the ratio of actual demand relative to average seasonal demand in that year and averaging the ratios across years.

A simpler method for finding seasonal relatives is the **annual average method**. To find the seasonal relatives using this method, we follow the procedure below:

1. For each year, compute its total annual demand and average seasonal demand.

2. For each year, for each season, compute the ratio of the actual demand relative to average seasonal demand.

3. For each season, average the ratios across years to get seasonal relatives.

4. Fit a linear trend to the total annual demand series.

5. Extend the model into the future to get next year's total annual demand.

6. Divide the forecast of next year's total annual demand by 4 to get the forecast of next year's average seasonal demand.

7. For each season, multiply the forecast of next year's average seasonal demand by the season's seasonal relative.

Consider the same data as Example 3-9.

a. Compute the seasonal relative for each quarter using the annual average method.

b. Forecast the sales of ice cream in each quarter of 2017.

◀ **EXAMPLE 3-10**

SOLUTION

a.

Quarter	2013	2014	2015	2016
1	33	39	34	34
2	52	60	55	52
3	47	55	45	50
4	29	34	29	30
Total	161	188	163	166
Average	40.25	47	40.75	41.50

Quarter	2013 Ratio	2014 Ratio	2015 Ratio	2016 Ratio	Average Ratio
1	$33/40.25 = 0.82$	0.83	0.83	0.82	$\dfrac{(0.82 + 0.83 + 0.83 + 0.82)}{4} = 0.83$
2	$52/40.25 = 1.29$	1.28	1.35	1.25	$\dfrac{(1.29 + 1.28 + 1.35 + 1.25)}{4} = 1.29$
3	$47/40.25 = 1.17$	1.17	1.10	1.20	$\dfrac{(1.17 + 1.17 + 1.10 + 1.20)}{4} = 1.16$
4	$29/40.25 = 0.72$	0.72	0.71	0.72	$\dfrac{(0.72 + 0.72 + 0.71 + 0.72)}{4} = 0.72$

$$0.83 + 1.29 + 1.16 + 0.72 = 4$$

Year	Annual Demand
2013	161
2014	188
2014	163
2015	166

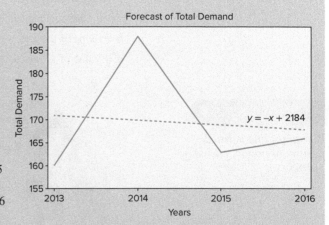

Forecast of Total Demand

$y = -x + 2184$

b. Forecast for 2017 1ˢᵗ Quarter $= \dfrac{(-2017 + 2184)}{4} \times 0.83 = 34.65$

Forecast for 2017 2ⁿᵈ Quarter $= \dfrac{(-2017 + 2184)}{4} \times 1.29 = 53.86$

Forecast for 2017 3ʳᵈ Quarter $= \dfrac{(-2017 + 2184)}{4} \times 1.16 = 48.43$

Forecast for 2017 4ᵗʰ Quarter $= \dfrac{(-2017 + 2184)}{4} \times 0.72 = 30.06$

Techniques for Cycles

Cycles are wavelike movements, similar to seasonal variations, but of longer duration—say, two to six years between peaks. When cycles occur in time series data, their irregularity makes it difficult or impossible to project them from past data because turning points are difficult to identify. A short moving average or a naïve approach may be of some value, although both will produce forecasts that lag cyclical movements by one or several periods.

The most commonly used approach is associative models: Search for another variable that relates to, and *leads*, the variable of interest. For example, the number of housing starts (i.e., permits to build houses) in a given month often is an indicator of demand a few months later for products and services directly tied to construction of new homes (e.g., sales of new major appliances; new demands for shopping, transportation, schools). Thus, if an organization is able to establish a high correlation with such a *leading variable* (i.e., changes in the variable precede changes in the variable of interest), it can develop an equation that describes the relationship, enabling forecasts to be made. It is important that a persistent relationship exist between the two variables. Moreover, the higher the correlation, the better the chances that the forecast will be accurate.

Associative Models

Associative models rely on identification of related variables that can be used to predict values of the variable of interest. For example, sales of beef are related to the price of beef and the prices of substitutes such as chicken, pork, and lamb; sales during promotions depend on the discount and size of the ad; and crop yields are related to soil conditions and the amounts and timing of rain and fertilizer applications.

The essence of associative models is the development of an equation that summarizes the effects of **predictor variables** on the variable of interest. The primary method of analysis is **regression**.

predictor variables
Variables that can be used to predict values of the variable of interest.

regression Technique for fitting a line to a set of points.

least squares line Minimizes the sum of the squared deviations around the line.

Simple Linear Regression

The simplest and most widely used form of regression involves a linear relationship between two variables. A plot of the values might appear like that in Figure 3-8. The objective in linear regression is to obtain an equation of a straight line that minimizes the sum of squared vertical deviations of data points (x, y) from the line. This **least squares line** has the equation

$$\hat{y} = a + bx \tag{3-8}$$

where

$\hat{y}$ = Predicted (dependent) variable

x = Predictor (independent) variable

b = Slope of the line

a = Value of $\hat{y}$ when $x = 0$ (i.e., the height of the line at the y intercept)

FIGURE 3-8 ▶

A straight line is fitted to a set of points, each a pair (x, y).

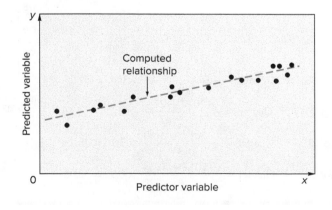

(*Note:* It is conventional to represent values of the predicted variable on the *y* axis and values of the predictor variable on the *x* axis.) Figure 3-9 illustrates the linear regression equation.

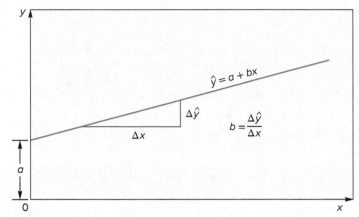

The line intersects the *y* axis where $\hat{y} = a$. The slope of the line $= b$.

◀ FIGURE 3-9

Equation of a straight line.

The coefficients *a* and *b* of the line are computed using these two equations:

$$b = \frac{n(\sum xy) - (\sum x)(\sum y)}{n(\sum x^2) - (\sum x)^2}$$ (3-9)

$$a = \frac{\sum y - b\sum x}{n} \text{ or } \bar{y} - b\bar{x}$$ (3-10)

where

n = Number of paired observations

(x, y) = The symbols showing a pair of observations

◀ EXAMPLE 3-11

Healthy Hamburgers has a chain of 12 stores. Revenue and profit for the stores are given below. Obtain a regression line for the data, and predict profit for a store with revenue of $10 million.

Revenue, x	Profit, y
(in millions of dollars)	
7	0.15
2	0.10
6	0.13
4	0.15
14	0.25
15	0.27
16	0.24
12	0.20
14	0.27
20	0.44
15	0.34
7	0.17

SOLUTION

First, plot the data and decide if a linear model is reasonable (i.e., do the points seem to scatter around a straight line? Figure 3-10 suggests they do). Next, compute the quantities $\sum x$, $\sum y$, $\sum xy$, and $\sum x^2$ and substitute into Formula 3-9 and Formula 3-10 to find:

$$b = \frac{n(\sum xy) - (\sum x)(\sum y)}{n(\sum x^2) - (\sum x)^2} = \frac{12(35.29) - 132(2.71)}{12(1,796) - 132(132)}$$

$$= 0.01593$$

$$a = \frac{\sum y - b(\sum x)}{n} = \frac{2.71 - 0.01593(132)}{12} = 0.0506$$

FIGURE 3-10 ▶

A linear model seems reasonable for Example 3-11.

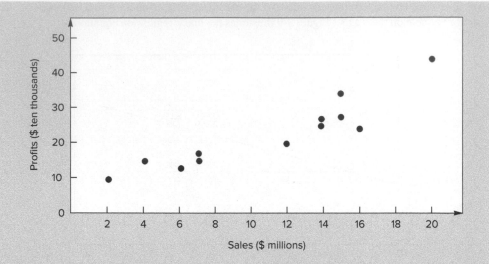

Thus, the regression equation is: $\hat{y} = 0.0506 + 0.01593x$. For revenue of $x = 10$ (i.e., $10 million), estimated profit is: $\hat{y} = 0.0506 + 0.01593(10) = 0.2099$, or $209,900. (It may appear strange that substituting $x = 0$ into the equation produces a predicted profit of $50,600 because it seems to suggest that profit will occur with no sales. However, the value of $x = 0$ is *outside the range of observed values*. The regression line should be used only for the range of values from which it was developed; the relationship may be nonlinear outside that range. The purpose of the a value is simply to establish the height of the line where it crosses the y axis.)

The Excel template of this problem on Connect2 is shown in Table 3-2. The symbol r represents correlation between x and y, and will be described next. The regression coefficients b and a can also be directly obtained in Excel using "=slope(RangeY,RangeX)" and "=intercept(RangeY,RangeX)" functions, respectively, where RangeY is the range of Excel cells containing the y values and RangeX is the range of Excel cells containing the x values.

TABLE 3-2 ▼

Excel template for Example 3-11.

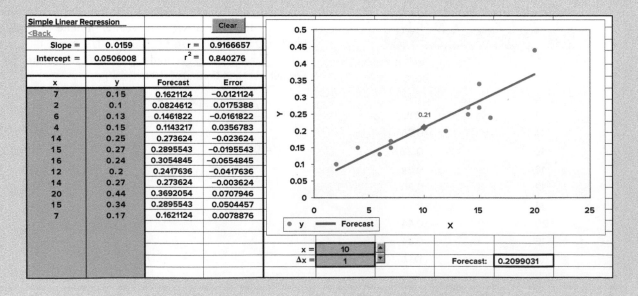

Correlation Coefficient

Correlation coefficient measures the strength of relationship between two variables, and can range from −1.00 to +1.00. A correlation coefficient of +1.00 indicates that changes in one variable are always matched by changes in the other variable in the same direction; a correlation coefficient of −1.00 indicates that increases in one variable are matched by decreases in the other variable; and a correlation coefficient close to zero indicates little *linear* relationship between two variables. If a causal model is to be used to forecast the demand for an item (y), it is important that the relationship between x and y variables is strong. The correlation coefficient between two variables can be computed using the equation:

> **correlation coefficient**
> A measure of the strength of relationship between two variables.

$$r = \frac{n(\sum xy) - (\sum x)(\sum y)}{\sqrt{n(\sum x^2) - (\sum x)^2} \cdot \sqrt{n(\sum y^2) - (\sum y)^2}} \tag{3-11}$$

The square of the correlation coefficient, r^2, provides a measure of the proportion of variability in the values of y that is "explained" by the independent variable. The possible values of r^2 range from 0 to 1.00. The closer r^2 is to 1.00, the greater the proportion of explained variation. A high value of r^2, say 0.80 or more, would indicate that the independent variable is a good predictor of values of the dependent variable. A low value, say 0.25 or less, would indicate a poor predictor, and a value between 0.25 and 0.80 would indicate a moderate predictor.

The correlation coefficient can be obtained in Excel using the "=CORREL(RangeY,RangeX)" function, where RangeY is the range of Excel cells containing the y values and RangeX is the range of Excel cells containing the x values. Similarly, r^2 can be obtained in Excel using the "=RSQ(RangeY,RangeX)" function.

Monthly sales of LCD television sets in a store and the unemployment rate in the region are shown below for 11 months. Determine if unemployment levels can be used to predict demand for LCD TVs and, if so, derive the correlation coefficient and the predictive equation.

◄ EXAMPLE 3-12

Month.............	1	2	3	4	5	6	7	8	9	10	11
Units sold (y)........	20	41	17	35	25	31	38	50	15	19	14
Unemployment % (x)...	7.2	4.0	7.3	5.5	6.8	6.0	5.4	3.6	8.4	7.0	9.0

SOLUTION

1. Plot the data to see if a linear model seems reasonable. In this case, a linear model seems somewhat appropriate.

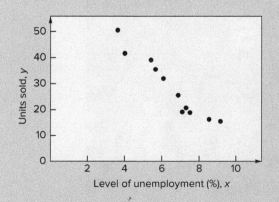

2. Compute the correlation coefficient:

$$r = \frac{11(1{,}750.8) - 70.2(305)}{\sqrt{11(476.3) - (70.2)^2} \cdot \sqrt{11(9{,}907) - (305)^2}} = -0.966$$

This is a high negative correlation, indicating a strong downward-sloping linear relationship.

3. Compute the regression line:

$$b = \frac{11(1{,}750.8) - 70.2(305)}{11(476.4) - 70.2(70.2)} = -6.91$$

$$a = \frac{305 - (-6{,}9145)(70.2)}{11} = 71.85$$

$$y = 71.85 - 6.91x$$

Note that the equation pertains only to unemployment levels in the range 3.6–9.0 percent, because sample observations cover only that range.

Multiple Regression

Simple linear regression may prove inadequate to handle certain problems because more than one predictor variable is needed. Models that involve more than one predictor require the use of multiple regression. While this is beyond the scope of this text, you should be aware that it is often used. The computations lend themselves more to computers than to hand calculation. It is necessary to weigh the additional cost and effort against potential improvements in accuracy of predictions. See the "Mark's" OM in Action for an interesting forecasting application.

 OM in Action   www.marks.com

Mark's

Mark's Work Wearhouse started as a work wear store in Calgary in 1977 but has since taken a new name, going simply by Mark's, and has expanded its merchandise to include casual, business, sports, and outdoor apparel for both men and women. It now has over 385 stores throughout Canada, more than 6,300 employees, and revenue of over $1 billion a year. Such a drastic expansion has put considerable strain on its supply chain management software to forecast demand accurately and have the right merchandise in the right store at the right time.

Every region has different apparel needs. For example, in downtown Toronto, work wear is khaki pants and a golf shirt, but in the oil fields around Edmonton, guys covered head-to-foot in oil will jump out of pick-up trucks in search of new clothes. Mark's sells a lot more rain wear in Vancouver than in Saskatoon. Sizes also vary regionally. Mark's stores in British Columbia cater to a significant Asian population and smaller sizes are

a steady part of the mix in the stores. In Gallic Quebec, customers tend to be of average stature, while in the prairie and mountain provinces, they "grow 'em big."

These are the reasons why Mark's needs good forecasting, fulfillment, and merchandising software. In the 1990s, Mark's was using INFOREM, IBM's inventory and forecasting software which ran on an IBM mainframe computer. However, the forecasting module was not used effectively and INFOREM did not have the analytics and merchandising capabilities Mark's needs. Mark's was incurring significant costs for free delivery of out-of-stock merchandise to its customers' homes under Mark's Fastfind program. Since then, Mark's has bought and installed various software from JDA. These include JDA Demand, JDA Size Scaling, and JDA Fulfillment. JDA Demand is the forecasting module. JDA Size Scaling uses store-level data on sizes of apparel purchased to determine which size fits each store. It also determines what percentage of merchandise should be distributed at season-opening and what percentage should be kept in the Mark's distribution centres (DCs)

Yelena Rodriguez/Dreamstime.com

for in-season replenishment. JDA Fulfillment is basically distribution requirements planning (DRP)—that is, using each store's weekly time-phased forecast for the coming season, it works backward and plans the distribution of apparel, the required inventory in Mark's DCs, and the required replenishments from Mark's suppliers (more on DRP in Chapter 12).

The demand for most of Mark's products, such as winter clothing and boots or summer shorts, is affected by the season. Mark's started using weather intelligence information from Planalytics to fine-tune its seasonal merchandising, assortment, and allocation planning for some of its products. Mark's buyers have found this information useful. For example, recently a men's buyer had to decide on the discount price for shorts for a Father's Day flyer to be printed in May. Usually, all shorts would have been offered at a 50 percent discount. However, the prediction from Planalytics was for a colder-than-usual spring and

warmer-than-usual summer. Based on this, the buyer took a chance and discounted only some types of the shorts 25 percent. The weather prediction came true, resulting in fewer sales of shorts in spring; however, all the remaining shorts were sold in the summer at full price. This action resulted in $50,000 more profit. Also, because the forecast called for a warmer summer in Western Canada, 8,000 additional shorts were diverted to the Western Canada stores, and all were subsequently sold.

In another example, winter was predicted to be less severe. This resulted in Mark's buying more removable-liner jackets and fewer fixed-liner jackets. Planalytics also provides how much more or less a product will sell during a season; for example, 20 percent more demand for cotton fleece.

Sources: Inforem User's Manual; J. K. Speer, "Rain or Shine, Mark's Work Wearhouse Has the Right Stuff," *Apparel* 48(2) Oct 2006, pp. 20–22.

Accuracy and Control of Forecasting Process (L07)

Accuracy and control of the forecasting process are vital aspects of forecasting. Forecasting accuracy is the degree of correctness of the forecasts generated by the forecasting process. The large number of factors usually influencing the demand for a product or spare part, and random variations, make it almost impossible to correctly predict future values of demand on a regular basis. Consequently, it is important to include the extent to which the forecast might deviate from the actual value. This will allow the forecast user to better prepare for probable values of demand, provided that this deviation is not too large (i.e., the forecasting process is accurate enough).

Accurate forecasts are necessary for the success of daily activities of every organization. Forecasts are the basis for an organization's schedules, and unless the forecasts are accurate enough, schedules will be generated that may provide for too few or too many resources, too little or too much output, the wrong output, or the wrong timing of output, all of which can lead to additional costs, dissatisfied customers, and headaches for managers.

A related concept is control of the forecasting process. Assuming that a forecasting process was initially accurate enough, it is important to monitor forecast errors through time to ensure that the errors remain within reasonable bounds (i.e., the forecasting process remains accurate enough). If they are not, it will be necessary to take corrective action. Both accuracy and control of the forecasting process require measurement of forecast errors. **Forecast error** is the difference between the value that actually occurs and the value that was forecasted for a given time period. Hence, Forecast error = Actual value − Forecast value:

$$e_t = A_t - F_t \tag{3-12}$$

Positive errors result when the forecast is too low relative to the actual value, whereas negative errors result when the forecast is too high relative to the actual value. For example, if actual demand for a month is 100 units and forecast demand was 90 units, the forecast was too low; the forecast error is $100 - 90 = +10$.

Accuracy of the Forecasting Process

Accuracy (or better, inaccuracy) of the forecasting process is measured using three alternative forecast-error summaries: **mean absolute deviation (MAD)**, **mean squared error (MSE)**, and **mean absolute percent error (MAPE)**. MAD is the average absolute forecast error, MSE is the average

---

forecast error Difference between the actual value and the forecast value for a given period.

mean absolute deviation (MAD) The average of absolute value of forecast errors.

mean squared error (MSE) The average of squared forecast errors.

mean absolute percent error (MAPE) The average absolute percent forecast error.

of squared forecast errors, and MAPE is the average absolute percent forecast error. The formulas used to compute MAD, MSE, and MAPE are:[3]

$$\text{MAD} = \frac{\sum |\text{Actual} - \text{Forecast}|}{n} \tag{3-13}$$

$$\text{MSE} = \frac{\sum (\text{Actual} - \text{Forecast})^2}{n} \tag{3-14}$$

$$\text{MAPE} = \frac{\sum \left[\frac{|\text{Actual} - \text{Forecast}|}{\text{Actual}} \times 100 \right]}{n} \tag{3-15}$$

where n is the number of periods. MAD and MSE are similar to the standard deviation and variance of the forecast error, respectively. Example 3-13 illustrates the calculation of MAD, MSE, and MAPE.

EXAMPLE 3-13 ▶

Calculate MAD, MSE, and MAPE for the following data.

Period	Actual	Forecast	Forecast (A−F) Error	Forecast |Error|	|Error|²	$\frac{|\text{Error}|}{\text{Actual}} \times 100$
1. . . .	217	215	2	2	4	0.92%
2. . . .	213	216	−3	3	9	1.41
3. . . .	216	215	1	1	1	0.46
4. . . .	210	214	−4	4	16	1.90
5. . . .	213	211	2	2	4	0.94
6. . . .	219	214	5	5	25	2.28
7. . . .	216	217	−1	1	1	0.46
8. . . .	212	216	−4	4	16	1.89
			−2	22	76	10.26%

SOLUTION

Using the numbers shown in the above table,

$$\text{MAD} = \frac{\sum |e|}{n} = \frac{22}{8} = 2.75$$

$$\text{MSE} = \frac{\sum e^2}{n} = \frac{76}{8} = 9.5$$

$$\text{MAPE} = \frac{\sum \left[\frac{|e|}{\text{Actual}} \times 100 \right]}{n} = \frac{10.26\%}{8} = 1.28\%$$

From a computational standpoint, the difference between these three measures is that MAD weighs all errors equally, MSE weighs errors according to their *squared* values, and MAPE weighs errors relative to their actual values.

Because MAD and MSE depend on the scale of data, it is not meaningful to compare the MAD or MSE of two different time series variables. However, we can compare the accuracy of two different forecasting techniques for the same time series variable: A lower value for MAD or MSE implies a more accurate forecasting technique. For an example, see Solved Problem 8.

MAPE can be used to measure forecasting accuracy irrespective of the specific time series data used. For example, the accuracy of the forecasting process resulting in the forecasts given in Example 3-13 is 100 − MAPE = 100 −1.28 = 98.72%, a very accurate forecasting process. In practice, accuracy above 70 percent is considered satisfactory. A related concept to forecasting accuracy is the sum of forecast errors, sometimes called **bias**. A persistently positive bias implies that forecasts frequently underestimate the actual values, and a persistently negative bias implies that forecasts frequently overestimate the actual values. Bias occurs because either demand pattern has changed or the way forecasts are determined is flawed. For example, if forecasts are based on salespeople's opinions, the way their budget is determined tends to influence their forecasts: for new products they tend to underestimate the demand, and for declining products they tend to overestimate the demand.[4]

bias The sum of forecast errors.

---

[3] The absolute value, represented by the two vertical lines in Formula 3-13, ignores minus signs; all data are treated as positive values. For example, −2 becomes +2.

[4] H. Petersen, "Integrating the Forecasting Process With the Supply Chain: Bayer Healthcare's Journey," *Journal of Business Forecasting Methods & Systems* 22(4), Winter 2003/2004, pp. 11–16.

The above statements about MAD, MSE, and MAPE assume negligible bias. If bias is substantial, it will reduce the accuracy of the forecasting process. For Example 3-13, bias = −2, which is very small relative to the scale of demand (over 210). It is important to reduce the bias in order to improve the accuracy of the forecasting process.

Controlling the Forecasting Process

It is necessary to monitor forecast errors to ensure that the forecasting process is performing adequately and remains accurate enough. If not, corrective action should be taken.

Monitoring forecast errors is usually accomplished by either a control chart or a tracking signal.

Control Chart A **control chart for forecast errors** is a time series plot of forecast errors where they are compared to two predetermined values, or *control limits*. Forecast errors that fall outside either control limit signal that corrective action is needed.

Also, corrective action is needed if there is strong evidence against the following two assumptions:

1. Forecast errors are randomly distributed around a mean of zero (i.e., there is no bias).

2. The distribution of forecast errors is normal. See Figure 3-11.

> **control chart for forecast errors** A time series plot of forecast errors that has limits for individual forecast errors.

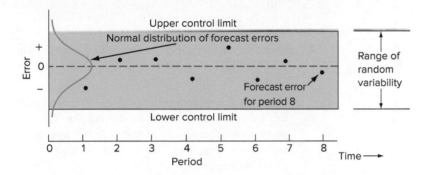

◀ **FIGURE 3-11**

Conceptual representation of a control chart.

The control limits are usually chosen as a multiple of the standard deviation of forecast errors. The square root of MSE is used in practice as an estimate of the standard deviation of forecast errors.[5] That is,

$$s = \sqrt{\text{MSE}} \qquad (3\text{-}16)$$

Recall from your statistics course that for a normal distribution, approximately 95 percent of the values (forecast errors in this case) fall within limits of $0 \pm 2s$ (i.e., 0 ± 2 standard deviations), and approximately 99.7 percent of the values fall within $\pm 3s$ of zero. Hence, if the forecasting process is "in control," 99.7 percent or 95 percent of the forecast errors should fall within the control limits, depending on whether $3s$ or $2s$ control limits are used.

Compute $2s$ control limits for forecast errors when the MSE is 9.0.

◀ EXAMPLE 3-14

SOLUTION

$$s = \sqrt{\text{MSE}} = \sqrt{9} = 3$$
$$\text{UCL} = 0 + 2(3.0) = +6.0$$
$$\text{LCL} = 0 - 2(3.0) = -6.0$$

---

[5] The actual value could be computed as $s = \sqrt{\frac{\Sigma(e - \bar{e})^2}{n-1}}$ (where e = forecast error and $\bar{e}$ = sample average of forecast errors).

EXAMPLE 3-15 ▶

Monthly sales of leather jackets at a store for the past 24 months, and forecasts and forecast errors for those months, are shown below. Determine if the forecasting technique is satisfactory using a control chart with $2s$ limits. Use data from the first eight months to develop the control chart, then evaluate the remaining data with the control chart.

Month	A (Sales)	F (Forecast)	A − F (Error)
1	47	43	4
2	51	44	7
3	54	50	4
4	55	51	4
5	49	54	−5
6	46	48	−2
7	38	46	−8
8	32	44	−12
9	25	35	−10
10	24	26	−2
11	30	25	5
12	35	32	3
13	44	34	10
14	57	50	7
15	60	51	9
16	55	54	1
17	51	55	−4
18	48	51	−3
19	42	50	−8
20	30	43	−13
21	28	38	−10
22	25	27	−2
23	35	27	8
24	38	32	6
			−11

SOLUTION

1. Make sure that the average forecast error is approximately zero:

$$\text{Average error} = \frac{\sum \text{errors}}{n} = \frac{-11}{24}$$
$$= -0.46 \sim 0 \text{ relative to magnitude of sales.}$$

2. Compute the standard deviation of forecast errors using the first eight months:

$$s = \sqrt{\text{MSE}} = \sqrt{\frac{\sum e^2}{n}}$$
$$= \sqrt{\frac{\sum 4^2 + 7^2 + 4^2 + 4^2 + (-5)^2 + (-2)^2 + (-8)^2 + (-12)^2}{8}}$$
$$= 6.46$$

3. Determine $2s$ control limits:

$$0 \pm 2s = 0 \pm 2(6.46) = -12.92 \text{ to } +12.92$$

4. **i.** Check that all forecast errors are within the control limits. Month 20's forecast error (−13) is just below the lower control limit (−12.92).

   ii. Check for nonrandom patterns. Note the runs of positive and negative errors in the following plot. This suggests nonrandomness (and that a better forecasting technique is possible). (We present more on control charts in Chapter 10.)

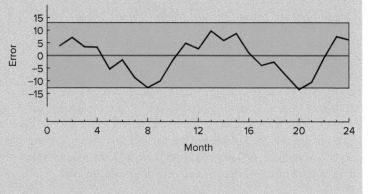

tracking signal A measure used to control the forecasting process: sum of forecast errors divided by mean absolute forecast error.

Tracking Signal   An alternative measure to control the forecasting performance is a **tracking signal**:

$$\text{TS} = \frac{\sum e}{\text{MAD}}$$

When TS values exceed 4 in absolute value,[6] the analyst should study the model and make changes. For example, reset the initial values to eliminate the bias (the top of the TS ratio), change parameters such as smoothing constant α to make the forecasting technique more responsive, use a different forecasting technique, etc.

---
[6] G.W. Plossl and O.W. Wight. *Production and Inventory Control.* Upper Saddle River, NJ: Prentice Hall, 1967.

Choosing a Forecasting Technique

Many different kinds of forecasting techniques are available, and no single technique works best in every situation. When selecting a technique for a given situation, the manager or analyst must take a number of factors into consideration.

The two most important factors are *cost* and *accuracy*. Cost is affected by the preparation time and complexity. Questions to ask are: How much money is budgeted for generating the forecast? What are the possible costs of errors, and what are the benefits that might accrue from an accurate forecast? Generally speaking, the higher the accuracy, the higher the cost, so it is important to weigh cost–accuracy trade-offs carefully. The best forecast is not necessarily the most accurate or the least costly; rather, it is some combination of accuracy and cost deemed best by the management. Other factors to consider in selecting a forecasting technique include the availability of historical data, the forecasting horizon, and pattern of data.

Some techniques are more suited to long-term forecasts, while others work best for the shorter term. For example, moving average and exponential smoothing are essentially short-term techniques, since they produce forecasts for the *next* period. Regression trend models can be used to project over much longer time periods. If there is a strong and stable cause-and-effect relationship, then causal regression models could be used. Also, if the objective of forecasting is to understand what drives sales, then regression should be used. Several of the judgmental techniques are well suited for long-term forecasting because they do not require historical data. The Delphi method and executive opinion methods are often used for long-term planning. New products and services lack historical data, so forecasts for them must be based on subjective estimates. Table 3-3 provides a guide for selecting an appropriate forecasting method. Table 3-4 provides additional perspectives on forecasts in terms of the forecasting horizon.

▼ TABLE 3-3

A guide to selecting an appropriate forecasting method.

Forecasting Method	Amount of Historical Data	Data Pattern	Forecasting Horizon	Preparation Time	Complexity
Simple exponential smoothing	5 to 10 observations	Data should be stationary	Short	Short	Little sophistication
Trend-adjusted exponential smoothing	10 to 15 observations	Trend	Short to medium	Short	Moderate sophistication
Regression trend models	10 to 20 observations	Trend	Short, medium, long	Short	Moderate sophistication
Seasonal	Enough observations to see two peaks and troughs	Seasonal patterns	Medium	Short to moderate	Moderate sophistication
Causal regression models	10 observations per independent variable	Can handle complex patterns	Medium or long	Long	Considerable sophistication

Source: J. Holton Wilson and D. Allison-Koerber, "Combining Subjective and Objective Forecasts Improves Results," *Journal of Business Forecasting Methods & Systems* 11(3), Fall 1992, p. 4.

◀ TABLE 3-4

Forecast perspectives, by forecasting horizon.

Factor	Short Term	Medium Term	Long Term
1. Frequency	Daily, weekly	Monthly, quarterly	Annual
2. Level of aggregation	Item	Product family	Total output
3. Type of model	Smoothing, trend, regression	Trend and seasonal regression	Managerial judgment, trend, regression
4. Degree of management involvement	Low	Moderate	High
5. Cost per forecast	Low	Moderate	High

Source: C. L. Jain, "Benchmarking Forecasting Models," *Journal of Business Forecasting Methods & Systems,* Fall 2002, pp. 18–20, 30.

In some instances, a manager might use more than one forecasting technique to obtain independent forecasts. If the different techniques produced approximately the same predictions, that would give increased confidence in the results; disagreement among the forecasts would indicate that additional analysis may be needed. The chosen forecasting technique should be tested before use to ascertain the level of accuracy.

The Institute of Business Forecasting and Planning (http://www.IBF.org) surveyed over 5,000 companies about their forecasting practices. Time series techniques are popular (61 percent use them), especially moving average (15 percent), exponential smoothing (15 percent), and linear trend (21 percent). Also used are regression (16 percent) and surveys (7 percent).[7]

Using Forecast Information

A manager can take a *reactive* or a *proactive* approach to a forecast. A reactive approach views forecasts as probable descriptions of future demand, and a manager reacts to meet that demand (e.g., adjusts production rates, inventories, the workforce). Conversely, a proactive approach seeks to actively influence demand (e.g., by means of advertising, pricing, or goods/service changes).

Generally speaking, a proactive approach requires either a causal model (e.g., regression) or a subjective assessment of the influence on demand. It is possible that a manager might use two forecasts: one to predict what will happen under the status quo, and a second one based on a "what-if" approach.

Computers in Forecasting

Computers play an important role in preparing forecasts based on quantitative data. Their use allows managers to develop and revise forecasts quickly and without the burden of manual calculations. There is a wide range of software packages available for forecasting.[8]

Installing an enterprise software solution (including the forecasting module) is a large undertaking and many things can potentially go wrong. For two examples, see the "Nike" OM in Action below and "Target Pulls Out of Canada" in Chapter 11.

 OM in Action

Nike

A few years ago, Nike CEO Philip Knight launched a blistering attack on i2 Technologies (now part of JDA Software) for implementation issues relating to a demand forecasting application. The forecasting application did not perform as expected, resulting in severe shortages of some popular shoe models and excess stock of slow-selling models. Nike chose to work with software vendor i2 as part of a $400 million overhaul designed to streamline communications and collaborate forecasting with upstream suppliers and downstream retail stores. The software failed to meet expectations, both in performance and in functionality. Some orders were placed twice, once by the old system and once by the new system. In addition, the application consistently failed to submit new orders for new shoe models, forcing Nike to expedite the production of those models at the last minute and ship them by airfreight. Nike's stock dropped nearly 20 percent on the news.

Source: InformationWeek, "i2 Says: 'You Too, Nike,'" March 1, 2001, www .informationweek.com/i2-says—you-too-nike-/d/d-id/1010113.

Summary

- Forecasts are vital inputs for the design and operation of the productive systems because they help managers anticipate the future.
- Forecasting horizons are classified into long, medium, and short term.
- Forecasting techniques can be classified as judgmental or quantitative.

- Judgmental methods rely on judgment, experience, and expertise of executives, sales staff, experts, or consumers to formulate forecasts.
- The judgmental methods include executive opinions, sales force estimates, consumer surveys, historical analogies, and expert opinions.

---

[7] C.L. Jain, "Benchmarking Forecasting Models," *Journal of Business Forecasting Methods & Systems* 21(3), Fall 2002, pp. 18–20, 30.

[8] For a survey, see http://www.orms-today.org/surveys/FSS/fss-fr.html.

- Quantitative techniques use precise numerical calculations to develop forecasts.
- Two major quantitative approaches are described: time series and associative (causal) techniques.
- The time series techniques rely strictly on the examination of historical data; predictions are made by projecting past patterns of a variable into the future, which includes averaging techniques (moving average and exponential smoothing), linear trend, and time series decomposition for seasonal data.
- Trend can be forecasted using simple regression and trend-adjusted exponential smoothing.
- Seasonal relatives can be computed using centred moving average or annual average.

- Associative techniques such as regression attempt to explicitly identify influencing factors and to incorporate that information into equations that can be used for predictive purposes.
- Measures of forecast accuracy include mean absolute deviation (MAD), mean squared error (MSE), and mean absolute percent error (MAPE).
- Control of forecasts involves deciding whether a forecast is performing adequately, using, for example, a control chart.
- When selecting a forecasting technique, a manager must choose a technique that will serve the intended purpose at an acceptable level of cost and accuracy.

Table 3-5 lists the formulas used in the forecasting techniques and in the methods of measuring their accuracy.

▼ **TABLE 3-5**

Summary of formulas.

Technique	Formula	Definitions
Naïve forecast for stable data	$F_t = A_{t-1}$	F = Forecast A = Actual data t = Index of time period
Moving average forecast	$F = \dfrac{\sum_{i=1}^{n} A_i}{n}$	n = Number of periods
Exponential smoothing forecast	$F_t = F_{t-1} + \alpha(A_{t-1} - F_{t-1})$	α = Smoothing constant
Linear trend forecast	$\hat{y} = a + bt$ where $b = \dfrac{n\sum ty - \sum t \sum y}{n\sum t^2 - (\sum t)^2}$ $a = \dfrac{\sum y - b\sum t}{n}$ or $\bar{y} - bt$	a = Intercept b = Slope y = Demand value $\hat{y}$ = Trend line value t = Index of time period
Trend-adjusted exponential smoothing forecast	$TAF_{t+1} = S_t + T_t$ where $S_t = TAF_t + \alpha(A_t - TAF_t)$ $T_t = T_{t-1} + \beta(S_t - S_{t-1} - T_{t-1})$	TAF_{t+1} = Trend-adjusted forecast for next period ($t+1$) S_t = Smoothed series at the end of current period (t) T_t = Smoothed trend at the end of current period (t) β = Smoothing constant for trend
Linear regression forecast	$\hat{y} = a + bx$ where $b = \dfrac{n(\sum xy) - (\sum x)(\sum y)}{n(\sum x^2) - (\sum x)^2}$ $a = \dfrac{\sum y - b\sum x}{n}$ or $\bar{y} - b\bar{x}$	x = Predictor (independent) variable
MAD	$MAD = \dfrac{\sum_{}^{n}|e|}{n}$	MAD = Mean absolute deviation e = Forecast error = $A - F$
MSE	$MSE = \dfrac{\sum_{}^{n} e^2}{n}$	MSE = Mean squared error
MAPE	$MAPE = \dfrac{\sum\left[\dfrac{|e|}{Actual} \times 100\right]}{n}$	MAPE = Mean absolute percent error
Control limits	$UCL = 0 + z\sqrt{MSE}$ $LCL = 0 - z\sqrt{MSE}$	$\sqrt{MSE}$ = Standard deviation z = Number of standard deviations; 2 and 3 are typical values
Tracking signal	$TS = \dfrac{\sum e}{MAD}$	

Key Terms

adaptive (or variable response) exponential smoothing

annual average method

associative models

bias

centred moving average (CMA)

control chart for forecast errors

correlation coefficient

cycles

Delphi method

demand forecast

exponential smoothing

forecast error

forecasting horizon

irregular variations

judgmental methods

least squares line

level (average)

linear trend equation

mean absolute deviation (MAD)

mean absolute percent error (MAPE)

mean squared error (MSE)

moving average

naïve forecast

predictor variables

random variations

regression

seasonal relatives

seasonal variations

seasonality

time series

time series models

tracking signal

trend

trend-adjusted exponential smoothing

weighted moving average

Solved Problems

Problem 1

Forecasts based on averages. Given the following data:

Period	Number of Complaints
1	60
2	65
3	55
4	58
5	64

Prepare a forecast using each of these approaches:

a. The appropriate naïve approach.

b. A three-period moving average.

c. A weighted average using weights of 0.50 (most recent), 0.30, and 0.20.

d. Exponential smoothing with a smoothing constant of 0.40.

Solution

a. This time series is stable. Therefore, the most recent value of the series can be used as the next forecast: 64.

b. $MA_3 = \dfrac{55 + 58 + 64}{3} = 59$

c. $F_6 = 0.50(64) + 0.30(58) + 0.20(55) = 60.4$

d.

Period	Number of Complaints	Forecast	Calculations
1	60		[The actual value of series in
2	65	60	Period 1 is used as the forecast for
			Period 2]
3	55	62	$60 + 0.40(65 - 60) = 62$
4	58	59.2	$62 + 0.40(55 - 62) = 59.2$
5	64	58.72	$59.2 + 0.40(58 - 59.2) = 58.72$
6		60.83	$58.72 + 0.40(64 - 58.72) = 60.83$

You can also obtain the exponential smoothing forecasts using the Excel template on Connect2:

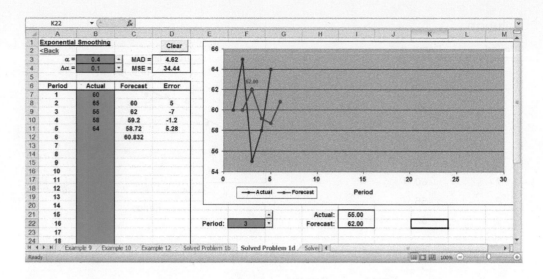

Problem 2

Using seasonal relatives. An orchard ships boxed fruit regionally. Using the following information, forecast shipments for the first four months of next year.

Month	Seasonal Relative	Month	Seasonal Relative
January	1.2	July	0.8
February	1.3	August	0.6
March	1.3	September	0.7
April	1.1	October	1.0
May	0.8	November	1.1
June	0.7	December	1.4

The monthly trend forecast equation is estimated to be:

$$y_t = 402 + 3_t$$

where

  $t = 0$ corresponds to January of two years ago

  $y_t =$ Trend value (number of boxes of fruits to ship) in month t

Solution

a. Determine trend amounts for the first four months of next year: January, $t = 24$; February, $t = 25$; etc. Thus,

$$Y_{Jan} = 402 + 3(24) = 474$$
$$Y_{Feb} = 402 + 3(25) = 477$$
$$Y_{Mar} = 402 + 3(26) = 480$$
$$Y_{Apr} = 402 + 3(27) = 483$$

b. Multiply each monthly trend by the corresponding seasonal relative for that month.

Month	Seasonal Relative	Forecast
January	1.2	474(1.2) = 568.8
February	1.3	477(1.3) = 620.1
March	1.3	480(1.3) = 624.0
April	1.1	483(1.1) = 531.3

Problem 3

Linear trend line. Plot the following data on a graph, and verify visually that a linear trend line is appropriate. Develop a linear trend equation. Then use the equation to predict the next two values of the series.

Solution

Period	Demand
1	44
2	52
3	50
4	54
5	55
6	55
7	60
8	56
9	62

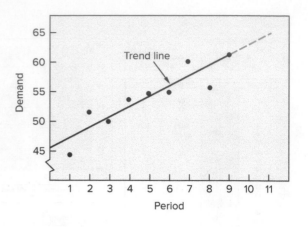

A time series plot of the data indicates that a linear trend line is appropriate:

Period, t	Demand, y	ty	t^2
1	44	44	1
2	52	104	4
3	50	150	9
4	54	216	16
5	55	275	25
6	55	330	36
7	60	420	49
8	56	448	64
9	62	558	81
45	488	2,545	285

$$b = \frac{n\sum ty - \sum t \sum y}{n\sum t^2 - (\sum t)^2} = \frac{9(2{,}545) - 45(488)}{9(285) - 45(45)} = 1.75$$

$$a = \frac{\sum y - b\sum t}{n} = \frac{488 - 1.75(45)}{9} = 45.47$$

Thus, the trend equation is $y_t = 45.47 + 1.75t$. The next two forecasts are:

$$y_{10} = 45.47 + 1.75(10) = 62.97$$
$$y_{11} = 45.47 + 1.75(11) = 64.72$$

You can also use the Excel template on Connect2 to obtain the regression coefficients and plot. Simply replace the existing data in the template with your data.

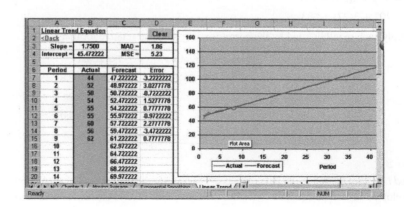

Problem 4

Calculating seasonal relatives. Obtain estimates of quarterly relatives for these data:

Year:		1				2				3				4
Quarter:	1	2	3	4	1	2	3	4	1	2	3	4	1
Demand:	14	18	35	46	28	36	60	71	45	54	84	88	58

Solution

Year	Quarter	Demand	CMA$_4$	CMA$_2$	Demand/CMA$_2$
1	1	14			
	2	18	28.25		
	3	35	31.75	30.00	1.17
	4	46	36.25	34.00	1.35
2	1	28	42.50	39.38	0.71
	2	36	48.75	45.63	0.79
	3	60	53.00	50.88	1.18
	4	71	57.50	55.25	1.29
3	1	45	63.50	60.50	0.74
	2	54	67.75	65.63	0.82
	3	84	71.00	69.38	1.21
	4	88			
4	1	58			

	Quarter			
	1	2	3	4
			1.17	1.35
	0.710	0.790	1.18	1.29
	0.740	0.820	1.21	
	0.145	0.161	3.56	2.64
Average for the quarter:	0.725	0.805	1.187	1.320

The sum of these relatives is 4.037. Multiplying each by 4.00/4.037 will scale the relatives, making their total equal 4.00. The resulting relatives are quarter 1, 0.718; quarter 2, 0.798; quarter 3, 1.176; quarter 4, 1.308.

Problem 5

Causal regression analysis. A large retailer has developed a graph that displays the effect of advertising expenditures on sales volume. Using the graph, determine an equation of the form $\hat{y} = a + bx$ that describes this relationship.

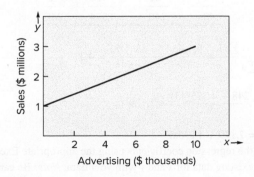

Solution

The linear equation has the form $\hat{y} = a + bx$ where a is the value of $\hat{y}$ when $x = 0$ (i.e., where the line intersects the y axis) and b is the slope of the line (the amount by which $\hat{y}$ changes for a one-unit change in x).

Accordingly, $a = 1$ and considering the points $(x = 0, y = 1)$ and $(x = 10, y = 3)$, $b = (3 - 1)/(10 - 0) = 0.2$, so $\hat{y} = a + bx$ becomes $\hat{y} = 1 + 0.2x$. [*Note:* $(3 - 1)$ is the change in y, and $(10 - 0)$ is the change in x.]

Problem 6

Causal regression analysis. The owner of a small hardware store has noted a weekly sales pattern for door locks that seems to move in parallel with the number of break-ins reported each week in the newspaper. The data are:

Sales:	46	18	20	22	27	34	14	37	30
Break-ins:	9	3	3	5	4	7	2	6	4

a. Plot the data to determine which type of equation, linear or nonlinear, is appropriate.

b. Obtain a linear regression equation for the data.

c. Estimate sales if the number of break-ins in a week is five.

Solution

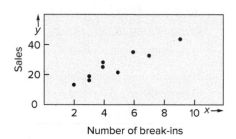

Number of break-ins

a. The graph supports a linear relationship.

b. The computations for a straight line regression equation are:

x	y	xy	x^2
9	46	414	81
3	18	54	9
3	20	60	9
5	22	110	25
4	27	108	16
7	34	238	49
2	14	28	4
6	37	222	36
4	30	120	16
43	248	1,354	245

$$b = \frac{n(\sum xy) - (\sum x)(\sum y)}{n(\sum x^2) - (\sum x^2)} = \frac{9(1{,}354) - 43(248)}{9(245) - 43(43)} = 4.275$$

$$a = \frac{\sum y - b(\sum x)}{n} = \frac{248 - 4.275(43)}{9} = 7.129$$

Hence, the equation is: $\hat{y} = 7.129 + 4.275x$.

You can also obtain the regression coefficients using the appropriate Excel template on Connect2. Simply replace the existing data for x and y with your data. *Note:* Be careful to enter the values for the variable you want to predict as *y* values. In this problem, the objective is to predict sales, so the sales values are entered in the *y* column.

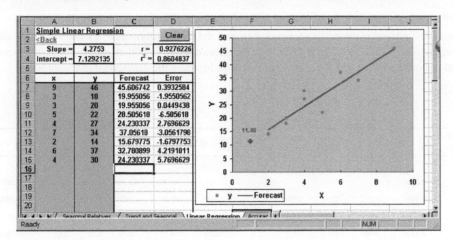

For $x = 5$, $\hat{y} = 7.129 + 4.275(5) = 28.50$ units.

Problem 7

Control chart. Given the following demand data for a product, prepare a naïve forecast for periods 2 through 10. Then determine each forecast error, and use those values to obtain 2*s* control limits. If demand in the next two periods turns out to be 125 and 130 units, can you conclude that the forecasting process is not in control?

Period:	1	2	3	4	5	6	7	8	9	10
Demand:	118	117	120	119	126	122	117	123	121	124

Solution

For a naïve forecast, each period's demand becomes the forecast for the next period. Hence, the forecasts and forecast errors are:

Period	Demand	Forecast	Error	Error^2
1	118	—	—	—
2	117	118	−1	1
3	120	117	3	9
4	119	120	−1	1
5	126	119	7	49
6	122	126	−4	16
7	117	122	−5	25
8	123	117	6	36
9	121	123	−2	4
10	124	121	3	9
			+6	150

The average forecast error (+6/9) is fairly small relative to size of demand (over 110).

$$s = \sqrt{\frac{\sum \text{error}^2}{n}} = \sqrt{\frac{150}{9}} = 4.08 \ (n = \text{Number of errors})$$

The control limits are $\pm 2 \times (4.08) = \pm 8.16$.

The forecast for period 11 is 124. Demand turned out to be 125, for a forecast error of $125 - 124 = +1$. This is within the limits of ± 8.16. The next demand turned out to be 130 and the naïve forecast is 125 (based on the period 11 demand of 125), the forecast error is +5. Again, this is within the limits, so you cannot conclude that the forecasting technique is not in control. With more values—at least five or six—you could plot the forecast errors as a time series plot in a control chart to see whether you could detect any patterns suggesting the presence of nonrandomness or non-Normality.

Problem 8

Accuracy and control of forecasting process. Compare the error performance of these three forecasting techniques using MAD, MSE, and MAPE: a naïve forecast, a two-period moving average, and exponential smoothing with $\alpha = 0.10$ for periods 3 through 11, using the data shown in Example 3-3.

Solution

		Naïve					Two-period MA					Exponential Smoothing				
Period, t	Demand	Forecast	Forecast Error	(A–F) |Error|	Forecast Error^2	$\frac{\|Error\|}{Actual} \times 100\%$	Forecast	Forecast Error	(A-F) |Error|	Forecast Error2	$\frac{\|Error\|}{Actual} \times 100\%$	Forecast	Forecast Error	(A-F) |Error|	Forecast Error2	$\frac{\|Error\|}{Actual} \times 100\%$
1	42	–														
2	40	42	−2	2	4	5.00%						42.00	−2.00	2.00	4.00	5.00%
3	43	40	3	3	9	6.98%	41.00	2.00	2.00	4.00	4.65%	41.80	1.20	1.20	1.44	2.79%
4	40	43	−3	3	9	7.50%	41.50	−1.50	1.50	2.25	3.75%	41.92	−1.92	1.92	3.69	4.80%
5	41	40	1	1	1	2.44%	41.50	−0.50	0.50	0.25	1.22%	41.73	−0.73	0.73	0.53	1.78%
6	39	41	−2	2	4	5.13%	40.50	−1.50	1.50	2.25	3.85%	41.66	−2.66	2.66	7.05	6.81%
7	46	39	7	7	49	15.22%	40.00	6.00	6.00	36.00	13.04%	41.39	4.61	4.61	21.26	10.02%
8	44	46	−2	2	4	4.55%	42.50	1.50	1.50	2.25	3.41%	41.85	2.15	2.15	4.62	4.88%
9	45	44	1	1	1	2.22%	45.00	0.00	0.00	0.00	0.00%	42.07	2.93	2.93	8.61	6.52%
10	38	45	−7	7	49	18.42%	44.50	−6.50	6.50	42.25	17.11%	42.36	−4.36	4.36	19.00	11.47%
11	40	38	2	2	4	5.00%	41.50	−1.50	1.50	2.25	3.75%	41.92	−1.92	1.92	3.70	4.81%
				28	130	67.45%				21.00	91.50	50.77%			22.48	69.89	0.539
MAD			3.11						2.33						2.50		
MSE			14.44						10.17						7.77		
MAPE			7.49%						5.64%						5.99%		

If lowest MAD is the criterion, the two-period moving average forecast has the greatest accuracy; if lowest MSE is the criterion, exponential smoothing works best; and if lowest MAPE is the criterion, the two-period moving average method is again best. Of course, with other data, or with different values of α for exponential smoothing, and different moving averages, the best performers could be different.

Discussion and Review Questions

Note: An asterisk indicates that a question or problem may be more challenging.

LO1 **1.** What are the differences between quantitative and judgmental approaches to forecasting? What are the advantages and disadvantages of each approach?

LO1 **2.** Name and explain, if not obvious, one feature common to all forecasts.

LO1 **3.** Name one element of a good forecast and, if not obvious, explain why it is important.

LO1 **4.** What are the three forecasting horizons? For each forecasting horizon, name one operations management decision that needs the forecast.

LO1 **5.** Briefly describe the steps of the forecasting process.

LO1 *6. How can *shipments* to a customer differ from *demand* by the customer?

LO1 **7.** Explain how flexibility in production systems relates to the forecasting horizon and accuracy.

LO1 **8.** What are some of the consequences of poor forecasts? Explain.

LO1 **9.** Contrast the terms *sales* and *demand*.

LO2 **10.** Pick one judgmental method and describe it.

LO3 **11.** What is a time series?

LO3 **12.** Generally, how do time series models forecast?

LO3 **13.** How does the naïve method forecast a seasonal time series such as sales dollars during every hour of a particular day in a fast-food restaurant?

LO3 **14.** Describe the moving average and exponential smoothing techniques, and explain why they are not suitable for seasonal or trend forecasting.

LO3 **15.** What advantages does exponential smoothing have over moving average?

LO3 **16.** How does the number of periods in a moving average affect the responsiveness of the forecast?

LO3 **17.** How does the size of the smoothing constant in exponential smoothing affect the responsiveness of the forecast?

LO4 **18.** How is regression used in forecasting linear trend?

LO4 *19. Explain the equation for an exponential trend.

LO4 *20. Explain the three formulas used in trend-adjusted exponential smoothing.

LO5 **21.** What is a seasonal relative? Give a numerical example and interpret it.

LO5 **22.** Describe the centred moving average method and explain how it eliminates seasonality from a time series.

LO5 **23.** Describe how seasonal relatives are determined using the centred moving average method.

LO5 **24.** List the steps of time series decomposition for a seasonal time series with trend.

LO6 **25.** Describe how the causal (associative) regression model is used for forecasting.

LO6 **26.** What is the correlation coefficient, and how is it used in associative regression model? What does it mean if correlation coefficient is negative?

LO7 **27.** What is forecasting accuracy and how is it measured?

LO7 **28.** Define and contrast MAD, MSE, and MAPE.

LO7 **29.** Define *control chart for forecast errors*. What is the purpose of establishing control limits for forecast errors?

LO7 *30. What factors would you consider in deciding whether to use a wide or narrow range of acceptable variation in a control chart?

LO7 **31.** What is the tracking signal? Contrast it with the control chart.

LO7 *32. Explain how a control chart and a tracking signal can be used to monitor bias.

LO8 **33.** Contrast the reactive and proactive approaches to forecasting. Give an example of an organization or situation in which each type is used.

LO8 *34. Choose a forecasting technique appropriate for predicting:
   a. Demand for Mother's Day greeting cards.
   b. Popularity of a new television series.
   c. Demand for vacations on the moon.
   d. Demand for toothpastes in a particular supermarket.

LO2 **35.** List the specific weaknesses of each of these approaches to developing a forecast:
   a. Consumer surveys.
   b. Sales force composite.
   c. Committee of managers or executives.

Taking Stock

LO3 **1.** Explain the trade-off between responsiveness and stability in a forecasting system that uses time-series data.

LO1 **2.** Who needs to be involved in preparing forecasts?

LO8 **3.** How has technology had an impact on forecasting?

LO2 *4. Forecasts are sometimes manipulated by managers to accomplish goals such as higher budget, capacity increases, etc. Also, salespeople may underestimate the demand in order to beat it to receive a bonus, or they may overestimate it to keep their job. How can a company combat these unethical behaviours?[9]

Critical Thinking Exercises

LO2 **1.** Omar has heard from some of his customers that they will probably cut back on order sizes in the next quarter. The company he works for has been reducing its sales force due to falling demand and he worries that he could be next if his sales begin to fall off. Believing that he may be able to convince his customers not to cut back on orders, he turns in an optimistic forecast of his next quarter sales to his manager. What are the pros and cons of doing that?

LO3 **2.** It has been said that forecasting using time series exponential smoothing is like driving a car by looking in the rear view mirror. What are the conditions that would have

to exist for driving a car that are analogous to the assumptions made when using exponential smoothing?

LO1 **3.** When a new business is started, or a patent idea needs funding, venture capitalists or investment bankers will want to see a business plan that includes forecast information related to a profit and loss statement. What type of forecasting information do you suppose would be required?

LO8 **4.** Explain the trade-off between cost and accuracy in a forecasting system.

[9] A. Michail, "How to Identify and Correct Politically Motivated Forecasts," *Journal of Business Forecasting Methods & Systems* 23(4), Winter 2004/2005, pp. 3–9.

Experiential Learning Exercises

L05 **1.** Go to https://www.xe.com/currencycharts/?from=USD& to=CAD&view=5Y and examine the one-year, two-year, and five-year timeframes. Is there any obvious seasonality pattern in the value of the currencies? Is there any obvious positive or negative trend?

L07 **2.** Obtain next-day temperature forecasts (daily highs) in your town/city for three days (you can visit http://www .theweathernetwork.com, choose your city, and click View Forecasts). Compare the accuracy of the next-day forecasts with naïve forecasts. Interpret your result.

L07 **3.** Gather data on one-, two-, and three-day temperature forecasts (daily highs) and actual highs in your town/city for four days and compare the accuracy of each one-, two-, and three-day temperature forecast (you can visit http://www.theweathernetwork.com, choose your city, click View Forecasts, scroll down to the middle of the web page). Interpret your results.

L08 **4.** Pick your favourite stock on the Toronto Stock Exchange and choose a forecasting method to forecast its next-day closing price. Repeat this for each of the next three days. (*Hint:* Go to http://www.tmx.com, click Get Quote at top right, click Symbol Lookup (if you don't know the symbol), find out the symbol for your company, then enter it under Get Quote, and click Go. You can also get past prices (to choose and fine-tune your forecasting method) by clicking the Price History tab.) Are you satisfied with the results? Explain why you feel the forecasting method you chose worked or didn't work.

Internet Exercise

L06 Visit http://www.stockexshadow.com/crude-oil-usdcad-correlation-chart and comment on the relationship between oil prices and the price of the Canadian dollar. Can oil prices be used to forecast the Canadian dollar?

Problems

L03 **1.** A commercial bakery has recorded sales (in dozens) for three products during the last 15 workdays:

Workday	Blueberry Muffins	Cinnamon Buns	Cupcakes
1	30	18	45
2	34	17	26
3	32	19	27
4	34	19	23
5	35	22	22
6	30	23	48
7	34	23	29
8	36	25	20
9	29	24	14
10	31	26	18
11	35	27	47
12	31	28	26
13	37	29	27
14	34	31	24
15	33	33	22

a. Plot the three time series variables to determine their pattern.

b. Forecast workday 16 sales for each of the products using an appropriate naïve method.

c. If you could use a more sophisticated method than naïve, what technique would you use for each variable?

L03 & 4 **2.** A can opener manufacturer has had monthly sales for a seven-month period as follows:

Month	Sales (000 units)
February	19
March	18
April	15
May	20
June	18
July	22
August	20

a. Plot the data.

b. Forecast September's sales volume using each of the following:

   i. A linear trend equation. (Use of Excel's Trendline, with display Equation on chart option, is recommended.)

   ii. A four-month moving average.

   iii. Exponential smoothing with a smoothing constant of 0.10, assuming a March forecast of 19(000).

   iv. The naïve approach.

   v. A weighted average using 0.50 for August, 0.30 for July, and 0.20 for June.

c. Which method seems *least* appropriate? Why?

d. What does use of the term *sales* rather than *demand* presume?

3. A dry cleaner uses exponential smoothing to forecast equipment usage as a percentage of capacity (i.e., utilization) at its main plant. August usage was forecast to be 88 percent of capacity, whereas actual usage turned out to be 89.6 percent of capacity. A smoothing constant of 0.2 is used.

    a. Prepare a forecast for September.

    b. Assuming actual September usage of 92 percent, prepare a forecast for October's usage.

L03 **4.** An electrical contractor's records during the last five weeks indicate the following numbers of job requests:

Week:	1	2	3	4	5
Requests:	20	22	18	21	22

Predict the number of requests for week 6 using each of these methods:

    a. Naïve.

    b. Four-week moving average.

    c. Exponential smoothing with $\alpha = 0.30$.

L04 **5.** Freight car loadings during an 18-week period at a port are:

Week	Number	Week	Number	Week	Number
1	220	7	350	13	460
2	245	8	360	14	475
3	280	9	400	15	500
4	275	10	380	16	510
5	300	11	420	17	525
6	310	12	450	18	541

    a. Compute a linear trend line for freight car loadings. (Use of Excel's Trendline is recommended. Make sure to select the display equation option.)

    b. Use the trend equation to predict loadings for weeks 19 and 20.

    c. The manager intends to install new equipment when the volume reaches 700 loadings per week. Assuming the current trend continues, the loading volume will reach that level in approximately what week?

L03 **6.** Suppose it is the beginning of 2008 and you are trying to help the forecaster at Case New Holland, an international agricultural and construction equipment manufacturer, to forecast total agricultural equipment industry sales in Canada for the year. You have accessed Statistics Canada's CANSIM 2 database and found the agricultural equipment manufacturing industry's GDP (in 2002 constant prices) in series v41881336. The data between 2000 and 2007 are as follows:

Year	Agricultural Equipment Manufacturing Industry's GDP (in billion 2002$)
2000	9.8
2001	10.3
2002	11.4
2003	9.8
2004	10.5
2005	10.0
2006	9.4
2007	9.8

    a. Plot the time series data.

    b. Identify its patterns and suggest a forecasting technique.

 7. a. Develop a linear trend equation for the following data on demand for white bread loaves at a bakery (use of Excel's Trendline, with display equation on chart option, is recommended), and use it to forecast demand on day 16.

Day	Loaves	Day	Loaves	Day	Loaves
1	200	6	232	11	281
2	214	7	248	12	275
3	211	8	250	13	280
4	228	9	253	14	288
5	235	10	267	15	310

    b. The variations around the linear trend line seem to have above- and below-the-line runs. Therefore, use trend-adjusted exponential smoothing with $\alpha = 0.3$ and $\beta = 0.2$ to model the bread demand. Use the first four days to estimate the initial smoothed series (use the average of the first four days) and smoothed trend (use the increase from day 1 to day 4 divided by 3). Start forecasting day 5. What is the forecast for day 16?

L03 & 4 ***8.** The agronomist in charge of canola seed production for a major seed-producing and marketing company is wondering if the forecast for production of seed #1234 for 2008, made by the head office, is a little too low. The sales of seed #1234, in thousand tonnes, for the past eight years are shown below. The company regularly improves its seeds, and has recently introduced a new seed. Given the life-cycle decline in the sales of #1234, the head office's 2008 forecast sales for #1234 is 10 percent lower than 2007 sales. Fit an appropriate model to the data and forecast sales of #1234 in 2008. Do you agree with the head office's forecast? Explain.

Year	#1234 sales
2000	0.1
2001	2.1
2002	2.8
2003	3.1
2004	3.9
2005	3.7
2006	3.5
2007	3.4
2008	

 9. After plotting the following demand data, a manager has concluded that a trend-adjusted exponential smoothing model is appropriate to predict future demand. Use period

1 to 4 to estimate the initial smoothed series (use the average of the first four periods) and smoothed trend (use the increase from day 1 to day 4 divided by 3). Use $\alpha = 0.5$ and $\beta = 0.4$ to develop forecasts for periods 5 through 10.

Period, t	A_t Actual
1	210
2	224
3	229
4	240
5	255
6	265
7	272
8	285
9	294
10	

LO5 **10.** A manager of a store that sells and installs hot tubs wants to prepare a forecast for the number of hot tubs demanded during January, February, and March of next year. Her forecasts are a combination of trend and seasonality. She uses the following equation to estimate the trend component of monthly demand: $y_t = 70 + 6t$, where $t = 0$ in June of last year. Seasonal relatives are 1.10 for January, 1.02 for February, and 0.95 for March. What demands should she forecast?

LO5 **11.** A gift shop in a tourist centre is open only on weekends (Friday, Saturday, and Sunday). The owner–manager hopes to improve scheduling of part-time employees by determining seasonal relatives for each of these days. Data on recent activity at the store (sales transactions per day) are shown in the following table:

	Week					
	1	2	3	4	5	6
Friday	149	154	152	150	159	163
Saturday	250	255	260	268	273	276
Sunday	166	162	171	173	176	183

a. Develop seasonal relatives for each day using the centred moving average method.

b. Deseasonalize the data, fit an appropriate model to the deseasonalized data, project three days ahead, and reseasonalize the projections to forecast the sales transactions for each day, Friday to Sunday, of next week.

LO5 **12.** The manager of a fashionable restaurant open Wednesday through Saturday says that the restaurant does about 35 percent of its business on Friday night, 30 percent on Saturday night, and 20 percent on Thursday night. What are the seasonal relatives for each day?

LO3 & 4 **13.** Coal shipments from a mine for the past 18 weeks are:

Week	Tonnes Shipped	Week	Tonnes Shipped
1	405	10	440
2	410	11	446
3	420	12	451
4	415	13	455
5	412	14	464
6	420	15	466
7	424	16	474
8	433	17	476
9	438	18	482

a. Plot the data as time series, determine the pattern, and explain why an averaging technique would not be appropriate in this case.

b. Use an appropriate technique to develop a forecast for week 19.

LO5 **14. a.** Calculate daily seasonal relatives for the number of customers served at a restaurant, given the following data. (*Hint:* Use a seven-day centred moving average.)

b. Deseasonalize the data, fit an appropriate model to the deseasonalized data, project it seven days ahead, and reseasonalize the projections to forecast daily demand next week.

Day	Number Served	Day	Number Served
1	80	15	84
2	75	16	77
3	78	17	83
4	95	18	96
5	130	19	135
6	136	20	140
7	40	21	37
8	82	22	87
9	77	23	82
10	80	24	98
11	94	25	103
12	125	26	144
13	135	27	144
14	42	28	48

LO5 ***15.** Echlin Inc. is an after-market supplier of automotive spare parts.[10] A part is usually made specifically for a particular model of a car. In order to forecast the demand for a part, Echlin tries to use the following process: (a) determine the total number of new vehicles using this part sold each

[10] See J.A.G. Krupp, "Forecasting for the Automotive Aftermarket," *Journal of Business Forecasting Methods & Systems* 12(4), Winter 1993–94, pp. 8–12.

year, (b) determine the replacement probability by age for the first replacement, second replacement, and so on of the part for current and future years, (c) calculate the total number of replacement units for each year, (d) break this down into original equipment manufacturer market and after-market manufacturer market, (e) calculate Echlin's annual share using its market share, and, finally (f) break down the annual forecast into quarterly and monthly sales forecasts using seasonal relatives.

Consider a specific part. Echlin makes brake calipers for a particular car model first introduced in 1986. Suppose it is now the end of 1992 and, using steps *a* to *e* above, Echlin has forecasted its own sales of this caliper for 1993.

Year	Echlin's Sales of Calipers
1990	10,444
1991	10,319
1992	8,477
1993	6,334 (forecast)

Echlin also has quarterly sales of these calipers for the past three years.

Quarter	1990	1991	1992
Q_1	2,370	2,641	2,281
Q_2	2,058	2,198	1,814
Q_3	2,778	2,518	2,127
Q_4	3,238	2,962	2,255
Total	10,444	10,319	8,477

a. Use the 1990–92 quarterly data above to determine the quarterly seasonal relatives.
b. Use your answer to part *a* and 1993 forecast sales (6,334 units) to forecast quarterly sales for 1993.
c. Deseasonalize the data, fit an appropriate model to the deseasonalized data, project it four quarters ahead, and reseasonalize the projections to forecast quarterly demand in 1993. Contrast your results with part *b*.

 16. A pharmacist has been monitoring sales of a certain over-the-counter (i.e., no prescription is needed) pain reliever. Daily sales during the last 15 days were:

Day:	1	2	3	4	5	6	7	8	9
Number sold:	36	38	42	44	48	49	50	49	52

Day:	10	11	12	13	14	15
Number sold:	48	52	55	54	56	57

a. If you learn that on some days the store ran out of this pain reliever, would that knowledge cause you any concern regarding the use of sales data for forecasting demand? Explain.
b. Assume that there were no stock-outs. Plot the data. Is the linear trend model appropriate for this item? Explain.
c. Using trend-adjusted exponential smoothing with initial smoothed series and trend determined from days 1 to 8 and $\alpha = \beta = 0.3$, develop forecasts for days 9 through 16.

 17. New-car sales of a dealer during the past year are shown in the following table, along with monthly seasonal relatives.

Month	Units Sold	Seasonal Relative	Month	Units Sold	Seasonal Relative
Jan	640	0.80	Jul	765	0.90
Feb	648	0.80	Aug	805	1.15
Mar	630	0.70	Sept	840	1.20
Apr	761	0.94	Oct	828	1.20
May	735	0.89	Nov	840	1.21
Jun	850	1.00	Dec	800	1.21

a. Plot the data. Does there seem to be a trend?
b. Deseasonalize the new car sales.
c. Plot the deseasonalized data on the same graph as the original data. Comment on the two plots.

 18. The following data shows a small tool and die shop's quarterly sales (in $000s) for the current year. What sales would you predict for the first quarter of next year? Quarterly seasonal relatives are $Q_1 = 1.10$, $Q_2 = 0.99$, $Q_3 = 0.90$, and $Q_4 = 1.01$. (*Hint:* First deseasonalize the data, then observe the trend and project it ahead one quarter, and finally reseasonalize.)

Quarter:	1	2	3	4
Sales:	88	99	108	141

 19. A farming cooperative's manager wants to forecast quarterly grain shipments for each quarter of next year (Year 6), based on the data shown below (quantities are in metric tonnes):

Year	Quarter 1	Quarter 2	Quarter 3	Quarter 4
1	200	250	210	340
2	210	252	212	360
3	215	260	220	358
4	225	272	233	372
5	232	284	240	381

a. Determine quarterly seasonal relatives using the centred moving average method.
b. Deseasonalize the data, fit an appropriate model to the deseasonalized data, extend it four quarters, and finally reseasonalize the projections.

L05 *20. Federated Cooperatives Limited (FCL) is the largest wholesaler of grocery, hardware, and agricultural supplies in Western Canada, and operates warehouses in Saskatoon, Edmonton, Calgary, and Winnipeg. In the Calgary warehouse, a particular golf club is carried in stock. The demand for this golf club during each month of the period 2003–2005 is listed below (note that FCL uses weekly time buckets, but for simplicity we have combined these into monthly data):

Month	2003	2004	2005
Jan	0	2	3
Feb	52	8	20
Mar	29	44	12
Apr	49	74	31
May	47	75	61
Jun	58	87	28
Jul	0	145	107
Aug	64	11	57
Sep	3	24	21
Oct	17	9	10
Nov	10	5	0
Dec	1	6	1

a. Determine the monthly relatives using the 12-period centred moving average method.

b. Deseasonalize the data, fit an appropriate model to the deseasonalized data, project it 12 months ahead, and reseasonalize the projections to forecast monthly sales for 2006. (These forecasts will be used to plan purchases of the golf club from the manufacturer.)

L05 **21.** The following data are quarterly sales of natural gas in Saskatchewan by SaskEnergy (in petajoules ≈ 1 billion cubic feet) from Q1 of 2005 to Q3 of 2009.

Year	Q1	Q2	Q3	Q4
2005	49	24	18	37
2006	42	20	20	43
2007	48	24	20	40
2008	51	25	19	43
2009	51	24	15	

a. Compute the seasonal relative for each quarter using the centred moving average method.

b. Deseasonalize the data, fit an appropriate model to the deseasonalized data, extend the model four quarters, and reseasonalize these in order to forecast the sales of natural gas by SaskEnergy from Q4 2009 to Q3 2010.

L05 *22. For planning production in the medium term, vehicle manufacturers need to forecast the demand for new motor vehicle sales. The following data are the numbers (in thousands) of Honda Ridgeline trucks manufactured by Honda during each quarter, starting from the first quarter of 2005 (when Ridgeline was introduced) until the third quarter of 2008.[11] Assume that all Ridgelines produced in a quarter were sold in the same quarter.

Year	Q1	Q2	Q3	Q4
2005	11.5	19.2	17.4	12.7
2006	11.9	15.1	17.4	12.1
2007	10.6	19.1	13.9	11.5
2008	10.2	6.2	5.6	

a. Compute the seasonal relative for each quarter using the centred moving average method.

b. Deseasonalize the data, fit an appropriate model to the deseasonalized data, extend the model four quarters, and reseasonalize these in order to forecast the sales of Ridgeline trucks in the fourth quarter of 2008, and first, second, and third quarters of 2009.

L05 *23. Mountain Aquaculture and Producers Association (MA&PA) is a small trout producers' cooperative in West Virginia.[12] Its main product is boned, head-removed trout sold to local stores. One of the problems MA&PA is facing is that the demand for its products is seasonal (see the sales in pounds of boned, head-removed trout from Q1 1997 to Q3 2000 below). The manager would like to plan production better.

Year	Q1	Q2	Q3	Q4
1997	664	1,338	1,170	1,069
1998	422	1,098	1,939	843
1999	803	1,430	1,206	724
2000	698	1,076	1,149	

a. Compute the seasonal relative for each quarter using the centred moving average method.

b. Deseasonalize the data, fit an appropriate model to the deseasonalized data, extend the model four quarters, and reseasonalize these in order to forecast the sales of boned, head-removed trout from the fourth quarter of 2000 to third quarter of 2001.

L05 **24.** Compute seasonal relatives for this data using the annual average method:

Quarter	Year 1	Year 2	Year 3	Year 4
1	2	3	7	4
2	6	10	18	14
3	2	6	8	8
4	5	9	15	11

L06 **25.** The manager of a seafood restaurant wants to establish a price on shrimp dinners. Experimenting with prices produced the following data:

Average Number Sold per Day, y	Price, x	Average Number Sold per Day, y	Price, x
200	$6.00	155	$8.25
190	6.50	156	8.50
188	6.75	148	8.75
180	7.00	140	9.00
170	7.25	133	9.25
162	7.50		
160	8.00		

a. Plot the data as a scatter plot, determine the regression equation, and plot the regression line on the same graph as data. (You may use Excel's "=slope(RangeY,RangeX)"

[11] CANSIM series V429850230.
[12] R.M. Fincham. A Break-Even Analysis of Trout Processing in West Virginia: A Case Study Approach, M.S. thesis, West Virginia University, 2001.

and "=intercept(RangeY, RangeX)" to obtain the regression coefficients b and a, respectively, where RangeY is the range of Excel cells containing the y values and RangeX is the range of Excel cells containing the x values. Alternatively, use Trendline in the Layout menu.)

   b. Determine the correlation coefficient and interpret it. (You may use Excel's "=CORREL (RangeY,RangeX)" to determine r.)

L06 **26.** The following data were collected during a study of consumer buying patterns.

Observation	X	Y	Observation	X	Y
1	15	74	8	18	78
2	25	80	9	14	70
3	40	84	10	15	72
4	32	81	11	22	85
5	51	96	12	24	88
6	47	95			
7	30	83			

   a. Plot the data as a scatter plot.
   b. Obtain a linear regression line for the data. (You may use Excel's "=slope(RangeY,RangeX)" and "=intercept(RangeY,RangeX, where RangeY is the range of Excel cells containing the y values and RangeX is the range of Excel cells containing the x values)" to obtain the regression coefficients b and a, respectively. Alternatively, use Trendline in the Layout menu.)
   c. What percentage of the variation is explained by the regression line? (You may use Excel's "=RSQ(RangeY,RangeX)" to obtain r^2.)
   d. Use the equation determined in part b to predict the value of y for $x = 41$.

L06 **27.** A lawn and garden centre intends to use sales of lawn fertilizer to predict lawn mower sales. The store manager wishes to determine the relationship between fertilizer and mower sales. The pertinent data are:

Period	Fertilizer Sales (tonnes)	Number of Mowers Sold	Period	Fertilizer Sales (tonnes)	Number of Mowers Sold
1	1.6	10	8	1.3	7
2	1.3	8	9	1.7	10
3	1.8	11	10	1.2	6
4	2.0	12	11	1.9	11
5	2.2	12	12	1.4	8
6	1.6	9	13	1.7	10
7	1.5	8			

   a. Determine the correlation between the two variables. Does it appear that a relationship between these vari-

ables will yield good predictions? Explain. (You may use Excel's "=CORREL (RangeY,RangeX)" to determine r, where RangeY is the range of Excel cells containing the y values and RangeX is the range of Excel cells containing the x values. You also need R^2, RSQ(RangeY,RangeX).)

   b. Obtain a linear regression line for the data. (You may use Excel's "=slope(RangeY,RangeX)" and "=intercept(RangeY,RangeX)" to obtain the regression coefficients b and a, respectively. Alternatively, use Trendline in the Layout menu.)
   c. Predict lawn mower sales, given fertilizer sales of 2 tonnes.

L06 **28.** Columbia Gas Company of Ohio distributes natural gas to residential, business, and industrial customers in Ohio.[13] In order to secure enough gas supply, Columbia Gas forecasts daily demand for the next five days using regression. It has identified the average daily temperature as the most important explanatory variable for daily demand for natural gas. The regression is estimated using daily data from the past two years. For brevity, we consider only a subset of this period as follows.

   a. Plot the average temperature and demand data for the past 10 days. Does there appear to be a linear relationship?
   b. Estimate the regression coefficients. (You may use Excel's "=slope(RangeY,RangeX)" and "=intercept(RangeY,RangeX)" to obtain the regression coefficients b and a, respectively, where RangeY is the range of Excel cells containing the y values and RangeX is the range of Excel cells containing the x values.)
   c. If the average temperature tomorrow is expected to be 54 degrees Fahrenheit, what is the forecast for demand for natural gas tomorrow?

Day	Avg. Temp (F)	Demand (thousand dekatherm)
−10	33	1005
−9	46	501
−8	41	612
−7	47	499
−6	37	692
−5	36	709
−4	32	951
−3	34	1053
−2	38	746
−1	43	458

L07 **29.** An analyst must decide between two different forecasting techniques for weekly sales of inline skates: a linear trend equation and the naïve approach. The linear trend equation is $y_t = 124 + 2t$, and it was developed using data

[13] Based on A.H. Catron, "Daily Demand Forecasting at Columbia Gas," *Journal of Business Forecasting* 19(2) Summer 2000, 10–15.

from periods 1 through 10. Based on data for periods 11 through 19 as shown below, which of these two methods has greater accuracy? (You can use any one of the three measures of forecast errors.)

t	Units Sold	t	Units Sold
11	147	16	152
12	148	17	155
13	151	18	157
14	145	19	160
15	155		

L07 **30.** The manager of a large manufacturer of industrial pumps must choose between two alternative forecasting techniques to forecast the demand for its top-selling pump. Both techniques have been used to prepare forecasts for a six-month period. Using MAD as a criterion, which technique produces more accurate forecasts?

		Forecast	
Month	Demand	Technique 1	Technique 2
1	492	488	495
2	470	484	482
3	485	480	478
4	493	490	488
5	498	497	492
6	492	493	493

L07 **31.** Two different forecasting techniques were used to forecast demand for cases of bottled water in a store. Actual demand and the two sets of forecasts for seven periods are as follows:

		Forecast Demand	
Period	Demand	F1	F2
1	68	66	66
2	75	68	68
3	70	72	70
4	74	71	72
5	69	72	74
6	72	70	76
7	80	71	78

a. Calculate the MAD for each set of forecasts. Which technique appears to be more accurate?
b. Calculate the MSE for each set of forecasts. Which technique appears to be more accurate?
c. Calculate the MAPE for each set of forecasts. Which technique appears to be more accurate?
d. Do all three measures of forecast errors provide the same conclusion (i.e., are they consistent) in this case? Do you expect consistent results for every case? Explain.

e. In practice, *either* MAD, MSE, or MAPE would be employed to compute a measure of forecast errors. What factors might lead a manager to favour one?

L07 **32.** Two independent sets of forecasts based on judgment and experience have been prepared each month for the past 10 months. The forecasts and actual demand are as follows:

Month	Demand	Forecast 1	Forecast 2
1	770	771	769
2	789	785	787
3	794	790	792
4	780	784	798
5	768	770	774
6	772	768	770
7	760	761	759
8	775	771	775
9	786	784	788
10	790	788	788

a. Calculate the MSE, MAD, and MAPE for each forecast. Does one forecast seem superior? Explain.
b. Do all three measures of forecast errors provide the same conclusion (i.e., are they consistent) in this case? Do you expect consistent results in every case? Explain.
c. Calculate $2s$ control limits for each forecast and determine if each forecasting process is in control. Explain.

L07 **33.** The classified department of a monthly magazine has used a combination of quantitative and judgmental methods to forecast sales of advertising space. The forecast errors over an 18-month period are as follows:

Month	Forecast Error	Month	Forecast Error
1	−8	10	−4
2	−2	11	1
3	4	12	6
4	7	13	8
5	9	14	4
6	5	15	1
7	0	16	−2
8	−3	17	−4
9	−4	18	−8

a. Using the first half of the data (Months 1 to 9), construct a control chart with $2s$ limits.
b. Plot the last nine forecast errors on the control chart. Is the forecasting process in control? Are the forecast errors random? Explain.

LO4 & 7 **34.** A textbook publishing company has compiled data on total annual sales of its business textbooks for the preceding eight years:

Year:	1	2	3	4	5	6	7	8
Sales (000):	40.2	44.5	48.0	52.3	55.8	57.1	62.4	69.0

a. Plot the data and fit an appropriate model to it. Forecast the preceding eight years, and determine the forecast errors. Finally, construct a 2s control chart.

b. Using the model, forecast textbook sales for each of the next five years.

c. Suppose actual sales for the next five years turn out as follows:

Year:	9	10	11	12	13
Sales (000):	73.7	77.2	82.1	87.8	90.6

Calculate the forecast errors for Years 9 to 13. Is the forecasting process in control? Explain.

LO7 35. A manager has just received an evaluation from an analyst on two potential forecasting methods. The analyst is indifferent between the two methods, saying that they should be equally accurate and in control. The demand and the forecasts using the two methods for nine periods follow:

Period:	1	2	3	4	5	6	7	8	9
Demand:	37	39	37	39	45	49	47	49	51
Method 1:	36	38	40	42	46	46	46	48	52
Method 2:	36	37	38	38	41	52	47	48	52

a. Calculate the MSE for each method and compare the two methods.

b. Construct a 2s control chart for each method and interpret them. Do you agree with the analyst? Explain.

LO4 & 7 36. A manager uses this equation to predict demand for landscaping services: $F_t = 10 + 5t$. Over the past eight periods, demand has been as follows:

Period, t:	1	2	3	4	5	6	7	8
Demand:	15	21	23	30	32	38	42	47

Is the forecast performing adequately? Explain.

LO3 & 4 *37. Consider the usage of item #14-46-506: 4 ft. Supersaver fluorescent lamps in Sterling Pulp Chemicals (now part of ERCO Worldwide) in the first 10 months of 2008.

Month	2008
Jan	10
Feb	10
Mar	66
Apr	32
May	34
June	18
July	24
Aug	9
Sep	14
Oct	48

Fit a model to the data using each of the following techniques and forecast the November usage in each case. Also,

plot the two moving average forecasts and the actual, the two exponential smoothing forecasts and the actual, and the linear trend and the actual (three graphs altogether).

a. Three-month moving average.

b. Five-month moving average.

c. Exponential smoothing with smoothing constant = 0.1.

d. Exponential smoothing with smoothing constant = 0.3.

e. Linear trend (regression).

f. Just by observing the plots, which of the above techniques would you use to forecast the usage of fluorescent lamps and why? (*Hint:* The plot overall closest to actual demand will be most accurate.)

g. Alternatively, compute the MAD for each forecasting technique and determine the most accurate technique.

LO3 & 4 *38. Consider the total production (and sales) of ice cream in Canada (in millions of litres) for the period 1995 until 2007 (from left to right):[14]

341, 331, 317, 315, 321, 278, 298, 311, 302, 302, 335, 320, 285

Fit a model to ice cream production data using each of the following techniques and forecast the 2008 production in each case. Also, plot the two moving average forecasts and the actual, the two exponential smoothing forecasts and the actual, and the linear trend and the actual (three graphs altogether).

a. Two-year moving average.

b. Four-year moving average.

c. Exponential smoothing with smoothing constant = 0.2.

d. Exponential smoothing with smoothing constant = 0.4.

e. Linear trend (regression).

f. Just by observing the plots, which of the above techniques would you use to forecast the ice cream production and why? (*Hint:* The plot overall closest to actual demand will be most accurate.)

g. Alternatively, compute the MAD for each forecasting technique and determine the most accurate technique.

LO3–5, 7 & 8 *39. The numbers of Toyota Corollas produced in the Cambridge, Ontario, plant during each month of January 2008 to December 2009 period were as follows:[15]

Month	No. Produced	Month	No. Produced
2008–01	4,959	2009–01	6,733
2008–02	8,463	2009–02	1,006
2008–03	11,706	2009–03	9,328
2008–04	9,907	2009–04	9,072
2008–05	9,354	2009–05	8,738
2008–06	11,297	2009–06	12,259
2008–07	8,905	2009–07	9,519
2008–08	12,249	2009–08	12,113
2008–09	19,160	2009–09	14,044
2008–10	14,264	2009–10	16,650
2008–11	13,687	2009–11	16,912
2008–12	8,657	2009–12	13,851

[14] CANSIM 2 database series v108517.
[15] CANSIM 2 series v42190663.

Assume that the cars are sold in the same month they are produced. Identify an appropriate forecasting technique, briefly state the reason(s) you chose it, and forecast Corolla demand in January 2010.

 40. A cosmetics manufacturer's marketing department has developed a linear trend equation that can be used to predict annual sales of its popular hand cream.

$$\hat{y}_t = 80 + 15t$$

where $\hat{y}_t$ = Annual sales (000 bottles) and t is the index of time periods

a. Are annual sales increasing or decreasing? By how much?

b. Predict annual sales for year 6 using the equation.

 41. Long-Life Insurance has developed a linear model that is used to determine the amount of term life insurance a family of four should have, based on the current age of the head of the household. The equation is:

$$y = 850 - 0.1x$$

where y = Insurance needed ($000) and x = Current age of head of household

a. Plot the relationship on a graph.

b. Use the equation to determine the amount of term life insurance to recommend for a family of four if the head of the household is 30 years old.

 MINI-CASE http://acadianbakers.com/

Acadian Bakers

Acadian Bakers is a small sweets bakery in Houston, Texas. One of its products is a croissant. Acadian buys frozen croissants and bakes them. For the sake of quality, the company doesn't want to store its frozen goods for more than one week. For orders of more than 576 cases, the delivery is free (saving $15 per order). A case contains 144 frozen croissants. Acadian has collected its total weekly sales for croissants (in cases) for the last 10 weeks. Management believes that the sales of croissants are increasing.

Week	Sales
1	461
2	450
3	463
4	458
5	476
6	492
7	482
8	491
9	488
10	488

Question
Can Acadian take advantage of the quantity discount, and if so when?

Chapter 4
Product Design

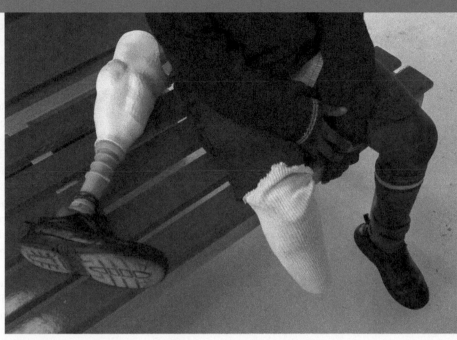

ISAAC KASAMANI/Getty Images

LEARNING OBJECTIVES

After completing this chapter, you should be able to:

LO1 Introduce product design and describe the design process.

LO2 Name some sources of ideas for new or revised designs.

LO3 Discuss key issues in product design.

LO4 Discuss special considerations for service design.

LO5 Describe and perform quality function deployment (QFD).

LO6 Discuss the Kano model.

LO7 Discuss FMEA Analysis.

3D printing has the potential to transform the healthcare industry. Numerous medical applications exist, including the production of inexpensive medical prosthetics. To this end, Professor Matt Ratto at the University of Toronto is using 3D printing technology to produce low-cost yet customized lower-leg prosthetics for children in the developing world.

Traditional prosthetics are time-consuming and costly to produce. In addition, frequent modifications to existing prosthetics are needed as children grow and this means new moulds need to be constantly produced. The cost of each prosthetic can be as high as $40,000 and therefore represents a significant barrier to those without substantial financial resources. With 3D printing, what used to take weeks can now be done in days. Once the CAD file is created, the limb can be printed using as little as $50 worth of plastic. Such a drastic reduction in the cost of production will undoubtedly help to make these life-changing prosthetics more easily accessible to lower-income patients throughout the world.

Sources: https://www.fastcompany.com/3039329/finally-a-good-use-for-3d-printing-prosthetic-limbs; https://www.usatoday.com/story/tech/nation-now/2017/02/17/students-build-3-d-printed-prosthetic-hands-kids/98071192/

(LO1) Introduction and Product Design Process

The essence of any business organization is the goods and services it offers, and every aspect of the organization and its supply chain is structured around those goods and services. There is an obvious link between the *design* of those goods and services and the *success* of the organization. Hence, organizations have a strategic interest in product and service design. Product or service design should be closely tied to an organization's strategy. It is a major factor in cost, quality, time-to-market, customer satisfaction, and competitive advantage. Consequently, marketing, finance, operations, accounting, IT, and HR need to be involved. Demand forecasts and projected costs are important, as is the expected impact on the supply chain. It is significant to note that an important cause of operations failures can be traced to faulty design. Designs that have not been well thought out or correctly implemented, or instructions for assembly or usage that are wrong or unclear, can be the cause of product and service failures, leading to lawsuits, injuries and deaths, product recalls, and damaged reputations. The quality of the product is mainly, perhaps as much as 80 percent, determined during the design. Hence, organizations have a vital stake in achieving good product design.

The introduction of new products, or changes to product designs, can have impacts throughout the organization and the entire supply chain. Some processes may change very little, while others may have to change considerably in terms of what they do or how and when they do it. New processes may have to be added, and some current ones may be eliminated. New suppliers and distributors may need to be found and integrated into the system, and some current suppliers and distributors may no longer be an appropriate fit. Moreover, it is necessary to take into account projected impact on demand as well as financial, marketing, and distribution implications. Because of the potential for widespread effects, taking a "big picture" systems approach early and throughout the design or redesign process is imperative to reduce the chance of missing some implications and costs, and to understand the time it will take. Likewise, input from engineering, operations, marketing, finance, accounting, and supply chains is crucial.

Product design involves the determination of the form and function of the product. Business organizations select the products they want to offer based on their expected profit contribution. In most cases, products are redesigned to invigorate their demand and to take advantage of new technology.

Design thinking is a systems approach to product design. See the "Steelcase and Design Thinking" OM in Action.

In this chapter, you will find many insights into goods and services design. Among the topics covered are the steps involved in product design or redesign; sources of ideas for design or redesign; some design issues; service design; and quality function deployment, a method for translating the "voice of customers" into design attributes.

Product design—or redesign—should be closely tied to an organization's strategy. It is a major factor in customer satisfaction and competitive advantage.

product design
Determining the form and function of the product.

Product Design Process

Successful organizations use four elements to rapidly create new goods and services and bring them to consumers. These are (1) the product approval committee, (2) core teams, (3) phase reviews, and (4) the structured development process.

The product approval committee consists of top management and oversees and directs the design/development activities. It is responsible for authorizing new products, reviewing their progress at phase (or stage) review points, allocating resources across different projects, and ensuring consistency between company strategy and design/development projects.

Core teams are cross-functional teams empowered to plan and lead the design/development projects from idea to commercialization. This involves resolving issues and conflicts, making trade-off decisions, and directing other support staff. Every function involved in the design/development should be represented in the core team, but the team should not be large (maximum of eight members) in order to be effective. It is important to clearly define every core member's role and responsibility, and those of the functional managers, to ensure that the core team is empowered. The limits of authority of the core team should be defined. Many core teams also include a legal and regulatory member.

Steelcase and Design Thinking

Design thinking is a systems approach to product design that starts with a thorough understanding of what people want and need in their lives and how they feel about the manner in which products are designed, produced, supported, and recycled. Design ideas are then iteratively prototyped and redesigned based on direct observation of user experiences. Design thinking has been promoted by IDEO, a major international design and consulting firm (www.ideo.com) as a key avenue for achieving and sustaining a competitive advantage.

Steelcase and IDEO have been collaborating and using design thinking for more than 25 years. Their relationship has influenced furniture design across a wide range of environments—including office workspaces, student classrooms, and hospitals—and has resulted in numerous design awards for products such as the Node Chair and the Leap WorkLounge. Steelcase is now shifting its focus away from the traditional office cubicle toward furniture that is more architectural and open after noticing that the way people worked was changing from static work in offices to more fluid and technology enabled workspaces. This insight has led to two recent collaborations: Room Wizard, a meeting room booking system, and media:scape, a meeting and conferencing workspace (see photo). Steelcase believes that the modern workplace needs to provide users with choice and control over where and how they work. These workplaces need to be designed to support the physical, cognitive, and emotional well-being of workers.

Courtesy of Steelcase Inc.

Source: https://hbr.org/2008/06/design-thinking; https://www.ideo.com/case-study/redesigning-where-we-work-and-learn.

Phase reviews (or stage-gates) are milestones during a new product design/development project when the progress of the core team is reviewed by the product approval committee. The decision will be to approve, cancel, or redirect the project. Reviews help top management better understand the project, guide the project, and force closure of issues arising during each phase of the project. Phase reviews result in recognizing the problems and making necessary changes earlier, reducing the cost of changes and time to market. Cost of changes tends to multiply with each phase—changing a sketch is a lot easier than changing a prototype, and changing a prototype is a lot easier than changing the first production unit. This is called the "escalator effect."[1]

The structured development process is the use of project management techniques. It involves breaking each phase (stage) into steps and each step into activities, determining their precedence relationships, scheduling, and execution and control. The steps are most critical and are planned and managed by the core team. An activity relates to one functional area and is planned and managed by

---

[1]See, for example, B. Huthwaite and G. Spence, "The Power of Cost Measurement in New Product Development," *National Productivity Review*, Summer 1989, 8(3), pp. 239–248.

the core team member from that function. Activities may be broken down into day-to-day tasks. It is important that the amount of structure be just right: too much structure results in bureaucracy and too little structure results in an ineffective design/development process.

The usual phases (stages) for product design, and a brief description for each, are:

1. Idea generation and preliminary assessment (or scoping): Ideas can come from customers' feedback, research and development staff, suppliers, and competitors. Preliminary assessment involves market, technical, and financial evaluation.

2. Building a business case: Determine what customers want ("voice of the customer"), determine the nature of the product and assess its technical feasibility, establish product goals and objectives (performance, price, quality, quantity, launch date, etc.), plan the nature of the production process (determine the inputs, process objectives, and production process in general), and perform a complete financial analysis.

3. Development of product and process: Translate the "voice of the customer" into technical (physical) product specifications, such as product size, features, and so on. As part of this, several concepts (sketches of the product) are developed. Each concept represents a slightly different product form and/or function, and its components. Choose one concept and complete the design. Build product prototypes, test, and revise the design if necessary. Design the production/service delivery process: develop a few process concepts (sketches), evaluate them and choose one concept and complete the design, build a prototype of the process and evaluate it, and revise the process if necessary. Determine the machines and equipment, plant layout, and work centre designs.

4. Testing and validation: Perform external testing, finalize the product and process specifications, and buy the machines and equipment and start trial runs.

5. Launch the product.

A core team usually consists of a product manager, product designers (usually stylists, also called industrial designers, and engineers), and manufacturing/operations representatives. The team is expanded during each phase of design with marketing representatives (at the start and at the end), accountants (to establish cost goals), process engineers (for process design, tooling/equipment), quality control, and purchasing and supplier representatives (component design and manufacturing).

This team-based approach of simultaneously designing the product and process is called *concurrent engineering*. In contrast, in the past, because of time pressure and the "silo" mentality, each functional area performed its part of design in isolation and "threw" the work "over the wall" to the next department in design. The order was (1) marketing, (2) product design/engineering, (3) manufacturing, and (4) purchasing. This frequently resulted in late launches and costly design revisions. Concurrent engineering is further discussed later in the chapter. The new product design/development process is illustrated in Figure 4-1 (the stage-gate model).

In the stage-gate model, *Scoping* involves preliminary market, financial, and technical assessment; *Building Business Case* involves determining customer requirements, competitive analysis, detailed financial and technical analysis, product definition, and operations assessment; *Development* involves further developing the product concept, making and testing prototypes, and operations process development; and *Testing and Validation* involves further in-house testing and customer trials, acquisition of production equipment, and operations trials.

FIGURE 4-1 ▼

The stage-gate model of the new product design and development process.

Source: Stage-Gate® © Product Development Institute Inc. www.prod-dev.com /stage-gate.php.

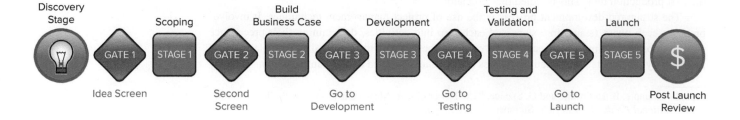

Traditionally, product design has been conducted by members of the design team who are located in one facility or a few nearby facilities. However, organizations that operate globally are discovering advantages in global product design, which uses the combined efforts of a team of designers who work in different countries and even on different continents. Such teams can provide a range of comparative advantages over traditional teams—such as engaging the best human resources from around the world without the need to assemble them all in one place, and operating on a 24-hour basis, thereby decreasing the time-to-market. The use of a **global team** also allows for customer needs assessment to be done in more than one country with local resources, opportunities, and constraints to be taken into account. Global product design can provide design outcomes that increase the marketability and utility of a product. The diversity of an international team may yield different points of view and ideas and information to enrich the design process. However, care must be taken in managing the diversity, because if it is mismanaged, that can lead to conflict and miscommunication.

global team A team of designers who work in different countries.

Advances in information technology have played a key role in the viability of global product design teams by enabling team members to maintain continual contact with each other and to instantaneously share designs and progress, and to transmit engineering changes and other necessary information. See the "Draganfly Innovations" OM in Action for an interesting example of product design.

 OM in Action   www.draganfly.com

Draganfly Innovations

Saskatoon-based Draganfly Innovations Inc. designs and builds unmanned aerial vehicles (UAVs). Commonly known as drones, UAVs have a host of potential military and civilian applications. For instance, the RCMP in Saskatoon have been using UAVs like the Draganflyer X4ES system since 2011 in support at crime scenes, and for traffic accident reconstruction, tactical support, and search and rescue.

Careful design decisions made by Draganfly engineers ensure that the drones excel at providing fast and reliable situational awareness wherever needed. Available four-engine and six-engine designs provide the power that Draganfly drones need to field a wide range of payload options. When on-site, the drones help provide law enforcement with situational awareness and the capability to take aerial surveillance video and shoot high-resolution photos.

Courtesy of Draganfly Innovations, Inc., www.draganfly.com

Source: http://www.rcmp-grc.gc.ca/sk/news-nouvelle/video-gallery/video-pages/search-rescue-eng.htm.

Sources of Ideas for New or Redesigned Products

Ideas for new or redesigned goods and services can come from a wide range of sources, both from within the organization and from outside it: front-line employees, the suppliers and purchasing function, customers and sales/marketing functions, competitors (through reverse engineering), and the research and development (R&D) function.

Front-line employees—those who make the goods or deliver services to customers—have seen the problems in manufacturing/assembly operations or service delivery system caused by faulty design of the parts and products. Their feedback could improve the redesigned product. Suppliers of materials and parts/components and their contacts within the organization, the purchasing agents, can be a rich source of ideas about the design/redesign of purchased items. Customers and their contacts within the organization, the customer service and marketing/sales employees, are aware of problems with products. Similarly, product failures and warranty claims indicate where improvements are needed. Marketing employees are often sources of ideas based on their studies of markets and buying patterns, and their familiarity with demographics. Also, marketing can help craft a vision of what customers are likely to want in the future. Customers may submit suggestions for improvements of existing products or need for new products, or they may be queried through the use of surveys or focus groups.

One of the strongest motivators for new and improved products and services is competitors' products and services. By studying a competitor's products or services and how the competitor operates (pricing policies, return policies, warranties, location strategies, etc.), an organization can glean many ideas. Beyond that, some companies purchase a competitor's product and dismantle it to discover what it is composed of and how the components work, searching for ways to improve their own product. This is called **reverse engineering**. The following are some examples of reverse engineering. Xerox, despite inventing the copy machine, came under competitive pressure from cheaper Japanese copiers such as Toshiba in the 1980s. Xerox tore down the competitors' copiers and learned their secrets. When IBM created its personal computer in the 1980s, the only component that was not publicly available was the ROM-Bios chip. Its competitors, such as Compaq, did not take too long to produce a similar chip and make IBM clones. Ford Motor Company used reverse engineering in developing its highly successful Taurus model: it examined competitors' automobiles, searching for best-in-class components (e.g., best hood release, best dashboard display, best door handle). Sometimes reverse engineering can enable a company to "leapfrog" the competition by developing an even better product. Suppliers are still another source of ideas, and with increased emphasis on supply chains and supplier partnerships, suppliers are becoming an important source of ideas. See the "Vlasic on a Roll With Huge Pickle Slices" OM in Action for an application.

Research is another source of ideas for new or improved products and services. **Research and development (R&D)** refers to organized efforts that are directed toward increasing scientific knowledge and product or process innovation. Most of the advances in semiconductors, medicine, communications, and space technology can be attributed to R&D efforts at colleges and universities, research foundations, government agencies, and private enterprises.

R&D efforts may involve basic research, applied research, or development.

- *Basic research* has the objective of advancing the state of knowledge about a subject without any near-term expectation of commercial applications.
- *Applied research* has the objective of achieving commercial applications.
- *Development* converts the results of applied research into useful commercial applications.

Basic research, because it does not lead to near-term commercial applications, is generally underwritten by the government and large corporations. Conversely, applied research and development, because of the potential for commercial applications, appeals to a wide spectrum of business organizations.

reverse engineering Dismantling and inspecting a competitor's product to discover what it is composed of and how the components work, searching for own product improvements.

research and development (R&D) Organized efforts that are directed toward increasing scientific knowledge and product or process innovation.

Vlasic on a Roll
With Huge Pickle Slices

Many were skeptical of Frank Meczkowski's plan to develop a pickle so big that a single slice could cover a hamburger. After all, who had ever seen a pickle that big—except maybe in the Guinness book of world records? Meczkowski and his team of food researchers at Vlasic Foods International were convinced the project—given the code name Frisbee—could fly.

For about four years, they laboured to cultivate a jumbo cucumber with the taste, shape, and crunch to be a perfect pickle. To develop Hamburger Stackers, Meczkowski worked with seed researchers and others to scour the globe looking for oversized varieties of cucumbers. Most weren't in commercial production. Vlasic's team grew different varieties in greenhouses, looking for one that would get big enough yet still make a good pickle. It had to taste like a regular cucumber, stay crisp when pickled, have a small seed cavity, and be straight enough so that it could be cut mechanically.

Eventually, Vlasic officials found what they were looking for—a now-patented cucumber that grows 3.25 inches

Courtesy of Pinnacle Foods Corporation.

The Hamburger Stacker on the burger at left dwarfs a traditional pickle slice at right.

in diameter, easily reaches 12 to 16 inches in length, and weighs about five pounds. Hamburger Stackers are about 10 times bigger than traditional pickle chips.

Source: Based on *Rochester Democrat and Chronicle*, December 13, 1999.

The benefits of successful R&D can be tremendous. Some research leads to patents, with the potential of licensing and royalties. However, many discoveries are not patentable, or companies don't wish to divulge details of their ideas so they avoid the patent route. Even so, the first organization to bring a new product or service to the market generally stands to profit from it before the others can catch up. Early products may be priced higher because a temporary monopoly exists until competitors bring out their versions.

The costs of R&D can be high. Large companies in the automotive industry (such as Magna International), computer industry (such as IBM Canada), communications industry (such as BCE), aerospace industry (such as Bombardier Inc.), and pharmaceutical/biotech industry (such as Apotex) spend a lot of money on R&D. For a list of Canada's top 100 R&D spenders, see https://www.researchinfosource.com/pdf/CIL%20Top%20100%20R%20and%20D%202016.pdf. For a list of the top 20 R&D spenders worldwide, see https://www.strategyand.pwc.com/innovation1000#GlobalKeyFindingsTabs2.

R&D also contributes to a company by developing the prototypes, testing the prototypes in engineering labs, and improving the products' reliability.

It is interesting to note that some companies are now shifting from a focus primarily on *products* to a more balanced approach that explores both product and *process* R&D. Also, there is increasing recognition that technologies often go through life cycles, in the same way that many products do. This can impact R&D efforts on two fronts. Sustained economic growth requires constant attention to competitive factors over a life cycle, and it also requires planning to be able to participate in the next-generation technology.

The "Searching for New Product Ideas" OM in Action illustrates some market-related sources of ideas for product design. See "BlackBerry Limited" for an interesting application.

OM in Action

Searching for New Product Ideas

What is the best way to find new product ideas? Consider the following approaches that have shown success in the past.

1. Listening to the Market Complaints

Many companies have made their products successful by listening to consumer complaints about products already on the market. Complaints about the inadequacies of two-ply tissues inspired Kimberly-Clark to create three-ply Cold Care Tissues, and Gillette found it could satisfy customers with complaints about white residue from its deodorants by creating the Clear Stick.

An equivalent complaint about lipstick smearing on coffee cups and shirt collars resulted in Lancôme's transfer-resistant Rouge Idôle lipsticks.

2. Gaps in the Market

3M used focus groups to create its Pop-Up Tape Dispenser—it noticed that consumers were one hand short of being able to hold wrapping paper, scissors, and tape when wrapping gifts. The new patented creation fit like a wristwatch, precutting tape strips and otherwise giving gift-wrappers a hand up. Black & Decker introduced its cordless DeWalt power tools for professionals who needed powerful equipment (such as drills) and could get this only from corded tools. The Black & Decker Snakelite twistable flashlight allows for hands-free use during repairs in tight-fitting spaces such as bathrooms or furnace rooms.

John Deere's "Gator" is an inexpensive, six-wheel, off-road all-terrain utility vehicle suitable for transporting everything from personnel and equipment to farming debris to wounded soldiers from the battlefield. The Gator simply doesn't have any direct competitors.

3. Exploring Niche Markets

For drivers who have been dropped by their insurance carriers because they are considered risky, Kingsway

Financial Services Company of Mississauga, Ontario, provides an unparalleled service. Offering car insurance to drivers like these, Kingsway has seen its annual revenue rocket from less than $20 million to more than $92 billion in a mere 10 years.

Coleman, traditionally a manufacturer of camping gear, found a lucrative niche in the market when it produced smoke detectors with large "broom button" alarm testers. Using a broom handle to shut off nuisance alarms triggered by burnt toast appealed especially to the elderly and gave Coleman a 40 percent market share as a result.

4. Using New Technology

Many new products have found that they could attract the attention of the market by exploiting a new science or art, whether it is a once-a-month pill to rid cats and dogs of fleas (Novartis), or frosted windows that turn clear with the flip of a switch (3M). The founders of Research In Motion (RIM) managed to use their capability with pagers to invent the BlackBerry, a portable email communicator, in the late 1990s at the peak of the high-tech boom.

5. Creating New Market Space

WestJet started by targeting a new market, the "friends and relatives" visitors who normally drive to visit. Sony Walkman created a new market of personal portable stereos for joggers and commuters. Starbucks emphasizes the emotional value of drinking coffee by providing a chic "caffeine-induced oasis." Body Shop did the reverse by selling natural ingredients and healthy living instead of glamour and beauty.

Sources: Adapted from Allan J. Magrath, "Mining for New Product Successes," *Business Quarterly* 62(2), Winter 1997, pp. 64–68; "The Edison Best New Product Awards," *Marketing News* 31(6), March 17, 1997, pp. E4–E12; W.C. Kim & R. Mauborgne, "Creating New Marketplace," *Harvard Business Review* 77(1), January/February 1999, pp. 83–93.

 # Key Issues in Product Design

Designers must take into account issues such as product life cycle, standardization, mass customization, product reliability, robust design, legal and ethical issues, design for environment, material selection, concurrent engineering of product and production process, computer-aided design, design for manufacturing and assembly, and component commonality. These topics are discussed in this section. We begin with the life cycle.

OM in Action

BlackBerry Limited

BlackBerry Limited of Waterloo, Ontario, is a Canadian wireless telecommunications company that at one time dominated the North American smartphone market. In 1999, the company leveraged its extensive experience with pager technology and designed an enterprise oriented two-way pager with powerful email capabilities and encryption. One key distinguishing feature of this device was the ability to automatically synchronize with a central server whenever emails were read or sent, a revolutionary innovation at the time. BlackBerry devices gained widespread acceptance by governmental agencies and businesses alike, allowing the company to capture more than half of North American smartphone sales.

BlackBerry's prominence continued to rise well into the late 2000s when its revenues reached $20 billion and its employment exceeded 10,000 employees. Unfortunately, the emergence of competing products from Apple and Samsung, and BlackBerry's embarrassing service outages, along with a lack of new innovation and losing its competitive advantage to text messaging,

Leszekkobusinski/Dreamstime.com

resulted in a sharp and sudden drop in sales. In 2013, John Chen was brought in as CEO, all manufacturing was outsourced to China, and employment was cut in half. In 2017, BlackBerry Limited had 4,500 employees and $2 billion in revenues.

Sources: https://en.wikipedia.org/wiki/BlackBerry_Limited.

Product Life Cycle

The decision to design a new substitute product or to redesign an existing product, and its timing, depends on the nature and length of the product's life cycle. Most products go through a **life cycle**: incubation, growth, maturity, saturation, and decline.

> **life cycle** Incubation, growth, maturity, saturation, and decline.

Incubation. When an item is introduced, it may be treated as a curiosity. Demand is generally low because potential buyers are not yet familiar with the item. Many potential buyers recognize that all of the bugs have probably not been worked out and that the price may drop after the introductory period. Production methods are generally designed for low volumes.

Growth. With the passage of time, design improvements usually create a more reliable and less costly product. Demand then grows for these reasons and because of increasing awareness of the product. Higher production volume will involve automated production methods and contribute to lower costs.

Maturity. There are few, if any, design changes, and demand levels off.

Saturation. Saturation leads to a decline in demand.

Decline. In decline, companies attempt to prolong the useful life of a product by improving its reliability, reducing costs of producing it (and, hence, the price), redesigning it, or introducing a new substitute product. These stages are illustrated in Figure 4-2.

FIGURE 4-2 ▶

Most products exhibit a life cycle over time.

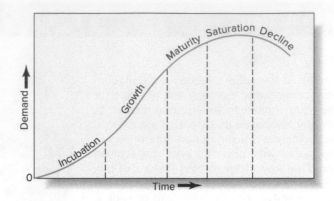

Consider the portable computer data storage products in various stages of the life cycle: Memory keys are in the growth stage, DVDs are in the saturation stage, and CDs are in the decline stage.

Some products do not exhibit life cycles: wooden pencils; paper clips; nails; knives, forks, and spoons; drinking glasses; and similar items. However, most new products do.

Services, too, experience life cycles. For example, in banking, using tellers is in the saturation stage, using ABMs is in its maturity, and Internet banking is in its growth stage.

Wide variations exist in the amount of time a particular product takes to pass through a given phase of its life cycle: some pass through various stages in a relatively short period; others take considerably longer. Often it is a matter of the basic *need* for the item and the *rate of technological change*. Some toys, novelty items, personal computers, and style items have a life cycle of less than one year, whereas other items, such as clothes washers and dryers, may last for decades before yielding to technological change.

Standardization

standardization Extent to which there is absence of variety in a part or product.

Standardization refers to the extent to which there is absence of variety in a part or product, that is, having limited types, sizes, and colours. Standardized products are made in large quantities of identical items; paper, gasoline, and 2 percent milk are examples. Standardized service implies that every customer or item processed receives essentially the same service. An automatic car wash is a good example; each car, regardless of how clean or dirty it is, receives the same service.

Large-volume production and purchase of only a few types of standardized parts would reduce costs due to economies of scale. For example, auto manufacturers have standardized key components of their automobiles across similar product lines; components such as brakes, electrical systems, and other "under-the-skin" parts would be the same. By reducing variety, they save time and money while increasing quality and reliability in their products.

Another benefit of standardization is reduced time and cost to train employees. Similarly, inventory, purchasing, and accounting activities become much more routine. WestJet's using only Boeing 737 airplanes is an example, where costs of training the pilots and maintenance workers, and inventory of spare parts, are reduced.

Lack of standardization can at times lead to serious difficulties and competitive struggles, particularly when systems are incompatible. For example, lack of standardization in computer software and operating systems (Apple versus IBM) has presented users with hard choices because of the difficulty in switching from one system to the other.

Standardization also has disadvantages. A major one relates to the reduction in variety. This can limit the range of customers to whom a product appeals. Another disadvantage is that a manufacturer may lock in obsolescence and resist modification of a part.

Employees on the production line at the Dell Chengdu Global Operation Facility in China. With the capacity of 7 million units a year, the site manufactures electronics for the Chinese market as well as markets in Europe and North America.

©Liu Zheng/ColorChinaPhoto/ AP Images

Mass Customization

Companies like standardization because it enables them to produce high volumes of relatively low-cost products, albeit products with little variety. Customers, on the other hand, typically prefer more variety, although they like the low cost. The question for producers is how to resolve these issues without (1) losing the benefits of standardization and (2) incurring the problems that are often linked to variety. The answer, at least for some companies, is **mass customization**, a strategy of producing standardized goods or services but incorporating some degree of customization in the final product. (See the "Fast-Food Chains Adopt Mass Customization" OM in Action.) Several tactics make this possible. One is *delayed differentiation,* and another is *modular design.*

Delayed differentiation is a *postponement* tactic: the process of producing but not quite completing a product until customer preferences or specifications are known. In the case of goods, almost-finished units might be held in inventory until customer orders are received, at which time customized features are incorporated according to customer requests. For example, furniture makers can produce dining room sets but not apply stain, allowing customers a choice of stains. Once the choice is made, the stain can be applied in a relatively short time. Another example is HP printers, made in Singapore, for the European market. By postponing country-specific customization (e.g., labels, packaging, and manuals), and doing this in its distribution centre in Stuttgart, HP saved 25 percent in total costs of manufacturing, shipping, and inventory costs. Finally, manufacturers of men's clothing produce dress pants that have legs that are unfinished, allowing the customers to choose the exact length.

> **mass customization**
> Producing basically standardized goods or services but incorporating some degree of customization.
>
> **delayed differentiation**
> Producing, but not quite completing, a product until customer preferences are known.

 OM in Action

Fast-Food Chains Adopt Mass Customization

Pulled pork sandwiches are proving popular at many chain restaurants, including Wendy's, Buffalo Wild Wings, and Burger King. Because pulled pork typically takes about four hours to cook, it's not a food most folks are likely to cook at home. And once cooked, sandwiches can easily be assembled to order (i.e., delayed differentiation) using any of a large number of sauces or seasonings. Customer appeal is obvious. And advantages for fast-food restaurants include simplified menus, minimal training requirements, and little need for new equipment.

Source: Based on "Fast-Food Chains Are Pigging Out," *Business Week*, October 12–October 18, 2015, pp. 22–3.

modular design Parts are grouped into modules that are easily replaced or interchanged. The product is composed of a number of modules or components instead of a collection of individual parts.

Modular design is the grouping of parts into modules that are easily interchanged or replaced. The product is composed of a number of modules or components instead of a collection of individual parts. One familiar example of modular design is computers with modular components that can be replaced if they become defective. By arranging modules in different configurations, different computer capabilities can be obtained. This is the major reason that Dell can assemble and have custom-ordered computers delivered to its Internet customers in a matter of days. For mass customization, modular design enables producers to quickly assemble modules to achieve a customized configuration for an individual customer, avoiding the long customer wait that would occur if individual parts had to be assembled.

Another advantage of modular design is that failures are often easier to diagnose and remedy because modules can be tested individually. Other advantages include simpler purchasing, inventory control, and assembly operations. The main disadvantage of modular design is the inability to disassemble some modules in order to replace a faulty part; the entire module must be scrapped—usually at a higher cost.

A relatively new means of mass customization uses computer technology. For example, Amazon.com uses a software program that analyzes a customer's browsing history and suggests other items that people with similar interests have bought.

For an example of modular design, see the "Magna International" OM in Action.

OM in Action   www.magna.com

Magna International

Magna International is the largest automobile parts manufacturer in North America and one of Canada's largest companies. Its operating groups include Magna Powertrain, Magna Exteriors, Magna Seating, Magna Closures, Magna Mirrors, Magna Electronics, and Cosma (body and chassis). Magna also provides original equipment manufacturers (OEMs) with product development services including concept design, development, prototyping, and testing. Magna's operating groups are constantly looking to reduce the number of parts in their products. This door module provides significant reductions in assembly time, which in turn results in cost savings.

Courtesy of Magna International

Product Reliability

Reliability is a measure of the ability of a product, a part, or an entire system to perform its intended function under normal conditions.

Reliability is always specified with respect to certain conditions, called **normal operating conditions**. These can include load, temperature, and humidity ranges as well as operating procedures and maintenance schedules. Failure of users to heed these conditions often results in premature failure of parts or complete systems. For example, using a passenger car to tow heavy loads will cause excess wear and tear on the drive train; driving over potholes or curbs often results in untimely tire failure; and using a calculator to drive nails might have a marked impact on its usefulness for performing mathematical operations.

Reliability can be improved in a number of ways. Because overall system reliability is a function of the reliability of individual components, improvements in their reliability can increase system reliability. Unfortunately, inadequate production or assembly procedures can negate even the best of designs, and this is often a source of failures. System reliability can be increased by the use of backup components. Failures in actual use often can be reduced by upgrading user education and refining maintenance recommendations or procedures. Finally, it may be possible to increase the overall reliability of the system by simplifying the system (thereby reducing the number of components that could cause the system to fail) or altering component relationships (e.g., increasing the reliability of interfaces).

A fundamental question concerning improving reliability is: How much reliability is needed? Obviously, the reliability needed for a household light bulb isn't in the same category as the reliability needed for an airplane. So the answer to the question depends on the potential benefits of improvements and on the cost of those improvements. Generally speaking, reliability improvements become increasingly costly. Thus, although benefits initially may increase at a much faster rate than costs, the opposite eventually becomes true. The optimal level of reliability is the point where the incremental benefit received equals the incremental cost of obtaining it. In the short term, this trade-off is made in the context of relatively fixed parameters (e.g., costs). However, in the longer term, efforts to improve reliability and reduce costs can lead to higher optimal levels of reliability.

The term **failure** is used to describe a situation in which an item does not perform as intended. This includes not only instances in which the item does not function at all, but also instances in which the item's performance is substandard or it functions in a way not intended. For example, a smoke alarm might fail to respond to the presence of smoke (not operate at all), it might sound an alarm that is too faint to provide an adequate warning (substandard performance), or it might sound an alarm even though no smoke is present (unintended response).

New products are tested to find their breaking points. If this is low, the reliability of the product must be improved. For example, laptop and notebook computers need to be tough enough to absorb unintentional drops, and trucks, cars, and motorcycles need to endure bumps in the roads for many years. For more on reliability, see the supplement to Chapter 4.

Robust Design

Some products will function as designed only within a narrow range of conditions, while others will perform over a much broader range of conditions. The latter have **robust design**. Consider a pair of fine leather boots—obviously not made for trekking through mud or snow. Now consider a pair of heavy rubber boots—just the thing for mud or snow, as well as other conditions. The rubber boots have a design that is more *robust* than the fine leather boots.

The more robust a product is, the less likely it is to fail due to a change in the environment in which it is used. Hence, the more designers can build robustness into the product, the better it should hold up, resulting in a higher level of customer satisfaction.

Taguchi's Approach. Japanese engineer Genichi Taguchi's approach is based on robust design. His premise is that it is often easier to design a product that is insensitive to environmental factors, either in manufacturing or in use, than to control the environmental factors.

The central feature of Taguchi's approach—and the feature used most often by North American companies—is *parameter design*. This involves determining the specification settings for the product that will result in robust design in terms of manufacturing variations, product deterioration, and conditions during use.

reliability The ability of a product, part, or system to perform its intended function under normal conditions.

normal operating conditions The set of conditions under which an item's reliability is specified.

failure Situation in which a product, part, or system does not perform as intended.

robust design Design that can function over a broad range of conditions.

The Taguchi approach modifies the conventional statistical methods of experimental design. Consider this example. Suppose a company intends to use 11 chemicals in a new product. There are two suppliers for these chemicals, and the chemical concentrations vary slightly between the two suppliers. Classical design of experiments would require $2^{11} = 2{,}048$ test runs to determine which combination of chemicals would be optimum. Taguchi's approach would involve testing only 12 combinations.[2]

Legal and Ethical Issues

Designers must be careful to take into account a wide array of legal and ethical considerations. Organizations have been faced with many government (federal, provincial, municipal) acts and regulations, administered by government agencies and boards designed to regulate their activities. Among the more familiar ones are the *Food and Drugs Act* (Health Canada), the *Canadian Environmental Protection Act* (Environment Canada), the *Motor Vehicle Safety Act* (Transport Canada), and the *Hazardous Products Act* (Industry Canada). Bans or regulations on materials such as saccharin, CFC, phosphate, and asbestos have sent designers scurrying back to their drawing boards to find alternative designs acceptable to both government regulators and customers. Similarly, automobile pollution standards and safety features—such as seat belts, air bags, safety glass, and energy-absorbing bumpers and frames—have had a substantial impact on automotive design. Much attention also has been directed toward toy design to remove sharp edges, small pieces that can cause choking, and toxic materials. In construction, government (municipal) regulations require access to public buildings for persons with disabilities, and standards for insulation, electrical wiring, plumbing, and fire protection.

Designers should not infringe on patents, trademarks, and copyright of competitors. If the product is not significantly different from a patented/copyrighted product in functional and operational characteristics or appearance (if this results in undeserved benefit), the company can be sued.[3]

Product liability can be a strong incentive for design improvements.

Product liability means that a manufacturer is liable for any injuries or damages caused by a faulty product because of poor workmanship or design. Many business firms have faced lawsuits related to their products, including Ford Motor Company, General Motors, tobacco companies, and toy manufacturers.

The suits and potential suits have led to increased legal and insurance costs, expensive settlements with injured parties, and costly recalls. Moreover, increasing customer awareness of product safety can adversely affect product image and subsequent demand for a product.

> **product liability** A manufacturer is liable for any injuries or damages caused by a faulty product.

Volkswagen sold more than 100,000 vehicles with the 2.0-litre TDI engine between 2000 and 2015 which featured emissions-cheating software. The software would automatically change performance parameters when the car was under formal emissions testing in order to reduce emissions. Under normal driving conditions, another set of parameters would be used and emissions were more than 10 times the advertised limit.

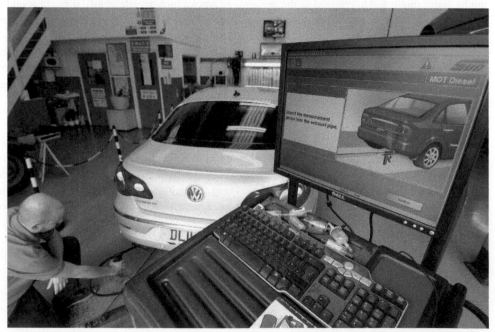

PA Images/Alamy Images

[2]See, for example, http://controls.engin.umich.edu/wiki/index.php?title=Design_of_experiments_via_-taguchi_methods:_orthogonal_arrays&printable=yes (accessed April 19, 2010).
[3]See, for example, W.M. Fitzpatrick and S.A. DiLullo, "Attack of the Clones: Reverse Engineering, R&D, and the Law," *Competition Forum*, 2006, 4(2), pp. 501–514.

Thus, it is extremely important to design products that are reasonably free of hazards. When hazards do exist, it is necessary to install safety guards or other devices for reducing accident potential, and to provide adequate warning notices of risks. Consumer groups, business firms, and various government agencies often work together to develop industry-wide standards that help avoid some of the hazards.

Ethical issues often arise in the design of products. Designers are often under pressure to speed up the design process and to cut costs. These pressures often require them to make trade-off decisions, many of which involve ethical considerations. One example is, should a software company release a product as scheduled when it struggles with bugs in the software, or wait until most of the bugs have been removed?

Design for Environment

Design for environment (DFE) is an umbrella term describing techniques used to incorporate environmental concerns (including the three Rs of *reduce, reuse, and recycle*) into product design. See the "Best Buy Wants Your Junk" OM in Action for an application. The most common DFE practices include:

- Design for energy efficiency of product and energy used in manufacturing.
- Design for hazardous material minimization, including emissions and wastes in manufacturing.
- Design for biodegradable disposal, including packaging.
- Design for reuse, including packaging.
- Design for disassembly and remanufacture.
- Design for recycling, including packaging.

Madartists/Dreamstime.com/GetStock.com

We will expand on some of these. **Remanufacturing** refers to refurbishing used products by replacing worn-out or defective components, and reselling the products. This can be done by the original manufacturer, or another company. Among products that have remanufactured components are automobiles, printers, copiers, cameras, computers, and telephones.

> **remanufacturing**
> Refurbishing used products by replacing worn-out or defective components.

 OM in Action

Best Buy Wants Your Junk

Electronic junk, that is. The giant electronics retailer sees its recycling program as a way to get customers into its stores while building a green reputation. While old TVs, desktop computers, and other outmoded electronics come in, out go flat-screen TVs, netbooks, and iPhones.

The company decided that being a good corporate citizen makes business sense. Best Buy's commitment to corporate responsibility fits nicely with the company's strategy and business model. To set itself apart from its biggest competitors—Walmart and Amazon—the company wants to do more than sell consumer electronics. It would like to help customers get better use out of technology, whether they are buying, installing, fixing, or disposing of their hardware. Since 2009, when Best Buy began offering free recycling of electronic equipment, millions of pounds of "in-store take-back" (ISTB) have found their way to the company's stores, making Best Buy North America's biggest collector of electronic junk.

Best Buy's interest in the social and environmental impact of electronic goods that had reached the end of their useful life came at the urging of its workers and customers. Employees wanted to know what Best Buy was doing to become more environmentally sustainable. Some customers—enough to matter—said they preferred buying from retailers that demonstrated an interest in their community. The company audits the factories of its suppliers to make sure they don't exploit workers or

pollute the environment; it actually severed ties with 26 of about 200 factories in 2008. Best Buy's CEO, Brian Dunn, strives to stay connected to staff and customers, posting questions on an employee website called "The Water Cooler," tracking consumer sentiment on Facebook and Twitter (BBY-CEO), attending focus groups, and inviting customers to the company's leadership meetings.

TVs account for the majority of items. This is somewhat of a mixed blessing. TVs with picture tubes can't be resold; they have to be taken away and disassembled before the materials are melted down for reuse. Unlike plastics, which might end up in lawn furniture or other products, the innards of TVs aren't of much value. In many provinces and states, manufacturers are required by take-back laws to help finance recycling, and companies like Dell, Samsung, and Sony share the costs of disposing of old TVs.

Even though there may not be a clear economic case for doing so, at least for TVs, the take-back program could also be beneficial by encouraging innovative design and new business models. Manufacturers that know they will be responsible for the end of life of their products will design them so that they can be disassembled and recycled easily. Computer maker Dell, for instance, reduced the number of screws in its computers to make them easier to dismantle.

Sources: Based on "Best Buy Wants Your Electronic Junk," *Fortune*, December 7, 2009; http://www.bestbuy.ca/en-CA/electronics-recycling.aspx?NVID=footer;product%20support;electronics%20recycling;en.

design for disassembly (DFD) Design so that used products can be easily taken apart.

recycling Recovering materials for future use.

cradle-to-grave assessment The assessment of the environmental impact of a product or service throughout its useful life.

Designing products so that they can be taken apart more easily is **design for disassembly (DFD)**, which includes using fewer parts and less material; using snap-fits and fewer screws, nuts, and bolts; and using no glue. It also means using accessible screws and bolts, and requiring only common hand tools to disassemble.

Recycling means recovering materials for future use. This applies not only to manufactured parts but also to materials used during production, such as lubricants and solvents. Reclaimed metal or plastic parts may be melted down and used to make different products. Recycling requires using materials that can be recycled (e.g., thermoset plastics vs. thermoplastics), not adding fillers in plastics, and identifying the material on the part.

Cradle-to-grave assessment is the assessment of the environmental impact of a product or service throughout its useful life, focusing on such factors as global warming (the amount of carbon dioxide released into the atmosphere), smog formation, oxygen depletion, and solid waste generation. For products, cradle-to-grave analysis takes into account impacts in every phase of a product's life cycle, from raw material extraction from the earth, or the growing and harvesting of plant materials, through fabrication of parts and assembly operations, or other processes used to create products, as well as the use or consumption of the product, and final disposal at the end of a product's useful life. It also considers energy consumption, pollution and waste, and transportation in all phases. Although services generally involve less use of materials, cradle-to-grave assessment of services is nonetheless important, because services consume energy and involve many of the same or similar processes that products involve. The goal of cradle-to-grave assessment is to choose products and services that have the least environmental impact while still taking into account economic considerations. See the "Paper or Plastic?" OM in Action for an interesting example.

Material Selection

Careful consideration for material selection is always important for achieving the performance and cost objectives of any product. For example, plastic may be used for the dashboard of a car due to its economical

---

 OM in Action

Paper or Plastic?

Should you ask for a paper or plastic bag at the checkout counter? There's no easy answer. The materials needed to make either bag come from our natural resources.

- Paper comes from wood, which comes from trees, which grow in the earth's soil.
- Plastic is made from petroleum, also known as fossil fuel. Petroleum is made by the decomposition (breaking down) of ancient plants and animals inside the earth.

The trees needed to make paper are considered renewable resources. That means more trees can be planted to take the place of trees that are cut down to make paper and other products. But, trees take many years to replace because they grow slowly. Once paper is made, it can be recycled and used to create more paper goods. Making it into new paper, however, uses water and energy.

Petroleum needed to make plastic is considered a non-renewable resource. Like aluminum, tin, and steel, petroleum is not renewable because it is the result of geological processes that take millions of years to complete. When used up, the earth's petroleum reserves will be gone for a long, long time.

©Jack Star/Photolink/Getty RF

While plastic bags are easy to reuse, they're seldom recycled, and lots and lots of them get dumped into landfills.

The best solution is to use a cloth bag or knapsack for grocery shopping, or to bring your old plastic or paper bag back to the store when you shop again. If you only purchase one or two items, you might not need a bag at all.

Source: Excerpted from https://www3.epa.gov/recyclecity/market.htm

nature, but it lacks strength and should never be used on the car body. Similarly, if a product is used primarily outdoors, one should always consider the damaging effects of ultraviolet light. If material selection is not done properly, the performance and life expectancy of a product may be highly unpredictable.

One must first define the product requirements in terms of mechanical, thermal, environmental, electrical and chemical properties. Once this is complete, the choice of material can be narrowed down by the method of elimination. Production techniques also have a major impact on material selection. Material property data sheets may be used to guide the process of material selection; however, actual performance must be assessed based on experimentation. Depending on the specific application, different materials may need to be assessed for tensile, bend, impact, and compressive strengths; fatigue; endurance; deformation; and stress-relaxation properties.

A design may look good on paper but fail to work properly in real world situations. For instance, a product may be subjected to a higher than expected load. Consequently, the materials engineer must have the ability to predict this ahead of time and design the product to withstand these types of demands. It is generally a good idea to produce several alternative designs and expose each to various environmental conditions in order to find the most appropriate material.[4]

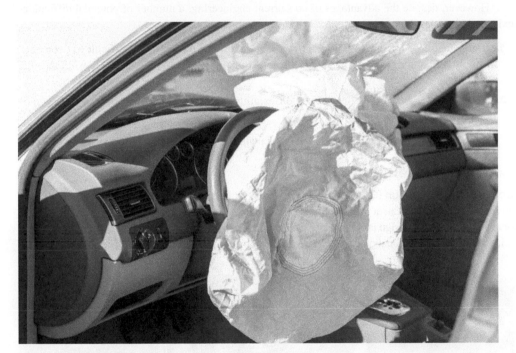

Viamax001/Dreamstime.com

Takata Corporation, one of Japan's largest airbag suppliers, was fined over $1 billion and ordered to recall over 50 million vehicles because of defective airbags that can explode with significantly more force than needed. The company made the mistake of using the chemical ammonium nitrate as an ignitor in its airbags, a substance which can be easily damaged by extreme temperature fluctuations and high humidity (such as the climate in Florida where most of the defects occurred). None of the other big airbag suppliers took a chance on ammonium nitrate.[5]

Concurrent Engineering of Product and Production Process

To achieve a smoother transition from product design to production, and to decrease product development time, many companies are using *simultaneous development,* or concurrent engineering. In its narrowest sense, **concurrent engineering** means bringing design and manufacturing engineers together early in the design phase to simultaneously develop the product and the processes for creating the product. More recently, this concept has been enlarged to participative design/engineering, which includes manufacturing, marketing, and purchasing personnel in a cross-functional team. In addition, the views of suppliers and customers are frequently sought. The purpose is to achieve product designs that reflect customer wants as well as manufacturing capabilities.

Traditionally, designers developed a new product without any input from manufacturing, and then turned over the design to manufacturing, which would then have to develop a process for making the new product. This "throw-over-the-wall" approach created tremendous challenges for

concurrent engineering
Bringing engineering design, manufacturing engineers, and staff from marketing, manufacturing, and purchasing together early in the design phase.

---

[4]http://www.brighthubengineering.com/manufacturing-technology/57192-why-is-selection-of-engineering-materials-important/
[5]https://www.nytimes.com/2014/12/10/business/compound-in-takata-airbags-is-inquirys-focus.html?_r=0

manufacturing, generating numerous conflicts and greatly increasing the time needed to success-fully produce a new product. It also contributed to an "us versus them" mentality.

For these and similar reasons, the simultaneous development approach has great appeal. Among the key advantages of this approach are the following:

1. Manufacturing engineers and personnel are able to identify production capabilities and capacities. Very often, there is some latitude in design in terms of selecting suitable materials and processes. Knowledge of production capabilities can help in this selection. In addition, cost and quality considerations can be greatly influenced by design, and conflicts during production can be greatly reduced.

2. There are early opportunities for design or procurement of critical machines or components, some of which might have long lead times. This can result in a major shortening of the product development process, which could be a key competitive advantage.

3. The technical feasibility of a particular design or a portion of a design can be assessed early on. Again, this can avoid serious problems during production.

4. The emphasis can be on *problem* resolution instead of *conflict* resolution.

However, despite the advantages of concurrent engineering, a number of potential difficulties exist in this co-development approach. Two key ones are the following:

1. Long-standing boundaries between design and manufacturing can be difficult to overcome. Simply bringing a group of people together and thinking that they will be able to work together effectively is probably naïve.

2. There must be extra communication and flexibility if the process is to work, and these can be difficult to achieve.

Hence, managers should plan to devote special attention if this approach is to work.

Computer-Aided Design (CAD)

computer-aided design (CAD) Product design using computer graphics.

Computer-aided design (CAD) uses computer graphics for product design. The designer can modify an existing design or create a new one on a display unit by means of a light pen, a keyboard, a joystick, or a mouse. Once the design is entered into the computer, the designer can manoeuvre it on the screen as if it was a three-dimensional object: It can be rotated to provide the designer with different perspectives,

An architect is using an iPad CAD (computer-aided design) application to model a 3D layout design of a new house.

it can be split apart to give the designer a view of the inside, and a portion of it can be enlarged for closer examination. The designer can obtain a printed version of the completed design and file it electronically, making it accessible to people in the firm who need this information (e.g., marketing, operations).

A growing number of products are being designed in this way, including transformers, automobile parts, aircraft parts, integrated circuits, and electric motors.

A major benefit of CAD is the increased productivity of designers. No longer is it necessary to laboriously prepare manual drawings of products or parts and revise them repeatedly to correct errors or incorporate revisions. A rough estimate is that CAD increases the productivity of designers threefold to tenfold. A second major benefit of CAD is the creation of a database for manufacturing that can supply needed information on product geometry and dimensions, tolerances, material specifications, and so on. It should be noted, however, that CAD needs this database to function and that this entails a considerable amount of effort.

Some CAD systems allow the designer to perform engineering and cost analysis on proposed designs. For instance, the computer can determine the weight and volume of a part and do stress analysis as well. When there are a number of alternative designs, the computer can quickly go through the possibilities and identify the best one, given the designer's criteria. For a tour of capabilities of the SolidWorks 3D CAD software, see http://www.solidworks.com/sw/products/simulation/finite-element-analysis.htm. CAD that includes finite element analysis (FEA) capability can greatly shorten the time to market of new products. It enables developers to perform simulations that aid in the design, analysis, and commercialization of new products. Designers in industries such as aeronautics, biomechanics, and automotives use FEA. See the "CAD and 3D Printing Push Medical Boundaries" for an interesting application.

Design for Manufacturing and Assembly

Designers need to clearly understand the capabilities of the production function (e.g., equipment, skills, types of materials, and technologies). This will help in choosing designs that match capabilities. When opportunities and capabilities do not match, management must consider the potential for expanding or changing capabilities to take advantage of those opportunities.

Manufacturability is a key concern for manufactured goods: ease of fabrication and/or assembly is important for cost, productivity, and quality.

The term **design for manufacturing (DFM)** is used to indicate the designing of products that are compatible with manufacturing capabilities. A related concept is **design for assembly (DFA)**. Design for assembly focuses on reducing the number of parts in an assembly, as well as on the assembly methods and sequence that will be employed.

Component Commonality

Companies can realize significant benefits when a component can be used in multiple products. For example, car manufacturers use the same chassis (platform) and internal components, such as engines

> **design for manufacturing (DFM)** Takes into account the organization's manufacturing capabilities when designing a product.
>
> **design for assembly (DFA)** Focuses on reducing the number of parts in a product and on assembly methods and sequence.

 OM in Action

CAD and 3D Printing Push Medical Boundaries

Imagine printing off a fully functional human kidney or heart with a simple click of a mouse. This may sound like something out of a science fiction novel, but medical researchers have already taken the initial steps toward producing transplantable organs using 3D printers. As a matter of fact, researchers have already produced prosthetic limbs and even a human ear. Ultimately, the goal is to create human organs for a particular patient using his own cells. It is hoped that this will solve a serious rejection problem where the body produces an immune response to attack the newly transplanted organ. Successful implementation of this technology could extend human life by numerous years—if not decades.

A 3D printer works in the same way that a standard inkjet printer does, with a cartridge that deposits successive layers of material in different shapes. Each printed layer is only half the width of a human hair and corresponds to a cross-section read from a CAD model.

Sources: CBC, www.cbc.ca/strombo/technology-1/printed-on-the-body-3d-printers-create-bones-organs.html.

and transmissions, on several models. In addition to the savings in design time, companies reap benefits through standard training for assembly and installation, increased opportunities for savings by buying in bulk from suppliers, and commonality of parts for repair, which reduces the inventory dealers and auto parts stores must carry, as well as the training needed by technicians. Computer software often comprises a number of modules that are commonly used for similar applications, thereby saving the time and cost to write the code for major portions of the software. Tool manufacturers use a design that allows tool users to attach different power tools to a common power source.

Hewlett-Packard's Design-for-Supply-Chain program includes a simple quantitative decision-making tool for designers to make commonality trade-off decisions.[6] The trade-off is between annual holding cost saved by using commonality versus extra cost of manufacturing to provide commonality. An example of a unique part is a power adapter that works with 110V electricity (for North America), and another that works with 220V electricity (for Europe). If commonality is used, the universal power adapter will work with either 110V or 220V electricity. To make the decision whether a universal power adapter will be cheaper in terms of both manufacturing and after-sale service, an analysis similar to the following is used: Based on number of products sold that need this adapter (e.g., 10,000), number of service locations throughout the world (e.g., 400), and annual failure rate of the adapter (e.g., 1 percent), it follows that average annual demand for this power adapter in a service location will be $10,000(0.01)/400 = 0.25$ unit. Given replenishment lead time of four days (from the supplier or other locations), average demand during lead time is only $0.25(4)/365 = 0.003$ unit. Therefore, to provide, for example, a four-hour service response, keeping one unit of this adapter in stock at each service location is more than sufficient. Now, if one universal adapter is kept in stock instead of two unique adapters, there will be a saving of one unit at each service location. If each adapter costs $100 and annual holding cost rate is 20 percent of unit cost, the savings in the annual holding cost will be $(400)(1)(\$100)(0.20) = \$8,000$. If the extra cost of manufacturing a universal adapter (relative to a unique adapter) is $0.50 per unit, annual additional cost will be $\$0.50 \times 10,000 = \$5,000$. Because $\$5,000 < \$8,000$, using the universal adapter is cheaper than using two unique adapters.

LO4 Differences in Designing Services

Most of this chapter so far also applies to service design. However, there are some key differences between goods and services that warrant special consideration for service design:

1. Goods are generally tangible; services are intangible. Consequently, service design often includes secondary factors such as peace of mind, ambiance, and convenience. Another consequence of this is that it is hard to sketch a service. A new service must rely on faith and trust of customers; thus, the importance of image.

2. In many instances, services are created and delivered at the same time. For example, if a bus company makes changes to the bus schedule, or the bus routes, or the types of buses used, those changes will not be hidden from the riders. Obviously, this service redesign could not be done realistically without considering the *process* for delivering the service. In such instances, there is less latitude in finding and correcting errors *before* the customer has a chance to discover them. Consequently, training, process design, and customer relations are particularly important; hence, the increased role of operations. Quality is measured by measuring customer satisfaction.

3. Most services involve some degree of customization (variety). Because of this, there will be variability in length of service. When there is little or no contact, service can be much more standardized, whereas high contact provides the opportunity to tailor the service to the precise needs of individual customers. For example, see Figure 4-3, which shows different types of clothes retailing.

4. Services have lower barriers to entry and exit. Even in capital-intensive services such as air travel, introducing a new service (e.g., a new type of ticket with new restrictions on its use) is relatively easy because it uses the current resources of the airline. The disadvantage of this is that the company cannot easily measure the cost of introducing the service because of the shared resources. Too many similar services will no doubt increase the complexity and cost of

---

[6]J. Amaral and B. Cargille, "How 'Rough-Cut' Analysis Smooths HP's Supply Chain," *Supply Chain Management Review* 9(6), September 2005, pp. 38–45.

operations. This places pressure on service design to be innovative but selective. Because of its relative ease of introduction, many new services are copies of competitors' services.

5. Location is often important to service design, with convenience as a major factor. Hence, design of services and choice of location are often closely linked.

To illustrate service design process further, let's look at the service design process in the financial sector.

The Service Design Process in the Financial Sector

The financial services sector is one of the largest service sectors in Canada and introduces most new services. In a survey of 82 North American financial institutions (banks; insurance, trust, leasing, reinsurance, and mutual fund companies), it was discovered that some financial institutions do not perform some of the activities given in the product design process. In particular, few do "detailed market study/market research" and "pre-commercialization business analysis." The reason for this is that most new services offered by a company are copies of successful services offered by a competitor or the company itself.

In comparing high and low performers, it was found that the difference is "better idea screening," "preliminary market assessment," "market research," "service development," and "post-launch review."

Service Design Guidelines

A number of simple but highly effective rules are often used to guide the design of services:

1. Have a single, unifying theme, such as convenience or speed. This will help personnel work together rather than at cross-purposes.

2. Ensure that the service delivery system has the capability to handle any expected variability in service requirements.

3. Include design features and checks to ensure that service will be reliable and will provide consistently high quality.

4. Design the service delivery system to be user-friendly. This is especially true for self-service systems.

Service Blueprinting

A useful tool for conceptualizing a service delivery system is the service blueprint, which is a method for describing and analyzing a service process. A **service blueprint** is much like an architectural drawing, but instead of showing building dimensions and other construction features, a service blueprint shows the basic customer and service actions involved in a service operation. Figure 4-4 illustrates a simple service blueprint for a restaurant. At the top of the figure are the customer actions, and just below are the related actions of the direct contact service people. Next are what are sometimes referred to as "backstage contacts"—in this example, the kitchen staff—and below those are the support, or "backroom," operations. In this example, support operations include the reservation system, ordering of food and supplies, cashier, and the outsourcing of laundry service. Figure 4-4 is a simplified illustration; typically time estimates for actions and operations would be included.

 ervice

service blueprint A method used in service design to describe and analyze a proposed service.

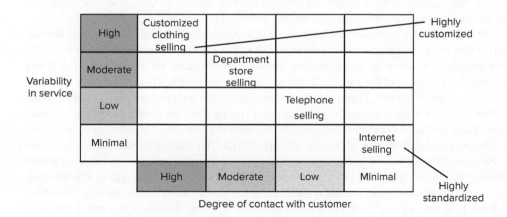

◀ FIGURE 4-3

The relationship between service variability and customer contact in retail clothes selling.

Customer actions	Arrive	Seated	Order	Eat		Pay and leave	
line of information							
Contact persons	Greeted by hostess Hostess checks reservation Hostess escorts customers to their table	Greeted by server Server provides menus Server fills water glasses	Server describes specials Server takes orders	Dinners are served	Server occasionally checks to see if any problems	Server brings the check Server receives payment	Busboy clears table
line of visibility							
Backstage contacts			Kitchen staff prepares food				Dishes are washed
line of internal interaction							
Support	Reservation system		Ordering food			Cashier	Laundry service

FIGURE 4-4 ▲

A simple service blueprint for a restaurant.

The major steps in service blueprinting are as follows:

1. Establish boundaries for the service and decide on the level of detail needed.
2. Identify and determine the sequence of customer and service actions and interactions. A flow-chart can be a useful tool for this.
3. Develop time estimates for each phase of the process, as well as time variability.
4. Identify potential failure points and develop a plan to prevent or minimize them, as well as a plan to respond to service errors.

(L05) Quality Function Deployment

quality function deployment (QFD) A structured approach that integrates the "voice of the customer" into product design.

Quality function deployment (QFD) is a structured approach for integrating the "voice of the customer" into product design. The purpose is to ensure that customer requirements are factored into every aspect of the process. Listening to and understanding the customer is the central feature of QFD. Customer requirements often take the form of a general statement such as, "It should be easy to adjust the cutting height of the lawn mower." Once the customer requirements are known, they must be translated into measurable technical terms. For example, a statement about changing the height of the lawn mower may be translated into the characteristics of the mechanism used to accomplish that (e.g., tightness of the spring that controls the mechanism). For manufacturing purposes, these must be related to the materials, dimensions, and equipment used for processing.

The structure of QFD is based on a set of matrices. The main matrix relates customer requirements (what) to their corresponding technical requirements (how); this matrix is illustrated in Figure 4-5. The matrix provides a structure for data collection. Technical requirements are measurable physical and functional characteristics of the product. Additional features are usually added to the basic matrix to broaden the scope of analysis. Typical additional features include competitive evaluation of customer requirements, a correlation matrix for technical requirements (this can reveal conflicting technical requirements), and target values (product specs) for technical requirements. The matrix is often referred to as the *house of quality* because of its house-like appearance. This concept is illustrated in Figure 4-6.

An example of a house of quality is shown in Figure 4-7. The data relate to a commercial printer (customer) and the company that produces the paper rolls. At first glance, the display appears complex. It contains a considerable amount of information for product and process planning. Therefore, let's break it up into separate parts and consider them one at a time. To start, a key part is the list of

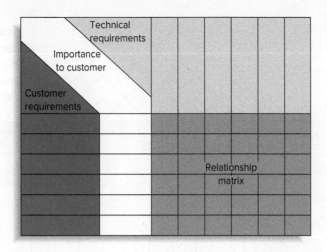

◀ **FIGURE 4-5**

An example of the house of quality: the main QFD matrix.

Source: Ernst and Young Consulting Group, Total Quality (Homewood, IL: Dow-Jones Irwin, 1991), p. 121. Reprinted by permission.

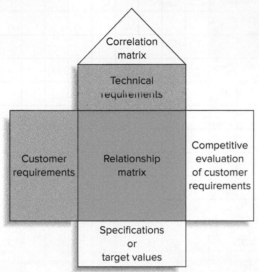

◀ **FIGURE 4-6**

The house of quality.

customer requirements on the left side of the figure. Next, note the technical requirements, listed vertically near the top. The key relationships and their degree of importance are shown in the centre of the figure. The circle with a dot inside it indicates the strongest relationship; that is, it denotes the most important technical requirement(s) for satisfying the customer requirement (see the lower right-hand side for relationship weights). Now look at the "customer requirements importance" weights that are shown next to each customer requirement (3 is most important). Designers will take into account the importance values and the strength of correlation in determining where to focus the greatest effort.

Next, consider the correlation matrix at the top of the "house." Of special interest is the strong negative correlation between "paper thickness" and "roll roundness." Designers will have to find some way to overcome that or make a trade-off decision.

On the right side of the figure is the competitive evaluation of customer requirements, comparing the paper roll manufacturing company's performance on the customer requirements with each of its two key competitors (A and B). For example, the company (X) is worst on the first customer requirement and best on the third customer requirement. A line connects the X performances. Ideally, design will cause all of the Xs to be in the highest positions.

Across the bottom of Figure 4-7 are technical requirements importance weights, target values, and competitive evaluations of technical requirements, which can be interpreted in a manner similar to that of the competitive evaluation of customer requirements (note the line connecting the Xs). The target values typically contain technical specifications that are the result of the design process.

A technical value (or specification) may have a norm (midpoint) and a tolerance (±). A tolerance is established to (a) make the fabrication and/or assembly of the product easier and (b) enable the product to perform its function with minimum adjustment. Usually, these two objectives are in conflict. Too tight a tolerance can ensure functional requirements, but is not cost-effective. Too loose

FIGURE 4-7 ▶

An example of the house of quality for paper rolls used by a commercial printer.

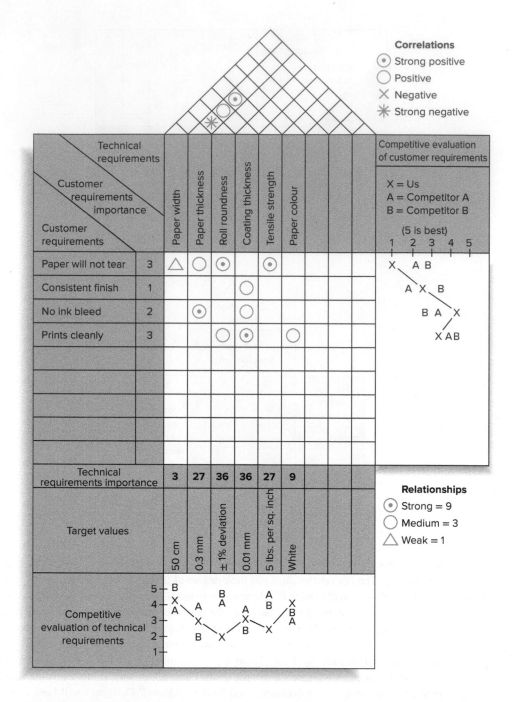

a tolerance can reduce fabrication and assembly costs, but requires frequent rework to maintain the product's performance. Technical requirements importance weights are the sums of values assigned to the relationships multiplied by customer requirements importance. For example, the 3 in the first column is the product of the importance to the customer, 3, and the weak (Δ) relationship, 1. These help designers focus on important technical requirements. In this example, the first technical requirement has the lowest importance while the next four technical requirements all have high importance.

The house of quality approach involves a sequence of "houses," beginning with house of quality (Figure 4-6), which determines the product design characteristics and target values (House 1), which in turn leads to specific component design characteristics and target values (House 2), which in turn leads to production process design characteristics and target values for each component (House 3), and finally, a quality plan for each production process (House 4). This sequence is illustrated in Figure 4-8. The construction of House 2 to House 4 is basically similar to construction of House 1, but the details are beyond the scope of this textbook.

The "A QFD Snapshot" OM in Action contains another example of house of quality.

OM in Action

A QFD Snapshot ervice

How a pencilmaker sharpened up its product by listening to "the voice of the customer" through quality function deployment.

Devised by Japan's Professor Yoji Akao, QFD has been winning adherents since it was transplanted to North America in the late 1980s. In this example of how it works, Writesharp Inc. is imaginary, but the technique in the accompanying diagram is real.

First, Writesharp's customers were surveyed to determine what they value in a pencil and how they rate the leading brands. Each wish list item was correlated with a pencil's physical and functional characteristics. Reverse engineering—tearing down a competitor's product to see its components and their workings—produced the competitive evaluation of technical requirements.

An analysis of the matrix quickly revealed that the improvement with the biggest potential was "point lasts"

(see competitive evaluation of customer requirements). This is largely correlated with "time between sharpenings" and "lead dust." It was determined that these characteristics could be improved by using a better quality of lead. An interdepartmental team was assigned the task of evaluating new lead formulations that would last longer and generate less dust. The lead-formulation team organized its work with a similar matrix, segmented to show the physical and functional contributions of the ingredients in pencil lead. This revealed that the binder, or glue, used in forming the lead was the key variable. Tests found a polymer that dramatically reduced dusting by retaining more moisture and also wore down more slowly. While this binder was more expensive, better production controls promised to reduce waste enough to trim total per-pencil manufacturing costs by $0.01.

Technical requirements
- ⊙ Strong correlation
- △ Possible correlation
- ○ Some correlation

Competitive evaluation of customer requirements
Scale: 1 to 5 (5 = best)

Customer requirements		Pencil length (inches)	Time between sharpenings (written lines)	Lead dust (particles per line)	Hexagonality	Customer requirements importance rating (5 = highest)	Writesharp (now)	Competitor X	Competitor Y	Writesharp (target)
	Easy to hold	○			○	3	4	3	3	4
	Does not smear		○	⊙		4	5	4	5	5
	Point lasts	△	⊙	○		5	4	5	3	5
	Does not roll	△			⊙	2	3	3	3	4
Competitive evaluation of technical requirements	Writesharp (now)	5	56	10	70%		Writesharp (now)	Competitor X	Competitor Y	Writesharp (target)
	Competitor X	5	84	12	80%					
	Competitor Y	4	41	10	60%					
	Writesharp (target)	5.5	100	6	80%					
	Market price						15¢	18¢	14¢	16¢
	Market share						16%	12%	32%	20%
	Profit per unit						2¢	3¢	2¢	4¢

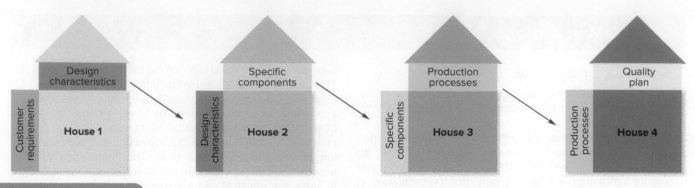

FIGURE 4-8 ▲

The house of quality sequence.

LO6

The Kano Model

The Kano model is a theory of product and service design developed by Noriaki Kano, a Japanese professor, who offered a perspective on customer perceptions of quality different from the traditional view that "more is better." Instead, he proposed different categories of quality and posited that understanding them would better position designers to assess and address quality needs. His model provides insights into the attributes that are perceived to be important to customers. The model employs three definitions of quality: basic, performance, and excitement.

Basic quality refers to customer requirements that have only a limited effect on customer satisfaction if present, but lead to dissatisfaction if not present. For example, putting a very short cord on an electrical appliance will likely result in customer dissatisfaction, but beyond a certain length (e.g., 4 feet), adding more cord will not lead to increased levels of customer satisfaction. Performance quality refers to customer requirements that generate satisfaction or dissatisfaction in proportion to their level of functionality and appeal. For example, increasing the tread life of a tire or the amount of time house paint will last will add to customer satisfaction. Excitement quality refers to a feature or attribute that was unexpected by the customer and causes excitement (the "wow" factor), such as a voucher for dinner for two at the hotel restaurant when checking in. Figure 4-9a portrays how the three definitions of quality influence customer satisfaction or dissatisfaction relative to the degree of implementation. Note that features that are perceived by customers as basic quality result in dissatisfaction if they are missing or at low levels, but do not result in customer satisfaction if they are present, even at high levels. Performance factors can result in satisfaction or dissatisfaction, depending on the degree to which they are present. Excitement factors, because they are unexpected, do not result in dissatisfaction when they are absent or at low levels, but have the potential for disproportionate levels of satisfaction if they are present.

Over time, features that excited become performance features, and performance features soon become basic quality features, as illustrated in Figure 4-9b. The rates at which various design elements are migrating is an important input from marketing that will enable designers to continue to satisfy and delight customers and not waste efforts on improving what have become basic quality features.

The lesson of the Kano model is that design elements that fall into each aspect of quality must first be determined. Once basic needs have been met, additional efforts in those areas should not be pursued.

FIGURE 4-9A ▶

The Kano model.

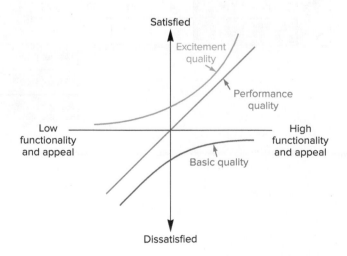

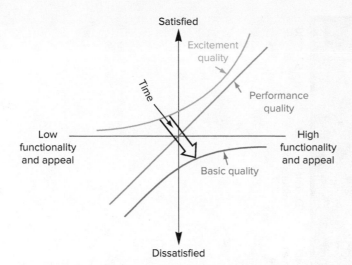

◀ **FIGURE 4-9B**

As time passes, excitement factors become performance factors, and performance factors become basic factors.

For performance features, cost–benefit analysis comes into play, and these features should be included as long as the benefit exceeds the cost. Excitement features pose somewhat of a challenge. Customers are not likely to indicate excitement factors in surveys because they don't know that they want them. However, small increases in such factors produce disproportional increases in customer satisfaction and generally increase brand loyalty, so it is important for companies to strive to identify and include these features when economically feasible.

The Kano model can be used in conjunction with QFD as well as in Six Sigma projects (see Chapter 10 for a discussion of Six Sigma).

FMEA Analysis

Failure modes and effects analysis (FMEA) is a structured method for identifying possible failures in a product or process and then assessing their effects in order to find opportunities for improvement. The *failure modes* portion of FMEA refers to the various ways in which failures can occur, and asks the question: "What can go wrong?" The *effects analysis* portion refers to studying the results of those failures, and asks: "What would be the consequences of failure for the customer?" FMEA is typically used to evaluate a new product or process prior to implementation, but can also be useful when considering a redesign. The following steps are required to perform the analysis:

1. Identify the functions of the product or process. Write down its intended purpose.
2. For each function, identify all the ways failure could happen. List these potential failure modes.
3. For each failure mode, identify all the effects of failure for the customer.
4. For each effect, determine the severity rating, S, which is typically on a scale from 1 (insignificant) to 10 (catastrophic).
5. For each failure mode, determine all the causes of the failure.
6. For each cause, determine the occurrence rating, O, which is typically on a scale from 1 (extremely unlikely) to 10 (inevitable).
7. For each cause, determine the control mechanism currently in place to detect the failure.
8. For each control, determine the detection rating, D. This rating estimates how likely it is that the failure can be detected before the customer is affected. Detection is typically rated on a scale from 1 (detection is absolutely certain) to 10 (no detection).
9. Calculate the risk priority number (RPN) for each cause based on the severity of the effect, frequency of occurrence, and detection rating, by multiplying $S \times O \times D$.
10. List the RPN in descending order. This highlights the cause with the greatest need for improvement.
11. Identify recommended actions to lower severity or occurrence of failures, or improve their detection.
12. As actions are completed, update the S, O, and D ratings and new RPNs.

See Table 4-1 for an example of FMEA for an ATM.[7]

---

[7] Based on http://asq.org/learn-about-quality/process-analysis-tools/overview/fmea.html.

▼ TABLE 4-1

FMEA for an ATM

Function	Potential Failure Mode	Potential Effects of Failure	S	Potential Causes of Failure	O	Current Process Control	D	RPN	Recommended Action	Responsibility and Target Completion Date	Action Taken	S	O	D	RPN
Dispense cash for customers	Dispenses no cash or not enough cash	Decreases customer satisfaction	8	Out of cash	5	Low-cash alert	5	200	Increase bill holder size	Designer, as soon as possible	Doubled holder size	8	2	5	80
				Jams	3	Jam alert	5	120							
				Electricity outage	2	Battery backup	2	32							
	Dispenses too much cash	Decreases profitability	6	Bills stuck together	2	Riffle cash	7	84							
				Denominations in wrong trays	3	Auto image verification	1	18							

Summary

- The design process involves market/competitor analysis, goal setting (product, performance, cost, quality), quality function deployment, concept design, product specification, and building and testing prototypes.
- The idea for a new or redesigned product can come from customers, employees, suppliers, competitors, and the research and development department.
- The stage of life cycle of a product influences the nature of its redesign.
- Using standard parts and common modules saves operating costs, but it is possible to provide some mass customization by allowing customers options on modules and postponement.
- The reliability of well designed products has to be extensively tested and improved.
- It may be cheaper to design robust products that perform consistently in varied production and use conditions.
- It is faster and less costly for the product team to perform both product and process designs concurrently.

- Research and development efforts can play a significant role in product and process innovations.
- CAD has helped reduce the design time significantly. It is cheaper overall to design products that have fewer parts and are easier to manufacture and assemble.
- Services need to deal with customer presence and involvement, and the inherent variability in service requirements.
- Service blueprinting is a useful tool for showing how a service is performed and includes inputs, processes, and outputs.
- QFD is a multi-functional process for product design that starts with the "voice of the customer" and ends with its translation into product characteristics.
- The Kano model is a way of understanding product and service quality based on the dimensions of basic, performance, and excitement attributes.
- FMEA is a technique for identifying failures to find opportunities for improvement.

Key Terms

computer-aided design (CAD)
concurrent engineering
cradle-to-grave assessment
delayed differentiation
design for assembly (DFA)
design for disassembly (DFD)
design for manufacturing (DFM)
failure

global team
life cycle
mass customization
modular design
normal operating conditions
product design
product liability
quality function deployment (QFD)

recycling
reliability
remanufacturing
research and development (R&D)
reverse engineering
robust design
service blueprint
standardization

Solved Problems

Problem 1

Service blueprint. Prepare a service blueprint on how to apply for a home equity loan from a bank.

Solution

Customer actions line of information	Customer calls in for appointment	Arrives and waits in line if necessary	Greets service rep and follows to cubicle	Tells service rep type of loan wanted		Customer leaves
Contact persons line of visibility	Phone rep schedules time for customer		Service rep greets customer and leads to cubicle	Service rep asks for necessary documents and checks to see if customer qualifies	Service rep fills out necessary database records	Service rep informs customer of decision
Backstage contacts line of internal interaction				Credit agency provides information		
Support				Database records	Records updated	

Problem 2

Examine and compare one of the following product sets. Base your comparison on such factors as features, costs, convenience, ease of use, and value.

   a. Online shopping versus "bricks and mortar" shopping

   b. Standard gasoline automobile engines versus hybrids

   c. Satellite television versus cable

Solution

   a. Online shopping requires that a customer have online access—bricks and mortar shopping does not. Online shopping allows a customer to place orders from any location—bricks and mortar shopping requires that a customer place orders at the bricks and mortar location. Online shopping normally does not allow easy access to a salesperson—bricks and mortar shopping does. Online shopping still is cheaper due to lower costs. Online shopping offers a wider variety of products than does bricks and mortar shopping; however, customers must be willing to wait for their products to be delivered. Online shopping is more convenient given that a customer can be at any location to place an order. Customers may find higher value in the online experience given the convenience, the wider product selection, and lower (or equal) prices.

   b. Standard gasoline automobile engines versus hybrids: Standard gasoline engines offer greater power than hybrids do. However, standard engines create more emissions and provide lower gas mileage. Standard engines cost less and are arguably more convenient when trying to merge on to a highway. Value depends on the user's driving habits and environmental concerns. For example, a user who has high concern for protecting the environment will perceive higher value in the hybrid.

c. Satellite television versus cable: Satellite television receives the transmission from a dish on the customer's roof—cable receives the transmission from a cable outside connected to a cable box in the customer's home. Satellite television may not offer some of the local stations (e.g., public access) that cable offers. Satellite television is subject to outages during bad weather (is less convenient)—cable is not. Cost and value of both options depend on the service options selected by customers.

Discussion and Review Questions

Note: An asterisk indicates that a question or problem may be more challenging.

LO1   **1.** What are some of the factors that cause organizations to redesign their products?

LO1   **2.** What are the stages (phases) of the product design process?

LO6   **3.** Select an electronic device you are familiar with. What standard feature does it have that was once a "wow" feature? What "wow" feature does it have that you think will soon be a standard feature on new versions?

LO3   **4.** What is *CAD*? Describe some of the ways a product designer can use it.

LO3   **5.** What is *standardization*? Give an example. Name some of the main advantages and disadvantages of standardization.

LO3   **6.** What is *modular design*? Give an example. What are its main advantages and disadvantages?

LO3   **7.** Explain the terms *design for manufacturing* and *design for assembly,* give an example of each, and briefly explain why they are important.

LO3   **8.** What is *concurrent engineering* and what are some of the competitive advantages of concurrent engineering?

LO1   **9.** What is the *stage-gate or phase-review model*? What are the stages?

LO3   **10.** What is meant by the term *life cycle?* Give an example. Why would this be a consideration in product design?

LO2   **11.** Name some ways in which the R&D department of a company contributes to produce design.

LO3   **12.** What is *mass customization?* What is *delayed differentiation?* Give an example.

LO4   **13.** Name two factors that make service design different from goods design.

LO3   **14.** Explain the term *robust design.* Give an example.

LO5   **15.** Explain what *quality function deployment* is, how it is done, and what its objective is.

LO2   **16.** What is *reverse engineering*? Give an example. Do you feel it is unethical?

LO4   **17.** Name a service organization and describe the basic service(s) it provides.

LO2   **18.** Contrast applied research and basic research.

Taking Stock

LO5   **1.** Describe some of the trade-offs that are encountered in product design.

LO1   **2.** Who needs to be involved in the design of products? Explain.

LO2 & 3   **3.** How has technology had an impact on product design?

LO3   **4.** Is designing products that are not refurbishable or recyclable, such as computers and electronics that end up in city garbage dumps, unethical? Discuss.

Critical Thinking Exercises

LO3   **1.** Think of a new or revised good or service that you would like to see on the market. Discuss the implications of designing and producing that product relative to legal, profitability, competitiveness, design, and production issues.

LO3   **2.** The speed of product development has continued to increase because of technological advances such as CAD. Do you expect this trend to continue?

LO1–3   **3.** In wintry conditions, highway safety is improved by treating road surfaces with substances that will provide traction and/or melt snow and ice. Sand and rock salt are two widely used substances. Recently, a combination of beet juice and rock salt started being used in some parts of the country to treat road surfaces. Suppose you have been asked to provide a list of factors to consider for a switch from rock salt alone to using a combination of beet juice and rock salt. Name the major considerations you would take into account in making a decision in the following categories: cost considerations; environmental considerations, both positive and negative; and other considerations.

Experiential Learning Exercise

 LO1 & 5 Visit http://www.baddesigns.com/examples.html and read about some bad designs. Describe one example from your own experience.

Internet Exercises

 LO1 **1.** Visit http://solutions.3m.com/wps/portal/3M/en_US/3M -Company/Information/Resources/History/ to read the history of 3M. List two innovative products that the company has invented.

 LO3 **2.** Visit https://ultimaker.com/en/stories?filter[category]=315 and read one of the provided product design stories. Summarize the article and discuss the pros and cons of 3D printing technology.

 LO3 **3.** Visit http://www.iihs.org/iihs/ratings to obtain recent crash-safety ratings for passenger vehicles. Next, answer these questions:

  a. Which vehicles received the highest ratings?
  b. What product design features help promote vehicle safety?
  c. What type of customer values safety most?

Problems

 LO4 **1.** Prepare a table similar to Figure 4-3 and place each of these banking transactions in the appropriate cell of the table:
  a. Make a cash withdrawal from an automated banking machine (ATM).
  b. Make a savings deposit using a teller.
  c. Open an account.
  d. Apply for a mortgage loan.

LO4 **2.** Prepare a table similar to Figure 4-3. Then place each of these transactions in the appropriate cell of the table:
  a. Buy stamps from a postal clerk.
  b. Mail a package that involves checking different rates.
  c. Send money using Western Union.

 LO3 **3.** Examine and compare one of the following product sets. Base your comparison on such factors as features, costs, convenience, ease of use, and value.
  a. GPS versus maps
  b. Cellphones versus landlines
  c. Online course versus classroom

LO4 **4.** Prepare a service blueprint for each of these post office transactions:
  a. Buy stamps from a machine.
  b. Buy stamps from a postal clerk.

LO5 **5. a.** Refer to Figure 4-7. What two technical requirements have the highest impact on the customer requirement "Paper will not tear"? Explain why.

  b. The following table presents technical requirements and customer requirements for the output of a laser printer. First, decide if any of the technical requirements relate to each customer requirement.

| Customer Requirements | TECHNICAL REQUIREMENTS | | |
	Type of Paper	Internal Paper Feed	Print Element
Paper doesn't wrinkle			
Prints cleanly			
Easy to use			

Decide which technical requirement, if any, has the greatest impact on that customer requirement.

LO5 **6.** Prepare a house of quality for chocolate chip cookies made in a bakery. List what you believe are the three most important customer requirements and the three most relevant technical requirements. Next, indicate by a checkmark which customer requirements and which technical requirements are related. Finally, determine the target values. There is no need to fill in the other parts of the house.

LO5 **7.** Determine a house of quality for a ballpoint pen. In the house of quality, fill in three customer requirements. Determine one technical requirement for each customer requirement and fill it in. Relate the pair by a checkmark, and determine a reasonable target value for each technical requirement and fill it in.

 LO5 ***8.** In 2002, Wilson Sporting Goods wanted to enter the market for youth baseball batting helmets with a durable, strong, stylish youth batting helmet with improved ventilation and a quick and simple adjustment feature for a one-size-fits-all youth batting helmet. Wilson commissioned the product design firm Designconcepts to design and develop the helmet. Designconcepts's sketch for the adjustment mechanism of the helmet is shown below.[8] The finished helmet is now marketed as Cat Osterman's Signature Series.

For each of the five customer requirements given above, find a measurable technical requirement and enter both in a house of quality. Relate them by placing a checkmark at their intersection. Also fill in the target value (specification) for each technical requirement.

Courtesy of Calor   Courtesy of Calor

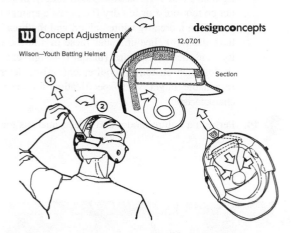

Design Concepts, Inc., www.design-concepts.com/portfolio /industry/sports-recreation/wilson-youth-batting-helmet.

*9. In 2004, Calor (T-Fal)—a member of Groupe SEB of France, the world's largest kitchen products and small appliances manufacturer—commissioned the product design firm of SeymourPowel to redesign its mid-line steam iron (http://onlinelibrary.wiley.com /doi/10.1111/j.1948-7169.2005.tb00004.x/epdf). The market for irons was in a slump and Calor wanted to reinvigorate the market. Like its predecessor, Avantis, Aquaspeed was desired to be attractive, easy to handle and ergonomic, and light, but had two additional requirements: (a) a larger hole and less messy process for putting water in the reservoir, and (b) more stability to reduce the chance of toppling off the ironing board. Avantis, like other irons, had a small water hole in the front part of the handle. The result of the redesign, Aquaspeed, is shown below (front and back views). In a house of quality, fill in five customer requirements. Determine one technical requirement for each customer requirement and fill it in. Relate the pair by a checkmark, and determine a reasonable target value for each technical requirement and fill it in.

*10. In the mid-2000s, DeWalt, a Black and Decker brand, saw the need of carpenters and do-it-yourselfers for a cordless battery-operated nailer.[9] At that time, the only automatic nailers in the market were pneumatic ones that were cumbersome because of the need for a compressor and a hose. DeWalt consulted and observed carpenters at work and determined the following customer requirements: speed, run time (length of time until the battery needs recharging), power (nail penetration), ease of loading nails, ergonomics (size, weight, and balance), being able to see the nail going in, and being able to work in tight spots. One of the eight related nailers in the designed family is shown. In a house of quality, fill in five customer requirements. Determine one technical requirement for each customer requirement and fill it in. Relate the pair by a checkmark, and determine a reasonable target value for each technical requirement and fill it in.

Courtesy of Dewalt

*11. Puritan-Bennett is a manufacturer of medical test equipment.[10] In the early 1990s, its PB900A spirometer (equipment to measure lung capacity) was rapidly losing market share to a competitor's product, which was simpler and half its price. Puritan-Bennett decided to use Quality Function Deployment to redesign PB900A. It surveyed its customers (pulmonologists, allergists, and nurses) to identify customer needs. A total of

---

[8]D. Franchino, "Delivering Success Through Design: Reinventing the Batting Helmet," *Design Management Review* 18(1), Winter 2007, pp. 22–27.
[9]J. Watson, "Building the Perfect Product: The Story of DeWalt Cordless Nailer," *Design Management Review* 17(1), Winter 2006, pp. 21–27.
[10]J.R. Hauser, "How Puritan-Bennett Used the House of Quality," *Sloan Management Review* 34(3) Spring 1993, pp. 61–70.

26 customer needs were identified. Puritan-Bennett's product design team translated these into 56 design attributes (technical requirements). Here, we will consider a small subset of the customer needs. The following customer needs were most important (importance is in brackets): product is affordable (150), provides accurate readings (100), eliminates technician (administrator) variability (140), is easy to operate (130), and is sanitary (108). Prepare a house of quality with five customer requirements. Determine one technical requirement for each customer requirement and fill it in. Relate the pair by a checkmark. Determine a reasonable target value for each technical characteristic and fill it in.

 *12. Ford and other automakers regularly use a house of quality to translate the voice of customers (customer requirements) into design characteristics (technical requirements) in areas such as rust prevention (body durability) and car door design.[11] Some of the most important customer requirements for a car door are the following: easy to close, stays open on a hill, easy to open, does not leak in rain, and doesn't allow road noise in. In a house of quality, fill in these five customer requirements. Determine one technical requirement for each customer requirement and fill it in. Relate the pair by a checkmark, and determine a reasonable target value for each technical requirement and fill it in.

 13. The following five customer requirements are considered important for a loaf of bread:[12] crust should be golden brown, inside should be "light" (i.e., have the right size and even distribution of holes), inside should not be too moist or too dry (i.e., elastic enough), inside should be a creamy white colour, and the bread should have the right flavour. Enter these in a house of quality, and determine one (unique) design characteristic for each customer requirement. Also, determine a reasonable target value/specification for each design characteristic.

LO7 14. Perform a failure modes and effects analysis for a truck tire.

🔍 MINI-CASE www.harveys.ca

Open Wide and Say "Ultra"

In fourth place behind McDonald's, A&W, and Burger King, Harvey's, the Canadian quick-service hamburger chain with more than 340 restaurants, needed a new idea in the mid-1990s. Harvey's is part of Cara Operations Ltd., the airline food services company that also owns the Swiss Chalet chain of restaurants, approximately 100 Air Terminal Restaurants, and Summit Food Services Distributors. Harvey's had had new ideas before (open grill and fresh vegetables, for one), but these had become old hat by 1995. Gabe Tsampalieros, Cara's new president, who was a major franchisee with 60 Harvey's and Swiss Chalet restaurants, started working on the idea in October 1995, and by the following month the mission was clear: "Create Canada's best-selling hamburger." Tsampalieros and Harvey's vice-president planned the launch of the new burger for May 1996.

Harvey's began polling burger lovers across Canada in January 1996, first by telephone and later in focus groups of 8 to 12 people. While the tradition of burgers had so far led to flattened-out, Frisbee-like burgers that hung over the edges of the buns (giving customers the impression that they were getting more for their money), feedback from the market produced another idea: go thicker, juicier, chewier, and tastier. To bring this simple idea to life, Harvey's brought in chef Michael Bonacini, whose upscale Toronto restaurants had been a big hit.

Bonacini's challenge was not only to produce a tasty burger, but also to produce a burger that could handily survive the fast-food process (mechanically produced, frozen for weeks, and shipped around the country). Bonacini produced 12 "taste profiles"—from the bland to the bizarre—and introduced them to the Harvey's executives at a suburban Harvey's training centre. This would be the first in a long series of tasting exercises. (Bonacini thinks he ate 275 bite-sized burgers in a four-month period.)

Each of Harvey's executives tasted a portion of the 12 unlabelled patties and ranked it for "mouth feel," taste, linger, fill factor, and bite. Exotic offerings (Cajun, Oriental, Falafel, and so forth) were rejected, leaving three simply seasoned burgers on the short list.

McCormick Canada Inc., Harvey's spice supplier, was employed to determine the final proportions of seasonings and secret ingredients to replicate the taste of Bonacini's samples in a way that could survive the fast-food process. "They [the meat packagers] would give us a 500-pound batch—that's 2,000 burgers—and we would taste them a couple of days after they had been mixed. Then we would also taste them at one-, two-, three-, and four-week intervals to see how the flavours would change," said Bonacini. McCormick's food technologists varied the seasonings by slight amounts with different results, and each change was followed by testing. For two months, all of Harvey's head-office workers gathered before breakfast to test the newest batches; it became clear that the May launch date was unrealistic, so they bumped back the launch to mid-September.

Though missing deadlines is rarely advisable, in this case it was fortuitous. On May 9, exactly one week before the

---

[11]J.R. Hauser and D. Clausing, "*The House of Quality*," *Harvard Business Review*, May–June 1988, pp. 63–73.
[12]http://www.1920-30.com/cooking/bread/scoring-bread.html

original launch date, McDonald's introduced the Arch Deluxe with the most aggressive marketing campaign yet seen from McDonald's.

As the burger making neared completion, Harvey's turned its attention to choosing a name for the new burger. The company considered several (the Ultimate, the Canadian, the Big Burger, the One and Only), but settled wisely on the Ultra, a bilingual name. The company chose a foil packaging for better heat retention (and because the traditional box would appear larger than the burger itself), and re-initiated the advertising campaign, promoting a $1.88 price. Testing the burger in Calgary, Sudbury, and Quebec, Harvey's found customer reaction to be very positive ("It's more like a home-made burger," "It has a steak-like bite"), but went through five more adjustments to the amounts and mixing time of the ingredients.

On September 16, 1996, Ultra was launched and resulted in record sales, transaction counts, and restaurant visits. With over a million sold in the first two weeks, the Ultra resulted in more than 85 percent of Harvey's sales.

Since then, Harvey's has introduced other types of hamburgers such as bacon and cheese, veggie burger, and Big Harv Angus, as well as a chicken sandwich.

Big Harv, introduced in 2003, was an attempt to buck the trend of low-fat, low-calorie burgers offered by the other fast-food restaurants. It had double the calories and fat of the Original burger. Big Harv targeted male customers craving thick home-made barbecued burgers.

Cara has expanded its full-service restaurant offerings by purchasing the Kelsey's chain and the Second Cup chain. In 2004, Cara bought back its outstanding shares and became a private company. In 2006, Cara sold Second Cup to Gabe Tsampalieros's new company, Dinecorp Hospitality.

Questions

1. Identify the steps of the product design process used by Harvey's. (Specifically, consider market analysis, concept development, prototype development, and (external) testing and validation).
2. Did Harvey's use any other concepts discussed in the chapter?
3. Prepare a house of quality for Ultra's design. Fill in four customer requirements. For each customer requirement, determine a technical requirement and relate the pair using a check mark. For each technical requirement, determine a reasonable target value.

Sources: Adapted from P. Roy, "Open Wide and Say 'Ultra' (Harvey's Had a Brilliant Idea About Burgers)," *Canadian Business* 69(12), December 1996, pp. 26–30; "Stay Hungry: Gabe Tsampalieros Knows the Food Business From the Kitchen Floor Up (Will That Be Enough for Cara?)," *Canadian Business* 69(11), September 1996, pp. 104–110; Cara Operations Annual Reports, 1999–2003, http://www.cara.com.

 ## Operations Tour

3twenty Modular

What is the best approach for building a temporary yet sturdy camp at a remote mining site, in the middle of nowhere? According to Bryan McCrea and Evan Willoughby, the founders of 3twenty Modular, the answer lies with the use of heavily modified shipping containers. Their inherent durability, portability, widespread availability, and low cost make these containers ideal for the job.

Holes are cut out for windows and doors. After that, the subfloor is installed and the unit is framed. Then electrical lines and plumbing (if necessary) are installed. Next, it is spray-foam–insulated to provide an effective building envelope for protection from brutal Canadian winters. Then, it is finished up with drywall and finally a fresh coat of paint. From start to finish, each container (or module) can be built within a few weeks.

Each module can be shipped or trucked to any remote location. Once all the modules are on site, they can be quickly stacked together to form office complexes, workforce housing, or anything else a customer might need.

Images courtesy of 3twenty Modular

Given the recent downturn in the oil and gas and mining industries, 3twenty Modular decided it was time to expand its operations to other markets. Fortunately, there was strong demand for relocatable classrooms, driven by rapid population growth.

3twenty Modular is currently the largest and fastest growing manufacturer of modular relocatable buildings in Saskatchewan. Bryan and Evan are continuing to innovate and now have their eyes on another promising market: relocatable luxury cottages.

Sources: https://static1.squarespace.com/static/5873e8b8a5790a59c9155a99/t/58adf9fae58c62d5649d86a9/1487796738141/SIMSA+-+3twenty+Case+Study.pdf; Haddock 10th Anniversary presentation at Edwards School of Business, March 2017.

To access "Reliability," the supplement to Chapter 4, please visit *Connect2*.

Chapter 5
Strategic Capacity Planning

erkanatbas/Shutterstock.com

LEARNING OBJECTIVES

After completing this chapter, you should be able to:

LO1 Define capacity, explain the importance of long-term capacity, know how to measure capacity, understand two related performance measures, know overall equipment effectiveness, and describe factors influencing effective capacity.

LO2 Describe the strategic capacity planning process in organizations, know long-term demand patterns and calculate capacity requirements, and discuss major considerations for developing capacity alternatives.

LO3 Describe the break-even analysis approach for evaluating capacity alternatives, and use it to solve problems.

$\mathbf{L}$ ike other major automobile manufacturers, Ford has a highly systematic process in place to ensure that its key suppliers are capable of delivering the required quantities of parts and components at the right times. Capacity planning and analysis are performed at two specific points of time before the start of production (called Job 1): between 23 and 17 months before Job 1 (23MBJ1–17MBJ1), then six months before Job 1 (6MBJ1). A third analysis is performed immediately after production starts.

Capacity planning and analysis involves: (a) drawing a process flow diagram (PFD, see Chapter 6) for the component, and for each part going into the component, (b) determining the quantity of good parts required at each operation while adjusting for scrap loss in each of the following operations, (c) calculating the required overall equipment effectiveness (OEE, defined in this chapter) at each operation, (d) estimating the demonstrated OEE at each operation, and finally (e) ensuring that the demonstrated OEE is larger than the required OEE at each operation.

The quantity of good parts needed has two values: average weekly production, and maximum weekly production. The demonstrated OEE 23MBJ1–17MBJ1 is based on the performance of similar (surrogate) operations (during 25 or so weeks) because at that time the operation has not begun and the value is still unknown. The demonstrated OEE 6MBJ1 is based on the actual test production of a small sample (e.g., 100 units).

Source: http://www.ghsp.com/uploads/CAR_2013_Capacity_Analysis_Training.pdf.

Capacity, Measures, Efficiency, Utilization, and Effective Capacity

capacity The upper limit on the workload that an operating unit can handle.

Capacity is the upper limit on the workload that an operating unit can handle. An operating unit might be a plant, department, machine, store, or worker.

Capacity is usually measured as maximum production rate or throughput (e.g., the maximum number of motorcycles that can be assembled in a particular plant per shift, or the maximum number of customers who can be served in a particular restaurant per day). If output is hard to measure, a major input can be used (e.g., size (square footage) or number of seats in a particular restaurant).

Capacity decisions have different time frames: long-term, medium-term, or short-term. *Long-term* usually refers to one to five years into the future. We need to make long-term capacity decisions such as determining the plant size and major machines and equipment. *Medium-term* usually refers to the next 12 months, and medium-term capacity decisions include determining the nature and level of the workforce, which in turn determines the aggregate operations plan. *Short-term* relates to the next few days and weeks, usually up to 12 weeks ahead, and short-term capacity decisions include determining the nature and level of staffing and work shifts, which in turn determines the production schedule of products or capacity of service.

If production or service delivery is to be outsourced, then there is usually no need to create the capacity in-house. Outsourcing has been increasingly used by many organizations to reduce costs, gain flexibility (for variable demand), and take advantage of suppliers' expertise (quality). For example, Canadian toy company Spin Master usually outsources the production of its toys to China. The downside is reduced control. It is also possible to outsource part(s) of a good/service or a segment of production/service process. For example, many restaurants buy prepared/partially cooked frozen/vacuum-packed food ingredients. **Strategic capacity planning** is the systematic determination of facility and major machine/equipment requirements to meet long-term demand for goods and services. Organizations become involved in capacity planning for various reasons. Among the chief reasons are changes in demand, changes in technology, changes in the environment, and perceived threats or opportunities. A gap between current and desired capacity will result in capacity that is out of balance. Overcapacity causes operating costs that are too high, while undercapacity causes strained resources and possible loss of customers.

strategic capacity planning Systematic determination of facility and major machine/equipment requirements to meet long-term demand for goods and services.

Because of uncertainties, some organizations prefer to delay capacity investment until demand materializes. However, such strategies often inhibit growth because adding capacity takes time and customers won't usually wait. Conversely, organizations that add capacity in anticipation of growth often discover that the new capacity actually attracts growth. Some organizations "hedge their bets" by making a series of small changes and then evaluating the results before committing to the next change.

In this chapter, we study mainly long-term capacity planning, while deferring medium-term capacity decisions to Chapter 13 and short-term capacity decisions to Chapter 16 and Chapter 18. Note that a capacity decision usually has a location dimension. For example, suppose a long-term-care facility needs to increase its number of beds. It can expand its current facility, open up another facility somewhere else to supplement the current facility, or close the current facility and open up a larger facility somewhere else. Note that services should be located close to their customers because location convenience is part of the service. Location decisions are covered in Chapter 8.

The Importance of Long-Term Capacity

For a number of reasons, long-term capacity decisions are among the most fundamental of all design decisions that managers must make.

1. Capacity has a real impact on the ability of the organization to meet future demand for products; capacity essentially limits the rate of output (throughput) possible. Having capacity to satisfy demand allows a company to exploit opportunities. When Microsoft introduced its new Xbox in late 2005, there was insufficient supply, resulting in lost sales and unhappy customers. And shortages of flu vaccine in some years due to production problems have affected capacity, limiting the availability of the vaccine.

2. Capacity affects operating costs. Ideally, capacity and demand requirements should be matched. A production level exceeding capacity is costlier, requiring overtime, expediting deliveries, lost sales, etc.

3. Capacity is usually a major determinant of initial capital cost. Typically, the greater the capacity of a productive unit, the greater is its capital cost.

4. Capacity involves long-term commitment of resources and, once they are committed, it may be difficult to modify them without incurring major costs.

5. Capacity can affect competitiveness. If a company has excess capacity, or can quickly add capacity, that fact may serve as a barrier to entry of other companies. Then, capacity can affect delivery speed, which can be a competitive advantage.

6. Capacity affects ease of management; having appropriate capacity makes management easier than when capacity is mismatched.

7. Globalization has increased the importance and the complexity of capacity decisions. Far-flung supply chains and distant markets add to the uncertainty about capacity needs.

8. Because capacity decisions often involve substantial financial and other resources, it is necessary to plan for them far in advance. For example, it may take years for a new crude oil refinery to be constructed and become operational. This increases the risk that the designated amount of capacity will not match actual demand when the capacity becomes available.

Measuring Capacity and Some Related Performance Measures

In selecting a measure of capacity, it is better to choose one that does not require updating. Dollar amounts are often a poor measure of capacity (e.g., a restaurant may have capacity of $1 million of sales a year) because price changes over time necessitate updating of that measure.

Where only one product is involved, the capacity of the productive unit is expressed in terms of that item. However, when multiple products are involved, as is often the case, using a simple measure of capacity based on units of output can be misleading. For example, an appliance manufacturer may produce a combination of refrigerators and freezers. Because their resource usages and costs are different, it would not make sense to simply state the capacity in units of appliance. One possible solution is to state capacities in terms of each product. Thus, the company may be able to produce 100 refrigerators per day *or* 160 freezers per day. Sometimes this approach is helpful, sometimes not. For instance, if an organization has many different products, it may not be practical to list all of the relevant capacities. A better way is to choose a major product, and represent each other product in equivalent units of the major product (more in Chapter 13). Alternatively, one can use the *availability of a major input* as capacity. Thus, a hospital has a certain number of beds, a job shop has a certain number of labour hours available per week, and a bus has a certain number of seats.

A simple method for estimating the throughput capacity of a productive unit from its size is to divide the size by the average time a product spends in the productive unit (this is called *Little's formula*):

Throughput capacity = Size/Average cycle time

For example, if a reactor in a steel mill has size of 28 tonnes and iron ore needs to spend 15 minutes in the reactor, then throughput capacity of the reactor equals 28/0.25 hour = 112 tonnes per hour.

No single measure of capacity will be appropriate in every situation. Rather, the measure of capacity must be tailored to the situation. Table 5-1 provides some examples of commonly used measures of capacity.

There are two definitions of capacity:

1. **Design capacity**: the maximum output rate under ideal conditions.

2. **Effective capacity**: the maximum output rate that can be sustained given work breaks, scheduling difficulties and expected delays, machine/equipment maintenance, etc. (also known as standard output rate).

> **design capacity** The maximum output rate under ideal conditions.
>
> **effective capacity** The maximum output rate that can be sustained given work breaks, product mix, scheduling difficulties and expected delays, machine/equipment maintenance, etc. (also known as standard output rate).

TABLE 5-1 ▶

Some examples of commonly used measures of capacity.

Business	Inputs	Outputs
Auto manufacturing		Number of cars per shift
Steel mill		Tonnes of steel per day
Oil refinery	Barrels of crude oil used per day	Barrels of gasoline produced per day
Farming	Number of acres	Bushels of grain per acre per year, litres of milk per day
Restaurant	Number of tables, number of seats	Number of meals served per day
Theatre	Number of seats	Number of tickets sold per day
Retailer	Floor space, sales per square foot	Revenue generated per day

Effective capacity is less than design capacity owing to realities of changing product mix, periodic maintenance of machines/equipment, lunch and coffee breaks, problems in scheduling and balancing operations, and similar circumstances. Actual output rate cannot exceed effective capacity and is often less because of machine/equipment breakdowns, absenteeism, shortages of materials, and quality problems, as well as other factors that are outside the control of the operations manager.

Two measures of performance are commonly used: efficiency and utilization. **Efficiency** is the ratio of actual output rate to effective capacity. *Utilization* is used in two ways. **Utilization of a unit of a resource during a period** measures how intensely the unit was used during the period. It is the ratio of uptime to available time. **Utilization of many units of a resource at a point in time** measures the percentage of units being used at the time.

efficiency The ratio of actual output rate to effective capacity.

utilization of a unit of a resource during a period Uptime divided by available time.

utilization of many units of a resource at a point in time Percentage of units used at the time.

$$\text{Efficiency} = \frac{\text{Actual output rate}}{\text{Effective capacity}} \qquad (5\text{-}1)$$

$$\text{Utilization of a resource during a period} = \frac{\text{Uptime}}{\text{Available time}} \qquad (5\text{-}2)$$

$$\text{Utilization of many units of a resource at a point in time} = \text{Percentage of units used at the time} \qquad (5\text{-}3)$$

EXAMPLE 5-1 ▶

Minco (now part of 3M) produces silica (http://www.3m.com/3M/en_US/company-us/all-3m-products/~/All-3M-Products/Advanced-Materials/Advanced-Ceramics/Fused-Silica/?N=5002385+8745513+8710684+8711017+8719579+3294857497&rt=r3). To process silica, eight furnaces are used. Each furnace has 2,200 pounds/hour capacity. Minco works 24 hours a day, five days a week. During a typical week, preventive maintenance takes 65 hours and other downtimes take 39 hours in total. Effective capacity is 1,700,000 pounds and actual production is 1,600,000 pounds of silica per week. Calculate total design capacity per week, average utilization of silica furnaces during a week, and efficiency of silica furnaces.

SOLUTION

Available furnace hours per week = 8(24)(5) = 960

Total design capacity per week = 2,200(960) = 2,112,000 pounds

Uptime furnace hours per week = 960 − 65 − 39 = 856

Average utilization during a week = Uptime furnace hours/Available furnace hours = 856/960 = 0.89 or 89%

Efficiency = Actual output rate/Effective capacity = 1,600,000/1,700,000 = 0.94 or 94%

Note: Effective capacity = 1,700,000 < Average utilization × Design capacity = 0.89(2,112,000) = 1,879,680

Both efficiency and utilization are normally less than 100 percent. As utilization approaches 100 percent, wait time in the system increases disproportionately (this will be shown in Chapter 18 on waiting-line analysis). This drastically increases the number of jobs/people waiting, and if there is limited space for waiting, will actually reduce the throughput rate (capacity). For an example of a case where utilization has sometimes reached 100 percent, see the "Utilization in Canadian Hospitals" OM in Action. For capacity measure and utilization used by airlines, see the "Airline Capacity" OM in Action.

Increasing both efficiency and utilization are important for an organization. Increasing efficiency (e.g., by improving quality, material availability, and maintenance) reduces costs and thus increases profits. Increasing utilization (e.g., by increasing machine uptime) usually increases profit (if there is demand for more units). Further, because effective capacity acts as a lid on actual output, increasing effective capacity should also increase the profit.

 OM in Action

Utilization in Canadian Hospitals

Until the early 1990s, the Canadian health care system was the envy of the world. Then came a recession and federal government deficits, which were passed to provinces in the form of drastic cuts in social services transfer payments. In turn, provinces cut hospital budgets. The number of hospital beds in Canada dropped by over 32 percent from 176,000 in 1989 to fewer than 120,000 in 2002. The bed reductions were followed by hospital closures and amalgamations. For example, Calgary General Hospital was demolished in 1998. As a result, there is little slack in the system now, especially during the peak flu season. For example, in Alberta average utilization rate (the percentage of beds occupied) rose from 70 percent to 95 percent by 2008.

Most hospitals in Canada are examples of operations where utilization has reached 100 percent some days. The Royal Columbian Hospital in Vancouver is an example. In peak season, the emergency room fills because there are no beds in the hospital to move patients to. The average stay in the emergency room increases up to three days from the customary two hours. Another example is Campbell River Hospital on Vancouver Island where, during some days in October 2008, 83 patients crowded the 59-bed hospital, forcing cancellation of two cancer surgeries. The same story holds for most other hospitals such as the Foothills Hospital in Calgary, Pasqua and Regina General Hospitals, York Central and Sunnybrook Health Sciences Centre of Toronto, Ottawa Hospital, and the Queen Elizabeth II Health Sciences Centre of Halifax.

As a result, nurses, physicians, and other health care providers are stressed, and some people requiring emergency care are dying. Examples include a heart attack victim in Weyburn, Saskatchewan; an asthmatic teenager in Toronto; and a construction worker who fell six storeys in Mississauga. In all these cases, the ambulance was turned away by the hospitals because the emergency rooms were completely full. Furthermore, patients are waiting excessively long for most non-emergency surgeries, which can result in death. For example, three women have died waiting for urinary tract surgery in Alberta.

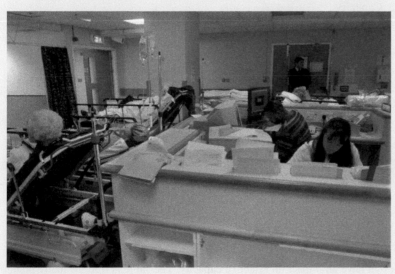
PA Images/Alamy Stock Photo

Sources: http://www.cbc.ca/health/story/2007/01/26 /hospitals-emerg.html; Hospital Trends in Canada, Canadian Institute for Health Information 2005, http://secure.cihi.ca/cihiweb/dispPage.jsp?cw_page =AR_1215_E; http://www.cbc.ca/health/story/2008/10/29 /bc-hospital-surgeries-cancelled-campbell-river.html?ref =rss; http://www.canada.com/topics/news/national/story .html?id=496f0573-e309-403a-8c3d-0768ccb7a372; http://en.wikipedia.org/wiki/Calgary_General_Hospital; R. M. Gerst, "Full House," *ASQ Six Sigma Forum Magazine*, May 2013, 12(3), 8–13.

⚙ OM in Action

Airline Capacity

Capacity in the airline industry is measured by *available seat miles* (the sum over all planes of the number of their seats multiplied by the number of miles each normally flies per year). Capacity utilization is measured by *passenger load factor*, which is the average percentage of seats occupied. Air Canada, with 381 aircraft, had 92.7 billion available seat miles and 82.5 percent passenger load factor in 2016. A related measure is *revenue passenger miles*, which is passenger load factor multiplied by available seat miles. In 2016, Air Canada's revenue passenger miles were equal to 92.7 billion × 0.825 = 76.5 billion.

Sources: Air Canada's Annual Report, 2016, http://www.aircanada.com/en /about/investor/documents/2016_ar.pdf;

Overall Equipment Effectiveness (OEE) A popular composite measure of performance is OEE:

$$\text{OEE} = \text{Utilization} \times \text{Efficiency} \times \text{Quality ratio} \tag{5-4}$$

or

$$\text{OEE} = \frac{\text{Uptime}}{\text{Available time}} \times \frac{\text{Total parts run}}{\text{Uptime/Cycle time}} \times \frac{\text{Total good parts}}{\text{Total parts run}} \tag{5-5}$$

or

$$\text{OEE} = \frac{\text{Cycle time} \times \text{Total good parts}}{\text{Available time}} \tag{5-6}$$

Cycle time is the maximum time allowed at the operation to complete its tasks on one unit.

EXAMPLE 5-2 ▶

Consider the casting operation needed for a lever (see slide 42 of http://www.ghsp.com/uploads/CAR_2013_Capacity _Analysis_Training.pdf). The average required weekly production of good parts is 2,727 units. The pattern of work will be five days a week, with three shifts of eight hours each per day. Cycle time is expected to be 240 seconds per unit. There will be three identical machines in parallel. Therefore, one unit will be produced every 240/3 = 80 seconds.

a. Calculate the required OEE.

b. If the average weekly number of good parts produced at a surrogate operation is 1,900 units, cycle time is 110 sec-onds, and available time is 120 hours, calculate the demonstrated OEE.

c. Will this operation be capable to meet the requirement?

Solutions

a. Required OEE $= \dfrac{\text{Cycle time} \times \text{Total good parts}}{\text{Available time}}$

$= \dfrac{80 \times 2,727}{5 \times 3 \times 8 \times 3,600} = 0.505 \; or \; 50.5\%$

b. Demonstrated OEE $= \dfrac{110 \times 1,900}{120 \times 3,600} = 0.484 \; or \; 48.4\%$

c. No, because 48.4% < 50.5%. May need to reduce the planned cycle time or increase the available time.

Check out www.oee.com/calculating-oee.html for more examples.

Factors Influencing Effective Capacity

Many aspects of design have an impact on effective capacity. The same is true for many planning and operating decisions.

Facilities and Machines The design of facilities, including floor space and layout, directly influences effective capacity. Layout of the work area often determines how smoothly work can be performed, and environmental factors such as heating, cooling, lighting, and ventilation also play a significant role. Further, machine and equipment speed and their state directly influence capacity, which means their maintenance is important.

Product Mix When items are similar, the ability of the system to produce those items is much greater than when successive items differ. There is less need for product change-over and machine/equipment setup. Thus, a restaurant that offers a limited menu can usually prepare and serve meals at a faster rate than a restaurant with an extensive menu. The more uniform the output, the more opportunities there are for standardization of machines, methods, and materials, which leads to greater effective capacity.

Workers The tasks that make up a job, the variety of activities involved, and the training, skill, and experience required to perform a job all have an impact on the potential output. In addition, employee motivation has a very basic relationship to effective capacity, as do absenteeism and labour turnover.

Planning and Operational Factors Scheduling problems may occur when there are differences in equipment capabilities or differences in job requirements. Effective capacity may be constrained by a bottleneck operation, inventory decisions, late deliveries from suppliers, acceptability of purchased materials and parts, and quality control procedures.

Supply Chain Factors Supply chain factors must be taken into account in capacity planning if substantial capacity changes are involved. Key questions include: What impact will the changes have on suppliers, warehousing, transportation, and distributors? If capacity will be increased, will these elements of the supply chain be able to handle the increase? Conversely, if capacity is to be decreased, what impact will the loss of business have on these elements of the supply chain?

External Factors Product standards, especially minimum quality and performance standards, can restrict management's options for increasing effective capacity. Also, pollution standards on products and equipment often reduce effective capacity, as does paperwork required by government regulatory agencies. A similar effect occurs when a union contract limits the type of work an employee may do.

©Mark Richards/PhotoEdit

In only 48 hours, Solectron in San Jose, California, can build to order, ship, and install a complex computer system. Suppliers hold inventory until it is pulled, thereby increasing manufacturing flexibility.

©Brand X Picture/PunchStock/Getty Images RF

Making a violin requires precision and skill from an artisan. Capacity is highly limited when items are specialized and produced one at a time.

Strategic Capacity Planning Process in Organizations

Capacity decisions in organizations are usually part of the annual strategic planning process. They directly influence capital budgeting. The steps taken are as follows:

1. Forecast demand for products one to five years, or more, ahead.

2. Calculate capacity requirements to meet the forecasts.

3. Measure capacity now, and decide if and how to bridge the gap in capacity in the future.

    a. Generate technically feasible alternatives varying in nature (plant, machines/equipment, sub-contract, lease), size, location, price changes, etc.

    b. Evaluate each alternative economically.

        i. Initial investment? Annual revenues? Annual operating expenses? Life of investment?

        ii. Method of evaluation: Break-even analysis, payback period, or net present value.

    c. Consider non-economic aspects too (e.g., ease of use, reliability, etc.).

    d. Choose the best alternative and implement it.

In the rest of this chapter, we will briefly describe Steps 1 and 2, provide some considerations for performing Step 3a, and describe use of breakeven analysis for Step 3b.

For an application of capacity planning and utilization, see the "Cisco's IT Network Capacity Planning" OM in Action.

 ## OM in Action

Cisco's IT Network Capacity Planning

Cisco has over 140 offices in North America, each with staff who use their computers to do their work. The offices are connected to the Internet (and hence together) using wide area network (WAN) lines with various bandwidths. The capacity or bandwidth initially chosen for each office (in megabits per second [Mbps]) was based on the number of employees (headcount) using the office. To increase the reliability of the system, a secondary circuit is usually made available.

Headcount	Primary WAN Bandwidth	Secondary WAN Bandwidth
1–10	1.5 Mbps	None
11–40	1.5 Mbps	1.5 Mbps
41–100	3 Mbps	3 Mbps
101–150	4.5 Mbps	4.5 Mbps
151–200	6 Mbps	6 Mbps
201–500	45 Mbps	6 Mbps
501+	155 Mbps	45 Mbps

However, the increasing use of applications and database synchronization and backup, including the use of voice over Internet protocol (VoIP) telephony and video on demand, soon created congestion during some periods of the day, reducing productivity. Cisco uses the following utilization (percentage of bandwidth used) thresholds as triggers for watching and adding capacity to the WAN bandwidth of an office. These depend on whether there is a same-size backup line, or half-capacity line, or no backup.

Primary/Backup WAN Bandwidth	Utilization[1] (Watch/Analyze)	Utilization[2] (Upgrade)
100/100[3]	60%	80%
100/50[4]	40%	50%
50/50[5]	40%	50%

[1]Average utilization of 10 percent or more of 15-minute intervals during local business hours in a month exceeds threshold
[2]Average utilization of 20 percent or more of 15-minute intervals during local business hours in a month exceeds threshold
[3]Primary circuit handles 100 percent of the traffic until failure, when the backup takes over
[4]Primary circuit handles 100 percent of the traffic until failure, when the backup takes over with 50 percent of the capacity of the primary
[5]Primary and backup circuits load-share until a failure occurs

For example, for a 100/100 office (same size backup line), if utilization exceeds 60 percent during more than 10 percent of the business hours, the utilization is watched and analyzed, whereas if utilization exceeds 80 percent during more than 20 percent of the business hours, the capacity planning team puts a request to the networks operations for increased capacity. The analysis requires that the reason for traffic is legitimate. For example, backups can be done overnight and personal recreational use of the Internet during busy times is discouraged. The WAN bandwidth utilization is monitored by Cisco's Netflow software, which is installed in its routers. Of course, the user performance expectations regarding quality of service are balanced against capital budget as bandwidths are expensive.

Source: http://www.cisco.com/web/about/ciscoitatwork/downloads/ciscoitatwork/pdf/Cisco_IT_Case_Study_Capacity_Planning.pdf.

Forecasting Long-Term Demand

Figure 5-1 illustrates some basic long-term demand patterns. In addition to basic patterns, there are more complex patterns, such as a combination of cycles and trends.

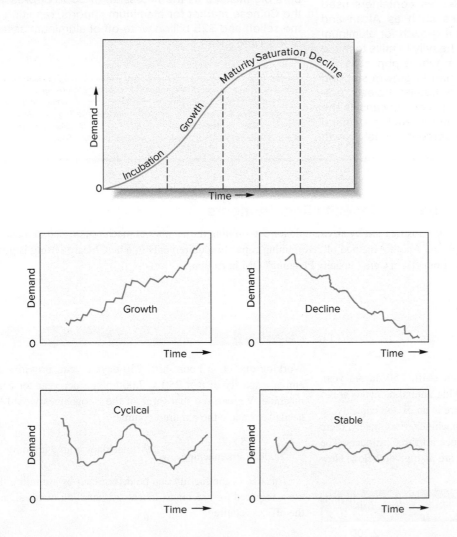

◀ **FIGURE 5-1**

Common long-term demand patterns.

When trends are identified, the fundamental issues are (1) how long the trend might persist and (2) the slope of trend. If a cycle is identified, interest focuses on (1) the approximate length of the cycle, and (2) the amplitude of the cycle (i.e., deviation from average).

Long-term forecasting techniques include judgmental and regression. For details, please refer back to Chapter 3.

The link between marketing and operations is crucial. Through customer contacts and demographic analysis, marketing can supply vital information to operations.

For an example where technology changed a trend unexpectedly, see the "Capacity in the Aluminum Industry" OM in Action.

 OM in Action

Capacity in the Aluminum Industry

Making capacity decisions is hard. Consider the aluminum industry. In the 1970s and 1980s, aluminum can sales were growing at over 10 percent per year. This occurred when aluminum pop cans grabbed market share from glass bottles as containers used to hold soft drinks. Companies such as Alcan and Alcoa saw no end to the market growth for aluminum cans. Therefore, they invested heavily in mills to make rolled sheets of aluminum from which pop cans are made. But in the early 1990s, market growth stopped because PET (polyethylene terephthalate) plastic bottles grabbed market share from aluminum cans. In the 2000s, the strong, seemingly never-ending demand for aluminum by China (with 9 percent annual growth

rate), and its inadequate future electricity supply to process aluminum, resulted in takeover frenzy within major Western aluminum companies looking for available production capacity. For example, Alcan warded off Alcoa's takeover bid only to accept the $38 billion takeover bid of Rio Tinto, a large British/Australian mining company, in late 2007. However, this turned out to be a big mistake as the recession of 2008 depressed the Chinese market for aluminum imports, resulting in the selloff and $25 billion write-off of aluminum assets of Rio Tinto Alcan.

Source: M. Brooks, president, Alcan Rolled Products, "Insights on the Global Aluminum Industry," December 5, 2003, http://www.alcan.com /web/publishing.nsf/Content/Insights+on+the+Global+Aluminum+Industry, accessed 2005; S. Silcoff, "Chinese Aluminum Demand Triggered Alcan Takeover," CanWest News, October 26, 2007, p. 1; J. W. Miller, "Digging Out of a $38 Billion Hole," *Wall Street Journal*, February 12, 2013.

Calculating Capacity Requirements

We will illustrate this by an example for determining the number of machines needed to make some products. Another method of determining capacity requirements in a health care setting is given in the "Long-Term Care Capacity Planning" OM in Action.

EXAMPLE 5-3 ▶

A department works one eight-hour shift, 250 days a year. Three new products with the following annual demands are to be produced in the department. There is no excess capacity, so the department needs to buy new machines. Fortunately, there is a type of machine that can produce all three products. The expected processing times per unit are also given below. How many machines are needed?

Product	Annual Demand	Standard Processing Time per Unit (Hr)	Processing Time Needed (Hr)
1	400	5.0	2,000
2	300	8.0	2,400
3	700	2.0	1,400
			5,800

SOLUTION

Working one eight-hour shift, 250 days a year, provides an annual capacity of $8 \times 250 = 2{,}000$ hours per year for each machine. We can see that three of these machines would be needed to handle the required volume:

$$\frac{5{,}800}{2{,}000 \text{ hours/machine}} = 2.90 \text{ machines (round up to 3)}$$

The size of the facility can be determined by summing the areas required for machines, inventory, handling material, and the offices required.

OM in Action

Long-Term Care Capacity Planning

As baby boomers approach old age, the percentage of the population over age 65 increases from approximately 15 percent to 25 percent. This will cause a significant increase in demand for long-term care (LTC) provided by nursing homes. Thus, provincial governments and regional health authorities (RHA), being responsible for provision of health care in Canada, are concerned about LTC capacity issues. The most common measure of demand for LTC is number of beds per 1,000 population aged 75+. This number varies among RHAs but averages around 100 beds per 1000 people over 75 years old. However, many patients needing LTC are younger than 75, and it is a fact that there is a shortage of beds, resulting in many patients needing alternative levels of care and taking beds in hospitals. Using the above ratio is simple but will underestimate the demand for LTC, which will result in very long waits for LTC in the near future.

Sources: http://www.cfhi-fcass.ca/sf-docs/default-source/planning-for-the-aging-population-files/10-15-10-Carriere.pdf?sfvrsn=0; http://www4.hrsdc.gc.ca/.3ndic.1t.4r@-eng.jsp?iid=33; http://www.longwoods.com/content/22881.

Major Considerations for Developing Capacity Alternatives

1. Design Flexibility Into the System The long-term nature of capacity decisions and the risks inherent in long-term forecasts suggest potential benefits from designing flexible systems. For example, provision for future expansion in the original design of a structure frequently can be obtained at a small price compared to what it would cost to remodel an existing structure that did not have such a provision. Hence, if future expansion of a restaurant seems likely, water lines, power hookups, and waste disposal lines can be put in place initially so that if expansion becomes a reality, modification to the existing structure can be minimized. Similarly, a new golf course may start as a nine-hole operation, but if provision is made for future expansion by obtaining options on adjacent land, it may progress to a larger (18-hole) course.

2. Differentiate Between New and Mature Products Mature products tend to be more predictable in terms of capacity requirements, and they may have predictable life spans. This means less risk of choosing an incorrect capacity and length of life for the investment. New products tend to carry higher risk because of the uncertainty often associated with predicting the quantity and duration of demand. These uncertainties are due to unknown and changing reactions of customers, evolving technologies, and uncertain competitor reactions. Flexibility and starting small is more important in this case.

3. Take a "Big Picture" Approach to Capacity Changes When developing capacity alternatives, it is important to consider how parts of the system interrelate. For example, when making a decision to increase the number of rooms in a motel, one should also take into account probable increased demands for parking, entertainment and food, and housekeeping. This is sometimes called *capacity balance.* Capacity *imbalance* results in *bottlenecks,* which restrict the capacity of the whole system. To increase the capacity of the system, the capacity of the bottleneck operation should be increased. A **bottleneck operation** is an operation in a sequence of operations whose capacity is lower than the capacities of other operations in the sequence. As a consequence, the capacity of the bottleneck operation limits the system capacity; the capacity of the system is reduced to the capacity of the bottleneck operation. Figure 5-2 illustrates this concept: Four operations generate work that must then be processed by a fifth operation. The four different operations each have a capacity of 10 units per hour, for a total capacity of 40 units per hour. However, the fifth operation can only process 30 units per hour. Consequently, the output of the system will only be 30 units per hour. If the other operations operate at capacity, a line of units waiting to be processed by the bottleneck operation will build up at the rate of 10 per hour.

> **bottleneck operation**
> An operation in a sequence of operations whose capacity is lower than that of the other operations.

FIGURE 5-2 ▶

Bottleneck operation.

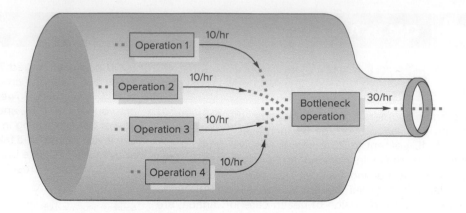

EXAMPLE 5-4 ▶

The first product created by toy company Spin Master, now the third largest toy manufacturer in North America, was Earth Buddy, a grass head.[1] Spin Master was hoping to produce and sell 8,000 Earth Buddies for Mother's Day and had one week to produce them. The Earth Buddy assembly consisted of the following operations: A: Fill grass seeds and sawdust in a nylon stocking (average time 90 seconds); B: Form ears and nose using elastic bands (average time 48 seconds); C: Stick on the eyeglasses and eyes (average time 24 seconds; eyeglasses were formed off line); and D: Paint the mouth (average time 15 seconds). Finally, Earth Buddies are left to dry overnight and then packed. There are six workers doing A, three doing B, two doing C, and one doing D. There is enough space for inventory between operations so that they can work fairly independently. Determine the bottleneck operation and capacity of the "line" for a 40-hour week. Is the line balanced? Can Spin Master meet its production goal?

SOLUTION

	Fill	Form	Eyes	Paint
Time per unit per worker (sec)	90	48	24	15
No. of units per minute per worker	60/90 = 2/3	60/48 = 1.25	60/24 = 2.5	60/15 = 4
Number of workers	6	3	2	1
Capacity per minute	6(2/3) = 4	3(1.25) = 3.75	2(2.5) = 5	4(1) = 4
Capacity per hour	4(60) = 240	3.75(60) = 225	5(60) = 300	4(60) = 240
		Bottleneck		

Line capacity = 225 units per hour. Yes, the line is fairly balanced because capacity per hour values for the operations are all close.

Productive hours required to make 8,000 units = 8,000/225 = 35.6 hours.

Yes, Spin Master should be able to meet its target production goal of 8,000 units provided employees work approximately 36 hours (excluding breaks).

4. Choose Capacity Timing and Increments Consider whether capacity is to be installed before, during, or after demand occurs. If before, it is called *leading strategy* and if after, *lagging strategy* (see Figure 5-3). Most organizations plan to have capacity available just before demand occurs because construction of capacity takes a long time. Leading competitors is more risky, but it has greater potential for rewards. If cost of capacity excess and cost of capacity shortage can be estimated, they can be used to make the timing decision. Also, consider whether incremental small expansions or a single big expansion is more appropriate. Using small expansions is less risky because it allows adjustment of the capacity based on demand changes over time, but it is usually more expensive overall. If goods are involved, any short-term mismatch between capacity and demand can be bridged by carrying inventory.

---

[1] "Company, About Us, Video Biography," http://www.spinmaster.com; https://globenewswire.com/news-release/2014/09/09/664758/10097837/en/Spin-Master-Celebrates-Its-20th-Anniversary.html .

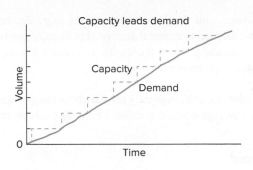
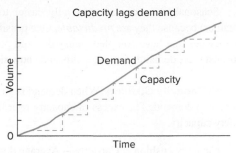

Leading and lagging capacity strategies.

5. Prepare to Deal With Capacity "Chunks" Capacity increases are often acquired in fairly large chunks rather than smooth increments, making it difficult to achieve a match between desired capacity and actual capacity. For instance, the desired capacity of a certain Air Canada Jazz route may be 75 seats, but aircraft available (Bombardier CRJ 700 NextGen and 900 NextGen) have 70 and 88 seats, respectively. One CRJ 700 would cause capacity to be five seats short of what is needed, but one CRJ 900 would result in an excess capacity of 13 seats. Most airlines would choose the larger aircraft in this case, because cost of shortage (lost profit) is usually larger than cost of excess capacity. This decision becomes more difficult when demand has a trend or cycle.

In some instances, capacity choices are made very infrequently; in others, they are made regularly, as part of an ongoing process. Generally, the factors that influence this frequency are the stability of demand, the rate of technological change in equipment and product design, and competitive factors. Other factors relate to the type of product or service and whether style changes are important (e.g., automobiles and clothing). In any case, management must review product and service choices periodically to ensure that the company makes capacity changes when they are needed for cost, competitive effectiveness, or other reasons.

6. Attempt to Smooth Out Capacity Requirements Unevenness in capacity requirements can create certain problems. For instance, during periods of inclement weather, public transportation ridership tends to increase substantially relative to periods of pleasant weather. If capacity is set slightly above normal demand, the system tends to alternate between underutilization and overutilization. Again, the best capacity basically depends on expected cost of shortage versus expected cost of excess capacity. If the service is critical, spare capacity should be available or be arranged for peak periods. Another solution in some cases such as electricity generation is demand management—persuading some customers to shift their demand from peak periods to off-peak periods by differential pricing.

Capacity requirements are affected by seasonal variations. One approach to smooth out capacity requirements is to identify products with complementary seasonal demand patterns such as water skis and snow skis.

©PictureNet/CORBIS RF   © Royalty-Free/CORBIS

Seasonal variations are generally easier to cope with than random variations (e.g., due to weather) because they are *predictable*. One possible solution to seasonal demand is to identify goods or services that have complementary demand patterns and produce them with the same resources. For instance, demands for water skis and snow skis complement each other.

7. Use Capacity Cushion   When demand is variable, capacity is usually chosen above the average (forecast) demand. The excess of capacity over the average demand is called **capacity cushion** or safety capacity.

> **capacity cushion** The excess of capacity over the average demand.

Capacity cushion = Capacity − Average demand

The size of capacity cushion again depends on the trade-off between cost of capacity shortage and cost of capacity excess. See Figure 5-4, where a Normal (bell-shaped) demand distribution is assumed. For vital services such as electricity, the chosen capacity should be larger than normal *peak* demand. There should be a large (positive) capacity cushion because customers cannot wait too long for critical services (e.g., electricity to heat the home in cold winters). For an application of this and some other capacity considerations, see the "Ontario's Planned Supply Mix" OM in Action.

FIGURE 5-4 ▶

Capacity cushion.

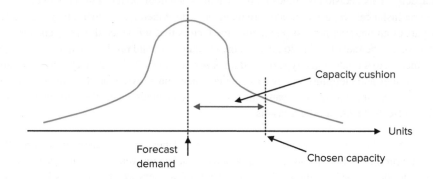

8. Identify the Optimal Operating Level   Production units typically have an ideal or optimal level of operation in terms of average unit cost of output. At the **optimal operating level**, average cost per unit is the lowest for that production unit; larger or smaller rates of output will result in a higher unit cost (i.e., the average cost curve is "U" shaped). Figure 5-5 illustrates these concepts.

> **optimal operating level** The level of production that has the lowest average unit cost.

FIGURE 5-5 ▶

Production units have an optimal rate of output for minimum cost.

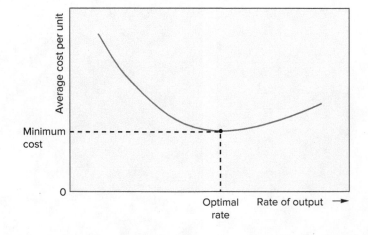

The explanation for the shape of the cost curve is that, at low levels of output, the investment costs of facility and machines/equipment must be absorbed (paid for) by very few units. Hence, the cost per unit is high. As output is increased, there are more units to absorb the "fixed" cost of facility and machines/equipment, so unit cost decreases. However, beyond a certain point, unit cost will start to rise. Reasons for this include worker fatigue; equipment breakdown; the loss of flexibility, which leaves less of a margin for error; and, generally, greater difficulty in coordinating operations.

Both optimal operating level and the amount of the minimum average unit cost tend to be a function of size of the operating unit. As the size of a plant increases, the optimal operating level increases and the minimum average cost per unit decreases. Thus, larger plants tend to have a larger optimal operating level and lower average cost per unit than smaller plants. Figure 5-6 illustrates this point, called *economies of scale*. However, beyond a certain size, the plant will be too large, expensive, and complex to manage. This is called *diseconomies of scale*.

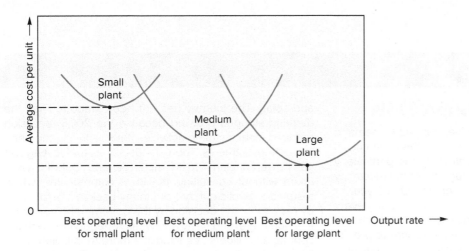

◀ FIGURE 5-6

Average cost per unit and optimal operating level are functions of size of a production unit (graph shows economies of scale).

In choosing the capacity of an operating unit, management must take these relationships into account along with the availability of financial and other resources and forecasts of demand.

Planning Service Capacity

While the foregoing discussion relates generally to capacity planning for both goods and services, it is important to note that capacity planning for services can present special challenges due to the nature of services. Three very important factors in planning service capacity are (1) the potential need to be near customers, (2) the inability to store services, and (3) the degree of volatility of demand.

Convenience for customers is often an important aspect of service. Generally, a service must be located near customers. For example, hotel rooms must be where customers want to stay; having a vacant room in another city won't help. Thus, capacity and location are closely tied.

Capacity also must be matched with the timing of demand. Unlike goods, services cannot be produced in one period and stored for use in a later period. Thus, an unsold seat on an airplane, train, or bus cannot be stored for use on a later trip. Similarly, inventories of goods allow customers to immediately satisfy wants, whereas a customer who wants a service may have to wait. This can result in a variety of negatives for an organization that provides the service. Thus, speed of delivery, or customer waiting time, becomes a major concern in service capacity planning. For example, deciding on the number of police officers and fire trucks to have on duty at any given time affects the speed of response and brings into question the cost of maintaining that capacity. Some of these issues are addressed in the chapter on waiting lines.

Demand volatility presents problems for capacity planners. Demand volatility tends to be higher for services than for goods, not only in timing of demand, but also in the amount of time required to service individual customers. For example, banks tend to experience higher volumes of demand on certain days of the week, and the number and nature of transactions tend to vary substantially for different individuals. Then, too, a wide range of social, cultural, and even weather factors can cause major peaks and valleys in demand. The fact that services can't be stored means service systems cannot turn to inventory to smooth demand requirements on the system the way goods-producing systems are able to. Instead, service planners have to devise other methods of coping with demand volatility and cyclical demand. For example, to cope with peak demand periods, planners might consider hiring extra workers, hiring temporary workers, outsourcing some or all of a service, or using pricing and promotion to shift some demand to slower periods.

In some instances, demand management strategies can be used to offset capacity limitations. Pricing, promotions, discounts, and similar tactics can help to shift some demand away from peak periods and into slow periods, allowing organizations to achieve a closer match in supply and demand.

 OM in Action

Ontario's Planned Supply Mix

Strategic capacity planning involves long-term demand forecasting and supply planning. One of the most critical services is electricity. Planning electricity is particularly challenging because it is not enough that total electricity generated equals total electricity demanded in a year or even a month. Supply should equal demand during every second. This means that the installed capacity should meet peak demand. But, peak demand is hard to predict (in terms of both size and timing) and peak capacity is rarely used throughout the year. Ontario Power Authority (OPA) is the agency responsible for long-term electricity capacity planning in Ontario. Since its creation in 2004, OPA has restructured Ontario's electricity supply away from coal dependency and toward less polluting sources (such as natural gas) and renewables (such as wind

and solar). The journey has not been smooth. First, the demand stopped growing because the 2008 recession reduced manufacturing activities, thus reducing the need for early investments. Then, the decisions for locating two gas-powered plants in Mississauga and Oakville were taken without consulting the local communities, which resulted in public outcry ("not in my backyard"), followed by reversal of the decision by the government (due to re-election scare) and hasty and weak renegotiation with the contracted builders (resulting in a more than billion-dollar loss), and finally hiding some of the facts. Despite all this, few dispute that electricity capacity planning is vital.

Sources: http://www.powerauthority.on.ca/sites/default/files/planning/LTEP_2013_English_WEB.pdf; http://www.auditor.on.ca/en/reports_en/mississaugapower_en.pdf; http://www.auditor.on.ca/en/reports_en/oakville_en.pdf.

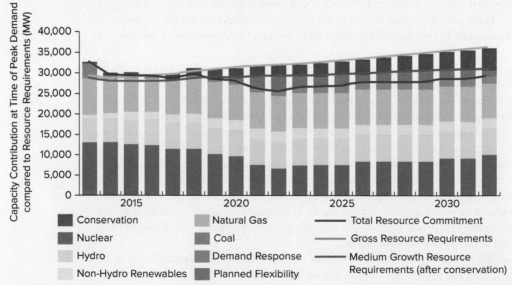

Source: Achieving Balance: Ontario's Long-Term Energy Plan. Figure 18, p. 42. (c) Published by the Ministry of Energy, Toronto, Ontario. Queen's Printer for Ontario, 2013. Reproduced with permission.

Evaluating Alternatives

An organization needs to evaluate alternatives for future capacity from a number of different perspectives. Most obvious are economic considerations: Will an alternative be economically feasible? How much will it cost? What will operating and maintenance costs be? What will the revenue be? What will its useful life be? There are also other considerations: Will it be compatible with present personnel and operations? What is the personal preference of managers?

Less obvious, but nonetheless important, is possible negative public opinion. Any option that could disrupt lives and property (noise, traffic, pollution) is bound to generate hostile reactions. Construction of new facilities may necessitate moving personnel to a new location. Embracing a new technology may mean retraining some people and terminating some jobs. Relocation can cause unfavourable reactions, particularly if a town is about to lose a major employer.

A number of techniques are useful for evaluating capacity alternatives from an economic standpoint. Some of the more common are break-even analysis, payback period, and net present value. Break-even analysis is described in this chapter.

Break-Even Analysis

Break-even analysis focuses on the relationship between costs, revenue, and volume (i.e., quantity) of output. The purpose of break-even analysis is to determine the quantity at which the initial investment starts to make a profit. Another name for break-even analysis is *cost–volume–profit analysis*.

Use of break-even analysis requires identification of all costs related to the production of a given product. These costs are then classified as fixed or variable costs. *Fixed costs* tend to remain constant regardless of quantity of output. Examples include facility lease (or amortized land and building) cost, property tax, machine/equipment cost, heating and cooling expenses, and certain administrative costs such as supervisors' salaries. *Variable costs* vary directly with quantity of output. The major components of variable costs are generally materials and labour costs. We will assume that variable cost per unit remains the same regardless of quantity of output.

Table 5-2 summarizes the symbols used in the break-even analysis formulas. All amounts, except v and R, have a unit of time such as a month or a year. These have been mainly omitted in this section due to simplicity.

$FC =$	Fixed cost
$VC =$	Total variable cost
$v =$	Variable cost per unit
$TC =$	Total cost
$TR =$	Total revenue
$R =$	Revenue per unit (i.e., price)
$Q =$	Quantity or volume of output
$Q_{BEP} =$	Break-even quantity
$P =$	Profit

◀ **TABLE 5-2**

Break-even analysis symbols.

The total cost associated with a given quantity of output is equal to the sum of the fixed cost and the variable cost per unit times quantity:

$$TC = FC + VC \qquad (5\text{-}7)$$
$$VC = Q \times v \qquad (5\text{-}8)$$

Figure 5-7a shows the relationship between quantity of output and fixed cost, total variable cost, and total (fixed plus variable) cost.

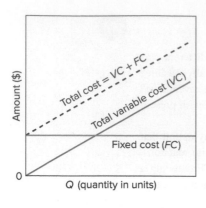

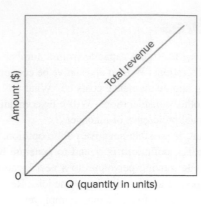

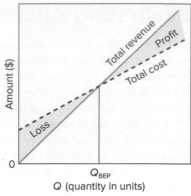

(a) Fixed, variable, and total costs

(b) Total revenue increases linearly with output

(c) Profit = TR − TC

FIGURE 5-7 ▲

Break-even relationships.

Revenue per unit, like variable cost per unit, is assumed to be the same regardless of quantity of output. Assuming that all output can be sold, total revenue will have a linear relationship to output, as illustrated in Figure 5-7b. The total revenue associated with a given quantity of output, Q, is:

$$TR = R \times Q \tag{5-9}$$

Figure 5-7c describes the relationship between profit, which is the difference between total revenue and total cost, and quantity of output. The quantity at which total cost and total revenue are equal is referred to as the **break-even point (BEP)**. When quantity is less than the break-even point, there is a loss; when quantity is greater than the break-even point, there is a profit. The greater the deviation from this point, the greater the profit or loss. Total profit can be calculated using the formula:

break-even point (BEP) The quantity of output at which total cost and total revenue are equal.

$$P = TR - TC = R \times Q - (FC + v \times Q)$$

Factorizing Q, we have

$$P = Q(R - v) - FC \tag{5-10}$$

Solving for Q, the required quantity needed to generate a specified profit P is:

$$Q = \frac{P + FC}{R - v} \tag{5-11}$$

A special case of this is the quantity of output needed for total revenue to equal total cost: that is, when profit $P = 0$. This is the break-even point:

$$Q_{BEP} = \frac{FC}{R - v} \tag{5-12}$$

If demand is expected to be greater than the break-even point, then we conclude that it is a good capacity investment decision (i.e., will make a profit). Otherwise, it is not (i.e., will make a loss).

EXAMPLE 5-5 ▶

The management of a large bakery is contemplating making pies, which will require leasing new equipment for a monthly cost of $6,000. Variable cost will be $2.00 per pie and retail price will be $7.00 each.

a. How many pies must be sold per month in order to break even?

b. What would the profit (loss) be if 1,000 pies were made and sold in a month?

c. How many pies must be sold to realize a profit of $4,000 per month?

d. If demand is expected to be 1,500 pies per month, is this a good investment?

SOLUTION

$FC = \$6{,}000$ per month, $v = \$2$ per pie, $R = \$7$ per pie

a. $Q_{BEP} = \dfrac{FC}{R - v} = \dfrac{\$6{,}000}{\$7 - \$2} = 1{,}200$ pies/month

b. For $Q = 1{,}000$, $P = Q(R - v) - FC = 1{,}000 (\$7 - \$2) - \$6{,}000 = -\$1{,}000$ (i.e., loss of $1,000)

c. $P = \$4{,}000$; solve for Q using Formula 5-11:

$$Q = \frac{\$4{,}000 + \$6{,}000}{\$7 - \$2} = 2{,}000 \text{ pies}$$

d. Because $1{,}500 > 1{,}200 = Q_{BEP}$, this is a good investment.

Break-even analysis can also be used for (1) make-or-buy decisions, and (2) deciding between two or more capacity alternatives (cost-vs.-cost analysis). See Figure 5-8.

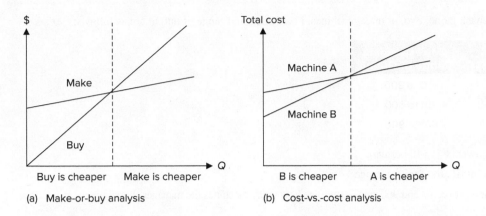

◀ FIGURE 5-8

Two other types of analysis.

(a) Make-or-buy analysis   (b) Cost-vs.-cost analysis

The make-or-buy decision involves deciding whether to buy a machine (fixed cost) and make the product in-house (variable cost), or to buy the product (variable cost with no fixed cost). See Figure 5-8a. Let v_m – Per unit variable cost of make and v_b – Per unit variable cost of buy (i.e., purchase price). Then, the indifference point will be:

$$Q = FC/(v_b - v_m) \tag{5-13}$$

The cost-vs.-cost decision involves two (or more) "make" options: Machine A vs. Machine B. Each machine will have a fixed cost and a variable cost. See Figure 5-8b. Let FC_A and v_A be fixed cost and unit variable cost of Machine A, and FC_B and v_B be fixed cost and unit variable cost of Machine B. Then, the indifference point will be:

$$Q = (FC_A - FC_B)/(v_B - v_A) \tag{5-14}$$

Break-Even Problem With Step Fixed Cost

Capacity alternatives may involve *step costs,* which are costs that increase stepwise as range of output increases. For example, a company may have the option of purchasing one, two, or three machines. Each additional machine increases the fixed cost, although perhaps not equally (see Figure 5-9a). In this case, *multiple break-even quantities* may occur, possibly one for each range. This is illustrated in Figure 5-9b, where there is a break-even point in the second and another in the third range. In order to decide how many machines to purchase, a manager must compare forecast demand to the break-even points and choose the most appropriate number of machines, as Example 5-6 shows.

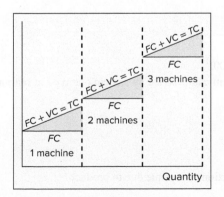

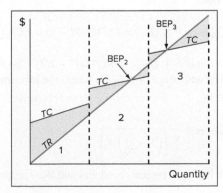

◀ FIGURE 5-9

Break-even problem with step fixed cost.

(a) Step fixed costs and variable costs   (b) Multiple break-even points

EXAMPLE 5-6 ▶

A manager has the option of purchasing one, two, or three machines. Fixed costs and range of output are as follows:

Number of Machines	Total Annual Fixed Cost ($)	Corresponding Range of Output
1	9,600	0 to 300
2	15,000	301 to 600
3	20,000	601 to 900

Variable cost is $10 per unit, and revenue is $40 per unit.

a. Determine the break-even point (if any) for each range.

b. For any value of annual demand between 0 and 900 units, determine how many machines the manager should purchase.

SOLUTION

a. Calculate the break-even point for each range using the formula $Q_{BEP} = FC/(R-v)$.

For one machine $Q_{BEP} = \dfrac{\$9,600}{\$40/\text{unit} - \$10/\text{unit}} = 320$ units [not in the range, so there is no *BEP*]

For two machines $Q_{BEP} = \dfrac{\$15,000}{\$40/\text{unit} - \$10/\text{unit}} = 500$ units

For three machines $Q_{BEP} = \dfrac{\$20,000}{\$40/\text{unit} - \$10/\text{unit}} = 666.67$ units

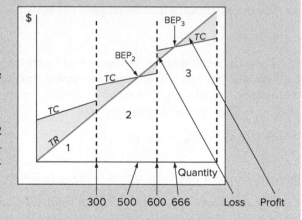

b. For demand $\leq 499 \rightarrow$ use 0 machines (because the first feasible break-even point is 500 units)

For $500 \leq$ demand $\leq 600 \rightarrow$ use 2 machines

For $601 \leq$ demand $\leq 766 \rightarrow$ do not use 3 machines, but use 2 machines and produce 600 units because profit(600) = 600($40 – $10) – $15,000 = $3,000 > profit($Q$), $601 \leq Q \leq 766$. For example, Profit(766) = 766($40 – $10) – 20,000 = $2,980.

For $767 \leq$ demand $\leq 900 \rightarrow$ use 3 machines

Break-Even Point in Dollars

Suppose the decision maker wishes to know the BEP in dollars, $Q_{BEP\$}$—that is, how much should the sales revenue $Q \times R$ be before the initial investment starts to make a profit? $Q_{BEP\$}$ can easily be determined from $Q_{BEP} = FC/(R-v)$. Simply multiply both sides by R and simplify the right-hand side:

$$Q_{BEP\$} = R \times Q_{BEP} = R(FC)/(R-v) = FC/(1 - v/R)$$

For Example 5-4, $Q_{BEP\$} = \$6,000/(1 - 2/7) = \$8,400$.

The advantage of $Q_{BEP\$}$ is where the investment can produce more than one type of output. In this case,

$$Q_{BEP\$} = \dfrac{FC}{\sum\left[\left(1 - \dfrac{v_i}{R_i}\right)W_i\right]}$$

Where index i represents product i and W_i = proportion of revenue due to product i.

EXAMPLE 5-7

The managers of the bakery in Example 5-5 think that they can also use the new equipment to make quiche. Quiche will have variable cost of $3 and will sell for $10 each. Management estimates that pies and quiche will bring approximately the same amount of revenue. Recall that leasing the equipment will cost $6,000 per month, and that the variable cost of a pie is $2.00 and its sales price is $7.00. Calculate the break-even point in dollars.

SOLUTION

$$Q_{BEPS} = \frac{FC}{\sum\left[\left(1 - \frac{v_i}{R_i}\right)W_i\right]} = \frac{6,000}{\left(1 - \frac{2}{7}\right)0.5 + \left(1 - \frac{3}{10}\right)0.5}$$

$$= \$8,484.85$$

As with any quantitative tool, it is important to verify that the assumptions on which the break-even analysis is based are reasonably satisfied for a particular situation. Note that revenue per unit or variable cost per unit is not always constant. Also, break-even analysis requires that fixed and variable costs be separated, and this is sometimes exceedingly difficult to accomplish.

Payback is a crude but widely used method that focuses on the length of time it will take for an investment to return its original cost. For example, an investment with an original cost of $6,000 and a monthly net cash flow of $1,000 has a payback period of six months. For an example, see the "Solar Power" OM in Action.

 ## OM in Action

Solar Power

In 2016, electricity generation by solar power became cheaper than coal for the very first time. This is the result of exponential gains in efficiency within the past five years, during which solar panel yield jumped from about 15 percent to 22 percent efficiency. A consequence of these efficiency gains is a significant reduction in the cost of solar power, from $300 per megawatt-hour to less than one-third of that. According to Natural Resources Canada, the cost of electrical generation from solar has become economical enough to reach grid parity.

Even before these gains, installing solar panels in Ontario had become economical because the government agreed to buy electricity from solar power producers at a premium price (44.3 cents per kilowatt-hour). The Sarnia solar farm, owned by Enbridge, is Canada's largest with an installed capacity of 80 megawatts of AC power. It was completed in 2010 at a cost of $400 million. First Solar developed, engineered, and constructed the facility, and is operating it for Enbridge under a long-term contract. Enbridge is selling the power to the Ontario Power Authority pursuant to 20-year power purchase agreements. The plant covers 1,100 acres and contains about 635 acres of solar panels, which is about

Glen Ogilvie/Wrecked Film and Spent Photographers

1.3 million thin-film panels. The expected annual energy yield is about 120,000 megawatt-hours. This is equivalent to 1500 hours (= 120,000/80) of electricity generation at maximum capacity.

Assuming that the annual operating cost was part of the initial construction cost, the payback period to Enbridge is $400 million/$0.443 × 120,000 × 1000 = 7.5 years.

Sources: https://www.nrcan.gc.ca/sites/www.nrcan.gc.ca/files/canmetenergy /pdf/2016-019_EN.pdf; http://www3.weforum.org/docs/WEF_Renewable _Infrastructure_Investment_Handbook.pdf; https://en.wikipedia.org/wiki /Sarnia_Photovoltaic_Power_Plant.

Summary

- Design capacity is the theoretical maximum output rate, but effective capacity is limited by work break hours, maintenance, etc.
- Efficiency is the ratio of actual output rate to effective capacity.
- Utilization of a unit is the proportion of the available time it is operating. Utilization of many units of the same resource at a point in time is the percentage of units operating at that time.
- Overall equipment effectiveness provides a picture of how well your manufacturing process is running, and helps to track improvements over time.
- A variety of factors can influence effective capacity. These include facility design and layout, human factors, product factors, equipment maintenance, scheduling problems, and quality considerations.
- Capacity planning is the process of determining alternatives to meet long-term forecast of demand.

- Development of capacity alternatives is enhanced by considering the life cycle of the product, designing systems with flexible capacity, timing the capacity plan before demand occurs, taking a systems approach to planning, recognizing that capacity increments are often acquired in chunks, practising demand management and complementary products, using capacity cushion, and choosing the right capacity and optimal operating level.
- One or more constraints can adversely affect the overall capacity of a system. Capacity increases can only be achieved by loosening the bottleneck(s), not by increasing other resources.
- In evaluating capacity alternatives, a manager must consider both quantitative and qualitative aspects. Quantitative analysis usually reflects economic factors, and qualitative considerations include intangibles such as operational fit and personal preferences of managers.
- Break-even analysis determines that quantity beyond which profit will be attained.

Key Terms

bottleneck operation
break-even point (BEP)
capacity
capacity cushion

design capacity
effective capacity
efficiency
optimal operating level

strategic capacity planning
utilization of a unit of a resource during a period
utilization of many units of a resource at a point in time

Solved Problems

Problem 1

A manager must decide whether to make or buy a certain item used in the production of vending machines. Cost and demand estimates are as follows:

	Make	Buy
Annual fixed cost	$150,000	$0
Variable cost/unit	$60	$80
Annual demand (units)	12,000	12,000

a. Given these numbers, should the company buy or make this item?

b. There is a possibility that demand could change in the future. At what quantity would the manager be indifferent between making and buying?

Solution

a. Determine the annual cost of each alternative:

Total cost = Fixed cost + Quantity × Variable cost

Make: $150,000 + 12,000($60) = $870,000

Buy: $0 + 12,000($80) = $960,000

Because the annual cost of making the item is less than the annual cost of buying it, the manager should make the item.

b. To determine the quantity at which the two choices would be equivalent, set the two total costs equal to each other, and solve for quantity: $TC_{make} = TC_{buy}$. Thus, $150,000 + Q(\$60) = \$0 + Q(\$80)$. Solving for Q, we get $Q = 7,500$ units. Alternatively, one can use Formula 5-13: $Q = FC/(v_b - v_m) = \$150,000/(\$80 - \$60) = 7,500$ units. Therefore, at 7,500 units a year, the manager would be indifferent between making and buying. For lower demand the choice would be to buy, and for higher demand the choice would be to make.

Problem 2

A toy company wants to make electric turtles. The line will have a monthly fixed cost of $42,000 and variable costs of $3 per turtle. Turtles would sell for $7 each. Prepare a table that shows total revenue, total variable cost, fixed cost, total cost, and profit for monthly demands of 10,000, 12,000, and 15,000 units. In what range do you expect the break-even point to lie? Calculate the break-even point.

Solution

Revenue = $7 per unit
Variable cost = $3 per unit
Fixed cost = $42,000 per month
Profit $= Q(R - v) - FC$
Total cost $= FC + v \times Q$

Demand	Total Revenue	Total VC	Fixed Cost	Total Cost	Profit
10,000	70,000	30,000	42,000	72,000	(2,000)
12,000	84,000	36,000	42,000	78,000	6,000
15,000	105,000	45,000	42,000	87,000	18,000

The break-even point would lie between 10,000 and 12,000 units per month (look at the profits).

$$Q_{BEP} = \frac{FC}{R - v} = \frac{\$42,000}{\$7 - \$3} = 10,500 \text{ units per month}$$

Problem 3

Refer to Problem 2. Develop an equation that can be used to calculate monthly profit for any quantity. Use that equation to determine profit when quantity equals 22,000 units per month.

Solution

Profit $= Q(R - v) - FC = Q(\$7 - \$3) - \$42,000 = \$4Q - \$42,000$
For $Q = 22,000$, profit is $\$4(22,000) - \$42,000 = \$46,000$

Problem 4

A manager must decide which type of machine to buy, Type A or Type B, and how many of each. Type A machine costs $15,000 each, and Type B machine costs $11,000 each. The machines are operated eight hours a day, 250 days a year. The variable cost of using either machine is negligible.

Either machine can be used to perform two types of chemical analysis, C1 and C2, but the processing times will be different. Annual quantities (i.e., number of analyses) and processing times are shown in the following table. The goal is to minimize total purchase cost but meet annual requirements within the available hours.

Analysis Type	Annual Quantity	Processing Time per Analysis (hr)	
		A	B
C1	1,200	1	2
C2	900	3	2

Solution

Total processing time (annual quantity multiplied by processing time per analysis) needed by the type of equipment is:

Analysis Type	A	B
C1	1,200	2,400
C2	2,700	1,800
Total	3,900	4,200 hrs

Total processing time available per machine is 8 hours/day × 250 days/year = 2,000 hours per year. Hence, one machine can handle 2,000 hours of analysis, two machines can handle 4,000 hours, etc.

Given the total processing requirements, two Type A machines would be needed for a total cost of 2 × $15,000 = $30,000, or three Type B machines would be needed for a total cost of 3 × $11,000 = $33,000. Thus, two machines of Type A would have lower cost than three Type B machines.

Problem 5

A new machine will cost $2,000, but it will result in savings of $500 per year. What is the payback time in years?

Solution

Initial cost = $2,000   Annual savings = $500

The payback time is initial cost divided by annual savings. Thus, the payback time is

$$\text{Payback time} = \frac{\text{Initial cost}}{\text{Annual savings}} = \frac{\$2,000}{\$500/\text{yr}} = 4 \text{ years}$$

Problem 6

What is the capacity (attainable output) of this system where the product is made on two parallel lines (1-2-3 and 4-5-6) that join for finishing in operation 7?

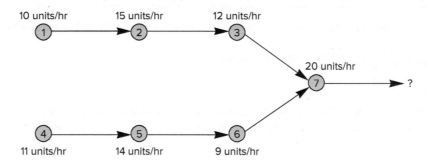

Solution

The attainable output of each portion of the system is equal to the output of the slowest operation. So the output of the upper portion is 10 units per hour and the output of the lower portion is 9 units per hour. Together the two portions can produce 10 + 9 = 19 units per hour. Although operation 7 can handle 20 units per hour, only 19 units per hour come from the two previous portions of the system, so the system output can be only 19 units per hour.

Discussion and Review Questions

Note: An asterisk indicates that a question or problem may be more challenging.

LO1 **1.** What is capacity? Give an example.

LO1 **2.** How do long-term, medium-term, and short-term capacity decisions differ?

LO1 **3.** Why is the long-term capacity decision important? Give three reasons.

LO1 **4.** Contrast design capacity and effective capacity.

LO1 **5.** Propose measures of capacity for a hospital and for an airline. In what way are the measures similar and different?

LO1 **6.** Contrast efficiency and utilization.

LO1 & 2 **7.** What is capacity planning and how is it done?

LO2 **8.** How can long-term capacity requirements be determined?

LO2 **9.** Give one example of building flexibility into system capacity.

LO2 **10.** What is a bottleneck operation? Name two places/operations in an airport that are usually bottlenecks.

LO2 **11.** What is meant by the term *capacity chunks*? Give an example. What are leading and lagging strategies for timing capacity increases? Should essential services such as utilities use the leading or lagging strategy? Explain.

LO2 **12.** What are economies of scale? Give an example. Is there a limit to it? Explain.

LO2 **13.** How do electrical utilities meet abnormal peak demand? Name three ways.

LO1 **14.** What influences effective capacity?

LO2 **15.** What is the optimal operating level for a machine and why is it usually less than its design capacity?

LO2 **16.** What is capacity cushion? Give an example of an industry sector that should have capacity cushion.

LO2 **17.** Discuss how capacity planning for essential services such as utilities differs from capacity planning for other services.

LO1 & 2 ***18.** When Air Canada emerged from bankruptcy protection in 2004, its top management decided to replace some of its older planes with new ones. In particular, several relatively small Embraer and Bombardier planes (with fewer than 90 seats) and several large Boeing 777s and 787s (with more than 200 seats) were ordered. These are much more fuel efficient than the planes they replace. However, Air Canada operations are still not as low cost as WestJet's. An available seat mile costs Air Canada approximately $0.17 whereas it costs WestJet approximately $0.14. Recall that WestJet is non-unionized, runs only one type of plane (Boeing 737, which seats 119–166 passengers), and is financially stronger (see the WestJet Mini-Case at the end of Chapter 2). Discuss the pros and cons of Air Canada's decision.

LO3 **19.** What is break-even analysis and how is it used?

LO1 **20.** What are some capacity measures for each of the following?
a. University.
b. Hospital.
c. Computer repair shop.
d. Farm.

LO2 **21.** Why is it important to adopt a big-picture approach to capacity planning?

LO2 **22.** Why is capacity planning for services more challenging than it is for goods production?

LO2 **23.** What kinds of capacity problems do many elementary and secondary schools periodically experience? What are some alternatives used to deal with those problems?

Taking Stock

LO2 **1.** What are two major trade-offs in capacity planning?

LO1 **2.** Who needs to be involved in capacity planning? Why?

LO2 **3.** In what ways has technology had an impact on capacity planning? What are the upsides and the downsides?

LO2 **4.** When Air Canada went into bankruptcy in 2003–2004, a new holding company, ACE, was formed with the goal of breaking up various business units of Air Canada such as the Aeroplan customer loyalty plan, the maintenance department, and the regional subsidiary airline Jazz. ACE managed to achieve its goals against the opposition of Air Canada employees, especially its pilots. Air Canada employees were put into a weak bargaining position. What was left of Air Canada was practically worthless. Is what has happened to Air Canada unethical? Explain.

Critical Thinking Exercises

LO1 **1.** An agricultural machinery manufacturer can potentially make eight units per day. Its effective capacity, however, is four units per day, and its actual output is three units per day. The manager would like to increase the output per day. Which of the following factors would you recommend that the manager investigate first: quality problems, absenteeism, or scheduling and balancing? Explain your reasoning.

LO2 **2.** Compared to manufacturing, capacity planning for services is more location dependent and time dependent. Why is this true?

Experiential Learning Exercises

 1. Estimate the hourly capacity of the following two service systems by obtaining their processing times.

    a. An automatic car wash.

    b. A cashier in a supermarket, a teller in a bank, or a similar service operation. Obtain the processing times for approximately six customers.

 2. How confident are you of your estimates for Exercise 1*a* and 1*b*? Explain.

 3. Next time you visit your doctor's office, take note of the various steps you go through and the associated processing times. For example, how long did check-in take? When it was your turn, how long did your doctor spend with you? Use this information to estimate the capacity of the medical clinic.

Internet Exercises

 1. Go to the following websites related to the Airbus A380, the biggest passenger plane ever built (525 passengers or more on two floors, with a range of 15,700 km, and a wing-span of 80 metres): http://www.airbus.com/aircraftfamilies /passengeraircraft/a380family/airlines-destinations/; http://centreforaviation.com/analysis/where-the-airbus -a380-will-fly-next-59245. Pick an airline flying the A380, and try to explain its choice on a route.

 2. The proposed TransCanada Pipelines Keystone XL will have a diameter of 36 inches and the crude oil in it will have a velocity of 6.3 km/h (based on the number and power of the pump stations planned). It is claimed that it will be able to transport 830,000 barrels of oil per day. You are wondering if this is right. Calculate the flow rate or capacity of the pipeline (in barrels per day) using:

    a. Geometry. (*Hint:* First, calculate how many barrels fit in a 6.3 km long pipe, where volume of a pipe with diameter d and length L is $(d/2)^2 \pi L$. *Note:* 18 inches = 0.4572 metre; 1 cubic metre = 8.3864 barrels.)

    b. http://www.1728.org/flowrate.htm (to check your answer in part *a*).

Problems

 1. a. Calculate the utilization and efficiency in each of these situations:

    i. A bank loan officer processes an average of seven loans per day. She works an eight-hour shift, but takes one hour off for lunch break. The effective capacity is eight loans per day.

    ii. A furnace repair team services an average of four furnaces a day. The team is idle an average of two hours in an eight-hour shift. The effective capacity is five furnaces a day.

    b. Would you say that systems with higher efficiency will have higher utilization than other systems? Explain.

2. In a job shop, effective capacity is only 50 percent of design capacity, and actual output is 80 percent of effective capacity. What design capacity would be needed to achieve an actual output of eight jobs per week?

 3. A producer of pottery is considering the addition of a new factory to absorb the backlog of demand that now exists. The primary location being considered will have fixed cost of $9,200 per month and variable cost of $0.70 per unit produced. Each item is sold to retailers at a price that averages $0.90.

    a. What quantity per month is required in order to break even?

    b. What profit would be realized on a monthly quantity of 61,000 units? 87,000 units?

    c. What quantity is needed to obtain a profit of $16,000 per month?

    d. What quantity is needed to provide revenue of $23,000 per month?

    e. Plot the total cost and total revenue lines against quantity per month.

 4. A small company intends to increase the capacity of its bottleneck operation by adding a new machine. Two alternatives, A and B, have been identified, and the associated costs and revenues have been estimated. Annual fixed costs would be $40,000 for A and $30,000 for B; variable costs per unit would be $10 for A and $12 for B; and revenue per unit would be $15 for A and $16 for B.

    a. Determine each alternative's break-even point.

    b. At what quantity would the two alternatives yield the same profit?

    c. If expected annual demand is 12,000 units, which alternative would yield higher profit?

LO3 **5.** The selling price for a type of felt-tip pen is $1 per pen. Fixed cost of the operation is $25,000 per month and variable cost is 50 cents per pen.
   a. Find the break-even quantity.
   b. How many pens must be sold to obtain a monthly profit of $15,000?
   c. What is the BEP$?
   d. Another type of marker with the following characteristics can also be produced by the machine: Selling price = $2 each, Variable cost = $0.75 each, and Proportion of revenue = 30%. Calculate the BEP$.

LO3 **6.** Natalie is considering the purchase of a cellphone service plan. There are two service plans to choose from. Plan A has a monthly charge of $20 plus $0.45 a minute for daytime calls and unlimited evening/night/weekend calls. Plan B has a flat rate of $50 with 200 daytime minutes of calls allowed per month and a cost of $0.40 per daytime minute beyond that, and unlimited evening/night/weekend calls.
   a. Determine the total charge under each plan for this case: 120 minutes of daytime calls a month.
   b. Prepare a graph that shows total monthly cost for each plan vs. daytime call minutes.
   c. Over what range of daytime call minutes will each plan be optimal?

LO3 **7.** A company plans to begin production of a new small appliance. The manager must decide whether to purchase the motor for the appliance from a vendor at $7 each or to produce them in-house. Either of two processes could be used for in-house production; one would have an annual fixed cost of $160,000 and a variable cost of $5 per unit, and the other would have an annual fixed cost of $190,000 and a variable cost of $4 per unit. Determine the range of annual quantity for which each of the alternatives would be best.

LO3 **8.** A manager is trying to decide whether to purchase a certain part or to have it produced internally. Internal production could use either of two processes. One would entail a variable cost of $16 per unit and an annual fixed cost of $200,000; the other would entail a variable cost of $14 per unit and an annual fixed cost of $240,000. Three vendors are willing to provide the part. Vendor A has a price of $20 per unit for any annual quantity up to 30,000 units. Vendor B has a price of $22 per unit if demand is 1,000 units or less, but $18 per unit (for all units) if demand is greater. Vendor C offers a price of $21 per unit for the first 1,000 units, and $19 per unit for additional units.
   a. If the manager anticipates an annual demand of 10,000 units, which alternative would be best from a cost standpoint? For 60,000 units, which alternative would be best?
   b. Determine the range for which each alternative is best. Are there any alternatives that are never best? If so, which ones?

LO2 **9.** A company manufactures a product using two identical machines. Each machine has a design capacity of 250 units per day and an effective capacity of 230 units per day. At present, actual output averages 200 units per machine, but

the manager estimates that productivity improvements soon will increase output to 225 units per day. Annual demand for the product is currently 50,000 units, but it is expected that within two years annual demand will triple. How many machines should the company plan to have to satisfy the forecasted demand? Assume 240 workdays per year.

LO2 **10.** A manager must decide which type of machine to buy, A, B, or C. Machine fixed costs are:

Machine	Cost/Year
A	$40,000
B	$30,000
C	$80,000

The company makes four products. Product demand forecasts and unit processing times on each machine are as follows:

Product	Annual Demand	Processing Time Per Unit (Minutes)		
		A	B	C
1	16,000	3	1	2
2	12,000	4	4	3
3	6,000	5	6	4
4	30,000	2	2	1

   a. How many machines of each type would be needed in order to meet annual demand for all the products? Based on annual fixed costs, which type of machine and how many will cost least to satisfy the demand? Machines operate 10 hours a day, 250 days a year.
   b. Consider this additional information: The machines differ in terms of hourly operating costs: The A machines have an hourly operating cost of $10 each, B machines have an hourly operating cost of $11 each, and C machines have an hourly operating cost of $12 each. Which alternative machine should be selected, and how many would be necessary to minimize total cost while satisfying processing requirements?

LO2 **11.** A company must decide which type of machine to buy, and how many units of that type, given the following information:

Type	Cost
1	$10,000
2	$14,000

Product demand and processing times for the equipment are:

Product	Annual Demand	Processing Time Per Unit (Minutes)	
		1	2
1	12,000	4	6
2	10,000	9	9
3	18,000	5	3

a. How many machines of each type would be required to handle demand if the machines will operate eight hours a day, 250 days a year, and what annual capacity cushion in processing time would result for each?

b. With high certainty of annual demand, which type of machine would be chosen if that was an important consideration? With low certainty, which type of machine would be chosen?

c. If purchasing and operating costs are taken into account, which type of machine would minimize total costs, given your answer for part *a*? Operating costs are $6/hr for type 1 and $5/hr for type 2.

LO3 **12.** A manager must decide how many machines of a certain type to purchase. Each machine can process 100 customers per day. One machine will result in a fixed cost of $2,000 per day, while two machines will result in a fixed cost of $3,800 per day. Variable costs will be $20 per customer, and revenue will be $45 per customer.

a. Determine the break-even points for one machine and two machines.

b. If estimated demand is 90 to 120 customers per day, how many machines should be purchased?

LO3 **13.** The manager of a car wash must decide whether to have one or two wash lines. One line will have a fixed cost of $4,000 a month, and two lines will have a fixed cost of $7,000 a month. Each line would be able to process 15 cars an hour. Variable cost will be $1 per car, and revenue will be $3 per car. The manager projects average demand of between 14 and 18 cars an hour. Assume extra demand for one line will be lost. Would you recommend one or two lines? The car wash will be open 300 hours a month.

LO2 **14.** The total demand for polypropylene, a type of plastic, in North America is approximately 11 billion pounds. H. Patrick Jack, VP of Fina Oil & Chemical Co., predicts (based on the previous 10 years) that total demand will grow anywhere between 5 percent and 8 percent annually. The total capacity is currently 12.3 billion pounds. In addition, a total of 4.5 billion pounds of new capacity is under construction by eight companies in eight locations and will be ready for production within the next four years. Would total capacity be enough to meet expected demand four years from now?[2]

LO3 **15.** A parts manufacturer plans to replace its existing facility with a new one. The management is considering two possible capacities for the new facility: 200,000 or 250,000 units per year. The 200,000-unit plant would have an annual fixed cost of $4 million and a per unit production cost of $20. The 250,000-unit plant would have an annual fixed cost of $6 million and a per unit cost of $15. The parts will be sold for an average price of $60 per unit.

a. Calculate the break-even point for each capacity alternative.

b. Suppose that the company projects its sales to be 220,000 units per year. Which alternative would you recommend? (*Hint:* Calculate the annual profit in each case.)

LO3 **16.** The fixed cost of running a gift store (wages, rent, etc.) in a particular mall is $250,000 per year.[3] The gross margin (i.e., Sales – Cost of goods sold, or alternatively, Revenue – Variable cost) is 45 percent of sales. Assuming that the store is open 364 days a year,

a. What are the minimum daily sales dollars to break even?

b. If the owner's profit target is 10 percent of sales, what are the minimum daily sales dollars?

c. If the owner's profit target is $100,000 per year, what are the minimum daily sales dollars?

LO3 ***17.** One of the first Internet-based grocery home-delivery businesses was Homegrocer.com. In 1998, Mike Donald (president of Concord Sales, one of the largest food brokers in British Columbia) and two partners thought of starting such a business in Vancouver. However, they had to move it to Seattle in order to get financing from the U.S. financiers. Mike thought that because Microsoft and Boeing are located in Seattle, the proportion of households with Internet would be high. After raising approximately $4 million and using it to lease a large warehouse, purchase 10 trucks, set up the web page and software, and advertise, Homegrocer.com had fewer than 1,000 regular customers. Mike estimated that an average regular customer purchased three times a month and bought approximately $75 each time (below $75, Homegrocer.com charged a delivery fee of $10). The gross margin (i.e., Sales – Cost of goods sold, or alternatively, Revenue – Variable cost) was around 20 percent, and total monthly labour and overhead costs were approximately $300,000.

a. How many regular customers did Homegrocer.com need in 1998 to break even?

Despite the slow initial business, Homegrocer.com persevered and even expanded into Portland, Oregon. In the frenzy of the dot.com era in 1999, private investors, including Amazon.com, invested approximately $100 million in Homegrocer.com. Homegrocer.com used the money to further expand, trying to compete with Webvan, a California-based competitor. At the beginning of 2000, Homegrocer.com raised over $250 million by issuing shares to the public, and kept on expanding to more cities in the United States. However, its share prices started to decline due to increasing losses. In mid-2000, Webvan bought Homegrocer.com for over $1 billion. Webvan itself went bankrupt in 2001.

b. Why would a startup company want to expand so fast? Why did most Internet grocery businesses fail?[4]

---

[2] D. Richards, "Polypropylene Capacity Soars But All of It May Be Needed," *Chemical Market Reporter* 251(12), March 24, 1997, pp. 7, 9.

[3] G. Cunningham, "Breakeven Analysis Key to Profits: The Next Century Promises More Stress and Retail Unpredictability," *Gifts & Tablewares* 25(1), January 2000, p. 58.

[4] J. Schreiner, "Net Grocer Debuts With Little Fanfare, Big Backers ...," *National Post*, March 11, 2000, p. C03;
J. Greenwood, "Canadians Break Bread With Amazon Online Grocery Store," *National Post*, May 19, 1999, p. C01.

LO3 *18. A few years ago, the Toronto plant of a multinational soup producer was in competition with its U.S. sister plant to supply the Northeastern U.S. market. However, its cost of production was not competitive. One source of its cost disadvantage was the tin cans. The Toronto plant bought its tin cans for approximately $6.00 per case of 48 cans, whereas the U.S. plant made its own cans at the cost of $5.00 (in Canadian dollars) per case. The manager estimated that installing an automatic can line would cost $2 million for building expansion and $12 million for equipment. The can line would have a variable production cost of $5.50 per case.

a. Assuming a useful life of 10 years, no salvage value, and straight-line depreciation, calculate the annual fixed cost of the canning line.

b. Calculate the annual break-even quantity between buying and making the cans in-house.

c. Draw a graph of the annual cost of buying and annual cost of making (try to make it to scale), and determine which option is better if the annual requirement of the Toronto plant was 5 million cases of cans.

LO2 19. Suppose your friend is thinking of opening a new restaurant, and she hopes that she will have around 20 groups of (on average) four customers on a typical busy evening. Each meal will take around 1.5 hours and it is expected that on average a table will be used twice in an evening. Each table and its surroundings will require four square metres of space.

a. Calculate the required seating area.

b. If each meal will take an average of 12 minutes to cook on a heating element, and each stove will have four elements, how many stoves would the restaurant require? Assume that all 10 "tables" could come at the same time and that the kitchen should be able to cook the meal for them during their first hour of the visit.

LO3 *20. Corner Tavern is a small-town bar that sells only bottled beer. The average price of a bottle of beer at the tavern is $3.00 and the average cost of a bottle of beer to the tavern is $1.00. The tavern is open every night. One bartender and two to three servers are on duty each night. The fixed costs (salaries, rent, tax, utilities, etc.) total $260,000 per year.

a. The owner wishes to know how many bottles of beer the tavern must sell during the year to start making a profit.

b. What is the revenue at the break-even quantity found in part a?

c. Draw the annual revenue and total annual cost vs. the number of bottles of beer sold per year. Make sure that the y axis is to scale. Identify the important points on the graph.

d. Using the graph in part c, answer the following question: If Corner Tavern sold 140,000 bottles of beer a year, would it make a profit? Explain.

e. The owner thinks $50,000 is a reasonable annual profit. How many bottles of beer should the tavern sell to make $50,000 profit?

f. An available option is to open the tavern earlier on the weekends. The attraction would be a discount of $0.50 off the regular price. The extra salaries of servers and bartender for the whole year are estimated to be $30,000. How many extra bottles of beer must the tavern sell in order to break even in this option?

LO3 *21. A small brewery reuses its own empty bottles, but it does not have a bottle-cleaning machine. The empty bottles are collected from liquor stores and bars, and brought back to the brewery. Once enough empty bottles accumulate, they are trucked to a cleaning facility and clean bottles are brought back. The cleaning facility charges $0.10 to wash a bottle, and cost of trucking is $0.02 per bottle. Management is thinking of buying an automated bottle-cleaning machine. The machine costs $1 million and has a useful life of 10 years. The machine will be used only when enough empty bottles accumulate. The operating cost of the machine is expected to be $108 per hour, washing 60 bottles per minute.

a. How many bottles per year would have equal total annual cost of doing the cleaning in-house versus outsourcing the cleaning? Use straight-line depreciation.

b. What is the total annual cost at the quantity found in part a?

c. Draw the two total annual costs vs. the quantity of bottles per year. Make sure that the y axis is to scale. If the brewery is expected to have 1 million bottles per year to wash, which decision is less costly?

LO2 22. The following diagram shows a four-step process that begins with Operation 1 and ends with Operation 4. The rate shown with each box represents the effective capacity of that operation.

a. Determine the capacity of this process.

b. Which of the following three actions would yield the greatest increase in process capacity? (i) increase the capacity of Operation 1 by 15 percent; (ii) increase the capacity of Operation 2 by 10 percent; or (iii) increase the capacity of Operation 3 by 10 percent.

Diagram for Problem 22

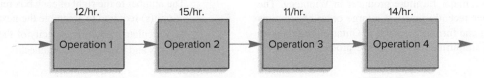

LO1 **23.** The mine hoist at a Mosaic Potash mine and mill in Saskatchewan had the following performance measures during a month.[5] Determine the utilization of the hoist.

> Total available time = 24 hours a day × 30 days × 60 minutes per hour = 43,200 minutes
>
> Scheduled hoist downtime (due to planned maintenance) = 5,820 minutes
>
> Unscheduled hoist downtime (due to breakdown) = 1,530 minutes

Idle time due to upstream (mine) delays (mine bin empty) = 2,817 minutes

Idle time due to downstream (mill) delays (mill bin full) = 4,578 minutes

LO2 **24.** Given the following diagram,
   a. What is the capacity of this process?
   b. If the capacity of one operation could be increased in order to increase the output of the process, which operation should it be, and what amount of increase? *Note:* The upper line and lower line both produce the same product.

Diagram for Problem 24

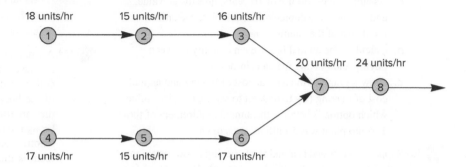

LO2 **25.** Find the capacity of this process:

Diagram for Problem 25

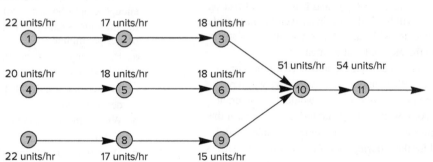

LO2 **26.** The following diagram describes a service process where customers go through either of two parallel sets of three steps and then merge into a single line for two final steps. The capacity of each step is shown on the diagram.
   a. What is the current capacity of the entire process?

   b. If you could increase the capacity of only one operation through process improvement efforts, which operation would you select, how much additional capacity would you strive for, and what would be the resulting capacity of the process?

Diagram for Problem 26

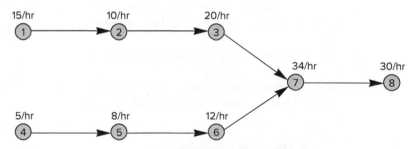

LO2 ***27.** Jamesco is a major furniture producer in Winnipeg. The company has recently received a large order of armoires from a high-end furniture reseller in Ontario. The diagram below is a simplified version of the production process.

The number to the right of each box represents the number of unit(s) required to assemble the next item.
   a. Calculate the hourly capacity of the production process and identify the bottleneck.

---

[5] R. Chadha, "Hoist Help," *Quality Progress*, February 2014, 47(2), 34–39.

Diagram for Problem 27

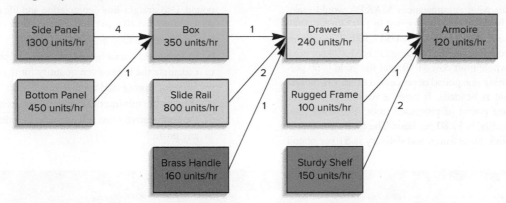

b. If the capacity of the bottleneck in part *a* is doubled, what is the new hourly capacity and bottleneck?

c. If the capacity of the bottleneck in part *b* is increased by 50 percent, what is the new hourly capacity and bottleneck?

d. If any non-bottleneck process is increased, will the capacity of the assembly line ever increase?

LO2 *28. The diagram below represents a simplified version of the steel production process at a steel mill and the capacity of each operation in tonnes per day (tpd). The outputs from iron ore processing, limestone processing, and coking coal oven need to be combined in a ratio of 4:1:2 into the blast furnace. Output of blast furnace equals the output of iron ore processing; limestone and coke are only for purifying and burning. The outputs from the blast furnace and recycled steel need to be combined in a ratio of 2:1 for the oxygen furnace. Output of oxygen furnace = Output of blast furnace + Output of recycled steel. The remaining processes have a ratio of 1:1 with their downstream process.

a. Calculate the daily capacity of the production process and identify the bottleneck.

b. If the capacity of the bottleneck in part *a* is increased by 50 percent, what is the new daily capacity and bottleneck?

c. What further improvements are needed to bring plant production to 2,700 tpd?

Diagram for Problem 28

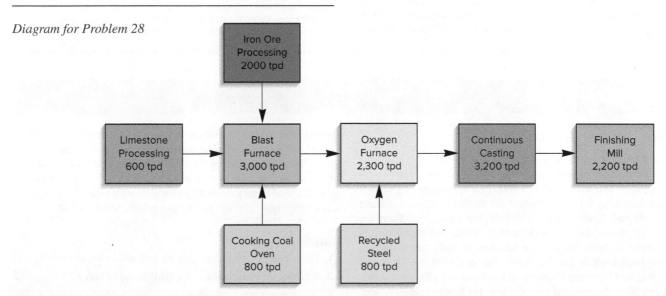

LO3 29. A new piece of equipment will cost $12,000 and will result in a reduced operation cost of $1,500 per year. What will the payback time be in years?

LO3 30. A new machine will cost $18,000, but results in savings of $2,400 per year. What will the payback time be in years?

LO3 31. Remodelling an office will cost $25,000 and will generate savings of $3,000 the first year, $4,000 the second year, and $5,000 per year thereafter. How long will it take to recoup the initial cost of remodelling?

LO3 32. Mountain Aquaculture and Producers Association (MA&PA) is a small trout producers' cooperative in West Virginia.[6] Its main product is boned, head-removed trout sold to local stores. Unfortunately, the cooperative has not made any profit since it was started in 1992 and has to rely

[6] R. M. Fincham. A Break-Even Analysis of Trout Processing in West Virginia: A Case Study Approach, M.S. thesis, West Virginia University, 2001.

on donations and government grants. The manager wants to know under what circumstances MA&PA would make a profit. The building was constructed in 1992 for $49,000, and the processing equipment cost $37,500. The utilities cost $6,800 per year, and the building tax is $1,100 per year. A pound of whole trout cost $1.40, and the yield is 60 percent (i.e., to make one pound of processed trout, 1.67 pound of whole trout is needed). It takes a worker 12 minutes to produce one pound of processed trout. The wage rate, including benefits, is $7.80 per hour. The total cost of processing supplies, advertising, and delivery is $1 per pound of processed trout. The processed trout is sold for $6.00 per pound. Use straight-line depreciation and life of 20 years for the building and 10 years for the processing equipment.

a. Calculate the total annual fixed cost.
b. Calculate the variable cost per pound of processed trout.
c. Calculate the break-even quantity for the number of pounds of processed trout sold per year.
d. What is the minimum amount of processed trout that the cooperative must sell per year in order to make any profit?

 MINI-CASE

W. C. Wood

W. C. Wood was the largest freezer manufacturer in Canada. It had two plants in Guelph, Ontario; one in the United States; and another in Mexico. In the early 2000s, some appliance manufacturers, such as Whirlpool, had converted from using cardboard box packaging to using plastic stretch wrap with corner padding (called clear-view packaging). The VP of manufacturing was wondering whether to also convert. The damage warranty rate for cardboard box packaging (1–3 percent depending on the type of freezer) was expected to remain the same with clear-view packaging. For simplicity, we consider only one of the Guelph plants with one line. Whereas a cardboard box required two workers to box an appliance, the clear-view packaging would be automated. Labour and material costs would be reduced by $0.50 and $1.50 per unit, respectively. However, electricity costs would increase by $10,000 per year. The stretch wrap equipment by MSK Covertech cost $130,000. The fitting of corner posts on each freezer required another machine, which cost $140,000. In addition, all lift truck arms had to be converted to clamp type at a total cost of $30,000.

Questions

a. What is the total variable cost saving per freezer?
b. What is the total investment cost per year if all pieces of equipment are expected to last 10 years (use straight-line depreciation)?
c. How many freezers per year should the Guelph plant produce in order to break even in the clear-view packaging conversion?

Sources: http://www.hp.com/hpinfo/newsroom/press_kits/2008/ipgcon-ference/images/clear-view-packaging-horizontal.jpg; http://www.tradekorea.com/product-detail/P00290675/Bale_clamp.html.

 MINI-CASE

Shoes for Moos

Jim Wells, the owner of a farm supply store in Elmira, Ontario, was thinking of introducing a new product: shoes for cows with foot (hoof) infection (rot). Jim had been approached by several farmers asking for it. He studied the market and found nothing durable and effective at the $40–$100 per shoe range. There are over 13 million dairy cows in North America, and approximately 2 percent of them develop foot infection annually (beef cows are slaughtered when this happens). Jim designed the shoe and approached Kaufman Footwear in Kitchener to make some prototypes. Next, he gave the prototypes to his farmer friends to test. After one year of design improvements, Jim was wondering whether to go ahead with marketing of the shoe. The cost of the mould to be used by the shoe factory was $10,000, and the mould was expected to last five years (use straight-line depreciation). The cost of Jim's time promoting the shoe, including attending farm shows, was approximately $10,000 per year. The cost of shoe inventory and space in Jim's store was estimated to be $1,000 per year. The shoe factory wanted $20 per shoe with a minimum order size of 100 shoes. Jim was thinking of pricing a shoe at $40.

Questions

1. How many shoes per year must Jim sell to break even?
2. What is the annual cost at the BEP found in part *a?*
3. If Jim could sell 2,000 shoes per year, should he go ahead with this venture? Why?

Source: Shoes for Moos, http://www.youtube.com/watch?v=VIqAQf4j7ql.

To access "Decision Analysis," the supplement to Chapter 5, please visit *Connect2*.

Chapter 6
Process Design and Facility Layout

Bloomberg/Getty Images

Ford F150 had been the best selling vehicle in North America for decades, so Ford did not have to change it much. Nevertheless, in order to reduce its weight and increase its fuel mileage, Ford took a big chance in 2015 by changing many of its body panels, including the cargo bed, from steel to high-strength aluminum. The 700 pound weight reduction was approximately 15 percent of the total weight of F150. Previously only the hood was made of aluminum. Another advantage of aluminum is that it is corrosion-resistant.

Ford decided to insource many of the stampings to control the production quality. This required new press lines. Also, aluminum has a much lower melting point than steel and therefore cannot be spot welded consistently. Just like aircraft which are made of aluminum, the new F150 required 2,000 rivets (instead of 5,000 spot welds) to join the pieces together. This required robots that rivet instead of weld. Ford decided to replace the hundreds of old floor-mounted spot-welding robots with 500 six-axis smaller robots that are mounted on overhead rails. According to the chief engineer for body construction, "Without welding guns, the plant is now quieter and cleaner, and we don't have to worry about all the welding sparks and splatter. I no longer end up with lots of holes in my shirts."

Other than self-piercing rivets, Ford uses flow-drill screws when there is limited access to the back side of a panel. Also, more than 350 feet of structural adhesive is used throughout the F150 body to add strength and block noise and moisture.

The factory changeover took five years to plan and only one month to implement on a fast-track basis, and cost over a billion dollars. Also, the aluminum supplier Alcoa had to find a new way to mass-produce stronger but more formable aluminum sheets. Another supplier was selected to recycle aluminum scraps.

Sources: https://www.bloomberg.com/news/articles/2015-10-19/ford-s-f-150-lots-of-aluminum-plenty -of-awesome; http://www.assemblymag.com/articles/92728-assembling-fords-aluminum-wonder -truck;http://www.assemblymag.com/articles/92764-video-how-the-new-f-150-is-assembled.

(L01) Introduction and Production Process Types

All work in organizations is performed as part of some process. A *process* is a sequence of activities, usually performed by more than one person, which achieves a desired result. There are three types of processes in an organization: core, support, and managerial.

A **core process** is a customer-ending process that must exist for the organization to function properly. Core processes include fulfilling customer orders, producing products, designing/ developing products, servicing customers, and purchasing supplies.

A **support process** is a process that assists the operations of an organization. Support processes include recruiting and training employees, purchasing and maintaining equipment, paying invoices, issuing invoices, and receiving payment. Note that the latter three processes can be part of larger core processes of purchasing and order fulfillment.

A **managerial process** is a process that manages the operations of an organization, including setting goals, planning, controlling, and leading. Managerial processes include strategic and tactical planning, and daily management of core and support processes.

The way an organization divides its activities into processes is called **enterprise/organization architecture.** The architecture is dynamic as the business environment changes. It also depends on the industry in which the company operates. For example, Coors' core processes[1] include: source, manufacture, deliver, develop brand, manage product life cycle, manage key accounts, support customers, and manage sales performance; Coors' support processes include HR, IT, legal, finance, and safety/health/environment; and Coors' managerial processes include strategic management and planning of the above processes.

In contrast, Deere's enterprise business model[2] consists of these core processes: customer acquisition, product development, order fulfillment, and customer support; support/enabling processes: channel management, supply management, HR, IT, and business acquisition; and managerial processes of leadership and business measurement.

Note that a large process is usually broken down into sub-processes. For example, Deere's customer support[3] includes product setup/delivery, adjust-repair-replace, parts procurement, dealer development, contact management, and problem resolution processes. In turn, contact management[4] includes request acknowledgement, assessment, response, and follow-up activities.

Process design determines the structure of a process—that is, the sequence of operations (the workflow), resources, and controls needed for a particular process. In this chapter, we will mainly focus on design of production/service processes.

Production/service process design has major implications for layout of facilities and design of work/jobs. It is important because it determines the efficiency and effectiveness of how work is done in the organization. It occurs as a matter of course when new products are being designed or existing

core process A customer-ending process that must exist for the organization to function properly.

support process A process that assists the operations of an organization.

managerial process A process that manages the operations of an organization, including setting goals, planning, controlling, and leading.

enterprise/organization architecture The way an organization divides its activities into processes.

process design Determining the structure of a process—that is, the sequence of operations (the workflow), resources, and controls needed for a particular process.

---

[1] Business Process Management, American Productivity & Quality Center, 2005, Figure 33.
[2] Ibid, Figure 41.
[3] Ibid, Figure 43.
[4] Ibid, Figure 44.

products are redesigned. However, it also occurs due to technological changes in equipment and material, and methods/quality improvement.

The very first step in production/service process design is to consider whether to **make or buy** some or all of a product or a segment of the production/service process. If a decision is made to buy a part/product or a segment of the production/service process, this eliminates the need to produce the part/product or perform that segment of production/service process in-house. Make-or-buy decisions, also called insourcing/outsourcing, are often strategic, based on existing or desired core capabilities. Other factors include available capacity, quality, whether demand is steady or temporary, the secrecy of technology, and cost.

Another important consideration for manufacturing processes is the use of inventories. Three **production/inventory strategies** are: make-to-stock, make-to-order, and assemble-to-order.

- **Make-to-stock** strategy means producing and holding items in inventory for fast delivery to customers. This reduces purchase lead time for customers. This strategy is feasible for standardized products that have high predictable demand.
- **Make-to-order** strategy means producing a variety of products to customer specifications. This usually involves low-demand customized products produced with complex but flexible processes resulting in long production lead time.
- **Assemble-to-order** strategy means producing a large variety of products after customer orders are received from few standardized sub-assemblies and components which are held in inventory. This results in fast delivery as well as high variety. The large number of possible options with hard-to-predict demand makes stocking finished products uneconomical. Final assembly is postponed until an actual order for the final product is received.

Process design and facility layout (i.e., the arrangement of the workplace) are closely tied, and for that reason these two topics are presented in a single chapter. The first part of this chapter covers basic production process types, technology/automation, and process design methodology, whereas the second part is devoted to types of layout, assembly-line balancing, and designing process (functional) layouts.

Every production process is different because the choice of operations depends on the material used and the product's shape, size, quantity, and variety. However, there are certain similarities between production processes based on quantity and variety of the products that are produced by the process, and the flexibility of the process. This enables us to classify production processes into four basic types: job shop, batch, repetitive (assembly line), and continuous. Projects are discussed in Chapter 17.

Job Shop

A **job shop** process is used when a low quantity of high-variety customized goods or services will be needed. The process is *intermittent*; work shifts from one small job to the next, each with somewhat different requirements. High flexibility of equipment and skilled workers are important characteristics of a job shop. A manufacturing example of a job shop is the process used by a custom spring maker that is able to produce one-of-a-kind springs. A service example is the process used in the surgery department of a hospital that is able to perform a variety of procedures.

The managerial challenge in a job shop is to schedule the jobs so that the due dates are met and the resources are utilized as much as possible.

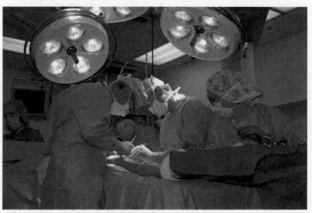

A job shop process: A hospital medical team performs a diagnostic procedure involving a cardiac catheterization.
©Royalty-Free/Corbis

make or buy Decide whether to make a part or product in-house or to buy it or a segment of the production/service process from another company.

production/inventory strategies Approaches for using inventories in manufacturing processes: make-to-stock, make-to-order, and assemble-to-order.

make-to-stock Producing and holding items in inventory for fast delivery to customers.

make-to-order Producing a variety of products to customer specifications.

assemble-to-order Producing a large variety of products after customer orders are received from few standardized sub-assemblies and components which are held in inventory.

job shop A process type used when a low quantity of high-variety customized goods or services is needed.

EXAMPLE 6-1 ▶

Hi-Bek Precision Spring company is a small job shop located in the centre of Hamilton, Ontario. Owned and operated by R.J. Hick, Hi-Bek fills a niche market, making custom springs for a variety of distributors and manufacturers, such as the springs in Jolly Jumper® baby exercisers, Delta faucet products, and chain-link fence. Each spring requires a unique design.

Many of Hi-Bek's customers specify the design of the spring they need, sending a blueprint or a sample of the spring with their request, which includes (1) number of pieces desired (varying anywhere from 50 to 500,000 units); (2) type of material required, gauge of wire, any finishing required, etc.; and (3) the date by which the order is required.

All of these factors are taken into consideration by Hick, who personally quotes on all orders. Naturally, it is easier for Hick to quote on jobs that Hi-Bek has done before. The quoted price is based on cost of raw material, time required to run the job, and the delivery dates (rush orders command higher margins).

After a quote has been accepted by a customer, the job order is sent to the shop floor. The shop operates from 7:30 a.m. to 5:00 p.m., Monday to Friday, employing between six and nine workers depending on the demand. Hick handles prioritization of orders and scheduling of machines and personnel along with the shop foreman. Production on a given job begins with the setup of the appropriate machine. Coiling machines can be custom configured for specific jobs, allowing for alterations to the gauge (thickness) and type of wire, the circumference and length of the spring, the number of coils in the spring, and the length of the spring ends. As well, the machine can be set to wind springs at varying speeds, depending on the level of quality required. Depending on the complexity of the product, a job being run in the machine may or may not require the full-time attention of an operator, and the time required for quality checking by the operator and foreman will vary accordingly. The setup of the job will cost the customer between $140 and $300, depending on complexity, and the skilled labour required to set up the job will cost $35 to $40 per hour. As well, customers are charged a "burden rate"—essentially a cost per hour for use of the machine during setup—of about $12 per hour. Finally, customers are charged for the operator's time to process the job, anywhere from $18 to $40 per hour.

Some jobs are quite simple, and springs are transported directly from the coiling machine to the oven on large metal racks where the steel is heated to temper it, giving the spring its tension (or its bounce, in the case of compression springs). Different springs require different temperatures (from 120°C for phosphor bronze—a low grade of wire—to 315°C for stainless steel), and a different length of time in the oven. The oven must also be scheduled for use for each individual job.

In the simplest jobs, after cooling, the springs can be packaged and arranged for shipping. In most cases, however, there are additional steps both before and after firing in the furnace.

Before firing, some springs require precision adjustments for their custom usage. The coiled springs are transported from the coiling machine to the precision-adjustment area of the shop in metal pails or large plastic drums, depending on the size of the job. An extension spring (the kind you stretch) or a torsion spring (the kind you twist) may require particularly crafted ends to suit its use. Each of these adjustments is done by hand, using a grinder or a press set for the specific job. Like the coiling machine, each press requires a certain amount of setup time and time for a shop worker to actually make the adjustments, all of which is factored into the price of the order. In the case of a press, a customer will be billed the same $140 to $300 per hour for setup though the customer is typically charged less for the labour required in the actual adjustment ($18 to $20 per hour) and the burden rate for the press (about $2 per hour).

Following the furnace, springs may undergo grinding or finishing, for either practical or aesthetic reasons. In some cases, springs are electroplated with zinc. This is a complex process involving electricity and acid or alkaline solutions, and for this reason is outsourced. Depending on the needs of the job, it may be outsourced to a company as near as Cambridge, Ontario (60 km away), or as far as Buffalo, NY (more than 100 km away). In other cases, springs are coated with oil or painted with "Black Japan" (a coating of linseed oil and Gilsonite varnish) for durability, depending on their eventual use. Unlike electroplating, these operations can be done in-house at a competitive rate.

Finally, the product is packaged and readied to be shipped. This, too, can take a good deal of time (10,000 springs can take a half day or more to pack).

The layout of the shop is shown in the following diagram on the left and the production process for three types of springs on the right. The colours and icons correspond to the departments of the shop.

Job A is the type of compression spring used inside a ballpoint pen. Here, after the coiling machine is set up, the springs are wound, then heat-treated in the furnace and shipped to the customer.

Job B is a typical machine spring, which undergoes the same basic steps as the ballpoint pen spring, but has its ends

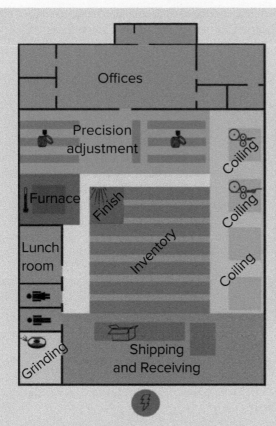

ground and is coated with oil in the finishing stage to add durability to the spring before shipping.

Job C is Jolly Jumper® springs. In this case, the coiling machine requires a special setup, because the Jolly Jumper®

springs require tapered ends. After this, each spring must be precision adjusted to give it a specially looped end. It is heat treated, but before shipping is sent to an outside company to be electroplated. The springs then are returned to Hi-Bek and are shipped to the customer.

Batch

Batch process is used when a moderate quantity/volume and variety of goods or services is desired, and a batch (lot) is made at a time. The equipment need not be as flexible as in a job shop, but process is still intermittent. The skill level of workers doesn't need to be as high as in a job shop because there is less variety in the jobs. Manufacturing examples of batch process include the process used by small bakeries that make bread, cakes, or cookies in batches; large restaurants that make batches of dishes and desserts; breweries; and clothing manufacturers. Service examples include movie theatres that show a movie to a group (batch) of people, and airlines that carry a planeload (batch) of people from airport to airport.

> **batch process** Used when a moderate quantity and variety of goods or services is desired, and a batch (lot) of product is made at a time.

The managerial challenge in a batch process is scheduling batches in

A batch process: Menu items are prepared in batches, in the kitchen of a large restaurant.

©Don Tremain/Photodisc/Getty Images RF

order to meet planned production and demand while utilizing the resources at a high level. Capacity issues and technology management are more important than in job shops.

EXAMPLE 6-2 ▶

Great Western Brewing Company (GWB) was formed in 1989 when Molson decided to close its Saskatoon brewery. Its employees bought the plant and reopened it as a private company. GWB produces lager, light, Pilsner, Pilsner Light, and six other specialty beers, and packages them in glass and plastic bottles, cans, and kegs.

The main ingredient in beer is malt, which is partially sprouted barley. Other ingredients are grains such as corn or wheat, and hops, which produces its bitter taste.

The production process for beer can be divided into four stages: brewing, fermentation, finishing, and packaging. Brewing starts with mixing ground malt and water in the mash mixer and heating it to 150°F. Then, the mash (solid) and the wort (malt sugar liquid) are separated (by filtering) in the lauter tun. Next, the wort is boiled in the brew kettle for approximately 1.5 hours while hops are added. Hops and other solids are separated from wort (by centrifuge) in the hot liquor tank. Then, the brew is aerated and cooled in the cold liquor tank. So far, the process has taken approximately five hours. The batch size in the brewing part of the process is approximately 20,000 litres.

Fermentation starts in one of the many fermenters where yeast is added. Yeast converts the wort sugar into alcohol and carbon dioxide (CO_2). Fermentation is complete in nine days and the fermented beer is now cooled and pumped into one of many primary aging tanks. The yeast, which settles in the fermenter, is recovered and reused in subsequent batches.

Finishing involves cold aging of the beer (at about 0°C) for a minimum of one week in a primary aging tank and then filtering and re-cooling it in a secondary aging tank where it rests a further week. The beer is then ready to be filtered and cooled again and pumped to a bright beer (packing) tank where it is now ready to be packaged. Carbon dioxide that has been collected during fermentation is injected into the beer each time it is moved, to ensure a specific level of carbon dioxide in the final product.

The bottles used are empty bottles collected from liquor stores. They are washed, machine inspected, filled with beer, and crowned. Then they move slowly through a pasteurizer, and are labelled, packed, and palletized (approximately 100 cases per pallet). The canning process is similar but uses only new cans, which do not require washing or labelling. GWB's packaging capacity is 360 bottles and 480 cans per minute. Overall capacity of GWB is 45 million litres of beer per year.

Different types of beer differ in terms of taste, colour, and alcohol content. These are influenced by the ingredients, temperature, and length of each step of the process, yeast, hops, separation, and filtration. The chemistry of brewing is very complex and is still not fully understood. The equipment is specialized, with all beer following the same processing route. The remotely activated pumps and gauges are controlled by a central control room. Changeover from one type of beer to another requires washing the tanks, which takes approximately half an hour. The process flow diagram and plant floor plan (layout) are displayed on the next page.

The brew kettle. *The lauter tun.*

All Photos: Photos courtesy of the Great Western Brewing Company, Saskatoon, SK, Canada

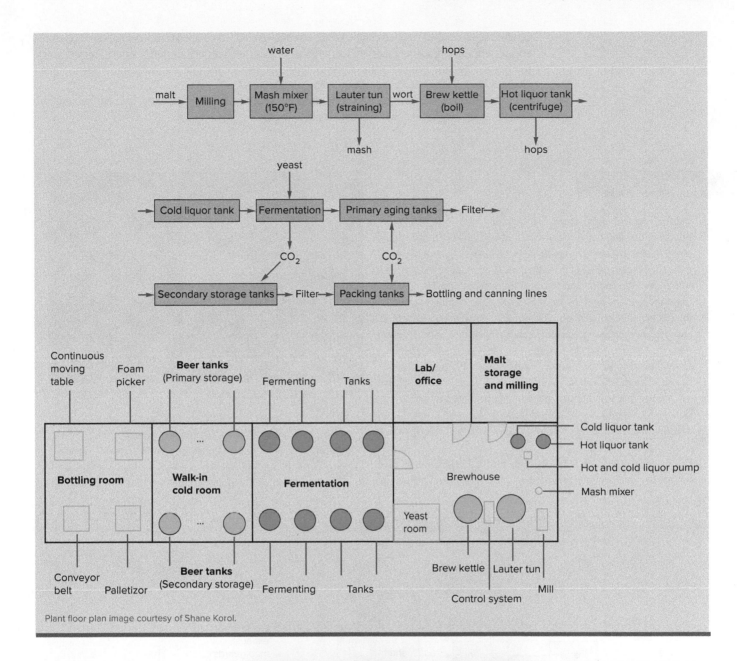

Plant floor plan image courtesy of Shane Korol.

Repetitive

When higher quantities of more standardized goods or services are needed and each unit follows the same production sequence, **repetitive process** is used. The standardized output means only slight flexibility of equipment is needed. Skill of workers is generally low. Examples of this type of process include a **production line** and an **assembly line**. A production line is a sequence of machines/workstations that perform operations on a part/product. An assembly line is a production line where parts are added to a

A repetitive process: Motorcycles on an assembly line with parts added in a sequential order.

©Keith Dannemiller/Corbis

repetitive process Used when higher quantities of more standardized goods or services are needed, and each unit follows the same production sequence.

production line A sequence of machines/workstations that perform operations on a part/product.

assembly line A production line where parts are added to a product sequentially.

product sequentially. The line can be either *machine-paced* (same speed) or *worker-paced* (variable speed). Familiar products made by this type of process include automobiles, trucks, motorcycles, television sets, and computers. Examples of repetitive service include automatic car washes, cafeteria lines, and ticket collectors at sports events and concerts.

The managerial challenges in a production/assembly line are capacity balance, technology management, quality, and materials management.

EXAMPLE 6-3 ▶

Paccar Trucks builds some of its high-end Kenworth and Peterbilt medium- and heavy-duty trucks at its 360,000 ft² assembly plant in Sainte-Thérèse, Quebec. A truck has two major sub-assemblies: chassis and cab. The chassis is made up of the bottom frame, the engine and power train, wheels, etc. The Quebec plant receives its engines from Paccar's U.S. engine plants and Paccar buys the other major components from its suppliers. The cab and hood are purchased already fabricated. The Quebec plant paints them and stores them in a buffer area on the second floor. This is to let the paint dry and because it is more efficient to use a batch process for painting (i.e., a large number of the same colour cabs and hoods are painted one after another). Sixty hoods and 30 cabs can be stored in the buffer area. Typically, a cab and hood are painted two to five days before they are used.

Four out of every five trucks are white. However, the different interior, engine, chassis length, and brand result in

approximately 40 different products. In addition, several options are available. Paccar constantly introduces new models offering better technologies such as no-idle solution (to provide heating or cooling to the sleeper cabin while the truck engine

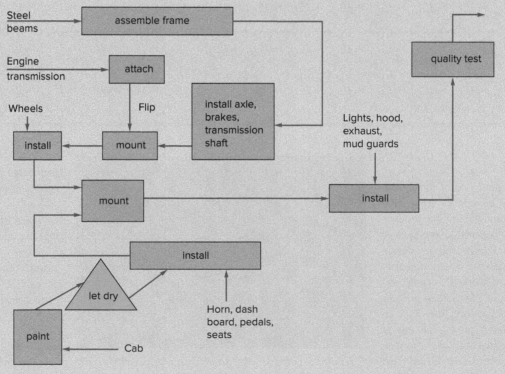

Based on: T. Feare, "Truck Plant Shifts Into Overdrive," *Modern Materials Handling*, 55(2), February 2000, pp. 73–76.

is turned off) and hybrid engines (built by Eaton Corporation of Cleveland). The equipment is specialized but flexible. Most material handling is by overhead conveyors. Workers appreciate this in the frame shop where they assemble beams that are heavy (1–2.5 tonnes) and long (6–13 metres). The overhead conveyors also save floor space.

The parts and components are received just in time and delivered straight to the point of use. There are 31 receiving docks near the points of use. The two sub-assembly lines (chassis and cab) join in the middle of the left side of the plant and the truck is hauled to the final assembly and test area on the right. Capacity of the plant is 40 trucks per eight-hour shift, which means that, at capacity, every 12 minutes a truck moves up one workstation. The Quebec plant periodically changes its employment level to match its production with North American demand for its trucks. In recent years, 60 to 70 trucks have been assembled per day during two shifts.

Continuous

When a very high volume of highly standardized output is desired, and the product is in continuous motion during production, **continuous process** is used. There is almost no variety in output and, hence, no need for equipment flexibility. As in repetitive process, workers are generally low skilled (except for maintenance technicians). Product is also usually continuous (i.e., it cannot be counted). Examples of products made using continuous process include gasoline, steel, paper, sugar, flour, and salt. Continuous services include utilities and the Internet.

> **continuous process** Used when a high volume of highly standardized output is required, and the product is in continuous motion during production.

A continuous process: An oil refinery performs a continuous process, mixing and separating crude oil into gasoline, fuel oil, jet fuel, and some other products.
©Royalty-Free/CORBIS

The managerial challenges in a continuous process are the same as in a repetitive process, but because of faster speed of production, greater care is required for automated control of the flow, and start and stop of production are more challenging.

Redpath Sugar Refinery is located on the Toronto waterfront. The refinery, Canada's largest, is owned by ASR Group, employs 250 people, and runs 24 hours a day, seven days a week.

Sugar cane is grown on large plantations in Latin America and processed in huge mills close to the fields by crushing the cane stalks and extracting the juice (sap). Boiling the juice crystallizes it into "raw sugar," which is purchased by Redpath Sugar and shipped to Toronto in large cargo ships.

Raw sugar is brought to the refinery in loads of up to 25,000 tonnes (the limit of ships passing through the St. Lawrence Seaway) and unloaded into a hopper and then transferred by conveyor belt to the refinery's raw sugar shed. This building has a capacity of 65,000 tonnes and has a floor the size of two football fields. This is necessary because the seaway closes in the winter (December to March) and raw sugar must be brought in and stored before then to ensure continuous production year-round.

Although the raw sugar is of a relatively high quality, it still contains a residue of original cane-trash, ash, and waxes, as well as any additional solids or other impurities that might have contaminated the cargo during transportation. Refining is designed to remove all of these unwanted elements and to leave only pure sucrose at the end.

The "mingler."
Courtesy of Redpath Sugar, Ltd.

Vacuum vessels used for recrystallization.
Courtesy of Redpath Sugar, Ltd.

The Redpath Sugar Refinery in Toronto, Ontario.
Courtesy of Redpath Sugar, Ltd.

The process commences with the transfer of the raw sugar into the refinery building, where it is weighed and fed into a mixing trough called a "mingler." Blended together with a solution of molasses and warm water, the resultant slurry ("magma") is spun at high speed in one of a set of oversized washing machines ("affination centrifugals"). The spun-off syrup is recycled, while the crystal ("washed raw sugar") is melted and dissolved in hot water to produce a syrup ("raw liquor"), which is then passed through a sequence of filters to remove the impurities.

Starting with a simple mechanical sieve ("strainer") that removes the larger visible solids, the liquor passes through a "carbonation" and "sweetland" system, whereby chalk (calcium carbonate) encapsulates the remaining solids, making them larger so that they can be removed by fine cloth filters in the sweetland presses. The final filtration, to remove the undesirable yellow colouration in the liquor, is done by the use of absorption in large tanks filled with commercial resin and carbon-based filtration agents, similar to those used in municipal water purification systems. The end result of this series of filtrations is a clear, colourless syrup ("fine liquor") consisting of nothing but sucrose and water.

The fine liquor is now recrystallized by boiling it for an hour under vacuum. The resultant "white massecuite" (a combination of recrystallized sucrose, uncrystallized sucrose syrup, and water) is spun in the "white sugar centrifugals" to separate the liquid from the crystals. While the syrups are recycled to create additional crystals, the crystals of pure white sucrose are dried in large rotary dryers ("granulators") to reduce their moisture content to less than 0.03 percent.

The granular sugar is either packaged in a range of weights or sold in larger "bulk" loads and shipped out in road or rail tanker loads (of up to 100 tonnes) for further use in a variety of industrial and commercial applications.

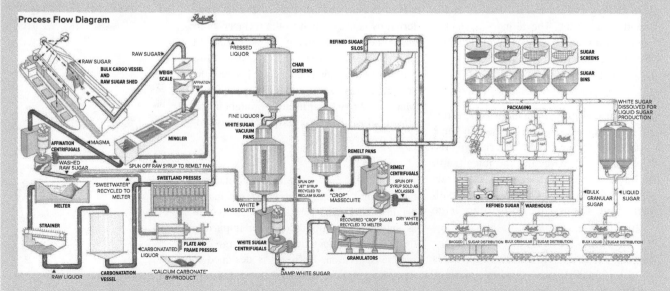

Courtesy of Redpath Sugar, Ltd.

	Job Shop	Batch	Repetitive/Assembly	Continuous
Product variety	Customized	Semi-standardized	Standardized	Highly standardized
Quantity/volume	Low	Low–moderate	High	Very high
Equipment flexibility	Very high	Moderate	Low	Very low
Equipment technology	General purpose (adjustable)	⟶		Special
Scale of equipment	Many small units	⟶		One large unit
Equipment arranged by	Function	⟶		Product need
Linking of process steps	Loose	⟶		Tight
Flexibility	High	⟶		Low
Operation of equipment	Intermittent (stop & go)	⟶		Continuous
Worker skill level	High	⟶		Low
Flow pattern	Jumbled	⟶		Linear
Fixed cost	Low	⟶		High
Variable cost	High	⟶		Low
Challenge	Scheduling	⟶		Capacity, technology
Inventory	Mostly work-in-process	⟶		Mostly raw material
Notion of capacity	Vague	⟶		Clear

▲ TABLE 6-1

Major characteristics of the four types of production process.

Comparison of Production Process Types

Table 6-1 provides an overview of major characteristics of the four types of production process. Note that by the nature of the market, higher variety implies smaller demand for each variation, and lower variety implies larger demand for each variation.

Selecting a Production Process Type

The ideal is to have production process capabilities such as equipment flexibility, linkages (loose vs. automated and tight), and flow (jumbled vs. one dominant) match product requirements such as product variety and quantity/volume. This relationship is displayed as the shaded main diagonal of the **product–process matrix** of Figure 6-1.

Failure to match product requirements and production process characteristics can result in inefficiencies and higher costs than are necessary, perhaps creating a competitive disadvantage. For example, using a batch process when there is only one product is usually inefficient because the process does not use enough automation. On the other hand, when there are many products produced on a continuous or repetitive process, the frequent product switches will result in long changeover times, which are nonproductive. Recently, however, some companies have managed to handle high

product–process matrix A matrix that shows the combination of a product's quantity and variety, and the flexibility of the processes that make it.

◀ FIGURE 6-1

The product–process matrix.

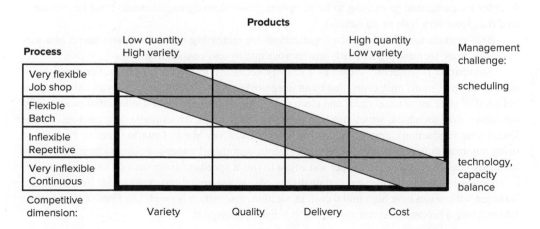

quantity and high variety on the same process (e.g., the "made-for you" system of McDonald's or Dell Computer's mass customization).

Another consideration is that products often go through a *life cycle* that begins with low quantity and increases as the product becomes better known. When that happens, a manager must know when to shift from one type of production process (e.g., job shop) to the next (e.g., batch).

The processes discussed above do not always exist in their "pure" forms. It is not unusual to find hybrid processes—processes that have elements of other process types embedded in them.

Within each production process, many individual operations are performed. The choice of operations used in a process depends on nature, shape, size, quantity, variety, and other competitive attributes of the products to be produced by the process. Examples of types of materials include metal, plastic, glass, wood, food ingredients, and yarn. Examples of shape include round, square, and with cavity. Examples of operations include forming (e.g., casting, forging), reshaping (e.g., drilling, cutting, bending, cold-drawing), and assembly (e.g., welding, bolting, gluing).

 # Technology

Technology is application of scientific discoveries to the development and innovation of goods and services and/or the processes that produce them.

> **technology** Application of scientific discoveries to the development and improvement of goods and services and/or the processes that produce them.

Process technology and information technology can have a major impact on costs, productivity, and competitiveness (including speed of delivery). *Process technology* includes robotics and automation on the factory floor. *Information technology (IT)* is the science and use of computers and other electronic equipment to store, process, and send information. This includes software such as enterprise resource planning (ERP), the use of bar codes to identify and track goods, data transmission, the Internet, email, and more.

To properly integrate technology into an organization, it is essential to understand what the technology will and won't do. Also, there are economic considerations (initial cost, space, cashflow, maintenance, consultants), integration considerations (cost, time, resources), and human considerations (training, safety, job loss).

Automation

Automation is using machinery/equipment with sensing and control devices that enable it to operate automatically (i.e., automation is automatic control). If a company decides to automate, the next question is by how much. Automation can range from factories that are completely automated to a single automated operation.

> **automation** Using machinery/equipment with sensing and control devices that enable it to operate automatically.

Automation offers a number of advantages over human labour. It has low variability, whereas it is difficult for a human to perform a task in exactly the same way, rapidly, and on a repetitive basis. In a production setting, variability is detrimental to quality and to meeting schedules. Moreover, automated machines do not get bored or distracted or injured, nor do they go on strike, ask for higher wages, or file labour grievances. Still another advantage of automation is reduction of variable costs. In order for automated processing to be an option, job-processing requirements must be *standardized* (i.e., have very little or no variety).

Both manufacturing and service organizations are increasing their use of automation as a way to reduce costs, increase productivity, and improve quality and consistency.

Automation is frequently touted as a strategy necessary for competitiveness. For example, in steel-making, a "mini" mill, controlled by an integrated computer system, produces an uninterrupted hot band of steel using scrap metal and electrical charge. Mini-mills have a substantial productivity advantage over foundries, which use iron ore in blast furnaces. An example of a mini-mill is the Direct Strip Production Complex of Algoma Steel in Sault Ste. Marie, Ontario. Another example of using automation for competitiveness is the gigantic automated paper-making machines that automatically sense the thickness of paper and adjust to run at speeds of more than 60 km per hour.

http://www.essarsteelalgoma
.com/facilities/dspc

However, automation also has certain disadvantages and limitations compared to human labour. To begin with, it can have high initial cost. In addition, automation is much less flexible than human labour. Once a process has been automated, it is hard to change it.

Management must carefully examine whether to automate and to what degree to automate, so that everyone clearly understands all the ramifications. Also, much thought and careful planning are necessary to successfully integrate automation into a production process. Otherwise, it can lead to major problems. Moreover, automation has important implications not only for cost and flexibility, but also for the fit with overall strategic priorities. If the decision is made to automate, care must be taken to remove waste from the system prior to automating, to avoid building the waste into the automated system. Table 6-2 has a list of questions for organizations that are considering automation.

1. What level of automation is appropriate? (Some operations are more suited to being automated than others, so partial automation can be an option.)
2. How would automation affect the flexibility of a process?
3. How can automation projects be justified?
4. How should changes be managed?
5. What are the risks of automating?
6. What are some of the likely effects of implementing automation on market share, costs, quality, customer satisfaction, labour relations, and ongoing operations?

◀ **TABLE 6-2**

Automation questions.

Generally speaking, there are three kinds of automation: fixed, programmable, and flexible.

Fixed automation is the most rigid of the three types. The concept was perfected by the Ford Motor Company in the early 1900s, and it has been the cornerstone of mass production in the auto industry. It uses high-cost, specialized equipment for a fixed sequence of operations. Low unit cost and high volume are its primary advantages; minimal variety and the high cost of making major changes in either product or process are its primary limitations.

Programmable automation involves the use of high-cost, flexible equipment controlled by a computer program that provides both the sequence of operations and specific details about each operation. Changing the process is as easy (or difficult) as changing the computer program. This type of automation has the capability of economically producing a fairly wide variety of low-quantity products in small batches. Numerically controlled (N/C) machines and some robots are examples of programmable automation.

©Brand X Pictures/PunchStock/Getty Images RF

numerically controlled (N/C) machines Machines that perform operations by following mathematical processing instructions.

Numerically controlled (N/C) machines are programmed to follow a sequence of processing instructions based on mathematical relationships that tell the machine the details of the operations to be performed. The instructions are stored on a device such as a computer disk, magnetic tape, or microprocessor. Individual machines may have their own computer; this is referred to as *computer numerical control* (*CNC*). Or one computer may control a number of N/C machines, which is referred to as *direct numerical control* (*DNC*). The computer can directly use the dimensions of the item from the CAD software to accelerate machine programming. This is part of computer-aided manufacturing (CAM), which is using software to control machines. For an application, see the "Redline CNC" OM in Action.

⚙ OM in ACTION   www.redlinecnc.com

Redline CNC

Redline CNC is a small (7,000 ft²) machine shop in Surrey, British Columbia. To program its complex CNCs, Redline bought GibbsCAM software, which translates the CAD data for each part into machine instructions for tool paths. The CAM software is especially useful as Redline has started to use its CNCs unattended during the night. There is an automatic pallet changer on a track that loads and unloads the CNCs.

Source: http://www.westcam.co/successstories/downloads/Redline-MLR149.pdf.

Courtesy of Redline CNC, www.redlinecnc.com

industrial robot A machine consisting of a mechanical arm, a power supply, and a controller.

N/C machines are best used in cases where part geometry is complex, close tolerances are required, mistakes are costly, and there is the possibility of frequent changes in the design. The main limitations of N/C machines are the higher skill levels needed to program the machines and their high initial cost.

An **industrial robot** consists of three parts: a mechanical arm, a power supply, and a controller. Unlike movie versions of robots, which vaguely resemble human beings, industrial robots are much less glamorous and much less mobile; most robots are stationary except for their movable arms.

Aliments Putter's of Sainte-Sophie, Quebec, makes pickles. In its plant, it uses this Motoman palletizing robot to arrange its cases of pickle jars into pallets (which can then be moved efficiently by forklift). Before installing the robot, the palletizing step was a bottleneck in the process. Also, the heavy cases were difficult to handle manually.[5]
Aliments Putter's Food of Sainte-Sophie, QC

Robots can handle a wide variety of tasks including welding, assembly (mainly surface mounting for circuit boards), loading to and unloading from machines, painting, and testing. They relieve humans of heavy, dirty, and unsafe work and often eliminate drudgery.

Some uses of robots are fairly simple; others are much more complex. At the lowest level are robots that follow a fixed set of instructions. Next are programmable robots, which can repeat a set of movements after being led through the sequence. These robots "play back" a mechanical sequence much as a camcorder plays back a visual sequence. At the next level up are robots that follow instructions from a computer. At the top are robots that can recognize objects and make simple decisions. Robots can be powered pneumatically (by air), hydraulically (by fluids), or electrically.

Flexible automation evolved from programmable automation. It uses equipment that is more customizable than programmable automation. A key difference between the two is that flexible automation requires significantly less changeover time. This permits almost continuous operation of equipment *and* product variety without the need to produce in batches.

In practice, flexible automation is used in several different formats. A *machining centre* is a machine capable of performing a variety of machining operations such as milling, turning, and drilling on parts. The machine is numerically controlled.

[5] http://www.motoman.com/casestudies/acs-081.php.

A **flexible manufacturing system (FMS)** is a group of machining centres, controlled by a computer, with automatic material handling, robots, or other automated equipment. They can produce a variety of *similar* products. A FMS may have two to a dozen machines. They are designed to handle intermittent processing requirements with some of the benefits of automation and some of the flexibility of individual, or stand-alone, machines (e.g., N/C machines). A FMS offers reduced labour costs and more consistent quality compared with more traditional manufacturing methods, lower capital investment and higher flexibility than fixed automation, and relatively quick changeover time. A FMS appeals to managers who hope to achieve both the flexibility of job shop and the productivity of repetitive process.

A FMS also has some limitations. One is that this type of system can handle a relatively narrow range of part variety, so it must be used for a family of similar parts requiring similar machining. Also, a FMS requires longer planning and development times than more conventional processing equipment because of its increased complexity and cost. Furthermore, companies sometimes prefer a gradual approach to automation, but FMS represents a sizable chunk of technology.

The suitability of these systems to a production environment primarily depends on the variety and quantity of products. See Figure 6-2.

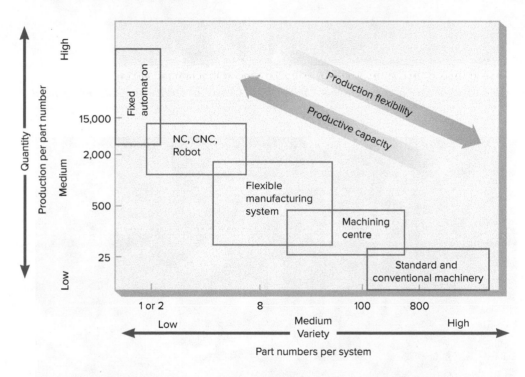

> **flexible manufacturing system (FMS)** A group of machining centres controlled by a computer, with automatic material handling, robots, or other automated equipment.

> ◀ **FIGURE 6-2**
>
> *Applicability of automated process technology based on product quantity and variety.*
>
> **Source:** Roger G. Schroeder, *Operations Management*, 1st ed., (Boston: McGraw-Hill/Irwin, 2000), p. 96. Reproduced with permission of The McGraw-Hill Companies, Inc.

Computer-integrated manufacturing (CIM) uses an integrated computer system to control the entire production process, and is linked to engineering, design, and production planning and control. More encompassing CIM systems can link order taking, scheduling, purchasing, inventory control, shop control, and distribution to manufacturing.

Service Automation. Automated services are becoming increasingly popular. Examples include ATMs, online banking, online journals and databases, electronic airplane tickets, self-service store checkout, automated toll payments, automatic meter reading, and automated package sorting and mail processing.

Green Technologies

A **green technology** is a technology that mitigates or reverses the effects of human activity on the environment. Companies are facing increasing pressure to use green technologies that are non-polluting while conserving energy and natural resources. Chemical hazards are to be eliminated, CO_2 (carbon footprint) is to be reduced, and wastes are reduced, eliminated, or recycled. An example in the grocery industry is the practice of charging customers for plastic bags to reduce their use.

> **computer-integrated manufacturing (CIM)** Uses an integrated computer system to control the entire production process, and is linked to engineering, design, and production planning and control.

> **green technology** A technology that mitigates or reverses the effects of human activity on the environment.

©Oleksiy Maksymenko/Alamy

PhotoInc/Getty Images RF

From self check-in at the airport to depositing a cheque from anywhere, automation speeds up service and reduces the need to stand in line.

McDonald's Canada is adding self-serve touch-screen kiosks inside restaurants, allowing diners to order custom-made burgers with a long list of new toppings. It's adding hostesses identified by the red bandanas around their necks who can help at the kiosks, and staff who deliver the ordered food to tables for those who don't want to stand around waiting for their food. The new program has been implemented across most of the 1,400 restaurants in Canada at a cost of about $200,000 per restaurant.

Source: https://www.thestar.com /business/2015/09/30/mcdonalds -canada-introduces-self-serve -ordering.html

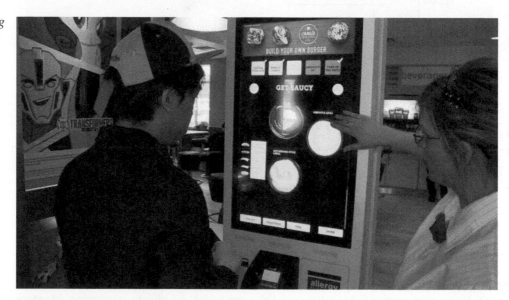

Permission of CTV-Ottawa and Bell Media Inc.

Another example is that companies such as Xerox and HP are recycling and reusing parts of their products. See, for example, the "Lavergne Groupe" OM in Action.

Coal-fired power plants are a major source of greenhouse gases, and many are using scrubbers to remove SO_2 emissions from their exhaust chimneys. The federal government has introduced a regulation to limit CO_2 emissions from these plants. An experimental method to reduce CO_2 emissions is carbon capture. The recent Boundary Dam power station carbon capture project[6] in Estevan, Saskatchewan, is testing the economic viability of carbon capture. However, the utilities plan to close most of these coal-fired plants and are investing in renewable resources such as solar panels and wind turbines, and in natural-gas powered plants.

---

[6] www.saskpower.com/our-power-future/carbon-capture-and-storage/

OM in ACTION   http://lavergne.ca/en/

Lavergne Groupe

Lavergne Groupe of Montreal is a relatively small plastics recycler, but its influence in plastics recycling has been enormous. Founder Jean Luc Lavergne started research on recycling PET (polyethylene terephthalate) plastic bottles in 1984. After decades of experiments, Lavergne has developed a unique plastics recycling expertise, so much so that in 2000 Hewlett-Packard partnered with Lavergne to recycle the PET plastics in its inkjet cartridges. However, it took more than a decade of experiments to get the quality of recycled PET to a level that allowed HP to reuse the recycled PET in its injection moulding machines to build new inkjet cartridges.

Through its recycling program called HP Planet Partners, HP receives a good portion of its inkjet cartridges back after use from consumers. In its Nashville recycling plant, inkjet cartridges are disassembled, and the plastics are shredded and shipped to Lavergne's Montreal plant. Each day a large container of shredded plastics (approximately 30,000 pounds) arrives. There, the HP shredded plastic is mixed with a larger amount of shredded PET made out of recycled pop bottles and some additives in a large V-shaped blender for more than three hours. Then the mixture goes through a hot extruder, which creates spaghetti-like strands at 575°F. The strands are cooled with water, chopped, treated, packed, and shipped back to Nashville. Of course, details of the recycling process are secret.

HP has produced over 1 billion new ink cartridges using Lavergne's recycled PET. Lavergne is an example of a successful company that has used its process design not only to profit but also to help the environment.

Sources: http://www.youtube.com/watch?v=5WMAORbFMtE; http://www.canadianmanufacturing.com/sustainability/canadian-innovation-changes-way-hp-recycles-plastic-products-101312; http://www.hp.com/hpinfo/globalcitizenship/environment/pdf/idc223180HPsupplies.pdf.

©79mtk/Shutterstock

©macka/Shutterstock

Process Design   LO3

Process design determines the structure of a process—that is, the sequence of operations (the workflow), resources, and controls needed for a particular process.

In this section, we will first present a methodology for production process design, then explain the differences for service design, and finally describe the design of processes that span functional areas, the subject of business process management.

We assume that this is a new production process for a new product. More often, production processes are only redesigned, by either automating one part of the process or replacing a machine with a newer one. In this case, only some of the following steps need to be performed.

Methodology for Production Process Design

Production process design is part of the product design methodology of Chapter 4, and, as such, was briefly mentioned there. Here, we will expand on it.

Given the product quantity, variety, cost, quality, delivery speed (lead time), and product specifications (nature, shape, size, components, and how they fit together),

1. **Define the production process** (performed in the "Build business case" stage of the stage-gate model—Figure 4-1)

   - Determine how completed the input materials should be. These are make-or-buy decisions. (See the "Tim Hortons' Par-Baking" OM in Action for an example.)
   - Set production process objectives:
     - Capacity (or production speed)
     - Type of process (job shop, batch, repetitive, continuous)
     - Cost (fixed, variable)
     - Process capability
     - Technology/extent of automation
     - Production start date
   - Determine the nature of process in general.

2. **Production process development** (performed in the "Development" stage of the stage-gate model—Figure 4-1)

   2.1 Conceptualize the design

   How do you get from inputs (materials) to output? What is the sequence of major operations needed?

   - Develop a few alternative process concepts (sketches). Two approaches can be used:
     - Incremental: do one step at a time from start to end.
     - Hierarchical (top down): break the whole job into two operations, then divide each into sub-operations until the desired level of detail is reached.
   - Usually a *process flow diagram* is used to show the operations and the movement of material between the operations.
   - Evaluate each alternative process concept.

   2.2 Make an embodiment of the design

   - Choose one process concept and complete the design.
   - Build a prototype process (can use computer modelling) and test it. This is called a pilot plant.
     - Determine the resources (machines, equipment, and labour) needed, in general.
     - Estimate the costs, quality, etc., and compare with the objectives.
   - Refine the process and re-evaluate it.

   2.3 Create a detailed design

   - Finalize the process specifications.
     - Determine the machines, equipment (their capacities and make), and labour.
     - Design the plant layout.
     - Design the work centres.

3. **Buy the machines and equipment, recruit workers, and start trial runs** (performed in the "Testing and validation" stage of the stage-gate model—Figure 4-1)

process flow diagram
Shows the operations and movement of material between the operations.

Drawing a **process flow diagram** starts with identifying the boundaries of the process (inputs and outputs) and the level of detail required. The incremental approach involves following the flow of material (or the customer, in services) through the transformation process, and identifying the operations and resources (machines, labour, and their capabilities) required and their sequence. Experience with a similar process is useful. For technical products, expertise of process/manufacturing engineers is required. Examples 6-1 to 6-4 earlier each displayed a different process flow diagram.

Example 6-5 illustrates the basics of process design.

◀ **EXAMPLE 6-5**

A company wants to diversify into mass-production of bread loaves. It needs to design the production process.

SOLUTION

We start with the common recipe for making a loaf of bread:

1. Mix flour, salt, yeast, and water to obtain dough.

2. Knead the dough.

3. Shape the dough into a ball, put in a pan, and leave to rise.

4. Bake in oven.

5. Let bread cool and remove from pan.

Because of the large quantity of flour needed (and the economy of quantity buying), a raw material storage room (or silo) will be used. Because mixing large quantities of ingredients by hand is difficult, a mixing machine is required. The same reason applies to kneading. As it happens, a machine exists that does both mixing and kneading. To automate the shaping, the easiest method is to dump the big lump of dough into a hopper that cuts and drops small pieces of dough into

bread pans, which are then transported on a conveyor belt for a while to let bread rise and then into an open-ended oven (like an automated car wash). Next, the pans are transported on a conveyor belt for a while to cool down. Finally, bread loaves are taken out of the pans, sliced, and bagged.

The following process flow diagram is a good first step:

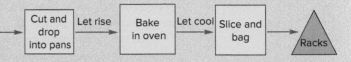

Note that storage is shown by a triangle and an operation is shown by a rectangle. Also note that flows (arrows) are usually from left to right. If there is a need to show the information flows (for control purposes), they could be shown as dashed arrows. In practice, time (or capacity) of each operation is estimated and displayed in or near its box. A similar tool is value stream mapping (Chapter 15) which focuses on delay reduction.

 OM in ACTION   www.timhortons.com

Tim Hortons' Par-Baking

In 2001, Tim Hortons' management decided to revise the production process of all its baked goods (e.g., doughnuts, muffins, soups, and baguettes) from made-in-store to par-bake. *Par-baking* is the process in which the goods are prepared and partially baked in a central location, flash frozen, shipped to the restaurants, and then reheated when a customer orders. Tim Hortons went into a joint venture with a European bakery manufacturing technology company, Cuisine de France, that had invented par-baking. The partners built a 230,000 ft² facility at a cost of $125 million in Brantford, Ontario. Although the cost of material to a Tim Hortons franchisee increased a little, it relieved the restaurant of having to employ trained bakers. For example, before 2002, it cost a franchisee approximately $0.07 to buy a doughnut from Tim Hortons, whereas after par-baking the cost went up to $0.18 per doughnut. Although some franchisees have complained about this, their sales and profits (which mainly come from selling coffee) have been increasing steadily over the years, making Tim

B. O'Kane/Alamy Stock Photo

Hortons the leader in the quick serve industry in Canada. Tim Hortons calls par-baking "always fresh."

Sources: http://www.timhortons.com/ca/en/corporate/news-release.php?id=7506; http://www.macleans.ca/economy/business/rolling-in-dough/.

Service Process Design

Service process design is similar to production process design except that, instead of material, the flow of the customer or something belonging to the customer should be followed. The focus is on customer experience, and the service process is usually measured by the value it creates for the customer. If the customer is not present, a service process is very similar to a manufacturing process (e.g., cheque processing).

If the customer is present, a range of service delivery processes exist based on degree of customization and interaction of customer and server. The higher the customization, the more extensive the service delivery process needs to be. This requires higher server skills but costs more money. Production efficiency goes down but sales opportunity goes up. For example, getting a mortgage requires customization and involvement from a mortgage officer, and costs more to the bank than if a customer uses an ATM for cash withdrawal. However, there is more sales opportunity for the bank during mortgage application; for example, the loan officer can entice the borrower to also get a line of credit or the bank's credit card. The self-service nature of the ATM reduces costs to the bank but service variety has to be limited.

The service can easily be changed by varying the degree of customization and involvement of customers at any step of the service. For example, a restaurant can require reservations or not; serve complimentary hot bread or not; take orders at the table or give customers an iPad to place their own order; increase or decrease the number of appetizers, entrees, desserts, and/or drinks; and allow credit card payments or not.

Service Blueprint. The process flow diagram for services is called a service blueprint. Service blueprinting was introduced in Chapter 4. Here, we will describe a more detailed example. Recall that a service blueprint shows how a service is to be provided. Its focus is the customer. In it, the employees can see how their role affects the service process. It can also be used to improve the service process. In the more detailed version, the activities involved in a service are separated: (a) those performed by the customer, (b) those performed by the server and visible to the customer, (c) those performed by the server and not visible to the customer, and (d) those performed by support staff and processes. Physical aspects of service such as facilities, room, food, etc., are also important and can be represented on the top row of the blueprint. These groups of activities are separated by lines of interaction, visibility, and internal interaction, respectively. Arrows/links show the flow of information and material. A double-sided vertical arrow shows a pair of shared activities. Figure 6-3 shows a blueprint for an overnight hotel stay. Note that time flows from left to right.

Services are especially vulnerable to quality and delivery problems because the customer is usually present during service delivery and there is little time to fix any problems. That is why there is a need to identify potential failure points and incorporate features that minimize the chance of failure. Every link that crosses the line of interaction (called the line of information in Service Blueprinting of Chapter 4) represents a "moment of truth." The customer's overall impression of the quality of service is formed based on moments of truth.

Customer Perception in Service Process Design. Another difference from manufacturing is that a service is usually varied and intangible. This raises the customer perception issue. Some suggestions to improve customer perception in services are:

- Do not raise customer expectations too high in the beginning. This is because customers compare their expectation and the actual service they receive in order to judge the quality of service.

- End the service positively, because customers better remember the end.

- If the service is pleasurable, divide it into segments. For example, two short rides in an amusement park may be better than one long ride.

- If the service is painful, combine the segments. For example, cleaning teeth in a one-hour session may be better than two half-hour sessions.

- Let customers control part or all of the process. For example, self-services such as ATMs are preferred by most people. In this case, it is important to make the process user-friendly.

- Communicate the evidence of quality to customers.

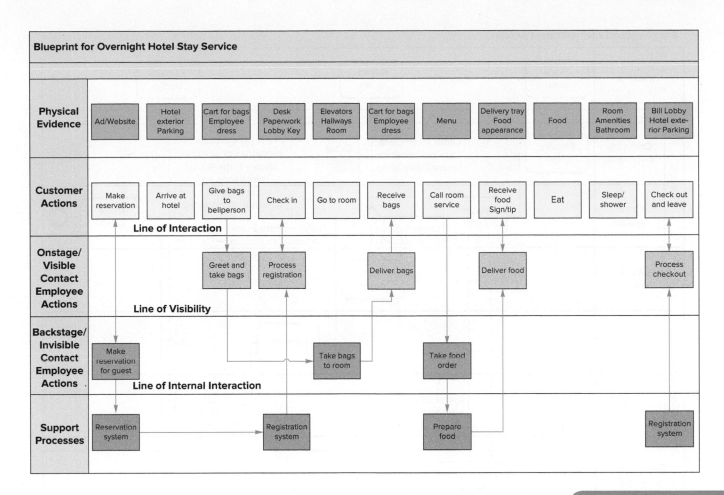

▲ **FIGURE 6-3**

Blueprint for an overnight hotel stay.

Source: M. J. Bitner, A. L. Ostrom, and F. N. Morgan, "Service Blueprinting: A Practical Technique for Service Innovation," *California Management Review* 50(3), Spring 2008.

Design of Processes With Interaction

This section deals with design of processes where a lot of interdepartmental interactions could cause excessive delays or other inefficiencies. An example is the purchasing process in which the purchasing department, the using department (such as engineering), and accounts payable need to collaborate.

In this case, the process design/redesign involves a lot of politics because various functions which perform part of the process tend to protect their own resources. Therefore, a top manager, the sponsor, needs to be directly involved. Also, a process owner/manager has to be appointed, similar to a project manager for a project. The difference is that the process owner's role is permanent.

A *process map* similar to a service blueprint is used by the multi-functional process design/ redesign team to display the activities/operations comprising the process. However, the grouping of activities is more precise; it is by function and even by roles within a function. This map is called a **swim lane diagram**, because each function/role's activities are in its row/lane. An example of an "automated" order fulfillment process for books from an online bookseller is displayed on the next page. Note that the diamond shape represents a decision, and time flows from left to right.

Objectives for a process—such as targets for time, cost, and quality—should be determined. These should support the organization's objectives/goals. A process should allocate the appropriate level of resources: IT and employees. The performance of the process should be regularly measured and compared with its target objectives. If performance is unsatisfactory, a minor improvement change or a major process redesign should be undertaken.

See the "Yellow Freight" OM in Action for an application of service improvement and design.

swim lane diagram A process map in which each function/role's activities are in its row/lane.

Books-online: order fulfillment process

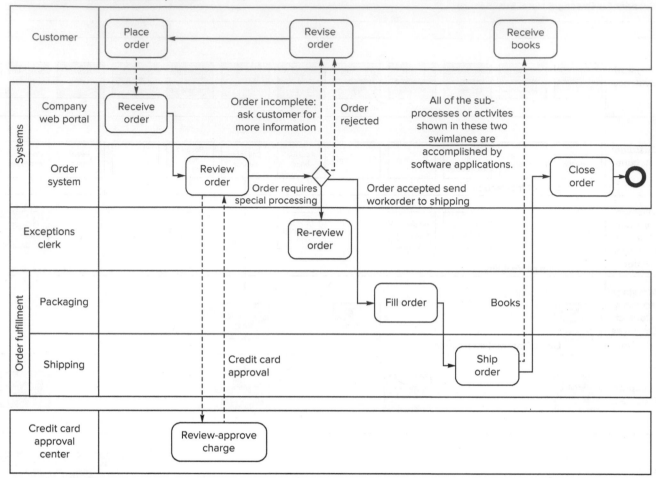

Reprinted from *Business Process Change*, 3e, Paul Harmon, Morgan Kaufman Publishers, Fig. 9.8, 2014, with permission from Elsevier.

⚙️ **OM in ACTION**   http://yrc.com

Yellow Freight

Yellow Freight (YRC) is the largest less-than-truckload (small freights) transportation company in North America. However, in the 1990s, it was one of the least admired. Shipments were picked up late, delivered damaged or wrong, misbilled, or lost 50 percent of the time.

To improve the delivery service, top management instituted a new customer-focused vision, enabled by an effective customer-feedback process, service recovery and complaint management, and huge investments in technology support. Also, input from the employees (including 20,000 teamster truck drivers) was sought.

A delivery service blueprint was created which led to the recognition of importance

Courtesy of YRC Worldwide

of the "driver touch points." The drivers were really the "face of Yellow" to its customers. Changes were made in their training and uniforms. Also, the importance of support by internal customer service, terminal personnel, and sales teams was recognized. Managers participated in workshops. For example, one group addressed issues related to "missed pick-ups." A team looked for ways to avoid missed pick-ups and another looked at service recovery following a missed pick-up.

Another initiative was the introduction of a new service, Exact Express, a premium service that guarantees on-time delivery of shipments within a specified time window. The process started with blueprinting an ideal service from the customer's point of view and comparing that to the existing as well as competitors' service blueprints. The blueprints revealed the need for customization in terms of customer access (e.g., online, fax, phone) and importance of certain "moments of truth." Today, Exact Express is the company's most profitable service.

Source: M. J. Bitner, A. L. Ostrom, and F. N. Morgan, "Service Blueprinting: A Practical Technique for Service Innovation," *California Management Review* 50(3), Spring 2008.

Types of Layout

Layout is the location of departments, work centres, or equipment in the facility/factory/plant. A good layout facilitates flow of work, whereas a bad one results in congestion. This section describes the main types of layout design.

The need for layout planning arises both in designing new facilities and in redesigning existing facilities. The most common reasons for redesign of layouts include inefficient operations (e.g., excessive material handling/delay), changes in the design of a product, changes in the quantity or mix of products, and changes in methods or equipment.

There are generally two types of layout—product (line) layout (for repetitive and continuous processes), and process (functional) layout (for job shop and batch processes).

> **layout** Location of departments, work centres, or equipment in the facility/factory/plant.

Product (Line) Layout

In a **product layout**, production resources are arranged linearly according to the progressive steps by which a product is made. Product layout is used to achieve a smooth and rapid flow of large quantities of goods or customers through the process. This is made possible by highly standardized goods or services that allow highly standardized continuous production. The work is divided into a series of standardized tasks, permitting specialization of both labour and equipment. Because only one or a few very similar items are involved, it is feasible to arrange an entire layout to correspond to the production requirements of the product. For instance, if a portion of a manufacturing process requires the sequence of cutting, sanding, and painting, the appropriate pieces of equipment would be arranged in that sequence. And because each item follows the same sequence of operations, it is often possible to utilize fixed-path material-handling equipment such as conveyors to transport items between operations. The resulting arrangement forms a line like the one in Figure 6-4.

In manufacturing environments, *line* refers to a production line or an assembly line, depending on the type of activity involved. In services, *line* may or may not be used. It is common to refer to a cafeteria line as such but not a car wash, although from a conceptual standpoint the two are nearly identical. Figure 6-5 illustrates the layout of a typical cafeteria line. Examples of this

> **product layout** Arrangement of production resources linearly according to the progressive steps by which a product is made.

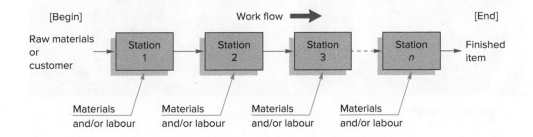

◀ **FIGURE 6-4**

A product (line) layout.

FIGURE 6-5 ▶

A cafeteria line.

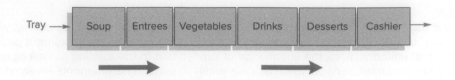

type of layout are less common in services because service requirements usually exhibit too much variability to make standardization feasible. Without high standardization, many of the benefits of a repetitive process are lost. When lines are used, certain compromises must be made. For instance, an automatic car wash provides equal treatment to all cars—the same amount of soap, water, and scrubbing—even though cars may differ considerably in cleaning needs. As a result, very dirty cars may not come out completely clean, and relatively clean cars go through the same system with considerable waste of soap, water, and energy.

Product layouts achieve a high degree of labour and equipment utilization, which tends to offset their high equipment cost. Because items move quickly from operation to operation, the amount of work-in-process is often minimal. Consequently, operations are so closely tied to each other that the entire system is highly vulnerable to being shut down because of mechanical failure or absenteeism. *Preventive maintenance*—periodic inspection and replacement of worn parts or those with high failure rates—reduces the probability of breakdowns during the operation. Of course, no amount of preventive maintenance can completely eliminate failures, so management must take measures to provide quick repair. These include maintaining an inventory of spare parts and having repair personnel available to quickly restore equipment to normal operation.

Advantages of product layout include low-cost production and simplified accounting, purchasing, and inventory control.

Disadvantages of product layout include higher equipment cost; dull, repetitive jobs; repetitive stress injuries; and inflexibility in response to changes in the quantity of output or in product mix.

A Ford assembly line.

© Bill Pugliano/Getty Images

Process Layout
(*functional*)
Used for Intermittent Processing
Job Shop and **Batch Processes**

| Dept. A | Dept. C | Dept. E |
| Dept. B | Dept. D | Dept. F |

Product Layout
(*sequential*)
Used for Repetitive Processing
Repetitive and **Continuous Processes**

Workstation 1 → Workstation 2 → Workstation 3 →

◄ FIGURE 6-6

Comparison of process and product layouts.

Process (Functional) Layout

In a **process layout**, production resources are arranged according to similarity of function. It processes items that have a variety of production requirements. The variety of jobs requires frequent adjustments to equipment. This causes a discontinuous workflow, which is referred to as *intermittent processing*. A manufacturing example of a process layout is a *machine shop*, which has separate departments for milling, grinding, drilling, and so on. Items that require these operations are moved in lots or batches to the departments in a sequence that varies from job to job. Consequently, variable-path material-handling equipment (forklift trucks, skids on wheels, tote boxes, etc.) is needed. The use of *general-purpose equipment* provides the flexibility necessary to handle a wide range of production requirements. Workers who operate the equipment are usually skilled. Figure 6-6 compares process and product layouts.

> **process layout** Arrangement of production resources according to similarity of function.
>
> **cellular layout** Different machines are arranged in a cell that can process items that have similar processing requirements.

Process layouts are quite common in services. Examples include various departments of a hospital, a grocery store, and an auto repair shop. For instance, a hospital has emergency rooms, X-ray rooms, surgery rooms, etc.

Because equipment in a process layout is arranged by type rather than by production sequence, and there is spare equipment, the system is much less vulnerable to shutdown caused by mechanical failure or absenteeism. Maintenance costs tend to be lower because the equipment is less specialized than that of product layout, and the grouping of machinery permits repair personnel to become skilled in handling that type of equipment. Machine similarity reduces the necessary investment in spare parts.

On the negative side, routing and scheduling must be done on a continual basis to accommodate the variety of production requirements. Material handling is inefficient and handling costs are higher than in product layout. In-process inventories can be substantial due to batch processing. Furthermore, it is not uncommon for such systems to have equipment utilization rates under 50 percent because of routing and scheduling complexities related to the variety of production requirements being handled.

Cellular Layout

In a **cellular layout**, different machines are arranged in a *cell* that can process items with similar processing requirements, called a *part family*. A cell is a small version of a product layout; it may have no conveyorized movement of parts between machines, or may have a conveyor (automatic transfer). Figure 6-7 compares a typical functional (process) layout and a cellular layout. Observe that in the cellular layout, machines are arranged to handle all of the operations necessary for a group (family) of similar parts. Thus, all parts in the same family follow the same route, although minor variations (e.g., skipping an operation) are possible. In contrast, the functional (process) layout involves multiple paths for these parts. Table 6-3 compares the characteristics of cellular and functional layouts.

StandardAero provides a variety of maintenance, repair, and overhaul services to the aviation industry, including repair of gas turbine engines. It has over 4,000 employees and a dozen major locations in Winnipeg, the United States, Europe, Australia, and Asia. In the 1990s, among other things, StandardAero reorganized its repair facilities into a cellular layout. Instead of a job shop layout where similar machines are bunched together, StandardAero segmented the repair process and also grouped similar parts into same cells. Each cell is operated by a self-managed team whose performance is measured and displayed in front of the cell. StandardAero has become so proficient at conversion into cellular layout that it started a division that sells this service to other engine repair facilities. StandardAero is now owned by Veritas Capital.

Courtesy of StandardAero

FIGURE 6-7 ▶

Comparison of functional (process) and cellular layouts.

Adapted from D. Fogarty and T. Hoffmann, *Production and Inventory Management* (Cincinnati-South-Western Publishing, 1983), p. 472.

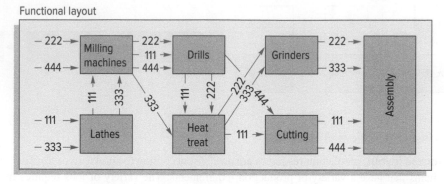

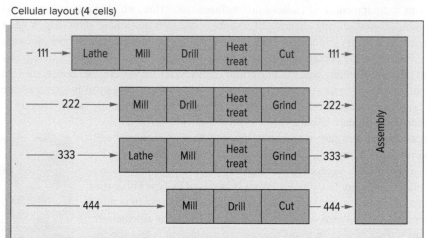

TABLE 6-3 ▶

Comparison of characteristics of functional (process) and cellular layouts.

Dimension	Functional	Cellular
Number of moves between departments	Many	Few
Travel distances	Longer	Shorter
Travel paths	Variable	Fixed
Job waiting time	Greater	Shorter
Throughput time	Higher	Lower
Amount of work in process	Higher	Lower
Supervision difficulty	Higher	Lower
Scheduling complexity	Higher	Lower
Equipment utilization	Lower	Higher

A cell is usually U-shaped (see Figure 6-8). A U-shaped line permits increased communication among workers on the line, thus facilitating teamwork. Also, flexibility in work assignments is increased because workers can handle not only adjacent stations but also stations on opposite sides of the line.

group technology Grouping items with similar design or manufacturing characteristics into part families.

Grouping of similar items is known as **group technology** and involves identifying items with similarities in either design or manufacturing characteristics, and grouping them into families. Design characteristics include size, shape, material, features (holes, slots, notches, grooves), and function; manufacturing characteristics involve the type/sequence of operations and tolerance (precision) required. Figure 6-9 illustrates a group of parts with similar characteristics.

Once similar items have been identified, items can be classified according to their families and coded, and a system can be developed that facilitates retrieval of these codes from the database for purposes of design and manufacturing. For instance, a designer can use the system to determine if there is an existing part similar or identical to the one that needs to be designed. It may happen that an existing part, with some modification, is satisfactory. This greatly enhances the productivity of design. Similarly, planning the manufacturing of a new part can include matching it with one of the part families in existence, thereby alleviating much of the burden of specific processing details.

The conversion to group technology is often a major undertaking; it is a time-consuming job that involves the analysis of a considerable amount of data. Three primary methods for accomplishing this are visual inspection, examination of design and production data, and production flow sequence and routing analysis.

▲ FIGURE 6-8

A U-shaped cell.

◀ FIGURE 6-9

A group of parts with similar characteristics.

Source: © McGraw-Hill Education/Mark Dierker, photographer

Some variations/combinations of line and cellular layouts are possible. For example, see Figure 6-10. The decision between line layout and cellular layout depends on room (line requires larger space), lot size (larger lots favour line), nature of workforce (temporary workers do better with the simpler, shorter tasks of a line), required flexibility (cells are better for dissimilar products of various lot sizes), and budget (line requires roller or belt conveyors).

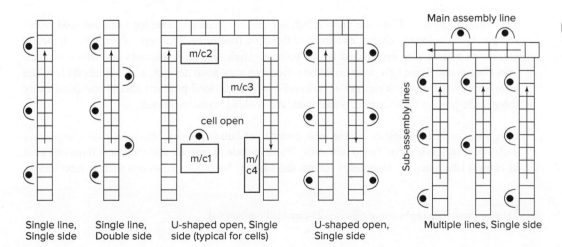

◀ FIGURE 6-10

Some variations/ combinations of line and cellular layouts.

Methodology for Layout Design

The objectives of manufacturing layouts are cost minimization and product flow. The following steps are used in manufacturing layout design. Other layout designs follow similar steps.

- Determine the location of receiving and shipping.
- For "product layout," fit the process flow diagram onto a sketch of the factory floor, starting from receiving and ending in shipping. Determine the approximate location of each part of the process.
- For "process layout," determine the expected workflow between pairs of departments, and place the two departments with the highest workflows closest to each other. Continue until all departments are located.
- Keep special requirements of machines in mind (e.g., a heavy press needs a strong foundation, the paint department needs a clean environment).
- Allow space for machines, in-feeds, out-feeds, workers, and carts/forklifts.
- Keep rearranging the plan using feedback from workers until you find what works best.
- On the factory floor, paint an outline of machines and in-feed and out-feed spaces.
- Walk through the normal sequence of activities.
- Install the electricity and other lines, and move the machines in.

Some Service Layouts

Most service layouts are process (functional) type.

Warehouse Layout. The design of a warehouse is based on a different set of factors than the design of factories. Items requiring cold storage are stored together in freezers and coolers. Other items that are ordered frequently and in large amounts should be placed near the shipping area. Any correlation between items is also significant (e.g., item A is usually ordered with item B), suggesting that placing those two items close together would reduce the cost and time of order picking.

Retail Layout. For retail layouts such as department stores, supermarkets, and specialty stores, the primary objective is to influence sales (maximize revenues). Some large retail chains use standard layouts for all of their stores. For an example, see the "Apple Store" OM in Action.

Office Layout. Office layouts underwent a transformation as the flow of paperwork was replaced with electronic communication. That means that there is less need to place office workers in a layout that optimizes the physical transfer of information or paperwork. A new trend is to create an image of openness; office walls are giving way to low-rise partitions.

Restaurant Layout. There are many different types of restaurants, ranging from fast food to full service. Many belong to chains, and some of those are franchises. That type of restaurant typically adheres to a floor plan established by the company. Independent restaurants and bars have their own floor plans. Some have what could be considered very good designs, while others do not. The most important element is process workflow. Food and non-food products should transition easily through the process from storage, preparation, and cooking, to the customer.

Hospital Layout. Hospitals are the most complex of building types.[7] Each hospital comprises a wide range of services and functional units. These include diagnostic and treatment functions such as clinical labs, imaging, emergency rooms, and surgery; hospitality functions such as food service

---

[7] https://www.wbdg.org/building-types/health-care-facilities/hospital

OM in ACTION www.apple.com/ca

Apple Store

Apple stores are designed to make customers spend more money, raking in more money per square foot (over $5,000) than any other stores, including jewellery stores. There are over 490 Apple stores worldwide. An Apple store is laid out in three zones starting from the entrance: (1) Product displays and sales, (2) Family zone (training and personal setup), and (3) Genius bar (tech support and repairs). The open layout allows free flow of customers. All devices are connected to the Internet and are ready to be

used. The store is well illuminated. Staff use an iPhone or iPad to process sales transactions (there is no cash register). Children's accessories are placed at their height. The Genius bar is modelled after the Ritz-Carlton hotel chain concierge station. Some stores have glass staircases and walls to make them impressive.

Source: http://www.businessinsider.com/apple-store-layout-makes-you-spend-2014-9. **Source:** http://www.businessinsider.com/apple-store-layout-makes-you-spend-2014-9.

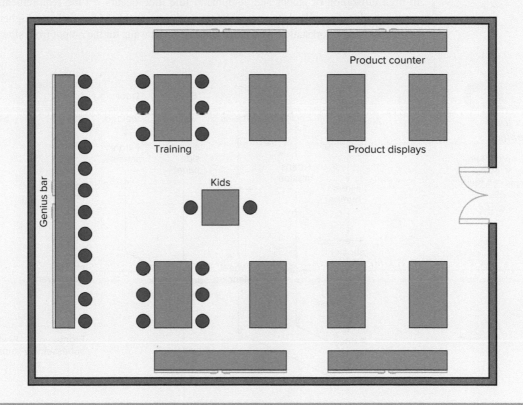

and housekeeping; and the fundamental inpatient care or bed-related function. The functional units within the hospital can have competing needs and priorities. Physical relationships between these functions determine the configuration of the hospital.

In a large hospital, the form of the typical nursing unit is a principal element of the overall configuration because it is repeated many times. Compact rectangles, modified triangles, and even circles have been used in an attempt to shorten the distance between the nursing station and the patient's bed.

A hospital layout should minimize walking distance of staff and patients, be designed on a modular basis, be easy to expand, provide a therapeutic and aesthetic environment, be easy to clean and maintain, provide accessibility to all areas, control circulation of people and goods, be secure and safe, and be sustainable.

LO5 Assembly-Line Balancing

Assembly lines range from fairly short, with just a few operations, to long lines that have a large number of operations. Automobile assembly lines are examples of long lines. Figure 6-11 illustrates the assembly chart for a typical automobile.

Many of the benefits of a product (line) layout relate to the ability to divide the required work into a series of tasks (e.g., "assemble parts C and D") that can be performed quickly and routinely by low-skilled workers or specialized equipment. The durations of these tasks typically range from a few seconds to a few minutes. Most time requirements are so brief that it would be impractical to assign only one task to each worker. Instead, tasks are usually grouped into manageable bundles and assigned to workstations staffed by one or two operators.

Assigning tasks to workstations in such a way that the workstations have approximately equal time requirements is called **line balancing**. This minimizes the idle time along the line and results in high utilization of labour and equipment. Idle time occurs if time requirements are not equal among workstations. Workstations with less work are capable of producing at higher rates than others. These "fast" workstations will experience periodic waits for the output from slower workstations

> **line balancing** Assigning tasks to workstations in such a way that the workstations have approximately equal time requirements.

FIGURE 6-11 ▶

Assembly chart for a typical automobile.

Adapted from R. U. Ayres, Morris A. Cohen, and Uday M. Apte, *Manufacturing Automation*, (Burr Ridge, IL: McGraw-Hill, 1997), p. 175.

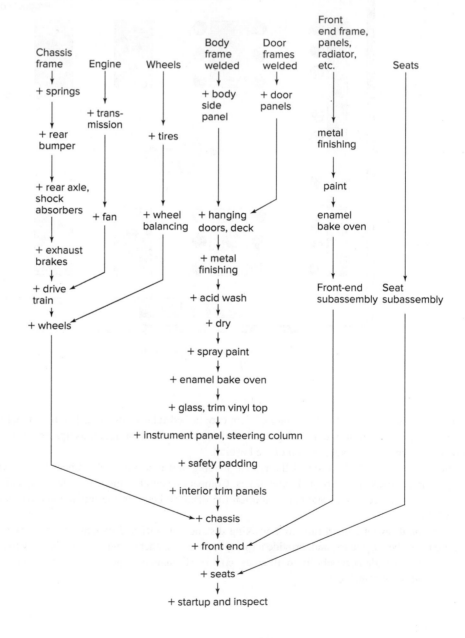

or to avoid build-ups of work in downstream workstations. Unbalanced lines are undesirable in terms of inefficient utilization of labour and equipment and because they may create morale problems at the slower workstations for workers who must work continuously.

The major obstacle to attaining a perfectly balanced line is that forming task bundles with the same duration is difficult, for several reasons. (1) It may not be feasible to combine certain activities into the same bundle, either because of differences in skill or equipment requirements or because the activities are not compatible (e.g., risk of contamination of paint from grinding). (2) Differences among task lengths cannot always be overcome by grouping the tasks. (3) The technological sequence may prohibit otherwise desirable task combinations.

Consider a series of three operations that have durations of two minutes, four minutes, and two minutes, as shown in the following diagram. Ideally, the first and third operations could be combined at one workstation and have a total time equal to that of the second operation. However, it may not be possible to combine the first and third operations. In the case of an automatic car wash, scrubbing and drying operations could not realistically be combined at the same workstation due to the need to rinse cars between the two operations.

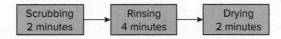

Usually, each workstation has one worker who handles all of the tasks at that workstation, although an option is to have two workers at a single workstation. For purposes of illustration, however, all of the examples and problems in this chapter have workstations with one worker.

A manager could decide to use anywhere from one to five workstations to handle five tasks. With one workstation, all tasks would be done at that workstation; with five workstations, one task would be assigned to each workstation. If two, three, or four workstations are used, some or all of the workstations will have multiple tasks assigned to them. How does a manager decide how many workstations to use?

The primary determinant is the line's **cycle time** (also called *takt time*), the *maximum* time allowed at each workstation to perform its assigned tasks before the unit moves on. The cycle time also establishes the output rate of a line. For instance, if the cycle time is two minutes, units will come off the end of the line at the rate of one every two minutes.

As a general rule, the cycle time is determined by:

$$CT = \frac{OT}{D}$$ (6-1)

where

CT = Cycle time
OT = Operating time per day
D = Desired output per day (i.e., demand)

For example, suppose that the desired output rate is 480 units per day, and the line will operate for eight hours per day (480 minutes). Using Formula 6-1, the necessary cycle time is

$$\frac{480 \text{ minutes per day}}{480 \text{ units per day}} = 1.0 \text{ minute per unit}$$

The number of workstations that will be needed is a function of the cycle time, the sum of task times, and our ability to combine tasks into workstations. We can determine the *theoretical minimum* number of workstations necessary, given a cycle time, as follows:

$$N_{\min} = \frac{\sum t}{CT}$$ (6-2)

where

$N_{\min}$ = Theoretical minimum number of workstations
$\sum t$ = Sum of task times

cycle time The maximum time allowed at each workstation to complete its set of tasks on a unit.

precedence network
Diagram of activities and their sequential relationships, using nodes and arrows.

Given cycle time of 1 minute per unit, if sum of task times is 2.5 minutes, the minimum number of workstations required to achieve this goal is:

$$N_{\min} = \frac{2.5 \text{ minutes per unit}}{1 \text{ minute per unit per workstation}} = 2.5 \text{ workstations}$$

Because 2.5 workstations is not feasible, it is necessary to *round up* (because 2.5 is the minimum) to three workstations. Thus, the actual number of workstations used will equal or exceed three, depending on how successfully the tasks can be grouped into work bundles.

A very useful tool in line balancing is a **precedence network**. Figure 6-12 illustrates a simple precedence network. It visually portrays the tasks that are to be performed along with the *precedence* requirements; that is, the *order* in which tasks may be performed. The network is read from left to right, so the initial task(s) are on the left and the final task is on the right. In terms of precedence relationship, we can see from the diagram, for example, that the only requirement to begin task *b* is that task *a* must be finished. However, in order to begin task *d*, tasks *b* and *c* must *both* be finished.

Now let's see how a line is balanced. This involves assigning tasks to workstations. Generally, no technique is available that guarantees an optimal set of assignments. Instead, managers employ *heuristic* (intuitive) rules, which provide good sets of assignments. A number of line-balancing heuristics are in use, three of which are described here for purposes of illustration:

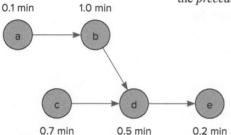

1. Assign the task with the longest time.
2. Assign the task with the most followers.
3. Assign the task with the largest *positional weight* (the sum of the task's time plus the time of all the following tasks).

You would encounter the following tasks by tracing all the paths (in the direction of arrows) from the task in question through the precedence network to the end node (final task).

The general procedure used in line balancing is described in Table 6-4.

FIGURE 6-12 ▲

A simple precedence network.

TABLE 6-4 ▶

Line balancing procedure.

1. Identify the cycle time and the minimum number of workstations.

2. Make assignments to workstations in order, beginning with workstation 1. Tasks are assigned to workstations moving from left to right through the precedence network. Start each workstation with Time left = Cycle time.

3. Before each assignment, use the following criteria to determine if a task (a) is eligible and (b) will fit:
   a. A task is eligible if all its preceding tasks in the precedence network have been assigned.
   b. A task will fit if its time does not exceed the time left at the workstation.
   If no eligible tasks will fit, set Idle time = Time left, and move on to the next workstation.

4. Assign tasks (and break ties) using one of these heuristic rules:
   a. Assign the task with the longest time.
   b. Assign the task with the most followers.
   c. Assign the task with the largest positional weight.

5. After each task assignment, update the time left at the workstation by subtracting the time of assigned task from time left.

6. Continue until all tasks have been assigned to workstations. Calculate total idle time.

Assign the tasks shown in Figure 6-12 to workstations using a cycle time of 1.0 minute. Use the heuristic rule "Assign the task with the most followers."

SOLUTION

Workstation	Time Left	Eligible	Will Fit	Task (time)	Idle Time
1	1.0	a, c	a, c*	a (0.1)	
	0.9	b, c	c	c (0.7)	
	0.2	b			0.2
2	1.0	b	b	b (1.0)	
	0.0	d	–		0.0
3	1.0	d	d	d (0.5)	
	0.5	e	e	e (0.2)	
	0.3	–		–	0.3
					0.5

*Task *a* was assigned because it has more followers (three, vs. two for task *c*).

Comment: The initial time left for each workstation is equal to the cycle time. For a task to be eligible, tasks preceding it on the precedence network must have been assigned, and for it to fit, the task's time must not exceed the workstation's time left. The following is a graphical representation of the determined work bundles.

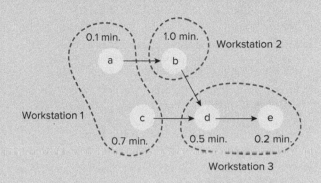

Two widely used measures of effectiveness of the result of line balancing are:

1. The **percentage idle time** of the line, sometimes referred to as the *balance delay*:

$$\text{Percentage idle time} = \frac{\text{Sum of idle times per unit}}{N_{\text{actual}} \times \text{Cycle time}} \times 100 \qquad (6\text{-}3)$$

where N_{actual} = Actual number of workstations.

For the preceding example:

$$\text{Percentage idle time} = \frac{0.5}{3 \times 1.0} \times 100 = 16.7\%$$

percentage idle time One hundred multiplied by the sum of idle times per unit divided by the product of actual number of workstations multiplied by cycle time.

2. The *efficiency* of the line:

Efficiency = 100 − Percentage idle time

In the preceding example, Efficiency = 100% − 16.7% = 83.3%.

$$(6\text{-}4)$$

EXAMPLE 6-7 ▶

Design an assembly line for assembling the oak accessory table shown in the following photos. Assume that the top and the legs come as sub-assemblies and that both leg assemblies need to be screwed to the top before leg braces (cross-bars) can be assembled. The steps of assembly and their estimated times are:

Task	Time (seconds)
a. Place top sub-assembly upside down on the work surface.	4
b. Place a leg sub-assembly over the top sub-assembly as shown in the left-hand photo, insert a screw in the predrilled hole, align, and drive the screw in.	20
c. Insert another screw in the other predrilled hole and drive the screw in.	13
d. Place another leg sub-assembly over the other side of the top sub-assembly, insert a screw in the predrilled hole, align, and drive the screw in.	20
e. Insert another screw in the other predrilled hole and drive the screw in.	13
f. Place a leg brace between two leg sub-assemblies as shown in the right-hand photo, insert a screw in the predrilled hole, align, and drive the screw in.	20
g. Insert another screw in the other side's predrilled hole and drive the screw in.	13
h. Place another leg brace between two leg sub-assemblies on the other side, insert a screw in the predrilled hole, align, and drive the screw in.	20
i. Insert another screw in the other side's predrilled hole and drive the screw in.	13
j. Tighten all screws.	32

Photos courtesy of Oakswings.com

1. Draw the precedence network.

2. Assuming that we need to assemble one table per minute, assign the tasks to workstations using the "Assign the task with the most followers" heuristic rule, breaking a tie with the "Assign the task with the longest time" heuristic rule. If there is a further tie, break it randomly (i.e., you can choose any one of the tasks tied).

SOLUTION

1. Drawing the precedence network is not difficult. Begin (from the left) with the activity(ies) with no predecessor. Then place the immediate followers and draw arrows to them. Note that an activity may require completion of two or more activities. For example, to be able to start f or h (installing a leg brace), both leg sub-assemblies should be already installed (c and e). That is why there are two arrows into f and h from c and e.

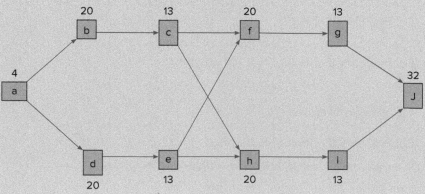

2.

WS	Time Left (seconds)	Eligible	Will Fit	Assign (time)	Idle Time
1	60	a	a	a (4)	
	56	b, d	b, d*	b (20)	
	36	c, d	c, d**	d (20)	
	16	c, e	c, e***	c (13)	
	3	e	—	—	3
2	60	e	e	e (13)	
	47	f, h	f, h****	f (20)	
	27	g, h	g, h*****	h (20)	
	7	g, i	—	—	7
3	60	g, i	g, i******	g (13)	
	47	i	i	i (13)	
	34	j	j	j (32)	
	2	—	—	—	2
					12

*b is assigned randomly—both b and d have 6 followers and their time is tied at 20 s also.

**d is assigned because it has 6 followers, more than 5 followers of c.

***c is assigned randomly—both c and e have 5 followers and their time is tied at 13 s also.

****f is assigned randomly—both f and h have 2 followers and their time is tied at 20 s also.

*****h is assigned because it has 2 followers, more than 1 follower of g.

******g is assigned randomly—both g and i have 1 follower and their time is tied at 13 s also.

If the last workstation has a large idle time and the desired output rate is flexible, it might be worthwhile to increase the cycle time slightly and see if the number of workstations can be reduced by 1, thus saving significant labour cost.

Variable Task Times

Although it is convenient to treat assembly operations as if their time will be the same in each repetition, it is more realistic to assume that task times will be variable. The reasons for the variations are numerous, including worker fatigue, boredom, material shortages, defects, mechanical problems, and product differences.

The following example shows the effect of variation in task times on output. If three workstations each take 3 minutes to perform their tasks, then the output of the line will be 20 units per hour, with Percentage idle time = 0 (see case *a* in the following figure). However, if each workstation's time ranges from 2 to 4 minutes uniformly, assuming that there is no room for inventory between the workstations, it can be shown using simulation that the output of the line drops to 17.4 units per hour, with Percentage idle time = 13 percent (see case *b* in the figure below). Note that the average workstation time is still 3 minutes; however, workstations 1 and 2 are blocked if their successor workstation(s) takes longer and workstations 2 and 3 are starved if their predecessor workstation(s) takes longer.

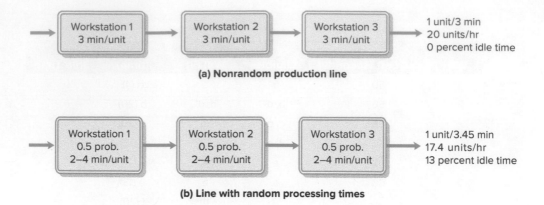

(a) Nonrandom production line

(b) Line with random processing times

Solutions to the variable task times include:

- Reducing the variability (e.g., by designing the work better, by using high-quality material, and by doing preventive maintenance).
- Using buffer inventory between workstations.
- Leaving some idle time in workstations that have variable time.
- Cross-training workers so that an adjacent worker can assist a worker who is temporarily over-burdened.

Treatment of Bottleneck Workstation

Several solutions are used to deal with a bottleneck workstation. First, one or more tasks in the bottleneck workstation can be automated or made easier using equipment such as a tool balancer. Second, if the bottleneck occurs because of only some products, the tasks for these products can be done offline or online by a special crew of "floaters." Third, use parallel workstations, which increase the workflow and provide flexibility.

Consider the following example. A job has four tasks; task times are 1 minute, 1 minute, 2 minutes, and 1 minute. Assume each task is assigned to a different workstation and there are no buffer inventories between the workstations. The cycle time for the line will be 2 minutes per unit and the output rate will be 30 units per hour:

$$\frac{60 \text{ minutes per hour}}{2 \text{ minutes per unit}} = 30 \text{ units per hour}$$

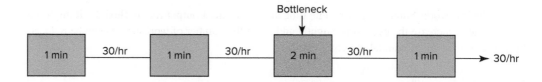

Using parallel workstations for the third task would result in a cycle time of 1 minute per unit because the output rate at the parallel workstations would total 60 units per hour, and this allows an output rate for the line of 60 units per hour:

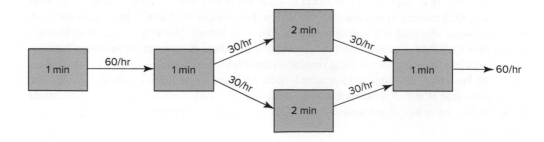

Designing Process (Functional) Layouts

LO6

In a process layout, similar resources are grouped in a department. Design of process (functional) layouts involves determining the position of the departments on the facility floor. For example, in Figure 6-13, departments 1 to 6 must be assigned to locations A to F on the facility floor. In general, some departments benefit from having adjacent locations, whereas others should be separated. For example, a lab with delicate equipment should not be located near a department with strong vibrations. Conversely, two departments that share some equipment would benefit from being close together.

The ideal situation is to first develop a layout and then design the physical structure (building) around it, thus permitting maximum flexibility in design. This procedure is commonly followed when new facilities are constructed. However, many layouts must be developed in existing structures where the shape of the floor, the dimensions of the building, and the location of entrances and elevators, reinforced flooring, and other similar factors must be carefully weighed in designing the layout. Multi-level structures are more challenging for layout planners.

Customers or materials in a process layout may require different operations and different sequences of operations, which causes them to follow different paths through the facility. Because transportation cost, distance, or time can be significant, one of the major objectives in process layout design is to minimize total transportation cost, distance, or time.

Locations			Departments to be assigned
A	B	C	1
			2
			3
D	E	F	4
			5
			6

▲ **FIGURE 6-13**

In process layout, departments are assigned to locations on the facility floor.

Minimizing Total Transportation Distance, Cost, or Time

The inputs to process layout design are:

1. A list of departments or work centres, their approximate dimensions, and the dimensions of the building that will house the departments.

2. Current and forecast of future workflows between the various departments.

3. The distance between centres of locations and the cost or time per unit of distance to move loads between locations.

4. A list of any special considerations (e.g., departments that must be close to each other or that must be separated).

It can be helpful to summarize the necessary data in *from–to* charts like those in Table 6-5 and Table 6-6. Table 6-6 displays current or forecast work flow (loads per day) between departments. Table 6-5 displays the distance between centres of locations. For instance, a trip from the centre of location A to the centre of location B will involve a distance of 20 metres. Oddly enough, the length of a trip between centres of two locations may differ depending on the *direction* of the trip, due to one-way routes, elevation, or other factors. To simplify the discussion, we assume the same distance between centres of any two locations regardless of direction. However, it is not realistic to assume that interdepartmental workflows are equal. For example, several departments may send goods to the packaging department, but packaging may send goods only to the shipping department.

Transportation costs (or times) can also be summarized in from–to charts, but we shall avoid that complexity, assuming instead that costs (or times) are a direct, linear function of distance.

In practice, there are a large number of possible assignments. For example, 14 departments can be assigned to 14 locations in more than 87 billion different ways (equal to $14 \times 13 \times 12 \times 11 \times 10 \times 9 \times 8 \times 7 \times 6 \times 5 \times 4 \times 3 \times 2 \times 1$, which is called "14 factorial," and written as "14!"). This makes finding an optimal solution difficult. Often planners must rely on a heuristic to obtain a good, but not necessarily optimal, solution. A reasonable heuristic is to locate departments with high interdepartmental workflow as close together as possible.

◀ **TABLE 6-5**

Distance between centres of locations (metres).

From	To	Location		
		A	B	C
A		–	20	40
B		20	–	30
C		40	30	–

◀ **TABLE 6-6**

From–to departmental workflow (loads per day).

From	To	Department		
		1	2	3
1		–	10	80
2		20	–	30
3		90	70	–

EXAMPLE 6-8 ▶

Assign the three departments shown in Table 6-6 to locations A, B, and C, which are separated by the distances shown in Table 6-5, in such a way that total transportation cost is minimized. Assume that the cost per metre to move any load is $1. Assume that distances between centres of departments are independent of direction of flow (i.e., the from–to distance chart is symmetrical).

SOLUTION

Sum the workflows between pairs of departments in each direction and sort the pairs of departments by the total workflow (largest first):

Department Pair	Workflow	
3–1	90	⎫ 170
1–3	80	⎭
3–2	70	⎫ 100
2–3	30	⎭
2–1	20	⎫ 30
1–2	10	⎭

You can see that departments 1 and 3 have the highest interdepartmental workflow. Also note that centres of locations A and B are the closest. Thus, it seems reasonable to consider assigning departments 1 and 3 to locations A and B, although it is not yet obvious which department should be assigned to which location. Further inspection of the workflow list reveals that departments 2 and 3 have higher interdepartmental workflow than departments 1 and 2, so departments 2 and 3 should be located more closely than departments 1 and 2. Hence, it would seem reasonable to place department 3 between departments 1 and 2. The resulting assignments might appear as in Figure 6-14.

Because the cost per metre to move any load is $1, we can compute the total daily transportation cost for this solution by multiplying each pair of departments' number of loads by the distance between their centres, and summing those quantities:

Department	Number of Loads to:	Location	Distance Between Centres:	Loads × Distance
1	2: 10	A	C: 40	10 × 40 = 400
	3: 80		B: 20	80 × 20 = 1,600
2	1: 20	C	A: 40	20 × 40 = 800
	3: 30		B: 30	30 × 30 = 900
3	1: 90	B	A: 20	90 × 20 = 1,800
	2: 70		C: 30	70 × 30 = 2,100
				7,600

At $1 per load metre, the cost for this assignment is $7,600 per day.

FIGURE 6-14 ▶

Solution to Example 6-8.

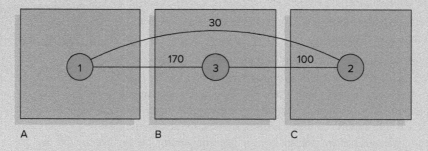

Heuristic

1. Assign the pair of departments with the greatest interdepartmental workflow to locations whose centres are closest to each other, keeping the future assignments in mind.

2. Then pick the pair with second highest workflow and assign them to two available locations whose centres are the next two closest, keeping their relationship with those already assigned and future assignments in mind.

3. Continue until all departments have been assigned.

Closeness Ratings

The preceding approach assumes that there is only one objective, the total transportation cost. Richard Muther developed a more general approach that uses the importance of closeness or remoteness of each pair of departments to managers.[8] This information is then summarized in a grid like that shown in

---

[8] Richard Muther and John Wheeler, "Simplified Systematic Layout Planning," *Factory* 120, nos. 8, 9, and 10 (August, September, October, 1962) pp. 68–77, 111–19, 101–13.

Department 1

Department 2

Department 3

Department 4

Department 5

Department 6

Code	Degree of closeness
A	Absolutely necessary
E	Very important
X	Undesirable

Figure 6-15. The letters represent the importance of closeness for each department pair, with A being absolutely necessary, E being very important, and X representing an undesirable pairing. Thus, in the grid in Figure 6-15 it is "absolutely necessary" to locate departments 1 and 2 close to each other because there is an A at the intersection of those departments on the grid. On the other hand, departments 1 and 4 should not be close together because their intersection has an X. In practice, the letters on the grid are often accompanied by numbers that indicate the reason for each closeness rating; they are omitted here to simplify the illustration. Muther suggests the following reasons for closeness/remoteness:

1. Use same equipment or facilities.
2. Share the same personnel.
3. Sequence of workflow.
4. Ease of communication.
5. Unsafe or unpleasant conditions.
6. Similar work performed.

Muther suggests that closeness ratings in the grid be first used to draw a relationship graph, using the A and X ratings, but keeping E ratings in mind. Then this graph is fitted onto the floor plan. Example 6-9 illustrates this heuristic.

Assign the six departments in Figure 6-15 to a 2 × 3 set of locations.

EXAMPLE 6-9

SOLUTION

Prepare a list of A and X ratings by referring to the grid in Figure 6-15:

A	X
1–2	1–4
1–3	3–4
2–6	3–6
3–5	
4–6	
5–6	

Next, form a cluster of A links, beginning with the department that appears most frequently in the A list (in this case, department 6):

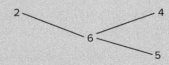

Take the remaining departments in order of number of appearance in the A list, and add them to the above main cluster, rearranging the cluster as necessary. Form separate clusters for departments that do not link with the main cluster. In this case, all departments link with the main cluster.

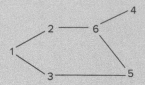

Next, graphically portray the Xs as "separation" cluster(s):

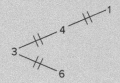

Finally, fit the As cluster into a 2×3 arrangement, keeping X separations in mind:

1	2	6
3	5	4

Note that alternative solutions are possible. For this solution, the E rating has also been satisfied, even though no attempt was made to explicitly consider it. Naturally, not every problem will yield the same results, so it may be necessary to do some additional adjusting to see if improvements can be made, keeping in mind that the A and X assignments deserve the greatest consideration.

Note that departments may be considered close not only when they touch side to side, but also when they touch corner to corner. However, side-by-side departments are closer.

Computer Software

www.plm.automation
.siemens.com/en_us
/products/tecnomatix
/manufacturing-planning
/factory-design/index
.shtml; www.autodesk
.com/suites/factory-design
-suite/overview

The difficulty and significant time required to accurately draw and visualize factory equipment and flows and to analyze the production process has led to the development of a number of computer software programs.

One example is the Plant Design & Optimization module of the Tecnomatix software of Siemens. This family (FactoryCAD, FactoryFlow, and Plant Simulation) provides icons for graphical display, calculates total material flow distances, uses several heuristics to determine a good layout, performs simulation of material flow, and provides 3-D walk-through. Another module is Robcad (Robot CAD) which simulates the operations of a robot.[9] Atomic Energy of Canada Limited uses Robcad and Siemens' Solid Edge (CAD) to digitally model a robot in a reactor to simulate safe and fast maintenance of the reactor. Another application of Tecnomatix is given in the "Magna Steyr" OM in Action.

Another software is Factory Design module of Autodesk, which does similar visualization and analysis to the Siemens software. In particular, it has icons for equipment that easily snap together and unsnap, facilitates new equipment drawing, allows easy 2D (AutoCAD) to 3D (Inventor) conversion, and helps identify interferences (e.g., a pillar blocking product movement).

 OM in ACTION www.magna.com/capabilities/ vehicle-engineering-contract-manufacturing

Magna Steyr

Magna Steyr, the Austrian subsidiary of Magna International, produces BMW X3 for BMW in its plant in Graz. In 2010, BMW also commissioned Magna Steyr to produce MINI Countryman on the same line. In order to model the inclusion of MINI on the line, the staff used Siemens Tecnomatix software to digitally model the robotics part of bodyshell manufacturing. The objective was to shorten the production line planning and reduce downtime. First, they made a 3D scan of the robots on the factory floor. These were loaded in Tecnomatix. Then, the welding requirements of MINI were loaded in the software. The result was surprisingly good: the software used as much as 95 percent of current robots for MINI.

Source: https://www.plm.automation.siemens.com/en_us/about_us/success/case_study.cfm?Component=123503&ComponentTemplate=1481.

---

[9] https://www.mayahtt.com/wp-content/uploads/2013/04/Atomic-Energy-of-Canada-Solid-Edge-Case-Study.pdf

Summary

- Process design determines the structure of a process—the sequence of operations (the workflow), resources, and controls needed for a particular process.
- There are three types of process: core, support, and managerial.
- Enterprise/organizational structure (that is, the way an organization divides its activities into processes) depends on the industry of the organization and the business environment.
- Production process types include job shop, batch, repetitive, and continuous flow. Job shop is used for many low-quantity customized products, batch process is used for few medium-quantity standard products that are produced in batches, and repetitive and continuous processes are used for one or two high-quantity/volume standard products.
- The product–process matrix relates the product quantity and variety to the process type and its flexibility.
- Automation is used to reduce the production costs and improve quality and speed. Examples include numerically controlled machines.
- Green technologies involve creation of goods using processes that are non-polluting while conserving energy and natural resources.
- Process design methodology involves finding a sequence of operations to produce the good or service, testing it, and finalizing it by determining the machines and plant layout. A process flow diagram is used to display the sequence of operations on materials in manufacturing.

- A service blueprint is similar to a process flow diagram, but follows the flow of customers.
- A swim lane diagram is similar to a service blueprint, but it groups the operations/activities by functions/roles.
- Facility layout design is used to determine the location of the machines and departments on the facility floor. A product layout is for a high-volume standardized product. Workers and equipment are arranged according to the technological sequence required by the product. Emphasis in design is on workflow through the system, and specialized processing and handling equipment is used.
- Process layouts group similar activities into departments or work centres. They can handle a wide range of processing requirements. However, this necessitates continual routing and scheduling. The rate of output is generally much lower than that of product layouts.
- Cellular layouts use a cell that processes a group of similar products or parts using different machines arranged in a "U" shape.
- The main effort in product layout design is assembly-line balancing, which focuses on bundling assembly tasks so that the time requirements for the workstations are as equal as possible.
- In process layout design, efforts focus on the relative positioning of departments to minimize total transportation cost or to meet other requirements concerning the closeness of certain department pairs.

Key Terms

assemble-to-order
assembly line
automation
batch process
cellular layout
computer-integrated manufacturing (CIM)
continuous process
core process
cycle time
enterprise/organization architecture
flexible manufacturing system (FMS)
green technology

group technology
industrial robot
job shop
layout
line balancing
make or buy
make-to-order
make-to-stock
managerial process
numerically controlled (N/C) machines
percentage idle time
precedence network

process design
process flow diagram
process layout
product layout
product–process matrix
production/inventory strategies
production line
repetitive process
support process
swim lane diagram
technology

Solved Problems

Problem 1

The tasks shown in the following precedence network are to be assigned to workstations with the intent of minimizing percentage idle time. Management desires an output rate of 275 units per day. Assume 440 minutes are available per day.

a. Determine the appropriate cycle time.

b. What is the minimum number of workstations possible?

c. Assign the tasks using the "Assign the task with the largest positional weight" heuristic rule.

d. Calculate efficiency.

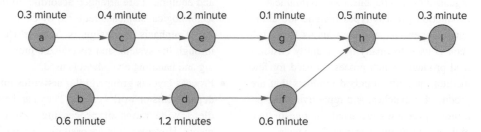

Solution

a. $CT = \dfrac{\text{Operating time}}{\text{Desired output}} = \dfrac{440 \text{ minutes per day}}{275 \text{ units per day}} = 1.6$ minutes per unit per workstation

b. $N_{min} = \dfrac{\sum t}{\text{Cycle time}} = \dfrac{4.2 \text{ minutes per unit}}{1.6 \text{ minutes per unit per workstation}}$

$= 2.625$, round up to 3 workstations

c. Add positional weights (task time plus the sum of all the following times) to the diagram. Start at the right end and work backward:

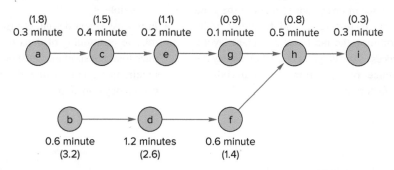

Workstation	Time Left*	Eligible	Will Fit	Assign Task (time)	Idle Time
1	1.6	a, b	a, b	b (0.6)	
	1.0	a, d	a	a (0.3)	
	0.7	c, d	c	c (0.4)	
	0.3	e, d	e	e (0.2)	
	0.1	g, d	g	g (0.1)	
	0.0	d	—	—	0.0
2	1.6	d	d	d (1.2)	
	0.4	f	—	—	0.4

(continued)

Workstation	Time Left*	Eligible	Will Fit	Assign Task (time)	Idle Time
3	1.6	f	f	f (0.6)	
	1.0	h	h	h (0.5)	
	0.5	i	i	i (0.3)	
	0.2	—	—	—	0.2
					0.6

* The initial time for each workstation is the cycle time calculated in part *a*.

The resulting assignments are shown below.

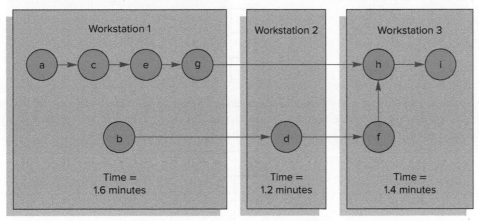

d. Efficiency = $100\% -$ Percent idle time $= 100\% - \dfrac{0.6 \text{ min.}}{3 \times 1.6 \text{ min.}} 100 = 87.5\%.$

Problem 2

Assign nine automobile service departments to bays in a 3 × 3 floor grid so that the closeness ratings in the following Muther grid are satisfied. Only A and X ratings are shown. The location of department 4 must be in the middle right-hand side of the floor grid.

Department 1
Department 2 A
   A
Department 3   A
   X A
Department 4   A
   A
Department 5   E   A
   X
Department 6   X
Department 7 X X
Department 8
Department 9

Solution

Department 1 has most A ratings, so make it the centre position in the cluster. After connecting all the other departments with A rating to department 1 and adding the other A ratings, we get the cluster:

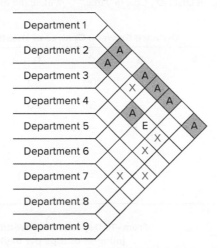

Next, we can identify the clusters of departmental pairings that should be avoided:

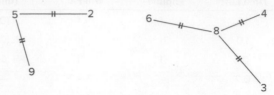

The departments in each X cluster should be spaced around the perimeter of the grid. Placing the A cluster on the floor plan with department 1 in the centre room and arbitrarily starting with department 6 in the top right room, we get:

2	3	6
9	1	4
7	5	

Now, using the X clusters, it follows that we should move departments 5 and 7 one room to the right and place department 8 in the bottom left room, so that department 5 is not close to department 9 and department 8 is not close to department 4. The following final floor plan results:

2	3	6
9	1	4
8	7	5

Problem 3

Five departments, 1 to 5, are to be assigned to locations B–F in the grid on the next page. For technical reasons, department 6 must be assigned to location A. Transportation cost is $2 per metre. The objective is to minimize total transportation cost. Information on from–to departmental workflows and distances between centres of locations is shown in the following tables. Use the heuristic given in the section "Minimizing Total Transportation Distance, Cost or Time." Calculate the total transportation cost.

		Distance Between Centres of Locations (metres)					
From	To	A	B	C	D	E	F
A		—	50	100	50	80	130
B			—	50	90	40	70
C				—	140	60	50
D					—	50	120
E						—	50
F							—

		From–To Departmental Workflows (number of trips per day)					
From	To	1	2	3	4	5	6
1		—	90	25	23	11	18
2		35	—	8	5	10	16
3		37	2	—	1	0	7
4		41	12	1	—	4	0
5		14	16	0	9	—	3
6		32	38	13	2	2	—

	A	B	C
	Dept. 6	B	C
	D	E	F

Solution

First, determine the total interdepartmental workflows (e.g., for 1–2 the flow is $90 + 35 = 125$) because the distances are symmetric. Then, arrange them from high to low.

Pair of Departments	Workflow	Pair of Departments	Workflow
1–2	125	2–4	17
1–4	64	4–5	13
1–3	62	2–3	10
2–6	54	5–6	5
1–6	50	3–4	2
2–5	26	4–6	2
1–5	25	3–5	0
3–6	20		

From this, we can see that departments 1 and 2 have the greatest interdepartmental workflow, so they should be closest, perhaps at B and E (which have the smallest between-centres distance). However, since workflow between 2 and 6 is larger than between 1 and 6, place department 1 in location E and department 2 in location B. Next, workflow between 1 and 4 is highest. The workflow between 4 and 6 is low, suggesting that they need not be close. Therefore, place department 4 in F. Next, workflow between 1 and 3 is highest. Hence, place department 3 in location D. Finally, department 5 has to be placed at location C.

	A	B	C
	Dept. 6	Dept. 2	Dept. 5
	D	E	F
	Dept. 3	Dept. 1	Dept. 4

Total cost:

Pair of Dept.	b Distance	c Workflow	(b × c × $2) Cost
1–2	(B–E) 40	125	$10,000
1–3	(D–E) 50	62	6,200
1–4	(F–E) 50	64	6,400
1–5	(E–C) 60	25	3,000
1–6	(A–E) 80	50	8,000
2–3	(B–D) 90	10	1,800
2–4	(B–F) 70	17	2,380
2–5	(B–C) 50	26	2,600
2–6	(A–B) 50	54	5,400
3–4	(F–D) 120	2	480
3–5	(D–C) 140	0	0
3–6	(A–D) 50	20	2,000
4–5	(C–F) 50	13	1,300
4–6	(A–F) 130	2	520
5–6	(A–C) 100	5	1,000
			$51,080

Discussion and Review Questions

LO1 1. Define process design and describe its importance.

LO1 2. Briefly describe the four production process types and give a manufacturing example for each that is not mentioned in the chapter.

LO1 3. Give a service example for each of the four production process types.

LO2 4. List the advantages and disadvantages of automation in production.

LO2 5. List and briefly describe computer-aided approaches to production.

LO2 6. What is a numerically controlled machine?

LO1 7. What is the product–process matrix? What is its purpose?

LO3 8. Describe the methodology for process design.

LO3 9. What is a process flow diagram?

LO3 10. What are the differences between process design for services versus goods?

LO4 11. Describe the general approach for layout design.

LO4 12. Relate process and product layout to production process types.

LO4 13. What are the main advantages of a product layout? The main disadvantages?

LO4 14. What are the main advantages of a process layout? The main disadvantages?

LO4 15. Why are routing and scheduling continual problems in process layouts?

LO4 16. Compare machine/equipment maintenance strategies in product and process layouts.

LO4 17. Briefly outline the impact that job operations sequence has on each of the layout types.

LO4 18. A city transportation planning committee must decide whether to begin a long-term project to build a subway system or to upgrade the present bus service. Suppose you are an expert in fixed-path and variable-path material-handling equipment, and the committee seeks your counsel on this matter. What are the advantages and limitations of the subway and bus systems?

LO4 19. Why are product layouts atypical in service environments?

LO1 & 4 20. According to a study, it costs more than three times the original purchase price in parts and labour to fix a totally wrecked automobile. Explain the reasons for this large discrepancy.

LO4 21. How can a layout help or hinder productivity?

LO4 22. What is a cellular layout? What are its main benefits and limitations?

LO4 23. What is group technology?

LO5 24. What is the goal of line balancing? What happens if a line is unbalanced?

LO5 25. Explain the consequence of task-time variability on line balancing and how to deal with it.

LO6 26. What is the main objective of process layout?

LO1 27. What is a process and what are the three types of processes? Give an example of each.

LO1 28. What is enterprise/organization architecture?

LO2 29. What is a green technology?

LO3 30. What is a service blueprint?

LO3 31. What is a swim lane diagram and when should it be used?

LO2 32. How has McDonald's changed its service process recently?

LO2 33. Give an example of a green technology.

LO3 34. What is par-baking and how has it helped Tim Hortons restaurants?

LO3 35. How is the layout of an Apple store different from the layout of another store such as Best Buy?

Taking Stock

LO3 & 5 1. Name a major trade-off in (a) production process design and (b) each type of layout design.

LO3 & 4 2. Who needs to be involved in production process design? Layout design?

LO2 & 6 3. In what ways does technology have an impact on production process design? Layout design?

LO3 4. Use of efficient production processes in raising animals for meat has resulted in factory farms where animals (pigs, hens, etc.) are kept in confinement at high stocking density. For example, female pigs are impregnated and kept in gestation crates (2 feet by 7 feet) for the whole four months of pregnancy. This process is repeated after the delivery. Many people consider this practice unethical. In fact, it has been banned in Europe. Smithfield Foods, the largest U.S. pork producer, under pressure from McDonald's, has decided to stop the use of gestation crates in its 187 pig nurseries.[10] Where in the process design methodology should this kind of ethical issue be considered?

---

[10] M. Kaufman, "Largest Pork Processor to Phase Out Crates," *Washington Post*, January 26, 2007, p. A06.

Critical Thinking Exercises

LO2 **1.** When would automation be feasible?

LO4 **2.** Layout decisions affect a wide range of facilities, from factories, grocery stores, offices, department stores, and warehouses, to malls, parking lots, and kitchens. Layout is also important in the design of some products such as the interiors of cars and computers. Select three different items from above and list one or two key considerations (objectives) for the item's layout design.

LO2 **3.** What is the risk of automating a production process? Give an example.

Experiential Learning Exercises

LO1 **1.** Visit a supermarket and identify an area of the store that has the characteristics of each of these production process types: job shop, batch, and repetitive.

LO4 **2.** Compare the layout of a supermarket to the layout of a convenience store. Explain the differences you observe.

LO3 **3.** Design an assembly line for preparing a turkey sub (lettuce, tomato, mayonnaise, and turkey). Use about six workstations. Begin with "cut the bun open," and end with "close the bun and cut the sub in half." Estimate the time needed (in seconds) for each workstation.

LO4 **4.** Compare the layouts of two gas stations. Which is better?

5. Buy a few copies of a Lego product, such as a Lego Racer (8119), and form a team of at least two.

    a. Disassemble the car and familiarize yourself with the pieces.

    b. Assemble the car according to the instruction sheet (in the box) a few times until you learn how to do it from memory.

    c. Assign tasks to individual members, and make an assembly line.

    d. Run the assembly line until all cars of your group are assembled, while timing the total time.

    e. Discuss various ways of reducing your time without causing quality problems.

    f. Disassemble all cars.

    g. Implement your improvement, run the line again, and time it.

    h. Summarize what you learned from this exercise.

Internet Exercises

LO3 **1.** View the video(s) of the following companies and draw their process flow diagram:

    a. AirBoss of America   http://www.airbossofamerica .com/tour

    b. Lego   http://www.youtube.com /watch?v=wnRRDIFNxoM

    c. Potash Corp   http://minetour.potashcorp.com

    d. Dofasco   https://www.youtube.com /watch?v=fPQHsoCEujU

LO3 **2.** Visit http://manufacturing.stanford.edu, click on "How Everyday Things Are Made," choose a product from the left column (e.g., airplane, motorcycle, cars, jelly beans, bottles, wool, denim), click on it, watch the video, and draw the process flow diagram.

LO1 **3.** Read http://www.bptrends.com/publicationfiles/11-05-WP -BoeingATBPM-Garretson-Harmon.pdf. Name one each of core, support, and managerial process of Boeing's Airlift and Tanker division.

LO2 **4.** Visit http://www.nitalabelingequipment.com/products /synerg-xp-series-automatic-labeling-systems and http:// www.assemblymag.com/articles/92399-motor-drives -ensure-precise-label-placement, and decide what type of automation (fixed, programmable, or flexible) Nita's Synergy labelling machine is. Explain.

LO1 **5.** View https://www.youtube.com/watch?v=kQmqNOuRzb0, and explain the difference between Boeing's old and new method of assembly of 777s.

LO4 & 5 **6.** View https://www.youtube.com/watch?v=c50_lAIfzsk, and explain how workers help each other in a manufacturing cell of Denimatrix.

LO3 **7.** Watch the Noodles & Company video http://canmedia .mheducation.ca/college/olcsupport/stevenson/5ce/videos /VidPlayer.php?vid=Noodles_and_Company_Service _Process_Design, and draw its service blueprint.

LO3 **8.** Read http://www.interfacing.com/uploads/File/bombardier .pdf and describe how the business aircraft division of Bombardier improved its customer support process.

Problems

LO5 **1.** An assembly line with 17 tasks is to be balanced. The longest task is 2.4 minutes, and the total time for all tasks is 18 minutes. The line will operate for 450 minutes per day.
   a. What is the minimum number of workstations needed if the output rate is to be 180 units per day?
   b. What cycle time will provide an output rate of 125 units per day?
   c. What output will result if the cycle time is
   (i) 9 minutes? (ii) 15 minutes?

LO5 **2.** A manager wants to assign tasks to workstations to achieve an hourly output rate of 33 units. Assume that the shop works 60 minutes per hour (i.e., no breaks).
   a. Assign the tasks shown in the following precedence network (times are on the nodes and are in minutes) to workstations using the following heuristic rules:
   (i) "Assign the task with the most followers."
   (ii) Tiebreaker: "Assign the task with the longest time."
   b. What is the efficiency?

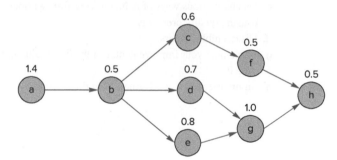

LO5 **3.** A manager wants to assign tasks to workstations in order to achieve an hourly output rate of four units. The department uses a working time of 56 minutes per hour.
   a. Assign the tasks shown in the following precedence network (times are on the nodes and are in minutes) to workstations using the following heuristic rules:
   (i) "Assign the task with the largest positional weight."
   (ii) Tiebreaker: "Assign the task with the longest time." If a tie still exists, choose randomly.
   b. What is the efficiency?

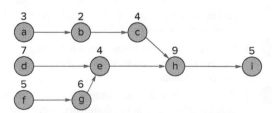

LO5 **4.** A large manufacturer of pencil sharpeners is planning to add a new sharpener, and you have been asked to balance the assembly line, given the following task times and precedence relationships. Assume that cycle time is 1.3 minutes per unit.

Task	Duration (minutes)	Immediate Follower
a	0.2	b
b	0.4	d
c	0.3	d
d	1.3	g
e	0.1	f
f	0.8	g
g	0.3	h
h	1.2	–

   a. Do each of the following:
   i. Draw the precedence network.
   ii. Assign the tasks to workstations using the heuristic rule "Assign the task with the most followers." Break ties using the heuristic rule "Assign the task with the longest time."
   iii. Determine the percentage idle time.
   iv. Calculate the rate of output that could be expected for this line assuming a 420-minute working day.
   b. Answer these questions:
   i. What is the shortest cycle time that will permit the use of only two workstations? Identify the tasks you would assign to each workstation.
   ii. Determine the percentage idle time that would result if two workstations were used.
   iii. What is the daily output under this arrangement?

LO5 **5.** As part of a major plant renovation project, the industrial engineering department has been asked to balance a revised assembly line to achieve an output rate of 240 units per eight-hour day. Task times and precedence relationships are as follows:

Task	Duration (minutes)	Precedes Task
a	0.2	b
b	0.4	d
c	0.2	d
d	0.4	g
e	1.2	f
f	1.2	g
g	1.0	–

   a. Draw the precedence network.
   b. Determine the required cycle time.
   c. Determine the minimum number of workstations needed.
   d. Assign the tasks to workstations using the heuristic rule "Assign the task with the most followers." Use

222

2222

222

the heuristic rule "Assign the task with the longest time" as a tiebreaker. If a tie still exists, choose randomly.

e. Calculate the percentage idle time for the assignments in part *d*.

L05 **6.** Twelve tasks, with times and precedence requirements as shown in the following table, are to be assigned to workstations using a cycle time of 1.5 minutes. Heuristic rule "Assign the task with the most followers" will be tried. The tiebreaker will be the heuristic rule "Assign the task with the longest time."

Task	Duration (minutes)	Follows Task	Task	Duration (minutes)	Follows Task
a	0.1	—	g	0.4	f
b	0.2	a	h	0.1	g
c	0.9	b	i	0.2	h
d	0.6	c	j	0.7	i
e	0.1	—	k	0.3	j
f	0.2	d, e	l	0.2	k

a. Draw the precedence network.
b. Assign tasks to workstations.
c. Calculate the percentage idle time.

L05 **7.** For the following tasks:
a. Develop the precedence network.
b. Determine the cycle time (in seconds) for a desired output rate of 500 units in a seven-hour day.
c. Determine the minimum number of workstations for an output rate of 500 units per day.
d. Balance the line using the "Assign the task with the most followers" heuristic rule. Break ties with "Assign the task with the longest time" heuristic rule. Use a cycle time of 50 seconds.
e. Calculate the percentage idle time for the line.

Task	Task Time (seconds)	Immediate Predecessors
A	45	—
B	11	A
C	9	B
D	50	—
E	26	D
F	11	E
G	12	C
H	10	C
I	9	F, G, H
J	10	I
	193	

L05 **8.** A shop works a 400-minute day. The manager of the shop wants an output rate of 200 units per day for the assembly line that has the tasks shown in the following table. Do the following:
a. Construct the precedence network and calculate the cycle time.
b. Assign tasks according to "Assign the task with the most followers" rule. In the case of a tie, use "Assign the task with the longest time" heuristic rule.
c. Calculate the balance delay.

Task	Immediately Precedes Task(s)	Task Time	Task	Immediately Precedes Task(s)	Task Time
a	b, c, d	0.5	g	h	0.4
b	e	1.4	h	k	0.3
c	e	1.2	i	j	0.5
d	f	0.7	j	k	0.8
e	g, j	0.5	k	m	0.9
f	i	1.0	m	—	0.3

L06 **9.** Arrange six departments into a 2 × 3 floor grid so that these conditions are satisfied: 1 is close to 2; 5 is close to 2, 4, and 6; and 3 is not close to 1 or 2.

L06 **10.** Using the information given in the preceding problem, develop a Muther grid using the letters A and X. Leave any pair of combinations not mentioned blank.

L06 **11.** Using the information in the following Muther grid, determine the department locations on the following floor plan. Note that departments 1 and 7 must be in the locations shown.

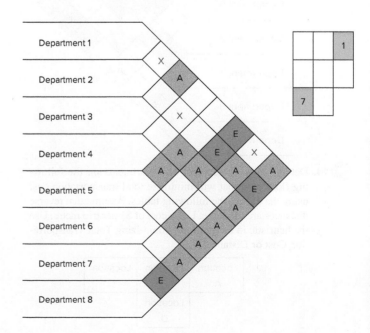

L06 **12.** Arrange the eight departments shown in the following Muther grid into a 2 × 4 floor plan. *Note:* Department 2 must be in the location shown.

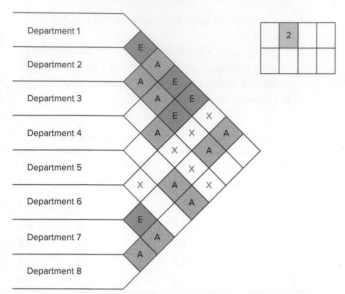

L06 **13.** Arrange nine departments into a 3 × 3 floor grid so that they satisfy the conditions shown in the following Muther grid. Place department 5 in the lower left corner of the 3 × 3 floor grid.

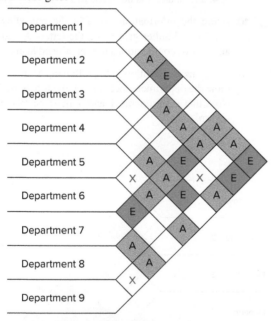

L06 **14.** Determine the placement of departments on the following floor plan that will minimize total transportation cost using the data in the following tables. Assume that reverse distances are the same. Use a cost of $1 per trip metre. Use the heuristic in the section "Minimizing Total Transportation Cost or Distance."

Location A	Location B	Location C
	Location D	

Distance Between Centres of Locations (metres)

From	To	A	B	C	D
A		–	40	80	70
B			–	40	50
C				–	60
D					–

Number of Trips per Day From–To Departments

From	To	1	2	3	4
1		–	10	20	30
2			–	40	40
3				–	25
4		50	50	30	–

L06 **15.** Eight work centres must be arranged in an L-shaped building. The locations of work centres 1 and 3 have already been assigned as shown in the following diagram. Assuming that transportation costs are $1 per load per metre, develop a suitable layout that minimizes total transportation cost using the information given below. (Assume the reverse distances are the same.) Use the heuristic in the section "Minimizing Total Transportation Cost or Distance."

A B		
1		
C	D	E
		3
F	G	H

Distance (metres)

From	To	A	B	C	D	E	F	G	H
A		–	40	40	60	120	80	100	110
B			–	60	40	60	140	120	130
C				–	45	85	40	70	90
D					–	40	50	40	45
E						–	90	50	40
F							–	40	60
G								–	40
H									–

Loads per Day

From	To	1	2	3	4	5	6	7	8
1		–	10	5	90	365	135	125	0
2		0	–	140	10	0	35	0	120
3		0	220	–	110	10	0	0	200
4		0	110	240	–	10	0	0	170
5		5	40	100	180	–	10	40	10
6		0	80	40	70	0	–	10	20
7		0	45	20	50	0	40	–	20
8		0	0	0	20	0	0	0	–

16. Develop a process layout that will minimize the total distance travelled by patients at a medical clinic, using the following information. Assume a distance of 35 feet between the reception area and each other location A to F. Assume that the reverse distances are the same. Use the floor plan shown below. Use the heuristic in the section "Minimizing Total Transportation Cost or Distance."

Distance Between Centres of Locations (feet)

From	To	A	B	C	D	E	F
A		–	20	60	80	120	160
B			–	40	60	80	120
C				–	40	60	80
D					–	40	60
E						–	40
F							–

Trips From–To Departments (per day)

From	To	1	2	3	4	5	6	Reception
Reception		10	10	200	20	0	100	–
1		–	0	0	80	20	40	10
2		0	–	0	0	0	20	40
3		40	0	–	10	190	10	10
4		30	50	0	–	10	70	0
5		60	40	60	30	–	20	10
6		10	100	0	20	0	–	30

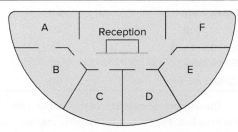

 17. Ten labs should be assigned to the circular floor plan shown below.

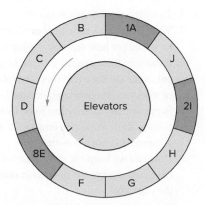

Recalling a similar layout's congestion in the halls, the new lab manager has requested an assignment that will minimize traffic between offices, but movement in the hall is restricted to a counterclockwise route.

Develop a suitable layout using the following information. Assign Lab 1 to Location A, Lab 2 to Location I, and Lab 8 to Location E.

Number of Trips per Day From–To Labs

From	To	1	2	3	4	5	6	7	8	9	10
1		—	40	1	20	20	4	0	2	6	5
2		0	—	2	15	25	10	2	12	13	6
3		50	35	—	10	13	4	0	4	7	1
4		6	1	8	—	0	14	10	20	22	11
5		3	2	7	35	—	22	5	9	19	10
6		5	5	10	0	2	—	15	0	1	20
7		20	16	50	4	9	2	—	1	3	0
8		10	6	14	2	4	44	13	—	1	25
9		5	5	18	1	2	40	30	42	—	32
10		30	30	35	20	15	5	40	10	15	—

 18. For the process of conducting a bank transaction using a teller in your bank, draw a service blueprint. Use only the customer and a (visible) teller.

 19. Based on your experience, draw a swim lane diagram for a customer of McDonald's buying a cheeseburger, fries, and drink. Show the cheeseburger assembly by just one box with 60 seconds of time. Try to specify the times for each box. Assume "to go."

 20. Draw a process flow diagram for preparing a personal income tax return.

 21. Draw a process flow diagram for mass producing potato chips. Start with trucks bringing potatoes to the plant. (*Hint:* First imagine how this can be done at home on a small scale and then try to convert the process to large-scale mass production. You may watch www.youtube.com/watch?v=ho-Az4mhaXY.)

 22. Draw a process flow diagram for batch production of bagels, as done by, for example, Great Canadian Bagel Company. (*Hint:* First imagine how this can be done at home (it is similar to making bread) and then try to convert the process to batch production at a store.)

 23. a. A pencil is made from a graphite rod and wooden body (plus a metal band and eraser at one end). Given the graphite rod, come up with two different ways (concepts) of manufacturing a pencil (ignore the metal band and eraser).

b. Draw a process flow diagram for mass producing a pencil. You may use the photos and descriptions from http://www.generalpencil.com/how-a-pencil-is-made.html.

General Pencil Company, Jersey City, NJ, http://www.generalpencil.com

 24. Draw a process flow diagram for making yarn (thread) from fleece (sheep wool). Use approximately four major steps. You may use http://www.blackberry-ridge.com/prosdscr.htm as a source.

LO3 25. a. Chocolate is toasted, ground (and heated), refined, and moulded seeds of cocoa beans. Draw a process flow diagram (approximately five operations) for making chocolate from cocoa beans at home. State what equipment (if any) you plan to use for each operation.

b. View the video at https://www.youtube.com/watch?v=0TcFYfoB1BY and draw the process flow diagram for mass producing milk chocolate with almond (approximately eight operations).

LO3 26. Paper is made from wood pulp. Wood pulp is made from wood chips by either cooking it with chemicals (called Kraft pulp) or grinding the wood chips into its fibres (called thermo-mechanical pulp). Pulp is cleaned and possibly bleached before papermaking. If one were to make paper at home, the following process could be used:

"The pulp is poured into a large tub and the fibres are suspended in the water. A framed screen is dipped into the water and is lifted to the surface, catching the fibres onto the screen. The screen can either be left in the sun to dry, or be pressed, smoothed and then dried."[11]

Design a continuous process for mass producing paper. Assume pulp has already been made. Draw the process flow diagram.

LO3 27. Audio Innovations of Stillwater, Oklahoma, makes car speaker cabinets and enclosures. Before 2001, it made 12,000 cabinets per month using 130 workers and a labour-intensive process. Then it was purchased by Rockford Corp of Arizona, which increased its capacity and productivity.

Before the change the process was as follows: 5/8 inch–thick medium density fiberboard (MDF) was cut into individual sides of the cabinet using a beam saw (a circular saw on a table guided by beams). Then, for each piece a router was used to machine the slanted edges. Next, to cover the four sides a strip of carpet was cut, and the four sides were glued to the strip. Then, the strip ends were glued together. Finally, the front and back pieces were glued.

The process change involved both the nature of operations and their automation. A machine (called a laminator) was bought to glue carpet to the whole sheet of MDF. Then, the carpeted board was cut into a piece the size of the four sides using the beam saw. A computerized grooving line was purchased to make three V-grooves where the piece will be folded to form the sides of the box. After this, a worker glued the strip ends together. Finally, the front and back pieces were glued.

As a result of the change, the company can make 20,000 cabinets per month using the same number of workers.

1. Draw the process flow diagram before the change.
2. Draw the process flow diagram after the change.

3. Determine the productivity before and after the change.[12]

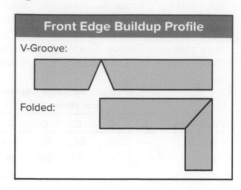

L. Ohm, "Automation Boosts Production 65 Percent," FDM—*The Magazine of Woodworking Production Management,* Aug 2003, 75(12), pp. 48–54.

LO3 28. Draw a process flow diagram for packing six 227-gram cartons of baby cereal into cardboard cases. Assume that filled cartons arrive from the manufacturing process on a conveyor, collapsed cases are on a nearby cart, and packed cases are put on a conveyor to the palletizing area.[13]

LO5 29. The tasks performed in a cafeteria to serve a customer and the average service times are as follows:

Tasks	Service Time per Customer (seconds)
Serve vegetables	25
Serve entree	30
Serve soup	20
Serve dessert	15
Serve drink	10
Collect money	60

The only precedence relationship is that "collect money" has to be last. The current layout performs these tasks in the sequence given; each task is performed by one worker except that only one worker serves both dessert and drink.

a. i. Draw the precedence network.
ii. What is the maximum number of customers who can be served per hour (capacity) using the current layout?
iii. Assuming that capacity in part *ii* equals desired output, what are the cycle time and minimum number of workstations (workers) needed?
iv. Suppose that capacity has to be increased. Where can the sixth worker be employed, assuming that equipment is not a constraint?
v. How can we keep the same number of workers (five) but change the process in order to increase the capacity?

---

[11] http://www.hqpapermaker.com/paper-history
[12] L. Ohm, "Automation Boosts Production 65 Percent," *FDM—The Magazine of Woodworking Production Management*, August 2003, 75(12), pp. 48–54.
[13] An automated case packer can be seen at http://www.trinamics.com/616sl.html and its use in H. J. Heinz is described in J. Mans, "Servos Increase Case-Packing Efficiency," *Packaging Digest*, 43(7), July 2006, pp. 26–29.

b. Using Cycle time = 35 seconds and "Assign the task with the longest time" as the heuristic rule, balance the assembly line, and calculate the percentage idle time.

L05 **30.** Suppose you need to assemble 67 Quickline Guest tables in one hour (see the photos beneath the table). The assembly activities and their standard times are listed below.

Using common sense, draw a precedence network and calculate the cycle time. Then, perform assembly-line balancing using the "Assign the task with the longest time" heuristic rule, breaking ties using the "Assign the task with the most followers" heuristic rule. Any further ties can be broken randomly.

Activity	Standard Time (seconds)
A. Lay the top face down on a clean surface.	10
B_1. Attach a mounting bracket to a corner of the top using three screws.	35
C_1. Add a compression ring on the bracket.	5
D_1. Slide one end of a leg over the compression ring and turn it so that the hole is aligned with the Allen screw.	10
E_1. Tighten the screw with the Allen wrench.	15
B_2. Attach another mounting bracket to another corner of the top using three screws.	35
C_2. Add another compression ring.	5
D_2. Slide one end of another leg over the compression ring and turn it.	10
E_2. Tighten with the Allen wrench.	15
B_3. Attach another mounting bracket to another corner of the top using three screws.	35
C_3 Add another compression ring.	5
D_3. Slide the end of another leg over the compression ring and turn it.	10
E_3. Tighten with the Allen wrench.	15
B_4. Attach another mounting bracket to another corner of the top using three screws.	35
C_4. Add another compression ring.	5
D_4. Slide the end of another leg over the compression ring and turn it.	10
E_4. Tighten with the Allen wrench.	15
F. Turn the table over on its legs.	30

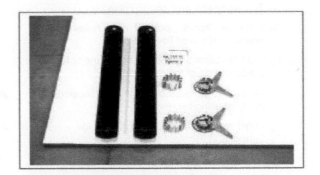

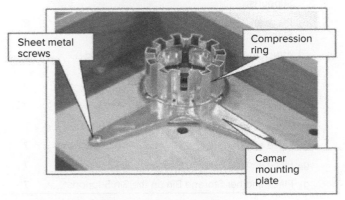

Sheet metal screws · Compression ring · Camar mounting plate

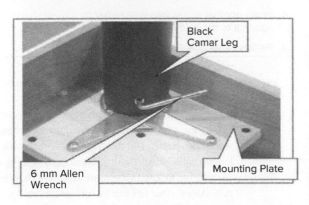

Black Camar Leg · 6 mm Allen Wrench · Mounting Plate

All photos courtesy of Harris Corporation

L05 31. Consider the Scoot & Go Rider shown at right, made by the Processed Plastic Company (PPC). Suppose that PPC has received a rush order from Walmart for 8,800 units to be shipped in five days.

a. Assuming 16-hour workdays, calculate the cycle time.

b. Start with the body on the table, and assume all parts are within reach. Also assume that the steering wheel sub-assembly has already been made. Using common sense, draw a precedence network for the following activities, which are required to assemble a Scoot & Go Rider.

Activity	Standard Time (seconds)
a. Insert the steering wheel sub-assembly into the body.	7
b. Hammer the front (short) axle into a pal nut (using the pal nut tool).	10
c. Slide a wheel into the component resulting from b.	5
d. Pass component resulting from c through the steering shaft hole.	5
e. Slide a wheel into component resulting from d.	4
f. Hammer the component resulting from e into a pal nut (using the pal nut tool).	12
g. Hammer the rear (long) axle into a pal nut (using the pal nut tool).	10
h. Slide a wheel into the component resulting from g.	6
i. Pass component resulting from h through the body's rear axle holes.	7
j. Slide a wheel into component resulting from i.	4
k. Hammer the component resulting from j into a pal nut (using the pal nut tool).	13
l. Place walker bar on the body and attach using one screw.	15
m. Insert another screw into walker bar to attach it to the body.	11
n. Insert another screw into walker bar to attach it to the body.	11
o. Insert another screw into walker bar to attach it to the body.	11
p. Perform final quality check and box it.	30

c. If the cycle time is 33 seconds, what is the minimum number of workstations needed?

d. Perform assembly-line balancing using 33 seconds of cycle time, the standard times, and the precedence network from part b. Use the "Assign the task with the longest time" heuristic rule, breaking ties using the "Assign the task with the most followers" heuristic rule. Any further ties can be broken arbitrarily.

#17300/#17360
Go & Scoot Rider™/MC
A Tim Mee Toy by
Processed Plastic Co.
1001 Aucutt Road
Montgomery, IL 60538

#17300
#17360
ASSEMBLY INSTRUCTIONS

#	DESCRIPTION	Qty
A	BODY	1
B	WALKER BAR	1
C	WHEEL	4
D	PAL NUT	4
E	PAL NUT TOOL	2
F	SHORT AXLE	1
G	LONG AXLE	1
H	3/4" SCREW	4

PARTS LIST

Note: Pal nut tools (E) are used for assembly, then discarded.

Processed Plastic Co., www.processedplastic.com

L05 32. Consider the Playskool Storage Studio that follows. We wish to design an assembly line to assemble several units. The assembly tasks and their standard times (in seconds) are as follows.

Tasks	Standard Time (seconds)
a. Place the Toy Chest (A), with the Lid/Art Board (F) already attached, on the conveyor.	8
b_1. Slide one Side Support (B) in the holes on one side of top of Toy Chest.	9
b_2. Slide the other Side Support (B) in the holes on the other side of top of Toy Chest.	9
c_1. Attach one Bin Support (C) to Side Supports in the front using two pins (D).	20
c_2. Attach another Bin Support (C) to Side Supports in the front using two pins.	20
d. Insert four pins in the Brace (G).	15
e_1. Place one Bin Support (C) in the back on Side Supports.	8
e_2. Place another Bin Support (C) in the back on Side Supports.	8
f. Attach the Brace (with pins) to the Bin and Side Supports in the back.	40
g_1. Place a Storage Bin (E) on the Bin Supports.	7
g_2. Place another Storage Bin on the Bin Supports.	7
g_3. Place another Storage Bin on the Bin Supports.	7
g_4. Place another Storage Bin on the Bin Supports.	7
g_5. Place another Storage Bin on the Bin Supports.	7
g_6. Place another Storage Bin on the Bin Supports	7

The parts are to be assembled according to the following precedence network:

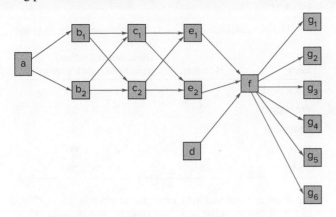

a. Calculate the cycle time if 75 units per hour are to be assembled.

b. What is the minimum number of workstations?

c. Using your answer to part *a*, perform assembly-line balancing using the "Assign the task with the longest time" heuristic rule, breaking any ties using the "Assign the task with the most followers" rule. If there is still a tie, break it randomly.

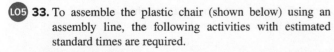

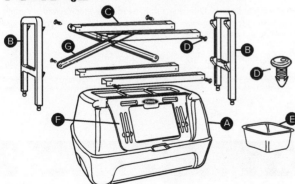

Processed Plastic Co., www.processedplastic.com

L05 33. To assemble the plastic chair (shown below) using an assembly line, the following activities with estimated standard times are required.

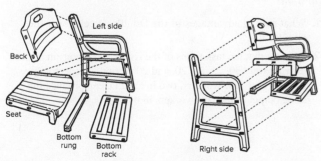

Processed Plastic Co., www.processedplastic.com

Activity	Standard Time (seconds)
A. Place left side inside up on the work area.	5 seconds
B. Tap back in.	8
C. Tap seat in.	13
D. Tap bottom rung in.	7
E. Tap bottom rack in.	9
F. Align all slots and tap right side in.	15

a. Draw a precedence network for this assembly.

b. If the desired output rate of the assembly line is 120 chairs per hour, what is the minimum number of workstations required?

c. Using a cycle time of 30 seconds per chair, and the "Assign the task with the longest time" heuristic rule, design the assembly line (i.e., balance the line).

L05 34. A large centralized food production (i.e., kitchen) facility is to be constructed for 29 hospitals. A small consulting firm has been contracted to design the facility. The firm has determined that the production process should be decomposed into the following departments and desired area for each, in addition to departments given on the following layout diagram (which has 200 ft by 150 ft floor space). Using common sense, determine the location of the unassigned departments on the layout:

Department	Desired Area (ft^2)
Vegetable fridges	2,700
Dry storeroom and dairy fridges	2,300
Poultry and meat freezers	1,500
Cook–chill area	3,800
Finished products coolers and fridges	2,800

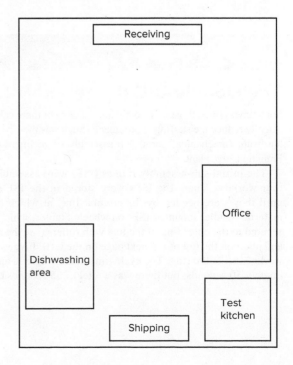

MINI-CASE

School Chairs

School chairs are usually made of plastic and metal, costing anywhere from $30 to $100 each. You wish to evaluate the idea of manufacturing wooden chairs for sale to schools, churches, etc. You have found the following design for a chair.

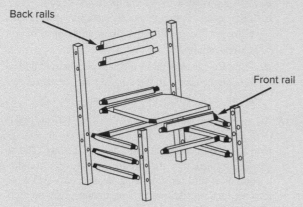

Back rails

Front rail

Source: Based on H. Quesada and R. Gazo, "Development of a Manufacturing System for Construction of School Furniture," *Forest Products Journal* 53(9), September 2003, pp. 47–54.

Most wooden chairs are made of hardwoods such as oak, maple, cherry, or cedar. Suppose that cedar is the cheapest where you live.

The dimensions of the parts of the chair are as follows:

Item	Number	Dimension (inches; thickness, width, length)
Back post	2	2 × 2 × 36
Front post	2	2 × 2 × 18
Cross-bar	10	1 × 1 × 14
Rails	3	2 × 1 × 14
Seat	1	1 × 16 × 16

The most economical size of cedar lumber is 2″ × 4″ × 8′ (i.e., 2 inches thick by 4 inches wide by 8 feet long). Therefore, you intend to buy only this size.

Questions

1. Calculate the number of pieces of this lumber that you will need per chair.

2. Determine the operations needed to make the chair and draw a process flow diagram. Note that the cross-bars and rails have a tenon (a small round tip) on each end that will go in the mortise (the hole) of the posts. These have to be made. Also, the seat's corners have to be cut to allow for the posts.

Source: Based on H. Quesada and R. Gazo, "Development of a Manufacturing System for Construction of School Furniture," *Forest Products Journal* 53(9), September 2003, pp. 47–54.

Q **MINI-CASE**

The Double-D Cell

Sometimes converting an assembly line into two or more cells will actually reduce the staffing requirements. Such was the case in the hardware (mechanical parts) sub-assembly of recliners in the Franklin Corp. plant.

The initial sub-assembly frames (ISF) were assembled by four workers. Then, the ISFs were stored in the ISF queue until they were needed by the circular line, at which time a material handler mounted ISFs on wheeled tables, which were secured to the outer ring of the line with rollers (see the sketch and photo at the top of the next page on the left). Five workers worked inside the ring. The cycle time in the ring was approximately 30 seconds, but there was a total of 35 seconds of idle time per sub-assembly assembled in the ring. There were four types of sub-assemblies but they were similar.

In order to improve the efficiency of the circular line, the Double-D layout was proposed (see the sketch and photo at the top of the next page on the right).

Questions

1. What are the advantages of the Double-D cells over the circular line?

2. Suppose that the task times of the five workstations in the ring were 30, 25, 20, 20, and 20 seconds, respectively. Explain how four workers, two in each D, can produce the same output as the five workers in the ring.

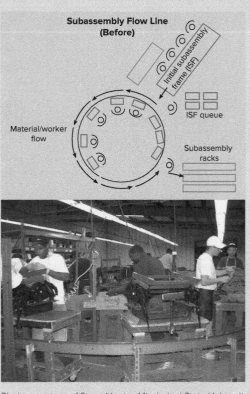

Subassembly Flow Line
(Before)

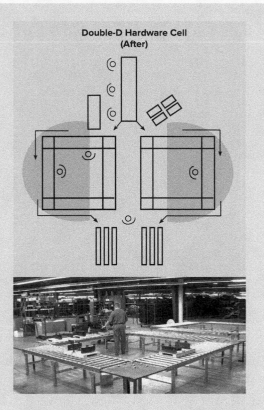

Double-D Hardware Cell
(After)

Photos courtesy of Steve Hunter, Mississippi State University

Q MINI-CASE

Lego Car

The precedence network for assembling the Lego Racer (8119) is shown at right. For example, the black rectangle (19) can be attached only after the yellow rectangle (12) and the two sides (2 and 3) are attached. Note that in order to reduce the size of problem (and possibly make assembly easier), items 5–9 and 13–16 are sub-assemblies.

Questions

1. We wish to assemble 240 cars in one hour. What should be the cycle time (in seconds)?

2. The following are the standard times (in seconds) of attaching each piece to its immediate predecessor(s). (*Note:* For items 5–9 and 13–16, the time includes time of assembling the sub-assemblies. Time of the first piece is for reaching and grasping it.) What is the theoretical minimum number of workstations needed if Cycle time = 15 seconds?

Task	1	2	3	4	5	6	7	8	9	10	11	12	13	14	15	16	17	18	19	20	21	22
Time	1	1	1	1	3	3	2	2	5	1	1	1	1	2	2	3	7	1	1	1	1	1

3. Pick an appropriate heuristic and cycle time of 15 seconds, and perform assembly-line balancing.

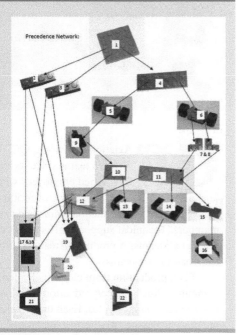

Precedence Network:

To access "Linear Programming," the supplement to
Chapter 6, please visit *Connect2*.

Chapter 7
Work/Job Design

Jim R. Bounds/Bloomberg via Getty Images

GE Aviation–Bromont, QC, has used participative management involving self-directed teams since its start in 1982. It employs approximately 630 hourly and 80 salaried employees who make 450 models of compressor and turbine blades (airfoils) for GE jet engines using over 500 CNCs and over 100 robots.

There are six production teams and two service teams (maintenance and tooling). The production teams consist of 55–140 members. Technical support staff such as engineers are assigned to a production team. Functions such as HR, finance, and IT support all teams. A production team is further divided into sub-teams (e.g., grinders, inspection). For example, titanium (Titan) team has 11 sub-teams.

Each production team elects its leaders for specific roles for a period of time, usually two years. Team leader, management committee, line balance/production planning, quality, new product introduction, environment/health/safety, and preventive maintenance are common roles. Each team makes these and other decisions such as work assignments, schedules, overtime/vacation policies, hiring, process improvement, and purchasing equipment by consensus.

There is only one job classification. Each member is expected to become multi-skilled (perform four jobs). There are 120 hours of training per year. Everyone emphasizes the importance of trust, respect, humility, and accountability. Employees are guardians of this culture. There is no union.

There are also 14 plantwide standing committees (or councils) such as plant, compensation/gain-sharing, hiring, training, and dispute resolution, which have representatives from each production team and support staff such as HR and the plant leader. These committees act both as decision makers and as a source of information, and make recommendations to each team.

Information about production, quality, and delivery performance is electronically available to everyone, which motivates members of each team to work together to meet their targets. Each team has to be competitive with 70 other plants of GE Aviation and outside suppliers to receive work from GE Aviation. There is peer observation to reduce accidents and improve quality. The Bromont plant is a model of productivity in GE Aviation and is a centre for robotics and automation.

Sources: Rasheedah Jones, "Teaming at GE Aviation," *Management Innovation eXchange*, July 2013; http://www.managementexchange.com/story/teaming-ge-aviation; www.geaviation.com.

Approaches to Work/Job Design

(L01)

Work/job design is the last step in process design. We are assuming that the organizational architecture and its processes are logical, and organizational goals, process sub-goals, resources, and interfaces are effectively managed. We now need to construct roles for employees and others to make the processes work.

Work/job design involves determining work/job content and work method, work environment/conditions, time standards, and compensation. Work/job design is one of the most fundamental activities in operations management and was the focus of the scientific management (later called industrial engineering), pioneered by Frederick Taylor at the beginning of the last century.

A set of related tasks makes up the **work/job**. For example, a UPS parcel delivery driver's work/job involves many tasks, one of which is the task of carrying a parcel from the truck to a customer's residence door. Scientific management breaks a **task** into a sequence of elements (e.g., pick up the parcel) and each **element** into a sequence of motions (e.g., reach for the parcel). The objective of work/job design is to assign the required organizational tasks to employees so that long-term goals of the organization are achieved.

According to the *Human Performance System*,[1] the following six job design and management factors are required for effective and efficient performance of a job:

1. *Performance specification.* Reasonable performance standards for the job (i.e., its goals) should be established and communicated to the worker.
2. *Task support.* A well structured job (as part of a well structured process) contains easily recognized, high-quality inputs (raw materials, forms, assignments, customer requests, etc.), minimal interference (distractions), logical procedures, and adequate resources (equipment and working conditions) to do the job.
3. *Consequences.* The consequences to the employee (e.g., bonus, recognition, complaint, disciplinary action, etc.) must support efficient achievement of job goals, be meaningful to the employee, and occur quickly enough to provide an ongoing incentive.
4. *Feedback.* The employee should receive relevant, accurate, timely, specific, and easy-to-understand performance feedback as to how well he/she is doing.
5. *Skills/knowledge.* The employee should have the necessary skills and knowledge to perform the job, and know why they are required. If not, training is required.
6. *Individual capacity.* The employee should have the physical (strength, energy, precision, and speed of movements), mental (information processing speed and accuracy), and emotional capacity to perform the job.

Lack of any of the above factors represents an opportunity for performance improvement. Rummler and Brache[2] have found that approximately 80 percent of performance improvement opportunities reside in the environment (Factors 1 to 4), 15–20 percent in Factor 5 (skills/knowledge), and less than 1 percent in Factor 6 (individual capacity).

> **work/job design** Specifying the content and method of the work or job, the work environment, and work/job's standard time and compensation.
>
> **work/job** A set of related tasks.
>
> **task** A sequence of elements (e.g., pick up the parcel).
>
> **element** A sequence of motions (e.g., reach for the parcel).

---

[1] G. A. Rummler and A. P. Brache. *Improving Performance: How to Manage the White Space on the Organization Chart*, Second Edition, Jossey-Bass, 1995, Figure 6.3.
[2] Ibid.

Organization and process improvements will not take root if they are not built into jobs. If jobs are not designed to support process steps, and if job environments are not structured to enable people to make their maximum contributions to process effectiveness and efficiency, then organization and process goals will not be met.

Current practice in work/job (re)design is based on two basic approaches. The first is the **efficiency approach**, which is a refinement of scientific management that emphasizes labour cost reduction in work design. The second is the **behavioural approach**, which emphasizes satisfaction of psychological and social wants and needs of workers as a motivator for increased productivity.

The behavioural approach emerged during the 1950s and includes initiatives such as job enlargement, enrichment, rotation, and teams. It is noteworthy that specialization is a primary issue of disagreement between the efficiency and behavioural approaches.

Efficiency Approach

The efficiency approach includes specialization, methods analysis, time standards, and compensation. We will discuss specialization here, and cover the rest later in the chapter.

Specialization focuses work/jobs to a narrow scope. Examples range from assembly-line jobs to medical specialties. For instance, an assembly-line worker could be installing windshields the whole shift (i.e., hundreds of them), repeating the same task every minute. College/university professors often specialize in teaching certain courses, some auto mechanics specialize in transmission repair, and some bakers specialize in wedding cakes. The main rationale for specialization is the ability to concentrate one's efforts and thereby become proficient at that type of work.

Unfortunately, some of these jobs (e.g., assembly-line jobs) can be monotonous and boring. The advantages and disadvantages of assembly-line specialization for a company and a worker are summarized in Table 7-1.

efficiency approach A refinement of scientific management that emphasizes labour cost reduction in work design.

behavioural approach An approach to work design that emphasizes satisfaction of psychological and social wants and needs of workers as a motivator for increased productivity.

specialization Focusing the work/job to a narrow scope.

TABLE 7-1 ▶

Advantages and disadvantages of assembly-line specialization.

Advantages	
For a company:	For a worker:
1. Simplified training	1. Low education and skill requirements
2. High productivity (faster times, less tool change)	2. Minimal responsibilities
3. Relatively low wages	3. Little mental effort

Disadvantages	
For a company:	For a worker:
1. Difficult to motivate	1. Monotonous/boring work
2. Worker dissatisfaction, possibly resulting in absenteeism, high turnover	2. Limited opportunities for advancement
	3. Little control over work
	4. Little opportunity for self-fulfillment

The seriousness of the problems with assembly-line specialization resulted in the creation of the behavioural approach.

Behavioural Approach

People work for a variety of reasons (beyond monetary compensation). These include socialization, self-actualization (fulfillment of one's talents and potential), status, and a sense of purpose and accomplishment. Awareness of these factors can help management develop a motivational framework that encourages workers to respond in a positive manner to the goals of the organization.

Most employees want to do a good job. It is important to motivate and inspire employees, create a culture of high performance, treat employees well, remove fears of failure, provide individual autonomy, and make employees feel that they are part of something bigger than themselves.[3]

An important factor is *trust*. In an ideal work environment, there is a high level of trust between workers and managers. When managers trust employees, there is a greater tendency to give employees added responsibilities. When employees trust management, they are more likely to respond positively to changes and be loyal to the organization.

---

[3] https://www.youtube.com/watch?v=R8TzmG-Pr40

New management approaches such as total quality management (TQM) are based on employee involvement in decision making (deciding how work is done and how its quality can be improved). This is also called *employee empowerment* or *high performance work system*.

The behavioural approach includes job enlargement, job rotation, job enrichment, and self-directed teams.

Job enlargement means giving a worker a larger portion of the total activity of making a good or providing a service. This is referred to as *horizontal loading* because additional tasks are on the same level of skill and responsibility as the original job. The goal is to make the work/job more interesting by increasing the variety of skills required and by letting the worker make a more recognizable contribution to the overall output (called *task identity*). For example, an assembly-line worker's work/job might be expanded so that he/she is responsible for a longer *sequence* of tasks. Two examples of job enlargement from the City of Winnipeg are the elimination of the distinction between welders and blacksmiths, and combining the jobs of vehicle-frame straightener and painter as body repairman.

> **job enlargement** Giving a worker a larger portion of the total activity.

Job rotation means having workers in the same work area periodically exchange jobs. A company can use this approach to avoid having an employee stuck in a monotonous or repetitive job. Job rotation allows workers to broaden their learning experience and enables them to fill in for others in the event of illness or absenteeism. Also, repetitive motion injuries may be avoided by periodically doing a different type of physical work. A good example of job rotation from Honda is when an assembly-line worker (called an associate) exchanges jobs with one of his/her teammates (who work nearby) every hour.

> **job rotation** Workers in the same work area periodically exchange jobs.

Job enrichment involves an increase in the level of employee responsibility for planning, execution, and control of the job. It is sometimes referred to as *vertical loading*. An example of this is an operator who is also responsible for the maintenance, setup, and quality control of the machine or process he/she uses. An example of job enrichment from the Shell Refinery in east Montreal occurred when the job of operator was expanded to include minor maintenance, completing time sheets, planning rotation/overtime/vacation/shutdown, writing operations and training manuals, training, and participating in reliability groups.

> **job enrichment** Increasing employee responsibility for planning, execution, and control of the job.

A **self-directed team**, sometimes referred to as a *self-managed* or *autonomous team,* is a group of employees who perform the same function or produce a family of products, and are empowered to make decisions involving their own work (e.g., membership, work assignment, pace of work, training, and quality). This is different from other forms of work teams such as quality circles (in Chapter 9) which have little decision making authority and are not permanent. The underlying concept for self-directed teams is that the workers, who are closest to their work and have the best knowledge of it, are better suited than management to make decisions involving their own work. Moreover, they are more engaged and motivated, and will work harder to achieve better results. Another benefit is that fewer middle managers/supervisors are necessary, and they no longer command and control, instead taking the role of team leader and coach. The structure of organizations using self-directed teams is flat rather than top-down with many levels. Furthermore, the organization requires a different culture, and team members must be trained in new skills, including communication, problem solving, and leadership. The chapter opener to this chapter is an example of a plant made up of self-directed teams.

> **self-directed team** A group of employees who perform the same function and are empowered to make certain decisions and changes in their work.

Other new initiatives in work/job design include flexible work hours and locations (see, for example, http://hrcouncil.ca/hr-toolkit/workplaces-flexible.cfm).

Role of Unions

Labour unions can affect all aspects of work/job design and how work is accomplished. In approximately 30 percent of organizations (more public than private, more in manufacturing and construction than in banking and retail), labour unions represent employees in negotiating and executing labour contracts (collective agreements). A collective agreement determines the wages, benefits (extended health care, vacation, pension, etc.), security of jobs/limits to outsourcing and hiring temporary workers, hiring/layoff/promotion/seniority, safety standards/working conditions, work rules, job classification, scheduling, and grievance procedures.

Unionized workplaces have approximately 20 percent higher wages and benefits than comparable non-union organizations. This is the main reason why companies such as Walmart and McDonald's have opposed unions in their facilities. Another reason for opposition to unions is that they promote rigid work rules and excessive job classification.

In Canada, once the majority of workers vote to have a union, all workers in that workplace will have to pay union dues. Forming a union is regulated by the Canada Labour Code and its provincial counterparts (e.g., the Labour Relations Act of Ontario). Provincial labour boards oversee the process of collective agreement and dispute resolution.[4]

While a minority of management–labour relationships are antagonistic,[5] most are cooperative. An example is the agreement between Magna International and the Canadian Auto Workers (now Unifor) called the Framework of Fairness Agreement in 2007 and renewed recently.[6] This agreement provides workers with competitive wages and helps with formation of unions in return for union agreement for arbitration to solve disputes and depoliticization of the workplace. This agreement is in effect in three Canadian Magna plants.

Most collective agreements are between a company and the union(s) representing its employees. But some are between an association of companies and a trade union in a province, as, for example, with Construction Labour Relations–Alberta (representing construction companies in Alberta) and the United Brotherhood of Carpenters and Joiners of Alberta.[7]

Many smaller unions are local to a particular workplace, but large ones are usually part of a national or international union. Examples include the Canadian Union of Public Employees, the National Union of Public and General Employees, and Unifor;[8] United Food and Commercial Workers Canada; United Steelworkers, which also represents some mining, forestry, and rubber company workers; Teamsters Canada, which represents truck drivers and also rail company workers; International Association of Machinists & Aerospace Workers; Construction & Specialty Workers Union; Bakery, Confectionery, Tobacco Workers and Grain Millers Union; and International Union of Operating Engineers. For more information about union coverage and unions in Canada, see http://www.labour.gc.ca/eng/resources/info/publications/union_coverage/union_coverage.shtml, and Fiona A. E. McQuarrie, *Industrial Relations in Canada*, 4th ed, 2015, Wiley, Toronto.

Role of Information and Communication Technologies

information and communication technologies The Internet, wireless networks, smartphones, and the software and applications that use those technologies.

Information and communication technologies (ICTs) include computers, the Internet, wireless networks, smartphones, and the software and applications that use those technologies.[9] ICTs have had a significant effect on all aspects of work/job design and how work is accomplished. ICTs are inherently more flexible than older industrial technologies. The utility of a machine tool is limited, whereas, for example, a smartphone has the ability to make phone calls; send text messages and email; browse the Internet; and take photographs and record videos. In the current information age, ICTs have changed the nature of work in many industries.

There is less demand for newspapers, but more demand for 24-hour Internet and TV news channels. Office work has become paperless. Employees write and store their own documents. Wi-Fi networks are commonplace. Business administration has become paperless. For example, instead of accounting clerks, business software keeps track of financial records. Payroll departments deposit employees' compensation electronically into their bank accounts. People are using ATMs, online banking and, more recently, mobile apps instead of interacting with a human teller in a bank branch. Customer service is performed by call centres, many of which are overseas. Many online services are provided 24/7, so some employees have to work irregular hours. Others prefer to work flexible hours. As a result, leisure time and work–life balance is blurred. There are fewer letters but more emails, and there are more packages to deliver. Computer literacy is a must. ICT training has become a booming industry.

---

[4] See, for example, http://www.lrb.bc.ca.

[5] See, for example, Best Western Seven Oaks and United Food and Commercial Workers Canada, http://leaderpost.com/news/local-news/hotel-strike-enters-fifth-month.

[6] See Labour Relations in the most recent SEC Form 40-F in http://www.magna.com/investors/financial-reports-public-filings?rpt=tax.

[7] http://negotech.labour.gc.ca/eng/agreements/02/0257411s.shtml

[8] Created from a recent merger of the Canadian Auto Workers Union and Communications, Energy and Paperworkers of Canada.

[9] http://www.teach-ict.com/gcse_new/work_employment/employment_ict/miniweb/index.htm; http://documents.worldbank.org/curated/en/290301468340843514/pdf/809770WP0Conne00Box379814B00PUB LIC0.pdf; McIlwain, Brianna. From Clocks to iPhones: Technology, Time and Temporality in Contemporary Society. MA Major Essay, Queen's University, 2015.

The "always on" character of these digital technologies provides employees with new opportunities for flexible coordination. ICTs are redefining the boundaries between work and home. Much work can now be done online and from anywhere. Business can be done while shopping, sitting at a coffee shop, or even standing in line.

One task can now be done by teams that are dispersed geographically. Online contracting services such as Upwork have millions of jobs posted. Information technology (IT) jobs—such as web design, software development, and data entry—make up the majority of the jobs. However, jobs in other areas—such as graphic design; animation; music, blog, and article writing; and even legal services—are also growing.

Microwork, disaggregating a large task into small pieces that are farmed out to a large number of workers, has generated significant opportunities for many workers worldwide. Examples of microwork include market research, data input, sentiment analysis, data verification, copywriting, graphic design, translation, and even software testing. CastingWords is an online, ICT-enabled transcription service that uses the Amazon Mechanical Turk platform to rapidly transcribe speech into text. The service is being used by many large organizations including the *Wall Street Journal* and the BBC. CrowdFlower allows users to access an online workforce to clean, label, and enrich data.

Methods Analysis

LO2

Methods analysis, also known as operations analysis, breaks each job into a sequence of tasks/elements/motions and tries to make it more efficient.

methods analysis Breaks the job into a sequence of tasks/elements/motions and improves it.

If methods analysis is done for an existing job, the analyst should observe the job as it is currently being performed by the worker in the workplace, ask several questions, and then devise improvements. For a new job, the analyst must rely on the method being used for similar jobs.

The basic procedure in methods analysis is:

1. Identify the job to be studied. A candidate job for study has high labour content, is done frequently, is unsafe/tiring/unpleasant/noisy, causes quality problems, and/or is a bottleneck.
2. Gather all pertinent facts about the worker (age, gender, size, experience, motivation, satisfaction, education, fitness), parts (sketch/drawing, size, shape, weight, material, tolerances), tasks (how parts flow in/out, what happens, motions, fixtures, machines/equipment, tools, layout, awkward motions, lifting, fatigue, sensory input, cycle time, standard time), workplace (location, layout, light, glare, noise, heat, vibration, protective equipment), and administrative factors (wage incentive, job rotation/team, enlargement, enrichment, training, policy).
3. Document and analyze the present method, and discuss the job/facts with the worker and supervisor.
4. Question the present method and propose a new method.

Analyzing and questioning the method and proposing a new method (sometimes called *work simplification*) requires careful thought about the what, why, when, where, and who of the job. Questions to ask include:

- Can a task/element/motion be eliminated? Combined with another?
- Can the sequence of tasks/elements/motions be changed?
- Are close tolerances necessary?
- Can cheaper material be substituted?
- Can material handling equipment be improved? Can distance moved be reduced?
- Can setup time be reduced? Can fixtures and tools be improved?
- Can any delay, storage, or inspection be eliminated?
- Can the part be redesigned for easy manufacturing/assembly?
- Are working conditions satisfactory?
- Is the work area arranged well?
- Can worker motions be improved or made more ergonomic?
- Does the worker have the right skill level?
- Can technology assist in the method improvement?

Documenting, analyzing, and improving methods is facilitated by the use of various charts, such as *a flow process chart* and *a worker–machine process chart.*

A **flow process chart** is used to collect and review the sequence of steps performed in a process. Each step is categorized as one of operation, movement, inspection, delay, and storage. *Delay* means waiting to be processed (a few hours), whereas *storage* is a much longer wait (a few days). A flow process chart is helpful in identifying the nonproductive steps of the process (e.g., delays, distances travelled). Figure 7-1 illustrates a flow process chart for "Requisition of petty cash" in a company. The petty cash is used for minor expenses such as buying a hand tool. For this example, after considering the amount of work involved in petty cash requisition, a solution may be to issue a corporate credit card (with a limit) to the department heads.

> **flow process chart** Chart used to collect and review the sequence of steps performed in a process.

FIGURE 7-1 ▶

Example of a flow process chart.

Source: Elias M. Awad, *System Analysis and Design,* 4th ed. (Burr Ridge, IL: Richard D. Irwin), p. 113. ©by Richard D. Irwin, Inc. Reprinted by permission of the McGraw-Hill Companies Inc.

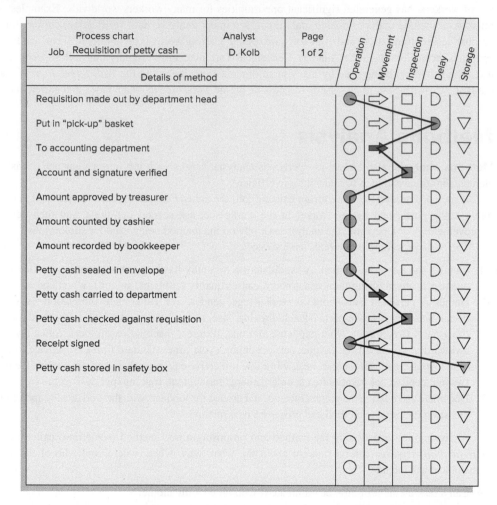

A **worker–machine chart** is a chart used to describe or plan the interactions between a worker and his/her machine(s) over time. The analyst can easily see when the worker and machine are working independently and when their work overlaps. One use of this type of chart is to determine how many machines the operator can manage.

Figure 7-2 presents an example of a worker–machine chart where the operator runs two machines in a staggered way (times are in fractions of an hour). As is evident from the figure, it is hard to improve the synchronization of the work—each machine is used approximately $0.0096/0.0134 = 0.72$ or 72 percent of the time and the worker is used 100 percent of the time.

> **worker–machine chart** A chart used to describe or plan the interactions between a worker and his/her machine(s) over time.

Motion Study

> **motion study** Systematic study of the motions used to perform a task/element.

Motion study is the systematic study of the motions used to perform a task/element. The purpose of motion study is to eliminate unnecessary motions and to identify the best motions for maximum efficiency. Hence, motion study can be an important tool for methods analysis and productivity improvement.

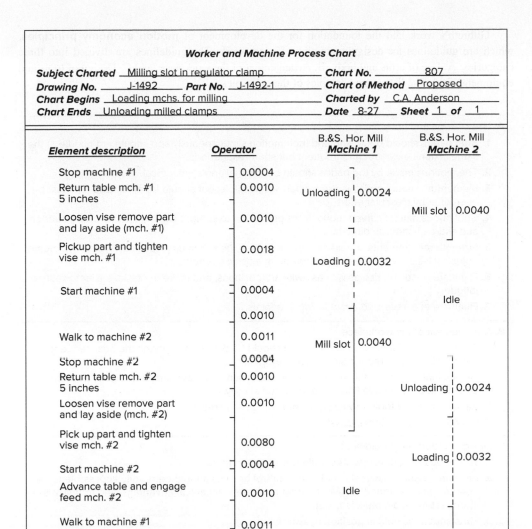

◀ FIGURE 7-2

Example of a worker–machine process chart.

Source: A. Freivalds, *Niebel's Methods, Standards, and Work Design*, 13e. Figure 2.14, p. 40. ©2013. Reprinted with permission of the McGraw-Hill Companies Inc.

Worker and Machine Process Chart

Subject Charted __Milling slot in regulator clamp__   Chart No. _____807_____

Drawing No. ____J-1492____ Part No. __J-1492-1__   Chart of Method __Proposed__

Chart Begins __Loading mchs. for milling__   Charted by __C.A. Anderson__

Chart Ends __Unloading milled clamps__   Date _8-27_ Sheet _1_ of _1_

Element description	Operator	B.&S. Hor. Mill Machine 1	B.&S. Hor. Mill Machine 2
Stop machine #1	0.0004		
Return table mch. #1 5 inches	0.0010	Unloading 0.0024	
Loosen vise remove part and lay aside (mch. #1)	0.0010		Mill slot 0.0040
Pickup part and tighten vise mch. #1	0.0018	Loading 0.0032	
Start machine #1	0.0004		
	0.0010		Idle
Walk to machine #2	0.0011	Mill slot 0.0040	
Stop machine #2	0.0004		
Return table mch. #2 5 inches	0.0010		Unloading 0.0024
Loosen vise remove part and lay aside (mch. #2)	0.0010		
Pick up part and tighten vise mch. #2	0.0080		Loading 0.0032
Start machine #2	0.0004		
Advance table and engage feed mch. #2	0.0010	Idle	
Walk to machine #1	0.0011		

Idle man time per cycle	0.0000	Idle hours machine #1	0.0038
Working man time per cycle	0.0134	Productive hours mch. #1	0.0096
Man-hours per cycle	0.0134	Machine #1 cycle time	0.0134

Idle hours machine #2		0.0038
Productive hours mch. #2.		0.0096
Machine #2 cycle time		0.0134

Present practice evolved from the work of Frank Gilbreth, who originated the concept in the bricklaying trade early in the twentieth century. Motion study was used by Gilbreth to increase the number of bricks laid per hour by a bricklayer by a factor of three.

Common motions includes *reach*, *grasp*, *move*, and *disengage*. Breaking a task/element into motions is the first step in motion study. This usually involves a substantial amount of work. However, for short, repetitive tasks it may be justified.

Usually, motion study is performed before time study (described later). You can watch this video for more information about the origin of motion study: "Frank Bunker Gilbreth (1868–1924), Original Films (motion study)," https://www.youtube.com/watch?v=xdnhEZ-tkOg.

The most popular motion study techniques/tools are:

1. Motion economy principles.
2. Slow-motion video study.
3. Simo or two-hand process chart.

motion economy principles Guidelines for designing motion-efficient work.

Gilbreth's work laid the foundation for the development of **motion economy principles**, which are guidelines for designing motion-efficient work. The guidelines are divided into three categories: A. Use of arms and body, B. Arrangement of the workplace, and C. Design of tools and equipment. Table 7-2 lists some examples of the principles.

TABLE 7-2 ▶

Examples of motion economy principles.

A. Use of arms and body:
1. Both hands should begin and end their motion simultaneously and should not be idle at the same instant, except during frequent but short rest periods.
2. The motions made by the hands should be minimal and symmetrical.
3. Momentum should assist workers wherever possible, but should be minimized if it must be overcome by muscular effort.
4. Continuous natural curved motions are preferable to straight-line motions involving sudden and sharp changes in direction.
5. Strength requirements should be much less than the maximum available. Avoid lifting heavy objects. Use slow movements for maximum muscle strength.
6. Eliminate bend and rise as well as awkward positions, and make the tasks easier to reduce fatigue.
7. Eliminate eye travel and avoid losing eye focus.

B. Arrangement of the workplace:
1. Fixed locations for all tools and material should be provided to permit the best sequence and to eliminate or reduce search and selection.
2. Gravity bins and drop delivery should reduce reach and move times; wherever possible ejectors should remove finished parts automatically.
3. All materials and tools should be located within easy reach.
4. Provide a chair or stool if possible.

C. Design of tools and equipment:
1. Where possible, power tools should replace hand tools.
2. All levers, handles, wheels, and other control devices should be readily accessible to the operator and designed to give the best possible mechanical advantage and to utilize the strongest available muscle group.
3. Parts should be held in position by fixtures.

Source: Adapted from Benjamin W. Niebel, *Motion and Time Study*, 8th Ed (Burr Ridge, IL: Richard D. Irwin, Inc.), pp. 206–207. Reprinted with permission of the McGraw-Hill Companies Inc.

slow motion study Use of motion pictures and slow motion to study motions that otherwise would be too rapid to analyze.

simo chart A chart that shows the motions performed by each hand, side-by-side, over time.

Frank Gilbreth and his wife, Lillian, an industrial psychologist, were also responsible for introducing motion pictures for studying motions, called **slow motion study**. This approach is applied not only in industry but also in some other areas such as sports. Use of camera and slow-motion replay enables analysts to study motions that would otherwise be too rapid to see. In addition, the resulting films provide a permanent record that can be referred to, not only for training workers and analysts, but also for settling disputes involving standard times.

Motion-study analysts may use a two-hand process chart or **simo chart** to study the motions performed by each hand, side-by-side, through time. In Figure 7-3a the methods analyst studied a trim/blanking task on a hand-operated press with an accompanying die. He/she broke the task down into a right- and left-hand process chart (aligned through time). A review of the process chart shows that delays are occurring because the motions of the right and left hands are not balanced: the left hand is waiting while the right hand raises the handle of the press, again while the right hand removes the part from the die, and again when the right hand regains control of the press handle. If the operator did not have to remove the finished piece from the die, he/she would be freed from the action of re-grasping the press handle. The improved method is shown in Figure 7-3b. A fixture was developed to blow the part off of the die into the gravity chute while the press is raised. Simo charts are invaluable in studying operations such as data entry, sewing, surgical and dental procedures, and certain fabrication and assembly operations.

See the "UPS" OM in Action for an application of methods analysis.

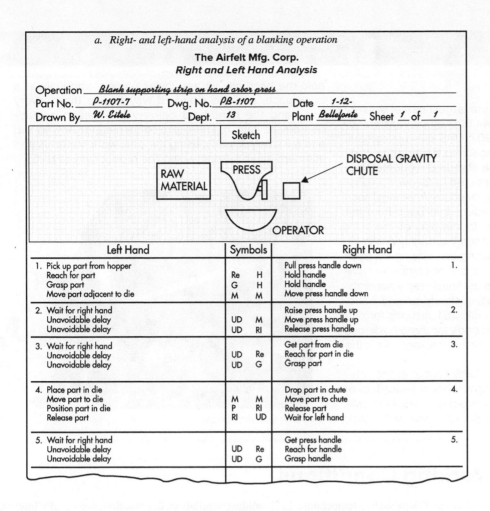

a. Right- and left-hand analysis of a blanking operation

The Airfelt Mfg. Corp.
Right and Left Hand Analysis

Operation __Blank supporting strip on hand arbor press__
Part No. __P-1107-7__   Dwg. No. __PB-1107__   Date __1-12-__
Drawn By __W. Eitele__   Dept. __13__   Plant __Bellefonte__ Sheet __1__ of __1__

Left Hand	Symbols		Right Hand	
1. Pick up part from hopper Reach for part Grasp part Move part adjacent to die	 Re G M	 H H M	Pull press handle down Hold handle Hold handle Move press handle down	1.
2. Wait for right hand Unavoidable delay Unavoidable delay	 UD UD	 M RI	Raise press handle up Move press handle up Release press handle	2.
3. Wait for right hand Unavoidable delay Unavoidable delay	 UD UD	 Re G	Get part from die Reach for part in die Grasp part	3.
4. Place part in die Move part to die Position part in die Release part	 M P RI	 M RI UD	Drop part in chute Move part to chute Release part Wait for left hand	4.
5. Wait for right hand Unavoidable delay Unavoidable delay	 UD UD	 Re G	Get press handle Reach for handle Grasp handle	5.

b. Right- and left-hand analysis of a blanking operation in which avoidable delays have been omitted

The Airfelt Mfg. Corp.
Right and Left Hand Analysis

Operation __Blank supporting strip on hand arbor press__
Part No. __P-1107-7__   Dwg. No. __PB-1107__   Date __1-12-__
Drawn By __W. Eitele__   Dept. __13__   Plant __Bellefonte__ Sheet __1__ of __1__

Left Hand	Symbols		Right Hand	
1. Get part from hopper Reach for part Grasp part Move part to die	 RE G M	 H M	Pull press handle down Hold handle Move press handle down	1.
2. Place part in die Move part to die Position part Release part	 M P RI	 M M H	 Raise press handle up Move handle up Hold handle	2.

◀ **FIGURE 7-3**

A simo or two-hand process chart.

Source: B. W. Niebel, *Motion and Time Study*, 5th ed. (Homewood, IL: Richard D. Irwin). ©1976. Figure 7.15, p. 201 and Figure 7.16, p. 202. Reprinted by permission.

OM in Action   www.ups.com

UPS

United Parcel Service (UPS) is the largest parcel delivery company in the world (with 444,000 employees worldwide). Since its founding in 1907, UPS executives have emphasized a structured approach to running the company. A large part of this is the standard work methods that all UPS employees are expected to follow.

There are more than 340 procedures/methods, such as the 12-step unloading procedure that goes from the driver parking the delivery truck to stepping off the truck with the parcel.[10] This task has been thoroughly analyzed, non-essential steps such as opening and closing the truck side door have been removed, and time standards have been established for each of its essential steps/elements. For example, the 12-step unloading should take 15.5 seconds for one package from a shelf, 25.1 seconds for one package from the floor, 29.6 seconds for three packages from a shelf, and 65.5 seconds for five packages from the rear door.

There is even a hands-on UPS school called Integrad (http://www.youtube.com/watch?v=cTuqgr8vd7o) that teaches future drivers (in a five-day course) the safe way to drive, get off the truck (three points of contact:

hold the handrail), lift and lower parcels, and walk at a brisk pace, and the standard way to use the delivery truck and the hand-held delivery information acquisition device (DIAD). There is also training for how to slip and fall safely. Clearly, using the best work methods and standard times has increased the productivity of UPS.

Kevin Wheal/Alamy Images

L03 Working Conditions

Working conditions such as temperature and humidity, ventilation, illumination, noise and vibration, work hours, work breaks, safety, ergonomics, and a healthy workplace, including mental well-being, can have a significant impact on worker performance in terms of productivity and product quality. Government has played an important role in the regulation of the work environment.

Government Regulation of the Workplace. The creation of factories in the nineteenth century was the start of increasing workplace health and safety problems. To address these problems, the government passed worker protection acts that required guards on the machines, fire safety, boiler and elevator inspection, sanitation, ventilation, and adequate heating and lighting. The Canada Labour Code of 1966 included safety as well as other employment/work standards such as minimum wage and a 40-hour workweek. In 1978, the Labour Code was amended to give three rights to workers: (a) to refuse dangerous work, (b) to participate in improving safety and health problems (through joint management/labour committees), and (c) to know about hazards in the workplace In 1988, (c) was shaped into the requirement for a Workplace Hazardous Materials Information System (WHMIS), which mandates proper labelling of hazardous materials and making the material safety data sheets available. See http://laws-lois.justice.gc.ca/eng/acts/L-2 for details of the Canada Labour Code, which contains acts for (1) industrial relations (unions), (2) occupational health and safety, and (3) standard hours, wages, vacations and holidays. The Canada Labour Code applies to federally regulated organizations, those whose activities cross provincial boundaries. Each province has its own version of labour and employment standards for provincially regulated organizations (e.g., https://www.labour.gov.on.ca/english/es/).

---

[10] The 12 steps are as follows: 1. Shift into the lowest gear. 2. Turn the ignition off and engage the parking brake. 3. Release the seat belt with your left hand. 4. Open the inside door. 5. Place key on ring finger. 6. Select package without stepping through door (if possible). 7. Only select packages from selection area. 8. Close the inside door. 9. Pick up the DIAD. 10. Fasten DIAD to belt clip. 11. Look both ways before stepping into the street. 12. Hold on to the handrail and exit truck. Source: http://archive.fortune.com/magazines/fortune/fortune_archive/2007/11/12/101008310/index.htm

Temperature and Humidity. Many operations are performed in high temperatures, such as in a foundry or a mine, and some others are performed in low temperatures, such as in a slaughterhouse. Although human beings can function under a fairly wide range of temperatures, work performance tends to be adversely affected if air temperatures are outside a very narrow *comfort band*. That comfort band depends on humidity, wind speed, and how strenuous the work is. For example, for office work (no wind) in winter (warm clothing) and relative humidity of 60 percent, the comfort band is 20°C to 24°C.[11] Solutions range from selection of suitable clothing to space heating or cooling devices.

Ventilation. Some factories (such as lumber mills and grinding operations) create large amounts of dust; some others (such as pulp and paper mills) generate gases and foul odours. These are unhealthy and unpleasant. Large fans and air conditioning equipment are commonly used to exchange and recondition the air.

Illumination. The optimal amount of lighting in a workplace depends largely on the type of work being performed; the more detailed the work, the higher the level of illumination needed for adequate performance. Other important considerations are the amount of glare and contrast.

Sometimes natural daylight can be used as a source of illumination. It not only is free, but also provides some psychological benefits. Workers in windowless factories may feel cut off from the outside world and experience various psychological problems. On the downside, the inability to control natural light (e.g., cloudy days) can result in dramatic changes in light intensity.

Noise and Vibrations. Noise is caused by the movement and vibrations of machines and equipment. Noise can be annoying or distracting, leading to errors and accidents. It can also damage or impair hearing if it is loud enough. Figure 7-4 illustrates the loudness level of some typical sounds.

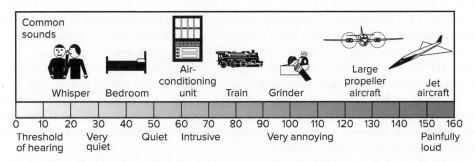

◀ **FIGURE 7-4**

Decibel values of typical sounds.

Source: From Benjamin W. Niebel, *Motion and Time Study*, 8th ed. Copyright ©1988 Richard D. Irwin, Inc. Used by permission of McGraw-Hill Companies, Inc., p. 248.

Successful sound control begins with measurement of the offending sounds. In a new operation, selection and placement of equipment can eliminate or reduce many potential problems. In the case of existing equipment, it may be possible to redesign or substitute equipment. In some instances, the source of noise can be isolated from other work areas. If that isn't feasible, acoustical walls and ceilings that deflect sound waves may prove useful. Sometimes the only solution is to provide earplugs or earmuffs for those in the immediate vicinity.

Vibrations can be a factor in work/job design even without a noise component. Vibrations can come from tools, machines, vehicles, air conditioning systems, pumps, and other sources. Corrective measures include padding, stabilizers, shock absorbers, cushioning, and rubber mountings.

Work Hours. Reasonable (and sometimes flexible) work hours can provide a sense of freedom and control over one's work. This is useful in situations where the emphasis is on completing work on a timely basis and meeting performance objectives rather than being "on duty" for a given time interval, as is the case for most retail and manufacturing operations.

The most common flexible work hours are (a) flexi-time schemes (e.g., working from 10 a.m. to 6 p.m. rather than from 9 a.m. to 5 p.m.), (b) compressed workweek (e.g., four 10-hour days or a nine-day fortnight), and (c) job sharing.[12]

Shift work (working nights) is mostly required for services such as health care. Though necessary, it can cause medical and social problems.

---

[11] https://www.ccohs.ca/oshanswers/phys_agents/thermal_comfort.html

[12] http://hrcouncil.ca/hr-toolkit/workplaces-flexible.cfm

Work Breaks. The frequency, length, and timing of work breaks (i.e., rests) can have a significant impact on both productivity and product quality. Efficiency generally declines as the day wears on, but breaks for lunch and rest can cause an upward shift in efficiency.

An important variable in the rate of decline of efficiency and potential effects of work breaks is the amount of physical and/or mental requirements of the job. Steelworkers, for instance, may need rest breaks of 15 minutes per hour due to the strenuous nature of their jobs. In fact, one of Frederick Taylor's experiments showed that for men carrying 92-pound pig-irons up a ramp, maximum output was achieved when the workers rested 58 percent of the time. For 40-pound pig-irons, optimal rest was 48 percent of the time. People working in front of computer monitors also need periodic breaks, and students need study breaks.

Safety. Worker safety is one of the most important issues in work/job design and needs constant attention from management and employees or the union. Workers cannot be motivated if they feel they are in physical danger.

From an employer standpoint, accidents are undesirable because they are expensive (workers' compensation insurance premiums will increase, and they may also get fined) and are bad publicity.

Two basic causes of accidents are worker carelessness and unsafe working conditions. Carelessness includes unsafe acts such as failing to use protective equipment, overriding safety controls (e.g., taping control buttons down), disregarding safety procedures, using tools (e.g., saws) and equipment (e.g., rollers, conveyors) improperly, and failing to use reasonable caution in danger zones (e.g., walking in front of or behind a forklift, touching hot parts or equipment).

Unsafe working conditions include unprotected pulleys, chains, material-handling equipment, and machinery; working at heights without a tether; items stored at heights that could fall, and so on. Also, poorly lit or slippery walkways, stairs, and loading docks constitute hazards. So do toxic wastes, gases and vapours, and radiation. Having faulty or inadequate equipment (e.g., using a two-person suspended platform for five window cleaners) is also an unsafe working condition.

Protection against hazards involves the use of proper equipment and lighting, clearly marked danger zones, use of protective equipment (hardhats, welding masks, goggles, earmuffs, gloves, steel-toed footwear, and clothing), safety devices (machine guards, dual-control switches that require an operator to use both hands), emergency equipment (emergency showers, fire extinguishers, fire escapes), and thorough instruction and training in safety procedures. Housekeeping (clean floors, open aisles, waste removal) is another important safety factor. Management must enforce safety procedures and the use of safety equipment.

Occupational health and safety regulations require the use of inspectors to ensure that the regulations are adhered to. Inspections are carried out both at random and to investigate complaints of unsafe conditions. The inspectors are empowered to issue warnings, to impose fines, and even to order shutdown of a facility because of unsafe conditions.

A more effective way to deal with management of safety issues is to incorporate it into the company's management planning and control activities, just as quality is managed. A safety management system based on the guidelines of BS OHSAS 18001 can be used. This is similar to ISO 9001 (for quality systems) and ISO 14001 (for environmental systems).

The OHSAS 18001 requires that health and safety activities be planned.[13] This process requires that, after an annual risk assessment, realistic objectives and targets be set and that the roles, responsibilities, and timelines necessary to achieve the targets be clearly communicated to—and understood by—all those involved in achieving them. Operational controls (procedures) and emergency plans must be developed and documented for those risks found to be intolerable. Employees must be trained. Performance and compliance with system requirements must be measured in order to ensure that they are controlled. Any incident, accident, or other non-conformance within the system needs to be investigated at a level appropriate to its impact on the system. The resulting corrective and preventive action developed from this process ensures that the standards of practice are complied with and are adequate. Finally, senior management must periodically review the system (e.g., internal or external audits every six months) to ensure that it is meeting the objectives stated in its policy and that it is effectively implemented. Improvements in the overall system are identified and implemented through the planning process.

---

[13] J. J. Janssen, "Another @#$%& Standard?" *OH&S Canada* 18(1), January/February 2002, p. 58; http://www.aims.org.pk/wp-content/uploads/2014/08/OHSAS-18001-2007-Standards.pdf.

Ergonomics. **Ergonomics** involves fitting the job to the worker's capability and size. It can include both physical and mental (cognitive) aspects of work. *Physical ergonomics* tries to remove awkward reaching and bending, forceful gripping of tools, heavy lifting, and endless repetition of motions. *Cognitive ergonomics* tries to speed up the mental aspects of work and reduce human errors. Much of it is about human/machine (control panels) and human/computer (software) interface.

> **ergonomics** Fitting the job to the worker's capability and size.

We will focus on physical ergonomics here. Physical ergonomics prevents common workplace injuries such as back injuries and repetitive motion injuries. Workers vary in their physical dimensions, and some activities when continually repeated result in strains in muscles and joints (called *musculo-skeletal injuries, repetitive motion injuries,* or *cumulative trauma disorders*). Most ergonomic problems are unintentional mistakes that develop because no one had the knowledge or the time to design the work properly.

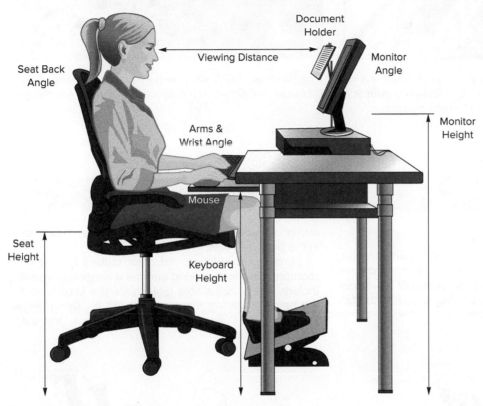

Components of a comfortable workstation.

Source: Copyright 2007 Bennett, Coleman & Co. Ltd. All rights reserved.

Ergonomic problems can also occur in the office. A common problem in using the computer mouse is that it is usually placed beside the keyboard. This results in the need for constant reaching and stretching of the arm, which can result in long-term joint and nerve damage such as carpal tunnel syndrome. A solution is using a rotating platform for the mouse so that it can be moved closer to the body. The arm should be at a right angle and close to the body and the wrist should not be bent.

Another common problem is bad sitting posture. An ergonomic chair that can be adjusted for the user's body dimensions should be used. The user's back should be completely supported (with a slight angle). An angled foot rest provides support for legs. The display monitor should be just below the horizontal eyesight so that there is no need for slouching. It should be approximately 60–80 cm from the eyes. Because monitors emit light, one should look away from the screen every few minutes for a few seconds (preferably at distant objects). Also, because monitors act like mirrors, their angle should be adjusted to avoid glare. For more information on ergonomics, see https://www.ccohs.ca/oshanswers/ergonomics/.

An industrial application of ergonomics is described in the "Supermarket Meat Department" OM in Action, and some ergonomics products are mentioned in the "NexGen Ergonomics" OM in Action.

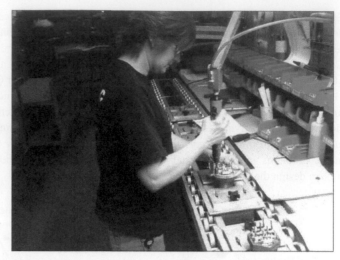

On the left, the worker was using a pistol grip driver in a vertical application, which was placing her in a position of poor shoulder posture. She was experiencing increasing pain in her right shoulder. On the right, by using a hanged palm-grip driver, the worker is now in a good shoulder posture.

Courtesy of Peak Ergonomics. www.HealthyWorkSolutions.com

 OM in Action

Supermarket Meat Department

The workers in a supermarket's meat department cut, package, and wrap the meat in a cold environment (10°C). Cutting involves bringing a large box of meat from cold storage, cutting it into big pieces, removing the fat, and slicing or grinding the pieces.

Awkward body positions and forceful movements can cause repetitive motion injuries in the neck and shoulder. Low room and meat temperatures affect dexterity and increase the required effort. Also, heavy lifting

and prolonged standing on a hard floor can cause strain in the back and feet.

Ergonomic solutions for meat cutters (besides job rotation with meat packing and meat wrapping workers) include use of adjustable tables (see the sketch on the left below), wearing meat cutters' gloves, using proper knives (see the sketch on the right below), and using anti-fatigue mats.

Workers' Well-Being and a Healthy Workplace

Many organizations have begun to realize that the productivity of their employees depends on their general health and well-being. The National Quality Institute (now Excellence Canada) in cooperation with Health Canada developed the Healthy Workplace Award in 1998 to recognize organizations that have a holistic system for a healthy workplace, including physical, mental, safety, personal, and social aspects.

The criteria for the Healthy Workplace Award include four "drivers" of a healthy workplace: leadership role (having a policy and management involved in a healthy workplace program); planning

OM in Action   www.nexgenergo.com

NexGen Ergonomics

NexGen Ergonomics is a well known Canadian company, located in Montreal, that is involved in the production of software and reselling of ergonomic products. The products include a virtual mannequin that can be dimensioned according to average or extreme sizes of a male or female body. The mannequin is used in testing CAD drawings of products that directly interact with a human body. Also, NexGen sells force/pressure and motion sensors and measurement products such as DataLOG (see the photo below), video analysis software, and many types of medical and safety equipment.

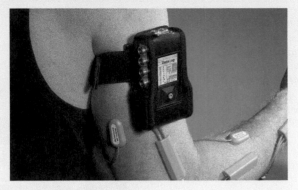

Courtesy of NexGen Ergonomics, Inc., www.nexgenergo.com.

process (needs assessment, setting goals, designing a program); fostering worker involvement (to use the program); and process management (collecting and using feedback). The outcomes—the results of a healthy workplace program such as reduction in absenteeism, turnover, and accident rates—are measured and compared with goals.

The program can affect the physical environment (safety, cleanliness, protective equipment, ergonomics, lighting, air quality, noise, wheelchair accessibility, etc.), health practices (assistance to give up smoking and alcohol abuse, promoting healthy nutrition in the cafeteria, a fitness facility, etc.), and social environment (developing self-respect and a sense of belonging and control over work, protection against harassment and workplace violence, coping with stress, fairness in job assignment and evaluation, reasonable pace of work, flexible hours, benefits plan, etc.). For an application of Healthy Workplace, see the "North York General Hospital's Healthy Workplace" OM in Action.

OM in Action   www.nygh.on.ca

North York General Hospital's Healthy Workplace

North York General Hospital (NYGH) is affiliated with the University of Toronto and has 611 beds and over 5,000 staff, physicians, and volunteers located across three sites.

NYGH takes the health and safety of its staff, physicians, and volunteers very seriously. Not only does the hospital have an occupational health, safety, and wellness department, but it also has a culture-changing People Plan as part of its human resources strategy which encourages employee engagement.

Programs available include physical fitness (e.g., onsite gym and yoga class), partnerships with YMCA and GoodLife Fitness, regular blood pressure checks, smoking cessation assistance, employee assistance program, and regular ergonomic assessments. For example, a $400,000 investment in overhead ceiling lifts was made to make it safer for staff to transfer immobile patients.

NYGH was a recipient of the highest level of Canada Awards for Excellence in Healthy Workplace in 2013 and the bronze award for Mental Health at Work in 2014.

Source: http://www.nygh.on.ca/Default.aspx?cid=2137&lang=1; http://www.youtube.com/watch?v=x9-IW5SNnes

Mental Health at Work

Excellence Canada has recently introduced a new award category called Mental Health at Work, to acknowledge the importance of mental health in recent years. The criteria for the award are based on the National Standard for Psychological Health and Safety in the Workplace, which was created in 2013. Research has shown that unmet human needs can result in psychological distress, and that these human needs can be addressed by 13 workplace factors: (1) honest/trustworthy/fair organization culture, (2) psychological support, (3) clear leadership and expectations, (4) civility and

The work environment at Google makes it an appealing place to work. Google provides its employees with a number of free perks, including therapeutic massages, gourmet meals, haircuts, arcade access, and other benefits.

Google and the Google logo are registered trademarks of Google Inc., used with permission.

respect, (5) fitness of job to employee competence, (6) growth and development, (7) recognition and reward, (8) involvement and influence, (9) appropriate workload, (10) engagement and belonging, (11) work–life balance, (12) psychological protection (no harassment, etc.), and (13) physical safety.

The required Psychological Health and Safety management system is similar to ISO 9001 (for quality). The objectives are identification and elimination of psychological hazards, control of risks that cannot be eliminated, and promotion of psychological health. The management system requires top management leadership with policy/commitment/resources, planning (identifying hazards, establishing processes, for example, to increase awareness and reduce stigma of mental illness, etc.), implementation, evaluation and corrective action, and management review and continual improvement. For the standard, see http://www.csagroup.org/documents/codes-and-standards/publications/CAN_CSA -Z1003-13_BNQ_9700-803_2013_EN.pdf, and for more information on mental health, see http:// www.mentalhealthcommission.ca/English and the "Bell's Mental Health at Work" OM in Action.

 OM in Action   http://letstalk.bell.ca/en

Bell's Mental Health at Work

Bell helped fund the National Standard for Psychological Health and Safety at Work. It is also funding Bell's Let's Talk Day (January 27) to facilitate open discussion and awareness of mental health and to reduce the stigma attached to it.

Bell has designed a training program for its managers to be able to help their employees with mental health issues. This program is mandatory for Bell's managers and over 6,000 have gone through it. Bell has also made this program available to other organizations through Queen's University and Bell's Employee Assistance Program provider. Also, the union and health and safety reps take advantage of this program.

Bell has set up an online site for its employees that contains information, videos, and a 30–45 minute tutorial on mental health in the workplace. It has set up a committee of HR professionals who hear complex mental health-related cases that are referred to them by its front-line HR consultants. Lessons learned (best practices) are incorporated into procedures that deal with mental health.

Bell has organized over 500 mental health events and seminars for its employees across Canada since 2011. It is employing return-to-work specialists to facilitate the return of employees who went on disability due to mental health. It received Excellence Canada's Mental Health at Work Gold Award in 2014.

Sources: https://www.excellence.ca/en/awards/2014-cae-recipients /2014-cae-profiles/2014-caeprofile-bell; https://www.youtube.com /watch?feature=player_embedded&v=5Gfb123632s#t=0.

Time Studies

LO4

A time study or work measurement involves various methods to determine the *length of time* needed to complete a task. Task times are vital inputs for personnel planning, estimating labour costs, assembly-line balancing, and designing incentive and performance-based pay.

A **standard time** is the amount of time it should take a qualified worker to complete a specified task, working at a sustainable rate, and using given methods, tools and equipment, raw materials, and workplace arrangement. Whenever a standard time is developed for a task, it is essential to provide a complete description of the parameters of the task because the actual time to do the task is dependent on all of these factors; changes in any one of the factors can affect the time requirement. For instance, changes in product design or changes brought about by methods analysis should trigger a new time study to update the standard time. As a practical matter, though, minor changes do not justify the expense of restudying the task. Consequently, the standard time for many tasks may be slightly inaccurate. Periodic time studies may be used to update the standard times.

Organizations develop standard times in a number of ways. The most commonly used methods are:

1. Stopwatch time study.
2. Predetermined time standards.
3. Work sampling.

> **standard time** The amount of time it should take a qualified worker to complete a specified task, working at a sustainable rate, and using given methods, tools and equipment, raw materials, and workplace arrangement.

Stopwatch Time Study

Stopwatch time study is used to develop a standard time for a task based on timing one worker over a number of cycles (repetitions of the task). The standard time is then applied to the work of all other workers in the organization who perform the same task. The basic steps in a stopwatch time study are:

1. Define the task to be studied and inform the worker who will be studied.
2. Determine the number of cycles (repetitions) to observe.
3. Time the task and rate the worker's performance.
4. Calculate the standard time, allowing for rest periods.

> **stopwatch time study** Development of a standard time based on timing one worker over a number of cycles.

The analyst who studies the task should be thoroughly familiar with it because it is not unusual for workers to attempt to include extra motions during the study in the hope of gaining a time standard that allows more time per piece. Furthermore, the analyst will need to check that the task is being performed efficiently (i.e., a methods analysis has been performed on the task) before setting the standard time.

In most instances, an analyst will break all but very short tasks down into elements and obtain times for each element. There are several reasons for this. First, some elements are not performed in every cycle and the breakdown enables the analyst to get a better perspective on them. Second, the worker's proficiency may not be the same for all elements of the task. Third, it is desirable to build a file of element times that can be used to set times for other tasks.

Workers sometimes feel uneasy about being studied and fear changes that might result. The analyst should make an attempt to discuss this issue with the worker prior to the study to reduce such fears and to enlist the worker's cooperation.

The number of cycles (repetitions) that must be timed is a function of three things: (1) the variability of observed times, (2) the desired accuracy, and (3) the desired level of confidence for the estimated task time. Very often the desired accuracy is expressed as a *percentage of the mean* of the observed times. For example, the goal of a stopwatch time study may be to achieve an estimate that is within 10 percent of the actual mean. The sample size needed to achieve this goal can be determined using:

$$n = \left(\frac{zs}{a\bar{x}}\right)^2 \tag{7-1}$$

where

z = Number of Normal standard deviations needed for the desired confidence
s = Sample standard deviation

$$s = \sqrt{\frac{\sum(x_i - \bar{x})^2}{n-1}} \text{ where } x_i = i\text{th time}$$

a = Maximum acceptable error proportion (= Percentage/100)
$\bar{x}$ = Sample mean
n = Number of observations (= Sample size)

Typical values of z used are:[14]

Desired Confidence (%)	z Value
90	1.65
95	1.96
95.5	2.00
98	2.33
99	2.58

Of course, the value of z for any desired confidence can be obtained from the Normal table in Appendix B, Table A, working backward (first divide the desired confidence by 200). For example, if a 97 percent confidence is required, then $97/200 = 0.485$, which relates to $z = 2.17$ in the table.

To make a preliminary estimate of sample size, it is typical to take a small number of observations (i.e., 10 to 20) and calculate values of $\bar{x}$ and s to use in the formula for n. Toward the end of the study, the analyst may want to recalculate n using revised estimates of $\bar{x}$ and s based on the increased data available.

An alternative formula used when the desired accuracy is stated as an *amount* (e.g., within one minute of the true mean) instead of a proportion is:

$$n = \left(\frac{zs}{e}\right)^2 \tag{7-2}$$

where

e = Accuracy amount or maximum acceptable error amount

EXAMPLE 7-1 ▶

An industrial engineer wants to estimate the time required to perform a certain task. A preliminary study yielded a mean of 6.4 minutes and a standard deviation of 2.1 minutes for the task. The desired confidence is 95 percent. How many observations will she need (including those already taken) if the maximum acceptable error is:

a. ±10 percent of the sample mean?

b. 0.5 minute?

SOLUTION

a. $s = 2.1$ minutes $z = 1.96$ for 95% confidence
$\bar{x} = 6.4$ minutes $a = 0.10$

$$n = \left(\frac{zs}{a\bar{x}}\right)^2 = \left(\frac{1.96(2.1)}{0.10(6.4)}\right)^2 = 41.36 \text{; round up to 42}$$

b. $e = 0.5$, $n = \left(\frac{zs}{e}\right)^2 = \left(\frac{1.96(2.1)}{0.5}\right)^2 = 67.77 \text{; round up to 68}$

---

[14] Theoretically, a t rather than a z value should be used because the population standard deviation is unknown. However, the use of z is simpler and provides reasonable results when the number of observations is 30 or more, as it generally is. In practice, z is used almost exclusively.

Development of a standard time actually involves calculation of three times: *observed time* (*OT*), *normal time* (*NT*), and *standard time* (*ST*).

Observed Time. The **observed time** is simply the average of the recorded times. Thus,

$$OT = \frac{\sum x_i}{n} \tag{7-3}$$

where

OT = Observed time

$\sum x_i$ = Sum of recorded times

n = Number of observations

> **observed time** The average of the recorded times.

Normal Time. The **normal time** is the observed time adjusted for the worker's performance. This is called performance levelling. It is calculated by multiplying the observed time by a *performance rating*. That is,

$$NT = OT \times PR \tag{7-4}$$

where

NT = Normal time

PR = Performance rating

> **normal time** The observed time adjusted for the worker's performance.

This assumes that a single performance rating has been determined for the entire task. If ratings are made on an element-by-element basis, the normal time is obtained by multiplying each element's average time by its performance rating and then summing those values:

$$NT = \sum (\bar{x}_j \times PR_j) \tag{7-5}$$

where

$\bar{x}_j$ = Average time for element j

PR_j = Performance rating for element j

The reason for including this adjustment factor is that the worker being observed may be working at a rate different from a "normal" rate, either to deliberately slow the pace, or because his or her natural abilities (skills) differ from the norm, or because the working conditions are different from the norm. For this reason, the analyst assigns a performance rating to adjust the observed times to a "normal" pace. A normal performance rating is 1.00. A performance rating of 0.9 indicates a pace that is 90 percent of normal, whereas a rating of 1.05 indicates a pace that is slightly faster than normal. For long tasks, each element may be rated; for short tasks, a single rating may be made for an entire task.

When assessing performance, the analyst must compare the observed performance to his/her concept of normal. Obviously, there is room for debate about what constitutes normal performance, and performance ratings are sometimes the source of considerable conflict between labour unions and management. Although no one has been able to suggest a way around these subjective evaluations, sufficient training and periodic recalibration of analysts using training films can provide a high degree of consistency in the ratings of different analysts.

Standard Time. Normal time is the length of time a worker should take to perform a task if there are no delays or rest breaks. It does not take into account factors such as personal needs (getting a drink of water or going to the washroom), unavoidable delays (machine adjustments and repairs, talking to a supervisor, waiting for materials), or rest breaks to recover from fatigue. The standard time for a task is the normal time multiplied by an **allowance** for these factors.

$$ST = NT \times AF \tag{7-6}$$

where

ST = Standard time

AF = Allowance factor

> **allowance** Factors such as personal needs (getting a drink of water or going to the washroom), unavoidable delays (machine adjustments and repairs, talking to a supervisor, waiting for materials), or rest breaks to recover from fatigue.

Allowance can be based on either task time or workday. If allowance is based on the *task time*, the allowance factor must be calculated using the formula

$$AF_{task} = 1 + A, \quad A = \text{Allowance proportion based on task time} \tag{7-7}$$

This is used when different tasks have different allowances. If allowances are based on the *workday*, the appropriate formula is

$$AF_{day} = \frac{1}{1-A}, \quad A = \text{Allowance proportion based on workday} \tag{7-8}$$

This is used when tasks are the same or similar and have the same allowance factor.

EXAMPLE 7-2 ▶

Calculate the allowance factor for these two cases:

a. The allowance is 20 percent of *task* time.

b. The allowance is 20 percent of *workday*.

$A = 0.20$

SOLUTION

a. $AF_{task} = 1 + A = 1.20$, or 120%

b. $AF_{day} = \frac{1}{1-A} = \frac{1}{1-0.20} = 1.25$, or 125%

Table 7-3 displays some typical allowances. In practice, the allowance may be based on the judgment of the analyst or negotiations between labour unions and management.

EXAMPLE 7-3 ▶

A time study of an assembly task yielded the following observations for a task for which the analyst gave a performance rating of 1.13. Using an allowance of 20 percent of task time, determine the standard time for this task.

i Observation	Time, *x* (minutes)
1...................	1.12
2...................	1.12
3...................	1.16
4...................	1.12
5...................	1.15
6...................	1.18
7...................	1.14
8...................	1.14
9...................	1.19
Total	10.35

SOLUTION

$n = 9, PR = 1.13, A = 0.20$

a. $OT = \frac{\sum x_i}{n} = \frac{10.35}{9} = 1.15$ minutes.

b. $NT = OT \times PR = 1.15(1.13) = 1.30$ minutes.

c. $ST = NT \times (1 + A) = 1.30(1.20) = 1.56$ minutes.

Time-Study Observation Sheet. A standard form is typically used to record the observations in a stopwatch time study. Alternatively a handheld device with time study software and an internal stopwatch can be used. In the following example, the task is attaching 24 inch by 36 inch chart sheets together. The task has been decomposed into four elements (the left column). Under each element

	Percent
A. Constant allowances for work breaks:	
1. Personal...	5
2. Basic fatigue...	4
B. Variable allowances:	
1. Standing...	2
2. Abnormal position...	
a. Awkward (bending)...	2
b. Very awkward (lying, stretching)...........................	7
3. Use of force or muscular energy (lifting, pulling, or pushing):	
Weight lifted (in pounds):	
5	0
10	1
15	2
20	3
25	4
30	5
35	7
40	9
45	11
50	13
60	17
70	22
4. Bad light:	
a. Well below..	2
b. Very inadequate...	5
5. Atmospheric conditions (heat and humidity, cold)—variable.............	0–10
6. Close attention required:	
a. Fine or exacting..	2
b. Very fine or very exacting..................................	5
7. Noise level:	
a. Intermittent—loud	2
b. Intermittent—very loud	5
c. High-pitched—loud	5
8. Mental strain:	
a. Fairly complex process......................................	1
b. Complex or wide span of attention	4
c. Very complex	8
9. Monotony:	
a. Medium..	1
b. High..	4
10. Tediousness:	
a. Tedious	2
b. Very tedious..	5

◀**TABLE 7-3**

Allowance percentages for different working conditions recommended by the International Labour Organization, a UN agency.

Source: A. Freivalds and B. W. Niebel, *Niebel's Methods, Standards, and Work Design,* 13th ed., Table 11.9, p. 466. ©2014 Reprinted with permission of the McGraw-Hill Companies Inc.

in parentheses is the event that signifies the end of the element. For example, grasping the stapler signifies the end of Element 1. Focusing on these events makes measuring the times easier. Also note that to the right of each element are two rows. The top row is the individual time of the element in each of the 10 cycles, whereas the bottom row is the cumulative times. For example, for Element 2 in Cycle 1, the cumulative time is 0.23 minute. The individual time for this element is therefore $0.23 - 0.07 = 0.16$ minute, where 0.07 was the (cumulative) time at the end of Element 1 in Cycle 1. The cumulative time steadily advances as more cycles are timed. However, the minute digit of the cumulative time has been omitted in order to save recording time. For example, the cumulative time for Element 4 in Cycle 2 is actually 1.09, but only ".09" is shown. It is clearly easier, faster, and more accurate to record the cumulative times first, and then calculate the individual times after the completion of the study.

Adapted from R. B. Chase et al., *Operations Management for Competitive Advantage*, 10th ed. (Boston: McGraw-Hill, 2004). Reprinted with permission of The McGraw-Hill Companies, Inc.

Time Study Observation Sheet															
Identification of operation		ASSEMBLE 24" × 36" CHART BLANKS										Date *10/9*			
Began Timing: *9:26* Ended Timing: *9:32*		Operator 109					Approval				Observer				
Task description and Breakpoint		Cycles										Summary			
		1 .00	2	3	4	5	6	7	8	9	10	ӿT	T	PR	NT
1	Fold over end (grasp stapler)	.07	.07	.05	.07	.09	.06	.05	.08	.08	.06	.68	.07	.90	.06
		.07	.61	.14	.67	.24	.78	.33	.88	.47	.09				
2	Staple five times (drop stapler)	.16	.14	.14	.15	.16	.16	.14	.17	.14	.15	1.51	.15	1.05	.16
		.23	.75	.28	.82	.40	.94	.47	.05	.61	.24				
3	Bend and insert wire (drop pliers)	.22	.25	.22	.25	.23	.23	.21	.26	.25	.24	2.36	.24	1.00	.24
		.45	.00	.50	.07	.63	.17	.68	.31	.86	.48				
4	Dispose of finished chart (touch next sheet)	.09	.09	.10	.08	.09	.11	.12	.08	.17	.08	1.01	.10	.90	.09
		.54	.09	.60	.15	.72	.28	.80	.39	.03	.56			.55	
5														normal minute for cycle	
6															
10															

Normal cycle time *.55* + Allowance *(.55 × .143)* or .08 = Std. time *.63 min/pc.*

Note: If an abnormally short time has been recorded, it would typically be assumed to be an observation error and thus discarded. If one of the observations in Example 7-3 had been 0.10, it would have been discarded. However, if an abnormally *long* time has been recorded, the analyst would want to investigate that observation to determine whether some irregularly occurring aspect of the task (e.g., speaking to the supervisor) exists, and if it should be factored into the task time.

Despite the obvious benefits that can be derived from a stopwatch time study, some limitations also must be mentioned. One limitation is that it disrupts the normal work routine. Another is that workers tend to dispute the performance rating judged by the time study analyst.

An easier method than using a stop watch and a paper form is to use a smartphone that is programmed for time study (see the "UMT Plus" OM in Action).

Predetermined Time Standards

predetermined time standards Published data based on extensive research on motion times.

methods-time measurement A set of tables of predetermined time standards for elements, developed by the Methods Engineering Council.

If an organization lacks its own historical element standard times, it can use **predetermined time standards**, which are published motion times determined by frame-by-frame analysis of motion picture films of various operations.

A commonly used set of tables of element times is **methods-time measurement** (MTM), which was developed in the late 1940s by the Methods Engineering Council. To use this approach, the analyst must divide the task into elements and each element into its motions (e.g., reach, grasp, move, turn, disengage), measure the distances involved, rate the difficulty of the motion (e.g., "move" has three levels of difficulty: move against stop; move to approximate location; and move

OM in ACTION   www.laubrass.com/umtplus

UMT Plus®

UMT Plus® is a software program that helps collect element times. The elements can be preprogrammed in a smartphone app. Then all that the time analyst has to do is to press the element's icon as the worker starts that element. UMT Plus is made by Laubrass INC., located in Montreal, Quebec. One of UMT Plus' applications was the continuous improvement department at a truck manufacturing plant in Montreal for a kaizen event. Before using smartphones with the UMT Plus app, they used a stopwatch and a paper form to collect data. But, it was hard to time and record simultaneously. The production coordinator decided to use five time analysts, each equipped with a smartphone with the UMT Plus app. Each analyst received two hours of training. They timed 70 assembly workers in three days. The results were easily uploaded to a computer. Using smartphones with the UMT Plus app was easier than using a stopwatch and paper form, and less intimidating to workers. In addition, the results were more accurate. The following image shows UMT Plus app for a car service shop.

Source: http://www.laubrass.com/assets/case_studies/en/UmtPlus_Beyond_the-Stopwatch.pdf

Courtesy of Laubrass

to exact location), and then refer to the appropriate table of data to obtain the time for that motion. The time for an element is obtained by adding the times for all of the motions, measured in terms of the **time measurement unit** (TMU); one TMU equals 1/100,000 of an hour or 0.036 second. The analyst needs a considerable amount of skill to adequately analyze the task and develop realistic time estimates. Table 7-4 presents the MTM table for "move" to give you an idea of the kind of information the MTM tables provide. These times incorporate performance ratings but do not include any allowance.

> **time measurement unit** 1/100,000 of an hour or 0.036 second.

For example, suppose that a motion is to move a tape measure that is in your hand 12 inches to the end of a plank of lumber that is on the table in front of you. This is a Case B move: move object to approximate location. It is not an exact move (Case C) because there are many possible locations at the end of the plank. The table says that this move should take 13.4 TMUs or approximately 0.5 second.

The weight allowances on the right of the table are for moving heavier objects. In this case, the formula for calculating the predetermined time is:

Predetermined time = Static constant + Dynamic factor × Time from the left of table

For example, suppose a hammer weighing 3 pounds is to be moved 12 inches (to strike a nail). Because 2.5 < 3 < 7.5, the second category on the right of the table applies. Hence,

Predetermined time = 2.2 + 1.06 × 13.4 = 16.4 TMUs or 0.6 second

A high level of skill is required to generate a predetermined time. Analysts take training or certification courses to develop the necessary skills to do this kind of work.

There are many MTM tables. There is a table for each of reach, move, turn, apply pressure, grasp, position, release, disengage, eye travel and eye focus, and body, leg, and foot motions. Each table has various values depending on the distance, difficulty (e.g., reach to fixed location or to variable location, etc.), whether the hand was in motion before or not, weight carried, degree turned, and size of object. Obviously, using the MTM tables is very time consuming and requires many years of experience.

Since its creation, there have been several variations of MTM to make it easier to use by making it less detailed. These include the simplified MTM in the 1960s, MTM-2 in the 1970s, and Maynard Operation Sequence Technique (MOST) in the 1980s. MTM is now called MTM-1. For more information, see http://www.mtm.org/ and watch the "MTM - First time right!" video at https://www.youtube.com/channel/UCCnoyNIhier1qfQ4oYXIuvA.

Time (TMU)					Weight Allowance			
Distance Moved (inches)	A	B	C	Hand in Motion B	Weight (pounds) up to:	Dynamic Factor	Static Constant TMU	Case and Description
$3/4$ or less	2.0	2.0	2.0	1.7	2.5	1.00	0	
1	2.5	2.9	3.4	2.3				
2	3.6	4.6	5.2	2.9	7.5	1.06	2.2	A. Move object to other hand or against stop.
3	4.9	5.7	6.7	3.6				
4	6.1	6.9	8.0	4.3	12.5	1.11	3.9	
5	7.3	8.0	9.2	5.0				
6	8.1	8.9	10.3	5.7	17.5	1.17	5.6	
7	8.9	9.7	11.1	6.5				
8	9.7	10.6	11.8	7.2	22.5	1.22	7.4	
9	10.5	11.5	12.7	7.9				B. Move object to approximate or indefinite location.
10	11.3	12.2	13.5	8.6	27.5	1.28	9.1	
12	12.9	13.4	15.2	10.0				
14	14.4	14.6	16.9	11.4	32.5	1.33	10.8	
16	16.0	15.8	18.7	12.8				
18	17.6	17.0	20.4	14.2	37.5	1.39	12.5	
20	19.2	18.2	22.1	15.6				
22	20.8	19.4	23.8	17.0	42.5	1.44	14.3	C. Move object to exact location.
24	22.4	20.6	25.5	18.4				
26	24.0	21.8	27.3	19.8	47.5	1.50	16.0	
28	25.5	23.1	29.0	21.2				
30	27.1	24.3	30.7	22.7				

Source: MTM Association for Standards and Research. Copyrighted by the MTM Association for Standards and Research. No reprint permission without written consent from MTM Association, 1111 E. Touhy Ave., Des Plaines, IL 60018.

TABLE 7-4 ▲

The MTM table for "move."

> **simplified MTM table** A table which contains approximate times for the motions.

Here, we will use the **simplified MTM table**, Table 7-5, which contains approximate times for the motions. This table requires the following explanations: in Type 2 reach or move, hand is in motion at the beginning or end of reach or move; loose-close-exact in position and disengage represent the amount of pressure required to join/separate two items; an example of complex grasp is pickup of a cloth or paper from a stack; Case 1 in side step or turn body ends when leading leg touches the floor, and Case 2 ends when lagging leg is brought into position. Release load has been left out of the table because its time is negligible.

As mentioned in Table 7-2, both hands should be used *simultaneously* as much as possible. In this case, the motion that takes longer is the limiting motion and only its time should be used. The same principle applies when a hand/arm motion and a leg/body motion are performed simultaneously. For example, a side step (Case 1, 20 TMUs) and a reach (for 12 inches, 4 + 12 = 16) occurring at the same time will have a time of 20 TMUs, not 20 + 16 = 36 TMUs.

EXAMPLE 7-4 ▶

Suppose a carpenter needs a 2-foot-long section out of a 2" × 4" × 8' piece of lumber that is located on his work table in front of him. First he needs to mark the 2-foot location from one end of the piece of lumber. His retractable measuring tape is in his left pocket, and his pencil is in his right pocket. After marking the lumber, both pencil and tape should be returned to the respective pockets. Decompose this marking element into motions and determine a standard time for marking the lumber using Table 7-5.

SOLUTION

Motion	Standard Time (TMU)
Reach (assume 12 inches) for the measuring tape in left pocket using left hand	4 + 12 = 16
Grasp (re-grasp: can't see, must feel for it)	6
Move (assume 12 inches) tape to the end of the lumber	4 + 12 = 16
Reach (assume 12 inches) and grasp (simple) the end of the tape using right hand	(4 + 12) + 2 = 18
Position (loose, symmetrical) the end of tape at the end of lumber using right hand	10
Move the measuring tape left across the lumber using left hand, and stop (eye time) just after the two-foot mark	(3 + 24) + 10 = 37
Release the end of tape (right hand), and reach (assume 12 inches) and grasp (re-grasp) pencil in the right pocket	0 + (4 + 12) + 6 = 22
Move (assume 12 inches) pencil close to the location of the two-foot mark on the tape	4 + 12 = 16
Position the pencil (close, asymmetric) next to the two-foot mark on the tape, and mark lumber (move pencil 1 inch)	25 + 2 = 27
Move the pencil back into the pocket (right hand), release, and return hand	(4 + 12) + 0 + (4 + 12) = 32
Grasp (simple) end of tape with right hand, disengage it from lumber (soose), and wait until it retracts into its case (assume 1 second = 28 TMU retracting time)	2 + 5 + 28 = 35
Move the tape back into the pocket (left hand), release, and return hand	(4 + 12) + 0 + (4 + 12) = 32
	267
	TMUs or 9.6 seconds

Note that a skilled carpenter does not need to use his/her right hand to position the end of tape at the end of lumber, and also that he/she can perform the reach and move of the right and left hands simultaneously. These would reduce the total time from 9.6 seconds to approximately 6 seconds. This demonstrates the importance of conducting methods analysis before doing time study.

**METHODS-TIME MEASUREMENT
APPLICATION DATA**

SIMPLIFIED DATA

(All times on this Simplified Data Table include 15% allowance)

HAND AND ARM MOTIONS			BODY, LEG, AND EYE MOTIONS	
REACH or MOVE		TMU		TMU
1″		2	Simple foot motion	10
2″		4	Foot motion with pressure	20
3″ to 12″ 4 + length of motion			Leg motion	10
over 12″ 3 + length of motion				
(For TYPE 2 REACHES AND MOVES use length of motion only)			Side step case 1	20
			Side step case 2	40
POSITION			Turn body case 1	20
Fit	Symmetrical	Other	Turn body case 2	45
Loose	10	15		
Close	20	25	Eye time	10
Exact	50	55		
			Bend, stoop or kneel on	
TURN—APPLY PRESSURE			one knee	35
TURN		6	Arise	35
APPLY PRESSURE		20		
			Kneel on both knees	80
			Arise	90
GRASP				
Simple		2	Sit	40
Regrasp or Transfer		6	Stand	50
Complex		10		
			Walk per pace	17
DISENGAGE				
Loose		5		
Close		10	1 TMU = .00001 hour	
Exact		30	= .0006 minute	
			= .036 second	

Source: Harold Maynard, *Industrial Engineering Handbook*, 2nd ed. (New York: McGraw-Hill, 1963). Reprinted with permission of the McGraw-Hill Companies.

◀ **TABLE 7-5**

The simplified methods-time measurement (MTM) table.

Work Sampling

work sampling A sampling technique for estimating the proportion of time that a worker spends on each task or is idle.

Work sampling is a technique for estimating the proportion of time that a worker spends on each task or is idle.

Unlike a time study, work sampling does not require timing a task, nor does it even involve continuous observation of the task. Instead, an observer makes brief observations of a worker at random intervals and simply notes the nature of the task. For example, a secretary may be typing, filing, talking on the telephone, and so on; and a carpenter may be carrying supplies, taking measurements, cutting wood, and so on. The resulting data are *counts* of the number of times each task or idle time was observed.

Although work sampling is occasionally used to set standard times, its primary use is for analysis of non-repetitive jobs. In a *non-repetitive job*, such as secretarial work or maintenance, it may be important to establish the percentage of time an employee is doing a particular task or is idle. Work sampling can also be an important tool in developing the job description.

Work sampling estimates include some degree of error. Hence, it is important to treat work sampling estimates as approximations of the actual proportion of time devoted to a given task. The goal of work sampling is to obtain an estimate of the proportion that provides a specified confidence of not differing from the true value by more than a specified error proportion. For example, we may desire an estimate of the idle time that will provide a 95 percent confidence of being within 4 percent of the actual percentage. Hence, work sampling is designed to produce a value, $\hat{p}$, which estimates the true proportion, p, within some acceptable error proportion, a: $\hat{p} \pm a$. The variability associated with sample estimates of p tends to be approximately Normal for large sample sizes.

The amount of acceptable error proportion is a function of the sample size, the desired level of confidence, and sample proportion. For large samples, the acceptable error proportion a can be calculated using the formula

$$a = z \sqrt{\frac{\hat{p}(1 - \hat{p})}{n}} \qquad (7\text{-}9)$$

where

z = Number of standard deviations needed to achieve the desired confidence

$\hat{p}$ = Sample proportion (the number of occurrences divided by the sample size)

n = Sample size

a = Maximum acceptable error proportion

In most instances, management will specify the desired confidence level and amount of acceptable error proportion, and the analyst will be required to determine a sample size sufficient to obtain these results. The appropriate value for n can be determined by solving Formula 7-9 for n, which yields

$$n = \left(\frac{z}{a}\right)^2 \hat{p}(1 - \hat{p}) \qquad (7\text{-}10)$$

EXAMPLE 7-5 ▶

The manager of a small supermarket wants to estimate the proportion of the time the stock clerks spend placing price stickers on merchandise. The manager wants a 98 percent confidence that the resulting estimate will be within 5 percent of the true value. What sample size should she use?

SOLUTION

$a = 0.05$, $z = 2.33$ (for 98% confidence), $\hat{p}$ is unknown

When no sample estimate of p is available, a preliminary estimate of sample size can be obtained using $\hat{p} = 0.50$. After 20 or so observations, a new estimate of $\hat{p}$ can be obtained from those observations and a revised value of n calculated using the new $\hat{p}$. It would be prudent to recalculate the value of n at two or three points during the study to obtain a better indication of the necessary sample size. Thus, the initial estimate of n is:

$$n = \left(\frac{2.33}{0.05}\right)^2 (0.50)(1 - 0.50) = 542.89, \text{ or } 543 \text{ observations}$$

Suppose that, in the first 20 observations, stock clerks were found to be placing price stickers twice, making $\hat{p} = 2/20 = 0.10$. The revised estimate of n at that point would be:

$$n = \left(\frac{2.33}{0.05}\right)^2 (0.10)(1 - 0.10) = 195.44, \text{ or } 196$$

Suppose a second check is made after a total of 100 observations, and $\hat{p} = 0.11$ at this point (including the initial 20 observations). Recalculating n yields:

$$n = \left(\frac{2.33}{0.05}\right)^2 (0.11)(0.89) = 212.60, \text{ or } 213$$

The overall procedure for work sampling consists of the following steps:

1. Clearly identify the worker to be studied.
2. Notify the worker of the purpose of the study to avoid arousing suspicion.
3. Calculate an initial estimate of sample size using a preliminary estimate of p, if available (e.g., from analyst's experience or past data). Otherwise, use $\hat{p} = 0.50$.
4. Develop a random observation schedule.
5. Begin taking observations. Recalculate the required sample size several times during the study.
6. Determine the estimated proportion of time spent on the specified task.

Observations must be spread out over a period of time so that a true indication of variability is obtained.

Determination of a random observation schedule involves the use of a random number table (see Table 7-6). Any number of digits can be read as one number. The digits are in groups of four for convenience only. The basic idea is to obtain numbers from the table and to convert each one so that it corresponds to an observation time. There are a number of ways to accomplish this. In the approach used here, we will obtain three sets of numbers from the table for each observation: the first set will correspond to the *day*, the second to the *hour*, and the third to the *minute* when the observation is to be made. The number of digits necessary for any set will relate to the number of days in the study, the number of hours per day, and minutes per hour. For instance, if the study covers 47 days, a two-digit number will be needed to generate random days; if the task is performed for eight hours per day, a one-digit number will be needed for hours. Of course, since each hour has 60 minutes, a two-digit number will be needed for minutes. A study requiring observations over a seven-day period in an office that works nine hours per day needs one-digit numbers for days, one-digit numbers for hours, and two-digit numbers for minutes.

	1	2	3	4	5	6
1	6912	7264	2801	8901	4627	8387
2	3491	1192	0575	7547	2093	4617
3	4715	2486	2776	2664	3856	0064
4	1632	1546	1950	1844	1123	1908
5	8510	7209	0938	2376	0120	4237
6	3950	1328	7343	6083	2108	2044
7	7871	7752	0521	8511	3956	3957
8	2716	1396	7354	0249	7728	8818
9	2935	8259	9912	3761	4028	9207
10	8533	9957	9585	1039	2159	2438
11	0508	1640	2768	4666	9530	3352
12	2951	0131	4359	3095	4421	3018

◀ TABLE 7-6

A portion of a random number table.

Suppose that three observations will be made in the last case (i.e., seven days, nine hours, 60 minutes). We might begin by determining the days on which observations will be made, then the hours, and finally the minutes. Let's begin with the first row in the random number table and read across (from left to right): The first number is 6, which indicates day 6. The second number is 9. Since it exceeds the number of days in the study, it is simply ignored. The third number is 1, indicating day 1, and the next is 2, indicating day 2. Hence, observations will be made on days 6, 1, and 2. Next we determine the hours. Suppose we read the second row of column 1, again obtaining one-digit numbers. We find 3 (= 3rd hour), 4 (= 4th hour), and 9 (= 9th hour). Moving to the next row and reading two-digit numbers (from left to right), we find 47 (= 47th minute), 15 (= 15th minute), and 24 (= 24th minute). Combining these results yields the following:

Day	Hour	Minute
6	3	47
1	4	15
2	9	24

This means that on day 6 of the study, an observation is to be made during the 47th minute of the 3rd hour; on day 1, during the 15th minute of the 4th hour; and on day 2, during the 24th minute of the 9th hour. For simplicity, these times can be put in chronological order by day. Thus,

Day	Hour	Minute
1	4	15
2	9	24
6	3	47

A complete schedule of observations might appear as follows, after all numbers have been arranged in chronological order, assuming 10 observations per day for two days:

	DAY 1				DAY 2		
Observation	Time	Busy(√)	Idle(√)	Observation	Time	Busy(√)	Idle(√)
1	8:15			1	8:04		
2	9:24			2	9:15		
3	9:02			3	9:24		
4	9:31			4	9:35		
5	9:48			5	10:12		
6	10:05			6	10:27		
7	10:20			7	10:38		
8	11:02			8	10:58		
9	1:13			9	11:50		
10	3:55			10	1:14		

The general procedure for using a random number table is to read the numbers in some sequence (across rows, down or up columns), discarding any that fall outside the study period.

It is possible to have work sampling self-administered, provided that the employees are motivated to cooperate and see no negative consequences from the study. In this case, observation during random times is not necessary—the employee can record the start time of each activity during the period of study. For an application of self-administered work sampling, see the "Scotiabank's Work Sampling" OM in Action.

OM in Action

Scotiabank's Work Sampling

The TimeCorder® time tracking system is a calculator-like device that keeps track of activity times of an employee. It is self-administered: when the employee starts a new activity, he/she pushes the associated code in the TimeCorder. After two or more weeks, the device is returned to Pace Productivity Inc. in Toronto and an anonymous report is issued to the employer. Scotiabank used the TimeCorder to find out what percentage of the time its personal banking officers actually spent selling. This was discovered to be only 29 percent. The rest of the time was spent on administrative duties, such as documenting calls, reviewing reports, servicing, planning, and sales management. After centralizing some administrative work and performing some training, the TimeCorder was used again. This time it showed that selling percentage went up to 37 percent of the employees' time.

Source: http://www.paceproductivity.com/results.htm.

©Pace Productivity/TimeCorder® Time Tracking System

Compensation

It is important for organizations to develop suitable monetary **compensation** plans for their employees. If wages are too low, the organization may find it difficult to attract and retain competent workers. If wages are too high, the increased costs may result in lower profits, or may force the organization to increase its prices, which might adversely affect demand for the organization's products.

Organizations compensate their employees using one or a combination of the following two forms: *time-based pay* and *output-based pay*. **Time-based pay** is either hourly pay or a salary. Hourly pay or a **wage** compensates an employee for the hours he/she works. A **salary** compensates an employee for being an employee. A full-time employee is usually required to work 40 hours a week. Time-based pay is determined by classifying the jobs according to their importance to the organization and labour market.

Output-based pay compensates employees according to the amount of output they produce, thereby tying pay to performance. **Piece rate** and **commission** represent two forms of output-based pay. *Bonus*, both individual and group, is also a form of output-based pay. A common example of bonus is the year-end (Christmas) bonus.

Time-based pay is more widely used than output-based pay, particularly for office and managerial employees, but also for blue-collar workers, for several reasons. First, calculation of compensation in time-based pay is straightforward. Second, employees often prefer time-based pay because the pay is steady and they know how much compensation they will receive for each pay period; employees may resent the pressures of the output-based pay. Third, many jobs do not lend themselves to the use of output-based pay. In some cases, it may be difficult or impossible to measure output. For example, jobs that require creative or mental work cannot be easily measured on an output basis. Other jobs may include irregular activities or have so many different forms of output that measuring output and determining pay are fairly complex. Fourth and finally, *quality* considerations may be as important as *quantity* considerations. In health care, for example, emphasis is placed on both the quality of patient care and the number of patients processed.

On the other hand, situations exist where output-based pay is desirable. It rewards workers for their output, causing some workers to produce more than they might under time-based pay. Note that only acceptable-quality output should be counted. Piece rate is still used by some clothing manufacturers and assembly operations. See the "Lincoln Electric" OM in Action for a successful application of piece rate.

compensation The money received by an employee from an employer as a salary or wages.

time-based pay Compensation based on length of time an employee works.

wage Hourly pay.

salary Compensation of an employee for being an employee. A full-time employee is usually required to work 40 hours a week.

output-based pay Compensation based on amount of output an employee produces. Two forms of output-based pay are piece rate and commission.

piece rate Compensation for producing a unit of output.

commission A fee paid to an employee based on a percentage of the sale price.

OM in Action www.lincolnelectric.com

Lincoln Electric

Lincoln Electric (LE), founded in Cleveland over 120 years ago, is the world's largest manufacturer of arc welding solutions. It has 63 plants in 23 countries including Canada, employs over 11,000 people, and sells in over 160 countries.

LE is well known in academic circles because of its unique incentive management system, which uses piece-rate compensation for many of its employees. It has no unions, but maintains a good worker–management relationship based on trust and open communication achieved through regularly scheduled employee advisory–management meetings. Piece rate adjustments are non-adversarial. Management receives no "perks." LE is an example of a high-involvement culture. Productivity and worker compensation are among the highest in North America—especially during peak portions of an economic cycle due to the incentive management system's profit sharing bonus plan, which is distributed according to a worker's merit rating. Labour turnover is low and there have been no layoffs

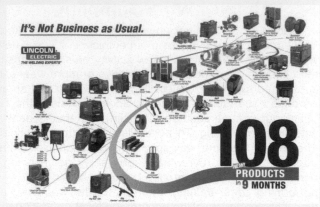

Courtesy of Lincoln Electric

since 1948. Workers are guaranteed at least 30 hours of work a week.

Sources: Richard J. Long, Strategic Compensation in Canada, 5th Ed, 2014, Nelson, Toronto, pp. 151-2; http://www.canadianmanufacturing.com /manufacturing/manufacturing-turnaround-lincoln-electric-keeps-production -canada-138305/.

In the past, output-based pay was fairly popular. Now minimum-wage legislation makes it somewhat impractical. Even so, many of the compensation plans currently in use represent variations of output-based pay. They typically incorporate a time-based pay that serves as a floor: workers are guaranteed that amount as a minimum, regardless of output. The time-based pay is tied to an output standard. If the worker produces more than that, he/she will receive a *bonus*. See the "Bonus Pay in a Distribution Centre" OM in Action for an example.

> **skills/knowledge-based bonus pay** Rewarding workers who undergo training to increase their skills/knowledge.

Skills/Knowledge-Based Bonus Pay. Organizations are increasingly setting up bonus plans to reward workers who undergo training to increase their skills/knowledge. This is referred to as **skills/ knowledge-based bonus pay**. Skills/knowledge has three dimensions: *horizontal skills* reflecting

 OM in Action

Bonus Pay in a Distribution Centre

When Bruce Ennis was tasked with increasing the productivity and accuracy of order picking at an industrial products distribution centre in Edmonton, order pickers were paid a modest hourly wage, irrespective of their productivity or accuracy. After intense deliberation and consultation with the order pickers, Bruce decided to introduce a bonus plan. Each picker's output was measured by the number of items picked per day (while adjusting for the size of items) times the percentage of

accuracy. This output measure for each order picker was posted in a prominent location on a daily basis. Those pickers whose output fell into the second quartile were paid a bonus of $2.63 per day. Those whose output fell into the third and fourth quartiles received a bonus of $5.26 and $10.53 per day, respectively. At first, Bruce was concerned about whether management would be able to recoup these extra labour expenses. However, through instigating an increase of 25 percent in productivity, this bonus plan has more than paid for itself.

Source: www.distributiongroup.com/articles/drivinghigherworkplaceper formance.pdf.

the variety of tasks the worker is capable of performing; *vertical skills* reflecting managerial tasks the worker is capable of; and *depth skills* reflecting quality and productivity results.

An example of skills/knowledge-based bonus pay is used in the Molson Breweries (Montreal) plant, where a multi-skill premium of $4 per day is paid to client service truck drivers and a $0.50 per hour premium is paid to multi-skilled brewing operations employees. Team leaders in the warehouse, shipping, and garage operations receive a team leader premium of $15 per week.[15]

Group Bonus Plans. A variety of group bonus/incentive plans, which stress sharing of output/ profit/productivity gains with the employees, are in use. Some focus exclusively on output (called goal sharing or group incentive), while others reward employees for reductions in costs (called gain sharing), or increases in profit (called profit sharing).

Employee share purchase plans are a form of group bonus. For example, WestJet employees can contribute up to 20 percent of their wages toward a share purchase plan that is matched by the company.

Summary

- Work/job design involves determining the content of work as well as the method, working conditions, time studies, and compensation.
- According to the human performance system, the following six factors are required for effective and efficient performance of a job: performance specification, task support, consequences, feedback, skills/knowledge, and individual capacity.
- In the past, work/job design was focused primarily on efficiency, but now there is an increasing use of the behavioural approach. This includes job enlargement, rotation, enrichment, and teamwork.
- Labour unions and information/communication technologies have affected all aspects of work/job design and how work is accomplished.
- Analysts often use methods analysis and motion-study techniques to make the job/task/ element more efficient. Charts such as the flow process chart, worker–machine chart, and simo chart are used to document and improve how work is done.

- Working conditions such as temperature, illumination, and work breaks affect productivity and the health and safety of workers.
- Ergonomics (fitting the job to the worker's capabilities) is also important.
- Mental health has recently become an important part of a healthy workplace.
- Time studies are concerned with determining the time needed to complete a task (i.e., its standard time). Commonly used approaches include stopwatch time study and predetermined time standards. A related technique is work sampling, which is used to estimate the proportion of time a worker spends on a certain aspect of the job. Table 7-7 provides a summary of the formulas used in stopwatch time study and work sampling.
- Time-based (hourly, salaried) pay is most common. Output-based (piece rate, commission) pay is used in some industries. Bonus plans are a form of output-based pay. Group bonus plans such as profit sharing and skills/ knowledge-based bonus pay are becoming more common.

Stopwatch Time Study		Work Sampling	
A. Sample size		A. Maximum acceptable error proportion	
$n = \left(\frac{zs}{a\bar{x}}\right)^2$	(7-1)	$a = z\sqrt{\frac{\hat{p}(1-\hat{p})}{n}}$	(7-9)
$n = \left(\frac{zs}{e}\right)^2$	(7-2)		
B. Observed time		B. Sample size	
$OT = \frac{\sum x_i}{n}$	(7-3)	$n = \left(\frac{z}{a}\right)^2 \hat{p}(1-\hat{p})^2$	(7-10)

◀ **TABLE 7-7**

Summary of formulas.

---

[15] S. Payette, "What's New in Workplace Innovations?" *Workplace Gazette* 3(1), 2000, pp. 110–119.

C. Normal time

$$NT = OT \times PR \qquad (7\text{-}4)$$

$$NT = \Sigma(\bar{x}_i \times PR_i) \qquad (7\text{-}5)$$

D. Standard time

$$ST = NT \times AF \qquad (7\text{-}6)$$

E. Allowance factor

$$AF_{task} = 1 + A \qquad (7\text{-}7)$$

$$AF_{day} = \frac{1}{1-A} \qquad (7\text{-}8)$$

Symbols:

a = Maximum acceptable error proportion

A = Allowance proportion

e = Maximum acceptable error amount

n = Number of observations needed

NT = Normal time

OT = Observed time

PR = Performance rating

$\hat{p}$ = Sample proportion

s = Standard deviation of observed times

ST = Standard time

x_i = Time for ith observation (i = 1, 2, 3, . . . , n)

z = No. of standard deviations needed to achieve desired confidence

Key Terms

allowance

behavioural approach

commission

compensation

efficiency approach

element

ergonomics

flow process chart

information and communication
   technologies

job enlargement

job enrichment

job rotation

methods analysis

methods-time measurement

motion economy principles

motion study

normal time

observed time

output-based pay

piece rate

predetermined time standards

salary

self-directed team

simo chart

simplified MTM table

skills/knowledge-based bonus pay

slow motion study

specialization

standard time

stopwatch time study

task

time measurement unit

time-based pay

wage

work/job

work/job design

work sampling

worker–machine chart

Solved Problems

Problem 1

A time-study analyst timed an assembly task for 30 cycles, and then computed the average time per cycle, which was 18.75 minutes. The analyst assigned a performance rating of 0.96 to the operator, and decided that an appropriate allowance was 15 percent based on the *workday*. Determine the observed time (OT), the normal time (NT), and the standard time (ST) for this task.

Solution

$OT = 18.75$ minutes, PR = 0.96, A = 0.15

$NT = OT \times PR = 18.75$ minutes $\times$ 0.96 = 18 minutes

$AF = \dfrac{1}{1-A} = \dfrac{1}{1-0.15} = 1.176$

$ST = NT \times AF = 18 \times 1.176 = 21.17$ minutes

Problem 2

A time-study analyst wants to estimate the number of observations that will be needed to achieve a specified maximum error, with a confidence of 95.5 percent. A preliminary study yielded a mean of 5.2 minutes and a standard deviation of 1.1 minutes for the task. Determine the number of observations needed for these two cases:

a. A maximum acceptable error of $\pm6\%$ of the sample mean.

b. A maximum acceptable error of 0.40 minute.

Solution

a. $\bar{x} = 5.2$ minutes $z = 2.00$ for 95.5% confidence
$s = 1.1$ minutes $a = 0.06$

$$n = \left(\frac{zs}{a\bar{x}}\right)^2 = \left(\frac{2.00(1.1)}{0.06(5.2)}\right)^2 = 49.72; \text{ round up to 50 observations}$$

b. $e = 0.40$

$$n = \left(\frac{zs}{e}\right)^2 = \left(\frac{2.00(1.1)}{0.40}\right)^2 = 30.25; \text{ round up to 31 observations}$$

Problem 3

Work sampling. An analyst has been asked to prepare an estimate of the proportion of time that a lathe operator spends adjusting the machine, with a 90 percent confidence level. Based on previous experience, the analyst believes the proportion will be approximately 30 percent.

a. If the analyst uses a sample size of 400 observations, what is the maximum possible error percentage that will be associated with the estimate?

b. What sample size would the analyst need in order to have maximum error proportion of no more than ±5 percent?

Solution

a. $\hat{p} = 0.30$, $z = 1.65$ (For 90 percent confidence) $n = 400$

$$a = z\sqrt{\frac{\hat{p}(1-\hat{p})}{n}} = 1.65\sqrt{\frac{0.3(0.7)}{400}} = 0.038 \text{ or } 3.8\%$$

b. $a = 0.05$, $n = \left(\frac{z}{a}\right)^2 \hat{p}(1-\hat{p}) = \left(\frac{1.65}{0.05}\right)(0.3)(0.7) = 228.69$, or 229

Problem 4

A supervisor timed a hotel maid performing the four main tasks necessary to clean a room. These times (in minutes) for five rooms and the performance rating of the maid for each task are given below. Assuming a 10 percent allowance factor based on task time, calculate the standard time for cleaning a room.

		Room				
Task	**Performance Rating**	**1**	**2**	**3**	**4**	**5**
Replenishing the mini-bar	100	2	2.5	1.5	1	2
Making the bed	90	2.5	3	4	3	2.5
Vacuuming the floor	110	3	4	2.5	3	2.5
Cleaning the bathroom	80	4	4.5	3.5	4	6

Solution

$A = 0.1$, $AF = 1 + A = 1.1$

Task	Performance Rating PR	Observations X_i (min. per cycle)					$OT = (X_1 + \cdots + X_5)/5$	$NT = OT$ (PR)	$ST = NT$ (AF)
		1	**2**	**3**	**4**	**5**			
1	100%	2.0	2.5	1.5	1.0	2.0	1.80	1.8	1.98
2	90%	2.5	3.0	4.0	3.0	2.5	3.00	2.7	2.97
3	110%	3.0	4.0	2.5	3.0	2.5	3.00	3.3	3.63
4	80%	4.0	4.5	3.5	4.0	6.0	4.40	3.52	3.87
								Standard Time:	12.45

Discussion and Review Questions

LO1 1. What is job design and why is it important?

LO1 2. What are some of the main advantages and disadvantages of specialization from a company's perspective? From a worker's perspective?

LO1 3. Contrast the meanings of the terms *job enlargement* and *job enrichment*.

LO1 4. What is the purpose of the behavioural approach to job design?

LO1 5. What is a self-directed work team? What are some potential benefits of using these teams?

LO1 6. Some Japanese companies have a policy of rotating their managers among different managerial jobs. In contrast, North American managers are more likely to specialize in a certain area (e.g., finance or operations). Discuss the advantages and disadvantages of each of these approaches. Which one do you prefer? Why?

LO2 7. Name some reasons methods analysis is needed. How is methods analysis linked to productivity improvements?

LO2 8. How are tools such as a flow process chart and a worker–machine chart useful?

LO2 9. What are the motion economy principles?

LO4 10. What is a standard time? What does it assume?

LO4 11. What are the main uses of standard times?

LO4 12. Could problems with determining a performance rating be avoided by studying a group of workers and averaging their times? Explain briefly.

LO4 13. If an average worker could be identified, what advantage would there be in using that person for a stopwatch time study? What is a reason an average worker might not be studied?

LO4 14. What are the main limitations of stopwatch time study?

LO4 15. Comment on the following. "At any given instant, the standard times for many tasks will not be strictly correct."

  a. Why is this so?
  b. Does this mean that those standard times are useless? Explain.

LO4 16. Why do workers sometimes resent stopwatch time studies?

LO4 17. What is work sampling? How does it differ from stopwatch time study?

LO5 18. What are the key advantages and disadvantages of:
  a. Time-based pay (i) for management and (ii) workers?
  b. Output-based pay (i) for management and (ii) workers?

LO5 19. Explain skills/knowledge-based bonus pay.

LO3 20. The temperature in the meat department of a grocery store is usually kept at about 10–11°C. The activities in this department include cutting, packing, and wrapping the meat. Explain how the workers could cope with this low temperature.

LO3 21. Why should a company care about the health and safety of its workers? Is it possible to operate profitably without this concern? Give an example of a company that cares about its workers and another that doesn't.

LO3 22. What is ergonomics? Give an example.

LO3 23. What is a healthy workplace? Give an example.

LO3 24. What is cognitive ergonomics? Give an example.

LO3 25. What is a mentally healthy workplace? Give an example.

LO4 26. During timing, the subject of a stopwatch time study drops his tool. Should the time to retrieve the tool count toward the standard time? Briefly explain.

LO1 27. Describe the six job design factors recommended by the human performance system.

LO1 28. What do labour unions do for their members?

LO1 29. How have information and communication technologies caused jobs to change?

LO3 30. What are the 13 factors of mental health at work?

Taking Stock

1. What are the trade-offs in each of these situations?
  LO1 a. Using self-directed work teams.
  LO4 b. Deciding how often to update standard times.
  LO4 c. Deciding between stopwatch time study and work sampling.

LO4 2. Who uses the results of time studies in an organization?

LO1, 3 & 4 3. In what ways has technology impacted job design?

LO3 4. In Canada, the health and safety of workers are protected by the Occupational Health and Safety Act of each province, which is enforced by the ministry (or department) of labour of the province. The website http://www.labour.gov.on.ca/english/news/courtbulletins.php describes recent court cases brought under the OHSA in Ontario. As can be seen from reading some of the cases, the employer is responsible for any accident; for example, a mechanic's hand being pulled between rollers of a conveyor while greasing it from underneath, an explosion inside a tank due to methane gas when a welder started to work in it, or a load of steel bars falling on a delivery driver helping a forklift driver to unload it. In addition, lack of procedures, training, and warning signs also

makes the employer responsible for any injuries to the worker. An employee not wearing a hardhat, or having a low level of light that can cause a fall, is grounds to fine the company. Moreover, a supervisor can personally be fined if he/she did not inform an employee of the right procedure. Discuss whether you think that the Occupational Health and Safety Act is now being unfair to companies and supervisors.

Critical Thinking Exercises

 1. Can work design be of strategic importance to a company? Explain and give examples.

 2. What approach—efficiency or behavioural—do you think McDonald's has used for its job design? Briefly explain why this is the case.

 3. What is the worst job you know? Why? How can it be improved?

Experiential Learning Exercises

 1. Select one of the following tasks and prepare a worker–machine chart that displays the elements and their estimated times:
   a. Visit an ATM and make a withdrawal.
   b. Visit a gas station and fill up.

 2. Develop a standard time for the task of preparing a ham and cheese sandwich:

a. List the steps (elements) required to prepare the sandwich.
b. Observe the task for several repetitions and make improvements if necessary.
c. Time each element for several repetitions.
d. Assign a performance rating to the overall task.
e. Develop the standard time.

Internet Exercises

 1. Visit the Association of Canadian Ergonomists website (https://www.ace-ergocanada.ca/about/about_ergonomics/ergonomics.html) and identify the types of activities ergonomists undertake.

 2. Visit http://www.ergoweb.com/casestudies, find an interesting ergonomics case study, and summarize it.

 3. Visit https://www.osha.gov/dts/osta/oshasoft/index.html, choose an industry etool, then choose an application area/task, and identify a safety or ergonomic lesson for work design in that industry.

 4. Visit http://www.youtube.com/watch?v=S9D2hmOtRio and describe how Ford's ergonomics staff help its job design.

 5. Visit http://excellence.ca/en/awards/2016-cae-recipients/2016-cae-profiles/2016-caeprofile-lassonde and describe Lassonde Industries' healthy workplace program.

 6. Visit https://www.excellence.ca/en/awards/2014-cae-recipients/2014-cae-profiles/2014-caeprofile-amd and describe ArcellorMittal Dofasco's healthy workplace program.

 7. Visit https://www.excellence.ca/en/awards/2012-cae-recipients/2012-cae-profiles/2012-caeprofile-hwcsb and describe Hamilton-Wentworth Catholic Schools' Mental Health at Work program.

 8. Visit http://www.laubrass.com/assets/case_studies/en/UmtPlus-Douglas-Time-Study.pdf and describe how the Douglas Mental Health University Institute in Montreal used Laubrass's UMT Plus software.

Problems

LO4 **1.** An analyst has timed a metal-cutting task for 50 cycles. The average time per cycle was 10.40 minutes, and the standard deviation was 1.20 minutes for a worker with a performance rating of 125 percent. Assume an allowance of 16 percent of task time. Calculate the standard time for this task.

LO4 **2.** A task was timed for 60 cycles. It took an average of 1.2 minutes per cycle. The performance rating was 95 percent, and workday allowance is 10 percent. Determine each of the following:

   a. Observed time.

   b. Normal time.

   c. Standard time.

LO4 **3.** A time study was conducted on a task that consists of four elements. The observations and performance ratings for six cycles are shown in the following table.

		Observations (minutes per cycle)					
Element	Performance Rating	1	2	3	4	5	6
1.............	90%	0.44	0.50	0.43	0.45	0.48	0.46
2..........	85	1.50	1.54	1.47	1.51	1.49	1.52
3..........	110	0.84	0.89	0.77	0.83	0.85	0.80
4............	100	1.10	1.14	1.08	1.20	1.16	1.26

   a. Calculate the average time for each element.

   b. Calculate the normal time for each element.

   c. Assuming an allowance factor of 15 percent of workday, calculate the standard time for this task.

LO4 **4.** Given these observations (in minutes) for four elements of a task, determine the observed time (OT) for each element. (*Note:* The second element occurs only in every other cycle.)

	Cycle					
Element	1	2	3	4	5	6
1	4.1	4.0	4.2	4.1	4.1	4.1
2	—	1.5	—	1.6	—	1.4
3	3.2	3.2	3.3	3.2	3.3	3.3
4	2.7	2.8	2.7	2.8	2.8	2.8

LO4 **5.** Given these observations (in minutes) for five elements of a task, determine the observed time (OT) for each element. (*Note:* Some of the elements occur only periodically.) Also, using a performance rating of 90 percent for each element and allowance of 15 percent of task time, calculate the standard time for the task. Why does your answer overestimate the task time? How can a better task time estimate be derived?

	Cycle					
Element	1	2	3	4	5	6
1	2.1	2.0	2.2	2.1	2.1	—
2	—	1.1	—	1.0	—	1.2
3	3.4	3.5	3.3	3.5	3.4	3.3
4	4.0	—	—	4.2	—	—
5	1.4	1.4	1.5	1.5	1.5	1.4

LO4 **6.** Using Table 7-3, develop an allowance percentage for a task that requires the worker to lift a weight of 10 pounds while (1) standing, (2) in light that is well below recommended standards, and (3) with intermittent loud noises occurring. The monotony for this task is high. Include a personal allowance of 5 percent and a basic fatigue allowance of 4 percent.

LO4 **7.** A worker–machine operation was found to involve 3.3 minutes of machine time per cycle. In the course of 40 cycles of a stopwatch time study, the worker's time loading and unloading the machine averaged 1.9 minutes per cycle, and the worker was given a rating of 120 percent. Assuming an allowance factor of 12 percent of task time, determine the standard time for this operation (including the machine time).

LO4 **8.** A recently negotiated union contract allows workers in a shipping department a total of 24 minutes for rest, 10 minutes for personal time, and 14 minutes for delays for each four-hour shift worked. A time-study analyst observed a task in the shipping department that is performed continuously and found an average time of 6.0 minutes per cycle for a worker she rated at 95 percent. What standard time is applicable for that task?

LO4 **9.** The following data were obtained by observing three elements of a financial manager's task.

   a. Using the data and an allowance of 10 percent of task time, determine a standard time for the task.

   b. Determine the number of observations that would be required to estimate the mean time for the first element within 4 percent of the true value with a confidence of 98 percent.

   c. How many observations would be needed to estimate the mean time for element C to within 0.10 minutes of its actual value with a confidence of 90 percent?

		Observations (minutes per cycle)				
Element	Performance Rating	1	2	3	4	5
A	90%	1.40	1.42	1.39	1.38	1.41
B	120	2.10	2.05	2.00	1.85	1.80
C	110	1.60	1.40	1.50	1.45	1.55

LO4 **10.** The data in the following table represent time-study observations for a woodworking task.

   a. Based on the observations, determine the standard time for the task, assuming an allowance of 20 percent of task time.

   b. How many observations would be needed to estimate the mean time for Element 1 within 1 percent of its true value with a 95.5 percent confidence?

   c. How many observations would be needed to estimate the mean time for Element 1 within 0.01 minute of its true value with a 95.5 percent confidence?

Element	Performance Rating	Observations (minutes per cycle)					
		1	2	3	4	5	6
1	110%	1.20	1.17	1.16	1.22	1.24	1.15
2	115	0.83	0.87	0.78	0.82	0.85	1.32*
3	105	0.58	0.53	0.52	0.59	0.60	0.54

*Unusual delay, disregard time.

 11. How many observations should a stopwatch time-study analyst plan for in a task that has a standard deviation of 1.5 minutes per piece if the goal is to estimate the mean time per piece to within 0.4 minute with a confidence of 95.5 percent?

 12. How many work cycles should be timed to estimate the average cycle time to within 2 percent of the sample mean with a confidence of 99 percent if a pilot study yielded these times (in minutes): 5.2, 5.5, 5.8, 5.3, 5.5, and 5.1?

 13. In an initial survey designed to estimate the percentage of time air-express cargo loaders are idle, an analyst found that loaders were idle in 6 of the 50 observations.
   a. What is the estimated percentage of idle time?
   b. Based on the initial results, approximately how many observations would you require to estimate the actual percentage of idle time to within 4 percent with a confidence of 95 percent?

 14. An analyst made the following observations about whether customer service representatives were busy (B) or idle (I):
   a. What is the percentage of idle time?
   b. Given these results, how many observations would be needed to estimate the actual percentage of idle time to within 6 percent with a confidence of 90 percent?

Diagram for Problem 14

Observation	1	2	3	4	5	6	7	8	9	10	11	12	13	14	15	16	17	18	19	20
Busy or idle	B	B	I	B	I	B	B	B	I	B	B	B	B	I	B	B	B	B	B	I

 15. A job in an insurance office involves telephone conversations with policy holders. The office manager estimates that about half of the employee's time is spent on the telephone. How many observations are needed in a work sampling study to estimate that time percentage to within 4 percent and have a confidence of 95 percent?

 16. A hospital administrator thinks that the X-ray equipment is only in use about 20 percent of the time. What number of observations in a work sampling study would be needed to estimate the true percentage of time to within 5 percent with a confidence of 98 percent?

 17. Design a schedule of work sampling observations in which eight observations are made during one eight-hour day (use 0:00 to 7:59). Using Table 7-6, read the *last digit* going down column 4 for hours (e.g., 1 7 4 4 6 . . .), and read across row 3 from left to right in sets of two for minutes (e.g., 47 15 24 86 . . .). Arrange the times chronologically.

 18. The manager of a large office intends to conduct a work sampling of the time the staff spends on the telephone. The observations will be taken over a period of 50 workdays. The office is open five days a week for eight hours a day (use 0:00 to 7:59). Although the study will consist of 200 random observations, in this problem you will be asked to determine times for 11 observations. Use random numbers from Table 7-6.
   a. Determine times for 11 observations. For days, read sets of two-digit numbers going across row 4 from left to right (e.g., 16 32 15 46 . . .), and do the same in row 5.
   b. For hours, read one-digit numbers going *down,* using the first digit of column 1 (e.g., 6 3 4 1 . . . then column 2).
   c. For minutes, read two-digit numbers going *up* column 4 using the first two digits (e.g., 30 46 10 . . .), and then repeat for the second two digits going *up* column 4 (e.g., 95 66 39 . . .).
   d. Arrange the combinations chronologically by day, hour, and minute.

   e. Assume March 1 is a Monday and that there are no holidays in March, April, or May.
   Convert your observation days to dates in March, April, and May.

 19. A work sampling study is to be conducted on rush-hour traffic (4:00 p.m. to 6:59 p.m.) five days per week. The study will encompass 40 days. Determine the day, hour, and minute for 10 observations using the following procedure and Table 7-6:
   a. Read two-digit numbers going *down* the first two digits of column 5 (e.g., 46 20 38 . . .), and then down the second two digits of that column (e.g., 27 93 56 . . .) for days.
   b. For hours, read one-digit numbers going from left to right across row 1 and then across row 2. (Read only 4s, 5s, and 6s.)
   c. For minutes, read two-digit numbers going *down* column 6, first using the *last* two digits (e.g., 87 17 64 . . .) those numbers, repeat using the first two digits of that column (e.g., 83 46 00 19 . . .).
   Arrange your times chronologically by day, then hour, and then minute.

 20. The killing and disassembly of a hog in a slaughter plant is very labour intensive, because the tasks cannot easily be automated. This is because each hog is slightly different and the carcasses cannot in general be held in place in a consistent way in order to automate the work. To achieve the target production (which is high in order to make a profit), tasks need to be very specialized. For example, one task is called "snatching guts." Suppose you are helping the industrial engineer to determine the standard time for this task. The videotape of five cycles revealed the following task times (in seconds): 14, 13, 13, 12, and 14. Assume a performance rating of 0.90 and allowance of 15 percent of task time. Calculate the standard time for this task.[16]

---

[16] Based on J.S. Moore and A. Garg, "Participatory Ergonomics in a Red Meat Packing Plant, Part II: Case Studies," *American Industrial Hygiene Association Journal* 58(7), July 1997, pp. 498–508.

21. The following two activities are commonly used to train stopwatch time-study analysts to get a feel for an average performance rating (i.e., performance rating of 1.0).

 a. Walk at 3 miles per hour (= 80 metres per minute = 1.34 metres per second).

 b. Deal a deck of 52 cards into four equal piles one foot apart (make a square) in 0.5 minute.

 Choose one of these and time yourself trying to achieve these times. If you are too slow, repeat the exercise faster until you reach these speeds. Do you believe that these times are sustainable? Explain.

22. You wish to estimate the time for installation of new shingles on your house. To start, you will try to time driving one nail into a shingle. Assume that the shingle is already in place. You are kneeling on your roof facing the shingle. The hammer is on the roof on the right of the shingle. Nails are in your left pocket. Use the simplified MTM table (Table 7-5) to determine the time of driving one nail into the shingle. End with placing the hammer back on the roof.

23. Using the simplified MTM times given in Table 7-5 and the "Made for You" McDonald's video (available as a streaming video from http://bevideos.mhhe.com/business/video_library/0072917776/swf/Clip_08.html), estimate the time it should take a McDonald's employee to:

 a. Pick up a bun from the rack and drop its two sides into the toaster (minutes 9:19–9:22 of the video).

 b. Squirt the second condiment on the bun, side step, and place small pieces of the first vegetable on the bun. Start from just after the first condiment dispenser is put back in its place and end just after the first vegetable pieces are placed on the bun (minutes 9:42–9:48 of the video).

If you have access to the non-streaming video (Volume 08, OM McGraw-Hill Video Library), you can slow down the video by choosing "Full screen" in view menu, then right-clicking and setting play speed to Slow.

24. In the bottle-recycling department of Labatt's Brewery (now part of Anheuser-Busch InBev) in St. John's, Newfoundland, the "throw on" task involves lifting cases of empty bottles from a pallet and throwing them on a conveyor.[17] A case weighs approximately 6 kg. "Throw on" sometimes involves reaching up above shoulder-height or bending and lifting elements (see the two sketches below). Each "throw on" takes between two and five seconds, and the pallet is unloaded in about three minutes. Even though the workers rotate out of this task every half hour, there is still a chance of repetitive motion injuries and lower back pain. Propose an ergonomic solution for this problem.

Diagram for Problem 24

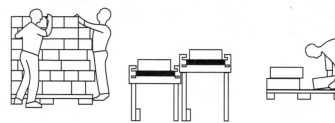

Source: www.distributiongroup.com/articles/drivinghigherworkplaceperformance.pdf

25. In the assembly operation of Mother Hubbard's Kitchens in Dartmouth, Nova Scotia, the worker holds the tool with his operating hand and the piece of cabinet with the other hand (see the three sketches below), and the work requires reaching and bending, exerting force from the shoulder, and awkward positions for the arms and the body.[18] There is a chance of repetitive motion injuries and shoulder and lower back pain. Propose an ergonomic solution for this problem.

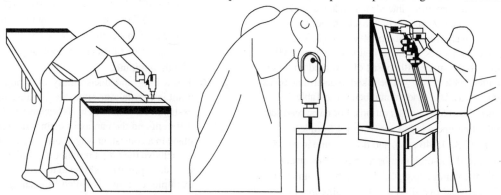

Source: Canadian Centre for Occupational Health and Safety. "Cabinet Manufacturing." http://www.ccohs.ca/oshanswers/occup_workplace/cab_manu.html

---

[17] Canadian Centre for Occupational Health and Safety. "Bottle Recycling Department of a Brewery," http://www.ccohs.ca/oshanswers/occup_workplace/brewery.html.

[18] Canadian Centre for Occupational Health and Safety. "Cabinet Manufacturing," http://www.ccohs.ca/oshanswers/occup_workplace/cab_manu.html.

L03 **26.** In the Buttered Sole line of Burin's Secondary Processing plant of Fishery Products International (later High Liner), in Newfoundland, the "spreading" operation involved spreading the sole on the conveyor belt.[19] The job involved standing in a stooped position and reaching. Propose an ergonomic solution for this problem.

Source: Canadian Centre for Occupational Health and Safety. "Cabinet Manufacturing." http://www.ccohs.ca/oshanswers/occup_workplace/cab_manu.html.

🔍 MINI-CASE

Earthwise Pallet Recyclers

Earthwise Pallet Recyclers (EPR) is a small business that refurbishes damaged wood pallets in Saskatoon. Gary Wurst founded EPR in 1996 after he saw so many unwanted damaged pallets lying around in construction sites. He started collecting them, fixing them, and selling them at a low price ($3–$5 each) to local manufacturers and distributors that use pallets. Currently he has about 12 employees, including approximately 4 "nailers." The company takes in approximately 2,800 pallets each week and produces approximately 2,000 refurbished pallets. Pallets that are in poor condition are dismantled and their pieces are used to refurbish other pallets. Each nailer produces approximately 130 refurbished pallets per day (8-hour shift). Gary would like to see this number increase to 160 pallets per day. Nailer responsibilities include assessing a damaged pallet (called a core), taking damaged boards off, nailing replacement boards in, and repairing the frame using a scab (a piece of 2" × 4" lumber with a notch cut out of it) or a block (a piece of 2" × 4" lumber).

A more detailed list of elements and time measurements (in seconds) for five cycles of a nailer fixing a pallet are given below. Also given is a layout diagram of the EPR shop. Occasionally a nailer runs out of good boards and has to walk to the chop saw workstation or other good-board bins to retrieve good boards. Part of the problem is that there are different sizes of pallets so nailers need different sizes of good boards. Nailers are also responsible for moving both the core stacks and the finished stacks to and from their workstation, and moving bad core stacks to the dismantler. They use a manual pallet jack to do so. Each leg of these trips takes approximately two minutes. There are only two pallet jacks in the shop. Cores and fixed pallet stacks are transported in and out of the shop using a forklift.

Questions

What is the processing time of a pallet? What suggestions can you make to Gary to increase EPR's productivity?

Building a pallet (times in seconds)	1	2	3	4	5
Pick pallet from cores pile (in workstation) and put on nail table	8	9	9	7	10
Assess pallet: if bad, put it aside; if good, proceed	6	7	4	14	8
Hit nails down with hammer	2	5	6	4	3
Rip off broken boards with crowbar	8	12	10	5	8
Remove broken boards by hand	6	11	8	12	11
Throw broken boards in garbage bin (on the left)	1	2	2	2	1
Grab good boards from good-board bin (on the right)	11	10	48	25	21
Place good boards on pallet	8	5	3	17	3
Nail good boards in with nail gun	3	7	10	6	6
Place block/scab in	3	10	9	8	3
Hammer in block/scab	6	4	31	3	9
Flip pallet	2	2	10	4	2
Hit nails down with hammer	7	11	20	15	5

---

[19] Canadian Centre for Occupational Health and Safety. "Fish Processing," http://www.ccohs.ca/oshanswers/occup_workplace/fish_pro.html. This plant closed in December 2012.

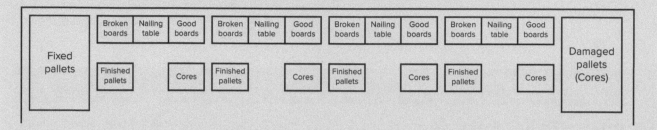

Rip off broken boards with crowbar	9	6	13	14	8
Remove broken boards by hand	11	14	9	18	13
Throw broken boards in garbage bin	1	1	1	2	2
Grab good boards from good-board bin	48	6	5	4	3
Place good boards on pallet	13	3	10	5	7
Nail good boards in with nail gun	17	6	10	8	6
Move pallet to finished pallet pile (in workstation)	9	9	8	8	8

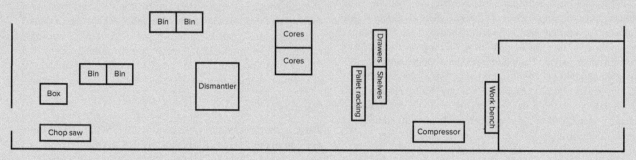

Source: Joy-Anne Caswell, "Earthwise Pallet Recyclers" (term paper), Dec 2004, COMM 205: Introduction ement.

To access "Learning Curves," the supplement to Chapter 7,
please visit *Connect2*.

Chapter 8
Location Planning and Analysis

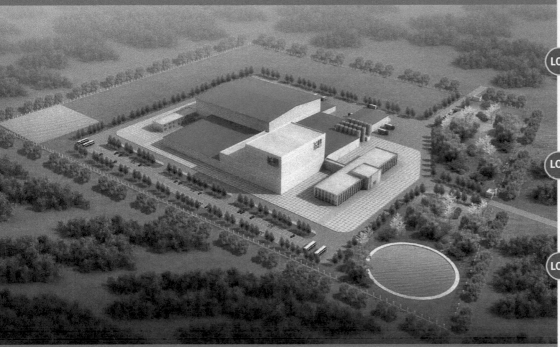

Courtesy of the City of Kingston and Feihe International

LEARNING OBJECTIVES

After completing this chapter, you should be able to:

LO1 Explain the nature and importance of location decisions, and outline the process for making such decisions.

LO2 Describe some of the major factors that affect location decisions, and discuss why a foreign company would want to locate in Canada.

LO3 Use various techniques to evaluate location alternatives.

Kingston, Ontario, has just been chosen by China's Feihe International to be the first goat milk infant formula manufacturing facility in North America. The 300,000 square foot plant is expected to open in early 2019 and will bring with it more than 200 full-time jobs to the city of over 160,000. The facility will cost an estimated $225 million and represents one of the largest foreign investments in the city. Once complete, the plant will be one of the world's most advanced infant formula production facilities utilizing a wet blending process, specifically targeting the North American and Asian markets. Proximity to a talent pool, Queen's University, Royal Military College, and St. Lawrence College was one deciding reason the Chinese firm was attracted to the city.

Location decisions represent a key part of the strategic planning process of any organization. This chapter begins with a brief overview of why businesses must make location decisions. We will then discuss the nature of these decisions, and finally explore different techniques for developing and evaluating location alternatives.

Sources: http://www.thewhig.com/2016/12/01/baby-formula-company-to-generate-hundreds-of-jobs.

LO1 Importance of Location

New companies obviously need a plant or store/office in which to make or provide their new goods or services. Existing organizations may also need to make location decisions for a variety of reasons. Companies such as banks, fast-food chains, supermarkets, and retail stores view location as part of their marketing strategy and look for locations that will help them expand their markets. Basically, the location decisions in those cases reflect the *addition* of new locations to an existing system. A similar situation occurs when an organization experiences a growth in demand for its products or services that cannot be satisfied by expansion at an existing location. The addition of a new location to complement an existing system is often a realistic alternative.

Some companies face location decisions because of depletion of their basic input. For example, fishing and logging operations are often forced to relocate due to the exhaustion of fish and forests at a given location. Mining and petroleum operations face the same sort of situation.

For other companies, a shift in market causes them to consider relocation, or the cost of doing business at a particular location reaches a point where other locations begin to look more attractive. Another reason may be centralizing dispersed locations to gain economies of scale.

There are several reasons that location decisions are an important part of production or service systems design. First, they entail a long-term commitment that makes mistakes difficult to overcome. Second, location decisions impact investment requirements, operating costs, and revenues. Third, a poor choice of location might result in a shortage of qualified labour, inadequate supplies of raw materials, or some similar condition that is detrimental to operations.

Because, by its nature, a location decision is usually based on many factors, no single location may be significantly better than the others. There may be numerous acceptable locations from which to choose, as shown by the wide variety of locations in which successful organizations can be found.

Location factors can depend on where a business is in the *supply chain*. For instance, at the retail end of a chain, site selection tends to focus more on accessibility, consumer demographics (population, age distribution, average income), traffic patterns, and local customs. Businesses at the beginning of a supply chain, if they are involved in supplying raw materials, are often located near the source of the raw materials. Businesses in the middle of a chain may locate near suppliers or near their customers, depending on a variety of circumstances. For example, businesses involved in storing and distributing goods often choose a central location to minimize distribution costs. However, web-based and phone-based businesses are much less dependent on location decisions; they can exist just about anywhere.

Location Decision Process

The way an organization approaches location decisions often depends on its size and the nature and scope of its operations. New or small organizations tend to adopt a rather informal approach to location decisions. New companies typically locate in a certain area simply because the owner lives there. Similarly, managers of small companies often want to keep operations in their backyard, so they tend to focus almost exclusively on local alternatives. Large, established companies, particularly those that already operate in more than one location, tend to take a more formal approach. Moreover, they usually consider a wider range of geographic locations. The discussion here pertains mainly to a formal approach to location decisions.

Whether a company chooses to use a location/site selection consultant or assign the project to someone in-house, the basic steps to a successful location decision will be similar:

1. Identify important search parameters and factors, such as location of markets or raw materials. The factors will differ depending on the type of facility.

2. Gather information on appropriate sites (e.g., through telephone and Internet inquiries, reading literature, etc.).

3. Eliminate some to obtain a shortlist of three or four sites.

4. Visit the shortlisted sites, meeting with local authorities and real estate agents.

5. Evaluate the alternatives and make a selection.

Typically, the process will take six months to a year. See the "Red Light Camera" OM in Action for an example of how locations for red light cameras are chosen.

 OM in Action

Red Light Camera

Within the last few years, we have seen a proliferation of red light cameras at busy intersections in many cities throughout Canada. The reason local and provincial governments have continued to support their use is because red light cameras appear to be very effective at preventing accidents. For instance, a recent study of the benefits of red light cameras in British Columbia has revealed a 14 percent reduction in collisions resulting in injuries. Considering the resounding success of red light cameras in reducing the frequency and severity of accidents, it was decided that their use should be further expanded. The following are some of the factors that were considered to be critical for deciding on the locations of new red light cameras.

©mathieukor/iStock.com

- *Potential for improvement.* This is the difference between the total number of observed collisions and what is considered to be the normal frequency of collisions at any particular intersection. Clearly, the higher the number of recorded collisions at any intersection, the more dangerous it is, and the larger the potential for improvement.

- *Severity of collisions.* The overall goal of any red light camera program is to mitigate the severity of life-threatening collisions. Consequently, it is important to identify intersections with the most severe collisions. To help identify the most dangerous intersections, a collision severity index was created by simply weighing collision frequency with collision severity. In British Columbia, the collision weights are 100 for collisions with a fatality, 10 for an injury, and 1 for property damage.

- *High proportion of collision types.* Evidence shows that red light cameras are best for reducing 90 degree, "T-bone" type collisions; side-impact collisions; and head-on collisions. Intersections with a high proportion of these collision types are given more weight.

- *Low proportion of rear-end collisions.* The literature suggests that red light cameras can actually increase the likelihood of rear-end type collisions. Consequently, those intersections with a low proportion of such collision types are recommended as good candidate locations.

Source: Paul de Leur and Mark Milner, "Site Selection Process and Methodology for Deployment of Intersection Safety Cameras in British Columbia, Canada," *Transportation Research Record: Journal of the Transportation Research Board,* March 2012, Vol. 2265, pp. 129–136.

Factors That Affect Location Decisions

Many factors influence location decisions. However, often one or a few factors are so important that they dominate the decision. For example, in manufacturing, the potentially dominating factors may include availability of abundant energy and proximity to raw materials (e.g., aluminum production needs large amounts of electricity). Cost of transportation to market can be a major factor (e.g., most soft drinks are produced in local bottling plants). In service organizations, possible dominating factors are market related. For example, car rental agencies locate in airports and downtown areas where their customers are.

This section contains a description of regional/country factors, community and site factors, and advantages of Canadian locations for foreign companies.

Regional/Country Factors

The primary regional factors involve raw materials, markets, and labour considerations. Positive country factors such as natural resources, cheap labour costs, and new markets make foreign locations an attractive possibility, but the potential negatives must also be considered.

Location of Raw Materials. Companies locate near or at the source of their raw materials for three primary reasons: necessity, perishability, and transportation costs. Mining operations, farming, forestry, and fishing fall under *necessity*. Obviously, such operations must locate close to the raw materials. Companies involved in canning or freezing of fresh fruit and vegetables, processing of dairy and meat products, and so on must consider *perishability* when considering location. *Transportation costs* are important in industries where processing eliminates much of the bulk connected with a raw material, making it much less expensive to transport after processing. Examples include potash, lumber, and pulp and paper production. Being close to raw materials is the reason many forest-products companies such as Catalyst Paper and Canfor have plants in British Columbia. Many petrochemical plants are located in Alberta, many farms are located in the prairies, and many fish-processing plants are located in the Atlantic provinces. Transportation costs are often the reason that companies locate near their major customers. Moreover, regional warehouses are used by supermarkets and other retail operations to supply multiple outlets, so often the choice of new locations and additional warehouses reflects the locations of existing warehouses or retail outlets.

Service   **Location of Markets.** Retailers and service providers are usually found near the centre of the markets they serve. Examples include fast-food restaurants, gas stations, and supermarkets. Quite often their products and those of their competitors are so similar that they rely on convenience to attract customers. Hence, these businesses seek locations with high population densities or traffic. This is also true for banks, drugstores, and convenience stores. Other factors include distribution costs or the perishability of a finished product.

Competitive pressure on retail operations can be extremely high. In some cases, the market served by a particular location may be too small to justify two competitors (e.g., one burger franchise per block), so the search for potential locations tends to concentrate on locations without competitors. The opposite also might be true; it could be desirable to locate near competitors. Large department stores often locate near each other, and small stores like to locate in shopping centres that have large department stores as anchors. The large stores attract large numbers of shoppers who become potential customers in the smaller stores or in the other large stores.

Some companies must locate close to their markets because of the perishability of their products. Examples include bakeries, flower shops, and fresh seafood stores. For other types of companies, distribution (transportation) costs are the main factor in closeness to market (for example, sand and gravel retailers and bottling plants). Another example is regional warehouses used by supermarkets and other retail operations to supply multiple outlets. Still other companies require close customer contact, so they too tend to locate within the area they expect to serve. Typical examples are custom tailor shops, home remodellers, home repair services, rug cleaners, lawn and garden services, and component suppliers to just-in-time manufacturers.

Location of many government services should be near the centre of the markets they are designed to serve. Police and emergency health care locations are frequently selected on the basis of client needs. For instance, police patrols often concentrate on high-crime areas, and emergency health care facilities are usually found in central locations to provide ready access from all directions.

Another trend is just-in-time manufacturing techniques (see Chapter 15), which encourage suppliers to locate near their customers to reduce supplier lead times. For this reason, some Canadian firms are reconsidering decisions to locate offshore. Moreover, in light manufacturing (e.g., electronics), low-cost labour is becoming less important than nearness to markets; users of electronics components want suppliers that are close to their manufacturing facilities. One offshoot of this is the possibility that the future will see a trend toward smaller factories located close to markets. In some industries, a small, automated **microfactory** with a narrow product focus will be located near major markets to reduce response time.

microfactory Small factory with a narrow product focus, located near major markets.

It is likely that advances in information technology will enhance the ability of manufacturing firms to gather, track, and distribute information that links purchasing, marketing, and distribution with design, engineering, and manufacturing. This will reduce the need for these functions to be

A worker inspects cans of Coca-Cola on the production line overseas. Coke is mainly made up of water, so it should be manufactured in or close to its markets. Globally, Coca-Cola has more than 900 bottling and manufacturing facilities (http://www.coca-colacompany.com/stories/offices-bottling-plants).

© Richard J. Greenman/Alamy

located close together, thereby permitting a strategy of locating production facilities near major markets.

Labour Factors. Primary labour considerations are availability of workers, the wage rates and labour productivity, attitudes toward work, and whether unions are a potential problem. Large plants usually locate in or near population centres. Some companies target regions with high unemployment in order to draw from the large pool of unemployed workers.

Labour costs are very important for labour-intensive companies and they can differ significantly across regions. Labour rates are related to the cost of living, which also varies across regions. Internationally, Canadian average hourly compensation is close to that in the United States, lower than in many European countries, but higher than in Mexico and Asian countries.[1]

Skills of potential employees may be a factor, although some companies prefer to train new employees rather than rely solely on previous experience. Increasing specialization in many industries makes this possibility even more likely than in the past. Although most companies concentrate on the supply of blue-collar workers, some companies are more interested in scientific and technical people as potential employees, and they look for areas with high concentrations of those types of workers.

Worker attitudes toward turnover, absenteeism, and similar factors may differ among potential locations—workers in large urban centres may exhibit different attitudes than workers in small towns or rural areas. Furthermore, worker attitudes in different parts of the country or in different countries may be markedly different.

Other Factors. Electric power sometimes plays a role in location decisions. For instance, many aluminum smelting plants are located in Quebec because they use a large amount of electricity, which is inexpensive in Quebec. The same is true for British Columbia.

Also, both business and personal taxes in some provinces can reduce or enhance a province's attractiveness to companies seeking new locations. Check out this weblink for tax refunds and

---

[1] See https://en.wikipedia.org/wiki/List_of_countries_by_average_wage

credits for Canada, http://canadabusiness.ca/grants-and-financing/government-grants-and-financing/tax-refunds-and-credits/. Many provinces have used lower taxes to attract companies. Federal and provincial governments give tax incentives to encourage more research and development, manufacturing, and investment. For examples, see the "Some Examples of Subsidies" OM in Action.

 OM in Action

Some Examples of Subsidies

A recent example of governmental subsidies includes $200 million from Ontario and the Canadian federal government to support Ford's Canadian operations in 2017. The money will be invested at a Ford engine plant in Windsor, Ontario, to help keep the facility "innovative and cutting edge," and is expected to create more than 300 new jobs for the province. Subsidies have now become a fact of life in the auto industry, with southern U.S. states being a prime example of securing funding by this means.

Justin Trudeau's government recently announced that it will provide $372.5 million in loans to Bombardier without interest over four years to support CSeries projects. The government hopes that the loan will help to create well paying jobs.

By permission of Bombardier Aerospace

Sources: http://www.bnn.ca/trudeau-government-ontario-to-invest-200m-into-ford-s-canadian-operations-1.710200; https://www.thestar.com/business/2017/02/07/bombardier-announcement-expected-in-montreal.html.

Land and building costs are also usually significant and can differ across regions. The presence of unions usually results in higher wages and less flexible work rules. Therefore, many companies prefer to locate in regions where unions are not strong.

 Foreign Locations. Some Canadian companies are attracted to foreign locations to exploit their natural resources. Others view foreign locations as a means of expanding their markets. Many developing countries offer an abundant supply of cheap labour. For example, many North American companies have plants in China.

A company contemplating a foreign location must carefully weigh the potential benefits against the potential problems. It is harder to manage a foreign location. Another factor is the stability of a country's government and its attitude toward foreign companies. Some of the problems of a foreign location can be caused by language and cultural differences. One factor that has negatively impacted the bottom line of some Canadian companies operating plants in foreign countries is the level of corruption (i.e., abuse of entrusted power for private gain). Transparency International, a nonprofit international organization based in Germany, annually publishes a Corruption Perception Index for over 170 countries.[2] Canada is one of the least corrupt countries. See the "Starbucks Location Selection" OM in Action for an example of a foreign location decision.

Community/Site-Related Considerations

Usually workers live close to their place of work. Blue-collar workers tend not to relocate to find a job. Therefore, companies ensure that there are sufficient numbers of potential applicants living near a site. If there are other large employers in the vicinity, then the pool of available workers will be smaller. Large employers usually locate in or around a big city for this reason. Companies employing office workers, engineers, lab researchers, and specialized trades need the services of a college,

---

[2] https://www.transparency.org/news/feature/corruption_perceptions_index_2016

university, or technical institution in the community. White-collar employees may relocate, but they usually require a higher quality of life.

From a company standpoint, a number of factors determine the desirability of a community as a place for its workers and managers to live. They include facilities for education, shopping, recreation, transportation, entertainment, and medical services.

Many communities actively try to attract new businesses because they are viewed as potential sources of future tax revenues and new job opportunities. Communities offer tax abatements, low-cost loans, and grants for worker training. However, communities do not, as a rule, want companies that will create pollution problems or otherwise lessen the quality of life in the community. Examples of this include community resistance to airport expansion, changes in zoning, construction of nuclear facilities, "factory farms," and highway construction.

For heavy industries, it is important to be close to a railway line, just at the edge of a city or town, usually on a green-field site (i.e., on a vacant out-of-town lot). Light industries usually need to be close to highways. Offices may want to be close to airports. Call and data centres need to be close to major telephone and data transmission lines.

The primary considerations related to sites are land and access. Usually a company first estimates the size of land and building required. In many cases, both vacant buildings and undeveloped sites are considered. Other site-related factors include room for future expansion, utility and sewer capacities, and sufficient parking space for employees and customers. In addition, for many companies, access roads for trucks or rail spurs are important.

Industrial parks may be worthy alternatives for companies involved in light manufacturing or assembly, warehouse operations, and customer-service facilities. Typically, the land is already developed—power, water, and sewer hookups have been attended to, and zoning restrictions do not require special attention.

Service and Retail Locations. Services and retailers are typically governed by somewhat different considerations than manufacturers in making location decisions. For one thing, proximity to raw materials is not a factor. Customer access is sometimes a prime consideration, as it is with banks and supermarkets, but not a consideration in others, such as call centres, catalogue sales, and online services. Manufacturers tend to be cost focused, and concerned with labour, energy, and material costs and availability, as well as distribution costs. Services and retailers tend to be profit or revenue focused, concerned with demographics such as age, income, and education; population/drawing area; competition; traffic volume/patterns; and customer access/parking.

Retail and service organizations typically place traffic volume and convenience high on the list of important factors. Generally, retail businesses prefer locations that are near other retailers (although not necessarily competitors) because of the higher traffic volumes and convenience to customers. Thus, restaurants and specialty stores often locate in and around malls, benefiting from the high traffic.

Medical services are often located near hospitals for patients' convenience. Doctors' offices may be located near hospitals, or grouped in other, centralized areas with other doctors' offices.

Good transportation and/or parking facilities can be vital to retail establishments. Downtown areas have a competitive disadvantage in attracting shoppers compared to malls because malls offer ample free parking and proximity to residential areas.

Competitors' locations can be important. In some cases, services and retailers will want to locate near competitors to benefit from the concentration of potential customers. Mall stores and auto dealers are good examples. When businesses locate near similar businesses, it is referred to as **clustering**. In other cases, it is important *not* to be near a competitor (e.g., another franchise operation of the same fast-food chain).

> **clustering** Similar types of businesses locate near each other.

Among the questions that should be considered to make a location decision for a multi-facility service or retail company are the following:

1. How can sales, market share, and profit be optimized for the entire set of locations? Solutions might include some combination of upgrading facilities, expanding some sites, adding new outlets, and closing or changing the locations of some outlets.

2. What are the potential sales to be realized from each potential solution?

3. Where should outlets be located to maximize market share, sales, and profits without negatively impacting other outlets? This can be a key cause of friction between the operator of a franchise store and the franchising company.

4. What probable effects would there be on market share, sales, and profits if a competitor located nearby?

For an example of retail location, see the "Liquor Store Location" OM in Action.

⚙️ OM in Action

Liquor Store Location

In a study of survival of Alberta liquor stores since privatization in 1993, it was discovered that location, among other factors such as population of trade area and age of the store, is an important determinant of a liquor store's survival. Those liquor stores located near a grocery store had an almost 100 percent chance of survival. The next best location was in shopping centres. Locating in a downtown area or near pubs did not help with survival.

Source: A. Eckert and D. S. West, "Firm Survival and Chain Growth in a Privatized Retail Liquor Store Industry," *Review of Industrial Organization*, February 2008, 32(1), pp. 1–18.

Why Should Foreign Companies Locate in Canada?

Foreign companies locate plants in Canada to shorten delivery time and reduce delivery costs to markets in Canada and the United States, as well as to exploit Canadian natural resources and use Canadian skilled labour. Notable Canadian natural resources are energy (oil, gas, electricity), forestry (lumber, newsprint, pulp), and minerals (nickel, copper, zinc, aluminum, gold, diamond, potash, uranium).

Canadian workers are educated, basic health care is free, and the country is politically stable with little corruption. Canada is generally safe and secure, energy costs are low, and governments provide R&D tax incentives. Canada has good phone and Internet infrastructure. According to a recent study

Apple establishes its stores in key locations with above-average household income and plenty of retail traffic. This store is located in Toronto.

Dubes Sonego Junior/Dreamstime.com

by KPMG,[3] Canada is one of the cheapest of nine major industrialized countries in which to operate a plant. According to country competitiveness rankings (based on a survey of executives' opinions in each country) by World Economic Forum (a nonprofit organization), Canada ranks 14th in the world.[4]

Many companies, mainly from the United States, have set up plants in Canada over the last century, thus helping to industrialize Canada. One industry greatly benefiting Canada is the auto industry. The Big Three U.S. automakers, Toyota, and Honda have several assembly and component plants in Canada, mainly in Southern Ontario. See the "Canadian Competitiveness" OM in Action for reasons why Canada is an ideal location.

 OM in Action

Canadian Competitiveness

KPMG has recently released a study on the relative cost of doing business and other competitiveness factors in 14 developed and developing countries across the Americas, Europe, and Asia. The key cost factors being considered include labour, facility, utilities, transportation, and taxes. Numerous noncost factors that influence global competitiveness such as labour availability and skills, infrastructure, regulatory environment, and cost of living have also been considered. The final analysis shows that

Canada is one of the most competitive locations in which to conduct business in the world and is more competitive than the United States in many major industries. Specifically, Canada has a cost advantage of 10.7 percent in the field of research and development, an 8.3 percent cost advantage in services, and a 3.5 percent cost advantage in manufacturing as compared to the United States.

Source: http://www.competitivealternatives.com/reports/2012_compalt_report_vol1_en.pdf, KPMG, Competitive Alternatives KPMG's Guide to International Business Location Costs, 2012.

Every province has something to offer. For example, Quebec has been promoting the development of its high-tech industries (which include ecommerce, multimedia, and biotech firms) for decades. It gives a 40 percent income tax credit for employee salaries of high-tech firms, and also a 40 percent tax credit on specialized machinery. This entices innovative companies to locate in Quebec and to take more risk in developing high-tech products. See the "First Commercial Rocket Launch Site" OM in Action for why Nova Scotia is an excellent location for rocket launches.

---

[3] http://www.competitivealternatives.com/highlights/international.aspx.
[4] www3.weforum.org/docs/GCR2013-14/GCR_Rankings_2013-14.pdf.

OM in Action

First Commercial Rocket Launch Site

The eastern coast of Nova Scotia is set to host the first commercial spaceport in Canada. Maritime Launch Service Limited plans to begin construction of a rocket launch pad facility near the town of Canso, Nova Scotia, as early as 2018. The $226 million facility would include a launch pad, processing building, and remote control centre. The entire facility is scheduled for completion in 2020 and will begin to deliver commercial satellites to low Earth orbit shortly thereafter using Ukrainian-built Cyclone rockets.

The site was selected from among 14 competing locations across North America. It was chosen primarily for its ideal flight trajectory and low population density. Rockets will be launched directly toward the Atlantic Ocean and will pose minimal risk to local communities. The proposed site is located on Crown property so approval from governmental officials must be secured before plans are finalized. Thus far, the local community

Courtesy of Maritime Launch Services

and provincial government have both expressed interest in the project. Once complete, the facility will provide high-paying jobs for scientists and engineers and will also draw tourists to the province.

Source: https://www.thestar.com/news/canada/2017/03/14/small-nova-scotia-community-picked-as-launch-site-for-rockets.html.

LO3 Evaluating Location Alternatives

A number of techniques are helpful in evaluating location alternatives. They include locational break-even analysis, transportation method, factor rating, the centre of gravity method to determine trade areas, and location analysis software.

Locational Break-Even Analysis

> **locational break-even analysis** Identifies the least (fixed and variable) cost location choice based on quantity to be produced.

Locational break-even analysis identifies the least (fixed and variable) cost location choice based on quantity to be produced. The analysis can be done numerically or graphically. The graphical approach will be demonstrated here because it enhances understanding of the concept and indicates the ranges over which one of the alternatives is superior to the others.

The procedure for locational break-even analysis involves these steps:

1. Determine the fixed and variable costs associated with each location alternative.
2. Plot the total-cost lines for all location alternatives on the same graph.
3. Determine which location will have the lowest total cost for the expected level of output.

This method assumes that fixed and variable costs are constant for the range of probable output, and only one product is involved.

The total cost for each location is represented mathematically as:

$$\text{Total cost} = FC + v \times Q \qquad (8\text{-}1)$$

where

FC = Fixed cost
v = Variable cost per unit
Q = Quantity of output

Fixed and variable costs for four potential plant locations are shown below:

Location	Fixed Cost per Year	Variable Cost per Unit
A	$250,000	$11
B	100,000	30
C	150,000	20
D	200,000	35

a. Plot the total-cost lines for these locations on a single graph.

b. Identify the range of output for which each alternative is superior (i.e., has the lowest total cost).

c. If the expected output at the selected location is 8,000 units per year, which location would provide the lowest total cost?

SOLUTION

a. To plot the total-cost lines, select an output that is approximately equal to the expected output level (e.g., 10,000 units per year). Calculate the total cost for each location at that level:

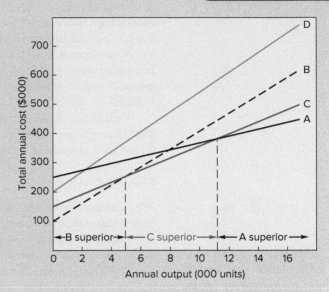

	Fixed Cost	+	Variable Cost	=	Total Cost
A . . .	$250,000	+	$11(10,000)	=	$360,000
B . . .	100,000	+	30(10,000)	=	400,000
C . . .	150,000	+	20(10,000)	=	350,000
D . . .	200,000	+	35(10,000)	=	550,000

Plot each location's fixed cost (at Output $= 0$) as a point and the total cost at 10,000 units as another point; and connect the two points with a straight line. (See the graph.)

b. The *approximate* ranges for which the various alternatives will yield the lowest total cost are shown on the graph. Note that location D is never superior. The *exact* ranges can be determined by finding the output level at which lines B and C and lines C and A cross. To do this, set their total cost equations equal and solve for Q, the break-even output level. Thus, for B and C:

$$\text{(B)} \qquad\qquad \text{(C)}$$
$$\$100,000 + \$30Q = \$150,000 + \$20Q$$

Solving, you find $Q = 5,000$ units per year.

For C and A:

$$\text{(C)} \qquad\qquad\qquad \text{(A)}$$
$$\$100,000 + \$20Q = \$250,000 + \$11Q$$

$$\text{Solving, } Q \qquad = 11,111 \text{ units per year.}$$

c. From the graph you can see that for 8,000 units per year, location C provides the lowest total cost.

Similar analysis can be performed using profit instead of total cost. Note that if the selling price and demand is the same across the sites, then the answer will be the same as when using total cost.

For a profit analysis, calculate the total profit for each location:

$$\text{Total profit} = Q(R - v) - FC \tag{8-2}$$

where

$R =$ Revenue per unit

Solved Problem 2 at the end of the chapter illustrates profit analysis.

Where the expected level of output is close to the middle of the range over which one alternative is superior, the choice is readily apparent. If the expected level of output is very close to the edge of a range, it means that the two alternatives will yield comparable annual costs, so management would be indifferent in choosing between the two *in terms of total cost*. However, it is important to recognize that, in most situations, other factors besides production cost must also be considered (such as transportation cost and availability of labour).

Transportation Method

Transportation costs sometimes play an important role in location decisions. These stem from the movement of raw materials and finished goods. When there is only one facility, the company can include the transportation cost in the locational break-even analysis by incorporating the transportation cost per unit into the variable cost per unit.

When there is more than one facility, the company should use the *transportation method* of linear programming. This is a special-purpose algorithm used to determine the shipments in order to minimize total transportation cost subject to meeting the demands and not exceeding the capacities of facilities.

Various models can be run, each adding one of the potential sites to the set of existing facilities. The site resulting in minimum total transportation cost will be chosen. See the chapter supplement for further description of the transportation model.

Factor Rating

A typical location decision involves both qualitative and quantitative factors, which tend to vary from situation to situation depending on the needs of each organization.

Factor rating involves scoring the factors (both quantitative and qualitative) and determining the weighted score for each location, and choosing the location with the highest weighted score.

The following procedure is used in factor rating:

factor rating Involves scoring the factors (both quantitative and qualitative) and determining the weighted score for each location, and choosing the location with the highest weighted score.

1. Determine which factors are relevant (e.g., location of market, labour supply, parking facilities, revenue potential).

2. Assign a weight to each factor that indicates its relative importance compared with all other factors. Typically, weights sum to 1.00.

3. Decide on a common scale for all factor scores (e.g., 0 to 100).

4. Score all factors for each location.

5. Multiply the factor weight by the score for each factor, and sum the results for each location.

6. Choose the location that has the highest composite score.

This procedure is illustrated by the next example.

EXAMPLE 8-2 ▶

A photo processing company intends to open a new branch store. The following table contains information on two potential locations. Which is the better alternative?

SOLUTION

Factor	Weight	Scores (Out of 100) Alt. 1	Alt. 2	Weighted Scores Alternative 1	Alternative 2
Proximity to existing store	0.10	100	60	0.10(100) = 10.0	0.10(60) = 6.0
Traffic volume	0.05	80	80	0.05(80) = 4.0	0.05(80) = 4.0
Rental costs	0.40	70	90	0.40(70) = 28.0	0.40(90) = 36.0
Size	0.10	86	92	0.10(86) = 8.6	0.10(92) = 9.2
Layout	0.20	40	70	0.20(40) = 8.0	0.20(70) = 14.0
Operating costs	0.15	80	90	0.15(80) = 12.0	0.15(90) = 13.5
	1.00			70.6	82.7

Alternative 2 is better because it has the higher composite score.

In some cases, managers may prefer to establish minimum *thresholds* for composite scores. If an alternative fails to meet that minimum, they can reject it without further consideration. If none of the alternatives meets the minimum, this means that additional alternatives must be identified.

Centre of Gravity Method

The **centre of gravity method** determines the location of a distribution centre/warehouse that will minimize total distribution cost. It treats distribution cost as a linear function of the distance and the quantity shipped.

The method uses a map that shows the locations of destinations (demand points). The map must be accurate and drawn to scale. A coordinate system is overlaid on the map to determine relative locations. The location of the (0, 0) point of the coordinate system, and its scale, are unimportant. Once the coordinate system is in place, you can determine the coordinates of each destination. (See Figures 8-1a and b.)

> **centre of gravity method** Method for locating a distribution centre/warehouse that minimizes total distribution cost.

a. Map showing destinations

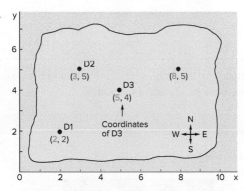

b. Add a coordinate system

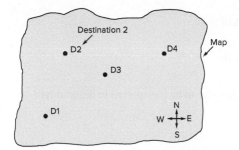

c. Centre of gravity

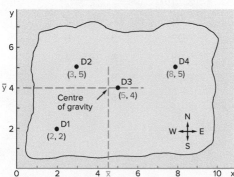

◀ **FIGURE 8-1**

Centre of gravity method.

If distance is rectilinear (i.e., travel is east–west and north–south only), then we can decompose the problem into *x* axis and *y* axis problems and solve them independently. We assume that distance is rectilinear.

If the quantities to be transported to every destination are *equal,* you can obtain the coordinates of the centre of gravity (i.e., the location of the distribution centre/warehouse) by finding the average of the *x* coordinates and the average of the *y* coordinates (see Figure 8-1c).

These averages can be easily determined using the following formulas:

$$\bar{x} = \frac{\sum x_i}{n}$$

$$\bar{y} = \frac{\sum y_i}{n}$$

(8-3)

where

x_i = *x* coordinate of destination *i*

y_i = *y* coordinate of destination *i*

n = Number of destinations

When the number of units to be transported is not the same for all destinations, which is usually the case, a *weighted average* must be used to determine the centre of gravity, with the weights being the *quantities* to be transported.

The appropriate formulas in this case are:

$$\bar{x} = \frac{\sum x_i Q_i}{\sum Q_i}$$

$$\bar{y} = \frac{\sum y_i Q_i}{\sum Q_i}$$

(8-4)

where

Q_i = Quantity to be transported to destination *i*

EXAMPLE 8-3 ▶

Determine the coordinates of the centre of gravity for the problem that is depicted in Figure 8-1a. Assume that the shipments from the centre of gravity to each of the four destinations will be equal quantities.

SOLUTION

The coordinates of the destinations can be obtained from Figure 8-1b:

Destination	x	y
D1	2	2
D2	3	5
D3	5	4
D4	8	5
	18	16

$$\bar{x} = \frac{\sum x_i}{n} = \frac{18}{4} \qquad \bar{y} = \frac{\sum y_i}{n} = \frac{16}{4}$$
$$= 4.5 \qquad\qquad\quad = 4$$

Hence, the centre of gravity is at (4.5, 4), which places it just west of destination D3 (see Figure 8-1c).

Suppose that the shipments for the problem depicted in Figure 8-1a are not all equal, but instead are the following:

Destination	x, y	Weekly Quantity
D1	2, 2	800
D2	3, 5	900
D3	5, 4	200
D4	8, 5	100
		2,000

Determine the centre of gravity in this case.

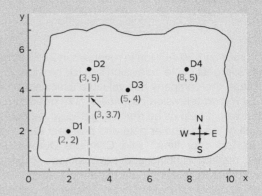

SOLUTION

Because the quantities to be shipped differ among destinations, you must use the weighted average formulas.

$$x = \frac{\sum x_i Q_i}{\sum Q_i} = \frac{2(800)+3(900)+5(200)+8(100)}{2,000}$$

$$= \frac{6,100}{2,000} = 3.05[\text{round to } 3]$$

$$y = \frac{\sum y_i Q_i}{\sum Q_i} = \frac{2(800)+5(900)+4(200)+5(100)}{2,000}$$

$$= \frac{7,400}{2,000} = 3.7$$

Hence, the coordinates of the centre of gravity are approximately (3, 3.7). This would place it south of destination D2.

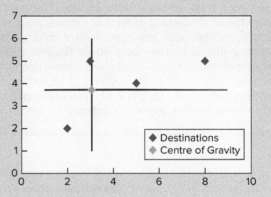

Location Analysis Software

Two types of software are used in location analysis: geographic information system and modelling/optimization. A **geographic information system (GIS)** is a computer-based tool for collecting, storing, retrieving, and displaying location-dependent demographic data on maps. A GIS relies on an integrated system of computer hardware, software, data, and trained personnel to make available a wide range of geographically referenced information. The data might involve age, incomes, type of employment, type of housing, or other similar data deemed useful for the decision at hand. The intuitive graphical maps facilitate communication of facts and hence decision making. Companies providing GIS software and services are MapInfo (now part of Pitney Bowes) and ESRI. For some applications involving MapInfo and ESRI software, see the "GIS Case Studies" OM in Action. Internet mapping programs used to obtain travel directions are an example of a GIS.

geographic information system (GIS) A computer-based tool for collecting, storing, retrieving, and displaying location-dependent demographic data on maps.

OM in Action

GIS Case Studies

Rogers

With more than $20.4 billion in revenues in 2015, Rogers is Canada's largest cable television service provider. Due to its success, the company has valuable user data on more than 2.3 million television customers. "We needed a solution that would help us be really targeted so we could leverage all of the customer data and prospect data we had accumulated over time," said Charlotte Durand, senior director, market planning and development. Rogers and Pitney Bowes Business Insight used the MapInfo Envinsa platform to develop MapMart, an interactive mapping application with a user-friendly web interface. The application is capable of processing millions of records from multiple sources and provides managers with a cohesive spatial database that is rich in detail about Rogers' customers throughout the country. Employees have recently used MapMart to monitor the effectiveness of promotional campaigns in real time. If a certain area has a low response rate, adjustments can be made accordingly to further entice customers. The ability to visualize markets and customer information on maps in real time helps managers to make decisions both better and faster.

Source: http://www.pbinsight.co.in/files/resource-library/resource-files/Rogers.pdf.

Levi Strauss

In the mid-2000s, Levi Strauss decided to maximize its distribution by also selling its jeans in specialty stores such as workwear and western apparel outfitters. In order not to impact the sales of its existing retailers, Levi Strauss purchased BusinessMAP and Business Analyst Online services from ESRI. For each existing retailer, the software determines a one-, three-, and five-mile ring (or square if driving distance is used) around the retailer (similar to Voronoi polygons). Any new potential retailer is also geocoded, and if it is too close to an existing retailer, it will not be approved.

Source: http://www.esri.com/library/casestudies/levistrauss.pdf.

Many countries have an abundance of GIS data that can be accessed. For location analysis, a GIS makes it relatively easy to obtain detailed information on factors such as population density, age, incomes, ethnicity, traffic patterns, competitor locations, educational institutions, shopping centres, crime statistics, transportation resources, utilities, recreational facilities, maps and images, and a wealth of other information associated with a given location. Local governments use a GIS to organize, analyze, plan, and communicate information about community resources. And job seekers can use GISs for their searches.

Here are some of the ways businesses use GISs:

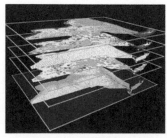

A geographic information system (GIS) is a tool that can be used for location planning. This graphic combines information from different databases to answer demographic questions about a region. This information also can be broken down into smaller units.

Visualization: Chris Pelkie, Cornell Theory Center, for New York State GAP

- Logistics companies use GIS data to plan fleet activities such as routes and schedules based on the locations of their customers.
- Publishers of magazines and newspapers use GISs to analyze circulation and attract advertisers.
- Real estate companies rely heavily on GISs to make maps available online to prospective home and business buyers.
- Banks use GISs to help decide where to locate bank branches and to understand the composition and needs of different market segments.
- Insurance companies use GISs to determine premiums based on population distribution, crime figures, and likelihood of natural disasters such as flooding in various locations, and to manage risk.
- Retailers are able to link information about sales, customers, and demographics to geographic locations in planning locations. They also use GISs to develop marketing strategies and for customer mapping, site selection, sales projections, promotions, and other store portfolio management applications.
- Utility companies use GISs to balance supply and demand, and to identify problem areas.
- Emergency services use GISs to allocate resources to locations to provide adequate coverage where they are needed.

Modelling/optimization software packages are also available for location analysis. Many packages employ linear programming or a variation called mixed integer programming algorithms. In addition, some software packages use heuristic approaches to obtain reasonable solutions to location problems. A modelling/optimization location software is LogicNet (http://www.llamasoft.com/).

Summary

- Location decisions confront both new and existing organizations.
- Growth, market shifts, depletion of raw materials, and the introduction of new products are among the reasons organizations are concerned with location decisions.
- The importance of location decisions is underscored by the long-term commitment necessary and by their impact on costs.
- A common approach to location analysis is to first identify a country or region that seems to satisfy overall needs and then identify a number of community/site alternatives for more in-depth analysis.
- The major influences on location decisions are location of raw materials, labour supply,

market considerations, tax credit, and community factors.
- Most retailers decide on a site far from their other stores and the competitors' stores, taking potential sales into account.
- Foreign locations may be attractive in terms of labour cost, abundance of raw material, or potential markets for a company's products.
- Canada is one of the best locations for foreign investment, because it is close to the U.S. market, and has an educated labour force, plenty of land, and abundant natural resources.
- A variety of methods are used to evaluate location alternatives. Those described in the chapter include locational break-even analysis, factor rating, and the centre of gravity method.

Key Terms

centre of gravity method
clustering

factor rating
geographic information system (GIS)

locational break-even analysis
microfactory

Solved Problems

Problem 1

Locational break-even cost-vs.-cost analysis. A manufacturer that sells its products in Saskatchewan is looking for a production location there. There are three potential locations: Saskatoon, Regina, and Yorkton. Saskatoon would involve a fixed cost of $4,000 per month and a variable cost of $4 per unit; Regina would involve a fixed cost of $3,500 per month and a variable cost of $5 per unit; and Yorkton would involve a fixed cost of $5,000 per month and a variable cost of $6 per unit. Use of the Saskatoon location would decrease the manufacturer's distribution costs by $19,000 per month, Regina by $22,000 per month, and Yorkton by $18,000 per month. Which location would result in the lowest total cost to distribute 800 units per month in Saskatchewan?

Solution

Given: Quantity = 800 units per month

	FC per Month	Variable Cost per Unit, *v*	Decrease in Distribution Cost per Month
Saskatoon	$4,000	$4	$19,000
Regina	3,500	5	22,000
Yorkton	5,000	6	18,000

Monthly total cost = *FC* + *VC* − Decrease in distribution cost

$$Saskatoon: \quad \$4,000 \ + \ \$4 \text{ per unit} \ \times \ 800 \text{ units} \ - \ \$19,000 \ = \ -\$11,800$$
$$Regina: \quad 3,500 \ + \ 5 \text{ per unit} \ \times \ 800 \text{ units} \ - \ 22,000 \ = \ -14,500$$
$$Yorkton: \quad 5,000 \ + \ 6 \text{ per unit} \ \times \ 800 \text{ units} \ - \ 18,000 \ = \ -8,200$$

Hence, Regina would have the lowest total cost.

Problem 2

Locational break-even profit-vs.-profit analysis. A manufacturer is about to lose its lease, so it must move to another location. Two locations are currently under consideration. Fixed costs would be $8,000 per month at location A and $9,400 per month at location B. Variable costs are expected to be $5 per unit at location A and $4 per unit at location B. Monthly demand has been steady at 8,800 units for the last several years and is not expected to deviate from that amount in the foreseeable future. The product sells for $6 per unit. Determine which location would yield higher profit under these conditions.

Solution

Profit $= Q(R - v) - FC$

Location	Q	R	v	Q(R—v)	FC	Monthly Profit
A.....	8,800	$6	$5	$8,800	$8,000	$ 800
B.....	8,800	$6	$4	$17,600	$9,400	$8,200

Hence, location B is expected to yield higher monthly profit.

Problem 3

Factor rating. Determine which location, A or B, has a higher composite score given the following information:

Factor	Weight	Score A	B
Cheap labour cost	0.50	20	40
Low material cost	0.30	10	30
Reasonable transportation cost	0.20	50	10
	1.00		

Solution

Multiplying the weights with the location scores and adding, we can see that location B has higher composite score:

Factor	Weight	Score A	B	Weighted Scores A	B
Cheap labour cost	0.50	20	40	0.50(20) = 10	0.50(40) = 20
Low material cost	0.30	10	30	0.30(10) = 3	0.30(30) = 9
Reasonable transportation cost	0.20	50	10	0.20(50) = 10	0.20(10) = 2
	1.00			23	31

Problem 4

Centre of gravity. Determine the centre of gravity location for these destinations:

Destination	(x, y) Coordinate	Weekly Quantity
D1	3,5	20
D2	6,8	10
D3	2,7	15
D4	4,5	15
		60

Solution

Because the weekly quantities are not all equal, we must use the formulas in Formula 8-4.

$$\bar{x} = \frac{\sum xQ}{\sum Q} = \frac{3(20)+6(10)+2(15)+4(15)}{60} = \frac{210}{60} = 3.5$$

$$\bar{y} = \frac{\sum yQ}{\sum Q} = \frac{5(20)+8(10)+7(15)+5(15)}{60} = \frac{360}{60} = 6.0$$

Hence, the centre of gravity has the coordinates $x = 3.5$ and $y = 6.0$.

Discussion and Review Questions

LO1 **1.** In what ways can the location decision have an impact on the production system?

LO1 **2.** Respond to this statement: "The importance of the location decision is often vastly overrated; the fact that virtually every type of business is located in every region of the country means that there should be no problem in finding a suitable location."

LO1 **3.** Outline the general approach for developing location alternatives.

LO2 **4.** What regional/country factors influence location decisions?

LO2 **5.** What community/site-related factors influence location decisions?

LO2 **6.** How are manufacturing and service location decisions similar? Different?

LO2 **7.** What are the potential benefits of locating in foreign countries? Potential drawbacks?

LO3 **8.** What is the factor rating method, and how does it work?

LO3 **9.** What are the basic assumptions in locational break-even analysis?

LO3 **10.** What is the centre-of-gravity method, and when should it be used?

LO3 **11.** The problem of finding a hub for an airline or for a package delivery service such as FedEx (for which Memphis is the hub) can be modelled and solved by the centre-of-gravity method. Explain how.

LO2 **12.** Crude oil in Canada that was first explored near Sarnia, Ontario, is long gone by now. Still, Sarnia is known as the Chemical Capital of Canada, having 16 chemical and three major oil refineries. Explain what advantage Sarnia has relative to locations in Alberta that are closer to oil and petrochemical feedstock production.

LO2 **13.** Discuss recent trends in location and possible future strategies.

LO2 **14.** Determine the main factors that might be used for locating each of the following facilities:
  a. hospital.
  b. chemical factory.
  c. fire station.
  d. high-end hotel.
  e. motel.

Taking Stock

LO2 **1.** What trade-offs are involved in deciding to have a single large centrally located facility instead of several smaller dispersed facilities?

LO1 **2.** Who needs to be involved in facility location decisions?

LO3 **3.** Name two ways in which technology has had an impact on location decisions.

LO2 **4.** Canada ranks in the top 10 "least corrupt countries" in the world, according to the Corruption Perceptions Index. In what ways does this help attract businesses to Canada?

Critical Thinking Exercises

LO2 & 3 **1.** The owner of a franchised fast-food restaurant has exclusive rights to operate in a city. The owner currently has a single outlet, which has proven to be very popular and there are often waiting lines of customers. The owner is therefore considering opening one or more other restaurants in the area. What are the key factors that the owner should investigate before making a final decision?

LO2 **2.** Corruption and bribery are common in some countries. Would you avoid   locating in such a country, or locate there and deal with it? If the latter,   how would you deal with it?

LO2 **3.** Immigration, Refugees and Citizenship Canada is moving its processing centre for immigration, student visas, etc., from Vegreville to Edmonton. Numerous people are employed at the Vegreville processing centre and many others are employed in businesses such as banks, personal services, restaurants, shopping centres, and supermarkets that will all suffer a decline in business. Is there a social responsibility to factor into this decision? Explain your reasoning.

Experiential Learning Exercises

 1. Identify a nearby location that has seen several businesses fail. Visit the location and try to determine the reasons for failures. Alternatively, visit a new business in your area and determine why it located there.

 2. Identify a company that is successful near where you live or work. Visit the company and find out how the location contributed to its success.

Internet Exercises

 1. Visit http://www.pitneybowes.com/us/location-intelligence/geographic-information-systems/mapinfo-pro.html. View the MapInfo video and read about its features and capabilities, then briefly summarize what the software does.

 2. Visit http://www.SiteSelection.com, type "Canada" in the search box on the top right, and press Enter. Find an article about a location decision involving Canada and summarize it.

 3. Visit http://www.hexagonsafetyinfrastructure.com/case-studies and summarize one case on the use of GIS.

Problems

 1. A newly formed company must decide on a plant location. There are two alternatives under consideration: locate near the major raw materials or locate near the major customers. Locating near the raw materials will result in lower fixed and variable costs than locating near the market, but the owners believe that there would be a loss in sales volume because customers tend to favour local suppliers. Revenue per unit will be $180 in either case. Using the following information, determine which location would produce greater profit.

	Near Raw Materials	Near Customers
Annual fixed costs ($ millions)	$1.2	$1.4
Variable cost per unit	$36	$47
Expected annual demand (units) . . .	8,000	12,000

 2. The owner of a sandwich shop hopes to add one new outlet. She has studied three locations. Each would have the same labour and materials costs (food, serving containers, napkins, etc.) of $1.76 per sandwich. Sandwiches sell for $2.65 each in all locations. Rent and equipment costs would be $5,000 per month for location A, $5,500 per month for location B, and $5,800 per month for location C.
   a. Determine the quantity necessary at each location to realize a monthly profit of $10,000.
   b. If expected sales at locations A, B, and C are 21,000, 22,000, and 23,000 sandwiches per month, respectively, which location would yield the greatest profit?

 3. A manufacturer of industrial machines wants to move to a larger plant, and has identified two alternatives. Location A has annual fixed cost of $800,000 and variable cost of $14,000 per unit; location B has annual fixed cost of $920,000 and variable cost of $12,000 per unit.
   a. At what quantity of output would the two locations have the same total cost?
   b. For what range of output would location A be superior? For what range would B be superior (i.e., have lower total annual cost)?

 4. A company that produces pleasure boats has decided to expand one of its lines. The current facility is insufficient to handle the increased workload, so the company is considering three alternatives: A (new location), B (subcontract), or C (expand existing facility).
   Alternative A would involve substantial fixed cost but relatively low variable cost: fixed cost would be $250,000 per year and variable cost would be $500 per boat. Subcontracting would involve a cost per boat of $2,500, and expansion would require an annual fixed cost of $50,000 and a variable cost of $1,000 per boat.
   a. Find the range of output for each alternative that would yield the lowest total cost.
   b. Which alternative would yield the lowest total cost for an expected annual quantity of 150 boats?
   c. What other factors might be considered in choosing between expansion and subcontracting?

 5. Rework Problem 4b using this additional information: Expansion would result in an increase of $70,000 per year, subcontracting would result in an increase of $25,000 per year, and adding a new location would result in an increase of $40,000 per year in transportation costs.

 6. A company that has recently experienced growth is seeking to lease a small plant in Winnipeg, Montreal, or Toronto. Prepare an economic analysis of the three locations given the following information: annual cost for building, equipment, and administration would be $40,000 for Winnipeg, $60,000 for Montreal, and $100,000 for Toronto. Labour and materials are expected to be $8 per unit in Toronto, $4 per unit in Winnipeg, and $5 per unit in Montreal. The Montreal location would increase total transportation cost by $50,000 per year, the Winnipeg location by $60,000 per year, and the Toronto location by $25,000 per year. Expected annual quantity is 10,000 units.

 7. A retired auto mechanic hopes to open a rustproofing shop. Customers would be local dealers. Two locations are being considered, one in the centre of the city and one in the outskirts. The central city location would involve fixed monthly cost of $7,000 and labour, materials, and transportation costs of $30 per car. The outskirt location would have fixed monthly costs of $4,700 and labour, materials, and transportation costs of $40 per car. Price at either location will be $90 per car.

a. Which location will yield the greatest profit if monthly demand is (i) 200 cars? (ii) 250 cars?

b. At what quantity of cars will the two sites yield the same monthly profit?

L02 **8.** For each of the four types of organizations shown below, rate the importance of each factor given in the left column in terms of making location decisions using L = low importance, M = moderate importance, and H = high importance.

Factor	Local Bank	Steel Mill	Grocery Warehouse	Public School
Convenience for customers	____	____	____	____
Attractiveness of building	____	____	____	____
Proximity to raw materials	____	____	____	____
Large amounts of power	____	____	____	____
Labour cost and availability	____	____	____	____
Transportation cost	____	____	____	____
Construction cost	____	____	____	____

L03 **9.** Using the following factor ratings (100 points is the maximum), determine which location for a clothing store—A, B, or C—should be chosen.

Factor	Weight	Location A	B	C
Convenience of access ..	0.15	80	70	60
Parking facility	0.20	72	76	92
Frontage	0.18	88	90	90
Shopper traffic..........	0.27	94	86	80
Operating cost	0.10	98	90	82
Neighbourhood	0.10	96	85	75
	1.00			

L03 **10.** Determine which location has the highest composite score:

Factor	Weight	East #1	East #2	West
Initial cost	8	100	150	140
Traffic	10	40	40	30
Maintenance	6	20	25	18
Dock space	6	25	10	12
Neighbourhood	4	12	8	15

L03 **11.** A manager has received an analysis of several cities being considered for a new office complex. The data (10 points is the maximum) are:

Factor	Location A	B	C
Business services	9	5	5
Community services	7	6	7
Construction cost	5	6	5
Cost of living	4	7	8
Personal taxes	5	5	4
Commuting ease	6	7	8

a. If the manager weighs the factors equally, how would the locations compare?

b. If business services and construction cost are given weights that are double the weights of the other factors, how would the locations compare?

L03 **12.** A toy manufacturer distributes its toys from five distribution centres (DCs) throughout the country. A new plant is to be built for a new line of toys. The monthly quantities to be shipped to each DC are approximately the same. A coordinate system has been established and the coordinates of each DC have been determined as shown below. Determine the optimal coordinates of the plant.

Location	(x, y)
A	3,7
B	8,2
C	4,6
D	4,1
E	6,4

L03 **13.** A clothing manufacturer produces women's clothes at four locations. A coordinate system has been determined for these four locations as shown below. The location of a central warehouse for rolls of cloth must now be determined. Weekly quantities to be shipped to each location are shown below. Determine the coordinates of the location that will minimize total transportation cost.

Location	(x, y)	Weekly Quantity
A	5,8	15
B	6,9	20
C	3,9	25
D	9,4	30

L03 **14.** A company that handles hazardous waste wants to open up a central disposal centre. The objective is to minimize the total shipping cost to the disposal centre from five receiving stations it operates. Given the locations of the receiving stations and the volumes to be shipped daily below, determine the location of the disposal centre.

Location of Receiving Station, (x, y)	Volume, Tonnes per Day
10, 4	26
4, 1	9
4, 7	25
2, 6	30
8, 7	40

 15. An analysis of sites for a distribution centre has led to two possible sites (L1 and L2 on the map). The sites are comparable on every key factor. The one remaining factor is the centre of gravity. Use the centre of gravity method

to select the better site. Monthly shipments will be the quantities listed in the table.

Destination	Quantity
D1	900
D2	300
D3	700
D4	600
D5	800

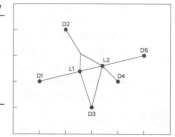

MINI-CASE   https://www.walmart.ca/en

Hello, Walmart?

Walmart is one of the largest corporations in the world, and it has obviously enjoyed tremendous success. But while many welcome its location in their communities, others do not. Some complain that its presence has too many negative effects on a community, ranging from traffic congestion to anti-union sentiment to unfair competition. Suppose Walmart has announced plans to seek approval from the planning commission of a small town to build a new store.

Questions

1. Develop a list of the main arguments, pro and con, that could be presented at a public hearing on the matter by members of each of these groups:
   a. Owners of small businesses located nearby
   b. Town residents, and residents of nearby towns
2. How might a Walmart representative respond to the negative criticisms that might be brought up, and what other benefits could the representative offer the planning board to bolster Walmart's case for gaining the board's approval?

MINI-CASE   http://acadianbakers.com

Acadian Bakers

Acadian Bakers is a small but well known bakery, making and selling cakes and croissants in Houston. Its major customers, their locations on a coordinate system, and their weekly purchases are listed below. Acadian's coordinates are (27, 36).

Question

Is Acadian centrally located to serve its customers?

Customer	Coordinates		Weekly Purchases ($)
	X	Y	
B. Catering	22	31	80
B. Bar & Grill	38	38	70
H's	38	36	90
H Club	38	37	120
H.C. Club	30	33	90
J's Hideaway	−10	12	60
M's	38	36	140
M. Club	−10	44	140
N.M.	47	33	300
K.S. Catering	33	33	50

Palliser Furniture

Palliser Furniture is the largest furniture manufacturer in Canada, but it grew out of the basement of its founder, A.A. DeFehr, who made simple wood products in Winnipeg in the 1940s. It grew steadily until 1963 when it moved to a 40 acre site in McLeod Industrial Park in northeast Winnipeg, the location of most of its current plants. Palliser's revenue was approximately $50 million and it employed approximately 800 workers in 1963.

The growth was steady but the furniture market in Canada was limited. In 1968, Palliser bought a bankrupt furniture upholsterer in Airdrie, north of Calgary, and started selling in the United States. However, it did not have much success there. In 1981, Palliser opened a furniture factory in Fargo, North Dakota, near Winnipeg, to make selling in the United States easier. In 1985, seeing the surge of cheap imports from Asia, Palliser got into wholesale trade by creating the World Trade division, which bought furniture from the Far East and sold it to North American furniture retailers.

Later, Palliser opened a particle board plant on its site in Winnipeg, becoming more vertically integrated in order to control quality and costs. In 1991, Palliser bought a bankrupt North Carolina furniture plant. Then, seeing the attractive prices for leather sofas and chairs, it started making more leather furniture. It also started a line of furniture for children's bedrooms, called Logic. Palliser had grown to 1,800 employees and $200 million revenue.

After NAFTA, in 1994, Palliser took advantage of free trade with the United States by doubling its sales and employees. It also built a plant in Mexico to reduce its costs and to get closer to the southern U.S. market for leather furniture. Mexico was chosen over a plant in China because Palliser chose to follow the customization and fast (2−4 weeks) delivery strategies, knowing that the transport time from China would be 6−8 weeks for its competitors, even though labour cost would

be cheaper there. Also, because of NAFTA, there would be no duties for goods produced in Mexico.

In 2001, Palliser introduced a line of trendy furniture for youth, called EQ3, and got into retailing furniture. Later, the rising Canadian dollar and cheap imports from China put pressure on solid wood furniture businesses, forcing Palliser to differentiate itself by making veneer products on machine-driven processes in Canada, but buying labour-intensive traditional wood products from the Far East. To reduce costs, Palliser built more factories in Mexico, and shifted more of the production of leather furniture from Winnipeg to Mexico.

After the collapse of the U.S. housing market in 2008, the North American residential furniture market suffered as well. Palliser is no longer in the plain-brown leather sofa market, and you won't find its product at The Brick or Leon's. Now it is primarily a leather furniture company offering a growing number of mid-market niche retailers customized ordering and up-market design. Some of its largest customers are Sears Canada and Winnipeg-based Dufresne group. In the U.S., its product is sold at national chains such as JC Penney.

Currently it has three factories in Mexico employing approximately 1,100 and one factory in Winnipeg employing approximately 600.

Question

How has Palliser competed internationally, and how have its location strategies helped it?

Sources: J. Rusen, "From Humble Beginnings . . .," *Manitoba Business,* September 1988, 10(7), Sec. 1, p. 6; J. E. Watson, "Entrepreneur of the Year," *Manitoba Business,* May 1, 2000, 22(4), p. 7; M. J. Knell, "Palliser to Shift Some Leather Mfg. to Mexico," *Furniture Today,* April 4, 2005 (http://www .furnituretoday.com/article/28738-Palliser_to_shift_some_leather _mfg_to_Mexico.php); M. J. Knell, "Palliser Restructures Into Five Operating Companies," *Furniture Today,* August 10, 2006 (http://www.furnituretoday .com/article/36914-Palliser_restructures_into_five_operating_companies .php?q=Palliser).

To access "The Transportation Model," the supplement to Chapter 8, please visit *Connect2*.

Chapter 9
Management of Quality

Courtesy of the Transportation Board of Canada

LEARNING OBJECTIVES

After completing this chapter, you should be able to:

LO1 Discuss evolution of quality management, dimensions and determinants of quality, various benefits and costs of quality, Taguchi loss function, and philosophies of quality gurus.

LO2 Describe ISO 9001.

LO3 Describe HACCP.

LO4 Describe the Canada Awards for Excellence and total quality management (TQM).

LO5 Describe methodology of problem solving and process improvement, including plan-do-study-act and seven basic quality tools.

On July 5, 2013, at about 10:50 p.m., a Montreal, Maine, & Atlantic Railway (MMA) train carrying Bakken, North Dakota, crude oil in 72 class 111 tank cars, destined for the Irving Oil Refinery in Saint John, New Brunswick, arrived at Nantes, Quebec. In keeping with MMA's practice, the locomotive engineer parked the train on the main track for the night, where the downhill grade is only 1.2 percent. After shutting down four of the five locomotives, the engineer applied seven hand brakes on five locomotives and two tank cars (less than MMA's rule of nine). Canadian Rail Operating Rules require that the hand brakes alone must be capable of holding a train, and this must be verified by a test. That night, however, the locomotive air brakes were left on during the test, meaning the train was being held by a combination of hand brakes and air brakes. The engineer then contacted MMA's rail traffic controller in Farnham, Quebec, to let him know that the train was secure. He also contacted MMA's rail traffic controller in Bangor, Maine, to discuss the smoke coming out of the lead locomotive and the problems it might cause for the next crew. As the smoke was expected to settle, it was agreed to leave the train as it was and deal with it the next morning.

Shortly after the engineer left for the night, the Nantes fire department responded to a 911 call of a fire on the lead locomotive. Firefighters extinguished the blaze by shutting off the fuel. After discussing the situation with MMA's rail traffic controller in Farnham and an MMA track foreman who had been dispatched to the scene, they turned off the electrical breakers and everyone left.

With all the locomotives shut down, the air brake system began to lose pressure and the brakes gradually became less and less effective. About an hour later, just before 1:00 a.m., the air pressure dropped to a point where the combination of air brakes and hand brakes could no longer hold the train. The train then began to roll downhill toward Lac-Megantic seven miles away. As it moved down the grade the train picked up speed, reaching a top speed of 65 miles per hour. The train derailed just past the Frontenac Street crossing, near the centre of town. Sixty-three tank cars derailed and almost all were damaged and breached, letting about 6 million litres of crude oil pour out into the streets. The fire began almost immediately and the ensuing blaze and explosions left 47 people dead and much of the downtown destroyed.

The total cost of this accident is expected to reach $2 billion. MMA declared bankruptcy in August 2013 and its assets were sold off. While accidents such as this are rare, they have tragic consequences for many, in this case including the victims, MMA, and the engineer who is also being sued for negligence. The investigation by the Transportation Safety Board of Canada has blamed MMA for:

- operating a poorly maintained locomotive (the lead locomotive was in the MMA repair shop eight months before the accident due to an engine failure, but was only repaired with an epoxy).
- failing to secure the unattended train properly.
- lack of training of its employees and a weak quality and safety culture.

Clearly, it is important to properly manage quality in order to prevent safety issues and to satisfy customers. That is the topic of this chapter.

Sources: https://www.youtube.com/watch?v=wVMNspPc8Zc; http://www.tsb.gc.ca/eng/rapports -reports/rail/2013/r13d0054/r13d0054-r-es.asp.

Introduction

Broadly defined, **quality** refers to the ability of a good or service to consistently meet or exceed customer expectations. Prior to the increased level of Japanese competition in the North American marketplace in the 1980s, quality was not uppermost in the minds of management. They tended to focus on quantity, cost, and productivity rather than on quality. It wasn't that quality was *un*important; it just wasn't *very* important.

> **quality** The ability of a good or service to consistently meet or exceed customer expectations.

Partly because of this thinking, foreign companies, many of them Japanese, captured a significant share of the North American market. In the automotive sector, leading Japanese manufacturers Toyota and Honda became major players in the North American market.

Many North American companies changed their views about quality after that. Stung by the success of foreign competitors, they embraced quality in a big way. They hired consultants, sent their people (including top executives) to Japan, and initiated a vast array of quality improvement programs. These companies clearly recognized the importance of quality and the fact that quality isn't something that is tacked on as a special feature, but is an *integral part* of a good or service. In the 1990s, North American automakers began to close the quality gap.

Evolution of Quality Management

Prior to the Industrial Revolution, skilled craftsmen performed all stages of production. Pride of workmanship, peer assessment, and reputation often provided the motivation to see that a job was done right. Lengthy guild apprenticeships caused this attitude to carry over to new workers. Moreover, one person or a small group of people was responsible for an entire product.

Division of labour in factories made each worker responsible for only a small portion of a product. Consequently, pride of workmanship became less meaningful for the workers. However, producing to standards became more important because of requirements for interchangeable parts. The responsibility for **quality control** (monitoring, testing, and correcting quality problems after they occur) shifted to the foremen and full-time quality inspectors. In many instances, 100 percent inspection was performed at the end of the production line.

> **quality control** Monitoring, testing, and correcting quality problems after they occur.

quality assurance Ensuring that a product's quality will be good by preventing defects before they occur.

quality management system (QMS) A structured and documented management system describing the policy, responsibilities, and implementation plan for ensuring quality.

continuous improvement Never-ending improvements to key processes as part of total quality management.

In the 1930s, Dodge, Romig, and Shewhart developed statistical procedures for sampling and quality control.

During the 1950s, the quality movement started to evolve into **quality assurance**, which is ensuring that a product's quality will be good by preventing defects before they occur. Operators were given more responsibility for quality during the production process. Various quality gurus such as Deming, Juran, Feigenbaum, and Crosby contributed to the evolution of quality assurance.

In the 1970s, NASA and the Pillsbury company created a **quality management system (QMS)** to assure and control food safety. A QMS is a structured and documented management system describing the policy, responsibilities, and implementation plan for ensuring quality. Later, the International Organization of Standards created the ISO 9001 standards for a quality management system.

In the 1980s, quality management become more strategic and was renamed *total quality management (TQM)*. This approach places greater emphasis on customer satisfaction and involves all levels of management and workers in a continuing effort to increase quality (**continuous improvement**).

Now, some organizations are pursuing a problem solving/process improvement approach called Six Sigma, which uses sophisticated statistical tools. Six Sigma will be discussed further in this chapter.

Dimensions of Quality

The term *quality* is used in a variety of ways. Sometimes it refers to the characteristics of material or grade of a product, such as Canada Choice apple juice or Canada Grade A eggs. At other times, it refers to workmanship, or performance, or reliability, or special features such as "waterproof" or "subtle aroma." We first describe product quality and then service quality.

The implication in these various connotations of quality is that customers value certain aspects of a good or service, and therefore associate those aspects with the quality that they perceive a good or service has.

dimensions of quality of goods Performance, aesthetics, special features, conformance, reliability, durability, perceived quality, and service after sale.

Quality of Goods. The aspects or **dimensions of quality of goods** include:[1]

- *Performance*—main characteristics or function of the product.
- *Aesthetics*—appearance, feel, smell, taste.
- *Special features*—extra characteristics or secondary functions.
- *Conformance*—how well a product corresponds to its design specification.
- *Reliability*—consistency of performance over time (not failing for a certain length of time).
- *Durability*—long life.
- *Perceived quality*—subjective evaluation of quality (e.g., reputation, image).
- *Service after sale*—handling of complaints or repairs.

These dimensions are illustrated for a car in Table 9-1.

TABLE 9-1 ▶

Examples of quality dimensions for a car.

Dimension		Example
1.	Performance	Everything works, ride, handling, leg room
2.	Aesthetics	Interior design, soft touch, fit and finish, grade of materials used
3.	Special features	
	Convenience	Placement of gauges and controls
	High tech	GPS, Bluetooth
	Safety	Anti-lock brakes, airbags, self-stopping
4.	Conformance	Car matches manufacturer's specification
5.	Reliability	No breakdowns in the first five years
6.	Durability	Long life, resistance to rust and corrosion
7.	Perceived quality	Top-rated car (e.g., Lexus)
8.	Service after sale	Warranty, handling of complaints, maintenance

[1] Adapted from David Garvin, "Competing on the Eight Dimensions of Quality," *Harvard Business Review* 65, no. 6 (1987).

In a broader sense, the term *fitness for use* is used to define quality. This means quality is whatever the customer requires in his/her particular use of the product. This point can be illustrated by looking at various uses of Velcro:[2] in the shoe industry, hook-and-loop (Velcro) on a pair of kids' sneakers isn't especially important because the shoes are used for a short time. But for a $600 knee brace, the quality of the hook-and-loop closure and cleanliness are important. For the textile customer aesthetics is important, but the automakers want durability, reliability, and uniform performance. With government, the specification is important.

Service Quality. The dimensions of quality of goods don't adequately describe service quality. Instead, service quality is often described using the following dimensions:[3]

- *Tangibles*—the physical appearance of facility, equipment, personnel, and communication materials.
- *Convenience*—the availability and accessibility of the service.
- *Reliability*—the ability to perform a service dependably, consistently, and accurately for a certain length of time.
- *Responsiveness*—the ability of the server to help customers in unusual situations and to deal with problems.
- *Timeliness*—the speed with which service is delivered.
- *Assurance*—the ability of server to convey trust and confidence; service guarantee.
- *Courtesy/empathy*—showing respect, and understanding and sharing the feelings of the customer.

Table 9-2 illustrates the dimensions of service quality for car repair.

Dimension	Examples
1. Tangibles	Clean facilities and neat personnel
2. Convenience	Convenient location and open late hours
3. Reliability	Problem fixed right every time
4. Responsiveness	Willing and able to answer questions
5. Timeliness	Short wait time
6. Assurance	Knowledgeable staff, service warranty
7. Courtesy/empathy	Polite and friendly treatment of customers

◀ **TABLE 9-2**

Examples of service quality dimensions for car repair.

We have already seen the dimensions of product quality in the customer requirements of quality function deployment (Chapter 4).

Customers evaluate a good or service's quality relative to their expectation. If the quality, as perceived by a customer, is higher than expected, he/she will be delighted; if it is the same, the customer is satisfied, but if it is less, he/she will be dissatisfied. See the Kano Model of Chapter 4 for a refinement of this idea.

Determinants of Quality

A product's quality is determined during:

1. Product design
2. Production process design
3. Production
4. Use

[2] https://hbr.org/1989/09/how-velcro-got-hooked-on-quality
[3] Adapted from Valerie A. Zeithhaml, A. Parasuraman, and Leonard L. Berry, *Delivering Quality Service and Balancing Customer Expectations*, New York: The Free Press, 1990; and J. R. Evans and W. M. Lindsey, *The Management and Control of Quality*, 3rd ed., St. Paul, MN: West Publishing, 1996.

The product design phase is the starting point for the level of quality eventually achieved. Product design involves decisions about the characteristics and specification of a product such as size, shape, and material. Note that quality is what the customers require. Quality function deployment (house of quality in Chapter 4) is used to translate the customer requirements into technical attributes of the product and their target values (specification). For example, in creating a new burger, the customer requirement of "juicy" can be translated into "moisture content of a burger" with target value of "1 millilitre."

During production process design, technical (product) characteristics are translated into process characteristics and specifications. For example, "moisture content = 1 mL" can be translated into "use a grill capable of maintaining 350 ± 10 degrees Fahrenheit" (which will be used for 8 minutes (4 minutes per side) to grill a meat patty). The "± 10 degrees F" is the *tolerance* allowed.

Conformance to design specification during production refers to the degree to which the produced good or service is defect-free (complies with the specification of the designer). This is affected by factors such as documentation of processes and procedures, the skills and training of operators, the stability and monitoring of processes, taking corrective actions (e.g., through problem solving) when necessary, communication and meeting of staff, record keeping and verification (audits), and having good quality suppliers.

During use, ease of use and user instructions are important. Manufacturers must ensure that directions for unpacking, assembling, using, maintaining, and adjusting the product—and what to do if something goes wrong (e.g., flush eyes with water, disconnect from electricity immediately)—are clearly visible and easily understood. If a product does not perform as expected, it is important to remedy the situation immediately through recall and repair, replacement, or refund.

> **conformance to design specification during production** The degree to which the produced good or service complies with the specification of the designer.

Benefits of Good Quality

Organizations with good quality products tend to be more profitable compared to those with poor quality because profitability is driven by both the quality of product design and conformance to design specifications. Improved quality of design will help the organization differentiate its product from competitors and enhance its reputation for quality, allowing the organization to charge premium prices and increase market share. On the other hand, improved conformance to design specifications leads to lower manufacturing and warranty expenses.

Costs of Quality

Cost of quality is a methodology to determine the resources used to prevent poor quality, appraise the quality of the products, and deal with internal and external failures. Cost of quality was introduced to show the importance of dealing with quality issues and to manage them. Those costs can be classified into four categories: internal failure costs, external failure costs, appraisal (detection) costs, and prevention costs.

Internal failure costs relate to part or product failures discovered during production. Internal failures occur for a variety of reasons, including defective material from suppliers, incorrect machine settings, faulty equipment, incorrect methods, incorrect processing, and faulty or improper material handling equipment or procedures. The costs of internal failures include lost production time, scrap and rework, possible equipment damage, and possible employee injury.

External failure costs relate to part or product failures discovered after delivery to the customer. They include handling of complaints, recall, replacement, liability/litigation, payments to customers or discounts used to offset the inferior quality, loss of customer goodwill, and opportunity costs related to lost sales.

Appraisal (detection) costs relate to inspection, testing, and other activities intended to uncover defective products. They include the cost of inspectors, testing, test equipment, labs, and quality audits.

> **cost of quality** A methodology to determine the resources used to prevent poor quality, appraise the quality of the products, and deal with internal and external failures.
>
> **internal failure costs** Relate to part or product failures discovered during production.
>
> **external failure costs** Relate to part or product failures discovered after delivery to the customer.
>
> **appraisal (detection) costs** Costs of inspection and testing.

Improved quality of product design → Better reputation → Premium prices and increased market share → Higher profitability

Improved conformance to design specifications → Lower manufacturing and warranty expenses → Higher profitability

Prevention costs relate to attempts to prevent defects from occurring. They include costs such as market research, product design verification, quality planning and administration, statistical process control, working with suppliers to improve quality of purchased materials and parts, standard operating procedures, and training.

Internal and external failure costs represent costs related to poor quality, whereas (some) appraisal and prevention costs represent investments for achieving good quality. It is generally accepted that spending $1 on prevention may save as much as $10 on detection and as much as $100 on fixing failures.

prevention costs Costs of preventing defects from occurring.

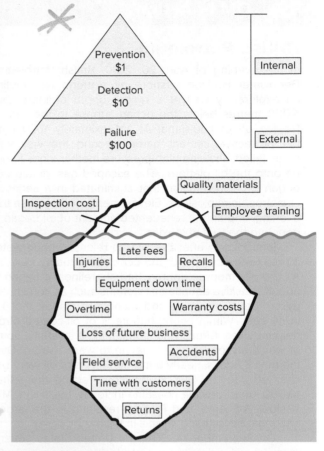

Hidden Costs of Quality. When managers think about the costs of quality, those categories that typically come to mind are the most visible ones, such as the costs associated with buying high quality materials, investing in employee training, and paying for inspections. However, this is just the tip of the iceberg. When managers attempt to cut costs by choosing lower quality materials, reducing employee training, or reducing inspections, the hidden costs of poor quality become larger. The use of lower quality materials is known to cause more product defects and lower production yields, which may require employees to put in extra hours to rework those defects. Since new employees are not sufficiently trained, senior employees may need to spend more of their time dealing with dissatisfied customers. If products are not sufficiently inspected, more defects are likely to be passed on to customers, which results in costly returns and loss of future business. Other examples of hidden costs include equipment downtime due to lack of preventive maintenance, injuries, accidents, product recalls, field service costs, late fees, and extra warranty expenses caused by mistakes. For every dollar that is cut from the tip of the iceberg, much more would need to be spent on the bottom of the iceberg. This is why quality is actually free, when one considers the hidden costs of poor quality.

©Tim Boyle/Bloomberg via Getty Images

A technician prepares to remove the accelerator assembly in a recalled Toyota Avalon. These "sticky" accelerator pedals have been known to cause unintended vehicle acceleration. In addition to paying out billions in civil lawsuits, the company was also fined $1.2 billion.

Source: *https://www.washingtonpost .com/business/economy/toyota -reaches-12-billion-settlement-to -end-criminal-probe/2014/03/19 /5738a3c4-af69-11e3-9627 -c65021d6d572_story.html?utm _term=.f79cb5f59d43*

For an example of costs of poor quality, see the "British Petroleum" OM in Action.

OM in Action

British Petroleum

In the evening of April 20, 2010, British Petroleum's Deepwater Horizon offshore oil platform was drilling an exploratory well at a record depth of more than 4,000 metres below the ocean surface in the Gulf of Mexico off of Louisiana. At approximately 9:50 p.m., the protective cement barrier around the well suddenly failed, allowing high-pressure methane gas to rise up onto the oil platform. The escaped gas ignited and began a chain reaction that culminated in a series of catastrophic explosions. Eleven men lost their lives that evening, and an unprecedented amount of oil began to pour into the Gulf of Mexico.

Immediately after the oil was released underwater, it rose to the surface of the ocean as a foamy mousse. As the oily mousse approached shorelines, it began to engulf sensitive aquatic ecosystems such as coral reefs, oyster beds, marshes, and mangrove stands that lay in its path. Within hours, hundreds of oil-coated birds, dolphins, sea turtles and other marine animals, some of which are endangered, began to wash ashore. Over the next 87 days, nearly 5 million barrels of oil were discharged into the Gulf of Mexico, affecting more than 10,000 km of pristine coastline in Texas, Louisiana, Mississippi, Alabama, and Florida, resulting in the largest and most devastating oil spill in history.

On September 14, 2011, the United States government issued a detailed report placing responsibility for the oil spill on British Petroleum and its partners—oil rig operator Transocean and contractor Halliburton. The report attributes the central cause of the blowout to the failure of the cement barrier around the well, which allowed the pent-up gas and oil to gush out of the oil platform. BP and its partners failed to perform the cement job in accordance with industry-accepted standards.

In addition, they attempted to work faster and more cheaply by cancelling an independent diagnostic test used to test the strength of the cement. The test would have detected the problems with the cement seal at a cost of only $140,000. In sharp contrast to this modest sum, BP ultimately had to pay out more than $46 billion in fines to restore the damaged shoreline and compensate the millions of people who lived and worked in the region. The tragic loss of life and the subsequent pollution of the Gulf of Mexico were the results of poor management decisions, based on a lack of understanding of the costs of quality.

Source: US Department of Interior, "Report Regarding the Causes of the April 20, 2010, Macondo Well Blowout," http://docs.lib.noaa.gov/noaa_documents /DWH_IR/reports/dwhfinal.pdf. Accessed February 10, 2014.

Courtesy of US Coast Guard

Taguchi Quality Loss Function

> **Taguchi quality loss function** The graphical representation of how an increase in deviation from the target value leads to a faster rate of increase in customer dissatisfaction.

Most measurable characteristics of a product are specified by the designer as a range of values between a lower specification (spec) limit and an upper spec limit. For example, a 3 inch screw may have [2.99, 3.01] design spec limits. Any unit that measures between these two limits is said to be acceptable (see the top figure on the next page). However, customers tend to prefer products that measure as close to the target value as possible. For the screw example, the target is 3 inches. The quality worsens as measurement deviates from the target. Taguchi called this quality deterioration **Taguchi quality loss function**, and claimed that the quality loss increases at a faster rate the farther the measurement is from the target (illustrated in the bottom figure on the next page). This concept is said to be the reason for the popularity of continuous improvement and Six Sigma, because it implies that quality keeps improving the better and more accurate the production process becomes.

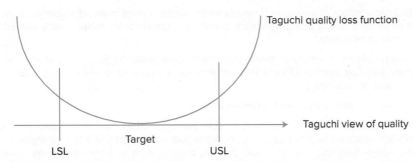

Traditional vs. Taguchi's view of quality.

Quality Gurus

A number of quality experts have shaped modern quality practices. Among the most famous, other than Taguchi, are Deming, Juran, Feigenbaum, and Crosby. Together, they have had a tremendous impact on the management of quality and the way companies operate.

W. Edwards Deming. A statistics professor at New York University in the 1940s, Deming went to Japan after the Second World War to assist the Japanese in improving their quality and productivity. His contributions were so much appreciated that an annual quality award, the Deming Prize, was established in his name in 1951.

Although the Japanese revered Deming, he was largely unknown to business leaders in North America. In fact, he worked with the Japanese for almost 30 years before North American companies turned their attention to Deming, embraced his philosophy, and requested his assistance in setting up quality improvement programs.

Deming compiled a list of 14 points that he believed were the prescription needed to achieve quality in an organization (see Table 9-3). His message is basically that the cause of inefficiency and poor quality is the *system*, not the employees. Deming felt that it was *management's responsibility* to correct the system to achieve the desired results. He stressed the need to reduce variation in output, which can be accomplished by distinguishing between *special causes* of variation (i.e., correctable) and *common causes* of variation (i.e., random). This is the foundation of statistical process control (SPC), which is covered in the next chapter. Deming also promoted the plan-do-study-act (PDSA) cycle of problem solving (covered later in this chapter).

Deming believed that workers want to create and learn, but that management unintentionally often does things (such as establishing rating systems) that rob workers of their internal motivation. He believed that management's greatest challenge in achieving quality was in motivating workers to contribute their collective efforts to achieve a common goal.[4]

W. Edwards Deming.
©Richard Drew/AP Images

http://www.juran.com

Joseph M. Juran. Juran, like Deming, taught Japanese manufacturers how to improve the quality of their goods, and he too can be regarded as a major force in Japan's success in quality. He made his first trip to Japan a few years after the publication of his *Quality Control Handbook* in 1951.

Juran viewed quality as fitness for use. He also believed that roughly 80 percent of quality defects are controllable; thus, management has the responsibility to correct these deficiencies. He described quality management in terms of a *trilogy* consisting of quality planning, quality control,

---

[4] For a three-part video about Deming, see http://www.youtube.com/watch?v=GHvnIm9UEoQ, http://www.youtube.com/watch?v=mKFGj8sK5R8, and http://www.youtube.com/watch?v=6WeTaLRb-Bs.

TABLE 9-3 ▶

Deming's 14 points.

1.	Create constancy of purpose toward improvement of goods and services with a plan to become competitive and to stay in business. Decide to whom top management is responsible.
2.	Adopt the new philosophy. We are in a new economic age. We can no longer live with commonly accepted levels of delays, mistakes, defective materials, and defective workmanship.
3.	Cease dependence on mass inspection. Require instead statistical evidence that quality is built in. (*Prevent* defects rather than *detect* defects.)
4.	End the practice of awarding business on the basis of price. Instead, depend on meaningful measures of quality along with price. Eliminate suppliers that cannot qualify with statistical evidence of quality.
5.	Find problems. It is management's job to work continually on the system (design, incoming materials, composition of material, maintenance, improvement of machines, training, supervision, retraining).
6.	Institute modern methods of training on the job.
7.	The responsibility of foremen must be changed from sheer numbers to quality . . . [which] will automatically improve productivity. Management must prepare to take immediate action on reports from foremen concerning quality barriers such as inherent defects, machines not maintained, poor tools, and fuzzy operational definitions.
8.	Drive out fear so that everyone may work effectively for the company.
9.	Break down barriers between departments. People in research, design, sales, and production must work as a team to foresee problems of production that may be encountered with various materials and specifications.
10.	Eliminate numerical goals, posters, and slogans for the work force, asking for new levels of productivity without providing methods.
11.	Eliminate work standards that prescribe numerical quotas.
12.	Remove barriers that stand between the hourly worker and his right to pride of workmanship.
13.	Institute a vigorous program of education and retraining.
14.	Create a structure in top management that will push every day on the above 13 points.

Source: Deming, W. Edwards, *Out of the Crisis*, pp. 23–24: 14 Points, © 2000 Massachusetts Institute of Technology, by permission of The MIT Press.

and quality improvement. According to Juran, quality planning is necessary to establish processes *capable* of meeting quality standards; quality control is necessary in order to know when corrective action is needed; and quality improvement will help to find better ways of doing things. A key element of Juran's philosophy is the commitment of management to continuous improvement.

Juran is credited as one of the first to measure the cost of quality, and he demonstrated the potential for increased profits that would result if costs of poor quality could be reduced.

Armand Feigenbaum. Feigenbaum was director of manufacturing operations at General Electric (1958–1968) and its top expert on quality. He recognized that quality was not only a collection of tools and techniques, but also a "total field"; he called it total quality control. He saw that when improvements were made in a process, other areas of the company also achieved improvements. Feigenbaum's understanding of systems theory led him to create an environment in which people could learn from each other's successes, and his leadership and open work environment led to cross-functional teamwork.

> **quality at the source** Avoid passing defective products to the following workstation, and stop and fix the problem. This is called *jidoka* in Japanese.

Also, he introduced the concept of **quality at the source**, or seeking to avoid passing defective products to the following workstation, and to stop and fix the problem. Quality at the source is called *jidoka* in Japanese. We will see more on this in Chapter 15.

> **zero defects** The philosophy that any level of defects is too high.

Philip B. Crosby. Crosby worked at Martin Marietta Company in the 1960s. While he was there, he developed the concept of *zero defects* and popularized the phrase "Do it right the first time." He stressed prevention and argued against the idea that "there will always be some level of defectives."

In accordance with the concept of **zero defects**, Crosby believed that any level of defects is too high, and that management must install programs that help the organization move toward zero defects. Among some of his key points are the following:[5]

---

[5] Philip Crosby, *Quality Without Tears: The Art of Hassle-Free Management,* New York: McGraw-Hill, 1984.

1. Top management must demonstrate its commitment to quality and its willingness to give support to achieve good quality.

2. Management must be persistent in efforts to achieve good quality.

3. Management must spell out clearly what it wants in terms of quality and what workers must do to achieve that.

4. Make it (or do it) right the first time.

Unlike the other gurus, Crosby maintained that achieving quality can be relatively easy. Crosby's "quality is free" concept is based on the following: costs of poor quality are much greater than traditionally recognized, and these costs are so great that, rather than viewing quality efforts as costs, organizations should view them as a way to reduce costs, because the improvements generated by quality efforts will more than pay for themselves.

Table 9-4 provides a summary of the important contributions of the gurus to modern quality management. To see how one hotel chain works for quality, see the "Delta Hotels" OM in Action.

Contributor	Key Contributions
Deming	14 points; special versus common causes of variation, SPC, PDSA cycle
Juran	Quality is fitness-for-use; quality trilogy
Feigenbaum	Total quality control; quality at the source
Crosby	Quality is free; zero defects

◄ **TABLE 9-4**

A summary of key contributions to quality management.

 OM in Action

Delta Hotels

With more than 7,000 employees and 38 hotels distributed across Canada, Delta Hotels is one of Canada's top hotel chains. Delta's quality journey began in 1996. Guest and employee satisfaction are its two core values. Delta has developed a strong quality culture and procedures for its daily operations based on Excellence Canada's Criteria for Canada Awards for Excellence.

Problem-solving teams regularly monitor processes for improvement opportunities. One result of these improvements is Delta's "one-minute check-in guarantee" for Delta Privilege members. Delta empowers its employees to remove all barriers to "wow" the guests. Its power-to-please program empowers employees to have control over a guest's experience. Guest loyalty is regularly measured. Consistency of service and service guarantees have been found to be key factors for guest loyalty. Guest needs are identified using guest comment cards and other methods. Guest callbacks (to front desk and housekeeping) are monitored to identify commonly needed items. For example, irons and ironing boards were introduced to all guestrooms as a result of this tracking mechanism. Customer concerns are promptly responded to. There is a direct 1-800 number for guests to contact Delta's president. Each concern is responded to within 24 hours. Guest satisfaction is measured and monitored monthly.

Delta trains internal assessors to conduct individual hotel assessments and develop a quality improvement plan. Every two years, a hotel will undergo an assessment to ensure that ongoing quality measures are incorporated into the hotel's culture and all aspects of its operations. Employees can also participate in the guest satisfaction committees, and are involved in the development of all plans. There is a process for employee suggestions. In addition to regular communications, senior leaders of Delta personally visit each hotel. Outside consultants are used to evaluate hotels' services, guest loyalty, and brand.

From their first days, employees are told what is expected of them, the key service standards, Delta's culture, that they are the key to the hotel's success because they directly influence guest satisfaction, and that their opinions matter. There is orientation, technical, and guest service training, including online training. Trust between management and employees has developed to the extent that an employee can walk into her manager's office and say, "I think this really needs to be changed" or "This is what I need in order to get my job done." Employee and team accomplishments are recognized during regular department and "town hall" meetings. Hotels share best practices. On-the-spot standing ovations are used to praise deserving employees. There is also an annual review of each employee's performance.

Employees receive an additional week's pay if they participate in a certain number of training hours per year. Delta internally delivers over 40 programs for employee development on topics ranging from conflict resolution to health and wellness. There is an annual employee opinion survey, and an employee assistance program (to deal with personal problems). Employees have access to hotels' fitness rooms. There are pre-shift morning stretches for the housekeeping teams.

Managers are also trained. Delta has created management development reviews, including 360° feedback, that examine specific managerial competencies such as flexibility, ability to handle stress, ability to work with a team, and interpersonal sensitivity. The results, including employee and guest satisfaction, are tied to managers and senior leaders' bonuses.

As a result of all these initiatives, Delta Hotels has won the highest level of Canada Award for Excellence in Quality and in Healthy Workplace. Delta Hotels was bought by Marriott International in 2015.

Source: http://www.excellence.ca/assets/files/legacy/NQI_Best_Practices _Brochure_Vol2.pdf.

ISO 9001

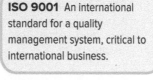
ISO 9001 An international standard for a quality management system, critical to international business.

http://www.iso.org

The purpose of the International Organization for Standardization (called ISO for short in all languages, not as an acronym) is to promote worldwide standards that will improve operating efficiency and productivity, and reduce costs. ISO is composed of the national standards bodies of over 100 countries. The Canadian representative body is the Standards Council of Canada. ISO's work is conducted by approximately 180 technical committees. Two of the most well known standards are ISO 9001 (quality) and ISO 14001 (environment).

ISO 9001 is an international standard for a quality management system. A company wanting to be certified as having implemented the standard must document its processes and procedures, and undergo an external on-site assessment by accredited auditors. The implementation and certification processes often take 12–18 months. Certification is required in some industries (e.g., parts suppliers to automakers). More than 1 million companies are ISO 9001 certified worldwide.[6]

The ISO 9001 review process involves considerable self-appraisal, resulting in problem identification and improvement. Certified companies face an ongoing series of audits, and they must be recertified every three years. The ISO 9001 standard is reviewed every five years and revised if needed. The most recent revision was in 2015, and the one before that was in 2008. A graphical representation of major ISO 9001:2015 elements and their interaction is shown below.

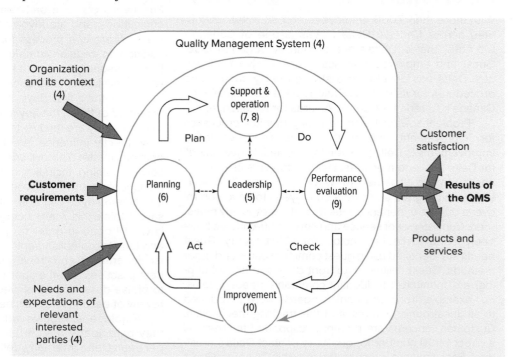

Permission to use extracts from ISO 9001:2015 was provided by the Standards Council of Canada (SCC). No further reproduction is permitted without prior written approval from SCC.

[6] https://www.iso.org/files/live/sites/isoorg/files/standards/conformity_assessment/certification/doc/survey _executive-summary.pdf

The following list is a summary of requirements for ISO 9001:2015:[7]

1. **Scope** (of ISO 9001)
2. **Normative References** (to Fundamentals and Vocabulary document)
3. **Terms and Definitions**
4. **Context of the Organization**
   1. **Understanding the organization and its context** (legal, technological, competitive)
   2. **Understanding the needs and expectations of interested parties** (customers, suppliers, regulators)
   3. **Determining the scope of the Quality Management System (QMS)** (locations, goods/services covered)
   4. **QMS and its processes**
5. **Leadership**
   1. **Leadership and commitment**
      I. **General.** Hold managers accountable for effectiveness of QMS, establish quality policy and objectives, provide resources, communicate importance of QMS, promote its improvement.
      II. **Customer focus.** Determine, understand, and meet requirements and risks and opportunities that can affect conformity of goods and services.
   2. **Policy**
      I. **Establishing the quality policy**
      II. **Communicating the quality policy** (document)
   3. **Organizational roles, responsibilities, and authorities** (quality manager, process managers)
6. **Planning**
   1. **Actions to address risks and opportunities** (to effectiveness of QMS)
   2. **Quality objectives and planning to achieve them** (document)
   3. **Planning of changes**
7. **Support**
   1. **Resources** (people, infrastructure, work environment [social, psychological, physical], monitoring and measuring resources [document calibration], organizational knowledge)
   2. **Competence** (of employees, train; document)
   3. **Awareness** (of employees of QMS)
   4. **Communication** (plan)
   5. **Documented information** (create, control, and update properly)
8. **Operation**
   1. **Operational planning and control** (of needed processes; document)
   2. **Requirements for goods and services**
      I. **Customer communication** (inquiries, orders, feedback)
      II. **Determining the requirements**
      III. **Requirements review** (make sure they can be met; document)
      IV. **Changes to requirements** (document and inform relevant people)

---

[7] *ISO 9001:2015 Quality Management Systems–Requirements, Fifth Edition 2015-09-15,* Ch. de Blandonnet 8 • CP 401 CH-1214 Vernier, Geneva, Switzerland.

   3. **Design and development of goods and services**

     I. **General** (establish, implement, and maintain a process)

     II. **Planning** (plan and document design process)

     III. **Inputs** (complete and unambiguous documented requirements)

     IV. **Controls** (reviews to meet desired results; document)

     V. **Outputs** (specifications, including measurement requirements; document)

     VI. **Changes** (identify, review, and control design changes)

   4. **Control of externally provided processes, goods and services**

     I. **General** (ensure conformance to requirements, provide supplier evaluation criteria; document)

     II. **Type and extent of control** (define the controls)

     III. **Information for external providers** (adequate requirements, required competence, verification at supplier site)

   5. **Production and service provision**

     I. **Control** (produce under controlled conditions, provide product specs, monitoring and measuring equipment, infrastructure and environment, competent operators, quality control, prevent human error)

     II. **Identification and traceability** (identify defective items, if required identify each item, trace its production; document)

     III. **Property belonging to customers or external providers** (Protect customer or supplier-owned property)

     IV. **Preservation** (protect the product)

     V. **Post-delivery activities** (meet requirements for warranty, maintenance, recycling, disposal)

     VI. **Control of changes** (to production; document)

   6. **Release of goods and services** (only if requirements are met; document)

   7. **Control of nonconforming outputs** (correct, segregate, inform customer, ship under concession; keep documents)

9. **Performance Evaluation**

   1. **Monitoring, measurement, analysis, and evaluation**

     I. **General** (what, method, when; document)

     II. **Customer satisfaction** (survey, feedback, meet in person, warranty claim, etc.)

     III. **Analysis and evaluation** (goods and services, customer satisfaction, QMS, suppliers, etc.)

   2. **Internal audit** (of QMS, periodically; document)

   3. **Management review**

     I. **General** (review the QMS)

     II. **Inputs** (status of previous actions, changes in issues, performance of QMS, adequacy of resources, opportunities for improvement)

     III. **Outputs** (decisions on improvements, changes to QMS, resource needs; document)

10. **Improvement**

   1. **General** (goods and services, corrective and preventive actions, QMS)

   2. **Nonconformity and corrective action** (take action and contain, eliminate cause, change QMS if necessary; document)

   3. **Continual improvement** (of QMS)

There are usually three types of documents created for ISO 9001: a quality manual, a procedures manual, and detailed work instructions and other supporting documents. The procedures manual includes all critical processes of the organization, and for each process a description (in general terms) of how it is to be done (using a process flow diagram) and what to do if there is a problem. For two applications of ISO 9001, see the "ERCO Worldwide" and "Holland College" OM in Action boxes.

 OM in Action   www.ercoworldwide.com

ERCO Worldwide

ERCO Worldwide, headquartered in Toronto, is a major international supplier of chemicals and chlorine dioxide technology. The company has a 115-year history of providing products and services to major industries including water treatment, food processing, fertilizers, agriculture, and oil and gas, as well as the pulp and paper industry. ERCO Worldwide is the second largest producer of sodium chlorate in the world, and has six manufacturing facilities in Canada (including one in Saskatoon), two in the United States, and one in Chile. ERCO facilities were ISO 9001 certified over two decades ago to ensure product quality for their customers. ERCO is currently in the process of upgrading its quality management system (QMS) certification from ISO 9001:2008 to ISO 9001:2015 standard.

ERCO's quality policy is: "ERCO Worldwide, through continual improvement and the commitment of its people, provides quality products, technology and services that meet our customer requirements. We will accomplish this by monitoring customer satisfaction to ensure we meet customer requirements, [and] continually improving the quality management system using innovation in work processes."

Quality objectives for 2017 in the Saskatoon plant were aimed at meeting or exceeding the Customer Satisfaction Index, and completing internal quality audits as per the audit plan.

ERCO Saskatoon's QMS comprises nine areas: internal audit, chloralkali, chlorate, document control, engineering and maintenance, purchasing, quality system, technical services (lab), and training. ERCO Saskatoon's QMS consists of approximately 250 controlled documents/records, including standard operating procedures (SOPs), forms, and reference charts.

Managing the QMS involves (1) document revisions/changes, (2) creating employee awareness of

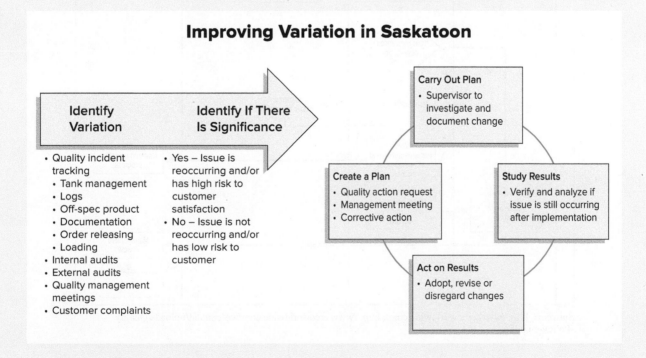

Improving Variation in Saskatoon

Identify Variation
- Quality incident tracking
  - Tank management
  - Logs
  - Off-spec product
  - Documentation
  - Order releasing
  - Loading
- Internal audits
- External audits
- Quality management meetings
- Customer complaints

Identify If There Is Significance
- Yes – Issue is reoccurring and/or has high risk to customer satisfaction
- No – Issue is not reoccurring and/or has low risk to customer

Carry Out Plan
- Supervisor to investigate and document change

Study Results
- Verify and analyze if issue is still occurring after implementation

Act on Results
- Adopt, revise or disregard changes

Create a Plan
- Quality action request
- Management meeting
- Corrective action

the QMS by training, setting area objectives and communication, and (3) identifying improvements in the QMS by analyzing quality near-misses, internal audits, external audits, quality management meetings, and addressing customer complaints in an effective and timely manner. As a Responsible Care® company,

ERCO follows the plan-do-study-act process improvement methodology.

Internal quality auditing is a major part of the quality coordinator's role and responsibilities. ERCO uses a process similar to the following internal audit process map, for internal auditing:

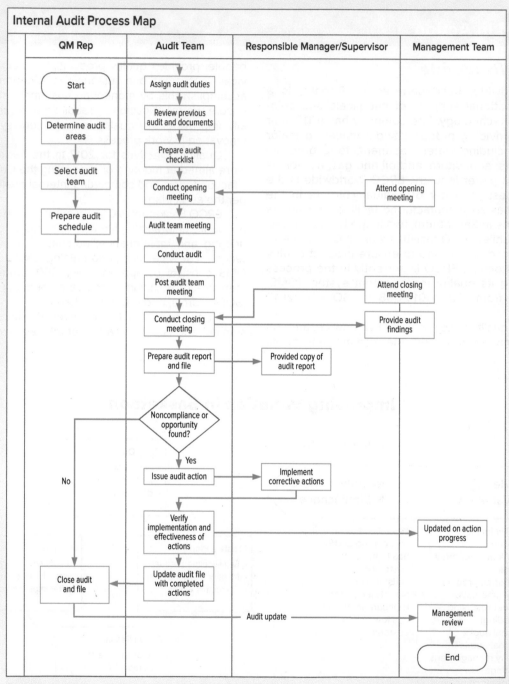

Internal Audit Process Map

QM Rep	Audit Team	Responsible Manager/Supervisor	Management Team

Sources: http://www.ercoworldwide.com/; http://www.ercoworldwide.com/wp-content/uploads/Quality -Policy-en.pdf.

OM in Action

Holland College

Holland College is a large community college with campuses in seven towns in Prince Edward Island. Holland College offers both competency-based (career-oriented) diploma/certificate programs and continuing education. It considers its products to be the programs it offers. Its primary customers are the students, while its secondary customers are the future employers of the students. Holland College is one of the few colleges/universities in Canada that is ISO 9001 certified.

The quality management system (QMS) set up by Holland College includes quality policies (e.g., involve industry/business leaders in development and evaluation of the programs) and quality objectives (e.g., more than 80 percent of students should recommend their program to someone they know). QMS also includes a quality manual that delineates how Holland College provides and manages its resources, and designs, delivers, controls, and improves its programs. It has set up several processes for its major activities. The processes and other information/instructions are described in a set of procedures. A procedure has the following sections: purpose, scope, related procedures/documents/definitions, responsibilities, procedure guidelines and instructions, and possibly a process flow diagram.

Adequate funding is provided for resources such as staff and faculty salaries, and buildings and equipment (e.g., computers and audiovisuals). There is a procedure for recruiting qualified staff/faculty based on education, training, skills, and experience. There are several procedures for appraisal and training of employees to improve their services to the students and to maintain the relevance and appeal of the programs. Computers are periodically replaced with new ones.

To design and deliver its programs and services, and to deal with its customers (the students), Holland College has several processes: Marketing and recruitment, admissions and registration, student exit and graduation, career counselling/accommodation/disability services, design and development of programs and curriculum, delivery of programs and courses, purchasing of equipment, and library/bookstore/computer services/student-finance services. These processes are provided under conditions controlled through using course outlines, taking attendance, assessing students, using transcripts, dealing with student misconduct, and maintaining and repairing equipment, as well as other procedures.

The programs are measured, analyzed, and improved by getting feedback from students and employers. Instructors and managers continuously review the performance of their programs and take corrective action. The executive committee annually reviews the programs' performance against the objectives and prescribes action plans to improve them.

For a list of links to Holland College QMS, visit https://sam.hollandcollege.com/shared/QMS/General/QMS-Welcome.pdf.

Sources: Holland College, PEI. www.hollandc.pe.ca/quality; https://sam.hollandcollege.com/AngelUploads/Content/Quality_Management_System/_assoc/9F99DA3D6BED484E8C5DBA903BBDB366/HC_Quality_Manual.pdf.

ISO 14001

ISO 14001 is an international standard for assessing a company's environmental performance. It is concerned with what an organization should do to minimize the harmful effects of its operations on the environment. The ISO 14001 standard[8] is very similar to the ISO 9001 standard (it has the same 10 requirements), but instead of quality it relates to environment.

> **ISO 14001** An international standard for assessing a company's environmental performance.

Hazard Analysis Critical Control Point (HACCP)

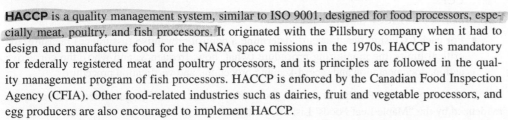

HACCP is a quality management system, similar to ISO 9001, designed for food processors, especially meat, poultry, and fish processors. It originated with the Pillsbury company when it had to design and manufacture food for the NASA space missions in the 1970s. HACCP is mandatory for federally registered meat and poultry processors, and its principles are followed in the quality management program of fish processors. HACCP is enforced by the Canadian Food Inspection Agency (CFIA). Other food-related industries such as dairies, fruit and vegetable processors, and egg producers are also encouraged to implement HACCP.

> **HACCP** Hazard Analysis Critical Control Point; a quality management system designed for food processors.

---

[8] For a copy of ISO 14001:2015 requirements, Google "ISO 14001:2015 requirements ga.hfu.edu.tw" and download the top pdf result.

HACCP deals with food safety, in particular, biological, chemical, and physical hazards.[9] In an organization, HACCP is implemented by a multidisciplinary team, including a HACCP coordinator, a food microbiologist, a sanitation expert, and representatives from production, engineering, quality assurance, etc. As in ISO 9001, top management's commitment is essential.

First, the HACCP team inspects various construction and/or sanitary aspects of the plant, equipment, and personnel. For example, the land should have good drainage and water source, and no garbage or odours. The building should be pest-proof and have easy-to-clean walls, floors, and ceilings; sloped floors to drains; screened windows; close-fitting doors; self-closing washroom doors; and good ventilation.

If there is any shortcoming, corrective action is undertaken. Also, the team ensures that there is a regular system of work instructions, inspection, and prevention in place for the building, equipment, and personnel. Guidelines and standard operating procedures (SOPs) are provided by the CFIA and other government agencies. Further, there should be a procedure for product recall (i.e., a product coding system and records).

The following product and process background information is required:

1. Describe the product, source of raw material, product characteristics, ingredients, packaging, how the product is used, shelf life, where the product will be sold, labelling instructions, and distribution control.

2. Draw the process flow diagram and number the steps of the process. Also, draw the plant layout diagram, identifying each operation by its number and showing the material flows by arrows.

3. Identify all of the regulatory action points (RAP), which are the points in the process where safety control is mandated by the government. These usually include the receiving point(s) of raw material(s) and the shipping point of the products, but may also include other critical points such as where thawing of fish and the labelling of fish cans take place. SOPs are provided for most of these activities, specifying parameters such as time and temperature. If there is no SOP for a RAP, the company needs to define one. The RAP plan specifies the control measures (such as SOPs), the inspection (detection) procedures (what, how, frequency, and who), and corrective actions.

There are three main HACCP steps:

1. Perform hazard analysis:

   - For each ingredient/processing step, identify potential hazard(s). To do this, one can use the reference database of CFIA; books on microbiology, food processing, and plant sanitation; Health Canada reports on illnesses, recalls, and complaints; and scientific papers. Hazards are classified into biological, chemical, and physical.

   - Determine if the potential hazard is significant and provide justification.

   - Provide preventive measures for significant hazards in process design (e.g., include pasteurization operation).

2. Determine the critical control points (CCPs):

   - For every ingredient/processing step with one or more significant hazard(s), if there will not be a subsequent step that would eliminate the hazard, then this step is a CCP. The receiving point of raw material, the closing point of the cans, and the sterilization point are typical CCPs.

3. Establish the HACCP plan:

   - For each CCP/significant hazard, determine a control/preventive (assurance) measure, the critical limits, the monitoring procedure (what, how, frequency, and who), the corrective action, documentation and record-keeping procedure, and verification procedure.

Even though HACCP helps to prevent food safety issues, it cannot guarantee food safety, as evidenced by the "Maple Leaf Foods' Listeria Outbreak" OM in Action.

---

[9] http://www.inspection.gc.ca/english/fssa/polstrat/haccp/haccpe.shtml; http://www.omafra.gov.on.ca/english /food/foodsafety/processors/haccp.htm.

OM in Action   www.mapleleaf.com/

Maple Leaf Foods' Listeria Outbreak

In the summer of 2008, 57 people got sick with Listeria and 22 of them died. Listeria is a little-known bacterial disease that can develop in cold-cut ready-to-eat meats and raw vegetables such as coleslaw. Cooking these to high temperatures will kill the bacteria. Listeria is very dangerous to older people (typically living in long-term care homes) and those with chronic illness.

The source of the 2008 Listeria outbreak was traced back to Sure Slice roast beef and corned beef produced in the Bartor Road, Toronto, plant of Maple Leaf Foods. Even though this plant had a food safety program (daily hygiene and sanitation as part of good manufacturing practice) and was HACCP certified, these did not stop the Listeria.

Investigation showed that microbiologists using swabs in their daily environmental sampling of production lines and equipment had occasionally (every two to three weeks) found Listeria starting a year earlier. In this case, the workers just sanitized all contact surfaces, but the quality assurance (QA) staff did not look for the root cause of Listeria. The sanitizing would temporarily remove the bacteria.

There was no product (meat) testing for Listeria. Nor did the QA staff inform the Canadian Food Inspection Agency (CFIA) inspectors about Listeria findings. They

Maple Leaf Foods' meat slicing machine being sanitized.
Source: http://www.cpha.ca/uploads/history/achievements/09-lirs -rpt_e.pdf.
Steve Russell/Getty Images

were more concerned with frequently found bacteria such as Salmonella and Escherichia coli.

After the outbreak, intense testing pointed toward two huge industrial Formax meat slicers on lines 8 and 9. It turned out that the bacteria were lodged deep inside the machines in meat residue. In order to completely sanitize the machines, they had to be completely disassembled, which took over one day and hence was never done.

▶ **EXAMPLE 9-1**

The product description is chunk-style tuna, canned in small cans, sealed at the bottom and top, packaged in brine (salt water) or oil, ready-to-eat, with a five-year shelf life, and sold in retail stores.

The company buys the cans, with the bottom already sealed to the wall, but separate can tops. For simplicity, we assume that the tuna is canned fresh (if the tuna is frozen, it has to be thawed first). The process briefly is as follows: after receiving, the fish's head and tail are cut off, and racks of fish are precooked in order to make skinning and deboning easier. Then, the automated canning line cuts the fish into chunks, fits a chunk in a can, adds ingredients, and vacuum-seals the top. Next, baskets of fish cans are sterilized and cooked

further in pressurized steam rooms, washed, dried, and individually weighed and labelled. See the process flow diagram on the next page.

Government regulations require that the tuna not be tainted or decomposed (i.e., should be safe and wholesome), and the can should be accurately labelled with a product code (including the date canned). In addition to sanitation and hygiene of the plant, equipment, and operators, HACCP requirements can be satisfied by the following critical control points and quality control and assurance plans:

Critical Control Point	Quality Assurance Plan	Quality Control Plan
Receiving	Check vessel's records of cooling	Visually inspect and test for toxins (60 fish per lot)
Precooking	Set up standard operating procedures (SOPs), including cooking time and temperature	
Cans and tops	Check manufacturing record of material and SOP	Visually inspect
Close cans		Visually (every half hour) and using tear down test (every four hours) inspect the seams
Pasteurize	Set up SOP, including temperature, time, pressure	
Wash with chlorine		Test residual chlorine in water
Label		Inspect continuously for accuracy

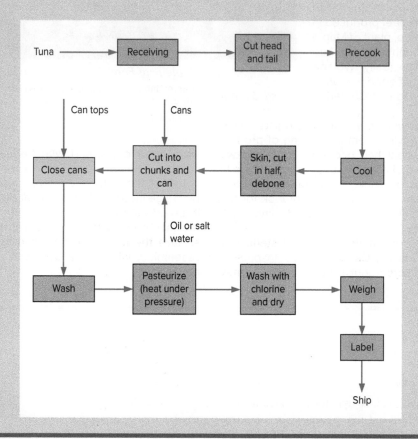

L04 Canada Awards for Excellence (CAE) and Total Quality Management (TQM)

Canada Awards for Excellence recognize outstanding excellence by Canadian organizations in various areas such as quality, healthy workplace, innovation, and mental health. These awards are administered annually by Excellence Canada (formerly the National Quality Institute), an independent not-for-profit organization. Excellence Canada has developed a set of criteria for organizational excellence that also provide a framework for continuous improvement. The six main categories of the criteria, called drivers of excellence, are displayed below. Note that quality is embedded in strategic management of the organization (that is, all functions of the organization are engaged in quality management).

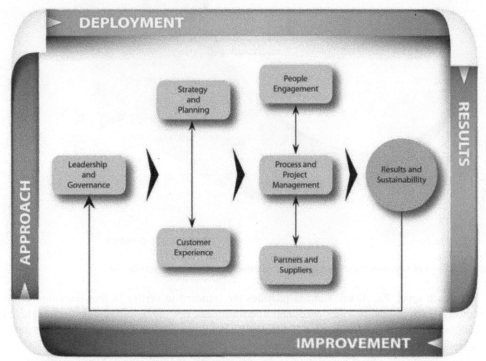

Source: Excellence Canada, page 4 of http://excellence.ca/assets/files/resources/EIW_Brochure.pdf.

These drivers are briefly explained below.[10]

Leadership and governance focuses on creating the culture, values, and overall direction for success. Leadership is about demonstrating good governance and innovation, and fulfilling the organization's legal, ethical, and societal obligations.

Strategy and planning incorporates developing business and improvement plans across all drivers, and monitoring, evaluating, and reporting on the progress in meeting defined strategic goals, as well as goals within all plans. All plans are linked to the organization's strategic plan.

Customer experience examines how the organization engages the customers for satisfaction and success. It includes listening, acting, and reporting on Voice of the Customer feedback.

People engagement examines how workers are treated, encouraged, supported, and enabled to contribute to the organization's overall success. It includes the wellness of employees and their families, including mental and physical wellness and a safe environment.

Process and project management includes a disciplined and common approach toward analyzing and solving process problems and project management across the organization. This facilitates a prevention-based (rather than correction-based) approach to process management.

Partners and suppliers examines the organization's external relationships with other organizations, institutions, and/or alliances that are critical to meeting the strategic objectives. Such working relationships can include suppliers, partnerships (both financial and non-financial) and joint ventures/projects.

To make pursuit of excellence easier, Excellence Canada has divided its certification into four stages or levels with progressively higher expectation for results. As shown in the following figure, the Progressive Excellence Program includes: Level 1: Foundation, Level 2: Advancement, Level 3: Role Model, and Level 4: Sustained World Class Performance.

---

[10]http://www.excellence.ca/assets/files/products/EIW%20Overview.pdf

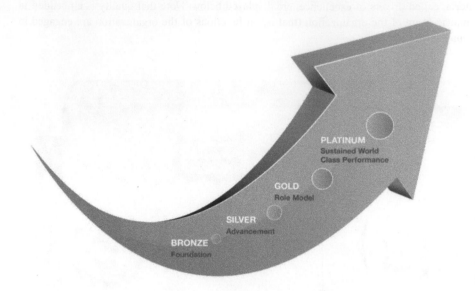

Source: Page 4 of http://www.excellence.ca/assets/files/products/EIW%20Overview.pdf.

For each level, Excellence Canada provides the standard to certify in that level for various frameworks such as quality, excellence-innovation-wellness, healthy workplace, and mental health at work, with minor differences between different types of organizations such as private and public organizations, small businesses, projects, educational institutions, and hospitals.

The following is a brief description of the requirements and key outcomes and results at each level for quality.[11]

Level 1, Bronze, demonstrates a clear commitment to quality. The organization is in the early stages of implementing a long-term strategic focus on quality that promotes good principles and practices as outlined in this standard. There is a commitment to continuous improvement with awareness and education on the standard, and using internal and/or external assessment, either in a pilot project or across the organization, to assist the process of establishing priorities for improvement. The key outcomes are: (a) broad support of the vision, mission, and values, (b) recognition of the importance of embedding quality principles in decision making at all levels of the organization, and (c) policy statements related to quality.

Level 2, Silver, builds on the commitment and foundation established in Bronze. A solid methodology is in place across the organization based on the standard, and has been implemented in key areas. The organization is in transition from a focus on "reacting" to issues to a more "proactive" approach. Positive results are being achieved from improvement efforts in some areas. The key outcomes are: (a) a wider understanding by employees of the organization's strategic approach to quality, (b) having strategic and operational plans in place, and (c) establishment of baseline indicators, measures, and related goals for quality.

Level 3, Gold, builds on the solid implementation of quality established in Silver. There is organization-wide implementation of the strategic focus on quality through the understanding and application of the standard. A sound, systematic approach to quality is in place. The key outcomes are: (a) positive achievements in meeting and exceeding strategic goals, (b) an organization-wide focus on quality issues, (c) positive results across all drivers, across all areas/departments of the organization, and (d) widespread quantifiable improvement as a result of moving from reactive to proactive approaches and practices.

Level 4, Platinum, builds on the achievements and outcomes from the previous three levels with a focus on establishing sustainable practices. The organization has achieved good to excellent results and positive trends from its efforts for overall improvement in quality. The organization can clearly identify sustained improvements against specific objectives and goals. The key

---

[11]Based on pp. 5–6, http://www.excellence.ca/assets/files/products/EIW%20Overview.pdf.

outcomes are: (a) a sound, systemic approach to quality, (b) continuous improvement as a "way of life" with full integration into culture and systems, (c) sustained positive improvements in all areas over at least three years (trend data required), and (d) the organization is viewed as a leader within its sector regarding quality, in terms of knowledge sharing, industry and benchmark leadership, and best practices.

Since the 1980s, the Canada Awards for Excellence have honoured more than 100 Canadian organizations for outstanding quality achievement.[12] For three examples, see the "Michael Garron Hospital" and "Diversicare" OM in Action boxes below, and the "Delta Hotels" OM in Action earlier in this chapter.

 OM in Action

Michael Garron Hospital

Michael Garron Hospital or MGH (formerly Toronto East General Hospital) has about 400 beds, over 2,600 staff, 500 physicians and midwives, and 500 volunteers. It is a full-service teaching hospital affiliated with the University of Toronto. MGH has been awarded the highest level of Canada Awards for Excellence in Quality and Healthy Workplace and, recently, Mental Health at Work.

MGH performs strategic planning every five years. Both strategic plans and annual reviews are shown on the MGH website for patients and employees to see. The performance measures are compared with other Toronto and Ontario hospitals as benchmarks. For those measures that require improvement, action plans are determined

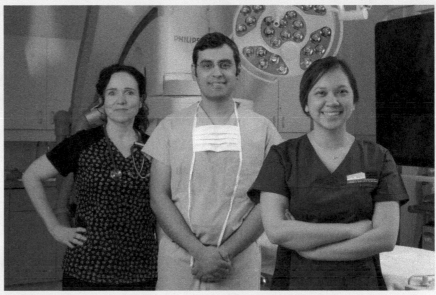

Courtesy of Michael Garron Hospital

and assigned to a corporate support manager. These priorities are well disseminated and reinforced across the organization at operations meetings (weekly) and unit huddles (daily) where patient stories and videos ensure that the voice of the patient is heard, improvement opportunities are identified, and performance of improvement projects are monitored. Unit huddles ("Gemba" walk or "rounding") are part of a daily management system in which leaders visit front line teams/workers and engage in daily problem solving.

This strong culture of continuous improvement is fostered and supported by senior leadership who created the MGH Operational Excellence (OpX) Team of quality facilitators in 2011. Through part-time cross-appointments of clinical staff and support staff (e.g., lab technicians) in OpX and vice versa, and developing venues like the annual Research and Innovation Fair, the team has facilitated many process improvement initiatives.

Several projects have been undertaken. The workplace violence prevention program has reduced staff injuries. The coordinated-care team model improved quality outcomes. The antimicrobial stewardship program promotes the appropriate use of antibiotics. Another project has achieved the lowest emergency department wait times for admitted patients in the local health integration network. Another project has reduced the length of stay for patients with chronic obstructive pulmonary disease by 46 percent.

MGH has designed and documented many processes and procedures—for example, patient flow (to reduce patient stay), continuity of care (to reduce the time until a patient is transferred to the right place for care), patient preparation for various tests or surgeries, a "Good Catch" program for staff to identify errors or safety risks before they occur, and standards for service delivery, appearance, etc.

Sources: http://www.excellence.ca/en/awards/2014-cae-recipients/2014 -cae-profiles/2014-caeprofile-tegh; https://www.researchgate.net /publication/262111813_Creating_and_sustaining_value_Building_a _culture_of_continuous_improvement.

---

[12] http://excellence.ca/en/awards/All_CAE_Recipients_Alpha-1; http://excellence.ca/en/awards/All_CAE _Recipients_Alpha-2

Total Quality Management

total quality management (TQM) An approach that involves everyone in an organization in quality management and continual effort to improve quality and customer satisfaction.

Total quality management (TQM) is an approach to quality management that involves everyone in an organization in quality management and a continual effort to improve quality and customer satisfaction. TQM has three key features: (1) a never-ending push to improve quality, which is referred to as *continuous improvement;* (2) the *involvement of everyone* in the organization in quality management; and (3) the goal of ever-increasing *customer satisfaction.*

We can describe the TQM approach as follows:

1. Find out what customers want. This might involve the use of surveys, focus groups, interviews, or some other technique that integrates the customer's voice in the decision-making process.

2. Design a product that will meet (or exceed) what customers want.

3. Design processes that facilitate doing the job right the first time (called "quality at the source" or *jidoka*). Determine where mistakes are likely to occur and try to prevent them; in this strategy called *poka-yoke*, we incorporate process design elements that prevent mistakes. A simple mistake-proofing aid is a checklist, as used by pilots and some surgeons. Another is the use of bar codes (see the "Medical Barcodes" OM in Action). When mistakes do occur, find out why, and implement corrective actions so that they are less likely to occur again.

4. Keep track of results (TQM is data driven), and use them to guide improvement in the system. Never stop trying to improve (aim for "continuous improvement").

5. Extend these concepts to suppliers/partners.

The iPod Shuffle stops playing music when the earphone jack is unplugged. When the earphone jack is plugged back in, the music resumes right where it left off. This keeps the battery from running down and is an example of poka-yoke.

©Paul Sakuma/AP Images

OM in Action

Medical Barcodes ervice

A report released by the Canadian Institute for Health Information estimates that preventable medical errors kill up to 24,000 Canadians each year. In addition, patients spend more than 1 million extra days in hospital being treated for complications related to their care. One of the most common types of preventable medical errors relates to medication. One in nine adults reported receiving an incorrect dose or type of medication. Health care is a complex environment in which even small errors can maim or kill. Consequently, it is critical for hospitals to find the root causes of these medical errors and then determine how to prevent them from reoccurring.

To address this issue, some hospitals are now using bar codes. With bar code technology, a nurse scans each patient's wristband as well as the medications to be given. This allows nurses who administer drugs to check to make sure the drug, dosage, and timing are all appropriate. If the patient and medication do not match, the nurse will be given a warning. Such innovations hold great promise for reducing the frequency of medication errors.

©Fuse/Getty Images

Source: Health Care in Canada 2004 booklet, Canadian Institute for Health Information, https://secure.cihi.ca/free_products/hcic2004_e.pdf.

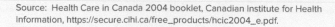

Many companies have successfully implemented TQM. Management must be totally committed and involved by becoming educated in quality, setting and enforcing improvement goals, providing resources, and reviewing progress. If it isn't, TQM will become just another fad that quickly dies and fades away. The above five steps should remind you of the criteria for the Canada Awards for Excellence, described earlier.

It would be incorrect to think of TQM as merely a collection of techniques. Rather, TQM reflects a whole new attitude toward quality. It is about the *culture* of an organization. To truly reap the benefits of TQM, the culture of an organization must change.

Table 9-5 illustrates the differences between cultures of a TQM organization and a more traditional organization.

Aspect	Traditional	TQM
Overall mission	Maximize return on investment	Meet or exceed customer expectations
Objectives	Emphasis on short-term	Balance of long-term and short-term
Management	Not always open; sometimes inconsistent objectives	Open; encourages employee input; consistent objectives
Role of manager	Issues orders; enforces	Coaches, removes barriers, builds trust
Customer requirements	Not highest priority; may be unclear	Highest priority; important to identify and understand
Problems	Assign blame; punish	Identify and resolve
Problem solving	Not systematic; individuals	Systematic; teams
Improvement	Erratic	Continuous
Supplier relations	Adversarial	Partners
Jobs	Narrow, specialized; much individual effort	Broad, more general; much team effort
Focus	Product-oriented	Process-oriented

◀ **TABLE 9-5**

Comparing the cultures of TQM and traditional organizations.

 OM in Action

Diversicare

Achieving customer and employee satisfaction in the retirement and nursing home industry is not an easy task. Diversicare—based in Mississauga, Ontario, and now called Verve Senior Living—operates 35 retirement homes and long-term-care facilities in Ontario and the West. Some of these are owned by Diversicare and the others are managed by Diversicare, some with staff from another company. Before 1993, there were huge discrepancies in services offered across its facilities and a lot of staff turnover. In 1993, a committee of Diversicare employees was formed to identify how to improve the quality of operations. The result was the "Continuous Quality Improvement" (CQI) initiative, designed to encourage employees to achieve excellence in quality of care.

CQI has four crucial elements:

1. *Key indicators:* Continual measuring and monitoring of specific health care issues to ensure the effectiveness of programs and services.

2. *Human resources:* Training of management and staff, and development of management systems to achieve optimal use of human resources.

3. *Commitment:* Active encouragement of individual initiatives to implement improvements in the quality of care.

4. *Empowerment:* Empowering caregivers to review existing mechanisms and to make recommendations to improve the quality of life for residents.

CQI involves focus not only on the customers but also on the processes. In order to achieve quality goals, a common mission and vision was created. The company focused its quality initiative on improving customer satisfaction and employee recruitment, development, and reward. For example, Diversicare looked at recruitment, selection, and retention processes. Each home identified the best workers and set up a "talent team." The talent teams took a central role in recruitment and selection, and mentored the new staff. Management took a cheerleader role, encouraging staff to participate in the CQI program.

CQI has 16 key indicators that measure a host of employee and resident concerns such as safety (e.g., falls, bedsores, work injuries). The company also added eight quality of life indicators, including a "key wish" for residents. Diversicare constantly looks for ways to improve these indicators. Initiatives from all levels within the organization are celebrated and shared through an annual CQI conference, which promotes the exchange of best practices within the organization.

In 2015, the company rebranded itself as Verve (meaning spirited effort), added the new position of executive chef, upgraded its financial system, and introduced a management training program. Diversicare (Verve) has won the highest level of Canada Awards for Excellence in Quality.

Sources: http://www.excellence.ca/en/awards/2012-cae-recipients/2012-cae-profiles/2012-caeprofile-dcms; http://excellence.ca/en/awards/2012-cae-recipients/2012-caevideo-dcms; http://excellence.ca/en/awards/2015-cae-recipients/2015-cae-profiles/2015-caeprofile-diversicare.

Courtesy of Diversicare Canada Mangement Services Co.

L05 Problem Solving and Continuous Improvement

Problem solving is one of the basic activities in quality improvement. In order to be successful, problem solving should follow a standard approach. Table 9-6 describes the basic steps used in the problem solving.

TABLE 9-6 ▶

Basic steps in problem solving.

Step 1 Recognize and define the problem.
Recognize the problem. Form a quality improvement team. Define the problem. Develop performance measure(s).
Step 2 Collect data.
The solution to the problem must be based on facts.
Step 3 Analyze the problem.
Determine possible causes.
Step 4 Generate potential solution(s).
Address the root cause.
Step 5 Choose a solution and implement it.
Use the performance measure(s) and select the best solution.
Step 6 Implement the solution.
Put the solution into effect. Keep everyone informed.
Step 7 Monitor the solution to see if it accomplishes the goal.
If the results are acceptable, *standardize* the new solution. If not, modify the solution or return to Step 2.

A similar methodology is the **plan-do-study-act (PDSA) cycle**, which is testing a change by developing a *plan* to test the change, carrying out the test (*do*), observing and learning from the consequences (*study*), and determining what modifications should be made to the test (*act*). The cycle, also referred to as the *Deming cycle,* is illustrated in Figure 9-1. Representing the improvement process with a circle underscores its continuing nature.

> **plan-do-study-act (PDSA) cycle** Testing a change by developing a *plan* to test the change, carrying out the test (*do*), observing and learning from the consequences (*study*), and determining what modifications should be made to the test (*act*).

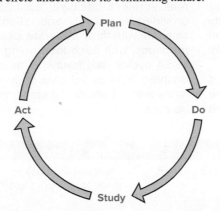

◀ **FIGURE 9-1**

The PDSA cycle.

See the "Royal University Hospital Emergency Department" OM in Action for an application of PDSA.

 OM in Action   www.saskatoonhealthregion.ca

Royal University Hospital Emergency Department

An in-depth study of emergency department wait times and service times was conducted at multiple hospitals throughout Saskatchewan in an effort to reduce inefficiencies and improve patient flow. Flow data collected from 1,728 patients reveals that on average each patient spent close to five hours in the emergency department, of which nearly half was spent in service. This is highly problematic because not only do long wait times prolong patient suffering, but they can also lead to further deterioration of a patient's condition.

When a patient arrives at an emergency department, he/she is first seen by a triage nurse who will perform a preliminary assessment and assign one of five Canadian Triage and Acuity Scale classifications. Acute cases are given higher priority. The following patient flowchart displays the flow of a patient through a typical hospital emergency department:

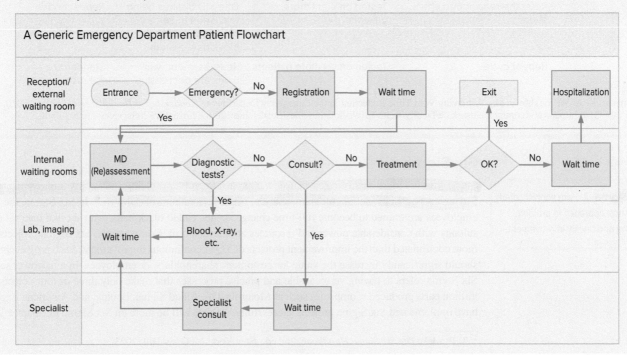

The flow data also showed the following: The initial wait time for non-urgent cases was approximately 1 hour; the longest wait times, other than the initial wait, were for (a) a hospital bed (3.5 hours), (b) a specialist consultation (2 hours), and (c) a physician (MD) reassessment (0.5 hour). Due to budgetary constraints, the quality improvement team decided to focus its investigation on the process of MD reassessment at Saskatoon's Royal University Hospital (RUH).

During MD reassessment, one frequently observed problem involved nurses who spent too much time attempting to find the assigned physician for a given patient. There was no whiteboard or other visual tool to indicate which physicians were assigned to which patients, leading to widespread confusion. MDs also did not know whether their patients were ready for reassessment because laboratory results were not provided in a timely and reliable manner. The team came up with three separate ideas for alleviating these problems, with each idea going through two or three PDSA cycles (see below). This problem-solving effort enabled RUH to achieve large reductions in waiting times with no additional staff and only minimal materials cost.

Idea	Cycle	Plan	Do	Study	Act
1	1	Create a colour code for the MDs. Write patient's name on a whiteboard, and mark colour of MD after it.	Carried out as planned	Clerk was too busy to mark. Markers got lost.	Try different colour-coding system
	2	Provide coloured dots.	Carried out as planned	One clerk adopts well; second stops process	Retrain the second clerk
	3	Also, train MD to identify own patients with coloured dots.	Carried out as planned	Process well accepted by MDs and clerks	Try next change idea
2	1	Create visual reminder of "ready for reassessment" on whiteboard. Use magnet reminder.	Magnets do not stick well (whiteboard is covered with plexiglas)	Not able to carry out the plan	Put sticky metal strips on plexiglas
	2	Retry magnets	Carried out as planned	Nurses forget to use magnet	Need a solution
3	1	Create a check sheet for nurses to keep track of times and remind them to use magnets	Tested on four patients	Nurses like the check sheet. MDs want check sheet to note when a resident sees the patient first	Redesign check sheet to show resident information
	2	Retry the redesigned check sheet	Tested on eight more patients	One MD dislikes being told when to see a patient, but doesn't block new system	Repeat cycle
	3	Repeat cycle	Tested on six more patients	Reassessment wait times are decreasing	Standardize the process

Source: K. A. Willoughby et al., "Achieving Wait Time Reduction in the Emergency Department," *Leadership in Health Services, 23*(4), 2010, pp. 304–319; http://www.commerce.usask.ca/faculty/Keith%20Willoughby/files/Leadership%20in%20Health%20Services%202010.pdf.

Six Sigma

Six Sigma A more sophisticated statistical approach to problem solving and quality improvement.

Six Sigma is a more sophisticated statistical approach to problem solving and quality improvement. Six Sigma has five steps: define, measure, analyze, improve, and control (DMAIC). In Six Sigma, the best employees are trained to become full-time change agents, called black belts, who act like internal consultants with considerable power and resources at their disposal. Consequently, Six Sigma projects are more coordinated than the improvement projects of TQM/continuous improvement. Each project chosen should significantly increase the value for customers, shareholders, or employees. In a narrower sense, Six Sigma refers to having very capable and precise processes that make only three or four defects per million parts produced. Companies such as Motorola, GE, Allied Signal, Boeing, and American Express have implemented Six Sigma projects successfully.[13] There will be more on Six Sigma in Chapter 10.

[13] T. Pyzdek, *The Six Sigma Handbook,* 2nd ed., New York: McGraw-Hill, 2003.

Basic Quality Tools

A quality improvement team can use a number of quality tools that aid in data collection and interpretation, and provide the basis for decision making. The following seven tools are often referred to as the *seven basic quality tools:* process flow diagram, check sheet, histogram, Pareto chart, scatter diagram, control chart, and cause-and-effect diagram. Figure 9-2 provides a quick overview of the seven tools.

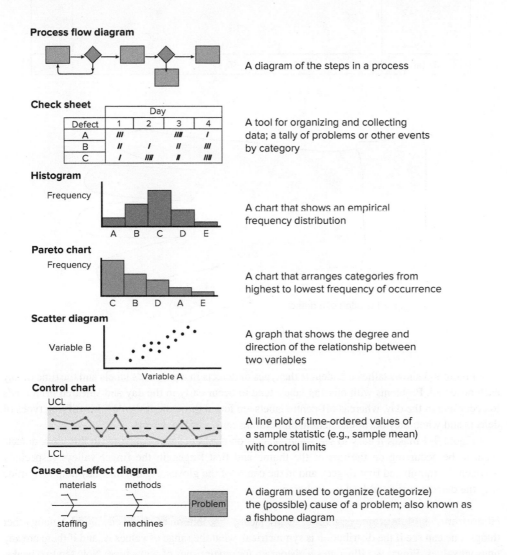

Process flow diagram

A diagram of the steps in a process

Check sheet

Defect	Day			
	1	2	3	4
A	///		////	/
B	//	/	//	///
C	/	////	//	////

A tool for organizing and collecting data; a tally of problems or other events by category

Histogram

Frequency

A B C D E

A chart that shows an empirical frequency distribution

Pareto chart

Frequency

C B D A E

A chart that arranges categories from highest to lowest frequency of occurrence

Scatter diagram

Variable B

Variable A

A graph that shows the degree and direction of the relationship between two variables

Control chart

UCL

LCL

A line plot of time-ordered values of a sample statistic (e.g., sample mean) with control limits

Cause-and-effect diagram

materials   methods

Problem

staffing   machines

A diagram used to organize (categorize) the (possible) cause of a problem; also known as a fishbone diagram

◀ **FIGURE 9-2**

The seven basic quality tools.

Process Flow Diagram. A *process flow diagram* is a diagram of the steps in a process and the movement of material between the steps. Its variations include a flowchart, service blueprint, and swim lane diagram. Another name for this chart is *process map.* As a problem-solving or quality improvement tool, a process map can help investigators identify possible points in a process where problems or opportunities for improvement occur. Process maps were described in Chapter 6.

Check Sheet. A **check sheet** is a sheet of paper that provides a format for recording and organizing data in a way that facilitates collection and analysis. Check sheets are designed on the basis of what the users are attempting to learn by collecting data. Many different formats can be used for a check sheet and there are many different types of check sheets. One frequently used form of check sheet deals with types of defects and when they occur (Figure 9-3), another with location of defects (Figure 9-4).

check sheet A sheet of paper that provides a format for recording and organizing data in a way that facilitates collection and analysis.

FIGURE 9-3 ▶

An example of a check sheet identifying the type and time of defect occurring in a product's labels.

Day	Time	Type of Defect					
		Missing label	Off-centre	Smeared print	Loose or folded	Other	
M	8–9	IIII	II				6
	9–10		III				3
	10–11	I	III	I			5
	11–12		I		I	I (Torn)	3
	1–2		I				1
	2–3		II	III	I		6
	3–4		II	HHI			8
Total		5	14	10	2	1	32

FIGURE 9-4 ▶

A check sheet that identifies the location of defects on a rubber glove.

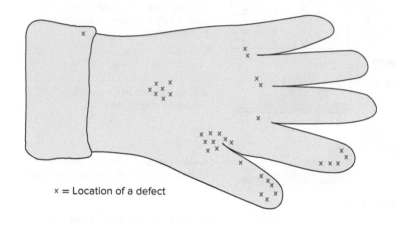

× = Location of a defect

Figure 9-3 shows tallies that denote the types of defects in a product's labels and the time of day each occurred. Problems with missing labels tend to occur early in the day and smeared print tends to occur late in the day, whereas off-centre labels are found throughout the day. Identifying types of defects and when they occur can help in pinpointing causes of the defects.

Figure 9-4 makes it easy to see where defects on a product are occurring. In this case, defects seem to be occurring on the tips of the thumb and first finger, in the finger valleys (especially between the thumb and first finger), and in the centre of the gloves. Again, this may help determine why the defects occur and lead to a solution.

histogram A chart of the frequency distribution of observed values.

Histogram. A **histogram** is a chart of the frequency distribution of observed values. Among other things, one can see if the distribution is symmetrical, what the range of values is, and if there are any unusual values. Figure 9-5 illustrates a histogram for repair times of a machine. Note the two peaks. A possible cause might be that there are two types of breakdowns: those requiring minor repairs, and others requiring major repairs.

FIGURE 9-5 ▶

A histogram of a machine's repair times.

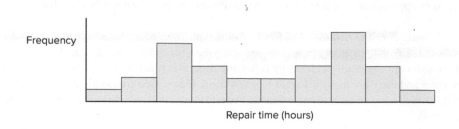

Repair time (hours)

Pareto Analysis. Pareto analysis is a technique for focusing attention on the most important problem (or opportunity for improvement). The Pareto concept is that relatively few factors account for a large percentage of the total problems (e.g., complaints, defects), thus making these few factors important. More specifically, the Pareto concept states that approximately 80 percent of the problems are from 20 percent of the types of problems. For instance, 80 percent of machine breakdowns are from 20 percent of the types of breakdowns, and 80 percent of the product defects are from 20 percent of the types of defects. The idea is to focus on resolving the most important problems first.

Often, it is useful to prepare a chart that shows the number of occurrences by category (type), arranged in order of frequency. Figure 9-6 illustrates such a chart corresponding to the check sheet shown in Figure 9-3. The dominance of off-centre labels becomes apparent. Presumably, the manager and employees would first focus on trying to resolve this problem. Once they accomplish that, they could address the remaining defects in a similar fashion.

Pareto analysis Technique for focusing attention on the most important problem (or opportunity for improvement).

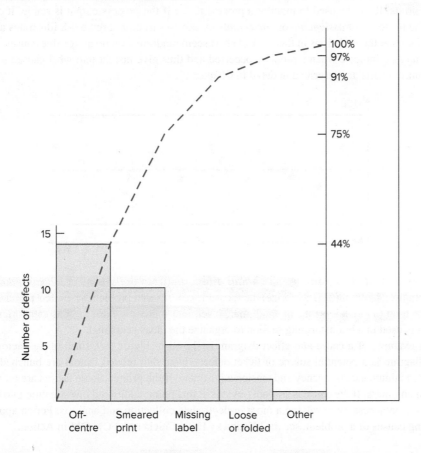

◀ **FIGURE 9-6**

A Pareto chart based on data in Figure 9-3.

Sometimes each defect type has a different consequence, and the company may assign a different weight to each. Then, the weighted value (Weight × Frequency) will be used in the Pareto analysis. For example, an overnight package delivery company may have a lower number of lost packages than number of abandoned calls to its call centres due to busy operators, but the lost package error is much more serious.

Scatter Diagram. A scatter diagram is a plot of pairs of observations of two variables that can show the correlation between the two variables. A correlation may point to a cause of a problem. In the scatter diagram of Figure 9-7 there is a *positive* (upward-sloping) relationship between the humidity and the number of errors per hour. High values of humidity result in high numbers of errors. On the other hand, a *negative* (downward-sloping) relationship would mean that when the value of one variable is high, the value of the other variable is low.

The higher the correlation between the two variables, the less scatter in the points; the points will tend to line up. Conversely, if there were little or no relationship between two variables, the points would be completely scattered. In Figure 9-7, the correlation between humidity and errors is high, because the points appear to scatter closely along an imaginary relationship line.

scatter diagram A plot of pairs of observations of two variables that can show the correlation between the two variables.

FIGURE 9-7 ▶

A scatter diagram.

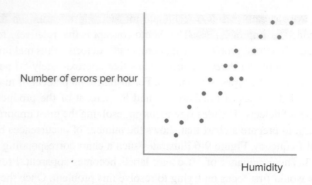

Number of errors per hour

Humidity

control chart A time-ordered plot of a sample statistic with control limits.

Control Chart. A **control chart** is a line plot of time-ordered values of a sample statistic with control limits. It can be used to monitor a process to see if the process output is stable. It can help detect the presence of *assignable* or *correctable* causes of variation. Figure 9-8 illustrates a control chart. Note that the variations in this control chart seem random, with no assignable causes. Control charts can also indicate when a problem occurred and thus give insight into what caused the problem. Control charts are described in detail in Chapter 10.

FIGURE 9-8 ▶

A control chart.

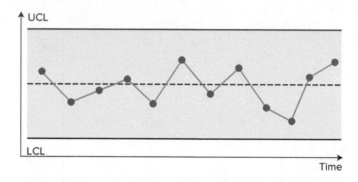

UCL

LCL

Time

cause-and-effect diagram A diagram used to organize (categorize) the (possible) causes of a problem (the effect); also called a fishbone or Ishikawa diagram.

Cause-and-Effect Diagram. A **cause-and-effect diagram** or *fishbone* or *Ishikawa diagram* is a diagram used to organize (categorize) the (possible) causes of a problem (the effect). Usually, four Ms—machine (and equipment), method, manpower, and materials—are used as categories. Often this tool is used in a brainstorming session to organize the ideas generated.

An example of a cause-and-effect diagram is shown in Figure 9-9. Each of the factors listed in the diagram is a potential source of ticket defects. Note that related factors are bunched up; for example, maintenance frequency and tension adjustment of the printer. Some factors are more likely causes than others. If the cause is still not obvious at this point, additional investigation into the *root cause* may be necessary, involving a more in-depth data collection and analysis. For an application of finding causes of a problem, see the "Kentucky Fried Chicken (KFC)" OM in Action.

FIGURE 9-9 ▶

Cause-and-effect diagram for ticket defects.

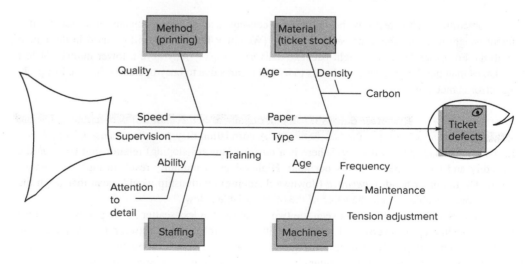

OM in Action

Kentucky Fried Chicken (KFC)

In the 1990s, KFC implemented an improvement program in its four Oklahoma City restaurants to reduce the drive-through service times, which were considered excessive. KFC bought and installed electronic timers to measure wait times. The window "hang time" was about two minutes on average. The regional manager set a goal to reduce this time by 10 percent at a time. When the window hang time exceeded the goal, a buzzer would go off and the employee had to write down the reason for the delay in a "blocker log."

The more frequent causes were identified and solutions were sought for them by the improvement team.

For example, sufficient working headsets and spare batteries were provided, layout was changed to reduce the distance employees walked, and rarely ordered items were discontinued and variety of desserts was reduced. This process of continuous improvement was continued for about a year (several more solutions were implemented such as pricing items so that they cost whole dollars after tax) until the average hang time was reduced to one minute.

Source: U. M. Apte and C. C. Reynolds, "Quality Management at Kentucky Fried Chicken," *Interfaces* 25(3), May/June 1995, pp. 6–21.

In addition to the seven basic quality tools above, another useful tool is the run chart.

Run Chart. A **run chart** is a time plot that can be used to track the values of a variable over time. This can aid in identifying trends or other patterns that may be occurring. Figure 9-10 provides an example of a run chart showing a decreasing trend in accident frequency over time.

> **run chart** A time plot that can be used to track the values of a variable over time.

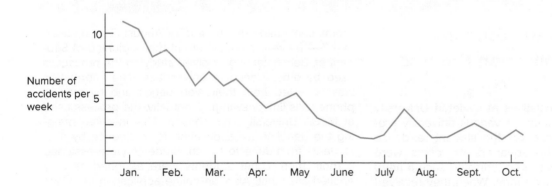

◀ **FIGURE 9-10**

A run chart.

Methods for Problem Solving and Continuous Improvement

Some useful methods for problem solving and quality improvement are brainstorming, affinity diagram, quality circle, interviewing, benchmarking, 5W2H, 5 Whys, and reaching consensus.

Brainstorming. **Brainstorming** is a technique for generating a free flow of ideas on finding causes and solutions, and implementing the solutions in a group of people. In successful brainstorming, criticism is absent, no single member is allowed to dominate sessions, and all ideas are welcomed.

Affinity Diagram. An **affinity diagram** shows the relationships among large numbers of ideas. The process of constructing an affinity diagram is as follows. Each participant writes each of his/her ideas on a sticky note. Then, all stickers are posted on a wall or board and moved around to form similar groups. An example of its use was a project to identify ways to speed up flow of passengers at the security screening stations of airports.

> **brainstorming** Technique for generating a free flow of ideas on finding causes and solutions, and implementing the solutions in a group of people.

> **affinity diagram** Shows the relationship among large amounts of ideas.

quality circle A group of workers in the same department who meet to discuss ways of improving the products or processes.

Quality Circle. A **quality circle** is a group of workers in the same department who meet to discuss ways of improving the products and processes. Quality circles are not only a valuable source of worker input, but also can motivate workers by demonstrating management interest in worker ideas. Quality circles are usually less structured and more informal than quality improvement teams. The major distinction is the amount of authority. Typically, quality circles have had very little authority to implement any but minor changes; quality improvement teams are sometimes given a great deal of authority.

Interviewing. Interviewing is used to collect information about a problem (or opportunity for improvement). Internal problems may require interviewing employees; external problems may require interviewing customers and suppliers.

benchmarking Process of measuring an organization's performance against the best organization in the same or another industry.

Benchmarking. **Benchmarking** is the process of measuring an organization's performance against the best organization in the same or another industry. Its purpose is to establish a standard against which performance is judged, and to possibly learn how to improve. Once a benchmark has been identified, the goal is to meet or exceed that standard through improvements.

Selecting an industry leader provides insight into what competitors are doing. However, competitors may be reluctant to share this information. Selecting organizations in other industries is an alternative. For example, Xerox uses many benchmarks: for employee involvement, Procter & Gamble; for quality process, Florida Power & Light and Toyota; for high-volume production, Kodak and Canon; for bill collection, American Express; for research and development, AT&T and Hewlett-Packard; for order filling and distribution, L.L. Bean and Hershey Foods; and for daily scheduling, Cummins Engine. For an example of benchmarking, see the "Benchmarking the Student Residence Application Process at Carleton University" OM in Action.

 OM in Action

Benchmarking the Student Residence Application Process at Carleton University

The Office of Quality Initiatives at Carleton University uses benchmarking to improve various university processes. One such project was the student residence application process. Three-quarters of rooms were reserved for new students who indicated such a need in their entrance application form. When they received conditional acceptance in February, they also received a form for residence. However, they had until June to apply. Other students could also apply but were put on a waiting list. All applicants were assigned to residences in July in a batch operation. However, reassignment of rooms continued until the end of August. This resulted in a 3–4 percent vacancy rate at the beginning of September. Benchmarking involved studying the processes used by other Canadian universities. The information was collected from their web pages and by making phone calls (interviewing). Eventually, the process used at McGill University was chosen. This involved bringing the deadline for application for residence by new students from June to March. Students were assigned a room then. Other students were assigned as they applied after that. Also, an online application form was created to make the process easier. The new process resulted in a vacancy rate of less than 1 percent at the beginning of September.

Sources: M. J. Armstrong, "Benchmarking Goes to School," *Quality Progress,* May 2007, 40(5), pp. 54–58; http://www.carleton.ca/qualityinitiatives.

5W2H A method of asking questions about a problem that begin with *what, why, where, when, who, how,* and *how much.*

5W2H. Asking questions about the problem (or opportunity for improvement) can lead to important insights about the cause of the problem, as well as potential ways to improve it. One method, called **5W2H**, asks questions about a problem that begin with *what, why, where, when, who, how,* and *how much.*

Sometimes posing the questions in a negative way may help. For example, in addition to asking, "Where is the defect on the object?" also ask, "Where else could the defect have been on the object, but isn't?" In addition to asking, "When did the defect occur?" also ask, "When else could the defect have occurred, but didn't?"

5 Whys. **5 Whys** involves systematically drilling down to a real root cause of a problem by asking "Why?" five times. It is important not to skip levels of questions, but to ask logical questions summarizing the observations from earlier questions. If there is more than one answer for a *why* question, each answer should be subjected to another *why* question. You reach the true root cause when the answer to your question is a process, policy, or person. Sometimes, this may take more or fewer than five times. Sometimes, there is more than one root cause. The following figure shows an example of 5 Whys analysis of "Getting caught speeding."

> **5 Whys** Systematically drilling down to a real root cause of a problem by asking "Why" five times.

Five whys analysis example / ONLINE FIGURE 1

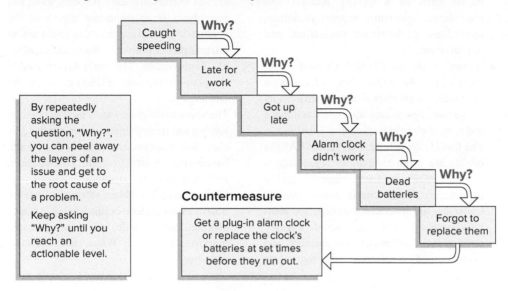

A, Vidyasagar. (Quality Progress, February 2015). "The Art of Root Cause Analysis", 48 (2). Online Figure 1, Five why analysis example. Permission granted by ASQ.

Reaching Consensus. The team approach works best when it reaches decisions on the best solution based on consensus. This may be achieved using one or more of the following methods:

1. *List reduction* is applied to a list of possible solutions. Its purpose is to clarify and reduce the list of items by posing questions about affordability, feasibility, and likelihood of solving the problem (or improving the quality).

2. A *balance sheet* approach lists the pros and cons of each item and focuses discussion on important issues.

3. *Paired comparisons* is a process by which each item on a list is compared with every other item, two at a time. For each pair, team members select the preferred item. This approach forces a choice between items. It works best when the list of items is small—say, five or fewer.

Summary

- Quality has evolved from an artisan's workmanship to quality control inspectors, to quality assurance and prevention of defects, and finally to incorporation of quality in the company strategy as total quality management.
- Quality of goods is defined according to various dimensions such as performance, aesthetics, reliability, and durability.
- Service quality dimensions include convenience, responsiveness, timeliness, assurance, and courtesy/empathy.

- Quality is determined during product design, process design, production, and use.
- Costs of quality include external and internal failure, detection, and prevention costs.
- Failure cost increases the closer the product gets to the customer.
- Traditionally most measurable characteristics of a product are specified by the designer as a range of values between the lower spec limit and upper spec limit. A unit is considered defective if its characteristic falls outside the

spec limits. However, according to Taguchi quality loss function, customer dissatisfaction increases at a faster rate the larger the deviation of the characteristic from the target value.

- The chapter includes a description of the key contributors (gurus) to quality management: Deming, Juran, Feigenbaum, and Crosby.
- ISO 9001 is a standard for a quality management system (QMS). It is made up of requirements such as a quality manual and procedures, leadership, support resources, operations, performance evaluation, and improvement.
- Hazard Analysis Critical Control Point (HACCP) is also a QMS, but its focus is on food safety. It involves finding control points for hazards and setting up quality assurance and control plans at each control point.
- The Canada Awards for Excellence (CAE) in quality are given annually to organizations that have shown great achievement in quality management. Their criteria involve areas of leadership and governance, strategy and planning, customer experience, people engagement, process and project management, and partners and suppliers. The Progressive

Excellence Program has divided the certification into four levels to make it easier to achieve it. CAE requirements lead to total quality management.

- Total quality management (TQM) is a never-ending pursuit of higher quality that involves everyone in an organization. The driving force is customer satisfaction and a key activity is continuous improvement. Training of managers and workers in quality concepts, tools, and procedures is an important aspect of the approach. Quality improvement teams are an integral part of problem solving and continuous improvement. The methodology used is the plan-do-study-act (PDSA) cycle (or the Deming cycle).
- The seven basic quality tools used in problem solving and quality improvement are the process flow diagram, check sheet, histogram, Pareto chart, scatter diagram, control chart, and cause-and-effect diagram.
- Methods used in problem solving and quality improvement include brainstorming, affinity diagram, quality circle, interviewing, benchmarking, 5W2H, 5 Whys, and reaching consensus.

Key Terms

5 Whys	control chart	quality assurance
5W2H	dimensions of quality of goods	quality at the source
affinity diagram	external failure costs	quality circle
appraisal (detection) costs	HACCP	quality control
benchmarking	histogram	quality management system (QMS)
brainstorming	internal failure costs	run chart
cause-and-effect diagram	ISO 9001	scatter diagram
check sheet	ISO 14001	Six Sigma
conformance to design specification during production	Pareto analysis	Taguchi quality loss function
continuous improvement	plan-do-study-act (PDSA) cycle	total quality management (TQM)
cost of quality	prevention costs	zero defects
	quality	

Solved Problems

Problem 1

A town's local police issued the following 20 traffic tickets on a winter's weekend. Make a check sheet and a Pareto chart for the types of infractions tickets were issued for. If the police want to reduce the number of traffic infractions, what type of traffic infraction should they focus on?

Ticket Number	Infraction	Ticket Number	Infraction
1	Excessive speed	11	Expired licence
2	Expired licence	12	DUI
3	Improper turn	13	Improper turn
4	Excessive speed	14	DUI
5	DUI	15	Excessive speed
6	DUI	16	DUI
7	Excessive speed	17	DUI
8	DUI	18	DUI
9	Improper turn	19	Excessive speed
10	DUI	20	DUI

Solution

Check sheet (list the types of infractions, tally, frequencies):

Infraction	Tally	Frequency
Excessive speed	卌	5
Expired licence	//	2
Improper turn	///	3
Driving under influence (DUI)	卌 卌	10

Pareto diagram (array infractions from highest frequency to lowest):

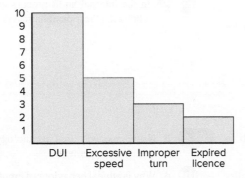

The police should focus on reducing driving under the influence (DUI), which accounts for 50 percent of all traffic infractions.

Problem 2

A friend of yours has told you that no matter how much she studies, she does badly in exams. Help her set up a cause-and-effect diagram for her problem.

Solution

The "effect" is "does not do well in exams." The possible causes can be categorized as four Ms: machine, method, manpower, and material. Some of the causes under each category are:

Machine:	Does not know how to use computer/Internet/library effectively to study.
Method:	Does not know how to study effectively; does not spend enough time studying.
Manpower:	Does not have the right background (e.g., lacks math skills); has problems memorizing things.
Material:	Does not know what is important to study (types of questions in the exam); does not have the textbook and study guide.

Discussion and Review Questions

LO1 **1.** List and briefly explain the dimensions of goods and service quality.

LO1 **2.** Explain the term *conformance to design specification during production.*

LO1 **3.** Contrast quality assurance, control, and improvement.

LO1 **4.** Use the dimensions of quality to describe typical characteristics of these goods and services:
   a. A television set.
   b. A restaurant meal (a good).
   c. A restaurant meal (a service).
   d. Painting a house.

LO1 **5.** Describe the cost of quality, and its categories. Give an example for each category for a fast-food restaurant.

LO1 **6.** Describe the evolution of quality management.

LO1 **7.** Select one of the quality gurus and briefly describe his contributions to quality management.

LO2 **8.** What is ISO 9001 and why is it important for global businesses to have ISO 9001 certification?

LO2 **9.** Briefly describe the important requirements of ISO 9001.

LO3 **10.** Describe HACCP.

LO4 **11.** Briefly describe the criteria for the Canada Awards for Excellence in quality.

LO4 **12.** What are the three key features of TQM?

LO5 **13.** Briefly describe each of the seven basic quality tools.

LO5 **14.** Briefly explain each of these tools:
   a. Brainstorming.
   b. Benchmarking.
   c. Run chart.

LO5 **15.** Explain each of these methods:
   a. The plan-do-study-act (PDSA) cycle.
   b. The 5W2H approach.

LO5 **16.** List the steps of problem solving.

LO5 **17.** Is there a specific set and sequence of basic quality tools used in problem solving and quality improvement?

LO2–4 **18.** Contrast ISO 9001, ISO 14001, HACCP, and CAE.

LO2 **19.** Why is ISO 14001 more important now than ever?

LO3 **20.** Why didn't Maple Leaf Foods' HACCP system prevent the Listeria outbreak?

LO5 **21.** What is an affinity diagram and how is it constructed?

LO5 **22.** Why is the word *cycle* in "PDSA cycle"?

LO2 **23.** In the internal audit process map of ERCO Worldwide, who is the "responsible manager/supervisor"?

Taking Stock

LO1 **1.** What trade-offs are involved in deciding how much to spend on quality improvement?

LO4 **2.** According to TQM, who needs to be involved in quality management?

LO1–5 **3.** Name one way that technology has had an impact on quality management.

LO4 **4.** Why is ethical behaviour of employees important in TQM?

Critical Thinking Exercises

LO1 & 5 **1.** Consider an auto assembly operation. What kinds of quality problems can arise during assembly? Name one or two. How can each be fixed? Prevented?

LO1 **2.** A few years ago, Ford asked Mazda to build some of the transmissions for a car it was selling in North America.[14] Both Ford and Mazda were supposed to build to identical specifications. Ford adopted the traditional view of quality, that a part is good if its dimension falls within spec limits. Mazda adopted the Taguchi quality loss function view of quality. After the cars had been on the road for a while, it became clear that Ford's transmissions were generating far higher warranty costs and many more customer complaints about friction noise and vibration. Ford disassembled and carefully measured samples of transmission gears made by both companies. Both companies' gear dimensions were within the spec limits but Ford's were uniformly distributed within the spec limits whereas Mazda's were Normally distributed centred on the targets. Explain how two randomly chosen Ford interacting gears would have higher probability of causing friction or vibration than two randomly chosen Mazda interacting gears.

---

[14] https://hbr.org/1990/01/robust-quality.

Experiential Learning Exercises

 1. Identify a bad-quality product you recently bought. Describe the quality problem and suggest how it could have been avoided.

 2. Identify a problem you have faced that doesn't seem to have an obvious root cause. Use the 5 Whys method to find the root cause.

Internet Exercises

 1. Visit http://www.theacsi.org/customer-satisfaction-benchmarks/benchmarks-by-industry, choose Automobiles & Light Vehicles industry, and observe the customer satisfaction scores of the companies in this industry. Do the indices agree with your knowledge of the quality of the cars? Explain.

 2. Look into Holland College's quality manual https://sam.hollandcollege.com/shared/QMS/QualityManuals/HC-QualityManual.pdf and quality procedures https://sam.hollandcollege.com/shared/QMS/General/Quality Procedures.pdf and answer the following questions.
 a. Who are the primary customers?
 b. What is the "product"?

 c. State one quality objective.
 d. Name one non-conformance.
 e. Name one document controlled.

 3. View the video, "HACCP – Making Food Products Safe, Part 1," https://www.youtube.com/watch?v=7nbjd_TnU8o. Compare it with HACCP coverage in the chapter and point out the differences.

 4. View the video, "HACCP Training for Food Handlers," https://www.youtube.com/watch?v=mE-q9W4jqQg. At what temperature range can food become unsafe?

Problems

 1. Make a check sheet and then a Pareto chart for the following car service repair shop data.

Ticket No.	Work	Ticket No.	Work	Ticket No.	Work
1	Tires	11	Brakes	21	Lube & oil
2	Lube & oil	12	Lube & oil	22	Brakes
3	Tires	13	Battery	23	Transmission
4	Battery	14	Lube & oil	24	Brakes
5	Lube & oil	15	Lube & oil	25	Lube & oil
6	Lube & oil	16	Tires	26	Battery
7	Lube & oil	17	Lube & oil	27	Lube & oil
8	Brakes	18	Brakes	28	Battery
9	Lube & oil	19	Tires	29	Brakes
10	Tires	20	Brakes	30	Tires

Key to Problem 2 table

Problem type:
 N = Noisy
 F = Equipment failure
 W = Runs warm
 O = Odour

Customer type:
 C = Commercial customer
 R = Residential customer

2. The manager of an air-conditioning repair department has compiled data on the primary reason for 41 service calls during the previous week, as shown below. Using the data, make a check sheet for the problem types for each customer type, and then construct a Pareto chart for each type of customer.

Job Number	Problem/ Customer Type	Job Number	Problem/ Customer Type	Job Number	Problem/ Customer Type
301	F/R	315	F/C	329	O/C
302	O/R	316	O/C	330	N/R
303	N/C	317	W/C	331	N/R
304	N/R	318	N/R	332	W/R
305	W/C	319	O/C	333	O/R
306	N/R	320	F/R	334	O/C
307	F/R	321	F/R	335	N/R
308	N/C	322	O/R	336	W/R
309	W/R	323	F/R	337	O/C
310	N/R	324	N/C	338	O/R
311	N/R	325	F/R	339	F/R
312	F/C	326	O/R	340	N/R
313	N/R	327	W/C	341	O/C
314	W/C	328	O/C		

LO5 3. Prepare a run chart for the number of defective computer monitors produced in a plant as shown below. Workers are given a 15-minute break at 10:15 a.m. and 3:15 p.m., and a lunch break at noon. What can you conclude?

Interval Start Time	Number of Defects	Interval Start Time	Number of Defects	Interval Start Time	Number of Defects
8:00	1	10:45	0	2:15	0
8:15	0	11:00	0	2:30	2
8:30	0	11:15	0	2:45	2
8:45	1	11:30	1	3:00	3
9:00	0	11:45	3	3:30	0
9:15	1	1:00	1	3:45	1
9:30	1	1:15	0	4:00	0
9:45	2	1:30	0	4:15	0
10:00	3	1:45	1	4:30	1
10:30	1	2:00	1	4:45	3

LO5 4. Prepare a run chart for the following 911 call data. Use five-minute intervals (i.e., count the calls received in each five-minute interval, and use intervals of 0–4, 5–9, etc.). *Note:* Two or more calls may occur in the same minute; there were three operators on duty this night. What can you conclude from the run chart?

Call	Time	Call	Time	Call	Time
1	1:03	15	1:43	29	2:03
2	1:06	16	1:44	30	2:04
3	1:09	17	1:47	31	2:06
4	1:11	18	1:48	32	2:07
5	1:12	19	1:50	33	2:08
6	1:17	20	1:52	34	2:08
7	1:21	21	1:53	35	2:11
8	1:27	22	1:56	36	2:12
9	1:28	23	1:56	37	2:12
10	1:29	24	2:00	38	2:13
11	1:31	25	2:00	39	2:14
12	1:36	26	2:01	40	2:14
13	1:39	27	2:02	41	2:16
14	1:42	28	2:03	42	2:19

LO5 5. Suppose that a table lamp fails to light when turned on. Prepare a cause-and-effect diagram to analyze possible causes. Use categories such as lamp, cord, etc.

LO5 6. Prepare a cause-and-effect diagram to analyze why a machine has produced a defective part.

LO5 7. Prepare a scatter diagram for each of the following pairs of variables and then express in words the apparent relationship between the two variables. Put the first variable on the horizontal axis and the second variable on the vertical axis.

a. Age	Days Absent	b. Temperature (°C)	Error Rate
24	6	18	1
30	5	17	2
22	7	22	0
25	6	19	0
33	4	28	3
27	5	14	3
36	4	24	1
58	1	30	5
37	3	25	2
47	2	18	1
54	2	26	3
28	5		
42	3		
55	1		

LO5 8. The RCMP has responded to a vehicle accident along a stretch of highway. Prepare a cause-and-effect diagram for this accident. Use categories such as vehicle, driver, weather, etc.

LO1 9. Suppose you are going to have a prescription filled at a local pharmacy. Referring to the dimensions of service quality, for each dimension, give an example of how you would judge the quality of the service.

LO3 10. Prepare an HACCP analysis for burgers made in a fast-food restaurant such as McDonald's.

LO3 11. Consider the processing of northern (cold water) shrimp. They are caught off the east and west coasts, beheaded at sea and frozen or iced, and then further processed on shore. Consider a process that results in cooked, peeled, and frozen small shrimps. Government regulations require that product not be tainted (rancid; bad taste and odour) or unsafe, or decomposed (rotten), and the bag/box should be accurately weighed and labelled with a product code (including place and date of processing). A process flow diagram for processing shrimp is given on the layout diagram that follows. Identify hazards/defects, and determine a critical control point and a quality assurance and control plan for each hazard/defect.[15]

---

[15] http://www.inspection.gc.ca/english/anima/fispoi/qmp/files/cookshrp.doc (accessed 2006).

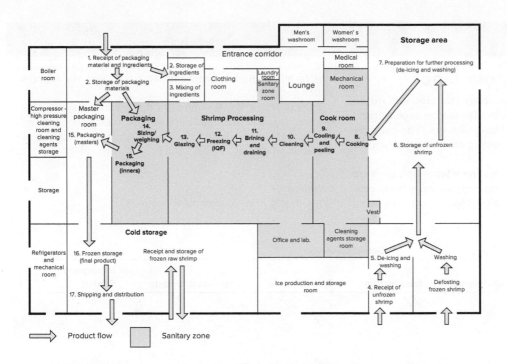

Product flow ⟹   Sanitary zone ▢

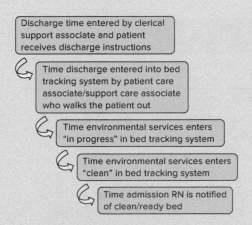

MINI-CASE

North Shore University Hospital

A few years ago, the North Shore University Hospital in New York initiated some improvement projects in order to accommodate the increasing number of patients. One project involved reducing the turnaround time of patient-discharge to bed-ready process, displayed below.

The process seemed to take many hours with significant variations. To study this process, the times between pairs of consecutive steps of the process for 195 patient discharges were determined and plotted (see the chart below). For example, discharge to bed tracking system (Step 1 to Step 2) took from 200 to 850 minutes.

Discharge time entered by clerical support associate and patient receives discharge instructions

Time discharge entered into bed tracking system by patient care associate/support care associate who walks the patient out

Time environmental services enters "in progress" in bed tracking system

Time environmental services enters "clean" in bed tracking system

Time admission RN is notified of clean/ready bed

Pellicone, B.; Martocci, M. (*Quality Progress*, March 2006). "Faster Turnaround Time," 39 (3), pp. 31–36. Figure 1, High Level Process Map, p. 32. Permission granted ASQ.

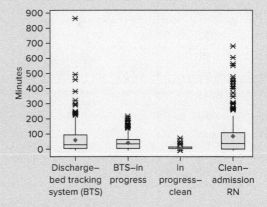

Pellicone, B.; Martocci, M. (*Quality Progress*, March 2006). "Faster Turnaround Time," 39 (3), pp. 31–36. Figure 4, Turnaround Time By Each Step in Process, p. 34. Permission granted by ASQ.

Question

Which part(s) of the process could be targeted for time reduction? Suggest some solutions.

Source: Pellicone, B.; Martocci, M. (*Quality Progress*, March 2006). "Faster Turnaround Time," 39 (3), pp. 31–36. Figure 1, High Level Process Map, p. 32 and Figure 4, Turnaround Time By Each Step in Process, p. 34. Permission granted by ASQ.

MINI-CASE

Chick-n-Gravy Dinner Line

The operations manager of a company that produces frozen dinners had received numerous complaints from supermarkets about the company's Chick-n-Gravy dinners. The manager asked her assistant, Ann, to investigate the matter and to report her recommendations.

Ann's first task was to determine what problems were generating the complaints. The majority of complaints centred on five defects: underfilled packages, a missing item, spilled/mixed items, unacceptable taste, and improperly sealed packages.

Next, she took 800 samples of dinners from the two production lines and examined each sample, making note of any defects that she found. A summary of those results is shown in the table below.

Question
What should Ann recommend to her boss?

				Defect Observed			
Date	Time	Line	Underfilled	Missing Item	Spilled/Mixed	Unacceptable Taste	Improperly Sealed
5/12	0900	1		✓✓	✓	✓✓✓	
5/12	1330	2			✓✓		✓✓
5/13	1000	2				✓	✓✓✓
5/13	1345	1	✓✓		✓✓		
5/13	1530	2		✓✓	✓✓✓		✓
5/14	0830	1		✓✓✓		✓✓✓	
5/14	1100	2	✓✓		✓	✓✓	
5/14	1400	1			✓		✓
5/15	1030	1		✓✓✓		✓✓✓✓✓	
5/15	1145	2			✓	✓✓	
5/15	1500	1	✓		✓		
5/16	0845	2				✓✓	✓✓
5/16	1030	1		✓✓✓	✓	✓✓✓	
5/16	1400	1					
5/16	1545	2	✓	✓✓✓✓✓	✓	✓	✓✓

 MINI-CASE

Tip Top Markets

Tip Top Markets is a regional chain of supermarkets. On July 28, Karen Martin, manager of one of the stores, was disturbed by the large number of recent complaints from customers at her store, particularly on Tuesdays, so she obtained complaint records from the store's customer service desk for the last three Tuesdays. These are shown below.

Question
Analyze the data. What can you recommend to Karen?

July 13

wrong price on spaghetti	overcharged
water on floor	out of brown rice
store looked messy	out of mushrooms
store too warm	overcharged
checkout lines too long	checkout wait too long
cashier not friendly	shopping cart broken
out of feta cheese	couldn't find Aspirin
overcharged	out of brown lunch bags
out of Saran Wrap	out of straws
out of Haagen-Dazs Bars	

July 20		**July 27**	
out of low-salt pickles	out of large eggs	out of dill pickles	open milk carton found in fridge
checkout lines too slow	out of cran-apple juice	reported accident in parking lot	store too warm
broken glass on floor	out of pretzels	wrong price on cran-apple juice	oatmeal spilled in bulk section
lost keys	out of apricot jam	out of carrot juice	telephone out of order
wrong price on sale item	telephone out of order	out of licorice sticks	out of soap
overcharged on corn	out of cocktail sauce	out of chocolate milk	water on floor
wrong price on baby food	water on floor	out of Lava Bars	out of glazed doughnuts
out of 500 mL Tide	out of frozen onion rings	windows dirty	out of baby carrots
out of green tea	out of frozen squash	out of iceberg lettuce	spaghetti sauce on floor
checkout lines too long	out of powdered sugar	store decorations are dated	out of Skippy crunchy peanut butter
out of romaine lettuce	out of nonfat peanut butter	out of St. John's wort	out of butter
		out of vanilla soy milk	

🔍 MINI-CASE

Staples' Extended Service Warranty Process

Ron bought a Toshiba laptop with a two-year extended warranty from a Staples store on November 8. The laptop developed a problem in January: a broken wire in the AC power supply. At the beginning of February, Ron went to the store with his power supply and showed the staff the problem. They said that he should call the Toronto service centre to get a claim number. Ron called the Toronto service centre and explained the problem. After about 10 minutes he received a repair number. He found out that he has to also turn in the laptop even though the problem was only with the power supply. On February 11, Ron took his laptop and power supply, in the original box, to the store. It took the employee about 20–25 minutes to issue a repair depot technician service request (he had difficulty completing the form on the computer).

Ron waited until March 23, when he went to the store at around 1 p.m. He told the employee that it had been more than six weeks since he turned in his laptop and power supply, and he was wondering what had happened. First, the employee brushed off Ron's question by saying that repairs may take two to six weeks. Ron pointed out that it had been more than six weeks and the repair was a simple replacement of a common power supply. Reluctantly, the employee tried to pull up the service request on the computer. He had

trouble locating it. After five minutes, he found the service request, which appeared to be cancelled. The employee couldn't explain what had happened and said that Ron should return and talk to Dylan after 4:00 p.m. Unfortunately, Ron didn't have time to do that. The next day, he went to the store around 7:00 p.m., and asked for Dylan. The manager, Jen, said that Dylan wasn't working then. Ron asked Jen if she could help. She couldn't find the service request on her computer, so she checked in her office in the back. After 10 minutes, she returned and said that the laptop had been shipped last Friday from Winnipeg and should arrive soon.

On April 3, Ron received a phone call from the store saying that the laptop had arrived. Ron went there the next day. An employee gave him his laptop and power supply. Ron pointed out that he had also turned in the box (which contained some manuals). She read the service request form and said that she didn't think that was correct. Ron left the store with his laptop and power supply. On April 9, Ron received a phone call from the store saying that his laptop box was there to be picked up.

Questions

1. State the quality problems incurred during the extended service warranty process described above.

2. For each quality problem, determine a quality assurance plan that could have prevented it in the first place.

Chapter 10
Statistical Quality Control

Trek Bikes - Madone 9.9

LEARNING OBJECTIVES

After completing this chapter, you should be able to:

LO1 List and explain various elements of the statistical process control planning process.

LO2 Explain how control charts are designed and the concepts that underlie their use, and solve typical problems.

LO3 Assess and solve problems involving process capability.

LO4 Describe Six Sigma quality and design of experiments.

Trek has a well earned reputation for building some of the most technologically advanced bikes in the world. The company has gotten to where it is by relentless innovation and continuous improvement of its production processes. Its most important innovation is known as Optimum Compaction Low Void (OCLV) Carbon, which is a carbon fibre production process that yields an extremely light-weight frame that still maintains the strength, stiffness, and aerodynamic properties that world-class competitors demand. If the $10,000+ price tag is any indication of quality, one can only imagine the amount of work and attention to detail that goes into each of these rolling pieces of art.

The patented production process begins with military-grade carbon fibre that is legally prohibited from being exported outside of NATO countries. The carbon fibre is then layered along with resin into a series of piles and then compressed in a way that minimizes the voids that exist between layers. The optimal ratio of fibre to resin and the exact combination of pressure and heat that is used is a closely guarded industry secret. At each key step in the production process, precise measurements of the frame are taken, including the dimensions of its length, width, and diameter, and the location of any machined holes. These measurements were previously recorded using pencil and paper, which is a time consuming and error prone process. However, Trek has recently purchased a statistical process control solution called ProFicient™ from InfinityQS. Once the solution is connected to a measurement device, it collects the data directly and provides quality analysis in real time. This automation saves the quality control department more than $19,000 per year in just the cost of paper.

Sources: http://www.qualitymag.com/articles/85472-case-studies-spc-automates-quality-control; https://www.bikerumor.com/2013/03/11/factory-tour-trek-bicycle-companys-waterloo-headquarters-part-1/

Introduction

LO1

The best companies emphasize *designing quality into the process* (e.g., by undertaking continuous improvement and Six Sigma quality projects), *thereby greatly reducing the need for inspection.* The least progressive companies rely heavily on receiving and shipping inspections. As you might expect, different business organizations are in different stages of this evolutionary process. Inspection alone is generally not sufficient to achieve a reasonable level of quality. Most companies occupy a middle ground that involves some inspection and a great deal of process control. The most progressive have achieved an inherent level of quality so that they can avoid any inspection/test and process control. That is the ultimate goal.

©Jim Richardson/Getty

Food inspectors examine cooked hamburger meat for food safety at McDonald's. All sandwich meats are cooked with a patented clamshell grill. The grill has specific time and temperature requirements and cannot be opened until sensors detect that requirements have been reached. In addition to in-restaurant quality control, McDonald's has extensive quality assurance requirements for its suppliers.[1]

Statistical quality control uses statistical techniques and sampling in monitoring and testing of quality of goods and services.

The part of statistical quality control that relies primarily on inspection of previously produced items is referred to as *acceptance sampling.* This is described in the chapter supplement, which can be accessed on Connect2. The part of statistical quality control that occurs during production is referred to as statistical process control, and we examine it in this chapter (see Figure 10-1 for phases of statistical quality control in a company, and Figure 10-2 for location of use of acceptance sampling and statistical process control within production).

> **statistical quality control**
> Use of statistical techniques and sampling in monitoring and testing of quality of goods and services.

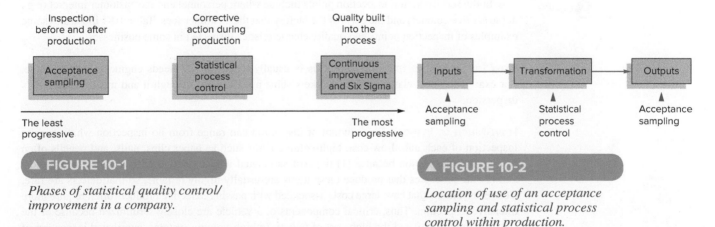

▲ **FIGURE 10-1**

Phases of statistical quality control/ improvement in a company.

▲ **FIGURE 10-2**

Location of use of an acceptance sampling and statistical process control within production.

---

[1] See http://www.foodsafetymagazine.com/magazine-archive1/februarymarch-2006/mcdonalds-usa-a-golden -arch-of-supply-chain-food-safety/.

Statistical quality control is important because it provides an economical way to evaluate the quality of products and meet the expectations of the customers.

Inspection is an appraisal activity that compares the quality of a good or service to a standard. Inspection is a vital but often unappreciated aspect of quality control. Although for well designed processes little inspection is necessary, inspection cannot be completely eliminated. To determine whether a process is functioning as intended or to verify that a batch or lot of raw materials or final products does not contain more than a specified percentage of defective goods, it is necessary to physically examine at least some of the items in question.

> **inspection** Appraisal of a good or service against a standard.

Statistical Process Control Planning Process

Effective statistical process control requires the following planning steps:

1. Define the quality characteristics important to customers, and how each is measured.
2. For each characteristic,
   a. Determine a quality control point.
   b. Plan how inspection is to be done, how much to inspect, and whether centralized or on-site.
   c. Plan the corrective action.

Define the Quality Characteristics. The first step is to define, in sufficient detail, what is to be controlled. It is not enough, for example, to simply refer to a painted surface. The paint can have a number of important characteristics such as its colour, gloss, thickness, and resistance to fading or chipping. Different characteristics may require different approaches for control purposes. Only those characteristics that can be measured are candidates for control. Thus, it is important to consider how measurement will be accomplished. There must be a standard that can be used to evaluate the measurement. This relates to the level of quality being sought.

Determine a Quality Control Point. Many operations have numerous possible inspection points. Because each inspection adds to the cost of a product, it is important to restrict inspection efforts to the points where they can do the most good. In manufacturing, some of the typical inspection points are:

1. *At the beginning of the process.* There is little sense in paying for goods that do not meet quality standards and in spending time and effort on material that is bad to begin with.
2. *At the end of the process.* Customer satisfaction and company's image are at stake here, and repairing or replacing products in the field is usually much more costly than doing it at the factory.
3. *At the operation where a characteristic of interest to customers is first determined.* In particular, before a costly, irreversible, or covering (e.g., painting) operation.

The HACCP system described in the previous chapter also provides some guidelines for determining the quality control points.

Service

In the service sector, inspection points include where personnel and the customer interact (e.g., at the service counter) and the parts of the facility that the customer sees. Table 10-1 illustrates some examples of inspection points and quality characteristics inspected in some businesses.

How Inspection Is to Be Done. This is usually technical and needs engineering knowledge. For example, to test clarity of beer, workers shine a white light through it and measure the light's dispersion.

How Much to Inspect. The amount of inspection can range from no inspection whatsoever to inspection of each unit. Low-cost, high-volume items such as paper clips, nails, and pencils often require little inspection because (1) the cost associated with passing defective items is quite low and (2) the processes that produce these items are usually highly reliable, so that defects are rare. Conversely, items that have large costs associated with passing defective products often require more intensive inspection. Thus, critical components of a vehicle are closely scrutinized because of the risk to human safety and the high cost of failure. In high-volume systems, automated inspection of each unit is one option that may be employed.

Type of Business	Inspection Points	Quality Characteristics
Fast food	Service counter	Appearance, friendliness of server, waiting time
	Eating area	Cleanliness
	Building and grounds	Appearance, safety hazards
	Kitchen	Cleanliness, quality of food, temperature and time of food storage, temperature and time of cooking, health regulations, and hygiene
Supermarket	Cashiers	Accuracy, courtesy, waiting time, productivity
	Aisles and stockrooms	Clutter
	Shelf stock	Availability, rotation of perishables, appearance
	Shopping carts	Good working condition, availability, theft/vandalism
	Building and parking lot	Appearance, safety, good lighting
Brewery	Hot/cold liquor tanks	Bitterness
	Filtering	Clarity
	Fermentation tank	Alcohol content

◄ **TABLE 10-1**

Examples of inspection points and quality characteristics in some businesses.

©Omron Electronics LLC

Food and beverage companies use Omron Electronics' fibre optic sensors to monitor processes and to perform quality inspections such as checking beverage content levels and presence of caps.[2] This is an example of automated inspection of each unit.

The majority of quality control applications lie somewhere between the two extremes. Most require some inspection, but it is neither possible nor economically feasible to examine every product. The cost of inspection and resulting interruptions of a process (if inspection is not automated) typically outweigh the benefits of 100 percent inspection. However, the cost of letting undetected defects slip through is sufficiently high that inspection cannot be completely ignored. The amount of inspection needed is governed by the costs of inspection and the expected cost of passing defective items.

As illustrated in Figure 10-3, if inspection activities increase, inspection costs increase, but the cost of passing defectives decreases. The goal is to minimize the sum of these two costs. In other words, it may not pay to attempt to catch every defect, particularly if the cost of inspection exceeds the penalties associated with letting some defects get through.

---

[2] See https://echannel.omron247.com/marcom%5Cpdfcatal.nsf/PDFLookupByUniqueID/442D956B37E1187586256F62007B6E9B/$File/B10InspectionSolutions1104.pdf?OpenElement.

FIGURE 10-3 ▶

*The amount of
inspection is optimal
when the sum of the
costs of inspection and
passing defectives is
minimized.*

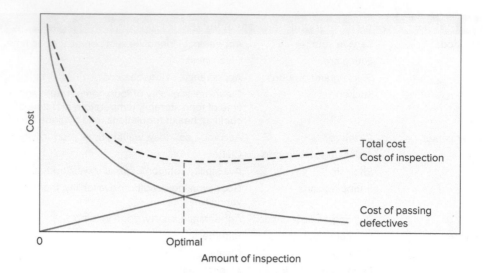

As a rule of thumb, operations with a high proportion of human involvement necessitate more inspection than mechanical operations, which tend to be more reliable. The frequency of inspection depends largely on the rate at which a process may go out of control. A stable process will require only infrequent checks, whereas an unstable one or one that has recently given trouble will require more frequent checks. Likewise, many small lots will require more samples than a few large lots because it is important to obtain sample data from each lot. For high-volume, repetitive operations, computerized automatic inspections at critical points in a process are cost effective. Also, when quality issues increase, the frequency of inspection should also increase. See the "Random Inspections of Medical Cannabis" OM in Action.

 OM in Action

Random Inspections of Medical Cannabis

Health Canada has just announced it will begin conducting random inspections of medical cannabis products from its 38 licensed marijuana producers. This comes after a series of product recalls due to contaminated marijuana that has sickened nearly 25,000 customers. The source of the contamination has been traced to the use of banned pesticides such as myclobutanil,

bifenazate, and pyrethrins. While these chemicals may be used for crops, they are strictly forbidden in the production of medical cannabis. These newly imposed random inspections supplement regular unannounced inspections of licensed producer facilities.

Sources: http://www.hc-sc.gc.ca/dhp-mps/marihuana/info/licencedproducer-producteurautorise/pesticides-eng.php; https://www.theglobeandmail.com/news/national/health-canada-mandates-pesticide-testing-for-medical-cannabis-producers/article34913001/.

 Centralized Versus On-Site Inspection. Some situations require that inspections be performed on-site. For example, inspecting the hull of a ship for cracks requires inspectors to visit the ship. If the test is simple enough (e.g., measuring dimensions), it can be done by a handheld caliper or micrometer. Alternatively, automated inspection (e.g., using a vision system or laser gauge) can be installed on the machine (which can perform 100 percent inspection). At other times, specialized tests need to be performed and can best be performed in a lab (e.g., medical tests, analyzing food and water samples, testing metals for hardness or paper for tensile strength and tear resistance, running viscosity tests on lubricants, measuring dimensions that require large, expensive coordinate measuring machines, and destructive tests).

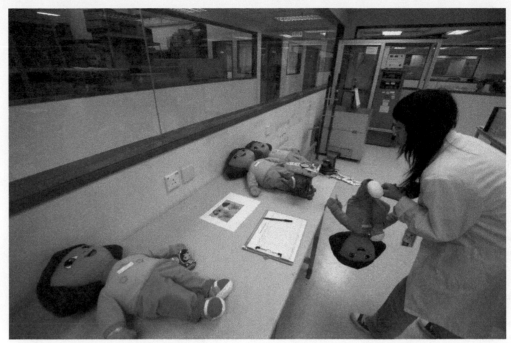

A Mattel technician in a lab of a manufacturing plant in China does a pulling test with a Dora the Explorer doll in the name of product safety. Mattel has 10 labs in six countries and has set up strict requirements for vendors because of past safety recalls (http://www .nytimes.com/2007/07/26 /business/26toy.html).

©Chang W. Lee/The New York Times/Redux

The central issue in the decision concerning on-site or lab inspections is whether the advantages of specialized lab tests are worth the time and interruption needed to obtain the results. Specialized equipment, skilled quality control inspectors, and a more favourable test environment (less noise, vibrations, and dust) offer strong arguments for using a lab. More companies are now relying on self-inspections by operators on-site.

Plan the Corrective Action. When a process is judged out of control for an important characteristic, the process should be stopped and corrective action must be taken. This involves uncovering the cause (e.g., worn-out tool bits, or failure to follow specified procedures) and correcting it. Also, any potentially off-specification (i.e., defective) parts or products should be tested, and if defective, should be either reworked or scrapped. To ensure that corrective action is effective, the output of a process must be monitored for a sufficient period of time to verify that the problem has been eliminated. See the "Nestlé Waters Canada" OM in Action for an example.

 OM in Action   http://www.nestle-waters.ca/en

Nestlé Waters Canada

Nestlé Waters Canada uses a rigorous 10-step quality process to ensure that the highest standards of quality for drinking water are met in a sustainable and environmentally friendly manner (shown below).

Step 1 is to ensure quality at the source. This is achieved by selecting springs only from sustainable sources that are free from contamination.

In Step 2, the spring water is transported directly to processing plants through food-grade pipelines or stainless steel tankers.

In Step 3, the spring water is tested multiple times for compliance with specifications and held in food-grade storage tanks.

In Step 4, pharmaceutical grade micro-filters remove any contaminants from the raw spring water.

In Step 5, the spring water gets ultraviolet light and ozone disinfection to destroy any bacteria that might be present.

In Step 6, the bottling of the water is done using state-of-the-art equipment designed to prevent contamination from the environment and then each bottle

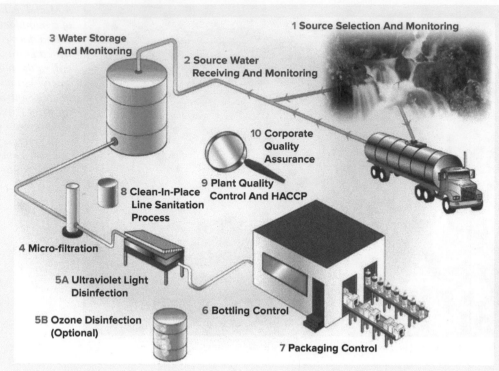

1 Source Selection And Monitoring

3 Water Storage And Monitoring

2 Source Water Receiving And Monitoring

10 Corporate Quality Assurance

9 Plant Quality Control And HACCP

8 Clean-In-Place Line Sanitation Process

4 Micro-filtration

5A Ultraviolet Light Disinfection

5B Ozone Disinfection (Optional)

6 Bottling Control

7 Packaging Control

Nestlé is a registered trademark of Société des Produits Nestlé S.A., Vevey, Switzerland. Used by permission.

is marked to identify the production line, plant location, and time produced in compliance with international guidelines set by the World Health Organization.

In Step 7, packing is conducted and each bottle is carefully monitored and controlled under some of the strictest food-safety regulations in the world.

Step 8 is clean-in-place, which is an automated cleaning process that circulates detergents and sanitizing solutions throughout the production process.

Step 9 is to ensure plant-level quality control by using a prevention-based HACCP program. The program identifies potential hazards to the production process, determines critical control points, and monitors each control point for chemical characteristics such as lead, arsenic, pH balance, chlorine, chloride; microbiological characteristics such as coliform, bacteria, viruses, and pathogenic protozoa; and taste and smell. The chemical tests are performed hourly and microbiological tests

are performed daily. Every Nestlé Waters facility has its own sensory expert panel. Human sensory capacities are highly adept at detecting certain quality issues and come closest to the end-consumer experience. People can detect chemicals that are undetectable under laboratory testing. For instance, a molecule such as trichloroanisole can be detected by people at a concentration of 0.2 nanograms per litre, while chromatographic devices are only able to detect it at a concentration of 0.5 nanograms per litre.

Finally, Step 10 is a corporate quality assurance program that makes sure each processing plant is staffed with fully qualified and experienced personnel, and is equipped with state-of-the-art testing laboratories.

Sources: http://www.nestle-waters.com/brands/water-quality/water -quality-analysis; http://www.nestle-waters.ca/content/documents /nwna_10_step_sw_process.pdf; http://www.wqpmag.com/house-quality -control-testing-bottled-water-plants.

LO2 Statistical Process Control

statistical process control (SPC) Statistical evaluation of the product in the production process.

A major part of statistical quality control is **statistical process control (SPC)** which is concerned with statistical evaluation of the product in the production process. To do SPC, the operator takes periodic samples from the process and compares them with predetermined limits. If the sample results fall outside the limits, the operator stops the process and takes corrective action. If the sample results fall within the limits, the operator allows the process to continue.

Types of Variations

All processes that produce a good or service exhibit a certain amount of "natural" variation in their output. The variations are created by the combined influences of countless minor factors, each one so unimportant that even if it could be identified and eliminated, the decrease in process variability would be negligible. In effect, this variability is inherent in the process. It is often referred to as a *chance* or **random variation**. In Deming's terms, this is referred to as *common variability* of the process. The amount of random variation differs from process to process. For instance, older machines generally exhibit a higher degree of random variation than newer machines, partly because of worn parts and partly because new machines may incorporate design improvements that lessen the variability in their output.

A second kind of variability in process output is nonrandom and is called **assignable variation**. In Deming's terms, this is referred to as *special variation*. Unlike random variation, the main sources of assignable variation can usually be identified (assigned to a specific cause) and eliminated. Excessive tool wear, equipment that needs adjustment, defective materials, and human errors (e.g., failure to follow correct procedures) are typical sources of assignable variation.

The main task in SPC is to distinguish assignable from random variation. Taking a sample of two or more observations and calculating a sample statistic such as sample mean makes the task easier. This is because random variations are reduced in sample statistics.

> **random variation** Natural variation in the output of a process, created by countless minor factors.
>
> **assignable variation** Nonrandom variability in process output; a variation whose cause can be identified.

Sampling and Sampling Distributions

In statistical process control, periodic samples of process output are taken and sample statistics, such as sample means or the number of occurrences of a certain type of outcome, are determined. The sample statistics can be used to judge randomness of process variations. The sample statistics exhibit variation, just as processes do. The variability of a sample statistic is described by its *sampling distribution,* which is the theoretical distribution of the values of the statistic for all possible samples of a given size from the process. Consider the process for filling bottles with soft drink. If the amount of soft drink in a large number of bottles is measured accurately, we would discover slight differences among the bottles. If these amounts were arranged on a graph, the frequency distribution would reflect the *process variability.* The values would be clustered close to the process average (e.g., 2 litres), but some of the values would vary somewhat from the mean.

If we take *samples* of three bottles at a time and compute, for example, the *mean* amount of soft drink in each sample, we would discover that these values also vary, just as the *individual* values varied. However, the distribution of the sample mean is more concentrated around process mean (2 litres) than the distribution of process. Figure 10-4 illustrates a sampling distribution and a process distribution (i.e., individual bottles).

Sampling distribution of the sample mean

Process distribution

Value of characteristic

Process mean

◀ **FIGURE 10-4**

The sampling distribution of the sample mean, for a given sample size, has less variability than the process.

The sampling distribution of the sample mean exhibits less variability (i.e., it is less spread out) than the process distribution. This reflects the *averaging* that occurs in computing the sample means: high and low values in samples tend to offset each other, resulting in less variability among sample means than among individual values. Note that both distributions have the same mean. Finally, note that the sampling distribution is approximately *Normal*. This is true even if the process distribution is not Normal.

central limit theorem The distribution of sample averages tends to be Normal regardless of the shape of the process distribution.

In the case of sample means, the **central limit theorem** states that as the sample size increases, the distribution of sample averages approaches a Normal distribution regardless of the shape of the sampled population. This tends to be the case even for fairly small sample sizes. For other sample statistics, the Normal distribution serves as a reasonable approximation to the shape of the actual sampling distribution.

Figure 10-5 illustrates what happens to the shape of the sampling distribution relative to the sample size. The larger the sample size, the narrower the sampling distribution. This means that the likelihood that a sample statistic is close to the true value in the population is higher for large samples than for small samples.

FIGURE 10-5 ▶

The larger the sample size, the narrower the sampling distribution.

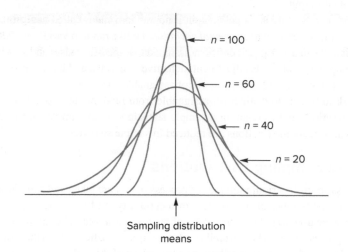

A sampling distribution serves as the theoretical basis for distinguishing between random and assignable variation of a sampling statistic. Very simply, limits are selected within which most values of a sample statistic should fall if its variations are random. The limits are stated in terms of number of standard deviations from the distribution mean. Typical limits are ±2 standard deviations or ±3 standard deviations. Figure 10-6 illustrates these possible limits and the probability that a sample statistic would fall within those limits if only random variations are present. Conversely, if the value of a sample statistic falls outside those limits, there is only a small probability ($1 - 0.9974 = 0.0026$ for ±3 limits, and $1 - 0.9544 = 0.0456$ for ±2 limits) that the value reflects random variation. Instead, we can conclude that the process most likely has shifted, and hence there is an assignable cause.

FIGURE 10-6 ▶

Percentage of values under the curve within given ranges in a Normal sampling distribution of the sample mean.

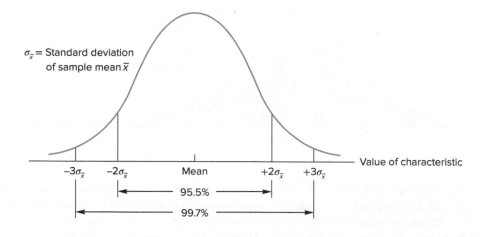

Visit   https://www.khanacademy.org/math/statistics-probability/sampling-distributions-library for more practice with sampling distributions.

Control Charts

An important tool in statistical process control is the control chart, which was developed by Walter Shewhart. A control chart is a *time-ordered* plot of a sample statistic, with limits. It is used to distinguish between random and assignable variation (or equivalently no shift and a shift in the process). It has upper and lower limits, called control limits. A control chart is illustrated in Figure 10-7. The purpose of a control chart is to monitor process output to see if it is random. A necessary (but not sufficient) condition for a process to be deemed "in control," or stable, is for all the data points to fall between the upper and lower control limits. Conversely, a data point that falls outside either limit would be taken as evidence that the process most likely has shifted, and hence there is an assignable cause; therefore, it is not "in control." If that happens, the process would be halted to find and correct the cause of the nonrandom variation. The essence of statistical process control is to assure that the output of a process is random so that *future output* will be random.

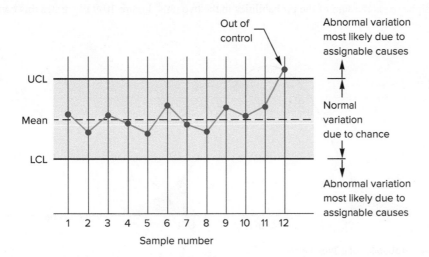

◀ **FIGURE 10-7**

The components of a sample mean control chart.

The basis for a control chart is the sampling distributions, which essentially describes random variability. There is, however, one minor difficulty relating to the use of a normal sampling distribution. The theoretical distribution extends in either direction to *infinity*. Therefore, *any* value is theoretically possible, even one that is a considerable distance from the mean of the distribution. However, as mentioned before, we know that 99.7 percent of the values will fall within ±3 standard deviations of the mean of the distribution. Therefore, we could decide to set the limits at ±3 standard deviations from the mean, and conclude that any value that was farther away from the mean than these limits reflects a shift in the process, and hence an assignable variation.

In effect, these limits are called **control limits**. Figure 10-8 illustrates how control limits for a sample mean control chart are based on the sampling distribution of the sample mean.

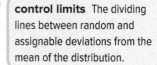

control limits The dividing lines between random and assignable deviations from the mean of the distribution.

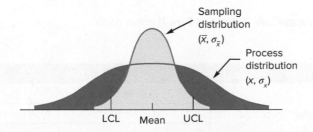

◀ **FIGURE 10-8**

Control limits are based on the sampling distribution of the sample mean.

Control charts have two limits that separate random and assignable variations. The larger value is the *upper control limit* (UCL), and the smaller value is the *lower control limit* (LCL). A sample statistic that falls between these two limits suggests random variation (i.e., no process shift), while a value outside or on either limit suggests assignable variation (i.e., the deviation from the longstanding known process mean is so large that the process must have shifted).

Note that the control limits are not directly related to specification limits. Control limits are based on the characteristic of the process, whereas the specification limits are based on the desired characteristic of the product. The process is capable if the process values fall within the specification limits. However, control limits are for sample statistics, so they should fall well within the specification limits. This will be further explained in the "Process Capability" section later in the chapter.

It is important to recognize that because any control limits will leave some area in the *tails* of the distribution, there is a small probability that a sample statistic value will fall outside the limits *even though only random variations are present* (i.e., there is no process shift). For example, if ±2 Sigma (standard deviation) limits are used, they would include 95.5 percent of the values. Consequently, the complement of that number (100 percent – 95.5 percent = 4.5 percent) would not be included. That percentage (or *probability*) is sometimes referred to as the probability of a **Type I error**, where the "error" is concluding that a process has shifted (i.e., an assignable variation is present) when it has not (i.e., only random variation is present). This is also referred to as *alpha* risk, where alpha (α) is the sum of the probabilities in the two tails. Figure 10-9 illustrates this concept.

> **Type I error** Concluding that a process has shifted (i.e., an assignable variation is present) when it has not (i.e., only random variation is present).

FIGURE 10-9 ▶

The probability of a Type I error.

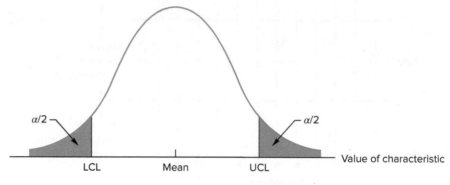

α = Probability of a Type I error

Using wider limits (e.g., ±3 Sigma limits) reduces the probability of a Type I error because it decreases the area in the tails of the distribution. However, wider limits make it more difficult to detect assignable variations (i.e., a shift in the process) *if* they are present. For example, the process might shift (an assignable cause of variation) enough to be detected by Two Sigma limits, but not enough to be readily apparent using Three Sigma limits. That could lead to a second kind of error, known as a **Type II error**, which is concluding that a process has not shifted (i.e., only random variation is present) when it has (i.e., an assignable variation is present). In theory, the costs of making each error should be balanced by their probabilities. However, in practice, Two Sigma limits and Three Sigma limits are commonly used without specifically referring to the probability of a Type II error.

> **Type II error** Concluding that a process has not shifted (i.e., only random variation is present). when it has (i.e., an assignable variation is present)

Table 10-2 illustrates how Type I and Type II errors occur.

TABLE 10-2 ▶

Type I and Type II errors.

		And the conclusion is that it is:	
		In Control	Out of Control
If a process is actually:	In control	No error	Type I error (producer's risk)
	Out of control	Type II error (consumer's risk)	No error

Each sample is represented by a single value (e.g., the sample mean) on a control chart. Moreover, each value is compared to the extremes of the sampling distribution (the control limits) to judge if it is within the acceptable range. Figure 10-10 illustrates this concept.

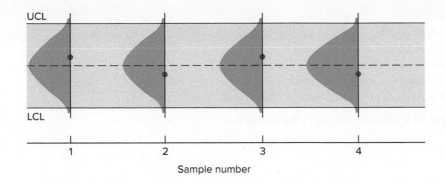

Each sample mean (a red dot) is compared to the control limits.

What is the probability that x will be within ± 1.5 from the mean of a standard normal distribution?

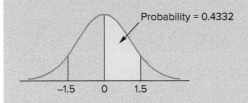

Probability = 0.4332

−1.5   0   1.5

◀ EXAMPLE 10-1

To find the area under the curve between −1.5 and 1.5, we look up 1.5 from Appendix B, Table A. Since the table shows the areas from 0 to 1.5, in order to find the probability that x will be within ± 1.5, we need to double the value listed in the table, which gives us $0.4332 \times 2 = 0.8664$. (See figure.)

Designing Control Charts. The following steps are usually taken to design control charts:

1. Determine a sample size n (usually between 2 and 20). The choice of n depends on the cost of inspection versus the expected cost of Type II error. The larger n *is,* the smaller the probability of Type II error.
2. Obtain 20 to 25 samples of size n. Compute the appropriate sample statistic for each sample (e.g., sample mean).
3. Establish preliminary control limits using appropriate formulas (given in following sections), and graph them.
4. Plot the sample statistic values on the control chart, and note whether any points fall outside the control limits.
5. If you find no points outside control limits, assume that there is no assignable cause and therefore the process is stable and in control (other cases showing instability will be illustrated at the end of this section). If not, investigate and correct assignable causes of variation; then repeat the process from Step 2 on.

Sample Mean and Range Control Charts

The **sample mean ($\bar{x}$) control chart**, sometimes referred to as an $\bar{x}$ chart, is used to monitor the process mean. The centre line used in an $\bar{x}$ chart represents the process mean. This is estimated by taking a few samples, computing their mean, and then averaging these means. These samples are used to ensure that the process is stable and in control. It can be shown that the average of means is the mean of all the observations in the samples, and hence is called the grand mean. The control limits can be determined in two ways. The choice depends on what information is available.

> **sample mean ($\bar{x}$) control chart** The control chart for sample mean, used to monitor the process mean.

The first approach to calculating the control limits is to use the standard deviation of the process, σ.

$$\text{Upper Control Limit (UCL}_{\bar{x}}) = \bar{\bar{x}} + z\sigma_{\bar{x}}$$
$$\text{Lower Control Limit (LCL}_{\bar{x}}) = \bar{\bar{x}} - z\sigma_{\bar{x}}$$

(10-1)

where

$\sigma_{\bar{x}}$ = Standard deviation of the sampling distribution of the sample mean = $\sigma/\sqrt{n}$
σ = Process standard deviation
n = Sample size
z = Standard Normal deviate (usually $z = 3$)
$\bar{x}$ = Average of sample means = Grand mean

Example 10-2 illustrates the use of these formulas.

EXAMPLE 10-2 ▶

A quality inspector took five samples, each with four observations, of the length of a part (in centimetres). She computed the mean of each sample (see table below).

a. Use the following data to obtain Three Sigma (i.e., $z = 3$) control limits for sample mean. Is the process in control?

b. If a new sample (Sample 6) has values 12.10, 12.19, 12.12, and 12.14, using the sample mean control chart in part a, has the process mean changed (i.e., is there an assignable variation)?

It is known from previous experience that the standard deviation of the process is 0.02 cm.

		Sample				
		1	2	3	4	5
	1	12.11	12.15	12.09	12.12	12.09
	2	12.10	12.12	12.09	12.10	12.14
Observation	3	12.11	12.10	12.11	12.08	12.13
	4	12.08	12.11	12.15	12.10	12.12
	$\bar{x}$	12.10	12.12	12.11	12.10	12.12

SOLUTION

a. $\bar{\bar{x}} = \dfrac{12.10 + 12.12 + 12.11 + 12.10 + 12.12}{5} = 12.11\,\text{cm}$

Using Formula 10-1, with $z = 3$, $n = 4$ observations per sample, and $\sigma = 0.02$, we find:

$$\text{UCL}_{\bar{x}}: 12.11 + 3\left(\frac{0.02}{\sqrt{4}}\right) = 12.14$$

$$\text{LCL}_{\bar{x}}: 12.11 - 3\left(\frac{0.02}{\sqrt{4}}\right) = 12.08$$

Because all five sample means fall between the control limits (12.08 and 12.14), the process is in control.

b. $\bar{x}_6 = \dfrac{12.10 + 12.19 + 12.12 + 12.14}{4} = 12.1375\,\text{cm}$

Because $12.08 < 12.1375 < 12.14$, the process mean has not changed (i.e., there is only random variation).

Note: The fact that some of the *individual* measurements fall outside the control limits (e.g., the first observation in Sample 2, the last observation in Sample 3, and the second observation in Sample 6) is irrelevant. You can see why by referring back to Figure 10-8: *individual* values are represented by the process distribution, a large portion of which lies outside the control limits for the sample *mean*.

A second approach to calculating the control limits is to use the sample *range* (i.e., Maximum value – Minimum value in the sample) as a measure of process variability (instead of σ). The appropriate formulas for sample mean control limits in this case are:

$$\text{UCL}_{\bar{x}} = \bar{\bar{x}} + A_2\bar{R}$$
$$\text{LCL}_{\bar{x}} = \bar{\bar{x}} - A_2\bar{R}$$

(10-2)

where

A_2 can be obtained from Table 10-3
$\bar{R}$ = Average of sample ranges of a few samples

Number of Observations in Sample, n	Factor for $\bar{x}$ Charts, A_2	Factors for R-Charts	
		Lower Control Limit, D_3	Upper Control Limit, D_4
2	1.88	0	3.27
3	1.02	0	2.57
4	0.73	0	2.28
5	0.58	0	2.11
6	0.48	0	2.00
7	0.42	0.08	1.92
8	0.37	0.14	1.86
9	0.34	0.18	1.82
10	0.31	0.22	1.78
11	0.29	0.26	1.74
12	0.27	0.28	1.72
13	0.25	0.31	1.69
14	0.24	0.33	1.67
15	0.22	0.35	1.65
16	0.21	0.36	1.64
17	0.20	0.38	1.62
18	0.19	0.39	1.61
19	0.19	0.40	1.60
20	0.18	0.41	1.59

◀ **TABLE 10-3**

Factors for Three Sigma control limits for $\bar{x}$ - and R-charts.

Source: Adapted from Eugene Grant and Richard Leavenworth, *Statistical Quality Control,* 4th ed. (New York: McGraw-Hill, 1972), p. 645.

Twenty samples of $n = 8$ have been taken of the weight of a part. The average of sample ranges for the 20 samples is 0.016 kg, and the average of sample means is 3 kg. Determine Three Sigma control limits for sample mean of this process.

◀ **EXAMPLE 10-3**

SOLUTION

$\bar{x} = 3, \bar{R} = 0.016, A_2 = 0.37$ for $n = 8$ (from Table 10-3)

$\quad \text{UCL}_{\bar{x}} = \bar{\bar{x}} + A_2\bar{R} = 3 + 0.37(0.016) = 3.006 \, \text{kg}$

$\quad \text{LCL}_{\bar{x}} = \bar{\bar{x}} - A_2\bar{R} = 3 - 0.37(0.016) = 2.994 \, \text{kg}$

Sample Range Control Chart. The **sample range (R) control chart** is used to monitor process dispersion or spread. Although the underlying sampling distribution is not Normal, the concept for design and use of the sample range control chart is much the same as that for the $\bar{x}$ chart. Control limits for the sample range control chart are found using these formulas:

$\quad \text{UCL}_R = D_4\bar{R}$

$\quad \text{LCL}_R = D_3\bar{R}$

(10-3)

sample range (R) control chart The control chart for sample range, used to monitor process dispersion or spread.

where values of D_3 and D_4 are obtained from Table 10-3.

In Example 10-4, a sample range of 0.0178 centimetre or more would suggest that the process variability has increased. A sample range of 0.0022 cm or less would imply that the process

EXAMPLE 10-4

Twenty-five samples of $n = 10$ observations have been taken from a milling process. The average of sample ranges is 0.01 centimetre. Determine upper and lower control limits for the sample range.

SOLUTION

$\bar{R} = 0.01$ cm, $n = 10$

From Table 10-3, for $n = 10$, $D_4 = 1.78$ and $D_3 = 0.22$

$\text{UCL}_R = 1.78(0.01) = 0.0178$ cm

$\text{LCL}_R = 0.22(0.01) = 0.0022$ cm

variability has decreased. In the former case, this means that the process is producing too much variation; we would want to investigate this in order to remove the assignable cause of variation. In the latter case, even though decreased variability is desirable, we would want to determine what is causing it: Perhaps an improved method has been used, in which case we would want to identify it.

If the standard deviation of process σ is not known but the average of sample ranges $\bar{R}$ is known, then σ can be estimated from $\bar{R}$ as follows: Equate the two UCLs in Formulas 10-1 and 10-2, substitute 3 for z, and simplify:

$$\bar{\bar{X}} + 3\sigma_{\bar{x}} \approx \bar{X} + A_2\bar{R}$$
$$3\sigma_{\bar{x}} \approx A_2\bar{R}$$
$$3\frac{\sigma}{\sqrt{n}} \approx A_2\bar{R} \tag{10-4}$$
$$\sigma \approx \frac{\sqrt{n}}{3}A_2\bar{R}$$

Why Use Both Sample Mean and Sample Range Control Charts? Sample mean and sample range control charts provide different perspectives on a process. Sample mean control charts are sensitive to shifts in the process mean, whereas sample range control charts are sensitive to changes in process dispersion or spread. Because of this difference in perspective, both charts must be used to monitor a process. The logic of using both is readily apparent from Figure 10-11. In Figure 10-11a, the sample mean control chart picks up the shift in the process mean, but because the dispersion is not changing, the sample range control chart fails to indicate a problem. Conversely, in Figure 10-11b, a change in process dispersion is not detected by the sample mean control chart, but is detected by the sample range control chart. Thus, use of both control charts provides more information than either chart alone.

Individual Unit and Moving Range Control Charts

When the rate of production is low, testing is expensive, or there is no reason to expect additional information by taking more observations, only one unit (i.e., $n = 1$) is used for inspection. In this case, the sample mean control chart reduces to **individual unit (X) control chart**, and its control limits can be determined by:

$$\text{UCL}_x = \bar{X} + z\sigma$$
$$\text{LCL}_x = \bar{X} - z\sigma \tag{10-5}$$

where $\bar{X}$ is the mean of a few individual observations (that estimates the process mean), σ is the process standard deviation, and z is the standard Normal deviate. It is important to note that the above formulas assume a Normal process distribution.

The "sample" range cannot be calculated in the usual way in this case because there is only one observation in each sample. Instead, the differences between consecutive observations, called moving range (MR), are calculated and used in the **moving range (MR) control chart** to control the dispersion or spread. We can still use the formula for the sample range control limits (Formula 10-3) but determine D_4 and D_3 from Table 10-3 using $n = 2$. Thus, the control limits for the moving range control chart are:

$$\text{UCL}_{\text{MR}} = 3.27\bar{R}$$
$$\text{LCL}_{\text{MR}} = 0\bar{R} = 0 \tag{10-6}$$

where $\bar{R}$ is the average of the moving ranges (the absolute value of the difference between two consecutive observations). It is important to note that consecutive moving range values are not independent and that this fact has to be considered when analyzing the moving range control chart.

individual unit (X) control chart Control chart for individual unit, used to monitor single observations ($n = 1$).

moving range (MR) control chart Control chart for moving range (i.e., the difference between consecutive observations), used to monitor the dispersion or spread when $n = 1$.

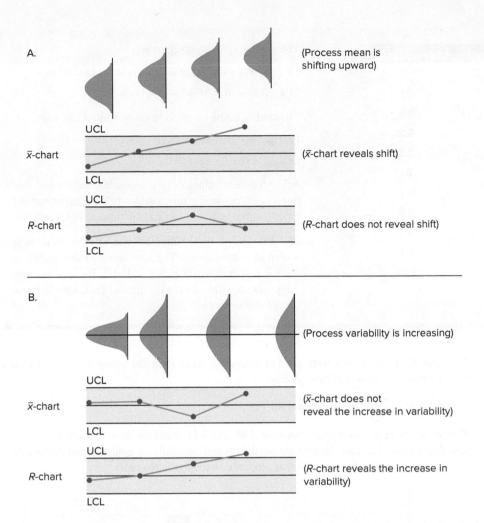

Sample mean and sample range control charts used together complement each other.

The following data are the (Brinell) hardness measures of 10 individual steel screws produced by a screw machine.

◀ EXAMPLE 10-5

a. Determine the Three Sigma control limits for the X-chart and the moving range control chart. Is the process in control?

b. If the 11th observation is 38.7, using the control charts in part *a*, is the process still in control?

SOLUTION

a. We have to compute the average and standard deviation of the individual observations (estimate of process standard deviation). Also, we need to calculate the difference of consecutive observations (absolute value) to obtain the moving ranges, and then average these to get $\bar{R}$. These are displayed as follows:

Sample Number	Hardness
1	36.3
2	28.6
3	32.5
4	38.7
5	35.4
6	27.3
7	37.2
8	36.4
9	38.3
10	30.5

Sample Number	Hardness	Moving Range
1	36.3	–
2	28.6	7.7
3	32.5	3.9
4	38.7	6.2
5	35.4	3.3
6	27.3	8.1
7	37.2	9.9
8	36.4	0.8
9	38.3	1.9
10	30.5	7.8
Average =	34.12	5.51
Std dev =	4.11	

The control limits for X-chart are:

$$UCL_x = \bar{X} + z\sigma = 34.12 + 3(4.11) = 46.45$$
$$LCL_x = \bar{X} - z\sigma = 34.12 - 3(4.11) = 21.79$$

The control limits for moving range control chart are:

$$UCL_{MR} = 3.27(5.51) = 18.02$$
$$LCL_{MR} = 0$$

All 10 hardness values fall within the X-chart control limits and all nine moving range values fall within the moving range control limits. Therefore, the process is in control.

b. $21.79 < 38.7 < 46.45$, therefore the 11th observation is within its control limits. The new moving range $= 38.7 - 30.5 = 8.2$. Because $0 < 8.2 < 18.02$, the new moving range is also within its control limits. Therefore, the process is still in control.

Note that if Formula 10-4 were used to estimate σ from $\bar{R}$ in the above example instead of calculating it directly, we would have obtained:

$$\sigma \approx \frac{\sqrt{n}}{3} A_2 \bar{R} = \frac{\sqrt{2}}{3}(1.88)(5.51) = 4.88$$

The relatively large discrepancy between 4.88 and 4.11 (estimate of σ derived directly from samples) is due to the fact that the data are not distributed Normally, as evident from the histogram below (note that Formula 10-4 assumes that process distribution is Normal).

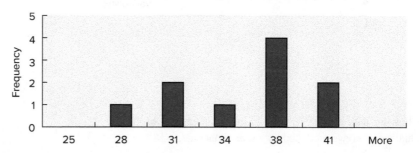

Control Charts for Attributes

Control charts for attributes are used when the process characteristic is *counted* rather than measured—that is, when an item in a sample is either defective or not. There are two types of attribute control charts: one for the fraction of defective items in a sample (*p*-chart), and one for the number of defects per unit (*c*-chart). A *p*-chart is appropriate when the data consist of two categories of items. For instance, if glass bottles are inspected for chipping and cracking, both the good bottles and the defective ones can be counted. However, one can count the number of accidents that occur during a given period of time but not the number of accidents that did not occur. Similarly, one can count the number of scratches on a polished surface, the number of bacteria present in a water sample, and the number of crimes committed during the month of August, but one cannot count the number of non-occurrences. In such cases, a *c*-chart is appropriate. See Table 10-4.

p-chart Control chart for sample proportion of defectives, used to monitor the proportion of defective items generated by a process.

p-**Chart.** The *p*-chart is the control chart for the sample proportion of defectives, and is used to monitor the proportion of defective items generated by the process. The theoretical basis for a *p*-chart is the binomial distribution, although for large sample sizes the Normal distribution

The following tips should help you select the type of control chart—a p-chart or a c-chart—that is appropriate for a particular application:

Use a p-chart:	Use a c-chart:

1. When observations can be placed into one of *two* categories. Examples include items (observations) that can be classified as
   a. Good or bad.
   b. Pass or fail.
   c. Operate or don't operate.
 	
 2. When the data consist of multiple samples of *n* observations each (e.g., 15 samples of *n* = 20 observations each).
	When only the number of occurrences per unit of measure can be counted; non-occurrences cannot be counted. Examples of occurrences and units of measure include
	   a. Scratches, chips, dents, or errors per item.
	   b. Cracks or faults per unit of distance (e.g., metres, miles).
	   c. Breaks or tears, per unit of area (e.g., square yard, square metre).
	   d. Bacteria or pollutants per unit of volume (e.g., gallon, cubic foot, cubic yard).
	   e. Calls, complaints, failures, equipment breakdowns, or crimes per unit of time (e.g., hour, day, month, year).

provides a good approximation to it. Conceptually, a p-chart is constructed and used in much the same way as an $\bar{x}$-chart.

The centre line on a p-chart is the average proportion of defectives in the population, *p*. The standard deviation of the sampling distribution of the sample proportion, when *p* is known, is

$$\sigma_p = \frac{\sqrt{p(1-p)}}{n}$$

Control limits for p-chart are calculated using the formulas

$$UCL_p = p + z\sigma_p$$
$$LCL_p = p - z\sigma_p$$

(10-7)

If *p* is unknown, it can be estimated from a few samples. That estimate, $\bar{p}$, replaces *p* in the preceding formulas, as illustrated in the following example.

Note: Because Formula 10-7 is an approximation, sometimes LCL_p will be negative. In this case, zero should be used as the lower control limit.

A quality inspector counted the number of defective parts a prototype machine made in samples of 100 taken every hour during a 20-hour period.

a. Using the following data, construct a Three Sigma control chart for the sample proportion of defectives.
b. Is the machine producing a stable proportion of defectives?

Sample	Number of Defectives	Sample	Number of Defectives	Sample	Number of Defectives
1	4	8	22	15	21
2	10	9	13	16	10
3	12	10	10	17	8
4	3	11	8	18	12
5	9	12	12	19	10
6	11	13	9	20	16
7	10	14	10		220

SOLUTION

a. $\bar{p} = \dfrac{\text{Total number of defectives}}{\text{Total number of observations}} = \dfrac{220}{20(100)} = 0.11$

$\hat{\sigma}_p = \sqrt{\dfrac{\bar{p}(1-\bar{p})}{n}} = \sqrt{\dfrac{0.11(1-0.11)}{100}} = 0.03$

Control limits are:

$UCL_p = \bar{p} + z(\hat{\sigma}_p) = 0.11 + 3(0.03) = 0.20$
$LCL_p = \bar{p} - z(\hat{\sigma}_p) = 0.11 - 3(0.03) = 0.02$

b. Plotting the control limits and the sample proportion of defectives, you can see that the process is not in control: sample 8 ($\frac{22}{100} = 0.22$) and sample 15 ($\frac{21}{100} = 0.21$) are above the upper control limit. Therefore, the machine operation should be investigated for assignable causes and, after corrective action, new data should be collected and new p-control limits should be calculated.

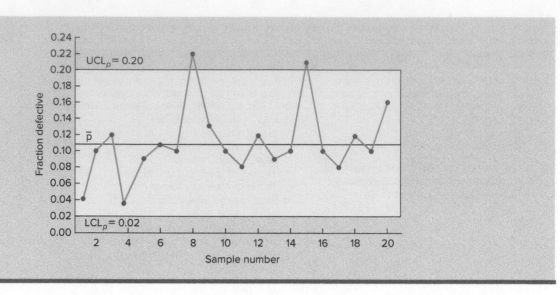

c-Chart. When the goal is to control the number of *occurrences* of defects *per unit product*, a c-chart (the control chart for the sample number of defects per unit product) is used. A unit might be an automobile, a hotel room, a typed page, or a roll of carpet. In this case, there is no sample size, and only occurrences may be counted: the non-occurrences cannot be. The underlying sampling distribution is the Poisson distribution. Use of the Poisson distribution assumes that defects occur over some *continuous* region and that the probability of more than one defect at any particular spot is negligible. The mean number of defects per unit product is c and the standard deviation is $\sqrt{c}$. For practical reasons, the Normal approximation to the Poisson is used. The control limits are:

> **c-chart** Control chart for sample number of defects per unit product, used to monitor the number of defects per unit product.

$$\begin{aligned} \text{UCL}_c &= c + z\sqrt{c} \\ \text{LCL}_c &= c - z\sqrt{c} \end{aligned}$$

(10-8)

If the value of c is unknown, as is generally the case, the average of number of defects per unit product from a few samples, $\bar{c}$, is used in place of c (that is, $\bar{c}$ = Total number of defects ÷ Total number of samples).

When the lower control limit is negative, it is set to zero.

EXAMPLE 10-7 ▶

Rolls of coiled wire are monitored using a c-chart. Eighteen rolls have been examined, and the number of defects per roll has been recorded in the following table.

a. Is the process in control? Plot the values on a c-chart using three standard deviation control limits.
b. Suppose a new roll has seven defects. Using the c-chart of part *a*, is the process still in control?

Sample	Number of Defectives	Sample	Number of Defectives
1..........	3	10..........	1
2	2	11...........	3
3	4	12..........	4
4	5	13..........	2
5	1	14..........	4
6	2	15..........	2
7	4	16..........	1
8	1	17..........	3
9	2	18..........	1
			45

SOLUTION

a. $\bar{c} = 45/18 = 2.5$

$\text{UCL}_c = \bar{c} + 3\sqrt{\bar{c}} = 2.5 + 3\sqrt{2.5} = 7.24$

$\text{LCL}_c = \bar{c} - 3\sqrt{\bar{c}} = 2.5 - 3\sqrt{2.5} = \rightarrow 0$

As shown in the c-chart that follows, the process is in control.

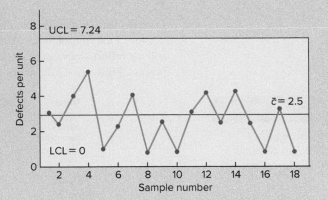

b. Because $0 < 7 < 7.24$, the process is still in control.

Managerial Considerations Concerning Control Charts

Using control charts adds to the cost and time needed to obtain output. Ideally a process is so good that the desired level of quality could be achieved without the use of any control charts. The best organizations strive to reach this level, but many are not yet there, so they employ control charts at various points in their processes. In those organizations, managers must make a number of important decisions about the use of control charts:

1. At what points in the process to use control charts
2. What size samples to take
3. What type of control chart to use (i.e., variables or attribute)
4. How often samples should be taken

The decision about where to use control charts should focus on those aspects of the process that (1) have a tendency to go out of control and (2) are critical to the successful operation of the product or service (i.e., variables that affect product or service characteristics).

Sample size is important for two reasons. The first reason is that cost and time are functions of sample size; the greater the sample size, the greater the cost to inspect those items (and the greater the lost product if destructive testing is involved) and the longer the process must be held up while waiting for the results of sampling. The second reason is that smaller samples are more likely to reveal a change in the process than larger samples because a change is more likely to take place *within* the large sample, but *between* small samples. Consequently, a sample statistic such as the sample mean in the large sample could combine both "before-change" and "after-change" observations, whereas in two smaller samples, the first could contain "before" observations and the second "after" observations, making detection of the change more likely.

In some instances, a manager can choose between using a control chart for variables (a mean chart) and a control chart for attributes (a p-chart). If the manager is monitoring the diameter of a drive shaft, either the diameter could be measured and a mean chart used for control, or the shafts could be inspected using a "go, no-go gauge"—which simply indicates whether a particular shaft is within specification without giving its exact dimensions—and a p-chart could be used. Measuring is more costly and time-consuming per unit than the yes–no inspection using a go, no-go gauge, but because measuring supplies more information than merely counting items as good or bad, one needs a much smaller sample size for a mean chart than a p-chart. Hence, a manager must weigh the time and cost of sampling against the information provided.

Sampling frequency can be a function of the stability of a process and the cost to sample.

Run Tests

Control charts test for points that are too extreme to be considered random (e.g., points that are outside of the control limits). However, even if all points are within the control limits, the data may still not reflect a random process. In fact, any sort of pattern in the data would suggest a nonrandom process. Figure 10-12 illustrates some patterns that might be present.

FIGURE 10-12 ▶

Some examples of nonrandom patterns in control chart plots.

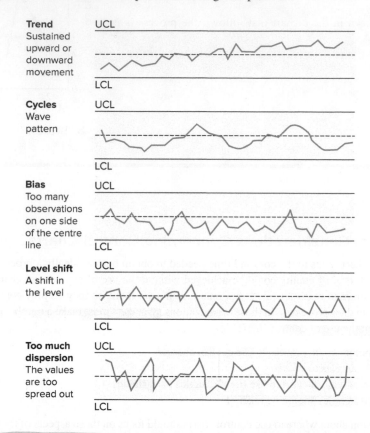

Trend
Sustained upward or downward movement

Cycles
Wave pattern

Bias
Too many observations on one side of the centre line

Level shift
A shift in the level

Too much dispersion
The values are too spread out

run test A test for patterns in a sequence.

run Sequence of observations with a certain characteristic.

Analysts often supplement control charts with a **run test**, which checks for patterns in a sequence of observations. This enables an analyst to do a better job of detecting abnormalities in a process and provides insights into correcting a process that is out of control. A variety of run tests are available; this section describes two that are widely used.

When a process is stable or in statistical control, the output it generates will exhibit random variability over a period of time. The presence of patterns (such as trends, cycles, or bias in the output) indicates that assignable, or nonrandom, causes of variation exist. Hence, a process that produces output with such patterns is not in a state of statistical control. This is true even though all points on a control chart may be within the control limits. For this reason, it is usually prudent to subject control chart data to run tests to determine whether patterns can be detected.

A **run** is defined as a sequence of observations with a certain characteristic, followed by one or more observations with a different characteristic. The characteristic can be anything that is observable. For example, in the series A A A B, there are two runs: a run of three As followed by a run of one B. Underlining each run helps in counting them. In the series AA BBB A, the underlining indicates three runs.

Two useful run tests involve examination of the number of runs up and down and runs above and below the *median*.[3] In order to count these runs, the data are transformed into a series of Us and Ds (for up and down) and into a series of As and Bs (for above and below the median). Consider the following sequence, which has a median of 36.5. The first two values are below the median, the next two are above it, the next to last is below, and the last is above. Thus, there are four runs:

---

[3] The median and mean are approximately equal for control charts. The use of the median depends on its ease of determination; use the mean instead of the median if it is given.

25	29		42	40		35	38
B	**B**		**A**	**A**		**B**	**A**

In terms of up and down, there are three runs in the same data. The second value is up from the first value, the third is up from the second, the fourth is down from the third, and so on:

25		29	42		40	35		38
-		**U**	**U**		**D**	**D**		**U**

(The first value does not receive either a U or a D because nothing precedes it.)

If a plot is available, the runs can be easily counted directly from the plot, as illustrated in Figure 10-13 and Figure 10-14.

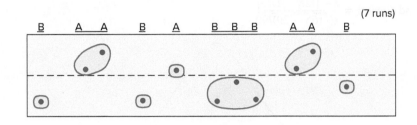

(7 runs)

◀ **FIGURE 10-13**

Counting above/ below median runs

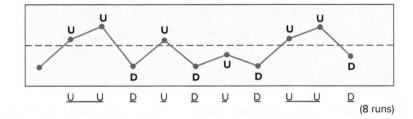

(8 runs)

◀ **FIGURE 10-14**

Counting up/down runs

To determine whether any patterns are present in control chart data, one must transform the data into both As and Bs and Us and Ds, and then count the number of runs in each case. These numbers must then be compared with the number of runs that would be expected in a completely random series. For both the median and the up/down run tests, the expected number of runs is a function of the number of observations in the series. The formulas are

$$E(r)_{med} = \frac{N}{2} + 1 \qquad \text{(10-9a)}$$

$$E(r)_{u/d} = \frac{2N - 1}{3} \qquad \text{(10-10a)}$$

where N is the number of observations or data points, and $E(r)$ is the expected number of runs.

The actual number of runs in any given set of observations will vary from the expected number, due to chance and any patterns that might be present. Chance variability is measured by the standard deviation of runs. The formulas are

$$\sigma_{med} = \sqrt{\frac{N - 1}{4}} \qquad \text{(10-9b)}$$

$$\sigma_{u/d} = \sqrt{\frac{16N - 29}{90}} \qquad \text{(10-10b)}$$

Distinguishing chance variability from patterns requires use of the sampling distributions for median runs and up/down runs. Both distributions are approximately Normal. Thus, for example, 95.5 percent of the time a random process will produce an observed number of runs within two standard deviations of the expected number. If the observed number of runs falls in that range, there are probably no nonrandom patterns; for observed numbers of runs beyond such limits, we begin to suspect that patterns are present. Too few or too many runs can be an indication of nonrandomness.

In practice, it is often easiest to compute the number of standard deviations, z, by which an observed number of runs differs from the expected number. This z value would then be compared to the value ±2 (z for 95.5 percent) or some other desired value (e.g., ±1.96 for 95 percent, ±2.33 for 98 percent). A test z that exceeds the desired limits indicates patterns are present. (See Figure 10-15.) The computation of z takes the form

$$z_{test} = \frac{\text{Observed number of runs} - \text{Expected number of runs}}{\text{Standard deviation of number of runs}}$$

For the median and up/down tests, one can find z using these formulas:

Median: $z = \dfrac{r - [(N/2) + 1]}{\sqrt{(N-1)/4}}$ (10-11)

Up and down: $z = \dfrac{r - [(2N-1)/3]}{\sqrt{(16N-29)/90}}$ (10-12)

FIGURE 10-15 ▶

A sampling distribution for runs is used to distinguish chance variation from patterns

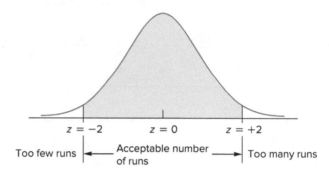

where

N = Total number of observations

r = Observed number of runs of either As and Bs or Us and Ds, depending on which test is involved.

It is desirable to apply both run tests to any given set of observations because each test is different in terms of the types of patterns it can detect. Sometimes both tests will pick up a certain pattern, but other times only one will detect nonrandomness. If either does, the implication is that some sort of nonrandomness is present in the data.

EXAMPLE 10-8 ▶

Twenty sample means have been taken from a process. The means are shown in the following table. Use median and up/down run tests with $z = 2$ to determine if assignable causes of variation are present. Assume the median is 11.0.

SOLUTION

The means are marked in the chart on the next page according to above/below the median and up/down. The solid lines represent the runs.

The expected number of runs for each test is

$$E(r)_{med} = \frac{N}{2} + 1 = \frac{20}{2} + 1 = 11$$

$$E(r)_{u/d} = \frac{2N-1}{3} = \frac{2(20)-1}{3} = 13$$

The standard deviations are

$$\sigma_{med} = \sqrt{\frac{N-1}{4}} = \sqrt{\frac{20-1}{4}} = 2.18$$

$$\sigma_{u/d} = \sqrt{\frac{16N-29}{90}} = \sqrt{\frac{16(20)-29}{90}} = 1.80$$

The z_{test} values are

$$z_{test} = \frac{10-11}{2.18} = -0.46$$

$$z_{u/d} = \frac{17-13}{1.80} = +2.22$$

Although the median test does not reveal any pattern, because its z_{test} value is within the range ±2, the up/down test does; its value exceeds $+2$. Consequently, nonrandom variations are probably present in the data and, hence, the process is not in control.

If ties occur in either test (e.g., a value equals the median or two values in a row are the same), assign A/B or U/D in such a manner that z_{test} is as large as possible. If z_{test} still does not exceed ±2 (±1.96, etc.), you can be reasonably confident that a conclusion of randomness is justified.

Sample	A/B	Mean	U/D	Sample	A/B	Mean	U/D
1	B	10.0	-	11	B	10.7	D
2	B	10.4	U	12	A	11.3	U
3	B	10.2	D	13	B	10.8	D
4	A	11.5	U	14	A	11.8	U
5	B	10.8	D	15	A	11.2	D
6	A	11.6	U	16	A	11.6	U
7	A	11.1	D	17	A	11.2	D
8	A	11.2	U	18	B	10.6	D
9	B	10.6	D	19	B	10.7	U
10	B	10.9	U	20	A	11.9	U

A/B: 10 runs

U/D: 17 runs

Using Control Charts and Run Tests Together

Although for instructional purposes most of the examples, solved problems, and problems focus on either control charts or run tests, ideally both control charts and run tests should be used to analyze process output, along with a plot of the data. The procedure involves the following three steps:

1. Compute control limits for the process output.
    1. Determine which type of control chart is appropriate (see Figure 10-18 in the chapter summary).
    2. Compute control limits using the appropriate formulas. If no probability is given, use a value of $z = \pm 3.00$ to compute the control limits.
    3. If any sample statistics fall outside of the control limits, the process is not in control. If all values are within the control limits, proceed to Step 2.
2. Conduct median and up/down run tests. Use $z = \pm 3.00$ for comparing the test scores if no other value is specified. If either or both test scores are not within $z = \pm 3.00$, the output is probably not random. If both test scores are within $z = \pm 3.00$, proceed to Step 3.
3. *Note*: If you are at this point, there is no indication so far that the process output is nonrandom. Plot the sample data and visually check for patterns (e.g., cycling). If you see a pattern, the output is probably not random. Otherwise, conclude the output is random and that the process is in control.

What Happens When a Process Exhibits Possible Nonrandom Variation?

Nonrandom variation is indicated when a point is observed that is outside the control limits, or a run test produces a large z-value (e.g., greater than ± 3.00). Managers should have response plans in place to investigate the cause. It may be a false alarm (i.e., a Type I error), or it may be a real indication of the presence of an assignable cause of variation. If it appears to be a false alarm, resume the process but monitor it for a while to confirm this. If an assignable cause can be found, it needs to be addressed. If it is a good result (e.g., an observation below the lower control limit of a p-chart, a c-chart, or a range chart would indicate unusually good quality), it may be possible to change the process to achieve similar results on an ongoing basis. The more typical case is that there is a problem that needs to be corrected. Operators can be trained to handle simple problems, while teams or a supervisor may be needed to handle more complex problems. Problem solving often requires the use of various tools, described in Chapter 9, to find the root cause of the problem. Once the cause has been found, changes can be made to reduce the chance of recurrence.

L03 Process Capability

Once the stability of a process has been established (i.e., no nonrandom variations are present), it is necessary to determine if the process is capable of producing output that is within an acceptable range. The variability of a process becomes the focal point of the analysis. Three terms relate to the process capability: design specification, control limits, and process variability. Each term represents a slightly different aspect of variability, so it is important to differentiate these terms.

Design specification, established by engineering design or customer requirements, is a range of values into which a product must fall in order to be acceptable.

Control limits are statistical limits that reflect the extent to which *sample statistics* such as mean and range can vary due to randomness alone.

Process variability is the actual variability in a process for a product.

Control limits and process variability are directly related: control limits are based on sampling distribution variability, and sampling distribution variability is a function of process variability. On the other hand, there is no direct link between design specification and either control limits or process variability. The output of a process may or may not conform to design specification, even though the process may be statistically in control. That is why it is also necessary to take into account the *capability* of a process. The term **process capability** refers to the ability of a process to meet the design specification. Measuring this capability is called capability analysis.

design specification A range of acceptable values established by engineering design or customer requirements.

process variability Actual variability in a process for a product.

process capability The ability of a process to meet the design specification.

Capability Analysis

Capability analysis determines whether the process output falls within the design specification. If it is within the design specification for all its output, then the process is said to be "capable." If it is not, the process is said to be incapable and the manager must decide how to correct the situation.

Consider the three cases illustrated in Figure 10-16. In Case A, process output and design specification are well matched, so that nearly all of the process output can be expected to meet the design specification. In Case B, 100 percent of the output is within the design specification limits. In Case C, however, the design specification is tighter than what the process is capable of, so a few percentages of the output fail to meet the design specification.

FIGURE 10-16 ▶

Process output and design specification may or may not match.

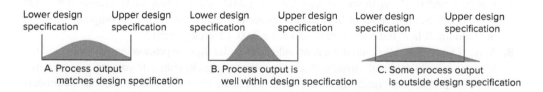

Lower design specification — Upper design specification

A. Process output matches design specification

Lower design specification — Upper design specification

B. Process output is well within design specification

Lower design specification — Upper design specification

C. Some process output is outside design specification

In instances such as Case C in Figure 10-16, a manager might consider a range of possible solutions: (1) redesign the process or reduce its variability by, for example, performing experiments to find the best settings for the controllable factors; (2) use an alternative process that can achieve the desired accuracy; (3) retain the current process but attempt to eliminate unacceptable output using 100 percent inspection; and (4) examine the design specification to see whether it could be relaxed without adversely affecting customer satisfaction.

Process variability is typically measured as the interval ± 3 standard deviations from the process mean. To determine whether the process is capable, compare this ± 3 standard deviations value to the acceptable range of variation (i.e., design specification range or width), assuming that the process mean is centred at the midpoint of design specification. For example, suppose that the ideal length of time to perform a service is 10 minutes, and an acceptable range of variation around this time is ± 1 minute. If the process has a standard deviation of 0.5 minute, it would not be capable because ± 3 standard deviations would be ± 1.5 minutes, which exceeds ± 1 minute.

An alternative way is to compare six standard deviations of the process with the design specification width (Upper design specification – Lower design specification). For the above example, Six Sigma of the process is $6(0.5) = 3$ minutes, and the design specification width is $2(1) = 2$ minutes.

EXAMPLE 10-9

A manager has the option of using any one of three machines—A, B, or C—for making a part. The machines and their standard deviations of outputs (in millimetres) are listed below. Determine which machines are capable if the design specification for the part's length is between 101.00 mm and 101.60 mm.

Machine	Standard Deviation (mm)
A	0.10
B	0.08
C	0.13

Machine	Standard Deviation (mm)	Machine Variability = 6σ
A	0.10	0.60
B	0.08	0.48
C	0.13	0.78

We can see that both machine A and machine B are capable of producing output that is within the specification (assuming they can be centred at the midpoint of the design specification 101.30), but that machine C is not, because its variability of 0.78 exceeds the design specification width of 0.60. See Figure 10-16 for a visual portrayal of these results.

SOLUTION

Determine the output variability of each machine (i.e., six standard deviations) and compare that value to the specification width of 0.60 mm (= 101.60 – 101.00).

C_p

To express the capability of a machine or process, some companies use the ratio of the design specification width to the process width (which equals six sigma). This can be calculated using the following formula:

$$\text{Process capability ratio, } C_p = \frac{\text{Design specification width}}{\text{Process width}}$$

$$= \frac{\text{Upper design specification} - \text{Lower design specification}}{6\sigma} \quad (10\text{-}13)$$

EXAMPLE 10-10

Calculate the process capability index for each machine in Example 10-9.

SOLUTION

The design specification width in Example 10-9 was 0.60 mm. Hence, to determine the capability index for each machine, divide 0.60 by the process width (i.e., six standard deviations) of each machine. The results are:

Machine	Standard Deviation (mm)	Machine Capability	C_p
A	0.10	0.60	0.60/0.60 = 1.00
B	0.08	0.48	0.60/0.48 = 1.25
C	0.13	0.78	0.60/0.78 = 0.77

Using the capability ratio, you can see that for a process to be capable, it must have a capability ratio of at least 1.00. A ratio of 1.00 implies that 99.74 percent of the output of a process can be expected to be within the design specification limits, hence only 0.26 percent, or 2,600 parts per million, fall outside the design specification. Moreover, the greater the process capability ratio, the greater the probability that the output of a machine or process will fall within design specification.

C_{pk}

If a process is not centred between design specification limits, or if there is no design specification limit on one side, a slightly different measure is used to calculate its capability. This ratio is represented by the symbol C_{pk}. It is calculated by finding the difference between each of the specification limits and the process mean, dividing that difference by three standard deviations of the process, and identifying the smaller ratio. Thus, C_{pk} is equal to the *smaller* of:

$$\frac{\text{Upper design specification} - \text{Process mean}}{3\sigma} \qquad (10\text{-}14)$$

and

$$\frac{\text{Process mean} - \text{Lower design specification}}{3\sigma}$$

EXAMPLE 10-11 ▶

A process's output has a mean of 9.20 kg and a standard deviation of 0.30 kg. The lower design specification is 8.00 kg and the upper design specification is 10.00 kg. Calculate the C_{pk}.

1. Calculate the ratio for the lower design specification:

$$\frac{\text{Process mean} - \text{Lower design specification}}{3\sigma} = \frac{9.20 - 8.00}{3(0.30)}$$

$$= \frac{1.20}{0.90} = 1.33$$

2. Calculate the ratio for the upper design specification:

$$\frac{\text{Upper design specification} - \text{Process mean}}{3\sigma} = \frac{10.00 - 9.20}{3(0.30)}$$

$$= \frac{0.80}{0.90} = 0.89$$

The smaller of the two ratios is 0.89, so this is the C_{pk}. Because the C_{pk} is less than 1.00, the process is *not* capable. Note that if C_p had been used, it would have given the false impression that the process was capable:

$$C_p = \frac{\text{Upper design specification} - \text{Lower design specification}}{6\sigma}$$

$$= \frac{10.00 - 8.00}{6(0.30)} = \frac{2.00}{1.80} = 1.11 > 1.00$$

LO4 Six Sigma Quality

Six Sigma quality A more advanced version of problem solving/continuous improvement. It also refers to the goal of achieving process variability so small that the half-width of design specification equals six standard deviations of the process.

Six Sigma quality is a more advanced version of problem solving/continuous improvement that was discussed in the previous chapter. It also refers to the goal of achieving process variability so small that the half-width of design specification equals six standard deviations of the process. That means that the process capability ratio equals 2.00, resulting in an extremely small probability (0.00034 percent, or 3.4 units per million) of getting any output outside design specification. This is illustrated in Figure 10-17.[4]

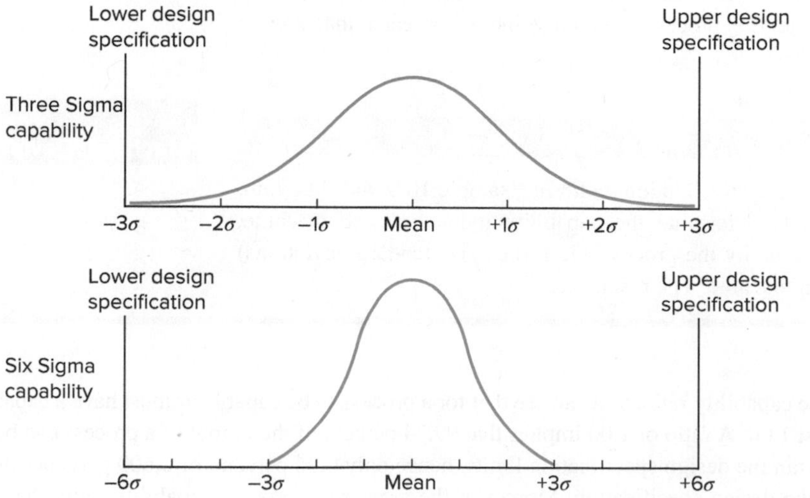

FIGURE 10-17 ▶

Three Sigma versus Six Sigma capability. (Blue curves show the process output; note horizontal axis scales are different in the two charts.)

---

[4] Actually 3.4 defects per million corresponds to 4.5σ. The other 1.5σ is to allow the process mean to be off-centre by up to 1.5σ.

The differences of Six Sigma quality and continuous improvement are:[5]

	Six Sigma Quality	Continuous Improvement
Objective	Product and process perfection	Product and process improvement
Tools	Statistical (e.g., design of experiments and analysis of variance)	Simple data analysis (Pareto chart, cause-and-effect diagram)
Methodology	Define, measure, analyze, improve, control (DMAIC)	Plan, do, study, act (PDSA)
Team leader	Black belt	Champion
Training	Long/formal	Short/informal
Culture change	Usually enforced	Sometimes enforced
Project time frame	Months/years	Days/weeks

The Six Sigma improvement methodology DMAIC involves:

Define	Determine the customers and critical-to-quality procedures
Measure	Identify and measure the quality problem, determine the baseline Sigma, and identify possible influencing factors
Analyze	Test the influencing factors and identify the vital few
Improve	Select the solution method, prove its effectiveness, and implement it
Control	Develop a process control plan

EXAMPLE 10-12

The North Shore-Long Island Jewish Health System[6] consists of several hospitals and nursing homes around New York City. A central lab performs blood tests for the health system as well as for other private clinics. The Six Sigma consultants are housed in the Center for Learning and Innovation of the health system. Although the health system has a very large and capable quality management department, the Six Sigma group decided to remain separate. The Six Sigma group focuses on chronic issues that cannot be solved easily and uses systematic statistical and change management techniques.

One project the Six Sigma group worked on in 2002–2003 was the labelling of test specimens in the central lab. The tests are done by automated machines, so most errors occur before the test. The critical-to-quality procedures for labelling are (a) receiving the requisition of blood test and specimen, (b) entering patient information into the computer, (c) delivering the specimen to the automated machines, (d) obtaining results, and (e) sending the results to the requisitioner.

The Six Sigma team consisted of some members of the Six Sigma group, lab management, and representatives from the compliance, quality, and marketing departments. The objective was to reduce the errors and missing data. The data accompanying the specimens were patient name, social security number, date of birth, gender, physician's name, name of test, and a code name for the diagnosis.

The percentage of errors and omissions was 5 percent. The major problem was identified to be omission of the code name for diagnosis. The solution was rather simple: a pocket guide to the diagnosis code for the requisitioners. This reduced the error and omission rate to 0.7 percent.

To further reduce labelling errors and omissions, the next common error (approximately 50 percent of remaining errors or omissions) was identified as the social security number. A pattern was easily found: most of these errors originated from units that used a special set of codes (called addressograph) which presented the information in a confusing way. Again, an easy solution was discovered: peel off the bar code at the bottom of the patient's chart and attach it to the requisition.

The team also performed a benchmarking study of the productivity of the labelling staff (accessioners). A labeller prepared an average of 17 labels per hour, whereas the industry norm was 20. Although some workers were faster

---

[5] "Baldrige, Six Sigma, & ISO: Understanding Your Options," http://www.nist.gov/baldrige/publications/up-load/Issue_Sheet_SS.pdf, Summer 2002; J. Bossert et al., "Your Opinion: Are Six Sigma and Lean Manufacturing Really Different?," *ASQ Six Sigma Forum Magazine* 2(1), November 2002, pp. 38–43.

[6] N.B. Riebling et al., "Toward Error Free Lab Work," *ASQ Six Sigma Forum Magazine* 4(1), 2004, pp. 23–29.

than the others, there was no statistically significant difference in their productivity. The team decided to look at the method of labelling. A meeting of all staff was called. Their opinion was that there was quite a bit of walking and moving involved and sometimes it was confusing to find the right machines for the particular test needed for a specimen. Solutions suggested were (a) provide a colour-coded book of tests and machines that perform each, (b) put up same colour signs over machines, and (c) employ a runner to move the batch of specimens to the machines. The team decided to try these and also to create a position of lead labeller who would take 20 requisitions/specimens per hour to each labeller and answer any questions they might have.

An experiment was designed to measure the influence of (a) using barcodes, (b) expertise of individual labellers (accessioners), and (c) the new work process (called distribution) on the productivity of labellers. This was done by collecting data under various levels of the factors above. The results are shown in the figure below.

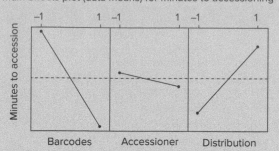

Main effects plot (data means) for minutes to accessioning

Source: N. Riebling, S. Condon, and D. Gopen. (*Six Sigma Forum Magazine,* November 2004). "Toward Error Free Lab Work," 4(1), pp. 23–29. Figure 6, Analyzing the Factorial Design, p. 28.

As can be seen, the use of barcodes (barcodes = 1) and the new work process (distribution = –1) reduces minutes to accession and thus increases productivity. Finally, the individual unit and moving range control charts were constructed to monitor the productivity of each labeller. Productivity has been improving and has exceeded 20 labels per hour per accessioner.

Design of Experiments

design of experiments
Performing experiments by changing levels of factors to measure their influence on output and identifying best levels for each factor.

Design of experiments involves performing experiments by changing levels of factors to measure their influence on output and identifying best levels for each factor. However, if this is done by changing the level of one factor at a time, while keeping the levels of other factors constant, an extremely large number of experiments will be required.

Factorial design suggests a more concise set of experiments by changing the level of more than one factor at a time. For example, suppose we have three factors, each having two levels. Then, if we change one factor's level at a time, in order to determine the best levels for each factor, we will need $2^3 = 8$ different experiments. However, factorial design suggests that, in this case, the following four experiments are adequate (the body of the table shows the level of each factor; this is called fractional factorial design):[7]

	Experiment			
Factor	**(i)**	**(ii)**	**(iii)**	**(iv)**
A	1	1	2	2
B	1	2	1	2
C	1	2	2	1

Runs	2	3	4	5	6	7	8	9
4	2^2	2^{2-1}_{III}						
8		2^3	2^{4-1}_{IV}	2^{5-2}_{III}	2^{6-3}_{III}	2^{7-4}_{III}		
16			2^4	2^{5-1}_{V}	2^{6-2}_{IV}	2^{7-3}_{IV}	2^{8-4}_{IV}	2^{9-5}_{III}
32				2^5	2^{6-1}_{VI}	2^{7-2}_{IV}	2^{8-3}_{IV}	2^{9-4}_{IV}
64					2^6	2^{7-1}_{VII}	2^{8-2}_{V}	2^{9-3}_{IV}
128						2^7	2^{8-1}_{VIII}	2^{9-2}_{VI}
256							2^8	2^{9-1}_{IX}
512								2^9

Courtesy of State-Ease, Inc.

[7] G.S. Peace, *Taguchi Methods*, Reading, Massachusetts: Addison-Wesley, 1993.

In general, the number of experiments (runs) one needs to perform, given the number of factors (at two levels), are given below, where white cells (and one black cell) are for full factorial experiments (which can also identify interaction between factors) and other colours show progressively more restrictive analyses (green, yellow, and red, respectively) whose results may be less reliable. For example, a full factorial experiment with four factors (at two levels) requires 16 experiments (runs).

EXAMPLE 10-13

In the early 1990s, Navistar's Indianapolis engine plant had a problem with the flatness of its cylinder heads (the top part of the engines). The specification width was a lot smaller than process variability, rendering the process incapable. The final machining operation shaved a small amount of metal from the top of cylinder heads. The variation in the flatness resulting from this operation needed to be reduced. Possible factors were thought to be:

1. Feed rate for broach that shaved the metal.
2. The thickness of metal removed.
3. The pressure of clamp holding the cylinder head down.

For each factor, two levels were determined:

a. (Level 1 = 80 feet/minute, Level 2 = 120 feet/minute)
b. (Level 1 = 0.020 inch, Level 2 = 0.0028 inch)
c. (Level 1 = 600 pounds, Level 2 = 500 pounds)

Four experiments were used (see the design given above). Each experiment (i) to (iv) was repeated six times in order to improve the accuracy of the results. For example, in the first experiment, all factors were set to Level 1. For each cylinder head produced, the height of 32 points on its flat surface was measured and the difference between the maximum height and the minimum height was calculated. This high–low difference was averaged over the six pieces produced using the same experiment. The results are:

	Experiment			
	(i)	(ii)	(iii)	(iv)
Average high–low difference (in 1/10,000 inch):	33.32	45.93	25.88	27.17

From these results, the influence of each level of each factor can be determined. For example, Factor 1, Level 1 was used in experiments (i) and (ii). Therefore, its average high–low difference is $(33.32 + 45.93)/2 = 39.63$. The other results were calculated in a similar manner:

Factor	Level 1	Level 2
1	39.63	26.53
2	29.60	36.55
3	30.25	35.90

It can be shown that the levels of all three factors have significant influence on average high–low difference. Therefore, to reduce the variation in cylinder head flatness, this operation should use Level 2 of Factor 1 (i.e., 120 feet/minute tool speed), Level 1 of Factor 2 (i.e., remove 0.020 inch metal), and Level 1 of Factor 3 (i.e., use 600 pounds of clamp pressure). This will reduce the variation in flatness as much as possible.

Source: Based on R. W. Schmenner, *Production/Operations Management*, 5th ed. (New York: MacMillan, 1993, pp. 118–119).

Summary

- Statistical process control focuses on detecting departures from stability in a process. Control charts are commonly used for this.
- There are two types of variations: random and assignable.
- Sample mean ($\bar{x}$) control charts are used to monitor the process mean.
- Sample range control charts are used to monitor process dispersion or spread.
- Individual unit X control charts are used to monitor single observations ($n = 1$).
- Moving range control charts are used to monitor the dispersion or spread of the differences between consecutive observations.
- p-charts are used to monitor the proportion of defective items generated by a process.
- c-charts are used to monitor the number of defects per unit product.
- If a sample statistic falls outside control limits or its series has a pattern, then the process is out of control.
- Run test is used to determine if a nonrandom pattern exists.

- Process capability analysis is used to determine if the output of a process will satisfy design specification.
- Six Sigma quality is the approach that improves process capability to very high levels (3.4 defects per million).

- Design of experiments is a major tool in Six Sigma quality. Factorial design provides an efficient method for design of experiments.
- Figure 10-18 can be used to choose the right control chart.
- Table 10-5 provides a summary of the formulas.

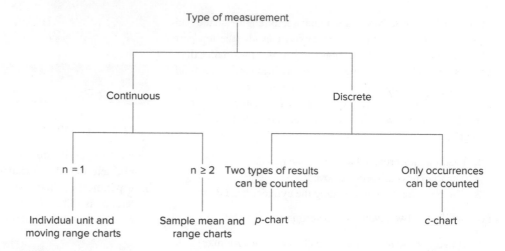

Control Charts		
Name	**Symbol**	**Control Limits**
Sample mean	$\bar{x}$	$\bar{x} \pm z\frac{\sigma}{\sqrt{n}}$ or $\bar{x} \pm A_2\bar{R}$
Sample range	R	$\text{UCL} = D_4\bar{R}, \text{LCL} = D_3\bar{R}$
Sample proportion of defectives	P	$\bar{p} \pm z\sqrt{\frac{\bar{p}(1-\bar{p})}{n}}$
Sample number of defects	C	$\bar{c} \pm z\sqrt{\bar{c}}$

Run Tests				
	Number of Runs			
Name	**Observed**	**Expected**	**Standard Deviation**	**z**
Median	r	$\frac{N}{2}+1$	$\sqrt{\frac{N-1}{4}}$	$\frac{r-[(N/2)+1]}{\sqrt{(N-1)/4}}$
Up/down	r	$\frac{2N-1}{3}$	$\sqrt{\frac{16N-29}{90}}$	$\frac{r-[(2N-1)/3]}{\sqrt{(16N-29)/90}}$

N = Number of observations

Process Capability		
Name	**Symbol**	**Formula**
Capability index for a centred process	C_p	$\dfrac{\text{Design specification width}}{6\sigma \text{ of process}}$
Capability index for a noncentred process	C_{pk}	Smaller of $\begin{cases} \dfrac{\text{Process mean} - \text{Lower design specification}}{3\sigma} \\ \dfrac{\text{Upper design specification} - \text{Process mean}}{3\sigma} \end{cases}$

Key Terms

assignable variation	moving range (MR) control chart	sample range (R) control chart
c-chart	p-chart	Six Sigma quality
central limit theorem	process capability	statistical process control (SPC)
control limits	process variability	statistical quality control
design of experiments	random variation	Type I error
design specification	run	Type II error
individual unit (X) control chart	run test	
inspection	sample mean ($\bar{x}$) control chart	

Solved Problems

Problem 1

Process distribution and sampling distribution. An industrial process makes 3 foot plastic pipes with an average inside diameter of 1 inch and a standard deviation of 0.05 inch.

  a. If you randomly select one piece of pipe, what is the probability that its inside diameter will exceed 1.02 inches, assuming that the process distribution is Normal?

  b. If you select a random sample of 25 pieces of pipe, what is the probability that the sample mean will exceed 1.02 inches?

  $\mu = 1.00, \sigma = 0.05$

Solution

  a. $z = \dfrac{x - \mu}{\sigma} = \dfrac{1.02 - 1.00}{0.05} = 0.4$

  Using Appendix B, Table A, $P(z > 0.4) = 0.5000 - 0.1554 = 0.3446$.

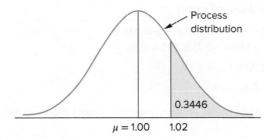

  b. $z = \dfrac{\bar{x} - \mu}{\sigma/\sqrt{n}} = \dfrac{1.02 - 1.00}{0.05/\sqrt{25}} = 2.00$

  Using Appendix B, Table A, $P(z > 2.00) = 0.5000 - 0.4772 = 0.0228$.

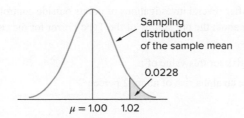

Problem 2

Control charts for sample mean and range. Processing new accounts at a bank is intended to average 10 minutes each. Five samples of four observations each have been taken. Use the sample data below in conjunction with Table 10-3 to construct upper and lower control limits for both sample mean and sample range control charts. Do the results suggest that the process is in control?

	Sample 1	Sample 2	Sample 3	Sample 4	Sample 5
	10.2	10.3	9.7	9.9	9.8
	9.9	9.8	9.9	10.3	10.2
	9.8	9.9	9.9	10.1	10.3
	10.1	10.4	10.1	10.5	9.7
Totals	40.0	40.4	39.6	40.8	40.0

Solution

a. Determine the mean and range of each sample.

$$\bar{x} = \frac{\sum x}{n}, \text{ Range} = \text{Largest} - \text{Smallest}$$

Sample	Mean	Range
1	40.0/4 = 10.0	10.2 − 9.8 = 0.4
2	40.4/4 = 10.1	10.4 − 9.8 = 0.6
3	39.6/4 = 9.9	10.1 − 9.7 = 0.4
4	40.8/4 = 10.2	10.5 − 9.9 = 0.6
5	40.0/4 = 10.0	10.3 − 9.7 = 0.6

b. Calculate the average sample mean and average sample range:

$$\bar{\bar{x}} = \frac{10.0 + 10.1 + 9.9 + 10.2 + 10.0}{5} = \frac{50.2}{5} = 10.4$$

$$\bar{R} = \frac{0.4 + 0.6 + 0.4 + 0.6 + 0.6}{5} = \frac{2.6}{5} = 0.52$$

Note that one can use Excel to compute these quantities. For average, "=average(cells)" should be used where "cells" includes the coordinates of cells where data are located. For example, if data are in cells A2 to A5, then use "=average(A2:A5)". Similarly, for range, "max(A2:A5)–min(A2:A5)" should be used.

c. Obtain factors A_2, D_4, and D_3 from Table 10-3 for $n = 4$: $A_2 = 0.73$, $D_4 = 2.28$, $D_3 = 0$.

d. Calculate upper and lower limits:

$$\text{UCL}_{\bar{x}} = \bar{\bar{x}} + A_2\bar{R} = 10.04 + 0.73(0.52) = 10.42$$
$$\text{LCL}_{\bar{x}} = \bar{\bar{x}} - A_2\bar{R} = 10.04 - 0.73(0.52) = 9.66$$
$$\text{UCL}_R = D_4\bar{R} = 2.28(0.52) = 1.19$$
$$\text{LCL}_R = D_3\bar{R} = 0(0.52) = 0$$

e. Plot sample means and ranges on their respective control charts, or otherwise verify that points are within limits.

All sample means (10.0, 10.1, 9.9, 10.2, 10.0) are larger than LCL of $\bar{X}$ (9.66) and smaller than UCL of $\bar{X}$ (10.42). Similarly, all sample ranges (0.4, 0.6, 0.4, 0.6, 0.6) are larger than LCL of R(0) and smaller than UCL of R(1.19). Hence, the process is in control.

Problem 3

Type I error (alpha risk). After several investigations of points outside control limits revealed nothing, a manager began to wonder about the probability of the Type I error for the control limits used, which were based on $z = 1.90$.

a. Determine the alpha risk for this value of z.

b. What z would provide an alpha risk of about 2 percent?

Solution

a. Using Appendix B, Table A, we find that the area under the curve between $z = 0$ and $z = +1.90$ is 0.4713. Therefore, the area (probability) of values within −1.90 to +1.90 is 2(0.4713) = 0.9426, and the area beyond these values is 1 − 0.9426 = 0.0574. Hence, the alpha risk is 5.74 percent.

b. Because half of the risk lies in each tail, the area under the curve between $z = 0$ and the value of z you are looking for is 0.49. The closest value is 0.4901 for $z = 2.33$. Thus, control limits based on $z = 2.33$ provide an alpha risk of about 2 percent.

Problem 4

p-chart and c-chart. Using the appropriate control chart, determine Two Sigma control limits for each case:

   a. An inspector found an average of 3.9 scratches in the exterior paint of each of the automobiles being prepared for shipment to dealers.

   b. Before shipping lawn mowers to dealers, an inspector attempts to start each mower and notes the ones that do not start on the first try. The lot size is 100 mowers, and an average of 4 did not start on the first try based on a few samples (4 percent).

Solution

The choice between these two types of control charts relates to whether *two* types of results can be counted (*p*-chart) or whether *only occurrences* can be counted (*c*-chart).

   a. The inspector can count only the scratches that occurred, not the ones that did not occur. Consequently, a *c*-chart is appropriate. The sample average is 3.9 scratches per car. Two Sigma control limits are found using the formulas:

$$UCL = \bar{c} + z\sqrt{\bar{c}}$$
$$LCL = \bar{c} - z\sqrt{\bar{c}}$$

where $\bar{c} = 3.9$ and $z = 2$. Thus,

$$UCL = 3.9 + 2\sqrt{3.9} = 7.85 \text{ scratches}$$
$$LCL = 3.9 - 2\sqrt{3.9} = -0.05, \text{ so the lower limit is } 0 \text{ scratches}$$

   b. The inspector can count both the lawn mowers that started and those that did not start. Consequently, a *p*-chart is appropriate. Two Sigma control limits can be calculated using the following:

$$UCL = \bar{p} + z\sqrt{\frac{\bar{p}(1-\bar{p})}{n}}$$
$$LCL = \bar{p} - z\sqrt{\frac{\bar{p}(1-\bar{p})}{n}}$$

where:

$$\bar{p} = 0.04$$
$$n = 100$$
$$z = 2$$

Thus,

$$UCL = 0.04 + 2\sqrt{\frac{0.04(0.96)}{100}} = 0.079$$
$$LCL = 0.04 - 2\sqrt{\frac{0.04(0.96)}{100}} = 0.001$$

Problem 5

Run tests. The number of defective items per sample for 11 samples is shown below. Determine if non-random patterns are present in the sequence for $z = \pm 2.00$.

	Sample										
	1	2	3	4	5	6	7	8	9	10	11
Number of defectives	22	17	19	25	18	20	21	17	23	23	24

Solution

Since the median isn't given, it must be estimated from the sample data. To do this, sort the data from low to high; the median is the middle value. (In this case, there is an odd number of values. For an even number of values, average the middle two values to obtain the median.) Thus,

17	17	18	19	20	21	22	23	23	24	25
	(5 below)				↑			(5 above)		
					median					

The median is 21.

Next, code the observations using A/B and U/D:

Sample	A/B	No. of defectives	U/D
1	A	22.0	-
2	B	17	D
3	B	19	U
4	A	25	U
5	B	18	D
6	B	20	U
7	tie	21	U
8	B	17	D
9	A	23	U
10	A	23	tie
11	A	24	U

Note that each test has tied values. How these are resolved can affect the number of observed runs. Suppose that you adhere to this rule: Assign a letter (A or B, U or D) so that the resulting difference between the observed and expected number of runs is as large as possible to be conservative. With this in mind, assign a B to sample 7 since the expected number of runs is

$$E(r)_{med} = \frac{N}{2} + 1 = \frac{11}{2} + 1 = 6.5$$

and the difference between the resulting number of runs, 5, and 6.5 is greater than between 6.5 and 7 (which occurs if A is used instead of B). Similarly, in the up/down test, a U for sample 10 produces six runs, whereas a D produces eight runs. Since the expected number of runs is

$$E(r)_{u/d} = \frac{(2N - 1)}{3} = \frac{(22 - 1)}{3} = 7$$

it makes no difference which one is used: both yield a difference of 1. For the sake of illustration, a D is assigned.

The computations for the two tests are summarized as follows. Each test has a z-value that is within the range of ± 2.00. Because neither test reveals nonrandomness, you may conclude that the data are random.

	Runs Observed	Expected	σ_r	z	Conclude
Median	5	6.5	1.58	−0.95	Random
Up/down	8	7.0	1.28	0.78	Random

Problem 6

Determine if these three processes are capable:

Process	Mean	Standard Deviation	Lower Spec	Upper Spec
1	7.5	0.10	7.0	8.0
2	4.6	0.12	4.3	4.9
3	6.0	0.14	5.5	6.7

Solution

Notice that the means of the first two processes are exactly in the centre of the upper and lower specs. Hence, the C_p index (Formula 10-13) is appropriate. However, the third process is not centred, so C_{pk} (Formula 10-14) is appropriate.

For processes 1 and 2: $C_p = \dfrac{\text{Upper spec} - \text{Lower spec}}{6\sigma}$

In order to be capable, C_p must be at least 1.0.

Process 1: $C_p = \dfrac{8.0 - 7.0}{6(0.10)} = 1.67$ (capable)

Process 2: $C_p = \dfrac{4.9 - 4.3}{6(0.12)} = 0.83$ (not capable)

For Process 3, C_{pk} must be at least 1.0. It is the lesser of these two:

$\dfrac{\text{Upper spec} - \text{Mean}}{3\sigma} = \dfrac{6.7 - 6.0}{3(0.14)} = 1.67$

$\dfrac{\text{Mean} - \text{Lower spec}}{3\sigma} = \dfrac{6.0 - 5.5}{3(0.14)} = 1.19$

Minimum $\{1.67, 1.19\} = 1.19 > 1.0 \rightarrow$ capable.

Discussion and Review Questions

Note: An asterisk indicates that a question or problem may be more challenging.

LO1 **1.** What is statistical quality control and why is it important?

LO1 **2.** List the steps in the statistical process control planning process.

LO1 **3.** Answer these questions about inspection:
   a. What level of inspection is optimal?
   b. What are the main considerations in choosing between centralized inspection and on-site inspection?
   c. What points are potential candidates for inspection?

LO2 **4.** What are the key concepts that underlie the construction and interpretation of control charts?

LO2 **5.** What is the purpose of a control chart?

LO2 **6.** Classify each of the following as either a Type I or a Type II error:
   a. Putting an innocent person in jail.
   b. Releasing a guilty person from jail.

LO2 **7.** Why is order of observation important in control charts?

LO2 **8.** What are the steps for designing a control chart?

LO2 **9.** Briefly explain the purpose of each of these control charts:
   a. $\bar{x}$
   b. R
   c. Individual unit
   d. Moving range
   e. p
   f. c

LO2 **10.** Why are $\bar{x}$ and R charts used together?

LO2 **11.** If all the observations are within control limits, does that guarantee that the process variation contains only randomness?

LO2 **12.** Identify a process in a bank and one in a retail store that control charts can be used to monitor.

LO2 **13.** What is a run? How are run charts useful in process control?

LO2 **14.** Why is it usually desirable to use both a median run test and an up/down run test on the same data?

LO2 **15.** If both run tests are used, and neither reveals nonrandomness, does that prove that the process is random? Explain.

LO3 **16.** Define and contrast control limits and design specification limits.

LO3 **17.** A customer has recently tightened the design specification for a part your company supplies. The design specification is now much tighter than the machine being used for the job is capable of. Briefly identify alternatives you might consider to resolve this problem.

LO3 **18.** Define and contrast C_p and C_{pk}.

LO3 **19.** Can the value of C_{pk} exceed the value of C_p for the same process and specification limits? Explain.

LO2 & 3 **20.** A process can be capable but out of control. Another process can be in control but incapable. Explain.

LO4 **21.** What is Six Sigma quality and how does it differ from continuous improvement's PDSA?

LO4 **22.** What is design of experiments and why is it useful for Six Sigma quality?

Taking Stock

1. What trade-offs are involved in each of these decisions?

LO2   **a.** Deciding whether to use Two Sigma or Three Sigma control limits.

LO1   **b.** Choosing between a large sample size and a smaller sample size.

LO3   **c.** Trying to increase the capability of a process that is barely capable.

LO1 **2.** Who needs to be involved in statistical process control (SPC)?

LO1 **3.** Name two ways in which technology has had an impact on SPC.

LO1 **4.** What kinds of ethical issues arise in SPC when the operators are put in charge of quality control at their own workstations? How can these concerns be addressed? Explain.

Critical Thinking Exercises

 1. A manufacturer of toys and board games has built a reputation on quality. However, sales have leveled off in recent years. The VP of sales has been concerned with customer complaints about the company's realistic line of working-model factories, farms, and service stations. The moving parts on certain models become disengaged and fail to operate or operate erratically. His assistant has proposed a trade-in program by which customers could replace malfunctioning models with new ones. He also proposes rebuilding the trade-ins and selling them at discounted prices in the company's retail outlet store. A production assistant has suggested increasing inspection of finished models before they are shipped. Take the role of a consultant who has been called in for advice by the company president. What do you recommend?

 2. Analysis of the output of a process has suggested that the variability was nonrandom on several occasions recently. However, each time the investigation has not revealed any assignable causes. What are some of the possible explanations for not finding any causes? What should the manager do?

 3. Many organizations use the same process capability standard for all their products or services (e.g., 1.33), but some companies use multiple standards: different standards for different products or services (e.g., 1.00, 1.20, 1.33, and 1.40). What reasons might there be for using a single measure, and what reasons might there be for using multiple standards?

 4. In repetitive operations, it is often possible to automatically check for quality and reject a part that is unacceptable. In those situations, does that mean that control charts aren't needed? Explain.

Experiential Learning Exercises

 1. Obtain approximately 10 small bags of M&M's (multi-coloured), or similar candies. Arrange the unopened bags in a single row, and treat each bag as a sample from an ongoing process, in the order you have placed them. Treat the yellow candies (or another colour that is the fewest in number in each bag) as defects.

   a. List the four or five steps needed to obtain sample information for each bag, beginning with opening the bag.

   b. Determine the upper and lower control limits for the sample proportion of defectives using Three Sigma

control limits. *Note:* the number of candies in each bag may not be exactly the same. You can ignore that.

   c. Is the process variation random? Explain how you reached your conclusion.

 2. Six Sigma means product specifications are six standard deviations away from the process mean. Without incorporating a shift of 1.5 standard deviations in the process mean, how many defective parts per million will be produced? When a 1.5 standard deviation shift is incorporated, how many defective parts per million will be produced?

Internet Exercises

 1. Visit http://www.qualitymag.com, search for "statistical quality control," find an application, and summarize it.

 2. Visit http://jobs.isixsigma.com, choose a job announcement related to Six Sigma quality, and describe the job description.

 3. Visit http://www.inspection.gc.ca/about-the-cfia/newsroom/food-safety-system/haccp/eng/1346306502207

/1346306685922 and read about what the Canadian Food Inspection Agency has to say about HACCP. What was the original purpose of HACCP? What are the seven principles?

4. Visit http://www.statease.com/pubs/breaddoe.pdf and summarize the design of an experiment to determine the ingredients for bread.

Problems

 1. Design specification for a motor housing states that it should weigh between 24 kg and 25 kg. The process that produces the housing yields a mean of 24.5 kg and a standard deviation of 0.2 kg. The distribution of output is Normal.

   a. What percentage of housings will not meet the design specification?

   b. Within what values should 95.44 percent of sample means of this process fall if samples of $n = 16$ are taken?

 2. An automatic filling machine is used to fill 2-litre bottles of cola. The machine's output is known to be approximately Normal with a mean of 2.0 litres and a standard deviation of 0.01 litre. Output is monitored using means of samples of five observations.

   a. Determine the upper and lower control limits that will include roughly 95.5 percent of the sample means.

   b. If the means for six samples are 2.005, 2.001, 1.998, 2.002, 1.995, and 1.999, is the process in control?

3. Process time at a workstation is monitored using sample mean and range control charts. Six samples of $n = 10$ observations have been obtained and the sample means and ranges computed (in minutes):

Sample	Mean	Range
1	3.06	0.42
2.........	3.15	0.50
3.........	3.11	0.41
4.........	3.13	0.46
5.........	3.06	0.46
6.........	3.09	0.45

   a. Using the factors in Table 10-3, determine the upper and lower limits for sample mean and range control charts.

   b. Is the process in control?

 4. Six samples of five observations each have been taken of 80 kg concrete slabs produced by a machine, and the results are displayed below.

   a. Using factors from Table 10-3, determine the upper and lower control limits for sample mean and range, and decide if the process is in control.

   b. A new sample results in the following slab weights: 81.0, 81.0, 80.8, 80.6, and 80.5. Use the control limits determined in part *a* to decide if the process is still in control.

		Sample			
1	**2**	**3**	**4**	**5**	**6**
79.2	80.5	79.6	78.9	80.5	79.7
78.8	78.7	79.4	79.4	79.6	80.6
80.0	81.0	80.4	79.7	80.4	80.5
78.4	80.4	80.3	79.4	80.8	80.0
81.0	80.1	80.8	80.6	78.8	81.1

 5. In a refinery, the octane rating of gasoline produced is measured by taking one observation from each batch. Twenty observations follow.

   a. Construct Three Sigma control charts for the individual unit and moving range. Is the process in control?[8]

   b. A new batch has an octane rating of 94.0. Using the control charts in part *a*, is the process still in control?

Observation Number	Octane Rating	Observation Number	Octane Rating
1	89.2	11	85.4
2	86.5	12	91.6
3	88.4	13	87.7
4	91.8	14	85.0
5	90.3	15	91.5
6	87.5	16	90.3
7	92.6	17	85.6
8	87.0	18	90.9
9	89.8	19	82.1
10	92.2	20	85.8

 6. Using four samples of 200 credit card statements each, an auditor found the following number of erroneous statements in each sample:

	Sample			
	1	**2**	**3**	**4**
Number of errors	4	2	5	9

   a. Determine the proportion of defectives in each sample.

   b. If the true proportion of defectives for this process is unknown, what is your best estimate of it?

   c. What is your estimate of the mean and standard deviation of the sampling distribution of the sample proportion of defectives for samples of 200?

   d. What control limits would give an alpha risk of 0.03 for this process?

   e. What alpha risk would control limits of 0.047 and 0.003 provide?

   f. Using control limits of 0.047 and 0.003, is the process in control?

   g. Suppose that the long term proportion of defectives of the process is known to be 2 percent. What are the values of the mean and standard deviation of the sampling distribution?

   h. Construct a *p*-control chart for the process, assuming a proportion of defectives of 2 percent, and Two Sigma control limits. Is the process in control?

 7. A medical facility does MRIs for sports injuries. Occasionally a test yields inconclusive results and must be repeated. Using the following 13 sample results for the number of retests in $n = 200$ observations each, construct a control chart for the proportion of retests using Two Sigma limits. Is the process in control?

	Sample												
	1	**2**	**3**	**4**	**5**	**6**	**7**	**8**	**9**	**10**	**11**	**12**	**13**
Number of retests	1	2	2	0	2	1	2	0	2	7	3	2	1

 8. The operations manager of a large manufacturer received a certain number of complaints during the last two weeks.

   a. Construct a control chart with Three Sigma limits for the number of complaints received each day using the following data. Is the process in control?

   b. If 16 complaints are received today (day 15), using the control chart of part *a*, is there a change in the average number of complaints per day?

	Day													
	1	**2**	**3**	**4**	**5**	**6**	**7**	**8**	**9**	**10**	**11**	**12**	**13**	**14**
Number of complaints	4	10	14	8	9	6	5	12	13	7	6	4	2	10

---

[8] Adapted from Amitava Mitra, Fundamentals of Quality Control and Improvement, 2nd ed., Englewood Cliffs, NJ: Prentice Hall, 1998.

9. a. Construct a control chart with Three Sigma limits for the number of scratches per 6 m × 2 m stainless steel sheet based on the following data. Is the process in control?

b. If a new sheet has five defects, using the control chart of part *a*, has the process changed?

	Observation													
	1	2	3	4	5	6	7	8	9	10	11	12	13	14
Number of scratches	2	3	1	0	1	3	2	0	2	1	3	1	2	0

 10. After a number of complaints about its directory assistance, a telephone company examined samples of calls to determine the frequency of wrong numbers given to callers. Each sample consisted of 100 calls. The manager stated that the error rate is about 4 percent. Construct a control chart using 95 percent limits and using $\bar{p} = 0.04$. Is the process in control? Is the manager's assertion about the error rate correct? Explain.

	Observation															
	1	2	3	4	5	6	7	8	9	10	11	12	13	14	15	16
Number of errors	5	3	5	7	4	6	8	4	5	9	3	4	5	6	6	7

11. Specification for the diameter of a metal shaft is much wider than the machine used to make the shafts is capable of. Consequently, the decision has been made to allow the cutting tool to wear a certain amount before replacement. The tool wears at the rate of 0.004 centimetre per metal shaft produced. The process has a natural variation, σ, of 0.01 centimetre and is Normally distributed. Specification for the diameter of the metal shafts is 15.0 to 15.2 centimetres. How many shafts can the process turn out before tool replacement becomes necessary (i.e., before the process makes an out-of-spec shaft)? (See the diagram below.)

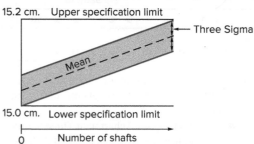

12. Design specification for the concrete slabs in Problem 4 is between 78 kg and 81 kg.

a. Based on the data given in Problem 4, is the specification being met?

b. Estimate the process standard deviation from the average range in Problem 4 using Formula 10-4. Then calculate the C_p. Is the process capable? Compare with your answer to part *a*.

13. The time needed for performing a machining operation is to be investigated. Historically, the process has had a standard deviation equal to 0.146 minute. The means (in minutes) of 39 samples of $n = 6$ are:

Sample	Mean	Sample	Mean	Sample	Mean
1.........	3.86	14.........	3.81	27.........	3.81
2.........	3.90	15.........	3.83	28.........	3.86
3.........	3.83	16.........	3.86	29.........	3.98
4.........	3.81	17.........	3.82	30.........	3.96
5.........	3.84	18.........	3.86	31.........	3.88
6.........	3.83	19.........	3.84	32.........	3.76
7.........	3.87	20.........	3.87	33.........	3.83
8.........	3.88	21.........	3.84	34.........	3.77
9.........	3.84	22.........	3.82	35.........	3.86
10.........	3.80	23.........	3.89	36.........	3.80
11.........	3.88	24.........	3.86	37.........	3.84
12.........	3.86	25.........	3.88	38.........	3.79
13.........	3.88	26.........	3.90	39.........	3.85

Construct an $\bar{x}$-chart for this process with Two Sigma limits. Is the process in control?

14. A company has just negotiated a contract to produce a part for another company. In the process of manufacturing the part, the inside diameter of successive parts becomes smaller and smaller as the cutting tool wears. However, the specification is so wide relative to machine capability that it is possible to set the diameter initially at a large value and let the process run for a while before replacing the cutting tool.

The inside diameter decreases at an average rate of 0.001 cm per part, and the process has a standard deviation of 0.01 cm and the variability is approximately Normally distributed. After how many parts must the tool be replaced if the design specification is between 3 cm and 3.5 cm, and the initial setting is three standard deviations below the upper design specification?

15. Refer to Solved Problem 2. Suppose that the design specification is between 9.65 minutes and 10.35 minutes. Based on the data given in Solved Problem 2, does it appear that the design specification is being met? If not, what should be done?

16. A technician in a quick oil change shop had the following service times (in minutes) for 20 randomly selected cars:

	Sample			
	1	2	3	4
	4.5	4.6	4.5	4.7
	4.2	4.5	4.6	4.6
	4.2	4.4	4.4	4.8
	4.3	4.7	4.4	4.5
	4.3	4.3	4.6	4.9

a. Determine the mean of each sample.

b. Estimate the mean and standard deviation of the process.

c. Estimate the mean and standard deviation of the sampling distribution of the sample mean.

d. What would Three Sigma control limits for the sample mean be? What alpha risk would they provide?

e. What alpha risk would control limits of 4.14 and 4.86 for the sample mean provide?

f. Using the control limits of 4.14 and 4.86, are any sample means beyond these control limits? If so, which one(s)?

g. Construct the control charts for sample mean and sample range using Table 10-3. Are any sample means and ranges beyond the control limits? If so, which one(s)?

h. Explain why the control limits are different for sample mean in parts *d* and *g*.

i. If the process has a known mean of 4.4 and a known standard deviation of 0.18, what would Three Sigma control limits be for a sample mean chart? Are any sample means beyond the control limits? If so, which one(s)?

 17. For each of the following control charts, analyze the data using both median and up/down run tests with $z = \pm1.96$ limits. Are nonrandom variations present? Assume the centre line is the long-term median.

Diagram for Problem 17

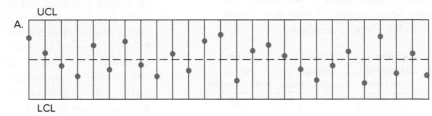

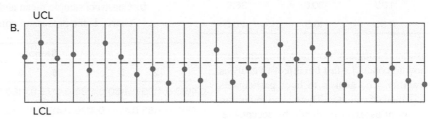

 18. Analyze the data in the following problems using median and up/down run tests with $z = \pm2$.

a. Given the following run test results of process output, what do the results of the run tests suggest about the process?

Test	z-score
Median	+1.37
Up/down	+1.05

b. Problem 9.

c. Problem 10.

 19. Use both types of run tests to analyze the daily expense voucher listed below. Assume a median of $31.

Day	Amount ($)	Day	Amount ($)	Day	Amount ($)	Day	Amount ($)
1	27.69	16	29.65	31	40.54	46	25.16
2	28.13	17	31.08	32	36.31	47	26.11
3	33.02	18	33.03	33	27.14	48	29.84
4	30.31	19	29.10	34	30.38	49	31.75
5	31.59	20	25.19	35	31.96	50	29.14
6	33.64	21	28.60	36	32.03	51	37.78
7	34.73	22	20.02	37	34.40	52	34.16
8	35.09	23	26.67	38	25.67	53	38.28
9	33.39	24	36.40	39	35.80	54	29.49
10	32.51	25	32.07	40	32.23	55	30.81
11	27.98	26	44.10	41	26.76	56	30.60
12	31.25	27	41.44	42	30.51	57	34.46
13	33.98	28	29.62	43	29.35	58	35.10
14	25.56	29	30.12	44	24.09	59	31.76
15	24.46	30	26.39	45	22.45	60	34.90

 20. (Refer to the data in Example 10-7.) Two additional observations have been taken. The first resulted in three defects, and the second had four defects. Using the set of 20 observations, perform run tests on the data. What can you conclude about the data?

21. A process screens a certain type of potash granule, resulting in a mean diameter of 0.03 cm and a standard deviation of 0.003 cm. The allowable variation in granule diameter is from 0.02 cm to 0.04 cm.

a. Calculate the capability ratio C_p for the process.

b. Is the process capable?

22. Given the following list of machines, the standard deviation for their output, and specification half-width for the job that may be processed on that machine, using C_p determine which machines are capable of performing the given jobs.

Machine	Standard Deviation (cm)	Job Half-Width Specification (6 cm)
001	0.02	0.05
002	0.04	0.07
003	0.10	0.18
004	0.05	0.15
005	0.01	0.04

23. Suppose your manager presents you with the following information about machines that could be used for a job, and wants your recommendation on which one to choose. The design specification width is 0.48 mm. Calculate the C_p index for each machine, and explain what additional information you will need to make a choice.

Machine	Cost per Unit ($)	Standard Deviation (mm)
A	20	0.079
B	12	0.080
C	11	0.084
D	10	0.081

(LO3) 24. Each of the processes listed below is noncentred with respect to the design specification. Calculate the C_{pk} index for each, and decide if the process is capable.

Process	Process Mean	Process Standard Deviation	Lower Design Specification	Upper Design Specification
H	15.0	0.32	14.1	16.0
K	33.0	1.00	30.0	36.5
T	18.5	0.50	16.5	20.1

(LO3) *25. As part of an insurance company's training program, participants learn how to conduct a fast but effective analysis of clients' insurability. The goal is to have participants achieve a time less than 45 minutes. There is no minimum time, but the quality of assessment should be acceptable. Test results for three participants were Armand, a mean of 38 minutes and a standard deviation of 3.0 minutes; Jerry, a mean of 37 minutes and a standard deviation of 2.5 minutes; and Melissa, a mean of 37.5 minutes and a standard deviation of 2.5 minutes.

Which of the participants would you judge to be capable? Explain.

(LO2) *26. The following data (in ohms) are the resistance of resistors made on an automated machine. The mean and range of each sample are given in the right two columns, and the mean of sample means and the mean of sample ranges are given below these.

a. Develop sample mean and sample range control charts for resistance of resistors using the first 10 samples. Is the process in control?

b. Use the control charts developed in part *a* to decide if the 11th sample (also given below) indicates an out-of-control situation.

Resistance of Resistors (in Ohms)

Sample	Obs 1	Obs 2	Obs 3	Obs 4	Mean	Range
1	1,010	991	985	986	993.00	25
2	995	996	1,009	994	998.50	15
3	990	1,003	1,015	1,008	1,004.00	25
4	1,015	1,020	1,009	998	1,010.50	22
5	1,013	1,019	1,005	993	1,007.50	26
6	994	1,001	994	1,005	998.50	11
7	989	992	982	1,020	995.75	38

Resistance of Resistors (in Ohms)

Sample	Obs 1	Obs 2	Obs 3	Obs 4	Mean	Range
8	1,001	986	996	996	994.75	15
9	1,006	989	1,005	1,007	1,001.75	18
10	992	1,007	1,006	979	996.00	28
					1,000.03	22.30
11	996	1,006	997	989		

(LO2) *27. Essex Corp. of St. Louis is a small manufacturer of parts for Boeing's Aircraft and Missile Systems. In the late 1990s, Essex was trying to establish a statistical process control program. Part number 528003-N was typical. The following samples[9] of two were observed for a critical dimension of the part (in inches). The lower specification, nominal, and upper specification values were 0.4160, 0.4185, and 0.4210 inches, respectively.

a. Is the process capable?

b. Construct sample mean and sample range control charts. Is the process in control?

	Sample									
1	**2**	**3**	**4**	**5**	**6**	**7**	**8**	**9**	**10**
0.4190	0.4190	0.4180	0.4180	0.4175	0.4180	0.4175	0.4173	0.4183	0.4185
0.4190	0.4185	0.4180	0.4179	0.4175	0.4179	0.4175	0.4176	0.4184	0.4185

(LO2) *28. When Polaroid reduced the number of quality inspectors and increased operator responsibility for statistical process control in its R2 plant (which made instant film cartridges with 10 films in each) in Waltham, Massachusetts, in 1985, it encountered an unexpected result.[10] Instead of quality improving, it actually got worse. To identify the problem, Bud Rolfs, quality control manager, asked an operator from each shift to sample six observations of the critical characteristics of the product and report these to him. One important characteristic of instant films is the pod weight. A pod is a small capsule at the end of each film that contains chemicals. When the film is pulled out, the pod bursts and releases the chemicals that will develop the film. Too much chemical overdevelops the film and too little underdevelops it.

a. Use the following three samples of six observations each (in grams) from the first day of the data collection period to develop a sample mean and sample range control chart for the pod weight. Is the process in control?

b. The first sample from the second day is 2.841, 2.802, 2.802, 2.806, 2.807, and 2.807. Is the process still in control?

Sample	Shift	1	2	3	4	5	6	Average
1	A	2.800	2.799	2.760	2.802	2.805	2.803	2.795
2	B	2.750	2.820	2.850	2.740	2.850	2.790	2.800
3	C	2.768	2.807	2.807	2.804	2.804	2.803	2.799

[9] Data retrieved from S.K. Vermani, "SPC Modified With Percent Tolerance Pre-Control Charts," *Quality Progress* 33(10), October 2000, pp. 43–48.

[10] Process Control at Polaroid (A), 1987, HBS case: 9-693-047.

LO2 *29. A small manufacturer of metal ring seals for aircraft engines has been asked by its major customer to implement statistical process control. One major type of ring requires cutting a one-eighth inch wide slot using a milling machine. The following six samples of five observations each, taken every half hour, are the width of the slots (in inches) made by the milling machine on the rings.

1	2	3	4	5	6
0.1261	0.1259	0.1239	0.1225	0.1259	0.1255
0.1253	0.1263	0.1265	0.1249	0.1243	0.1273
0.1245	0.1247	0.126	0.1265	0.1242	0.1245
0.1249	0.124	0.1257	0.1248	0.1257	0.1268
0.1248	0.1251	0.1243	0.1256	0.1251	0.1263

   a. Set up the sample mean and range control charts for this operation. Is the process in control?
   b. The seventh sample contains the following values: 0.124, 0.1252, 0.1295, 0.1262, and 0.1275. Using the control charts from part *a,* is the process still in control?

LO3 *30. The management of a dried milk manufacturer wanted to evaluate the process capability of its packaging lines. A can line was studied for weight of filled cans. The specification is 974 grams plus or minus 14 grams (including the weight of the can itself). Thirty-five samples of six cans were weighed, and sample mean and range were calculated. The process was in control. The grand mean was 975.7 grams and process standard deviation was 4.7581 grams.
   a. Calculate the C_p and C_{pk} ratios. Is the filling line capable?
   b. After changing the wearable parts of the line, including the piston cylinders, workers weighed 46 samples of six cans. The grand mean was 976.19 grams and process standard deviation was 2.891 grams. Calculate the new values of C_p and C_{pk} ratios. Has the filling line become capable?

LO3 *31. Suppose a process capability study was conducted on a punch-press operation. One of the characteristics of interest is the width of the slot having a specification of 0.4040 ± 0.007 inch. Twenty-five samples of five pieces were obtained during a shift, and the sample means and ranges are plotted below. Determine if the process is capable of meeting the specification.[11]

Diagram for Problem 31

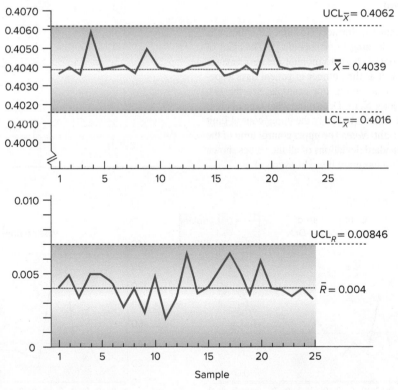

LO2 *32. Royal North Shore Hospital, a 650-bed teaching hospital in Sydney, Australia, uses control charts for quality management.[12] One control chart used shows the number of outpatients waiting more than 30 days for elective surgery (see below). Because the number was increasing (see the plot to the left of X up to three months before X), the hospital appointed a waiting list coordinator (three months before X) who helped reduce the number (see the plot between

[11] J. Heinricks and M.M.K. Fleming, "Quality Statistical Process Control at Cherry Textron," *Industrial Management*, May/June 1991, 33(3), pp. 7–10.
[12] H. E. Ganley and J. Moxey, "Making Informed Decisions in the Face of Uncertainty," *Quality Progress*, October 2000, 33(10), pp. 76–78.

three months before X and Y), and later reduced further by reducing the holidays for elective surgery from six weeks to three weeks during Christmas (see the plot to the right of Y). The control limit lines are three standard deviations of the values during each of the three sub-periods from their centre lines. Determine what type of control chart this is.

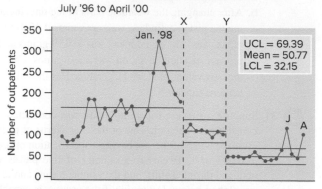

Number of outpatients waiting more than 30 days for elective surgery

July '96 to April '00

L02 *33. The Lexington, Kentucky, Shriners Hospital for children is a small hospital specializing in orthopedics.[13] The chief of staff uses various control charts to monitor the performance of the physicians, such as the number of patient days a specific doctor works in a month. For example, see the two charts below for Doctor X. (a) Determine what type of chart the left chart below is, and (b) verify the upper control limit for the chart on the right. *Note:* The upper control limit of the left chart is three standard deviations of all the values shown (Jan 02–July 03) from its centre line (the average).

L04 *34. A design of experiments was conducted to study the effect of various factors on the yield and taste of microwave popcorn.[14] The factors and their settings were as follows:

Table 1 *Factors and levels.*

Factor	Low (−1)	High (+1)
Price	Generic	Brand
Time	4 min.	6 min.
Power	Medium	High
Preheat	No	Yes
Elevate	No	Yes

Preheat involves heating water in the microwave for 1 minute prior to popcorn. *Elevate* means put a plate or something similar under the popcorn bag to raise the bag.

Fractional factorial design was used to obtain two responses: (a) Bullets = Weight of unpopped kernels, in ounces; and (b) Taste (a score between 1 and 10, 10 is best).

A	B	C	D	E	Bullets	Taste
−1	−1	−1	−1	1	1.5	7.5
1	−1	−1	−1	−1	1.4	8.0
−1	1	−1	−1	−1	1.9	9.0
1	1	−1	−1	1	0.6	6.5
−1	−1	1	−1	−1	1.8	7.0
1	−1	1	−1	1	0.3	7.5
−1	1	1	−1	1	0.2	2.5
1	1	1	−1	−1	0.9	1.0
−1	−1	−1	1	−1	1.7	7.0
1	−1	−1	1	1	0.8	6.0
−1	1	−1	1	1	0.6	4.5

Diagram for Problem 33

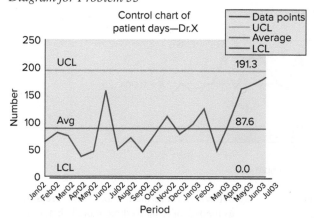

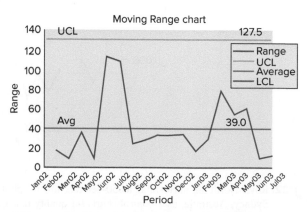

---

[13] D. E. Lighter and C. M. Tylkowski, "Case Study: Using Control Charts to Track Physician Productivity," *Physician Executive*, September/October 2004, 30(5), pp. 53–57.

[14] http://www.statease.com/pubs/popcorn.pdf.

A	B	C	D	E	Bullets	Taste
1	1	−1	1	−1	0.9	4.0
−1	−1	1	1	1	0.6	9.0
1	−1	1	1	−1	1.3	7.5
−1	1	1	1	−1	Missing	–
1	1	1	1	1	Missing	–

The last two experiments were botched and produced no results.

Determine the influence of each level of each factor on each response and prescribe the best levels for each response (Bullets to be minimized and Taste to be maximized).

LO4 *35. Stat-Ease Inc., the producer of a design of experiments software, performed an experiment a few years ago to identify the factors that were important in increasing the response rate of engineers to Stat-Ease workshop announcements. The factors and their levels were:[15]

Factor A: Number of colours (two vs. four)
Factor B: Postcard size (4″ × 6″ vs. 5.5″ × 8.5″)
Factor C: Paper stock (index vs. heavyweight)

Stat-Ease made eight types of its announcement postcard and sent each type to 1/8 of this mailing list of engineers. The levels of each type and number of fax responses received were:

Version	Factor A Number of Colours	Factor B Postcard Size	Factor C Postcard Thickness	Response
1	2-colour (−)	4″ × 6″ (−)	Index (−)	34
2	4-colour (+)	4″ × 6″ (−)	Index (−)	18
3	2-colour (−)	5.5″ × 8.5″ (+)	Index (−)	44
4	4-colour (+)	5.5″ × 8.5″ (+)	Index (−)	26
5	2-colour (−)	4″ × 6″ (−)	Heavyweight (+)	26
6	4-colour (+)	4″ × 6″ (−)	Heavyweight (+)	17
7	2-colour (−)	5.5″ × 8.5″ (+)	Heavyweight (+)	29
8	4-colour (+)	5.5″ × 8.5″ (+)	Heavyweight (+)	21

Determine the influence of each level of each factor on the response and prescribe the best levels for each factor. What do you recommend Stat-Ease should do?

LO3 *36. A chocolate manufacturer makes a variety of chocolate products including large chocolate bars (340 grams) and boxes of six smaller chocolate bars (170 grams in total).
   a. Specification for a large bar is 330 grams to 350 grams. What is the largest standard deviation (in grams) that the machine that fills the bar moulds can have and still be considered capable if its average fill is 340 grams?
   b. The machine that fills the bar moulds for the smaller bars has a standard deviation of 0.80 grams. The filling machine is set to deliver an average of 28.5 grams per bar. Specification for the six-bar box is 160 grams to 180 grams. Is the process capable? *Hint:* The variance of the box's weight is equal to six times the variance of each smaller bar's weight.
   c. What is the lowest setting (in grams) for the smaller-bar filling machine that will leave the process for the six-bar box capable?

LO2 37. An appliance manufacturer wants to contract with a repair shop to handle authorized repairs. The company has set an acceptable range of repair time of 50 minutes to 90 minutes. Two firms have submitted bids for the work. In test trials, one firm had a mean repair time of 74 minutes with a standard deviation of 4.0 minutes, and the other firm had a mean repair time of 72 minutes with a standard deviation of 5.1 minutes. Which firm would you choose? Why?

LO2 38. Boxes of 50 small packages of M&M's milk chocolate candies, produced by Mars, should weigh 625 grams. Therefore, Mars has to ensure that there are enough candies in each package. Suppose two packages of M&M's were sampled every hour from the packaging machine during a six-hour period and the number of candies in each package was:

			Sample			
	1	2	3	4	5	6
	14	15	15	16	13	14
	15	16	15	15	15	15

   a. Calculate the sample mean and sample range for each sample.
   b. Calculate the average of sample means and sample ranges.
   c. Calculate the control limits for sample mean and sample range control charts.
   d. Was the process in control? Why?
   e. Suppose that the above control limits were then used to control the process. The next day, two packages were sampled and they contained 17 and 14 candies, respectively. Was the packaging machine still in control? Why?

[15] http://www.statease.com/pubs/marketingvoodoo.pdf.

MINI-CASE

Cereal Manufacturer

The plant manager of a cereal manufacturer is wondering if the company could save some cereal by slightly lowering the cereal content of each box. Studying a major product, a 454 gram (net weight) ready-to-eat cereal, he discovers that four boxes are routinely taken from the filling machine every 10 minutes and weighed. Data for approximately 2.5 hours of inspection are shown below.

Questions

1. Is the process in control?
2. Determine what weight the filler head is likely set to.
3. If the *Weights and Measures Act* dictates that the tolerance for weight of a product of approximately 454 grams is 2 grams, what is the probability that an inspector will find a legally defined underweight box (i.e., weighing less than 452 grams)?
4. Has the filler head been set too conservatively? Discuss.

							Samples							
1	**2**	**3**	**4**	**5**	**6**	**7**	**8**	**9**	**10**	**11**	**12**	**13**	**14**	**15**
455.5	456.0	456.0	452.5	456.0	452.0	457.5	454.5	456.0	453.0	455.0	458.0	457.5	458.0	460.0
460.0	455.5	453.0	455.0	456.0	455.0	455.5	453.0	454.0	455.0	457.5	456.0	456.5	453.0	455.5
456.5	456.0	454.0	453.0	455.0	453.0	457.0	453.0	453.0	456.0	456.5	454.5	453.0	456.5	454.5
456.5	456.0	455.0	455.0	454.5	456.0	452.0	458.0	455.0	456.5	456.5	454.0	455.5	456.0	457.0

To access "Acceptance Sampling," the supplement to Chapter 10, please visit *Connect2*.

Chapter 11
Supply Chain Management

STORE PICKUP

Jim Gehrz/Minneapolis Star Tribune

LEARNING OBJECTIVES

After completing this chapter, you should be able to:

LO1 Explain what a supply chain is and why it is important; identify major supply chain activities; describe quick response, distribution requirement planning, global supply chains, and technologies used in supply chain management; and outline the key steps in creating an effective supply chain.

LO2 Explain the purchasing function in organizations, ecommerce, and supplier management and partnership.

LO3 Describe what logistics is, know how to select a transportation mode and solve problems, and discuss third-party logistics and reverse logistics.

Ecommerce has grown at an exponential rate within the last decade, bringing with it many benefits for both retailers and customers alike. For example, selling over the Internet allows retailers such as Best Buy and Walmart to offer a larger variety of products than was previously possible with traditional brick-and-mortar stores, which helps to increase the likelihood a customer will make a purchase. Customers have also benefited since online shopping increases convenience by eliminating the need to travel to a physical store.

Making a purchase from a brick-and-mortar store does have several advantages over making an online purchase. One of the main reasons many customers still prefer to purchase from brick-and-mortar stores is that doing so gives them the opportunity to touch and feel a product and determine its fit, which is especially important for product categories such as clothing and shoes. On top of that, an online purchase means there will be delivery time delays and additional shipping expenses, which makes online purchases less appealing to customers.

In theory, there is no reason why a retailer cannot have both channels at the same time. As a matter of fact, more and more retailers are leveraging their physical assets to offer an "online-to-store" channel to better serve their customers. This new distribution channel allows customers to place an order online, then pick up their product at a nearby store. Doing so allows customers to bypass the traditional online ordering process and pick up their products sooner. In addition, by travelling to a physical store, customers can save the additional shipping expenses which would have been incurred. This new distribution channel creates a win–win scenario for retailers and customers by increasing shopping convenience, offering a better selection, saving on shipping expenses, and improving profitability.

Source: "Impact of an 'Online-to-Store' Channel on Demand Allocation, Pricing and Profitability." *European Journal of Operational Research, 248*(1): 234–245.

LO1 **Fundamentals**

> **supply chain** Sequence of organizations—their facilities and activities—that are involved in producing and delivering a product.

A **supply chain** is the sequence of organizations—their facilities and activities—that are involved in producing and delivering a product. The sequence begins with suppliers of raw materials and extends all the way to the final customer (the consumer). Facilities include factories, warehouses/distribution centres, and retail outlets. Activities include forecasting, product design, scheduling, purchasing, transportation, inventory management/warehousing, production, distribution/delivery, and customer service. There are two kinds of movement in these systems: the physical movement of material (generally toward the end of the chain, the consumer) and the exchange of information and money (mainly toward the beginning of the chain, the source of material).

The term *chain* in supply chain signifies the importance of a close relationship and integration between a supplier and a customer such as a manufacturer and a retailer. This term was first used approximately three decades ago when automatic replenishment systems were introduced between Procter & Gamble and its retail chain customers.

Every organization is part of at least one supply chain, and many are part of multiple supply chains. Figure 11-1a illustrates a typical supply chain for a product. Figure 11-1b is the supply chain for Wavefarer Board Shorts by Patagonia, a Los Angeles–based clothing designer and distributor. Note that all of Patagonia's manufacturing activities are outsourced to Far East companies (this is called offshoring).

Supply chains are sometimes referred to as *value chains*, a term that reflects the concept that value is added as goods progress through the chain. Supply or value chains typically comprise separate organizations, rather than just a single organization. However, the objective of a supply chain is that these organizations integrate their activities so that the supply chain acts as one.

> **supply chain management** Collaboration of supply chain companies and coordination of their activities so that market demand is met as efficiently and effectively as possible.

Supply chain management is collaboration of supply chain companies and coordination of their activities so that market demand is met as efficiently and effectively as possible.

The same key purchasing criteria that were given for the products of a company in Chapter 2 are important for supply chains: price, timeliness, quality, and variety. Therefore, supply chains should be efficient (reduce costs) and effective (meet timeliness and quality requirements).

Supply chains are the lifeblood of any organization. They connect suppliers, producers, and final customers in a network that is essential to the creation and delivery of goods and services. Managing the supply chain is the process of planning, implementing, and controlling supply chain operations. The basic components are strategy, procurement and supply management, demand

FIGURE 11-1a ▶

A typical supply chain.

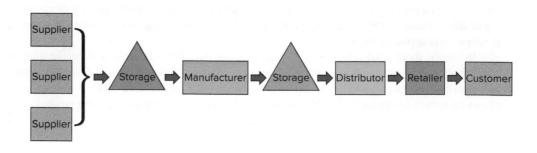

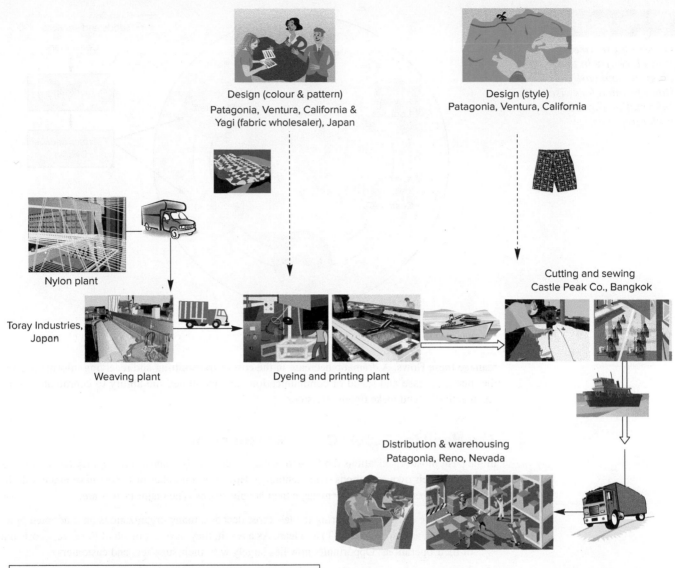

Design (colour & pattern)
Patagonia, Ventura, California &
Yagi (fabric wholesaler), Japan

Design (style)
Patagonia, Ventura, California

Nylon plant

Toray Industries,
Japan

Weaving plant

Dyeing and printing plant

Cutting and sewing
Castle Peak Co., Bangkok

Distribution & warehousing
Patagonia, Reno, Nevada

Legend: Information ▶ Trucking ⟶ Ocean Freight ⟹

▲ FIGURE 11-1b

*Supply chain for
Wavefarer Board Shorts
by Patagonia.*

management, and logistics. The goal of supply chain management is to match supply to demand as effectively and efficiently as possible. Key aspects relate to:

1. Determining the appropriate level of outsourcing
2. Managing procurement
3. Managing suppliers
4. Managing customer relationships
5. Being able to quickly identify problems and respond to them

An important aspect of supply chain management is flow management. The three types of flow that need to be managed are goods and services flow, information flow, and financial flow. See Figure 11-2 for an illustration. Product flow involves the movement of goods and services from suppliers to customers as well as handling customer service needs and product returns. Information flow involves sharing forecast and sales data, transmitting orders, tracking shipments, and updating order status. Financial flow involves credit terms, payments, and consignment and title ownership arrangements. Technological advances have greatly enhanced the ability to effectively

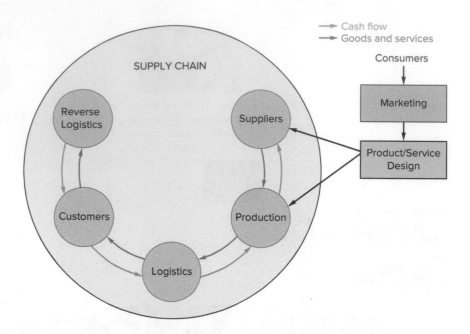

FIGURE 11-2 ▶

Goods and services flow clockwise in this diagram, and cash flows counterclockwise. Information flows in both directions.

manage these flows. A dramatic decrease in the cost of transmitting and receiving information and the increased ease and speed of communication have facilitated the ability to coordinate supply chain activities and make timely decisions.

The Need for Supply Chain Management

In the past, most organizations did little to manage their supply chains. Instead, they tended to concentrate on their own operations (silo mentality). However, a number of factors have made it desirable for organizations to actively manage their supply chains. The major factors are:

1. *Increasing competition.* During the last three decades, many organizations have adopted practices such as just-in-time (JIT) and lean. As a result, they have cut much of the excess costs out of their operations. Opportunity now lies largely with their suppliers and customers.

2. *Increasing outsourcing.* Organizations are increasing outsourcing by buying goods or services instead of producing or providing them in-house (called insourcing). As companies are reducing their costs and increasing their product quality, they are focusing on their core activities and subcontracting the others.

3. *Increasing globalization.* Globalization has extended the physical length of supply chains, and the quantity of materials and products being transported.

4. *Increasing ecommerce.* Increasing ecommerce has resulted in more Internet purchasing, which requires more and faster package delivery services.

5. *The need to manage orders and inventories across the supply chain.* Inventories play a major role in the success or failure of a supply chain, so it is important to coordinate inventory levels throughout a supply chain. Shortages can severely disrupt timely production or sales, while excess inventories add unnecessary holding costs. It would not be unusual to find inventory shortages in some parts of a supply chain and excess inventories in the other parts of the same supply chain.

bullwhip effect Demand/ order variability gets progressively larger the further back in a supply chain the company is.

The **bullwhip effect** or demand/order amplification is the phenomenon in which the demand/ order variability gets progressively larger the further up in the supply chain the company is. While the demand at a retail store for a particular product is usually fairly stable, the orders of the retailer from wholesaler/distributor are more variable. These variations are even more magnified in the orders of wholesaler/distributor from the manufacturer. Clearly, the bullwhip effect causes inefficiencies at the wholesaler/distributor and manufacturer, such as excess inventory holding cost and overtime, and shortage cost and lower customer service. This phenomenon was discovered by Jay Forrester at MIT many decades ago, where a business simulation game called the Beer Distribution Game was created to illustrate its existence. A typical result from playing this game is displayed in Figure 11-3. The bullwhip effect is illustrated in Figure 11-4.

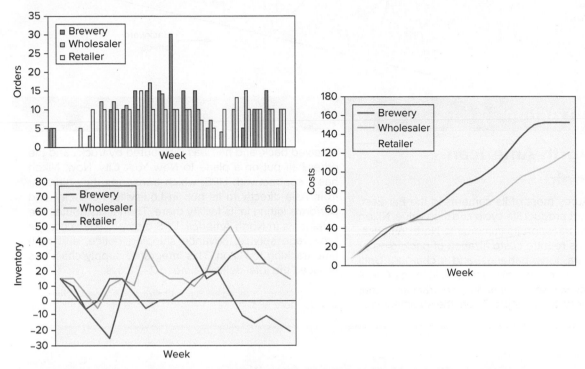

Generated from The Beergame Portal, http://www.beergame.org. Copyright © Dr. Kai Riemer

▲ FIGURE 11-3

Typical results from playing the Beer Distribution Game (http://www.beergame.org) showing the bullwhip effect. The supply chain consists of three stages: a brewery, a wholesaler, and a retailer. Consumer demand is five cases per week for the first four weeks and then is raised to 10 units per week (known only to the retailer). Each stage starts with 20 cases of inventory. Each stage plays once a week, receiving a shipment from its supplier (if its supplier had inventory), shipping to its customer (if it has inventory), receiving an order from its customer, and then placing an order to its supplier. There are two weeks of lag from issuing an order until receiving it. There is one week of lag in receiving an order. The cost of carrying inventory is $0.50 per case per week and cost of shortage is $1 per case per week. The game is played for 20 weeks. As can be observed, all stages are interdependent, and shipment lag makes decision making difficult. As the wholesaler develops a shortage in week 9, it places a larger order (17 cases) which causes a bigger shortage at the brewery (10 cases), which causes the brewery to order 30 cases next week.

The major cause of the bullwhip effect is slow and/or erratic reaction to a change in demand/order due to lack of end-of-line demand visibility, long lead times, inexperience, and lack of understanding of the impact of one's action on the supplier. Other causes are manufacturer price discounts that lead to surges in demand, and gaming by retailers when there is a shortage by inflating their orders in anticipation of receiving only a portion of them.

Effective supply chain management is a prerequisite for success in the marketplace, as demonstrated by companies such as P&G, Walmart, Apple, Amazon, Best Buy, HP, Cisco, Sony, and Campbell Soup. Also, package delivery companies such as UPS, FedEx, and Purolator have expanded their services to include warehousing, light assembly, and distribution. For an example, see the "Nikon's North American Supply Chain" OM in Action.

FIGURE 11-4 ▶

The bullwhip effect: demand variations begin at the customer end of the chain and become increasingly large as they radiate backward through the chain.

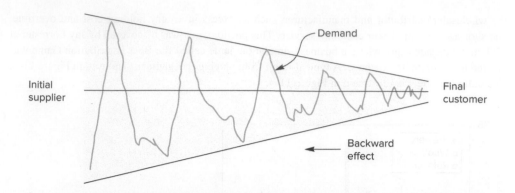

OM in Action

Nikon's North American Supply Chain

Nikon manufactures most of its cameras in the Far East. Because of a short product life cycle and high value, Nikon uses air cargo to transport its cameras to North America. Many retail chains require customization of packaging or a kit (e.g., camera, lens, batteries, and a charger). Until recently, after the air cargo arrived from Asia in Los Angeles, the shipment was sent to a nearby contract kitter that took days or weeks to do its job. Then, the shipment was received back, and half was distributed by trucks and the other half put on a plane to New York City. Now, Nikon has a contract with UPS, which transports the shipment from Asia directly to its hub in Louisville, Kentucky, and performs kitting in its facility there. Then it distributes the shipments in North America. UPS also provides customs brokerage service, advance shipping notice, and real-time tracking to Nikon. This integrated supply chain has reduced the total delivery time to 2–3 days.

Source: R. Morton, "Keeping the Supply Chain in Focus," *Logistics Today*, 48(7), July 2007, pp. 12–15.

Supply Chain Management Activities

Strategic (Design) Activities. Strategic decisions have long-term impacts on a supply chain. First, goals and competitive characteristics such as quality, cost, variety (flexibility), timeliness (speed), customer service, and fill rate (i.e., percentage of demand filled from stock on hand) should be agreed upon by the members of the supply chain. Then, products are designed/redesigned with these competitive characteristics in mind. Next, supply chains are designed/redesigned for these products, goals, and competitive characteristics. This involves determining the number, location, capacity, products to produce, and process types of the facilities. Information systems should also be able to communicate seamlessly. Determining the best supply chain network (i.e., the location and capacity of the facilities) is usually performed using linear programming based optimization (see supplements to Chapters 6 and 8). For smaller problems, heuristics such as "Locate a supplier factory close to customer's manufacturing factory" or "Locate a regional distribution centre close to major retail customers" are used. See the "At 3M, a Long Road Became a Shorter Road" for an example of supply chain design.

OM in Action

At 3M, a Long Road Became a Shorter Road

3M's many product lines include Command plastic hanging hooks. Not long ago, production of the Command hooks occurred at several widely scattered locations in the American Midwest. The process started in a Springfield, Missouri, plant that made adhesives. The adhesives were then shipped about 550 miles to a plant in Hartford City, Indiana, where they were applied to rolls of polyethylene foam. After that, the adhesive-backed foam was shipped another 600 miles to a contractor's plant near Minneapolis, Minnesota, where it was cut into individual pieces and imprinted with the 3M logo. Finally, the foam pieces were shipped to another contractor's plant in central Wisconsin, another 200 miles away, where they were bundled with Mexican-made plastic hooks and packaged for sale. This entire process took over a hundred days and over 1,000 miles to complete.

3M has recently consolidated its operations into a single plant in Hutchinson, Minnesota, where Scotch tape, Nexcare bandages, furnace filters, and other items are made. This move has reduced the processing time by two-thirds, from 100 days to 35 days, and eliminated all the transporting.

Situations like this can arise when a business acquires other companies and then elects to maintain their processing operations in their current locations.

Questions

1. Businesses sometimes acquire widely dispersed processing facilities through a number of mergers or acquisitions. What trade-offs might they face in considering consolidation?

2. This reading offers one possible reason for the existence of a long supply process. Can you think of some other possible reasons for long supply processes?

Source: "3M Begins Untangling Their Hairballs." *The Wall Street Journal*, May 17, 2012.

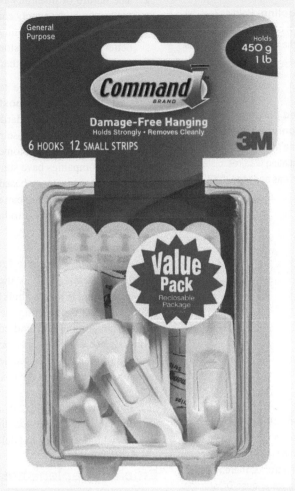

Courtesy of 3M Canada

Note that determining the extent of vertical integration (i.e., the ownership of a segment of supply chain) is also a strategic decision. Recently, instead of ownership, companies are outsourcing noncore parts of the supply chains, and customer–supplier partnerships are becoming more widespread.

Tactical (Planning)/Operational Activities. The important tactical/operational activities in supply chains relate to production planning and control, including forecasting, purchasing/ordering, transportation of material, inventory control/warehousing, scheduling of production and distribution/deliveries, and customer service. Questions such as, "Should a product be manufactured at this plant, today or later, or shipped from another location, today or later?" should be answered. Supply chain management involves getting agreement on decisions that affect other members of the supply chain or even jointly making decisions and performing the above activities. We will discuss some of these in the rest of this chapter.

Inventory in a Supply Chain. An important tactical/operational decision is where in a supply chain the inventory should be held. Two general rules apply to this decision:

1. The value of inventory increases as materials move down the supply chain toward the consumers, but the response (or lead) time to consumer demand decreases. Management must strike a balance between additional carrying cost (due to increased value) and better customer service (shorter lead time) to determine the location of inventory in the supply chain.

> **risk pooling** Holding (safety) stocks in one central location rather than in multiple locations.

2. The nature of inventory becomes more specific (thus it loses flexibility of use) as inventory moves down the supply chain. This reduces **risk pooling**: holding (safety) stocks in one central location rather than in multiple regional locations closer to customers. Risk pooling can provide better availability to customers, because the variations in demands in various regional locations typically cancel each other out for the central location.

However, it is possible to achieve risk pooling and hold inventory closer to customers by **delayed differentiation/postponement**, which is waiting until late in the process to add differentiating features to standard components and products. For example, in the paint industry, manufacturers send only white base paint to retail stores where a small amount of coloured paint is mixed into white to create the customer's desired colours when demanded.

> **delayed differentiation/ postponement** Waiting until late in the process to add differentiating features to standard components and products.

Some companies have started to use inventory optimization software that determines the optimal location of inventory based on the agreed-upon lead times and costs of carrying inventory. If a facility in the supply chain can replenish its own inventory and produce within the agreed-upon lead time, then it does not have to hold any inventory; otherwise, it has to keep either finished goods or raw material inventory.[1]

Warehousing/Transportation in a Supply Chain. Besides storage of goods, a warehouse/ distribution centre (DC) is used for consolidating (combining) shipments of customers' orders, deconsolidating (breaking bulk) shipments of suppliers' products, and cross-docking. Consolidating shipments means collecting the incoming shipments from various geographic areas headed toward another geographic area and combining them into a larger shipment in order to take advantage of economies of scale in transportation. Deconsolidating shipments is the opposite: splitting a large incoming shipment into smaller shipments that are headed to different customers. There will be more on warehousing in the next chapter and more on transportation at the end of this chapter as part of logistics.

> **cross-docking** Loading goods arriving at a warehouse/ DC from a supplier directly onto outbound trucks, thereby avoiding warehouse/DC storage.

In **cross-docking**, goods arriving at a warehouse/DC from a supplier are directly loaded onto outbound trucks, thereby avoiding warehouse/DC storage. Walmart initiated cross-docking to reduce inventory holding costs and delivery lead times.

Efficient Replenishment Methods

Just-in-time (JIT) replenishment started in the auto industry in the 1980s, and for an automobile manufacturer it means that parts/components are received in small lots and frequently, only a few hours before they will be used. At about the same time, JIT replenishment was modified and applied to apparel/textile and wholesale/retail sectors under the name "quick response."

> **quick response (QR)** Just-in-time replenishment system used in retailing where orders are based on actual sales, not periodic orders by retailers.

Quick response (QR) involves making sales information available to vendors. The purpose is to create a JIT replenishment system that is automated and keyed to consumer buying patterns, as opposed to periodic orders by retailers. Another name for quick response is *continuous product replenishment*. QR results in frequent small-lot shipments.

Quick response has several benefits. Among them are reduced dependency on forecasts and the ability to achieve a closer match between supply and demand, which results in savings in inventory holding and shortage costs. For an application, see the "Nygård" OM in Action.

> **efficient consumer response (ECR)** An expanded version of quick response, used in the grocery industry, which includes further collaboration.

Efficient consumer response (ECR), initiated by Procter & Gamble, is an expanded version of quick response, used in the grocery industry. In addition to continuous product replenishment, ECR includes further collaboration on forecasting, planning of store assortments, promotions, and product introductions. ECR is continued by collaborative planning, forecasting, and replenishment (CPFR), which is described later in the chapter.

> **vendor-managed inventory (VMI)** An agreement in which the supplier has access to the customer's inventory and is responsible for maintaining the inventory levels required by the customer.

Vendor-managed inventory (VMI) is a related, though not necessarily fast, replenishment method where the vendor's sales/account manager periodically visits the buyer's premises (or uses electronic means), counts the inventories of her company on the buyer's shelves (or in the computer database), and has them replenished to the previously agreed-upon levels. VMI has been used by soft drink companies supplying convenience stores, electrical distributors supplying small maintenance warehouses, etc.

---

[1] See, for example, http://www.logility.com/solutions/inventory-optimization/voyager-inventory-optimization.

OM in Action

Nygård

Nygård International is the largest women's fashion clothing company in Canada (with estimated revenue of over $1 billion). Its design facilities are in Winnipeg (also its headquarters) and New York City (its new U.S. HQ); its production facilities are mainly in southeast Asia now (its last Winnipeg sewing shop closed in 2008); its sales offices are in Winnipeg, Toronto, and New York; and it has large distribution (service) centres in Winnipeg (155,000 ft²), Vaughan, Ontario (300,000 ft²), and Los Angeles (800,000 ft²). Nygard also has over 200 stores in Canada.

Founder Peter J. Nygård is a visionary in the apparel industry and the use of technology. Starting in the 1980s, Nygård computerized all its operations including design and production activities using computer-assisted design, computerized cutting, planning/control, and receiving and shipping. All the programming—equivalent to a full-blown enterprise resource planning software—was done in-house. In the mid-1990s, Nygård turned his attention to the supply chain. He asked his major customers, such as Hudson's Bay Company, to let an EDI software be installed on their computer system so that when an item was sold at a store, this information was immediately relayed to Nygård. Nygård guaranteed

24-hour response time, from the time of receiving an order to shipment (any item short was shipped the following day free). This quick response/continuous replenishment system was and is revolutionary in the apparel industry, where the usual lead time is at least two weeks. Nygård's system also has electronic data interchange connections to its major suppliers of fabric, zippers, buttons, etc. Nygård spent over $66 million on its information technology in the 1980s and 1990s, and $10 million per year since then.

In the mid-2000s, Nygård partnered with Dillard's, Inc., a major U.S. clothing retail chain, to implement collaborative planning, forecasting, and replenishment. This involved both merchandise planning/forecasting and replenishment. The IT applications in the two companies had to be integrated to enable this (synchronized data). Results were positive in all test stores. One of the largest stores experienced a 40 percent sales increase while carrying 20 percent less inventory. Time from replenishment order to goods-on-selling floor was cut from 16 to 7 days.

Sources: http://corporate.nygard.com/scf/News.aspx?id=7984&terms=Quick%20Response; http://corporate.nygard.com/scf/News.aspx?id=10986&terms=quick%20response; http://corporate.nygard.com/scf/News.aspx?id=7964&terms=Quick%20Response; http://corporate.nygard.com/scf/News2007.aspx?id=12286.

Distribution Requirements Planning

Distribution requirements planning (DRP) is a system for synchronizing replenishment schedules across the supply chain. It is especially useful in multi-echelon distribution networks (hierarchical levels of factory, regional warehouses/DCs, and retail stores). It uses a concept similar to material requirements planning (see Chapter 14) for distribution. Starting with forecast demand at the end of the distribution network (retail stores), DRP works backward through the network to obtain time-phased replenishment schedules for moving goods from the factory through each level of the distribution network. Note that DRP is a push system (it produces and ships based on demand forecasts and plans), whereas quick response is a pull system (it produces and ships based on actual demand).

> **distribution requirements planning (DRP)** Starts with the forecast demand at the end of the distribution network (retail stores), and works backward through the network to obtain time-phased replenishment schedules for moving goods from the factory through each level of the distribution network.

Global Supply Chains

As international trade barriers fall, more companies are expanding their global operations. This is presenting tremendous opportunities and opening up previously untapped markets for raw materials, goods, and services. The ability to export to other countries, as opposed to making the product there, has allowed multinational companies to centralize the production of families of their products in one location. Also, increasing ecommerce has resulted in increasing global package deliveries.

Managing a global supply chain that may have far-flung customers and/or suppliers magnifies some of the challenges of managing a domestic supply chain. Obviously, distances and lead times increase as the supply chain becomes longer. In addition, there is the possibility of having to deal with different languages, cultures, and currencies; additional modes of transportation (resulting in additional shipment changing hands); intermediaries such as freight forwarders (consolidators of small shipments; for example, http://www.tslnz.com/index.htm) and customs brokers; and risk of damage, disruption, and terrorism.

Cargo trucks carry containers in and out of the Port of Singapore. The terminal is the world's second busiest (now surpassed by the Port of Shanghai), handling about one-fifth of the world's total container transshipments. It connects with 200 shipping lines with connections to 600 ports in 123 countries. This includes daily sailings to every major port in the world.

William Cho/Creative Commons

Canada's most significant trading partner by far is the United States, and bulk goods are transported between these two nations mainly by rail whereas other goods are transported by truck. Most overseas trade involves ocean transport and is mainly through the Port of Vancouver. However, perishable, lightweight, and expensive goods are transported by air cargo. For an example, see the "Grower Direct" OM in Action.

OM in Action

Grower Direct

Grower Direct is a major flower importer and retail franchise chain in Canada. It is a privately held company started by Skip Kerr in 1986 in Edmonton (http://www.growerdirect.com/our-people). Most Grower Direct flowers, as well as those of other North American flower distributors, are imported from Colombia and Ecuador. The North American flower industry has made long-term arrangements with the flower farmers there to supply flowers as needed in North America, especially to meet the peak demand days of Mother's Day and Valentine's Day.

Planted rose bushes flower after six to eight months and thereafter for approximately nine years. The blooming of rose flowers is curtailed during the low season by "pinching" the buds. The harvest is so well timed that flowers arrive just before peak-demand days. The transport takes about one week, during which time the roses are kept fresh by being cooled to just above freezing (approximately 1 degree Celsius) just after cutting and processing (immersing in citric acid, removing some foliage and thorns, grading by type, colour, length, and head size, bundling in bunches of 25, and being hydrated for 6–24 hours) and are kept dormant at that temperature throughout the long journey. All modes of transport are refrigerated.

The flower boxes are air lifted to Miami International Airport and go through U.S. customs in 24 hours (each box is X-rayed). Those for Grower Direct are picked up and transported to a Grower Direct facility in Miami and packed in refrigerated trucks destined for each region

© Yasonya/iStock.com

of Canada. The trucks are driven by a team of two drivers who drive in shifts. The trucks are pre-cleared by the Canada Border Services Agency and cross the border in a matter of minutes, and are in flower shop coolers approximately four to six days after they are cut. Given their life of three weeks, they will last another two weeks.

Sources: http://www.growerdirect.com/a-cut-flowers-journey; http://www.supplychain247.com/article/the_logistics_of_delivering_fresh_roses_in_time_for_valentines_day/c.h._robinson.

Small Businesses

Small businesses do not always give adequate attention to their supply chains. However, there are many benefits for small businesses to actively managing their supply chains, including increased efficiencies, reduced costs, reduced risks, and increased profits. And size can actually be a competitive advantage for small businesses because they often are more agile than larger companies, enabling them to make decisions and changes more quickly when the need arises.

Three aspects of supply chain management that are often of concern to small businesses are:

- Inventory management
- Reducing risks
- International trade

Inventories can be an issue for small businesses. They may carry extra inventory as a way to avoid shortages due to supply chain interruptions. However, that can tie up capital and take up space. An alternative is to have backup suppliers for critical items. Similarly, having backups for deliveries from suppliers and deliveries to customers can help overcome disruptions. Because it can take a fair amount of time to set up accounts, it is prudent to have these systems in place before they are needed to maintain operations.

Another area that often needs attention is risk management. The key to reducing risks is managing suppliers. Important steps are:

- Use only reliable suppliers.
- Determine which suppliers are critical; get to know them, and any challenges they have.
- Measure supplier performance (e.g., quality, reliability, flexibility).
- Recognize warning signs of supplier issues (e.g., late deliveries, incomplete orders, quality problems).
- Have plans in place to manage supply chain problems.

Exporting can offer opportunities for small business producers to greatly expand their businesses, although they typically lack the knowledge to do so, which can cause unforeseen problems. For instance, exporting nonconforming goods or packaging can result in shipments being held up at a port of entry, which can be costly and time-consuming, and can lead to dissatisfied customers.

Supply Chain Management Information System

Data and information are used in supply chains for transaction processing (execution), including visibility (tracking of shipments), making planning/design decisions, and collaboration (an example of collaboration in forecasting CPFR will appear later in the chapter). It is said that information "replaces" inventory. This means that an organization can reduce the inventory it carries if it has relevant, accurate, and timely information.

To be cost effective, an information system should be based on an open systems concept (i.e., be non-proprietary) and use the Internet (for communication). Relevant accurate data should be collected and data should be synchronized (i.e., be updated without delay across the supply chain).

Information technology (IT) comprises tools that are used to gather (e.g., for tracking), access, analyze (for decision making), and share information (for linking the supply chain). IT includes computers (hardware and software) and communication devices. IT enables supply chain processes/activities to be performed cheaper, faster, and more accurately. IT automates flow of information.

Supply chain planning software can be classified into strategic (e.g., network design optimization), tactical (e.g., production planning such as sales and operation planning explained in Chapter 13, and distribution planning), and operational (e.g., forecasting/demand management, production scheduling, transport planning).

Supply chain execution software includes order taking, purchasing/replenishment/order fulfillment, a warehouse management system (WMS; see Chapter 12), and a transport management system (TMS; selecting carriers, vehicle routing, dispatch, visibility/tracking, etc.).

A more general type of software is enterprise resource planning (ERP) or enterprise software, which was originally focused on managing and coordinating all the resources and functions of an organization from a shared database (more in Chapter 14).

Initially, supply chain management software produced by companies such as Manugistics and i2 Technologies (both now part of JDA) had to work with the ERP software of an organization to be able to function seamlessly. Through acquisition, general business modules/software were added to their suite, thus getting closer to an ERP.

At the same time, ERP software producers such as SAP and Oracle added supply chain modules to their ERPs to make them more suitable for supply chain management. These modules usually facilitate interaction with suppliers (called supplier relationship management, SRM) and with customers (called customer relationship management, CRM).

Supply chain software tends to change over time. A new application is event management software that monitors the supply chain for out-of-tolerance (exception) events (for example, a delay of shipment) and notifies the relevant person. This software is related to visibility and tracking.

The use of tracking can be observed in online shopping where the parcel delivery or trucking company assigns a unique number/bar code to a shipment and makes it available to the customer who can monitor the status of shipment as it flows in the supply chain. The carrier uses bar code readers to update the status of the shipment (more on bar codes in the next chapter). A more sophisticated approach is to use radio frequency identification (RFID) which reads the identity of the item electronically rather than by scanning required for a bar code.

ervice

A recent trend in software purchase option is to use a software as a service (SaaS) product, which involves using the Internet to access the computer of an application service provider that maintains the customer's data. The advantage of SaaS is that it requires no initial investment and the service can usually be terminated with a month's notice.

One technical difficulty in supply chain information systems is data standardization, which allows easier interconnectivity and economies of scale. The computer languages used for this purpose include electronic data interchange (EDI) for electronic communication and, more recently, extensible mark-up language (XML) used for designing web pages.

Another technical difficulty in supply chain information systems is application integration—the ability of supply chain member information systems to easily communicate with each other's application software. Efforts in this regard include developing service-oriented architecture (SOA) such as Microsoft.NET and Java. See the "Target Pulls Out of Canada" OM in Action for an example of ERP.

⚙ OM in Action

Target Pulls Out of Canada

Target Canada filed for bankruptcy protection merely two years after starting its business, putting an end to a debacle that cost its American parent company nearly $3 billion. From the very beginning, the company suffered from crippling supply chain problems which were exacerbated by an overly ambitious launch schedule. Target paid $1.8 billion for the leases to the entire Zellers chain and was forced to adopt an extremely aggressive expansion schedule to utilize more than 120 properties before they were fully ready. One of the most serious operational problems was that products could not move efficiently along the supply chain, leaving store shelves poorly stocked.

SAP was the software Target used to manage inventory along the company's entire supply chain. While SAP is generally regarded as best in class, the system was not able to function properly because the inexperienced personnel made an astounding number of mistakes inputting data. For example, product dimensions were often inputted in the wrong order (width by length and not length by width), or inputted in inches instead of centimetres, or inputted in pounds instead of kilograms. As a result, products could not fit into shipping containers and clear customs in a timely fashion. Merchandise that eventually made

it to the distribution centres on pallets could not be split up and processed for delivery to individual stores because UPC codes were riddled with errors. When orders were eventually delivered to stores, many items came with the wrong quantities and some could not fit properly onto store shelves.

Target's expansion into Canada was nothing short of a disaster. Shopping malls throughout the country were left without a major anchor and 17,600 people lost their jobs.

Source: http://www.canadianbusiness.com/the-last-days-of-target-canada/.

Electronic Data Interchange. **Electronic data interchange (EDI)** is direct, computer-to-computer transmission of interorganizational transactions and information, including purchase orders, sales data, advance shipping notices, invoices, engineering drawings, and more. Among the reasons companies use EDI are:

- Reduction in clerical labour (no need for receiving and entering data manually).
- Reduction of paperwork.
- Increased accuracy (avoids re-entry of data, thus reducing errors).
- Increased speed.

See, for example, the "QLogitek" OM in Action.

> **electronic data interchange (EDI)** The direct transmission of interorganizational transactions and information, computer-to-computer, including purchase orders, sales data, advance shipping notices, invoices, and engineering drawings.

 OM in Action

QLogitek

QLogitek is a B2B-EDI supply chain solutions provider in Toronto. QLogitek's set of nine supply chain software programs are mainly used as software-as-a-service, and are based on Microsoft's BizTalk server platform. The service allows a company to connect with its suppliers over the Internet using QLogitek's servers, instead of directly. Over 20,000 companies in 170 countries use the service. More than 80,000 users made 3.7 billion transactions last year.

HMV (Canada) used QLogitek's supplier order management SaaS, which allowed HMV's approximately 113 stores to send purchase orders to and receive invoices from its small suppliers. The larger suppliers and all the stores use EDI directly.

Hudson's Bay Company used QLogitek's inbound management SaaS to receive advance shipping notices and invoices from its small suppliers. QLogitek was acquired by Smart Employee Benefits, a Toronto employee-benefits software company.

Source: http://www.qlogitek.com/company.

In most JIT systems, EDI is used to signal a replenishment to the supplier. There are many applications of EDI in retailing involving electronic communication between retailers and vendors. Walmart has a satellite network for EDI that allows its retail store point-of-sale data to be downloaded every night to its main database, which vendors can also access through RetailLink. This enables the vendors to manage their own inventory; Walmart saves money and fill rates are up. For more information, see the "Walmart" OM in Action.

Radio Frequency Identification. **Radio frequency identification (RFID)** is a technology that uses radio waves to identify objects such as goods in a supply chain. This is done through the use of an RFID tag that is attached to an object. The tag has an integrated circuit chip and an antenna that emits information to network-connected RFID readers using radio waves. The illustration below shows an RFID tag. It looks like a label, although the centre of the middle layer contains a microchip surrounded by a thin metal object, which acts as antenna.

> **radio frequency identification (RFID)** A technology that uses radio waves to identify objects such as goods in a supply chain.

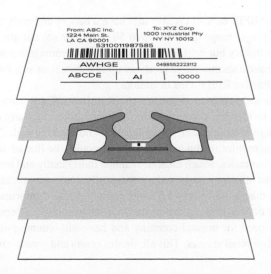

OM in Action

Walmart

Walmart uses a satellite to transmit store point-of-sale and other data (shelf space and local sales decisions captured by handheld devices from store staff) to Walmart's computers in Bentonville, Arkansas, several times a day. There are three supply chains: (1) Some suppliers (of mainly soft lines such as apparel, footwear,

etc.) have access to the POS data through Retail Link and perform vendor-managed inventory and replenish the stores directly. (2) Other suppliers receive orders from Walmart and ship to the distribution centres, which cross-dock most items to the retail stores. (3) Walmart replenishes fast-moving items in the stores according to its POS data from inventory kept in the distribution centres. See the following diagram for Walmart Canada.

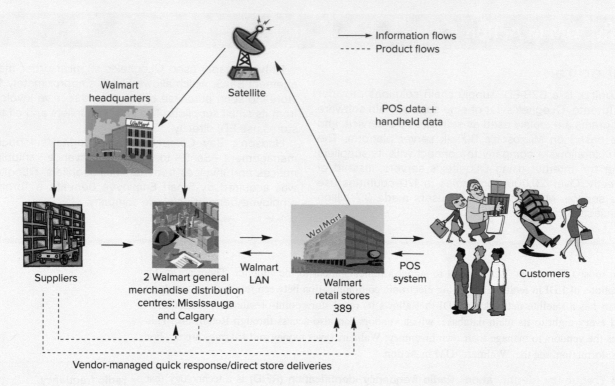

Adapted from F.A. Kuglin, *Customer-Centered Supply Chain Management*. New York: AMACOM (American Management Association), 1998, p. 175; "IS in Action—Walmart Supply Chain," by Dennis Galletta, http://www.youtube.com/watch?v=SUe-tSabKag

Sources: http://www.youtube.com/watch?v=SUe-tSabKag; F. A. Kuglin, *Customer-Centered Supply Chain Management*. New York: AMACOM (American Management Association), 1998, p. 175.

There are two kinds of RFID tags: (1) Active tags have a battery and emit radio waves by themselves; hence they have a longer range (perhaps up to 50 metres or so) but are more expensive; (2) passive tags do not have a battery but work by responding to electromagnetic waves emitted by the RFID reader; hence they have a shorter range (perhaps up to 5 metres or so). For more information, see the "Active RFID vs. Passive RFID" OM in Action.

RFID tags can be attached to pallets, cases, or individual items. They provide unique identification, enabling businesses to identify, track, monitor, or locate practically any object in the supply chain that is within the range of a tag reader. These tags are similar to bar codes, but have the advantage of conveying much more information and they do not require the line-of-sight reading that bar codes require. And unlike bar codes, which must be scanned individually and usually manually, multiple RFID tags can be read simultaneously and automatically. Furthermore, an RFID tag provides more precise information than a bar code: RFID tags contain detailed information on each object, whereas bar codes convey only an object's classification, such as its stock keeping unit (SKU).

RFID eliminates the need for manual counting and bar-code scanning of goods at receiving docks, in warehouses, and on retail shelves. This eliminates errors and greatly speeds up the process.

OM in Action

Active RFID vs. Passive RFID

There are two fundamentally different approaches to RFID—active and passive. Active RFID uses an internal battery while passive RFID uses radio frequency energy transferred wirelessly from a reader. Active RFID allows low level signals to be received and the tag can generate high level signals back to the reader. This increases range and signal penetration. Active tags can also initiate communications with a reader when certain conditions on the temperature, humidity, or motion are met.

On the other hand, passive RFID requires stronger signals from the reader, the return signal strength is very low, and there is no ability to initiate communication. The benefit of passive RFID lies primarily with its low price—around $0.15 to $5.00, whereas active RFID tags cost around $15 to $100. The price is critical considering some supply chain applications require the tagging of millions of units.

Source: http://www.atlasrfid.com/jovix-education/auto-id-basics/active-rfid-vs-passive-rfid/.

The costs involved in setting up an RFID system include the cost of the tags themselves as well as the cost of programming and fixing individual tags to the objects, the cost of readers, and the cost of hardware and software to transmit and analyze the data generated. Other than the cost (currently a passive RFID tag costs approximately 10 cents), the downside of RFIDs is that the radio waves are affected by the nature of some objects (e.g., liquid and metal objects interfere with the proper working of the RFID tags).

Other applications of RFID include credit cards with chips, books with chips, and even cows with chips (see the "Robotic Milking System With RFID Technology" OM in Action.

Creating an Effective Supply Chain

Successful supply chain management requires forming close relationships, effective communication and coordination of activities, supply chain visibility and information sharing, event management capability, and performance metrics.

Forming Close Relationships. It is important for the members of a supply chain to form close relationships (even partnerships). This requires trust, willingness to cooperate, sharing similar goals, and confidence that they will take actions that are mutually beneficial.

Modern credit cards feature embedded RFID capabilities.

David Izquierdo/Dreamstime.com

The Saskatoon Public Library is using RFID technology to make the process of borrowing books easier than ever before. Traditionally, each book had a unique barcode that needed to be manually scanned by a barcode reader in order for the computer to register the loan. With RFID technology, an entire stack of books can be placed onto a special surface on these self-service machines, and a radio frequency scanner will read the tag of each book and process them simultaneously. These two white Bibliotheca machines are located in the Stonebridge area of Saskatoon.

Courtesy of Saskatoon Public Library

 OM in Action

Robotic Milking System With RFID Technology

Pure Holsteins farm in Little Rapids, Newfoundland and Labrador, was the first in the province to introduce a robotic milking system with RFID technology. Each cow has an identification collar around her neck with an RFID tag. The computer system keeps a record of each cow's health conditions, milking history, volume, and quality. A grain feeder is used to entice cows to enter the system and stay. If the cow is due for milking, the system identifies the position of the cow using lasers and 3D cameras. The robotic system starts by first using a set of brushes to disinfect the cow's teats, then air dries them, and next attaches plugs to the udder to begin milking. After the milking is finished, the plugs detach from the cow, food is withdrawn, the door opens, and the cow exits.

The robotic milking system is completely automated and operates reliably 24 hours a day, seven days a week.

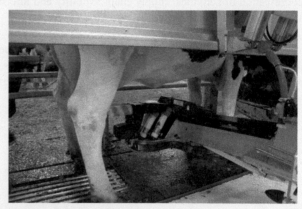

Geraldine Brophy/The Western Star

Effective Communication and Coordination of Activities. Effective supply chains require close and regular communication among members at all levels in order to coordinate activities for effective operations. This requires integrated information systems and standardized ways and means of communicating among members. One example is collaborative planning, forecasting, and replenishment (CPFR), explained later.

supply chain visibility A member can connect to any part of the supply chain to access data in real time.

Supply Chain Visibility and Information Sharing. **Supply chain visibility** means that a member can connect to any part of the supply chain to access data in real time on forecasts and sales, inventory levels, shipment status, impending shortages, and other problems that could impact the timely flow of products through the chain. Thus, instead of each organization in a supply chain making plans based on forecast of demand of its immediate customer, by sharing data on end-customer sales on a real-time basis, each organization in the supply chain can develop plans that contribute to synchronization across the supply chain.

Event Management Capability. **Event management** is the ability to detect and respond to unplanned events such as delayed shipment or a warehouse running low on a certain item.

> **event management** The ability to detect and respond to unplanned events.

Performance Metrics. Performance metrics are necessary to confirm that the supply chain is functioning as expected, or that there are problems that must be addressed. A variety of measures can be used. These are presented later in this section.

Risk Management and Resiliency

Risk management involves identifying risks, assessing their likelihood of occurring and their potential impact, and then developing strategies for addressing those risks. Strategies can pertain to risk avoidance, risk reduction, and risk sharing with supply chain partners. *Risk avoidance* includes avoiding suppliers in a certain area, *risk reduction* includes replacing unreliable suppliers, and *risk sharing* includes contractual arrangements with supply chain partners that spread the risk. **Resiliency** is the ability of a business to recover from an event that negatively impacts the supply chain. *Recovery* is a function of the severity of the impact and the plans that are in place to cope with the event. Organizations can reduce, but not eliminate, the need for resiliency by managing risks.

> **resiliency** The ability of a business to recover from an event that negatively impacts the supply chain.

The first step in risk management is to identify potential risks. Supply chain risks fall into several categories. One is disruptions, which can come from natural disasters such as fires, flooding, hurricanes and the like that either disrupt shipping or affect suppliers directly (by damaging production or storage facilities) or indirectly (by impacting access to facilities or impacting employees in other ways). Other disruptions can occur as a result of supplier issues such as labour strike, production problems, and issues with their suppliers, including bankruptcy. Another source of risk is quality issues, which can disrupt supplies and may lead to product recalls, liability claims, and negative publicity. Still another risk is the potential for suppliers to divulge sensitive information to competitors that weakens a competitive advantage.

Steps in Creating an Effective Supply Chain

Creation of an effective supply chain entails several key steps:

1. Develop strategic objectives. These will guide the process.

2. Integrate and coordinate activities inside the organization. This requires (a) overcoming barriers caused by functional thinking that lead to attempts to optimize a subset of a system rather than the system as a whole, and (b) sharing data and coordinating activities.

Supply chain disruptions can reduce revenue and threaten production and distribution. A risk from accidents is shown here with containers falling from the deck of a damaged cargo ship after a collision between two cargo ships.

Dinodia Photos/Alamy Stock Photo

© Voluntary InterIndustry Commerce Standards Association, http://www.vics.org

3. Coordinate activities with suppliers and with customers. This involves addressing supply and demand issues.

4. Coordinate planning and execution across the supply chain. This requires a system for sharing data across the supply chain, allowing access to data to those who engage in operations to which it will be useful.

5. Consider the possibility of forming *strategic supplier/customer partnerships*. A **strategic supplier/customer partnership** occurs when a buyer and a supplier agree to collaborate so that each may realize a strategic benefit. There are different degrees of partnership. A basic version occurs when a supplier agrees to hold inventory for a customer, thereby reducing the customer's cost of holding the inventory, in exchange for the customer agreeing to a long-term commitment, thereby relieving the supplier of the costs of continually looking for new customers, negotiating prices and services, and so on. It is important that the number of partners in a supply chain be small and the number of chains a company belongs to be limited so that working relationships and trust can be established.

Collaborative Planning, Forecasting, and Replenishment (CPFR)

Collaborative planning, forecasting, and replenishment (CPFR) is the latest effort to increase the effectiveness and efficiency of supply chains. It moves efficient consumer response one step further by establishing a process for communicating and agreeing on forecasts and orders between the manufacturer and the customer (the distributor/retail chain). For collaborative forecasting, a two-step process is usually used. In the first step, the retailer/distributor collects POS data, forecasts sales, and electronically shares them with the manufacturer, which compares the sales forecasts with capacity. If there will be any significant shortfall (called "exception"), the manufacturer tries to resolve the difference. If this is not possible, the manufacturer contacts the retailer/distributor (usually by making a phone call), and the two try to reconcile the difference. After the two agree on the sales forecast, the second step involves the order forecast (which considers the sales forecasts and the inventories, etc.). A similar process to Step 1 is used to create the order forecast.

For more details, see the diagram in http://www.copilotes.eu/images/CPFR_1.gif. Companies such as Best Buy, Sony, Motorola, HP, and Whirlpool regularly use CPFR with their major distributor/retailer customers.

Performance Metrics

The following attributes/metrics are commonly used to measure performance of a supply chain (note their similarity with the competitive priorities of Chapter 2):

1. Cost (unit cost, inventory turnover, logistics costs).
2. Variety/flexibility (speed of production and product changes).
3. Delivery (lead time, percentage of on-time delivery).
4. Customer service (item fill rate).

Inventory turnover refers to the rate at which inventory (material) goes through the supply chain. Faster is better: The quicker that materials pass through the supply chain, the lower inventory costs will be, and the quicker that products will be delivered to the customer. **Item fill rate** is the percentage of demand for an item filled from stocks on hand.

A similar set of performance attributes/metrics has been proposed by the Supply Chain Council (now part of APICS), a not-for-profit association of organizations and consultants interested in supply chain management. The metrics are part of the Supply Chain Operations Reference (SCOR) model[2] and the top-level attributes/metrics are shown in Table 11-1. The SCOR model reflects an effort to standardize measurement of supply chain performance. Perfect order fulfillment is the percentage of orders on time, complete, and with accurate invoice. Cost of goods sold (COGS) is the material, direct

---

strategic supplier/customer partnership A buyer and a supplier agree to collaborate so that each may realize a strategic benefit.

collaborative planning, forecasting, and replenishment (CPFR) A process for communicating and agreeing on forecasts and orders between the manufacturer and the customer (distributor/retailer).

inventory turnover Ratio of annual cost of goods sold to average inventory investment.

item fill rate Percentage of demand for an item filled from stocks on hand.

---

[2] For more details, see http://www.apics.org/docs/default-source/scc-non-research/apicsscc_scor_quick_reference_guide.pdf.

Attribute	Metric
Reliability	Perfect order fulfillment
Responsiveness	Lead time
Agility	Upside flexibility/adaptability
Costs	Supply chain management cost COGS
Assets management	Cash-to-cash cycle time; return on fixed assets; return on inventory

Based on information made available at http://www.supply-chain.org by the Supply Chain Council

◀ **TABLE 11-1**

Supply Chain Operations Reference (SCOR) model 10.0: attributes and top-level metrics.

labour, and indirect labour costs. Cash-to-cash cycle time is the number of days of working capital tied up in the supply chain. It is calculated by adding the number of days of inventory on hand to number of days of receivables (sales) outstanding and subtracting the number of days of payables outstanding.

Purchasing

The purchasing department is responsible for buying the raw materials, manufacturing parts, supplies and spare parts, machines and equipment, and services needed to produce a good or provide a service. Purchasing is a major part of supply chain management. You can get some idea of the importance of purchasing when you consider that most of the cost of many finished goods comes from purchased parts and materials. Furthermore, all goods sold by retailers and wholesalers have to be purchased first (retail/wholesale buying also requires merchandising skills). Nonetheless, the importance of purchasing is more than just the cost of goods purchased; other important factors include the *quality* of goods and services, and *timing* of deliveries of goods or services, both of which can have a significant impact on operations. Also, purchasing plays the central role in forming partnerships.

The basic goal of purchasing is to develop and implement purchasing plans for goods and services that support the business plan. Among the duties of a buyer (the professional who does the purchasing) are identifying sources of supply, negotiating contracts, maintaining a database of suppliers, obtaining goods and services that meet operations' requirements in a timely and cost-efficient manner, managing suppliers, establishing partnerships, and acting as liaison between suppliers and various internal departments/functions.

Purchasing is taking on increased importance as organizations place greater emphasis on supply chain management, quality improvement, JIT, and outsourcing.

Purchasing's Interfaces. Purchasing interfaces with a number of other functional areas within an organization, as well as with outside suppliers (see Figure 11-5).

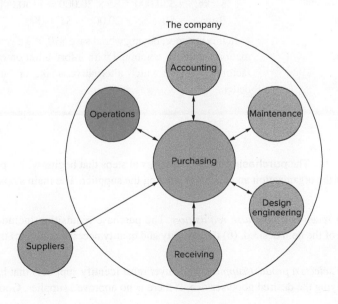

◀ **FIGURE 11-5**

Purchasing's interfaces.

The *operations* department constitutes the main source of requests for purchased materials (manufacturing parts and operating supplies). *Accounting* is responsible for handling payments to suppliers. Another user of purchasing services is the *maintenance* department, which requires spare parts and repair supplies. New machines and equipment are requisitioned by manufacturing engineers. *Design engineering* requests new material/parts. *Receiving* staff check incoming shipments and receive them, and material handling staff move the goods to their destination (the requisitioner).

Make-or-Buy and Insourcing–Outsourcing Decisions. A make-or-buy decision applies when a company can both produce and purchase a part. The question is whether to manufacture the part or buy it from a supplier. Some companies buy most of parts they need. For example, personal computer manufacturers buy most of their parts from suppliers and merely assemble the computers. Likewise for automobile manufacturers. Note that custom parts are usually designed by the buying company and only its manufacturing is contracted out.

Insourcing is bringing the performance of a major business function (e.g., IT, HR, manufacturing) in-house, whereas outsourcing is paying a supplier to perform it.

Organizations may buy/outsource for a variety of reasons: a supplier may have lower cost (due to economies of scale, etc.), more expertise and knowledge, or a patent; demand may be temporary or seasonal; or the company may not have idle capacity. Buying/outsourcing carries some risk: namely reduction in control and expertise. Strategic considerations may outweigh other factors: organizations should make/insource those parts or processes that are or should be their core competencies (long-term organizational capabilities that help the organization to compete).

In some cases, a company might do both: make a portion of the quantity needed in-house and pay a supplier to make the rest. The benefits include maintaining expertise and flexibility, and hedging against loss of a supplier or higher prices.

The following simple example (Example 11-1) illustrates how one might compare the costs of make versus buy of a part.

EXAMPLE 11-1

Analyze the following data to determine the total annual cost of making or buying a part.

	Make	Buy
Expected annual quantity	20,000 units	20,000 units
Variable cost per unit	$5.00	$6.00
Annual fixed costs	$30,000	

SOLUTION

Total annual cost = Fixed cost + Variable cost per unit × Estimated annual quantity

Make: $30,000 + $5 \times 20,000 = $130,000$

Buy: $0 + $6 \times 20,000 = $120,000$

In this instance, buying would save $10,000 a year. This information should be combined with information on other relevant factors to decide which alternative, make or buy, would be better.

purchasing cycle A series of steps that begins with a request for purchase and ends with paying the supplier.

Purchasing Cycle. The **purchasing cycle** is a series of steps that begins with a purchase requisition from within the organization and ends with paying the supplier. The main steps in the purchasing cycle are:

1. *Purchasing receives a purchase requisition.* The purchase requisition includes (a) a general description of the item desired, (b) the quantity and quality necessary, and (c) the desired delivery date.

2. *Purchasing selects a product/supplier.* The buyer must identify suppliers that have the capability of supplying the desired good/service. If there is no approved supplier, Google can be used

to search for a source. Potential suppliers may be prequalified (by, for example, testing a proto-type part made by them) and then asked to quote a price. If the order is not well defined, potential suppliers are asked to submit a proposal saying how they will meet the need.

3. *Purchasing decides how the good or service is purchased.* High-value customized manufacturing parts are negotiated using long-term contracts/partnership. Low-value standard items such as supplies (e.g., stationery) are purchased by blanket purchase (or standing) orders. This involves annual negotiation of prices for a total annual purchase dollar value, with deliveries subject to operating units' direct request throughout the year. Many companies have EDI connection with their suppliers. Electronic purchasing is referred to as *eprocurement.* Low-value one-time purchases should be handled directly between the operating unit and the supplier using corporate credit cards.

4. *Monitoring orders (and expediting).* Routine follow-up, especially for orders with lengthy lead times, allows the buyer to prevent delays.

5. *Receiving shipments.* Receiving staff must check the incoming shipment against the purchase order and notify the purchasing and accounting departments by preparing a receiving report. If the quality of the incoming shipment is in doubt, quality control staff must inspect the shipment. If the goods are not satisfactory, the supplier should be notified without delay.

6. *Paying the supplier.* Upon receipt of the shipment, accounts payable must pay the invoice. If a discount is given for early payment, this should be taken advantage of.

> **value analysis** Examination of the function and design of a part/product in an effort to reduce its cost.

Value Analysis. **Value analysis** refers to the examination of the *function* and design of a part/product in an effort to reduce its cost. Typical questions that are asked are included in Table 11-2.

1. Select a part/product that has a high annual dollar value.
2. Identify the basic function of the item (in a verb–noun form, e.g., a bolt "joins things.")
3. Obtain answers to these kinds of questions:
   a. Can the function be performed in another way?
   b. Could another material or part be used instead?
   c. Can specifications be made less stringent?
   d. Can two or more parts of the item be combined?
   e. Can a different manufacturing process be used?
   f. Do suppliers have suggestions for improvement?
   g. Can packaging be made less costly?
4. Evaluate the answers obtained, and make a recommendation.

◄ TABLE 11-2

The value analysis process and questions.

A team is formed with representatives from design engineering, manufacturing, and cost accounting to work with purchasing to conduct the value analysis.

Determining Prices. Prices are determined in one of three ways: published price list, competitive bidding, and negotiation.

Standard items that are bought infrequently and/or in small quantities are purchased at a fixed market price (published price list). Large orders of standard items receive a price break (due to quantity discount). To begin the process, the buyer should get at least two to three quotes or use *competitive bidding.* The buyer calls (in the informal version) or sends written requests (in the formal version) for bids to potential suppliers, asking them to quote a price. Large government purchases of goods or services are usually made through formal competitive bidding. Usually, the lowest quote or bid wins the contract. Commodities have volatile prices and could be purchased ahead of the need in order to hedge against price increase. Future prices provided by futures markets could be used to forecast future prices.

Price negotiation is used for customized goods or services, or when only a few potential sources exist. A take-it-or-leave-it approach or one that capitalizes on the weaknesses of the supplier will have detrimental effects later. The most reasonable approach is one of give and take (referred to as win–win).

centralized purchasing
Purchasing is handled by a central purchasing department.

decentralized purchasing
Individual departments or separate locations handle their own purchasing requirements.

Centralized Versus Decentralized Purchasing. **Centralized purchasing** means that purchasing is handled by a central purchasing department. **Decentralized purchasing** means that individual departments or separate locations handle their own purchasing requirements.

The purchasing department may be able to obtain lower prices than decentralized units if the higher volume created by combining orders enables the company to take advantage of quantity discounts offered on large orders. It may also be able to obtain better service and closer attention from suppliers. In addition, centralized purchasing enables companies to assign certain categories of items to specialist buyers who tend to become more efficient and skilled. For an application of purchasing centralization, see the "Teck" OM in Action.

OM in Action   http://www.teck.com

Teck

Teck is a copper and zinc mining company based in Vancouver, but has expanded into oil and coal mining recently. Teck's mines are in British Columbia, Alberta, the United States, Chile, and Peru. When, in 2008, Teck bought six coal mines in B.C., the spare parts inventory management functions of the six mines were run independently using six independent software programs not connected to the legacy mainframe in Vancouver. To be able to coordinate purchasing and buy spare parts as a group,

Teck's information systems department oversaw the purchase and installation of Microsoft Dynamics, a Tier 2 ERP software. Now, there is a centralized database that can be accessed by each mine and the head office. Purchase orders are accumulated over the six mines and inventory is controlled more efficiently.

Sources: http://www.microsoft.com/en-ca/dynamics/customer-success-stories-detail.aspx?casestudyid=4000008850. Microsoft Dynamics, "Teck's Coal Business Unearths Stronger Procurement Processes With Microsoft Dynamics," http://www.microsoft.com/en-ca/dynamics/customer-success-stories-detail.aspx?casestudyid=4000008850.

Decentralized purchasing has the advantage of awareness of differing "local" needs and being better able to respond to those needs. Where locations are widely scattered, decentralized purchasing may be able to save on transportation costs by buying locally.

Some organizations manage to take advantage of both centralization and decentralization by permitting individual units to buy certain items while other items are bought centrally. For example, small orders and rush orders are handled locally or by departments, while centralized purchasing is used for high-volume, high-value items/commodities or corporate services such as payroll, personnel, information systems, legal, etc.

Spend Analysis. Many organizations fail to collect accurate and useful purchasing data. This is because (1) different codes may be used to describe the same supplier or item in different plants, (2) there may not be an easy way to relate and aggregate similar items using their stock codes and description (no product classes or types are defined), or (3) relationships between suppliers may have been missed. *(Note:* Expenditure with all subsidiaries of a company should be aggregated when negotiating quantity discounts.) These problems can be rectified by undertaking spend analysis.

spend analysis Collecting, cleansing, classifying, and analyzing expenditure data with the purpose of reducing procurement costs, improving efficiency, and monitoring compliance with purchasing policies.

Spend analysis involves collecting, cleansing (i.e., amending or removing data that is incorrect, incomplete, improperly formatted, or duplicated), classifying, and analyzing (e.g., using charts) expenditure data with the purpose of reducing procurement costs, improving efficiency, and monitoring compliance with purchasing policies. Spend analysis can provide answers to questions such as, "What was bought? From which suppliers? What is the total expenditure on a part? How much is the total expenditure with a supplier?"

It is important that deficiencies of data collection and/or purchasing practice be fixed (e.g., using a spend analysis software) so that the need for spend analysis in the future is diminished. For example, maverick buying (users buying from non-approved suppliers) should be minimized. Companies have realized up to 5 percent reduction in their total expenditure by performing spend analysis.[3]

---

[3] http://www.supplychainbrain.com/content/index.php?id=5032&cHash=081010&tx_ttnews[tt_news]=1406.

Ethics. Ethical behaviour is particularly important in purchasing, where buyers are authorized to spend significant amounts of the organization's funds and also may be tempted to use their position for personal gain. Furthermore, salespeople are often eager to make a sale and may resort to unethical behaviour such as giving gifts to buyers. See Table 11-3 for guidelines for ethical behaviour in the management of supply chains.

SCMA Standards of Conduct
Members will conduct themselves in a manner that a reasonable and informed third party would conclude as being appropriate to a professional in supply chain management.

1. **Avoidance of conflicts of interest**
   Members should exercise professional judgment and discretion in order to avoid any apparent or actual conflict of interest when performing their duties. Should a conflict of interest arise, the member is required to disclose their interests to their employer and/or other impacted parties as soon as possible. Members should consider removing themselves from any decisions in which they have a conflict of interest until express direction from the appropriate authority is obtained.

2. **Protection of confidential or sensitive information**
   Where a member has been privy to confidential or sensitive information, it is their responsibility to ensure that it remains so. Such information must not be used for any personal gain or advantage. Information given in the course of a member's professional activity should be forthright and not intended to mislead or deceive others.

3. **Business relationships**
   Members should maintain relationships with suppliers and third parties in a manner that contributes to and promotes fair competition in the market and protects the interests and reputation of his or her employer. Members should not use their position to garner personal favours or advantages.

4. **Gifts, gratuities, and hospitality inducements**
   When permitted by employing organizations, members must ensure that the objectivity of their decisions is not compromised or unduly influenced by the acceptance of gifts, gratuities, or hospitalities of any kind. Members should be discerning in their business and social relationships and activities and, through them, seek to enhance the integrity of the profession.

5. **Environmental and social responsibilities**
   Members shall exercise their responsibilities in a manner that promotes and provides opportunities for the protection and preservation of the natural environment. Members shall favour the use and distribution of resources in an efficient, effective, and ethical manner. Members will be cognizant of the social rights extended to all people, including the conventions of the International Labour Organization with respect to labour standards, and will encourage and support supplier diversity. These attributes of sustainability should guide members in their decisions, and in implementing the policies and values of the organizations they represent.

◀ **TABLE 11-3**

Guidelines for ethical behaviour in managing supply chains.

Source: Reprint http://scma.com/en/about-scma/join-scma/code-of-ethics

Companies often expect ethical behaviour from their suppliers. An organization known for its ethical purchasing is Mountain Equipment Co-op (see the OM in Action).

⚙ OM in Action

Mountain Equipment Co-op

Mountain Equipment Co-op (MEC) was established in 1971 by six mountaineers in Vancouver who wanted to have quality mountain climbing equipment available for sale in Canada. It is a consumers' cooperative and its profits are distributed to its members based on their purchases. Lifetime membership is only $5 and there are over 3 million members. MEC now has stores in 22 Canadian cities and over $366 million in revenue. MEC designs and manufactures approximately 60 percent of the items it sells. Other items are purchased from high-quality manufacturers.

MEC has a strong sustainability policy for environmentally friendly and ethical sourcing. The environmental efforts involve using greener material (e.g., PVC-free, organic cotton, recycled polyester), green buildings, waste reduction (e.g., no hang tags, poly bags, paper), and using greener logistics (inter-modal instead of truck for shipping from Vancouver to the east, no overseas air cargo). MEC is a member of 1% For the Planet and donates 1 percent of its gross sales to environmental causes.

The ethical sourcing policy is the MEC Supplier Code of Conduct, which requires suppliers to have respect for the environment and the health and safety of their workers. It requires that a supplier not employ children under the age of 15 or use forced labour such as prisoners. The supplier should not abuse its workers, prevent unions, or force its workers to work more than 48 hours of regular time and 12 hours of overtime per week. Workers should have at least one in seven days off and should be paid fairly. Workplace health and safety norms should be followed, such as use of earplugs and dust masks. There should be no discrimination or harassment. New potential suppliers and current suppliers (every 1.5 years) are audited by a MEC team or external auditors. This entails a one-day visit. MEC publishes the identity of its supplier–manufacturers, called the Factory List, which contains approximately 80 names, mostly in China and other Southeast Asian countries.

Sources: https://www.mec.ca/en/explore/about-mec; https://www.mec.ca/en/explore/our-environmental-commitment; http://images.mec.ca/media/Images/pdf/supplier_conduct_v1_m56577569830523401.pdf; https://www.mec.ca/media/Images/pdf/annualreport/MEC_2015_AnnualReport_rev_v2_m56577569836610940.pdf.

There are many examples of unethical behaviour involving supply chains. They include bribing government or company officials to secure permits or favourable status; "exporting smokestacks" to developing countries; claiming a "green" supply chain when in reality the level of "green" is only minimal; ignoring health, safety, and environmental standards; violating basic rights of workers (e.g., paying substandard wages; using sweatshops, forced labour, or child labour); mislabelling country of origin; and selling goods abroad that are banned at home.

Every company should develop an ethical supply chain code to guide behaviour. A code should cover behaviours that involve customers, suppliers, contract negotiation, recruiting, and the environmental issues.

A major risk of unethical behaviour is that when such behaviour is exposed in the media, consumers tend to blame the major company or brand in the supply chain associated with the ethical infractions that were actually committed by legally independent companies in the supply chain. The problem is particularly difficult to manage when supply chains are global, as they often are in manufacturing operations. Unfortunately, many companies lack the ability to quickly contact most or all of the companies in their supply chain, and communicate with suppliers on critical issues of ethics and compliance. Although monitoring of supply chain activities is essential, it is only one aspect of maintaining an ethical supply chain. With global manufacturing and distribution, supply chain scrutiny should include all supply chain activities from purchasing, manufacturing, assembly, and transportation, to service and repair operations, and eventually to proper disposal of products at the end of their useful life.

Key steps companies can take to reduce the risk of damages due to unethical supplier behaviour are to choose those that have a reputation for good ethical behaviour; incorporate compliance with labour standards in supplier contracts; develop direct, long-term relationships with ethical suppliers; and address quickly any problems that occur.

Ecommerce

ecommerce The use of computers and the Internet to conduct buying and selling activities.

Ecommerce refers to the use of computers and the Internet to conduct buying and selling. Ecommerce involves business-to-business (B2B) and business-to-consumer (B2C) commerce. Table 11-4 lists some of the numerous advantages of ecommerce.

There are two essential features of ecommerce businesses: the website, and order fulfillment. Companies often invest considerable time and effort in front-end design (the website, its visual appeal, and ease and speed of product search). Visit Shopify.ca to build a simple and easy-to-use ecommerce website. **Order fulfillment** involves order processing, scheduling, inventory management, warehousing, packaging, billing, and delivery.

order fulfillment Involves order processing, scheduling, inventory management, warehousing, packaging, billing, and delivery.

Order fulfillment and its lead time varies by the nature of work required. For items made ahead and kept in stock (make-to-stock), fulfillment simply involves assigning the order to the nearest distribution centre (DC), whereas for make-to-order, the order has to be scheduled for production first. For assemble-to-order items, components have already been made and only final assembly has to be scheduled. Finally, for engineer-to-order items, the item needs to be designed first according to the customer's specifications.

Companies have a global presence and customers have global choices and easy access to information.	
Companies can improve competitiveness and quality of service by allowing access to their services at any time.	
Companies can analyze the interest in various products based on the number of hits and requests for information.	
Companies can collect detailed information about clients' choices, which enables mass customization and personalized products. An example is the purchase of Dell Computers over the web, where the buyer specifies the final configuration.	
Supply chain response times are shortened. The biggest impact is on products that can be delivered directly on the web, such as software.	
The roles of the intermediary and sometimes the traditional retailer or service provider are reduced or eliminated entirely in a process called *disintermediation*. This process reduces costs and adds alternative purchasing options.	
Substantial cost savings and price reductions related to the reduction of transaction costs can be realized. Companies that provide purchasing and support through the web can save significant personnel costs.	
Ecommerce allows the creation of virtual companies that distribute only through the web, thus reducing costs. Amazon.com and other etailers can afford to sell for a lower price because they do not need to maintain retail stores.	
The playing field is levelled for small companies, which lack significant resources to invest in infrastructure and marketing.	

◀ **TABLE 11-4**

Advantages of ecommerce.

David Simchi-Levi, Philip Kaminsky, and Edith Simchi-Levi, *Designing and Managing the Supply Chain: Concepts, Strategies, and Case Studies*, New York: Irwin/McGraw-Hill, © 2000, p. 235.

In the early days of Internet selling, many organizations thought that they could avoid bearing the costs of holding inventories by acting solely as intermediaries, having their suppliers ship directly to their customers. But this approach failed as sales increased because suppliers ran out of certain items. Industry giants such as Amazon built large warehouses so they could maintain greater control over their inventories.

Traditional retailers (called "brick-and-mortar") have now added online shopping (now called "click and mortar" or "bricks and clicks")—for example, Walmart.ca or BestBuy.ca. These use the web in a different way, offering low-volume, slow-moving items online. This complements their in-store products. They fulfill online orders from their regular distribution centres (DCs) (if total online dollar amounts are small) or have dedicated DCs for online orders (if total online dollar amounts are large). Also, instead of parcel delivery, the goods are made available in the nearest store for the consumer to pick up (the goods are prepared for the consumer at a DC or at the store). To facilitate B2B ecommerce, some emarketplaces or exchanges have been created. See Table 11-5 for some examples. An important industry-led non-profit organization is GS1 Canada, which is trying to advance ecommerce by standardizing communication between trading partners and improving

Type	Description	Website
Buyer-Initiated Exchanges		
CareNet Services Inc.	Has over 450 hospitals using EDI for ordering and receiving invoices from more than 95 health care vendors.	http://www.gs1ca.org/pages/n /sectors/hc/index.asp
Avendra	Set up by Marriott and Hyatt; buys for about 5,000 hotels, resorts, and restaurants from 800 suppliers.	http://www .avendra.com
Seller-Initiated Exchange		
Global Healthcare Exchange	Set up by a few large pharmaceutical and medical/surgical equipment suppliers. Over 4,100 health care providers and 400 manufacturers in North America use GHX.	http://www.ghx.com /ghxcanada/canada.aspx

◀ **TABLE 11-5**

Examples of e-exchanges.

data accuracy. GS1 was the founder of bar codes many decades ago and controls the assignment of bar codes in Canada.

Supplier Management and Partnership

Reliable and trustworthy suppliers are a vital link in an effective supply chain. Timely deliveries of high-quality goods or services contribute to effective operations. A buyer functions as an "external operations manager," working with suppliers to coordinate the supplier's operations and the buyer's needs.

Choosing Suppliers. In many respects, choosing a supplier involves taking into account many of the same factors associated with making a major purchase (e.g., a car). A person considers price, quality, availability of product or timely delivery, the supplier's reputation, past experience with the supplier, and service after sale. The factors a company takes into account when it selects a product/supplier and typical questions to ask are outlined in Table 11-6.

TABLE 11-6 ▶

Factors and typical questions to ask when selecting a product/supplier.

Factor	Typical Questions
Quality	Is the supplier technically capable of achieving the desired quality?
	What procedures does the supplier have for quality control?
Flexibility	How flexible is the supplier in handling changes in delivery schedules, quantity, and product or service?
Location	Is the supplier nearby?
Price	Are prices reasonable?
Financial stability and reputation	What is the reputation of the supplier? Is the supplier financially stable?
Lead time	What lead time can the supplier provide?
	What policies does the supplier have for keeping items in stock? Is the supplier reliable?
Other customers	Is the supplier heavily dependent on other major customers, causing a risk of giving priority to their needs over ours?
Service after sale	How much after-sale support does the supplier provide?

Because different factors are important for different organizations, purchasing must decide, with the help of the requisitioner, the importance of each factor (i.e., how much weight to give to each factor), and then rate potential products/suppliers according to how well they can be expected to perform against this list. This process is called **supplier analysis**. The information required can be obtained from the potential supplier, its current customers (reference), and business intelligence vendors such as Dun & Bradstreet. If the potential supplier was used before, its performance should be evaluated and used in decision making.

supplier analysis Evaluating a supplier in terms of factors such as price, quality, delivery, and service.

Supplier Relationship. In the past, many organizations regarded their suppliers as adversaries. One lesson learned from the Japanese manufacturers is that numerous benefits derive from a good supplier relationship, including supplier flexibility in terms of accepting changes in delivery schedule, quality, and quantity. Moreover, suppliers can often help identify improvements in the design of an item (value analysis). In fact, they can be involved in the design of new products (called *early supplier involvement*).

Many Japanese companies rely on only one or two suppliers to handle their needs for an item. The advantages of single-sourcing/partnership include lower number of orders, deliveries, and invoices, and being able to work with the supplier to reduce lead time, improve quality, and reduce the price.

Supplier Partnership. More and more organizations are seeking to establish partnerships with their suppliers. This implies fewer suppliers, longer-term relationships, sharing of information (sales date, forecasts, problems), and cooperation in planning.

Supplier partnerships are required for initiatives such as JIT, quick response, VMI, and CPFR, where both sides need to invest time and money in a long-term relationship.

Professor D.M. Lambert has developed a partnership model that has been used dozens of times.[4] The partnership model is as follows. After the number of suppliers is reduced, those that provide key materials/services and with whom a company does a lot of business are approached for partnership discussion. Top executives and managers from functional areas from each company are invited to a retreat, facilitated by a third-party consultant.

During 1.5 days, each company's managers first determine the key reasons they should get into partnership (e.g., cost reduction, customer service enhancement, etc.), provide a metric and target for each reason, and then share these with the other company's managers. There should be frank discussions to clarify the issues. These key expectations are called partnership drivers.

Next, if both sides agree that partnership will likely meet their expectations, they proceed to identify the so-called facilitators. These include compatibility of cultures and management philosophy, and other factors that influence the ease of coordination of activities required for partnership.

Then, if coordination appears to be reasonably easy, based on the level of expectation of benefits of partnership (i.e., attainment of partnership drivers), the intended partnership can be classified as Type I (low benefits), Type II (moderate benefits), or Type III (high benefits).

Finally, based on the type of intended partnership, both sides have to identify the extent of cooperation in planning, control, communication, and risk/reward sharing, and implement activities to achieve this. For example, joint planning can range from ad hoc (sharing plans for a project) to regularly scheduled meetings (joint planning for key processes). Performance measures can range from separate (but shared) to joint (i.e., joint performance). Communication can range from ad hoc (one way) to linked electronic communication system (two ways). Short-term loss tolerance can range from low to high, and desire to help the other party gain financially can range from limited to high. For two examples of partnership, see the "OfficeMax Grand & Toy" and "Cargill Value Added Meats–Canada" OM in Action boxes.

 OM in Action

OfficeMax Grand & Toy

Grand & Toy Company is one of the largest office supply distributors in Canada. It carries approximately 6,000 stock-keeping units in its eight regional distribution centres. It had 75 retail locations but recently has been closing them to focus on online order-taking and delivery. Grand & Toy provides EDI service to its customers using its own wide area network, computers, and an ERP software. It also allows its customers to order over the Internet (using its OrderPoint system), where they can use Grand & Toy's electronic catalogue. Grand & Toy keeps records of customers' purchase quantities and allows them to access this data, in effect providing inventory record keeping for its customers. Grand & Toy offers next-day delivery in major cities, and has an in-stock rate of 98 percent. Grand & Toy also helps organizations develop EDI connections with their other suppliers. In return the customer organization agrees to use Grand & Toy as the sole source for its office product needs for a certain number of years. This is an example of supplier partnership. In 1996, Grand & Toy was purchased by Boise Cascade, which later changed its name to OfficeMax. More recently, OfficeMax merged with Office Depot, and Grand & Toy's name has been changed to OfficeMax.

Source: https://www.officemaxcanada.com/en/sites/core/aboutUs_ corporateProfile.aspx.

Supplier Certification. Supplier certification is a detailed examination of the policies and capabilities of a supplier. The certification process verifies that a supplier meets or exceeds the requirements of a buyer. This is generally important in supplier relationships, but it is particularly important

---

[4] D.M. Lambert and A.M. Knemeyer, "We're in This Together," *Harvard Business Review*, December 2004, pp. 114–122.

OM in Action

Cargill Value Added Meats— Canada

Cargill Value Added Meats–Canada (CVAM–Canada) supplies McDonald's Canada with beef and chicken. The relationship is exclusive: CVAM–Canada is the only beef and chicken supplier to McDonald's Canada, and McDonald's Canada is the only customer of CVAM–Canada. This relationship started in January 2002 for chicken. The London, Ontario, chicken processing facility employs approximately 900 people and processes 80,000 chickens each day. The hatchery in Jarvis, Ontario, has 70 employees and, on average, produces 150,000 chicks per day. The beef partnership started in September 2004. The beef patty-processing facilities in Spruce Grove, Alberta, and Brampton, Ontario, employ a total of 120 people, and produce approximately 1.5 million pounds of beef patties each week.

CVAM–Canada's annual business planning process is conducted together with McDonald's Canada. The output from this process is used to form CVAM–Canada's three-year strategic plan. Annual and monthly meetings are conducted with McDonald's Canada to review the strategic-plan progress and customer needs and expectations. A formal supplier performance review is conducted jointly every two years. The tight approach to determine current and future customer needs and expectations ensures daily interactions between CVAM– Canada and McDonald's Canada. As a result, CVAM– Canada has won four supplier excellence awards from McDonald's Canada, and the Spruce Grove facility has won a food safety award for its complaint reductions and food safety.

Source: http://www.excellence.ca/en/awards/2011-cae-recipients/2011-cae -profiles/2011-caeprofile-cvam.

when buyers are seeking to establish a long-term relationship with suppliers. Certified suppliers are sometimes referred to as world class suppliers. One advantage of using certified suppliers is that the buyer can eliminate much or all of the inspection and testing of delivered goods. And although problems with supplier goods or services might not be totally eliminated, there is much less risk than with non-certified suppliers.

Rather than develop their own certification programs, some companies rely on standard industry certifications such as ISO 9001, perhaps the most widely used international certification.

Importing. Importing can have many benefits. Here are some useful tips for using foreign suppliers:[5]

- Work with someone who has expertise to help oversee foreign suppliers, preferably someone who spends a good deal of time in that country. Also, a licensed customs broker can help with laws and regulations, necessary documents, and working with importers and exporters.
- Describe your buying patterns and schedules to set expectations for demand and timing.
- Don't rely on a single supplier; a backup supplier can reduce risk and provide bargaining leverage.
- Building goodwill can have benefits in negotiations and resolving problems when they arise.
- Consider using domestic suppliers if the risks or other issues with foreign suppliers are formidable. Advantages can involve lower shipping times and costs, closer interactions with suppliers, and increased agility.

 # Logistics

logistics The movement and warehousing of materials/ products and information.

Logistics refers to the transport and warehousing of incoming materials/parts and outgoing distribution of products. It also includes the use of information to control the activities. In the past, inbound logistics was controlled by purchasing/manufacturing and outbound logistics was controlled by marketing/sales. However, more and more organizations are integrating these two to reduce costs. Logistics management is a major part of supply chain management.

---

[5] U.S. Small Business Administration, "5 Tips for Managing an Efficient Global Supply Chain," *Small Business Operations*, March 12, 2013.

Logistics costs (mainly transportation and warehousing/inventory holding cost) in Canada usually range between 3 percent and 8 percent of a product's sales price: pharmaceuticals/chemicals have the highest and petroleum/motor vehicles have the lowest logistics costs relative to their sales price.

We will cover inventory control/warehousing/material handling in the next chapter.

Traffic management is involved in transport planning and overseeing transport execution and control (the delivery of incoming and outgoing goods). This function handles schedules and decisions on delivery methods and times, taking into account costs of various alternatives, government regulations, the needs of the organization relative to quantities and timing, and external factors such as potential delivery delays or disruptions (e.g., highway construction, truckers' strikes).

traffic management
Involved in planning and overseeing the delivery of incoming and outgoing goods.

Transport Planning

Given the quantity and speed-of-delivery requirements of the expected shipments, an organization has to make the following decisions:

- Decide whether to outsource the transportation.
- Select the mode of transportation.
- Select the carrier.
- Negotiate the transport rates.

If the quantity to be shipped is small and shipment is infrequent, a common carrier (for hire) can be used as the transport need arises. However, most manufacturers have ongoing transportation needs. They can either employ professionals or outsource the transportation (or even logistics) function to a third-party logistics (3PL) service provider. Similarly, they can purchase (or lease) and manage their own trucks (private fleet) or contract with transport companies (contract carrier).

Third-Party Logistics (3PL). A 3PL service provider is a logistics service management company. It can own its own transport equipment (trucks, planes, ships) or it can be only a logistics management company. So, a third-party logistics company can employ a transport company (the second party). Many transport companies also provide 3PL services, as do package delivery companies such as UPS (its 3PL service division is called UPS Supply Chain Services). One possible reason for outsourcing logistics is a desire to concentrate on the core business. Employing a company that specializes in logistics provides other benefits, such as a well developed logistics information system, experienced logistics personnel, customs clearance facilities, foreign locations, and the ability to provide lower transportation rates.

Modes of Transportation. **Modes of transportation** used for delivery include pipelines, ships, trains, trucks, and airplanes. The order of modes given above is from least costly to most costly and from slowest to fastest. The most common delivery method inland is trucking (which is most flexible), followed by railways, which are used for bulk transport of heavy goods over long distances. Ocean freight is used for bulk transport of goods or ocean containers (20 or 40 feet long) on oceans. Some cargo ships are used on the Great Lakes, and pipelines transport crude oil and natural gas. Air cargo is used for expensive, light, urgent products. Most air cargo is transported by passenger airlines (in the cargo hold). Some logistics companies use a combination of these modes. For example, parcel delivery companies such as UPS use air and trucks. The use of intermodal transport of large containers (e.g., truck → train → truck) is increasing (the container is put onto the back of a flat-bed truck, transported to a rail station, trans-loaded onto a flat-bed rail car, transported to the destination rail station, and trans-loaded back onto another flat-bed truck).

modes of transportation
The equipment used for delivery, including pipelines, ships, trains, trucks, and airplanes.

The trucking industry in North America is very efficient. There are many trucking companies, including small, one-person owner–operator businesses. Trucking service is categorized into "truckload (TL)," when approximately 15,000 pounds or more is shipped, and "less-than-truckload (LTL)" when between 150 and 15,000 pounds is shipped. Less than 150 pounds is considered a small package and is shipped by package delivery companies. In TL, the whole truck is hired and a direct delivery can be made, whereas LTL involves several pickups and deliveries in order to increase the utilization of the capacity of the truck. Trucking companies are moving toward offering both TL and LTL, and package delivery companies are increasing their maximum shipment weight (e.g., FedEx now has a ground freight service).

CN and CP are the main rail carriers in Canada, and because they are a natural monopoly, they are regulated by the federal government. Laying new rail track is very expensive, so their capacity is fixed. Because there are not enough pipelines out of Alberta, Saskatchewan, and North Dakota, oil companies have started using crude oil railcars to ship their oil to refineries/ports. This has caused delays for other users of rail such as grain exporters and farmers.

In terms of delivery reliability, the order from most to least reliable is air cargo, trucking, railway, and ocean freight (same order as speed because the longer the trip, the more likely there will be delays). Because of low delivery reliability, until recently JIT manufacturers have been hesitant to use ocean freight for their inbound logistics from Southeast Asia.

Selecting a Transportation Mode. Mode selection factors include pickup/delivery accessibility, transit time, reliability, product safety (including theft), product characteristics (weight, size, fragility, temperature sensitivity, and perishability), value (low-value product needs low-cost mode), and freight cost. For some shipments, one or more of the above factors dictates a particular mode of transport. However, companies sometimes must make a choice between rapid (but more expensive) delivery such as overnight or second-day air and slower (but less expensive) alternatives such as using a truck. The decision in such cases often focuses on the total transportation and in-transit inventory holding cost of each alternative. An important assumption is that the buyer takes ownership at the supplier's location and pays for delivery, which is the case in some purchases. Initially, we make the assumption that the two alternative modes of transportation are equally reliable; hence they require the same level of safety stock (safety stocks are extra inventory kept when supply and/or demand are variable).

The in-transit inventory holding cost incurred by an alternative is calculated as:

$$\text{In-transit holding cost} = \frac{H(d)}{365} \tag{11-1}$$

where H = Annual holding cost of items being transported

d = Duration of transport (in days)

Total delivery cost = Transportation (freight) cost + In-transit holding cost

$$= \text{Transportation (freight) cost} + \frac{H(d)}{365}$$

EXAMPLE 11-2 ▶

Determine which delivery alternative—one day or three days—is best when the holding cost of the item is $1,000 per year, the one-day delivery transportation cost is $40, and the three-day delivery transportation cost is:

a. $35
b. $30

H = $1,000 per year

SOLUTION

Total cost of one-day delivery = $40 + $1,000(1/365) = $42.74

Total cost of three-day delivery

a. = $35 + $1,000(3/365)
    = $43.22 > $42.74

Therefore, one-day delivery is cheaper.

b. = $30 + $1,000(3/365)
    = $38.22 < $42.74

Therefore, three-day delivery is cheaper.

When the modes of transportation are different (e.g., air vs. ocean freight), the unequal reliability of these modes requires different levels of safety stocks. Therefore, the cost of holding safety stocks at the destination should also be included in the total cost of a mode.

Consider a part that is to be transported from China to Europe. The annual demand for the part is 23,000 units. Price is $210 per unit. Annual holding cost rate is 20 percent of unit price. There are two transportation options.

EXAMPLE 11-3

> Air cargo: Takes 7 days (door to door) and costs $52 per unit.
> Ocean freight: Takes 35 days and costs $10 per unit.

Because of variability of transportation time and demand, two weeks of demand will be kept at the destination as safety stock [(2/52) × (23,000) units] if air cargo is used. On the other hand, eight weeks of demand will be kept at the destination as safety stock if ocean freight is used. Assume that order quantity will be the same in either case. Calculate the total annual freight, in-transit holding, and safety stock costs for each mode, and choose the cheaper mode.

SOLUTION

Annual costs:

Air

$$\text{Freight} = \$52(23,000) = \$1,196,000.00$$
$$\text{In-transit holding} = 23,000(\$210)(0.20)(7/365) = 18,526.03$$
$$\text{Safety stock} = (2/52)(23,000)(\$210 + \$52)(0.20) = \underline{46,353.85}$$
$$\$1,260,879.88$$

Note: Cost of the part at the destination includes air transportation cost: $210 + $52.

Ocean

$$\text{Freight} = \$10(23,000) = \$230,000.00$$
$$\text{In-transit holding} = 23,000(\$210)(0.20)(35/365) = 92,630.14$$
$$\text{Safety stock} = (8/52)(23,000)(\$210 + \$10)(0.20) = \underline{155,692.31}$$
$$\$478,322.45$$

Note: Cost of the part at the destination includes ocean transportation cost: $210 + $10. Ocean is much cheaper.[6]

Selecting a Carrier. Relevant capability and service quality factors include transit time average and variation, on-time pick-up and delivery, vehicle availability and capacity, technical/information system capability, geographic coverage, damage protection, billing accuracy, responsiveness to emergencies/problem resolution, financial stability, and whether the product can be delivered direct (e.g., TL) or indirect (involving stops and transfers, e.g., LTL, rail). To be able to reduce costs and improve service, an organization should use only a limited number of carriers.

Negotiating a Transport Rate. If one is using a carrier regularly, it is advantageous to enter into a contract with the carrier in order to take advantage of price discounts. In doing so, some negotiation may be involved on transport cost (or freight rate). For this reason, one should be aware of how the rate is determined.

To simplify rate determination, postal code of origin and destination is usually used. Rate increases with distance, almost linearly, by zone. Rate of an LTL common carrier for a given origin–destination pair is usually in dollars per 100 pounds. (In North America, 100 pounds is known as a "hundredweight," and is abbreviated as "cwt" since C is the roman numeral for 100.) For a TL carrier, it is by dollars per mile, for a given truck capacity. For LTL, there are usually weight breaks reflecting economies of scale. For example, if the weight is less than 500 pounds, the rate is $47.94/cwt, if the weight is between 500 and 1000 pounds, the rate is $38.35/cwt, etc.

---

[6] T. Miller, "The International Modal Decision (Part 1)," *Chilton's Distribution*, 90(11), pp. 82–92; T. Miller, "Air vs. Ocean: Two Critical Factors (Part 2)," *Chilton's Distribution*, 90(12), pp. 46–52.

For LTL, the characteristics of the product (called its *transportability*) affect the rate. These include:

- Density
  - Weight/volume ratio
  - Lower density → higher rate
- Stowability
  - To allow compact packing (i.e., space utilization). For example, an assembled bicycle is not very stowable (i.e., will waste space).
  - More stowable → lower rate
- Difficulty of handling
  - Need for repacking, re-palletizing, special equipment
  - More difficult → higher rate
- Liability
  - For loss, damage (e.g., fragile, perishable), theft
  - Is also a function of value of product
  - Higher liability → higher rate

For LTL, to simplify rate determination, products are grouped into classes of same transportability. The National Motor Freight Traffic Association has created the National Motor Freight Classification (NMFC) used in North America. There are 18 classes, from 50 to 500. Class 100 is average transportability class. Class 200 is twice as hard. Class 50 is half as hard. Class 400 is four times harder. Note that packaging affects the class.

Product classes for railways are called uniform freight classification (there are 31 classes). Rates for railways are called commodity rates. Water carriers use weight or volume. Freight-all-kind rate is for a mixed shipment.

Transport Execution and Control

Transport execution and control involves load planning and consolidation, load tendering (selecting carrier(s)), appointment scheduling, checking carriers' legal compliance (safety, etc.), having in-transit visibility and tracking, freight payment, and measuring performance of carrier.

Some buyers ask their suppliers to use a particular carrier based on their location and weight of shipment. This is sometimes contained in a transportation routing guide, which may also have guidelines for packaging.

A bill of lading (BOL) is the transport contract. It provides all the information the carrier needs. It also specifies the carrier's liability for loss and damage. Furthermore, it acts as a receipt for when the carrier delivers the shipment to the buyer.

Carriers tend to use the shortest distance or time route between an origin and a destination. This is called route planning. A common technology used by truckers is PCMiler, which has a GPS and electronic maps.

Local delivery to drop off or load shipments also requires finding the shortest distance or time but the route starts and ends at a depot. There are also time window restrictions at various stops. This is called the vehicle routing problem.

Logistics of Returns

reverse logistics Backward flow of goods returned by consumers or retailers.

Reverse logistics is the backward flow of goods returned by consumers or retailers. Goods are returned because they are defective or unsold (excess inventory), or because customers simply changed their minds or don't know how to use them. Returns management includes processing returned goods, which generally involves sorting, examining/testing, restocking items that are in good condition, repairing defectives, reconditioning, recycling materials, and disposing of obsolete or hazardous materials. The goal of returns management is to recapture value in returned goods and to properly dispose of goods that cannot be resold.

Two key elements of reverse logistics are **gate keeping** and avoidance. Gate keeping oversees the acceptance of returned goods with the intent of reducing the cost of returns by screening returns at the point of entry into the system and refusing to accept goods that should not be returned or goods that are returned to the wrong destination. **Avoidance** refers to preventing returns by dealing with their causes. It can involve product design and quality assurance issues. It may also involve careful monitoring of forecasts during promotional programs to avoid overestimating demand.

gate keeping Screening returned goods at the point of entry into the system to prevent inappropriate acceptance of goods.

avoidance Preventing returns by dealing with their causes.

©Mark Richards/PhotoEdit

An Amazon employee inspects returned products at a distribution warehouse in Nevada. The returned goods are inspected for restocking if in pristine condition, forwarded to a repair centre if necessary, inventoried, and examined for potential product, process, or packaging improvements if they are defective.

Summary

- A supply chain consists of the sequence of organizations—their facilities and activities—that are involved in producing a product, from the initial suppliers of raw materials to the final consumer.
- Supply chain management (SCM) is the collaboration of members and coordination of activities of the supply chain so that market demand is met as efficiently and effectively as possible.
- Supply chain management offers the benefits of lower operating costs, reduced inventories (e.g., by avoiding the bullwhip effect), better product availability, and customer satisfaction.
- The need for SCM has increased due to increased outsourcing (buying as opposed to making), globalization, and ecommerce.
- Activities in supply chain management can be classified as strategic (e.g., network design), or tactical/operational (e.g., production and

distribution planning, inventory and transportation management, and fulfillment).
- Retailers/wholesalers and manufacturers have initiated efficient replenishment systems with their suppliers under the names of *quick response, efficient consumer response (ECR),* and *vendor managed inventory (VMI).*
- Global supply chains are long and have to deal with intermediaries, customs clearance, and shipments changing hands several times.
- Accurate and timely information is vital in supply chain management. Planning software includes network design, production planning, and forecasting. Execution software includes order management, warehouse management system, transportation management system, and tracking/visibility software. ERP software programs have been adding supply chain management modules to their suite. Electronic data interchange is used for

purchasing, order confirmation and payment, and arranging shipments. Radio frequency identification (RFID) is for fast identification of items.

- The key to an effective supply chain is to link companies, develop trust, align goals, share information, and measure performance. Collaborative planning, forecasting, and replenishment (CPFR) extends ECR further in forecasting by using a formal reconciliation process for forecasts and orders. The Supply Chain Operations Reference (SCOR) model is increasingly used for supply chain performance measurement.

- The purchasing function obtains materials, manufacturing parts, supplies and spare parts, equipment and machines, and services needed to produce a product. Purchasing selects suppliers, negotiates contracts, helps establish partnerships, and acts as liaison between suppliers and various internal departments.

- Organizations are outsourcing and buying more of their noncore services and parts. The purchasing cycle starts with a purchase requisition and ends with paying the invoice. Value analysis is used to provide the basic function of a part/product at minimum cost. Prices for many products are determined using competitive bidding and negotiation. Multiplant organizations use a hybrid system where common material and services are centralized and small purchases are bought locally.

- Spend analysis examines purchases in order to group them by item families and suppliers, so that price discounts can be obtained and purchases from unapproved suppliers are minimized. Ethics in purchasing is important because of the amount of money involved and because buyers may be enticed by salespeople to favour their company. Controlling ethical treatment of workers by overseas suppliers is part of ethical purchasing.

- Ecommerce is the use of computers and the Internet to conduct buying and selling. The use of ecommerce is rapidly expanding and has resulted in increasing need for small-package delivery services. Fulfillment is the process of order taking, scheduling, warehousing, order picking and packing, and delivery.

- Price, quality, and timely delivery are important factors for a product purchase. These plus technical and managerial capability, flexibility, service, and financial stability are important for choosing a supplier.

- In many organizations there is a move to reduce the number of suppliers and to establish and maintain longer-term relationships with suppliers. Supplier partnership is the closest form of relationship where both buyer and supplier benefit by assisting each other. The Lambert partnership model provides a process for deciding if partnership between a buyer and a supplier is desirable and, if so, to what extent.

- Logistics involves the movement and warehousing of goods, material, and information in a supply chain. This includes incoming materials and outgoing goods. Transportation planning involves an outsourcing decision, selecting a transport mode, choosing a carrier, and negotiating freight rates. A third-party logistics (3PL) service provider is a logistics management company that oversees the logistics function of the buyer organization. Transport modes include pipelines, ships, trains, trucks, and airplanes. Truckload (TL) involves a full truckload, and less-than-truckload (LTL) is a portion of a truck's capacity.

- In selecting a shipping mode, the tradeoff is between a faster mode with higher freight cost and a slower mode that is cheaper in terms of freight cost but results in higher in-transit holding cost. Selecting a carrier is like purchasing any other service. Transport rate depends whether it is TL or LTL. TL for a given truck capacity is charged by miles, and LTL is charged by origin–destination distance, weight, and transportability (density, stowability, difficulty of handling, and liability).

- Transport execution and control involves load planning and consolidation, load tendering, appointment scheduling, checking carriers' legal compliance, in-transit visibility and tracking, freight payment, and measuring performance of carrier.

- Reverse logistics is returns logistics and management. Gate keeping and returns avoidance are important.

Key Terms

avoidance
bullwhip effect
centralized purchasing
collaborative planning, forecasting, and
   replenishment (CPFR)
cross-docking
decentralized purchasing
delayed differentiation/postponement
distribution requirements planning (DRP)
ecommerce
efficient consumer response (ECR)
electronic data interchange (EDI)

event management
gate keeping
inventory turnover
item fill rate
logistics
modes of transportation
order fulfillment
purchasing cycle
quick response (QR)
radio frequency identification (RFID)
resiliency
reverse logistics

risk pooling
spend analysis
strategic supplier/customer partnership
supplier analysis
supply chain
supply chain management
supply chain visibility
traffic management
value analysis
vendor-managed inventory

Solved Problems

Problem 1

a. Determine which shipping alternative is best if the annual holding cost of an item is 25 percent of its unit price, and a single unit with a price of $6,000 is to be delivered, either by two-day delivery at a cost of $400 or by five-day delivery at a cost of $350.

b. At what unit price would two-day delivery be less costly?

Solution

a. $H = 0.25(\$6,000) = \$1,500$ per year

Total two-day delivery cost $= \$400 + \$1,500(2/365)$
$$= \$408.22$$

Total five-day delivery cost $= \$350 + \$1,500(5/365)$
$$= \$370.55 < \$408.22$$

Hence, use five-day delivery.

b. Let $p =$ Unit price. Total two-day delivery cost $= \$400 + 0.25p\,(2/365)$

Total five-day delivery cost $= \$350 + 0.25p\,(5/365)$.
Set the two total costs equal: $\$400 + 0.25p\,(2/365) = \$350 + 0.25p\,(5/365)$
Or $50 = 0.25p\,(3/365)$ or $p = 50(365)/3(0.25) = \$24,333.34$

Problem 2

Given the following data, determine the total annual cost of making and of buying from each of vendor A and B. Estimated demand is 15,000 units a year. Which alternative is best?

	Make	Vendor A	Vendor B
Variable cost per unit	$8	$11	$10
Annual fixed cost	$20,000	$0	$5,000 (annual charge)

Solution

Total annual cost = Fixed cost + Variable cost per unit × Estimated annual quantity

Make: $\$20,000 + \$8 \times 15,000 = \$140,000 \leftarrow$ lowest
Vendor A: $\$0 + \$11 \times 15,000 = \$165,000$
Vendor B: $\$5,000 + \$10 \times 15,000 = \$155,000$

Thus, making has the lowest total annual cost.

Discussion and Review Questions

LO1 1. What is a supply chain?

LO1 2. What is supply chain management?

LO1 3. What factors have made it desirable to manage supply chains? What are some potential benefits of doing so?

LO1 4. What is the bullwhip effect, and why does it occur? How can it be overcome?

LO1 5. Explain how the need to reduce inventory holding costs would be a good reason to (re)design a supply chain, and give an example.

LO1 6. What does supply chain design mean?

LO1 7. What are the advantages and disadvantages of pushing inventory downstream closer to consumers?

LO1 8. What is risk pooling? Delayed differentiation?

LO1 9. Explain quick response, efficient consumer response, and vendor-managed inventory.

LO1 10. What is cross-docking?

LO1 11. Why is global supply chain management more challenging?

LO1 12. Describe supply chain management information systems.

LO1 13. What is RFID? What are its advantages and disadvantages for a company?

LO1 14. What is EDI? What are its advantages and disadvantages for a company?

LO1 15. What are the requirements for effective supply chain management?

LO1 16. Name two supply chain performance metrics and explain them.

LO1 17. What is CPFR? What are its advantages and disadvantages?

LO1 18. Explain the importance of supply chain visibility.

LO1 19. Explain why each of these is critical for a successful supply chain operation:
    a. Integrated technology
    b. Information sharing
    c. Trust among trading partners
    d. Real-time information availability
    e. Event-response capability
    f. Procurement
    g. Risk management

LO2 20. Explain the importance of the purchasing function in organizations.

LO2 21. Describe what a buyer (in an organization) does. Name at least five activities.

LO2 22. Describe how purchasing interacts with two other functional areas of an organization.

LO2 23. When should a company outsource the production of a part or performance of a service? Give an example. What are the disadvantages?

LO2 24. How is price determined in B2B purchasing? Give an example for each way price is determined.

LO2 25. Describe value analysis.

LO2 26. Discuss centralization versus decentralization in purchasing. What are the advantages of each?

LO2 27. What is spend analysis? Why is it necessary?

LO2 28. What is ecommerce and what impact has it had on supply chain management?

LO2 29. What are some of the advantages of ecommerce?

LO2 30. What is fulfillment?

LO2 31. Describe supplier analysis. What are the common factors used in selecting a supplier?

LO2 32. Why are good supplier relations important?

LO2 33. What are the advantages and disadvantages of a partnership to the buyer? To the supplier?

LO2 34. Describe Lambert's partnership model.

LO3 35. What is logistics?

LO3 36. What is involved in transport planning?

LO3 37. What is a third-party logistics service? Give an example.

LO3 38. What are the transportation modes?

LO3 39. What is the trade-off in selecting a transportation mode?

LO3 40. What is involved in transportation execution and control?

LO3 41. What is reverse logistics?

LO3 42. Why is managing returns important?

Taking Stock

LO1–3 1. What trade-offs are involved in sharing information with a supplier? With a customer?

LO1–3 2. Who needs to be involved in supply chain management?

LO1 3. Name two different ways that information systems technology has improved the ability to manage supply chains.

LO2 4. Name one ethical issue related to a buyer's job, and explain it.

Critical Thinking Exercises

LO1 **1.** Describe an example of RFID that you have seen in your daily life or work.

LO1 & 2 **2.** For an item you recently bought, (a) try to determine its supply chain, and (b) describe the criteria you used to select the product/supplier.

LO1 **3.** Given the complexities and risks involved with supply chains, would it make sense for a business organization to vertically integrate and be its own supply chain? Explain.

Experiential Learning Exercise

LO1 The Beer Distribution Game is an activity that is designed to teach the distribution-side dynamics of a three-level or four-level supply chain. In the four-level game, the activity needs to be completed in teams of four students, where each student is assigned to be either the brewery, distributor, wholesaler, or retailer. The game generates end-customer demand. The brewery makes and sells cases of beer to the distributor, who sells to the wholesaler, who sells to the retailer. Each student needs to make a decision with respect to the number of cases of beer he or she would like to order from the person above him/her in the supply chain. In the case of a brewery, the decision is how many cases of beer to produce. Once the order has been placed, the shipment will be delivered after a certain amount of game time (e.g., two weeks), if there is enough inventory in stock. If there is not enough inventory, then the order is filled as much as possible. The party that does not have enough on-hand inventory will pay a backorder cost. Brewery orders will always be met. Finally, for every case of beer that is kept in inventory, there is an associated inventory holding cost. The objective is to end up with minimum total inventory holding and backorder cost. Visit http://www.beergame.org, learn more about the Beer Distribution Game, and set it up. Find three friends and play the game for a few rounds (e.g., 25 weeks) twice, first without sharing any information (except your order), and then with sharing end-customer demand and your inventory position with the person upstream. At the conclusion of the game, report what you have learned.

Internet Exercises

1. View http://www.youtube.com/watch?v=rqXIwjD3Cso and identify Pepsi's distribution channels.

LO1 **2.** View http://www.youtube.com/watch?v=KksQbzRMwvQ on LogicNet, a network design software, and summarize what it can do.

LO1 **3.** Visit https://www.youtube.com/watch?v=kfyYF0oIMIw&t = 26s and summarize how RFID is being used by Montreal Transit Authority.

LO1 **4.** Visit http://www.rfidjournal.com/case-studies, choose a case study, and state how RFID is used.

LO1 **5.** Visit https://www.sap.com/about/customer-testimonials .html, click Find Customer Stories, choose Canada as Region/Country, choose Supply Chain as Solution, read a testimonial, and summarize it.

LO1 **6.** The Supply Chain Management Association (SCMA) is Canada's largest association for supply chain management professionals. Visit http://scma.com/en/resources/supply-chain-success-stories and read one of the success stories and summarize it.

LO3 **7.** Visit http://www.ops.fhwa.dot.gov/publications/fhwa-hop09035/video.htm, view the video "Keeping the Global Supply Chain Moving," and summarize it.

LO2 **8.** Visit http://thepartnershipmodel.com/the-partnership-model/, find and watch the video of Dr. Lambert's overview of his partnership framework, and summarize it.

LO3 **9.** Visit http://www.nykwebcasting.com/profile/video/08_eng .htm, watch the video "NYK Group Profile," and summarize the supply chain/logistics services NYK Logistics performs for its customers.

LO3 **10.** Visit http://www.purolator.com/en/resources-and-support /about-us/annual-review/2012/enabling-success.page? and view and summarize a customer video.

LO3 **11.** The BBC attached an RFID tag to a 40-foot ocean container and tracked it and its contents for a year in order to get a sample of global trade. Use http://news.bbc.co.uk/2 /hi/in_depth/629/629/7600053.stm to identify each leg of the trip. (*Hint:* You may need to use Internet Explorer. Place the cursor on the blue discs to see the dates and follow the blue lines chronologically, shifting the map by pressing and holding the left mouse button.)

Problems

 1. A manager at Strateline Manufacturing must choose between two shipping alternatives: two-day freight and five-day freight. Using five-day freight would cost $135 less than using two-day freight. The primary consideration is holding cost, which is $10 per unit a year. Two thousand items are to be shipped. Which alternative would you recommend? Explain.

 2. a. Determine which delivery alternative would be most economical for 80 boxes of parts. Each box costs $200 and annual holding cost is 30 percent of cost. Assume 365 days per year. Freight costs are:

Alternative	Freight Cost (for all 80 boxes)
Overnight	$300
Two-day	260
Six-day	180

b. For what range of unit cost for a box would each delivery alternative be least costly?

 3. A manager must make a decision on delivery alternatives. There are two carriers, A and B. Both offer a two-day rate. In addition, A offers a three-day rate and a nine-day rate, and B offers a four-day rate and a seven-day rate. Three hundred boxes are to be delivered and the freight cost for the whole lot for each option is given below. Annual holding cost is 35 percent of unit cost, and each box has a cost of $140. Assume 365 days per year. Which delivery alternative would you recommend?

Shipper A		Shipper B	
Option	Freight Cost	Option	Freight Cost
2 days	$500	2 days	$525
3 days	460	4 days	450
9 days	400	7 days	410

 4. An appliance manufacturer has a plant near Toronto that receives small electric motors from a manufacturer located in Winnipeg. The demand for motors is 120,000 units per year. The cost of each motor is $120. The motors are purchased in lots of 3,000 units. The ownership of motors transfers to the appliance manufacturer in Winnipeg. The question is, which mode of transportation (truck or train) should the appliance manufacturer use to bring the motors from Winnipeg to Toronto? The railroad company charges $2 per motor, and it takes approximately seven days by train. The trucking company charges $4 per motor, but it takes only three days. The appliance manufacturer will keep 1,000 units as safety stock if a truck is used and 3,000 units as safety stock if a train is used for transportation. Assume 365 days per year. If the holding cost rate is 25 percent of unit cost per year, which mode of transportation will minimize total transportation and in-transit and safety holding cost? (*Hint:* The value of a motor in Toronto for calculating the safety stock holding cost is $120 plus cost of freight per unit.)

5. Pratt & Whitney, a major aircraft engine manufacturer, wants to re-evaluate the transportation mode it uses to send

unfinished parts to its joint-venture facility in Chengdu, China.[7] Annual demand is 2,900 units. At present the company uses air freight. It takes approximately six days from Los Angeles to Chengdu (including pick-up and delivery and customs delays). There are 20 parts in a lot, each weighing 30 kilograms. The air freight cost per part is $90. The pick-up and delivery charges at origin and destination add up to $15 per part. The alternative is to use an ocean liner to ship the parts to Shanghai and from there to use either a truck or a train (a 2,000 km distance). The ocean freight for this lot size will cost $30 per part and will take 15 days. The truck from Shanghai to Chengdu will cost $20 per part and will take six days (including pick-up and delivery and customs delays). Transportation by rail will cost $15 per part and will take 14 days (including pick-up and delivery, customs, and transfer delays). In addition, for rail there is a $10 per part charge for pick-up and delivery. The company's inventory holding cost rate is 12 percent per year, and the value of each part is $1,000. Assume 365 days per year.

Due to variability of lead times, at the destination, safety stocks of 60, 210, and 290 units will be kept if air, ship and truck, and ship and train are used, respectively. Determine the cheapest (total freight, delivery, and in-transit and safety holding cost) mode of transportation for these parts. (*Hint:* The value of a part in Chengdu for calculating the safety-stock holding cost should include the freight cost.)

 6. A brick maker (BM) in Alberta mixes dry ink into its bricks to make them brown.

BM's demand for dry ink is 60 tons per year. Currently, BM buys the dry ink from an import merchant that buys the ink from an East Coast U.S. manufacturer. The shipments arrive in lot size of 30 tons by rail. The current cost of dry ink is C$612.22 per ton, including rail transportation cost to BM's location. BM currently keeps 6 tons of dry ink as safety stock. BM's buyer has asked the import merchant to quote a price for truck deliveries in smaller lot sizes. The merchant has quoted C$567.78 per ton for a lot size of 20 tons.

In the meantime, BM's buyer has contacted the manufacturer directly and asked if BM could purchase dry ink directly from the manufacturer. The answer was affirmative and the cost would be US$386.89 per ton (assume US$1 = C$1.05). A common carrier has quoted a price of C$2,600 to haul a full truckload of dry ink (20 tons) from the manufacturer to BM's location in Alberta. The trip will take seven days.

The holding cost rate for BM is 20 percent of unit cost per year. For truck deliveries, BM will hold only 2 tons of safety stocks. Assume 365 days per year. Which alternative has the lowest total annual purchase, transport, in-transit, safety stock, and average cycle stock holding cost? (*Hint:* The value of dry ink in Alberta for calculating the safety stock and cycle stock holding cost of truck deliveries should include the freight cost.)

 7. Given the following data, determine the total annual cost of making with each of process A and B and of buying. Estimated demand is 10,000 units a year. Which alternative is best?

---

[7] Based on A. Z. Zeng and C. Rossetti, "Developing a Framework for Evaluating the Logistics Costs in Global Sourcing Processes," *International Journal of Physical Distribution & Logistics Management* 33(9/10), 2003, pp. 785–803.

	Make		
	Process A	Process B	Buy
Variable cost per unit	$50	$52	$51
Annual fixed cost	$40,000	$36,000	
Transportation cost per unit			$ 2

 8. For the previous problem, suppose that the operations manager has said that it would be possible to achieve a 10 percent reduction in the fixed cost of process B and a 10 percent reduction in B's variable cost per unit. Would that be enough to change your answer if the estimated annual cost to achieve those savings was $8,000? Explain.

 9. Juliette loves to eat ice cream and spends a fortune each week buying it. In an effort to save money, she is considering making her own ice cream at home. The cost of an ice cream maker is $150 and the cost of ingredients is $6 for each 1.5 L batch. The cost of the same 1.5 L is $10 at the store. If she eats three litres of ice cream per month, will she save money by making her favourite treat at home? Assume the ice cream maker has a one-year warranty and breaks immediately after.

 10. Potash Corp, through Canpotex, has an order for 5,000 tons of potash from Sinofert, the largest fertilizer importer and distributor in China. How should this shipment be delivered (in terms of supply chain)? Draw the supply chain. (*Hint:* You may find https://www.canpotex.com/our-business/logistics useful.)

 11. All products sold at the Co-op retail stores in Western Canada are purchased and distributed by Federated Cooperatives Ltd (FCL). The produce buyer for FCL purchases 13 loads of Chiquita bananas per week (a load is the contents of a 40-foot-long ocean container). Also, one load per week is purchased from Dole. Chiquita bananas usually come from Guatemala in Central America on a Great White Fleet (Chiquita) ship in refrigerated containers. FCL receives the bananas from Chiquita's (refrigerated) warehouses in three different ports in the United States.[8] The bananas are destined for each of FCL's food warehouses in Calgary, Edmonton, Saskatoon, and Winnipeg. For the Calgary warehouse, FCL receives three loads per week from Hueneme (just north of Los Angeles) and one load per week from San Diego. For the Saskatoon warehouse, FCL receives four loads per week from Hueneme. For the Edmonton warehouse, FCL receives three to four loads per week from Hueneme. And for the Winnipeg warehouse, FCL receives two loads per week from Freeport, Texas. A refrigerated company truck/trailer is sent down at regular intervals to pick up a load so that the ripening (ethylene) gas chambers in each DC are used evenly.

Is there a better way, in terms of supply chain management, to satisfy FCL's Chiquita banana demand? Briefly explain.

Q MINI-CASE   http://www.clearwater.ca

Clearwater Seafoods

Clearwater Seafoods Limited Partnership of Bedford, Nova Scotia (NS), near Halifax, founded in 1976, is one of the largest harvesters, processors, and distributors of shellfish in the world. It has a combined total of 10 company-owned and joint venture–operated vessels that harvest in the North Atlantic and off the coast of Argentina. It also has two subsidiaries: one in Argentina harvesting scallops off of the Argentinean continental shelf, and one harvesting prawns off of Newfoundland and Labrador (NL) and selling them worldwide. Its processing facilities are Pierce Fisheries (in Lockeport, NS, 200 km southwest of Halifax), which produces frozen scallops and lobster; a facility in St. Anthony, NL, which produces frozen shrimp; a facility in Grand Bank, NL, which produces clams; Highland Fisheries in Glace Bay, NS, which produces snow crab; a facility in Arichat, NS, which holds live lobsters in a dryland pound holding facility in the state of hibernation (8 million pounds per year go through Arichat); another live lobster holding facility in Bedford; and a third live lobster holding facility (with two 25,000 gallon saltwater tanks) in Louisville, Kentucky, for U.S. distribution. It also has cold storage facilities in the United Kingdom, France, and China, and ships globally out of Bedford.

The live lobsters are sold to many of the world's finest restaurants at short notice (24 hours)—over 30,000 pounds per week. Shipping live lobsters is a time-sensitive challenge. Clearwater ships live lobsters (in boxes) out of Halifax but this process was experiencing some difficulties because of delays due to paperwork mix-ups, technology interruptions, banning of gel

©Clearwater Seafoods LP

packs to chill the lobster in-transit after September 11, 2001, and customs backlogs. A solution to this problem for shipping to the United States was to truck live lobsters (a 36-hour journey) once or twice a week from Bedford to Louisville (the U.S. air hub of UPS) on special reefer trucks, hold the lobsters in Louisville in cold water in saltwater tanks waiting for customer orders, and then courier them via UPS.

Question

What are the advantages and disadvantages of opening up Louisville holding tanks versus shipping live lobsters out of Bedford to the United States?

Source: http://www.clearwater.ca.

---

[8] For the supply chain of bananas before getting to the port, you can view http://www.youtube.com/watch?v=SQ_gpZCvag.

🔍 **MINI-CASE** https://www.summerwood.com/

Summerwood

Summerwood is a high-end shed and gazebo manufacturer in Toronto. The majority of Summerwood's products are delivered to the customer in a kit (separate pieces of wood). Summerwood's customers are located all over North America. The website has enough information for a potential buyer to choose the model and size of the structure she wants, and to order it online. The website has extensive information under "ordering" and "delivery" to make the fulfillment process clear to the buyer in order to reduce customer misunderstanding and disappointment. The fulfillment process is summarized in the following process flow diagram (for delivery to outside Southern Ontario). Summerwood uses various trucking companies to deliver its products throughout North America. Depending on the size of the structure, the kit could weigh anywhere from a few hundred pounds to 3,000 pounds. The LTL shipment is transported under "standard motor freight," which is deliveries by semi-trailer truck that are offloaded by the buyer. Assistance with unloading can be

arranged (for approximately $200) through local employment agencies but this has to be specified days before the delivery so that it can be arranged (the truck driver won't help with unloading). Even though the delivery process is clearly stated on the website, some customers are taken by surprise (unprepared) when the truck arrives. They complain that given the high cost of the product, the unloading should have been included and they assumed this. Management is wondering what else to do to prevent these types of customer complaints.

A possible solution may be to include unloading as part of the delivery, but at a higher delivery cost. FedEx Ground Freight (FXF) provides unloading service as the default. Summerwood management wishes to compare its current delivery rates with FXF rate. As a sample, consider a small (5 foot × 7 foot) shed. The current carrier is asking $750 for freight from Summerwood's shop in Toronto (postal code M1H 2W7) to the postal code S7N 5A7. The pre-cut unassembled shed wrapped on a skid weighs 740 pounds with dimensions 88 inches × 52 inches × 29 inches.

Customer service calls customer to confirm order progress	←	Production schedules order, salesperson informs customer due week	←	Salesperson validates order and deposit	←	Customer enters order online, or calls

Carrier is booked. Carrier calls customer with due date	→	Product is received from production on skid	→	Truck is loaded, shipping document is generated, and truck leaves	→	Truck waits for unloading at customer site

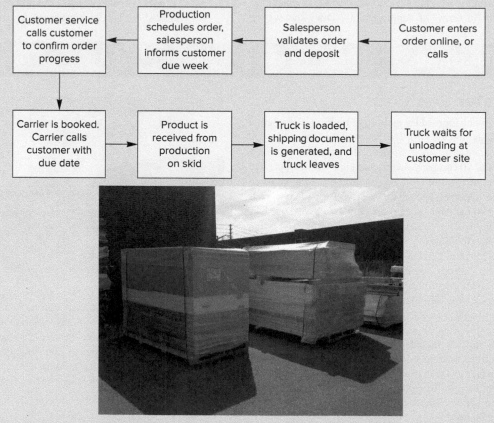

Courtesy of Summerwood Products, http://www.summerwood.com

Question

What is the FXF rate for this shipment? *Hint:* You need to determine the transportability class of this shipment (http://shipfreight.van.fedex.com/ClassificationTool.aspx). Then, you can get the rate from https://www.fedex.com/ratefinder/standalone?method=goToFreight &from=Package: Enter From, To, no. of skid (1), Weight (in pounds), and Class, and press "Get—rates and transit times" in the bottom.

Source: http://www.summerwood.com.

Q MINI-CASE

MasterTag

When MasterTag was founded in 1949, its founder, Ludwig Schmidt, set out to be a manufacturer of plastic fishing bobbers. Then, in 1950, Schmidt was approached by a local greenhouse owner and was asked if he could produce a line of horticultural labels for plants. At the time, these labels were made of wood. Schmidt adapted his machines to produce these labels. Later, plastic replaced wood and he has been manufacturing the plastic "tags" for plants ever since. Over the years, the labels have increased in quality and now feature full-colour pictures of the plants along with the name and planting and care instructions.

Many of MasterTag's largest customers are seed companies that sell their seeds to commercial growers. The large seed companies typically place one or two large orders with MasterTag at the beginning of the growing season. The seed companies then sell their seeds and the labels to their customers who grow the plants and sell them to the end consumer. The seed companies do not like ordering tags, but do so because their customers demand labels with their seeds.

There are several problems with this ordering process. The main issue stems from the fact that the exact quantities of tags that will be needed is difficult to predict due to possible crop failures and the introduction of new items. To avoid a shortage of tags, seed companies order and ship a large quantity of tags to their customers. Seed companies usually end up each year with huge numbers of leftover tags. In fact, MasterTag's largest customers often end up with millions of leftover tags.

When MasterTag's management became aware of all the unused labels and unhappy grower–customers, they decided they must come up with a better solution for achieving a match between supply and demand of the tags. One possible solution would be to make an initial, fairly large batch, which would be produced and shipped directly to the growers instead of the seed companies, as is now being done. Later, when the grower results became available, a second batch would be produced using information from growers on how many additional tags were needed. The second batch would then be shipped to the growers. (See figure for Before and After.)

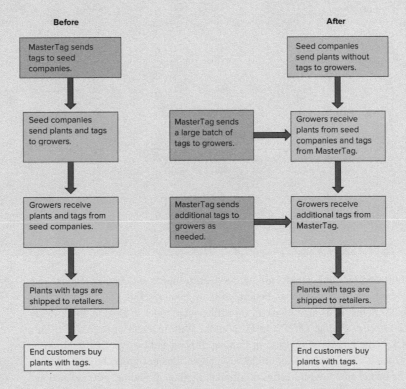

Questions

1. Explain the key benefit of the revised approach, and the reason for the benefit.

2. MasterTag has not yet decided to implement this plan. List the pros and cons you think should be considered.

Source: Mini-case by Nicole Foster, Grand Valley State University

Chapter 12
Inventory Management

Photo taken by James Cao. Federated Co-operatives warehouse in Saskatoon.

A food/grocery, home and building supply, animal feed, crop supply, and petroleum and propane wholesaler and distributor such as Federated Co-operatives Ltd. (FCL) moves and stores over 100,000 items. FCL also owns an oil refinery/upgrader in Regina and a fresh-produce wholesaler (The Grocery People (TGP)) in Edmonton. With revenue of over $10 billion and 3,000 employees, FCL is the largest wholesaler in Canada. It is owned by over 225 retail co-op associations in Western Canada that employ another 23,500 people. Besides group buying and distribution, FCL provides its owner stores with centralized marketing (e.g., branding, advertising) and administrative services (e.g., IT, facility development).

FCL has five distribution centres, six feed plants, 10 propane distribution facilities, a petroleum terminal near Calgary, 59 FCL-owned and 72 retail member–owned bulk petroleum storage facilities, one FCL-owned and 379 retail/co-op–owned gas bars, 225 semi-trailers, and 200 petroleum tankers.

FCL competes with grocery chains such as Loblaw, hardware and lumber stores such as Home Depot, crop supply companies such as Glencore, and gas/diesel distributors such as Esso, Shell, and Petro-Canada. How has Federated Co-op remained competitive? One important factor is good inventory management.

Until 2011, the small but efficient operations research (OR) team in FCL managed INFOREM—IBM's Inventory Forecasting and Replenishment Modules—for decades. Run on a mainframe IBM computer, INFOREM provided effective forecasting and inventory control service to over 30 FCL merchandise buyers located in the Saskatoon head office. The small and efficient industrial engineering group helps manage the five FCL distribution centres (DCs) in Calgary, Edmonton, Saskatoon, and Winnipeg. The OR group has also facilitated electronic ordering by the retail co-op stores and even provided them with space and shelf planning (planograms). Recently, FCL converted to JDA (Manugistics) demand forecasting and replenishment software and migrated away from the mainframe. FCL has always had good inventory turns (approximately 18 overall and up to 60+ in the produce category) and customer service level (item fill rate of 96–98 percent in the distribution centres depending on the category of the item). The new JDA software has further improved FCL's inventory performance, especially in fresh produce/perishables with the following results: 1.2 percent increase in service level, 2.6 more inventory turns, and 14 percent less perishability cost.

Sources: https://www.coopconnection.ca/wps/portal/fclretail/FCLInternet/AboutUs; http://www.youtube.com/watch?v=500G-h2nPhk.

Introduction

Good inventory management is important for the successful operation of most organizations, especially manufacturers and wholesalers, distributors, and retailers that hold a lot of inventory. Operations, marketing, and finance all have an interest in good inventory management. Poor inventory management holds operations back and diminishes customer satisfaction, in addition to costing money.

This chapter describes inventory management of finished goods, some raw materials, supplies and spare parts, and wholesale/retail items. The demand for these items is unknown and has to be forecasted. For this reason, these items are said to have **independent demand**. Management of manufacturing parts and components will be discussed in Chapter 14 on material requirements planning and Chapter 15 on just-in-time and lean production. Demand for manufacturing parts and components depends on the production schedule for the finished goods; for this reason, these items are said to have *dependent demand*. This chapter includes models for determining *how much* to order and *when* to order for independent demand items. Emphasis is on inventory analysis.

An **inventory** or stock is any material, part, or product sitting idle, not being used, usually in a warehouse or stockroom, and kept for use or sale in the future. Organizations typically store hundreds or even thousands of items in inventory, ranging from small items such as pencils, paper clips, screws, nuts, and bolts to large items such as equipment. A warehousing item that is unique and must be stored and accounted for separately from other items is called a **stock keeping unit (SKU)**. Naturally, many of the items a company holds in inventory relate to the kinds of activities it engages in. Thus, manufacturers hold inventories of raw materials, purchased manufacturing parts and components, partially finished items (i.e., **work-in-process (WIP)**), and finished goods, as well as spare parts for machines, tools, and other supplies. These are depicted in the following diagram:

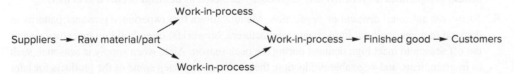

Retail stores hold inventories of items, mostly on their shelves, for resale. Hospitals stock drugs, surgical supplies, life-monitoring equipment, sheets and pillow cases, and more.

Inventory management is concerned with planning and controlling inventories.

Importance of Inventory

A typical company has approximately half of its *current* assets in inventory (the other half are in receivables and cash). One widely used measure of business performance is *return on assets* (ROA), which is profit after tax divided by total assets. Because inventory may represent a significant portion of total assets in the balance sheet, a reduction in inventory can result in a significant increase in ROA.

independent demand Demand that is unknown and has to be forecasted.

inventory An idle material, part, or product, usually in a warehouse or stockroom.

stock keeping unit (SKU) A warehousing item that is unique and must be stored and accounted for separately from other items.

work-in-process (WIP) Partially finished items.

inventory management Planning and controlling inventories.

Inventory also influences the income statement through the cost of goods sold (COGS). COGS is the sum of material, direct labour, and indirect labour costs. Material cost is the sum of Value of inventory at the start of the year + Total cost of material purchase during the year − Value of inventory at the end of the year. Accounting is interested in value of inventory. Management also uses value of inventory for decision making. For example, if total value of finished goods (FGs) is high, management will reduce production and sell some of the FGs at a discount.

It is important that the value of inventory represent the true worth of inventory. Accountants use various methods of inventory valuation: first-in-first-out (FIFO), last-in-first-out (LIFO), and weighted average cost. If value of inventory gives a wrong impression about the quantity of inventory (in units), this can lead management to make wrong decisions. An example involved the CEO and CFO of SunOpta (http://www.sunopta.com), the Toronto-based natural and organic food producer. They thought that they had more strawberries (by weight) in inventory than they actually did because the cost of growing strawberries was underestimated. Hence, they reduced the price of strawberry-based products. This error resulted in an unnecessary $11 million write-down. This caused a 30 percent drop in share price of SunOpta, which led to the executives' dismissal.[1]

The major source of revenue for retailers and wholesalers/distributors is the resale of merchandise (i.e., inventory). In fact, in terms of dollars, the inventory of goods held for resale is one of the largest assets of a merchandising business. Service companies do not carry as much inventory, although they do carry inventory of supplies and equipment.

To understand why organizations hold inventory, you need to be aware of the various functions (purposes) of inventory.

Functions (Purposes) of Inventory

Inventory serves a number of functions. Among the most important are the following:

1. *To wait while being transported.* Raw materials and parts from suppliers and finished goods from manufacturers heading to markets (being distributed) need to be transported. Depending on the mode of transportation, the freight could take up to a month to reach its destination. Items being transported are called **in-transit inventory**.

2. *To protect against stock-outs.* Delayed deliveries from suppliers and unexpected increases in customer demand increase the risk of stock-outs. Supply delays can occur because of weather conditions, supplier stock-outs, deliveries of wrong materials, quality problems, and so on. The risk of stock-out can be reduced by holding **safety stock**, which is stock in excess of average demand.

3. *To take advantage of economic lot size or to avoid future price increase.* To minimize purchasing, receiving, material handling, and accounts payable costs, an organization often buys in a quantity (called *economic order quantity*) that exceeds its immediate requirements. Also, it may buy a large quantity due to quantity discount or to avoid future price increase. These necessitate storing some of the purchased goods for later use. Similarly, it is usually economical to produce in a large quantity (called economic production quantity). As a result consecutive orders occur after some interval of time, called the *order cycle*. The resulting inventory, known as **cycle stock**, is replenished cyclically and is gradually depleted as demand occurs and is met.

4. *To smooth seasonal demand or production.* Manufacturers that experience seasonal patterns in demand (e.g., agricultural implement manufacturers, breweries) often build up inventory during the off season to meet high demand during the peak season. Also, when supply is seasonal, such as in grain, fruit, and vegetable production, the producer may keep some of the products for later sale (possibly after freezing/canning). These inventories are aptly named **seasonal inventory**.

5. *To decouple operations.* Manufacturers use **decoupling inventory** between successive operations in order to create independence between the two operations in case one of them breaks down temporarily. Decoupling inventory is made of WIP inventory, and its level fluctuates analogous to the level of water in a tank:

Workstation A →Supply rate→ WIP level   → Demand rate → Workstation B

---

in-transit inventory Items being transported.

safety stock Stock that is held in excess of expected demand due to variability of demand and/or supply.

cycle stock Inventory that is replenished cyclically and is gradually depleted as demand occurs and is met

seasonal inventory Inventory produced during the off season to meet peak season demand, or inventory produced during a growing season kept for later sale.

decoupling inventory Inventory between successive operations in order to create independence between the two operations in case one of them breaks down temporarily.

[1] S. Islam, "Strawberry Surprise," *Financial Post Magazine*, September 2008, p. 27.

The average supply rate and the average demand rate should be equal, or else the tank will be empty or will overflow. The average WIP inventory (L), average time a unit spends waiting in the inventory/tank (W), and average supply (or demand) rate (λ) are related through Little's formula: $L = \lambda W$ (more in Chapter 18, Formula 18-4).

6. *To meet anticipated above-average demand.* Demand will be higher than average during a sales promotion or when customers expect a future price increase. To meet this demand, and in anticipation to a plant shutdown, a manufacturer will build up its finished goods inventory, called **anticipation inventory**.

Objectives of Inventory Management

Inadequate management of inventory can result in both understocking of some items and overstocking of the others. Understocking results in missed deliveries, lost sales, dissatisfied customers, and production stoppage; overstocking unnecessarily ties up funds that might be more productive elsewhere and also ties up storage space. Although overstocking may appear to be the lesser of the two evils, the price tag for excessive overstocking can be staggering. It is not unheard of for managers to discover that their company has a 10-year supply of some item. (No doubt they got a good deal on it!)

Inventory management has two main concerns. One is the *level of customer service (item availability or fill rate)*; that is, to have the right goods, in sufficient quantities, in the right place, at the right time. The other is the inventory costs: the *costs of ordering and holding inventory*.

The overall objective of inventory management is to achieve satisfactory levels of customer service while minimizing inventory costs. Toward this end, a buyer or inventory analyst must make two decisions for each item: the *timing* and *size* of orders (i.e., when to order and how much to order). The greater part of this chapter is devoted to models that can be applied to assist in making these decisions.

Managers have a number of measures of performance to judge the effectiveness of their inventory management. The most obvious, of course, is customer satisfaction, which they might measure by the in-stock percent or *item fill rate* (i.e., the percentage of demand filled from stocks on hand).

Another measure is *inventory turnover*, which is the ratio of annual cost of goods sold (COGS) to average inventory investment. The inventory turnover ratio indicates how many times a year the inventory is sold or used. Generally, the higher the ratio the better, because that implies more efficient use of inventories. A benefit of this measure is that it can be used to compare companies in the *same* industry. For example, in the retail industry, supermarkets have high inventory turnover (more than 15 turns per year, because much of their goods are perishable), whereas furniture stores have low inventory turnover (approximately 3–6 turns per year)—see Figure 12-1.

A related measure is *days of inventory* on hand, a number that indicates the expected number of days of sales or usage that can be supplied from existing inventory.

> **anticipation inventory**
> Additional inventory to meet higher than average demand during a sales promotion or when customers expect a future price increase, and in anticipation of a plant shutdown

Reducing the Need for Inventory

Organizations can reduce their need for inventory without reducing customer service by addressing the purpose for holding inventory:

Inventory Purpose	Ways to Reduce the Need for Inventory
In-transit	Locate companies in a supply chain as close to each other as possible
	Cross-dock or eliminate the DC (e.g., ask manufacturer to drop-ship directly to consumers)
Safety	Establish close long-term relationships with suppliers and customers
	Ensure high quality material
Cycle	Reduce the ordering/setup times
Seasonal	Develop sources of supply and demand that collectively extend seasons
Decoupling	Reduce machine breakdown
	Cross-train workers
Anticipation	Don't use sales promotions; keep prices steady

FIGURE 12-1 ▶

Inventory turnover, by retail trade group.

Source: Industry Canada. Based on data from Statistics Canada (Annual Retail Trade Survey), 2010. http://www.ic.gc.ca/eic/site/retra-comde.nsf/eng/qn00282.html?Open&pv=1.

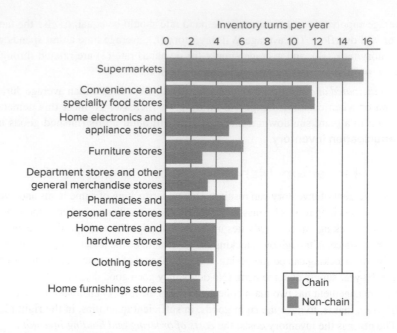

SYSPRO, a popular ERP software used by medium-sized companies, has an easy-to-use inventory module. See the "SYSPRO" OM in Action.

OM in Action

SYSPRO

A good enterprise resource planning (ERP) software for medium-sized companies is SYSPRO®. The first step in using the software is to define the inventory items. This is done by the Stock Codes program under Setup

of the Inventory module. Each item will have a file (see the screenshot below). The typical information needed is Stock code, Warehouse to use, Part category (Bought out or Made-in), Product class (e.g., raw material), and Lead time (Days) or Batching rule (e.g., Lot-for-lot).

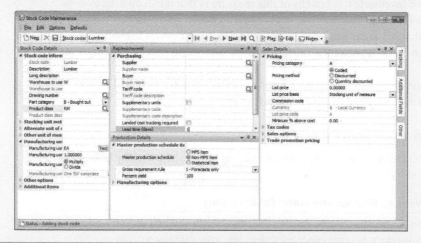

L02 Requirements for Effective Inventory Management

Effective inventory management requires:

1. Safe storage and handling of inventories.
2. Tracking inventory levels and using inventory control models.

3. Forecasting demands and lead times.

4. Estimating inventory costs.

5. Performing A-B-C classification.

Let's take a closer look at each of these requirements.

Safe Storage and Handling of Inventories

Most inventory items need to be protected from harsh outdoor environmental conditions, such as rain and snow. Therefore, inventory is usually stored indoors, in a warehouse or stockroom. Depending on the nature of the item, racks, shelves, or bins may be used to hold it. Heavy items or fast-moving items are stored on the floor. Each location should have an address code. To save moving items long distances, warehouses usually use the vertical space and have a very high ceiling (as high as three or four storeys). Forklifts are used to access the highest locations.

A warehouse/stockroom should be uncluttered so that items can be stored and retrieved easily. Depending on the flow of items into and out of the warehouse/stockroom, the right level of automation should be used. Most warehouses use forklifts, which move cases/boxes of items piled on a pallet (an approximately 4 foot by 4 foot wooden platform). Some use conveyors and some use carousel storage systems. A **warehouse management system (WMS)** is a computer software that controls the movement and storage of materials within a warehouse, and processes the associated transactions, including receiving, put-away, replenishment (bringing pallets and cases from a storage location to a pick location), picking, and shipping.

> **warehouse management system** A computer software that controls the movement and storage of materials within a warehouse, and processes the associated transactions

Basic warehouse activities for a wholesaler can be described as follows: A shipment arrives on board a semi-trailer. A receiver drives the pallets out of the trailer using a forklift truck, identifies the associated purchase order, and receives each pallet by scanning the bar code of the product (on a case) and entering the quantity in WMS. WMS generates a bar-code label that provides pallet tracking and also has the the address of the storage location. Usually a large warehouse has two locations for each item: a bulk (reserve) rack location (usually high up) and an individual-item pick location (reachable by a person without equipment). After receiving, the pallets are left in a staging area for a put-away forklift driver to move to their bulk storage location. WMS is informed of the moves and updates the location of pallet. Later, as a pick location runs out of units of an item, WMS issues a replenishment order to move a pallet of the item from the bulk location to the pick location.

As a customer order arrives, it is assigned to a specific order picker on a pallet jack. WMS then directs the order picker to retrieve the cases of the items in the order in the sequence that minimizes total distance travelled while picking heavy cases first. Once at the picking location, the order picker scans the location and product bar codes before picking the number of cases requested. After the cases are put on the pallet, the WMS directs the picker to move to the next pick location, and so on until all the cases in the order are picked. The pallet is then moved to a wrapping station, a label is printed and attached, and then it is moved to the shipping area. For an application, see the "Co-op Distribution Centre" Operations Tour at the end of this chapter.

It is also possible to automate both storage and picking operations by using an **automated storage and retrieval system (ASRS)**. For an application, see the "Sobeys' High-Tech Distribution Centres" OM in Action.

> **automated storage and retrieval system (ASRS)** A computer-controlled system for automatically placing and retrieving loads from defined storage locations.

 OM in Action

Sobeys' High-Tech Distribution Centres

Sobeys' Vaughan, Ontario, and Terrebonne, Quebec, distribution centres (DCs) are the most high-tech grocery DCs in Canada. They have automated storage and retrieval systems for pallets and cases of groceries. All storage, picking, conveying, and packing equipment is computer controlled, and made by WITRON. Each facility is approximately half a million square feet, is 65–70 feet high, and has daily receiving and picking capacity of approximately 300,000 cases, three times that of a non-automated DC of the same size.

As a wrapped pallet of cases of a product is unloaded from a trailer, it is placed on a pallet crane which moves and places it in a high-bay storage location. When the cases of a product in the case storage location need replenishing, a pallet is brought down by a crane from a high-bay storage location, then the contents are depalletized and dismantled automatically. Each case is put on a plastic tray, moved on an automated conveyor, and placed on a tray crane (one of 32), which stores it in one of the 350,000 case storage locations.

As a retail store orders, the computerized system identifies and retrieves the cases of products ordered from the case storage location using tray cranes, sequences and stacks them in one of 16 case order machines to build a pallet, stretch-wraps the pallet, and places the pallet in a staging area ready for shipment to the store. Sobeys uses this ASRS for 85 percent of products. The others have a larger or smaller package size than a case.

Automation has reduced picking errors and damages. The product aisle placement of a Sobeys store is used by the warehouse management system to custom build a pallet in the sequence that the shelves will be stocked in the store. The automated packing system reduces transportation cube volume requirements by

Juice Images/Alamy Stock Photo

5–10 percent by packing the cases more densely, perfectly square with no overhang, and higher. This results in fewer deliveries to a store.

Two new ASRSs are currently being added to the Vaughan DC to handle perishables and frozen foods.

Sources: https://www.youtube.com/watch?v=aSzACYXT0oQ; http://www.canadiangrocer.com/top-stories/inside-sobeys-high-tech-warehouse-28037.

The required warehouse capacity depends on yearly volume and frequency of inventory movements. For each item, the maximum space required at any time (including safety stock) should be determined. Also, the floor space needed for aisles and receiving/shipping, returns, etc., should be considered.

A warehouse is owned, rented, or leased (contracted). Ownership provides more control, but to be economical, demand should be high and stable. Public (rented) warehousing is for short-term needs and requires no capital or personnel. Contract warehousing is offered by a third-party logistics (3PL) service provider.

Food distributors require a warehouse that has cold rooms/zones for fresh produce and freezers for items such as ice cream. Some inventoried items are expensive, so access to the building should be controlled, and items that are prone to theft (e.g., small valuable items such as batteries and cigarettes) should be locked up in a secure area/room. Also, because full pallets are heavy, racks in the warehouse can be high, and forklifts and pallet jacks are large and fast moving, safety is an important issue in warehouse management.

A common problem in most warehouses/stockrooms is the existence of a considerable amount of obsolete items. These include parts for machines that no longer exist, wrong parts, excess material, used/old machines, etc. To be efficient, outdated items should be either sent back to the supplier or sold to a liquidator. Obsolete items are a drag on the company's assets and take space in the warehouse.

Tracking Inventory Levels and Using Inventory Control Models

If inventory is not continually tracked, then it must be periodically reviewed and counted. Some small retailers that do not use a computer use this approach: a manager periodically checks the shelves and the records to determine the **inventory position** for each item: Quantity on hand + On order − Back-ordered. "On order" relates to an order that has been received by a supplier but the shipment has not arrived yet. A *back order* is a shortage that the customer has agreed to wait for; it is a future inventory committed to a customer.

Then, the manager estimates how much of the item will be demanded from now until receipt of the next delivery (called the order-up-to level), and bases the order quantity on the difference between order-up-to level and inventory position. This replenishment model is called

inventory position Quantity on hand + On order − Back-ordered.

the **fixed-interval/order-up-to level model**. This model can also be used when a computer keeps track of inventory levels continually. An advantage of this model is that items from the same supplier are ordered at the same time, which results in economies in ordering, shipping, receiving, and paying. A disadvantage is the possibility of stock-out between reviews.

Perpetual or continual tracking keeps track of removals from and additions to inventory on a continuous basis, so the system can provide information on the current inventory position for each item at any time. Bank accounts are kept using this method; transactions such as deposits and withdrawals are instantly recorded and balance is determined continually. All modern inventory software keeps track of inventories continually. For example, see the "SYSPRO" OM in Action earlier in the chapter.

Another common inventory control model is the **economic order quantity/reorder point model (EOQ/ROP)**. This model works only with perpetual tracking. When the inventory position of an item drops down to or below a predetermined minimum called the reorder point (ROP), a fixed (economic) quantity of the item is ordered. Usually a computer keeps track of inventory for this model. An advantage of this model is that the probability or expected number of shortage can be controlled. Another advantage is that the order quantity is fixed; management can determine an optimal order quantity and use it for a few months, provided that demand does not vary seasonally or have a trend. A disadvantage of this model is the added cost of individual ordering.

This model is closely related to the popular Min/Max model: when inventory position drops to or below Min, an order equal to "Max − Inventory position" is placed. Finding the optimal values for Min and Max is a little more complex (it requires an iterative search procedure). Fortunately, we can approximate Min by ROP and Max by "ROP + EOQ" without a large cost penalty. This approximation slightly underestimates the optimal Min and Max.[2]

The above two models are appropriate if unused items can be carried over into subsequent periods and used or sold then. The single-period model is appropriate when items cannot be carried over (because they are perishable, for example).

A simple implementation of the economic order quantity/reorder point model that does not require perpetual inventory tracking is the **two bin system**. Items are withdrawn from the first bin until its contents are exhausted. It is then time to reorder. The second bin contains enough stock to satisfy expected demand until the order is filled plus safety stock. When the order arrives, the second bin is topped off and the remainder is placed in the first bin. Sometimes an order card is placed at the bottom of the first bin. For an application, see the "Logi-D's 2Bin-ID" OM in Action.

> **fixed-interval/order-up-to level model** An inventory control model that places orders at fixed time intervals to bring the inventory position up to the order-up-to level.
>
> **perpetual or continual tracking** Keeping track of removals from and additions to inventory continuously, thus providing the current inventory position of each item.
>
> **economic order quantity/ reorder point model (EOQ/ ROP)** An inventory control model that places a fixed optimal-size order when the inventory position of an item drops to or below a minimum quantity called the reorder point.
>
> **two bin system** A simple implementation of the economic order quantity/reorder point model that reorders when the first bin is empty, uses the second bin until the order arrives, then tops off the second bin and leaves the rest in the first bin.

 OM in Action   http://www.logi-d.net

Logi-D's 2Bin-ID

Logi-D (now part of TECSYS) is a Laval-based provider of point-of-use inventory management, traceability, cost capture, and patient charging technologies for hospitals. Logi-D's RFID-enabled two bin replenishment system, 2BIN-iD, is used by several hospitals in Quebec such as CHU de Québec-Université Laval and Centre hospitalier de l'Université de Montréal.

2BIN-iD begins with an established quantity of a given item divided into two batches and stored in primary and secondary compartments of a single storage module. When the primary compartment is empty, clinical staff transfer its identification tag (which contains an RFID transponder) to a wall-mounted RFID "reader" board located near the storage unit. They then begin using items from the secondary compartment, which holds a set number of days' worth of inventory. Placing

Courtesy of Logi-D

2 See, for example, E. A. Silver, D. F. Pyke, and R. Peterson. *Inventory Management and Production Planning and Scheduling*, 3rd Ed. New York: John Wiley and Sons, 1998, pp. 332–335.

the primary compartment's tag on the board triggers an automated replenishment request from the hospital's material management information system, which then generates a pick list for items from the hospital's central storage or a requisition for direct purchase.

During their delivery rounds, material management staff transfer the supplies to the primary compartment and replenish the secondary compartment while returning the corresponding RFID tag to the primary compartment.

---

bar code A number assigned to an item or storage location, made of a group of vertical black or white bars of different thicknesses that are readable by a scanner.

Most warehouses/stockrooms use bar code scanners that read bar codes assigned to items (cases/boxes, pallets, etc.) and the storage locations (racks, shelves, bins, etc.). A **bar code** is a unique number assigned to an item or a location, made of a group of vertical black and white bars that are read by a scanner. There are different types of bar codes. The standard grocery bar code is called a *universal product code (UPC)*, has 12 digits, and is illustrated below. The zero on the left of the bar code identifies this as a regular grocery item, the next five numbers (36000) indicate the manufacturer, the next five numbers (29145) indicate the specific item, and the last digit (2) is a check-digit, used by the computer to check the validity of the first 11 digits that the scanner read. Each digit is made of seven black or white bars. However, the colour of a bar depends on whether the digit is on the left of centre guard (L pattern) or on the right (R pattern). See the table below (1 = black, 0 = white). For example, 4 in the right is 1011100. This is done so that a scanner can read the UPC from left to right or from right to left (and still get the same digits). Bar-code scanners have increased the speed and accuracy of transactions significantly.

4 ▶ 1011100 ▶

036000 291452

Get It/Wikimedia Commons

Digit	Left Pattern	Right Pattern
0	0001101	1110010
1	0011001	1100110
2	0010011	1101100
3	0111101	1000010
4	0100011	1011100
5	0110001	1001110
6	0101111	1010000
7	0111011	1000100
8	0110111	1001000
9	0001011	1110100

Forecasting Demands and Lead Times

Inventory is used to satisfy future demand, so it is essential to forecast future demand for each SKU. Also, it is essential to know the **purchase lead time**, the time interval between ordering and receiving an order. Similarly, for a SKU produced in-house, it is important to know the *manufacturing lead time*, the time it will take for a batch of a part/product to be manufactured. In addition, managers need to know the extent to which demands and lead times might vary: the greater the potential variability, the greater the need for additional safety stock to reduce the risk of stock-out between deliveries. Thus, there is a crucial link between forecasting and inventory management.

purchase lead time Time interval between ordering and receiving the order.

A **point-of-sale (POS) system** electronically records actual sales at the time and location of sale, which, after accumulation into daily or weekly or monthly sales, are used in forecasting.

point-of-sale (POS) system Equipment for electronically recording sales at the time and location of sale.

Given the large number of SKUs of a typical organization, a simple time-series forecasting technique such as exponential smoothing (and its variants) is commonly used to forecast demand of SKUs.

Estimating Inventory Costs

Three basic costs, other than the purchase price, are associated with inventories: holding, ordering, and shortage costs.

Holding cost relates to physically having items in storage. Costs include warehousing costs (rent or building depreciation, labour, material-handling equipment depreciation, heating/cooling, light, etc.) and the opportunity cost associated with funds tied up in inventory. Other holding costs include insurance, obsolescence, spoilage, theft, and breakage.

The significance of some of the components of holding cost depends on the type of item. Items that are easily concealed or are fairly expensive are prone to theft. Perishable items such as meat and dairy are subject to rapid spoilage. Computers and electronics, and their parts, are subject to obsolescence.

Holding cost is stated in either of two ways: as a percentage of unit cost or as a dollar amount per unit. Typical annual holding cost rates are 20–40 percent of the cost of an item. In other words, to hold a $100 item for one year could cost from $20 to $40.

Ordering cost is the cost of placing an order (not including the purchase price), receiving it, and paying for it. This includes the time of purchasing/inventory control staff determining how much is needed, periodically evaluating sources of supply, preparing purchase orders, and the fixed-cost portion of transportation, receiving, inspection, and moving the goods to storage. It also includes the cost of time spent paying the invoice. Ordering cost is generally expressed as a fixed dollar amount per order, regardless of order size.

When a company produces its own parts instead of ordering from a supplier, the cost of machine setup is analogous to ordering cost; that is, it is expressed as a fixed charge per production run, regardless of the size of the run. Machine **setup** involves preparing the machine for the job by adjusting it, changing cutting tools, etc.

Shortage cost results when demand exceeds supply of inventory on hand. This cost can include the opportunity cost of not making a sale (i.e., unrealized profit), loss of customer goodwill, late charges, and expediting costs. Furthermore, if the shortage occurs in an item carried for internal use (e.g., to supply an assembly line), the cost of lost production or downtime is considered a shortage cost, which can easily run into hundreds of dollars a minute or more.

> **holding cost** Cost to keep an item in inventory.

> **ordering cost** Cost of placing an order (not including the purchase price), receiving it, and paying for it.

> **setup** Preparing the machine for the job by adjusting it, changing cutting tools, etc.

> **shortage cost** Cost of demand exceeding supply of inventory on hand; includes unrealized profit per unit, loss of goodwill, etc.

Performing A-B-C Classification

Items held in inventory are typically not of equal importance in terms of dollars invested, profit potential, annual sales or usage quantity, or shortage cost. For instance, a producer of electrical equipment might have electrical generators, coils of wire, and miscellaneous nuts and bolts among the items carried in inventory. It would be inefficient to devote equal attention to each of these items. Instead, a more reasonable approach would be to allocate control efforts according to the *relative importance* of various items in inventory.

The **A-B-C classification** groups inventory items into three classes according to some measure of importance, usually annual dollar value (i.e., cost per unit multiplied by annual usage or sales quantity), and then allocates inventory control efforts accordingly. The three classes are A (very important), B (moderately important), and C (least important). A items generally account for about 15–20 percent of the items (SKUs, not counting multiple units of the same item) in inventory but about 70–80 percent of the annual dollar value (ADV). At the other end of the scale, C items might account for about 50–60 percent of the SKUs but only about 5–10 percent of the ADV.

> **A-B-C classification** Grouping inventory items into three classes (A, B, or C) according to some measure of importance, and allocating inventory control efforts accordingly.

These percentages vary from company to company, but in most instances a relatively small number of items will account for a large share of ADV, and these items should receive a greater share of inventory control efforts. For instance, A items should receive close attention through better forecasting, more frequent ordering, and better safety stock determination. The C items should receive only loose control (e.g., using a two bin system, bulk orders), and the B items should have controls that lie between the two extremes.

EXAMPLE 12-1

Classify the following SKUs as A, B, or C based on annual dollar value (ADV):

SKU	Annual demand ×	Unit cost =	Annual dollar value (ADV)
1.......	3,000	$10	$30,000
2.......	9,000	3	27,000
3.......	1,000	710	710,000
4.......	2,500	250	625,000
5.......	1,900	500	950,000
6.......	400	200	80,000
7.......	500	100	50,000
8.......	1,000	4,300	4,300,000
9.......	200	210	42,000
10......	5,000	720	3,600,000
11.......	2,500	192	480,000
12.......	1,000	35	35,000

SOLUTION

Sort the rows by decreasing values of ADV and calculate the percentage of total ADV for each SKU:

SKU	Annual demand ×	Unit cost =	Annual dollar value (ADV)	% of total ADV	
8........	1,000	$4,300	$ 4,300,000	39.3	A
10........	5,000	720	3,600,000	32.9	
5........	1,900	500	9,50,000	8.7	
3........	1,000	710	7,10,000	6.5	B
4........	2,500	250	6,25,000	5.7	
11........	2,500	192	4,80,000	4.4	
6........	400	200	80,000	0.7	
7........	500	100	50,000	0.5	
9........	200	210	42,000	0.4	
12........	1,000	35	35,000	0.3	C
1........	3,000	10	30,000	0.3	
2........	9,000	3	27,000	0.3	
			$10,929,000	100.0	

Proceed down the list, adding percentage of total ADVs until you get close to 80 percent of total ADV. The first two items have 72.2 percent of total ADV and $2/12 = 17$ percent of SKUs, so it seems reasonable to classify them as A items. (Also note the sharp drop in ADV from the second to third rows.) The next four items have moderate ADV (25.3 percent of total ADV and $4/12 = 33$ percent of SKUs) and should be classified as B items. (Also note the sharp drop in ADV between the sixth and seventh rows.) The remainder are C items, based on their relatively low ADV (2.5 percent of total ADV and $6/12 = 50$ percent of SKUs).

Although annual dollar value may be the primary factor in classifying inventory items, a manager may take other factors into account in making exceptions for certain items (e.g., changing the classification of a C item to A). Factors may include the risk of obsolescence, the consequence of a stock-out, the distance of a supplier, long lead time, and so on.

Managers use the A-B-C concept in many different settings to improve operations. For example, the A-B-C concept is sometimes used to guide **cycle counting**, which is counting the items in inventory on a cyclic schedule (more frequently than annually). Determination of inventory quantity by actual count is called **physical inventory**. The purpose of cycle counting is to (1) reduce discrepancies between inventory records and the actual quantities of inventory on hand, and (2) investigate the causes of inaccuracy and fix them. Accuracy is important because inaccurate records can lead to wrong inventory control decisions, which then lead to disruptions in production, poor customer service, or unnecessarily high inventory holding cost.

The key questions concerning cycle counting for management are:

1. How much accuracy is needed?

2. How frequently should we count?

3. Who should do it?

APICS recommends the following guidelines for inventory record accuracy: ±0.2 percent for A items, ±1 percent for B items, and ±5 percent for C items. Therefore, A items should be counted more frequently than C items. For example, A items should be counted every month, B items quarterly, and C items annually. Some companies use regular stockroom personnel to do cycle counting during periods of slow activity, while others contract with outside companies to do it on a periodic basis. Use of an outside company provides an independent check on inventory and may reduce the risk of problems created by error-prone employees.

The "Cardinal Health Canada (CHC)" OM in Action features a company that uses the A-B-C classification for locating items in the warehouse.

> **cycle counting** Counting the items in inventory on a cyclic schedule (more frequently than annually).
>
> **physical inventory** Determination of inventory quantity by actual count.

http://www.apics.org

 OM in Action   www.CardinalHealthCanada.com

Cardinal Health Canada (CHC)

CHC is one of the two largest medical, surgical, and lab products distributors in Canada (the other is McKesson Canada). It offers over 80,000 items to its customers, which include hospitals, clinics, doctors' offices, nursing homes, clinical labs, etc. These items satisfy more than 85 percent of the customers' needs, and range from bandages to operating tables. CHC has over 600 suppliers, including 3M Canada, Procter & Gamble, and Kimberly-Clark.

CHC has a national supply centre (NSC), a 220,000 ft^2 warehouse/distribution centre, in Mississauga, Ontario, and seven regional warehouse/distribution centres (DCs), from Vancouver to St. John's. The regional DCs keep the high-demand SKUs in inventory and provide daily delivery service to customers. Other, less frequently used SKUs are kept only in the NSC, which holds approximately 30,000 SKUs. Very low demand items (e.g., equipment) are bought when necessary, and are either cross-docked via the NSC to the customer or directly shipped to the customer.

The materials management team forecasts customer demand, monitors and improves supplier delivery performance, and controls the levels of inventory in each facility. Any low or high levels are investigated to identify their cause and the problem is solved with the cooperation of suppliers and/or customers. For example, the cause for

a low inventory of an SKU may be an incorrect purchase order or a problem at a supplier. Using this method, CHC has reduced its inventories while increasing its fill rates.

Shipments from suppliers to the NSC are 30–35 full truckloads and 50–60 less-than-full truckloads per day. The NSC is divided into two parts: approximately 2,000 full case SKUs (A items) are kept on one side, and 28,000 other SKUs (B and C items) are kept on shelves on the other side. Radio frequency (RF) communication and bar code scanners are used for receiving, put away, replenishment, and order picking.

CHC has a JIT or *stockless* inventory arrangement with its customers. This means that an order received by EDI from, for example, a ward of a hospital is delivered the next day directly to the ward, hence relieving the hospital of the need for a stockroom. CHC's online ordering system (a B2B ecommerce portal) provides custom pricing and allows the use of a bar code scanner (the system is called OrderConnect) which makes ordering faster and easier. Also, rush deliveries are possible. The advanced customer logistics team works with customers to improve the efficiency and effectiveness of the supply system, for example, by performing product standardization. EDI is also used for communication within CHC and with its suppliers.

Sources: http://www.cardinalhealthcanada.com/en/pages/supply_chain. aspx; R. Robertson, "Saving Lives," *Materials Management and Distribution*, July/August 2003, 48(6), pp. 14–20.

Determining the Economic Order Quantity and Its Variants

In the economic order quantity/reorder point (EOQ/ROP) model, a fixed quantity of an SKU equal to EOQ is ordered when its inventory position (Amount on hand + On order − Back-ordered) drops to or below its reorder point. For simplicity, we decompose the determination of the order quantity and the reorder point. Even though the formulas we will obtain will not necessarily give the optimal values, they generally give close-to-optimal values (the worst case cost penalty is approximately 12 percent).[3] The **economic order quantity (EOQ)** is the order size that minimizes the total annual inventory control cost. Four EOQ-related models are described here:

economic order quantity (EOQ) The order size that minimizes total annual inventory control cost.

1. Basic economic order quantity (EOQ).
2. Economic production quantity (EPQ).
3. EOQ with quantity discount.
4. EOQ with planned shortage.

Basic Economic Order Quantity (EOQ)

The basic EOQ model for an item will minimize the sum of annual costs of holding and ordering inventory. The annual purchase price is not included because in the basic case it is assumed that unit purchase price is unaffected by the order size.

The basic EOQ model is based on a number of assumptions. They are listed in Table 12-1.

TABLE 12-1 ▶

Assumptions of the basic EOQ model.

1. Only one item is involved.
2. Annual demand is known.
3. Demand is spread evenly throughout the year so that the demand rate is reasonably constant.
4. Purchase lead time does not vary.
5. Each order is received in a single delivery.
6. There are no quantity discounts.
7. Shortage is not allowed.

Ordering, receiving, and usage occur in cycles. Figure 12-2 illustrates 2.5 order cycles for a specific SKU. A cycle begins with receipt of a shipment of Q units, which are then used at a constant rate over time. When the quantity on hand is just sufficient to satisfy demand during a purchase lead time, another purchase order for Q units is submitted to the supplier. Because it is assumed that both the demand rate and the lead time do not vary, the shipment will be received at the precise instant that the inventory on hand falls to zero. Thus, orders are timed to avoid both excess stock and shortage. Note that for simplicity, the profile is for inventory on hand, not inventory position. That is, the order quantity is not shown on the graph until it is actually received. The economic order quantity reflects a trade-off between total annual holding and ordering costs: If the order size is relatively small, the average inventory will be low, resulting in low annual holding cost. However, a small order size will necessitate frequent orders, which will drive up annual ordering cost. Conversely, ordering large quantities at infrequent intervals can reduce annual ordering cost, but would result in higher average inventory levels and therefore increased annual holding cost. Figure 12-3 illustrates these two extremes.

Thus, the ideal solution is an order size that is neither very large nor very small, but somewhere in between. The exact amount to order will depend on the relative magnitudes of holding and ordering costs and annual demand.

Annual holding cost is calculated by multiplying the average amount of inventory on hand by the cost to hold one unit for one year (even though any given unit would not be held for a year). The average inventory is simply half of the order quantity: The amount on hand decreases steadily from

---
[3] Y. S. Zheng, "On Properties of Stochastic Inventory Systems," *Management Science*, 38(10), 1992, pp. 87–103.

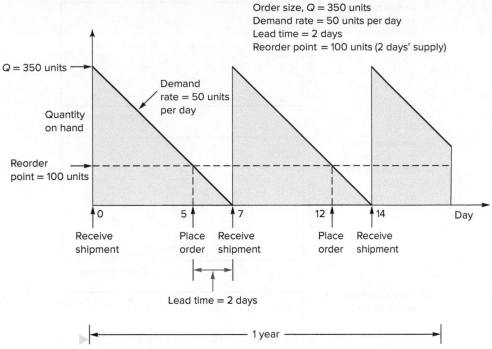

Order size, Q = 350 units
Demand rate = 50 units per day
Lead time = 2 days
Reorder point = 100 units (2 days' supply)

Order cycles: profile of inventory on hand over time.

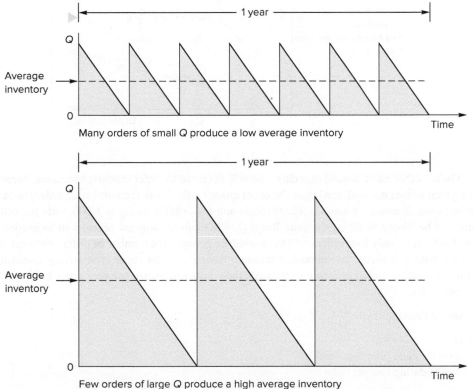

Average inventory on hand and number of orders per year are inversely related: as one increases, the other decreases.

Q units to 0, for an average of $(Q + 0)/2$, or $Q/2$. Using the symbol H to represent the annual holding cost per unit:

$$\text{Annual holding cost} = \frac{Q}{2}H$$

where:

Q = Order quantity (units per order)

H = Holding cost per unit per year

Annual holding cost is thus a linear function of Q: It increases in direct proportion to changes in the order quantity Q, as Figure 12-4A illustrates.

FIGURE 12-4 ▶

Annual holding, ordering, and total inventory control cost curves.

A. Annual holding cost is linearly related to order quantity

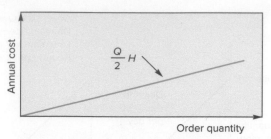

B. Annual ordering cost is inversely and nonlinearly related to order quantity

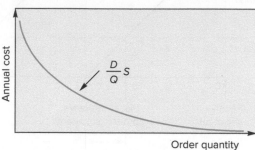

C. The total annual inventory cost curve is U-shaped, and at its minimum annual holding cost equals annual ordering cost

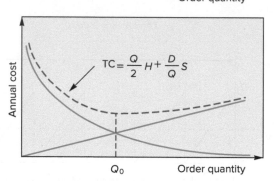

On the other hand, annual ordering cost will decrease as order quantity increases, because for a given annual demand, the larger the order quantity, the fewer the number of orders needed. For instance, if annual demand is 12,000 units and the order quantity is 1,000 units per order, there will be 12 orders during the year. But if $Q = 2,000$ units, only six orders will be needed; if $Q = 3,000$ units, only four orders will be needed. In general, the number of orders per year will be D/Q, where D = Annual demand. Because ordering cost per order is relatively insensitive to order quantity, *annual ordering cost* equals the number of orders per year times the ordering cost per order:

$$\text{Annual ordering cost} = \frac{D}{Q}S$$

where:

D = Demand (units per year)

S = Ordering cost per order

Because the number of orders per year, D/Q, decreases as Q increases (but not at a constant rate), annual ordering cost is inversely and nonlinearly related to order quantity, as Figure 12-4B illustrates.

The total annual inventory cost of holding and ordering inventory, when Q units are ordered each time, is:

$$\text{TC} = \text{Annual holding cost} + \text{Annual ordering cost} = \frac{Q}{2}H + \frac{D}{Q}S \tag{12-1}$$

Figure 12-4C reveals that the total-cost curve is U-shaped (i.e., a convex function, with one minimum) and that *it reaches its minimum at the quantity where annual holding and annual ordering*

costs are equal. An expression for the optimal order quantity, Q_0, can be obtained using calculus.[4]
The result is the formula:

$$EOQ = Q_0 = \sqrt{\frac{2DS}{H}} \qquad\qquad (12\text{-}2)$$

The minimum total cost is then found by substituting Q_0 for Q in Formula 12-1.
The length of an order cycle (i.e., the time between orders, if Q_0 is used) is:

$$\text{Length of order cycle (in years)} = \frac{Q_0}{D} \qquad\qquad (12\text{-}3)$$

◄ EXAMPLE 12-2

A tire store expects to sell approximately 100 all-season tires of a certain make, model, and size next year. Annual holding cost is $16 per tire and ordering cost is $20 per order. The store operates 360 days a year and has enough storage space in the back.

a. What is the EOQ?

b. How many times per year would the store reorder if EOQ units are ordered each time?

c. What is the length of an order cycle if EOQ units are ordered each time?

d. What is the total annual inventory control cost if EOQ units are ordered each time?

SOLUTION

$D = 100$ tires per year
$H = \$16$ per unit per year
$S = \$20$ per order

a. $Q_0 = \sqrt{\frac{2DS}{H}} = \sqrt{\frac{2(100)(20)}{16}} = 15.8$, round to 16 units

b. Number of orders per year: $D/Q_0 = \frac{100 \text{ tires/yr}}{16 \text{ tires each time}} = 6.25$ times per year

c. Length of order cycle: $Q_0/D = \frac{16 \text{ tires}}{100 \text{ tires/yr}} = 0.16$ year, which is 0.16×360, or 57.6 days or approximately 2 months.

d. TC = Annual holding cost + Annual ordering cost
$= (Q_0/2)H + (D/Q_0)S$
$= (16/2)16 + (100/16)20$
$= \$128 + \$125$
$= \$253$

Note that the annual ordering and holding costs are almost equal at the EOQ, as illustrated in Figure 12-4c.

Holding cost is usually stated as a percentage i of unit cost of an item rather than as a dollar amount per unit H. However, as long as this percentage is converted into a dollar amount by multiplying it by unit cost R, the EOQ formula is still appropriate.

◄ EXAMPLE 12-3

A distributor of security monitors purchases 3,600 monitors a year from the manufacturer at the cost of $65 each. Ordering cost is $30 per order and annual holding cost rate is 20 percent of the unit cost. Calculate the optimal order quantity and the total annual cost of ordering and holding the inventory.

SOLUTION

$D = 3,600$ monitors per year
$S = \$30$ per order

i = Holding cost rate per year = 20%
R = Unit cost = $65
$H = iR = 0.20(\$65) = \$13$

$Q_0 = \sqrt{\frac{2DS}{H}} = \sqrt{\frac{2(3,600)(30)}{13}} = 128.9$, round to 129 monitors

TC = Annual holding cost + Annual ordering cost
$= (Q_0/2)H + (D/Q_0)S = (129/2)13 + (3,600/129)30$
$= \$838.50 + \$837.21 = \$1,675.71$

---

[4] We can find the minimum point of the total-cost curve by differentiating TC with respect to Q, setting the result equal to zero, and solving for Q. Thus,

$$\frac{d\text{TC}}{dQ} = \frac{dQ}{2}H + d(D/Q)S = H/2 - DS/Q^2$$

$H/2 - DS/Q^2 = 0$ so $Q^2 = \frac{2DS}{H}$ and $Q = \sqrt{\frac{2DS}{H}}$

Note that the second derivative $\left(\frac{2DS}{Q_3}\right)$ is positive, which indicates a minimum has been obtained.

Comment. Holding cost per unit per year and ordering cost per order are estimated rather than precisely determined from accounting records. Consequently, the EOQ value should be regarded as an approximate rather than an exact quantity. Thus, rounding the calculated value is perfectly acceptable; stating a value to several decimal places would tend to give an unrealistic impression of the precision involved. An obvious question is: How good is this "approximate" EOQ in terms of minimizing total annual inventory control cost? The answer is that the EOQ is fairly robust; the total cost curve is relatively flat near the EOQ, especially to the right of the EOQ. In other words, even if the approximate EOQ differs from the actual EOQ, total cost will not increase much (see Figure 12-5). Also note that annual demand D is usually estimated by multiplying next month's forecast of demand by 12 or next week's forecast of demand by 52. If there is seasonality in demand, a lot sizing technique, described in Chapter 14, will be more appropriate than EOQ. However, a simple solution commonly used is to determine the length of order cycle for EOQ and set the order quantity equal to the expected demand during that period. For example, for Example 12-2 above, order the forecast demand for the next two months.

FIGURE 12-5 ▶

The total annual inventory cost curve is relatively flat near the EOQ.

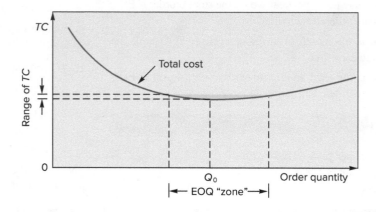

Economic Production Quantity (EPQ)

If we are producing an item in-house, to determine the optimal production lot size we can use the **economic production quantity (EPQ)**, the production lot size that minimizes total annual production setup and inventory holding cost.

The assumptions of the EPQ model are similar to those of the EOQ model, except that instead of shipments being received in a single delivery, units are received incrementally. Figure 12-6 illustrates how inventory on hand is affected by periodically producing a batch of a particular item that is received in storage and used incrementally.

economic order quantity (EOQ) The order size that minimizes total annual inventory control cost.

FIGURE 12-6 ▶

Inventory on hand when a batch of an item is produced periodically.

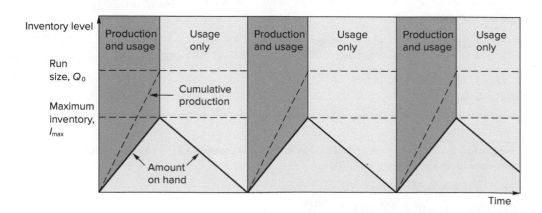

During the production phase of the cycle, inventory builds up at a rate equal to the difference between production and usage rates. For example, if the daily production rate is 20 units and the daily usage rate is 5 units, inventory will build up at the rate of $20 - 5 = 15$ units per day. As long as production continues, the inventory will grow; when production ceases, the inventory will begin to decrease. Hence, the inventory on hand will be maximum, denoted by I_{max}, when production ceases. When the amount of inventory on hand is exhausted, production is resumed and the cycle repeats itself. It can be seen that the average inventory on hand is $0.5I_{max}$.

Because the company makes the item itself, there is no ordering cost as such. Nonetheless, with every production run (batch), there is a setup cost—the cost to prepare the equipment for the job, such as cleaning, adjusting, and changing tools and fixtures. Setup costs are analogous to ordering costs because they are independent of the lot (run) quantity. They are treated in exactly the same way, and we use the same symbol, S, to denote setup cost per production run. The larger the run quantity, the fewer the number of runs needed per year and, hence, the lower the annual setup cost. The number of runs or batches per year is D/Q, and the annual setup cost is equal to the number of runs per year times the setup cost per run: $(D/Q) \times S$.

Total annual inventory control cost is:

$$TC = \text{Annual holding cost} + \text{Annual setup cost} = \left(\frac{I_{max}}{2}\right)H + (D/Q)S \qquad (12\text{-}4)$$

where

$I_{max} = $ Maximum inventory
$Q = $ Production run quantity
$S = $ Setup cost per production run

To calculate I_{max}, let
$p = $ Production rate (e.g., units per day)
$d = $ Usage or demand rate (e.g., units per day)

The production run quantity Q is consumed at the rate of d during the entire cycle (which is the time between the starting points of two consecutive production runs). Therefore,

$$\text{Cycle length} = \frac{Q}{d} \qquad (12\text{-}5)$$

The production run quantity Q is produced at the rate of p during the production run (the production phase of the cycle). Therefore,

$$\text{Production run length} = \frac{Q}{P} \qquad (12\text{-}6)$$

Therefore, the maximum inventory level I_{max} is

$$I_{max} = Q - d\left(\frac{Q}{P}\right) = \frac{Q}{P}(p - d) \qquad (12\text{-}7)$$

Substituting Formula 12-7 into Formula 12-4, taking derivatives with respect to Q, setting it equal to zero, and solving for Q, will result in:

$$Q_0 = \sqrt{\frac{2DS}{H}}\sqrt{\frac{p}{p - d}} \qquad \qquad \text{optimal run size} \qquad (12\text{-}8)$$

EXAMPLE 12-4

A toy manufacturer uses 48,000 rubber wheels per year for its popular dump truck series. The company can make its own wheels at a rate of 800 per day. The toy trucks are assembled uniformly over the entire year. Holding cost is $1 per wheel per year. Setup cost for a production run of wheels is $45. The company operates 240 days per year. Determine the:

a. Optimal production run quantity.

b. Minimum total annual cost for holding and setup.

c. Cycle length for the optimal production run quantity.

d. Production run length for the optimal production run quantity.

SOLUTION

$D = 48,000$ wheels per year
$S = \$45$ per production run
$H = \$1$ per wheel per year
$p = 800$ wheels per day
$d = 48,000$ wheels per 240 days, or 200 wheels per day

a. $Q_0 = \sqrt{\dfrac{2DS}{H}} \sqrt{\dfrac{p}{p-d}} = \sqrt{\dfrac{2(48,000)45}{1}} \sqrt{\dfrac{800}{800-200}}$
$= 2,400 \text{ wheels}$

b. TC_{min} = Annual holding cost + Annual setup cost =
$\left(\dfrac{I_{max}}{2}\right) H + (D/Q_0)S$

Thus, you must first calculate I_{max}:

$I_{max} = \dfrac{Q}{p}(p-d) = \dfrac{2,400}{800}(800-200) = 1,800 \text{ wheels}$

$TC_{min} = \dfrac{1,800}{2} \times \$1 + \dfrac{48,000}{2,400} \times \$45 = \$900 + \$900$
$= \$1,800$

Note again the equality of the annual costs (in this example, setup and holding costs) at the EPQ.

c. Cycle length $= \dfrac{Q}{d} = \dfrac{2,400 \text{ wheels}}{200 \text{ wheels per day}} = 12 \text{ days}$

Thus, a production run of wheels will be made every 12 days.

d. Production run length $= \dfrac{Q}{p} = \dfrac{2,400 \text{ wheels}}{800 \text{ wheels per day}} =$
3 days

Thus, each production run will take three days.

Note that in the above derivation, setup *time* is ignored. This is not a problem unless setup time is significant and the utilization of the production resource is close to 100 percent due to making other products. In this case, there is no choice but to increase the production run quantity, which will result in fewer setups and less setup time in a year, thus fitting in the limited time of the operation. However, inventory holding cost will increase.

EOQ With Quantity Discount

quantity discount Price reductions for large orders.

A **quantity discount** is a price reduction for large orders, offered to customers to induce them to buy in large quantities. For example, a surgical supply company published the price list shown in Table 12-2 for boxes of extra-wide gauze strips. Note that the price per box decreases as order quantity increases. In this section, we consider the *all-unit discount* case where the price of every unit is the price per unit given for the order quantity. For example, if 60 gauze strips are purchased, the total cost will be 60($1.70) = $102. The alternative method of discounting, the *incremental discount,* will charge $2.00 for the first 44, $1.70 for each unit above that up to the 69th unit, and $1.40 for each unit above that. For example, for an order of 60 units, 44($2.00) + 16($1.70) = $115.20 will be charged.

TABLE 12-2

Price list for boxes of extra-wide gauze strips.

Order Quantity	Price per Box
1 to 44	$2.00
45 to 69	1.70
70 or more	1.40

If a quantity discount is offered, the buyer must weigh the potential benefits of reduced pur-chase price and fewer orders that will result from buying in large quantities against the increase in holding cost caused by higher average inventory. The buyer's goal is to select the order quantity that will minimize total annual holding, ordering, *and* purchase cost:

$$TC = \text{Annual holding cost} + \text{Annual ordering cost} + \text{Annual purchase cost}$$

$$\left(\frac{Q}{2}\right)H \quad + \quad \left(\frac{D}{Q}\right)S \quad + \quad RD \qquad (12\text{-}9)$$

where
    R = Unit price

Recall that, in the basic EOQ model, determination of order quantity does not involve the pur-chase cost. The rationale for not including the purchase cost there is that, under the assumption of no quantity discount, annual purchase cost is not affected by the order quantity. A graph of total annual purchase cost versus order quantity would be a horizontal line. Hence, including purchase cost would merely raise the total cost curve (in Figure 12-4c) by the same amount (RD) at every point. That would not change the EOQ (see Figure 12-7).

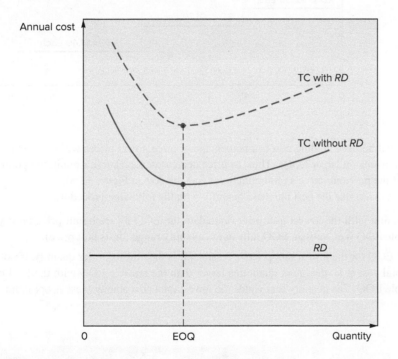

◄ FIGURE 12-7

Adding annual purchase cost RD doesn't change the EOQ if there is no quantity discount.

When an all-unit quantity discount is offered, there is a separate U-shaped total cost curve for each unit price. Again, including annual purchase price merely raises each curve by a constant amount. However, because the unit prices are all different, each curve is raised by a different amount: Smaller unit prices will raise the total cost curve less than larger unit prices. Note that no one curve applies to the entire range of order quantity; each curve applies to only a *portion* of the range (see Figure 12-8). Hence, the applicable or *feasible* total cost is initially on the curve with the highest unit price and then drops down, curve by curve, at the *break quantities*. Note that from Table 12-2, the break quantities for gauze strips are at 45 and 70 boxes. The result is a total cost curve with *steps* at the break quantities. Even though each curve has a minimum, those points are not necessarily feasible. For example, the minimum point for the $1.40 curve in Figure 12-8 appears to be around 65 units. However, the price list shown in Table 12-2 indicates that an order size of 65 boxes will receive a unit price of $1.70. The actual total cost curve is denoted by the solid red lines; only those price–quantity combinations are feasible. The objective of the quantity discount model is to identify an order quantity that will represent the lowest total annual cost for the solid lines.

FIGURE 12-8 ▶

The total cost curve with an all-unit quantity discount is composed of the solid red portion of the total cost curve for each unit price.

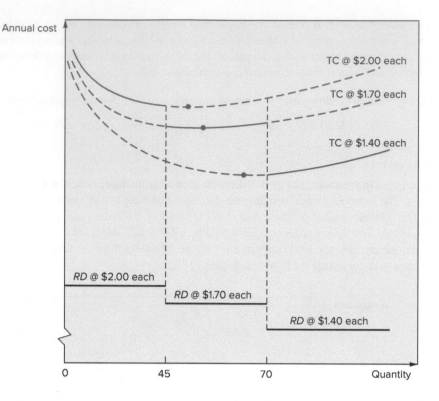

Note that because holding cost is a percentage of price, lower prices will lead to lower holding cost, which results in larger EOQs. Thus, as price decreases, each curve's minimum point will be to the right of the previous curve's minimum point (see the dots in Figure 12-8).

We can determine the best purchase quantity with the following procedure:

1. Beginning with the lowest unit price, calculate the EOQ for each unit price until you find a feasible EOQ (i.e., until an EOQ falls in the quantity range for its unit price).

2. If the EOQ for the lowest unit price is feasible, it is the optimal order quantity. If not, compare the total cost at all the break quantities larger than the feasible EOQ with the total cost of the feasible EOQ. The quantity that yields the lowest total cost among these is optimum.

EXAMPLE 12-5 ▶

A casino uses 4,000 light bulbs a year. Light bulbs are priced as follows: 1 to 499, 90 cents each; 500 to 999, 85 cents each; and 1,000 or more, 80 cents each. It costs approximately $30 to prepare a purchase order, receive, and pay for it, and holding cost rate is 40 percent of purchase price per year. Determine the optimal order quantity and the total annual cost.

SOLUTION

See Figure 12-9 for the graph of total annual cost.

$D = 4{,}000$ light bulbs per year, $S = \$30$, $H = 0.40R$, $R =$ unit price

Range	Unit Price R	H
1 to 499	$0.90	0.40(0.90) = 0.36
500 to 999	$0.85	0.40(0.85) = 0.34
1,000 or more	$0.80	0.40(0.80) = 0.32

Find the EOQ for each price, starting with the lowest price, until you locate a feasible EOQ.

$$EOQ_{0.80} = \sqrt{\frac{2DS}{H}} = \sqrt{\frac{2(4{,}000)30}{0.32}} = 866 \text{ light bulbs}$$

Because an order size of 866 light bulbs is fewer than 1,000 units, 866 is not feasible for the unit price of $0.80 per light bulb. Next, try $0.85 per unit.

$$EOQ_{0.85} = \sqrt{\frac{2(4{,}000)30}{0.34}} = 840 \text{ light bulbs}$$

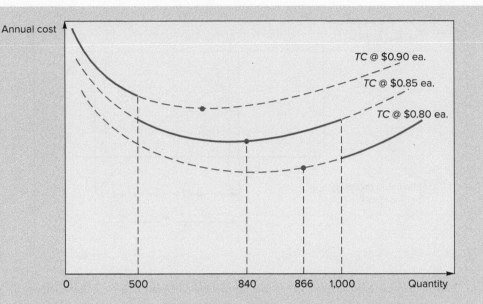

Total annual cost for Example 12-5.

This EOQ is feasible; it falls in the $0.85-per-light-bulb quantity range (500 to 999).

Now calculate the total cost for 840 order size, and compare it to the total cost of the break quantity larger than 840, which is 1,000 units.

TC = Annual holding cost + Annual ordering cost + Annual purchase cost

$$= \left(\frac{Q}{2}\right)H + \left(\frac{D}{Q}\right)S + RD$$

$$TC_{840} = \frac{840}{2}(0.34) + \frac{4,000}{840}(30) + 0.85(4,000) = \$3,686$$

$$TC_{1,000} = \frac{1,000}{2}(0.32) + \frac{4,000}{1,000}(30) + 0.80(4,000) = \$3,480$$

Because $3,480 < $3,686, the minimum-cost order quantity is 1,000 light bulbs.

Comment. Quantity discount may result from economies of scale in production as well as in transportation (a truckload is cheaper per unit weight of load than a less-than-truckload). Also, in practice it is also possible to get a discount for total *dollars* of all goods purchased during a year from a supplier.

EOQ With Planned Shortage

When holding cost per unit is large and the customer can wait, a company may decide to have a **planned shortage**, that is, to intentionally allow shortage. We assume that all shorted demand will be back-ordered (i.e., all customers will wait until the beginning of the next order cycle). However, the back-ordered demand will incur shortage cost proportional to the length of the time a unit is back-ordered (similar to inventory holding cost). We represent this cost and the number of units back-ordered as:

planned shortage
Intentionally allowing shortage.

B = Back-order cost per unit per year
Q_b = Quantity back-ordered per order cycle

We also make the same assumptions as in the basic EOQ model, except that we allow shortages which are all back-ordered. The inventory position in this case can be graphed as in Figure 12-10, where

T = Length of an order cycle (in days)
t = Time period (during an order cycle) when inventory position is non-negative
t_b = Time period (during an order cycle) when inventory position is negative (i.e., back-order occurs).

FIGURE 12-10 ▶

Applicability of Inventory position for the EOQ with planned shortage model.

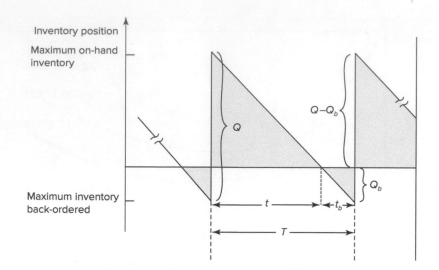

When the next order arrives, the back-ordered demand is satisfied first; the inventory position just after an order arrival will be $Q - Q_b$. Let d = Demand rate per day. Because $Q - Q_b$ units are used up at the rate of d units per day, then $Q - Q_b = d \times t$, or:

$t = \dfrac{Q - Q_b}{d}$. Similarly, $t_b = \dfrac{Q_b}{d}$ and $T = t + t_b = \dfrac{Q}{d}$. Hence,

$$\frac{t}{T} = \frac{\dfrac{Q - Q_b}{d}}{\dfrac{Q}{d}} = \frac{Q - Q_b}{Q} \text{ and } \frac{t_b}{T} = \frac{\dfrac{Q_b}{d}}{\dfrac{Q}{d}} = \frac{Q_b}{Q}$$

Therefore, average inventory on hand during the year is:

$$\frac{Q - Q_b}{2} \times \frac{t}{T} + 0\left(\frac{t_b}{T}\right) = \frac{(Q - Q_b)^2}{2Q},$$

and average level of back-orders during the year is:

$$\frac{Q_b}{2} \times \frac{t_b}{T} + 0\left(\frac{t}{T}\right) = \frac{Q_b^2}{2Q}$$

Finally, the total annual inventory control cost:

TC = Annual ordering cost + Annual holding cost + Annual back-order cost

$$= \left(\frac{D}{Q}\right)S + \left(\frac{(Q - Q_b)^2}{2Q}\right)H + \left(\frac{Q^2}{2Q}\right)B$$

Taking the derivative of TC with respect to Q_b, setting it equal to zero, and solving for Q_b, we get:

$$Q_b = Q\left(\frac{H}{H + B}\right) \tag{12-10}$$

Taking the derivative of TC with respect to Q, setting it equal to zero, multiplying it by $2Q^2$, and rearranging, we get:

$$-2DS + Q^2H - Q_b^2(H + B) = 0 \tag{12-11}$$

Substituting Formula 12-10 into Formula 12-11 and solving for Q, we get:

$$Q = \sqrt{\frac{2DS}{H}\left(\frac{H + B}{B}\right)} \qquad \text{optimal order quantity} \tag{12-12}$$

Annual demand for a particular model of refrigerator at an appliance store is 50 units. The holding cost per unit per year is $200. The back-order cost per unit per year is estimated to be $500. Ordering cost from the manufacturer is $10 per order. Determine the optimal order quantity and the back-order quantity per order cycle.

SOLUTION

$D = 50$ units per year
$H = \$200$ per unit per year
$B = \$500$ per unit per year
$S = \$10$ per order

$$Q = \sqrt{\frac{2DS}{H}\left(\frac{H+B}{B}\right)} = \sqrt{\frac{2(50)(10)}{200}\left(\frac{200+500}{500}\right)}$$
$= 2.65$, round to 3 units.

$$Q_b = Q\left(\frac{H}{H+B}\right) = 3\left(\frac{200}{200+500}\right) = 0.86, \text{ round to } 1.$$

This has the following interpretation: Allow the inventory level to drop to zero. Then, when there is a customer demand (for a unit), place an order of three fridges from the manufacturer.

Determining the Reorder Point

The **reorder point (ROP)** is the inventory position (Inventory position = On hand + On order − Back-ordered) at or below which an order should be issued.

If demand and purchase lead time are both constant, the reorder point is simply:

$$\text{ROP} = d \times \text{LT} \tag{12-13}$$

where

d = Demand rate (units per day or week or month)
LT = Lead time (in days or weeks or months)

> **reorder point (ROP)** The inventory position at or below which the item is reordered.

A patient takes two special tablets per day. The order is delivered to his home seven days after it is called in. At what point should the patient reorder?

SOLUTION

Usage = 2 tablets a day
Lead time = 7 days

ROP = Usage × Lead time
= 2 tablets per day × 7 days = 14 tablets

Thus, the patient should reorder when 14 tablets are left.

Note: Demand and lead time must have the same time units.

When variability is present in demand and/or lead time, it creates the possibility that the actual demand during a lead time will exceed the expected demand during a lead time. Consequently, it becomes necessary to carry additional inventory, called *safety stock*, to reduce the risk of running out of inventory (i.e., shortage) or to reduce the number of units short. The reorder point then is increased by the amount of the safety stock:

ROP = Expected demand during a lead time + Safety stock

For example, if the expected demand during a lead time is 100 units, and the desired amount of safety stock is 10 units, then the ROP would be 110 units.

Figure 12-11 illustrates how safety stock can reduce number of units short or risk of shortage during a lead time (LT). Note that for the EOQ/ROP model, shortage protection is needed only during purchase lead times.

FIGURE 12-11 ▶

Safety stock reduces the risk of shortage or the number of units short during a lead time.

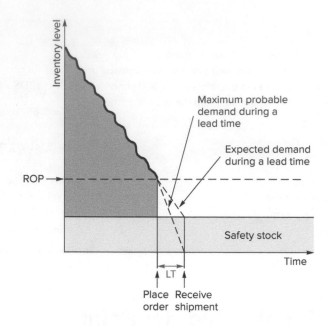

The amount of safety stock that is appropriate for an item depends on:

1. Demand and lead time variability.

2. The desired service level.

There are many ways to define the service level. We will focus on the following two:

1. Lead time service level.

2. Annual service level.

> **lead time service level** Probability that demand will not exceed inventory on hand during a lead time.

Lead time service level is the probability that demand will not exceed inventory on hand during a lead time; that is, the probability of no shortage during a cycle. It can be seen that lead time service level is also equal to the fraction of cycles with no shortage. **Annual service level** is the proportion of annual demand filled from stocks on hand, also called *fill rate*.

> **annual service level** The proportion of annual demand met from stocks on hand. Also called *fill* rate.

In this chapter, we assume that management has a desired service level for a group of items. Alternatively, shortage cost can be used to determine the appropriate service level. We will use the shortage cost only in the last section of this chapter on the single period model.

The formula commonly used to determine the safety stock, in the presence of demand and/or lead time variability, assumes that demand during a lead time is Normally distributed. Thus,

$$\text{Safety stock} = z \cdot \sigma_{d\text{LT}} \tag{12-14}$$

where

z = Safety factor; number of standard deviations above the expected demand

$\sigma_{d\text{LT}}$ = Standard deviation of demand during a lead time

In the above formula, z is related to the service level. However, the exact nature of this relationship depends on the type of service level used: lead time or annual. First, we will describe it for the lead time service level.

ROP Using Lead Time Service Level

Given a desired lead time service level, the value of z can be determined directly from the (standard) Normal probability table, Appendix B, Table B (see Figure 12-12). In this figure, the term *stockout* is equivalent to *shortage*. Note that the area under the curve is 1, so Stockout risk = 1 − Lead time service level. For example, if the desired lead time service level is 0.95, stock-out risk will be 0.05. Also note that the smaller the desired stock-out risk, the greater the value of z.

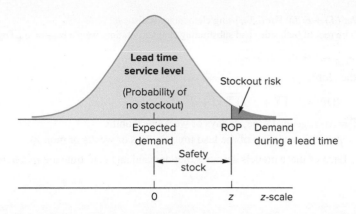

Distribution of demand during a lead time, lead time service level, and ROP.

EXAMPLE 12-8

The manager of a hardware store has determined from historical records that demand for a given type and size of bagged cement during its lead time could be described by a Normal distribution that has a mean of 50 bags and a standard deviation of 5 bags. Answer these questions, assuming that the manager is willing to accept a stockout risk of no more than 3 percent during a lead time:

a. What value of z is appropriate?

b. How many bags of safety stock should be held?

c. What reorder point should be used?

SOLUTION

Expected demand during a lead time = 50 bags

$$\sigma_{dLT} = 5 \text{ bags}$$

Stock-out risk = 3 percent

a. From Appendix B, Table B, using a service level of $1 - 0.03 = 0.97$, we obtain a value of $z = 1.88$.

b. Safety stock = $z\sigma_{dLT} = 1.88(5) = 9.40$ bags

c. ROP = Expected demand during a lead time + Safety stock = $50 + 9.40 = 59.40$; round to 59 bags

When data on demand during a lead time are not readily available, its mean and standard deviation are not directly available. Nevertheless, data are generally available on daily or weekly or monthly demand, and on the lengths of lead times. Using these data, a manager can determine whether demand and lead time are variable, and the related standard deviations. For these situations, one of the following formulas can be used:

If only demand is variable, then $\sigma_{dLT} = \sqrt{LT}\,\sigma_d$, and the reorder point is[5]

$$\text{ROP} = \bar{d}.\text{LT} + z\sqrt{LT}\,\sigma_d \tag{12-15}$$

where $\bar{d}$ = Average daily or weekly or monthly demand

σ_d = Standard deviation of daily or weekly or monthly demand

LT = Lead time in days or weeks or months

If both demand and lead time are variable, then[6]

---

[5] If daily demand d_i are independent and have the same variance σ_d^2, then it can be shown, using elementary statistics, that $\text{Var}(d_1+...+d_{LT}) = \text{Var}(d_1)+...+\text{Var}(d_{LT}) = LT\,\text{Var}(d)$. Taking square root of both sides and substituting chapter notation, we get $\sigma_{dLT} = \sqrt{LT}\sigma_d$.

[6] The result follows from the well known variance decomposition formula:

Given two random variables X and Y,

$\text{Var}\,X = E_X X^2 - (E_X X)^2$, by the definition of the variance; E = Expectations

$= E_Y(E_X(X^2|Y)) - E_Y(E_X(X|Y))^2$, conditioning on Y and then taking expectations with respect to Y

$= E_Y(\text{Var}_X(X|Y) + E_X(X|Y)^2) - E_Y(E_X(X|Y))^2$, by the definition of the first term

$= E_Y(\text{Var}_X(X|Y)) + E_Y(E_X(X|Y)^2) - E_Y(E_X(X|Y))^2$, expanding the first term

$= E_Y(\text{Var}_X(X|Y)) + \text{Var}_Y(E_X(X|Y))$, by the definition of the second term

Now let $X = d_1 + ... + d_{LT}$ and $Y = LT$. Then the variance decomposition formula becomes:

$$\text{Var}\left(\sum_{t=1}^{LT} d_t\right) = E_{LT}\left(\text{Var}\left(\sum_{t=1}^{LT} d_t | LT\right)\right) + \text{Var}_{LT}\left(E\left(\sum_{t=1}^{LT} d_t | LT\right)\right)$$

$$= E(\text{LT}) \operatorname{Var}(d_t) + E(d_t)^2 \operatorname{Var}(\text{LT}), \text{ using elementary statistics}$$

Taking square root of both sides and substituting chapter notation, we get $\sigma_{d\text{LT}} = \sqrt{\overline{\text{LT}}\sigma_d^2 + \bar{d}^2\sigma_{\text{LT}}^2}$

[handwritten margin note: if both demand and lead time are variable]

$$\sigma_{d\text{LT}} = \sqrt{\overline{\text{LT}}\,\sigma_d^2 + \bar{d}^2\,\sigma_{\text{LT}}^2}$$

and the reorder point is

$$\text{ROP} = \bar{d} \cdot \overline{\text{LT}} + z\sqrt{\overline{\text{LT}}\,\sigma_d^2 + \bar{d}^2\,\sigma_{\text{LT}}^2} \tag{12-16}$$

Where $\overline{\text{LT}} = $ *Average* lead time, in days or weeks or months

$\sigma_{\text{LT}} = $ Standard deviation of the lead time, in days or weeks or months

Note: Each of these models assumes that demand and lead time are *independent*.

EXAMPLE 12-9 ▶

A restaurant uses an average of 50 jars of a special sauce each week. Weekly usage of sauce has a standard deviation of 3 jars. The manager is willing to accept no more than a 10 percent risk of stock-out during a lead time, which is two weeks. Assume the distribution of usage is Normal.

a. Which of the above formulas is appropriate for this situation? Why?

b. Determine the value of z.

c. Determine the ROP.

SOLUTION

$\bar{d} = 50$ jars per week $\text{LT} = 2$ weeks

$\sigma_d = 3$ jars per week   Acceptable stock-out risk = 10 percent, so lead time service level is 0.90

a. Because only demand is variable (i.e., has a standard deviation), Formula 12-15 is appropriate.

b. From Appendix B, Table B, using a service level of 0.90, we obtain $z = 1.28$.

c. $\text{ROP} = \bar{d}.\text{LT} + z\sqrt{\text{LT}}\,\sigma_d = 50(2) + 1.28\sqrt{2}(3)$
$= 100 + 5.43 = 105.43$ round to 105 jars

Comment. The logic of Formula 12-15 may not be immediately obvious. The first part of the formula is the expected demand, which is the product of daily (or weekly or monthly) demand and the number of days (or weeks or months) of lead time. The second part of the formula is z times the standard deviation of demand during a lead time. Daily (or weekly or monthly) demand is assumed to be Normally distributed and has the same mean and standard deviation (see Figure 12-13). The standard deviation of demand for the entire lead time is found by summing the variances of daily (or weekly or monthly) demands and then taking the square root of that number. Note that, unlike variance, standard deviation is not additive. Hence, if lead time is, say, four days, the variance of demand during a lead time will equal the sum of the four daily variances, which is $4\sigma_d^2$. The standard deviation of demand during a lead time will be the square root of this, which is $2\sigma_d$. In general, this becomes $\sqrt{\text{LT}}\,\sigma_d$ and, hence, the last part of Formula 12-15.

FIGURE 12-13 ▶

Composition of the demand during a lead time.

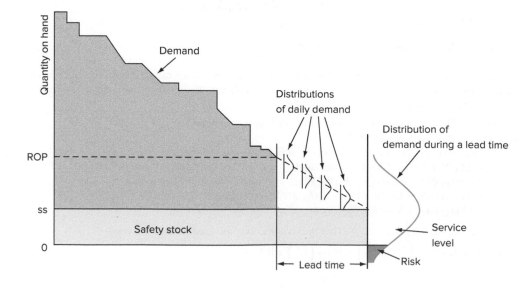

If daily demand is Normally distributed with a mean of 3 units and a standard deviation of 1 unit, and lead time is 2 days, then demand during a lead time will be Normally distributed with a mean of 6 units and a standard deviation of $\sqrt{1^2 + 1^2} = 1.41$ units (see the following charts where the

charts on the left side of the equation are the distributions of Day 1 and Day 2 demands and the right-hand-side chart is the distribution of the sum of Day 1 and Day 2 demands):

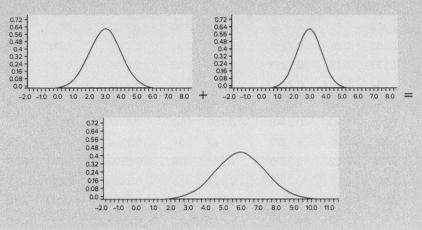

Also note that average demand is usually estimated using the forecast of demand, and standard deviation of demand is usually estimated using standard deviation of forecast error (i.e., square root of MSE or 1.25 × MAD; refer to Chapter 3).

Finally, we assumed that there is a desired service level from which z, and then safety stock and ROP, are determined. An alternative method to determine the ROP is based on cost of overstocking and cost of shortage. This analysis is similar to the single period model later in this chapter.

ROP Using Annual Service Level

Given a desired annual service level SL_{annual} (i.e., the proportion of demand filled directly from inventory on hand during the whole year; also known as the *item fill rate*), in order to find the required ROP, a three-step procedure should be used:

1. Calculate $E(z) = \dfrac{Q(1 - SL_{annual})}{\sigma_{dLT}}$ (12-17)

Where $E(z)$ = Standardized expected number of units short during an order cycle.[7]

2. Take the $E(z)$ to Table 12-3 and determine the associated z value.

3. Use the z value in the following general ROP formula or a specific one, such as Formula 12-15 or Formula 12-16:

     ROP = Expected demand during lead time + $z\sigma_{dLT}$

---

[7] SL_{annual} = (expected number of units filled during a cycle)(number of cycles per year)/annual demand
     = (expected number of units filled during a cycle)$(D/Q)/D$
     = expected number of units filled during a cycle/Q
     = $(Q$ − expected number of units short during a cycle$)/Q$, because average demand during an order cycle is Q. Multiplying both side by Q:
$Q(SL_{annual}) = Q$ − expected number of units short during a cycle
Rewriting:
Expected number of units short during a cycle = $Q(1 - SL_{annual})$
(Standardized expected number of units short during a cycle)$(\sigma_{dLT}) = Q(1 - SL_{annual})$,
This follows from statistics. Using $E(z)$ notation,
$E(z)(\sigma_{dLT}) = Q(1 - SL_{annual})$
$E(z) = \dfrac{Q(1 - SL_{annual})}{\sigma_{dLT}}$

TABLE 12-3 ▼

Lead time service levels and standardized expected numbers short during an order cycle for Normal distribution.

z	Lead Time Service Level	E(z)	z	Lead Time Service Level	E(z)	z	Lead Time Service Level	E(z)	z	Lead Time Service Level	E(z)
−2.40	0.0082	2.403	−0.80	0.2119	0.920	0.80	0.7881	0.120	2.40	0.9918	0.003
−2.36	0.0091	2.363	−0.76	0.2236	0.889	0.84	0.7995	0.112	2.44	0.9927	0.002
−2.32	0.0102	2.323	−0.72	0.2358	0.858	0.88	0.8106	0.104	2.48	0.9934	0.002
−2.28	0.0113	2.284	−0.68	0.2483	0.828	0.92	0.8212	0.097	2.52	0.9941	0.002
−2.24	0.0125	2.244	−0.64	0.2611	0.798	0.96	0.8315	0.089	2.56	0.9948	0.002
−2.20	0.0139	2.205	−0.60	0.2743	0.769	1.00	0.8413	0.083	2.60	0.9953	0.001
−2.16	0.0154	2.165	−0.56	0.2877	0.740	1.04	0.8508	0.077	2.64	0.9959	0.001
−2.12	0.0170	2.126	−0.52	0.3015	0.712	1.08	0.8599	0.071	2.68	0.9963	0.001
−2.08	0.0188	2.087	−0.48	0.3156	0.684	1.12	0.8686	0.066	2.72	0.9967	0.001
−2.04	0.0207	2.048	−0.44	0.3300	0.657	1.16	0.8770	0.061	2.76	0.9971	0.001
−2.00	0.0228	2.008	−0.40	0.3446	0.630	1.20	0.8849	0.056	2.80	0.9974	0.0008
−1.96	0.0250	1.969	−0.36	0.3594	0.597	1.24	0.8925	0.052	2.84	0.9977	0.0007
−1.92	0.0274	1.930	−0.32	0.3745	0.576	1.28	0.8997	0.048	2.88	0.9980	0.0006
−1.88	0.0301	1.892	−0.28	0.3897	0.555	1.32	0.9066	0.044	2.92	0.9982	0.0005
−1.84	0.0329	1.853	−0.24	0.4052	0.530	1.36	0.9131	0.040	2.96	0.9985	0.0004
−1.80	0.0359	1.814	−0.20	0.4207	0.507	1.40	0.9192	0.037	3.00	0.9987	0.0004
−1.76	0.0392	1.776	−0.16	0.4364	0.484	1.44	0.9251	0.034	3.04	0.9988	0.0003
−1.72	0.0427	1.737	−0.12	0.4522	0.462	1.48	0.9306	0.031	3.08	0.9990	0.0003
−1.68	0.0465	1.699	−0.08	0.4681	0.440	1.52	0.9357	0.028	3.12	0.9991	0.0002
−1.64	0.0505	1.661	−0.04	0.4840	0.419	1.56	0.9406	0.026	3.16	0.9992	0.0002
−1.60	0.0548	1.623	0.00	0.5000	0.399	1.60	0.9452	0.023	3.20	0.9993	0.0002
−1.56	0.0594	1.586	0.04	0.5160	0.379	1.64	0.9495	0.021	3.24	0.9994	0.0001
−1.52	0.0643	1.548	0.08	0.5319	0.360	1.68	0.9535	0.019	3.28	0.9995	0.0001
−1.48	0.0694	1.511	0.12	0.5478	0.342	1.72	0.9573	0.017	3.32	0.9995	0.0001
−1.44	0.0749	1.474	0.16	0.5636	0.324	1.76	0.9608	0.016	3.36	0.9996	0.0001
−1.40	0.0808	1.437	0.20	0.5793	0.307	1.80	0.9641	0.014	3.40	0.9997	0.0001
−1.36	0.0869	1.400	0.24	0.5948	0.290	1.84	0.9671	0.013			
−1.32	0.0934	1.364	0.28	0.6103	0.275	1.88	0.9699	0.012			
−1.28	0.1003	1.328	0.32	0.6255	0.256	1.92	0.9726	0.010			
−1.24	0.1075	1.292	0.36	0.6406	0.237	1.96	0.9750	0.009			
−1.20	0.1151	1.256	0.40	0.6554	0.230	2.00	0.9772	0.008			
−1.16	0.1230	1.221	0.44	0.6700	0.217	2.04	0.9793	0.008			
−1.12	0.1314	1.186	0.48	0.6844	0.204	2.08	0.9812	0.007			
−1.08	0.1401	1.151	0.52	0.6985	0.192	2.12	0.9830	0.006			
−1.04	0.1492	1.117	0.56	0.7123	0.180	2.16	0.9846	0.005			
−1.00	0.1587	1.083	0.60	0.7257	0.169	2.20	0.9861	0.005			
−0.96	0.1685	1.049	0.64	0.7389	0.158	2.24	0.9875	0.004			
−0.92	0.1788	1.017	0.68	0.7517	0.148	2.28	0.9887	0.004			
−0.88	0.1894	0.984	0.72	0.7642	0.138	2.32	0.9898	0.003			
−0.84	0.2005	0.952	0.76	0.7764	0.129	2.36	0.9909	0.003			

An inventory item has order quantity $Q = 250$ units, expected demand during a lead time $= 50$ units, and standard deviation of demand during a lead time $\sigma_{dLT} = 16$ units. Determine the ROP if the desired annual service level is (a) 0.997, and (b) 0.98.

SOLUTION

a. $E(z) = \dfrac{Q(1 - SL_{annual})}{\sigma_{dLT}} = \dfrac{250(1 - 0.997)}{16} = 0.047$

From Table 12-3, $E(z) = 0.047$ falls between $E(z) = 0.048$ with $z = 1.28$ and $E(z) = 0.044$ with $z = 1.32$. Therefore,

using interpolation, $z = 1.29$. Finally, ROP $= 50 + 1.29(16) = 70.64$; round to 71 units.

b. $E(z) = \dfrac{Q(1 - SL_{annual})}{\sigma_{dLT}} = \dfrac{250(1 - 0.98)}{16} = 0.3125$

From Table 12-3, $E(z) = 0.3125$ falls between $E(z) = 0.324$ with $z = 0.16$ and $E(z) = 0.307$ with $z = 0.20$. Therefore, using interpolation, $z = 0.19$. Finally, ROP $= 50 + 0.19(16) = 53.04$; round to 53 units.

Other Related Models

There are some variations of the EOQ/ROP or Min/Max models.

1. *Periodic review.* Instead of instantaneous review, inventory position is reviewed periodically— for example, every three days. Finding the optimal value for ROP or Min is complex.[8] Alternatively, simulation can be used. However, we can use the following conservative approximation. Let RP = Review period. To be safe, LT can be increased by RP. Then, when demand is variable and LT is constant, approximate values for Min and Max are:

$Min = \bar{d}(LT + RP) + z\sigma_d \sqrt{LT + RP}$ and

$Max = Min + EOQ.$

2. *Can-order model.* In this model, when an item's inventory position drops to or below its ROP, all related items (e.g., those bought from the same supplier) are investigated to see if their inventory position is at or below their can-order level. If so, they are ordered too (to bring their inventory level up to their Max).[9]

Fixed-Interval/Order-up-to Level Model and Coordinated Periodic Review Model

LO5

The *fixed-interval/order-up-to level model* is used when orders are placed at fixed time intervals (e.g., weekly, twice a month, etc.), and inventory position is brought up to the order-up-to level. This model is widely used by wholesalers/distributors and retailers, where all items from the same supplier are ordered at the same time. The order size tends to vary from interval to interval depending on demand during the previous interval. This is quite different from the EOQ/ROP model in which the order size remains fixed from cycle to cycle while the length of the cycle may vary (shorter if demand is above average and longer if demand is below average).

Grouping orders for items from the same supplier can produce savings in ordering, shipping, receiving, and paying costs. Furthermore, some situations do not readily lend themselves to continuous monitoring of inventory positions. Many retail operations (e.g., small drugstores, small grocery stores) fall into this category. The alternative for them is to use fixed-interval ordering, which requires only periodic checks of inventory positions.

Two decisions are needed to apply this model for a group of items from the same supplier: (1) the order interval, and (2) the order-up-to level for each item.

---

[8] See, for example, E. A. Silver, D. F. Pyke, and R. Peterson. *Inventory Management and Production Planning and Scheduling*, 3rd Ed. New York: John Wiley and Sons, 1998, pp. 336–341.

[9] See, for example, E. A. Silver, D. F. Pyke, and R. Peterson. *Inventory Management and Production Planning and Scheduling*, 3rd Ed. New York: John Wiley and Sons, 1998, pp. 434–435.

Determining the Order Interval

The order interval can be determined by minimizing the total annual holding and ordering costs of all the SKUs received from a particular supplier. The complication is that there are two components to the ordering cost: the cost of issuing a purchase order, and the cost of ordering each line item (SKU) in it. In the basic model, we assume that every SKU is ordered at every order time, no matter how small its order quantity is. Later, we present the case where not every SKU is ordered at every order time (called the *coordinated periodic review model*).

Let

OI = Order interval (in fraction of a year)

S = Fixed ordering cost per purchase order excluding line items (**purchase order ordering cost**)

s = Variable ordering cost per SKU included in the purchase order (**line item ordering cost**)

For simplicity, we assume s is the same for every SKU.

n = Number of SKUs purchased from the supplier

R_j = Unit cost of SKU_j, $j = 1, ..., n$

i = Annual holding cost rate

D_j = Annual demand of SKU_j, $j = 1, ..., n$

For each SKU_j from this supplier, we will purchase enough to last until the next order time; that is, $Q_j = D_j \cdot OI$.

$$\text{Total annual inventory control cost (TC)} = \sum \left(\frac{D_j \cdot OI}{2}\right) R_j \cdot i + (S + ns)\left(\frac{1}{OI}\right)$$

Taking the derivative of TC with respect to OI, setting it equal to 0, and solving for OI, we get the optimal order interval:

$$OI^* = \sqrt{\frac{2(S + ns)}{i \sum D_j R_j}} \tag{12-18}$$

purchase order ordering cost Fixed ordering cost per purchase order excluding line items.

line item ordering cost Variable ordering cost per SKU included in the purchase order.

EXAMPLE 12-12

Three parts are purchased from the same supplier. The basic cost of placing an order for one of the SKUs is $1.50. The inclusion of each additional SKU costs $0.50 more. The annual holding cost rate is 24 percent of unit cost. The annual demands (in units) and unit prices are given below. Assume that the buying company works 250 days a year. Calculate the optimal order interval.

SKU	Annual Demand	Unit Price
1	12,000	0.50
2	8,000	0.30
3	700	0.10

SOLUTION

$S = 1.50 - 0.50 = \$1.00$

$s = 0.50$

$i = 0.24$

$$OI^* = \sqrt{\frac{2(1.00 + 3(0.50))}{0.24(12,000 \times 0.50 + 8,000 \times 0.30 + 700 \times 0.10)}}$$

$= 0.0496$ year $= 12.4$ days

Round to 12 days.

Determining the Order-up-to Levels

The order-up-to level for an item should be enough so that the item lasts until the next shipment arrives (after an order interval plus a lead time). This fact is illustrated in the bottom chart in Figure 12-14, which also contrasts the fixed-interval model with the EOQ/ROP model. Note that the order quantity (the difference between order-up-to level and inventory position) for the fixed-interval model will vary from one order to another (depending on size of demand during the past interval).

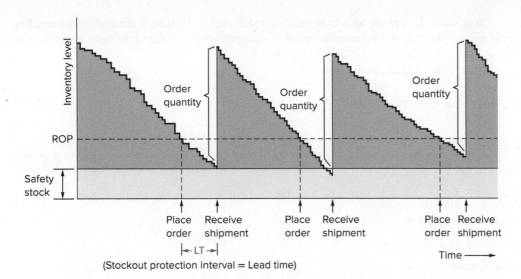

Comparison of the EOQ/ROP (on top) and the fixed-interval (on bottom) models.

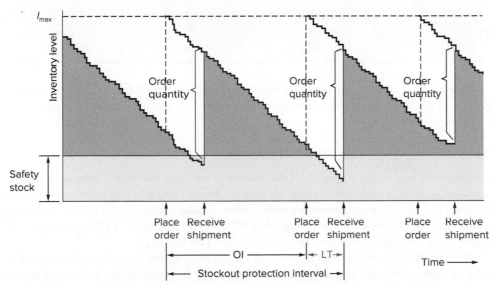

In the presence of demand and lead time variability, there is a need for safety stocks. The two models also differ in terms of safety stocks. The fixed-interval model must have stock-out protection until the *next* order arrives, but the EOQ/ROP model needs protection only during the lead time. Therefore, the fixed-interval model necessitates a larger amount of safety stock for a given service level.

Therefore, order-up-to level or I_{max} can be determined by:

$$I_{max} = \text{Expected demand during an order interval plus a lead time} + \text{Safety stock} \qquad (12\text{-}19)$$

Like the EOQ/ROP model, the fixed-interval model can have variations in demand and/or lead time. For the sake of simplicity and because it is the most frequently encountered situation, the discussion here will focus only on the *variable demand* and *constant lead time* case. As in the EOQ/ROP model, we assume that demand during an order interval and a lead time is Normally distributed.

Therefore, Formula 12-19 becomes

$$I_{max} = \bar{d}(\text{OI} + \text{LT}) + z\sigma_d\sqrt{\text{OI} + \text{LT}} \qquad (12\text{-}20)$$

where

$\bar{d}$ = *Average* daily or weekly or monthly demand

OI = Order interval (length of time between orders); in days or weeks or months

LT = Lead time in days or weeks or months

z = Safety factor; number of standard deviations above the expected demand

σ_d = Standard deviation of daily or weekly or monthly demand

Note that I_{max} does not have to be recalculated at each order time if demand has no trend or seasonality. Also note that because the period of vulnerability covers the whole order interval, there is only one definition of service level for this model.

Order quantity Q can be determined by:

$$Q = I_{max} - \text{Inventory position} \tag{12-21}$$

Given the following information for a SKU, determine its order-up-to level and amount to order (i.e., order quantity).

$\bar{d} = 30$ units per day; Desired service level = 99 percent

$\sigma_d = 3$ units per day; Inventory position at reorder time = 71 units;

LT = 2 days; OI = 7 days

SOLUTION

$z = 2.33$ for 99 percent service level (from Appendix B, Table B)

$$I_{max} = \bar{d}(OI + LT) + z\sigma_d\sqrt{OI + LT}$$
$$= 30(7 + 2) + 2.33(3)\sqrt{7 + 2}$$
$$= 291 \text{ units}$$

Amount to order = I_{max} — Inventory position = 291 — 71 = 220 units

Note that average demand is usually estimated using forecast of demand, and the standard deviation of demand is usually estimated using standard deviation of the forecast error (square root of MSE or $1.25 \times$ MAD).

Coordinated Periodic Review Model

In the fixed-interval model, it might cost less to order some items every two, three, or more order intervals than to order them at every interval, because their holding cost may be less than the line-item ordering cost. The **coordinated periodic review model** accommodates this by determining a common order interval OI for reviewing every SKU and a multiple m_i of OI for ordering stock keeping unit i, SKU$_i$ (this determines the order-up-to level for SKU$_i$).

coordinated periodic review model A variation of fixed interval model where an item is ordered to meet demand for a multiple m of a common order interval.

After planning the model (i.e., determining OI and m_is), during operation and control of the model, at a review time the inventory position of each SKU is compared with its forecast demand for the next OI plus lead time plus safety stocks (just like ROP), and if inventory position is less, a quantity that will bring the inventory position up to the SKU's order-up-to level is ordered. The order-up-to level for SKU$_i$ should cover its forecast demand during the next m_i order intervals plus a lead time plus safety stocks only for the next order interval plus lead time.

The determination of optimal values for OI and m_is is complicated. We will use a simple heuristic:[10]

1. Find the SKU with largest annual dollar value D_iR_i. Suppose, it is SKU$_k$. Let $m_k = 1$.

2. For every other SKU$_j$, calculate

$$m_j = \sqrt{\frac{s\,D_kR_k}{D_jR_j(S + s)}} \tag{12-22}$$

and round it to the nearest integer greater than or equal to 1.

3. Calculate OI using:

$$OI^* = \sqrt{\frac{2\left(S + s\sum_{j=1}^{n}\frac{1}{m_j}\right)}{i\sum_{j=1}^{n}m_jD_jR_j}} \tag{12-23}$$

---

[10] E.A. Silver, D.F. Pyke, and R. Peterson. *Inventory Management and Production Planning and Scheduling*, 3rd ed. New York: John Wiley and Sons, 1998, pp. 426–429.

The rationale for this heuristic is that both purchase order ordering cost (S) and line item ordering cost (s) are charged to the SKU_k because SKU_k will be ordered at every order interval. Then, m_j values for other SKUs are determined using Formula 12-22 relative to m_k. Finally, OI is calculated using Formula 12-23, which is very similar to Formula 12-18 but uses $m_j D_j$ as the demand for SKU_j.

◀ **EXAMPLE 12-14**

We use the same data as Example 12-12 in order to compare the coordinated periodic review model with the fixed-interval model. Recall that $S = \$1.00$, $s = 0.50$, and $i = 0.24$.

The annual demand and unit prices are repeated below. Calculate the m_js and OI.

SKU	Annual Demand (D_j)	Unit Price (R_j)	$D_j R_j$
1	12,000	0.50	$6,000
2	8,000	0.30	$2,400
3	700	0.10	$70

SOLUTION

The SKU with largest $D_j R_j$ is SKU_1. Therefore, $m_1 = 1$.

$$m_2 = \sqrt{\frac{0.5}{2{,}400}\frac{\$6{,}000}{1+0.5}} = 0.91; \text{round to 1. Therefore, } m_2 = 1.$$

$$m_3 = \sqrt{\frac{0.5}{70}\frac{\$6{,}000}{1+0.5}} = 5.35; \text{round to 5. Therefore, } m_3 = 5.$$

$$OI^* = \sqrt{\frac{2(1.00 + 0.5(1 + 1 + 0.20))}{0.24(1 \times 6{,}000 + 1 \times 2{,}400 + 5 \times 70)}}$$

$$= 0.0447 \text{ year} = 11.2 \text{ days}$$

(because the buyer works 250 days a year)

Thus, OI is only slightly smaller than in Example 12-12, but the plan for SKU_3, because of its small annual dollar usage and unit price, is to order it every five order times.

Suppose LT and safety stocks are negligible. Demand for SKU_3 during the next 11 work days $= 700(11)/250 = 30.8$ units. Therefore, the order-up-to level for SKU_3 should be set to $5(30.8) = 154$ units.

A Related Model

A common variation of the fixed-interval/order-up-to level model is when an order is placed at a review time only if the order quantity is larger than a minimum Q_{min}. Finding the optimal order-up-to level in this case is complex, but one can use the following conservative approximation:

$$I_{max} = \bar{d}(OI + LT) + z\sigma_d \sqrt{OI + LT} + Q_{min}$$

The Single Period Model

The **single period model** (sometimes referred to as the *news-vendor problem*) is used for ordering perishables (e.g., fresh fruits and vegetables, baked goods, seafood, cut flowers) and other items that have a limited useful life (e.g., newspapers, magazines, spare parts for specialized equipment). The *period* for a spare part is the life of the equipment, assuming that the part cannot be used for other equipment. What sets unsold or unused goods apart is that they are not typically carried over from one period to the next, at least not without penalty. Day-old baked goods, for instance, are often sold at reduced prices; leftover seafood may be discarded; and out-of-date magazines may be offered to used book stores at bargain rates. There may even be some cost associated with disposal of leftover goods.

single period model An inventory model for ordering perishables and other items with limited useful lives.

Analysis of the single period model generally focuses on two costs: shortage and excess. Shortage cost may include a charge for loss of customer goodwill as well as the opportunity cost of the lost sale (the unrealized profit per unit). Usually the latter is used:

$$C_{shortage} = C_s = \text{Revenue per unit} - \text{Purchase cost per unit}$$

We assume $C_s \geq 0$. If a shortage or stock-out relates to an item used in production or to a spare part for a machine, then shortage cost is the cost of lost production.

Excess cost pertains to items left over at the end of the period. In effect, excess cost is the difference between purchase cost and salvage value. That is,

$$C_{excess} = C_e = \text{Purchase cost per unit} - \text{Salvage value per unit}$$

If there is a cost associated with disposal of excess items, then the salvage value will be negative and will therefore *increase* the excess cost per unit. On the other hand, if salvage value is larger than the purchase cost, then C_e will be negative. However, in this case, we must have $C_s + C_e > 0$, because salvage value per unit must be less than revenue per unit.

> **excess cost** Difference between purchase cost and salvage value of an item left at the end of the period.

The goal of the single period model is to identify the order quantity, or stocking level, that will minimize the long-run (expected) total excess and shortage cost.

There are two general categories of problems that we will consider: those for which demand can be approximated by a continuous distribution (such as Uniform or Normal) and those for which demand can be approximated by a discrete distribution (such as historical frequencies or Poisson). The nature of the item can indicate which type of model might be appropriate. For example, demand for liquids and items whose individual units are small but whose demand is large (such as muffins or newspapers) tends to vary over some *continuous scale,* thus lending itself to description by a continuous distribution. Demand for spare parts, expensive flowers, and computers is expressed in terms of the *number of units* demanded and lends itself to description by a discrete distribution.

Continuous Stocking Levels

The concept of identifying an optimal stocking level (i.e., order quantity) is perhaps easiest to visualize when demand is Uniform. Choosing the stocking level is similar to balancing a seesaw, but instead of a person on each end of the seesaw, we have the excess cost per unit (C_e) on one end of the seesaw and the shortage cost per unit (C_s) on the other. The seesaw represents the Uniform distribution. The optimal stocking level is analogous to the fulcrum of the seesaw; the stocking level equalizes the cost weights, as illustrated in Figure 12-15. If actual demand exceeds the balance point S_o, there is a shortage; hence, C_s is on the right end of the seesaw. Similarly, if demand is less than S_o, there is an excess, so C_e is on the left end of the seesaw. When $C_e = C_s$, the optimal stocking level will be halfway between the endpoints of the seesaw. If one cost is greater than the other, S_o will be closer to the larger cost.

FIGURE 12-15 ▶

The optimal stocking level (i.e., order quantity) balances unit shortage and excess costs.

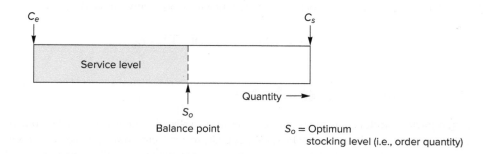

S_o = Optimum stocking level (i.e., order quantity)

The *service level* (SL) is the *probability* that demand will not exceed the stocking level. Calculation of the service level is the key to determining the optimal stocking level, S_o. It can be shown that in order to balance the seesaw on the fulcrum, service level should be chosen so that:

$$\text{Service level} = \frac{C_s}{C_s + C_e} \tag{12-24}$$

Therefore, the optimal stocking level, S_o, is that point in the demand distribution that satisfies: Probability (demand $< S_0$) = SL.

A cafeteria buys muffins daily. Demand varies Uniformly between 30 and 50 muffins per day. The cafeteria pays 20 cents per muffin and charges 80 cents per muffin. Unsold muffins are discarded at the end of the day. Find the optimal stocking level and the stock-out risk for that quantity.

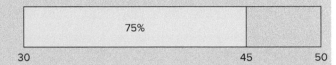

SOLUTION

C_e = Cost per unit − Salvage value per unit
  = \$0.20 − \$0
  = \$0.20 per unit

C_s = Revenue per unit − Cost per unit
  = \$0.80 − \$0.20
  = \$0.60 per unit

$$SL = \frac{C_s}{C_s + C_e}$$
$$= \frac{\$0.60}{\$0.60 + \$0.20} = 0.75$$

Thus, the optimal stocking level (i.e., order quantity) must satisfy 75 percent of demand. For the Uniform distribution, this will be at a point equal to the minimum demand plus 75 percent of the difference between maximum and minimum demands:

$$S_o = 30 + 0.75(50 - 30) = 45 \text{ muffins}$$

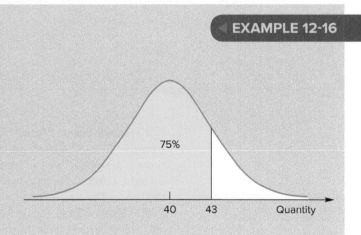

The stock-out risk at stocking level of 45 muffins is $1.00 - 0.75 = 0.25$.

A similar approach can be applied when demand is Normally distributed.

Suppose that the distribution of demand for muffins in the previous example was approximately Normal with a mean of 40 muffins per day and a standard deviation of 5 muffins per day. Find the optimal stocking level for the muffins. Recall that $C_s = \$0.60$, $C_e = \$0.20$, and SL = 0.75.

SOLUTION

This indicates that 75 percent of the area under the Normal curve must be to the left of the stocking level. Appendix B, Table B shows that a value of z between 0.67 and 0.68, say, 0.675, will satisfy this. Thus,

$$S_o = 40 + 0.675(5) = 43.375 \text{ or } 43 \text{ muffins.}$$

Discrete Stocking Levels

When stocking levels are discrete rather than continuous, the ratio $C_s/(C_s + C_e)$ usually does not coincide with the cumulative probability of a stocking level (e.g., the ratio may be *between* the cumulative probability of five and six units). The optimal stocking level in this case is the *higher level* (e.g., six units). In other words, choose the stocking level so that the cumulative probability equals or just *exceeds the ratio*. Figure 12-16 illustrates this concept.

FIGURE 12-16 ▶

The cumulative probability for optimal discrete stocking level must equal or just exceed the ratio $C_s/(C_s + C_e)$.

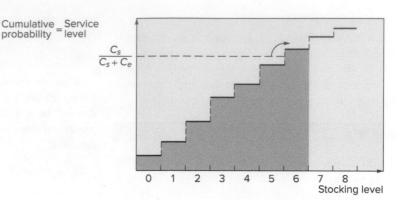

Cumulative probability = Service level

$$\frac{C_s}{C_s + C_e}$$

Stocking level

EXAMPLE 12-17 ▶

Historical records on the number of units of a spare part used during the life of an old press (shown in the following table) are to be used to estimate number of units of the spare part in a similar but new press. Stock-out cost involves downtime expenses and special ordering costs. These average $4,200 per unit short. The spare part costs $1,200 each, and an unused part has $400 salvage value. Determine the optimal stocking level for the spare part.

SOLUTION

$C_s = \$4,200$, $C_e = 1,200 - 400 = \$800$,

$$\text{SL} = \frac{C_s}{C_s + C_e} = \frac{\$4,200}{\$4,200 + \$800} = 0.84$$

The Cumulative Probability column indicates the fraction of time that demand was equal to or less than some amount. For example, Demand ≤ 1 unit occurred 60 percent of the time, or Demand ≤ 2 units occurred 90 percent of the time. Go down the table until cumulative probabilities just exceed service level of 84 percent. This is 0.90, which relates to 2 units.

Number of Units Used	Probability	Cumulative Probability
0................................	0.20	0.20
1................................	0.40	0.60
2................................	0.30	0.90
3................................	0.10	1.00
4 or more..................	0.00	
	1.00	

The logic behind Formula 12-24 can be seen by solving Example 12-17 using a *decision table* approach. Table 12-4 illustrates this approach. The table enumerates the expected cost of each combination of stocking level and demand. For instance, if the stocking level is three, and demand turns out to be zero (see the blue-shaded cell), that would result in an excess of three units, at a cost of $800 each. The probability of a demand of zero units is 0.20, so the expected cost of that cell is 0.20(3)($800) = $480. Similarly, if no units are stocked and demand is two (see the yellow-shaded cell), the expected cost is the probability of demand being two (i.e., 0.30) multiplied by two units

TABLE 12-4 ▼

Expected cost for each possible outcome.

	And the demand probabilities are				
If the stocking level is	0 prob. = 0.20	1 prob. = 0.40	2 prob. = 0.30	3 prob. = 0.10	The expected cost will be
0	$S = D$ $0	1 unit short 0.40(1) ($4,200) = $1,680	2 units short 0.30(2) ($4,200) = $2,520	3 units short 0.10(3) ($4,200) = $1,260	$5,460
1	1-unit excess 0.20(1) ($800) = $160	$S = D$ $0	1 unit short 0.30(1) ($4,200) = $1,260	2 units short 0.10(2) ($4,200) = $840	$2,260
2	2-unit excess 0.20(2) ($800) = $320	1-unit excess 0.40(1) ($800) = $320	$S = D$ $0	1 unit short 0.10(1) ($4,200) = $420	$1,060
3	3-unit excess 0.20(3) ($800) = $480	2-unit excess 0.40(2) ($800) = $640	1-unit excess 0.30(1) ($800) = $240	$S = D$ $0	$1,360

multiplied by the shortage cost per unit. Thus, the expected cost is 0.30(2)($4,200) = $2,520. For the cases in which the demand and stocking level are the same (the green-shaded cells), Supply = Demand, so there is neither a shortage nor an excess, and thus the cost is $0. The expected cost for each stocking level is the sum of the expected costs of each demand. For example, the expected cost of 0 stocking level is $0 + $1,680 + $2,520 + $1,260 = $5,400.

The lowest expected cost is $1,060, which occurs for the stocking level of two units, which agrees with the SL ratio approach in Example 12-17.

Example 12-18 illustrates how to solve a problem when demand is Poisson distribution.

EXAMPLE 12-18

Demand for long-stemmed red roses at a small flower shop on a slow day can be approximated by a Poisson distribution that has a mean of four dozen roses. Profit on the roses is $3 per dozen. Leftover roses are marked down and sold the next day at a loss of $2 per dozen. What is the optimal stocking level?

Demand (dozen)	Cumulative Probability
0	0.018
1	0.092
2	0.238
3	0.434
4	0.629
5	0.785
⋮	⋮

SOLUTION

Obtain the cumulative probabilities from the Poisson table (Appendix B, Table C) for a mean of 4.0:

$$C_s = \$3, \quad C_e = \$2, \quad SL = \frac{C_s}{C_s + C_e} = \frac{\$3}{\$3 + \$2} = 0.60$$

Compare the service level (ratio) to the cumulative probabilities. Go down the table until cumulative probability just exceeds SL = 0.60. This is 0.629, which relates to four dozen roses.

Multi-Echelon Inventory Management

L07

Usually inventory of a product is kept at more than one location in the outbound-distribution supply chain, for example, at the manufacturer's distribution centre (DC), at the retailer's warehouse, and at the retailer's store. Also, inventory of a part may be kept at various locations in the inbound supply chain, for example, at the supplier and at the manufacturer's plant. The single location inventory models described so far can be used at each location independently, but because demands are dependent in a **multi-echelon** supply chain, this will be suboptimal. Also, because of decentralized control, the total orders from the downstream facilities may be overwhelming (all "customers" ordering at the same time). In addition, the bullwhip effect of Chapter 11 can arise.

> **multi-echelon** A supply chain with multiple levels or stages.

Various methods are used for coordinated control of inventories in a supply chain:

- Multi-echelon control
- Distribution requirements planning
- Inventory optimization

Multi-Echelon Control

A distribution network is usually like a tree on its side (see Figure 12-17).

The warehouse echelon (level) is the warehouse and all the retailers it feeds (the dashed box in the figure). In multi-echelon control, retailers transmit their point of sale (POS) data to the warehouse. Retailers may use their own inventory control model (e.g., EOQ/ROP or fixed-interval

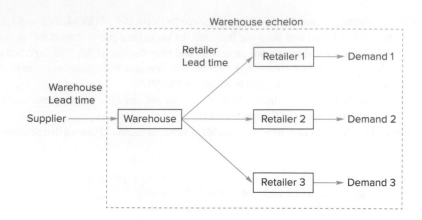

model). The warehouse determines its inventory control model parameters as follows: (1) its demand is forecasted based on total POS data; (2) its echelon lead time is equal to the sum of lead time from supplier to warehouse (warehouse lead time) and lead time of warehouse to a retailer (retailer lead time); and (3) its echelon inventory position is the total inventory at all retailers, warehouse, and en route to them minus any back orders to end customers. In other words, the warehouse plans for the whole warehouse echelon, which includes end-customer demands, not the orders of retailers from the warehouse.

Distribution Requirements Planning (DRP)

Distribution requirements planning (DRP) is a planning method that determines time-phased replenishment schedules between a manufacturer's facility and DCs (or between a DC and retail stores). DRP is like MRP (see Chapter 14) but is for distribution planning, not material planning. For each SKU, DRP starts with forecast demand at DCs and works backward in time, offsetting for replenishment lead times. DRP requires:

- Forecast of demand at each DC (usually done by the DC itself).
- Current inventory on hand and on order.
- Order quantities/batch sizes.
- Lead times.

Note: The manufacturer may not be able to meet the orders because of capacity limitation. Solutions include using overtime, outsourcing, and putting retailers on allocation. *Allocation* here means that the retailers will not receive all of their order. A common allocation method is called *fair share*, which bases allocation on Actual sales – Inventory on hand, and not order quantities (which may be inflated at the time of shortage).

Inventory Optimization

inventory optimization A method that determines the location and optimal level of inventory in the supply chain.

Inventory optimization is a method that determines the location and optimal level of inventory in the supply chain. It can be described as follows: given customer-promised LT, probability distribution of demand at each inventory location, cost of holding inventory at each location, processing time at each location, and transport times, determine committed LT (to the next location in supply chain) and amount of inventory to be kept at each location in order to minimize total inventory holding cost.

If a location does not hold inventory, its committed LT has to be met within its incoming raw-material lead time and processing time. The fixed-interval inventory model is used at each stocking location. A special type of optimization method called dynamic programming is used to solve this problem. For an application of inventory optimization, see the "Procter & Gamble" OM in Action.

Procter & Gamble

Procter & Gamble (P&G) is the world's largest consumer products company with core product categories of baby care, feminine care, family care, grooming, oral care, personal health care, hair care, skin and personal care, fabric care, and home care. P&G's billion dollar brands include Always, Braun, Crest, Fusion, Gillette, Head & Shoulders, Mach3, Olay, Oral-B, Pantene, Bounty, Charmin, Dawn, Downy, Gain, Pampers, and Tide.

Within each category, research and development, product supply, and the brand organization develop, manufacture, and market the products. P&G has over 125 P&G-owned manufacturing facilities in over 25 countries and over 200 contract manufacturers. Selling and marketing operations are divided into six regions (Asia Pacific; Europe; Greater China; India, the Middle East and Africa; Latin America; and North America), and reach consumers in over 180 countries. Functions provide specialized expertise in the areas of finance, HR, sales, communications, legal, and IT. Global business services provide shared services such as payroll, purchases, analytics and operations research, benefits, and facilities management. The analytics/OR group helps the business units plan material supply, production, distribution, and inventories.

Inventory management is clearly important for P&G. P&G has achieved two step-change improvements in inventory levels. The first improvement came from the broad application of spreadsheet-based inventory models. This work produced single stage tools for materials warehouses and finished goods distribution centres (DCs) using models similar to EOQ/ROP with fill rate service targets, and one two-stage DRP model for one central warehouse and remote DCs. These models locally optimized different portions of the supply chain. The second improvement integrated multi-echelon inventory optimization software in P&G's more-complex supply chains. In total, these tools have saved P&G over $1.5 billion in cash, while increasing service levels.

An example of a complex P&G supply chain is that for liquid makeup (a simplified model is shown below). The chain consists of 8 unique raw materials, 10 blank uncoloured WIPs, 24 coloured WIP materials, 150 packaging materials, 18 intermediate sub-assemblies, and 75 finished goods. The intermediate sub-assemblies also must satisfy demand for promotional items. In total, the model contained 500 SKU-locations and over 700 arcs.

Sources: Farasym, I., et al., "Spreadsheet Models for Inventory Target Setting at Procter & Gamble," *Interfaces* 38(4), 2008, pp. 241–250; Farasym, I., et al., "Inventory Optimization at Procter & Gamble: Achieving Real Benefits Through User Adoption of Inventory Tools," *Interfaces* 41(1), 2011, pp. 66–78.

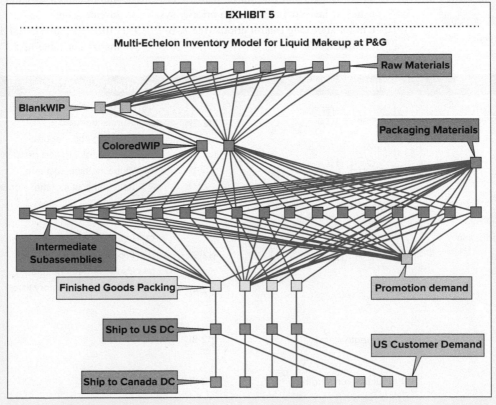

EXHIBIT 5

Multi-Echelon Inventory Model for Liquid Makeup at P&G

Supply Chain Management Review

Summary

- Inventory is any unused material, part, or product, usually stored in a warehouse or storeroom.
- Inventory management is important because holding inventory costs money, both for storage and the opportunity cost of money tied up in inventory, and shortage (stock-out) is costly too. Management measures efficient use of inventory by the inventory turnover ratio (Cost of goods sold/Average inventory investment).
- Inventories serve different functions (or purposes), including waiting while being transported (in-transit), protection against stock-out (safety stocks), to take advantage of economic lot size or to avoid future price increase (cycle stocks), to smooth seasonal demand or production, to decouple operations, and to meet anticipated above-average demand.
- Successful inventory management requires keeping and handling items safely, a system to keep track of inventory position (On hand + On order − Back-ordered) and using inventory control models, accurate information about demand and lead times, realistic estimates of inventory costs, and a priority system for allocating control efforts (the A-B-C classification).

- Three classes of models are described: economic order quantity/reorder point (EOQ/ROP), fixed-interval/order-up-to level, and the single period models. The first two are appropriate if unused items can be carried over into subsequent periods.
- EOQ models address the question of how much to order. They include the basic EOQ, economic production quantity, quantity discount, and planned shortage models.
- The ROP models address the question of when to order (in terms of inventory position) and are particularly helpful in dealing with situations that include variations in either demand or purchase lead time. They involve service level and safety stock considerations. Two types of service level are lead time and annual (fill rate) service levels.
- When the time between orders is fixed, the fixed-interval model is useful. Coordinated periodic review model is more general.
- Multi-echelon inventory management is management of inventory across various organizations in a supply chain. Methods used are multi-echelon inventory control, DRP, and inventory optimization.

The formulas presented in this chapter are summarized in Table 12-5.

TABLE 12-5 ▼

Summary of inventory formulas.

Model	Formula		Symbols
1. Basic EOQ	$EOQ = Q_0 = \sqrt{\dfrac{2DS}{H}}$	(12-2)	Q_0 = Economic order quantity D = Annual demand S = Ordering cost per order H = Annual holding cost per unit $= i \cdot R$ i = Annual holding cost rate R = Item unit cost (purchase price)
	$TC = \dfrac{Q}{2}H + \dfrac{D}{Q}S$	(12-1)	
	Length of order cycle $= \dfrac{Q_0}{D}$	(12-3)	
2. Economic production quantity	$Q_0 = \sqrt{\dfrac{2DS}{H}}\sqrt{\dfrac{P}{p-d}}$	(12-8)	Q_0 = Optimal production run quantity P = Production rate d = Usage or demand rate I_{max} = Maximum inventory level
	$TC = \dfrac{I_{max}}{2}H + \dfrac{D}{Q}S$	(12-4)	
	Cycle length $= \dfrac{Q}{d}$	(12-5)	
	Production run length $= \dfrac{Q}{p}$	(12-6)	
	$I_{max} = \dfrac{Q}{P}(p-d)$	(12-7)	

Model	Formula		Symbols
3. Quantity discount	$TC = \dfrac{Q}{2}H + \dfrac{D}{Q}S + RD$	(12-9)	
4. Planned shortage	$Q_b = Q\left(\dfrac{H}{H+B}\right)$	(12-10)	Q_b = Quantity back-ordered in an order cycle B = Annual back-order cost per unit
	$Q = \sqrt{\dfrac{2DS}{H}\left(\dfrac{H+B}{B}\right)}$	(12-12)	

5. Reorder point under:
  a. Constant demand and
    lead time
  b. Variable demand
  c. Variable lead time and
    demand
	$ROP = d(LT)$
	$ROP = \bar{d}(LT) + z\sqrt{LT}(\sigma_d)$
	$ROP = \bar{d}(LT) + z\sqrt{LT(\sigma_d^2) + \bar{d}^2(\sigma_{LT}^2)}$
		(12-13)
		(12-15)
		(12-16)
			LT = Lead time
			$\bar{d}$ = Average demand rate
			σ_d = Standard deviation of demand rate
			z = Standard Normal deviate
			$\overline{LT}$ = Average lead time
			σ_{LT} = Standard deviation of lead time

6. Annual service level	$E(z) = \dfrac{Q(1 - SL_{annual})}{\sigma_{dLT}}$	(12-17)	$E(z)$ = Standardized expected number short per
			    order cycle
			σ_{dLT} = Standard deviation of demand during a lead
			    time
			SL_{annual} = Annual service level (fill rate)

7. Fixed-interval	$OI^* = \sqrt{\dfrac{2(S + ns)}{i\sum D_j R_j}}$	(12-18)	OI = Order interval
			S = Group ordering cost (i.e., cost of a purchase
			    order)
			s = Individual item ordering cost (i.e., cost of a line
			    item in the purchase order)
			n = Number of SKUs ordered from same supplier
			D_j = Annual demand for SKU_j
			R_j = Unit cost of SKU_j

	$I_{max} = \bar{d}(OI + LT) + z\sigma_d\sqrt{OI + LT}$	(12-20)	
	$Q = I_{max}$ − Inventory position Inventory position = On hand + On order − Back-ordered	(12-21)	
8. Coordinated periodic review	$m_j = \sqrt{\dfrac{s}{D_j R_j}\dfrac{D_k R_k}{S + s}}$	(12-22)	m_j = Multiple of OI^* used for ordering SKU_j k = Index of the SKU with largest annual dollar value $D_j R_j$
	$OI^* = \sqrt{\dfrac{2\left(S + s\sum_{j=1}^{n}\frac{1}{m_j}\right)}{i\sum_{j=1}^{n}m_j D_j R_j}}$	(12-23)	
9. Single period	$SL = \dfrac{C_s}{C_s + C_e}$	(12-24)	SL = Service level C_s = Shortage cost per unit C_e = Excess cost per unit

Key Terms

A-B-C classification

annual service level

anticipation inventory

automated storage and retrieval system
(ASRS)

bar code

coordinated periodic review model

cycle counting

cycle stock

decoupling inventory

economic order quantity (EOQ)

economic order quantity/reorder point
model (EOQ/ROP)

economic production quantity (EPQ)

excess cost

fixed-interval/order-up-to level model

holding cost

independent demand

in-transit inventory

inventory

inventory management

inventory optimization

inventory position

lead time service level

line item ordering cost

multi-echelon

ordering cost

perpetual or continual tracking

physical inventory

planned shortage

point-of-sale (POS) system

purchase lead time

purchase order ordering cost

quantity discount

reorder point (ROP)

safety stock

seasonal inventory

setup

shortage cost

single period model

stock keeping unit (SKU)

two bin system

warehouse management system

work-in-process (WIP)

Solved Problems

Problem 1

Basic EOQ. A small computer manufacturer uses 32,000 computer chips annually. The chips are used at a steady rate during the 240 days a year that the plant operates. Annual holding cost is 60 cents per chip, and ordering cost is $24 per order. Determine:

  a. The optimal (or economic) order quantity.

  b. The number of workdays in an order cycle.

Solution

$$D = 32{,}000 \text{ chips per year}, \quad S = \$24$$

$$H = \$0.60 \text{ per unit per year}$$

  a. $Q_0 = \sqrt{\dfrac{2DS}{H}} = \sqrt{\dfrac{2(32{,}000)\$24}{\$0.60}} = 1{,}600 \text{ chips}$

  b. $\dfrac{Q_0}{D} = \dfrac{1{,}600 \text{ chips}}{32{,}000 \text{ chips/yr}} = \dfrac{1}{20} \text{year} \times 240 \text{ days} = 12 \text{ workdays}$

Problem 2

Economic production quantity. A company is both a producer and a user of brass couplings. The company operates 220 days a year and uses the couplings at a steady rate of 50 per day. Couplings can be produced at a rate of 200 per day. Annual holding cost is $1 per coupling, and machine setup cost is $35 per production run.

  a. Determine the economic production quantity.

  b. How many production runs per year will there be?

  c. Calculate the maximum inventory level.

  d. Determine the length of the pure consumption portion of the cycle.

Solution

$D = 50 \text{ units per day} \times 220 \text{ days per year} = 11{,}000 \text{ units per year}$

$S = \$35 \text{ per production run}$

$H = \$1$ per unit per year
$p = 200$ units per day
$d = 50$ units per day

a. $Q_0 = \sqrt{\dfrac{2DS}{H}}\sqrt{\dfrac{p}{p-d}} = \sqrt{\dfrac{2(11,000)35}{1}}\sqrt{\dfrac{200}{200-50}} = 1,013$ units.

b. Number of production runs per year: $D/Q_0 = 11,000/1,013 = 10.86$, or 11.

c. $I_{max} = \dfrac{Q_0}{p}(p-d) = \dfrac{1,013}{200}(200-50) = 759.75$ or 760 units.

d. Length of cycle $= \dfrac{Q_0}{d} = \dfrac{1,013 \text{ units}}{50 \text{ units per day}} = 20.26$ workdays

Length of production run $= \dfrac{Q_0}{p} = \dfrac{1,013 \text{ units}}{200 \text{ units per day}} = 5.06$ workdays

Length of pure consumption portion = Length of cycle − Length of production run
$= 20.26 - 5.06 = 15.20$ workdays

Problem 3

Quantity discount. A small manufacturer uses roughly 3,400 kg of a chemical dye a year. Currently the company purchases 300 kg at a time and pays $3/kg. The supplier has just announced that orders of 1,000 kg or more will be filled at the price of $2/kg. The manufacturer incurs a cost of $100 each time it replenishes and uses the annual holding cost rate of 17 percent of the purchase price.

a. Determine the order quantity that will minimize the total cost.

b. If the supplier offered the discount at 1,500 kg instead of 1,000 kg, what order quantity would minimize total cost?

Solution

$D = 3,400$ kg per year, $S = \$100$, $H = 0.17R$
The quantity ranges are:

Range	Unit Price (per kg)
1 to 999	$3
1,000+	$2

a. Calculate the EOQ for $2/kg price:

$$Q_{\$2} = \sqrt{\dfrac{2DS}{H}} = \sqrt{\dfrac{2(3,400)100}{0.17(2)}} = 1,414 \text{ kg}$$

Because this quantity falls in the $2/kg quantity range, it is optimal.

b. If the discount is offered at 1,500 kg, the EOQ for the $2/kg price is no longer feasible. Consequently, it becomes necessary to calculate the EOQ for $3/kg and compare the total annual cost for that order quantity with the total annual cost of using the break quantity (i.e., 1,500).

$$Q_{\$3} = \sqrt{\dfrac{2DS}{H}} = \sqrt{\dfrac{2(3,400)100}{0.17(3)}} = 1,155 \text{ kg}$$

$$TC = \left(\dfrac{Q}{2}\right)H + \left(\dfrac{D}{Q}\right)S + RD$$

$$TC_{1,155} = \left(\dfrac{1,155}{2}\right)(0.17)(3) + \left(\dfrac{3,400}{1,155}\right)100 + 3(3,400)$$
$$= \$294.53 + \$294.37 + \$10,200 = \$10,789$$

$$TC_{1,500} = \left(\dfrac{1,500}{2}\right)(0.17)(2) + \left(\dfrac{3,400}{1,500}\right)100 + 2(3,400)$$
$$= \$255 + \$226.67 + \$6,800 = \$7,282$$

Because it would result in a lower total annual cost, 1,500 kg is the optimal order quantity (see the following figure).

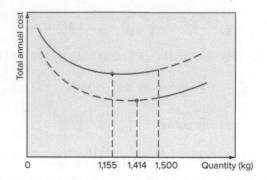

Problem 4

ROP for variable demand and constant lead time. The housekeeping department of a hotel uses approximately 400 towels per day. The actual number tends to vary with the number of guests on any given night. Usage can be approximated by a Normal distribution that has a mean of 400 and a standard deviation of 9 towels per day. A linen service company washes the towels with a lead time of three days. If the hotel policy is to maintain a stock-out risk of 2 percent for towels, what is the minimum number of towels that must be on hand at reorder time (i.e., the ROP), and how much of that amount can be considered safety stock?

Solution

$\bar{d} = 400$ towels per day, $LT = 3$ days

$\sigma d = 9$ towels per day, Stock-out risk = 2 percent, so Lead time service level = 98 percent

From Appendix B, Table B, the z value that corresponds to an area under the Normal curve to the left of z of 98 percent is about 2.055.

$$ROP = \bar{d}LT + z\sqrt{LT}\,\sigma_d = 400(3) + 2.055\sqrt{3}(9)$$
$$= 1,200 + 32.03 = 1,232.03, \text{ or } 1,232 \text{ towels}$$

Safety stock is 32 towels.

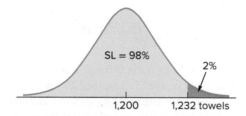

Problem 5

ROP for variable demand and variable lead time. The hotel replaces broken and stolen drinking glasses at a rate of 25 per day. In the past, this quantity has tended to vary Normally and has a standard deviation of three drinking glasses per day. Drinking glasses are ordered from a distant supplier. Lead time is Normally distributed with an average of 10 days and a standard deviation of 2 days. What ROP should be used to achieve a lead time service level of 95 percent?

Solution

$$\bar{d} = 25 \text{ drinking glasses per day}, \quad \overline{LT} = 10 \text{ days}$$
$$\sigma_d = 3 \text{ drinking glasses per day}, \quad \sigma_{LT} = 2 \text{ days}$$

Lead time SL = 95 percent, so $z = 1.645$ (from Appendix B, Table B)

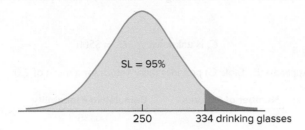

$$ROP = \bar{d}\bar{LT} + z \sqrt{\bar{LT}\sigma_d^2 + \bar{d}^2\sigma_{LT}^2}$$
$$= 25(10) + 1.645 \sqrt{10(3)^2 + (25)^2(2)^2} = 334 \text{ drinking glasses}$$

SL = 95%

250   334 drinking glasses

Problem 6

Annual service level. The manager of an office supply store has decided to set an annual service level (or fill rate) of 96 percent for a certain model of telephone answering machine. The store sells approximately 300 of this model a year. Holding cost is $5 per unit annually, ordering cost is $25 per order, average demand during a lead time is 20, and standard deviation of demand during a lead time is 7. Calculate the ROP, assuming EOQ is used as the order quantity.

Solution

$SL_{annual} = 96$ percent $D = 300$ units $H = \$5$ $S = \$25$ $\mu_{dLT} = 20$ $\sigma_{dLT} = 7$
First, we need to calculate the EOQ:

$$Q = \sqrt{\frac{2DS}{H}} = \sqrt{\frac{2(300)(25)}{5}} = 54.77 \text{(round to 55)}$$
$$E(z) = \frac{Q(1 - SL_{annual})}{\sigma_{dLT}} = \frac{55(1 - 0.96)}{7} = 0.314$$

Interpolation in Table 12-3 gives $z = 0.18$.
ROP = 20 + 0.18(7) = 21.26; round to 21 machines

Problem 7

Fixed-interval model. A lab orders a number of chemicals from the same supplier every 30 days. Lead time is five days. The assistant manager of the lab must determine how much of one of these chemicals to order. A check of stock revealed that eleven 25 mL jars are on hand and none are on order. Daily usage of the chemical is approximately Normal with a mean of 15.2 mL and a standard deviation of 1.6 mL. The desired service level for this chemical is 95 percent.
   a. What should be the amount of safety stock for the chemical?
   b. How many jars of the chemical should be ordered at this time?

Solution

$\bar{d} = 15.2$ mL per day, OI = 30 days, SL = 95% or $z = 1.645$
$\sigma_d = 1.6$ mL per day, LT = 5 days, Amount on hand = 11 jars × 25 mL per jar = 275 mL

a. Safety stock = $z\sigma_d \sqrt{OI + LT} = 1.645(1.6)\sqrt{30 + 5} = 15.57$ mL

b. Amount to order = I_{max} − Amount on hand
$$I_{max} = \bar{d}(OI + LT) + z\sigma_d\sqrt{OI + LT}$$
$$= 15.2(30 + 5) + 15.57 = 547.57 \text{ mL}$$

Amount to order = 547.57 − 275 = 272.57 mL

Convert this to number of jars:
$$\frac{272.57 \text{ mL}}{25 \text{ mL per jar}} = 10.90 \text{ or } 11 \text{ jars}$$

Problem 8

Single period model. A cable TV company uses a certain piece of equipment for which it carries two units of a spare part. The part costs $500 and has no salvage value. Part failures can be modelled by a Poisson distribution with a mean of two failures during the useful life of the equipment. Estimate the range of shortage cost per unit for which stocking two units of this spare part is optimal.

Solution

$$C_s \text{ is unknown} \qquad C_e = \$500$$

The Poisson table (Appendix B, Table C) provides these values for a mean of 2.0:

Number of Failures	Cumulative Probability
0.........	0.135
1.........	0.406
2.........	0.677
3.........	0.857
4.........	0.947
5.........	0.983
⋮	⋮

For the optimal discrete stocking level, the service level must be rounded up. Hence, we know that the service level must have been between 0.407 and 0.677 in order to make two units the optimal stocking level. By setting the service level first equal to 0.407 and then to 0.677, we can establish bounds on the possible range of shortage cost.

$$\frac{C_s}{C_s + \$500} = 0.407, \text{so } C_s = 0.407(\$500 + C_s)$$

Solving, we find $C_s = \$343.17$.
Similarly,

$$\frac{C_s}{C_s + \$500} = 0.677, \text{so } C_s = 0.677(\$500 + C_s)$$

Solving, we find $C_s = \$1,047.99$. Hence, the range of shortage cost per unit is $343.17 to $1,047.99.

Discussion and Review Questions

Note: An asterisk indicates that a question or problem may be more challenging.

LO1 **1.** What are the primary reasons for holding inventory?

LO1 **2.** What are some ways that a company can reduce its needs for inventories?

LO1 **3.** Why might it be inappropriate to use inventory turnover ratio to compare the inventory performance of companies in different industries?

LO2 **4.** What are the requirements for effective inventory management?

LO2 **5.** Define purchase lead time. What factors affect it?

LO2 **6.** What benefits do bar codes have for inventory management?

LO2 **7.** Briefly describe each of the costs associated with inventory.

LO2 **8.** Describe briefly the A-B-C classification.

LO3 **9.** How would you respond to the criticism that the EOQ model tends to provide misleading results because values of S and H are, at best, educated guesses?

LO3 **10.** Explain briefly how a higher holding cost should result in more frequent orders.

LO3 **11.** Explain how a decrease in machine setup time should lead to a decrease in the average amount of work-in-process inventory a company holds, and why that would be beneficial.

LO3 **12.** How are the economic production quantity and its model different from EOQ and its model?

LO3 **13.** Why would any company intentionally plan for shortage? Give an example.

LO4 **14.** What is safety stock and what is its purpose?

LO4 **15.** Under what circumstances should the amount of safety stock held be
   a. Large?
   b. Small?
   c. Zero?

LO4 **16.** What is meant by the term *lead time service level?* Generally speaking, how is lead time service level related to the amount of safety stock held?

LO4 **17.** What is annual service level and how is it related to z?

LO5 **18.** What is the difference between the fixed-interval/order-up-to level model and the economic order quantity/reorder point model? When would each be preferred?

LO5 **19.** What is the difference between the fixed-interval/order-up-to level model and the coordinated periodic review model? When would each be preferred?

LO6 **20.** What is the single period model, and under what circumstances is it appropriate?

LO6 **21.** Can the optimal stocking level in the single period model ever be less than median (i.e., 50th percentile) demand? Explain briefly.

LO7 **22.** Briefly describe the three methods used for multi-echelon inventory management.

LO2 **23.** What is an ASRS? Give an example.

LO7 **24.** What are the echelons in the liquid makeup supply chain of Procter & Gamble?

Taking Stock

LO2 **1.** What trade-offs are involved in each of these aspects of inventory management?
   a. Buying additional amounts to take advantage of quantity discount.
   b. Conducting actual (physical) inventory counts once a quarter instead of once a year.

LO1 & 2 **2.** Who needs to be involved in inventory decisions?

LO2 **3.** How has technology aided inventory management?

LO2 **4.** Employee theft of inventories can be a problem in a wholesaler/distributor/retailer warehouse. Name one thing a manager can do to combat this.

Critical Thinking Exercises

LO2 **1.** To be competitive, many fast-food chains have begun to expand their menus to include a wider range of meals. Although contributing to competitiveness, this has added to the complexity of operations, including inventory management. Explain why.

LO4 **2.** As a supermarket manager, how would you go about evaluating the criticality of an inventory shortage?

Experiential Learning Exercises

LO1 **1.** Give three examples of inventory in your personal life. How do you manage them?

LO3–6 **2.** Which inventory model would you use for each of the following activities? Which has the highest shortage cost?
   a. Buying gasoline for your car.
   b. Buying groceries.
   c. Getting cash from your bank account.

LO2 **3.** How can the grocery store you use improve its inventory management?

Internet Exercises

L02 **1.** View https://www.youtube.com/watch?v=gJixk7Yjc3E and briefly describe what Retail Pro 9 (the most popular retail software) can do.

L02 **2.** Visit http://mhi.org/mediaba nk/general.asp, choose a category, click on "videos," pick a video, view it, and describe the equipment shown and its advantages.

L02 **3.** Answer the following questions about the Montreal DC of Canadian Tire. You might want to use the following article http://www.mmh.com/images/site/MMH1011_SystemRptCanadianTire.pdf and video http://www.youtube.com/watch?v=deE6pDBHlTc.

    a. What is the difference between conveyable and non-conveyable items? Give an example of each.

    b. What type of order picking system is used in the DC? Radio frequency (RF), light, voice?

    c. What type of conveyor sorters are used in the DC?

L02 **4.** Read http://img.en25.com/Web/DematicCorp/%7B3af4ab7f-7233-463e-88ab-d96299f6a4c5%7D_NA_CS-1017_UBC.pdf and describe how Dematics' automatic storage and retrieval system is used by the UBC Library.

L07 **5.** Watch http://www.youtube.com/watch?v=4AcjAfWBVXg and summarize how SAP's SmartOps helped Celestica's supply chain inventory management.

L02 **6.** Watch Moose Jaw Hospital's kanban video https://www.youtube.com/watch?v=EQW-zcLC1lE and describe how its two bin system works.

Problems

L02 **1.** **a.** Perform A-B-C classification on these items:

Item	Unit Cost	Annual Volume (00)
1	$100	25
2	80	30
3	15	60
4	50	10
5	11	70
6	60	85
7	10	60

    b. Find the EOQ given this information: $D = 4,500$ units/year, $S = \$36$, and $H = \$10$ per unit per year.

    c. Find the economic production quantity given this information.

    $D = 18,000$ units/year, $S = \$100$, $H = \$40$ per unit per year, $p = 120$ units/day, and $d = 90$ units/day.

L02 **2.** The manager of an automobile repair shop hopes to achieve a better allocation of inventory control efforts by adopting A-B-C classification. Given the monthly usages and unit costs in the following table, classify the items into the A, B, and C categories according to monthly dollar value.

Item	Monthly Usage	Unit Cost
4021	50	$1,400
9402	300	12
4066	40	700
6500	150	20
9280	10	1,020
4050	80	140

Item	Monthly Usage	Unit Cost
6850	2,000	15
3010	400	20
4400	7,000	25
2307	1,958	14

L02 **3.** The following table contains the monthly usage and unit costs for a random sample of 15 items from a list of 2,000 inventory items at a health care facility.

Item	Unit Cost	Monthly Usage
K34	10	200
K35	25	600
K36	36	150
M10	16	25
M20	20	80
Z45	80	700
F14	20	300
F95	30	800
F99	20	60
D45	10	550
D48	12	90
D52	15	110
D57	40	120
N08	30	40
P05	16	500

    a. Develop an A-B-C classification for these items.

    b. How could the manager use this information?

    c. After reviewing your classification scheme, suppose that the manager decides to place item P05 into the A category. What are some possible explanations for this decision?

4. A large bakery buys flour in 25 kg bags. The bakery uses an average of 4,860 bags a year. Preparing an order, receiving the shipment, and paying the invoice costs $10 per order. Annual holding cost is $5 per flour bag.

    a. Determine the economic order quantity.

    b. What is the average number of bags on hand (i.e., average cycle inventory) if EOQ is used?

    c. How many orders per year will there be if EOQ is used?

    d. Calculate the total annual cost of ordering and holding flour for EOQ.

    e. If ordering cost were to increase by 50 percent per order, by what percentage would the EOQ change?

 5. A large law firm uses an average of 10 packages of copier paper a day. Each package contains 500 sheets. The firm operates 260 days a year. Holding cost for the paper is $1 per year per package, and ordering cost is $10 per order.

    a. What order quantity would minimize total annual ordering and holding cost?

    b. Calculate the total annual inventory control cost using your order quantity from part *a*.

    c. Except for rounding, are annual ordering and holding costs equal at the EOQ?

    d. The office manager is currently using an order quantity of 100 packages. The partners of the firm expect the office to be managed in a cost-efficient manner. Would you recommend that the office manager use the optimal order quantity instead of 100 packages? Justify your answer.

 6. A flower shop uses 250 clay pots a month. The pots are purchased for $2 each. Annual holding cost is estimated to be 30 percent of purchase cost, and ordering cost is $20 per order. The manager has been using an order quantity of 250 flower pots.

    a. Calculate the EOQ.

    b. Calculate the EOQ's total annual inventory control cost.

    c. What additional annual inventory control cost is the shop incurring by using the current order quantity?

 7. A fresh produce distributor uses 800 nonreturnable packing crates a month, which it purchases at a cost of $5 each. The manager has assigned an annual holding cost of 25 percent of the purchase price per crate. Ordering cost is $28 per order. Currently the manager orders 800 crates at a time. How much could the firm save annually in ordering and holding costs by using the EOQ?

 8. Demand for an item is projected to be 100 units per month. The monthly holding cost is $2 per unit, and it costs $55 to process an order.

    a. Determine the EOQ.

    b. If the vendor is willing to offer the manager a discount of $10 *per order* for ordering in multiples of 50 units (e.g., 50, 100), would you advise the manager to take advantage of the offer? If so, what order quantity would you recommend?

    c. Alternatively, if the demand can wait at the cost of $5 per unit per month, what should the order quantity and the amount short per order cycle be?

 9. A food processor uses approximately 27,000 glass jars a month. Because of storage limitations, a lot size of 4,000 jars has been used. Monthly holding cost is $0.01 per jar, and ordering cost is $20 per order.

    a. What penalty is the company incurring by using its present order quantity?

    b. The manager would like to justify the present order quantity. One possibility is to simplify order processing to reduce the ordering cost. What ordering cost would enable the manager to justify the current order quantity?

 10. A sausage factory can produce European wieners at a rate of 500 kg per day. It supplies wieners to local stores and restaurants at a steady rate of 100 kg per day. The cost to prepare the equipment for producing European wieners is $12. Annual holding cost is $4/kg of wieners. The factory operates 300 days a year. Calculate:

    a. The optimal production run quantity.

    b. The number of production runs per year.

    c. The length (in days) of a production run.

 11. A chemical plant produces sodium bisulfate in 100 kg bags. Demand for this product is 20 tonnes per day. The capacity for producing this product is 50 tonnes per day. Setup cost is $400, and holding cost is $200 per tonne per year. The company operates 200 days a year. (*Note:* 1 tonne = 1,000 kg)

    a. What is the optimal number of bags per production run?

    b. What would the average inventory level be for this lot size?

    c. Determine the approximate length of a production run, in days.

    d. About how many production runs per year would there be?

    e. How much could the company save annually in inventory control cost if the setup cost could be reduced to $200 per production run and the optimal production quantity is recalculated and used?

LO3 **12.** A company is about to begin production of a new product. The manager of a department that is asked to produce one of the components wants to know if there is enough machine time available. The machine will produce the item at a rate of 200 units a day. Eighty units will be used daily in assembling the final product. The company operates five days a week, 50 weeks a year. The manager estimates that it will take almost a full day to get the machine ready for a production run, at a cost of $300. Inventory holding cost will be $10 per unit per year.

   a. What production run quantity should be used to minimize total annual setup and holding cost?

   b. What is the length of a production run (in days)?

   c. During production, at what rate will inventory build up?

   d. If the manager needs to run another job between runs of this job, and needs a minimum of 10 days per cycle of this job for the other job, will there be enough time?

LO3 **13.** A company manufactures hair dryers. It buys some of the components, but it makes the heating element, which it can produce at the rate of 800 per day. Hair dryers are assembled 250 days a year, at a rate of 300 per day. Because of the disparity between the production and usage rates, the heating elements are periodically produced in batches of 2,000 units.

   a. Approximately how many batches of heating elements are produced annually?

   b. If production on a batch begins when there is no inventory of heating elements on hand, how much inventory will be on hand two days later?

   c. What will be the average level of inventory of the heating element, assuming each production cycle begins when there is no inventory on hand?

   d. The same equipment could also be used to make a component for another of the company's products. That job would require four days per cycle of the element. Setup time for making a batch of the heating elements is a half day. Is there enough time to do this job between production of batches of heating element? Explain.

LO3 **14.** A small mail-order company uses 18,000 boxes a year. Holding cost rate is 20 percent of unit cost per year, and ordering cost is $32 per order. The following quantity discount is available. Determine:

   a. The optimal order quantity.

   b. The number of orders per year.

Number of Boxes	Price per Box
1,000 to 1,999	$1.25
2,000 to 4,999	1.20
5,000 to 9,999	1.15
10,000 or more	1.10

LO3 & 4 **15.** A jewellery manufacturer buys semi-precious stones to make bracelets and rings. The supplier has quoted a price of $8 per stone for order quantities of 600 stones or more, $9 per stone for orders of 400 to 599 stones, and $10 per stone for smaller order quantities. The jewellery manufacturer operates 200 days per year. Usage rate is 25 stones per day, and ordering cost is $48 per order.

   a. If annual holding cost is 30 percent of unit cost, what is the optimal order quantity?

   b. If lead time is six workdays, at what inventory level should the company reorder?

LO3 **16.** A manufacturer of exercise equipment purchases pulleys from a supplier who lists these prices: less than 1,000, $5 each; 1,000 to 3,999, $4.95 each; 4,000 to 5,999, $4.90 each; and 6,000 or more, $4.85 each. Ordering cost is $50 per order, annual holding cost is 20 percent of purchase cost, and annual usage is 4,900 pulleys. Determine the order quantity that will minimize total cost.

LO3 **17.** The manager of a large electronics store wants to begin stocking a universal TV remote control device. Expected monthly demand is 800 units. The remote controls can be purchased from either supplier A or supplier B. Their price lists are as follows:

Supplier A		Supplier B	
Quantity	Unit Price	Quantity	Unit Price
1–199	$14.00	1–149	$14.10
200–499	13.80	150–349	13.90
500+	13.60	350+	13.70

Ordering cost is $40 per order and annual holding cost is 25 percent of unit price. Which supplier should be used and what order quantity is optimal if the intent is to minimize total annual cost?

LO3 **18.** A manager just received a new price list for boxes from a supplier. It will now cost $1.00 a box for order quantities of 801 or more, $1.10 a box for 200 to 800, and $1.20 a box for smaller quantities. Ordering cost is $40 per order and holding cost rate is 40 percent of unit cost per year. The company uses 3,600 boxes a year. The manager has suggested a "round number" order quantity of 800 boxes. The manager's rationale is that total annual inventory cost is U-shaped and fairly flat at its minimum. Therefore, the difference in total annual cost between 800 and 801 units would be small anyway. How would you reply to the manager's suggestion? What order quantity would you recommend?

LO4 **19.** A newspaper publisher uses roughly 800 metres of baling wire each day to secure bundles of newspapers. The paper is published Monday through Saturday. Lead time for purchase of wires is six workdays. The stock-out risk for various levels of safety stock is as follows: 1,500 metres, 0.10; 1,800 metres, 0.05; 2,100 metres, 0.02; and 2,400 metres, 0.01. What is the appropriate reorder point given that the company desires a lead time service level of 95 percent?

LO4 20. Given the following information:

Expected demand during a lead time = 300 units

Standard deviation of demand during a lead time = 30 units

Demand during a lead time is distributed Normally.

a. Determine the safety stock needed to attain a 1 percent risk of stock-out during a lead time.

b. Would a stock-out risk of 2 percent require more or less safety stock? Explain.

LO4 21. Given the following information:

Expected demand during a lead time = 600 kg

Standard deviation of demand during a lead time = 52 kg

Demand during a lead time is distributed Normally.

Acceptable stock-out risk during a lead time = 4 percent

a. What amount of safety stock is appropriate?

b. At what level of inventory should this item be reordered?

LO4 & 5 22. Demand for vanilla ice cream at a small ice cream shop can be approximated by a Normal distribution with a mean of 21 litres per week and a standard deviation of 3.5 litres per week. The ice cream is purchased from an ice cream producer. The store manager desires a lead time service level of 90 percent. Lead time from the producer is two days. The store is open seven days a week.

a. If the EOQ/ROP model is used for ordering the ice cream from the producer, what ROP would be consistent with the desired lead time service level?

b. If a fixed-interval model is used instead, what order quantity should be used if the order interval is seven days and 8 litres are on hand and none are on order at the time of order?

c. Suppose that the manager is using the EOQ/ROP model described in part *a*. One day after placing an order with the producer, the manager receives a call from the producer saying that the order will be delayed because of problems at the producer's plant. The producer promises to have the order there in two days. After hanging up, the manager checks the inventory of vanilla ice cream and finds that 2 litres have been sold since the order was placed. Assuming that the producer's promise is valid, what is the probability that the store will run out of vanilla ice cream before the shipment arrives?

LO4 23. The injection moulding department of a company uses an average of 30 litres of a special lubricant a day. The lubricant is replenished when the amount on hand is 170 litres. It takes four days for an order to be received. The current stock-out risk is 9 percent. What amount of safety stock would be needed if the acceptable risk of stock-out is to be reduced to 3 percent?

LO4 24. A large electronics repair shop uses an average of 85 capacitors a day. The standard deviation is 5 units per day. The buyer follows this rule: Order when the amount on hand and on order drops to 625 units. Orders are delivered approximately six days after being placed. The delivery time is Normal with a mean of six days and a standard deviation of 1.10 days. What is the probability that the inventory of capacitors will be exhausted before the shipment is received?

LO4 25. Demand for a particular tablet at an electronics store has recently surged, and the store manager must recalculate at what inventory level to replenish it. The manager wants a probability of at least 96 percent of not having a stock-out during a lead time. The manager expects demand to average a dozen units a day and to have a standard deviation of two units a day. Purchase lead time is variable, averaging four days with a standard deviation of one day. Assume demand during a lead time is Normal. At what inventory level (On hand + On order) should the manager reorder to achieve the desired service level probability?

LO3 & 4 26. The manager of a car wash has received a revised price list from the vendor of the liquid soap, and a promise of a shorter lead time for deliveries. Formerly the lead time was four days, but now the vendor promises a reduction of 25 percent in that time (i.e., new lead time is three days). Annual usage of soap is 4,500 litres. The car wash is open 360 days a year. Assume that daily usage of soap is Normal, and that it has a standard deviation of two litres per day. The ordering cost is $10 per order and annual holding cost rate is 40 percent of unit cost. The revised price list is shown below.

Quantity (litres)	Unit Price per Litre
1–399	$2.00
400–799	1.80
800+	1.60

a. What order quantity is optimal?

b. What ROP is appropriate if the acceptable risk of a stock-out is 1.5 percent?

LO3–5 27. Experience suggests that usage of copy paper at a small copy centre can be approximated by a Normal distribution with a mean of five boxes per day and a standard deviation of one-half box per day. Two days are required to fill an order for paper. Ordering cost is $10 per order, and annual holding cost is $10 per box.

a. Determine the economic order quantity, assuming 250 workdays a year.

b. If the copy centre reorders when the paper on hand and on order is 12 boxes, calculate the risk of a stock-out during a lead time.

c. If a fixed interval of seven days, instead of the EOQ/ROP model, is used for reordering, what shortage risk does the copy centre incur if it orders 36 boxes when the amount on hand is 12 boxes?

LO4 **28.** A bulk foods store sells unshelled peanuts by the kilogram. Historically, daily demand is Normally distributed with a mean of 8 kg and a standard deviation of 1 kg. The purchase lead time from the supplier also appears to be Normally distributed with a mean of eight days and a standard deviation of one day. What ROP would provide stock-out risk of 10 percent during a lead time?

LO3 & 4 **29.** A supermarket is open 360 days per year. Daily use of cash register tape averages 10 rolls, Normally distributed, with a standard deviation of two rolls per day. The cost of ordering tape is $10 per order, and holding cost is 40 cents per roll a year. Lead time is three days.
a. What is the EOQ?
b. What ROP will provide a lead time service level of 96 percent?
c. What ROP will provide an annual service level (i.e., fill rate) of 96 percent if order quantity equals EOQ is used?

LO3 & 4 **30.** A car service shop uses 1,200 cases of oil a year. Ordering cost is $20 per order, and annual holding cost is $3 per case. The shop owner has specified an *annual* service level of 99 percent.
a. What is the EOQ?
b. What level of ROP is appropriate if demand during a lead time is Normally distributed with a mean of 80 cases and a standard deviation of 5 cases?

LO3 & 4 **31.** A small school bus depot operates 250 days a year. Daily demand for diesel fuel at the depot is Normal with an average of 250 litres and a standard deviation of 14 litres. Holding cost for the fuel is $0.30 per litre per year, and ordering cost is $10 an order for more fuel. It takes one day to receive a delivery of diesel fuel.
a. Calculate the EOQ.
b. Determine the ROP needed if the manager wants an annual service level of 99.5 percent.

LO4 **32.** A hospital reorders size 7 surgical gloves when the supply on hand and on order falls to 18 units (pairs). Lead time for resupply is three days. Given the typical usage over the last 10 days below, what service level is achieved with the hospital's reorder policy?

Day	1	2	3	4	5	6	7	8	9	10
Units	3	4	7	5	5	6	4	3	4	5

LO5 **33.** A drugstore uses the fixed-interval model for many of the items it stocks. The manager wants a service level of 0.98. Determine the order quantity for the following items if the order interval is 14 days and lead time is 2 days:

Item	Average Daily Demand	Daily Standard Deviation	Quantity on Hand (none on order)
K033	60	5	420
K144	50	4	375
L700	8	2	160

LO3–5 **34.** A stockroom manager must set up inventory ordering procedures for two new items, P34 and P35. P34 can be ordered at any time, but P35 can be ordered only once every four weeks. The company operates 50 weeks a year, and the weekly usage rate for each item is Normally distributed. The manager has gathered the following information about the items:

	Item P34	Item P35
Average weekly demand	60 units	70 units
Standard deviation	4 units per week	5 units per week
Unit cost	$15	$20
Annual holding cost rate	30%	30%
Ordering cost per order	$70	$30
Lead time	2 weeks	2 weeks
Acceptable stock-out risk	2.5%	2.5%

a. At what inventory level should the manager reorder P34?
b. Calculate the economic order quantity for P34.
c. Calculate the order quantity for P35 if 110 units are on hand at the time the order is placed.

LO2 & 3 **35.** Given the following list of items,
a. Classify the items as A, B, or C.
b. Determine the economic order quantity for each item.

Item	Estimated Annual Demand	Ordering Cost	Holding Cost (%)	Unit Price
H4-010	20,000	$50	20	$ 2.50
H5-201	60,200	60	20	4.00
P6-400	9,800	80	30	28.50
P6-401	16,300	50	30	12.00
P7-100	6,250	50	30	9.00
P9-103	4,500	50	40	22.00
TS-300	21,000	40	25	45.00
TS-400	45,000	40	25	40.00
TS-041	800	40	25	20.00
V1-001	26,100	25	35	4.00

LO6 **36.** The distribution of demand (in dozens) for jelly doughnuts on Saturdays at a doughnut shop is shown in the following table. Determine the optimal number of doughnuts, in dozens, to make each Saturday morning if labour, materials, and overhead are estimated to cost $3.20 per dozen, doughnuts are sold for $4.80 per dozen, and leftover doughnuts at the end of each day are sold the next day at half price. What is the *resulting* service level?

Demand (dozens)	Relative Frequency
19	0.01
20	0.05
21	0.12
22	0.18
23	0.13
24	0.14
25	0.10
26	0.11
27	0.10
28	0.04
29	0.02

LO6 37. A public utility intends to buy a turbine as part of an expansion plan and must now decide on the number of spare parts to order. One part, X135, can be purchased for $100 each. Holding and disposal costs are estimated to be 145 percent of the purchase price over the life of the turbine. A stock-out is expected to cost $8,000 due to downtime, ordering, and "special purchase" factors. Historical records based on the performance of similar equipment operating under similar conditions suggest that demand for the spare part will tend to approximate a Poisson distribution with a mean of 3.2 units for the useful life of the turbine.

   a. What is the optimal number of units of this spare part to stock?

   b. Stocking six spare parts would be the best strategy for what range of shortage cost per unit?

LO6 38. A fish store buys fresh tuna daily for $4.20/kg and sells it for $5.70/kg. At the end of each day, any remaining tuna is sold to a producer of cat food for $2.40/kg. Daily demand for tuna at the fish store can be approximated by a Normal distribution with a mean of 80 kg and a standard deviation of 10 kg. What is the optimal stocking level?

LO6 39. A small grocery store sells fresh produce, which it obtains from local farmers. During the strawberry season, demand for fresh strawberries at the store can be reasonably approximated using a Normal distribution with a mean of 40 litres per day and a standard deviation of 6 litres per day. Excess cost is $0.35 per litre. The grocer orders 49 litres per day.

   a. What is the implied cost of shortage per litre?

   b. Why might this be a reasonable number?

LO6 40. Demand for Black Forest cake at the bakery of a supermarket can be approximated using a Poisson distribution with a mean of six per day. The manager estimates it costs $9 to prepare each cake. Fresh cakes sell for $12 each. Day-old cakes sell for $7 each. What stocking level is appropriate?

LO6 41. A large burger restaurant buys ground beef at $3/kg. The restaurant's policy is to use meat that is fresh daily. Any leftover meat at the end of each day is sold to the local zoo for $2/kg. Eight burgers can be prepared from each kilogram of meat. Burgers sell for $2 each. Labour, overhead, meat, buns, and condiments altogether cost $1 per burger. Demand for ground beef is Normally distributed with a mean of 400 kg per day and a standard deviation of 50 kg per day. What daily order quantity for ground beef is optimal?

LO6 42. The distribution of daily demand for carpet cleaning machines at a supermarket is shown in the following table. Machines are rented by the day only. Profit on a carpet cleaner is $10 per day. The store has four carpet cleaning machines.

Demand	Frequency
0	0.30
1	0.20
2	0.20
3	0.15
4	0.10
5	0.05
	1.00

   a. Assuming that the stocking decision is optimal, what is the implied range of excess cost per machine per day?

   b. Your answer from part *a* has been presented to the manager, who protests that the amount is too low. Does this suggest an increase or a decrease in the number of carpet cleaning machines she stocks? Explain.

LO6 43. A manager wants to purchase a new piece of processing equipment and must decide on the number of a spare part to order with the new equipment. The spares cost $200 each, and any unused spares will have an expected salvage value of $50 each. The probability of usage of parts can be described by the following distribution:

Number	0	1	2	3
Probability	0.10	0.50	0.25	0.15

If the part fails and a spare is not available, it will take two days to obtain a replacement and install it. The cost for idle equipment is $400 per day. The spare is expected to cost the same in the future ($200 per unit). What quantity of spares should be stocked?

LO6 44. A Las Vegas bakery must decide how many wedding cakes to prepare for the upcoming weekend. Cakes cost $33 each to make and sell for $60 each. Unsold cakes are reduced to half-price on Monday, and typically one-third of those are sold. Any that remain are donated to a nearby senior centre. Analysis of recent demand resulted in the following probability distribution:

Demand	0	1	2	3
Probability	0.15	0.35	0.30	0.20

How many cakes should be prepared?

LO6 **45.** Because there is a significant number of no-shows on a specific daily flight, the airline wants to intentionally over-book the flight. The number of no-shows can be described by a Normal distribution with a mean of 18 passengers and a standard deviation of 4.55 passengers. Profit per passenger is $99. If a passenger arrives but cannot board due to overbooking, the company policy is to provide a $200 coupon for any future flight on the airline. How many tickets should be overbooked to maximize expected profit?

LO3–5 *46. The South Texas Center for Pediatric Care in San Antonio wants to reduce its inventory costs. The centre carries vaccines (e.g., for whooping cough), noninjectable medical supplies (such as examining-table paper, alcohol swabs, tongue depressors), and office supplies (stationery, paper, and forms). Out of the 113 inventory items, seven vaccines account for approximately 70 percent of annual dollar value of $225,000. Approximately 210 whooping cough vaccines are needed per month. The office manager spends a total of approximately one half-hour finding out how much inventory of whooping cough vaccine is on hand and placing an order. She is paid approximately $17 an hour. The cost of capital for the centre is 8 percent per year, and the storage cost (including the use of freezers) is estimated to also be approximately 8 percent of item cost per year. A lot of 10 whooping cough vaccines costs an average of $160.[11]

    a. Calculate the EOQ for whooping cough vaccines.

    b. Suppose that the purchase lead time is two days and daily demand for whooping cough vaccines is Normally distributed with a mean of seven vaccines and a standard deviation of two vaccines. Calculate the reorder point if lead time service level of 98 percent is desired.

    c. Suppose that the office manager wants to make the replenishment of whooping cough vaccines easier for herself by ordering them every two weeks.

        i. Using the information in part b, what should the order-up-to level (I_{max}) be?

        ii. Suppose that the centre has 34 whooping cough vaccines on hand and none on order. What should the order quantity be, given your answer to part *i*?

LO3 **47.** The owner of a health food store has decided to intentionally allow shortage of a food supplement. The annual demand is 500 bottles, the ordering cost is $10 per order, and the holding cost is $1 per bottle per year. Cost of back-ordering one bottle is estimated to be $10 per bottle per year.

    a. What should be the order quantity?

    b. How many bottles should be short per order cycle?

LO6 *48. Hallmark sells "personal expression" cards and gifts worldwide through either its own stores or other retailers. Most products are single runs. Unsold products either are discounted and sold to discount retailers, or are discarded.

    A typical problem Hallmark faces is as follows: A Barbie stationery gift set—containing 16 notes, envelopes, and foil seals—is to be produced and marketed to celebrate the 55th year of Barbie. The price will be set at $12.99 per unit. The cost of production to Hallmark will be approximately $6 per unit. The product manager, based on previous sales of Barbie stationery products, estimates that demand and its probability for this product will be as follows:

Demand (in 1000s)	90	100	110	120	130
Probability	0.1	0.2	0.4	0.2	0.1

    Any units not sold through regular channels will be sold to discount retailers at $1 less than cost (i.e., $5 per unit). There is no penalty cost for being short. Determine the optimal order quantity for the Barbie stationery gift set.[12]

LO3 & 4 *49. Teck (Cominco)[13] is a Canadian metal mining and processing company with new investments in coal and oil. The company has several warehouses in Western Canada that store thousands of parts and supplies for the machines and equipment used in its mines and operations. The stocks in the warehouses are controlled using computers in the Vancouver head office. For spare parts, the EOQ/ROP model is used.

    The following data is the usage of specific spare part during a nine-month period:

Jan	Feb	Mar	Apr	May	Jun	Jul	Aug	Sep
2	5	10	4	12	0	8	16	4

    Suppose that now is the end of September and the next reorder point is coming up. The forecast for October is 6.7 units. The part costs Teck $15/unit. Holding cost rate is 20 percent of unit cost per year. Ordering cost is $2/order (due to EDI connection with the supplier). Purchase lead time for this part is 20 days. Assume 30 days in a month.

    a. What should the EOQ be? (*Hint:* Use the forecast for October multiplied by 12 to estimate next year's demand.)

    b. For how many days is the EOQ enough (i.e., what is order cycle for EOQ)?

    c. Calculate the total annual inventory control cost of the EOQ.

[11] D. M. Burns, M. J. Cote, and S. L. Tucker, "Inventory Analysis of a Pediatric Care Center," *Hospital Materiel Management Quarterly* 22(3), pp. 84–90.

[12] Based on F. H. Barron, "Payoff Matrices Pay Off at Hallmark," Interfaces 15(4), pp. 20–25.

[13] K. B. Hustwick and J. W. Merkley, "Cominco's Computerized Inventory Control System," *Canadian Institute of Mining Bulletin*, 75(843), pp. 136–141.

d. Suppose now this part is ordered seven at a time. How much more expensive is this?

e. Suppose there was no variability in demand or lead time. Determine the reorder point.

f. Suppose a 95 percent lead time service level is required. The standard deviation of monthly demand is 5.14 units. Determine the reorder point.

LO5 *50. Federated Cooperatives Limited (FCL) is the largest wholesaler/distributor of food and hardware in Western Canada. Until three years ago, FCL managed inventories using the Inforem forecasting and inventory control software on its mainframe computer, but has now switched to JDA (Manugistics) Demand and JDA (Manugistics) Order Optimization. FCL uses the fixed-interval model to order products for its four warehouses. Many of the order review intervals are predetermined by vendors (weekly or biweekly). As an illustration, consider the ordering of Energizer batteries for the Calgary warehouse. The purchase lead time is approximately 15 days. For simplicity, suppose that there are only two types of Energizer batteries in the warehouse: Item #0378422CA, 6V Lantern battery with annual demand of 5,767 units and price of $3.85 each, and Item #0378539CA, 6V Lantern battery with annual demand of 603 units and price of $7.54 each.

a. Suppose that the fixed cost of a purchase order for one SKU is $3.50 and the variable cost of each additional line item (SKU) is $0.50. Also, suppose that holding cost rate is 20 percent of unit cost per year. Determine the optimal order interval.

b. The forecast demand for Item #0378422CA is 138 units per week for the next few weeks and the standard deviation of demand is estimated to be 37 units per week. Currently there are 555 units on hand in the warehouse and none are on order. The service level for this SKU is desired to be 98.5 percent. Calculate the I_{max} (order up to level) for this battery, and determine the quantity to order.

c. If the weekly demand forecast for Item #0378422CA for the next five weeks was in fact 144.2, 144.2, 133.1, 133.1, and 122 units, respectively (i.e., this item has seasonality), how would your answer to part *b* change? Assume that the standard deviation of demand remains at 37 units per week.

LO3–5 *51. Sterling Pulp Chemicals (ERCO) in Saskatoon produces chemicals for processing wood pulp, such as caustic soda. In its maintenance stockroom, it keeps all the spare parts for its equipment as well as supplies such as light bulbs. For inventory control, it uses the Min/Max model, which is basically the EOQ/ROP model. Every day, the inventory staff is supposed to use the computer system to identify those stocks that have reached their Min (ROP) level and to order those items. For illustration, consider the usage of item #14-46-506: four-foot supersaver fluorescent light bulbs in the first ten months of a year: 10, 10, 66, 32, 34, 18, 24, 9, 14, and 48. The forecast for

November using exponential smoothing with $\alpha = 0.3$ is 27.48 units, and the standard deviation of monthly demand for these bulbs is 18.84 units. The lead time from the supplier, EECOL Electric, is 14 days, and the unit cost is $1.40. Holding cost rate for Sterling is estimated to be 20 percent of unit cost per year and ordering cost is $1 per order (because usually many items are ordered from the supplier together). Assume 30 days in a month.

a. Calculate the EOQ for this item. (*Hint:* estimate $D =$ Forecast for November $\times$ 12.)

b. For how many months is the EOQ enough (i.e., its order cycle)?

c. Calculate the total annual inventory control cost of the EOQ.

d. Now this part is ordered 30 units at a time. How much more costly is this?

e. Calculate the reorder point of these bulbs. Use a 97.5 percent lead time service level.

f. Given the noncriticality of this item, the new stockroom manager has suggested that it be reviewed only once a month. Calculate the Min and Max in this case. Use a 97.5 percent service level.

LO3–5 *52. The usage of Male Cord End (#14-20-391), purchased from EECOL Electric Ltd, by Sterling Pulp Chemicals (ERCO) during the June to October period of a year was 5, 1, 5, 9, and 8 units. Using Exponential Smoothing with $\alpha = 0.5$, the forecast usage for November is 7.25 units, and the standard deviation of monthly usage, using the above numbers, is 3.13 units. The price of one unit is $2.48. Suppose Sterling uses 20 percent as its holding cost rate per year, purchase lead time is approximately 14 days, and desired lead time service level is 97.5 percent. Assume 30 days in a month.

a. If this item is ordered individually using the EOQ/ROP model, and ordering cost is $1 per order, calculate the EOQ and ROP for it.

b. If this item is ordered using Min/Max and it is reviewed only once a month, determine the Min and Max.

c. Suppose Sterling uses the fixed-interval model and orders the Eagle Male Cord Ends jointly with other SKUs supplied by EECOL Electric. For simplicity, assume that there is only one other SKU, item #14-20-390, Eagle Female Cord End. The forecast for usage of Eagle Female Cord End for November is 2.23 units. The price of one Female Cord End is $5.06. The ordering cost per purchase order for one SKU is $3 and for another line item is $.50.

    i. Calculate the optimal order interval.

    ii. If currently there are 13 units of Male Cord End on hand and none on order, how many should be ordered now?

LO6 *53. A franchisee of Fuddruckers, a hamburger restaurant chain, has signed a contract to supply food for a day-long music festival. Fuddruckers distinguishes itself from other hamburger restaurant chains with on-premise butcher shop and bakery. It is now the Wednesday before the Saturday festival. Approximately 5,000 tickets have been sold so far, and this number should increase because the weather forecast is that Saturday will be sunny. Based on previous experience, the manager believes that the eventual number of people who will attend the festival, and the associated probabilities, are:

Numbers	6,000	7,000	8,000	9,000	10,000
Probability	0.1	0.2	0.4	0.2	0.1

The manager expects that on average, each person will eat one meal during the seven-hour festival. She has decided to limit the menu to just two meals: one-third-pound burgers and quarter-pound hot dogs. She estimates, based on regular restaurant sales, that 60 percent of people will buy the burger and 40 percent will buy the hot dog. The cost of one burger will be $2.25 and it will sell for $5, whereas the hot dog will cost $1.34 and will sell for $4 each. Unused food has to be discarded, and there is no penalty for being short. The meat, hot dogs, buns, and vegetables need to be ordered today (three days before the festival so that the shipment will arrive on the day of the festival). Determine the optimal order quantities for burgers and hot dogs.[14]

LO5 **54.** A distributor orders four products from a supplier. The fixed cost to place an order for one SKU is $23, and cost of each additional SKU added to the order is $3. The carrying cost rate is 24 percent per year. Purchase lead time is one week. Assume a 50-week year. The annual demand (units) and unit cost of the four SKUs are:

SKU	Annual Demand	Unit Cost
1	450	$ 8.00
2	2,000	12.50
3	200	3.52
4	3,000	33.30

The distributor wishes to use the coordinated periodic review model to plan ordering these SKUs. Calculate the multiples m_js and the optimal order interval OI*.

LO3–5 *55. Schaan Healthcare Products is a distributor of medical/surgical products in Saskatchewan. Schaan has a warehouse in Saskatoon that carries thousands of items, one of which is item #345-5870, Micro-Touch Surgical Glove, size 7. The demand for this item (in cases) during a September to November period was 25, 57, and 50, respectively. Schaan's inventory manager uses a three-month moving average to forecast next month's demand for the items. The three-month moving average forecast for December's demand for size 7 gloves is 44 cases. Suppose that he uses the EOQ/ROP model to replenish this item. The surgical gloves are purchased from Ansell Limited in cases of 200 units at a cost of $120

per case. Using the three-month moving average forecast for December, ordering cost of $15 per order, inventory holding cost rate of 15 percent per year, and purchase lead time of two days,

a. Calculate the EOQ for this item (rounded to a whole number).

b. Calculate the total annual holding and ordering cost if order quantity is 30 cases.

c. Using lead time service level of 96 percent and standard deviation of monthly demand of 16.82 cases, calculate the ROP (rounded to a whole number).

d. In fact, Schaan uses the fixed-interval model for replenishing this item. Calculate the order up to level (I_{max}) for this item (rounded to a whole number) if it is ordered every two weeks and the desired service level is 94 percent.

LO3 & 4 *56. A wholesale bottler and distributor of both imported and domestic alcoholic drinks purchases half its spirits in barrels, which it then blends and bottles (approximately 60 different types of spirits in up to five different bottle sizes). The most time-consuming activity is the changeover of the bottling line for a different bottle size. This takes one full day. Therefore, products that have the same bottle size are bottled one batch after another, saving the bottle-size changeover time (however, there is a smaller setup time for spirit, bottle, and label changeover). ROP of the one-litre bottles is set to one month of demand because they are usually bottled once a month. Each time, approximately 10 different spirits are run, one after another. The actual bottling time is negligible (only two days for all 10 spirits). Management wants the bottling batch size of each spirit to be equal to its EOQ. Note that because production rate is so much faster than the demand rate, we can use the EOQ formula instead of the economic production quantity formula.

Suppose now is the beginning of June, and there is going to be a changeover to the 1-L bottles tomorrow. The on-hand inventory of the 1-L bottles of vodka is only 144 cases, whereas the demand forecast of this SKU in June is 312 cases. Assume that the demand has no trend or seasonality. The setup cost per bottle run for vodka is $73.23. The cost per case of vodka is $29.31. The carrying cost rate is 15 percent of unit cost per year.

a. Calculate the optimal batch size (i.e., EOQ) for 1-L bottles of vodka.

b. After talking to the supervisor, it became clear that he does not use the EOQ to determine the batch size. Instead he produces enough 1-L bottles of a spirit so that this quantity plus any on-hand inventory is expected to last until the next production run for 1-L bottles, which is one month later. However, for items with uncertain demand such as vodka, he

---
[14] Based on S. M. Shafer, "Fuddruckers and the Crystal Coast Music Festival," *Case Research Journal* 22(2).

produces a quantity that, together with any on-hand inventory, is expected to meet two months of demand. Assuming that the standard deviation of monthly demand for vodka is 98 cases, what service level is the supervisor implicitly using?

LO6 *57. A high-end skiwear producer makes parkas for men, women, juniors, and preschoolers. For each gender, there are tens of styles, and for each style approximately five colours and four sizes. This results in hundreds of parka SKUs for each gender. This large variety plus the long lead time from design to distribution make the production planning of the skiwear producer very difficult.

The design starts in February, concepts are finalized by May, prototypes are made by July, designs are finalized by September, first-half production quantity is determined and fabrics are ordered by November, fabrics are received and production starts by February of next year, retailers place their orders by March, shipments of products arrive from manufacturers in Asia by July, retailers receive their orders by August, sales pick up by December, and unsold goods are discounted by February of the third year.

It is now November and the VP of operations has to decide on the first-half production quantities. The buying committee has met and each of the six members forecasted the first-half demand for the parkas. For each parka, the VP has averaged these forecasts and calculated the standard deviation. To be more conservative, he has doubled the standard deviation.

As an illustration, a specific women's parka has average forecast value of 2,150 units and standard deviation of 807 units (after doubling). Assume a Normal distribution for the demand. Each parka will be sold for $173 to retailers. The unit cost will be approximately $130. If any parkas are left after January two years later, they will be sold at $115 each. Determine the best production quantity for this parka.

LO3 *58. A commercial laundromat product manufacturer wants to consolidate the purchase of all the cardboard boxes it needs for the detergents, bleaches, and fabric softeners it sells to laundromats. The total demand for all these boxes is 10,000 units per year (a unit is equal to 1,000 packages). Assume that ordering cost is $50 per order and holding cost rate is 20 percent per year. Competitive bids have been solicited for this purchase. The following unit prices and the associated order quantity ranges are proposed by the most competitive bidder. If

this bidder is chosen, what should be the order quantity for the boxes?

Order Quantity Range	Unit Price
1–500 units	$29.50
501–750	26.87
751–1500	24.77
1,501–2,000	23.93

LO3 59. Bike Friday is a small manufacturer of high-end folding travel bicycles. The bikes can be folded and carried in a Travelcase. The controller of Bike Friday is looking into ways to cut costs. The company purchases the Travelcases in lot sizes of 100, at a unit price of $65 plus $4.50 for shipping expense. A lot would last a little more than one month. The purchase lead time is six to eight weeks. The controller has discovered that if the company ordered a full truckload of 500 Travelcases at a time, the unit price would be $50 plus $2.50 for shipping expense. However, Bike Friday would need a bigger storage space (350 square feet) which was not available in-house. Assuming that a nearby storage space could be leased for $400 a month, holding cost rate of 20 percent per unit per year, and ordering cost of $50 per order, determine if buying a truckload of Travelcases would have a lower total cost.[15]

Photo provided by Green Gear (Bike Friday)

LO6 60. A grain elevator not only buys grains from nearby farmers but also sells them seeds and chemicals. But how much of each item will be sold in a given year is uncertain, making the decision on the purchase quantity difficult. Consider the ordering of a particular herbicide by a specific grain elevator manager. Each unit weighs 50 kg. The selling price is $56.93 per unit, and the purchase cost (including the transportation cost) is $45.54. Any excess herbicide after the growing season is transported to a warehouse at the cost of $1.09 per unit, and held over winter at the holding cost rate of 10 percent of unit cost per year (which equals 5 percent for half a

---

[15] G. A. Horsfall, "How to Leverage a Bad Inventory Situation," *Hospital Materiel Management Quarterly* 20(2), pp. 40–46; http://www.bikefriday.com.

year—the approximate length of winter). It is estimated that 10 percent of shortage will be lost. The rest will incur $2.19 per unit in expediting cost from the supplier. The elevator manager estimates that the demand for this herbicide can take values of 100, 400, and 1,500 units with probabilities of 0.1, 0.5, and 0.4, respectively. What is the best stocking level?[16]

 61. A major Saskatchewan potash producer ships potash from mines in Saskatchewan to several warehouses in North America by rail. The objective is to prevent stock-out at the warehouses. The demand from the warehouses is very hard to predict. It is rarely the same every day and is often impacted by weather. In addition, the transit time is long and variable. The potash producer has to continually monitor demand and rail service patterns to avoid running out of product. Typically, there will be safety stock in the warehouses and the potash producer will also hedge its position by advancing trains when it is estimated that the busy season will start. The warehouses have limited capacity. There are situations where a train has to be held out of a site if they cannot handle it. There can be significant costs to holding a train. The other option is to divert a train to another location but that also results in additional costs.

Consider a specific problem. A customer's warehouse in Florida requires continuous replenishment with potash. The warehouse has a total storage capacity of 10,000 tonnes. There is a potash producer's mine in Saskatchewan that has 50,000 tonnes of inventory of the required product. Empty cars have to be staged at the mine two days before loading. The loading for up to 100

cars takes only one day. The train with up to 100 cars gets pulled by the originating rail carrier from the mine to Chicago, where some or all of the cars get interchanged to a US rail carrier for forwarding to Florida (the other cars, if any, go to a different customer). Then, the US carrier interchanges the cars to a short line carrier that provides local rail service to the warehouse in Florida. The rail transit from Saskatchewan to Florida takes on average 20 days (but could vary between 12 and 40 days). The short line can carry 20 cars per day to the warehouse. The warehouse can unload 20 cars per day and would typically unload the cars the same day they are delivered to the site. Each car has a capacity of 100 tonnes.

Suppose that the busy season has started and demand from the Florida warehouse is expected to be 700 tonnes per day on average for the next month or so. There are a total of 180 cars (18,000 tonnes of potash) already on the way to the Florida warehouse, shipped in two trains (9,000 tonnes each) that are expected to arrive at the warehouse in 4 days and 13 days, respectively. There will be no other shipments to the Florida warehouse during the next 28 days. There are currently 4,500 tonnes of potash in the warehouse.

a. What is the average time to replenish the warehouse with 10,000 tons of potash?

b. How many cars of potash should the potash producer dispatch to the Florida warehouse today? The potash producer would like to fill up the Florida warehouse to its limit. You may use Excel.

Q MINI-CASE

Cameco Promotional Items

Audrey Blondeau is in charge of the promotional (gift) items of Cameco, one of the largest uranium producers in the world. Promotional items include mugs and T-shirts printed with the company logo. Located in the investor, corporate, and government relations department, Audrey receives requests for gift items from supervisors and employees of Cameco for special events and also from local charities for donations of gifts.

Audrey had no system in place for receiving orders from the employees or for ordering the approximately 190 items her office carries. Most items are purchased from Impact Marketing (http://www.impactmarketing.ca), which will inscribe the company logo on the items. The reasons for carrying inventory are that the supplier requires a minimum order quantity, a

setup charge (depending on the type of item), and a lead time of two weeks for producing an item. Large orders from supervisors, over the minimum, are passed directly to the supplier for production. The supplier needs artwork approval for new items. The donation requests have to be approved for a budget and are met mostly from slow-moving stocked items.

To improve efficiency, Audrey created a simple employee request form and reduced the number of items she carried to 40. She also added 11 new items to replace old models of popular items such as mugs, bottles, and bags. Audrey is also trying to make her job easier by establishing a fixed-interval system with order interval of two months for the promotional items. She has collected the demand (from Cameco employees) for the promotional items during the last few months and has estimated the average monthly demand for the next few

---

[16] Based on D. J. Raby et al., "Inventory Management of Chemical Supplies at Alberta Wheat Pool," *Production and Inventory Management Journal* 32(1), pp. 1–6.

months and the standard deviation of monthly demand for the items. First, she is focusing on all-season items. Seasonal items such as golf balls and fleece vests will be replenished just before the season. Consider, for example, the following all-season items:

Item	Avg. Monthly Demand	Standard Dev. of Monthly Demand	On Hand	Min Order Quantity
Executive sports bag	12	4	0	25
Retro stainless steel mug	15	2	4	60
Lava pen	35	6	16	75
Heavyweight brushed cotton cap	60	6	6	72

Questions

a. What are the order-up-to level and the order quantity for these items? Audrey thinks that a lead time service level of 70 percent is adequate as large orders are passed to the supplier and the requisitioner is willing to wait two weeks.

b. In the case of the heavyweight brushed cotton cap, the supplier is offering the following quantity discount.

Quantity Range	Unit Price
72–143	$8.75
144–239	$7.95
240–575	$7.50

If holding cost rate is 12 percent per year and setup cost is $50 per setup, how many units should Audrey order?

Source: Audrey Blondeau, "Cameco's Promotional Item System: Employee Ordering" (term paper), Dec. 2006. COMM 205.

 MINI-CASE

Cameco Mine Supplies

Conor Shirley is a materials management (MM) intern in the supply chain management department of Cameco, one of the largest uranium producers in the world. Cameco has three mines (Rabbit Lake, MacArthur River, and Cigar Lake) and a mill (Key Lake), all in northern Saskatchewan. Each site has a warehouse containing supplies and spare parts. The data is maintained by the SAP software, which runs on a computer located in Cameco's head office in Saskatoon.

There are approximately 30,000 SKUs. Over 80 percent are bought from contracted suppliers. The inventory control module uses the Min/Max model. SAP checks the inventory position against the Min level every three days, and, if it is below, will automatically order enough stocks from contracted suppliers to bring inventory position up to the Max. A major initiative by the MM group is to reduce inventories by $10 million. This includes readjusting the Min and Max levels to their optimal levels.

Conor has picked four SKUs from two plants to study. The item code, description, price, and lead time from the supplier are as follows:

Code	Description	Price	Lead Time	Current Min	Current Max
20050008	Cable Hanger CAB826	$2.99	5 days	151	250
20073791	Grinding Wheel 5" ¼" 5/8" All Metal	$4.57	6	31	50
20126073	Pyrolon Coveralls XL Blue w/ HD Elastic	$8.05	8	4	75
20013742	Oil Pressure Gauge 2-1/2" 0-200 PSI	$44.75	14	1	3

Ordering cost per order is $10, holding cost rate per year is 20 percent, and lead time service level is 97.5 percent. The monthly total usage for each item during 2013 was as follows:

Month	Cable Hanger	Grinding Wheel	Coveralls	Oil Pressure Gauge
Jan	0	44	3	0
Feb	150	57	1	0
Mar	75	61	0	0
Apr	100	28	0	0
May	0	102	26	0
Jun	0	53	0	0
Jul	100	97	26	0
Aug	75	27	25	0
Sep	0	27	66	0
Oct	0	74	9	0
Nov	0	31	0	0
Dec	0	25	2	0

Conor has noticed that the demands for the cable hanger and coveralls are lumpy (there are many zero usage months) and that Normal distribution may be inappropriate for determining the Min or ROP. Therefore, he has also collected dates and quantities of transactions for these two items:

Cable Hanger

Posting Date	Quantity
Feb 8	25
Feb 18	25
Feb 23	100
Mar 14	25
Mar 14	25
Mar 26	25
Apr 4	25
Apr 5	25
Apr 13	25
Apr 25	25
Jul 4	75
Jul 30	25
Aug 10	50
Aug 10	25

Coveralls

Posting Date	Quantity
Jan 6	2
Jan 21	1
Feb 14	1
May 19	1
May 23	25
Jul 6	2
Jul 7	10
Jul 10	14
Aug 17	25
Sep 1	2
Sep 2	2
Sep 2	2
Sep 3	6
Sep 8	50
Sep 18	2
Sep 23	2
Oct 1	9
Dec 7	2

Question

Have the Min/Max values been set correctly?

Co-op Distribution Centre

Federated Co-operatives Limited (FCL) manages a sprawling 444,000 ft$_2$ distribution centre in Saskatoon, which distributes approximately 13,500 stock keeping units (SKUs) to retail co-op stores throughout the province. The distribution centre is partitioned into four distinct climate-controlled zones with one zone each for frozen, fresh (fridge), produce and dry grocery. There are approximately 2,000 industrial storage racks, which extend up to 30 feet in height. Each rack has up to five levels, with the two lowest levels within easy reach of order pickers (see the layout diagram below).

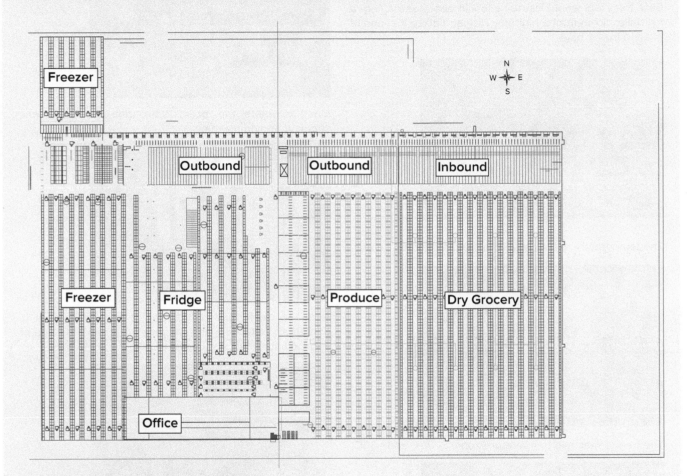

Kent Kostuk, Industrial Engineering Manager, FCL

Suppliers ship orders to the distribution centre using semi-trailer trucks. Once the trucks arrive, a forklift will move the product-laden pallets to the receiving area. The product is identified, and the quantity is verified and matched to the purchase order. To facilitate inventory tracking a pre-printed barcode is applied to the pallet and the inventory data is matched to this barcode within the Priya Warehouse Management System (WMS). Finally, it is put away into a high-bay storage rack. Whenever a pick location runs out of a SKU, the WMS would instruct a forklift operator to bring a full pallet down from a high-bay rack and place it in one of the two lower bays.

The temperature in the cooler is around 4 degrees Celsius.

The freezer has two temperature zones: −20C and −30C.

A typical retail co-op store will place orders two to three times each week. As orders come in, an order picker will put on a Honeywell Vocollect Talkman and follow voice instructions to pick the order in the most efficient manner.

Once complete, the order is brought to an automatic shrink wrapping machine.

After the pallet load is wrapped, a barcode sticker is printed and attached, and the pallet is brought to one of approximately 100 staging lanes.

Shipping trailers feature multi-temperature zones, so only one delivery needs to be made to each retail store, even though different types of products are ordered at the same time.

The distribution centre has approximately 70 pallet jacks, 23 high-reach forklifts and 55 Talkmans. Approximately 160 hourly employees take turns working in two shifts.

Bananas are green and inedible when they first arrive from Latin America. This location features seven ripening rooms which use ethylene gas to help the bananas ripen.

In recent years, this distribution centre was able to increase its labour productivity by implementing a labour management system (which is fully integrated with Priya) that uses predetermined time standards. The result was a 41 percent improvement in picking productivity (see the table below) and a reduction in the number of customer complaints by half.

Avg. no. of picks per hour

Area	2013	2014	2015	2016
Produce	114	141	165	166
Dry grocery	92	100	122	130
Fridge	83	116	155	160
Freezer	89	90	118	122

Chapter 13
Aggregate Operations Planning and Master Scheduling

Canada Post spends months planning for the busiest time of the year.
Fernando Morales/The Globe and Mail

LEARNING OBJECTIVES

After completing this chapter, you should be able to:

LO1 Explain what sales and operations planning and aggregate operations planning are, and identify the variables and strategies used in aggregate operations planning.

LO2 Develop a good aggregate production plan.

LO3 Discuss the differences with aggregate service planning.

LO4 Explain what master production scheduling is and how it is performed.

anada Post delivers approximately two-thirds of all parcels ordered online in Canada, and more than one-quarter of these are delivered in November and December. There are more than 20 days in November and December during which Canada Post delivers more than a million packages each day. And the online shopping trend is continuing to increase. How does Canada Post prepare for this delivery rush?

- It hires over 2,500 seasonal workers.
- It rents up to 900 local pickup and delivery vehicles.
- It deploys extra equipment in plants and depots.
- It extends its post office hours beginning in November.
- It delivers during the weekends in major urban centres starting in mid-November.

How organizations deal with the peaks and valleys of the demand for their goods and services is the topic of this chapter.

Sources: http://www.newswire.ca/news-releases/canada-post-readies-for-record-breaking-holiday-volumes-601552205.html; http://photos.newswire.ca/images/download/20161116_C2421_PHOTO_EN_820748.jpg.

Introduction

Organizations usually make capacity and production decisions on three levels: long term, intermediate term, and short term. Long-term decisions relate to product selection, facility size and location, major equipment, and layout of facilities. These long-term decisions essentially define the capacity constraints within which intermediate planning must function. Intermediate decisions relate to general level of employment, output, and inventories, which in turn define the boundaries within which short-term capacity and production planning must function. Short-term decisions involve determining the master production schedule (MPS), material requirements planning (MRP), and scheduling jobs and workers. The three levels of capacity and production decisions are depicted in Figure 13-1. This chapter covers intermediate capacity and production decisions, as well as MPS. These decisions are usually made in the context of an activity called *sales and operations planning*.

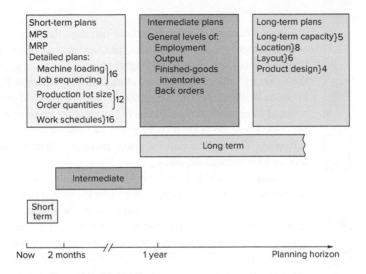

◀ **FIGURE 13-1**

Overview of planning levels (chapter numbers are shown).

Sales and Operations Planning

Sales and operations planning (S&OP) is the process of reconciling sales forecasts with operations plans at an aggregate (product family) level and tying them to the strategic plan. S&OP is for the intermediate term (usually the next 12 months), covering a horizon sufficient to plan for workforce and production changes. Figure 13-2 shows the hierarchy of production planning and the position of S&OP in it. This chapter covers the operations (or aggregate) planning part of S&OP, and master scheduling. Material requirements planning will be covered in Chapter 14, and detailed planning/scheduling and execution systems in Chapter 16.

sales and operations planning Process of integrating sales forecasts with operations plans.

Updating the Sales and Operations Plan. The sales and operations plan is usually updated monthly. The process of updating begins with recording the sales, production, and inventory levels of the previous month, updating forecasts for the next 12 months or so, seeing if the necessary production changes are feasible, and providing a summary of information to top management for making decisions.

The monthly process used by the S&OP team of Ingersoll-Rand (a diversified industrial manufacturer of air conditioners, pumps, compressors, etc.) is as follows:

Demand planning

> Day 1: Prepare sales data; perform baseline forecasts
>
> Day 3: Gather field intelligence (salespeople info)
>
> Day 7: Regional managers review forecasts and possibly modify them

Supply planning

> Days 11–15: Review forecasts, compare with capacity, identify constraints, and develop countermeasures

Partnership meeting

Day 16: Functional managers review and approve the forecasts, evaluate performance measures, analyze financial impact, try to work out the issues, and identify actions to balance demand and supply

Executive meeting

Day 18: Understand and react to misalignments, resolve remaining issues, approve one set of numbers (one plan), authorize actions to achieve the plan

Source: http://www.apics.org/industry-content-research/publications/apics-magazine/apics-magazine—landing-page—everyone/2013/09/09/s-op-step-by-step.

In the executive/top management meeting, the executives have time only to review a summary of sales, production, and inventory plans of a limited number (e.g., up to six to eight) families of products. An example of the summary information for a product family is shown in Figure 13-3. In Location A, the target fill rate of 99 percent and finished goods inventory target of 10 days of supply are shown. Note that for make-to-stock products, the company needs to keep safety stocks of finished goods to meet demand variability. The level of finished goods inventory directly affects customer service level through fill rate.

Locations B and E show the old forecast sales for the past three months, and old and new (after update) forecasts for the next six months and the two quarters after that. Locations C and F show the operations plan and the actual production during the past three months, and the old and new (after update) production plan for the next six months and two quarters after that. Locations D and G show the inventory plan and the actual levels during the past three months, and the projected inventory levels resulting from the given forecasts and production plans and the equivalent days of supply during the next six months and two quarters after that. Also shown is fill

---

FIGURE 13-2 ▲

Production planning hierarchy.

T. F. Wallace, *Sales & Operations Planning* (Cincinnati: T. F. Wallace & Co., 2001). Figures reprinted courtesy of T. F. Wallace & Co.

FIGURE 13-3 ▶

An example of the summary information for a product family used in the top management S&OP meeting.

T. F. Wallace, *Sales & Operations Planning* (Cincinnati: T. F. Wallace & Co., 2001). Figures reprinted courtesy of T. F. Wallace & Co.

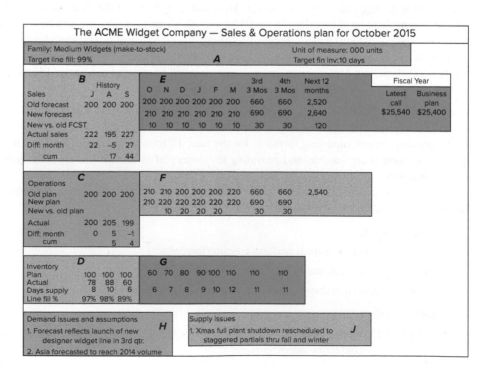

rate performance during the past three months. Finally, in Locations H and J, any major demand and production issues are pointed out.

See the "Red Wing Shoes' Journey to S&OP" OM in Action for details of the transformation process Red Wing Shoes underwent to set up an effective S&OP process.

 OM in Action

Red Wing Shoes' Journey to S&OP

Red Wing Shoes (RWS) is a private company founded over 100 years ago. It manufactures (in eight locations) and distributes (from six DCs) six brands of tough work boots and shoes (26,000 SKUs) and apparel (72,000 SKUs), globally. RWS is somewhat vertically integrated in that it has its own leather tannery, boot/shoe manufacturing plants, and few retail stores, but also has suppliers (especially for apparel) and mainly sells through other retailers such as Mark's.

Before 2008, there was no integrated S&OP in RWS. A planner from the supply chain department and a representative of new product development collected and entered huge amounts of data in Excel, and made a 12-month forecast for each SKU based on the previous year's actual sales. The planner updated the forecasts monthly by taking the actual sales out of the forecasts, without talking to sales managers to identify the causes for forecast discrepancy. Data collection and entry in Excel were manual and required two weeks. The forecasts were not communicated to the manufacturing plants or suppliers, but instead work orders and purchase orders for immediate needs were issued. Huge amounts of excess inventory were stored in trailers, resulting in significant demurrage charges.

Then in 2008, RWS hired a process improvement manager. She embarked on creating an effective S&OP process. By 2009, she had involved 12 representatives of sales of each brand, product development, manufacturing, supply chain, and a senior executive. The meetings (which took place once every two months) were long and looked at past performance rather than future plans. In 2010, she asked the IT department to create the sales data spreadsheets automatically from RWS's ERP. This saved two weeks and prevented errors of data entry and worksheet setup. It also provided a longer history of sales.

In 2011, she convinced senior management to create a demand planning department that is responsible for creation of sales forecasts. They communicate with brand managers, find the reasons for forecast discrepancies, oversee data collection and forecasting, and adjust forecasts. Also, the bimonthly long meeting was divided into smaller/shorter functional meetings every month: first, sales forecasts are generated, then they are approved by sales managers and next by the VP of business services, all in the first week of a month. Then the forecasts are transmitted to the supply chain (SC) department that checks their production/distribution feasibility; next, a consensus meeting between sales and SC occurs by the end of second week; and finally the executive review meeting (involving the president and all VPs) occurs by the third week.

In 2012, a forecasting and replenishment software (Logility) was purchased and installed, reducing the forecasting work and improving the accuracy of forecasts. Staff were also trained in statistical techniques and the use of the software. The results are a shorter and more effective S&OP process, better forecasts, forecast management-by-exception, shared forecasts and collaboration with manufacturing and suppliers, 27 percent reduction in inventory, 8–10 percent increase in customer fill rate, and 50 percent reduction in demurrage charges.

Source: http://www.scmr.com/plus/SCMR1405_F_RedWing.pdf.

Aggregate Operations Planning

Aggregate operations planning is monthly planning for the sum of all the products in the same family (produced in the same facility) for the next 12 months or so. It is particularly useful for organizations that experience seasonal fluctuations in demand. The goal of aggregate operations planning is to achieve a production plan that will satisfy total forecast demand at minimum cost. Planners must make decisions on employment levels and changes, production levels and changes, and the resulting inventory levels.

> **aggregate operations planning** Monthly planning for the sum of all the products in the same family (produced in the same facility) for the next 12 months or so.

The Concept of Aggregation

In aggregate operations planning, planners focus on a group of similar products produced in the same facility. For example, planners in an ice cream plant would not concern themselves with flavours and brands of ice cream. Instead, planners would lump all tubs (containers) of the same size together and deal with them as though they were a single product, e.g., a 2-litre tub of ice cream; hence, the term *aggregate*. If the products are very different, a typical product is chosen and all other products are represented in equivalent units of the chosen product. For example, if an ice cream line can make 2,000 11.4-litre tubs or 17,000 2-litre tubs per eight-hour shift, then an 11.4-litre tub is equivalent to 17,000/2,000 = 8.5 2-litre tubs.

Another example is space allocation in a department store. A manager might decide to allocate 40 percent of the available space in the clothing department to women's wear, 30 percent to juniors, and so on, without regard for what brand names will be offered or how much of juniors will be pants. The aggregate measure or equivalent unit might be racks of clothing.

For labour-intensive services, a common aggregate measure or equivalent unit is full-time equivalent (FTE) of workforce. For example, a half-time worker (working 20 hours a week) is counted as 0.5 FTE.

In each of these examples, an aggregate approach permits managers to make general decisions about intermediate-term capacity and production levels without having to deal with details.

Demand and Capacity Options

Management has a wide range of decision options at its disposal for sales and operations planning. These include demand-influencing actions such as changing prices, promotion, early orders, back orders, exporting, and producing complementary products during the off-season; and capacity-influencing actions such as hiring temporary workers, using overtime/idle time, hiring part-time workers, stockpiling finished-good inventory, and subcontracting. We assume that the organization usually keeps a number of year-round "permanent" workers and will replace them as they retire or resign. Hence, this is not included as a capacity option.

Demand-Influencing Options. The basic demand-influencing options, handled by marketing, are:

1. *Pricing.* Pricing differentials are commonly used to shift demand from peak periods to off-peak periods. For example, air fares are cheaper in the September to November period than in December.

2. *Promotion.* Advertising and other forms of promotion such as displays, direct marketing, and extending the payment period can sometimes be effective in shifting demand so that it conforms more closely to capacity.

3. *Early orders.* It might be possible to convince customers to place their order (may be an initial partial order) before the peak season.

> **back orders** Orders taken in one period but promised to be delivered at a later period.

4. *Back orders.* A company can shift demand to future periods by using **back orders**, which are orders taken in one period but promised to be delivered at a later period. The success of this approach depends on how willing customers are to wait for delivery. The costs associated with back orders include lost sales, annoyed or disappointed customers, and additional paperwork. Back orders can be thought of as negative inventory. Make-to-order companies carry an "inventory" of (back) orders as opposed to finished-goods inventory that is carried by make-to-stock companies. A form of back order is the appointment system, which is an acceptable way to regulate demand in services such as health care.

5. *Exporting.* It might be possible to export excess production during the off season to the southern hemisphere (for example, to Australia or Brazil), where the temperature cycle is the reverse.

6. *Complementary products during off season.* Manufacturers that experience seasonal demands for certain products (e.g., snow blowers) are sometimes able to develop a demand for a complementary product (e.g., lawn mowers) that makes use of their resources during the off season. The same is true for air conditioners and heaters.

Capacity-Influencing Options. The basic capacity-influencing options, handled by operations, are:

1. *Hiring temporary workers.* Organizations may hire a limited number of temporary full-time workers (who work 40 hours a week). For instance, if a factory usually uses 10 of its 14 production lines, crews for additional lines (up to four lines) could be added on a temporary basis during peak season.

   Furthermore, a company can add or reduce the number of shifts. For example, instead of working eight hours a day (i.e., one shift), a company can double its workforce on a temporary basis and operate in two shifts (i.e., work 16 hours a day) during peak season.

   Union contracts may restrict the number of temporary workers a company can hire. Another consideration is the skill level of workers. Highly skilled temporary workers are difficult to find.

   Hiring temporary workers entails certain costs. Hiring costs include screening, interviewing, recruitment, and training costs to bring new temp workers "up to speed." And quality may suffer. Some savings may occur if workers who have recently worked for the organization are rehired.

2. *Using overtime/idle time.* Overtime and idle time (i.e., nonproductive employment or slack time) of permanent workers can be implemented easily and quickly. Organizations use idle time for training, performing maintenance, problem solving, and process improvement. Overtime (i.e., working longer than 40 hours a week) permits the employees to increase their earnings (overtime pay is usually 1.5 times the regular-time pay).

   On the other hand, overtime often results in lower productivity, poorer quality, more accidents, and increased payroll costs, and idle time results in less efficient use of resources. Overtime is usually used to meet unexpected demand.

3. *Hiring part-time workers.* In many instances the use of part-time workers is a viable option—much depends on the nature of the work, training and skills needed, and union agreement. Part-time workers such as high school students typically work 20 hours a week or less, and usually do not receive fringe benefits such as dental insurance. Part-time workers are usually temporary.

4. *Stockpiling finished-good inventory.* The use of finished-good inventory allows companies to produce goods in an off-season period and sell them in a future peak-season period. Holding cost includes not only storage costs and the cost of money tied up in inventory, but also the cost of obsolescence, spoilage, and so on. This method is suitable for make-to-stock manufacturing.

5. *Subcontracting.* **Subcontracting** is asking another company to make the product or part of it. It is like employing temporary workers but the work is done offsite. Subcontracting may be cheaper than in-house production, however it has the disadvantages of reduction in control and possibly quality issues. Conversely, in periods of excess capacity, an organization may subcontract-in, that is, conduct work for another organization.

> **subcontracting** Asking another company to make the product or part of it.

Inputs To and Outputs From Aggregate Operations Planning

Effective aggregate operations planning requires good *information*. First, the production rates for various labour schemes (e.g., 40 hours a week regular time and 10 hours of overtime) must be known, and forecasts of demand must be available. Then planners must take into account organization policies; for example, regarding changes in employment level. Costs of various options should also be determined.

The output of aggregate operations planning is the level of production (output), which is determined from the level of employment, and in turn determines the amount of inventory at the end of each period (for make-to-stock manufacturers). All these contribute to the total cost of the plan.

Table 13-1 lists the major inputs to and outputs from aggregate operations planning.

TABLE 13-1 ▶

Aggregate operations planning inputs and outputs.

Inputs	Outputs
Resources	Total cost of the plan
Production rates (capacity) for various labour schemes	Projected levels of
Warehouse (inventory) capacity	Inventory
Demand forecasts	Output
Policy statements	Employment
Overtime (maximum)	
Maximum temporary/part-time workers	
Inventory levels (initial, safety stocks, desired ending)	
Costs	
Inventory holding	
Back order	
Hiring	
Wage rates (permanent, temporary, part-time)	
Overtime	

Basic Aggregate Operations Planning Strategies

In this chapter, we will concentrate on the capacity-influencing options. An organization might adopt one of the following aggregate operations planning strategies:

1. Maintain level output/workforce.

2. Change output to match demand period by period.

3. Use a combination.

level output/workforce strategy A production plan that maintains a steady rate of output and workforce while meeting variations in demand and changes in required safety stocks by inventories.

Under the **level output/workforce strategy**, a steady rate of output and workforce is maintained while variations in forecast demand and changes in required safety stocks are met by using seasonal finished-good inventory. This strategy only works for make-to-stock manufacturers. The "fixed" number of permanent workers is equal to the average full-time worker requirements during the planning horizon (e.g., next 12 months). Level output/workforce strategy assumes that inventoried products have a long shelf life. This is true for some products such as durable goods, but not for others such as ice cream (which has a freezer life of only three months).

chase demand strategy A production plan that varies the output of any period to equal the forecast of demand and changes in required safety stocks for that period.

Matching output to demand is **chase demand strategy**; the planned output for any period is equal to forecast of demand (and changes in required safety stocks for that period if it is feasible to hold finished-good inventory). Chase demand strategy uses a smaller number of permanent workers and meets peak demand using a combination of part-time/temporary workers, overtime, and subcontracting. Service organizations that cannot regulate their demand have to use chase demand strategy. For an application of chase demand strategy, see the "Lands' End" OM in Action.

 OM in Action www.landsend.com

Lands' End

Lands' End is a major phone/mail/Internet-order distributor of clothing and sewn goods located in the small town of Dodgeville, Wisconsin (population 4,000). Sales of Lands' End peak in November and December each year,

much like other retailers, due to the holiday shopping season. Lands' End does 40 percent of its business during the fourth quarter. The number of inquiries received jumps from 40,000 a day to more than 100,000 on the busiest days. During the other three quarters, there is also some variation in sales. Lands' End employs customer sales workers (for order taking), warehouse workers, and sewers who perform alterations. It employs approximately 3,500 permanent and 1,000 part-time workers year-round. How does the company meet its excess demand for labour hours during November and December?

First, it employs approximately 2,000 more temporary full-time and part-time workers. The supply of part-time temporary workers comes from high school, college, and university students who can work a six-hour shift after school (three times a week), and the supply of full-time temporary workers comes from some local cheese factories who end their busy season in October.

Second, Lands' End encourages its workers to cross-train so they can work in other jobs when they are needed (called job sharing). Third, employees can work extended schedules during November and December, up to 12 hours a day (the portion above eight hours is performed in a different department and is considered overtime). Approximately one-third of temporary workers return to work for Lands' End again the following year or later. A new hire receives six hours of orientation/training, but a rehire may receive only up to two hours of retraining.

Sources: J. J. Laabs, "Strategic Holiday Staffing at Lands' End," *Personnel Journal* 73(12), p. 28ff; K. Haegele, "Gearing Up for the Holiday Rush," *Target Marketing* 23(6), pp. 44–48ff.

Figure 13-4 illustrates the two strategies, using a seasonally varying demand pattern to highlight the differences in the two approaches.

A mixed strategy uses a combination of two strategies. For example, a company can have two levels of output—low in the off season and high in the peak season—and also use overtime, temporary workers, and finished-good inventory buildup.

For three applications, see the "Three Cases of Aggregate Production Plans" OM in Action.

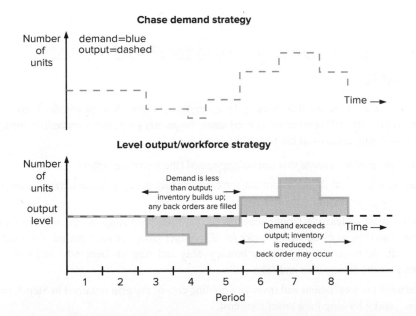

► FIGURE 13-4

Illustration of chase demand and level output/workforce strategies.

 OM in Action

Three Cases of Aggregate Production Plans

A Fridge Plant

This plant produces three brands of fridges in 15 sizes (models) and three colours. Summer months' sales are 20 percent higher than winter months', and there is a peak in November for Christmas sales. Monthly forecast sales for the next 12 months are aggregated at the brand level. There are two assembly lines that work one shift per workday. Holidays are two weeks at Christmas and two weeks in July. The company uses a chase demand strategy because fridges are large and expensive. The union has agreed that 25 percent of the workforce can be temporary, on a three-month contract. A new hire needs two to three days of training. Overtime is used only for emergencies.

A Chocolate Plant

This plant produces Easter eggs and Christmas chocolate novelties (300 SKUs). Therefore, the periods before Easter and Christmas are the busy periods (Easter is busier). There are several chocolate tanks, moulding machines, and foiling/wrapping machines. Change of chocolate type is very time consuming (one to four shifts). The company produces chocolate for Christmas based on forecasts in May and June, and based on firm orders in July and August. Similarly, for Easter, initial production is in September to November based on forecasts, and in December to February based on firm orders. The permanent employment is 120–140 workers (on two shifts but not all lines running). However, during the busiest months, October to January, up to 120–140 temporary workers on four- to 50-week contracts are employed on a third shift. The training period is short. Overtime is used for new product trials and emergencies.

An Air Conditioner and Gas Heater Manufacturer

These products are highly seasonal. The company originally made air conditioners (ACs) but bought a gas-heater producer nearby to complement its production. Two of six AC assembly lines can switch from ACs to heaters. When needed, the company uses casual workers who need only three hours of training in the assembly area. Jobs are rotated daily in order to increase the flexibility of workers for reassignment to bottleneck operations. The plants are closed for two weeks at Christmas, one week in April or June, and one week in September or October, depending on product demand. Forecast error is very high, so one to 2.5 months' worth of safety stocks are kept. Planners create rolling "rough-cut" monthly business plans for the next 12 months. Overtime is used as a last resort.

Source: G. Buxey, "Aggregate Planning for Seasonal Demand: Reconciling Theory With Practice," *International Journal of Operations & Production Management*, 25(11), pp. 1083–1100.

Techniques for Aggregate Production Planning

Two approaches are used for determining the aggregate production plan: trial-and-error and optimization. In practice, trial-and-error is used more frequently. A general procedure for aggregate production planning consists of the following steps:

1. Determine product groups that can be aggregated (the fewer the better).
2. Determine the total demand forecast for each product group in each period of the planning horizon (e.g., next 12 months).
3. Identify a set of feasible labour schemes so that total production meets or exceeds the total demand and the required safety stocks for all product groups in each period. For example, use one shift (40 hours a week) during January–May and August–December and two shifts (80 hours a week) during June and July.
4. Determine the total labour and inventory holding cost of the plan obtained in Step 3, and repeat Steps 3 and 4 looking for a lower total cost.

If optimization is used, the software will automatically find the lowest total-cost feasible plan; that is, it will perform Steps 3 and 4 repeatedly until the lowest-cost plan is obtained.

Trial-and-Error

Trial-and-error consists of developing simple *tables/worksheets* or *graphs* that enable managers to determine the production levels that meet forecast demand and safety stocks. The main disadvantage of trial-and-error is that it does not necessarily result in the optimal (i.e., lowest total cost) aggregate production plan.

Using Graphs. Very often, graphs are used to guide the development of alternative aggregate production plans. The obvious advantage of a graph is that it provides a visual portrayal of a production plan. Some planners prefer cumulative graphs, while others prefer to see a period-by-period break-down of a production plan (Figure 13-4 was an example of two period-by-period graphs). Figure 13-5A shows a cumulative graph for a production plan with level output/workforce (the slope of the dashed line represents the production rate) and seasonal finished-good inventory (the vertical difference between cumulative production and cumulative demand at any period) absorbing demand variations. Figure 13-5B is a cumulative graph used by Blue Bell (Wrangler) jeans (now part of VF Corp.) for a product line (e.g., men's corduroy jeans). Note that the cumulative demand is padded by safety stocks, seasonal inventory is called build-up stock, and target inventory is the sum of the two. The cumulative production line is chosen so that it meets the cumulative demand plus safety stock up to any month in the planning horizon. In this case, September of next year determines the slope of the cumulative production line, which is essentially linear, indicating a level output/workforce strategy.

a.

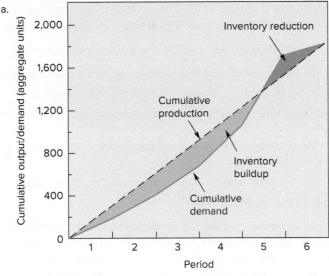

◀ **FIGURE 13-5A**

A cumulative graph for level output/ workforce strategy.

b.

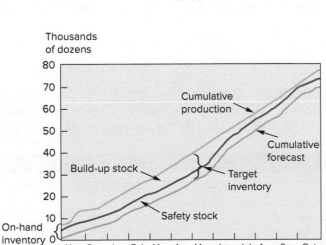

◀ **FIGURE 13-5B**

A cumulative graph for level output/ workforce strategy used by Blue Bell (Wrangler).

J.R. Edwards, et al., "Blue Bell Trims Its Inventory," *Interfaces* 15(1), Jan/Feb 1985, pp. 34–52. The Institute for Operations Research and the Management Sciences (INFORMS). Reproduced with permission. Copyright, INFORMS, http://www.informs.org

Using Tables/Worksheets. First, we make the following simplifying assumptions:

1. There is only one aggregate group. That is, all products can be represented in terms of an equivalent unit.

2. No allowance is made for statutory holidays, vacations, and different numbers of workdays in different months.

3. No allowance is made for safety stocks for each period. However, manufacturers can hold seasonal stocks and there is an initial and possibly desired end-of-planning-horizon inventory. In addition, back-orders are allowed during any period but must be cleared by the end of planning horizon.

4. All production is represented in terms of number of units of product, not the number of labour hours or workers.

5. The total cost for each of regular-time/temporary/overtime production, back orders, holding inventory, and new hires is a linear function of number of units of product; that is, it equals a constant unit cost times the number of units of product.

6. The production of a unit of product can be associated to a worker in terms of hours it will take and labour cost. Hence, unit cost of labour to make a unit product can be calculated using the wage rate and number of hours each unit will take a worker to make.

7. The hiring cost per unit product is the hiring cost per worker divided by the number of units of product a worker can make during one period, and is charged to his/her first period of employment.

8. Inventory holding cost is charged to the average level of inventory held during a period, but back-order cost is charged to the amount of back orders carried to the next period.

The following relationships are used in calculating inventory in each period.

1. To determine the ending inventory or back order in any period i, first calculate X:

$$X = \text{Beginning inventory}_i + (\text{Output} - \text{Forecast})_i - \text{Back order}_{i-1},$$

where Output is the sum of regular permanent, overtime, and part-time/temporary/subcontract production.

If $X \geq 0$, then Ending inventory$_i$ = X and Back order$_i$ = 0; whereas if $X < 0$, then Ending inventory$_i$ = 0 and Back order$_i$ = $-X$.

2. The average inventory for a period is equal to (Beginning inventory + Ending inventory)/2.

3. Beginning inventory$_i$ = Ending inventory$_{i-1}$

The three examples below illustrate the development and comparison of simple aggregate production plans using tables/worksheets. In Example 13-1, output/workforce is held level, with back order absorbing demand increases (Plan 1). In Example 13-2, back order is prevented by using overtime (Plan 2). Example 13-3 is similar, but uses temporary workers instead of overtime (Plan 3).

EXAMPLE 13-1 ▶

The planner for a company that makes garden tractors is about to prepare an aggregate production plan that will cover the next six months. She has collected the following information:

Month	1	2	3	4	5	6	Total
Forecast demand	2,000	2,000	3,000	4,000	5,000	2,000	18,000

Permanent workforce = 140
Production per month = 2,800 units or 20 per worker
Initial inventory = 1,000 units
Desired ending inventory at the end of sixth month = 1,000 units
Costs
  Labour
    Regular time permanent = $100 per tractor
    Overtime = $150 per tractor
    Temporary = $100 per tractor
Hire cost = $500 per temporary worker or $25 (= $500/20 units) per unit (charged to the first month of employment); assume that temporary workers have the same productivity as permanent workers.
Inventory = $10 per tractor per month (charged on the average inventory level)
Back order = $150 per tractor per month

The planner now wants to evaluate a production plan that calls for level output/workforce (with the current level of permanent workforce, 140), using inventory to absorb the uneven forecast demand but allowing some back order.

SOLUTION

The total regular-time output of permanent workers per month is 2,800 units. The filled worksheet for this level output/workforce strategy is shown below. The calculations are explained after the worksheet.

Month	1	2	3	4	5	6	Total
Forecast demand	2,000	2,000	3,000	4,000	5,000	2,000	18,000
Output							
Regular permanent	2,800	2,800	2,800	2,800	2,800	2,800	16,800
Temporary	–	–	–	–	–	–	
Overtime	–	–	–	–	–	–	
Output – Forecast	800	800	–200	–1,200	–2,200	800	–1,200
Inventory							
Beginning	1,000	1,800	2,600	2,400	1,200	0	
Ending	1,800	2,600	2,400	1,200	0	0	
Average	1,400	2,200	2,500	1,800	600	0	8,500
Back order	0	0	0	0	1,000	200	1,200
Costs							
Labour							
Regular perm (at $100/ unit)	$280,000	$280,000	$280,000	$280,000	$280,000	$280,000	$1,680,000
Temporary (at $100/unit)	–	–	–	–	–	–	
Overtime (at $150/unit)	–	–	–	–	–	–	
Hire temporary (at $25/ unit)	–	–	–	–	–	–	
Inventory (at $10/unit/ month)	14,000	22,000	25,000	18,000	6,000	0	85,000
Back order (at $150/unit/ month)	0	0	0	0	150,000	30,000	180,000
Total cost	$294,000	$302,000	$305,000	$298,000	$436,000	$310,000	$1,945,000

Starting with month 1, $(\text{Output} - \text{Forecast})_1 = 2,800 - 2,000 = 800$,
$X = \text{Beginning inventory}_1 + (\text{Output} - \text{Forecast})_1 - \text{Back order}_0$
$= 1,000 + 800 - 0 = 1,800$

Therefore, Ending inventory$_1$ = 1,800 and Back order$_1$ = 0. Also,
Average inventory$_1$ = (Beginning inventory$_1$ + Ending inventory$_1$)/2
$= (1,000 + 1,800)/2 = 1,400$

Then, Beginning inventory$_2$ = Ending inventory$_1$ = 1,800. Continue with the same formulas, but note that in month 5,
$X = \text{Beginning inventory}_5 + (\text{Output} - \text{Forecast})_5 - \text{Back order}_4$
$= 1,200 + (-2,200) - 0 = -1,000$

Therefore, Ending inventory$_5$ = 0 and Back order$_5$ = $-(-1,000)$ = 1,000. Also, in month 6,
$X = \text{Beginning inventory}_6 + (\text{Output} - \text{Forecast})_6 - \text{Back order}_5$
$= 0 + 800 - 1,000 = -200$

Therefore, Ending inventory$_6$ = 0 and Back order$_6$ = 200.
The costs were calculated as follows. Regular permanent cost in each month equals 2,800 units × $100 per unit, or $280,000. Inventory holding cost = Average inventory × $10 per unit. Back-order cost is $150 per unit times the number of back orders. The total cost for this plan (either sum the row totals of costs or sum the column totals of costs) is $1,945,000.

After reviewing Plan 1, developed in the preceding example, the planner noticed the large number of back orders in month 5 (1,000 units) and month 6 (200). Furthermore, the desired month 6 ending inventory of 1,000 units is not realized. Therefore, output has to increase by a total of 1,200 units during the planning horizon (the difference between total forecast and total regular permanent output, leaving the same amount of ending inventory as the initial inventory).

EXAMPLE 13-2 ▶

The planner has decided to investigate the use of overtime to make up for the shortage in Example 13-1. It is the policy of the company that the maximum amount of overtime output per month be 400 units. Develop an aggregate production plan in this case and compare it to Plan 1.

SOLUTION

The 1,200 units to be produced during overtime must be scheduled on and before month 5 (when shortage or back order starts to occur). Scheduling it earlier would increase inventory holding costs ($10/unit/month); scheduling it later would incur back-order cost ($150/unit/month), which is larger. That is why the maximum permitted overtime production should be used in months 3–5. The completed worksheet is given below.

Month	1	2	3	4	5	6	Total
Forecast	2,000	2,000	3,000	4,000	5,000	2,000	18,000
Output							
Regular permanent	2,800	2,800	2,800	2,800	2,800	2,800	16,800
Temporary	–	–	–	–	–	–	
Overtime	–	–	400	400	400	–	1,200
Output – Forecast	800	800	200	−800	−1,800	800	0
Inventory							
Beginning	1,000	1,800	2,600	2,800	2,000	200	
Ending	1,800	2,600	2,800	2,000	200	1,000	
Average	1,400	2,200	2,700	2,400	1,100	600	10,400
Back order	0	0	0	0	0	0	0
Costs							
Labour							
Regular perm (at $100/unit)	$280,000	$280,000	$280,000	$280,000	$280,000	$280,000	$1,680,000
Temporary (at $100/unit)	0	0	0	0	0	0	0
Overtime (at $150/unit)	–	–	60,000	60,000	60,000	–	180,000
Hire temporary (at $25/unit)	–	–	–	–	–	–	
Inventory (at $10/unit/month)	14,000	22,000	27,000	24,000	11,000	6,000	104,000
Back order (at $150/unit/month)	0	0	0	0	0	0	0
Total cost	$294,000	$302,000	$367,000	$364,000	$351,000	$286,000	$1,964,000

Note that, even though Plan 2 has a larger total cost than Plan 1, it produces 1,200 more units and leaves 1,000 units at the end of month 6.

Alternatively, the company can use temporary workers to meet the 1,200 units short in Example 13-1. The unit cost of temporary-worker production ($100) is lower than the unit cost of overtime production ($150), but there is a per unit hire cost of $25 for units produced during the first month of employment. Overall, using temporary workers is less costly than using overtime.

The third option is to use temporary workers during months of high demand. Suppose that temporary workers will be working during a second shift and enough of them are available. Develop an aggregate production plan in this case (Plan 3).

◀ EXAMPLE 13-3

SOLUTION

Dividing the number of short units (1,200) by the output rate of 20 per temporary worker, you find that 60 temporary worker-months are needed (e.g., 60 temporary workers for one month each, or 30 temporary workers for two months each, or 20 temporary workers for three months each, etc.).

Therefore, the planner tried each of the alternatives: hiring 60 temporary workers in month 5 on a one-month contract; or hiring 30 temporary workers starting in month 4 on a two-month contract; or hiring 20 temporary workers starting in month 3 on a three-month contract, and so on. The plan with the lowest total cost, including inventory holding cost, hires temporary workers starting in month 4 on a two-month contract. The completed worksheet for this plan is given below. Note that the hiring cost applies to only the first month of employment.

Month	1	2	3	4	5	6	Total
Forecast	2,000	2,000	3,000	4,000	5,000	2,000	18,000
Output							
Regular permanent	2,800	2,800	2,800	2,800	2,800	2,800	16,800
Temporary				600	600		1,200
Overtime	—	—	—	—	—	—	
Output forecast	800	800	−200	−600	−1,600	800	0
Inventory							
Beginning	1,000	1,800	2,600	2,400	1,800	200	
Ending	1,800	2,600	2,400	1,800	200	1,000	
Average	1,400	2,200	2,500	2,100	1,000	600	9,800
Back order	0	0	0	0	0	0	0
Costs							
Labour							
Regular perm (at $100/unit)	$280,000	$280,000	$280,000	$280,000	$280,000	$280,000	$1,680,000
Temporary (at $100/unit)				60,000	60,000		120,000
Overtime (at $150/unit)	—	—	—	—	—	—	
Hire temporary (at $25/unit)	0	0	0	15,000	0	0	15,000
Inventory (at $10/unit/month)	14,000	22,000	25,000	21,000	10,000	6,000	98,000
Back order (at $150/unit/month)	0	0	0	0	0	0	0
Total cost	$294,000	$302,000	$305,000	$376,000	$350,000	$286,000	$1,913,000

Overall, the total cost for this plan ($1,913,000) seems to be the lowest possible, so Plan 3 seems to be optimal.

Procedure for Trial-and-Error. From the three examples above, it is evident that one should follow these steps to obtain a low-cost aggregate production plan:

- Determine the production output by permanent workers (during regular time) for each period.
- Determine total units short and the periods short.
- Determine the cheapest way to meet the units short in periods short. For example,
  - Hire temporary and/or part-time workers.
  - Use permanent workers during overtime.

Trade-Off Analysis. It is possible to use the unit costs of labour, inventory, and back order in trade-off analysis in order to make good production planning decisions without having to recalculate the total cost of each plan. Let's look at some of the decisions we made in the above three examples. In Example 13-2, overtime should be used in the months when back orders will occur and, if more overtime production is needed, in the month(s) before them, not after, because back-order cost per unit ($150) is larger than inventory holding cost per unit ($10). Also, because holding inventory costs money, overtime should be used as close to the months with back order as possible. Therefore, our decision to produce the maximum of 400 units in each of the third, fourth, and fifth months during overtime.

Trade-off analysis would have been able to save us the trouble of even considering Plan 2. This is because the cost of a unit made during overtime is $150, whereas the cost of a unit made by a temporary worker (employed, say, for one month) is less ($100 + Hiring cost/Number of units produced in a month = $100 + $500/20 = $100 + $25 = $125).

Another example is the question of how to use the temporary workers in Plan 3. Consider, for example, employing 60 temporary workers for one month in month 5 versus 30 temporary workers for two months starting in month 4. As derived above, the cost of a unit produced by a temporary worker employed for one month is $125. However, the cost of a unit produced by a temporary worker employed for two months is only $100 + $500/(20 × 2) = $100 + $12.50 = $112.50. However, because a unit needs to be carried in inventory for one month (from the fourth to the fifth month), its total unit cost is $112.50 + $10 = $122.50, which is still less than $125. Therefore, using 30 temporary workers for two months starting in month 4 is cheaper than using 60 temporary workers for one month in month 5.

Now consider employing 20 temporary workers for three months starting in month 3. The cost of a unit produced by a temporary worker employed for three months is only $100 + $500/(20 × 3) = $100 + $8.33 = $108.33. However, because a unit needs to be carried in inventory for two months (from the third to the fifth month), its total unit cost is $108.33 + 2($10) = $128.33, which is larger than $125. Therefore, using 20 temporary workers for three months starting in month 3 is more expensive than using 30 temporary workers for two months starting in month 4.

Example 13-4 further illustrates the trade-off analysis.

EXAMPLE 13-4 ▶

A food company makes puddings in a plant.[1] It sells the puddings in cases (a case contains 48 pudding cups). The plant has 15 parallel production lines. The regular operating hours are eight hours a day, five days a week, 13 weeks a quarter. Each line is automated but needs six workers to operate it and can produce 200 units of output (each unit equals 1,000 cases) per quarter. Currently, only 11 production lines are used, for a total quarterly output of 2,200 units. The sales department has forecasted total demand for all flavours of puddings for the next five quarters as follows: 2,000, 2,200, 2,500, 2,700, and 2,200 units, respectively. Currently, there are no puddings in inventory other than some safety stocks in the warehouse. The company can increase production by hiring groups of six workers at a time (that is, by opening one to four additional production lines). Hiring one worker costs approximately $2,000. Each worker is paid an average of $19.23 per hour. Overtime costs 1.5 times regular time wage, and is limited to 20 percent of regular time production in any quarter. Holding inventory of a unit for a quarter will cost $50 (charged on the average level

[1] Based on Bradford Manufacturing case in F. R. Jacobs, R. B. Chase, and N. J. Aquilano, *Operations & Supply Chain Management*, 12th ed. (New York: McGraw Hill/Irwin, 2009), pp. 541–542.

of inventory in the quarter). Back order per unit per quarter is estimated to cost $200.

a. Determine all the relevant unit costs.

b. If the current number of workers is kept for the next five quarters, how many units will the company be short at the end of quarter 5?

c. Meet the forecast demands at minimum cost by

   i. Adding another production line.

   ii. Adding any number of production lines and/or using overtime.

You may use trade-off analysis to limit the number of plans considered.

SOLUTION

a. Labour cost per unit during regular time

  = Labour cost of one line for one quarter ÷ Production of the line in the quarter

  = Number of workers for the line × Cost per worker per quarter ÷ 200

  = 6 × Wage per hour × Hours per quarter ÷ 200

  = 6 × $19.23 × Hours per day × Days per week × Weeks per quarter ÷ 200

  = 6 × $19.23 × 8 × 5 × 13 ÷ 200

  = $299.99; round to $300

Labour cost per unit during overtime

  = 1.5 × Regular time cost

  = 1.5 × $300 = $450

Hiring cost per unit (charged to the first quarter employed)

  = Hiring cost per worker × Number of workers per line ÷ Production per line per quarter

  = $2,000 × 6 ÷ 200 = $60

b. Number short at the end of quarter 5

  = Total demand forecasts − 5 × Regular production per quarter

  = 11,600 − 5 (2,200) = 600 units

c. i. The 12th production line should work three quarters because the number short is 600 units (from part *b*) and the capacity of a line is 200 units per quarter. Note that the quarters with higher-than-average demand are Q3 and Q4. Therefore, the 12th production line should work during Q3 and Q4. It is evident that the 12th line should also work Q2 because holding a unit in inventory for two quarters (from Q2 to Q4) costs only 2 × $50 = $100 < $200 = Cost of back ordering a unit from Q5 back to Q4. The completed worksheet is displayed below. Note that the output of the 12th production line is shown in the "Temporary" row.

Aggregate plan using an additional production line (Q2–Q4)

Quarter	1	2	3	4	5	Total
Forecast	2,000	2,200	2,500	2,700	2,200	11,600
Output						
Permanent	2,200	2,200	2,200	2,200	2,200	11,000
Temporary		200	200	200		600
Overtime						
Output − Forecast	200	200	−100	−300	0	0
Inventory						
Beginning	0	200	400	300	0	
Ending	200	400	300	0	0	
Average	100	300	350	150	0	900
Back order	0	0	0	0	0	0
Costs per unit product						
Permanent @ $300	$660,000	$660,000	$660,000	$660,000	$660,000	$3,300,000
Temporary @ $300	0	60,000	60,000	60,000	0	180,000
Overtime @ $450	0	0	0	0	0	0
Hire temporary @ $60	0	12,000	0	0	0	12,000
Inventory @ $50	5,000	15,000	17,500	7,500	0	45,000
Back order @ $200	0	0	0	0	0	0
Total	$665,000	$747,000	$737,500	$727,500	$660,000	$3,537,000

ii. First we will show that using temporary workers is cheaper than using overtime: Cost of a unit made by a temporary worker hired and laid off after one quarter = $300 + $60 = $360 < $450 = Cost of a unit produced by a permanent worker during overtime.

Now, one way to reduce the total cost of the plan determined in part c_i above is to use two extra production lines during Q4. This will produce 400 units. To produce the remaining 200 units needed, it is clear that we need to start one of these two lines in Q3. As you can see in the worksheet below, the total cost in this case is lower than the plan in part c_i.

Aggregate plan using two additional production lines (Q4 and Q3–Q4)

Quarter	1	2	3	4	5	Total
Forecast	2,000	2,200	2,500	2,700	2,200	11,600
Output						
Permanent	2,200	2,200	2,200	2,200	2,200	11,000
Temporary			200	400		600
Overtime						0
Output – Forecast	200	0	−100	−100	0	0
Inventory						
Beginning	0	200	200	100	0	
Ending	200	200	100	0	0	
Average	100	200	150	50	0	500
Back order	0	0	0	0	0	0
Costs per unit product						
Permanent @ $300	$660,000	$660,000	$660,000	$660,000	$660,000	$3,300,000
Temporary @ $300	0	0	60,000	120,000	0	180,000
Overtime @ $450	0	0	0	0	0	0
Hire temporary @ $60	0	0	12,000	12,000	0	24,000
Inventory @ $50	5,000	10,000	7,500	2,500	0	25000
Back-order @ $200	0	0	0	0	0	0
Total	$665,000	$670,000	$739,500	$794,500	$660,000	$3,529,000

Note that producing 400 units in Q3 and 200 units in Q4 by extra lines will increase the total cost because 200 more units have to be carried in inventory from Q3 to Q4. Also, producing 600 units in Q3 and nothing in Q4 by the extra lines will increase the total cost because 400 more units have to be carried in inventory from Q3 to Q4, in addition to $60 × 200 extra hiring cost. Finally, producing nothing in Q3 and 600 units in Q4 by the extra lines will increase the total cost because 100 units have to be back ordered from Q4 to Q3, in addition to $60 × 200 extra hiring cost. Therefore, the above plan (starting one line in Q3 for two quarters and another line starting in Q4 for one quarter) is optimal.

Optimization

Linear Programming Model. In a linear programming model of aggregate production planning, a variable is assigned to each of the number of hires and the number of layoffs, amount of overtime, ending inventory, and back order in each period (e.g., month). All other unknown quantities are represented in terms of these variables. The total cost formula, consisting of the unit costs times the variables, is the linear objective function. Each relationship is represented as a linear equation or inequality constraint. Once the model is entered in a linear programming software, after some iterations, the optimal solution (the lowest cost feasible solution) is found (if it exists). Excel has an add-on program, called Solver, which solves linear programs. See the supplement to Chapter 6 for more information on linear programming.

Transportation Model. When there are no hirings or layoffs, the problem can be formulated as a transportation model, which is even simpler to solve than a linear programming model. See the supplement to Chapter 8 for more information on the transportation model. In order to use this approach, planners must identify the capacity (i.e., maximum supply) of regular time, overtime, and part-time/temp, and demand for each period, as well as related costs of production and inventory.

Table 13-2 shows the notation and format of a transportation table for aggregate production planning. There are n sets of production (supply) rows (e.g., $n = 12$) and n consumption (demand) columns. There is also a row for the beginning inventory (at the top) and a column for unused capacity (on the right). The production quantities, to be determined by the software, will be in each cell. Unit costs are in the little squares in the top right corner of each cell. Note the systematic way that costs change as you move across a row from left to right. Regular cost, overtime cost, and part-time/temporary costs are at their lowest when the output is consumed (i.e., delivered) in the same month as it is produced. If goods are produced in one month but carried over to later months (i.e., moving across a row to the right), inventory holding costs are incurred at the rate of h per month. Conversely, with back orders, the unit cost increases as you move across a row to the left. For instance, if some goods are produced in month 3 to satisfy back orders from month 2, a unit back-order cost of b is incurred. Unused capacity is generally given a unit cost of 0. Finally, beginning inventory is given a unit cost of 0 if it is used to satisfy demand in month 1. However, if it is held over for use in later months, a holding cost of h per unit is added for each month.

◀ **TABLE 13-2**

Transportation model and notation for aggregate production planning.

Example 13-5 illustrates the format and final solution of a transportation model of an aggregate production planning problem.

Given the following information, formulate the aggregate production planning problem as a transportation table and solve it:

◀ **EXAMPLE 13-5**

	Month 1	Month 2	Month 3
Demand forecast	550	700	750
Capacity (maximum)			
Regular	500	500	500
Overtime	50	50	50
Part-time	120	120	100
Beginning inventory	100		

Costs	
Regular time	$60 per unit
Overtime	$80 per unit
Part-time	$90 per unit
Inventory holding cost	$1 per unit per month
Back-order cost	$3 per unit per month

The transportation table and an optimal solution (using Excel's Solver) for the above problem (in yellow background colour) are shown in Table 13-3.

Thus, the demand of 550 units in period 1 will be met using 100 units from beginning inventory and 450 units obtained from regular time output in month 1. The 700 units demanded in month 2 are met by 50 units produced during regular time, 50 units during overtime, and 30 units of part-time in month 1 all carried to month 2; and 500 units produced during regular time, 50 units during overtime, and 20 units of part-time in month 2. The 750 units demanded in month 3 is met by 100 units of part-time in month 2 carried to month 3, and 500 units produced during regular time, 50 units during overtime, and 100 units of part-time in month 3. The total cost for this solution is $100(0) + 450(60) + 50(61) + 50(81) + 30(91) + 500(60) + 50(80) + 20(90) + 100(91) + 500(60) + 50(80) + 100(90) + 90(0) = \$124,730$.

TABLE 13-3 ▶

Transportation table and optimal solution for Example 13-5.

Supply from		Demand for				Total capacity available (supply)
		Month 1	Month 2	Month 3	Unused capacity	
Month / Beginning inventory		[0] 100	[1]	[2]	[0]	100
1 / Regular time		[60] 450	[61] 50	[62]	[0]	500
Overtime		[80]	[81] 50	[82]	[0]	50
Part-time		[90]	[91] 30	[92]	[0] 90	120
2 / Regular time		[63]	[60] 500	[61]	[0]	500
Overtime		[83]	[80] 50	[81]	[0]	50
Part-time		[93]	[90] 20	[91] 100	[0]	120
3 / Regular time		[66]	[63]	[60] 500	[0]	500
Overtime		[86]	[83]	[80] 50	[0]	50
Part-time		[96]	[93]	[90] 100	[0]	100
Demand		550	700	750	90	2,090

Where back orders are not permitted, the cell costs for the back orders can be made prohibitively high so that no back orders will appear in the optimal solution.

L03 Aggregate Services Planning

Service

Aggregate planning for production and aggregate planning for services share many similarities, but there are some important differences:

1. *Services occur when they are performed.* Unlike goods, services can't be inventoried or back ordered. Consequently, it becomes important to match capacity and demand during any month or quarter (i.e., we need to use the chase demand strategy).

2. For labour-intensive services, it may be easier to measure the aggregate plan in terms of time (e.g., hours) or number of workers (full-time equivalent, FTE) instead of an aggregate measure of output. See the "Banner Good Samaritan Medical Center" OM in Action, Example 13-6, and Example 13-7.

OM in Action

Banner Good Samaritan Medical Center

Banner Good Samaritan Medical Center, a 662-bed hospital, was in a difficult budgetary situation. Its nursing budget was based on level workforce (approximately 1,000 FTEs) throughout the year. Because there was little allowance for seasonality, the staff had idle time (approximately 20 percent) during summer months and the hospital employed temporary nurses, hired from external nursing agencies, during winter months. Overtime was also used in winter at 1.5 times the regular wage rate plus a premium of $7 per hour. These arrangements cost the hospital a great deal. In addition, the nurses were reluctant to serve as floats and be traded between units when there was a short-term imbalance in nurse requirements between units. Finally, when these extra costs reached $10 million, a consultant was hired to assist the new senior administrator for nursing.

Data were gathered on patient days during the year, and a time standard was set for the nursing hours required per patient day. Five levels of work for registered nurses (RNs) were established. Level 1 RNs,

comprising the majority of RNs, work only in one unit (do not float). The number of RNs in Level 1 was based on annual patient days divided by 365. Level 2 RNs, also full-time, work in three to four units that share similar skill requirements and are used to meet increases in patient numbers or acuity. Level 2 RNs were paid $0.75 per hour more. Level 3 RNs work in many units and are primarily per diem employees. They are used to fill in when regular RNs are sick or if help is needed during winter. Level 4 RNs are part-time, filling in shifts of two hours' duration. Level 5 RNs comprise external agency nurses. Further efforts to reduce the permanent nurses' availability in the summer months were instituted in the form of career enhancement programs, vacation, and voluntary leaves of absence.

The new staffing system was very successful. The cost of external agency temporary nurses and overtime declined to $2 million, flexibility increased, patient care improved, and nurses were happier.

Sources: S. Hollabaugh and S. Kendrick, "Staffing: The Five-Level Pyramid," *Nursing Management* 29(2), pp. 34–36; www.bannerhealth.com/Locations /Arizona/Banner+Good+Samaritan+Medical+Center/_Banner+Good +Samaritan+Medical+Center+Home.htm.

EXAMPLE 13-6

The nursing manager of a 28-bed acute care unit at Mount Sinai Hospital in Toronto does an annual exercise to plan for nursing needs.[2] On any day from 7:30 a.m. to 7:30 p.m., eight registered nurses (RNs) are needed, and from 7:30 p.m. to 7:30 a.m., the requirement is five. There are 12 days of statutory holidays and 20 days of vacation, and an average of seven sick days are expected. Given the number of replacements needed, the nursing director expects 2.1 FTE for orientation to introduce new RNs to their role in the unit, and 1.1 FTE of paid educational hours. Each FTE nurse works 40 hours a week. There are 260 workdays in a year. How many FTE RNs should the nursing manager ask for in her budget request?

SOLUTION

Number of RNs working 12 hours a day $= 8 + 5 = 13$

Number of FTE RNs needed to cover Mon–Fri $= 13 \, (12/8) = 19.5$

Number of FTE RNs needed to cover Sat–Sun $= 13 \, (12/8) \, (2/5) = 7.8$

Total FTE needed to cover shifts $= 19.5 + 7.8 = 27.3$

Number of FTE relief RNs needed to cover statutory holidays, vacations, and expected sick days $= 27.3 \, (12 + 20 + 7) / 260 = 4.1$

Total FTE RNs needed $= 27.3 + 4.1 + 2.1 + 1.1 = 34.6$

EXAMPLE 13-7

The director of nursing of a hospital needs to plan the nursing levels for each quarter of next year. She forecasted the average number of patients per day in each of the hospital wards throughout each quarter of next year. Then, she multiplied these numbers by 90 days a quarter and 24 hours a day and divided the result by the number of patients to be assigned to

each nurse in each ward (e.g., three patients per nurse in intensive care, etc.) to obtain the aggregate forecast for hours of nursing required in each quarter. Finally, these were converted

---

[2] https://www.mountsinai.on.ca/nursing/building-capacity/BestPracticeToolkit.pdf, Table 3a.

into number of full-time equivalent (FTE) nurses needed each quarter by dividing them by 480 hours per quarter, and rounding them to the nearest integer. These numbers are displayed as Forecast (FTE) in the following table. There are currently 140 permanent nurses, each working 480 hours a quarter, and being paid an average of $14 an hour. Overtime is allowed up to 50 percent of regular permanent FTEs and is compensated at 1.5 times the regular wage rate. Temporary nurses are available but hospital policy dictates that the maximum number of temporary nurses be at most 20 percent of permanent nurses. Temporary nurses are paid an average of $17 per hour, but no overtime is permitted. The hiring cost is $480 per temporary nurse. Being a service, no inventory or shortage (back order) is permitted. *Note:* The unit of product here is FTE of nursing service.

a. Determine all the relevant costs per FTE working a quarter.

b. Suppose one temporary nurse is hired for one quarter. Would this be cheaper than using a permanent nurse during overtime?

c. Determine the minimum cost aggregate service plan.

SOLUTION

a. Regular permanent wages = $14/hour × 480 = $6,720 per quarter; Temporary nurse wages = $17/hour × 480 = $8,160 per quarter; Overtime wages = 1.5 × $6,720 = $10,080 per FTE per quarter. Hiring cost per temporary FTE (charged to the first quarter hired) is $480.

b. Cost per FTE of temporary nurse kept for a quarter = Hire cost per nurse + Wages = $480 + $8,160 = $8,640 < $10,080 = Cost per FTE of overtime. Yes, using temporary nurses is cheaper than using permanent nurses during overtime.

c. Given the result in part *b*, use up to the maximum number of temporary nurses in each quarter so that total output (FTE) equals forecast (recall we cannot have inventory or shortage). Maximum number of temporary nurses = 0.20 × 140 = 28 FTE in any quarter. If there is any more need for nurses, we have to use permanent nurses during overtime. In this case, no overtime is necessary. The following aggregate service plan has minimum total cost. Note that the hiring cost applies only when the number of temporary nurses in a quarter is larger than in the previous quarter, and it equals $480 multiplied by the difference.

Quarter	1	2	3	4	Total
Forecast (FTE)	167	150	158	165	
Output (FTE)					
Reg. perm.	140	140	140	140	
Temporary	27	10	18	25	
Overtime					
Costs per FTE					
Reg. perm. @ $6,720	$940,800	$940,800	$940,800	$940,800	$3,763,200
Temporary @ $8,160	220,320	81,600	146,880	204,000	652,800
Overtime @ $10,080	0	0	0	0	0
Hire temporary @ $480	12,960	0	3,840	3,360	20,160
					$4,436,160

 # Master Production Scheduling

For the aggregate production plan to be translated into meaningful terms for production, it is necessary to *disaggregate* it. This involves breaking down the aggregate production plan into the specific products' production schedules.

    For example, suppose a lawn mower manufacturer's aggregate production plan is to produce 200 lawn mowers in January, 300 in February, and 400 in March. The company produces various models of lawn mowers. Obviously, there are some differences in the materials, parts, and operations that each model requires. Hence, the 200, 300, and 400 aggregate lawn mowers must be broken down into specific numbers of mowers of each model prior to actually scheduling operations and planning inventory requirements.

The result of disaggregating the aggregate plan is the **master production schedule (MPS)**, which shows the anticipated build schedule expressed in terms of the quantity and timing of production of each product for the next 12 weeks or so. It should be noted that, whereas the aggregate plan covers an interval of, say, 12 months (i.e., the intermediate term), the MPS covers only a portion of this (i.e., the short term). In other words, only the first three months or so of the aggregate plan are disaggregated. Moreover, the MPS must be updated weekly. Figure 13-6 illustrates the concept of disaggregating the aggregate plan for the lawn mower manufacturer. The process of determining the MPS is called *master scheduling*.

master production schedule (MPS) The anticipated build schedule stating which end items are to be produced, when, and in what quantities for the next 12 weeks or so.

Aggregate plan

Month	Jan.	Feb.	Mar.
Planned output*	200	300	400

*Aggregate units

Master production schedule

Month Planned output*	Jan.	Feb.	Mar.
Model A	100	100	100
Model B	75	150	200
Model C	25	50	100
Total	200	300	400

*Actual units—need to further disaggregrate into weekly planned output. It is assumed that all products are equivalent.

◀ FIGURE 13-6

Example of disaggregating an aggregate plan.

An important issue in master scheduling is the setup time involved for product changeover. These are wasted times and reduce the effective capacity of the production process. If the chosen lot sizes are smaller than assumed in aggregating production planning, there will be more setup times leading to the need for more labour hours than planned for in aggregate production planning. On the other hand, large lot sizes result in excess finished-good inventories and lower customer fill rates. The objective of master scheduling is to minimize the total inventory holding and setup cost subject to meeting each product's anticipated demand and safety stocks while not exceeding the capacity determined in the aggregate production plan.

Once a *tentative* MPS has been developed, a planner can do **rough-cut capacity planning (RCCP)** which converts the MPS into requirements for key resources in order to test the feasibility of a proposed MPS. This means checking capacities of production and warehouse facilities, labour, and vendors to ensure that no gross deficiencies exist that will render the MPS unworkable. Example 13-8 illustrates RCCP.

rough-cut capacity planning (RCCP) Converting the MPS into requirements for key resources in order to test the feasibility of a proposed master production schedule.

Suppose similar products (x, y, and z) have the following demand forecasts for January and February:

EXAMPLE 13-8

	January	February
x:	100	100
y:	80	160
z:	20	40

The company uses the chase demand strategy; the aggregate plan is 200 units for January and 300 units for February.

A possible master production schedule is:

	January				February			
Week	1	2	3	4	5	6	7	8
x:	25	25	25	25	25	25	25	25
y:	20	20	20	20	40	40	40	40
z:	20				20		20	

Note: It is not economical to produce very small batches of products; so produce 20 units of z at a time.

To see if this MPS is feasible, RCCP can be used as follows. Suppose there is only one (bottleneck) key machine, with Setup time = 1 hour, and Run time = 0.5 hour per unit of any product x, y, or z. Then the load on the machine in each week (in hours) will be:

Week	January				February			
	1	2	3	4	5	6	7	8
x:	1 + 25/2	1 + 25/2	1 + 25/2	1 + 25/2	1 + 25/2	1 + 25/2	1 + 25/2	1 + 25/2
y:	1 + 20/2	1 + 20/2	1 + 20/2	1 + 20/2	1 + 40/2	1 + 40/2	1 + 40/2	1 + 40/2
z:	1 + 20/2				1 + 20/2		1 + 20/2	
Hrs req'd	35.5	24.5	24.5	24.5	45.5*	34.5	45.5*	34.5
Planned	40	40	40	40	40	40	40	40

*In weeks 5 and 7 this machine will be overloaded. Possible solutions include using overtime, and changing the MPS (e.g., produce more z in January).

Alternatively, master scheduling can be done using linear programming, which will automatically find an optimal feasible MPS, thus sparing us the trial-and-error process of using RCCP. For an application, see the "Kellogg's" OM in Action.

 OM in Action   www.kelloggs.ca

Kellogg's

Kellogg's uses linear programming to perform both aggregate planning and master production scheduling. The Kellogg Planning System (KPS) was written in-house to plan production/packaging and distribution of Kellogg's products (hundreds of SKUs including 80 cereals). The operational version of KPS plans the next 30 weeks of production/packaging (approximately 90 production and 180 packaging lines in five Kellogg's plants in North America and 15 subcontractor or co-packer plants) and distribution (seven distribution centres (DCs)) for master scheduling. The linear program minimizes the production, inventory, and transportation costs subject to meeting the demand plus safety stocks (equal to two weeks of demand or four weeks of demand if the item is being promoted) at the DCs. The solution is used by the plant managers to schedule their production lines and by the logistics managers to schedule their inventories and transportation. The tactical version of KPS plans the next 18 months of production/packaging and distribution for aggregate planning. The results are used to determine plant budgets, inventory spaces required in distribution centres, etc. KPS also facilitates what-if questions. For example, should production of a product over time or in different plants be combined if its batch sizes are small.

Source: G. Brown et al., "The Kellogg Company Optimizes Production, Inventory, and Distribution," *Interfaces* 31(6), Nov/Dec 2001, pp. 1–15.

In the following section, we will show how one product's production schedule is determined in master scheduling.

MPS Inputs

Master scheduling has three inputs for each product: the beginning inventory, which is the quantity on hand from the preceding week; demand forecasts for each week of the schedule (next 12 weeks or so); and customer orders, which are quantities already *committed* to customers. We assume that production cycle time is small and a production order issued for a week will be received in the same week.

The master scheduler should work closely with the demand planner to obtain the (committed) customer order and forecast demand information, and to cooperatively determine the MPS.

Consider the following example. A company that makes industrial pumps wants to prepare a master production schedule for June and July. Marketing has forecasted demand of 120 pumps for June and 160 pumps for July for its major product. These will be evenly distributed over the four weeks in each month: 30 per week in June and 40 per week in July, as illustrated in Figure 13-7.

	Weeks							
	June				**July**			
	1	**2**	**3**	**4**	**5**	**6**	**7**	**8**
Forecast	30	30	30	30	40	40	40	40

◀ **FIGURE 13-7**

Weekly forecast demand for the pump.

Now, suppose that there are currently 64 units of the pump on hand, and that there are some customer orders that have been committed (booked) and must be filled (see Figure 13-8).

Beginning inventory	Weeks							
	June				**July**			
64	**1**	**2**	**3**	**4**	**5**	**6**	**7**	**8**
Forecast	30	30	30	30	40	40	40	40
Customer orders (committed)	33	20	10	4	2			

◀ **FIGURE 13-8**

The table for the pump showing forecast and (committed) customer orders for the next eight weeks, and the beginning inventory.

MPS Outputs

Master scheduling has three outputs for each week and each product: projected inventory (at the end of the week), planned production, and the resulting uncommitted planned inventory which is referred to as **available-to-promise (ATP)** . Knowledge of the uncommitted (ATP) inventory can enable the sales department to make realistic promises to customers about deliveries of new orders.

The first step for each product is to calculate the projected on-hand inventory (at the end of the week), one week at a time, until it falls below a specified limit (safety stock). In the above example, the specified limit is assumed to be zero. Hence, we will continue until the projected on-hand inventory (at the end of the week) becomes negative.

The projected on-hand inventory (at the end of the week) is calculated as follows:

available-to-promise (ATP) Uncommitted planned inventory.

$$\frac{\text{Projected on-hand}}{\text{inventory}} = \frac{\text{Inventory from}}{\text{previous week}} - \frac{\text{Current week's}}{\text{requirements}} \qquad (13\text{-}1)$$

where we use the convention that current week's requirements is the *larger* of forecast and customer orders (committed).

For the example, the projected on-hand inventory at the end of the first week equals beginning inventory minus the *larger of forecast and customer orders* in week 1. Because customer orders (33) is larger than the forecast (30), the customer orders amount is used. Thus, for the first week, we obtain:

Projected on-hand inventory (at the end of the week) = 64 − 33 = 31

Projected on-hand inventories for the first three weeks (i.e., until the projected on-hand becomes negative) are shown in Figure 13-9. When the projected on-hand inventory (at the end of the week) becomes negative, this is a signal that production will be needed to replenish inventory. Suppose that the economic production quantity is 70 units, and whenever production is called for, 70 units will be planned to be produced. (The determination of economic production quantity was described in Chapter 12.) Hence, the negative projected on-hand inventory at the end of third week will require production of 70 units in the third week, which will meet the projected shortfall of 29 units and leave 41 (i.e., $70 - 29 = 41$) units for future demand.

FIGURE 13-9 ▶

Projected on-hand inventory is calculated week by week until it becomes negative (assuming safety stocks are zero).

These calculations continue for the entire scheduling horizon. Every time projected on-hand inventory becomes negative, another production lot of 70 units is added to the table. Figure 13-10 illustrates the calculations. The result is the planned production and updated projected on-hand inventory for each week (see Figure 13-11).

FIGURE 13-10 ▶

Determining the planned production and projected on-hand inventory.

Week	Inventory From Previous Week	Requirements*	Net Inventory Before Planned Production		(70) Planned Production		Projected Inventory
1	64	33	31				31
2	31	30	1				1
3	1	30	−29	+	70	=	41
4	41	30	11				11
5	11	40	−29	+	70	=	41
6	41	40	1				1
7	1	40	−39	+	70	=	31
8	31	40	−9	+	70	=	61

* Requirements equals the larger of forecast and customer orders in each week.

It is now possible to determine the amount of inventory that is uncommitted and hence available to promise. Several methods are used in practice. The one we will use involves a "look-ahead" procedure: Sum customer orders week by week until (but not including) a week in which there is a planned production. For example, in the first week, this procedure results in summing customer orders of 33 (week 1) and 20 (week 2) and subtracting this from the beginning inventory of 64 pumps plus the planned production in week 1 (zero in this example). Thus, ATP for week 1 is:

$$64 + 0 - (33 + 20) = 11$$

Weeks

64	June				July			
	1	**2**	**3**	**4**	**5**	**6**	**7**	**8**
Forecast	30	30	30	30	40	40	40	40
Customer orders (committed)	33	20	10	4	2			
Projected on-hand inventory	31	1	41	11	41	1	31	61
Planned production			70		70		70	70

◀ **FIGURE 13-11**

Planned productions are scheduled whenever the projected on-hand inventory would have been negative without it. Then, the projected on-hand inventories are updated.

Weeks

64	June				July			
	1	**2**	**3**	**4**	**5**	**6**	**7**	**8**
Forecast	30	30	30	30	40	40	40	40
Customer orders (committed)	33	20	10	4	2			
Projected on-hand inventory	31	1	41	11	41	1	31	61
Planned production			70		70		70	70
Available-to-promise inventory (uncommitted)	11		56		68		70	70

◀ **FIGURE 13-12**

The available-to-promise inventory quantities have been added to the table.

This inventory is uncommitted and can be delivered in week 1 or 2. Note that the ATP quantity is calculated only for the first week and for any other week in which there is a positive planned production. See Figure 13-12.

For weeks other than the first week, the beginning inventory drops out of the calculation and ATP is the planned production quantity in that week minus the look-ahead customer orders. Thus, for week 3, the customer orders (committed) amounts are $10 + 4 = 14$ and the ATP is $70 - 14 = 56$. For week 5, customer orders (committed) are 2 (future customer orders have not yet been booked), and the ATP is $70 - 2 = 68$. For weeks 7 and 8, there are no customer orders, so for the present all of the planned production amount is available to promise. As additional orders are booked, these would be entered in the table, and the ATP amounts would be updated to reflect those orders. The sales department can use the ATP amounts to quote realistic delivery dates to customers.

Stabilizing the MPS

Changes to a master production schedule (i.e., the set of planned productions for all the products) can be disruptive, particularly the near-future changes. Typically, the farther out in the future a change is, the less it will cause problems.

The schedule horizon is often divided into three zones. The dividing lines between zones are referred to as **time fences**. The emergency zone (see Figure 13-13) is closest to the present time. Changes in the emergency zone may affect commitment of key resources and therefore require top

time fences Points in time that separate zones of a master production schedule.

management approval. Changes to the trading zone can be approved at a middle management level and generally involve trading one product's planned production for another product's, as opposed to the emergency change that usually sacrifices something in the short term. In the planning zone, changes are managed without management approval, usually by the master scheduler.

FIGURE 13-13 ▶

An example of zones in an MPS.

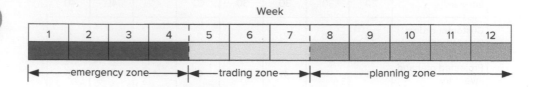

Week

| 1 | 2 | 3 | 4 | 5 | 6 | 7 | 8 | 9 | 10 | 11 | 12 |

|◀——emergency zone——▶|◀——trading zone——▶|◀——————planning zone——————▶|

MPS in Process Industries

Process industries use a raw material and process it into many products. Examples include food, beverage, chemical, and pharmaceutical industries. For example, in ice cream production, from a common base (for example, a white mix of pasteurized/homogenized/cooled milk), various flavours of ice cream such as vanilla and chocolate are produced. In process industries, products are grouped in families based on the type of raw material used—for example, white mix and frozen yogurt mix. Usually a large amount of a mix is produced and then a portion is used to produce a variety of products by adding various flavours/fruits. It turns out that a mix changeover/setup takes much more time and incurs much more cost than a flavour/fruit changeover/setup. Therefore, master scheduling in process industries is usually performed in two levels: first by family, then by SKUs within each family. That is, first families are scheduled, then within the time interval assigned to a family, individual members of the family are scheduled for production.

A similar approach is used in bottling beverages. It turns out that changeover of a bottle size takes a lot more time (e.g., an eight-hour shift) than changeover of the beverage type. Therefore, bottlers try to fill all products with the same bottle size one after the other, and then change to another bottle size.

For two examples of MPS in a process industry, see the "Scotsburn Dairy: The MPS Problem" and "Welch's" mini-cases.

Summary

- Sales and operations planning (S&OP) is the process of integrating sales forecasts with operations plans. This is usually done for the next 12 months and updated monthly. A systematic calendar-driven process is used to forecast demand, to check against capacity limits, to reconcile the differences, and to get approval of top management.

- Aggregate operations planning establishes general levels of employment, output, and inventories for the next 12 months or so. In the spectrum of planning, it falls between the broad decisions of long-term strategic planning and short-term planning/scheduling.

- A basic requirement of aggregate operations planning is the representation of a family of products by an "equivalent" unit. This permits planners to

consider overall levels of employment, output, and inventories without having to become involved with specific details that are better left to short-term planning.

- The planning variables include overtime, part-time/temporary workers, subcontracting, and carrying inventory.

- Planning strategies range from level output/workforce to chase demand.

- Planners often use informal (trial-and-error) graphic and table/worksheet techniques to develop plans, although optimization techniques such as linear programming and the transportation model are also used.

- Trade-off analysis, comparing unit costs of various options, saves planning time.

- Services cannot use inventory and thus rely on the chase demand strategy. They also usually use the amount of workforce (hours or FTE) as the equivalent unit.
- After the aggregate production plan has been developed, it is disaggregated into specific product production plans. This leads to the master production schedule, which is the planned production quantities and their timing for all the products. Inputs to the master production scheduling process are on-hand inventory amounts, forecasts of demand, and committed orders. The outputs are planned productions, projected on-hand inventories, and uncommitted inventories (available-to-promise).
- Rough-cut capacity planning determines the load on the production process of an MPS, thus checking its feasibility.
- Time fences are used to reduce last-minute changes to an MPS. The near future is frozen unless an emergency occurs.
- Process industries first schedule families of products, and then individual products within each family's allotted time.

Key Terms

aggregate operations planning
available-to-promise (ATP)
back orders
chase demand strategy

level output/workforce strategy
master production schedule (MPS)
rough-cut capacity planning
  (RCCP)

sales and operations planning
subcontracting
time fences

Solved Problems

Problem 1

A manager is attempting to put together an aggregate production plan for the coming nine months. She has obtained forecasts of aggregate demand for the planning horizon. The plan must deal with highly seasonal demand; demand is relatively high in months 3 and 4, and again in month 8, as can be seen below:

Month	1	2	3	4	5	6	7	8	9	Total
Forecast	190	230	260	280	210	170	160	260	180	1,940

The company has 20 permanent employees, each of whom can produce 10 units of output per month at a cost of $6 per unit. Inventory holding cost is $5 per unit per month, and back-order cost is $10 per unit per month. The manager is considering a plan that would involve hiring two people to start working in month 1, one on a temporary basis who would work until the end of month 5. The hiring of these two would cost $500. Beginning inventory is 0.

a. What is the rationale for this plan?

b. Determine the total cost of the plan, including production, inventory, and back-order costs.

Solution

a. With the current workforce of 20 people each producing 10 units per month, regular capacity is $20 \times 10 \times 9 = 1,800$ units during the nine months. That is 140 units less than total demand forecast. Adding one worker during the nine months would increase regular capacity to $1,800 + 10 \times 9 = 1,890$ units. That would still be 50 units short, or just the amount one temporary worker could produce in five months. Since one of the two seasonal peaks is quite early, it would make sense to start the temporary worker right away to avoid some of the back-order cost.

b. The worksheet for this strategy is as follows (here permanent and temp production are lumped together and hiring cost is accounted for separately):

Month	1	2	3	4	5	6	7	8	9	Total
Forecast	190	230	260	280	210	170	160	260	180	1,940
Output										
Regular	220	220	220	220	220	210	210	210	210	1,940
Overtime	—	—	—	—	—	—	—	—	—	—
Subcontract/part-time	—	—	—	—	—	—	—	—	—	—
Output – Forecast	30	−10	−40	−60	10	40	50	−50	30	0
Inventory										
Beginning	0	30	20	0	0	0	0	20	0	
Ending	30	20	0	0	0	0	20	0	0	
Average	15	25	10	0	0	0	10	10	0	70
Back order	0	0	20	80	70	30	0	30	0	230
Costs per unit										
Output										
Regular @ $6	$1,320	$1,320	$1,320	$1,320	$1,320	$1,260	$1,260	$1,260	$1,260	$11,640
Overtime										
Subcontract/part-time										
Inventory @ $5	$75	125	50	0	0	0	50	50	0	350
Backorder @ $10	0	0	200	800	700	300	0	300	0	2,300
Total	$1,395	$1,445	$1,570	$2,120	$2,020	$1,560	$1,310	$1,610	$1,260	$14,290

The total cost for this plan is $14,290 plus the $500 cost for two hirings, giving a total of $14,790. This plan is likely not the best (note the back orders in months 3–6 and 8). The manager would need to evaluate other plans before settling on the best.

You can also use the Excel template on *Connect2* to obtain the solution:

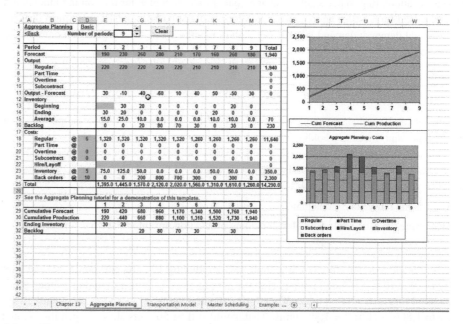

Problem 2

A self-employed seamstress forecasts the following demand (in units) for her products for the next eight months:

Period	1	2	3	4	5	6	7	8	Total
Forecast	1,200	1,200	1,400	3,000	1,200	1,200	1,200	1,200	11,600

She wants to hire two temporary workers to handle the extra workload in month 4. The cost for hiring and training a temp worker is $50 per worker, and she plans to hire and train them at the end of month 3 for work in month 4. Develop an aggregate production plan that uses steady output from the seamstress (1,200 units per month) with added output from the two temp workers (1,000 units per person per month) in month 4. The output rate for the temp workers is slightly less than that of the seamstress, so their cost per unit is higher. The cost per unit for the seamstress is $4 per unit, while cost per unit for the temp workers is $5 per unit. Back-order cost is $1 per unit per month. Determine the total cost of the plan, including production, inventory, and back-order costs.

Solution

Period			1	2	3	4	5	6	7	8	Total
Forecast			1,200	1,200	1,400	3,000	1,200	1,200	1,200	1,200	11,600
Output											
Regular			1,200	1,200	1,200	1,200	1,200	1,200	1,200	1,200	9,600
Temp						2,000					2,000
Overtime											0
Subcontract											0
Output - Forecast			0	0	−200	200	0	0	0	0	0
Inventory											
Beginning			0	0	0	0	0	0	0	0	
Ending			0	0	0	0	0	0	0	0	
Average			0.0	0.0	0.0	0.0	0.0	0.0	0.0	0.0	0
Backorder			0	0	200	0	0	0	0	0	200
Costs:											
Regular	@	4	4,800	4,800	4,800	4,800	4,800	4,800	4,800	4,800	38,400
Temp	@	5	0	0	0	10,000	0	0	0	0	10,000
Overtime	@		0	0	0	0	0	0	0	0	0
Subcontract	@		0	0	0	0	0	0	0	0	0
Hire		.05			100						100
Inventory	@		0.0	0.0	0.0	0.0	0.0	0.0	0.0	0.0	0.0
Backorders	@	1	0	0	200	0	0	0	0	0	200
Total			4,800.0	4,800.0	5,100.0	14,800	4,800.0	4,800.0	4,800.0	4,800.0	48,700.0

Problem 3

Prepare an MPS table like that shown in Figure 13-12 for the following situation. The forecast for each of the next four weeks is 70 units. The starting inventory is zero. The MPS rule is to schedule production if the projected inventory on hand will be negative. The production lot size is 100 units. The following table shows customer (committed) orders.

Week	Customer Orders
1	80
2	50
3	30
4	10

Solution

Starting Inv. = 0	Week 1	2	3	4
Forecast	70	70	70	70
Customer orders	80	50	30	10
Projected on-hand inventory	20	50	80	10
Planned production	100	100	100	
ATP	20	50	60	

The numbers for the projected on-hand inventories and planned productions were obtained as follows:

Week	(A) Inventory From Previous Period	(B) Requirement*	(C = B − A) Net Inventory Before Planned Production	Planned Production	(Planned Production + C) Projected Inventory
1	0	80	−80	100	20
2	20	70	−50	100	50
3	50	70	−20	100	80
4	80	70	10	0	10

* Requirements equal the larger of forecast and customer orders in each week.

Discussion and Review Questions

Note: An asterisk indicates that a question or problem may be more challenging.

LO1 **1.** What is sales and operations planning? How is it done?

LO1 **2.** What is aggregate operations planning? What is its purpose?

LO1 **3.** Why is there a need for operations planning?

LO1 **4.** What is an equivalent unit and why is it used?

LO1 **5.** What are the most common decision variables for aggregate operations planning in a manufacturing setting? In a service setting?

LO1 **6.** What options are available for changing the medium-term capacity of (a) a school, (b) an airline?

LO1 **7.** Under what circumstances would a company use the following strategies?
  a. Maintain level output/workforce and let inventories absorb changes in demand.
  b. Vary the size of the workforce to correspond to changes in demand.
  c. Maintain a constant workforce, but vary hours worked (through overtime and idle time) to correspond to changes in demand.

LO2 **8.** How does the trial-and-error approach for aggregate operations planning work?

LO2 **9.** Give an example of a product with highly seasonal demand and discuss how its manufacturer meets the demand.

LO3 **10.** What are the differences between aggregate operations planning for services and goods?

LO4 **11.** What is master production scheduling and how is it done?

LO4 **12.** What is RCCP and why is it useful?

LO4 **13.** What is ATP and how is it determined?

LO4 **14.** What is a time fence and why is it useful?

LO4 **15.** How is MPS for a process industry different?

LO3 **16.** What is FTE? Give an example.

Taking Stock

LO4 **1.** What general trade-offs are involved in master production scheduling for determining the length of the emergency zone of the schedule?

LO4 **2.** Who needs to interface with the master production schedule and why?

LO1–4 **3.** How has technology had an impact on aggregate operations planning?

LO2 & 3 **4.** Many companies are using temporary workers to meet their peak demand. Is using temps instead of permanent workers ethically wrong? Briefly discuss.

Critical Thinking Exercise

LO3 & 4 Discuss disaggregating an aggregate service plan, and give an example of it in an organization such as a hospital.

Experiential Learning Exercise

 Aggregate planning in operations is like budgeting in finance/accounting. Prepare a personal budget for next year following the concept of aggregate production planning. Forecast your need for money each quarter and identify the supply of money and its sources. Make sure supply (it could include a student loan) meets the demand.

Internet Exercises

 1. Visit http://info.steelwedge.com/rs/steelwedge/images/sw_sony_case_study_2014.pdf, and summarize how Sony Entertainment is using Steelwedge's planning software. Steelwedge was recently bought by E2open.

 2. Visit http://www.kinaxis.com/Global/resources/case-studies/supply-chain-responsiveness-mtd-case-study-kinaxis

.pdf, and summarize what RapidResponse is doing for MTD.

 3. Visit https://www.oliverwight-americas.com/system/files/clients/profiles/caterpillarna.pdf and http://oliverwight-americas.com/system/files/clients/profiles/caterpillarttt.pdf, and summarize how Caterpillar improved its planning.

Problems

 1. Calculate the total cost for each of the following aggregate production plans using these unit costs:

Regular output = $40
Overtime = $50
Subcontract = $60
Inventory per month = $10

a.

Month	Jan	Feb	Mar	Apr	May	Jun
Forecast	300	320	320	340	320	320
Output						
Regular	300	300	300	300	300	300
Overtime	20	20	20	20	20	20
Subcontract	0	0	0	0	0	0
Output – Forecast						
Inventory						
Beginning						
Ending						
Average						

b.

Month	Jul	Aug	Sep	Oct	Nov	Dec
Forecast	320	340	360	380	400	400
Output						
Regular	300	300	300	300	300	300
Overtime	20	20	20	20	30	30
Subcontract	20	30	40	40	60	70
Output – Forecast						
Inventory						
Beginning						
Ending						
Average						

c. (Refer to part *b*.) After complaints from some workers about working overtime every month during the first half of the year, the manager is now considering adding some temporary workers for the second half of the year, which would increase regular output to a steady 350 units a month, not using any overtime, and using subcontracting to make up the shortage. Determine the total cost of this plan.

 2. A manager would like to know the total cost of an aggregate production plan that meets the forecasts below using a steady regular production rate of 200 units a month, a maximum of 20 units per month of overtime, and subcontracting as needed to make up any shortages. The unit costs are:

Regular production = $35
Overtime = $70
Subcontracting = $80

Month	1	2	3	4	5	6
Forecast	230	200	240	240	250	240

 3. Determine the total cost for the following plan given the following forecasts:

Month	1	2	3	4	5	6
Forecast	380	400	420	440	460	480

Use steady regular output of 400 units per month, use overtime as needed for up to 40 units per month, and use subcontracting to make up any shortage. Unit costs are:

Regular output = $25
Overtime = $40
Subcontract = $60
Inventory per month = $15

4. a. Given the following forecasts and steady regular output of 550 every month, what total cost would result if overtime is limited to a maximum of 40 units a month, and subcontracting is limited to a maximum of 10 units a month? Unit costs are:

> Regular output = $20
> Overtime = $30
> Subcontract = $25
> Inventory per month = $10
> Back order per month = $18

Month	1	2	3	4	5	6
Forecast	540	540	570	590	600	580

b. Suppose back orders are not allowed. Modify your plan from part *a* to accommodate this as economically as possible. The limits on overtime and subcontracting remain the same.

5. Refer to Example 13-3. Suppose that the new union contract limits the number of temporary workers in any month to 28 (i.e., 20 percent of permanent workers). Recall from Example 13-2 that up to 400 units can be produced during overtime per month. Using trade-off analysis and trial-and-error, find the minimum cost plan in this case. (*Hint:* Hire 10 temps for three months and 15 temps for two months starting in month 3.)

6. A manufacturer of heavy truck engines must develop an aggregate production plan, given the following demand forecasts for engines. The company currently has 13 workers and makes 130 engines per month. Regular labour cost is $500 per engine. The beginning inventory is zero. Overtime labour costs $750 per engine. Hiring cost is $3,000 per worker. Inventory holding cost is $50 per engine per month, and back-order cost is $250 per engine per month. Develop the minimum cost plan for this company. (*Hint:* Start with a level output/workforce plan, and use trade-off analysis to show that changing this plan will only increase the total cost.)

Month	1	2	3	4	5	6	7	8	Total
Forecast	120	135	140	120	125	125	140	135	1,040

7. A fabric mill has developed the following forecasts (in hundred bolts of cloth). The mill has a normal capacity of 275 units (a unit equals one hundred bolts) per month, and employs 275 workers. Regular labour cost is $2,000 per unit and overtime labour cost is $3,000 per unit. Up to 50 units per month can be made during overtime. The beginning inventory is zero. Hiring cost is $1,500 per worker. The inventory holding cost is $1,000 per unit per month, and back-order cost is $5,000 per unit per month.

a. Develop a level output/workforce plan.

b. Starting with your answer to part *a*, use trade-off analysis to find the minimum cost plan.

Month	1	2	3	4	5	6	7	Total
Forecast	250	300	250	300	280	275	270	1,925

8. A small company produces recreational vehicles. The marketing manager has developed the following forecasts (in units):

Month	Mar	Apr	May	Jun	Jul	Aug	Sep	Total
Forecast	50	44	55	60	60	40	50	359

Use the following information:

Regular labour cost	$240 per unit
Overtime labour cost	$360 per unit
Regular capacity	40 units per month, using 5 workers
Overtime capacity	8 units per month
Holding cost	$30 per unit per month
Back-order cost	$100 per unit per month
Beginning inventory	0
Desired ending inventory	0
Hiring cost	$2,000 per worker

Develop the minimum cost production plan and compute its total cost. (*Hint:* Hire eight new workers and meet any shortages with overtime.)

9. A small distiller produces whisky. The salesperson has developed the following forecasts for demand (in cases) for the next six months.

Month	May	Jun	Jul	Aug	Sep	Oct
Forecast	4,000	4,800	5,600	7,200	6,400	5,000

Use the following information:

Regular labour cost	$20 per case
Regular labour capacity	5,000 cases per month using 50 workers
Overtime labour cost	$30 per case
Part-time labour cost	$40 per case
Holding cost	$2 per case per month
Back-order cost	$10 per case per month
Beginning inventory	0

Develop the minimum cost production plan using level output/workforce, supplemented with each of the following, and compute the total cost for each plan. Which plan has lower total cost?

a. Use overtime (up to 1,000 cases per month). (*Hint:* Use OT in a three-month period.)

b. Use a combination of overtime (500 cases per month maximum) and part-time labour (500 cases per month maximum). (*Hint:* Use OT in a five-month period, supplemented with part-time production.)

L02 10. A company produces sofas. The manager wants to prepare a plan for the next six months using the following information:

	Month					
	1	2	3	4	5	6
Forecast demand	160	150	160	180	170	140

Cost Per Unit	
Regular time	$100
Overtime	$150
Part-time	$120
Inventory, per month	$10
Back order, per month	$50

There are five workers, each making 30 sofas a month. The maximum number of sofas produced during overtime is 30 per month. Part-time workers can handle a maximum of 20 units per month. Beginning inventory is zero. Develop a production plan that minimizes total cost. No ending inventory or back orders are desired at the end of month 6.

L02 11. Refer to Solved Problem 1. Start with 20 permanent workers. Prepare a minimum cost plan that may use some combination of hiring ($250 per worker), subcontracting ($8 per unit, maximum of 20 units per month, must use for at least three consecutive months), and overtime ($9 per unit, maximum of 25 units per month). The ending inventory in month 9 should be zero with no back orders at the end. Compute the total cost. (*Hint:* Use max. overtime and subcontracting in months 2–4.)

L02 12. A spring-water bottling company has recently expanded into flavoured water. The marketing manager is predicting an upturn in demand based on the new offerings and the increased public awareness of the health benefits of drinking more water. She has prepared aggregate forecasts for the next six months (in truckloads):

Month	May	Jun	Jul	Aug	Sept	Oct	Total
Forecast	50	60	70	90	80	70	420

The production manager has gathered the following information:

Regular production cost	$1,000 per truckload
Regular production capacity	60 truckloads per month using 20 employees
Overtime production cost	$1,500 per truckload
Holding cost	$200 per truckload per month
Back-order cost	$5,000 per truckload per month
Beginning inventory	0

The regular production can be supplemented by up to 30 truckloads a month from overtime. Determine the production plan that has the lowest total cost. (*Hint:* Use overtime in August–October.)

L02 13. A niche bicycle manufacturer manufactures bicycles in two different sizes. David, the company's owner–manager, has just received the following forecasts for the next six months.

	16-inch	20-inch
Nov.	1,000 units	500 units
Dec.	900	500
Jan.	600	300
Feb.	700	500
Mar.	1,100	400
Apr.	1,100	600

a. Under what circumstances is it appropriate to develop just one plan rather than two (one for each size)?

b. Suppose forecasts for the two sizes are summed to obtain one forecast for each month. Currently David employs 27 full-time, highly skilled employees, each of whom can produce 50 bikes per month. Because skilled labour is in short supply in the area, David would like to keep them permanently. There is no inventory on hand at present, but David would like to have 300 units on hand at the end of April. A maximum of 200 bikes can be produced during overtime each month. Determine the minimum cost production plan using these unit costs:

Regular	$50	Inventory	$2.00 per month
Overtime	$75	Back order	$10.00 per month

(*Hint:* Use overtime in November, December, and April.)

L02 14. A sporting-goods manufacturer makes baseball and hockey gloves. Suppose now is the end of December and the manager wishes to plan production for the next three quarters. The forecasts for aggregate pairs of gloves are Q1: 9,400; Q2: 16,200; and Q3: 18,500. There are 26 permanent workers. Each works 480 hours a quarter and makes 1 pair of gloves per hour. The wage rate is $8 per hour, holding cost per unit per quarter is $1, and the back-order cost per unit per quarter is $10. The manager can hire full-time temporary workers at the cost of $960 per person. Temporary workers also receive $8 per hour and work 480 hours a quarter. Overtime by full-time workers is possible at 1.5 times the regular wage rate, up to a maximum of 20 percent of regular time production. Current inventory level is zero and there is no inventory expected at the end of the planning horizon.

a. If the 26 permanent workers are kept throughout the planning horizon, how many units will the company be short at the end?

b. Do trade-off analysis to show that using temporary workers will be cheaper than using permanent workers during overtime.

c. Find the production plan that minimizes total cost. (*Hint:* Hire seven temps for two quarters starting in Q2.)

LO2 **15.** MR is a manufacturer of industrial fridges, freezers, and air conditioners. In December, the production planner needs to submit a production plan to the plant manager for the next year. The aggregate forecast for each quarter of next year is Q1: 14,800; Q2: 26,400; Q3: 35,000, and Q4: 19,200 units. The beginning inventory in January is 0, and the year-end inventory in December of next year can be 0. It costs MR $24 to hold an appliance in inventory for one quarter. Shortages are undesirable. Assume that all shortage will be back-ordered, and that back-order cost is $100 per unit per quarter. There are 160 permanent workers who produce 19,200 units per quarter. In busy quarters, workers can produce up to 9,600 additional units during overtime. Regular time labour cost is $60 per unit appliance and overtime labour cost is $83 per unit. MR can hire up to 160 temporary workers for a second shift. Assume temporary workers have the same productivity and can produce up to 19,200 units per quarter. A unit produced by temporary workers also costs $60 in labour cost. However, there will be an extra hiring cost of $25 per unit during the first quarter of employment.

a. If permanent workers are used for the next four quarters during regular time, how many units will MR be short at the end of the year and in which quarters?

b. Meet units short by hiring temporary workers. Use trade-off analysis to choose the minimum cost plan in this case. (*Hint:* Hire approximately 78 temps for two quarters starting in Q2.)

c. Would using overtime (in addition to some temporary production) be less expensive? Use trade-off analysis to choose the overall minimum cost plan. (*Hint:* Hire approximately 38 temps for two quarters starting in Q2, supplemented with overtime.)

LO2 ***16.** MT makes small camping and snowmobile trailers. The demand for camping trailers occurs between January and June (mostly in April and May). MT makes camping trailers from January to June, shuts down in July and then makes snowmobile trailers from August to November. Suppose now is the end of December. For simplicity, we consider every two months as a period. The forecasts for camping trailers during each of the next three periods (six months) are:

Period 1	Period 2	Period 3
869	1,730	1,374

MT employs 40 permanent workers who are paid an average of $20 per hour (including fringe benefits) and work approximately 320 hours a period (two months). They make approximately 1,000 camping trailers per period during regular time. They can also work up to 50 percent more as overtime (i.e., up to 12 hours a day vs. the regular 8 hours a day) and will be paid 1.5 times the regular wage rate. Alternatively, MT can hire *up to* 40 additional temporary workers to work during a second shift. Hiring cost is $3,000 per temporary worker.

Assume temporary workers' wage rate and productivity are the same as permanent workers'. Also assume that temporary workers work only during regular time (no overtime) and are kept for whole periods (i.e., for two months or four months). Inventory holding cost per camping trailer per period is $180, and is charged to average inventory level during each period. Currently there are no camping trailers on hand, and the desired inventory at the end of period 3 is zero (although a small positive number is also acceptable). MT wishes to meet the total demand, but shortage during a period (except last) is acceptable, in which case the shortage is assumed to be back ordered at the cost of $600 per camping trailer per period.

a. Calculate all the relevant unit costs.

b. Suppose MT uses permanent workers during regular time and overtime. Determine the minimum cost plan in this case. (*Hint:* Use overtime in each period.)

c. Suppose MT hires temporary workers, but decides not to use permanent workers during overtime (just regular time). Determine the minimum cost plan in this case. (*Hint:* Hire 15 temps for two periods and nine temps for one period starting in period 2.)

d. Would overtime production by permanent workers and regular time production by temporary workers simultaneously result in a lower total cost? Do a trade-off analysis. What is the overall minimum cost plan?

LO2 **17.** Mity-Lite (ML) is a manufacturer of folding and stackable chairs and folding tables for social events. The demand for ML's products is seasonal, peaking in spring and summer. Suppose it is December now, and the production manager needs to prepare the production plan for the next 12 months (for simplicity we use four quarters). Also for simplicity, we aggregate all products. The forecast during each of the next four quarters is:

Q1	Q2	Q3	Q4
141,330	242,550	217,866	129,900

ML currently employs 348 "permanent" workers. The workers are paid $10 per hour and work 480 hours a quarter. The workers can make approximately 167,040 units per quarter during regular time (10 hours a day, four days a week). (*Note:* This works out to one hour per unit per worker.) They can also work up to 25 percent more as overtime (i.e., work 10 hours more on Fridays) and will be paid 1.5 times the regular wage rate. ML can hire up to 200 temporary workers for a second shift. The average hiring cost (searching, interviewing, and training) is estimated to be $480 per new employee. (*Note:* Hiring cost is charged to each unit produced during the first quarter of employment.) Temps are kept for one or two quarters. For simplicity, we assume that the productivity of a new temp worker is the same as a permanent worker. Also, a temp worker's wage rate is $10 per hour. The inventory holding cost rate per quarter is 3 percent of unit cost, and the unit cost is $90. There are no products on hand now, and the desired seasonal inventory at the end of the year is zero. (In reality, ML keeps the equivalent of two weeks of demand as safety stock; we can assume that these are kept separately.) ML wishes to meet all demand, but shortage during any quarter (except the last) is allowed, in which case assume that the shortage is back ordered at the cost of $15 per unit per quarter.

   a. Calculate all the relevant unit costs. Suppose ML uses permanent workers during regular time and nothing else. In the last quarter, ML will produce only what is needed and then will let workers go on vacation (i.e., they plan to produce 129,900 units). Determine the number of units short during each quarter.

   b. Suppose ML hires temp workers to meet the shortages of part *a*. Determine when and how many temp workers should be used. (*Hint:* Hire 104 temps for two quarters starting in Q2, and two temps for one quarter in quarter 3.)

   c. Using trade-off analysis, show why levelling (i.e., equalizing) the temp workers in Q2 and Q3 of the above solution is not cost-effective. (*Hint:* Show that producing one more unit in Q2 and one less unit in Q3 by temp workers is not cost-effective.)

   d. Using trade-off analysis, show why using permanent workers during overtime in part *b*'s solution is not cost-effective. (*Hint:* Show that producing one more unit in Q3 during OT and one less unit in Q3 by temp workers is not cost-effective.)

18. A small high-end swimwear manufacturer needs to plan for next year. Demand for swimwear (in units) follows a seasonal pattern:

Quarter	Demand Forecast
1	2,000
2	9,000
3	9,000
4	4,000

Given the following information:

Permanent workforce	5 workers
Overtime capacity	Maximum = 50% of regular production
Production rate per worker	750 units/quarter (perm or temp)
Regular wage rate	$15 per hour (480 hours per quarter)
Overtime wage rate	$22.5 per hour (only for perm)
Temp hiring cost	$1,500 per worker (charged to first quarter of employment)
Holding cost	$1.50 per unit/quarter
Back-order cost	$30 per unit/quarter
Beginning inventory	0

   a. Determine the unit costs.

   b. Determine how many units the company will be short during each quarter if only permanent workers are used during regular time.

   c. Do a trade-off analysis to determine if temp workers cost less than permanent workers during overtime.

   d. Find the lowest cost production plan. (*Hint:* Hire six temp workers for two quarters.)

19. The manager of an injection moulding shop is interested in using aggregate planning to determine the shop's production levels during each of the next four quarters. The shop uses eight moulding machines to produce approximately 150 different products, employing 18 permanent workers. Because of the variety of products, standard (production) hours are used to measure demand and production. The demand forecasts (in hundred standard hours) for the next four quarters are 84, 90, 58, and 69, respectively. Each worker provides 126 standard hours per month. Up to seven temp workers can be hired. Hiring cost is $870 per worker. Labour cost (permanent or temp) is $13.50 per standard hour and overtime labour cost (by permanent workers) is $23.50 per standard hour. Maximum overtime production is 20 percent of regular time production by permanent workers. The current inventory level is 0. Inventory carrying cost is $2.40 per standard hour per quarter, and shortage cost is $10.80 per standard hour per quarter. Assume all shortages are back ordered.

   a. Show that total production standard hours by 18 permanent workers is 6,804 per quarter.

   b. Show that maximum total temp standard hours is 2,646 per quarter.

   c. Show that maximum total overtime standard hours is 1,361 per quarter.

   d. Show that hire cost per standard hour during the first quarter of work is $2.30.

   e. Calculate the beginning and ending inventories and back orders for each quarter for the plan that only uses regular permanent standard hours.

   f. Using trade-off analysis, show that hiring temp workers will be cheaper than using permanent workers during overtime.

   g. Consider the following two temp options (in addition to permanent worker production): Plan A: 16 hundred standard hours in Q1 and 22 hundred standard hours in Q2; Plan B: 16 hundred standard hours in Q1 and 21 hundred standard hours in Q2. Using trade-off analysis, show why plan B is cheaper.

20. Refer to Example 13-5. Suppose that an increase in warehousing costs has increased the inventory holding cost to $2 per unit per month. All other costs and quantities remain the same. Determine a revised optimal solution to this transportation problem using Excel's Solver.

LO2 21. Refer to Example 13-5. Suppose that regular time capacity in month 3 will be reduced to 440 units to accommodate a company-wide safety inspection of equipment. Using Excel's Solver, what will the additional cost of the optimal plan be as compared to the one shown in Example 13-5? Assume all input data are the same as Example 13-5 except for the regular time capacity in month 3.

LO2 22. Using Excel's Solver, solve the previous problem with an inventory holding cost of $2 per unit per month.

LO4 23. Prepare an MPS table for the pumps of Figure 13-12 using the same inputs but change the MPS rule from "Schedule production when the projected on-hand inventory would be negative without production" to "Schedule production when the projected on-hand inventory would be less than 10 units without production."

LO4 24. Update the MPS table shown in Figure 13-12 given these inputs: It is now the end of week 1; customer orders are 35 units for week 2, 16 for week 3, 11 for week 4, 8 for week 5, and 3 for week 6. Inventory on hand is now 33 units. Use the MPS rule of ordering production when projected on-hand inventory would be negative without production.

LO4 25. Prepare an MPS table like Figure 13-12 using the following information: The forecast for each week of an eight-week schedule is 50 units. The MPS rule is to schedule production if the projected on-hand inventory would be negative without it. Customer orders (committed) are:

Week	Customer Orders
1	52
2	35
3	20
4	12

Use a production lot size of 75 units and no beginning inventory.

LO4 26. Verify the available-to-promise (ATP) quantities for each week of Solved Problem 3.

LO4 27. Prepare an MPS table like Figure 13-12 for the following situation: The forecast is 80 units for each of the first two weeks and 60 units for each of the next three weeks. The starting inventory is 30 units. The company uses lot size of 150 units. Also, the desired safety stock is 20 units. Committed orders are:

Week	Customer Orders
1	82
2	80
3	60
4	40
5	20

(*Hint:* If ATP in a week is negative, reduce the previous ATP by the same amount and make this ATP = 0.)

LO4 28. Minco Inc. is a small manufacturer of fused magnesia and silica.[3] Minco's continuous improvement efforts led to a capacity and production planning software. To prepare for the use of software, a spreadsheet was first used to determine the capacity requirements for the main equipment (the fusion furnaces) and the production schedule for the main products. A major product had the following forecast and committed orders (all in thousand pounds):

Week	January			February			
Week	2	3	4	1	2	3	4
Forecast	56	56	56	66	66	66	66
Committed order	44	0	18				

The initial inventory was 119,000 pounds and the minimum stock at the end of each week was to be 83,000 pounds.

a. Calculate the economic production quantity (EPQ) if the annual demand is 3,000,000 pounds, setup cost is $350 per setup, inventory holding cost rate is 20 percent per year, unit cost is $2 per pound, demand rate is 500 pounds per hour, and production rate is 1,000 pounds per hour. (*Hint:* Refer to Chapter 12.)

b. If EPQ = 100,000 pounds, prepare a production schedule for this product for the next seven weeks.

c. Determine the available-to-promise inventory for the next seven weeks.

LO4 *29. Owens Corning Fiberglas (OCF) makes several types, weights, and widths of Fiberglas mats from chopped strands of fibreglass for boat hulls on two production lines in a plant.[4]

Aggregate planning for OCF involves choosing a certain number of shifts (one to four shifts, or, equivalently, 40, 80, 120, or 160 hours of operation per week), depending on forecast demand. MPS is determined by optimization, minimizing product changeover, production, and inventory costs. Product changeover takes between 0.5 hour and 1 hour, and is sequence dependent, taking longest for fibreglass type change, and least for width change.

---

[3] W. S. Beversluis and H. H. Jordan, "Using a Spreadsheet for Capacity Planning and Scheduling," *Production and Inventory Management Journal* 36(2), pp. 12–16

[4] M. D. Oliff and E. E. Burch, "Multiproduct Production Scheduling at Owens-Corning Fiberglas," *Interfaces*, 15(5), pp. 25–34.

Changeover cost includes loss of profit, direct labour, and mat waste.

For simplicity, we will consider only one production line and two products: light (3/4 ounce/ft², 76 inches wide), and heavy (1.5 ounces/ft², 76 inches wide) mats. The forecast for the next eight weeks for light mats is 110,000 pounds, and for heavy mats is 120,000 pounds. Given the aggregate plan, the line can make 370,000 pounds of light or 185,000 pounds of heavy mats during each of the next eight weeks. Instead of optimization we will use the economic production quantity (EPQ) for each mat.

a. If product changeover cost from heavy to light is $1,100 and from light to heavy is $1,500, holding cost rate is 12 percent per year, price of light mats is $0.75 per pound, price of heavy mats is $0.50 per pound, and demand occurs 50 weeks a year, calculate the EPQ for each product.

b. If there are 230,000 pounds of light and 240,000 pounds of heavy mats on hand, determine which product will run out first.

c. Using the above results and safety stocks of 110,000 pounds of light and 120,000 pounds of heavy mats, plan production of the two products so that neither product's projected on hand dips below its safety stock level and their production lot sizes are as close to their EPQ as possible. That is, if light mats will be short, interrupt the production of heavy mats (at the end of the week) and start making light mats.

L03 30. Lands' End is a phone/mail/Internet-order retailer of outdoor clothes and shoes. Like other retailers, Lands' End's customer orders surge just before Christmas. Therefore, Lands' End requires more employees just before Christmas. Jobs include customer sales and service, warehouse operations, and seamstressing. The full-time equivalent (FTE) employee requirements for October to December of last year were as follows: October: 4,000 FTE; November: 6,600 FTE; and December: 7,100 FTE. Lands' End employs 4,000 FTE employees throughout the year (3,500 full-time and 1,000 half-time). During November and December, Lands' End can employ up to 1,000 additional full-time temp workers (idle workers from local cheese factories) and up to 1,000 half-time high school students. Also, Lands' End can use up to 2,000 FTE of overtime per month using its permanent and year-round part-time workers (e.g., working 12-hour shifts instead of 8-hour shifts). Each FTE permanent employee receives $3,000 a

month. Each FTE of overtime work receives $4,500 a month. Each FTE temp employee also receives $3,000 a month, and each half-time student receives $1,500 per month. However, new employees require two to six hours of training. This is estimated to cost $300 on average, and is charged to the first month of employment.

a. Set up this problem as a planning problem and determine the minimum cost plan. Briefly state the trade-off analysis you used.

b. What factors, other than cost, should be considered? Explain.

L03 31. Banner Good Samaritan Medical Center is a 662-bed hospital. Like other hospitals, the number of its patients increases in the winter. The full-time equivalent (FTE) nurse requirements for Q1 to Q4 of next year are forecasted to be Q1: 1,300 FTE; Q2: 1,000 FTE; Q3: 800 FTE; and Q4: 1,000 FTE. Banner Good Samaritan employs 1,000 FTE permanent nurses throughout the year. During peak season, it can employ up to 500 additional FTE temporary nurses from local temp agencies. Also, it can use up to 500 FTE of overtime (hours worked beyond an eight-hour shift in a day). Each FTE permanent nurse receives an average of $8,000 a quarter. Each FTE of overtime work receives $12,000 a quarter. Each FTE temp receives $8,000 a quarter, but needs an average of $1,000 for training (charged to the first quarter of employment).

a. Set up this problem as a planning problem and determine the minimum cost plan. Briefly state the trade-off analysis you used. Calculate the total cost. (*Note:* If demand is less than the number of permanent nurses in a quarter, the nurses will still be paid but the idle time will be used as paid holidays and/or for further training.)

b. What factors, other than cost, should be considered? Explain.

L04 32. Jet Spray Corp, now part of IMI Cornelius, manufactures dispensers for beverages. One of Jet Spray's best-known products is a two-product cold beverage dispenser, the twin Jet 3 (TJ3), which is made to stock. The following table shows part of the MPS record of TJ3 for the next seven weeks. Given initial inventory of 258 units, safety stock of 250 units, and lot size of 225 units, determine the production plan and available-to-promise quantities of TJ3 for each week.

Table for Problem 32

Begin date:	11/17/	11/24/	12/01/	12/08/	12/15/	12/22/	12/29/
Forecast	28	63	147	147	147	146	146
Committed	9	26	8	5	4	4	
Projected on hand (min =)							
Produce (lot size =)							
Available-to-promise							

MINI-CASE

Scotsburn Dairy

Scotsburn Dairy's plant in Truro, Nova Scotia, makes over 300 types and sizes of ice cream and frozen yogurt products. The process is in two stages. In the first stage, a type of mix such as premium white is made in one of the two large pasteurizing vats (with 5,400 litre and 7,500 litre capacities), homogenized, cooled, and stored in one of eight storage tanks. In the second stage, the mix is fed into one of the three lines where flavour(s)/fruit(s) are added and the mix is packaged in containers (tubs) of various sizes. All three lines feed into the spiral freezer and then the tubs are stored in the on-site warehouse. For simplicity, we assume that all the products can be aggregated and that the volume of the product determines its production speed and cost. The plant manager has received the following aggregate demand forecasts (in units, a unit equals 10,000 litres) for the next 12 months: **L02**

Jan	Feb	Mar	Apr	May	Jun	Jul	Aug	Sep	Oct	Nov	Dec
140	160	190	180	180	220	240	210	170	170	160	130

A major consideration is product changeover time. This is significant as a mix is changed and as a tub size is changed. The manager estimates that out of 4.3 weeks per month, on average one week is spent for changeovers.

Although production speed of a line in the second stage varies by product (and not as a linear function of products' tub size), the spiral freezer's speed is based on volume of ice cream going through it (10,000 litres per hour). For some products, the line is a bottleneck, but for most products, the spiral freezer is. For simplicity, we assume that the production capacity of the plant is determined by the capacity of the spiral freezer (one unit or 10,000 litres per hour).

The plant manager can use the following labour schemes: 40 hours a week (1 shift; 10 hours a day Monday–Thursday); 50 hours a week (40 + 10 hours of overtime on Fridays); and 80 hours a week (2 shifts; 10 hours a day each Monday–Thursday).

The initial inventory of products is 210 units (i.e., 2,100,000 litres). The manager would like to have safety stocks at the end of each month equal to the next month's forecast demand. Also, the ending inventory next December should be at least 170 units.

Scotsburn has on-site warehouse space for 6,500 pallets of products. Each pallet's load differs by tub size. For example, 550 two-litre tubs can be placed on a pallet. For simplicity, we will use this as a measure of on-site warehouse capacity (i.e., 6500(550)(2) = 7,150,000 litres or 715 units).

The production cost of the 40-hour-a-week labour scheme (requiring three freezer operators, nine freezer packers, one freezer bypass, five palletizers, one quality control lab supervisor, one lab technician, two wash-up staff, four mixers, one production supervisor, one maintenance manager, and four maintenance workers) is $78,408 per month. Overtime production cost is 1.5 times regular time production. A temp worker's production cost is the same as a permanent worker's.

The average hiring cost of 32 temp workers required to run the plant is $500 each, charged to the first month of employment.

Value of one litre of product is $1, cost of capital is 11 percent per year, each pallet holds 1,100 litres, and warehousing cost is $20 per pallet per month. From these, inventory holding cost per unit (10,000 litres) per month is 0.11($1) (10,000)/12 + 20(10,000/1100) = $273. Shortage/back order is highly undesirable. Assume a cost of $1,000 per unit per month back ordered.

Question

What is the minimum cost aggregate production plan for Scotsburn Dairy? (*Hint:* Use the second shift in May and June, supplemented by overtime in several months.)

Source: Andrea Cameron, Production Scheduling and Inventory Management for an Ice Cream Manufacturer Using Hierarchical Planning Models, M.Sc. thesis, Dalhousie University 2009.

MINI-CASE

Scotsburn Dairy: The MPS Problem

The master scheduling problem at Scotsburn is to determine the production quantity for the products during each week for the next 13 weeks subject to the limitation of production hours imposed by the aggregate production plan. Because some products have "joint" setup, it is more efficient to group them as a family if possible. For example, some products are made from the same base mix (e.g., no sugar) and some use the same tub size (e.g., two litres). Changing base mix on a line requires washing all the equipment, and changing the tub size requires physical adjustment to the filling and packaging equipment. Either action requires approximately a half-hour, and changing base mix also results in approximately $300 of wasted mix. Exceptions include multiflavour products (e.g., Neapolitan ice cream) which require tight coordination of flavours, and products containing a particular allergen (e.g., peanuts). In these cases, all sizes of these products should be included in their own family. Within a family, a flavour or fruit change requires approximately five minutes.

Scotsburn produces tens of families of ice cream and frozen yogurt on three lines. For simplicity, we assume two families, one line, and only three weeks. Suppose that the setup time for each family is one hour, cost of labour involved in changeover is $300 per hour, and cost of mix loss is $300. Holding cost rate is 30 percent per year, cost of one litre of ice cream is $1, and there are 50 workweeks per year.

The demand (in production hours) for each family per week (after adjusting for initial inventories and safety stocks) during the next three weeks are as follows:

Family	Week 1	Week 2	Week 3
F1	11	12	18
F2	13	16	24

The aggregate production plan has specified 40-hour weeks (four days of 10 hours each) during these three weeks.

Question

What feasible set of lot sizes for each family in each week will minimize total setup and holding cost? A feasible set of lot sizes will meet the demand during the next three weeks within 40-hour weeks. Assume that a week's demand for a family cannot be split between two weeks.

 MINI-CASE

Welch's

Welch's, a major producer of grape juice, packages a few families of the products on each line. In order to prepare the master production schedule, the planner first aggregates the demand and the required safety stock of each product in each family during the next four weeks. She also aggregates the initial inventory of each product to obtain the family initial inventory. Then, given the production hours available during the regular time and overtime, the production rates and the setup time for each family, and some other cost data, she uses a linear programming software to determine the production quantity of each family during the next four weeks in order to minimize the total cost of holding inventory, setup time, and overtime, such that after satisfying the demand, the ending inventories each week are greater than or equal to the required safety stocks.

On a particular line, four families are packaged. One of the families has three products in it. The forecast demand (in 1,000 cases), the safety stock, and the beginning inventory for each product during the next four weeks are as follows:

Demand Forecast	Week 1	Week 2	Week 3	Week 4
Product 1	6.7	6.78	6.78	6.78
Product 2	0.5	1.48	1.48	1.48
Product 3	2.0	1.88	1.88	1.88

Safety Stock	Week 1	Week 2	Week 3	Week 4
Product 1	17.99	19.03	17.12	16.73
Product 2	0.93	0.98	3.16	3.60
Product 3	3.02	3.16	5.72	6.23

Initial inventory	
Product 1	12.89
Product 2	2.66
Product 3	4.45

Questions

a. What are the aggregate demand forecast and aggregate safety stock for each week, and the aggregate initial inventory?

b. Using the result of part *a*, and available hours during regular time (80 hours per week) and overtime (36 hours per week), production rate of 1.14 hours per unit, setup time of eight hours, holding cost per unit per week of $150, setup cost of $400, and overtime cost of $212 per unit, and similar information about the other families, the linear programming software has determined the following quantities for this family for weeks 1 to 4: 11.14, 14.00, 10.34, and 10.70 units. What is the aggregate ending inventory in each week? Are they greater than or equal to the required aggregate safety stocks for each week?

c. The aggregate production quantities are next disaggregated by also using linear programming for each family. Given the production rates and setup time for each product, and some other cost data, the linear programming software determines the production quantity for each product during the next four weeks in order to minimize the total cost of holding inventory and setup time and the deviation of total production quantity from that derived in the aggregate model for each week, such that after satisfying the demand, the ending inventories each week are greater than or equal to the required safety stocks. Using the aggregate production quantities given in part *b*, production rates of 1.10, 1.21, and 1.12 hours per unit for products 1 to 3, respectively, setup time of 0.5 hour for each production run, holding cost per unit per week of $150, and setup cost of $100 per product run, the linear programming software has determined the following quantities for each product for weeks 1 to 4. What are the ending inventories for each product in each week? Are they greater than or equal to the required safety stocks for each product in each week?

Production	Week 1	Week 2	Week 3	Week 4
Product 1	12.44	7.24	5.43	5.77
Product 2	0	1.42	4.95	0
Product 3	1.69	5.34	0	5.00

Source: Based on S. J. Allen and E. W. Schuster, "Practical Production Scheduling With Capacity Constraints and Dynamic Demand: Family Planning and Disaggregation," *Production and Inventory Management Journal* 35(4), pp. 15–21.

Chapter 14
Material Requirements Planning and Enterprise Resource Planning

Courtesy of Progressive Turf Equipment

LEARNING OBJECTIVES

After completing this chapter, you should be able to:

LO1 Discuss material requirements planning (MRP) and the conditions under which its use is appropriate, including dependent demand.

LO2 Describe the inputs to MRP.

LO3 Describe the calculation of MRP, and solve typical problems.

LO4 Describe safety time, lot sizing methods, capacity requirements planning, and MRP II.

LO5 Describe enterprise resource planning (ERP).

Progressive Turf Equipment of Seaforth, Ontario, founded in 1990, designs and manufactures pull-behind rotary finishing mowers ranging from 10 feet to 36 feet in cutting width for turf grass producers, golf courses, and municipal/general use around the globe.

Over the years, the company has expanded with several additions to the manufacturing facility, adding state-of-the-art manufacturing machinery, the latest 3D CAD software, and an integrated ERP system. By 2000 Progressive was making eight different mowers that used both shared and model-specific components for domestic and export sales. Although Progressive fabricates all of the frames and mower decks in-house, it also purchases critical items such as gear boxes, bearings, and power take-off shafts. It's not surprising that some of those models had well over 300 parts. To manage this, it required a bill of material (BOM) structure up to six levels, and often resulted in a production lead time of five to six weeks. Getting all of the 300+ parts for each model at the right place at the right time for both fabrication and assembly was a constant challenge. Further, some of the European suppliers had lead times of six months, and an increasing field population meant the demands of a growing aftermarket parts business also had to be considered in the planning. As the business continued to grow, these factors created many challenges between shop floor staff and purchasing agents, and often caused unnecessary expediting costs.

Progressive initially installed SYSPRO ERP software in 2000. Over the subsequent years, Progressive streamlined its internal systems and processes, and realized the benefits of a structured and integrated "way of work." Before implementing the various MRP modules, there were shortages on the shop floor and in the three warehouses. Today, Progressive has managed to reduce its WIP and raw material inventory, despite growing the product portfolio to 25 models. The company now builds to forecast based on economic batch quantities while supporting an ever increasing field population of mowers that often exhibit life cycles approaching 20 years. As a result, Progressive can devote more time to other issues, such as new product development, continued production efficiency, and supporting its customers.

Sources: Luke Jamaat, founder, Progressive Turf Equipment; http://shea.ca/wp-content/uploads /2016/01/progressive-turf.pdf.

(L01) Introduction

material requirements planning (MRP) The activity that determines the plans for purchasing and production of dependent-demand components.

This chapter describes MRP and ERP. **Material requirements planning (MRP)** is a planning and scheduling technique used to manage production and purchase of the components of assembled items. In this chapter, a component refers to a raw material, part, or sub-assembly. *Enterprise resource planning (ERP)* or enterprise software is used to manage and coordinate all the resources, information, and functions of an organization from a shared database. ERP grew out of MRP software, and includes other business modules.

First we will show why production/purchase plans for components of products require a different treatment than production/purchase plans for finished goods, supplies, or spare parts.

Dependent Demand

dependent demand Demand (for a manufacturing part or component) that depends on the production schedule for the finished goods.

When demand for items is derived from plans to make certain products—as it is with components used in producing a finished product—those items are said to have **dependent demand**. For example, the components that go into the production of a particular model of automobile have dependent demand because the amounts needed are a function of the number of cars that is planned to be produced. Conversely, demand for the *finished* cars is *independent:* the customer demand for cars is not known before it occurs and has to be forecasted.

Independent demand of most finished goods and supplies is fairly steady once allowances are made for seasonal variations, but dependent demands tend to be sporadic or "lumpy"; large quantities are used at specific points in time with little or no usage at other times. For example, a company that produces lawn and garden equipment might make a variety of products such as lawn mowers and small tractors, but these are usually made in batches. Suppose that the products are produced as follows: in one month, gas mowers; in the next month, electric mowers; and in the third month, tractors. Some components may be used in most of the items (e.g., nuts and bolts, screws). It makes sense to have a continuous inventory of these supplies because they are always needed. On the other hand, some parts might be used for only one product. Consequently, demand for those parts occurs only when that product is being produced, which might be once every few months; the rest of the time, demand is zero. Thus, demand is "lumpy." Because of these tendencies, independent-demand items must be carried on a continuous basis, but dependent-demand items need only be stocked just prior to the time they will be needed in production. Moreover, the predictability of usage of dependent-demand items implies that there is little need for safety stock.

Figure 14-1 illustrates key differences between independent and dependent demand, and inventory levels resulting from using inventory control models of Chapter 12 vs. MRP. The inventory control models of Chapter 12 are used for purchasing or production of items with independent demand. In this chapter, we will use MRP for planning the purchasing or production of dependent-demand items.

Overview of MRP

In MRP, the production plan for a specified number of each product during the next 12 weeks or so (that is, the master production schedule (MPS)) is converted into the requirements for its components, working backward from the due dates of the production plan using lead times, and netting inventories on hand and on order. This determines when and how much to order for each

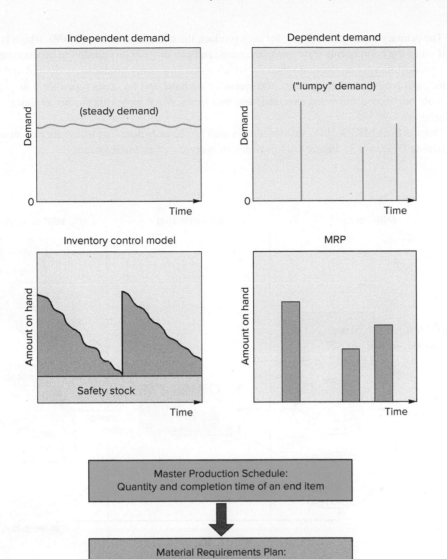

◄ **FIGURE 14-1**

Comparison of independent and dependent demand, and inventory levels resulting from using inventory control models of Chapter 12 vs. MRP.

◄ **FIGURE 14-2**

A material requirements plan indicates quantity and timing details needed to achieve the master production schedule.

component. Hence, requirements for end items generate requirements for lower-level items, so that ordering, fabrication, and sub-assembly of parts can be scheduled for timely completion of end items while inventory levels for parts are kept reasonably low. Thus, MPS leads into MRP (see Figure 14-2).

Historically, planning purchasing and production of components for assembled products suffered from two difficulties. One was the enormous task of setting up production schedules for products, keeping track of large numbers of components, and coping with plan changes. The other was a lack of differentiation between independent-demand and dependent-demand items. All too often, techniques designed for independent-demand items were used to handle dependent-demand items, which resulted in excess inventories.

Then, manufacturers began to recognize the importance of the distinction between independent- and dependent-demand items and to approach these two categories in different ways. Much of the burden of record keeping and determining material requirements in many companies has now been transferred to computers. A great deal of the credit for publicizing MRP and educating potential users goes to Joseph Orlicky,[1] George Plossl, Oliver Wight, and APICS.

Lectronic is a small Mississauga, Ontario–based company with an innovative product: a radio-controlled golf caddy (http://www .kaddy.com). Lectronic has been using the full version (including the MRP module) of the Business System from Minotaur Software of Brampton.

Courtesy of Lectronic Kaddy Corporation

---

[1] Orlicky is the author of *Material Requirements Planning* (New York: McGraw-Hill, 1975).

bill of materials (BOM) A listing of all of the components (raw materials, parts, and sub-assemblies) needed to produce one unit of a product.

The primary inputs to MRP are: for each product, the **bill of materials (BOM)**, which is a listing of all of the components (raw materials, parts, and sub-assemblies) needed to produce one unit of the product; master production schedule, which states how many products are desired and when; and for each product and component, the inventory on hand and on order (open shop or purchase orders already issued and being executed) and lead times. MRP inputs are further explained in the next section.

Outputs from MRP include various reports such as planned-order lists (these are explained later in Learning Objective 3). Figure 14-3 provides an overview of an MRP system.

FIGURE 14-3 ▶

Overview of an MRP system.

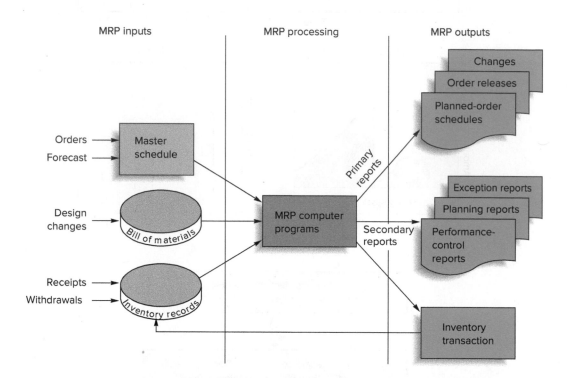

 OM in Action   www.uview.com

UView Ultraviolet Systems

UView Ultraviolet Systems of Mississauga, Ontario, makes innovative auto repair equipment and supplies such as an air conditioner leak-detection system. It has over 100 patents, 100 employees, and a 60,000 ft² plant. UView installed INDUSTRIOS ERP from INDUSTRIOS Software of Oakville, Ontario, to improve its inventory accuracy and reduce its inventories. UView especially uses the inventory, MRP worksheet, forecasting, production control, ATP, EDI, and shipment workbench of INDUSTRIOS. UView accountants use the MRP worksheet in INDUSTRIOS Test Environment to test forecasts/production plans.

Source: http://www.industrios.com/upload/New_UView_Success_Story.pdf.

L02 ## MRP Inputs

An MRP system has three major sources of information: the master production schedule; bills of materials; and inventories on hand, open orders, and lead times. Let's consider each of these inputs.

Master Production Schedule

The master production schedule (MPS) was introduced in Chapter 13. Here we will focus on an aspect of the MPS that is important for MRP. Figure 14-4 illustrates a portion of an MPS that shows planned production for the end item X for the planning horizon. The schedule shows that 100 units of X should be available (e.g., for shipments to customers) at the *start* of week 4 and that another 150 units should be available at the *start* of week 8.

Week number

Item: X	1	2	3	4	5	6	7	8
Quantity				100				150

◀ **FIGURE 14-4**

A portion of the master production schedule for the end item X.

It is important that the planning horizon be longer than the **cumulative lead time** necessary to produce the end item. This amounts to the sum of the lead times that sequential phases of the purchasing and production process require, as illustrated in Figure 14-5, where a total of nine weeks of lead time is needed from ordering components until final assembly is completed.

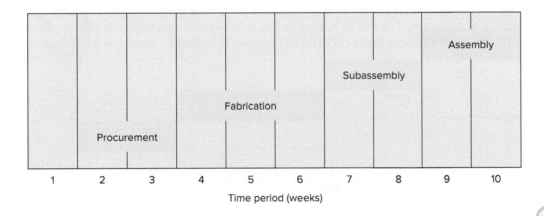

◀ **FIGURE 14-5**

The planning horizon must be longer than the cumulative lead time.

cumulative lead time The sum of the lead times that sequential phases of producing a product require, from ordering components to completion of final assembly.

Some sub-assemblies are also included in the MPS if they are made to stock (and later used to assemble the final product to order).

Bills of Materials

Each finished product has its own bill of materials (BOM). A BOM is related to the assembly diagram and **product structure tree**, which provide a hierarchical diagram of the components needed to assemble a product. Figure 14-6 shows an assembly diagram, the associated product structure tree, and the indented BOM for a chair. The end item (in this case, the chair, the finished product) is shown at the top. Just beneath the end item are the back and front sub-assemblies that must be put together with two cross-bars and a seat to make up the end item; beneath each sub-assembly are the parts for it. Note that the numbers in the product structure tree refer to the quantity of a component needed to complete one unit of the parent at the next higher level. For example, three back supports are needed for one back assembly. The number 1 is not shown, although one seat is needed per chair. For the indented BOM, the sub-assemblies are indented one tab to the right, and the components of each sub-assembly are listed under it and indented one tab farther to the right.

product structure tree A hierarchical diagram of the components needed to assemble a product.

FIGURE 14-6 ▶

Assembly diagram, product structure tree, and indented BOM for a chair.

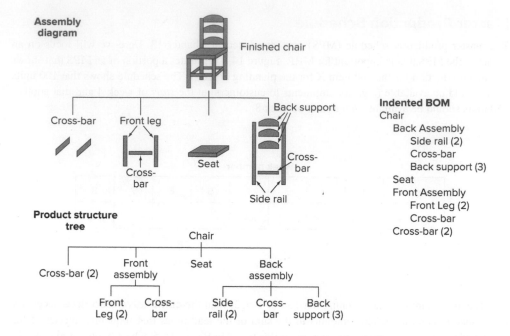

Indented BOM
Chair
    Back Assembly
        Side rail (2)
        Cross-bar
        Back support (3)
    Seat
    Front Assembly
        Front Leg (2)
        Cross-bar
    Cross-bar (2)

Let's consider the product structure tree shown in Figure 14-7. End item X is composed of two Bs and one C. Moreover, each B consists of three Ds and one E, and each D requires four Es. Similarly, each C is made up of two Es and two Fs. These *requirements* are listed by *level*, beginning with level 0 for the end item, then level 1 for the next level, and so on. The items at each level are children of the next level up and, as in a family tree, are *parents* of their respective children. For a software's use of BOM, see the "SYSPRO" OM in Action. Example 14-1 shows how a BOM can be used in MRP.

FIGURE 14-7 ▶

A product structure tree for end item X.

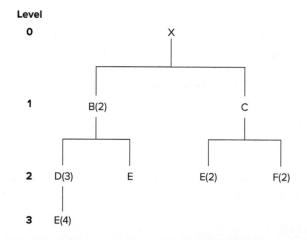

OM in Action

SYSPRO

SYSPRO is a reasonably priced MRP/ERP software that is easy to use. Suppliers, work centres, all the components (raw materials/parts/sub-assemblies), products, and customers must be defined first. Then, the structure and routing (operations) of each product and its sub-assemblies must be defined. This involves listing each operation to be performed on the item and the components used in that operation. Using these structures and routings, customer orders or master production schedule, and inventories, SYSPRO determines the requirements plans. Following is the BOM for a simple table.

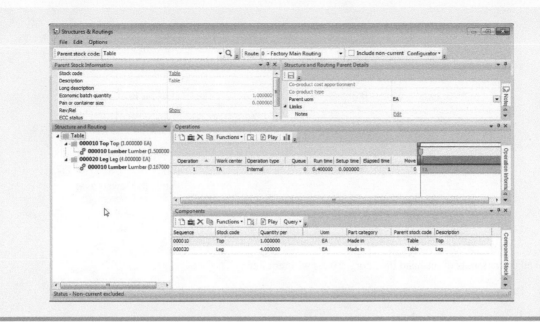

Use the information presented in Figure 14-7 to do the following:

a. Determine the quantities of B, C, D, E, and F needed to assemble one X.

b. Determine the quantities of these components that will be required to assemble 10 Xs, taking into account the following inventories on hand (and none on order):

Component	On Hand
B	4
C	10
D	8
E	60
F	5

SOLUTION

a.

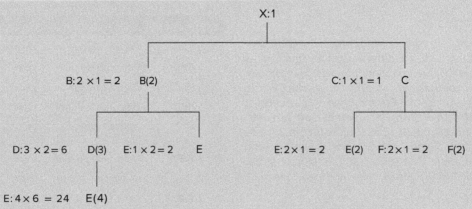

Thus, one X will require:

B:	2
C:	1
D:	6
E:	28 (Note that E occurs in three places, with requirements of $24 + 2 + 2 = 28$)
F:	2

b.

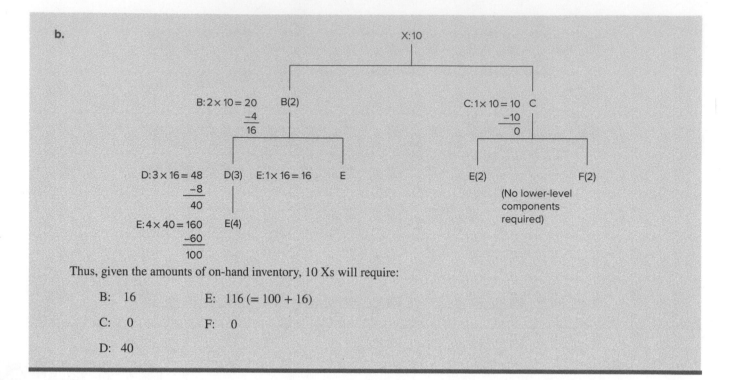

Thus, given the amounts of on-hand inventory, 10 Xs will require:

B: 16   E: 116 (= 100 + 16)

C: 0   F: 0

D: 40

Note that the amount on hand for each component is *netted out* (i.e., subtracted from the requirement) before determining the requirements of its children.

Determining net requirements is usually more complicated than Example 14-1 might suggest. The issue of *timing* is essential (i.e., when the components must be purchased or made) and must be included in the analysis.

> **planning bill** Also called a pseudo bill or a kit, is a combination of several BOMs.

Special Types of BOM. There are three special types of BOM. A **planning bill**, also called a pseudo bill or a kit, is a combination of several BOMs (see, for example, the "Aqua Lung" OM in

---

⚙ OM in Action

Aqua Lung

When there are very similar end products with only minor differences such as different-colour trims, it is possible to simplify the planning process by combining similar end products into an artificial product with a BOM called a planning bill. For example, Aqua Lung, a manufacturer of scuba diving equipment and wetsuits, uses the planning bill below. Each suit requires 2 yards of fabric. Roughly 75 percent of suits are black and 25 percent are blue. Therefore, in the planning bill, 1.5 yards of black and 0.5 yard of blue fabric are specified.

Component	Description	Unit	Qty	Level
1-7001	Fabric, Black	Yard	1.5	1
1-7002	Fabric, Blue	Yard	0.5	1
1-7500	Bind Tape, Black	Inch	300	1
1-7600	Bind Tape, Blue	Inch	100	1
1-1410	Velcro Hook, Black	Inch	33	1
1-1420	Velcro Hook, Blue	Inch	11	1
2-3510	Airway Assembly	Each	1	1
2-8-228	Tank Band Assembly	Each	1	1
1-2567	Foam Pad	Each	1	1
1-9001	Box, Spectrum	Each	1	1

Sources: G. H. French, "Linking Design, Marketing, and Shipping for Success: A Case Study in Integration," *Production and Inventory Management Journal*, 33(3), pp. 44–48; http://www.aqualung.com/us/gear/wetsuits.

Action). While it does not relate to a real product, its use will result in the calculation of the right number of components to be purchased or produced. Planning bills are used to reduce the number of BOMs necessary for planning when the products have various options.

A **modular bill** is a type of BOM for a module or option. Modular bills are used to reduce the number of BOMs when a product consists of many modules, each with a few options. For example, if there are 10 modules each with two options, the number of product configurations is $2^{10} = 1,024$, whereas there are only $10(2) = 20$ options. Thus, a company will use the 20 modular bills to plan the purchase or production of the modules and later will assemble the final products to order using the modules.

A **phantom bill**, also called a transient bill, is for an item that is usually not kept in inventory. However, it may be sometimes needed, as, say, a spare part or a work-in-process in an assembly line. A phantom item has zero lead time and special stock code so that it will not be regularly ordered. Use of a phantom bill makes planning easier.

Comment. It is important that the bill of materials accurately reflect the breakdown of a product, particularly since errors at one level will become magnified by the multiplication process used to determine quantity requirements of its components. As obvious as this might seem, many companies find themselves with incorrect bills of materials. This makes it impossible to effectively determine material requirements; moreover, the task of correcting these records can be complex and time consuming. Accurate records are a prerequisite for effective MRP.

> **modular bill** A type of BOM for a module or option.
>
> **phantom bill** Also called a transient bill, is for an item that is usually not kept in inventory.

Inventories On-Hand, Open Orders, and Lead Times

Each item in stock (product, sub-assembly, part, or raw material) should have a separate description file that contains information about the item and, if purchased, the purchase lead time. Also, the quantity on hand (inventory balance) of each item should be updated continuously as transactions (receipts and issues) occur, and be used to net the requirements as in Example 14-1b.

Each fabricated or assembled item will have a configuration file that shows the operations necessary and the components used. Each operation will have a standard time for setup and per-unit operation run time. Using these and the number of items to be produced, the total manufacturing lead time for a batch of the item is computed. Lead times will be used for timing orders.

Each open shop order and open purchase order (called *scheduled receipt* in MRP) has a quantity and due date and will be considered projected on-hand inventory on its due date (and used to net the requirements). For an application of MRP, see the "Atlas Hydraulics" OM in Action.

 OM in Action

Atlas Hydraulics

Atlas Hydraulics (AH) makes tubes and hoses for agriculture/forestry/construction equipment manufacturers in two plants in Canada, three plants in the United States, and one in Mexico. AH performs some of the operations (brazing, plating, and bending) in its main plant in Brantford, Ontario, and ships work-in-process to other plants. Scheduling and control of all operations in all plants are centralized in Brantford. AH uses Epicor's CMS (ERP for discrete manufacturers) to do so, especially the MRP module and the EDI. Before Epicor,

AH used Excel for planning, back-flushed inventory of components as products were shipped, and was able to do only one physical inventory per year. Now, AH does cycle counting 220 days/year, which has improved its inventory accuracy from 90 percent to 98.8 percent. The software has also allowed AH to meet the customer-promised one-week lead time for hoses and six-week lead time for tubes, despite long-distance shipments.

Sources: http://www.epicor.com/MRCPR/Atlas-Hydraulics-CS-ENS.pdf; http://www.atlashyd.com.

MRP Processing

MRP processing takes each end item's requirements specified by the MPS and "explodes" them into *time-phased* requirements for fabrication of parts or assembly of sub-assemblies, and purchase of purchased parts and raw materials using the bill of materials, offset by the lead times and netted for any inventories on hand or scheduled receipts (on order). You can see the time-phasing of requirements in the *assembly time chart* in Figure 14-8. For example, raw materials D, F, and I must be

FIGURE 14-8 ▶

Assembly time chart showing material purchase points and production start times needed to meet scheduled delivery of 100 units of the end item at the start of week 12.

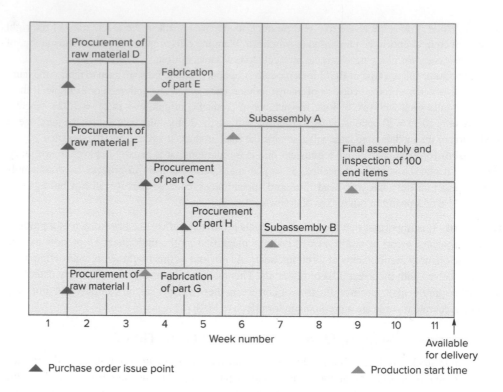

▲ Purchase order issue point   ▲ Production start time

purchased at the start of week 2, part C at the start of week 4, and part H at the start of week 5 in order for 100 units of the end item to be made and be available for delivery at the start of week 12. The figure also shows the planned fabrication or assembly start times of the manufactured items.

Note that the lengths of horizontal lines represent the lead times. For example, the purchase lead time for raw material D is two weeks, and the manufacturing lead time for 100 units of part E has been computed to be two weeks. This is based on the speed of the operation(s) involved in fabricating part E.

Each quantity generated by exploding a bill of materials is a **gross requirement**—the total demand without taking into account any inventory that is currently on hand or is due to be received (scheduled receipt). A material that a company must actually acquire to meet the demand generated by the MPS is a **net requirement**.

The determination of the net requirements (*netting*) is the core of MRP processing. One accomplishes this by subtracting from a gross requirement the sum of **projected on-hand** and any scheduled receipt, and then adding in any safety stock requirement, if applicable:

$$
\begin{array}{ccccc}
\text{Net} & \text{Gross} & \text{Projected on-} & \text{Scheduled} & \text{Safety} \\
\text{requirement in} = \text{requirement in} - \text{hand at the start} - \text{receipt in} + \text{stock} \\
\text{period } t & \text{period } t & \text{of period } t & \text{period } t & \text{in period } t
\end{array} \tag{14-1}
$$

If Formula 14-1 gives a negative value, then there is no net requirement (i.e., it is 0). For simplicity, we will omit safety stock from the calculations in the examples and most problems. It is convenient to subtract the safety stock from inventory on hand and exclude it from MRP processing as if it was locked up in a stockroom. Net requirements are sometimes adjusted to include an allowance for scrap, but for simplicity, this too will not be included in the examples or most problems.

The timing and sizes of orders (i.e., materials ordered from suppliers or work ordered within the company) is determined by a **planned-order release**. The timing of the receipts of these quantities is indicated by a **planned-order receipt**. Depending on the ordering policy, a planned-order release may have a minimum quantity, may be multiples of a specified quantity (e.g., 50 units), or may be equal to the quantity needed at that time (called *lot-for-lot ordering*). Example 14-2 will illustrate the difference between these ordering policies as well as the general concept of time-phasing material requirements in MRP. As you work through the example, you may find the following explanations helpful:

- **Gross requirement:** The total demand for an item *during* a time period (a week or a day) without regard to the amount on hand or on order. For an end item, this is the production plan from

gross requirement The total demand for an item during a time period without regard to inventory on hand and on order.

net requirement The actual amount needed in a time period.

projected on-hand Expected amount of inventory that will be on hand at the beginning of a time period.

planned-order release Quantity planned to be released (i.e., ordered) in the beginning of a period; that is, planned-order receipt offset by the lead time.

planned-order receipt Quantity planned to be received in the beginning of a period.

the MPS; for a component, this is equal to the planned-order release of its immediate "parent" multiplied by the number of the item used in one parent.

- **Scheduled receipt:** Open order, scheduled to arrive from a vendor or shop floor in the *beginning* of a period.
- **Projected on-hand:** The amount of inventory that is expected to be on hand at the *beginning* of a time period: it equals the scheduled receipt this period plus any ending inventory expected from the last period.
- **Net requirement:** The actual amount needed in a time period.
- **Planned-order receipt:** The quantity planned to be received in the *beginning* of a period. Under *lot-for-lot* ordering, it will equal the net requirement. Under lot-size ordering, it may exceed the net requirement. We assume that any excess is added to available inventory in the beginning of the *next* time period.
- **Planned-order release:** The quantity planned to be released (i.e., ordered) in the beginning of a period. It equals planned-order receipt offset by the lead time. This amount generates gross requirement(s) at the next level down in the BOM. When an order is executed (i.e., the planned-order release of week 1 is released), it is removed from planned-order releases and receipts rows, and is entered in the scheduled receipts row, a lead-time period later.

> **scheduled receipt** Open order scheduled to arrive from a vendor or shop floor.
>
> **net requirement** The actual amount needed in a time period.

These quantities are used in a time-phased plan in the following format. The column for period 0 is used to show beginning on-hand inventory.

Week or day number	0	1	2	3	4	5	6	7	8
Item:									
Gross requirements									
Scheduled receipts									
Projected on-hand									
Net requirements									
Planned-order receipts									
Planned-order releases									

Example 14-2 is useful for describing some of the main features of MRP processing, but it understates the enormity of the task of keeping track of material requirements, especially in situations where the same sub-assemblies, parts, or raw materials are used in different products. Differences in timing of demands, revisions caused by late deliveries, high scrap rates, and cancelled orders all have an impact on processing.

EXAMPLE 14-2

A company that produces wood shutters has received two orders for a particular model of wood shutter: 100 units are due for delivery at the start of week 4 and 150 units are due for delivery at the start of week 8. Each shutter consists of two frames and four slatted wood sections. The wood sections are purchased, and the purchase lead time is one week. The frames are also purchased, and the purchase lead time is two weeks. Assembly of the shutters requires one week for lot sizes of 100 to 200 shutters. There will be a previously arranged scheduled receipt of 70 wood sections from the vendor at the beginning of week 1. Currently, there is no inventory on hand. Determine the size and timing of planned-order releases necessary to meet delivery requirements under each of these conditions:

a. Lot-for-lot ordering (i.e., order sizes are equal to net requirements).

b. Lot-size ordering with a minimum lot size of 320 units for frames and multiples of 70 units for wood sections.

SOLUTION

The production schedule for the shutters is:

Week number:	1	2	3	4	5	6	7	8
Quantity:				100				150

Draw the product structure tree for a shutter:

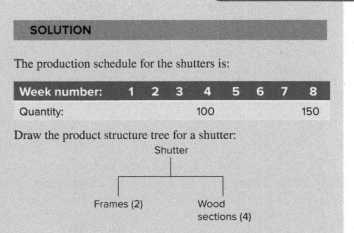

FIGURE 14-9 ▶

MRP tables with lot-for-lot ordering for Example 14-2.

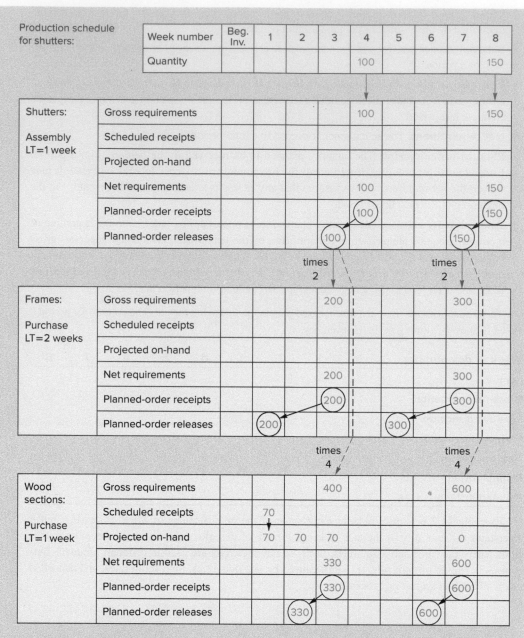

Production schedule for shutters:

Week number	Beg. Inv.	1	2	3	4	5	6	7	8
Quantity					100				150

Shutters: Assembly LT=1 week

	Beg. Inv.	1	2	3	4	5	6	7	8
Gross requirements					100				150
Scheduled receipts									
Projected on-hand									
Net requirements					100				150
Planned-order receipts					100				150
Planned-order releases				100				150	

times 2

Frames: Purchase LT=2 weeks

	Beg. Inv.	1	2	3	4	5	6	7	8
Gross requirements				200				300	
Scheduled receipts									
Projected on-hand									
Net requirements				200				300	
Planned-order receipts				200				300	
Planned-order releases		200				300			

times 4

Wood sections: Purchase LT=1 week

	Beg. Inv.	1	2	3	4	5	6	7	8
Gross requirements				400				600	
Scheduled receipts		70							
Projected on-hand		70	70	70				0	
Net requirements				330				600	
Planned-order receipts				330				600	
Planned-order releases			330				600		

At the start of week 4, the production schedule calls for 100 shutters to be ready for delivery and no shutters are projected to be on hand, so the net requirements are 100 shutters. Therefore, planned-order receipt for week 4 equals 100 shutters. Because shutter assembly for 100 units requires one week, this means a planned-order release for 100 units at the start of week 3. Using the same logic, 150 shutters must be assembled during week 7 in order to be available for delivery at the start of week 8.

The planned-order release of 100 shutters at the start of week 3 means that 200 frames (gross requirement) must be available at that time. Because none are expected to be on hand, this generates a net requirement of 200 frames and necessitates planned-order receipt of 200 frames by

the start of week 3. With a two-week purchase lead time, this means that the company must order 200 frames at the start of week 1. Similarly, the planned-order release of 150 shutters at the start of week 7 generates gross and net requirements of 300 frames for week 7 as well as planned-order receipt for that time. The two-week purchase lead time means that the company must order 300 frames at the start of week 5.

The planned-order release of 100 shutters at the start of week 3 also generates a gross requirement of 400 wood sections at that time. However, because 70 wood sections are expected to be received (scheduled receipt) at the start of week 1 and will be on hand, the net requirement is 400 − 70 = 330 for week 3. This means a planned-order receipt of 330 by the start of week 3. Since purchase lead time for wood sections is one week, the purchase order for 330 wood sections must be issued (planned-order release) at the beginning of week 2.

Similarly, the planned-order release of 150 shutters in week 7 generates gross requirement of 600 (= 150 × 4) wood sections at that time. Because no on-hand inventory of wood sections is projected for week 7, the net requirement is also 600, and planned-order receipt is 600 units at the start of week 7. Again, the one-week purchase lead time means 600 sections should be purchased (planned-order release) at the start of week 6.

b. Under lot-size ordering, the only difference is that planned receipts will exceed net requirements. The excess is recorded as projected on-hand inventory at the beginning of the

following week. For example, in Figure 14-10, the minimum order size for frames is 320 units, but the net requirement for week 3 is 200; thus, 320 units are ordered, resulting in an excess of 320 − 200 = 120 units, which become projected on-hand inventory at the start of the next week. Similarly, the net frame requirement is 300 − 120 = 180 units in week 7, thus 320 units are ordered, and the excess of 320 − 180 = 140 units becomes projected on-hand inventory at the start of week 8. The same thing happens with wood sections; the excess of planned-order receipts in weeks 3 and 7 is added to projected on-hand inventory at the start of weeks 4 and 8. Note that the order size for wood sections must be in *multiples* of 70; for week 3, it is 5 times 70 because 350 is the first multiple of 70 larger than 330, and for week 7, it is 9 times 70 because 630 is the first multiple of 70 larger than 580.

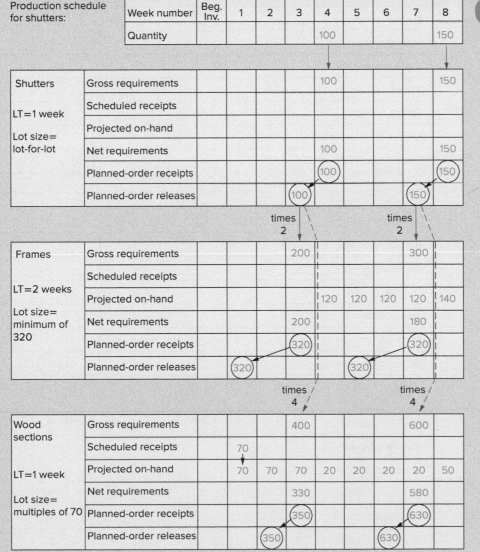

◀ **FIGURE 14-10**

MRP tables with lot-size ordering for Example 14-2.

EXAMPLE 14-3 ▶

Consider the two product structure trees shown in Figure 14-11. Note that both products A and C have D as a component. Suppose we want to develop a material requirements plan for D given this additional information: the demand for A is 80 units at the start of week 4 and the demand for C is 50 units at the start of week 5; there is a beginning inventory of 110 units of D on hand, all items have manufacturing or purchase lead times of one week, and we order D using lot-for-lot ordering. The plan is shown in Figure 14-12. Note that the requirements for B and E are not shown because they are not a "parent" of D.

FIGURE 14-11 ▶

Two different products (A and C) having D as a component.

FIGURE 14-12 ▶

Material requirements plan for component D of Example 14-3.

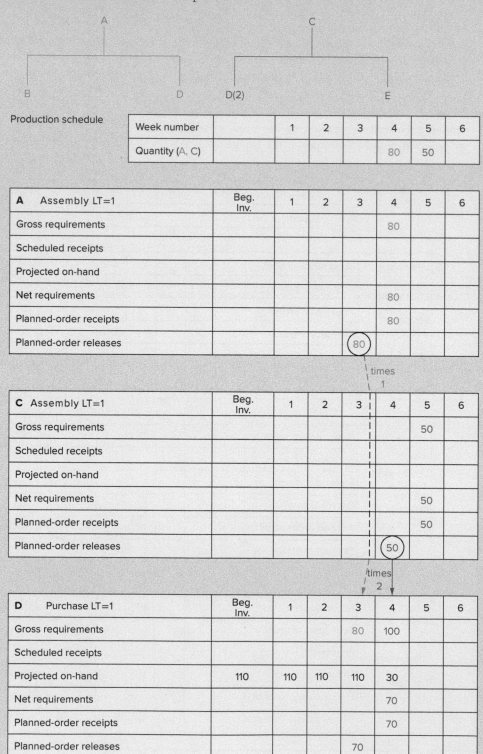

Production schedule

Week number			1	2	3	4	5	6
Quantity (A, C)						80	50	

A Assembly LT=1	Beg. Inv.	1	2	3	4	5	6
Gross requirements					80		
Scheduled receipts							
Projected on-hand							
Net requirements					80		
Planned-order receipts					80		
Planned-order releases				80			

times 1

C Assembly LT=1	Beg. Inv.	1	2	3	4	5	6
Gross requirements						50	
Scheduled receipts							
Projected on-hand							
Net requirements						50	
Planned-order receipts						50	
Planned-order releases					50		

times 2

D Purchase LT=1	Beg. Inv.	1	2	3	4	5	6
Gross requirements				80	100		
Scheduled receipts							
Projected on-hand	110	110	110	110	30		
Net requirements					70		
Planned-order receipts					70		
Planned-order releases				70			

The term **pegging** denotes working the MRP processing in reverse; that is, identifying the immediate parent items that have generated a given set of requirements for an item such as D. Although this may appear simple enough, when multiple products are involved, it is more complex. Pegging enables managers to determine which items will be affected if an order for an item such as D is late.

The importance of the computer becomes evident when you consider that a typical company would have hundreds of end items for which it needs to develop material requirements plans, each with its own set of components. Inventories on hand and on order, planned order releases, and so on must all be updated as changes and rescheduling occur. Without the aid of a computer, the task would be hopeless.

Updating the System

A material requirements plan is not static. As time passes, some purchase/work orders will have been completed and received, and new purchase/work orders will have to be released. In addition, there may have been changes to purchase/work orders, such as changes in quantity, delays, missed deliveries of parts or raw materials, and so on. In addition, MPS may have changed and new customer orders may have been received. Hence, a material requirements plan changes over time. And what we refer to as week 1 (i.e., the current week) is continually moving ahead; so what is now week 2 will soon become week 1. In a sense, requirements plans such as these have a *rolling horizon*, which means that plans are updated and revised so that they reflect the next set of weeks.

Two approaches are used to update MRP tables: *regenerative* and *net-change*. Regenerative MRP is run periodically (e.g., weekly); net-change MRP is run after each major change.

Regenerative MRP is a type of MRP processing that erases all the previous planned orders and computes them again, given any changes to MPS, inventories on hand, and scheduled receipts.

Net-change MRP is a type of MRP processing that only updates those planned orders that are affected by a change. For example, if some defective purchased parts had to be returned to a supplier, the manager can enter this information into the system as soon as it becomes known. Only the *changes* are "exploded" through the system, level by level; the entire plan would not be regenerated.

Regenerative MRP is best suited for fairly stable situations, whereas net-change MRP is best suited for situations that have frequent changes. The obvious disadvantage of regenerative MRP is the potential amount of lag between the time information becomes available and the time it can be incorporated into the material requirements plan. One way around this is to use a day as the time bucket (instead of a week) and rerun the MRP every night. However, regenerative MRP may take a few hours to process, much longer than net-change MRP.

A small change in requirement of an item at the top of the product structure tree can have large effects on items down the tree. This is referred to as **MRP system nervousness**. This is especially a problem if it results in changes in purchase or shop orders. MRP system nervousness is similar to the bullwhip effect in supply chains (see Chapter 11). As stated in Chapter 13, one solution to this problem is to freeze the master production schedule for the near future (e.g., next four weeks).

Back-flushing is exploding an end item's BOM periodically to determine the quantities of the components that must have been used to make the quantity of the item (and updating their inventory on-hand). This eliminates the need to collect detailed usage information on the shop floor.

MRP Outputs

MRP systems have the ability to provide management with a fairly broad range of outputs. These are often classified as *primary reports*, which are the main reports, and *secondary reports*, which are optional outputs.

---

pegging Identifying the immediate parent items that have generated a given set of requirements for an item.

regenerative MRP A type of MRP processing that erases all the previous planned orders and computes them again.

net-change MRP A type of MRP processing that only updates those planned orders that are affected by a change.

MRP system nervousness A small change in a requirement for an item at the top of the product structure tree has large effects on items down the tree.

back-flushing Exploding an end item's BOM to determine the quantities of the components that must have been used to make the item.

Primary Reports

1. *Planned-order schedules* list the amount and timing of future orders. These are divided into a list for purchase orders and another for job (work) orders.

2. *Order releases* authorize the execution of planned orders.

3. *Changes* to scheduled receipts, including revisions of due dates or order quantities and cancellations of orders. For example, in Example 14-2, the software would indicate postponing the 70-unit scheduled receipt of wood sections from week 1 to week 3.

Secondary Reports

1. *Performance-control* reports evaluate system operation. They aid managers by measuring deviations from plans, including missed deliveries and stock-outs.

2. *Planning* reports are useful in forecasting future inventory requirements. They include purchase commitments and other data that can be used to forecast future component requirements.

3. *Exceptions* reports call attention to major discrepancies such as late and overdue orders, reporting errors, and requirements for nonexistent parts.

See the "Kitchen Partners" OM in Action for an application of MRP in food services.

 OM in Action www.kitchenpartners.com

Kitchen Partners

Kitchen Partners Ltd (KPL) is a 90-employee food manufacturer in Edmonton. KPL makes around 100 custom private-label foods (soup, lasagna, cabbage rolls, etc.) for retail chains such as Sobey's and Costco, and ground beef toppings for pizza and taco salad at Boston Pizza restaurants.

KPL is growing fast (40 percent per year) and required a software to store all the recipes/bills of materials, perform MRP and MPS, trace ingredients and products, and enable EDI (required by Costco), as well as print labels for pallets stored in the offsite warehouse.

KPL chose Justfooderp software (from IndustryBuilt Software company of Mississauga), which is based on Microsoft Dynamics but has additional programs for food manufacturers such as government-regulation compliance, quality management (HACCP), lot traceability and recall, recipe management, etc.

The implementation team consisted of lead hands/supervisors from every area of business and the vice-president of SCM of KPL. The team pushed data entry to the shop floor and offsite warehouse, providing terminals for supervisors/employees.

As a result of using the ERP, inventory accuracy is up and inventory on hand is down. Receiving dates for ingredients are entered in the software and tracked. Justfooderp suggests the ingredient lots to be used based on the first-come-first-served rule.

Source: http://justfooderp.pixelshopdesign.net/JustFoodERPRefresh/media/JustFoodERP/PDF/Case%20Study/Kitchen-Partners-Ltd.pdf.

Courtesy of Kitchen Partners, Ltd., http://www.kitchenpartners.com

Some Related Concepts

LO4

Safety Time

Theoretically, inventory systems with dependent demand should not require safety stock below the end-item level. This is one of the main advantages of the MRP approach. Supposedly, safety stock is not needed because the manager can project the requirements once the MPS has been established. Practically, however, there may be quality issues causing scrap and/or shipments may be late or fabrication/assembly may take longer than expected.

MRP systems deal with these problems in several ways. The manager's first step is to identify activities or operations that are subject to variability and to determine the extent of that variability. It is important in general to make sure that lead times are accurate. When lead times are variable, the concept of safety *time* instead of safety *stock* is often used. **Safety time** is the amount of time an order is submitted earlier than expected because of lead time variation. If there are quality problems resulting in scrap, planned order release amounts can be increased by a percentage.

Lot Sizing

Determining a lot size for a purchase or production order is an important issue in inventory management for both independent- and dependent-demand items. This is called **lot sizing**. For independent-demand items, managers often use economic order quantity or economic production quantity. For dependent-demand systems, however, a wider variety of methods is used to determine lot sizes, mainly because no single method has a clear advantage over the others. Two common methods for lot sizing are described in this section.

A primary goal of inventory management for both independent- and dependent-demand items is to minimize the sum of annual ordering cost (or setup cost) and holding cost. With independent demand, the demand is frequently distributed evenly throughout the year. However, for dependent demand, the demand tends to be much more lumpy, and the planning horizon is shorter (e.g., three months), so economic lot sizes are usually much more difficult to identify. See Figure 14-13 for an example of lumpy demand for a part.

Managers can usually realize economies by grouping consecutive orders. This would be the case if the additional cost incurred by holding the extra units until they are used leads to a savings in setup or ordering cost. This determination can be very complex at times for two reasons. First, combining the demands for some of the periods into a single order, particularly for middle-level or end items, has a cascading effect down through the product structure tree; that is, in order to achieve this grouping, you must also group items at lower levels in the tree and incorporate their setup and holding costs into the decision. Second, the uneven period demands and the relatively short planning horizon require continual recalculation and updating of lot sizes.

The choice of a lot-sizing technique must take into account the pattern of demand over time, the relative importance of holding cost versus ordering (or setup) cost, and any other considerations that affect ordering. For example, considerations might be minimum and maximum order quantities established by management or supplier (e.g., do not order more than five months' supply), and operating or shipping constraints (e.g., 200 pieces per run or 12 dozen per shipment). Below are two of the more common lot sizing methods.

Fixed Interval Ordering. **Fixed interval ordering** is a type of lot sizing method that covers the requirements of a predetermined number of periods (e.g., two or three weeks). In some instances, the span is simply arbitrary; in other cases, a review of historical demand patterns may lead to a more rational designation of order interval. The rule can be modified when common sense suggests a better way. For example, take a look at the demand shown in Figure 14-13. Using two-period intervals, an order size of 120 units would cover the first two periods. However, the demand in period 3 is so small that it would make sense to combine it with the demand during the first two periods; that is, order 121 units for the first three periods.

safety time The amount of time an order is submitted earlier than expected because of lead time variation.

lot sizing Choosing a lot size for a purchase or production order.

	Period				
	1	2	3	4	5
Demand	70	50	1	80	4
Cumulative demand	70	120	121	201	205

▲ **FIGURE 14-13**

Lumpy demand for a part.

fixed interval ordering A type of lot sizing method that covers the requirements of a predetermined number of periods (e.g., two or three weeks).

part-period method A lot sizing method that sets the order horizon equal to the number of periods that most closely matches the total holding cost with the setup (or ordering) cost.

capacity requirements planning (CRP) The process of determining detailed capacity requirements of MRP.

Part-Period Method. This method provides a better way to determine the number of periods to order for at the same time. The part-period method, like the EOQ, attempts to balance setup (or ordering) and holding costs. The **part-period method** sets the order horizon equal to the number of periods that most closely matches the total holding cost with the setup (or ordering) cost. The term *part-period* refers to holding a part or parts over a number of periods. For instance, if 10 parts (or units) were held for two periods, this would be $10 \times 2 = 20$ part-periods. The *economic part-period* (EPP) can be calculated as the ratio of setup (or ordering) cost to the cost to hold a unit for one period:

$$EPP = \frac{Setup(or\,ordering)cost}{Unit\,holding\,cost\,per\,period} \tag{14-2}$$

To determine an order size that is consistent with the EPP, various order sizes equal to various cumulative demands are examined and each one's number of part-periods is determined. The one that comes closest to the EPP is selected as the best lot size. Example 14-4 illustrates this approach.

EXAMPLE 14-4

Use the part-period method to determine production run sizes for the following demands (i.e., net requirements) for a manufactured part:

	Period							
	1	2	3	4	5	6	7	8
Demand	60	40	20	2	30	–	70	50
Cumulative demand	60	100	120	122	152	152	222	272

Setup cost is $80 per production run for this item, and unit holding cost is $0.95 per period.

SOLUTION

1. First calculate the EPP: EPP = $80/$0.95 = 84.21, which rounds to 84 part-periods. This is the target.

2. Next, try the cumulative lot sizes, beginning with 60, until the part-periods approximate the EPP. The calculations of part-periods below indicate that 122 units should be ordered in period 1 to cover the demand for the first four periods. Repeat this process starting at period 5, which results in 100 units to be ordered in period 5 to cover periods 5–7. The next lot will be ordered in period 8, but there is insufficient information now to determine its size.

Period When Order Is Placed	Lot Size	Extra Inventory Carried	×	Periods Carried	=	Part-Periods	Cumulative Part-Periods
1	60	0		0		0	0
	100	40		1		40	40
	120	20		2		40	80
	122	2		3		6	86*
5	30	0		0		0	0
	100	70		2		140	140**
8	50	0		0		0	0

*Closer to 84 (than 80)
**Closer to 84 (than 0).

The part-period method worked well for the first lot size because the cumulative number of part-periods is close to the EPP, but the effect of lumpy demand is apparent for the second lot size of 100 (140 part-periods is not very close to 84 part-periods).

Capacity Requirements Planning

Capacity requirements planning (CRP) is the process of determining detailed capacity requirements of MRP. The inputs to CRP are planned-order releases of MRP for fabricated or assembled items, the current shop load, routing information, and processing times. The output of CRP is load reports for each work centre.

An MPS and the resulting MRP may not be feasible given the available capacities of the production process. It is often necessary to run the MRP through CRP in order to obtain a clearer picture of capacity requirements, which can then be compared to available capacities. If it turns out that the MRP are not feasible, management can either increase the capacity of overloaded work centre(s) (e.g., through overtime) or revise the MPS. In the latter case, this may entail several revisions, each of which is run through the CRP system until a feasible plan is obtained. At that point, the MPS and MRP are *frozen*, at least for the near term, thus establishing a firm schedule and requirements plan.

Figure 14-14 presents an overview of the capacity requirements planning process. The process begins with a proposed or tentative master production schedule that must be tested for feasibility and possibly adjusted before it becomes permanent. The proposed schedule is processed using MRP to determine the material requirements. These are then translated into resource (i.e., capacity) requirements for items made in-house involving assembly or fabrication. This is often in the form of a series of **load reports** for each department or work centre, which compares known and expected future capacity requirements with capacity availability.

Figure 14-15 illustrates the nature of a load report. It shows expected resource requirements for jobs currently being worked on and the future planned-order releases. Given load reports, the manager can more easily determine whether capacity is sufficient to satisfy the requirements. In the load report illustrated in Figure 14-15, planned-order releases in time period 4 will cause an overload. However, it may be possible to accommodate demand by shifting some orders to adjacent periods. In cases where capacity is insufficient, a manager may be able to increase capacity by scheduling overtime or transferring personnel from other areas if this is possible and

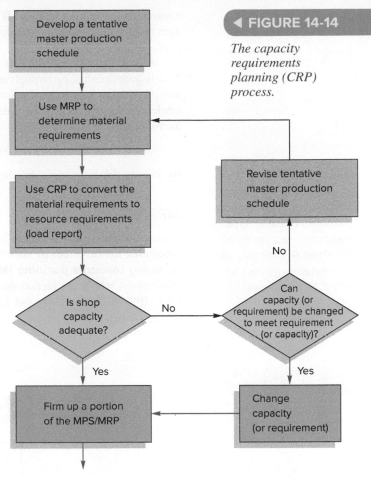

◀ **FIGURE 14-14**

The capacity requirements planning (CRP) process.

Stephen Love, *Inventory Control* (New York: McGraw-Hill, 1979), p. 164. Reprinted by permission

load reports Department or work centre reports that compare known and expected future capacity requirements with capacity availability.

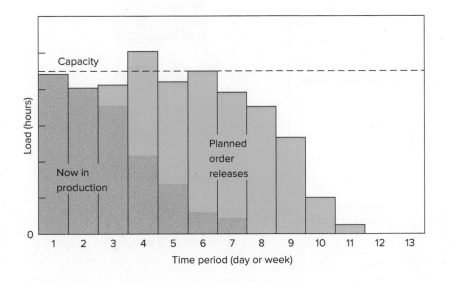

◀ **FIGURE 14-15**

An example of a work centre or department's load report.

economical, or revise the MPS. If the MPS must be revised, this generally means that the manager must assign priorities to orders because some orders will be finished later than originally planned.

An important aspect of CRP is the conversion of quantity requirements into time requirements. This is accomplished by multiplying each period's quantity requirements by processing time per unit plus a setup time per production run. For instance, if 10 units of product A are scheduled in the fabrication department and each unit has a processing time of 2 hours plus a setup time of 8 hours for the batch, then 10 units of A converts into:

$$10 \text{ units} \times 2 \text{ hours/unit} + 8 = 28 \text{ hours}$$

By the way, this is the manufacturing lead time for fabricating 10 units of A.

> **manufacturing resource planning (MRP II)** Expanded system for production planning and scheduling, involving sales and operations planning, MPS, MRP, CRP, and detailed scheduling.

MRP II

Material requirements planning has been expanded into a broader system for planning and scheduling the resources of manufacturing companies. This expanded system is called **manufacturing resource planning (MRP II)**. MRP II is a *closed-loop MRP*, which means that it involves the whole production planning process, starting with sales and operations planning; then MPS, MRP, and CRP; and finally detailed scheduling, with feedback going back up (see Figure 14-16).

FIGURE 14-16 ▶

An overview of MRP II process.

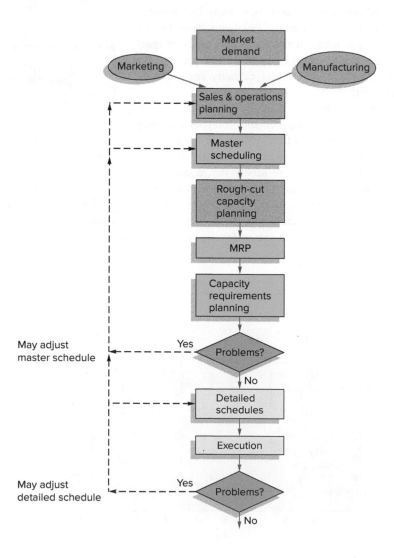

See the "Caterpillar" OM in Action for an example of the MRP II implementation.

 OM in Action   www.cat.com

Caterpillar

Caterpillar's construction industry (Cat) division makes bulldozers. A few years ago, Cat went through a long labour strike that destroyed labour–management trust. The new chairman instituted a common values program to restore trust, mutual respect, and teamwork. After a few years, there were still too many emergencies and too much time spent searching for parts, and unreliable deliveries of parts to dealers. Also, manufacturing did not trust marketing's forecasts, which frequently overestimated the demand. So the division was mandated to get certified by Oliver Wight International's Class A in Planning and Control. Oliver Wight was one of the originators of MRP and established a certification program so that companies could learn to perform effective

production planning (MRP II). To combat communication issues, Oliver Wight consultants served as change agents and independent observers. They instituted formal processes so that employees started meeting regularly and working together. The major initiative was sales and operations planning (S&OP, see Chapter 13). Classes were conducted for middle managers and planners/ schedulers on S&OP and developing valid schedules. Every operator was trained for two hours on inventory record and BOM accuracy. As a result, Cat's on-time delivery is now 98 percent, inventory of dealers is down, and use of overtime and expedited freight is down significantly.

Source: www.oliverwight-americas.com/system/files/clients/profiles /caterpillarttt.pdf.

Enterprise Resource Planning

Enterprise resource planning (ERP) or enterprise software is used to manage and coordinate all the resources, information, and functions of an organization from a shared database. ERP involves *standardized* record keeping that will facilitate *information sharing*.

ERP became popular when enterprises were revamping their legacy mainframe computer systems in anticipation of possible year 2000 (Y2K) problems. Tier 1 ERPs at that time—such as SAP, PeopleSoft, J.D. Edwards, BAAN, and Oracle—cost millions of dollars to buy and implement, and had a high annual maintenance fee. But top managers felt that they had no choice and jumped on the bandwagon. The implementation of most ERPs took many years because of their complexity and the software's thousands of features and settings. For example, Tier 1 ERPs are multi-currency and multi-language.

Tier 1 ERPs offered more capabilities than accounting software such as Great Plains and ACCPAC, which primarily keep track of transactions. Tier 1 ERPs included high-volume fast databases that could be connected to supplier systems, and modules to perform HR, manufacturing planning and control, materials management, customer relationship management (CRM), and ecommerce. They also provided industry-specific solutions and the ability to control workflow, such as enforcing the authorization requirement for a high-dollar purchase by a buyer. See Table 14-1 for a brief description of common ERP software modules.

Now, many mid-market accounting software products have expanded to become complete business systems, even including manufacturing modules. Microsoft has also entered this market by buying Great Plains, Navision, and Solomon accounting software, and has even introduced its own ERP software called Axapta. Now these software packages are called Microsoft Dynamics GP, Nav, Sl, and Ax, respectively.

The amount of difference between Tier 1 ERPs and some Tier 2 ERPs has shrunk. At the same time, many companies have realized the high cost and complexity of Tier 1 ERPs. As a result, ERP companies such as SAP are providing mid-market products such as SAP Business One. Also, there has been significant consolidation. For example, PeopleSoft bought J.D. Edwards, then Oracle bought PeopleSoft, and Baan is now part of Infor. For a list of ERP vendors and news, see http:// www.180systems.com/portals/erp.

enterprise resource planning (ERP) Also known as enterprise software, ERP is used to manage and coordinate all the resources, information, and functions of an organization from a shared database.

TABLE 14-1 ▶

An overview of some ERP software modules.

Module	Brief Description
Accounting/Finance	A central component of most ERP systems. It provides a range of financial capabilities, including general ledger, accounts payable, accounts receivable, payroll, income statement, and balance sheet.
Marketing	Supports lead generation, target marketing, and direct mail.
Human Resources	Maintains employee information such as date of hire, salary, contact information, and performance evaluations.
Purchasing	Facilitates supplier selection, price negotiation, issuing purchase orders, and receiving shipments.
Production Planning	Integrates information on forecasts, orders, production capacity, on-hand inventory quantities, bills of materials, work in process, schedules, and production lead times.
Inventory Management	Identifies inventory availability, replenishment rules, and inventory tracking.
Distribution	Contains information on third-party carriers, shipping and delivery schedules, and delivery tracking.
Sales	Information on orders, invoices, order tracking, and shipping.
Supply Chain Management	Facilitates supplier and customer management, supply chain visibility, and event management.
Customer Relationship Management	Contact information, buying behaviour, shipping preferences, contracts, payment terms, and credit history.

ERP Definition and Solutions[2]

ERP attempts to integrate all departments and functions of a company onto a single computer system that can serve all those different departments' particular needs. It's a tall order, building a single computer system that serves the needs of the people in finance as well as the people in human resources and in the warehouse. Each of these departments typically has its own computer system, each optimized for the particular ways in which the department does its work. But ERP combines them all into a single, integrated computer system that runs off a single database so that various departments can more easily share information and communicate with each other, and also it reduces redundant data entry.

The integrated approach can have a tremendous payback if companies install the system correctly. Take a customer order, for example. Typically in the past when a customer placed an order, that order began a mostly paper-based journey from in-basket to in-basket around the company, often being keyed and re-keyed into different departments' computer systems along the way. All that lounging around in in-baskets caused delays and lost orders, and all the keying into different computer systems invited errors. Meanwhile, no one in the company truly knew what the status of the order was at any given point in time because there was no way for the finance department, for example, to get into the warehouse's computer system to see whether the item had been shipped.

How Can ERP Improve a Company's Business Performance? ERP automates the tasks involved in performing a business process—such as order fulfillment, which involves taking an order from a customer, making it, shipping it, and billing for it. With ERP, when a customer service representative takes an order from a customer, he or she has all the information necessary to complete the order (the customer's credit rating and order history, the company's MPS and inventory levels, and the shipping/trucking schedule). Everyone else in the company also has access to the single database that holds the customer's new order. When one department finishes with the order, it is automatically routed using the ERP system to the next department.

---

[2] Most of this section is based on C. Koch and T. Wailgum, "ERP Definition and Solutions," http://www.cio .com/article/2439502/enterprise-resource-planning/erp-definition-and-solutions.html?page=1.

To find out where the order is at any time, one needs only to log on to the ERP system and track it down. Customers get their orders faster and with fewer mistakes than before. ERP can apply that same magic to the other major business processes, such as employee benefits or financial reporting.

That, at least, is the dream of ERP. The reality is much harsher. Let's go back to those in-baskets. That process may not have been efficient, but it was simple. Finance did its job, the warehouse did its job, and if anything went wrong outside the department's walls, it was somebody else's problem. Not anymore. With ERP, the customer service representatives are no longer just typists entering someone's name into a computer and hitting the Enter key. The ERP screen makes them businesspeople. It flickers with the customer's credit rating from the finance department and the product inventory levels from the warehouse. Will the customer pay on time? Will we be able to ship the order on time? These are questions that customer service representatives have never had to answer before and they affect the customer and every other department in the company. But it's not just the customer service representatives who have to wake up. People in the warehouse who used to keep inventory in their heads or on scraps of paper now need to put that information online. If they don't, customer service will see low inventory levels on their screens and tell customers that their requested item is not in stock. Accountability, responsibility, and communication have never been tested like this before.

To do ERP right, the ways a company does business will need to change and the ways people do their jobs will need to change too. Real transformational ERP implementation usually runs between one and three years.

Will ERP Fit the Way a Company Does Business? It's critical for companies to figure out if their ways of doing business will fit within a standard ERP package before the cheques are signed and the implementation begins. The most common reason that companies walk away from multimillion dollar ERP projects is that they discover that the software does not support one of their important business processes. At that point there are two things they can do: (1) They can change the business process to accommodate the software, which will mean deep changes in long-established ways of doing business and shaking up important people's roles and responsibilities. (2) They can modify the software to fit the process, which will slow down the project, introduce dangerous bugs into the system, and make upgrading the software difficult.

What Does ERP Really Cost? The total cost of ownership of ERP—including hardware, software, professional services, and internal staff costs (for one to two years after installation, which is when the real costs of maintaining, upgrading, and optimizing the system are felt)—usually ranges between $50,000 and a few million dollars, depending on the number of licences (seats) and the software.

The Hidden Costs of ERP. ERP practitioners point to the following areas as most likely to result in budget overrun:

1. *Training.* Training expenses are high because workers almost invariably have to learn a new set of processes, not just a new software.

2. *Integration and testing.* A typical manufacturing company may have add-on applications for logistics, production planning, and bar coding. If this laundry list also includes customization of the core ERP package, expect the cost of integrating, testing, and maintaining the system to skyrocket.

3. *Data conversion.* It costs money to move corporate information, such as customer and supplier records, product design data and the like, from the old system to a new ERP system.

4. *Consultants.* When users fail to plan for disengagement, consulting fees run wild.

How Do You Configure ERP Software? The packages are built from database tables, thousands of them, that programmers and end users must set to match their business processes; each table has a decision "switch" that leads the software down one decision path or another. By presenting only one way for the company to do each task—say, run the payroll or close the books—a company's individual operating units and far-flung divisions are integrated under one system. But figuring out precisely how to set all the switches in the tables requires a deep understanding of the existing processes being used to operate the business. As the table settings are decided, these business processes are re-engineered ERP's way. Most ERP systems are preconfigured, allowing just hundreds—rather than thousands—of procedural settings to be made by the customer.

For some applications of ERP, see the "Some SYSPRO Applications" OM in Action.

OM in Action

Some SYSPRO Applications

Hayward Gordon   www.haywardgordon.com

Hayward Gordon (HG) designs, manufactures, and distributes industrial pumps for mining, waste-water treatment, and other process industries. It has a head office and 50,000 sq. ft. plant in Toronto, two plants in the United States, and sales offices in Montreal, Calgary, and Vancouver. HG exports worldwide. In order to reduce costs, HG installed SYSPRO. Besides the Financials, HG uses the BOM, WIP, and Requirements Planning modules to plan and control production. SYSPRO also helps track operations/labour times on the shop floor. Furthermore, Microsoft's CRM is integrated in SYSPRO for order entry, credit check, etc.

Higginson Equipment   www.higginson.ca

Higginson Equipment (HE), founded in 1945, is a Canadian cylinder manufacturer and distributor that has been providing products and services to thousands of customers across Canada from its 50-employee facility in Burlington, Ontario. The company designs and manufactures hydraulic and pneumatic cylinders to National Fluid Power Association (NFPA) standards and custom specifications, and distributes more than 30 fluid power and industrial product lines. In 2009, management decided to replace its 15-year-old business software, which didn't have MRP. HE was using an Excel worksheet for each job and to calculate the product's dimensions. With the help of two grants, HE purchased SYSPRO, which automatically generates work orders from sales orders, stores BOMs and uses them in quotations, etc. Since the MRP software was installed, sales have more than doubled. The original office staff are still able to process all the orders and HE has had to add only manufacturing employees.

Quadco Equipment   www.quadco.com

Quadco Equipment (QE) designs and manufactures configurable saw tooth heads for wood harvesting equipment in the forestry industry. It is based in St. Eustache, Quebec, with two parts and service facilities in Canada and two in the United States. QE employs 200 employees and holds 40 patents. It has been using SYSPRO for over a decade.

Hayward Gordon

Higginson Equipment, Ltd.

QE uses all the programs in SYSPRO but finds the Product Configurator especially useful. This program allows QE to easily create a new product structure from existing components. SYSPRO generates a sales order/price quote and a work order automatically. Another useful feature of SYSPRO is that all the product information is available in one screen.

Arctic Manufacturing   www.arcticmfg.com

Arctic Manufacturing (AM) designs and manufactures log-hauling trailers. Its 35,000 sq. ft. shop is located in Prince George, British Columbia. AM has been using SYSPRO for over two decades. It uses most SYSPRO modules, but especially finds the WIP module useful for tracking costs. AM also finds the customizable screens useful.

Courtesy of Arctic Manufacturing

Sources: http://americas.syspro.com/resources/case_studies/ca/hayward_gordon_canada_syspro_case_study.pdf; http://www.syspro.com/resources/case_studies/ca/higginson_canada_syspro_case_study.pdf; http://www.syspro.com/resources/case_studies/ca/quadco_equipment_canada_syspro_case_study.pdf; http://www.syspro.com/resources/case_studies/ca/arcticmanufacturing_canada_syspro_case_study.pdf.

Courtesy of Quadco Equipment

Summary

- Material requirements planning (MRP) is the activity that determines the ordering of dependent-demand items (i.e., components of assembled products).
- The planning process begins with a master production schedule.
- Each end item is "exploded" using its bill of materials, then level-by-level for each component the inventory on-hand and on order (scheduled receipts) are netted, and planned-order releases are developed by offsetting for lead time. These show the quantity and timing for purchasing or producing the component.
- Little safety stock is used in MRP. Instead, safety time (ordering earlier) is used.

- Various lot-sizing methods are used in MRP such as the part-period method. However, the main approach is lot-for-lot ordering.
- Capacity requirements planning (CRP) uses the MRP shop order releases and operations times and routings to determine the capacity requirements from each work centre.
- MRP II is a second-generation MRP that adds a broader scope to planning because it links sales and operations planning, MPS, MRP, CRP, and detailed scheduling.
- ERP systems build on these linkages even further by integrating all functions of an organization in a single common database.

Key Terms

back-flushing
bill of materials (BOM)
capacity requirements planning (CRP)
cumulative lead time
dependent demand
enterprise resource planning (ERP)
fixed interval ordering
gross requirement
load reports

lot sizing
manufacturing resource planning (MRP II)
material requirements planning (MRP)
modular bill
MRP system nervousness
net requirement
net-change MRP
part-period method
pegging

phantom bill
planned-order receipt
planned-order release
planning bill
product structure tree
projected on-hand
regenerative MRP
safety time
scheduled receipt

Solved Problems

Problem 1

The following product structure tree shows the components needed to assemble one unit of product W. Determine the quantities of each component needed to assemble 100 units of W. (*Note:* For the procedure when there are on-hand inventories, see Example 14-1.)

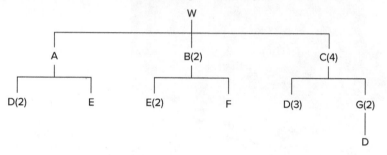

Solution

An easy way to calculate and keep track of component requirements is to first do it for one end item right on the tree, as shown by the subscripts in the following product structure tree.

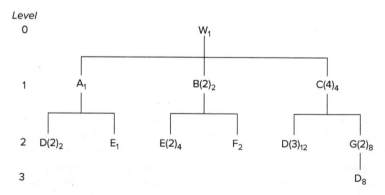

Summary:

Item	(1 W) Quantity	(100 W) Quantity
W	1	100
A	1	100
B	2	200
C	4	400
E	$5 = (1 + 4)$	500
F	2	200
G	8	800
D	$22 = (2 + 12 + 8)$	2,200

Problem 2

Material Requirements Plan Setup Guide

Twelve units of the end item End are needed at the beginning of week 6. Prepare a material requirements plan for component D given that there is a scheduled receipt of 10 units of sub-assembly A in week 3 plus the following information:

Item	End	A	B	C	D
Units on hand	2	6	4	32	15
Lead time (weeks)	1	2	1	2	2

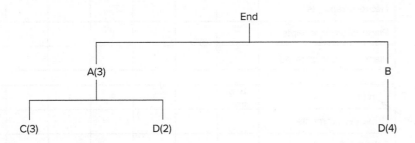

Steps

1. If a question asks for a material requirements plan for a component such as D in the product structure tree, circle all occurrences of that component so you will be sure to include them.

2. Label the spreadsheet sections, top to bottom, following the order shown in the product structure tree:

    Top section: End
    Next section: A
    Next section: B
    Last section: D

    (You don't need one for C because the problem asks for D, and C isn't needed for D.)

3. Add the LT (lead time) for the end item and each component next to the section labels.

4. Add any beginning inventory (on hand) for the end item and each component to their spreadsheet sections.

5. Place the desired end item quantity in the master schedule in the week it is needed, and in the gross requirements of the end item in that same week.

6. Complete the remainder of the plan.

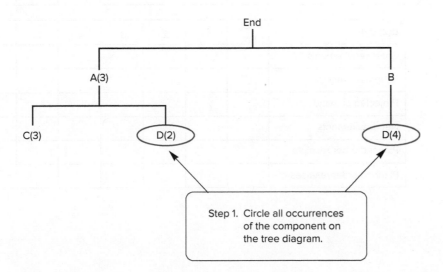

Step 1. Circle all occurrences of the component on the tree diagram.

Master	Week	1	2	3	4	5	6
Schedule	Quantity						

End	Beg. Inv.	1	2	3	4	5	6
Gross requirements							
Scheduled receipts							
Projected on hand							
Net requirements							
Planned-order receipts							
Planned-order releases							

A (3)	Beg. Inv.	1	2	3	4	5	6
Gross requirements							
Scheduled receipts							
Projected on hand							
Net requirements							
Planned-order receipts							
Planned-order releases							

Step 2. Label spreadsheet sections in the order shown in the product structure tree.

B	Beg. Inv.	1	2	3	4	5	6
Gross requirements							
Scheduled receipts							
Projected on hand							
Net requirements							
Planned-order receipts							
Planned-order releases							

D(2) D(4)	Beg. Inv.	1	2	3	4	5	6
Gross requirements							
Scheduled receipts							
Projected on hand							
Net requirements							
Planned-order receipts							
Planned-order releases							

Master	Week	1	2	3	4	5	6
Schedule	Quantity						

End	LT = 1	Beg. Inv.	1	2	3	4	5	6
Gross requirements								
Scheduled receipts								
Projected on hand								
Net requirements								
Planned-order receipts								
Planned-order releases								

A (3)	LT = 2	Beg. Inv.	1	2	3	4	5	6
Gross requirements								
Scheduled receipts								
Projected on hand								
Net requirements								
Planned-order receipts								
Planned-order releases								

B	LT = 1	Beg. Inv.	1	2	3	4	5	6
Gross requirements								
Scheduled receipts								
Projected on hand								
Net requirements								
Planned-order receipts								
Planned-order releases								

D(2) D(4)	LT = 2	Beg. Inv.	1	2	3	4	5	6
Gross requirements								
Scheduled receipts								
Projected on hand								
Net requirements								
Planned-order receipts								
Planned-order releases								

Step 3. Add lead times.

Master	Week	1	2	3	4	5	6
Schedule	Quantity						

End LT = 1	Beg. Inv.	1	2	3	4	5	6
Gross requirements							
Scheduled receipts							
Projected on hand	2						
Net requirements							
Planned-order receipts							
Planned-order releases							

A (3) LT = 2	Beg. Inv.	1	2	3	4	5	6
Gross requirements							
Scheduled receipts				10			
Projected on hand	6						
Net requirements							
Planned-order receipts							
Planned-order releases							

B LT = 1	Beg. Inv.	1	2	3	4	5	6
Gross requirements							
Scheduled receipts							
Projected on hand	4						
Net requirements							
Planned-order receipts							
Planned-order releases							

D(2) D(4) LT = 2	Beg. Inv.	1	2	3	4	5	6
Gross requirements							
Scheduled receipts							
Projected on hand	15						
Net requirements							
Planned-order receipts							
Planned-order releases							

Step 4. Enter specified beginning inventory and scheduled receipts quantities.

Master	Week	1	2	3	4	5	6
Schedule	Quantity						12

Step 5 . Enter the master schedule quantities and end item gross requirements in the specified week(s).

End LT = 1	Beg. Inv.	1	2	3	4	5	6
Gross requirements							12
Scheduled receipts							
Projected on hand	2						
Net requirements							
Planned-order receipts							
Planned-order releases							

A (3) LT = 2	Beg. Inv.	1	2	3	4	5	6
Gross requirements							
Scheduled receipts				10			
Projected on hand	6						
Net requirements							
Planned-order receipts							
Planned-order releases							

B LT = 1	Beg. Inv.	1	2	3	4	5	6
Gross requirements							
Scheduled receipts							
Projected on hand	4						
Net requirements							
Planned-order receipts							
Planned-order releases							

D(2) D(4) LT = 2	Beg. Inv.	1	2	3	4	5	6
Gross requirements							
Scheduled receipts							
Projected on hand	15						
Net requirements							
Planned-order receipts							
Planned-order releases							

Master	Week	1	2	3	4	5	6
Schedule	Quantity						12

End LT = 1	Beg. Inv.	1	2	3	4	5	6
Gross requirements							12
Scheduled receipts							
Projected on hand	2	2	2	2	2	2	2
Net requirements							10
Planned-order receipts							10
Planned-order releases							10

> Step 6. Complete the remainder of the plan, starting with the end item and working down, subtracting projected on hand from gross requirements to get net requirements. Planned order receipts = Net requirements, and all are in the same week.
> Planned order releases are always the same as planned order receipts, but earlier by lead time (one week in this case).

A (3) LT = 2	Beg. Inv.	1	2	3	4	5	6
Gross requirements						30	
Scheduled receipts					10		
Projected on hand	6	6	6	16	16	16	
Net requirements						14	
Planned-order receipts						14	
Planned-order releases					14		

> Subassemblies A and B both come under End in the product structure tree, so their gross requirements are in the same column as the End item's planned-order releases (Week 5), using the multiples given in the product structure tree:
> 3 times 10 for A = 30
> 1 times 10 for B = 10

B LT = 1	Beg. Inv.	1	2	3	4	5	6
Gross requirements						10	
Scheduled receipts							
Projected on hand	4	4	4	4	4	4	
Net requirements						6	
Planned-order receipts						6	
Planned-order releases					6		

> D(2) comes under A in the product structure tree, so its gross requirements are related to A's planned-order releases and in that same week:
> 2 times 14 = 28 in week 3
>
> D(4) comes under B in the product structure tree, so its gross requirements are related to B's planned-order releases and in that same week:
> 4 times 6 = 24 in week 4

D(2) D(4) LT = 2	Beg. Inv.	1	2	3	4	5	6
Gross requirements				28	24		
Scheduled receipts							
Projected on hand	15	15	15	15	0		
Net requirements				13	24		
Planned-order receipts				13	24		
Planned-order releases			13	24			

Problem 3

The product structure tree for end item E follows. The manager wants to know the material requirements for the purchased part R that will be needed to complete 120 units of E by the start of week 5. Manufacturing lead times for items of this order are one week for level 0 and level 1 items, and purchase lead time is two weeks for level 2 items. There is a scheduled receipt of 60 units of M at the *end* of week 1 and 100 units of R at the *start* of week 1. Lot-for-lot ordering is used, and there are no inventories on hand.

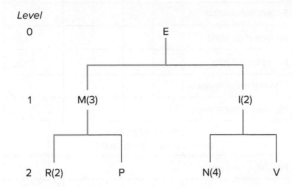

Solution

A partial assembly time chart that includes R and leads to completion of E by the start of week 5 looks like this:

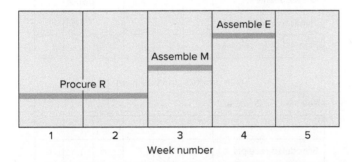

The relevant MRP tables are shown below. The table entries are arrived at as follows:

Production schedule for E: 120 units of E is to be available at the start of week 5.

Table for Item E: Gross requirement equals the quantity specified in the production schedule. Since there is no on-hand inventory, net requirement also equals 120 units. Using lot-for-lot ordering, 120 units must be scheduled to be available at the start of week 5. Because there is a one-week lead time for assembly of 120 units of E, shop order will need to be released (i.e., work started) at the beginning of week 4.

Table for Item M: The *gross* requirement for M is three times the planned-order release for E ($120 \times 3 = 360$), because each E requires three Ms. These must be available at the start of week 4. The net requirement is 60 units less due to the 60 units of scheduled receipt expected to be on hand at that time. Note that the 60 units expected at the end of week 1 are entered in week 2 because, according to our convention, scheduled receipts occur at the start of the week. Also note that according to our convention, the scheduled receipt goes into projected on-hand immediately. Hence, $360 - 60 = 300$ additional units of M must be available at the start of week 4. With the one-week lead time, there must be a shop order release for 300 Ms at the start of week 3.

Table for Item R: Because each M requires two units of R, 600 Rs will be needed to assemble 300 units of M. However, 100 units of R will be on hand because of the scheduled receipt of 100 units at the start of week 1, so only 500 units of R need to be ordered. Because there is a purchase lead time of two weeks, 500 Rs must be ordered at the start of week 1.

Production schedule for E

Week number	Beg. Inv.	1	2	3	4	5
Quantity						(120)

Item: E LT= 1 week						
Gross requirements						(120)
Scheduled receipts						
Projected on-hand						
Net requirements						120
Planned-order receipts						(120)
Planned-order releases					(120)	

Multiplied by 3
(see product structure tree)

Item: M LT= 1 week						
Gross requirements					(360)	
Scheduled receipts			(60)			
Projected on-hand			(60)	60	60	
Net requirements					300	
Planned-order receipts					(300)	
Planned-order releases				(300)		

Multiplied by 2
(see product structure tree)

Item: R LT= 2 weeks						
Gross requirements					(600)	
Scheduled receipts		(100)				
Projected on-hand		(100)	100	100		
Net requirements				500		
Planned-order receipts				(500)		
Planned-order releases		(500)				

Problem 4

Capacity requirements planning. Given the following planned-order releases and the production times for a component produced at a work centre, determine the labour hour requirements of the component each week. Are the planned-order releases feasible if capacity is 120 labour hours per week at the work centre?

Planned-Order Releases:

Week	1	2	3	4
Quantity	200	300	100	150

Production Times:

Processing	0.5 hour/unit
Machine setup	10 hours (assume one production run per week)

Solution

Convert the quantity requirements into labour requirements by multiplying the quantity requirements by the respective processing times and adding the setup time:

Week	1	2	3	4
Quantity	200	300	100	150
Processing hours	100	150	50	75
Machine setup hours	10	10	10	10
Total labour hours	110	160	60	85

Capacity in week 2 is insufficient because 160 labour hours required > 120 labour hours available.

Discussion and Review Questions

Note: An asterisk indicates that a question or problem may be more challenging.

 1. Contrast independent and dependent demand.

 2. What is MRP and when is it appropriate?

 3. How can the use of MRP contribute to profitability?

 4. Why should the planning horizon be at least as long as the cumulative lead time?

 5. What are planning and modular BOMs?

 6. Briefly define or explain each of these terms:
   a. Master production schedule.
   b. Bill of materials.
   c. Manufacturing lead time.
   d. Gross requirement.
   e. Net requirement.

 7. What is the difference between the determination of purchasing lead time and manufacturing lead time?

 8. Describe MRP processing.

9. Contrast planned-order receipts and scheduled receipts.

10. What is pegging and why is it used?

11. Contrast net-change and regenerative MRPs. What is MRP system nervousness?

12. What is back-flushing and why is it used?

13. What is safety time?

14. What is CRP? What can the planner do if the capacity of a work centre will be exceeded?

15. Briefly describe MRP II.

16. What is lot sizing and what is its goal?

17. Explain the part-period method.

18. How does an ERP system differ from MRP II software?

19. What are some unforeseen costs of the ERP implementation?

Taking Stock

 1. What trade-offs are involved in customizing an ERP software?

 2. Who in the organization needs to be involved in MRP?

 3. Why are each of the following considerations an ERP software important?

   a. Ease of use.
   b. Complete integration.
   c. Data reliability.

 4. Why should future users of MRP, MRP II, or ERP software be involved in its selection and implementation?

Critical Thinking Exercise

 Suppose you work for a furniture manufacturer, one of whose products is the chair depicted in Figure 14-6. Finished goods inventory is held in a central warehouse in anticipation of customer orders. Finished goods are controlled using an EOQ/ROP model. The warehouse manager has suggested using the same model for controlling component inventories. Write him a brief memo outlining your opinion on doing that.

Experiential Learning Exercise

 Select an assembled item that you can disassemble and has several parts (e.g., a stapler, pencil sharpener, toy car or truck). Develop a product structure tree for the item.

Internet Exercises

 1. Choose one of the following applications of MRP/ERP and determine the benefit of using the software:

   a. http://www.industrios.com/files/pdf/Success_Story_Cam_Tran.pdf

   b. http://www.epicor.com/Press-Room/Success-Story/CRS-Electronics.aspx

   c. https://www.microsoft.com/en-ca/search/result.aspx?q=Allan+Candy&form=MSHOME, using the "Allan Candy Company case study" document.

 2. Read http://www.ism.ws/files/RichterAwards/IBMSupportDocs2012.pdf about IBM's supply chain MRP, and explain its benefit to IBM.

Problems

 1. a. Given the following product structure tree for product E, determine the quantity of each component required to assemble one unit of E.

```
                        E
        ┌───────────────┼───────────────┐
      F(2)              G                H
    ┌───┴───┐        ┌───┴───┐        ┌───┴───────────┐
   J(2)    D(4)    L(2)     J(2)     A(4)            D(2)
```

 b. Draw the product structure tree for a stapler using its indented BOM below:

Item
Stapler
Top assembly
Cover
Spring
Slide assembly
Slide
Spring
Base assembly
Base
Strike plate
Rubber pad (2)

 2. The following table shows the components needed to assemble an end item, their manufacturing or purchase lead times for typical lot sizes, and amount on hand. The following product structure tree for the end item shows the number of each component per its immediate parent.

Item	End Item	B	C	D	E	F	G	H
LT (wk)	1	2	3	3	1	2	1	2
Amount on hand	0	10	10	25	12	30	5	0

```
                      End Item
        ┌───────────────┼───────────────┐
      B(2)              C                D(3)
    ┌───┴───┐        ┌───┴───┐        ┌───┴───┐
   E(2)    F(3)    G(2)     E(2)     H(4)    E(2)
```

a. If 20 units of the end item are to be assembled, how many additional units of E are needed? (You don't need to develop the MRP tables to determine this.)

b. An order for the end item is scheduled to be shipped at the start of week 11. What is the latest week that production or purchase of the components of the order can be started and the order still be ready to ship on time? (You don't need to develop the MRP tables for this part either.)

3. The following table lists the components needed to assemble an end item, the manufacturing or purchase lead times (in weeks) for typical lot sizes, amount on hand, and the direct components of each item and, in brackets, the number of each component for each parent.

Item	Lead Time	Amount on Hand	Direct Components
End item	1	—	L(2), C(1), K(3)
L	2	10	B(2), J(3)
C	3	15	G(2), B(2)
K	3	20	H(4), B(2)
B	2	30	
J	3	30	
G	3	5	
H	2	—	

a. Draw the product structure tree for the end item.
b. If 40 units of the end item are to be assembled, how many additional units of B are needed? (You don't need to develop the MRP tables.)
c. An order for 40 units of the end item is scheduled to be shipped at the start of week 8. What is the latest week that the components of the order can be started and the order still be ready to ship on time? (You don't need to develop the MRP tables.)

 4. Eighty units of product E are needed at the beginning of week 6. Three cases (30 units per case) of J have been ordered and one case is scheduled to arrive in week 3, one in week 4, and one in week 5. *Note:* J must be ordered by the case, and B must be produced in multiples of 120 units. There are 60 units of B and 20 units of J on hand now. Manufacturing lead times are two weeks each for E and B, and purchase lead time is one week for J.

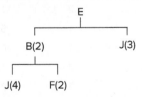

a. Prepare the material requirements plan for component J.
b. Suppose that now is week 4 and the quantity of E needed in week 6 has changed from 80 to 70. The planned order releases through week 3 and scheduled receipts have all been executed as in part *a*. How many more (relative to part *a*) Bs and Js will be on hand in week 6?

 5. a. One hundred twenty units of end item Z are needed at the beginning of week 7. Prepare a material requirements plan for component C. Take into account that on hand there are 40 units of Z, 70 units of A, 100 units of B, and 30 units of C. Also, there is a scheduled receipt of 20 units of component C in week 4. Lead times are two weeks for Z and B, and one week for the other

components. Lot-for-lot ordering will be used for all items.

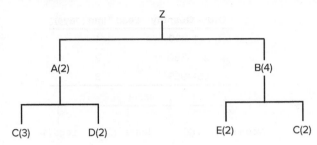

b. Ninety-five units of end item E are needed at the beginning of week 7. Prepare a material requirements plan *for component D.* Take into account that 5 units of E are currently on hand, as well as 50 units of B, 100 units of C, and 80 units of D. Also, 30 units of C have been outsourced and are expected to arrive in week 4. Lead times are two weeks for E and C, and one week for the other components. Assume lot-for-lot ordering except for D, where multiples of 40 must be used.

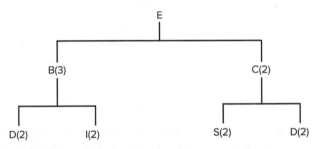

6. Product P is composed of three sub-assemblies: K, L, and W. Sub-assembly K is assembled using 3 Gs and 4 Hs; L is made of 2 Ms and 2 Ns; and W is made of 3 Zs. On-hand inventories are 40 Gs and 200 Hs. Scheduled receipts are 10 Ks at the start of week 3 and 30 Ks at the start of week 6. One hundred Ps must be shipped at the start of week 6, and another 100 at the start of week 7. Manufacturing lead times are two weeks for sub-assemblies and purchase lead times are one week for the components. Final assembly of P requires one week for 100 units. Include an extra 10 percent scrap allowance in each planned order of G. The minimum order size for H is 200 units. For other items, use lot-for-lot ordering. Develop each of the following:
a. The product structure tree.
b. The material requirements plan for P, K, G, and H.

7. A table is assembled using three components, as shown in the following product structure tree. The company that makes the table wants to ship 100 units at the beginning of day 4, 150 units at the beginning of day 5, and 200 units at the beginning of day 7. Receipts of 100 wood sections are scheduled at the beginning of day 2. There are 120 legs on hand. An additional 10 percent of the order size on legs is added as scrap allowance. There are 60 braces on hand. Lead time (in days) for all items is a function of each order quantity and is shown below. Prepare the material requirements plan using lot-for-lot ordering.

Order Quantity	Lead Time (days)
1–200	1
201–550	2
551–999	3

Table

Wood sections (2) Braces (3) Legs (4)

LO3 **8.** Eighty units of product X are needed at the beginning of week 6, and another 30 units are needed at the beginning of week 8. Prepare the material requirements plan for component D, B, and X. D can be ordered only in whole cases (50 units per case). One case of D is automatically received every other week, beginning in week 1 (i.e., week 1, 3, 5, 7). Also, there are 30 units of B and 20 units of D on hand now. Lead times for all items are a function of quantity: one week for up to 100 units, two weeks for 101 to 200 units, three weeks for 201 to 300 units, and four weeks for 301 or more units.

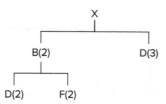

LO3 **9.** A company sells three models of radar detectors. It buys three basic units (E, F, and G) from a Japanese manufacturer and adds one, two, or four lights (component D) to further differentiate the models. D is bought from a domestic producer.

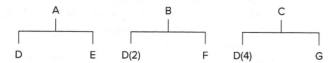

Lead times are one week for all items except C, which is two weeks. There are ample supplies of the basic units (E, F, and G) on hand. There are also 10 units of B, 10 units of C, and 25 units of D on hand. Lot sizing rules are lot-for-lot ordering for all items except D, which must be ordered in multiples of 100 units. There is a scheduled receipt of 100 units of D at the start of week 1.

The production schedule calls for 40 units of A to be available at the start of week 4, 60 units of B at the start of week 5, and 30 units of C at the start of week 6. Prepare the material requirements plan for D and its parents.

LO2 & 3 **10.** Assume that you are the manager of a shop that assembles power tools. You have just received an order for 50 chain saws, which are to be shipped at the start of week 8. Pertinent information on the chain saw is:

Item	Lead Time (weeks)	On Hand	Direct Components
Chain saw	2	15	A(2), B(1), C(3)
A	1	10	E(3), D(1)
B	2	5	D(2), F(3)
C	2	30	E(2), D(2)
D	1	20	
E	1	10	
F	2	30	

a. Draw the product structure tree for the chain saw and an assembly time chart for this order.

b. Develop the material requirements plan for component E and its parents using lot-for-lot ordering.

c. Suppose that capacity to produce part E is limited to a maximum of 100 units per week. Revise the planned-order releases for weeks 1–4 so that this maximum is not exceeded in any period, keeping in mind the objective of minimizing holding cost. The quantities need not be equal in every period. Note that the gross requirements for E will remain the same. However, quantities in some of the other rows will change. Determine the new values in those rows.

LO2 & 3 **11.** Assume that you are the manager of a robot manufacturer. You have just received an order for 40 units of an industrial robot, which is to be delivered at the start of week 7. Using the following information, determine how many units of part G to order and the timing of those orders, given that part G must be ordered in multiples of 80 units and all other components are ordered lot-for-lot. (*Hint:* You just need tables for Robot, C, and G.)

Item	Lead Time (weeks)	On Hand	Direct Components
Robot	2	10	B, G, C(3)
B	1	5	E, F
C	1	20	G(2), H
E	2	4	—
F	3	8	—
G	2	15	—
H	1	10	—

LO3 **12.** Determine the material requirements plan for parts N and V and sub-assembly I as described in Solved Problem 3 (see figure there) for each of the following situations:

a. Assume that there are currently 100 Ns on hand and scheduled receipts of 40 Is and 10 Vs are expected at the beginning of week 3. Suppose that 120 Es are needed at the start of week 5.

b. Assume on-hand and scheduled receipts are as in part *a*. Now suppose that 100 Es are needed at the start of week 5 and 50 at the start of week 7. Also, use multiples of these order sizes: N, 800; V, 200. Use lot-for-lot ordering for I and E.

c. Using your answer to part *a*, update the MRP for I, N, and V, using the following additional information for each of these cases: (1) one week has elapsed (making it the start of week 2), and (2) three weeks have elapsed (making it the start of week 4). *Note:* Start your revised plans so that the updated time in each case is designated as week 1. The updated production schedule now has an order for 100 units of E in week 8 of case 1 and in week 6 of case 2 (i.e., week 9 under the former production schedule). Assume all orders are released and received as planned.

LO2 & 3 13. Information concerning the product structure, lead times, and quantities on hand for an electric golf cart is shown in the following table. Use this information to do each of the following:

a. Draw the product structure tree.

b. Draw the assembly time chart.

c. Develop the material requirements plan that will provide 200 golf carts at the start of week 8, assuming lot-for-lot ordering.

Parts List for Electric Golf Cart	Lead Time (for Typical Order Size)	Quantity on Hand
Electric golf cart	1	0
Top	1	40
Base	1	20
Top		
Supports (4)	1	200
Cover	1	0
Base		
Motor	2	300
Body	3	50
Seats (2)	2	120
Body		
Frame	1	35
Controls	1	0
Wheels (4)	1	240

LO3 14. Refer to Problem 13. Assume that unusually mild weather has caused a change in the quantity and timing of orders for golf carts. The revised plan calls for 100 golf carts at the start of week 6, 100 at the start of week 8, and 100 at the start of week 9.

a. Determine the timing and quantities of orders for top and base.

b. Assume that equipment problems have reduced the manufacturer's capacity for assembling bases to 50 units per week. Revise your material requirements plan for base to reflect this, but still meet delivery dates.

LO4 15. A manufacturer buys a certain part in varying quantities throughout the year. Ordering cost is $11 per order, and holding cost is $0.14 per unit per month. Given the following demand (net requirements) for the part for the next

eight months, determine the order sizes and timing of purchase orders using the part-period method.

Month	Demand (units)
1	—
2	80
3	10
4	30
5	—
6	30
7	—
8	30

LO4 16. A company periodically produces a part that is a basic component of an assembled product. Each time the part is run, a fixed cost of $125 is incurred. The cost to hold one unit for a week is estimated to be $1.65. For the demand (net requirements) shown below, determine the quantity and timing of production runs using the part-period method.

Week	Demand (units)
1	40
2	20
3	100
4	20
5	—
6	20
7	80

LO4 17. A company that manufactures paving material for driveways and parking lots expects the following demand for its products for the next four months.

Month Number	1	2	3	4
Material (tonnes)	40	80	60	70

The company's machine standard time and available capacity are:

Machine standard time (hours per tonne)   3

Monthly production capacity (hours)   200

a. Determine the capacity requirement for each of the four months.

b. In which months do you foresee a problem? What options would you suggest to resolve any problems?

LO4 18. A company produces two products, A and B, that go through a three-step sequence of fabrication, assembly, and packaging. Processing requirements for the departments (hours per unit) are:

Product	Fabrication	Assembly	Packaging
A	2	1.5	1
B	1	1	1.5

Department capacities are all seven hours per day. The following production schedule is for the next three days:

Day	Mon	Tues	Wed
A	2	4	1
B	3	2	2

a. Develop, for each department and day, the capacity requirements for each product and the total load for each day. Ignore changeover time between A and B.

b. Evaluate the projected loads for each day. Is the schedule feasible? What do you suggest for balancing the load?

(LO3) *19. The IT department has a problem. Its computer died just as it spat out the following information: Planned-order release for item J27 = 640 units in week 2. The company has been able to reconstruct all the information it lost except the production schedule for the end item 565. The company is fortunate because J27 is used only in 565. Given the following product structure tree and the associated inventory on hand, lot sizing, and lead-time information, determine what production schedule entry for item 565 was exploded into the material requirements plan that killed the computer.

Part Number	On Hand	Lot Sizing	Lead Time
565	0	Lot-for-lot	1 week
X43	60	Multiples of 120	1 week
N78	0	Lot-for-lot	2 weeks
Y36	200	Lot-for-lot	1 week
J27	0	Lot-for-lot	2 weeks

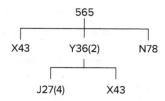

(LO2 & 3) 20. Using the drawing of a pair of scissors below, do the following:

a. Draw the product structure tree for the scissors.

b. Perform MRP for the scissors and all its components except the screw. Lead times are one day for buying each type of blade, assembling the blades with grips, and for final scissors assembly, but two days for buying each type of plastic grip. Six hundred pairs of scissors are needed on day 6. *Note:* There are 200 straight blades, 350 bent blades, and 40 top blade assemblies on hand.

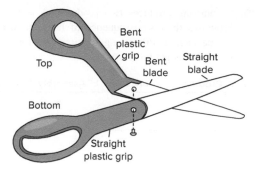

(LO3) 21. Develop the material requirements plan for component H of the end product A that has the following product structure tree. Lead times for A and each component except B are one week. The lead time for B is three weeks. Sixty units of A are needed at the start of week 8. There are currently 15 units of B and 130 units of E on hand, and 50 units of H are in production by a supplier and are scheduled to be received by the start of week 2.

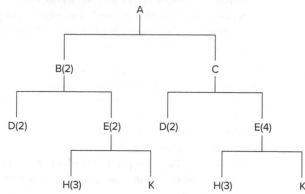

(LO3) *22. Promotional Novelties manufactures a wide range of novelty items for its corporate customers. It has just received an order for 20,000 toy tractor-trailers that will be sold by a gas station chain as part of a holiday promotion. The order is to be shipped at the beginning of week 9. The product structure tree below shows various components of the tractor-trailer and the way it is assembled.

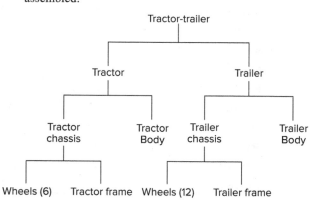

The company can complete final assembly of the tractor-trailers at the rate of 10,000 a week. Assembly time of tractors and trailers for this size order, in different departments, is one week each.

The tractors and trailers each have their own chassis departments that can produce chassis at the rate of 20,000 a week. Wheels are purchased from a supplier. Ordered wheels come in sets of 6,400. The lead time for delivery of wheels from the supplier is three weeks. Perform MRP for the wheels and its parents and answer the following questions:

a. How many wheels will the manager need to order?

b. When should the manager place the order?

c. How many wheels should the manager expect to have left over?

LO3 ***23.** A small furniture maker has just received an order to deliver 250 chairs at the beginning of week 6. The production/purchase planner needs to arrange for the assembly of sub-assemblies and purchase of parts required for the order. The product structure tree for the chair is displayed as follows. The chairs, leg assemblies, and back assemblies are to be assembled by one worker each. During an eight-hour day, 25 chairs, 25 leg assemblies, and 50 back assemblies can be assembled. The company operates five days a week. The seats, spindles, tops, legs, and rails are purchased from another company. Purchase lead time for this size order for each part is one week. The company has some inventory of parts from previous productions: 40 seats, 100 rails, 150 legs, 30 tops, and 80 spindles.

a. Calculate assembly lead times for chairs, leg assemblies, and back assemblies required for this order. Assume that an assembly will start only after the whole batch of its components is available.

b. Develop a material requirements plan for this order. Use lot-for-lot ordering. What action should you take now?

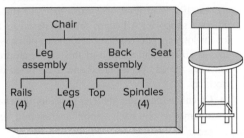

LO2 & 3 ***24.** A furniture maker has received an order for 100 units of its kitchen table to be delivered in six workdays. The table consists of one top and four legs, made from purchased lumber (2″ by 6″ by 6′). Each top is made from 1.5 units of lumber, and each leg is made from 1/6 unit of the lumber. Tops and legs can be made independently in two different workstations, and manufacturing time for one top is expected to be 12 minutes and for one leg is two minutes. All 100 tops and 400 legs should be made before any tables are assembled, and final assembly of one table is expected to take four minutes. The shop works eight hours a day, Monday to Friday. Currently, the company has 20 units of lumber in stock, and purchase lead time for lumber is one workday.

a. Calculate the manufacturing lead time for each operation (round up) and draw the product structure tree.

b. Perform material requirements planning for this order. What action should be taken now?

c. How would your answer for lumber change:
   i. If the safety stock for lumber is 20 units?
   ii. If lumber is purchased in batch size of 250 units?
   iii. If 250 units are scheduled to be received on the next workday?

LO2 & 3 ***25.** You need to plan the fabrication and assembly of an order of 40 side (accessory) tables (see Example 6-7 in Chapter 6) due in six workdays. See the product structure tree that follows. The raw material is planks of oak measuring one inch by four inches by six feet long. The product structure tree below shows that one end table is made of one top sub-assembly, two leg sub-assemblies, and two cross-bars. One top sub-assembly is made from one plank of oak, one leg sub-assembly is made from 0.5 plank of oak, and one cross-bar is made of 0.1 plank of oak. The cutting and assembly time of one top sub-assembly is 20 minutes. The cutting and assembly time of one leg sub-assembly is 10 minutes. The cutting time to make one cross-bar is two minutes. Lastly, the final assembly of one end table is 15 minutes. Assume that the shop works eight hours a day, five days a week. The purchase lead time for oak is one workday. Assume that each operation is performed by a different worker in a different work centre and each batch is to be completed before it is moved to the next work centre. Assume lot-for-lot ordering for all items, except that oak is bought in a batch of 150 planks. There are no inventories on hand or on order, except for 40 planks of oak on hand. Also, there are no safety stocks required, except 30 planks of oak.

a. Determine each of the manufacturing lead times for this order (round up to whole days).

b. Develop the MRP tables. What action should you take now?

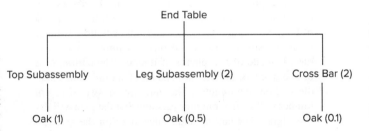

LO2 & 3 ***26.** Restaurants need to plan the purchase and production of their food ingredients and components based on the forecast of demand for each meal. Consider the following example for veal picante with linguini in a restaurant.[3]

The forecasts for demand for veal picante with linguini during each of the next four days are Thursday, 6; Friday, 10; Saturday, 9; and Sunday, 8. The product structure tree of one veal picante with linguini is as follows: The chef assembles the dish from one serving of cooked linguini and one piece of grilled veal steak. The assistant chef makes the cooked linguini using approximately 100 grams of uncooked linguini (takes approximately 15 minutes). The chef grills the veal steak from a marinated piece of veal (takes approximately 17 minutes). Marinating of a raw veal steak needs to be done the day before (by assistant chef) using some picante sauce, lime juice, oil, salt, and pepper (takes approximately five minutes but needs to rest in the fridge overnight). On hand, we have 1 kg of uncooked linguini, six marinated veal steaks, and 13 unmarinated veal steaks. All production lead times are negligible (zero days), except marinating veal steaks, which takes one day. All purchase lead times are one day. The restaurant orders uncooked linguini in 10 kg bags and unmarinated veal steaks in 20-piece boxes.

a. Draw the product structure tree for a veal picante with linguini.

b. Develop MRP tables for all items except picante sauce, lime juice, oil, salt, and pepper.

LO3 *27. Consider this magazine rack and its pieces shown below. The raw material is planks of oak lumber measuring one inch by six inches by six feet long. The six rails and handle are made from one plank of lumber, but to make the two ends and bottom, first two planks have to be glued together side-by-side.

Magazine rack

Pieces:
(Top: 2 end pieces and bottom piece; bottom: 6 rails and handle)

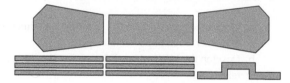

The product structure tree that follows shows that one kit of six rails and a handle is made from one plank of lumber, and one kit of two ends and a bottom is made from one side-by-side glued piece of lumber, which, in turn, is made of two planks of lumber. The cutting time of one plank of lumber into one kit of six rails and a handle will be five minutes. The glue time of two planks of lumber will be five minutes (assume that the glue will dry overnight). The cutting and router time (for the grooves) of one side-by-side glued piece of lumber into one kit of two ends and a bottom will be 10 minutes. Finally, the assembly of one kit of six rails and a handle and one kit of two ends and a bottom will take 15 minutes. The shop works eight hours a day, five days a week. The purchase lead time for lumber is one workday. The shop has just sold 80 magazine racks to a customer to be delivered in eight workdays. Assume that each operation is performed by a different operator and each batch should be completed before it is moved to the next operation.

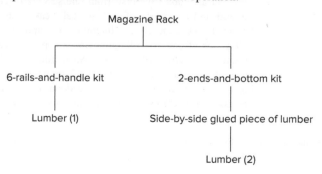

a. Calculate the manufacturing lead time for each operation to make this order.

b. Complete MRP tables for each item. Suppose we currently have 100 planks of lumber in stock. Assume lot-for-lot ordering for all items except lumber, which is purchased in lots of 200 planks.

c. What action should we take now?

LO3 *28. Consider the chair described in Figure 14-6. Suppose that the chair is made by a small furniture manufacturer that has just received an order to deliver 100 chairs in six workdays. The production/purchase planner needs to arrange for the purchase of parts and their assembly. The chairs, front assemblies, and back assemblies are to be built by one worker each. During an eight-hour day, 100 front assemblies and 50 back assemblies can be put together. After a batch of 100 front assemblies and 100 back assemblies are produced, the whole chair will be put together at the rate of 50 per eight-hour day. The company works five days a week. The seats, front legs, cross-bars, side rails, and back supports are purchased from another company. The purchase lead time for any order is one workday. The company has some inventory of parts from previous purchases: 100 front legs, 160 cross-bars, 40 side rails, and 90 back supports. All items are purchased or assembled lot-for-lot, except cross-bars, which are purchased in a lot size of 200. In anticipation of this order, an order of 100 seats has already been placed and is expected on the next workday.

a. Calculate the assembly lead times for the chairs, front assemblies, and back assemblies required for this order.

b. Develop the material requirements plan for this order. What action should you take now?

LO3 *29. Consider the School Chairs Mini-Case at the end of Chapter 6. Suppose the seat is made in a seat-fabrication work centre, all other parts (posts, cross-bars, rails) are made in a post/bar/rail work centre, and the chair is assembled in the chair-assembly work centre. Suppose that a chair takes 15 minutes to assemble and uses one seat and one kit of other parts (two front posts, two back posts, 10 cross-bars, and three rails). A seat takes five minutes to make from half a plank (a plank is two inches by four inches by eight feet). Assume that glue will be dried overnight. A kit of other parts takes 10 minutes to make from one plank. Suppose each work centre is staffed by one worker who works eight hours a day, five days a week (Mon–Fri), and that we promised 90 chairs to a school to be delivered in seven workdays.

a. Determine the manufacturing lead times (in days) for assembling 90 chairs, making 90 seats, and making 90 kits of other parts. Round up if a fraction of day is used.

b. There is no inventory on hand or on order, no safety stocks are needed, lot-for-lot ordering is used, and purchase lead time for lumber is one workday. Use

MRP to determine when and how many units of lumber to purchase, seats to make, other parts to make, and chairs to assemble.

c. What action should be taken now?

d. If we have 35 planks on hand, how would your answer change?

e. If we have 35 planks on hand and we order lumber in a batch size of 200 planks, how would your answer change?

LO3 30. DMD makes specialty bikes. The manager used to order enough bike parts for four months' worth of production, but parts were stacked all over the place, seriously reducing work space and hampering movement of workers. And no one knew exactly where anything was.

The manager heard about MRP, and wants to use it. DMD makes two types of bikes: Arrow and Dart. The manager wants to assemble 15 Arrows and 10 Darts each week from weeks 4 through 8. The product structure trees for the two bikes follow.

```
        Arrow                Dart
   ┌─────┼─────┐        ┌─────┴─────┐
   X     M     W       K(2)        F
   │                 ┌──┴──┐
   F               W(2)    Q
```

He has collected the following information on lead times, inventory on hand, and lot-sizing methods (established by suppliers and/or DMD):

Item	Lead Time (weeks)	On Hand	Lot-Sizing Method
Arrow	2	5	Lot-for-lot
Dart	2	2	Lot-for-lot
X	1	5	Q = 25
W	2*	2	Multiples of 12
F	1	10	Multiples of 30
K	1	3	Lot-for-lot
Q	1	15	Q = 30
M	1	0	Lot-for-lot

*LT = 3 weeks for orders of 36 or more units.

Scheduled receipts are:

Week 1: 20 Arrows, 18 Ws

Week 2: 20 Darts, 15 Fs

Develop the material requirements plan for all the items.

Q MINI-CASE

Zurn

Zurn makes various plumbing products such as fixtures, faucets, drainage equipment, and valves (under the Wilkins brand name). The plant manager is concerned with excessive amounts of inventory of parts in the plant. The materials manager has been tasked to identify if these inventories can be reduced. Zurn uses an accounting software, which also has an MRP module. The materials manager has chosen a popular and reliable pressure vacuum breaker valve (backflow preventer), Model 720A, to study.

Model 720A consists of various parts, most made in the plant but some bought from suppliers, both domestic and Asian. The BOM and assembly chart for 720A are displayed below.

Note that there is a repair kit for Model 720A (in the bottom of the BOM). This is used by some contractors to repair a faulty installed Model 720A and replaces only the internal parts of the pressure valve. The weekly forecast demands for 720A and repair kit for the next quarter (13 weeks) are fairly constant:

Item	720A	repair kit
Weekly demand (units)	1154	135

Courtesy of Zurn Industries, LLC., http://www.zurn.com/products/water-safety/backflow-prevention/model-720a

WILKINS
a **ZURN** *company*

MODEL 720A
Pressure Vacuum Breakers
1/2" to 1"

ITEM NO.	DESCRIPTION	PART NO.
1	CANOPY SCREW	721-11
2	CANOPY	721-3
3	BONNET	721-20
4	PLASTIC WASHER	721A-12
5	O-RING	WK-138N
6	LOAD NUT & GUIDE	721-90
7	LOAD WASHER	721-80
8	DISC UPPER	721A-34
9	POPPET	721-30
10	SPRING	721-33
11	SCREW	721-11A
12	LOWER DISC	721B-34
13	GUIDE SPIDER	721-31
14	NUT, HEX	721-9A
15	TEST COCK	18-860
16	BALL VALVE 1/2" TAP	12-850T
	BALL VALVE 3/4" TAP	34-850T
	BALL VALVE 1" TAP	1-850T
17	POPPET ASSEMBLY	721-300
18	SPIDER ASSEMBLY	721-310

REPAIR KITS

RK1-720A	REPAIR KIT MODEL 720A, 1/2", 3/4" & 1"	
PART NO.	QTY.	DESCRIPTION
721A-12	1	PLASTIC WASHER
WK-138N	1	O-RING
721-33	1	SPRING
721-300	1	POPPET ASSEMBLY
721-310	1	SPIDER ASSEMBLY

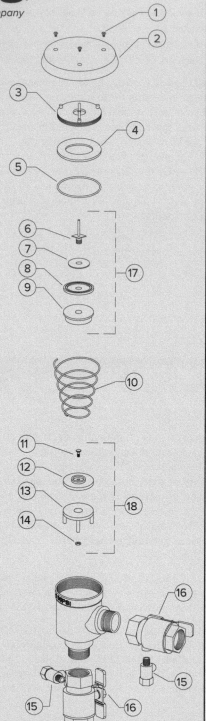

Courtesy of Zurn Industries, LLC., http://www.zurn.com/media-library/web_documents/pdfs/repairparts-(1)/720a_12-1-pdf

71

To save time, the materials manager has decided to look at the requirements plans for only the following components: body, plastic washer, and ball valves. In addition to Model 720A and repair kit, some of these components are used in other valves as well. The weekly forecast demands for these components for the next quarter (13 weeks) are fairly constant:

Item	body	plastic washer	ball valve
Weekly demand (units)	804*	2,265	12

* only weeks 9–13

Some more information about these five items is as follows:

Item	Lead Time (weeks)	Safety Stocks	Lot Size	Currently On Hand
Model 720A	0	0	L4L	8,600
Repair kit	1	360	L4L	434
Body	2	0	50,000	15,536
Plastic washer	5	9,000	55,000	16,680
Ball valve	8	0	10,300	9,387

Questions

a. What are the requirements for these five items for the next 13 weeks?

b. Is Zurn carrying too much inventory? (*Hint:* Look at on-hand, safety stocks, and lot sizes.)

Chapter 15
Just-in-Time and Lean Production

With permission of the Ministry of Education, Saskatchewan

Lean production, which was initially developed by the Japanese for the manufacture of automobiles, is making its way into the Canadian health care system. A recent comparison of 11 peer countries showed that Canadians were required to wait the longest before seeing a doctor or nurse, despite having the sixth highest per capita health care cost. Realizing the need for change, health care providers hope that lean can help them to better manage skyrocketing costs, reduce excessive wait times, and improve the quality of patient care.

Technically speaking, lean is both a philosophy and a set of methodologies which seek to eliminate wastes and improve efficiencies throughout an organization. In colloquial terms, lean simply means doing more with less. While the full benefits of lean implementation will take many more years to reveal themselves, we can already see some promising preliminary results throughout the West:

- 100 percent of severely ill mental health patients got appointments within 24 hours, up from 50 percent, in the Sunrise Health Region in Saskatchewan
- Time to get a new health card was reduced to two days, from 46 days, in Prince Albert, SK
- Time from referral to assessment for eating disorders was reduced from 66 days to 8.5 days and savings of $32,400 per year were obtained from elimination of 2,160 unnecessary blood tests at BC Children's Hospital

- Qu'Appelle Health Region, SK, was able to provide an additional 650 MRI scans without increased staffing because of improved efficiencies
- Wait times for patients in the lab were reduced by 76 percent in the Five Hills Health Region, SK
- Wait times for service after referral were reduced from 68 days to 14 days in the Northern Health Region, Manitoba
- $134 million was saved in the Saskatchewan Health Region from lean implementation

Sources: Current State of Lean in Canadian Health Care, The Conference Board of Canada, October 20, 2014; http://www.saskatchewan.ca/government/health-care-administration-and-provider-resources/saskatchewan-health-initiatives/lean, retrieved July 15, 2016.

Introduction

As organizations strive to improve efficiencies and reduce costs, they are continually seeking new and better ways of operating. For some, this means changing from the traditional ways of operating to what is now referred to as JIT/lean production. The term **just-in-time (JIT)** in a narrow sense, also called *little JIT,* refers to a production system in which both the movement of work-in-process (WIP) during production and deliveries of parts/modules from suppliers are carefully timed so that at each step of the process, the next (usually small, ideally one-unit) batch arrives for processing just as the preceding batch is completed—thus the name, *just-in-time.* The result is a system with few idle items waiting to be processed (i.e., inventory) and a balanced, rapid flow.

In a broader sense, JIT, also called *big JIT,* is a philosophy of "waste" reduction, be it inventory or resources (such as workers, equipment, or floor space), and continuous improvement. In this sense, JIT is identical to **lean production**.

JIT, in the narrow sense, is sometimes contrasted with material requirements planning (MRP; see Chapter 14). MRP relies on a computer-based *component-scheduling* system (using daily or weekly time periods) to trigger and "push" production and deliveries through the process, whereas JIT relies on visual signals to trigger and "pull" production and deliveries (usually hourly) through the process. MRP controls the work centre capacities, whereas JIT controls the inventory (through kanbans).

The JIT/lean approach was pioneered by Toyota's founder, Taiichi Ohno, and Shigeo Shingo as a much faster and less costly way of producing automobiles. JIT/lean is both a philosophy and a

just-in-time (JIT) Production system in which processing and movement of parts/modules/work-in-process occur just as they are needed, usually in small batches.

lean production JIT, in a broad sense, is a philosophy of waste reduction and continuous improvement.

© Alexandra Boulat/VII/Getty

A worker is assembling a Louis Vuitton handbag at the company's fine leather goods factory in the town of Ducey in France. To keep its brand exclusive and contain costs, the company monitors growth and incorporates lean production processes. It used to take 20 to 30 workers to produce each tote bag, over the course of eight days. Different workers would sew together leather panels, glue in linings, and attach handles. Today, clusters of 6 to 12 workers are utilized, with each performing several tasks. Assembly time has been reduced to a single day. (See http://www .post-gazette.com/business /businessnews/2006/10/09 /Louis-Vuitton-tries-modern -methods-on-factory-lines /stories/200610090118)

methodology that focuses on eliminating waste and streamlining operations by closely coordinating all activities. The development of JIT/lean in Japan was influenced by the fact that Japan is a crowded country with few natural resources. Not surprisingly, the Japanese are very sensitive to waste and inefficiency. They regard rework as waste and excess inventory as evil because it takes up space and ties up resources.

A stunning example of the potential of lean manufacturing was illustrated by the successful adoption of lean methods in the mid-1980s in a Fremont, California, auto plant. The plant was originally operated by General Motors (GM). However, GM closed the plant in 1982 because of its low productivity and high absenteeism. A few years later the plant was reopened as a joint venture of Toyota and GM, called NUMMI (New United Motor Manufacturing, Inc.). About 80 percent of the former plant workers were rehired, but the white-collar jobs were shifted from directing to supporting workers, and small teams were formed and trained to design, measure, and improve their performance. The result? By 1985 productivity and quality improved dramatically, exceeding all other GM plants, and absenteeism was negligible.

A few years later, more interest in lean production arose when *The Machine That Changed the World,* by Womack, Jones, and Roos, was published. Now JIT/lean is being promoted by numerous government programs, associations, and companies, and being used by most progressive organizations.

Just like the awards for quality, there is a prize for world-class lean systems, called the Shingo Prize. The principles and criteria for a lean system are given in the "Shingo Prize" OM in Action.

 OM in Action

Shingo Prize

The Shingo Prize for Operational Excellence was established in 1988 to recognize the achievement of companies worldwide that are implementing JIT/lean systems. It is named after the Japanese guru of lean manufacturing, Dr. Shigeo Shingo. The criteria currently used to judge a company are principle based. These are displayed in the following figure. The 10 guiding principles are the key concepts or foundations of the philosophy of JIT/lean according to the Shingo Prize. Note that "Flow & Pull Value" means shortening lead time and matching supply with demand. Four categories (or dimensions) of principles are shown, starting from the bottom:

THE GUIDING PRINCIPLES

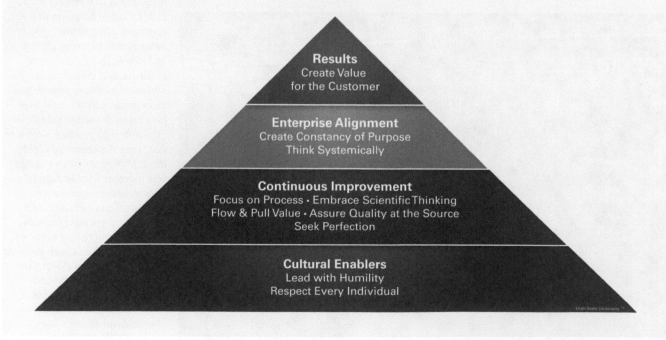

Results
Create Value
for the Customer

Enterprise Alignment
Create Constancy of Purpose
Think Systemically

Continuous Improvement
Focus on Process · Embrace Scientific Thinking
Flow & Pull Value · Assure Quality at the Source
Seek Perfection

Cultural Enablers
Lead with Humility
Respect Every Individual

Utah State University

Cultural Enablers, Continuous Improvement, Enterprise Alignment, and Results. Each category has some sub-categories, and each is assessed based on how the company has progressed from basic use of tools and techniques, to systems thinking (involving all parts of the company), to incorporating a lean approach as part of work principles. Category 2 (i.e., Continuous Improvement) is assessed in each of the business process areas: customer relations, product development, operations, supply, and management (other functions of business). Some explanation and the maximum points for each sub-category are given in the table below.

	Max. Points		Max. Points

1. Cultural Enablers
Leadership
People Development
  Education, training and coaching
  Empowerment and involvement
  Environmental and safety systems
	250	**Management**
		(alignment and integration of other functions in support of production value stream, value stream mapping of other processes, use of JIT/lean/quality improvement tools in other processes)	

2. Continuous Improvement Customer Relations (having a process for assessing voice of customer, order taking, invoicing, etc.) Product Development (QFD, concurrent engineering, benchmarking, new markets, DFM and DFA, component standardization and modularity, value analysis, innovations, involvement of suppliers/customers, etc.) Operations (one-piece flow, demand pull, value stream mapping, total preventive maintenance, SMED, poka-yoke, visual systems, cellular layout, kaizen, level loading, 5S, right-sized equipment/facilities, Six Sigma/SPC/design of experiments, tools for quality improvement, etc.) Supply (integration with suppliers, a process for making the linkage visible, transport and distribution alliances, respect for suppliers, commitment to supplier development)	350	**3. Enterprise Alignment** Enterprise thinking in a global environment (reporting of lean principles/policy, having common management/reporting system, using lean accounting, simple/visual information systems, etc.) Policy Deployment (scientific thinking, planning process for policy deployment, alignment of objectives, constancy of purpose, etc.) **4. Results** Quality (internal quality, quality to the customer, etc.) Delivery (lead time, on-time delivery, etc.) Cost/Productivity (labour productivity, asset productivity, inventory turns, etc.) Customer Satisfaction (customer survey, etc.) Safety/Environment/Morale (employee survey, etc.)	200 200

Source: http://www.shingoprize.org/files/ModelsGuidelines_v5.pdf, retrieved April 1, 2014.

A slightly different representation of the JIT/lean principles and tools, which better matches the chapters in this textbook, is given in Figure 15-1. Displayed are the goals and building blocks of JIT/lean systems. We will describe the goals and each of the building blocks (product design, process design, personnel/organization, and planning and control) in a separate section below.

The Goals of Lean Production

The ideal JIT/lean production system produces one piece at a time, defect-free, on demand, fast, without waste, and in a safe production environment. This can be achieved by a balanced rapid flow.

A Balanced Rapid Flow

A *balanced rapid flow* of a family of products is a smooth, even, swift flow of materials, information, or work through the steps of the production process. Here, "balanced" has the same interpretation as in the line balancing of Chapter 6, that the workload should be distributed evenly among the work-stations. This goal includes the elimination of unevenness (*mura* in Japanese) and overburden (i.e., using a resource in excess of its optimal operating rate; *muri* in Japanese). A balanced rapid flow

FIGURE 15-1 ▶

An overview of the goals and building blocks of JIT/lean systems.

Adapted from Thomas E. Vollmann, William L. Berry, and D. Clay Whybark. *Manufacturing Planning and Control Systems*, 4th ed. (McGraw-Hill/Irwin, 1997). Table 3.1, p. 77, and Figure 3.3, p. 75.

Ultimate Goal

A balanced, rapid flow

Supporting Goals

Elimination of disruptions
System flexibility

Elimination of waste
Continuous improvement

Product Design:
• Product quality
• DFM and DFA

Process Design:
• A balanced system
• A flexible system
• Small lot sizes
• Setup time reduction
• Cellular layout
• Process quality
• Standardized processes
• Little inventory

Personnel/Organizational Elements:
• Workers as assets
• Leadership
• Nonmanufacturing support

Planning and Control:
• Level loading
• Pull system and *kanban*
• Close supplier relationship
• Preventive maintenance and housekeeping

Building Blocks

A worker attaches wheels and hubcaps to an SUV on an assembly line. An assembly line is the best example of a balanced rapid flow.

© Marcos Issa/Bloomberg via Getty

can be achieved by four supporting goals: elimination of disruptions, system flexibility, elimination of waste, and continuous improvement.

Elimination of Disruptions. Disruptions upset the smooth flow of products through the production system and cause variability. Disruptions are caused by a variety of factors such as poor quality, equipment breakdowns, changes to the schedule/customer demand, and late deliveries of parts/components. All these sources of variability should be eliminated as much as possible.

System Flexibility. A *flexible system* is one that is robust enough to handle a mix of products and changes in the level of output, while still maintaining balance and throughput speed. Reduction of machine setup and lead time will increase system flexibility. Flexibility enables the system to meet changing demand.

Elimination of Waste. Waste (*muda* in Japanese) represents unproductive resources. Eliminating waste can free up resources and enhance production. In the JIT/lean system, wastes include:

1. Overproduction—excess inventory.

2. Unnecessary inventory—excess supplies and equipment.

3. Waiting—order waiting to be processed, requests for information awaiting answers.

4. Unnecessary transportation—inefficient routing.

5. Overprocessing—using a complex process instead of a simpler one; work that adds no value.

6. Inefficient work methods/excess motions—poor layout design, unnecessary steps, inadequate training.

7. Producing defective products—scrap and rework.

8. Underutilization of employee knowledge/skill—not using all of the mental and creative capabilities of workers.

The existence of these wastes is an indication that improvement is possible. For an implementation of JIT/lean in a service, including examples of waste, see the "RBC" OM in Action.

 OM in Action   www.rbc.com

RBC

RBC (Royal Bank of Canada) started using lean and Six Sigma tools to reduce waste and defects in 2003. However, the projects were led by outside consultants who did not fully transfer the knowledge of the improvement process to RBC staff. In 2007, RBC started employing master black belts and black belts who not only led improvement projects but also trained the staff on how to undertake improvement projects themselves.

One project was to make "skimming" fraud investigations more efficient. *Skimming* means using a counterfeit debit card. The team consisted of a master black belt, two fraud agents, and the manager of the National Fraud Detection Group in the Enterprise Operations of RBC. The project was in the form of a kaizen event (or blitz), which took five days. On day 1, the current skimming fraud investigation process was mapped, and the process was examined for wastes (versus value to client). On days 2 and 3, possible new processes were mapped

and examined. On day 4, the chosen process was implemented, and on day 5 its improvements were evaluated. Some of the waste reductions were (1) 20 percent reduction in unnecessary data entry, (2) elimination of emails to branches, (3) reduction in choices of general ledger accounts required for posting the transaction (from 30 to 2), (4) elimination of duplicate or fraudulent transaction checks, and (5) conversion of a manual paper-based process to an electronic filing process, which saves time needed to walk to the shared printer. The electronic filing process has also cut manual searches, and enabled catching of missed information (mandatory fields) earlier. This has helped to reduce the investigation time from three days to one day, resulting in happier customers who get their refund faster. It also saved 2,500 hours of work, 14,000 emails, 1,000 km of walking, and 315,000 sheets of printed paper per year.

Source: "RBC Embeds Black Belts in a Bid to Get Lean," *Plant*, 2008, pp. 42–46.

Continuous Improvement. *Kaizen* means *continuous improvement* to better the system. In operations, examples include reducing inventories, setup cost, and time; improving quality; increasing the output rate; and generally cutting wastes and disruptions. But kaizen also applies to customer-related processes such as order taking, product development processes such as quality function deployment, supply-related processes such as issuing purchase orders, and support processes such as hiring. Kaizen is based on the following tenets:

1. Improvement should be done gradually and continuously.

2. Everyone should be involved.

3. It does not require spending great sums of money on technology or consultants.

4. It can be applied anywhere.

5. It involves learning by doing, using scientific thinking.

6. Kaizen relies on direct observation and data collection.

One can think of kaizen as continuous problem solving (see Chapter 9). Thus, continuous improvement/problem solving becomes a way of life—a "culture" that must be assimilated into the mindset of everyone in the organization. It becomes a never-ending quest for improving processes as all members of the organization strive to improve the system. Improvements are made at all levels of the organization. Of particular importance are problems that interrupt the smooth flow of work. These must be dealt with quickly, usually by the employee with the help of his supervisor.

The tools (or building blocks) used to achieve the above goals are classified into four classes: product design, process design, personnel and organizational elements, and planning and control.

(LO3) Product Design

JIT/lean seeks to reduce wastes in all forms, especially excessive inventory. Therefore, there isn't much safety stock to use if the parts and materials are defective. Ensuring quality of parts and materials requires selecting capable suppliers and ensuring they have good quality control. This is easier if standard parts and materials are specified in the product design. These are readily available and can be resupplied quickly.

Quality function deployment (QFD) should be used to capture the "voice" of customers and deploy it in the product design. Value analysis may be used to identify the necessary functions of the product and to cut down product features not valued by the customers.

Concurrent engineering should be used to increase functional communications, reduce the need for engineering changes, and speed up the design process.

Products should be designed for easy manufacturing (called *design for manufacturability* (DFM)) and assembly (called *design for assembly* (DFA)). This will help to speed up operations. For example, products should be designed in such a way as to minimize tool setups, by designing products around commonly used tools. This will reduce setup times and reduce workstation clutter. Another example is fastener standardization. If screws can be standardized to one type per workstation, powered screwdrivers can be used without the need to change bits. The proliferation of excess parts and procedures contributes to mistakes and delays. The use of computer numerically controlled (CNC) machine tools along with CAD can reduce the need for machine setups.

For more information on these and other elements of product design that contribute to a JIT/lean system, see Chapter 4.

(LO4) Process Design

A Balanced System

In a balanced system, workload is distributed evenly among workstations (see line balancing in Chapter 6). Recall that the maximum time allowed at each workstation to complete its set of tasks on a unit is called cycle time or **takt time**. Takt time is changed periodically (e.g., daily) to meet changing demand.

> **takt time** The maximum time allowed at each workstation to complete its set of tasks on a unit. Also called cycle time.

Calculating cycle or takt time was covered briefly in Chapter 6. Here, we illustrate it in more detail. The procedure for obtaining the takt time is:

1. Determine the net time available per shift by subtracting any nonproductive time from total shift time.

2. If there is more than one shift per day, multiply the net time per shift by the number of shifts to obtain the net available time per day.

3. Calculate takt time by dividing the net available time by demand during the day.

EXAMPLE 15-1 ▶

Given the following information, calculate the takt time: Total time per shift is 480 minutes per day, and there are two shifts per day. There are two 20-minute rest breaks and a 30-minute lunch break per shift. Daily demand is 80 units.

SOLUTION

1. Calculate net time available per shift:

Total time	480 minutes
Rest breaks	−40 minutes
Lunch	−30 minutes
	410 minutes per shift

2. Calculate the net time available per day:

410 minutes per shift × 2 shifts/day = 820 minutes per day

3. Calculate the takt time:

$$\text{Takt time} = \frac{\text{Net time available per day}}{\text{Daily demand}}$$

$$= \frac{820 \text{ minutes per day}}{80 \text{ units per day}}$$

$$= 10.25 \text{ minutes per unit}$$

A Flexible System

Process design can increase *production flexibility* in a variety of ways. Table 15-1 lists some of the techniques used for this purpose.

1. Reduce changeover (setup) time.
2. Cross-train workers so they can help others facing overcapacity.
3. Use many small machines rather than a few large machines.
4. Use safety stocks.
5. Keep some idle capacity.

Adapted from Edward M. Knod, Jr., and Richard J. Schonberger, *Operations Management: Meeting Customers' Demands*, 7th ed. (New York: McGraw-Hill, 2001).

Small Lot Sizes

In a JIT/lean system, the ideal lot size is one unit, a quantity that may not always be realistic owing to practical considerations requiring minimum lot sizes (e.g., machines that process multiple items simultaneously, and machines with very long setup times). Nevertheless, the objective is to reduce the lot size as much as possible. Small lot sizes in both the production process and deliveries from suppliers yield a number of benefits that enable JIT/lean systems to operate efficiently. First, with small lots moving through the system, work-in-process (WIP) inventory is considerably less than it is with large lots. This reduces holding cost, space requirement, and clutter in the workplace. Second, inspection and rework costs are less when problems with quality occur, because there are fewer items in a lot to inspect and rework.

Small lots also result in greater system flexibility. Batch systems typically produce a small variety of products. This usually means long production runs of each product, one after the other. Although this spreads the setup cost for a run over many items, it also results in long cycles over the entire range of products. For instance, suppose a company has three product models, A, B, and C. In a batch system, there would be a long run of model A (e.g., covering two or three days or more), then a long run of model B, followed by a long run of model C before the sequence would repeat. In contrast, a JIT/lean system, using small lots, would frequently shift from producing A to producing B and C. This enables JIT/lean systems to respond more quickly to changing customer demands. The contrast between small and large lot sizes is illustrated in Figure 15-2. A summary of the benefits of small lot sizes is presented in Table 15-2.

A = units of product A
B = units of product B
C = units of product C

Small-lot JIT/lean approach

AAA   BBBBBBB   CC   AAA   BBBBBBB   CC   AAA   BBBBBBB   CC   AAA   BBBBBBB   CC

Time ⟶

Large-lot batch approach

AAAAAAAAAAA   BBBBBBBBBBBBBBBBBBBBBBBBBB   CCCCCCCCC   AAAAAAAAAA

Time ⟶

It is important to note that the use of small lot sizes is not in conflict with the EOQ approach; in JIT/lean, there is an emphasis on reducing the setup time (and hence cost), which reduces the optimal lot size.

TABLE 15-2 ▶

Benefit of small lot sizes.

Reduced inventory, lower carrying costs
Less space required to store inventory
Less rework if defects occur
Less inventory to "work off" before implementing product improvements
Increased visibility of problems
Increased production flexibility
Increased ease of balancing operations

Setup Time Reduction

Small lots and changing product mixes require frequent machine setups. An example of a machine changeover or setup is putting a different fixture in a machine to hold a different part or putting a different die in a press to "stamp" a different part. Another example of a machine changeover/setup is adjusting the heights of fillers and labellers on a beverage bottling line to fill different sized bottles. Unless setups are quick and relatively inexpensive, the time and cost to accomplish them can be prohibitive. In JIT/lean systems, workers are often trained to do their own setups. Moreover, tools and methods are used to reduce setup time.

Multipurpose equipment or attachments can help to reduce setup time. For instance, a machine with multiple spindles that can easily be rotated into place for different job requirements can drastically reduce job changeover time. Moreover, group technology (described in Chapter 6) may be used to reduce setup cost and time by capitalizing on similarities in recurring operations. For instance, parts that are similar in shape, materials, and so on, may require very similar setups. Processing them in sequence on the same equipment can reduce the need to completely change a setup; only minor adjustment may be necessary.

Another method for setup time reduction is to separate the internal setup activities (i.e., those that cannot be done offline in advance) from the external setup activities (i.e., those that can be done offline in advance), and to make as many setup activities as possible external; for example, bring the tools and fixtures to the machine before the setup, or preheat the injection mould. Yet another technique is to streamline the setup. For example, preset the desired settings (one-touch setting), use locator pins to prevent misalignment of a die on a press, reduce or eliminate tools, and make movements easier. Finally, train the operators and standardize the setup procedure.

 OM in Action ◀

Lean in Formula 1 Racing

In the exciting world of Formula 1 racing, the difference between first place and second is often measured in fractions of a metre. At racing speeds in excess of 370 km/hour, one extra second spent in the pit represents well over 100 metres on the racetrack. Multiply this by an average of two to three stops each race, and it becomes clear why pit crews try to minimize the time it takes to change a set of tires.

Using principles of lean production, Formula 1 pit crews have reduced the time required to completely change a set of four tires to under two seconds. Compare this number to the time it took to change a tire on your car. How do these race cars get in and out of the pit so quickly? While the process may appear complex, the method used is fairly simple. One of the keys to achieving such efficiency is the separation of the setup activities that can be done only when the race car stops from the setup activities that can be done before the car stops. This allows the pit crew to prepare as much as possible and ensure that the least amount of time is wasted after the car stops.

© kolvenback/Alamy

Source: http://www.redbull.com/ca/en/motorsports/f1/stories/1331621211398/red-bull-racing-pitstop-record, retrieved July 10, 2016.

Shigeo Shingo made a very significant contribution to lean operation with the development of what is called the **single-minute exchange of die (SMED)** system for reducing changeover time. It involves first categorizing changeover activities as either "internal" or "external" activities. Internal activities are those that can be done only while a machine is stopped (i.e., not running). Hence, they contribute to long changeover times. External activities are those that do not involve stopping the machine—they can be done before or after the changeover—hence, they do not affect changeover time. After activities have been categorized, a simple approach to achieving quick changeovers is to convert as many internal activities as possible to external activities and then streamline the remaining internal activities.

> **single-minute exchange of die (SMED)** A system for reducing changeover time.

The potential benefits that can be achieved using the SMED system were impressively illustrated in 1982 at Toyota, when the changeover time for a machine was reduced from 100 minutes to 3 minutes! The principles of the SMED system can be applied to any changeover operation.

Cellular Layout

Many JIT/lean systems have one or more *cells*. A cell contains the machines and tools needed to process a family of parts that have similar processing requirements (see Chapter 6). In essence, a cell is a highly specialized and efficient production centre.

Conversion to a cell requires:

- Determining a family of products.
- Mapping the current process for the family of products.
- Determining the operations required.
- Determining the capacity requirements.
- Rearranging the layout and bringing the necessary machines closer together, usually in a U-shaped configuration.
- Determining the capacity of the cell.

> **poka-yoke** Any mechanism that helps an equipment operator avoid mistakes. Its purpose is to eliminate product defects by preventing, correcting, or drawing attention to human errors as they occur.

- Upgrading the machines if the capacity is inadequate.
- Balancing the cell and determining labour requirements.
- Determining the WIP required between the machines/workstations in the cell.

The advantages of cells include faster throughput (i.e., shorter lead times), less material handling, reduced space requirement, and flexibility to increase/decrease the capacity by adding/subtracting workers. The disadvantages of cells are that the machines may not be fully utilized and bringing various machines close together may raise safety/ergonomic issues. For an example of a cell, see Figure 2 of the Mini-Case "Airline Manufacturing" at the end of this chapter.

OM in Action   www.sconatrailers.com

Scona Trailer Manufacturing

Scona Trailer Manufacturing of Edmonton, part of McCoy Corp., manufactures large, heavy-duty trailers. In 2003, the demand for trailers was soaring but Scona could not keep up with demand. The new president of McCoy, Jim Rakievich, heard about JIT/lean manufacturing and, with Scona plant manager Giorgio Overeem, started to study it. Jim brought in a consultant and Giorgio enrolled in a course on JIT/lean manufacturing at the Northern Alberta Institute of Technology. In the summer of 2005 they introduced JIT/lean production to Scona, starting with one cell. JIT/lean tools used included value stream mapping, identifying nonvalue steps and eliminating these wastes, identifying the bottleneck and rearranging the flow to improve the throughput, and tidying up the shop floor (5S). Eventually, the whole plant (25,000 ft²) was converted into three to four cells. The capacity of the plant has more than doubled. A trailer can now be produced in only three days (down from approximately 25 days before). McCoy sold Scona and its sister company, Peerless, to Manac, Canada's largest commercial trailer maker, in 2014.

Courtesy of Scona Trailer Manufacturing

Sources: K. Laudrum, "McCoy Gets Leaner and Doubles Productivity," *Plant*, March/April 2009, 4(2), p. 8; http://www.sequeirapartners.com/news/mccoy-corporation-divests-of-non-core-mobile-solutions-segment-2/.

> **autonomation** Intelligent automation: if an abnormal situation arises, the machine automatically stops, preventing production of defective products.

An ethernet cable has a clip to prevent users from connecting it upside down.

© anat chant/Shutterstock

Process Quality

Because of low inventories in JIT/lean systems, it is important to prevent defects from occurring; hence, the importance of a capable production process, statistical process control (SPC) including control charts to control and stabilize the production process, Six Sigma to reduce its variability, and poka-yoke to mistake-proof it.

A **poka-yoke** is any mechanism that helps an equipment operator avoid mistakes. Its purpose is to eliminate product defects by preventing, correcting, or drawing attention to human errors as they occur. Examples of poka-yoke include an alarm that sounds if the weight of a package is too low (indicating missing components), an ABM signal if a card is left in the machine, a connector that can be attached in only one way, and detectors at department stores that signal if a monitoring tag hasn't been removed from an item. Much of the credit for poka-yoke goes to Shigeo Shingo.

A related term is **autonomation** (note the extra syllable *no* in the middle of the word), meaning intelligent automation. It means that if an abnormal situation arises, the machine automatically stops, preventing production of defective products. Another related term is **jidoka**, meaning quality at the source: avoid passing defective products to the following workstation, and stop and fix the problem. Clearly, both poka-yoke and autonomation assist in jidoka.

An ATM provides an alert if a card is left in the machine.

Bloomberg/Getty Images

jidoka Japanese term for quality at the source: avoid passing defective products to the following workstation, and stop and fix the problem.

andon A set of lights used at each workstation to signal problems or slowdowns.

Some companies use lights to signal problems; in Japan, this is called **andon**. Each workstation is equipped with a set of three lights. A green light means no problems, an amber light means a worker is falling a little bit behind, and a red light indicates a serious problem. The purpose of the light system is to enable supervisors to immediately see where problems are occurring.

The andon board in the GM Powertrain Engine facility is a visual communication tool. It advises employees of the real-time status of each machine within the manufacturing lines, enabling the production system to be run more effectively.

General Motors LLC used with permission of GM Media Archive

Standardized Processes

Processes include customer-related processes such as invoicing, product development processes such as standardization and modularity, supply-related processes such as supplier qualification, and support processes such as capital budgeting. Here we will focus on the production process. The Toyota Production System has rigid rules for work, interaction, workflow, and improvement process.[1]

---

[1] S. Spear and H. K. Bowen, "Decoding the DNA of the Toyota Production System," *Harvard Business Review*, September/October 1999, pp. 97–106.

The content, sequence, timing, and output of every employee's work are fully specified, even for nonrepetitive work such as training or shifting equipment. The worker learns her job primarily by doing it. While in training, the supervisor constantly monitors the worker, compares her performance to the standards, and asks questions to make the worker think and learn her job (e.g., How do you know if you are doing the job right, and what do you do if there is a problem?).

Every connection or link (i.e., people–work interaction) is standardized and specified: it shows the people involved, the form and quantity of product to be supplied, the way the request is made, and the time it should take to meet the request. For example, when a worker cannot do her job, she is supposed to immediately inform her supervisor, and the supervisor should be there promptly to help her (if not, a specified alternative person should be available). Kanbans and andon are examples of tools used to establish a direct link.

Every product or piece of work flows along a simple, specified path (with no loops), not to the next available machine or workstation.

Improvement of all aspects of the work is done by the front-line person, with guidance and teaching of her supervisor, based on the scientific method. That is, a hypothesis is formed to predict the outcome of a solution to a problem, and experiments are performed by the worker to see if the hypothesis can be rejected. This will enforce decision making based on data and facts, rather than guesses.

The advantage of these standardizations is that they provide consistency and repeatability, hence the system can be learned and constantly improved. If there was no standard way to, say, install a vehicle seat, the variations across workers (and shifts) would confuse the results, making learning and improvement of the operation difficult.

Little Inventory

JIT/lean systems are designed to *minimize* inventory. Recall that in JIT/lean systems, inventory is a waste. Inventories are buffers that tend to cover up recurring problems that are never resolved, partly because they aren't obvious and partly because the presence of inventory makes them seem less serious. When a machine breaks down, it won't disrupt the system if there is sufficient inventory of the machine's output to feed into the next workstation. A better solution is to investigate the *causes* of machine breakdowns and focus on eliminating them. Similar situations occur with quality problems, unreliable vendors, and scheduling problems.

A useful analogy is a boat on a pond that has large, hidden rocks (see Figure 15-3). The rocks represent problems that can hinder production (the boat's movement). The water in the pond that covers the rocks is the inventory in the system. As the water level is lowered, the largest rocks are the first to appear. At that point, efforts are undertaken to remove these rocks from the water (resolve these problems). Once that has been accomplished, the lower water level (inventory) is adequate.

FIGURE 15-3 ▶

Large rocks (problems) are hidden by a higher water level (inventory) in A. Lower water level (B) reveals the rocks. Once the large rocks are removed, the lower water level (inventory) is adequate (C).

A

B

C

One way to minimize inventory of raw materials/parts in a JIT/lean system is to have deliveries from suppliers go directly to the production floor, which eliminates the need to store incoming parts and materials. At the other end of the process, completed units are shipped out as soon as they are ready, which minimizes storage of finished goods. Coupled with small manufacturing lot sizes resulting in low work-in-process inventory, these features result in systems that operate with very little inventory.

Personnel/Organization

Workers as Assets. A fundamental tenet of JIT/lean is that *workers are assets* and should be respected. Well trained and motivated workers with high morale are the heart of a JIT/lean system. Education, training, and coaching are essential to developing the workers, as is the promotion of their health and safety. They are given authority (are empowered) to make decisions. Workers are expected to participate (be involved) in continuous improvement (kaizen). In return, their contribution is recognized and rewarded. Workers are cross-trained to perform several steps of a process and operate a variety of machines. This adds to system flexibility because workers are able to help one another when bottlenecks occur or when a co-worker is absent.

Leadership. Top management should take leadership in conversion to JIT/lean because it involves culture change and affects the way workers do their job. Goals should be set to progress toward world-class JIT/lean status, their importance should be communicated to the employees to create constancy of purpose, and resources should be allocated so that progress toward JIT/lean is systematic. Employees should be both directed and encouraged to use tools and techniques of JIT/lean and incorporate its principles in their daily work. On the other hand, managers and supervisors are expected to be facilitators, not just order givers. JIT/lean encourages two-way communication between workers and managers. Leaders should lead with humility and seek input from everyone in the organization.

 OM in Action   www.cglmfg.com

CGL Manufacturing

CGL Manufacturing is a machining and fabrication company based in Guelph, Ontario. It started in 1977 as a job shop with five employees. Later, through quality and service, CGL expanded, producing parts for heavy equipment manufacturers such as Raymond for its lift-trucks.

In 2000, CGL had revenue of $10 million and employed approximately 100 workers, but a major customer unexpectedly demanded a 20 percent price cut. The general manager, David Deskur, knew that a major change in CGL had to occur. He attended a JIT/lean manufacturing seminar, was captivated, and acted as the JIT/lean champion.

All staff were educated in JIT/lean tools such as value stream mapping, cellular layout, teamwork, and

kaizen. The plant was reconfigured so that high-volume orders were made in five cells. During the first year, the distance travelled by forklifts was reduced by 1,000 km, revenues were up by 50 percent, inventories were down by 30 percent, and lead times were down by 20 percent.

David believes that the two most important keys to JIT/lean manufacturing are to (1) communicate its importance to all staff and (2) tie employee performance measures to their participation in continuous improvement projects.

CGL now has 12 facilities in Canada and China, with total square footage of 300,000 sq. ft. CGL is a role model for JIT/lean manufacturing.

Source: "Get Lean," *Plant*, 2008, pp. 55–64; http://www.cglmfg.ca/company -history.html.

Non-Manufacturing Support. Clearly, support is needed from sales/marketing for product design, from accounting for product costing, from HR for hiring and training good employees, and from quality assurance and control for improving the quality of products and processes. Further, finance needs to provide the cash for faster but more flexible equipment, purchasing needs to identify qualified JIT/lean suppliers and maintain a close relationship with them, and MIS needs to provide the information required to track performance measures and to provide data gathering/communication links. In addition, all these functions should reduce their own department's "wastes."

Planning and Control

LO6

Level Loading

JIT/lean places a strong emphasis on achieving a stable, level daily mixed-model schedule/sequence. This will result in *level capacity loading* (**heijunka** in Japanese).

> **heijunka** Japanese term for level loading.

When a company produces different products or models, it is desirable to produce in small lots (to minimize the work-in-process inventories and to maintain flexibility) and to spread out the production of different products or models throughout the day to achieve even, smooth production. The ideal case would be to produce one unit of one product or model, then one unit of another, then one unit of another, and so on.

The simplest method for determining a *level mixed-model sequence* is as follows:[2]

1. Determine a "due time" for each unit of each product or model so that the units of the product or model are evenly distributed throughout the day.

2. Sequence the units of all products or models based on their "due times" (from smallest to largest).

The "due times," based on daily demand for each model, are as follows:

Daily Demand	Due Times (start of day = 0, end of day = 1)
1	1/2
2	1/4, 3/4
3	1/6, 3/6, 5/6
4	1/8, 3/8, 5/8, 7/8
5	1/10, 3/10, 5/10, 7/10, 9/10
6	1/12, 3/12, 5/12, 7/12, 9/12, 11/12
7	1/14, 3/14, 5/14, 7/14, 9/14, 11/14, 13/14
8	1/16, 3/16, 5/16, 7/16, 9/16, 11/16, 13/16, 15/16
⋮	

In general, if daily demand is n for a product or model, the due times will be:

$$\frac{1}{2n}, \frac{3}{2n}, \frac{5}{2n}, \ldots \frac{2n-1}{2n}.$$

EXAMPLE 15-2 ▶

Determine a level mixed model sequence if daily demand for product A = 7, B = 16, and C = 5 units.

SOLUTION

1. The due times for each product are:

A: $1/14 = 0.071, 3/14 = 0.214, 5/14 = 0.357, 7/14 = 0.5,$ $9/14 = 0.643, 11/14 = 0.786, 13/14 = 0.929$

B: $1/32 = 0.031, 3/32 = 0.094, 5/32 = 0.156, 7/32 = 0.219, 9/32 = 0.281, 11/32 = 0.344, 13/32 = 0.406,$

$15/32 = 0.469, 17/32 = 0.531, 19/32 = 0.594, 21/32 = 0.656, 23/32 = 0.719, 25/32 = 0.781, 27/32 = 0.844, 29/32 = 0.906, 31/32 = 0.969$

C: $1/10 = 0.1, 3/10 = 0.3, 5/10 = 0.5, 7/10 = 0.7, 9/10 = 0.9$

2. Now, sequence the due times from the smallest to the largest. The smallest due time is 0.031 for a B, so the first unit to produce is B. The next smallest due time is 0.071 for an A, so the second unit to produce is A, and so on. The level mixed model sequence is:

B-A-B-C-B-A-B-B-C-B-A-B-B-A-C-B-B-A-B-C-B-B-A-B-C-B-A-B

Pull System and Kanban

The terms *push* and *pull* are used to describe two different approaches for making and moving items (raw material, parts, sub-assemblies, products) through a production process. In the traditional production environments that use MRP, a **push system** is used: A batch is started at a work centre according to the production plan derived from MRP. When the batch is finished at the work centre, the output is *pushed* to the next work centre or, in the case of the final operation, it is pushed on to the finished

push system Based on MRP plan, a batch of items is made and pushed to the next work centre as it is completed.

---

[2] R. R. Inman and R. L. Bulfin, "Sequencing JIT Mixed-Model Assembly Lines," *Management Science* 37(7), July 1991, pp. 901–904.

goods warehouse. Consequently, inventory will pile up at work centres. Conversely, in a **pull system**, control of moving the batch (preferably only one unit) rests with the following operation; each work centre *pulls* the output from the preceding work centre as it is needed; output of the final operation is pulled by customer demand. JIT/lean uses the pull system. See Figure 15-4 for an illustration.

pull system Based directly on customer demand, a work centre pulls items from the preceding work centre as they are needed.

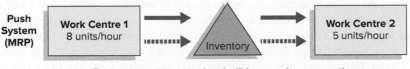

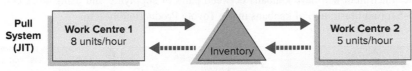

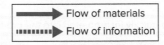

◀ **FIGURE 15-4**

Push vs. pull system.

In a pull system, communication moves backward through the system from work centre to work centre. Each work centre communicates its need for more items to the preceding work centre. The batch moves "just in time" to the next operation; the flow is thereby coordinated, and the accumulation of excessive inventories between operations is avoided. Of course, some buffer inventory is usually allowed because operations are not instantaneous. When the buffer inventory decreases to a certain level (i.e., the reorder point), this signals the preceding work centre to produce enough output to replenish the buffer supply. The size of the buffer supply depends on the lead time. If the lead time is short, the buffer can be small. The communication between the two work centres can be done in a variety of ways, including a shout or a wave, empty squares on the floor, empty carts or containers, and empty shelves/racks. However, the most commonly used method is the use of **kanban** cards. *Kanban* is Japanese for "signal" or "visual card." When a worker needs a batch of an item from the preceding work centre, she uses a kanban card. In effect, the kanban card is the *authorization* to make the batch. No item can be made without one of these cards.

kanban Card that communicates demand for a batch of an item to the preceding work centre.

Courtesy of TriState Industries, footage courtesy of MacLean Media, Inc.

At TriState Industries, a kanban system is in effect to move work through the production system. Shown here, a kanban card provides the authorization to move or work on parts.

Courtesy of TriState Industries, footage courtesy of MacLean Media, Inc.

Special carts were designed that, when filled, act as a visual signal that they are ready to be moved to the next work cell. An empty cart indicates that it is time to produce, in order to refill the cart.

The system works this way: A kanban card is affixed to each container. When a work centre needs to replenish its supply of a batch of an item, a worker goes to the area where these items are stored and withdraws one container of the item. Each container holds a predetermined quantity. The worker removes the kanban card from the container and posts it in a designated spot where it will be clearly visible to the operator of the producing work centre (e.g., a kanban board), and the worker moves the container to the using work centre. The posted kanban is later picked up by the operator of the producing work centre and another batch of the item is made. Usually because of significant setup time and the desire for high utilization of the producing work centre, a few kanbans are first accumulated before production is triggered. Similar withdrawals and replenishments—all controlled by kanbans—occur all the way up and down the line from vendors to the finished-goods warehouse. Each item will have kanbans between pairs of supplying and using work centres. See Figure 15-5 for an illustration of kanbans in the Toyota Production System.

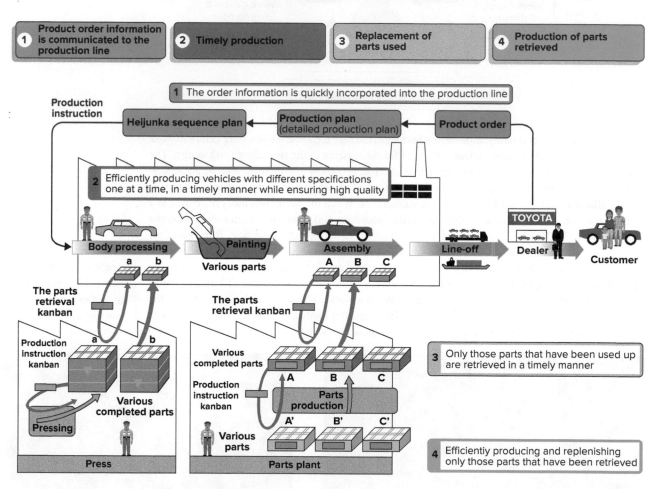

FIGURE 15-5 ▲

An illustration of kanbans in the Toyota Production System.

Source: http://www.toyota-global.com/company/vision_philosophy/toyota_production_system/illustration_of_the_toyota_production_system.html

If supervisors decide the system is too loose because inventories are building up, they may decide to withdraw some kanbans. Conversely, if the system seems too tight, they may introduce additional kanbans. It is apparent that the number of kanban cards in use is an important variable. One can calculate the ideal number of kanban cards for each item, between pairs of supplying and using work centres, by this formula:

$$N = \frac{DT(1 + X)}{C} \qquad (15\text{-}1)$$

where

N = Total number of kanbans (one kanban per container)
D = Average usage rate of using work centre
T = Average lead time for replenishment of one container (includes wait before production, setup, production, and transport times)

X = Policy variable set by the management that represents the safety stocks (as a proportion of average usage during lead time T)

C = Capacity of a standard container

Note that D and T must use the same time unit (e.g., hour, day). The concept underlying the above formula is the same as the concept underlying the reorder point in the EOQ–ROP inventory model (see Chapter 12): ROP = $DT(1 + X)$ = Average demand during a lead time plus safety stock, where safety stock is a proportion X of the average demand during a lead time.

◀ EXAMPLE 15-3

Usage at a work centre is 300 units of a specific part per day, and a standard container holds 25 units. It takes an average of 0.12 day from the time a kanban card is posted until the full container is received by the using work centre. Calculate the number of kanban cards needed for this part between these two work centres, if $X = 0.20$.

SOLUTION

$N = ?$
$D = 300$ units per day
$T = 0.12$ day
$C = 25$ units per container
$X = 0.20$

$$N = \frac{300(0.12)(1 + 0.20)}{25} = 1.728; \text{ round to 2 containers}$$

Note: Rounding up will cause the system to be looser, and rounding down will cause it to be tighter. Usually, rounding up is used.

For an application of kanbans, see the "Waterville TG" OM in Action.

OM in Action   www.wtg.ca

Waterville TG

Waterville TG (WTG), of Quebec, designs and manufactures insulation for doors, hoods, and trunks of cars from various types of rubber. Waterville TG is part of Toyoda Gosei Co. Ltd., a division of Toyota Motor Company. WTG has close to 385 different models of insulations designed for almost all types of automobiles. The raw material is synthetic powder rubber. The production process is four stages: mixing, extrusion, moulding, and finishing. WTG uses kanbans for pulling material through most of the production process, as shown below.

There are raw material (RM) kanbans, WIP extrusion (E) and moulding (M) kanbans, finished-goods production (P) kanbans, and shipping or expedition (E) kanbans. An example of a raw material kanban is shown at the top of the next page.

The use of bar codes on a kanban is not unusual. WTG uses the computer and bar codes to keep track of inventories and changes the number of active kanbans as demand varies. The bar codes make this easier. The card itself is printed on plain white paper and inserted in a protective clear plastic pouch that in

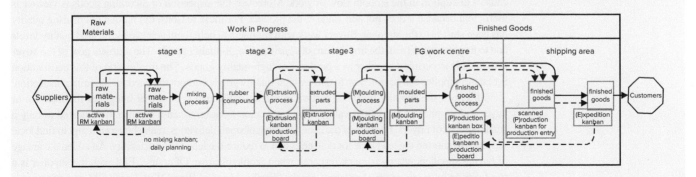

turn is placed in a self-adhesive pouch. This pouch is then attached to a container. Soon after a full container is moved to its point of use, the kanban is detached and moved back to the originating area. The punched hole in the top left corner is used to hang the card on the kanban boards.

The figure at right shows an example of a WIP E kanban. A zip-top seal was added to the pouch for easier maintenance. After trying out several versions of this card, WTG found that kanban maintenance was easier when cards included only information that changed little or not at all over time.

At the finished-goods level, two cards are used instead of one to allow some excess production (relative to shipment). These kanbans are similar to the WIP kanbans.

Source: S. Chausse, S. Landry, F. Pasin, and S. Fortier, "Anatomy of a Kanban: A Case Study," *Production and Inventory Management Journal* 41(4), Fourth Quarter 2000, pp. 11–16.

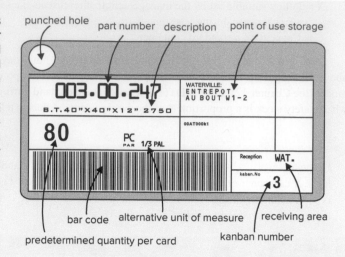

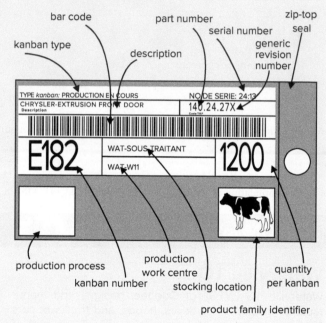

Close Supplier Relationship

JIT/lean companies typically have close relationships with their major suppliers, who are expected to provide frequent small deliveries of high-quality goods. Traditionally, the buying company has assumed the role of monitoring the quality of purchased goods, inspecting shipments for quality and quantity, and returning poor-quality goods to the vendor for rework. JIT systems have little slack, so poor-quality goods cause a disruption in the smooth flow of work. Moreover, the inspection of incoming goods is viewed as inefficient because it does not add value to the product. For these reasons, the burden of ensuring quality has been shifted to the supplier. Buyers work with suppliers to help them achieve the desired quality levels and to impress upon them the importance of consistent, high-quality goods. The ultimate goal of the buyer is to be able to certify a supplier as a producer of high-quality goods. The implication of this certification is that the supplier can be relied on to deliver high-quality goods without the need for incoming inspection.

In effect, the supplier becomes part of an extended JIT/lean system that integrates the facilities of buyer and supplier as part of the value chain. Integration is easier when a supplier is dedicated to only a small number of buyers. Because of the need for frequent small deliveries, many buyers attempt to find local suppliers to shorten the lead time for deliveries and to reduce the lead-time variability. An added advantage of having suppliers nearby is quick response when problems arise. Of course, EDI with the supplier is a must. For an interesting implementation, see the "Fresher Hospital Blood With Lean" OM in Action.

OM in Action

Fresher Hospital Blood With Lean

Canadian Blood Services uses lean principles to boost productivity and operational efficiency. One particular area of note is the method by which blood supplies are managed. Traditionally, two-thirds of inventory was kept in hospitals in order to protect against supply side disruptions such as reduced production because of bacterial and/or viral contamination, or even a harsh winter storm that shuts down roads and airports. The problem with carrying high levels of inventory in hospitals is that a significant proportion remains unused and eventually is discarded. Outdated blood products represent a major source of waste in the system.

Using lean principles developed by Toyota, management has pursued closer collaboration and streamlining of critical processes with suppliers across the entire supply chain. Closer collaboration with suppliers allows Canadian Blood Services to get a better picture of where blood supplies are and how much is available. Automated software systems help to streamline the ordering process by automatically placing orders with suppliers whenever on-hand inventory drops below a pre-programmed point. And after ordering, global positioning satellites track the movement of blood supplies and provide alerts whenever problems arise.

These changes have allowed hospitals to reduce the amount of inventory that is carried, while at the same time ensuring that patients receive fresher blood. The discard rate has been reduced from 8.4 percent in 2011–2012 to close to 6 percent today. The order packing time has been reduced by 40 percent. Lean has resulted in savings in excess of $50.3 million.

Source: http://globalnews.ca/news/1858856/sask-government-says-lean -saving-125-million; https://blood.ca/en/media/two-unlikely-partners-one -powerful-and-innovative-collaboration-toyota-teams-canadian-blood -services; https://www.blood.ca/sites/default/files/2013Review-MRTOC.pdf, retrieved July 12, 2016.

Ford is taking a page out of Toyota's JIT/lean book at its Chicago plant, which opened in 2004, by having some of its suppliers locate very close to its assembly plant. Ford leased production facilities on its 155 acres of land to approximately 10 key suppliers. Suppliers' parts and modules are carefully coordinated to feed directly into Ford's assembly line and match the sequence of vehicles Ford is producing, which can range from small cars to SUVs. Not only are suppliers nearby in case problems arise, but also the shortened travel distance and lead times yield tremendous savings in the in-transit inventories of parts and modules.

A key feature of many JIT/lean companies is the relatively small number of suppliers used. In traditional production, a manufacturer often deals with hundreds or even thousands of suppliers in a highly centralized arrangement, not unlike a giant wheel with many spokes. The manufacturer is at the hub of the wheel, and the spokes radiate out to suppliers, each of whom must deal directly with the manufacturer. In traditional systems, a supplier does not know the other suppliers or what they are doing. Each supplier works to specifications provided by the manufacturer. Suppliers have very little motivation for suggesting improvements. Moreover, as a manufacturer plays one supplier off against others, the sharing of information is more risky than rewarding. In contrast, lean manufacturers employ a tiered approach for suppliers: They use relatively few first-tier suppliers who work directly with the manufacturer to supply major sub-assemblies or modules. The first-tier suppliers are responsible for dealing with second-tier suppliers who provide components for the sub-assemblies, thereby relieving the manufacturer of dealing with a large number of suppliers.

The automotive industry provides a good example of this situation. Suppose a certain car model has an electric seat. The seat and its motor together might entail 250 separate parts. A traditional automobile manufacturer might use more than 30 suppliers for the electric seat, but a JIT/lean auto manufacturer will use a single (first-tier) supplier that has the responsibility for the entire seat unit. The auto manufacturer will provide some specification for the overall unit, but leave the details of the motor, springs, and so on, to the supplier. The first-tier supplier, in turn, might subcontract the motor to a second-tier supplier, the track to another second-tier supplier, and the cushions and fabric to another. The second-tier suppliers might subcontract some of their work to third-tier suppliers, and so on. Each tier has to deal with only those just above it and just below it. Suppliers on each level are encouraged to work with each other, and they are motivated to do so because that increases the probability that the resulting item (the seat) will meet or exceed the final buyer's expectations. Figure 15-6 illustrates the difference between the traditional and tiered (JIT/lean) supplier networks.

A: Traditional

B: Tiered

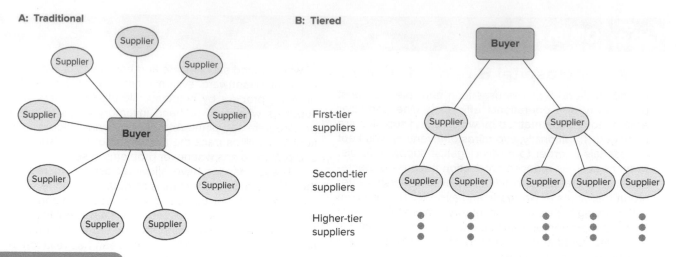

FIGURE 15-6 ▲

Traditional supplier network compared to supplier tiers used in JIT/lean.

A method of very close cooperation with suppliers, called JIT II, has been used by Bose Corporation, the manufacturer of luxury audio equipment, in which a supplier representative is located in Bose's facility and performs the functions of Bose's buyer. This reduces lead times. For another application, see the "Dana" OM in Action.

⚙ **OM in Action**   www.dana.com/

Dana

When Toyota decided to build a truck assembly plant in Princeton, Indiana, to make Tundra and Sequoia in the late 1990s, it chose Dana Corporation to build its truck frames. Dana built a 129,080 ft^2 plant employing about 300 people 73 miles away in Owensboro, Kentucky. To be as lean as possible, Dana makes the frames to the sequence of trucks planned in the Toyota plant. There are 14 frame models, which are sequenced in batch sizes of one. Therefore, the Dana plant has to be very flexible: it takes a maximum of only three seconds to change over from one model to another in any work centre on the production line. The order information comes via Internet (EDI) from the Toyota plant and is displayed on every work centre. About nine hours later, after operations such as welding, machining, and painting, the frames are trucked to the Toyota plant in batches of 25, about one truck every half hour.

Dana sold this and its other nine structural products factories to Metalsa, Mexico's largest vehicle frame and structures supplier, in 2010.

Courtesy of Dana Corporation

Sources: T. Vinas, "In Sync With the Customer," *IndustryWeek* 252(10), October 2002, pp. 46–48; http://www.lanereport.com/11579/2010/02/three-kentucky-dana-plants-in-spin-off-to-metalsa-s-a-de-c-v/.

---

preventive maintenance
Keeping equipment in good operating condition and replacing parts that have a tendency to fail before they do fail.

Preventive Maintenance and Housekeeping

Because JIT/lean systems have very little work-in-process inventory, equipment breakdowns can be extremely disruptive. To minimize downtime, JIT/lean companies use **preventive maintenance** programs, which emphasize maintaining equipment in good operating condition and replacing parts that have a tendency to fail before they do fail.

Even with preventive maintenance, occasional equipment failures will occur. Companies must be prepared for this, so they can quickly return equipment back to working order. This may mean maintaining supplies of critical spare parts and making other provisions for emergency situations, perhaps maintaining a small team of maintenance personnel or training workers to do certain repairs themselves.

Housekeeping involves keeping the workplace clean, because it facilitates discovery of problems. For example, clean floors will show oil leaks from a machine, which could result in a worker slipping, a safety hazard. Housekeeping also involves keeping the workplace free of anything that is not needed for production, because it takes up space and may cause disruption to the workflow. These and other principles of housekeeping are included in the *5S principles:*

- *Sort:* remove all objects that do not need to be in the workstation or area.
- *Set in order:* tidy up the objects needed and organize them such that they can be seen and therefore found quickly. For example, use a peg or shadow board for hand tools.
- *Shine:* clean the workstation completely and eliminate all signs of dust or grime on the floor, machines, and equipment.
- *Standardize:* set standards in cleanliness and organization, and audit the area for compliance.
- *Sustain:* train workers to perform housekeeping and continuously improve on the standards; make 5S part of the work culture.

housekeeping Keeping the workplace clean and free of unnecessary things.

http://www.lmsi.ca/5s.htm

Before and after 5S implementation at a bookstore backroom.
Courtesy of EZ Sigma Group

For an application, see the "Plains Fabrication & Supply" OM in Action.

 OM in Action

Plains Fabrication & Supply

Plains Fabrication & Supply (PF&S) is a metal shop in Calgary that makes custom industrial heaters, separators, and pressure vessels. It started with 16 people in 1988 and now employs over 100 workers. Low profit margins (4 percent) and an old plant brought PF&S to a crossroads in 2005: either it had to become more efficient, or it had to close down. It decided on the former and got help from a provincial government program called Productivity Alberta, which provided JIT/lean manufacturing

guidance at a low price. After a four-hour assessment, all employees were put through a four-hour workshop on JIT/lean manufacturing. One area of the shop, the small vessels area, was chosen for lean improvement. The improvements included use of visual and shadow boards, kanban cards and shelves, and cleaning and organizing the shop floor. After 12 months, the amount of inventory on the shop floor was reduced by 75 percent and lead time was reduced from 44 days to five days.

Sources: http://www.plant.ca/sustainability/making-the-most-of-time-and-space-9742/; http://www.oilfieldpulse.com/plains-fabrication-and-supply/.

JIT/lean systems have been described in the preceding pages. Table 15-3 provides a brief overview of JIT/lean versus traditional production systems. The next section lists JIT/lean implementation steps and an implementation tool called value stream mapping.

Factor	Traditional	JIT/Lean
Inventory	Much, to offset late deliveries, etc.	Minimal necessary to operate
Deliveries	Few, large	Many, small
Lot sizes	Large	Small
Setups, runs	Few, long runs	Many, short runs
Vendors	Adversaries	Partners
Workers	Replaceable	Assets

L07 Implementing JIT/Lean

The success of JIT/lean systems in Japan and the West has attracted keen interest among other traditional manufacturers. To increase the probability of a successful transition, companies should adopt a carefully planned approach.

Planning a Successful Conversion

1. Make sure top management is committed to the conversion and that they know what will be required. Make sure that management is involved in the process and knows what it will cost, how long it will take to complete the conversion, and what results can be expected.

2. Study the operations carefully; decide which parts will need the most effort to convert.

3. Obtain the support and cooperation of workers. Prepare training programs that include sessions in setups, maintenance of equipment, cross-training for multiple tasks, cooperation, and problem solving. Make sure workers are fully informed about what lean is and why it is desirable. Reassure workers that their jobs are secure.

4. Begin by trying to reduce setup times while maintaining the current system. Enlist the aid of workers in identifying and eliminating existing problems (e.g., bottlenecks, poor quality).

5. Gradually convert operations, beginning at the end of the process and working backward. At each stage, make sure the conversion has been relatively successful before moving on. Do not begin to reduce inventories until major problems have been resolved.

6. As one of the last steps, convert suppliers to JIT/lean and be prepared to work closely with them. Start by narrowing the list of suppliers, identifying those who are willing to embrace the lean philosophy. Give preference to suppliers who have long-term track records of reliability. Use suppliers located nearby if quick response time is important. Establish long-term commitments with suppliers. Insist on high standards of quality and adherence to strict delivery schedules.

7. Be prepared to encounter obstacles to conversion.

Obstacles to Conversion

Converting from a traditional system to JIT/lean may not be smooth. Cultures vary from organization to organization. Some cultures relate better to the lean philosophy than others. If a culture doesn't relate to lean, it can be difficult for an organization to change its culture within a short time. Also, manufacturers that operate with large amounts of inventory in order to handle varying customer demand may have difficulty acclimating themselves to less inventory.

Some other obstacles include the following:

1. Management may not be totally committed or may be unwilling to devote the necessary resources to conversion. This is perhaps the most serious impediment because the conversion is probably doomed without serious commitment.

2. Workers and/or management may not display a cooperative spirit. The system is predicated on cooperation. Managers may resist lean because lean shifts some of the responsibility from management to workers and gives workers more control over the work. Workers may resist lean because of the increased responsibility and stress.

3. Suppliers may resist for several reasons:

   a. Buyers may not be willing to commit the resources necessary to help them adapt to JIT/lean.

   b. They may be uneasy about long-term commitments to a buyer.

   c. Frequent, small deliveries may be difficult, especially if the supplier has other buyers who use traditional systems.

   d. The burden of quality control will shift to the supplier.

   e. Frequent engineering changes may result from continuing lean improvements by the buyer.

A Cooperative Spirit

JIT/lean requires a cooperative spirit among workers, management, and vendors. Unless that is present, it is doubtful that a truly effective lean system can be achieved. The Japanese have been very successful in this regard, partly because respect and cooperation are ingrained in the Japanese culture. In Western cultures, workers, managers, and vendors have historically been strongly at odds with each other. Consequently, a major consideration in converting to JIT/lean is whether a spirit of mutual respect and cooperation can be achieved. This requires an appreciation of the importance of cooperation and a tenacious effort by management to instill and maintain that spirit.

Finally, it should be noted that not all organizations lend themselves to a JIT/lean approach. It is best used for repetitive operations under fairly stable demand.

Despite the many advantages of JIT/lean production systems, an organization must take into account a number of other considerations when planning a conversion.

The key considerations are the time and cost requirements for successful conversion, which can be substantial. But it is absolutely essential to eliminate the major sources of disruption in the system. Management must be prepared to commit the resources necessary to achieve a high level of quality and to function on a tight schedule. That means attention to even the smallest of details during the design phase and substantial efforts to debug the system to the point where it runs smoothly. Beyond that, management must be capable of responding quickly when problems arise, and both management and workers must be committed to the continuous improvement of the system. Although each case is different, a general estimate of the time required for conversion is one to three years.

For implementations of JIT/lean, see the "Lean in Formula 1 Racing," "Scona Trailer Manufacturing," and "CGL Manufacturing" OM in Actions earlier in the chapter.

Value Stream Mapping

Value stream mapping (VSM) is a visual tool to systematically examine the flow of materials and information involved in bringing a product or service to a consumer. The technique originated at Toyota, where it is referred to as *material and information flow mapping.*

The map is a sketch of an entire process that typically ranges from incoming goods from suppliers to shipment of a product or delivery of a service to the customer. The map shows all processes in the value stream, from arrivals of supplies to the shipping of the product. The objective is to increase value to the customer, where value is typically defined in terms of quality, time, cost, or flexibility (e.g., rapid response or agility). Data collected during the mapping process might include times (e.g., cycle time, setup time, changeover time, touch time, lead time), distances travelled (e.g., by parts, workers, paperwork), mistakes (e.g., product defects, data entry errors), inefficient work methods (e.g., extra motions, excessive lifting or moving, repositioning), and waiting lines (e.g., workers waiting for parts or equipment repairs, orders waiting to be processed). Information flows are also included in the mapping process.

> **value stream mapping (VSM)** A visual tool to systematically examine the flow of materials and information.

You can get a sense of value stream mapping from the following tips for developing an effective mapping of a value stream:

1. Map the value stream in person.

2. Begin with a quick walk-through of the system from beginning to end to get a sense of the system.

3. Then do a more thorough walk-through following the actual pathway to collect current information on material or information flow.

4. Record elements of the system such as cycle times, scrap rates, amounts of inventory, downtimes, number of operators, distances between processes, and transfer times.

Value improvement for a product or a service embodies the lean principles described earlier and repeated here. It begins by specifying value from the customer's standpoint. You can see where value stream mapping can help process improvement:

1. Specify value from the standpoint of the end customer.

2. Identify all the steps in the value stream and create a visual (map) of the value stream.

3. Eliminate steps that do not create value to create flow.

4. Use next-customer-in-the-process demand to pull from each preceding process as needed to control the flow.

5. Repeat this process as long as waste exists in the system.

Once a value stream map is completed, data analysis can uncover improvement opportunities by asking key questions, such as:

- Where are the process bottlenecks?
- Where do errors occur?
- Which processes have to deal with the most variation?
- Where does waste occur?

For an interesting implementation, see "Canada Post's Calgary Plant" OM in Action.

 OM in Action

Canada Post's Calgary Plant

Canada Post has been increasing the efficiency of its operations (letter, parcel, express mail, and publication and advertising mail) since the mid-1990s. Before then, Canada Post used batch processing in many parts of its sorting/distribution plants. Two of the JIT/lean initiatives in its Calgary plant are described below.

- The publication and advertising mail is brought into the plant in 50- to 60-pound bags placed in large, wheeled metal containers. The containers used to be emptied onto a below-floor conveyor at the receiving area that took them to a sorting area where an employee read the tags and rerouted them to be piled up in another container, which was then taken to another part of the 350,000 ft² plant for further sorting. Altogether, a bag was handled four times. This inefficient process was replaced with one that takes the container to an "induction" area where a bag is picked up every 24 seconds (to match the

average number of bags arriving), the tag is read, and the bag is put onto one of the four conveyors (for Calgary, Southern Alberta, Eastern Canada, and needing further processing) depending on the information on the tag. Then the bags are opened and sorted on each conveyor. The whole process now requires six or seven employees (versus the 10–15 employees needed before the change) and the processing lead time has been reduced from two days to one day.

- Value stream mapping was used for most JIT/lean initiatives. An example is the value stream for the current state of express parcel mail processing (shown on the next page; PY = payroll). Again, the parcels are first sorted into East, Edmonton, BC, Others, and Calgary. After this sort, some of the mail is accumulated and moved to another location in the plant for further sorting. This added an average of two hours of waiting. In the future state, this wait time is eliminated and payroll is reduced by two employees.

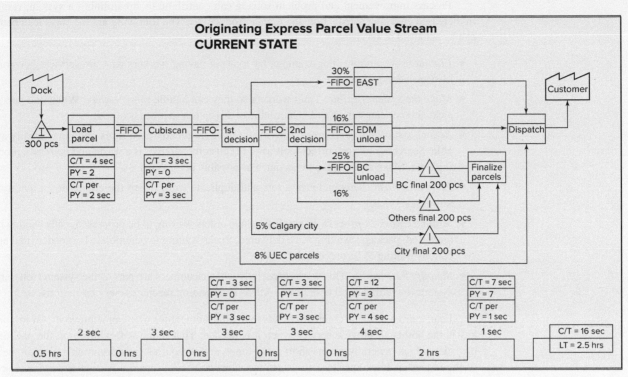

Originating Express Parcel Value Stream
CURRENT STATE

Lean Services

The discussion of lean up to this point has focused on manufacturing, simply because that is where it was developed and where it has been used most often. Nonetheless, services can and do benefit from many lean concepts. When just-in-time is used in the context of services, the focus is often on the time needed to perform a service—because speed is often an important order winner for services. Some services do have some inventories, so inventory reduction is another aspect of lean that can apply to services. Examples of speedy delivery ("available when requested") are McDonald's, UPS, Domino's Pizza, and emergency services.

In addition to speed, lean services emphasize consistent, high-quality, standard work methods; flexible workers; and close supplier relationships.

The Pyxis® ProcedureStation™ system provides rapid access to secured inventory in the operating room, cath and cardiac labs, and other specialty departments. Usage, inventory, and replenishment information is transmitted electronically, creating an efficient supply management and workflow process. It helps reduce inventory outages and facilitates charging supply usage directly to the billing system in real time.[3]

[3] http://www.bd.com/en-us/offerings/capabilities/medication-and-supply-management/medication-and-supply-management-technologies/pyxis-supply-technologies/pyxis-procedurestation-system

Process improvement and problem solving can contribute to streamlining a system, resulting in increased customer satisfaction and higher productivity. The following are the ways lean benefits can be achieved in services:

- *Eliminate disruptions.* For example, try to avoid having workers who are servicing customers also answer telephones.

- *Make the system flexible.* Train workers so they can handle more variety. When one person is sick, another can step in and help minimize disruption to process output.

- *Reduce setup times and processing times.* Have frequently used tools and parts readily available. Searching for the correct tools after the customer arrives is a waste and increases processing time. Make sure to prepare as much as possible beforehand.

- *Eliminate waste.* This includes errors and duplicate work. Keep the emphasis on quality and uniform service.

- *Minimize work-in-process.* Examples include orders waiting to be processed, calls waiting to be answered, packages waiting to be delivered, trucks waiting to be unloaded or loaded, and applications waiting to be processed.

- *Simplify the process.* This works especially when customers are part of the system (self-service systems including retail operations, ABMs and vending machines, service stations, etc.).

Lean can be a major competitive advantage for companies that can achieve it. An important key is the ability to provide service when it is needed. That requires flexibility on the part of the provider, which generally means short setup times, and it requires clear communication on the part of the requester. If a requester can determine when he/she will need a particular service, a server can schedule deliveries to correspond to those needs, eliminating the need for continual requests, and reducing the need for provider flexibility—and therefore probably reducing the cost of the service.

All organizations, whether they are primarily engaged in service or in manufacturing, can benefit by applying lean principles to their office operations. This includes purchasing, accounting, order entry, and other office functions. Office wastes might include:

1. Excess inventory: excess supplies and equipment.
2. Overprocessing: excess paperwork and redundant approvals.
3. Waiting times: orders waiting to be processed, requests for information awaiting answers.
4. Unnecessary transportation: inefficient routing.
5. Processing waste: using more resources than necessary to accomplish a task.
6. Inefficient work methods: poor layout design, unnecessary steps, inadequate training.
7. Mistakes: order entry errors, lost files, miscommunications.
8. Underused people: not using all of the mental and creative capabilities of workers.

World Class Manufacturing

World class manufacturing (WCM) includes just-in-time manufacturing, total quality management (TQM), total productive maintenance (TPM), and total industrial engineering (TIE). WCM was developed by Fiat Group and Professor Yamashina of Kyoto University. TPM is the use of both operator (called autonomous maintenance, including taking care of the machine and organizing the workplace) and maintenance technicians (called professional maintenance, including finding the root cause of failure and fixing it) to reduce machine breakdowns. TIE is the use of industrial engineering to reduce worker injuries and increase productivity. The power of WCM comes from employee involvement and teams.

The progress of a plant toward perfection (zero injuries, zero waste/loss/defects/breakdowns, and zero inventories) is measured by 10 technical criteria (called pillars) and 10 managerial criteria (foundations). These are displayed on the following diagram.

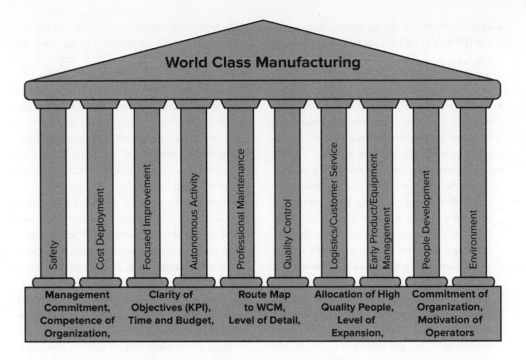

Cost deployment is costing each loss/waste. *Focused improvement* is selecting the most costly waste/loss to study and eliminate (according to Deming's plan–do–study–act continuous improvement method). *Early equipment management* is purchasing machines that are easy to run, safe, and reliable, and result in rapid and smooth plant startup. *Early product management* aims to shorten development lead times, with teams working on simultaneous activities so that startup can be achieved with zero defects.

People development involves measuring the skill level of employees, and training them as required. This is usually done by supervisors/managers. Chrysler (together with the United Automobile Workers) has set up a world class manufacturing academy that offers hands-on, fun exercises to develop advanced skills in its employees. WCM provides a standard language and tools across the plants. Each pillar has an owner/manager and the WCM as a whole also has a manager.

The managerial criteria include *clarity of objectives* (gathering and evaluating the necessary information to prioritize the problems), *time and budget* (developing timing charts of projects that teams are working on), *level of detail* (using logic appropriately), and *level of expansion* (working on improvements in maintenance and quality control).

The WCM implementation involves deployment and alignment of goals from plant manager down to area managers, supervisors, and workers. Performance is measured using *key performance indicators (KPI)*, which include weekly measures for safety, quality, absenteeism, suggestions per employee, delivery, manufacturing hours, inventory, etc. The KPI are regularly communicated to employees using various displays and boards in the plant. Achievements and knowledge are shared across plants.

Summary

- Just-in-time (JIT), in a narrow sense, is a system of production in which processing and movement of parts/modules/work-in-process occur just as they are needed, usually in small batches. JIT systems require very little inventory because successive operations are closely coordinated.
- JIT (which is also called lean production) is in a broad sense a philosophy of eliminating

  wastes, especially setup, lead times, and inventories, and continuous improvement.
- The goals of JIT/lean are a balanced rapid flow, elimination of waste and disruption, a flexible system, and continuous improvement.
- The building blocks of a JIT/lean system are various tools and methods used in product design, process design, personnel and organization, and planning and control.

- Products should be simple to make and assemble (DFM and DFA). Concurrent engineering and QFD should be used to ensure a fast product design process and that the voice of the customer is reflected in the product's quality.
- A JIT/lean system is balanced. One unit is produced every takt (or cycle) time to meet the demand. It is flexible (e.g., changeover times are fast) to meet the mix of products and changes in demand.
- Small production lot sizes are used in order to reduce the WIP, increase flexibility, and facilitate defect detection. Setup times should be reduced to render small lot sizes economical. Product families are identified and produced in dedicated cells; this reduces material handling and manufacturing lead times. JIT/lean requires the highest quality parts because there is little safety stock. Through jidoka or quality at the source, a defective item isn't passed through; workers stop and fix the problem. Standardized work, interaction, and workflow are required in order to learn and improve a JIT/lean system. In addition to WIP, raw material and finished goods inventories should also be minimized.
- Workers should be respected and empowered in order to participate in continuous improvement (kaizen), and be cross-trained in order to help with system flexibility. Top management should assign the necessary resources, communicate its importance, and direct the JIT conversion process. Other functions of business should support manufacturing to become lean, and they should also initiate waste reduction programs within their own departments.

- To reduce inventories, production of various products should be levelled. Level loads are achieved by mixed-model sequencing. Production is synchronized to demand by using kanbans to pull the minimum amount of parts and materials through the manufacturing process and from the suppliers. There is a need to integrate operations with the suppliers; hence, the number of suppliers should be reduced in order to establish close relationships and partnerships.
- Preventive maintenance is crucial for JIT/lean systems, because machine downtime may stop the whole plant's production. The 5S housekeeping method is also important because organized and clean workstations operate faster and help in discovering problems.
- A firm must redesign its facilities and rework labour contracts to implement JIT/lean. Teamwork and cooperation are important at all levels, as are problem-solving abilities of workers and an attitude of continuous improvement.
- A value stream map—which displays the process steps, and material and information flows—is an important and useful tool for implementing JIT/lean.
- Lean services is the application of lean concepts from manufacturing toward services. This is becoming more important as our economy shifts further toward being a service economy. Lean services emphasizes waste reduction in processing times, inventory reduction, and satisfying customers' expectations, among others.

TABLE 15-4 ▶

Overview of lean.

Lean systems are designed to operate with fewer resources than traditional systems. Elements of lean operation include:
    Smooth flow of work (the ultimate goal).
    Elimination of waste.
    Continuous improvement.
    Elimination of anything that does not add value.
    Simple systems that are easy to manage.
    Use of product layouts that minimize time spent moving materials and parts.
    Quality at the source: Each worker is responsible for the quality of his or her output.
    Poka-yoke: failsafe tools and methods to prevent mistakes.
    Preventive maintenance to reduce the risk of equipment breakdown.
    Good housekeeping: an orderly and clean workplace.
    Setup time reduction.
    Cross-trained workers.
    A pull system.
There are seven types of waste:
    Inventory.
    Overproduction.
    Waiting time.
    Excess transportation.
    Processing waste.
    Inefficient work methods.
    Product or service defects.

- World class manufacturing is based on 10 technical and 10 managerial pillars that help bring a company closer to operational excellence. WCM practitioners place a strong emphasis on being proactive to eliminate machine breakdowns and workplace injuries, and to reduce wastes and disruptions that hinder workflow, which helps to save time and money, and increases productivity.

Key Terms

andon	just-in-time (JIT)	pull system
autonomation	kanban	push system
heijunka	lean production	single-minute exchange of die (SMED)
housekeeping	poka-yoke	takt time
jidoka	preventive maintenance	value stream mapping (VSM)

Solved Problems

Problem 1

Determine the number of kanbans needed for a part in a workstation that uses 100 units of the part per hour if the time from posting a kanban until receiving a full container (wait, setup, fill, return) is 90 minutes. Assume a standard container holds 84 units and a safety factor of 0.10 is currently being used.

Solution

$N = ?$

$D = 100$ units per hour

$T = 90$ minutes (1.5 hours)

$C = 84$ units

$X = 0.10$

$$N = \frac{D(T)(1 + X)}{C} = \frac{100(1.5)(1 + 0.10)}{84} = 1.96, \text{ round to 2 kanbans.}$$

Problem 2

Determine a level mixed-model sequence for the following four products. Assume the plant operates five days a week.

Product	Weekly Quantity
A	20
B	40
C	30
D	15

Solution

Convert the weekly quantities to daily quantities:

Product	Daily Quantity = Weekly Quantity ÷ 5
A	20 ÷ 5 = 4
B	40 ÷ 5 = 8
C	30 ÷ 5 = 6
D	15 ÷ 5 = 3

The due times are:

A: $1/8 = 0.125$, $3/8 = 0.375$, $5/8 = 0.625$, $7/8 = 0.875$

B: $1/16 = 0.0625$, $3/16 = 0.1875$, $5/16 = 0.3125$, $7/16 = 0.4375$, $9/16 = 0.5625$, $11/16 = 0.6875$, $13/16 = 0.8125$, $15/16 = 0.9375$

C: $1/12 = 0.083$, $3/12 = 0.25$, $5/12 = 0.417$, $7/12 = 0.583$, $9/12 = 0.75$, $11/12 = 0.917$

D: $1/6 = 0.167$, $3/6 = 0.5$, $5/6 = 0.83$

Sort the due times from the smallest to the largest. The smallest due time is 0.0625 for B, so the first unit in the sequence should be B. The next smallest due time is 0.083 for C, so the second unit in sequence to produce should be C, and so on:

B-C-A-D-B-C-B-A-C-B-D-B-C-A-B-C-B-D-A-C-B

Problem 3

Cars are to be assembled on a moving assembly line. Five hundred cars are required per day. Production time per day is eight hours minus a half-hour for a lunch break. What is the takt time?

Solution

$8(60) = 480 - 30 = 450$ minutes per day

Takt time $= 450/500 = 0.9$ minute $= 54$ seconds

Discussion and Review Questions

Note: An asterisk indicates that a question or problem may be more challenging.

LO1 **1.** Distinguish between little JIT and big JIT.

LO1 **2.** Describe the philosophy that underlies JIT/lean. (That is, what is JIT/lean intended to accomplish?)

LO1 **3.** Explain briefly how a JIT/lean system differs from an MRP-based system.

LO1 **4.** What are the main benefits of JIT/lean? Name a company using JIT/lean, and describe how JIT/lean contributes to the company's competitive advantage.

LO1 **5.** Contrast the principles of the Shingo prize with the goals of JIT/lean given in Figure 15-1. Why can't a Shingo Prize winner's production process be unbalanced and slow? Explain.

LO2 **6. a.** What are the goals of a JIT/lean system?

LO2 **b.** What are the eight wastes?

LO3 **7.** What aspects of product design are important for JIT/lean?

LO4 **8.** What are (a) takt time, (b) SMED, (c) jidoka, and (d) poka-yoke?

LO4 **9.** What are the benefits and risks of (a) small lot sizes, (b) standardized process, and (c) low inventories?

LO5 **10.** What is the role of workers in JIT/lean?

LO6 **11.** What is a kanban?

LO6 **12.** Contrast push and pull systems of moving parts/modules/ work-in-process through the production system.

LO6 **13.** What is level mixed-model sequencing and why is it important?

LO6 **14.** Briefly discuss supplier relations in JIT/lean in terms of the following issues:
a. Why are they important?
b. How do they tend to differ from the more adversarial relations of the past?

LO6 **15.** What is 5S and why is it important?

LO7 **16.** What are some of the main obstacles that must be overcome in converting from a traditional system to lean?

LO7 **17.** What is value stream mapping and why is it important?

Taking Stock

LO1 **1.** What trade-offs are involved in shifting from an MRP system to a JIT/lean system?

LO7 **2.** Who in the company is affected by a decision to shift from an MRP system to a JIT/lean system?

LO4 & 6 **3.** To what extent has technology had an impact on JIT/ lean systems?

LO4 **4.** A cellular layout contains various machines in close proximity to one another. What kinds of health and safety issues can arise in a cell? Give an example. (*Hint:* See, for example, G. D. Brown and D. O'Rourke, "Lean Manufacturing Comes to China: A Case Study of Its Impact on Workplace Health and Safety," *International Journal of Occupational and Environmental Health,* 13(3), July/September 2007, pp. 249–257.)

Critical Thinking Exercises

LO1 1. In operations management, as in life, a balanced approach is often the best policy. One of the best examples of the benefits of this in operations management is the lean approach. Explain the basic factors that must be in place in order to achieve a balanced lean system.

LO3–6 2. Was the service of WestJet JIT/lean? (See the end of Chapter 2 for the Mini-Case on WestJet.) Explain.

LO6 3. In what way is a kanban system similar to the EOQ–ROP system of Chapter 12?

LO7 4. What are the key enablers for successful implementation of JIT/lean?

Experiential Learning Exercise

LO3–6 Visit a McDonald's restaurant and observe its production system. Is it using JIT/lean? Is the production schedule levelled? Is the system flexible (in terms of both equipment and workers)? Is there any visible waste? Does McDonald's use kanbans? Explain.

Internet Exercises

LO1 1. Visit http://www.shingoprize.org/awards, choose a recent recipient of the Shingo prize, and briefly summarize its JIT/lean program.

LO7 2. View http://www.youtube.com/watch?v=3mcMwlgUFjU &feature=related and describe value stream mapping.

LO1 & 2 3. Visit http://totalqualitymanagement.wordpress.com/2008/10 /28/lean-production-system, and compare the concepts of JIT/lean production system there with the information given in the chapter.

LO8 4. Visit http://www.cbc.ca/news/health/simple-hospital -innovation-saves-time-money-1.1298578 to see an application of lean in a hospital. What happened in the hospital?

Problems

LO6 1. A manager wants to determine the number of kanbans to use in a new process for a part. The process will have a usage rate of 80 pieces of the part per hour. Because the process is new, the manager has assigned a safety factor of 1.0. Each container holds 45 pieces and a kanban will take an average of 75 minutes to complete a cycle. How many kanbans should be used? As the system improves, will more or fewer kanbans be required? Why?

LO6 2. A JIT/lean system uses kanban cards to authorize production and movement of materials. In one portion of the system, a work centre uses an average of 100 pieces of a part per hour. The manager has assigned a safety factor of 0.50. Standard containers are designed to hold six dozen pieces each. The cycle time for a kanban is 105 minutes. How many kanbans are needed?

LO6 3. A cell uses 90 kg of a certain material each day. The material is transported in vats that hold 54 kg each. Cycle time for a kanban is about two hours. The manager has assigned a safety factor of 0.50. The plant operates on an eight-hour day. How many kanbans are needed?

LO6 4. Determine a level mixed-model sequence, given the following demand data:

Product	Daily Quantity
A	1
B	2
C	3
D	4

LO6 5. Determine a level mixed-model sequence, given the following demand data:

Product	Daily Quantity
A	2
B	12
C	4
D	5
E	9

LO6 **6.** Determine a level mixed-model sequence, given the following demand data:

Product	Daily Quantity
A	21
B	12
C	3
D	15

LO6 **7.** Determine a level mixed-model sequence, given the following demand data:

Product	Daily Quantity
A	9
B	8
C	5
D	6

LO6 **8.** Level Operations is a small company that produces a variety of security devices and safes. The safes come in several different designs. Recently, a number of new customers have placed orders, and the production facility has been enlarged to accommodate the increased demand for the safes. The production manager is currently working on a production plan for the safes. She has obtained the following information from the marketing department on projected average daily demand for each model:

Model	Daily Quantity
A	4
B	3
C	10
D	12
E	5

What might the production manager determine as the level mixed-model sequence for each day?

LO6 **9.** Toyota decided to make its minivan, Sienna, in the same plant as Camry and Avalon. Suppose that during a half-hour period, twelve Camrys, nine Avalons, and six Siennas are to be produced. Determine a level mixed-model sequence.

LO6 **10.** The Whirlpool factory in Oxford, Mississippi, makes built-in kitchen ovens.[4] In the 1990s, this plant re-engineered its processes to become JIT/lean. One of the parts of a particular oven, Part A, is processed by two 600 ton presses (in series), and then goes through a porcelain system to be coated. Finally, it is stored in the WIP storage location until it is used by the assembly lines. As a container of Part A is to be used, the kanban attached to it is taken to the press area and posted on the kanban post. Demand for Part A is 175 units per workday. A workday is 19 hours. The container size is 30 units. The setup time is one hour. Because of the large setup time, five kanbans are accumulated before production of A begins on the presses (approximately 16 hours of wait time). Production rate for A is 120 units per hour. The safety factor is 120 percent. Determine the number of kanbans required for Part A.

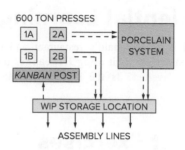

LO4 **11.** Calculate the takt time for a system where the total time per shift is 480 minutes, there is one shift, and workers are given two 15-minute breaks and 45 minutes for lunch. Daily demand is 300 units.

LO4 **12.** What takt time would match capacity and demand if demand is 120 units a day, there are two shifts of 480 minutes each, and workers are given three half-hour breaks during each shift, one of which is for lunch or dinner?

LO4 **13.** Calculate the takt time for a service system that is intended to perform a standardized service. The system will have a total work time of 440 minutes per day, two 10-minute breaks, and an hour for lunch. The service system must process 90 jobs a day.

LO6 ***14.** A motorcycle manufacturer produces three models: A, B, and C. This month's master production schedule, divided by 22 workdays, has resulted in daily production targets of 54 As, 42 Bs, and 30 Cs. The company works one shift per day, and effective production time is seven hours per day. Determine a level mixed-model sequence. (*Hint:* To reduce the size of the problem, divide each production target by the targets' greatest common divisor.)

---

[4] Based on J. D. Hall et al., "An Optimizer for the Kanban Sizing Problem: A Spreadsheet Application for Whirlpool Corporation," *Production and Inventory Management Journal* 39(1), First Quarter, 1998, pp. 17–22.

MINI-CASE

Airline Manufacturing

Airline Manufacturing is a 275,000 ft^2, 100-employee wood component manufacturer supplying upholsterers (e.g., sofa manufacturers), and is located in Columbus, Mississippi. When Judy Dunaway took the helm of the company following her father in 2000, the company had used a batch production system for 40 years. However, the threat of competition led her to start JIT/lean manufacturing. High-run (quantity) products were identified and grouped together if their required sequences of operations were identical. The machines required for each group were located close together in a dedicated cell (flow line). As a result, the amount of WIP inventory has been cut by more than half, the number of material-handling carts has been reduced from 3,000 to 1,000, and the number of material handlers has been reduced by half. Also, manufacturing lead time is down from four weeks to less than a week.

A high-run product is part #146-3843. Consider the production of a 2,900-unit customer order. Before the layout change, batches of approximately 1,000 units were transported from the warehouse to the CNC router, and from there batches of approximately 380 units were carried, when ready, from one machine to another by two workers using heavy carts. See the batch plant layout diagram in Figure 1. These workers returned the empty carts to the originating machine. After the final operation, dowel, the finished product was transported in batches of approximately 380 units to the finished goods warehouse using forklifts. The total worker-feet of movement using the forklifts (including the return to their origin) was approximately 5,300.

After the layout change, the only transport is by forklifts bringing in and taking out the product. The total worker-feet of movement using the forklifts has remained at approximately 5,300. However, the amount of machine-to-machine material handling has been greatly reduced because the machines are located close to each other. See the cellular layout, Figure 2. Due to elimination of delays waiting for material handling, the company can now make the 2,900-unit customer order in one day whereas it used to take six days.

Question

What are the benefits of the cellular layout to Airline Manufacturing?

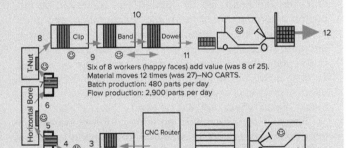

Figure 1

Figure 2

Sources: W. Duane Motsenbocker et al., "Wood Furniture Components: Implementation of Flow-Line Technology Based on Lean Manufacturing Concepts," *Research Bulletin,* Forest and Wildlife Centre, Mississippi State University; http://www.airlinemfg.com/capabilities.html. Figures courtesy of Mississippi State University.

Operations Tour

Boeing

The Boeing Company, headquartered in Chicago, Illinois, is one of two major commercial aircraft manufacturers in the world, the other being Airbus.

Boeing produces four models of aircraft in Everett, Washington: 747, 767, 777, and 787. The planes are all produced in the same building. At any one time, there may be as many as six planes in various stages of production. The building is so large that it covers over 98 acres and it is four storeys high, making it the largest building by volume in the world. The building has six huge doors along one side, each about 100 yards wide and 40 yards high—large enough to allow a completed airplane to pass through.

Boeing sells airplanes to airlines and countries around the globe. There isn't a set price for the planes; the actual price depends on what features the customer wants. Once the details have been settled and an order submitted, the customer requirements are sent to the design department. While any customization usually involves changes to equipment (such as seats), systems (such as navigation), and performance (such as cold weather), Boeing's improvement to the airframe of a model is ongoing.

Design

Design of a new aircraft is a very complex project, taking several years and involving hundreds of engineers. Boeing's 777 was the first passenger jet to be designed using CAD, in the mid-1990s. However, its $1 billion design cost was much lower than the $5 billion Boeing spent on the 787 Dreamliner, which used Dassault's CATIA 3D CAD to shape not only the aircraft's fuselage, but also every subsystem, and to plan its progress from conception through to eventual retirement. Apart from projecting wear and tear on the 787 over three decades, 3D was used to design the guts of the airliner so that a mechanic can climb in and reach every piece of equipment for repairs.

The Production Process

Once design has been completed and approved by the customer, production of the plane is scheduled, and parts and materials are ordered. Parts come to the plant by rail, airplane, and truck, and are delivered to the assembly area of the plane they will be used for. The parts are scheduled so they arrive at the plant just prior to when they will be used in assembly, and are immediately moved to a storage area close to where they will be used.

The partially assembled portions of the plane and, in later stages, the plane itself, move from station to station as the work progresses. Giant overhead cranes are used to move large sections from one station to the next, although once the wheel assemblies have been installed, the plane is towed to the remaining stations.

Finished planes are painted in one of two separate buildings. Painting usually adds 400 to 600 pounds to the weight of a plane. The painting process involves giving the airplane a negative charge and the paint a positive charge so that the paint will be attracted to the airplane.

Quality Control

Quality is critical for an aircraft manufacturer. Accordingly, quality can't be just an occasional act; it has to be a habit. Doing the work right the first time applies at all levels. The quest is for zero defects such as rework, bad work instructions, foreign object debris (FOD), and bad parts from suppliers. Boeing works hard to eliminate defects. For example, to address FOD, root-cause analyses have been conducted and ways to track tools and catch metal shavings have been identified. Employees are encouraged to speak up when something isn't right. And managers do what they can to make things right.

A funny example of a defect occurred when an airline investigated a loud rattle that came from the aft galley ceiling during flight. When the plane landed, a maintenance crew opened the ceiling and discovered a long wooden broom handle, apparently left there during production. Brooms now are part of the 5S process and always have a place.

Boeing personnel are embedded at supplier factories around the world to monitor quality, work with suppliers on process improvements, and ensure adherence to Boeing standards. Boeing also performs audits of supplier operations. When it comes to regulatory requirements, Boeing's external supplier network is an extension of Boeing factories. Boeing suppliers must certify that their production systems meet Boeing's quality management system requirements, and their systems must be approved by Boeing, the FAA, and an independent third party.

Lean Production

Boeing began its lean journey with the introduction of quality circles in the mid-1980s. This was followed by world class competitiveness training (a lean course based on top management Japan study tour), 5S, and JIT workshops. These were set up by John Black, who worked at Boeing from 1987 to 1999 as director of quality and then director of lean.

Learning to use individual lean tools like accelerated improvement workshops (kaizen) provided the foundation on which Boeing created an integrated lean strategy. The whole of Boeing was embracing lean by 1999. The strategy for becoming a lean operation is called the "Nine Tactics":

1. Perform value-stream mapping and analysis to define current and future states
2. Balance the line by distributing work evenly
3. Standardize work and instructions, eliminating non-value-added activity
4. Put visual controls or cues in place
5. Stage materials at point of use
6. Establish feeder and supply chain lines
7. Redesign major processes using breakthrough concepts
8. Convert processes to pulse-line configuration
9. Convert to a moving line with continuous flow

A pulse line is really a modification of the traditional assembly line. But instead of the object actually moving down a conveyor belt, it is moved from one work area to the next in a steady rhythm, like a pulse.

A 787 is made of 2.3 million parts and there are thousands of suppliers. Boeing has reduced the number of suppliers it deals with directly by using a few major Tier 1 component suppliers, called systems integrators, who in turn manage their own Tier 2 suppliers.

Examples of lean projects are too numerous. For some examples in the Everett plant, see https://www.epa.gov/lean/boeing-everett. In 2005, Boeing redesigned the production process into an assembly line. The assembly time of aircraft has been reduced significantly. For example, in 1998, it took Boeing 71 days to assemble a 777 aircraft—today, it takes just 17.

Bloomberg/Getty Images

Sources: https://roadtrippers.com/stories/boeing-factory; http://www.aircraftmonitor.com/uploads/1/5/9/9/15993320/commercial_aspects_of_aircraft _customization___v1.pdf; http://www.thenational.ae/business/industry-insights/technology/dassault-designs-path-to-success; https://www.youtube.com /watch?v=apDECxQFL-0; http://www.boeing.com/news/frontiers/archive/2009/august/aug09frontiers.pdf; http://787updates.newairplane.com/787-Suppliers /World-Class-Supplier-Quality; http://www.johnblackandassociates.com/uploads/2/0/7/8/20782048/the-lean-journey-at-boeing.pdf; https://www.youtube.com /watch?v=kQmqNOuRzb0.

To access "Maintenance," the supplement to Chapter 15,
please visit *Connect2*.

Chapter 16
Job and Staff Scheduling

ZUMA Press Inc/Alamy Stock Photo

Pier 1 Imports is a retailer specializing in imported home furnishings and decor. The chain operates over 1,000 stores in North America and employs 20,000 people. Before 2012, each Pier 1 Imports store created its own employee schedules using a mix of pen, paper, Excel, and Access. But store managers were prone to building schedules that were influenced by intuition and the people they were around, as opposed to the needs of the business. Also, manual scheduling resulted in the perception of preferential treatment.

In 2012, Pier 1 Imports implemented the Dayforce workforce management system as a software as a service, hosted by the software producer Ceridian. This allowed it to determine the optimal mix of full-time and part-time staff at each store. Now, instead of employing three to four full-time managers and assistant managers per store, Pier 1 staffs each store with a full-time store manager, a full-time assistant, and a part-time "sales lead" associate, in addition to several part-time associates. This has both reduced labour cost and improved customer service and sales.

Source: http://images.knowhow.ceridian.com/Web/CeridianCorporation/%7B62634dab-68d3
-4a05-8469-8c7a93c68b64%7D_CS-NA-EN-HCM-114332-000-Ceridian-PierOne.pdf.

Introduction

Job (or detailed) scheduling is establishing the start and end times of operations of jobs or orders. It involves assignment of jobs to work centres and to machines within each work centre, sequencing the jobs in front of each work centre/machine, and specifying their start and end times. A **work centre** is a production area consisting of one or more workers and machines with similar capabilities, which can be considered as one unit for purposes of scheduling.

In the production planning hierarchy, job scheduling is the final step before the actual output is produced (see the bottom box in Figure 13-2, called "Detailed planning and execution systems"). Many decisions have to be made long before job scheduling. They include strategic planning such as the capacity of the process and equipment, aggregate planning such as selection and training of workers, and master production scheduling (MPS) and material requirements planning (MRP). Consequently, job scheduling must be done within the constraints established by the above decisions, making it fairly narrow in scope and latitude.

In this chapter, we will also cover *shop-floor control*, which relates to execution of the schedule and involves maintaining, communicating, and monitoring the status of material, orders, and processes, and taking any necessary actions.

Recall that ordinary MRP does not take the load on the component work centres into account during its computation, and thus can result in overloaded machines. One has to perform capacity requirement planning to identify the capacity needs of MRP and accommodate them to make the MRP feasible. However, advanced planning and scheduling software has the ability to combine and automate these activities. For example, Taylor Scheduler is the capacitated version of MRP (and MPS). See the "Beaver Plastics" OM in Action.

> **job (or detailed) scheduling** Establishing the start and end times of operations of jobs or orders.
>
> **work centre** A production area consisting of one or more workers and machines with similar capabilities, that can be considered as one unit for purpose of scheduling.

OM in Action

Beaver Plastics

Beaver Plastics, based just outside of Edmonton, makes polystyrene construction and packaging products such as egg cartons. The production process starts with polystyrene beads that are cured and then fed into moulding machines. Large products may be cut using electric-heated wires. Some construction products such as insulated walls have reinforcement embedded in them. Beaver Plastics uses Taylor Scheduler (now called APS) to schedule the customer orders on its moulding machines and also to schedule the moulds. The schedule is updated every afternoon with new orders and order completions. The software is also used to help sales staff promise achievable due dates. Beaver Plastics uses Taylor Scheduler to enable sharing of some of its expensive moulds among its plants, in Edmonton, AB; Chilliwack, BC; and Mexico. Taylor Software is also based in Edmonton. Taylor Scheduler has the ability to use optimization (integer linear programming) to perform capacitated master scheduling and material requirements planning, thus ensuring that machine (and mould) capacities are not exceeded. Taylor is now part of Demand Solutions.

Source: http://www.taylor.com.hk/en/news/2006_beaver.htm; http://www.beaverplastics.com.

MRP schedules the planned order releases backward, starting from the due date for the product. This is an example of **backward scheduling**. However, often scheduling begins from the start time of a job and works forward into the future. This is called **forward scheduling**.

Staff scheduling involves determining the workdays, and start and end times on each workday, for each employee. (We will discuss this further, later in the chapter.) Job and staff scheduling are important because they affect customer-order completion dates and production costs through the utilization of resources.

> **backward scheduling** Scheduling backward from the due date.
>
> **forward scheduling** Scheduling ahead, beginning from the start date of a job.

Loading

Loading refers to the assignment of jobs to work centres and to various machines within each work centre. In cases where a job can be processed only by a specific line/machine, loading presents little difficulty, except for determining the time of the operation. However, a decision needs to be made

> **loading** The assignment of jobs to work centres and to various machines within each work centre.

when there are a number of work centres or machines within a work centre capable of performing the required work. In such cases, the scheduler needs some way of assigning jobs to the work centres or machines within each work centre.

When making an assignment, managers often choose a work centre or machine that (a) minimizes processing and setup costs, (b) minimizes idle time among work centres or machines, (c) allows an operator to run two or more machines simultaneously, or (d) is the least sophisticated work centre or machine that can do the job. The assignment model later in this section will select the best assignment for a set of jobs.

Load Gantt Chart

> **Gantt chart** A visual aid for loading, scheduling, and control purposes.
>
> **load Gantt chart** A Gantt chart that shows the loading and timing of jobs for each resource.

A visual aid called a **Gantt chart** is used for a variety of purposes related to loading, scheduling, and control. It derives its name from Henry Gantt, who pioneered its use for industrial scheduling in the early 1900s. There are two types of Gantt charts: the *load Gantt chart* and the *schedule Gantt chart* (described later in Section 4 in this chapter).

A **load Gantt chart** depicts the loading and timing of jobs for each resource such as a machine or work centre. This chart is used in services as well. Two examples are illustrated in Figure 16-1, which shows scheduling courses to classrooms and scheduling patients to a hospital's operating rooms. The purpose of a load chart is to organize and clarify the actual or intended use of resources over *time*. The time scale is represented horizontally and resources are listed vertically. The use of the resources is reflected in the body of the chart.

FIGURE 16-1 ▶

Examples of load Gantt charts used for scheduling facilities in services.

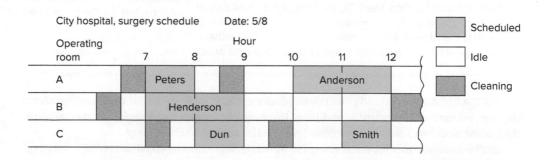

Classroom schedule: Fall   Friday

Room	8	9	10	11	12	1	2	3	4	5
A100	Stat 1	Econ 101	Econ 102	Fin 201	Mar 210	Acct 212			Mar 410	
A105	Stat 2	Math 2a	Math 2b			Acct 210	CCE — — — — —			
A110	Acct 340	Mgmt 250	Math 3		Mar 220					
A115	Mar 440		Mgmt 230			Fin 310	Acct 360			

City hospital, surgery schedule   Date: 5/8

Operating room	7	8	9	10	11	12
A		Peters			Anderson	
B	Henderson					
C		Dun			Smith	

□ Scheduled □ Idle ▨ Cleaning

Schedulers can use the load Gantt chart for trial-and-error schedule development. Thus, a tentative surgery schedule might reveal insufficient time allowance for a surgery that may take longer than expected. Use of the chart for classroom scheduling would help avoid assigning two different classes to the same room at the same time. Another example of a load Gantt chart is given in Figure 16-2A. This chart indicates that work centre 3 is completely loaded for the entire week, work centre 4 will be available from Tuesday on, and the other two work centres have idle time scattered

A.

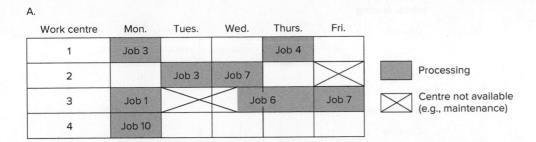

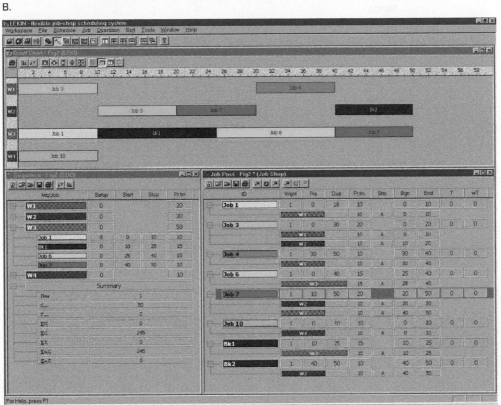

◄ FIGURE 16-2

A. Sample load Gantt chart. B. The same chart using the Lekin software which was developed at New York University and is available for free download.

Source: http://web-static .stern.nyu.edu/om/software /lekin/ © Pinedo and Feldman. Used with permission.

throughout the week. This information can help a manager rework loading to better utilize the work centres. For instance, if all work centres perform the same kind of work, the manager might want to free one work centre for a long job or a rush order.

Dealing With Infinite Loading

Sometimes it is easier or advantageous to first schedule jobs without capacity considerations. An example is MRP scheduling. This is called *infinite loading*. **Infinite loading** assigns jobs to work centres without regard to the available capacity of the work centres. However, most scheduling is done by finite loading. **Finite loading** assigns jobs to work centres, taking into account the available capacities of work centres and the processing times of jobs, so that the capacities are not exceeded. Schedules based on finite loading may have to be updated often, perhaps daily, due to processing delays at work centres, the addition of new jobs, and completion of current jobs. The following diagram contrasts finite versus infinite loading.

infinite loading Assigning jobs to work centres without regard to the available capacity of the work centres.

finite loading Assigning jobs to work centres, taking into account work centres' available capacities and jobs' processing times.

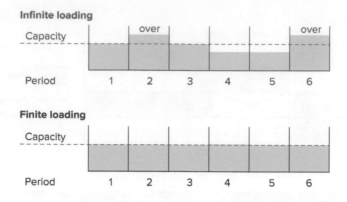

With infinite loading, a manager needs to respond to overloaded work centres. Among the possible responses are shifting work to other periods, working overtime, or contracting out a portion of the work. Example 16-1 illustrates some of these responses.

EXAMPLE 16-1 ▶

The work centre loads resulting from MRP for order #1, 100 units of a kitchen table due on day 6 (see Problem 24 of Chapter 14), can graphically be represented by the following load Gantt chart where a blue horizontal bar represents the duration of an operation. For example, Top Fab work centre is scheduled to produce table tops for this order during working hours (eight hours a day) of days 2 to 4:

Order #1	Day 1	Day 2	Day 3	Day 4	Day 5	Day 6	Day 7
Top Fab		▬	▬	▬			
Leg Fab			▬	▬			
Table Assembly					▬		

Also, suppose order #2, 50 units of a different table due on day 7, was also promised, with the following additional loads determined by MRP on the same work centres:

Order #2	Day 1	Day 2	Day 3	Day 4	Day 5	Day 6	Day 7
Top Fab				▬			
Leg Fab				▬			
Table Assembly					▬	▬	

Order #2 tables need less time for Top Fab but more time for Table Assembly. Note that order #2 needs only half a day in Top Fab, hence a red horizontal bar with half the length represents it. Capacity of work centres Top Fab and Leg Fab on day 4 and Table Assembly on day 5 are exceeded, because the total load (of both orders) exceeds eight hours in each case. What can the scheduler do?

SOLUTION

Many options are possible. Four are tried below. Choose the least expensive option.

1. Move due date for order #2 to day 8. This relieves the overload. However, order #2 will be one day late.

Order #1	Day 1	Day 2	Day 3	Day 4	Day 5	Day 6	Day 7
Top Fab		▬	▬	▬			
Leg Fab			▬	▬			
Table Assembly					▬		

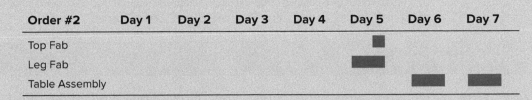

Order #2	Day 1	Day 2	Day 3	Day 4	Day 5	Day 6	Day 7
Top Fab					■		
Leg Fab					■		
Table Assembly						■	■

2. Move Leg Fab for order #1 to day 2 and day 3, if possible, and increase capacity of Top Fab on day 4 and Table Assembly on day 5. Neither order will be late but this will cost more.

Order #1	Day 1	Day 2	Day 3	Day 4	Day 5	Day 6	Day 7
Top Fab		■	■	■			
Leg Fab		■	■				
Table Assembly					■		

Order #2	Day 1	Day 2	Day 3	Day 4	Day 5	Day 6	Day 7
Top Fab				■			
Leg Fab				■			
Table Assembly					■	■	

3. Schedule order #2 first (i.e., change the sequence of scheduling). Order #1 will be half a day late but work centres are utilized more in the near future.

Order #1	Day 1	Day 2	Day 3	Day 4	Day 5	Day 6	Day 7
Top Fab		■	■	■	■		
Leg Fab			■	■			
Table Assembly					■	■	

Order #2	Day 1	Day 2	Day 3	Day 4	Day 5	Day 6	Day 7
Top Fab		■					
Leg Fab		■					
Table Assembly			■	■			

4. Use solution 3 and split Top Fab for order #1. (For example, move 50 tops to Table Assembly when 50 tops are ready, and start Table Assembly. Move the other 50 tops later when they are ready.) Neither order will be late and work centres are utilized more in the near future.

Order #1	Day 1	Day 2	Day 3	Day 4	Day 5	Day 6	Day 7
Top Fab		■	■	■	■		
Leg Fab			■	■			
Table Assembly					■		

Order #2	Day 1	Day 2	Day 3	Day 4	Day 5	Day 6	Day 7
Top Fab		■					
Leg Fab		■					
Table Assembly			■	■			

An example of a popular finite-capacity-loading scheduling software is Preactor, used by many companies. See, for example, the "Plastique Micron" OM in Action.

OM in Action   www.plastiquemicron.com

Plastique Micron

Plastique Micron (PM), located in Sainte Claire near Quebec City, is a medium-sized plastic-bottle manufacturer, primarily for the pharmaceutical and cosmetic industry. PM has 29 plastic moulding machines that use the blow moulding method. Each machine melts polyethylene pellets (four types in various colours), forms hollow cylinders of plastic in the right size (called preforms; there are hundreds of sizes), places the preforms in moulds (there are hundreds and they can also be custom made), blows air into the neck of preforms to expand them into the shape of the inside of the moulds, cools the bottles, and finally ejects them. There are several types/models of blow moulding machines, with different capabilities and speeds, some requiring specific moulds.

Before 2006, a customer service agent/planner scheduled the production, all based on his knowledge of the machines that could produce a particular order and the moulds available. Other required information for scheduling such as current load on machines was not easily available, despite having a computer system. A production schedule was determined and displayed on a board in the office on a daily basis. The production supervisors had to walk into the office several times a day to find out what they should produce on what machine using what mould. Consequently, customer order promises and follow-up were unsatisfactory and slow.

Then PM purchased the Preactor 300 scheduling software. The implementation team (the planner, the IT person, and a consultant) started to define the machines and moulds, and their relationships. Because of the large varieties and lack of any previous documentation, this process is taking a long time and is ongoing. Preactor 300 has brought order and speed to the scheduling of jobs, thus improving customer service.

© Courtesy of Plastique Micron

Source: http://www.preactor.com/Case-Studies/Case-Studies/Plastique -Micron#.WUEAYGjyvcs.

Assignment Model

assignment model A model for optimal assignment of tasks/ jobs to resources.

The **assignment model** is useful in situations that call for assigning tasks/jobs to resources. Typical examples include assigning jobs to machines or workers, territories to salespeople, and repair jobs to repair crews. The idea is to obtain an optimal *matching* of tasks/jobs and resources. Commonly used criteria include costs, profits, and performance.

Table 16-1 illustrates a typical problem, where four jobs are to be assigned to four workers. The problem is arranged in a format that facilitates evaluation of assignments. The numbers in the body of the table represent the value or cost associated with each job–worker combination. In this case, the numbers represent costs. Thus, it would cost $8 for worker A to do job 1, $6 for worker B to do job 1, and so on. If the problem involved minimizing the cost for job 1 alone, it would clearly be assigned to worker C, because that combination has the lowest cost. However, that assignment does not take into account the other jobs and their costs, which is important because the lowest-cost assignment for any one job may not be consistent with a minimum-cost assignment when all jobs are considered.

If there are to be n matches, there are $n!$ different possibilities. In this case, there are $4! = 4 \times 3 \times 2 \times 1 = 24$ different matches. One approach is to investigate each match and select the one with the lowest cost. However, if there were 12 jobs, there would be 479 million different matches! A much simpler approach is to use a procedure called the **Hungarian method** to identify the lowest-cost solution.

To be able to use the Hungarian method, a one-for-one matching is required. Each job, for example, must be assigned to only one worker. It is also assumed that every worker is capable of handling every job, and that the costs or values associated with each assignment combination are

TABLE 16-1 ▼

A typical assignment problem showing job costs for each job–worker combination.

		WORKER			
		A	B	C	D
	1	8	6	2	4
Job	2	6	7	11	10
	3	3	5	7	6
	4	5	10	12	9

known. The number of rows and columns must be the same. Solved Problem 1 at the end of the chapter shows what to do if they aren't the same.

Once the relevant cost information has been acquired and arranged in tabular form, the basic procedure of the Hungarian method is as follows:

> **Hungarian method** A simple method of assigning jobs to resources by a one-for-one matching at lowest cost.

1. Subtract the smallest number in each row from every number in the row. This is called a *row reduction.* Enter the results in a new table.

2. Subtract the smallest number in each column of the new table from every number in the column. This is called a *column reduction.* Enter the results in another table.

3. Test whether an optimum assignment can be made. You do this by determining the *minimum* number of lines (horizontal or vertical) needed to cover all zeros. If the number of lines equals the number of rows (or columns), an optimum assignment is possible. In that case, go to Step 6. Otherwise go on to Step 4.

4. If the number of lines is less than the number of rows, modify the table in this way:

   a. Subtract the smallest uncovered number from every uncovered number in the table.

   b. Add the smallest uncovered number to the numbers at the *intersections* of cross-out lines.

   c. Numbers crossed out (covered), but not at intersections of cross-out lines, carry over to the next table.

5. Repeat Steps 3 and 4 until an optimal table is obtained.

6. Make the assignments. Begin with rows or columns with only one zero. Use only one match for each row and each column. Eliminate both the row and the column after each match.

Determine the optimum assignment of jobs to workers for Table 16-1:

EXAMPLE 16-2

	WORKER				
	A	B	C	D	Row Minimum
1	8	6	2	4	2
Job 2	6	7	11	10	6
3	3	5	7	6	3
4	5	10	12	9	5

	WORKER			
	A	B	C	D
1	6	3	0	0
Job 2	0	0	5	2
3	0	1	4	1
4	0	4	7	2

SOLUTION

a. Subtract the smallest number in each row from every number in the row, and enter the results in a new table. The result of this row reduction is:

	WORKER			
	A	B	C	D
1	6	4	0	2
Job 2	0	1	5	4
3	0	2	4	3
4	0	5	7	4
Column Minimum	0	1	0	2

b. Subtract the smallest number in each column from every number in the column, and enter the results in a new table. The result of this column reduction is:

c. Determine the *minimum* number of lines needed to cross out all zeros. (Try to cross out as many zeros as possible when drawing lines.)

	WORKER			
	A	B	C	D
1	6	3	0	0
2	0	0	5	2
Job 3	0	1	4	1
4	0	4	7	2

d. Since only three lines are needed to cross out all zeros and the table has four rows (or columns), this is not the optimum. Note that the smallest uncovered value is 1.

e. Subtract the smallest uncovered value from every uncovered number, and add it to numbers that are at the intersections of covering lines. The results are as follows:

		WORKER			
		A	**B**	**C**	**D**
	1	7	3	0	0
Job	**2**	1	0	5	2
	3	0	0	3	0
	4	0	3	6	1

		WORKER			
		A	**B**	**C**	**D**
	1	7	3	0	0
Job	**2**	1	0	5	2
	3	0	0	3	0
	4	0	3	6	1

f. Determine the minimum number of lines needed to cover all zeros. One way to cover all the zeros with a minimum number of lines is displayed below, where four lines are used. Since this number equals the number of rows (or columns), you can make the optimum assignment.

		WORKER			
		A	**B**	**C**	**D**
	1	7	3	0	0
Job	**2**	1	0	5	2
	3	0	0	3	0
	4	0	3	6	1

g. Make assignments: Start with rows and columns with only one zero. Match jobs with workers that have a zero cost.

Assignment	Original Cost
1-C	$ 2
3-D	6
2-B	7
4-A	5
	$20

The assignment problem can also be solved using Excel's Solver or the Transportation model template on *Connect2*, as seen in Table 16-2. The ones in the solution matrix denote the assignments (e.g., assign job 1 to worker C), and the zeros denote no assignment for a worker and job combination.

TABLE 16-2 ▼

Excel solution to Example 16-2.

Input Matrix:

Job	Worker/Machine	A	B	C	D	E	F	G	H	
	1	8	6	2	4					1
	2	6	7	11	10					1
	3	3	5	7	6					1
	4	5	10	12	9					1
	5									0
	6									0
	7									0
	8									0
		1	1	1	1	0	0	0	0	

Total Jobs = 4

Do not change or delete unshaded cells.   Total Workers/Machines = 4

Solution Matrix:

Job	Worker/Machine	A	B	C	D	E	F	G	H	
	1	0	0	1	0	0	0	0	0	1
	2	0	1	0	0	0	0	0	0	1
	3	0	0	0	1	0	0	0	0	1
	4	1	0	0	0	0	0	0	0	1
	5	0	0	0	0	0	0	0	0	0
	6	0	0	0	0	0	0	0	0	0
	7	0	0	0	0	0	0	0	0	0
	8	0	0	0	0	0	0	0	0	0
		1	1	1	1	0	0	0	0	

Total Cost = 20

When profits instead of costs are involved, the profits can be converted to *relative costs* by subtracting every number in the table from the largest number and then proceeding as in a minimization problem.

It is worth knowing how to prevent undesirable assignments. For example, union rules may prohibit one person's assignment to a particular job, or a manager might wish to avoid assigning an unqualified person to a job. Whatever the reason, specific combinations can be avoided by assigning a relatively high cost to that combination. In the previous example, if we wish to avoid combination 1-A, assigning a cost of $50 to that combination will achieve the desired effect, because $50 is much greater than the other costs.

For an unusual sequencing problem, see the "Boarding an Airplane" OM in Action.

 OM in Action

Boarding an Airplane

The *turnaround time* is the time from when an airplane stops at a gate in an airport to the time it is ready to take off again. Minimizing turnaround time is of interest to airlines because it allows them to use their airplanes as much as possible. Airlines have tried to perform all activities required in a turnaround as quickly as possible. For the last two decades, unboarding, cleaning the cabin, and then boarding are the bottleneck (the longest) series of required activities in a turnaround. Out of these three activities, boarding can be shortened. For the last two decades, airlines and researchers have been trying to find the optimal method for boarding.

What slows boarding are two types of passenger-to-passenger interference: (a) *aisle interference*, which means that a passenger ahead is putting his/her luggage in the overhead bin, and (b) *seat interference*, which means there is a passenger already sitting in a middle or aisle seat of the row of your window seat. Theoretically, if passengers could line up at the gate in the order of their seat from the back of the airplane to the front, the total boarding time would be minimized. However, this is not possible.

All airlines allow first-class passengers, families with small children, and others who have difficulty boarding to board first. Many airlines use three to six groups or zones for their economy seats. However, Southwest Airlines has no seat assignment (i.e., a passenger can sit on any seat), but this causes hardship for passengers who wish to sit in the front because they have to arrive early. American Airlines has only one economy zone (i.e., all economy passengers board in any order), which makes it easy to administer but may result in large interference.

Almost all airlines find that aisle interference is more serious than seat interference, and therefore use the back-to-front zones method. However, United Airlines uses the outside-in zone method: first all passengers with window seats board, then all with middle seats,

and finally all with aisle seats. This has the disadvantage of temporarily separating families who sit in the same row.

Research has shown that the optimal boarding method is a combination of back-to-front and outside-in zones. This is called reverse pyramid. America West Airlines used it for a few years in the mid-2000s and reported savings of two minutes per flight. However, this practice was discontinued when America West was taken over by US Airways (which was itself taken over by American Airlines).

1	1	
1	1	
1	1	
4	5	6
4	5	6
4	5	6
4	5	6
3	4	6
3	4	6
3	4	6
3	4	6
3	4	6
2	4	6
2	4	6
2	4	6
2	4	5
2	3	5
2	3	5
2	3	5
2	3	5
2	3	5
2	3	5

1	1	
1	1	
1	1	
6	5	4
6	5	4
6	5	4
6	5	4
6	4	3
6	4	3
6	4	3
6	4	3
6	4	3
6	4	2
6	4	2
6	4	2
5	4	2
5	3	2
5	3	2
5	3	2
5	3	2
5	3	2
5	3	2

Reverse pyramid boarding method (front of the aircraft is at the top; board zone 1, then 2, etc.)

Source: F. Jaehn and S. Neumann, "Airplane Boarding," *European Journal of Operational Research*, 244(20), July 2015, pp. 339–359.

(L03) **Sequencing**

> **sequencing** Determining the order in which jobs will be processed in a work centre or machine.

Although loading decisions determine the machines or work centres that will be used to process specific jobs, they do not necessarily indicate the *order* in which the jobs waiting there are to be processed. **Sequencing** is concerned with determining the order of processing the jobs on a machine or work centre.

If work centres or machines are lightly loaded, or if the jobs all require the same amount of processing time, have the same due date, and setup time/cost is sequence independent, sequencing presents no particular difficulties. Otherwise, the order of processing can be important in terms of work centre/machine utilization/costs and order due dates. In this section, we will examine some of the ways in which jobs are sequenced.

Priority Rules and Performance Measures

> **priority rules** Simple heuristics used to select the order in which jobs will be processed.

Typically, a number of jobs will be waiting for processing. **Priority rules** or dispatching rules are simple heuristics used to select the order in which jobs will be processed. Some of the most common priority rules are listed in Table 16-3. The rules generally rest on the assumption that a job's setup time is *independent* of the processing sequence, and processing time for each job includes its setup time. Due dates may be the result of delivery times promised to customers, MRP planned order receipt dates, or warehouse replenishment due dates.

TABLE 16-3 ►

Common priority rules.

FCFS (first come, first served): Jobs are processed in the order in which they arrive at the machine/work centre.
SPT (shortest [imminent] processing time): Jobs are processed according to processing time at the machine/work centre, shortest job first.
SRPT (shortest remaining processing time): Jobs are processed according to sum of the processing times at all the remaining required machines/work centres for each job, smallest first.
EDD (earliest due date): Jobs are processed according to due date, earliest due date first.
MST (minimum slack time): Jobs are processed according to their **slack time** (i.e., time until due date minus remaining processing time), minimum first.
CR (critical ratio): Jobs are processed according to ratio of time until due date to remaining processing time, smallest first.
Rush: Emergency or preferred customers first.

> **slack time** Time until due date minus remaining processing time.

Performance Measures. The effectiveness of any given sequence is judged in terms of one or more *performance measures*. The most frequently used performance measures are average flow time, average hours or days late, the make-span, and average WIP. These are defined as follows:

> **job flow time** The length of the time a job is in a shop.

- **Job flow time** is the length of the time a job is in a shop. It includes not only the actual setup and processing time but also any time waiting to be processed, and movement time between operations. The *average flow time* for a group of jobs is equal to the total flow time for the jobs divided by the number of jobs.

- *Job lateness* is the length of time or number of days the job completion time/date exceeds the job due time/date. We assign zero lateness to jobs that are early. The *average hours or days late* for a group of jobs is equal to the total jobs lateness divided by the number of jobs.

- **Make-span** is the time needed to complete a *group* of jobs. It is the length of time between the start of the first job in the group and the end of the last job in the group.

> **make-span** Time needed to complete a group of jobs from the beginning of the first job to the end of the last job.

- Jobs that are in the shop are considered to be work-in-process (WIP) inventory. The *average WIP* for a group of jobs can be calculated using the following formula: Average WIP = Total flow time for the group/Make-span of the group.

Note that average WIP and average flow time are closely related. If a priority rule results in small average flow time, it will also result in small average WIP and vice versa. Of the priority rules, the FCFS and rush are quite simple and need no explanation. The other rules and the performance measures above are illustrated in the following one-machine shop example.

Processing times (including setup times) and due dates for six jobs that arrived today and are waiting to be processed at the only machine in a shop are shown in the table below. Determine the sequence of jobs, the make-span, the average flow time, average days late, and average WIP in the shop for each of these priority rules:

a. SPT.   **b.** EDD.   **c.** MST.   **d.** CR.

Job Sequence	Processing Time (days)	Due Date (days from today)
A	2	7
B	8	16
C	4	4
D	10	17
E	5	15
F	12	18

SOLUTION

a. Using the shortest processing time (SPT) rule, the job sequence is A-C-E-B-D-F. So, rearrange the job processing time and due date columns so that jobs appear in the SPT order in the Job Sequence column. Also add Completion Time and Days Late columns. See the table below. The Completion Time column shows the *cumulative* processing times. For example, job C's completion time is four days after job A's completion time (i.e., $2 + 4 = 6$). Job A is not late because it is completed at the end of the second day, before its due date, the end of day 7, but job C is late by two days because it is completed at the end of day 6, whereas its due date is the end of day 4. Summing the completion times gives the total flow time (108 days) and completion time of the last job, job F, is the make-span, which is 41 days. Note that for one-machine shops, make-span is the same no matter what priority rule is used. The resulting measures of performance are:

   i. *Average flow time:* $108/6 = 18$ days.
   ii. *Average days late:* $40/6 = 6.67$ days.
 iii. *Average WIP:* $108/41 = 2.63$ jobs.

Job Sequence	(i) Processing Time	(ii) Completion Time	(iii) Due Date	(ii) − (iii) Days Late [0 if negative]
A	2	2	7	0
C	4	6	4	2
E	5	11	15	0
B	8	19	16	3
D	10	29	17	12
F	12	<u>41</u>	18	<u>23</u>
		108		40

b. Using the earliest due date (EDD) rule, the job sequence is C-A-E-B-D-F. Repeating the steps in part *a* results in the table at the top of the next page. The resulting measures of performance are:

   i. *Average flow time:* $110/6 = 18.33$ days.
   ii. *Average days late:* $38/6 = 6.33$ days.
 iii. *Average WIP:* $110/41 = 2.68$ jobs.

Job Sequence	(i) Processing Time	(ii) Completion Time	(iii) Due Date	(ii) – (iii) Days Late [0 if negative]
C	4	4	4	0
A	2	6	7	0
E	5	11	15	0
B	8	19	16	3
D	10	29	17	12
F	12	<u>41</u>	18	<u>23</u>
		110		38

c. Using the minimum slack time (due date minus processing time) MST rule, the job sequence is C-A-F-D-B-E (see the slack times in the table below; for example, slack time of job C = 4 – 4 = 0 and slack time of job A = 7 – 2 = 5; note the sequence is in increasing size of slack time). Doing the calculations results in the table below. The measures of performance are:

i. *Average flow time*: 160/6 = 26.67 days.
ii. *Average days late*: 85/6 = 14.17 days.
iii. *Average WIP*: 160/41 = 3.90.

Job Sequence	(i) Slack Time	(ii) Processing Time	(iii) Completion Date	(iv) Due Date	(iii) – (iv) Days Late [0 if negative]
C	0	4	4	4	0
A	5	2	6	7	0
F	6	12	18	18	0
D	7	10	28	17	11
B	8	8	36	16	20
E	10	5	<u>41</u>	15	<u>26</u>
			133		57

d. Using the critical ratio (due date divided by processing time) CR rule, the job sequence is C-F-D-B-E-A (see the critical ratios in the table below; for example, CR for job C is 4/4 = 1, and CR for job F is 18/12 = 1.5; note the sequence is in increasing size of CR). Doing the calculations results in the following measures of performance:

i. *Average flow time*: 160/6 = 26.67 days.
ii. *Average days late*: 85/6 = 14.17 days.
iii. *Average WIP*: 160/41 = 3.90.

Job Sequence	(i) Critical Ratio	(ii) Processing Time	(iii) Completion Date	(iv) Due Date	(iii) – (iv) Days Late [0 if negative]
C	1.0	4	4	4	0
F	1.5	12	16	18	0
D	1.7	10	26	17	9
B	2.0	8	34	16	18
E	3.0	5	39	15	24
A	3.5	2	<u>41</u>	7	<u>34</u>
			160		85

The results of these four rules are summarized in Table 16-4. In this example, the SPT rule is the best according to average flow time and average WIP and a little worse than the EDD rule on average days late. The CR rule is the worst in every case. However, for a different set of processing times and due dates, the performance of priority rules will be different.

Rule	Average Flow Time (days)	Average Days Late	Average WIP
SPT	18.00	6.67	2.63
EDD	18.33	6.33	2.68
MST	22.17	9.5	3.24
CR	26.67	14.17	3.90

◀ TABLE 16-4

Comparison of performance measures of the four rules for Example 16-3.

Guidelines for Selecting a Priority Rule. The following results apply for every one-machine shop: SPT is always superior in terms of minimizing average flow time and, hence, average WIP; if all jobs are late, then SPT will always minimize average days late as well; however, EDD always minimizes the maximum days late.

For multi-machine, multi-stage shops, the following statements about the priority rules can be made. The primary limitation of FCFS is that long jobs may delay the following jobs which will increase idle times for downstream work centres. However, for service systems in which customers are directly involved, FCFS is by far the dominant priority rule, mainly because of the inherent fairness, but also because of the difficulty in obtaining realistic estimates of processing time for individual jobs. FCFS also has the advantage of simplicity.

SPT results in low average flow time and low average days late. In addition, because it involves low average WIP, there tends to be less congestion in the shop. SPT also minimizes downstream idle times. However, it doesn't use due dates and it tends to make long jobs wait, perhaps for rather long times (especially if new, shorter jobs are continually added to the shop). Various modifications of the SPT rule may be used in an effort to avoid this. For example, after waiting for a given time period, a long job is automatically moved to the head of the line.

EDD directly addresses due dates and usually results in low maximum days late. Although it has intuitive appeal, its main limitation is that it does not take processing times into account. One possible consequence is that it can result in a long job being processed first, resulting in other jobs waiting a long time, which adds to both WIP and shop congestion.

MST and CR have intuitive appeal. Both use both the due dates and remaining processing times. Although they had the poorest results in Example 16-3 for all three measures, they usually work quite well.

Sequencing Jobs Through Two Work Centres/Machines

Johnson's rule is a technique that schedulers can use to minimize the make-span for a group of jobs to be processed on two successive work centres/machines (referred to as a two-machine flow shop).[1] It also minimizes the total idle time at the second work centre/machine. For the technique to work, several conditions must be satisfied:

Johnson's rule Technique for minimizing make-span for a group of jobs to be processed on two successive work centres/machines.

1. Job time (setup and processing) must be known for each job at each work centre/machine.
2. Job times must be independent of the job sequence.
3. All jobs must follow the same two-step work sequence.
4. All units in a job must be completed at the first work centre/machine before the job is moved to the second work centre/machine (there is no job splitting).
5. There is adequate space for WIP before the second work centre/machine.

Determination of the optimal sequence involves these steps:

1. Select the job with the shortest time. If the shortest time is at the first work centre/machine, place that job first in the sequence; if the time is at the second work centre/machine, place the job last in the sequence. Break ties arbitrarily.
2. Eliminate the job and its times from further consideration.
3. Repeat Steps 1 and 2, working toward the centre of the sequence, until all jobs have been placed in the sequence.

[1] S. M. Johnson, "Optimal Two- and Three-Stage Production With Setup Times Included," *Naval Research Quarterly* 1, 1, pp. 61–68.

EXAMPLE 16-4

A group of six jobs is to be processed through a two work-centre flow shop. The processing times (including setup times) are shown in the following table. The first operation involves cleaning and the second involves painting.

a. Determine a sequence that will minimize the make-span for this group of jobs.

b. Determine the make-span and the idle times on work centre 2.

	Processing Time (Hours)	
Job	Work Centre 1	Work Centre 2
A	5	5
B	4	3
C	8	9
D	2	7
E	6	8
F	12	15

SOLUTION

a. Select the job with the shortest processing time. It is job D, with a time of two hours. Since this time is at the first work centre, place job D first in the sequence. Eliminate job D from further consideration. Job B has the next shortest processing time (three hours). Since it is at the second work centre, place it last in the sequence and eliminate job B from further consideration. We now have partially identified the sequence:

1st	2nd	3rd	4th	5th	6th
D					B

The remaining jobs and their times are:

Job	WC 1	WC 2
A	5	5
C	8	9
E	6	8
F	12	15

Note that there is a tie for the shortest remaining time (five hours): job A has the same time at each work centre. It makes no difference whether we place A toward the beginning or the end of the partially filled sequence. Suppose A is placed arbitrarily toward the end:

1st	2nd	3rd	4th	5th	6th
D				A	B

Eliminate job A's times. The shortest remaining time is six hours for job E at work centre 1. Thus, place job E toward the beginning of the partially filled sequence (after job D):

1st	2nd	3rd	4th	5th	6th
D	E			A	B

Eliminate job E's times. Job C has the shortest time of the remaining two jobs (eight hours). Since it is for the first work centre, place it third in the sequence. Finally, assign the remaining job (F) to the fourth position and the resulting sequence is:

1st	2nd	3rd	4th	5th	6th
D	E	C	F	A	B

b. One way to determine the make-span and idle times at work centre 2 is to construct a load Gantt chart:

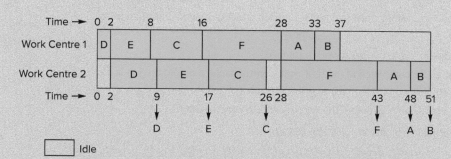

Note that work centre 2 has to wait until the end of the second hour for job D, because job D has to first finish work centre 1 (a job can't be in two places at the same time, unless it can be split). Similarly, after completing job C at the end of the 26th hour, work centre 2 has to wait for job F, because work centre 1 will not finish with job F until the end of the 28th hour. This group of jobs will take 51 hours to complete (i.e., Make-span = 51 hours), and the second work centre will wait two hours for its first job and also wait two hours after finishing job C.

When significant idle time at the second work centre occurs, *job splitting* at the first work centre, just prior to the occurrence of idle time, may alleviate some of the problem and also shorten the make-span. The use of transfer batches (i.e., splitting jobs) is an important tool in the theory of constraints described later in the chapter. Solved Problem 5 at the end of this chapter illustrates the use of job splitting.

Sequencing Jobs With Sequence-Dependent Setup Times

The preceding discussion and examples assumed that machine setup times are independent of processing order and can therefore be added to the processing times. However, in some situations this assumption is not true, which makes sequencing more difficult. The problem in this case is to determine the sequence which has the minimum total setup time.

Consider the following table, which shows setup times based on job order. For example, if job A is followed by job B, the setup time for B will be six hours. Furthermore, if job C follows job B, it will have a setup time of four hours. If a job is done first, its setup time is shown in the Initial Setup Time column to the right of the job. Thus, if job A is done first, its setup time will be three hours.

		Initial Setup Time (hours)	Resulting Following Job Setup Time (hours) Is		
			A	B	C
If the Preceding Job Is	A	3	–	6	2
	B	2	1	–	4
	C	2	5	3	–

The simplest way to determine which sequence will result in the smallest total setup time is to list each possible sequence and determine its total setup time. In general, the number of different alternatives is $n!$ (i.e., n factorial), where n is the number of jobs. Here, n is 3, so $n! = 3 \times 2 \times 1 = 6$. The six alternatives and their total setup times are:

Sequence	Setup Times Total
A-B-C	$3 + 6 + 4 = 13$
A-C-B	$3 + 2 + 3 = 8$
B-A-C	$2 + 1 + 2 = 5$ (smallest)
B-C-A	$2 + 4 + 5 = 11$
C-A-B	$2 + 5 + 6 = 13$
C-B-A	$2 + 3 + 1 = 6$

Hence, to minimize total setup time the scheduler would select sequence B-A-C.

This procedure is relatively simple to do manually when the number of jobs is small. However, as the number of jobs increases, the number of sequences increases exponentially. For example, six jobs would have 720 sequences. In such instances, a scheduler should employ a computer to generate the list and identify the best sequence or use a scheduling software.

Sequencing Jobs Through One Work Centre/Machine in Order to Minimize Number of Late Jobs

Moore's rule is a technique to minimize the number of late jobs for a group of jobs to be processed on one work centre/machine.[2] For the technique to work, the following conditions must be satisfied:

1. Job time (setup and processing) must be known for each job at the work centre/machine.

> **Moore's rule** A technique to minimize the number of late jobs for a group of jobs to be processed on one work centre/machine.

_____

[2] J. M. Moore, "An *N* Job, One Machine Sequencing Algorithm for Minimizing the Number of Late Jobs," *Management Science*, 15(1), September 1968, pp. 102–109.

2. Job times must be independent of the job sequence.

3. Job due dates must be known for each job.

Determination of the optimal sequence involves these steps:

1. Schedule the jobs by EDD rule.

2. Find the first late job in the current sequence. If none are late, go to Step 4.

3. Consider all jobs scheduled up to and including the first late job. Reject the job with the largest processing time (break ties arbitrarily), and remove it from the current sequence. Return to Step 2.

4. The optimal sequence is the current sequence followed by any rejected jobs (in any order).

EXAMPLE 16-5

Processing times (including setup times) and due dates for five jobs that arrived today and are waiting to be processed at the only machine in a shop are given below. Determine the sequence of jobs that will minimize the total number of late jobs.

Job	Processing Time (days)	Due Date (days from now)
A	2	5
B	8	8
C	5	12
D	6	10
E	1	4

SOLUTION

a. Using the earliest due date (EDD) rule, the job sequence is E-A-B-D-C. Using this sequence, calculate the completion date for each job and compare it with the job's due date. We stop the first time a job is late.

Job	Processing Time (days)	Completion Date	Due Date	Late?
E	1	1	4	no
A	2	3	5	no
B	8	11	8	yes
D	6		10	
C	5		12	

Job B is the first job late because its due date (8) is earlier than its completion date (11). Consider jobs E, A, and B. Job B has the largest processing time of these jobs: 8 = max {1, 2, 8}. Therefore, reject job B (that is, remove it from the EDD sequence).

b. Now, using the job sequence E-A-D-C:

Job	Processing Time (days)	Completion Date	Due Date	Late?
E	1	1	4	no
A	2	3	5	no
D	6	9	10	no
C	5	14	12	yes

The first job late is job C. Consider jobs E, A, D, and C. Job D has the largest processing time of these jobs: 6 = max {1, 2, 6, 5}. Therefore, reject job D. There are no more jobs. Optimal sequence is either E-A-C-B-D or E-A-C-D-B with two late jobs.

Sequencing Jobs Through Three or More Work Centres/Machines in Order to Minimize Make-Span

When the jobs have to be processed on three or more machines/work centres, the problem becomes very difficult to solve to optimality for any objective function including make-span. There are several heuristics to solve the flow shop (i.e., when the jobs have to go through the machines in the same order) version of the problem with the objective of minimizing the make-span. One heuristic that usually works well is the **CDS heuristic**.[3]

Let t_{ij} = Processing time of job i on machine j. The CDS heuristic is as follows:

1. Convert the m-machine, n-job problem into $m - 1$ surrogate two-machine n-job problems where the time of job i on machine 1 in surrogate problem k, $k = 1, \cdots, m - 1$, is $(t_{i1} + \cdots + t_{ik})$ and time of job i on machine 2 in surrogate problem k is $(t_{im} + \cdots + t_{i(m - k + 1)})$.

2. Solve each surrogate problem using Johnson's rule and determine the sequence.

3. Calculate the make-span of the original m-machine problem for each sequence derived in Step 2, and choose the one with smallest make-span.

> **CDS heuristic** A quick way to find a good solution to the problem of minimizing make-span of a set of jobs to be processed on three or more machines/work centres in the same order.

EXAMPLE 16-6

Processing times (including setup times) for four jobs that arrived today and are waiting to be processed in the same order on three machines in a shop are given below. Determine the sequence of jobs that will likely have minimum make-span.

Job	Processing Time (hours)		
	Machine 1	Machine 2	Machine 3
A	6	5	5
B	8	1	4
C	3	5	4
D	4	4	2

SOLUTION

a. Surrogate problem 1. Note: Times of Machine "1" = Machine 1, and times of Machine "2" = Machine 3.

Job	Processing Time (hours)	
	Machine "1"	Machine "2"
A	6	5
B	8	4
C	3	4
D	4	2

The optimal sequence that minimizes the make-span of the above surrogate problem, using Johnson's rule, is: C-A-B-D.

b. Surrogate problem 2. Note: Times of Machine "1" = Machine 1 + Machine 2, and times of Machine "2" = Machine 3 + Machine 2.

Job	Processing Time (hours)	
	Machine "1"	Machine "2"
A	11	10
B	9	5
C	8	9
D	8	6

The optimal sequence that minimizes the make-span of the above surrogate problem, using Johnson's rule, is: C-A-D-B.

c. The make-span of the original problem for sequence C-A-B-D, obtained for surrogate problem 1, is 27:

Sequence	Completion Time (hours)		
	Machine 1	Machine 2	Machine 3
C	3	8	12
A	9	14	19
B	17	18	23
D	21	25	27

The make-span of the original problem for sequence C-A-D-B, obtained for surrogate problem 2, is 26:

Sequence	Completion Time (hours)		
	Machine 1	Machine 2	Machine 3
C	3	8	12
A	9	14	19
D	13	18	21
B	21	22	26

Therefore, the CDS sequence is C-A-D-B, which has the lower make-span of 26 hours. This is likely the optimal sequence.

---

[3] H. G. Campbell, R. A. Dudek, and M. L. Smith, "A Heuristic Algorithm of the n-Job, m-Machine Sequencing Problem," *Management Science*, 1970, 16, pp. B630–B637.

For an example of assignment and sequencing problems, see the "Sivaco" OM in Action.

 OM in Action http://www.sivaco.com/sivacoquebec/

Sivaco

Sivaco, in Marieville, Quebec, produces steel wires for bed and garage springs, rivets, and various types of cables to customer order. Sivaco is part of Heico Wire Group, which itself is part of Heico companies, a $2 billion private conglomerate. The raw materials are spools of wires that are pickled (acid washed), possibly annealed (heat treated in ovens), cold drawn (pulled through an orifice to reduce their diameter in 40 nonidentical machines), galvanized (coated with zinc), and re-spooled. The assignment of the wire drawing machine for an order depends on setup time/cost, appropriateness and availability of machine, and due date of the job. Setup time/cost depends on the diameter of input to and output from drawing. Heat treatment in an oven is done in batches of spools based on the required temperature and duration (7–62 hours). Some jobs are simple and require only pickling and drawing, but others are complex, requiring, for example, pickling, annealing, re-pickling, drawing, and galvanizing.

Until 2002, Sivaco used a simple home-grown program (integrated in its ERP) for scheduling jobs, but many complex production rules, known only to the experienced schedulers, were not included in the software. Therefore, order promise dates were not accurate and the availability of the raw material was not considered in the schedule, resulting in borrowing raw material from other orders. Then Sivaco purchased and installed Preactor 400, a popular scheduling software (now part of Siemens). Because wire drawing is the bottleneck operation for Sivaco, it is scheduled before the other operations. Much time was spent identifying and incorporating the complex production rules into Preactor. The scheduling engine creates dynamic clusters of jobs for the wire drawing operation based on hierarchical product similarities that minimize sequence-dependent setup time/cost, but also considers the appropriateness and availability of machines and the due dates of jobs. Also, a bin packing program has been written in Preactor to maximize the number of similar spools used in each oven. Scheduling time is now reduced from one hour to five minutes.

Source: http://www.preactor.com/Case-Study/Case-Studies/Sivaco# .U6zNDE18P5o.

Shop-Floor Control

Shop-floor control, or production activity control, involves the execution of the job schedule; maintenance, communication, and monitoring of the status of material, orders, and process; and taking any necessary actions. Also, shop-floor control measures the efficiency and utilization of the workforce and machines.

Tools for shop-floor control include:

- *Daily dispatch list:* a list of jobs to be run in priority sequence for each work centre/machine. The dispatch list is also called the work centre/machine schedule.
- *Anticipated delay report:* a report issued by manufacturing and purchasing regarding late shop and purchase orders, causes of delay, actions taken, and new due dates.
- *Input/output control report:* a report used to manage the work inflows and outflows at each work centre/machine.
- *Schedule Gantt chart:* a chart used to monitor the progress of jobs.

Usually a manufacturing execution system generates the above list/reports/chart. A **manufacturing execution system (MES)** is a factory floor information and communication system capable of resource allocation, job scheduling, dispatching, performance analysis, reporting, etc. See, for example, the "Mattec MES" OM in Action.

shop-floor control Execution of the schedule; maintaining, communicating, and monitoring the status of material, orders, and process; and taking any necessary actions.

manufacturing execution system (MES) A factory floor information and communication system capable of resource allocation, job scheduling, dispatching, performance analysis, reporting, etc.

OM in Action

Mattec MES

Mattec Manufacturing Execution System (MES), now part of Epicor, is a popular production control software used especially by plastic injection moulding plants. It collects shop floor status information (on machines and jobs) both automatically from machines and through in-shop communication equipment used by the operators. Data includes whether a machine is running or is down (and the reason for this), its speed and quality (SPC data), number of good parts produced for a job, and how many hours are left to complete the job. The data also includes number of times a particular tool or die is used, so that it can be replaced in time. Mattec MES can display real-time status of all machines, and detailed production information for each machine/job. The Mattec scheduler can automatically schedule a job on the most efficient machine, assist in rescheduling jobs, and report tool conflicts. The real-time information is used by shop management to reduce scrap and improve quality, increase uptime (by performing corrective actions and preventive maintenance), and reduce cycle times. Canadian companies using Mattec MES include Canplas Industries of Barrie, ON, which makes plastic plumbing, ventilation, and vacuum fittings; Chrysler's die casting shop in Etobicoke, ON, which makes pistons, brackets, and housings; Lakeside Plastics of Oldcastle, ON, which makes thermoplastic trims for cars; and Starplex Scientific of Etobicoke, ON, which makes plastic food, beverage, and drug containers.

Sources: http://www.epicor.com/Company/PressRoom/Pages/Success Stories.aspx; mattecsupport.com/products/phepm/page2.htm.

Schedule Gantt Chart

A manager often uses a **schedule Gantt chart** to monitor the progress of a job. The vertical axis shows the activities, and the horizontal axis shows the time and the progress of activities. The chart indicates which jobs or their components are on schedule and which are behind or ahead. A typical schedule Gantt chart for a landscaping service is shown in Figure 16-3. It shows the planned and

schedule Gantt chart A Gantt chart that shows the progress of the activities and whether they are on schedule.

Component/Week	1	2	3	4	5	6	7
Drawings	[Approval]						
Site		[Preparation]					
Trees		[Order]		[Receive]	[Plant]		
Shrubs		[Order]		[Receive]		[Plant]	
Final Inspection							[Approval]

Scheduled   [   ]   Now

Actual progress

◀ FIGURE 16-3

Schedule Gantt chart for a landscaping job.

actual starting and finishing times for the five components of the job. The scheduled times are shown with red square brackets and actual times are shown with blue horizontal bars. The chart indicates that approval of the drawings and the ordering of trees and shrubs were on schedule. The site preparation was a bit behind schedule. The trees were received earlier than expected, and planting started ahead of schedule. However, the shrubs have not yet been received. The chart indicates some slack between scheduled receipt of shrubs and shrub planting, so if the shrubs arrive by the end of the week, the schedule can still be met.

Input/Output Control

Input/output (I/O) control is used to manage the work inflows and outflows at each work centre/machine. Without I/O control, demand (i.e., work inflow) may exceed processing capacity, causing an overload at the work centre/machine. Conversely, work may arrive slower than the rate a work centre/machine can handle, leaving the work centre underutilized ("starved"). Ideally, a balance can be struck between the input and output rates, thereby achieving effective use of work centre/machine capacity without experiencing excessive queues or starvation at the work centre/machine. See Figure 16-4 for a water tank analogy.

input/output (I/O) control Used to manage the work inflows and outflows at each work centre/machine.

FIGURE 16-4 ▶

Input/output control for a work centre/machine is like control of the input and output valves of a water tank so that there will be enough water in the tank for a continuous supply of water.

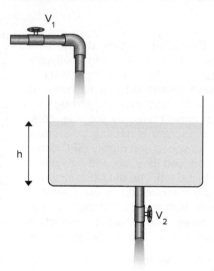

Input/output control is done by periodically generating planned inputs and outputs for each work centre/machine, comparing the actual inputs and outputs to them, and making changes if necessary. The planned inputs and outputs come from the capacity requirement planning system, and are then approved by manufacturing management. Comparing planned and actual inflow may indicate a problem with inflow, and comparing planned and actual outflow may indicate a problem with the work centre/machine production.

Figure 16-5 illustrates an input/output report for a work centre. A key portion of the report is the WIP waiting to be processed (in the bottom). The report highlights deviations from planned for both input and output. The deviations in each period are determined by subtracting "Planned" from "Actual." For example, in the first period, subtracting the planned input of 100 hours from the actual input of 120 hours produces a deviation of +20 hours. Similarly, in the first period, the planned and actual outputs are equal, producing a deviation of zero hours. The WIP for each period is determined by subtracting the actual output from the actual input and adjusting the WIP from the previous period by that amount. For example, in the first period, actual input exceeds actual output by 10 hours. Hence, the current WIP of 40 hours is increased by 10 hours to 50 hours. It appears that the production controller planned inputs lower than outputs, therefore reducing the WIP to zero, which is not usually desirable.

Period (week)

	1	2	3	4	5	6
Input Planned	100	100	90	90	90	90
Actual	120	95	80	88	93	94
Deviation	+20	−5	−10	−2	+3	+4
Cum. dev.	+20	+15	+5	+3	+6	+10

	1	2	3	4	5	6
Output Planned	110	110	100	100	100	95
Actual	110	105	95	101	103	96
Deviation	0	−5	−5	+1	+3	+1
Cum. dev.	0	−5	−10	−9	−6	−5

WIP*	40	50	40	25	12	2	0

*Note: Figures represent standard hours of processing time.

◀ **FIGURE 16-5**

An input/output report for a work centre.

Difficulty of Scheduling and Using the Bottleneck Operation

Why Scheduling Can Be Difficult

Scheduling can be difficult because of variability in setup and processing times, interruptions, and changes in the set of jobs. Another reason is that, except for very small problems, there is no practical method for identifying the optimal schedule. Job shops where each job may need a different sequence of operations are especially hard to schedule. See Example 16-7 for an illustration.

◀ **EXAMPLE 16-7**

A shop has one lathe, one milling machine, one grinding machine, and one vertical drill. Five jobs must be processed in the operations sequence given in the table below (from top down), with processing times given to the right of the machine name. For example, for job 1, first one hour on the drill is required, then two hours on the lathe, etc. The four machines are available starting tomorrow morning and there is no WIP in the shop. Also, the due hour of each job is at the end of tomorrow's shift; that is, at the end of hour 8. Hours 9 to 14 correspond to the first six hours of the day after tomorrow. Setup times are included in the processing times. It is possible to interrupt the processing of a job on a machine (without increasing its setup time). Determine the schedule that meets the due hours.

Operations Sequence	Job 1		Job 2		Job 3		Job 4		Job 5	
1.			Lathe	2	Grind	2	Drill	1	Mill	1
	Drill	1								
2.	Lathe	2	Mill	2	Drill	2	Grind	2	Drill	1
3.	Grind	1	Grind	1	Mill	2	Lathe	1	Lathe	1
4.	Mill	2	Drill	2	Lathe	2			Grind	2
Total (hours)	6		7		8		4		5	

SOLUTION

All five jobs have the same due hour, so EDD will not provide a specific sequence. The shortest remaining processing time (SRPT) rule results in the sequence 4-5-1-2-3. In the following table, first job 4 is scheduled all the way on all machines (this is called *job-based or horizontal scheduling*):

4-	Hours													
	1	2	3	4	5	6	7	8	9	10	11	12	13	14
Lathe				4										
Mill														
Grind		4	4											
Drill	4													

then job 5:

4-5-	Hours													
	1	2	3	4	5	6	7	8	9	10	11	12	13	14
Lathe			5	4										
Mill	5													
Grind			4	4	5	5								
Drill	4	5												

then job 1:

4-5-1-	Hours													
	1	2	3	4	5	6	7	8	9	10	11	12	13	14
Lathe			5	4	1	1								
Mill	5								1	1				
Grind			4	4	5	5		1						
Drill	4	5	1											

then job 2:

4-5-1-2-	Hours													
	1	2	3	4	5	6	7	8	9	10	11	12	13	14
Lathe	2	2	5	4	1	1								
Mill	5		2	2					1	1				
Grind			4	4	5	5	2	1						
Drill	4	5	1					2	2					

and finally job 3:

4-5-1-2-3	Hours													
	1	2	3	4	5	6	7	8	9	10	11	12	13	14
Lathe	2	2	5	4	1	1							3	3
Mill	5		2	2					1	1		3	3	
Grind	3	4	4	5	5	2	1	3						
Drill	4	5	1				2	2	3	3				

We observe that the above schedule results in job 3 being six hours late, and job 1 being one hour late. The minimum slack time (MST) rule results in the opposite sequence: 3-2-1-5-4. It can be shown that this sequence will have the following schedule (using job-based loading):

3-2-1-5-4	Hours													
	1	2	3	4	5	6	7	8	9	10	11	12	13	14
Lathe	2	2	1	1	5		3	3			4			
Mill	5		2	2	3	3	1	1						
Grind	3	3			2	1	5	5	4	4				
Drill	1	5	3	3	4	2	2							

Even though the MST rule performs better than the SRPT rule, its schedule still results in job 4 being three hours late.

As you can see in Example 16-7, scheduling in a job shop is very difficult. One needs to try various sequences and choose the best. The problem is that there are too many sequences. Note that we made many simplifying assumptions. In general, there is WIP in the shop, the processing time estimates may be inaccurate, a machine could break down, an operator may become ill, setup times may be sequence-dependent, and jobs could be split and transferred to the next operation in smaller batch sizes (called a *transfer batch*).

How to Reduce Scheduling Difficulty

- Set realistic due dates.
- Focus on the bottleneck operation: schedule the bottleneck operation first, and then schedule the non-bottleneck operations around the bottleneck operation. Don't interrupt the bottleneck operation. More on this in "Theory of Constraints" below.
- For non-bottleneck operations, consider lot-splitting for large jobs (transfer a portion of the job after it is done in a work centre/machine to the next operation).
- Use a scheduling software.
- Use shop-floor control and reschedule frequently, for example, every day.

Theory of Constraints

Theory of constraints (TOC) is a method for identifying the most important limiting factor (i.e., the bottleneck) that stands in the way of achieving maximum productivity and then systematically improving that constraint until it is no longer the limiting factor. TOC was developed by Eli Goldratt in the 1980s and illustrated in his book *The Goal*.[4]

TOC is based on the following observation: Because the output of a process is limited by the output of the bottleneck operation, it is essential to schedule the bottleneck operation first and then schedule the non-bottleneck operations in a way that minimizes the disruption to the bottleneck operation. Thus, idle times of non-bottleneck operations are not a factor in overall capacity of the system, as long as the bottleneck operation is used effectively. Note that TOC applies only when there is a permanent bottleneck operation. In many cases, the bottleneck operation changes as the product mix changes.

TOC uses the *drum-buffer-rope* concept to manage the process. The "drum" is the master schedule; it sets the pace of the production of the bottleneck operation. The "buffer" refers to inventory just before the bottleneck operation. The "rope" represents the synchronizing of non-bottleneck operations feeding the bottleneck operation to ensure that these non-bottleneck operations produce the right quantities of products and at the right times. The goal is to avoid costly and time-consuming multiple setups at the bottleneck operation.

> **theory of constraints (TOC)** A method for identifying the most important limiting factor (i.e., the bottleneck) that stands in the way of achieving maximum productivity and then systematically improving that constraint until it is no longer the limiting factor.

---

[4] Eliyahu M. Goldratt and Jeff Cox, *The Goal: Excellence in Manufacturing* (New York: North River Press), 1984. For a summary of the book, see http://maaw.info/ArticleSummaries/ArtSumTheGoal.htm.

TOC also uses varying batch sizes at non-bottleneck operations to achieve the greatest output of the bottleneck operation. The term *process batch* denotes the production lot size for a job, and *transfer batch* denotes a portion of the production lot that could be moved to the bottleneck operation. The "OFD (Oregon Freeze Dry)" OM in Action is an application of the drum-buffer-rope technique.

 OM in Action   www.ofd.com

OFD (Oregon Freeze Dry)

OFD has three plants on a 35 acre site (with 300 workers) that freeze-dry vegetables, fruits, and meats by removing their water at low temperature and pressure. After the product is frozen, the ice is evaporated without melting it into water in the low-pressure drying chambers. Freeze-drying retains the flavour, and the natural structure of the food is regained by adding water at the time of consumption. Production begins with wet processing of products—a labour-intensive operation involving activities such as cooking or heating. The next step is freezing. This is a capital-intensive operation that uses one of the six very large freezers. The product is then processed through one of 32 dryers (low-pressure chambers). The drying operation is also capital intensive and may take from 8 to 50 hours (depending on the product), although 14 to 20 hours is typical. The final step is dry processing—a labour-intensive step including activities such as blending, packaging, and boxing.

Before, the production was scheduled on a make-to-stock basis according to predetermined batch sizes and sequence. This resulted in large inventories of finished goods and WIP in the freezers, which increased the production lead times and caused the company to be slow in responding to customer orders that could not be satisfied from finished goods. In addition, it resulted in extensive costly overtime and disruptive expediting efforts. Meanwhile, the plants were overstocked with products for which there were no current orders.

Specifically, materials were released for processing according to production schedule, available wet-processing capacity, and available storage space

for the accumulated WIP (in the freezers). The wet-processing schedule drove all other operations as in a *push system*. There were no formal schedules for the freezers, dryers, or dry processing. Typically, about six to eight weeks' worth of demand for each product was processed. The highly variable production times created a "feast or famine" environment in the various operations in which periods of work overload were followed by periods in which there was nothing to do.

Then the company implemented the drum-buffer-rope technique. The capacity analysis clearly indicated that wet processing and dry processing were not constraints. The constraint (i.e., bottleneck) was drying. The dryer schedule was set based on market demand and dryer capacity. The schedules of all other departments were subordinated to the dryer schedule, which fully utilized dryer capacity. Specifically, materials were released to wet processing at the rate dictated by the dryer schedule (offset by lead times). See the process flow diagram with the drum-buffer-rope illustration. As a result, the wet-processing department could not overproduce and cause excess WIP inventory in the freezers. Furthermore, having a set schedule at the dryers resulted in a predictable product flow to downstream operation at dry processing. The dryer schedule provided greater visibility to future work schedules in wet and dry processing and made the labour requirements in these departments smoother and predictable. Monitoring the buffer inventory in the freezers highlights when the system is having a problem.

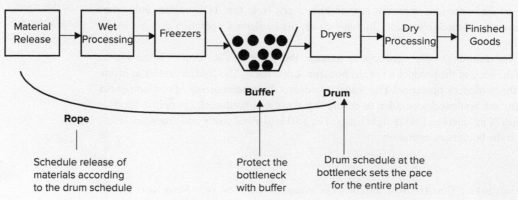

© Oregon Freeze Dry, Inc.

A bank of dryers at OFD.

Source: M. Umble et al., "Integrating Enterprise Resources Planning and Theory of Constraints: A Case Study," *Production and Inventory Management Journal* 42(2), pp. 43–48.

Staff Scheduling

Staff scheduling involves determining the workdays and the start and end times of work on each workday for each employee. Staff scheduling in a manufacturing company is usually easy: a typical company works eight hours a day (e.g., 9:00 a.m. to 5:00 p.m.) and five days a week (Mon–Fri), a total of 40 hours a week (i.e., full-time employment) for all its employees. If it is very busy, overtime or a second shift (e.g., 5:00 p.m. to 1:00 a.m., Mon–Fri) can be instituted. Some processing companies such as pulp and paper mills operate continuously: 24 hours a day, seven days a week. They use four sets of full-time shifts in a week, possibly rotating the shifts among employees so that everyone gets to work the unpopular night and weekend shifts.

> **staff scheduling**
> Determining the workdays, and start and end times on each workday, for each employee.

On the other hand, staff scheduling in services presents certain problems not generally encountered in manufacturing. This is due primarily to (1) the inability to store services, and (2) the random nature and timing of customer requests for service (unless appointments can be used). For this reason, in this section we will focus on staff scheduling in services such as a restaurant or an airline. Employment can be full-time (40 hours a week) or part-time (e.g., 20 hours a week). Three staff scheduling problems are considered in this section:

a. Many services operate every day (i.e., seven days a week). However, employees usually work only five consecutive days and then receive two days off. The problem is to determine the minimum number of full-time workers with five consecutive days of work and two consecutive days off that meets the daily staff requirements in a week.

b. Usually a service employee works during a given "shift" (i.e., a period with fixed start and end times). The problem is to determine a set of shifts with minimum total duration that meet the hourly staff requirements in a day.

c. A complex staffing problem arises while scheduling an airline's pilots (and, to a lesser degree, flight attendants). Besides time, location also plays a role because a pilot has a home base and needs to get back there after a few days.

For an application of staff scheduling software developed for law enforcement, see the "InTime Solutions" OM in Action.

 **OM in Action**

InTime Solutions

InTime Solutions is a Vancouver software developer for law-enforcement employee scheduling. The InTime Scheduling Engine (ISE) integrates with time and attendance equipment, the organization's ERP payroll program, and courts and subpoena databases. ISE is used by over 400 police departments in North America such as Calgary, Thunder Bay, and Saint John police services. ISE also has an employee self-service web portal that allows employees to sign up for overtime shifts, request leave, swap shifts, etc. ISE keeps track of overtime, the training and skill sets of employees, and equipment (assets such as rifles, laptops, and vehicles) assigned to each officer. ISE issues daily rosters, reports early/late employees, keeps work history, issues notifications, and estimates the cost of policing an event.

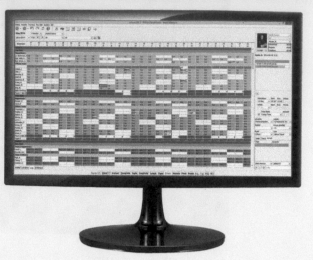

Source: http://www.intimesoft.com.

Courtesy of InTime Solutions

Scheduling Two Consecutive Days Off

First, based on forecast demand for service, we have to determine the number of staff needed per day. We assume that the weekly demand for staff is fairly stable from week to week, but daily demand for staff varies. For example, the daily full-time kitchen-staff requirements in a week for a small restaurant are as follows:

Day	Mon	Tue	Wed	Thu	Fri	Sat	Sun
Staff needs	2	4	3	4	6	5	5

A fairly simple but effective approach for determining the minimum number of workers needed (who work five consecutive days and then take two consecutive days off) is the following:[5]

1. Write "Worker 1" under "Staff needs" and rewrite the daily staff needs for worker 1 (see table below). Find two consecutive days with the lowest maximum daily staff needs. Here Mon–Tue, Tue–Wed, and Wed–Thu all have a maximum of four staff needs. Among these three pairs, choose the one with minimum sum of staff needs: min (2 + 4, 4 + 3, 3 + 4) = 6. Therefore, Mon–Tue should be the two consecutive days off for worker 1. Box those days. *(Note:* In case of a further tie, pick the pair whose previous day is not part of the pairs in the tie.)

Day	Mon	Tue	Wed	Thu	Fri	Sat	Sun
Staff needs	2	4	3	4	6	5	5
Worker 1	2	4	3	4	6	5	5

2. Write "Worker 2" under "Worker 1." Subtract one from each day's staff needs in the row of Worker 1, except for the boxed days, and write them in front of Worker 2. See the following table. These are the remaining staff needs. Assign worker 2's days off using the lowest maximum daily remaining staff needs of two consecutive days. Wed–Thu has the lowest maximum (3) of any consecutive pair of days of staff needs in front of Worker 2. Box those days.

---

[5] R. Tibrewala et al., "Optimal Scheduling of Two Consecutive Idle Periods," *Management Science* 19(1), pp. 71–75.

Day	Mon	Tue	Wed	Thu	Fri	Sat	Sun
Staff needs	2	4	3	4	6	5	5
Worker 1	2	4	3	4	6	5	5
Worker 2	2	4	2	3	5	4	4

3. Write "Worker 3" under "Worker 2." Subtract one from each day's remaining staff needs, except for the boxed days, and write them in front of Worker 3 (see table below). Assign worker 3's days off using the lowest maximum remaining staff needs of two consecutive days. In this case, Mon–Tue, Tue–Wed, Wed–Thu, Sat–Sun, and Sun–Mon all have a maximum remaining staff needs of three employees. The sum of Mon–Tue and Sun–Mon is the smallest $(1 + 3 = 4)$ among these five pairs. The day before Sun (i.e., Sat) is not part of these two tied pairs. Therefore, box Sun–Mon as the third employee's days off, and repeat the preceding steps for each additional worker until all staffing needs have been met (see below). *Note:* Don't subtract from zero.

Day	Mon	Tue	Wed	Thu	Fri	Sat	Sun
Staff needs	2	4	3	4	6	5	5
Worker 1	2	4	3	4	6	5	5
Worker 2	2	4	2	3	5	4	4
Worker 3	1	3	2	3	4	3	3
Worker 4	1	2	1	2	3	2	3
Worker 5	1	2	0	1	2	1	2
Worker 6	0	1	0	1	1	0	1
Worker 7	0	0	0	0	1	0	0
Number working:	4	5	5	5	6	5	5

To identify the days each worker is working, go across each worker's row to find the values that are not boxed. Similarly, to find the workers who are assigned to work during any particular day, go down that day's column to find the values that are not boxed. *Note:* Worker 6 is needed to work only three days, and worker 7 is needed only *one* day. Perhaps two part-time employees can be found to work these days.

Shift Scheduling

Many services have to meet uneven customer demand throughout a day. For example, restaurants have peak lunch and supper demands. To meet a peak demand but save on wages, short shifts (for example, three to four hours long, staffed by part-time workers) are commonly used. A part-time worker works up to five days a week, and usually has limitations on his availability times.

Usually, the work schedule is determined for the following week. It involves the following steps:

1. Forecast the amount of work that needs to be done during each hour of each day next week.

2. Convert the work into the number of workers required during each hour of each day.

3. Try to cover these requirements with a minimum number of shifts.

4. Assign the shifts to staff according to their skill, availability, and agreed-upon total weekly work hours. A common method is assign the shifts according to staff preference, staff ordered by seniority.

For Step 2, company standards may exist that specify labour hours required per sales dollar forecasted (this may be called a *manning chart*).

We will focus on Step 3 (called *shift scheduling*) and illustrate it with an example from McDonald's. We will focus on shifts for the part-time employees and leave out the scheduling of managers who are typically full-time and whose shifts are straightforward. For example, for a McDonald's restaurant that is open 24 hours a day, a manager's shift could be one of: 6:00 a.m. → 2:00 p.m., noon → 8:00 p.m., 2:00 p.m. → 10:00 p.m., or 10:00 p.m. → 6 a.m., five days a week. Note that peak times are covered by more than one manager.

While we will perform shift scheduling manually, McDonald's Canada uses a sophisticated software called ESP by ThoughtWorks, a Toronto software company. ESP also performs Step 1: Forecasting, Step 2: Converting the forecasts using manning charts, and Step 4: Assigning employees to the derived shifts using a complex heuristic procedure (called simulated annealing). See the "ESP by ThoughtWorks Inc." OM in Action.

OM in Action

ESP by ThoughtWorks Inc.

The employee scheduling program (ESP) of Thought-Works Software Solutions, of Dundas, Ontario, is used by major fast-food chains such as McDonald's. ESP allows the restaurant manager to enter the information on:

- Each employee, including skill level and qualifications to work at one or more of the stations (e.g., front counter, assembly board, fries), hours and days available, and maximum hours in a day or in a week he/she can work.

- Staffing requirements for each station based on expected sales during each hour of next week (called *positioning guide* or *manning chart*).

- Any fixed shifts (e.g., specific hours for receiving material) as deemed necessary by the manager.

- Operating hours, shift lengths and their desirability during various times of the day, and preferences such as desired average skill level for a station during a particular period, and fairness (giving part-time workers approximately equal numbers of hours in a week).

- Sales each hour of past weeks.

ESP will use the history of sales from the past few weeks or year to forecast next week's sales on an hourly basis (using the moving average method). Then, using the positioning guide, it will determine the number of staff (excluding the managers) required in each station. Next, using linear programming, ESP determines feasible shifts to cover the required staff every hour. Finally, ESP will assign the employees to the chosen shifts according to their availability, skill level, maximum hours and days, and fairness.

Source: http://www.thoughtworksinc.com.

Shift Scheduling Heuristic. Our manual shift scheduling heuristic technique for *three- to eight-hour*-long shifts is as follows:

1. Start from the opening hour:

   i. Determine the length of the shift as follows: Begin with a three-hour shift. Increase it by one hour if the number of staff required during the next hour is not smaller than the maximum number of staff required so far on the shift. Continue. Stop if the shift is eight hours long.

   ii. Set the number of workers on this shift equal to 1 and reduce the number of staff required for each hour of this shift by 1. Repeat Step (i) if the number of staff required (still not met) at the beginning of this shift is not zero.

2. Move to the next hour with a positive number of staff required (still not met). Repeat Steps 1(i) and (ii), and continue until all the requirements (still not met) are 0.

This heuristic is illustrated by Example 16-8.

A McDonald's restaurant uses the following manning chart (positioning guide) for the regular menu (we will focus on the 5:00 a.m. to 11:00 p.m. period):

Sales/Hour ($)	Counter	Drive-Through	CSA	Assembly Board	Grill	French Fries
0–162	1	1			1	
163–223	1	1		1	1	
224–338	1	2		1	1	
339–395	1	2		2	1	
396–492	2	2		2	1	
493–542	2	2		2	1	1
543–621	2	2		3	1	1
622–723	2	3		3	1	1
724–905	2	3	1	4	1	1
906–1,109	3	3	1	4	1	1
>1,110	3	3	1	5	1	1

The hourly forecast sales for a particular day, from 5:00 a.m. until 11:00 p.m., were:

5–6	6–7	7–8	8–9	9–10	10–11	11–noon	noon–1	1–2	2–3	3–4
$20	$90	$180	$320	$410	$410	$920	$1,260	$630	$420	$360

4–5	5–6	6–7	7–8	8–9	9–10	10–11
$590	$1,040	$1,040	$810	$390	$340	$240

a. Determine the number of drive-through (DT) staff required during each hour.

b. Determine the DT shifts (*three to eight hours* long) using the shift scheduling heuristic.

SOLUTION

a. The number of DT staff required during each hour is determined based on the hour's forecast sales and the manning chart (see the following table, the second column from the left). For example, between 8:00 a.m. and 9:00 a.m., the forecast sales are $320, which falls within the $224–$338 sales/hour range in the manning chart. Therefore, two DT employees are required then.

b. Shifts S_1, S_2, ... are created to meet or exceed the DT staff requirements determined in part *a*. S_1's length is the maximum eight hours because the number of DT staff required is not decreasing from 5:00 a.m. until 1:00 p.m. Set the number of DT staff on $S_1 = 1$, and calculate number of staff required, still not met, N_1:

N_1 = original requirement − 1,   during any hour of S_1
  = original requirement,   during any other hour.

Shift 2 (S_2) starts at 8:00 a.m. because that is the first hour when N_1 is positive. The length of S_2 is only six hours because N_1 starts decreasing after 2:00 p.m. Set the number of DT staff on $S_2 = 1$ and calculate the number of staff required, still not met, N_2:

$N_2 = N_1 − 1$, during any hour of S_2
  = N_1,   during any other hour.

Shift 3 (S_3) starts at 11:00 a.m. because that is the first hour when N_2 is positive. The length of S_3 is eight hours because N_2 does not decrease until 8:00 p.m. Set the number of DT staff on $S_3 = 1$ and calculate the number of staff required, still not met, N_3:

$N_3 = N_2 - 1$, during any hour of S_3

$\quad = N_2$, during any other hour.

Shift 4 (S_4) starts at 1:00 p.m. because that is the first hour when N_3 is positive. The length of S_4 is seven hours because N_3 starts decreasing after 8:00 p.m. Set the number of DT staff on $S_4 = 1$ and calculate the number of staff required, still not met, N_4:

$N_4 = N_3 - 1$, during any hour of S_4

$\quad = N_3$, during any other hour.

Shift 5 (S_5) starts at 5:00 p.m. because that is the first hour when N_4 is positive. The length of S_5 is six hours because N_4 does not decrease and 11:00 p.m. is assumed to be the end of the operating time. Set the number of DT staff on $S_5 = 1$ and calculate the number of staff required, still not met, N_5:

$N_5 = N_4 - 1$, during any hour of S_5

$\quad = N_4$, during any other hour.

Shift 6 (S_6) starts at 7:00 p.m. because that is the first hour when N_5 is positive. The length of S_6 is four hours because N_5 does not decrease and 11:00 p.m. is assumed to be the end of the operating time. Set the number of DT staff on $S_6 = 1$ and calculate the number of staff required, still not met, N_6:

$N_6 = N_5 - 1$, during any hour of S_6

$\quad = N_5$, during any other hour.

Because N_6 is all zeros, all staff requirements have been met. There is no need for another shift.

	Forecast Sales	DT Staff Required	S_1 1	N_1	S_2 1	N_2	S_3 1	N_3	S_4 1	N_4	S_5 1	N_5	S_6 1	N_6
5 am														
6	$20	1		0										
7	90	1		0										
8	180	1		0										
9	320	2		1										
10	410	2		1		0								
11	410	2		1		0								
Noon	920	3		2		1		0						
1 pm	1,260	3		2		1		0						
2	630	3		3		2		1		0				
3	420	2		2		2		1		0				
4	360	2		2		2		1		0				
5	590	2		2		2		1		0				
6	1,040	3		3		3		2		1		0		
7	1,040	3		3		3		2		1		0		
8	810	3		3		3		3		2		1		0
9	390	2		2		2		2		2		1		0
10	340	2		2		2		2		2		1		0
11	240	2		2		2		2		2		1		0

A very similar employee scheduling method is used by Hard Rock Cafe (see the OM in Action below).

 OM in Action

Employee Scheduling in Hard Rock Cafe

At the end of 2015, Hard Rock Cafe had 191 locations (restaurants, hotels, and casinos) in 59 countries, including one restaurant in Toronto. To schedule a particular restaurant's employee shifts for each day of a particular week, the manager first obtains sales from the same day of last year, and then adjusts it based on major concerts in town. Even the occupancy rates of nearby hotels are checked. From the forecast, she calculates the number of employees needed each day for kitchen, bar, host, and table service. Each week employees submit work request forms, including daily availability. This information, including the priority of employees (1 to 9 based on seniority and importance to the restaurant), is fed into the linear programming based employee scheduling software. The resulting employee schedules are posted. Shift trades are handled directly between employees.

Sources: J. Heizer et al., *Operations Management*, Canadian Ed., Pearson, Toronto, 2014, p. 619; https://www.youtube.com/watch?v=s-9XNXjxe6o; https://heizerrenderom.wordpress.com/2011/03/01/video-tip-scheduling-employees-at-hard-rock-cafe; https://www.hotschedules.com/news/hotschedules-receives-hard-rock-internationals-technology-vendor-of-the-year-award.

Airline Crew Scheduling

Airlines first schedule the flights for a period (e.g., for the next season) based on market demand, then assign their planes to the flight legs and schedule their maintenance, and finally schedule the crews. Crews are further divided into cabin (flight attendants) and cockpit (pilots and flight engineer). While cabin crew can be scheduled on any flight, cockpit crew is typically licensed for only one type/model of aircraft, so the problem can be decomposed by aircraft type/model for pilots.

The scheduling of pilots (for a given type/model of aircraft) is divided into two steps: (1) Determine good crew *pairings*, typically one to seven days long, and (2) String the pairings together to form a *bid line* or *roster* for one month.

In Step 1, a *pairing* (or rotation or trip) is a sequence of scheduled flights, with short connection times (one to four hours) and overnight layovers, starting from an airline base and ending in the same city. A pairing has to satisfy government, airline, and union rules. For example, the maximum hours of flying per day is eight hours, unless there are long rest periods before and after the flight. A feasible set of pairings covers each flight scheduled during a month. The best set of feasible pairings is the one that minimizes pilot idle times and layover times and costs.

In Step 2, *bid lines* or *rosters* are generated, each consisting of a string of the best feasible pairings from Step 1. Bid lines are determined in order to maximize the utilization of crew while satisfying government, airline, and union rules, and presumed preferences of the pilots. An example of a rule for rosters is that in seven days there has to be a continuous rest period of at least 24 hours. Also, there are rules for the maximum and minimum hours of flying per month, minimum number of days off, maximum number of trips, etc. Pilots seem to prefer long blocks of days off, crossing limited time zones, same-city layovers, long rest periods between night followed by day flying, etc.

The rosters are called bid lines because they are presented to pilots for bidding (choosing). If this is done by seniority (most common in North America) and bid lines are constructed according to the pilots' preferences, Step 2 is called a preferential bidding system.

Because of the rules, some of the pairings, called open or unassigned pairings, may not be included in any bid line. These should be limited to 1–5 percent of the pairings. The unassigned pairings, and those dropped by sick pilots, are given to backup or reserve pilots.

Two software companies that provide software for airline crew scheduling are AD OPT of Montreal (http://www.ad-opt.com) and Navtech Inc. of Waterloo (recently bought by Airbus).[6]

---

[6] S. Yan and J-C Chang, "Airline Cockpit Crew Scheduling," *European Journal of Operational Research*, 136, pp. 501–511; B. Gopalakrishnan and E. L. Johnson, "Airline Crew Scheduling: State-of-the-Art," *Annals of Operations Research*, 140, pp. 305–337; A. I. Z. Harrah and J. T. Diamond, "The Problem of Generating Crew Bidlines," *Interfaces*, 27(4), pp. 49–64; H. Achour, et al., "An Exact Solution Approach for the Preferential Bidding System Problem in the Airline Industry," *Transportation Science*, 41(3), pp. 354–365.

A similar problem is scheduling bus drivers. See the "GIRO" OM in Action.

 OM in Action

GIRO

GIRO is a Montreal-based public transport software producer. GIRO's HASTUS software is for public transport planning (routes and location of terminals and stops), analysis (run times and ridership data), scheduling (vehicles, drivers), operations (assigning drivers to runs, managing changes to schedule, collecting driver worktime data), and providing service information to customers.

GIRO's ACCES is for demand-responsive transport of disabled people (paratransit). Paratransit doesn't follow set routes, unlike regular public transport. Another GIRO software is GeoRoute for mail and parcel distribution. GIRO's software is used all over the world. In Canada, applications of HASTUS include the Montreal, Quebec City, Calgary, Edmonton, Ottawa, Winnipeg, and Mississauga public transport services, and applications of ACCES include Toronto, Montreal, and Calgary.

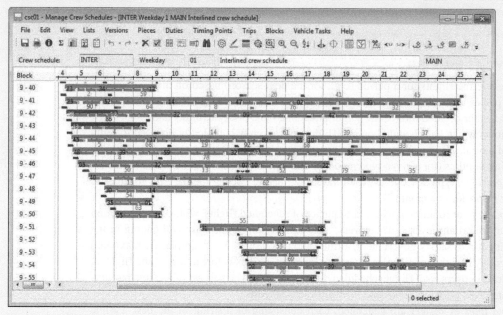

Courtesy of GIRO, Inc.

The horizontal axis is time of a day. For example, 4 means 4 a.m. and 25 means 1 a.m. A block is a sequence of trips to be operated by a bus; it starts by the vehicle pulling out of the depot and ends by the vehicle returning to the depot (pull in). Several drivers can operate the same block; they will relieve each other at a given time and location along the route. This graph combines information about the vehicles (blocks) and the crew (duties, pieces). For a given block, the upper horizontal bar shows the duty pieces defined on the block, with the corresponding duty number indicated above it; the lower portion shows the trips. A run is a sequence of duty pieces for a driver. As part of crew scheduling, the vehicle blocks are "cut" so pieces can be combined into crew duties that can be operated by drivers according to collective agreement rules. The vehicle will operate its complete block, but several drivers will operate the vehicle throughout the day. The black numbers on each bar (e.g., 23, 34, 12 on Block 9–40 bar) are the piece start/end time, indicated by the minutes relative to the hour of the grid: 4:23, 6:34, 9:12.

Sources: http://www.giro.ca; http://www.giro.ca/en/references/success-stories/giro-acces-a-successful-integration.

Some Other Scheduling Problems

Other scheduling problems include field service workforce scheduling and taxi dispatching. See the "ClickSoftware" and "Trapeze Group" OM in Actions.

OM in Action

ClickSoftware

ClickSoftware's ClickSchedule and ClickExpress are field service workforce management software programs used by many field service providers such as Bell Canada, Direct Energy (a furnace and air conditioner service and repair company in Ontario), Gas Metropolitan Plus (a gas appliance service and repair company in Quebec), and Ledcor Technical Services (which builds and services communication networks). The software assists in managing the whole field service process, from receiving an order for service to scheduling it, assigning it to a qualified technician, and keeping track of the location and time of technicians using GIS and a schedule Gantt chart. These companies have reported significant productivity gains due to using the software.

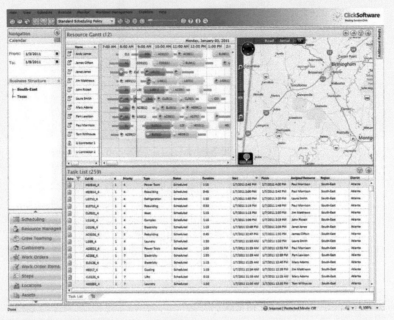

© Courtesy of ClickSoftware

Sources: http://www.clicksoftware.com; http://www.youtube.com/watch?v=tEbXYgBQWxM.

 OM in Action

Trapeze Group

Trapeze Group (based in Mississauga, ON) provides transport management systems for demand responsive (DR) services such as taxis and paratransit. The computerized dispatching system works with in-vehicle GPS-enabled computers to automate the operations.

The automatic order taking displays the customer's name and address as he/she calls, and the automatic dispatching identifies the closest available vehicle (which is centrally tracked using GPS). There is also an interactive voice response (IVR) function that allows customers to leave a message. The automation has resulted in reduction of order-taking and dispatching time from 5 minutes to 30 seconds. IntelliFleet can also

call customers as the taxi is approaching or has arrived at the customer's location. Trapeze in-taxi Ranger computers provide in-vehicle credit card verification and taximeters. IntelliFleet also includes IntelliClerk for driver account management.

Examples of taxi companies using Trapeze IntelliFleet include 650-vehicle Checker (Yellow) Cabs and 75-vehicle Mayfair Taxis of Calgary, 470-vehicle Toronto Co-op Cabs, and Saskatoon's United Blue-line.

The results are more efficient scheduling, routing, and reporting (e.g., a historical dashboard for each customer, on-time performance of vehicles). Automated dispatching also results in fair trip distribution among drivers.

Courtesy of Trapeze Group

Source: http://www.trapezegroup.com.

Another type of scheduling problem is multi-resource scheduling (see the "AltaLink Uses SAP's Multi-Resource Scheduling" OM in Action.)

 OM in Action

AltaLink Uses SAP's Multi-Resource Scheduling

AltaLink is Alberta's privately owned electric-power transmission company. It operates 12,000 km of power lines and poles, and 280 electrical substations through which it distributes electricity to customers. The service technicians are based in the major cities (Calgary, Edmonton, Red Deer, and Lethbridge). Even though AltaLink used SAP's Human Capital Management for personnel management and SAP's Enterprise Asset Management for substation management, the seven schedulers located in these major cities use their own independent Excel-based systems to manage and schedule preventive maintenance of substations. To improve efficiency, AltaLink centralized maintenance management and installed SAP's Multi-Resource Scheduling module in Calgary. The resources include the technicians and equipment such as cranes and scaffoldings. As a result, AltaLink could eliminate four scheduler jobs, and the remaining three schedulers are being used more efficiently by combining the work orders for the same substations.

Source: http://www.sap.com/bin/sapcom/en_us/downloadasset.2013-09-sep -17-10.altalink-improving-service-delivery-through-improved-maintenance -scheduling-pdf.html.

Summary

- Job scheduling involves determining the timing (i.e., start and end times) of operations for jobs or orders. Staff scheduling involves determining the timing (i.e., start and end times) of work of employees and the days they work.
- A major problem in job scheduling is assigning (loading) jobs to machines/work centres. A load Gantt chart is frequently employed to help managers visualize workloads on each machine/work centre.
- MRP uses infinite loading (i.e., workloads may exceed work centre/machine capacities), and the schedule has to be made feasible by either increasing the work centre/machine capacities or rescheduling.
- The Hungarian method for the assignment model assigns each job to a different machine in order to minimize total assignment time/cost of a group of jobs.
- An important activity in job scheduling is sequencing the jobs. Various priority rules can be used, such as shortest processing time (SPT), earliest due date (EDD), and minimum slack time (MST).
- Job scheduling is usually difficult but it can be solved (i.e., the sequence that results in the minimum make-span can be found) for two work centre/machine flow shop problems using Johnson's rule.

- Sometimes job setups are sequence-dependent. This makes sequencing more difficult.
- Moore's rule can be used to minimize the number of late jobs for a group of jobs to be processed on one work centre/machine.
- When the jobs have to be processed on three or more machines/work centres in the same order (i.e., a flow shop) and make-span is to be minimized, the CDS heuristic can be used.
- Shop-floor control involves execution of the job schedule; maintenance, communication, and monitoring of the status of material, orders, and process; and taking any necessary actions.
- A schedule Gantt chart or job progress chart is useful for shop-floor control.
- Input/output control is used to monitor the work inflows and outflows at work centres/machines.
- The theory of constraints focuses on the bottleneck operation to perform scheduling.
- Staff scheduling is a common problem in services. Determining two consecutive days off for full-time employees and daily shifts for part-time employees are common staff scheduling problems. Another common but complex staff scheduling problem is airline crew scheduling.

Key Terms

assignment model
backward scheduling
CDS heuristic
finite loading
forward scheduling
Gantt chart
Hungarian method
infinite loading
input/output (I/O) control

job flow time
job (or detailed) scheduling
Johnson's rule
load Gantt chart
loading
make-span
manufacturing execution system (MES)
Moore's rule
priority rules

schedule Gantt chart
sequencing
shop-floor control
slack time
staff scheduling
theory of constraints (TOC)
work centre

Solved Problems

Problem 1

The Hungarian method. The following table contains information on the cost to run three jobs on four available machines. Determine an assignment plan that will minimize total cost.

		MACHINE			
		A	B	C	D
	1	12	16	14	10
Job	**2**	9	8	13	7
	3	15	12	9	11

Solution

In order to be able to use the Hungarian method, the numbers of jobs and machines must be equal. To remedy this situation, add a *dummy* job with costs of 0, and then solve as usual.

		MACHINE			
		A	B	C	D
	1	12	16	14	10
Job	**2**	9	8	13	7
	3	15	12	9	11
(dummy)	**4**	0	0	0	0

a. Subtract the smallest number from each row. The results are:

		MACHINE			
		A	B	C	D
	1	2	6	4	0
Job	**2**	2	1	6	0
	3	6	3	0	2
	4	0	0	0	0

b. Subtract the smallest number in each column. (Because of the dummy zeros in each column, the resulting table will be unchanged.)

c. Determine the minimum number of lines needed to cross out (or cover) the zeros. One possible way is:

		MACHINE			
		A	B	C	D
	1	2	6	4	0
Job	**2**	2	1	6	0
	3	6	3	0	2
	4	0	0	0	0

d. Because the number of lines is less than the number of rows (or columns), modify the numbers.

   1. Subtract the smallest uncovered number (1) from each uncovered number.

   2. Add the smallest uncovered number to numbers at line intersections.

   The result is

		MACHINE			
		A	B	C	D
	1	1	5	4	0
Job	**2**	1	0	6	0
	3	5	2	0	2
	4	0	0	1	1

e. Test for optimality:

MACHINE

		A	B	C	D
	1	1	5	4	0
Job	**2**	—1———	0—	—6—	—0—
	3	5	2	0	2—
	4	—0———	0—	—1——	—1

Because the minimum number of lines needed equals the number of rows (or columns), an optimum assignment can be made.

f. Assign jobs to machines. Start with rows 1 and 3 because they each have only one zero (alternatively, start with columns A and C because they have only one zero). After each assignment, cross out all the numbers in that row *and* column. The result is:

MACHINE

		A	B	C	D
Job	**1**	1	5	4	[0]
	2	1	[0]	6	0
	3	5	2	[0]	2
	4	[0]	0	1	1

Notice that there is only one assignment in each row and only one assignment in each column.

g. Compute total costs, referring to the original table:

1-D	$10
2-B	8
3-C	9
4-A	0
	$27

h. The implication of assignment 4-A is that machine A will not be assigned a job. It may remain idle or be used for another job.

Problem 2

Priority rules. Job times (including setup) and due hours (from now) are shown in the following table for five jobs waiting to be processed in a one-machine shop:

Job	Job Time (hours)	Due Hour
a........	12	15
b........	6	24
c........	14	20
d........	3	8
e........	7	6

Determine the processing sequence that would result from each of these priority rules:

a. SPT.

b. EDD.

Solution

	a. SPT		b. EDD	
Job	Job Time	Processing Order	Due Hour	Processing Order
a	12	4	15	3
b	6	2	24	5
c	14	5	20	4
d	3	1	8	2
e	7	3	6	1

Problem 3

Priority rules. Using the job times and due hours from Solved Problem 2 above, determine each of the following performance measures for the FCFS sequence (a-b-c-d-e):

a. Make-span.

b. Average flow time.

c. Average hours late.

d. Average WIP.

Solution

Job	Job Time	Completion Time	Hour Due	Hours Late
a	12	12	15	0
b	6	18	24	0
c	14	32	20	12
d	3	35	8	27
e	7	42	6	36
Total		139		75

a. Make-span = 42 hours (= Largest completion time)

b. Average flow time $= \dfrac{\text{Total completion time}}{\text{Number of jobs}} = \dfrac{139}{5} = 27.80$ hours

c. Average hours late $= \dfrac{\text{Total hours late}}{\text{Number of jobs}} = \dfrac{75}{5} = 15$ hours

d. Average WIP $= \dfrac{\text{Total completion time}}{\text{Make-span}} = \dfrac{139}{42} = 3.31$ jobs

Problem 4

Sequencing jobs through two work centres/machines. Use Johnson's rule to obtain the sequence that minimizes the make-span for the jobs shown below through work centre 1 and 2 in the same order.

	Job Times (hours)	
Job	Work Centre 1	Work Centre 2
a.......	2.50	4.20
b.......	3.80	1.50
c.......	2.20	3.00
d.......	5.80	4.00
e.......	4.50	2.00

Solution

Identify the smallest time: job b (1.50 hours at work centre 2). Because the time is for work centre 2, sequence this job last, and eliminate job b times.

The next smallest time is job e (2.00 hours at work centre 2). Sequence job e next to last, and eliminate job e times.

The next smallest time is job c (2.20 hours at work centre 1). Because the time is for work centre 1, sequence job c first and eliminate job c times. At this point, we have: c, __, __, e, b.

The next smallest time is job a (2.50 hours at work centre 1). Because the time is for work centre 1, sequence job a after job c. The one remaining job (job d) fills the remaining slot. Thus, we have the sequence: c-a-d-e-b.

Problem 5

For Solved Problem 4 above, determine what effect splitting jobs c, d, e, and b in work centre 1 would have on the idle time of work centre 2 and on the make-span. Assume that each job is split into two equal parts.

Solution

The solution from the previous problem is shown in the following load Gantt chart. The chart below it shows reduced idle time at work centre 2 when splitting in half is used.

An inspection of these two charts reveals that make-span has decreased from 20.30 hours to 19.55 hours. In addition, the original idle time was 5.6 ($= 2.2 + 1.1 + 0.5 + 1.8$) hours. After splitting c, d, e, and b in half, idle time was reduced to 4.85 ($= 1.1 + 0.6 + 1.1 + 2.05$) hours, so some improvement was achieved. Note that processing times at work centre 2 are generally smaller than at work centre 1 for jobs toward the end of the sequence. As a result, jobs e and b at work centre 2 were scheduled so that they were *centred* around the finishing times of e and b, respectively, at work centre 1, to avoid having to break the jobs due to waiting for the remainder of the split job from work centre 1.

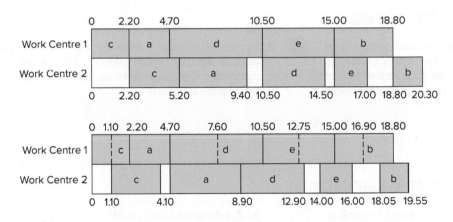

Discussion and Review Questions

Note: An asterisk indicates that a question or problem may be more challenging.

 1. What is job scheduling?

 2. What is a Gantt chart? Name two uses of Gantt charts in scheduling. What is the advantage of Gantt charts?

 3. What is loading?

4. MRP assumes infinite loading. Explain.

5. What is the assignment model? Briefly describe the Hungarian method for the assignment model.

 6. Briefly describe each of these priority rules:

   a. FCFS.

   b. SPT.

   c. EDD.

   d. MST.

   e. Rush.

 7. Why are priority rules needed?

8. Describe Johnson's rule.

 9. What is shop-floor control? Name two tools used in shop-floor control.

LO4 **10.** What is the input/output control?

LO5 **11.** What is the theory of constraints?

LO6 **12.** What is staff scheduling and what are the steps used in staff scheduling?

LO6 **13.** What is meant by scheduling two consecutive days off and how is it done?

 14. What is shift scheduling and how is it done, assuming three- to eight-hour shifts?

LO6 **15.** How is airline pilot scheduling done?

LO3 **16.** Describe Moore's rule.

LO3 **17.** Describe the CDS heuristic.

LO2 **18.** What is the fastest way to board the passengers on an aircraft?

Taking Stock

LO1 & 3 **1.** What trade-off is involved in job scheduling decisions?

LO1 **2.** Who needs to be involved in setting job schedules?

LO1 & 6 **3.** How has technology had an impact on scheduling?

 4. Some continuous 24/7 operations rotate the employee shifts on a weekly basis (e.g., day shift → evening shift → night shift → day shift, etc.), whereas others keep their employee shifts constant. What are the pros and cons of each approach? What ethical issues are involved in this decision?

Critical Thinking Exercises

 1. One approach that can be effective in reducing the impact on the bottleneck operation is to use smaller transfer lot sizes as in the theory of constraints. Explain how smaller transfer lot sizes can reduce the impact on the bottleneck operation.

LO6 **2.** Doctors' and dentists' offices frequently schedule patient visits at regularly spaced intervals. What problems can this create? Can you suggest an alternative approach to reduce these problems?

Experiential Learning Exercises

 1. Visit a fast-food restaurant, a supermarket, a hospital, or another service and ask a manager about staff scheduling, covering these questions:

    a. Who does it?

    b. How frequently is it done?

    c. Is any software used and, if so, which software?

    d. How easy or difficult is it?

    e. Are demand forecasts used?

    f. Is the manager generally satisfied with the outcome?

    g. Are employees satisfied?

 2. How do you schedule your homework assignments?

 3. How does your city sequence or prioritize snow plowing?

Internet Exercise

 Visit http://www.preactor.com/getdoc/bdd42227-1d4b-4660-ab8b-99b0005de92b/North-America.aspx. Choose a case study not used in the chapter and summarize it.

Problems

1. Use the Hungarian method to determine the best way to assign three workers to three jobs, given the following cost information. Calculate the total cost for your assignment.

		JOB		
		A	B	C
	1	5	8	6
Worker	2	6	7	9
	3	4	5	3

2. Rework Problem 1, treating the numbers in the table as profits instead of costs. Calculate the total profit.

3. Assign five trucks to five delivery routes so that total cost is minimized, given the cost data shown below. What is the total cost?

		ROUTE				
		A	B	C	D	E
	1	4	5	9	8	7
	2	6	4	8	3	5
Truck	3	7	3	10	4	6
	4	5	2	5	5	8
	5	6	5	3	4	9

4. Develop an assignment plan for three workers that will minimize total cost, given the information shown below, and interpret your answer.

		WORKER		
		A	B	C
	1	12	8	11
Job	2	13	10	8
	3	14	9	14
	4	10	7	12

5. Use the Hungarian method to obtain a plan that will minimize total processing cost in the following table under these conditions:
   a. The combination 2-D is undesirable.
   b. The combinations 1-A and 2-D are undesirable.

		WORKER				
		A	B	C	D	E
	1	14	18	20	17	18
	2	14	15	19	16	17
Job	3	12	16	15	14	17
	4	11	13	14	12	14
	5	10	16	15	14	13

6. The following table contains information concerning four jobs that are waiting for processing at a machine.

Job	Job Time (days)	Due Date (days)
A	14	20
B	10	16
C	7	15
D	6	17

   a. Sequence the jobs using priority rules (1) SPT, and (2) EDD.
   b. For each of the priority rules in part *a*, determine (1) the average flow time, and (2) the average days late.
   c. Is one priority rule superior to the other? Explain.

7. Using the information presented in the following table, identify the processing sequence that would result using priority rules (1) MST, (2) SPT, (3) EDD, and (4) CR. For each priority rule, determine (1) average flow time, (2) average hours late, and (3) average WIP. Is one priority rule superior to the others? Explain. (*Hint:* First determine the total job time for each job by calculating the total processing time for the job and then adding in the setup time. All times are in hours.)

Job	Processing Time (hr) per Unit	Units per Job	Setup Time (hr)	Due Hour
a	0.14	45	0.7	4
b	0.25	14	0.5	10
c	0.10	18	0.2	12
d	0.25	40	1.0	20
e	0.10	75	0.5	15

8. The following table shows orders to be processed at a machine.
   a. Determine the processing sequence using each of these priority rules: (1) CR, (2) MST, (3) SPT, (4) EDD.
   b. Determine the performance of each rule using (1) average flow time, (2) average days late.
   c. Is one rule superior to the others?

Job	Processing Time (days)	Due Date (days)
A	8	20
B	10	18
C	5	25
D	11	17
E	9	35

LO3 **9.** A production process uses a two-step operation. Tomorrow's work will consist of seven orders as shown below. Determine a job sequence that will minimize the total time required to fill the orders (i.e., the make-span) and determine the make-span.

Order	Time (hours)	
	Step 1	**Step 2**
A	1.20	1.40
B	0.90	1.30
C	2.00	0.80
D	1.70	1.50
E	1.60	1.80
F	2.20	1.75
G	1.30	1.40

LO3 **10.** The times required to complete each of five jobs in a two-machine flow shop are shown in the following table. Each job must begin with machine A and end with machine B.
   a. Determine a sequence that will minimize the make-span.
   b. Construct a load Gantt chart for the resulting sequence, and find machine B's idle time.
   c. For the sequence determined in part *a,* can machine B's idle time be reduced by splitting some jobs in half? If so, which jobs? Split jobs c and e and draw the new load Gantt chart.

Job	Time (hours)	
	Machine A	**Machine B**
a	6	5
b	4	3
c	9	6
d	8	7
e	2	9

LO3 **11.** Given the operation times in the two-work-centre flow shop below:
   a. Develop a job sequence that minimizes total idle time at work centre 2.
   b. Construct a load Gantt chart for the activities at the two work centres, and determine work centre 2's idle time.

Job Times (minutes)	A	B	C	D	E	F
Work Centre 1	20	16	43	60	35	42
Work Centre 2	27	30	51	12	28	24

LO3 **12.** A two-person shoe repair operation uses a two-step sequence that all jobs follow (first work centre A then work centre B). For the group of jobs listed below,
   a. Find the sequence that will minimize the make-span.
   b. Determine the amount of idle time for work centre B.

c. What jobs are candidates for splitting? Why? If jobs b and c are split in half, how much would the idle time of work centre B be reduced?

Job Times (minutes)	a	b	c	d	e
Work Centre A	27	18	70	26	15
Work Centre B	45	33	30	24	10

LO3 **13.** The following schedules (in hours) were prepared by the production manager of a metal shop. Note that all jobs first go through cutting, then polishing.

Job	CUTTING		POLISHING	
	Start	**Finish**	**Start**	**Finish**
A	0	2	2	5
B	2	6	6	9
C	6	11	11	13
D	11	15	15	20
E	15	17	20	23
F	17	20	23	24
G	20	21	24	28

Determine a sequence of jobs that will result in a shorter make-span. (*Hint:* First calculate the job times.)

LO3 **14.** A production manager must determine the processing sequence for seven jobs through the grinding and deburring departments. The same sequence will be followed in each department. The manager's goal is to move the jobs through the two departments as quickly as possible. The site supervisor of the grinding department wants the SPT rule to be used to minimize the work-in-process inventory in his department.

Job	PROCESSING TIME (HOURS)	
	Grinding	**Deburring**
A	3	6
B	2	4
C	1	5
D	4	3
E	9	4
F	8	7
G	6	2

   a. Prepare a schedule using the SPT priority rule for the grinding department (using the grinding times).
   b. What is the total flow time in the grinding department for the SPT sequence? What is the make-span for the seven jobs in both the grinding and deburring departments (using the sequence found in part *a*)?
   c. Determine a sequence that will minimize the make-span in both departments. Does using the SPT rule in the grinding department result in smallest make-span?

L03 15. Suppose a body and paint shop has to work on four cars (A, B, C, and D) of a car rental agency. The manager estimated the job times required (in hours) as follows:

Cars:	A	B	C	D
Body shop	6	9	7	8
Paint shop	3	5	4	6

The body and paint shop each have dedicated workers. A car has to finish body work before it can be painted. Assume that there are no other cars in the shops.

a. The rental agency is in a hurry to get its cars back. In what order should the shops work on the cars to minimize their make-span?

b. Draw a load Gantt chart for your sequence in part *a*, and determine the make-span.

L03 16. A foreman has determined the expected processing times at a machine for a set of jobs and now wants to sequence them. Given the following information, do the following:

a. Determine the processing sequence using (1) MST, (2) SPT, (3) EDD, and (4) CR. For each sequence, calculate the average days late, the average flow time, and the average WIP.

b. Which rule is the best?

Job	Job Time (days)	Due Date (days)
a	4.5	10
b	6.0	17
c	5.2	12
d	1.6	27
e	2.8	18
f	3.3	19

L03 17. Given the information in the following table, determine a processing sequence that will minimize the average flow time.

Job	Processing Time (days)	Due Date
A	5	8
B	6	5
C	9	10
D	7	12
E	8	10

L03 18. Given the following information on job times and due hours, determine the processing sequence using priority rules (1) MST, (2) SPT, (3) EDD, and (4) CR. For each rule, find the average flow time and the average hours late. Which rule is the best?

Job	Job Time (hours)	Due (hours)
A	3.5	7
B	2.0	6
C	4.5	18
D	5.0	22
E	2.5	4
F	6.0	20

L03 19. A shop specializes in heat-treating gears. At 8 a.m. when the shop opened today, five orders were waiting to be processed. Assume that only one unit at a time can be heat-treated.

Order	Order Size (units)	Per Unit Time in Heat Treatment (minutes/unit)	Due (minutes from now)
A	16	4	160
B	6	12	200
C	10	3	180
D	8	10	190
E	4	1	220

a. If the earliest due date (EDD) rule is used, what sequence should be used?

b. What will be the average minutes late for the sequence in part *a*?

c. What will be the average WIP in the shop for the sequence in part *a*?

d. Would the SPT rule produce better results in terms of average minutes late?

L03 20. A manufacturer has accepted the following jobs for July. Today is Thursday, and it is the end of June. The nonworking days in July are July 1, 2, 3, 10, 17, 24, 30, and 31.

Job	Date Order Received	Production Time Including Setup	Due Date	Due Date in Working Days From Now
A	6/4	6.25 days	11 July	7
B	6/7	2.5 days	8 July	5
C	6/12	8.25 days	25 July	19
D	6/14	3.5 days	19 July	14
E	6/15	9.5 days	29 July	23

Examine the following priority rules, summarizing your findings, and advise on which priority rule to use: FCFS, SPT, EDD, or CR.

L03 21. The following table contains order-dependent setup times for three jobs. Which processing sequence will minimize the total setup time?

		Initial Setup Time (hours)	Following Job's Setup Time (hours)		
			A	B	C
Preceding Job	A	2	—	3	5
	B	3	8	—	2
	C	2	4	3	—

L03 22. The following table contains order-dependent setup times for three jobs. Which processing sequence will minimize the total setup time?

	Initial Setup Time (hours)	Following Job's Setup Time (hours)		
		A	**B**	**C**
A	2.4	–	1.8	2.2
Preceding Job **B**	3.2	0.8	–	1.4
C	2.0	2.6	1.3	–

LO3 **23.** The following table contains order-dependent setup times for four jobs. For safety reasons, job C cannot follow job A, nor can job A follow job C. Determine the processing sequence that will minimize the total setup time. (*Hint:* There are 12 sequences.)

	Initial Setup Time (hours)	Following Job's Setup Time (hours)			
		A	**B**	**C**	**D**
A	2	–	5	×	4
Preceding Job **B**	1	7	–	3	2
C	3	×	2	–	2
D	2	4	3	6	–

LO4 **24.** Given the following standard hours of planned and actual inputs and outputs at a work centre, determine the WIP for each period. The beginning WIP is 12 hours of work.

Period

Input		1	2	3	4	5
	Planned	24	24	24	24	20
	Actual	25	27	20	22	24

Output		1	2	3	4	5
	Planned	24	24	24	24	23
	Actual	24	22	23	24	24

LO4 **25.** Given the following standard hours of planned and actual inputs and outputs at a work centre, determine the WIP for each time period. The beginning WIP is seven hours of work.

Period

Input		1	2	3	4	5	6
	Planned	200	200	180	190	190	200
	Actual	210	200	179	195	193	194

Output		1	2	3	4	5	6
	Planned	200	200	180	190	190	200
	Actual	205	194	177	195	193	200

LO6 **26.** During each four-hour period, a small town police force requires the following number of on-duty police officers: eight from midnight to 4:00 a.m.; seven from 4:00 a.m. to 8:00 a.m.; six from 8:00 a.m. to noon; six from noon to 4:00 p.m.; five from 4:00 p.m. to 8:00 p.m.; and four from 8:00 p.m. to midnight. Each police officer works two consecutive four-hour shifts. Determine how to minimize the total number of police officers needed to meet the town's daily police requirements.

LO6 **27.** Determine the minimum number of full-time workers needed and schedule their work given the following staffing requirements. Give the full-time workers two consecutive days off per week.

Day	Mon	Tue	Wed	Thu	Fri	Sat	Sun
Staff needed	2	3	1	2	4	3	1

LO6 **28.** Determine the minimum number of full-time workers needed and schedule their work given the following staffing requirements. Give the full-time workers two consecutive days off per week.

Day	Mon	Tue	Wed	Thu	Fri	Sat	Sun
Staff needed	3	4	2	3	4	5	3

LO6 **29.** Determine the minimum number of full-time workers needed and schedule their work given the following staffing requirements. Give the full-time workers two consecutive days off per week.

Day	Mon	Tue	Wed	Thu	Fri	Sat	Sun
Staff needed	4	4	5	6	7	8	4

LO6 ***30.** A small grocery store needs the following number of cashiers during each day of a week for day (8:00 a.m. to 4:00 p.m.) and evening (4:00 p.m. to midnight) shifts. The store prefers to employ full-time cashiers who work eight hours a day, five days a week, with two consecutive days off. A half-time cashier works four hours a day up to five days a week (with no requirement for consecutive days off). Note that for each unit of cashier requirement, two half-time cashiers are needed because the periods are eight hours long. Determine the mix of full-time and half-time cashiers and schedule their work in order to minimize the total number of cashiers employed but meet the daily cashier requirements below.

Cashiers needed	Mon	Tue	Wed	Thu	Fri	Sat	Sun
8:00 a.m.–4:00 p.m.	3	4	3	3	5	8	3

Cashiers needed	Mon	Tue	Wed	Thu	Fri	Sat	Sun
4:00 p.m.–12:00 a.m.	2	3	2	2	6	5	3

LO6 **31.** Refer to Example 16-8. Use the shift scheduling heuristic to determine shifts for:
a. Counter staff.
b. Assembly board staff.

L05 **32.** Refer to Example 16-7. Find the optimal solution (the sequence of jobs that satisfies the due hours (i.e., end of the eighth hour) for all five jobs). (*Hint:* Switch a pair of jobs in the MST sequence.)

L03 **33.** The following table shows jobs to be processed at a machine. Determine the processing sequence that will minimize total number of late jobs.

Job	Processing Time (days)	Due Date (days)
A	3	4
B	2	5
C	5	10
D	2	11
E	4	13
F	9	20

L06 **34.** Consider the host/seater job in a full-service restaurant. Suppose that it takes an average of 2.5 minutes to greet a group of customers, check their reservation, and seat them. The expected number of new groups arriving during each hour on a particular day is given below.

Time period	Noon–1 p.m.	1–2 p.m.	2–3 p.m.	3–4 p.m.	4–5 p.m.	5–6 p.m.
No. of new groups	20	60	20	8	14	14

Time period	6–7 p.m.	7–8 p.m.	8–9 p.m.	9–10 p.m.	10–11 p.m.	11 p.m.–Midnight
No. of new groups	40	30	50	40	30	14

a. Determine the number of hosts/seaters required during each hour. Round up if the number has a decimal. (*Hint:* You don't need more than three hosts/seaters for any hour.)

b. Schedule three- to eight-hour-long shifts to cover the host/seater requirements you derived in part *a*. Use the shift scheduling heuristic.

L03 **35.** Processing times (including setup times) for five jobs that arrived today and are waiting to be processed in the same order on three machines in a shop are given below. Determine the sequence of jobs that will likely minimize the make-span.

Job	Processing Time (hours) Machine 1	Machine 2	Machine 3
A	4	6	3
B	3	5	4
C	2	3	6
D	6	3	4
E	5	2	2

MINI-CASE

Scotsburn Dairy— Operational Sequencing

The production scheduler of Scotsburn Dairy in Truro, NS, has just received a list of products and their desired lot size (the first week of MPS) from the operations coordinator to be produced next week. The aggregate plan has specified a 40-hour week (four days of 10 hours each) for next week. In sequencing the production, she schedules the products in the same family (as determined during MPS), but also tries to assign allergens toward the end of a day and stronger flavours (e.g., mint) after weaker flavours, and to keep availability of ingredients in mind. Suppose the following families, products, and their quantities (in terms of hours of production) have been chosen to be sequenced for production on one of the three lines next week:

Family	Product	Quantity (in hours of production)
F1	Vanilla-1.89 L	9
	Butterscotch-1.89 L	3

Family	Product	Quantity (in hours of production)
F2	Neapolitan-1 L	2
	Neapolitan-1.65 L	2
	Neapolitan-1.89 L	4
F3	Maple walnut-1 L	2
	Peanut butter fudge-1.89 L	3
F4	Chocolate-1.89 L	5
	Chocolate mint chip fudge-1.89 L	2

The plant is running low on mint flavour but a shipment is expected later next week. Assume one hour of setup time between families and negligible setup time within families.

Question

How should the production scheduler sequence the production of these products?

Q MINI-CASE

Zappos

Zappos, the online shoe retailer with head office in Las Vegas, has over 200 call centre employees who work the customer service phones. At present, once per quarter after the required shifts are determined, the employees choose their preferred shifts in order of seniority by writing their names on sheets of paper listing the shifts. CEO Tony Hsieh noticed that the customer service centre's walls were covered—floor to ceiling—with sheets of printer paper listing the shifts. Hsieh is thinking of replacing the seniority-based system with a *computerized open market pay*

model where busier hours pay higher (like Uber's surge pricing model). Demand is especially high in the early hours of weekdays, when customers on the East Coast are placing calls before starting their workdays. Those calls and online inquiries land in Zappos' Las Vegas call centre before dawn, when few workers want to be on the clock. Employees manning the customer service centre during those hours will earn a higher hourly rate. By contrast, workers will receive less pay if they work on the weekends, when Zappos receives fewer customer inquiries.

Source: http://fortune.com/2015/01/28/zappos-employee-pay/

Tech Cocktail via Flickr/Creative Commons

Questions

1. What are the advantages of the computerized open market system for bidding for shifts?

2. What are the disadvantages of the computerized open market system for bidding for shifts?

Chapter 17
Project Management

Creative Commons/SH Hewitt

Hebron is an oil platform that has recently been deployed on the ocean floor in 93 metres of water, 350 kilometres southeast of St. John's, Newfoundland and Labrador. The lower part of the platform, the gravity based structure (GBS), is 120 metres high by 130 metres in diameter, weighs 370,000 tonnes, and consists of a concrete-reinforced steel shell designed to withstand icebergs. Inside the GBS, 1.2 million barrels of crude oil can be stored. GBS supports an integrated Topsides deck that includes a living quarters for 220 persons and facilities to perform drilling and production. Topsides measures 158 metres long by 70 metres wide by 110 metres high, and weighs 65,000 tonnes.

A substantial portion of Topsides was engineered and fabricated in Newfoundland and Labrador, but the derrick equipment set and the utilities/process module were made in Korea. The project included offshore surveys, engineering, procurement, fabrication, construction, installation, commissioning, development drilling, production, and maintenance. It started in 2010 and took approximately eight years to produce its first oil. It was on schedule and on budget ($14 billion). Hebron's major owners are ExxonMobil Canada (35.5 percent), Chevron Canada (29.6 percent), and Suncor (21 percent).

The vice-president of ExxonMobil Canada was the project manager. He used the famous *ExxonMobil Capital Project Management System* (ECPMS) to manage this complex construction and installation project. Other than the common project management tools and techniques that are described in this chapter, ECPMS involves the following:

- In project planning, ExxonMobil first decides if a project will be *routine* or *non-routine*. Then, the project manager and team best suited for the project are assigned.

- ExxonMobil eliminates uncertainty as early as possible to enhance project predictability for both cost and schedule performance.

- ExxonMobil locks down the development concept as soon as possible, and carefully manages each of the critical transitions, from front-end engineering to detailed design to construction, resolving all major issues before moving from one phase to the next.

- ExxonMobil uses an integrated approach across all of its upstream companies—exploration, development, and production, for both oil and gas. An example is how it integrates production personnel into the project team during front-end engineering to provide an operational perspective all the way through the commissioning and start-up phase.

- ExxonMobil uses a safe design, construction, and operation process called the Operations Integrity Management System.

- ExxonMobil's project lessons are shared systematically. Within 24 hours, it can apply lessons learned from one region to another.

- ExxonMobil selects contractors with the required core competency for the work, and will use them repeatedly for engineering, procuring equipment, fabricating facilities, hooking up modules, building ship hulls, performing precommissioning, and other work. ExxonMobil teams work alongside contractor teams in contractors' fabrication yards and design shops to ensure safety.

- ExxonMobil uses a *design-one, build-multiple* approach, which means it uses the same design in multiple locations. This increases learning. For example, the Hebron platform is identical to the Hibernia platform that was installed in the same area 20 years ago.

- The ECPMS has continuously been improved as ExxonMobil has completed more than 100 projects over the past 15 years.

Sources: http://www.hebronproject.com/; http://corporate.exxonmobil.com/en/company /multimedia/the-lamp/reputation-for-excellence.

 Introduction and Project Manager's Job

> **project** A unique, multi-person, large, one-time work designed to accomplish a specific objective (deliverable) in a limited time frame.
>
> **program** A set of projects.
>
> **project performance goals** Keeping the project within time/schedule, cost/ budget, and quality/scope guidelines.

A **project** is a unique, multi-person, large, one-time work designed to accomplish a specific objective (deliverable) in a limited time frame. Examples of projects include constructing a store, redesigning a business process, merging two companies, putting on a play, designing new goods or services, and designing an information system. In the above examples, the specific objective is the store, the redesigned business process, the merged company, the play, etc. A related term is *program*. A **program** is a set of projects.

Consider the Olympics. It involves a tremendous amount of planning and coordination. Athletes' living quarters and training facilities must be constructed, competition schedules must be developed, arrangements for televising events must be made, equipment and crews must be coordinated, transportation and hotel accommodations must be made, and many other activities that go on behind the scenes must be planned and managed so that everything goes off smoothly. A smaller project is a concert.

Projects may involve considerable cost. Some have a long time horizon, and some involve a large number of activities that must be carefully planned and coordinated. All projects are expected to achieve the following **project performance goals**: to be completed within time/schedule, cost/ budget, and quality/scope guidelines. To accomplish this, projects must be authorized, their objectives and scope must be established, a project manager should be appointed, and the project must be

© Matt Kent/Redferns/Getty

© Kevin Mazur/WireImage/Getty

The U2 360 Tour a few years ago was named after the 360-degree staging and audience configuration it used for shows. To accommodate this, they used a massive four-legged supporting rig that was nicknamed "The Claw." The tour crew consisted of 137 technicians supplemented by over 120 support personnel hired locally. Dismantling the massive set took 3½ days. First, sound and light equipment were packed into the fleet of trucks during the four hours following the concert; the remainder of the time was spent deconstructing the steel structures.

planned. Activities/tasks must be identified and their durations estimated. Once it is underway, the project's progress must be monitored to ensure that the project's performance goals will be achieved.

If during the execution of a project one of the performance goals (schedule, cost, quality) becomes unacceptable, then one or both of the other performance goals should be adjusted (traded off) to bring the project on track. This is known as the **project management triangle**.

> **project management triangle** A model of the three opposing performance goals or constraints of project management—cost, schedule (time), and quality (scope)— showing that they should be traded off.

The Project Management Triangle

Cost/Budget

Time/Schedule

Performance Objectives

Quality/Scope

Projects go through a life cycle or series of stages or **project phases** which include initiating the project (conception, feasibility study, etc.), planning and scheduling, execution and monitoring and controlling, and closing (see the following figure). During this life cycle, a variety of skills are needed. The circumstances are analogous to constructing a house. Initially an idea is presented and its feasibility is assessed, then plans must be drawn up by an architect and approved by the owner and the town's building permits department. Then a succession of activities occurs, each with its own skill requirements, starting with the site preparation; then laying the foundation; erecting the frame, roofing, constructing exterior walls; wiring and plumbing; installing kitchen and bathroom fixtures and appliances; and interior finishing and painting, and carpeting. Similar sequences occur on large construction projects, in R&D, in information technology projects, and in virtually every other instance where projects are being carried out.

> **project phases** Also known as project stages: initiating (conception, feasibility study/ selection), planning and scheduling, execution and monitoring and controlling, and closing.

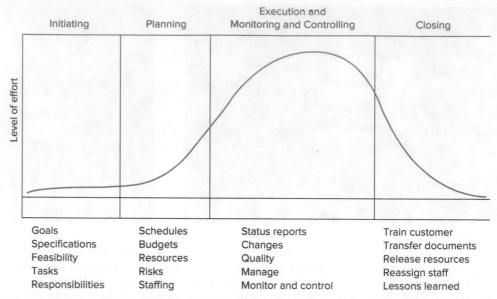

Initiating	Planning	Execution and Monitoring and Controlling	Closing
Goals	Schedules	Status reports	Train customer
Specifications	Budgets	Changes	Transfer documents
Feasibility	Resources	Quality	Release resources
Tasks	Risks	Manage	Reassign staff
Responsibilities	Staffing	Monitor and control	Lessons learned

Source: Adapted from Clifford F. Gray and Erik W. Larson, *Project Management: The Managerial Process,* 2nd ed., p. 6. Copyright © 2003 McGraw-Hill Companies, Inc.

In an organization, a project initiator/sponsor is usually a senior manager or vice-president. A project output or deliverable is a good (such as a building/software) or a service (such as merging two databases). A project is influenced by the company's strategy and policies, as well as its "environment" (e.g., culture, information systems, human resources). The major document used in project initiation is the **project scope**, the work that needs to be accomplished to deliver a good or service, the specified objective.

Deciding which projects to implement is called **project portfolio selection**. This involves factors such as budget, availability of personnel with appropriate knowledge and skill, cost–benefit considerations, financial benefits (e.g., return on investment and net present value), and how the project will contribute to the company's strategy. The following steps for project selection have been suggested:[1]

project scope The work that needs to be accomplished to deliver a good or service, the specific objective of the project.

project portfolio selection Deciding which projects to implement.

1. Establish a project council (e.g., the executive committee).

2. Identify some project categories (e.g., long-term vs. short-term, minor vs. major) and criteria (e.g., business value, customer satisfaction, process effectiveness, employee satisfaction).

3. Collect project data.

4. Assess resources (e.g., labour, dollars) availability.

5. Prioritize the projects within categories.

6. Select projects to be funded.

7. Communicate the results to stakeholders and provide the reasons for selection or non-selection of each project.

work breakdown structure (WBS) A hierarchical listing of components of a project.

Project planning determines how the project is to be undertaken, and includes breaking the job down into smaller components, called **work breakdown structure (WBS)**, determining the resources needed and estimating their costs, scheduling the activities involved or subcontracting the work, planning risk management, and planning material purchases.

Project execution involves purchasing the material, and using the team members and subcontractors to perform the activities/tasks. Project control involves observing the project's progress; issuing performance reports on time/schedule, cost/budget, and quality/scope; and making any necessary changes to the project.

[1] R. L. Englund and R. J. Graham: "From Experience: Linking Projects to Strategy," *Journal of Product Innovation Management*, January 1999, 16(1), pp. 52–64.

Projects bring various people together, from both inside and outside the organization. These stakeholders include the project team who perform the activities/tasks; the project sponsor/initiator who initiates and gets approval for the project; and customers/users. The project is headed by a project manager, guided by the project sponsor.

Most team members, who have diverse knowledge and skills, will remain associated with the project for less than its full life. Some people go from project to project as their contributions become needed, and others are "on loan," on either a full-time or a part-time basis, from their regular jobs.

Certain organizations frequently use projects; examples include consulting firms, architects, lawyers, publishers, and construction companies. In these organizations, it is not uncommon for some employees to spend virtually all of their time on projects. These companies have a **project-based organizational structure**.

However, most companies use a **matrix organization** that temporarily groups together specialists from different departments to work on special projects. Each staff member—for example, a structural engineer or an accountant—works on one or more project(s) part-time, but permanently belongs to his/her department. The project manager and the functional managers share the authority of assigning priorities and directing the work.

Finally, some organizations have set up a **project management office (PMO)**, which is a group or department within an organization that defines and maintains standards for project management within the organization. For an application, see the "Pacific Blue Cross" OM in Action.

> **project-based organizational structure** A type of organizational structure where a company's departments and personnel are organized around each particular project.
>
> **matrix organization** An organizational structure that temporarily groups together specialists from different departments to work on special projects.

 OM in Action

Pacific Blue Cross

Pacific Blue Cross provides extended health and dental insurance to residents of British Columbia. When the new vice-president (VP) of information technology (IT) was appointed in 2003, she put in a gate governance process for approving larger projects (lasting over one month), changed the review boards for smaller projects, and created a PMO. Each large project is now sponsored by a VP who takes it to the executive committee. If it passes the first gate, cost/benefit analysis is performed on it with the help of the PMO. This result is brought to the executive committee again. If it passes gate 2, it is approved. However, projects costing over half a million dollars need to also go through gate 3, and those costing more than $1 million need to also go through gate 4.

Post-implementation review is gate 5. Smaller projects are prioritized by the department review boards that include department managers. The PMO consists of a manager, three project managers, and two to five contract project managers. All information about processes to follow for a project has been put online. The PMO regularly reports the status of projects to the executives using a "traffic light" report which uses green, yellow, and red lights to show the status of each project in terms of time, budget, and quality. The reports are also put online.

Source: Dr. C. Aczel Boivie, "Red Light, Green Light; How One CIO Used Project Management Discipline and the Traffic Light Report to Align Her IT Department With Her Company's Business Goals," *CIO*, June 15, 2006, 19(17), p. 1.

Construction projects are delivered using various methods:[2]

- *Construction management* (owner hires a project management company who helps hire an architect and various contractors)

- *Design–build* (owner hires a builder who in turn hires the architect and subcontractors)

- *Engineer–procure–construct* (similar to design–build but for large engineering projects)

- *General contracting* (same as *design–bid–build*; owner hires an architect and then hires a general contractor who in turn hires subcontractors)

- *Public–private partnership* (a government department or agency hires a consortium of financier, designer, builder, and operator).

For an example of the design–build construction method, see the "Saskatoon Police Service Headquarters" OM in Action.

> **project management office (PMO)** A group or department within an organization that defines and maintains standards for project management within the organization.

---

[2] http://www.pcl.com/Services-that-Deliver/Delivery-Methods/Pages/default.aspx

OM in Action

Saskatoon Police Service Headquarters

A police building has specific functional requirements In addition to offices for supervisors, interrogation rooms, meeting rooms, a processing centre, and detention cells, it may have community rooms, classrooms, a 911 call centre, forensic labs and an exhibit holding area, an indoor firing range, a K9 facility, training rooms, a fitness centre, a gym, and a lounge. It also needs parking spaces.

In 2011, the Saskatoon city council authorized a five-storey, 390,000-square-foot, $101 million building for a new police headquarters. The old building was over 30 years old and was getting too small for the growing policing force.

A design–build type of request for proposal (RFP) was put out. This means that the proponent is responsible for both detailed design and construction. The RFP gives proponents latitude in how to achieve the performance standards. A proponent develops a preliminary design and submits a firm tender price. EllisDon was chosen out of the three short-listed proponents.

EllisDon is a major Canadian construction and building service company which is based in London, Ontario. EllisDon hired CS&P Architects of Toronto and aodbt architecture + interior design of Saskatoon to design the building. EllisDon created a building information model (a digital representation of physical and functional characteristics of the facility) to flush out coordination issues and find scope gaps as the design progressed.

Among the improvements EllisDon made in the police headquarters' plans was the refinement of the HVAC system's design. The RFP specification had called for multiple smaller air-handling units, serving different areas of the building. This has been replaced with a smaller number of larger units, which will use less energy and save on both maintenance and operating costs.

Another improvement was the decision to use curtain wall instead of windows. This cost EllisDon a little more money, but it will last longer. Vinyl windows would last only 20 to 25 years, whereas curtain wall could last up to 50 years.

EllisDon used approximately 50 to 60 subcontractors on the project. The project was completed in 2014 on schedule and a little over budget. The budget overrun occurred because the requirement for parking spaces was increased from 600 to 800 (including 200 secure spaces for police cars), which was accomplished using an underground parking area and a separate adjacent parkade.

Radharc Images / Alamy Stock Photo

Source: http://www.buildingandconstruction-canada.com/sections/community/520-ellisdon-saskatoon-saskatoon-police-service-headquarters; http://saskatoonpolice.ca/newhq/;http://www.ellisdon.com/project/saskatoon-police-services-headquarters/.

The Project Manager's Job

project manager The person responsible for planning, scheduling, executing, and controlling a project from inception to completion; meeting the project's requirements; and ensuring completion on time, within budget, and to the required quality standards.

The **project manager** is the person responsible for planning, scheduling, executing, and controlling a project from inception to completion; meeting the project's requirements; and ensuring completion on time, within budget, and to the required quality standards. The project manager bears the ultimate responsibility for the success or failure of the project. He or she must acquire adequate resources and personnel and be capable of working through the team members to accomplish the specific objective of the project. The project manager is responsible for effectively managing each of the following:

1. The *work,* so that all of the necessary activities are accomplished in the desired sequence, and performance goals are met.

2. The *human resources,* so that those working on the project have direction and motivation.

3. *Communications,* so that everybody has the information they need to do their work (usually through regular meetings), and the customer/sponsor is well informed. Logs of actions, issues, and risks should be kept to manage the project, and to have as project history.

4. *Quality,* so that the specific objective of the project is realized.

5. *Time,* so that the project is completed on schedule.

6. *Costs,* so that the project is completed within budget.

An effective project manager is organized, multitasks, motivates and directs team members and builds a team, makes trade-off decisions in project performance goals, expedites the work when necessary, deals with obstacles and team conflicts, puts out fires and solves problems, handles failures, is persistent, and monitors time, budget, and quality.

For projects that involve fairly well defined work, those qualities will often suffice. However, for projects that are less well defined, and thus have a higher degree of uncertainty, the project manager must also employ strong leadership skills. These include the ability to adapt to changing circumstances that may involve complex organizational decision-making structures, changes to project performance goals, technical requirements, and project team composition. As a leader, the project manager must be able not only to deal with these issues, but also to recognize the need for change, decide what changes are necessary in consultation with stakeholders, and work to accomplish them.

A project manager should accept and take advantage of the political nature of the organization, and should be politically sensitive, realizing that people are afraid of change because it might alter their established political relationships.[3]

The job of the project manager can be both difficult and rewarding. The manager must coordinate and motivate people who sometimes owe their allegiance to other managers in their functional areas. In addition, the people who work on a project possess specialized knowledge and skills that the project manager may lack. Nevertheless, the project manager is expected to guide and evaluate their efforts. Project managers often must function in an environment that is beset with uncertainties. Even so, budgets and time constraints are usually imposed, which can create additional pressures on project personnel.

The rewards of the job of project manager come from the creative challenges of the job, the benefits of being associated with a successful project (including promotion and monetary compensation), and the personal satisfaction of seeing it through to its conclusion.

Ethical issues often arise in connection with projects. Examples include the temptation to understate costs or to withhold information in order to get a project approved, and pressure to alter or make misleading statements on status reports, falsifying expenses, compromising workers' safety, and approving substandard work. It is the responsibility of the project manager to maintain and enforce ethical standards.

Project Planning

LO2

Project planning involves further elaboration of the project scope (the work to be done) including breaking the project down into smaller components (deliverables, sub-projects, work packages, and activities), planning for risk management (the identification, analysis, and response plans to what may go wrong), estimating the required resources for the activities (employees, equipment, material), estimating costs (for each activity) and budgeting (calculating total cost), human resource planning (including assigning team member roles and responsibilities), project scheduling (estimating activity durations, sequencing, and scheduling), and planning quality, communications, and purchases.

> **project planning** Analyzing the project into work packages and activities, risk management planning, estimating resources needed, budgeting, HR planning, scheduling, and quality, communication, and purchase planning.

It is important to determine the details of work to be done (the scope), to formally obtain acceptance of the detailed scope from the project customer/sponsor and later, during execution and control, to control the changes to the project scope.

We will describe risk management planning and work breakdown structure (WBS) below, and project scheduling in the following sections.

Quality planning involves determining how project quality is to be assured and controlled. It includes deciding on the quality policy, objectives, responsibilities, metrics, and tools such as checklists.

Communications planning involves determining the nature of information needed by stakeholders (including team members and subcontractors) and how to satisfy these needs. It includes plans for information collection/storage, the technology and media used, the nature of information distributed (e.g., project performance reports), and methods for accessing and updating the information. For an application, see the "Tim Hortons" OM in Action.

---

[3] For more details, see J. K. Pinto and O. P. Kharbanda, "Lessons for an Accidental Profession," *Business Horizon*, March/April 1995, pp. 41–50.

OM in Action www.timhortons.com

Tim Hortons

In the early 2000s, Tim Hortons was in the middle of an aggressive expansion plan and needed a faster way to develop new restaurants. Therefore, the engineering services department started using Expesite project management software, which allowed them to use the Internet to communicate project documents (e.g., blueprints), monitor the schedule, track costs, and receive bids.

The system cut the development process for a restaurant from 12 months to 11 months, and saved thousands of dollars a year for couriering blueprints back and forth between architects, engineers, and Tim Hortons' staff. The system has also increased process consistency and accountability (by regular reporting) across regions.

Source: M. Wilson, "Expediting Development," *Chain Store Age*, October 2006, 82(10), p. 92.

Purchase planning involves determining what to purchase, the statement of work or the specification of the item, supplier evaluation and selection, and the award of contract. The actual delivery and monitoring/controlling of supplier performance are part of the execution and control of the project.

Risk Management Planning

Risks are inherent in projects. They relate to the occurrence of events that can have undesirable consequences, such as delays, increased costs, inability to meet technical specifications (quality/scope), or even termination. Although careful planning can reduce risks, no amount of planning can totally eliminate them.

The probability of occurrence of risk events is highest near the beginning of a project and lowest near the end. However, the cost associated with risk events tends to be lowest near the beginning of a project and highest near the end:

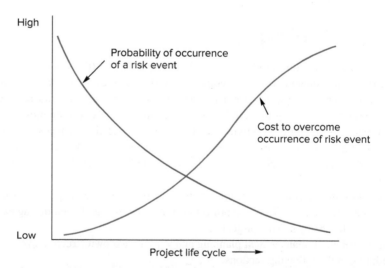

Source: Adapted from Clifford Gray and Erik W. Larson, *Project Management: The Managerial Process*, 4th ed., p. 198. Copyright © 2008 McGraw-Hill Companies, Inc.

Good risk management entails identifying as many potential risks as possible, analyzing and assessing those risks, and planning a response to avoid, transfer, or mitigate the risk. Much of this takes place during planning of a project, although it is not unusual for this process to be repeated during the execution of project as experience grows and new information becomes available.

The first step for risk management planning is to identify the risks. Typically, there are numerous sources of risks, although the more experience an organization has with a particular type of work, the fewer and more identifiable the risks will be. Everyone associated with the project should have responsibility for identifying risks. Brainstorming sessions and questionnaires can be useful in this regard. Another approach to risk identification is to review the documents and analyze the assumptions, looking for inaccuracies, inconsistencies, and incompleteness. The list of risks and other information obtained is usually stored in a *risk register*.

Once risks have been identified, each risk must be evaluated to determine its probability of occurrence and the potential consequences if it does occur. Both quantitative and qualitative approaches have merit. All stakeholders can contribute to this effort, and experts might also be called on. Experience with previous projects can be useful. Many tools might be applied, including scenario analysis, simulation, decision trees, and sensitivity analysis. There should be a response to risks with high probability and impact (cost).

Risk response can take a number of forms. Much depends on the nature and scope of a project. First, the root cause of a risk is identified. It will help to categorize risks, either by their source (this is called risk breakdown structure) or by the area of work (using the WBS). Risk response includes:

- Redundant (backup) systems, for example, an emergency generator could supply power in the event of an electrical failure.
- Using a less complex process or a more stable supplier.
- Frequent monitoring of critical project aspects with the goal of catching and eliminating problems in their early stages, before they cause extensive damage.
- Transferring risks, say by outsourcing a particular component of a project and requiring performance bonds.
- Risk-sharing, for example, as in an oil and gas consortium.
- Extending the schedule, creating contingency funds, reducing project scope, clarifying the requirements, obtaining information, and improving communications.

Work Breakdown Structure

A large project is usually decomposed into smaller components. **Work breakdown structure (WBS)** is a hierarchical listing of components of a project; it is for a project what the product structure tree is for a product. The first step is to identify the major components of the project. These are the Level 2 boxes in Figure 17-1. The next step is to identify the major sub-components for each of the major components—the Level 3 boxes. Then, if necessary each major sub-component may be broken down further—the Level 4 boxes, and so on. The rule is that a **work package** or **activity** in the bottom of the WBS should be small enough that it can be done by a subcontractor in a few days or weeks.

> **work breakdown structure (WBS)** A hierarchical listing of components of a project.
>
> **work package** A group of related tasks within a project. The smallest unit of work that a project can be broken down to when creating your work breakdown structure.
>
> **activity** Another name for a work package in a project.

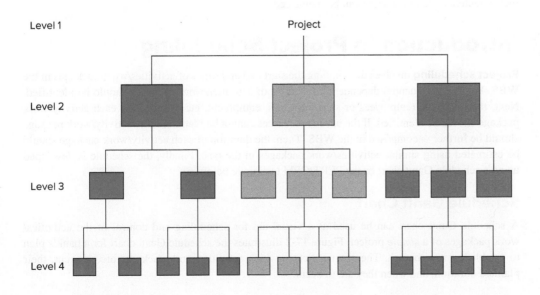

Level 1   Project

Level 2

Level 3

Level 4

◀ **FIGURE 17-1**

A schematic example of a work breakdown structure.

For example, building a house may have the following Level 2 components (e.g., foundation, framing, etc.) and Level 3 sub-components (e.g., excavate, concrete, etc.). Because horizontal space for Level 3 sub-components is limited, they are drawn below each other. Note that it is better to specify the elements of WBS as parts of the house, as opposed to work to be done. In this case, the blueprint of the house was already available so it was not included in the WBS. Also not included is the construction/project management work.

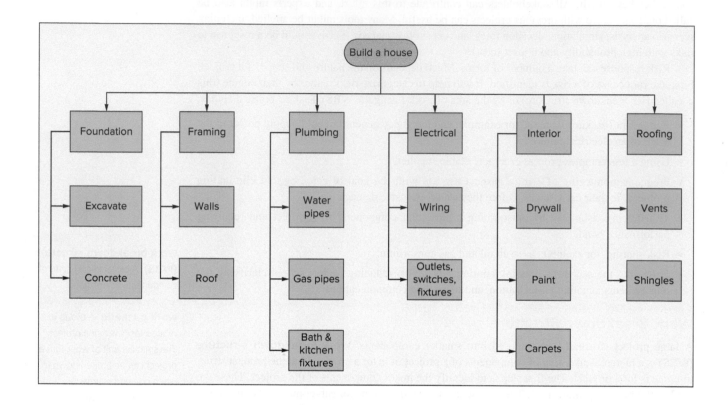

The work packages or activities in the bottom of the WBS are used for planning, including developing time and cost estimates. The details of a work package may not be known at the start of the planning stage but should be obtained from the subcontractor before the work package is implemented so that their work can be monitored.

LO3 Introduction to Project Scheduling

project scheduling
Determining the start and end times of activities/work packages in the work breakdown structure.

Project scheduling involves determining the start and end times of activities/work packages in the WBS. First, any sequential dependencies of pairs of activities/work packages should be identified. Next, the resources (employees or subcontractors, equipment, etc.) needed for each activity/work package should be identified. If the needed resources cannot be identified, the activity/work package should be further decomposed in the WBS. Then, the duration of each activity/work package should be estimated using similar activities/work packages in the past. Finally, the schedule is developed using a schedule Gantt chart or the PERT/CPM technique below.

Schedule Gantt Chart

A schedule Gantt chart can be used as a visual aid for scheduling and control of the activities/work packages of a *simple* project. Figure 17-2 illustrates the schedule Gantt chart for a bank's plan to establish a new branch. The chart indicates which activities/work packages are to occur, their planned duration, and when they are to occur.

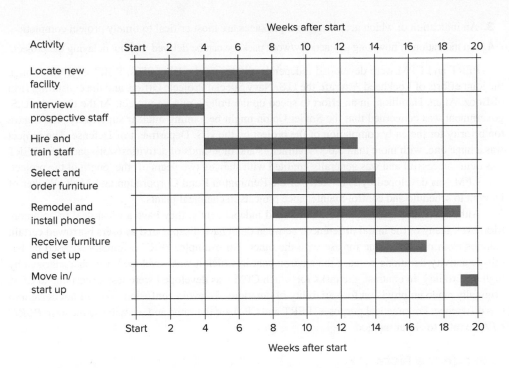

◀ **FIGURE 17-2**

A schedule Gantt chart for establishing a new bank branch.

Aside from being a visual tool, an advantage of a schedule Gantt chart is its simplicity. However, a schedule Gantt chart fails to reveal relationships among activities/work packages that can affect the performance of work. On more complex projects, a *precedence network,* described below, is used for scheduling purposes. For an example of using scheduling techniques to keep projects on schedule, see the "PCL" OM in Action.

 OM in Action   www.pcl.com

PCL

PCL is a major Canadian construction and construction management company. PCL ensures on-time completion of a project using the following scheduling techniques.

A master construction schedule outlines all key decision dates and key equipment delivery dates, and identifies the critical path of the project (the longest path from the start to the end). The master schedule will track all major on-site activities and will become the road map for the successful execution of the project. The master schedule will be updated by PCL on a weekly basis.

PCL also utilizes six-week look-ahead schedules. These short-duration schedules are updated and distributed to PCL's sub-trades on a weekly basis. This allows PCL to monitor the project's progress on a smaller scale, mapping out the individual steps to meeting the greater goals. These six-week look-ahead schedules allow PCL to identify small scheduling and sequencing concerns before they become larger, more complicated schedule risks.

PCL also monitors trade-specific progress on a quantity and man-hours basis. This feedback allows PCL to accurately measure the productivity achieved to date and forecast the duration of time to complete the remaining work.

Source: http://www.thunderbay.ca/Assets/City+Government/Event+Centre/docs/TBECC+Final+Phase+3+Report_Construction+Plan+$!26+GMP.pdf.

PERT/CPM

The **program evaluation and review technique (PERT)** and the **critical path method (CPM)** are two of the most widely used tools for scheduling and control of large-scale projects. By using PERT and CPM, managers are able to obtain:

1. A graphical display of project activities/work packages and their sequential relationship.
2. An estimate of how long the project will take.

program evaluation and review technique (PERT) A technique used for scheduling and control of large projects.

critical path method (CPM) Method used for scheduling and control of large projects.

3. An indication of which activities/work packages are most critical to timely project completion.

4. An indication of how long any activity/work package can be delayed without delaying the project.

PERT and CPM were developed independently during the late 1950s. PERT evolved through the joint efforts of Lockheed Aircraft, the U.S. Navy Special Projects Office, and the consulting firm of Booz, Allen, Hamilton, in an effort to speed up the Polaris missile project. At the time, the U.S. government was concerned that the Soviet Union might be gaining nuclear superiority, and it gave top priority for the early completion of the project by the U.S. Department of Defense. The project was a huge one, with more than 3,000 contractors and thousands of activities/work packages. PERT was quite successful and was generally credited with shaving two years off the length of the project.

CPM was developed by J. E. Kelly of the Remington Rand Corporation and M. R. Walker of DuPont to schedule and control maintenance projects in chemical plants.

Although PERT and CPM were developed independently, they have a great deal in common. Moreover, many of the initial differences between them have disappeared as users borrowed certain features from one technique for use with the other. For example, PERT originally stressed probabilistic activity durations because the environment in which it was developed was characterized by high uncertainty. In contrast, the tasks for which CPM was developed were less uncertain, so CPM originally made no provision for variability of durations. To avoid confusion, we will not delve into this difference. For practical purposes, PERT and CPM are the same and we will use the term *PERT/CPM* to refer to either method.

activity-on-arrow (AOA)
Network in which arrows designate activities.

activity-on-node (AON)
Network in which nodes designate activities.

Precedence Network

One of the main features of PERT/CPM is its use of a precedence network to depict project activities/work packages and their sequential relationships by use of arrows and nodes. There are two slightly different conventions for constructing these networks. Under the original convention, the *arrows* designate activities; under the new convention, the *nodes* designate activities. These are referred to as **activity-on-arrow (AOA)** and **activity-on-node (AON)** networks, respectively.

Both types of networks are illustrated in Figure 17-3, using the new bank branch example of Figure 17-2. In the AOA network, the arrows represent both the activities and the sequence in which they must be performed (e.g., *Interview* precedes *Hire and train*); in the AON network, the arrows show only the sequence in which activities must be performed, while the nodes represent the activities. Only AON precedence networks will be used in this chapter.

FIGURE 17-3 ▼

Precedence networks for establishing a new bank branch.

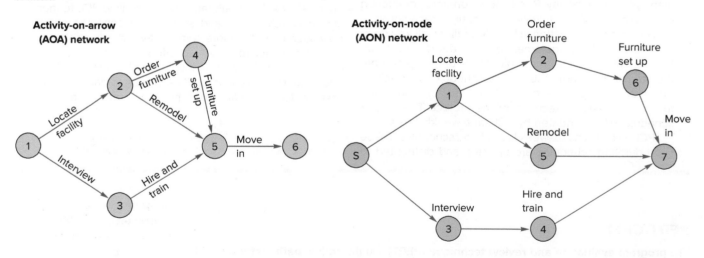

Note that the AON network has a start node, S, which is actually not an activity but is added in order to have a single starting node. Also, an AON network should have only one ending node.

The relationships shown in Figure 17-3 are all of the finish-to-start type (i.e., an activity/work package must finish before its immediate successor can start). Sometimes other types of relationships exist, such as start-to-start (an activity can start only after another has started), finish-to-finish, and start-to-finish. We will consider only finish-to-start relationships, which are most common, in this chapter. Developing and interpreting AON precedence networks requires some familiarity with network conventions; see Figure 17-4.

INTERPRETATION	NETWORK RELATIONSHIP

Activities must be completed in sequence: first *a*, then *b*, and then *c*.

Both *a* and *b* must be completed before *c* can start.

Activity *a* must be completed before *b* or *c* can start.

Both *a* and *b* must be completed before *c* or *d* can start.

Of particular interest are the *paths* or chains in a precedence network diagram. A **path** is a sequence of activities/work packages that leads from the start node to the end node. For example, in the AON network of Figure 17-3, S-1-2-6-7 is a path. Note that there are three paths in this network. One reason for the importance of paths is that they reveal *sequential relationships*. If one activity in a sequence is delayed (i.e., is late) or is done incorrectly, all of the following activities/work packages on that path will be delayed.

Another important aspect of a path is its length (i.e., duration). The length of a path can be determined by summing the expected duration of the activities on it. The path with the largest duration is of particular interest because it governs the project completion time. In other words, expected project duration equals the expected duration of the longest path. Moreover, if there are any delays along the longest path, there will be corresponding delays in the project completion time. Attempts to shorten project completion must focus on the activities/work packages on the longest path. Because of its influence on project completion time, the longest path is referred to as the **critical path**, and its activities/work packages are referred to as **critical activities**.

Paths that are shorter than the critical path can experience some delays and still not affect the overall project completion time as long as their duration does not exceed the length of the critical path. The allowable slippage for any path is called **path slack time**, and it reflects the difference between the length of the path and the length of the critical path. The critical path, then, has zero path slack time.

path A sequence of activities/work packages that leads from the start node to the end node.

critical path The longest path from start to end; determines the expected project duration.

critical activities Activities on the critical (longest) path.

path slack time Allowable slippage for a path; the difference between the length of the path and the length of the critical (longest) path.

LO4 Scheduling Using Deterministic Durations

deterministic durations
Durations that are fairly certain.

probabilistic durations
Durations that allow for random variation.

The main determinant of the way PERT/CPM networks are used is whether activity/work package durations are *probabilistic* or *deterministic*. If durations are fairly certain, we say that they are **deterministic durations**. If durations are subject to random variation, we say that they are **probabilistic durations**. This section deals with deterministic activity durations. The next section deals with probabilistic activity durations.

One of the best ways to gain an understanding of the nature of the precedence network and the critical path is to consider a simple example using an intuitive solution method.

EXAMPLE 17-1 ▶

Given the information provided below:

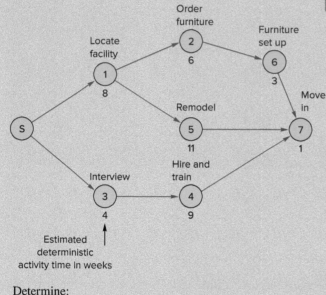

Determine:

a. The length (duration) of each path.

b. The critical path.

c. The expected duration of the project.

d. The slack for each path.

SOLUTION

a. As shown in the following table, the path durations are 18 weeks, 20 weeks, and 14 weeks.

b. The longest path (20 weeks) is S-1-5-7, so it is the critical path.

c. The expected duration of the project is equal to the length of the critical path (i.e., 20 weeks).

d. We find the slack for each path by subtracting its length from the length of the critical path, as shown in the Path Slack column of the following table.

Path	Duration (weeks)	Path Slack (weeks)
S-1-2-6-7	8 + 6 + 3 + 1 = 18	20 − 18 = 2
S-1-5-7	8 + 11 + 1 = 20*	20 − 20 = 0
S-3-4-7	4 + 9 + 1 = 14	20 − 14 = 6

*Critical path length.

PERT/CPM Solution Technique

Many real-life precedence networks are much larger than the simple network illustrated in Example 17-1; they often contain hundreds or even thousands of activities and exponentially more paths. Therefore, large networks are analyzed by a solution technique that avoids the need to enumerate all the paths. Instead, it determines four values for each activity:

- ES, the *earliest* time the activity can *start*.
- EF, the *earliest* time the activity can *finish*.
- LS, the *latest* time the activity can *start* and not delay the project.
- LF, the *latest* time the activity can *finish* and not delay the project.

Once these values have been determined, they can be used to find:

1. Expected project duration

2. Activity slack times

3. The critical path

First, we calculate the earliest start and finish times for each activity, starting from the left at the start node and moving to the right of the precedence network (called a *forward pass*), using the following two simple rules:

1. The earliest finish time for any activity/work package is equal to its earliest start time plus its expected duration, *t*:

$$EF = ES + t \tag{17-1}$$

2. ES for an activity/work package with one immediate predecessor is equal to the EF of that node. ES for an activity/work package with multiple immediate predecessors is equal to the largest EF of those nodes. Let ES of the start node be zero.

Calculate the earliest start time and earliest finish time for each activity in the network shown in Example 17-1.

◄ EXAMPLE 17-2

SOLUTION

Begin by enlarging each node and placing the activity number and duration inside it as follows:

We determine and place the earliest start time, ES, and the earliest finish time, EF, for the activity inside each node as follows:

ES of the start node is 0. The start node in this example has zero duration. Therefore, $EF_S = ES_S + t = 0 + 0 = 0$. The EF of the start node becomes the ES of the nodes immediately following it. Thus, $ES_1 = 0$ and $ES_3 = 0$:

Next, use $EF = ES + t$ for each of the nodes 1 and 3; $EF_1 = 0 + 8 = 8$ and $EF_3 = 0 + 4 = 4$:

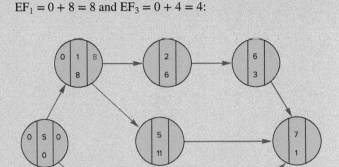

Now, because activity 1 has an EF of 8, both activities 2 and 5 (its immediate successor) will have an ES of 8. Similarly, activity 4 will have an ES of 4 because the EF of node 3, its immediate predecessor, is 4:

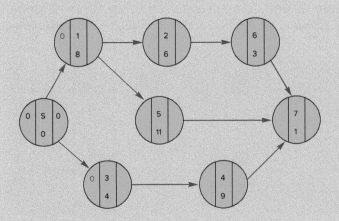

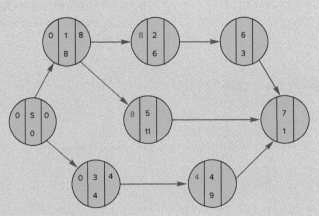

This permits calculation of the EFs for activities 2, 5, and 4: $EF_2 = 8 + 6 = 14$, $EF_5 = 8 + 11 = 19$, and $EF_4 = 4 + 9 = 13$.

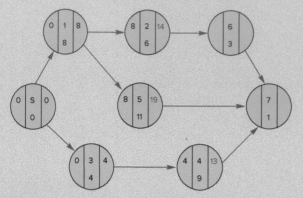

The ES for activity/work package 6 is the EF of activity 2 (its immediate predecessor) which is 14. Using this value, we find $EF_6 = 14 + 3 = 17$.

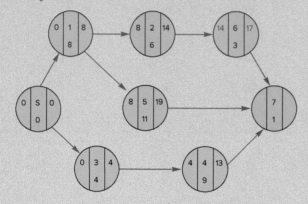

In order to determine the ES for activity 7, we must realize that it cannot start until *every* activity that immediately precedes it is finished. Therefore, the *largest* of the EFs for the three activities that immediately precede it determines ES_7. Hence, the ES for activity 7 is 19 (that is, $\max(17, 19, 13)$).

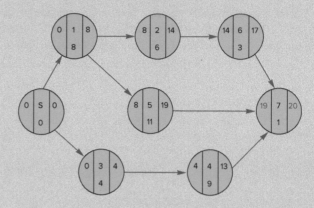

Finally, $EF_7 = 19 + 1 = 20$. Note that the EF for the end node is the expected project duration, 20 weeks.

Now, we calculate the latest start and finish times, starting from the right (i.e., the end node) and moving to the left of the precedence network (called a *backward pass*), using the following two simple rules:

1. The latest start time for any activity/work package is equal to its latest finish time minus its expected duration:

$$LS = LF - t \tag{17-2}$$

2. For a node with one immediate successor, LF equals the LS of that node. For a node with multiple immediate successors, LF equals the smallest LS of those nodes. Let LF of the end node equal its EF.

EXAMPLE 17-3 ▶

Calculate the latest finish and latest start times of activities for the precedence network shown at the end of Example 17-2.

SOLUTION

We will add the LS and LF times to the nodes just below the ES and EF times, respectively, determined in Example 17-2.

Begin by setting the LF of the last activity (node 7) equal to the EF of that activity. Thus,

$$LF_7 = EF_7 = 20 \text{ weeks}$$

Obtain the LS for activity 7 by subtracting its duration, t, from its LF:

$$LS_7 = LF_7 - t = 20 - 1 = 19:$$

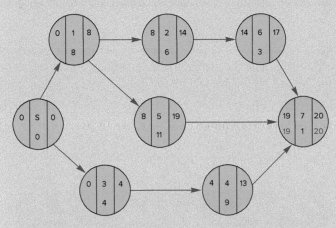

The LS of 19 for activity 7 now becomes the LF for each of the activities that immediately precede it. Thus, $LF_6 = LF_5 = LF_4 = 19$. Now subtract their activity time from their LF to obtain their LS. The LS for activity 4 is $19 - 9 = 10$, for activity 5 is $19 - 11 = 8$, and for activity 6 is $19 - 3 = 16$:

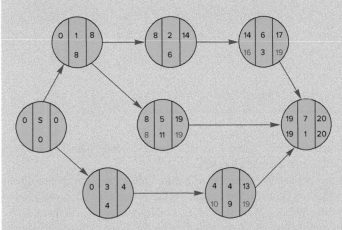

Next, the LS for activity 6, which is 16, becomes the LF for activity 2 (its immediate predecessor), and the LS for activity 4, which is 10, becomes the LF for activity 3 (its immediate predecessor). Using these values, we find the LS for each of these activities by subtracting their activity time from their LF. Therefore, LS for activity 2 is $16 - 6 = 10$, and for activity 3 is $10 - 4 = 6$:

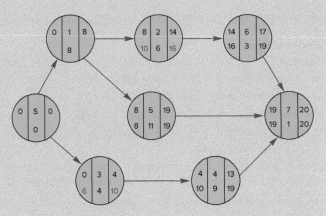

The LF for activity 1 is the *smaller* of the two LSs of the activities that immediately succeed it. Hence, the LF for activity 1 is 8 (that is, min(8, 10)). The reason you use the smaller time is that activity 1 must finish at a time that permits both of the immediately following activities to start no later than their LS.

Once we have determined the LF of activity 1, we find its LS by subtracting its time of 8 from its LF of 8. Hence, LS of activity 1 is 0:

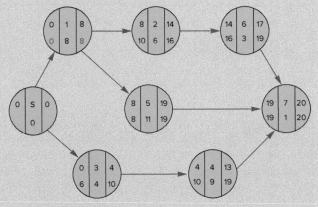

Next, the LF of activity S is the smaller of LS of activities 1 and 3; that is, $LF_S = min(0, 6) = 0$. Finally, $LS_S = LF_S - t = 0 - 0 = 0$:

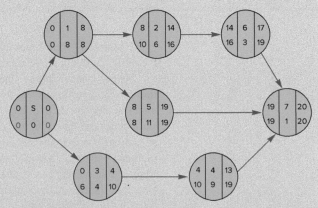

The rules for the above solution technique are reiterated in the following box.

Rules for the PERT/CPM Solution Technique

Forward Pass

Start at the left side of the precedence network (i.e., the start node) and work toward the right side.

For the start activity: ES = 0.

For each activity: ES + Activity duration = EF.

If an activity has a unique immediate predecessor: ES = EF of that activity.

If an activity has multiple immediate predecessors, set its ES equal to the largest EF of its immediate predecessors.

Backward Pass

Start at the right side of the precedence network (i.e., the end node) and work toward the left side.

Use the EF as the LF for the end activity.

For each activity: LS = LF − Activity duration.

If an activity has a unique immediate follower: LF = LS of that activity.

If an activity has multiple immediate followers, set the activity's LF equal to the smallest LS of the immediate followers.

> **activity slack time**
> The amount of time that an activity can be delayed without causing a delay to project completion date.

Calculating Activity Slack Times. **Activity slack time** is the amount of time that an activity can be delayed without causing a delay in the project completion date. An activity slack time can be calculated in either of two ways:

$$\text{Activity slack time} = \text{LS} - \text{ES} \quad \text{or} \quad \text{LF} - \text{EF} \qquad (17\text{-}3)$$

The critical path consists of the activities with zero slack time.

EXAMPLE 17-4 ▶

Calculate activity slack times for the precedence network at the end of Example 17-3.

SOLUTION

Either the start times or the finish times can be used. Suppose we use the start times. Using ES calculated in Example 17-2 and LS calculated in Example 17-3, activity slack times are:

Activity/Work Package	LS	ES	LS − ES (= Slack)
S	0	0	0
1	0	0	0
3	6	0	6
2	10	8	2
5	8	8	0
4	10	4	6
6	16	14	2
7	19	19	0

Example 17-4 indicates that activities S, 1, 5, and 7 are all critical activities, which agrees with the results of the intuitive approach demonstrated in Example 17-1.

Knowledge of activity slack times provides managers with information for planning the allocation of scarce resources and for directing control efforts toward those activities/work packages that are most susceptible to delaying the project. In this regard, it is important to recognize that activity slack times are based on the assumption that all of the activities on the same path will be started as early as possible and not exceed their expected times. Furthermore, if two activities are both on the same path (e.g., activities 2 and 6 in the preceding example) and have the same slack (e.g., two weeks), this will be the *total* slack available to both. In essence, the activities have *shared slack*. Hence, if the first activity uses all of the slack, there will be zero slack left for all of the following activities on that same path.

As noted earlier, this solution technique lends itself to computerization. This problem (Example 17-2, Example 17-3, and Example 17-4) will be solved using Microsoft Project at the end of chapter.

Probabilistic Durations

The preceding section assumed that activity/work package durations were known and not subject to variation. While this assumption is appropriate in some situations, there are many others where it is not. Consequently, these situations require a probabilistic approach.

The probabilistic PERT/CPM approach, called the **three-point estimation method**, involves *three* duration estimates for each activity/work package instead of one:

1. **Optimistic duration**: The length of time under the best conditions; represented by t_o.

2. **Pessimistic duration**: The length of time under the worst conditions; represented by t_p.

3. **Most likely duration**: The most probable length of time; represented by t_m.

Managers or others with knowledge about the activity/work package can make these duration estimates.

The **Beta distribution** is a family of continuous positive distributions used to describe the inherent variability of an activity/work package's duration (see Figure 17-5). Although there is no real theoretical justification for using the Beta distribution, it has certain features that make it attractive in practice: The distribution can be symmetrical or skewed to either the right or the left depending on its shape parameters; the mean and variance of the distribution can be readily obtained from the three estimates listed above; and shape parameters can be chosen so that the distribution is unimodal with a high concentration of probability surrounding the most likely duration estimate.

> **three-point estimation method** The probabilistic PERT/CPM approach that involves *three* duration estimates for each activity/work package instead of one: optimistic, most likely, and pessimistic.
>
> **optimistic duration** The length of time under the best conditions (t_o).
>
> **pessimistic duration** The length of time under the worst conditions (t_p).
>
> **most likely duration** The most probable length of time (t_m).

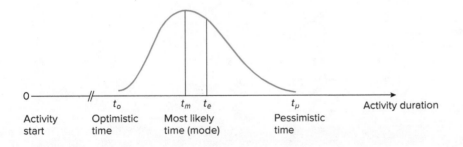

◀ FIGURE 17-5

A Beta distribution is used to describe the variability of an activity's duration.

Of special interest in probabilistic PERT/CPM are the average or expected duration for each activity/work package t_e, and the variance of each activity's duration, σ^2_{act}. The expected duration of an activity, t_e, is an unequally weighted average of the three estimates:

$$t_e = \frac{t_o + 4t_m + t_p}{6} \qquad (17\text{-}4)$$

> **Beta distribution** A family of continuous positive distributions used to describe the inherent variability in activity durations.

The expected (average) duration of a path is equal to the sum of the expected durations of the activities on it:

Path mean $= \Sigma$ (Expected durations of activities on the path)   (17-5)

The standard deviation of each activity's duration is estimated as one-sixth of the difference between the pessimistic and optimistic estimates. (Analogously, almost all of the area under a Normal distribution lies within three standard deviations of the mean, which is a range of six standard deviations.) We find the variance by squaring the standard deviation. Thus,

$$\sigma^2_{act} = \left[\frac{(t_p - t_o)}{6}\right]^2 \quad \text{or} \quad \sigma^2_{act} = \frac{(t_p - t_o)^2}{36} \qquad (17\text{-}6)$$

The size of the variance reflects the degree of uncertainty associated with an activity/work package's duration: The larger the variance, the greater the uncertainty.

It is also required to calculate the standard deviation of the duration of a *path*. We can do this by summing the variances of the activity durations on the path and then taking the square root of that number; that is,

$$\sigma_{path} = \sqrt{\sum[(\text{Variances of activity durations on path})]} \tag{17-7}$$

Example 17-5 illustrates these calculations.

EXAMPLE 17-5 ▶

The precedence network for a project is shown below, with the three duration estimates for each activity (in weeks) over each node.

a. Calculate the expected duration for each activity and the expected duration for each path.

b. Identify the critical path (based on the expected durations).

c. Calculate the variance of each activity's duration and the standard deviation of each path's duration.

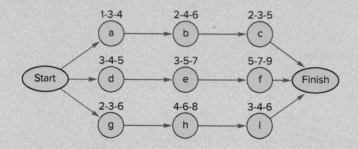

SOLUTION

a. Because the start and finish activities do not take any time in this example, we can ignore them in the following calculations:

Path	Activity	Durations t_o	t_m	t_p	$t_e = \dfrac{t_o + 4t_m + t_p}{6}$	Path Expected Duration
	a	1	3	4	2.83 ⎤	
a-b-c	b	2	4	6	4.00 ⎬	10.00
	c	2	3	5	3.17 ⎦	
	d	3	4	5	4.00 ⎤	
d-e-f	e	3	5	7	5.00 ⎬	16.00
	f	5	7	9	7.00 ⎦	
	g	2	3	6	3.33 ⎤	
g-h-i	h	4	6	8	6.00 ⎬	13.50
	i	3	4	6	4.17 ⎦	

b. The path that has the largest expected duration is the critical path. Because path d-e-f has the largest path expected duration, it is the critical path.

c.

Path	Activity	Durations t_o	t_m	t_p	$\sigma^2_{act} = \dfrac{(t_p - t_o)^2}{36}$	σ^2_{path}	σ_{path}
	a	1	3	4	$(4 - 1)^2/36 = 9/36$	$34/36 = 0.944$	0.97
a-b-c	b	2	4	6	$(6 - 2)^2/36 = 16/36$		
	c	2	3	5	$(5 - 2)^2/36 = 9/36$		
	d	3	4	5	$(5 - 3)^2/36 = 4/36$	$36/36 = 1.00$	1.00
d-e-f	e	3	5	7	$(7 - 3)^2/36 = 16/36$		
	f	5	7	9	$(9 - 5)^2/36 = 6/36$		
	g	2	3	6	$(6 - 2)^2/36 = 16/36$	$41/36 = 1.139$	1.07
g-h-i	h	4	6	8	$(8 - 4)^2/36 = 16/36$		
	i	3	4	6	$(6 - 3)^2/36 = 9/36$		

Knowledge of the path's expected duration and standard deviation of duration enables a manager to calculate probabilistic estimates of the project completion time, such as these:

- The probability that the project will be completed by a specified time.
- The probability that the project will take longer than its scheduled completion time.
- These estimates can be derived from the probability that various paths will be completed by the specified time or take longer than the scheduled completion time. Although activity/ work package durations are represented by Beta distribution, a path's duration is approximately a Normal distribution. This concept, called the central limit theorem, is illustrated in Figure 17-6.

▼ FIGURE 17-6

Activity-duration distributions and the path-duration distribution.

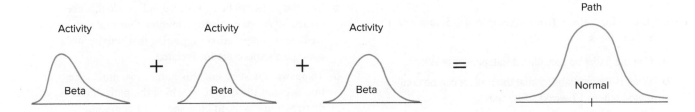

Determining Path Probabilities

The probability that a given path will be completed in a specified length of time can be determined using the following formula:

$$z = \frac{\text{Specified length of time} - \text{Expected path duration}}{\text{Standard deviation of path duration}} \qquad (17\text{-}8)$$

The resulting value of z indicates how many standard deviations of the path's duration the specified length of time is beyond the expected path duration. A negative value of z indicates that the specified time is *earlier* than the expected path duration. Once the value of z has been determined, it can be used in Appendix B, Table B, to obtain the probability that the path will be completed by the specified time. Note that the probability is equal to the area under the Normal curve to the left of z, as illustrated in Figure 17-7.

FIGURE 17-7 ▶

The path probability is the area under the Normal curve to the left of z.

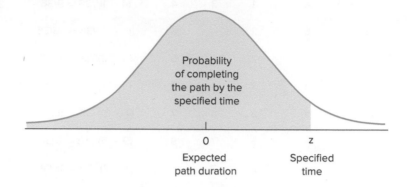

Probability of completing the path by the specified time

0
Expected path duration

z
Specified time

A project is not completed until *all* of its activities/work packages, not only those on the critical path, have been completed. It sometimes happens that another path ends up taking more time to complete than the critical path, in which case the project runs longer than expected. Hence, it can be risky to focus exclusively on the critical path. This requires determining the probability that *all* paths will finish by a specified time. To do that, find the probability that each path will finish by the specified time, and then multiply those probabilities. The result is the probability that the *project* will be completed by the specified time. This assumes independence of path durations. The assumption of *independence* of path durations requires two conditions: (a) that the activity/work package durations are independent of each other, and (b) that each activity/work package is on only one path. For activity/work package durations to be independent, the duration for one must not give any information about the duration of the other; if two activities/work packages were always early or late together, they would not be considered independent.

EXAMPLE 17-6 ▶

Using the information from Example 17-5, answer the following questions:

a. Can the paths be considered independent? Why?

b. What is the probability that the project can be completed within 17 weeks of its start?

c. What is the probability that the project will be completed within 15 weeks of its start?

d. What is the probability that the project will *not* be completed within 15 weeks of its start?

SOLUTION

a. Yes, the paths can be considered independent, since no activity/work package is on more than one path and we have no information suggesting that activity/work package durations are interrelated.

b. To answer questions of this nature, we must take into account the degree to which the path-duration distributions "exceed" the specified completion time. This concept is illustrated in the following figure, which shows the three path-duration distributions, each centred on that path's expected duration, and the specified completion time of 17 weeks.

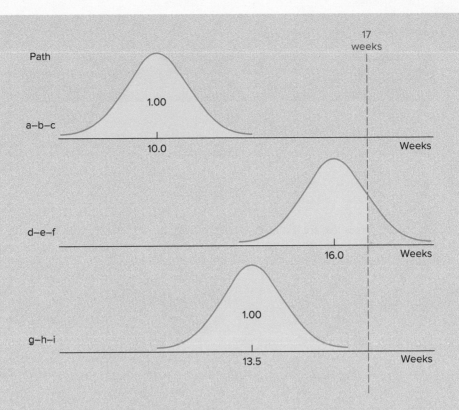

The coloured portion of each distribution corresponds to the probability that the path will be completed within the specified time. Observe that paths a-b-c and g-h-i are well enough to the left of the specified time that it is highly likely that both will be finished by week 17. In such cases, we essentially need to consider only the distribution of path d-e-f in assessing the probability of completion by week 17. To do so, we must first calculate the value of z using Formula 17-8 for this path:

$$z = \frac{17 - 16}{1.00} = +1.00$$

Turning to Appendix B, Table B with $z = +1.00$, we find that the area under the curve to the left of z is 0.8413. To check our intuition, the probabilities for the other two paths are also determined, and all three are summarized in the following table. *Note:* If the value of z exceeds $+3.50$, treat the probability of completion as being equal to 1.

Path	$z = \dfrac{17 - \text{Expected path duration}}{\text{Standard deviation of path duration}}$	Probability of Completion in 17 Weeks
a-b-c	$\dfrac{17 - 10}{0.97} = +7.22$	1.00
d-e-f	$\dfrac{17 - 16}{1.00} = +1.00$	0.8413
g-h-i	$\dfrac{17 - 13.5}{1.07} = +3.27$	0.9995

Thus, Prob(project finishes by week 17) = Prob(path a-b-c finishes by week 17) ×
Prob(path d-e-f finishes week 17) ×
Prob(path g-h-i finishes by week 17)
$= 1.00 \times 0.8413 \times 0.9995 = 0.8409 \sim 84\%$

c. For a specified time of 15 weeks, the z values are:

Path	$z = \dfrac{15 - \text{Expected path duration}}{\text{Standard deviation of path duration}}$	Probability of Completion in 15 Weeks
a-b-c	$\dfrac{15 - 10}{0.97} = +5.15$	1.0000
d-e-f	$\dfrac{15 - 16}{1.00} = -1.00$	.1587
g-h-i	$\dfrac{15 - 3.5}{1.07} = +1.40$	.9192

Paths d-e-f and g-h-i have z values that are less than +3.50. From Appendix B, Table B, the area to the *left* of $z = -1.00$ is 0.1587, and the area to the *left* of $z = +1.40$ is 0.9192. The path distributions are illustrated in the following figure. The joint probability of all paths finishing within 15 weeks is the product of their probabilities: $(1.00)(0.1587)(0.9192) = 0.1459$.

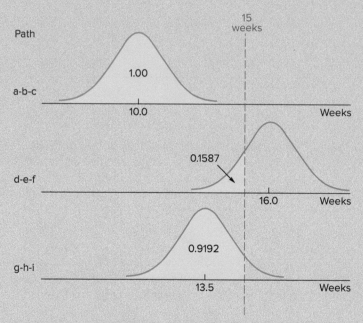

d. The probability of not finishing within 15 weeks is the complement of the probability obtained in part *c*: $1 - 0.1459 = 0.8541$.

Using Simulation. The above discussion assumed that the paths of the project were *independent*, which requires that no activity be on more than one path. If an activity was on more than one path and it happened that the completion time for that activity far exceeded its expected time, all paths that include that activity would be affected and, hence, their durations would not be independent. If only a few activities are on multiple paths, particularly if the paths are *much* shorter than the critical path, the independence assumption may still be reasonable.

Otherwise project schedulers often use *simulation* to find the desired probabilities. This amounts to a form of repeated sampling wherein many passes are made through the precedence network. In each pass, a random value for each activity/work package's duration is selected from the probability distribution of its duration. After each pass, the project duration is determined. After a large number of such passes (e.g., several hundred), there is enough information to prepare a frequency distribution of the project duration. A project scheduler can use this distribution to make a probabilistic assessment of the project duration.

Project Crashing

An estimate of an activity/work package's duration is usually made for a given level of resources. In many situations, it is possible to reduce the length of a project, which is called **crashing a project**, by using additional resources. The impetus to shorten projects may reflect efforts to avoid late penalties, to take advantage of monetary incentives for timely or early completion of a project, or to free resources for use on other projects. In new product development, shortening the time may lead to a strategic benefit: beating the competition to the market. In some cases, however, the desire to shorten the length of a project merely reflects an attempt to reduce the indirect costs associated with running the project, such as facilities, equipment, supervision, and personnel costs. Hence, a project manager may be able to shorten a project by increasing *direct* expenses to speed up the project, thereby realizing savings on indirect project costs. A *time–cost trade-off* can be used to identify those activities/work packages that will reduce the sum of the indirect and direct project costs.

> **crashing a project** Reducing the length of a project by using additional resources.

Only activities on the critical path are potential candidates for crashing (i.e., shortening), because shortening non-critical activities would not have an impact on the project duration. From an economic standpoint, critical activities should be crashed according to crashing cost per period: crash those with the lowest crash cost per period first. Moreover, crashing should continue as long as the cost to crash is less than the benefits derived from crashing. We assume that the indirect costs are a linear function of project duration. Also, we assume (direct) crashing cost per period increases faster the more you crash the project. Figure 17-8 illustrates the basic relationship between indirect, direct, and total project costs due to crashing.

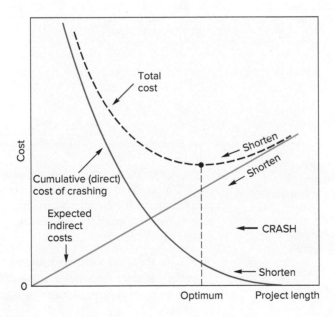

Costs related to crashing activities; crashing activities reduces the indirect project costs but increases direct costs; the optimum amount of crashing results in minimizing the sum of these two types of costs.

The general procedure for crashing is:

1. Obtain estimates of regular and crash durations and crash cost per period for each activity, and indirect project costs per period.
2. Determine the lengths of all paths.
3. Determine the critical activities.
4. Crash critical activities, starting from the cheapest, as long as crashing cost per period does not exceed the benefits of crashing. Note that two or more paths may become critical as the original critical path becomes shorter, so that subsequent improvements will require simultaneous shortening of two or more paths. In some cases, it will be more economical to shorten an activity that is on two (or more) of the critical paths than two (or more) activities on each critical path.

EXAMPLE 17-7 ▶

Using the following information and precedence network, develop the optimal project crashing. Indirect project costs are $1,000 per day.

Activity/ Work Package	Normal Duration (days)	Crash Duration (days)	Cost per Day to Crash
a	6	6	—
b	10	8	$500
c	5	4	300
d	4	1	700
e	9	7	600
f	2	1	800

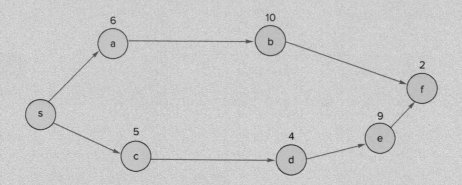

SOLUTION

a. Determine the critical path, its length, and the length of the other path:

Path	Length
s-a-b-f	6 + 10 + 2 = 18
s-c-d-e-f	5 + 4 + 9 + 2 = 20 (critical path)

b. Rank the critical activities in order of crashing cost per day, starting from the lowest, and determine the number of days for which each can be crashed.

Activity	Cost per Day to Crash	Available Days to Crash
c	$300	1
e	600	2
d	700	3
f	800	1

c. Begin shortening the project, one day at a time, and check after each reduction to see if the other path becomes critical. (After a certain point, the other path's length will equal the length of the shortened critical path.) Thus:

i. Shorten the activity with cheapest crash cost per day, activity c, one day at a cost of $300. The length of the critical path now becomes 19 days.

ii. Activity c cannot be shortened any more. Shorten the activity with next cheapest crash cost per day, activity e, one day at a cost of $600. The length of path s-c-d-e-f now becomes 18 days, which is the same as the length of path s-a-b-f.

iii. The paths are now both critical; further improvements will necessitate shortening both paths.

The remaining activities for crashing and their costs are:

Path	Activity	Crash Cost (per day)	Available Days
s-a-b-f	a	—	0
	b	$500	2
	f	800	1
s-c-d-e-f	c	—	0
	e	600	1
	d	700	3
	f	800	1

At first glance, it would seem that crashing activity f would not be advantageous, because it has the highest crashing cost per day. However, activity f is on both paths, so shortening activity f by one day would shorten *both* paths (and hence, the project) by one day for a cost of $800. The option of shortening the least expensive activity/work package on each path would cost $500 for activity b for s-a-b-f and $600 for activity e for s-c-d-e-f, or $1,100 in total. Thus, shorten activity f by one day. The project duration is now 17 days.

iv. At this point, no additional crashing is cost-effective. The cost to crash activities b and e is a total of $1,100, and that would exceed the indirect project costs of $1,000 per day.

The crashing sequence is summarized below:

Path	n = 0	1	2	3
		Length After Crashing n Days:		
s-a-b-f	18	18	18	17
s-c-d-e-f	20	19	18	17
Activity crashed		c	e	f
Crash cost		$300	$600	$800

Project Execution and Control

Project execution involves the actual performance of the activities/work packages that were planned in project planning. The project manager directs, coordinates, and manages project activities/work packages and team members. The budgeted funds are expended to accomplish the project objective. Resources are obtained, managed, and used.

> **project execution**
> Performance of planned activities/work packages of a project.

During execution, quality of the deliverable (product) is assured by applying the planned quality activities. Team members who are not yet assigned are chosen; their skills are assessed, needed training is instituted, and ground rules for team participation are set. Any purchases or subcontracting plans, whose suppliers are not determined yet, are finalized, and contracts are negotiated. In a construction project, bid packages (e.g., for foundation, frame, roofing, etc.) go out. The plan for information collection and distribution is executed using clear and timely information in appropriate form (written or oral, formal or informal, using software or manual, etc.). Unexpected requests for information by stakeholders are responded to.

An approach for project execution, especially when multiple projects are underway and require joint resources, is the *critical chain,* proposed by Eli Goldratt in 1997.[4] It is based on two psychological principles: (a) *student's syndrome* is that a student tends to delay the start of an assignment until the last possible time, and (b) *Parkinson's law* states that work expands to fill the time available for its completion. To combat these tendencies, which result in late projects, the critical chain approach does not disclose the due dates of activities to the project workers. Instead, activities are prioritized, scheduled accordingly, and done as soon as possible. Also, estimates of activity duration are examined to ensure that they are not being padded with safety time. Safety or buffer time is added at the end of the critical chain (critical path) and at the end of each feeder chain that feeds into the critical chain. Activity/work package (and chain) priorities are determined daily based on the percentage of buffer time used divided by the percentage of the chain work completed (the activity with a larger ratio gets a higher priority). See the "Warner Robins Air Logistics Complex" OM in Action.

---

[4] Eliyahu M. Goldratt, *Critical Chain*, Great Barrington, MA: North River Press, 1997, pp. 246.

⚙ OM in Action

Warner Robins Air Logistics Complex

Warner Robins Air Logistics Complex (WR-ALC) in Southern Georgia repairs and overhauls U.S. Air Force transport planes such as C-5 Galaxy, C-17 Globemaster, C-130 Hercules, and F-15 fighter jets. Before year 2004, WR-ALC took an average of one year to overhaul a C-5 (resulting in 16–17 planes in WIP), which was deemed to be too slow. Most of the time, a plane was waiting for mechanics, facilities, and/or parts. Then in 2004, WR-ALC implemented lean production, which reduced the throughput time to 240 days. However, this was still too long for the U.S. Air Force.

In 2005, WR-ALC implemented the critical chain project execution management. Aggressive times for each activity were determined, which added up to only 105 days, with 55 days of project buffer. Similarly, 100 or so non-critical chains each received their own buffers at their end (before feeding into the critical chain). Chains are prioritized daily based on the percentage of buffer time used divided by the percentage of the chain work completed. The activities on a chain receive the priority of their chain, and those with highest priorities are scheduled for the next five workdays. Support services, including parts needed, are prepared/acquired for the schedule.

Also, the WIP is reduced to seven C-5 planes (from 12 in 2004). "Fixer release control" points (i.e., the points at which the director could permit the aircraft to move from one phase to the next) have been put in place after each major phase to control the WIP. Also, there is now a "hold" phase of 20 days after the strip phase (i.e., disassembly) and repair phase to ensure that all parts needed have been refurbished before buildup (i.e., reassembly) phase can start. This will reduce the idle time and multitasking of mechanics. Supervisors roam the shop floor solving problems. Bottleneck activities/work packages are kaizened.

Source: M. M. Srinvasan, W. D. Best, and S. Chandrasekaran, "Warner Robins Air Logistics Center Streamlines Aircraft Repair and Overhaul," *Interfaces*, 37(1), January/February 2007, pp. 7–21.

---

project control Comparing a project's progress against plans and taking corrective action if necessary.

scope creep The problem of uncontrolled changes to a project's scope.

earned value analysis A standard method of measuring a project's progress at any given point in time, forecasting its completion date and final cost, and analyzing variances in the schedule and budget as the project proceeds.

Project control involves assessing a project's progress against plans and taking corrective actions, if necessary, in order to bring the project on track. Forecasts of costs and completion time are generated using trend analysis to determine the need for action.

Project control also involves controlling the changes to a project or to the project's scope. Replanning is usually necessary, but it should be kept to a minimum. Changes to the project's scope should be tightly controlled. If acceptable to the project manager, a change to the scope should be formally verified (i.e., authorized by the customer/sponsor). A common problem is that the customer/sponsor tends to frequently demand changes to the work required. The problem of uncontrolled changes to the project's scope is called **scope creep**.

To control a project's cost and schedule, various measures are used. Work performance information includes the completed and uncompleted activities/work packages, percentage of each activity/work package completed, costs authorized/incurred, cost estimates to project completion time, and so on.

Earned value analysis is a standard method of measuring a project's progress at any given point in time, forecasting its completion date and final cost, and analyzing variances in the schedule and budget as the project proceeds. After a project's duration and costs (including budget at completion (BAC)) are planned, the progress of the project at any time t is measured by budgeted cost of work performed up to t (called *earned value* (EV)), and not by budgeted cost of work scheduled up to t (called *planned value* (PV)). The scheduled *time overrun* (in dollars) at time t is measured by (PV − EV). Let the actual cost up to time t be AC. Then, *cost overrun* at time t is measured by (AC − EV), and cost *estimate at completion* (EAC) is given as follows: EAC = BAC/(EV/AC).

EXAMPLE 17-8 ▶

A project's budget at completion (BAC) is $200,000. At the midpoint of the time schedule, only 40 percent of the work is done. The budgeted cost of work done so far—that is, the earned value (EV)—is $80,000, the budgeted cost of work scheduled up to this time (PV) is $100,000, whereas the actual cost (AC) so far is $110,000. Determine the:

a. scheduled time overrun (in dollars).

b. cost overrun.

c. cost estimate at completion (EAC).

See Figure 17-9 for an overbudget project that is also behind schedule.

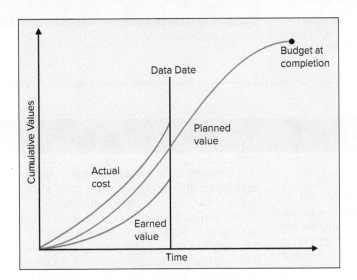

◀ **FIGURE 17-9**

Cumulative cost values for a project that is over budget and behind schedule.

Quality control involves using quality tools such as the control chart and cause and effect diagram in order to identify quality "variance," find its cause, and implement corrective actions.

The project team is managed by measuring team performance, providing feedback, resolving issues, and recognizing and rewarding good performance.

Software, email, and status review meetings, etc., are used to collect information and report on the project's performance through status reports, progress measurements, and forecasts. Communication with project stakeholders is managed by resolving issues promptly.

Risks are tracked and reassessed, and the response plans evaluated. Reserve analysis is performed to determine the adequacy of the contingency fund.

Contracts are managed by measuring suppliers' performance, comparing it with the contract requirements, and taking corrective action, if necessary. The relations with suppliers are managed by quickly resolving issues such as contested changes or late payments.

Finally, the project is completed and closed out. It is important to ensure that all contractors/teams have completed their work, and provided warranties and any other necessary paperwork. Also, it is important to review the project for lessons learned and document these for future reference. For examples of issues that can arise during project execution, see the "McGill University Health Centre" and "New Champlain Bridge" OM in Actions.

 OM in Action

McGill University Health Centre

In 2010, McGill University and the Government of Quebec awarded Groupe infrastructure santé McGill, composed of SNC-Lavalin and Innisfree Ltd., a $1.3 billion contract to finance, design, build, operate, and maintain a mega hospital complex on a 346,150 square-metre site in Montreal as part of a public–private partnership until 2044. McGill University Health Centre (MUHC) was to replace four distinct health care institutions and a research institute.

SNC-Lavalin is one of Canada's largest design, engineering, construction, and project management companies. Founded in 1911 in Montreal, SNC-Lavalin has

35 international offices and has performed hundreds of large projects.

For years, the Glen site was one of the largest construction sites in North America, with 900 professionals, nearly 12,000 workers, and 14 tower cranes in full swing. The project was completed in 2015.

SNC-Lavalin and its partner have launched a $330 million lawsuit against MUHC and the Government of Quebec over cost overruns. The extra costs stem from "the numerous instructions and changes made by the MUHC as well as the value of the additional work it requested."

Source: http://www.snclavalin.com/en/mcgill-university-health-centre
-glen-site; http://www.theglobeandmail.com/report-on-business/snc-and
-partner-file-330-million-lawsuit-against-mcgill-university-health-centre
/article29491164/.

© Meunierd/Dreamstime.com

 OM in Action www.newchamplain.ca

New Champlain Bridge

As the majority shareholder of the Signature on the Saint-Lawrence Group consortium, SNC-Lavalin has been tasked with the design, construction, and maintenance of Montreal's new Champlain Bridge as part of a public–private partnership agreement with Infrastructure Canada. With a 125-year design life, the new crossing includes a 3.4 km bridge across the St. Lawrence River, as well as a 470 metre bridge connecting Montreal to Ile-des-Soeurs. In addition, the 4.5 km federal portion of Highways 15 and 10 is being reconstructed and widened.

The new Champlain Bridge will replace the current bridge, one of the busiest in Canada, with 50 million vehicles passing over it each year. Aesthetic lighting is added on the main tower and bridge, and there is a multi-use path for cyclists and pedestrians.

The most significant challenge of the project is the compressed schedule affecting both design and construction. The 3.4 km crossing is required to be operable by December 1, 2018, just 42 months after the consortium was awarded the contract. Careful project planning—including tactics such as preparing permit applications in advance, large scale temporary jetties, and opting for significant offsite fabrication and precasting—makes it possible for the project to meet the schedule.

Durability is also a key design consideration, requiring high-performance materials. In addition, the structure has to satisfy seismic design standards.

An unresolved issue is that the consortium has launched a $124 million lawsuit against Infrastructure Canada. The lawsuit alleges that the consortium was not told that the existing bridge could not support more than 65 tonnes, whereas the weight needed to allow certain bridge components to be delivered to the new construction site is 80 tonnes. As a result, the project could be delayed and the consortium could be penalized.

Source: http://www.snclavalin.com/en/projects/champlain-bridge-corridor
-project.aspx, http://top100projects.ca/consortium-files-lawsuit-over
-champlain-bridge-project/.

Courtesy of Infrastructure Canada

 # Project Management Software

Many project management software programs are available, such as Microsoft Project. There are many advantages to using project management software, including:

- It imposes a methodology and common project management terminology.
- It provides a logical planning structure.

- It enhances communication among team members.
- It flags the occurrence of a problem.
- It automatically formats reports.
- It generates multiple levels of summary reports and detailed reports.
- It enables "what-if" scenarios.
- It generates various charts, including a basic schedule Gantt chart.

Using Microsoft® Project

Download a free 60-day trial version of *Project Professional 2016.*[5] After registering, downloading, and installing the software, open it:

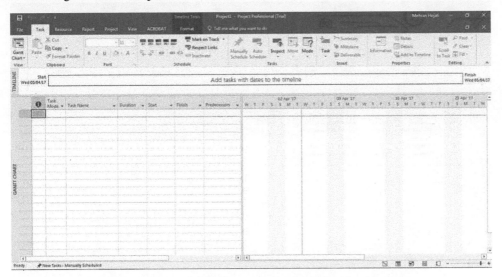

Next, enter the activity/work package (called task) names and their duration. We will enter the data from Example 17-1. Click the cell under the Task Name and type in "Locate Facility," and press the Enter key. Continue entering the task (activity/work package) names until all tasks are entered. Now, click on the cell below Duration and enter 8w (for 8 weeks), and press Enter. As you enter a duration, the Gantt chart on the right assigns a horizontal bar to the activity (task). Continue entering the durations until all durations are entered:

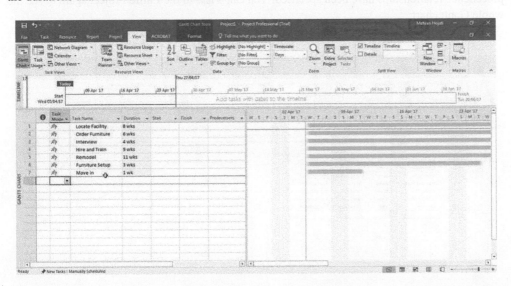

---

[5] https://www.microsoft.com/en-GB/evalcenter/evaluate-project-professional-2016.

In order to see the whole Gantt chart, click on the "View" tab on the top, then click "Entire Project." Note that the bars on the right and the pins under Task Mode are light blue. This indicates that the tasks are currently in Manually Scheduled Mode. This means that Microsoft Project will consider them as fixed tasks, and does not use them in its PERT/CPM solution method. We need to change the Task Modes to Auto Scheduled by clicking on the cell to the left of each task name, then clicking on the blue arrow-down square, and finally clicking on the Auto Scheduled. As you do this, the colour of the pin and the bar on the right will change to dark blue. After all task modes have been changed to Auto Scheduled, the screen looks as follows. Note that in the present form, all the activities/work packages (tasks) start the first day of the current week.

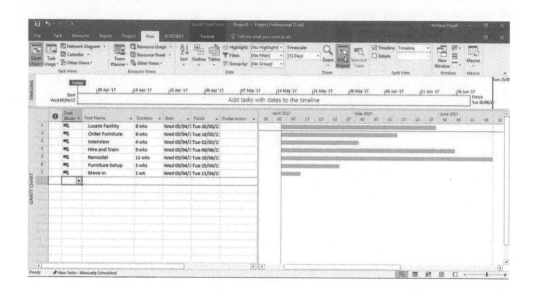

In order to enter the precedence relationships, click on the "Task" tab on the top, then select two activities with finish–start relationship (by keeping the control key pressed), and then clicking on the chain icon above the Schedule in the ribbon on the top to link the selected tasks. This will move the bar for the successor activity to the right of the bar for the Predecessor activity, and relate them with a short arrow. Continue with all the predecessor–successor pairs until all the precedence relationships have been specified. You can View to the Entire Project again to see the whole Gantt chart:

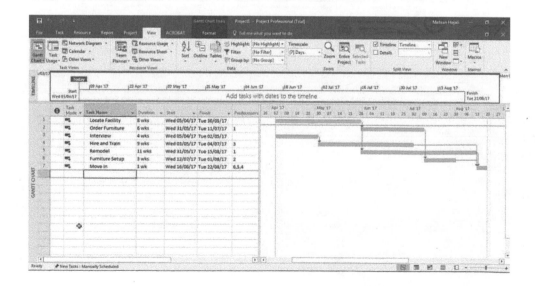

To see the precedence network, (in the "View" tab) click "Network diagram":

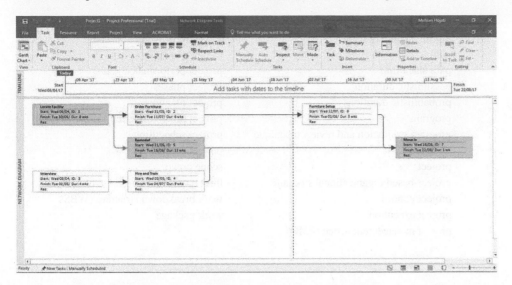

As you can see, the boxes for critical activities are pink. Microsoft Project also permits us to define resources (i.e., employees and equipment) and to assign these to the activities/work packages. This is done by clicking on the "Resources" tab on the top. Also, Microsoft Project allows us to track the progress of activities. This is done by clicking on the "Task" tab on the top, then on "Mark on Track," and finally "Update Tasks." As days pass, team members should enter the percentage of each activity completed. The software will indicate if any activity is behind schedule.

Summary

- A project is a unique, multi-person, large one-time job requiring special activities by different people, established to realize a specific objective (deliverable) in a limited time span.
- Projects go through a life cycle that involves initiation, planning and scheduling, execution and control, and close-out.
- Most organizations are structured as a matrix, with members working for both projects and a functional department.
- A project manager is responsible for all project activities from inception to close-out, including meeting the project performance goals of being on time/schedule and within quality/scope and cost/budget.
- Project planning involves finalizing the project scope, creating the work breakdown structure, risk management planning, scheduling, cost estimation and budgeting, and quality, communications, and purchase planning.
- Risk management planning involves risk identification, assessment, and response planning. Schedule Gantt charts are used to schedule and control simple projects.

- PERT/CPM is used to schedule complex projects. A precedence network depicts the sequential relationships that exist among activities/work packages. The solution reveals the longest (i.e., critical) path and the critical activities, which are those activities that must be completed on time to achieve timely project completion.
- For projects with variable activity/work package durations, the three-point estimation method can be used.
- It may be possible to shorten, or crash, the length of a project by shortening one or more of the critical activities. Typically, such gains are achieved by spending additional resources, but the shortening will save indirect project costs.
- Project execution involves putting the project plans into action, buying materials, assigning team members, and subcontracting the work.
- Project control means taking measurements of project performance and taking corrective action if necessary.
- Microsoft Project is a widely used project management software.

Key Terms

activity

activity-on-arrow (AOA)

activity-on-node (AON)

activity slack time

Beta distribution

crashing a project

critical activities

critical path

critical path method (CPM)

deterministic durations

earned value analysis

matrix organization

most likely duration

optimistic duration

path

path slack time

pessimistic duration

probabilistic durations

program

program evaluation and review technique
   (PERT)

project

project-based organizational structure

project control

project execution

project management office (PMO)

project management triangle

project manager

project performance goals

project phases

project planning

project portfolio selection

project scheduling

project scope

scope creep

three-point estimation method

work breakdown structure (WBS)

work package

Solved Problems

Problem 1

The following list contains information related to the major activities of a research project. Use the information given to do the following:

a. Draw the precedence network.

b. Find the critical path by identifying all the start-to-end paths and calculating their lengths.

c. What is the expected duration of the project?

Activity	Immediately Precedes	Expected Duration (days)
a	c, b	5
c	d	8
d	i	2
b	i	7
e	f	3
f...........	m	6
i	m	10
m	End	8
g	h	1
h	k	2
k	End	17

Solution

a. In constructing precedence networks, these observations can be useful.

   i. Use pencil.

   ii. Start and end with a single node.

   iii. Try to avoid having paths cross each other.

   iv. Have arrows go from left to right.

v. Activities with no predecessors are at the beginning (left side) of the network, immediately after the start node S.

vi. Activities with multiple predecessors are located at path intersections.

vii. Go down the activity list in order to avoid overlooking any activities.

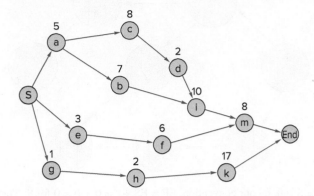

b. and c.

Path	Length (days)
s-a-c-d-i-m-End*..........	$5 + 8 + 2 + 10 + 8 = 33^†$
s-a-b-i-m-End	$5 + 7 + 10 + 8 = 30$
s-e-f-m-End	$3 + 6 + 8 = 17$
s-g-h-k-End	$1 + 2 + 17 = 20$

* Critical path.
† Expected project duration.

Problem 2

Using the PERT/CPM solution technique, determine the ES, EF, LF, LS, and slack times for each activity in the following precedence network (durations are in days). Identify the activities that are on the critical path.

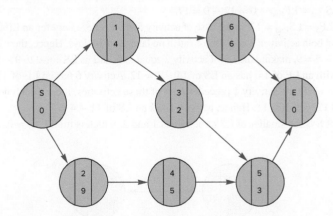

Solution

We will determine and place the ES, EF, LS, and LF times for each activity in its circle as follows:

We determine the earliest start and finish times, working from left to right, as shown in the following network. The explanations follow.

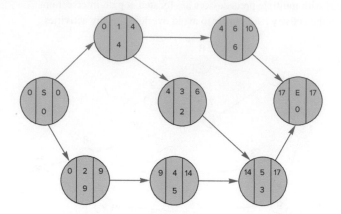

ES for the start node S is 0, by our convention. EF = ES + t = 0 + 0 = 0 for S. Then, activity 1 can start at 0 (i.e., its ES = 0). With a duration of 4 days, it can finish after 0 + 4 = 4 days (i.e., its EF = 4). Hence, activity 6 and 3 can start no earlier than day 4 (i.e., their ES = 4). Activity 6 has earliest finish of 4 + 6 = 10 days, and activity 3 has the earliest finish of 4 + 2 = 6 days. At this point, it is impossible to say what the earliest start is for activity 5; that will depend on which activity, 4 or 3, has the larger EF. Consequently, it is necessary to first calculate ES and EF along the lower path. Using an ES of 0 for activity 2, its EF will be 9, so activity 4 will have an ES of 9 and an EF of 9 + 5 = 14.

Considering that the two activities immediately preceding node 5 have EF times of 6 and 14, the earliest that activity 5 can start is the *larger* of these, which is 14. Hence, activity 5 has an EF of 14 + 3 = 17.

Now compare the EFs of the activities immediately preceding the End node. The larger of these, 17, is the ES_{End}, and EF_{End} = 17 + 0 = 17. This is also the expected project duration.

The LF and LS times for each activity can now be determined by working backward through the network (from right to left; see the following network). The LF for the End node is 17—the project duration. Then, $LS_{End} = LF_{End} - 0 = 17 - 0 = 17$.

Now, $LF_6 = LF_5 = LS_{End} = 17$. In the case of activity 5, the LS necessary for an LF of 17 is 17 − 3 = 14. This means that both activities 3 and 4 must finish no later than 14 days. Hence, their LF is 14. Activity 4 has an LS of 14 − 5 = 9, making the LF of activity 2 equal to 9, and its LS equal to 9 − 9 = 0.

Activity 3, with an LF of 14, has an LS of 14 − 2 = 12. Activity 6 has an LF of 17 and therefore an LS of 17 − 6 = 11. Since activity 1 precedes *both* of these activities, it can finish no later than the *smaller* of 11 and 12, which is 11. Hence, activity 1 has an LS of 11 − 4 = 7.

Finally, LF of S is the smaller of LS of activities 1 and 2, which is min(7, 0) = 0. Hence, LS of S is 0 − 0 = 0.

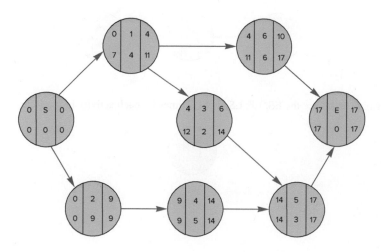

The slack time for an activity is the difference between either LF and EF or LS and ES. Thus,

Activity	LS	ES	Slack	or	LF	EF	Slack
S	0	0	0		0	0	0
1	7	0	7		11	4	7
6	11	4	7		17	10	7
3	12	4	8		14	6	8
2	0	0	0		9	9	0
4	9	9	0		14	14	0
5	14	14	0		17	17	0
E	0	0	0		0	0	0

The activities with zero slack times indicate the critical path. In this case the critical path is S-2-4-5-E.

When working on problems of this nature, keep in mind the following:

a. The ES time for a node with multiple immediate predecessors is the largest EF of the immediate predecessors.
b. The LF for a node with multiple immediate successors is the smallest LS of the immediate successors.

Problem 3

A path in a network has three activities. Their standard deviations are 1.50, 0.80, and 1.30. Find the path standard deviation.

Solution

Standard deviations cannot be added, but variances can be added. Square each standard deviation to obtain its variance, and then add the resulting variances to obtain the path variance:

Standard Deviation	Variance
1.50	2.25
0.80	0.64
1.30	1.69
	4.58 (path variance)

The square root of the path variance is the path standard deviation:

$$\sqrt{4.58} = 2.14 \text{ (path standard deviation)}$$

Problem 4

Expected durations (in weeks) and variances for the major activities of an R&D project are depicted on the following precedence network. Determine the probability that the project completion time will be:

a. Less than 50 weeks.
b. More than 50 weeks.

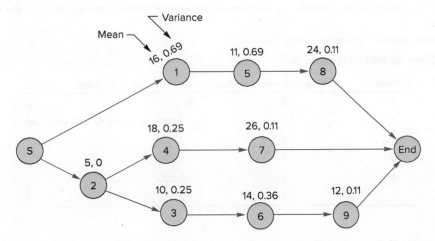

Solution

Because S and End have zero duration, we can ignore them in the following calculations. The mean and standard deviation for each path are:

Path	Expected Time (weeks)	Standard Deviation (weeks)
S-1-5-8-End	16 + 11 + 24 = 51	$\sqrt{0.69 + 0.69 + 0.11} = 1.22$
S-2-4-7-End	5 + 18 + 26 = 49	$\sqrt{0.00 + 0.25 + 0.11} = 0.60$
S-2-3-6-9-End	5 + 10 + 14 + 12 = 41	$\sqrt{0.00 + 0.25 + 0.36 + 0.11} = 0.60$

a. Calculate the z value for each path for the length specified. Use: $z = \dfrac{50 - t_{path}}{\sigma_{path}}$

The probability that each path will be completed in 50 weeks or less is shown on the following charts (probabilities are from Appendix B, Table B). The probability that the project will be completed in 50 weeks or less depends on all three paths being completed in that time. Because z for path S-2-3-6-9-End is greater than +3.50, it is treated as having a probability of completion in 50 weeks of 1.00. The probability that *both* other paths will not exceed 50 weeks is the *product* of their individual probabilities of completion within 50 weeks. Thus, 0.2061(0.9525) = 0.1963.

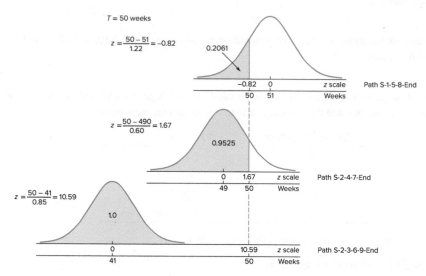

b. The probability that the project will exceed 50 weeks is the complement of this number, which is 1.000 − 0.1963 = 0.8037. (Note that this is not the product of the path probabilities of exceeding 50 weeks.)

Problem 5

Indirect cost for a project is $12,000 per week for as long as the project lasts. The project manager has supplied the crash cost and potential information and precedence network shown below. Use the information to:

a. Determine an optimum crashing plan.

b. Graph the total costs for the plan.

Activity	Crashing Potential (weeks)	Cost per Week to Crash
a	3	$11,000
b	3	3,000 first week, $4,000 after that
c	2	6,000
d	1	1,000
e	3	6,000
f	1	2,000

Solution

a. i. Calculate path lengths and identify the critical path:

Path	Duration (weeks)
s-a-b-End	24 (critical path)
s-c-d-End	19
s-e-f-End	23

ii. Rank critical activities according to crash costs:

Activity	Cost per Week to Crash	Available Weeks to Crash
b	$3,000 first week, $4,000 after that	3
a	11,000	3

Activity b should be shortened one week since it has the lower crashing cost per week. This would reduce indirect costs by $12,000 at a direct cost of $3,000, for a net savings of $9,000. At this point, paths s-a-b-End and s-e-f-End would both have length of 23 weeks, so both would be critical.

iii. Rank activities by crashing cost on the two critical paths:

Path	Activity	Cost per Week to Crash	Available Weeks to Crash
s-a-b-End	b	$4,000	2
....	a	11,000	3
s-e-f-End	f	2,000	1
....	e	6,000	3

Choose one activity (the least costly) on each path to crash: b on s-a-b-End and f on s-e-f-End, for a total cost of $4,000 + $2,000 = $6,000 and a net savings of $12,000 − $6,000 = $6,000. *Note:* There is no activity common to the two critical paths.

iv. Check to see which path(s) might be critical: s-a-b-End and s-e-f-End would be 22 weeks in length, and s-c-d-End would still be 19 weeks.

v. Rank activities on the critical paths:

Path	Activity	Cost per Week to Crash	Available Weeks to Crash
s-a-b-End	b	$4,000	1
....	a	11,000	3
s-e-f-End	e	6,000	3
....	f	(no further crashing possible)	0

Crash b on path s-a-b-End and e on path s-e-f-End one week each for a cost of $4,000 + $6,000 = $10,000, for a net savings of $12,000 − $10,000 = $2,000.

vi. At this point, no further reduction is cost-effective: paths s-a-b-End and s-e-f-End would be 21 weeks in length, and one activity from each path would have to be shortened. This would mean activity a at $11,000 and e at $6,000 for a total of $17,000, which exceeds the $12,000 potential savings in indirect costs. Note that no further crashing for activity (b) is possible.

b. The following table summarizes the results, showing the length of the project after crashing n weeks:

Path	n = 0	1	2	3
s-a-b-End	24	23	22	21
s-c-d-End	19	19	19	19
s-e-f-End	23	23	22	21
Project crashed		b	b, f	b, e
Crashing costs ($000)		3	6	10

A summary of costs for the preceding schedule would look like this:

Project Length	Weeks Shortened	Cumulative Crashing Costs ($000)	Cumulative Indirect Costs ($000)	Total Costs ($000)
24	0	0	24(12) = 288	288
23	1	3	23(12) = 276	279
22	2	3 + 6 = 9	22(12) = 264	273
21	3	9 + 10 = 19	21(12) = 252	271
20	4	19 + 17 = 36	20(12) = 240	276

The graph of total cost is as follows.

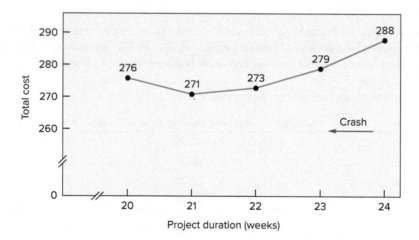

Discussion and Review Questions

Note: An asterisk indicates that a question or problem may be more challenging.

LO1 **1.** What are the phases of a project?

LO1 **2.** Explain the difference between matrix-based and project-based organizational structure.

LO1 **3.** How should a company select its projects?

LO1 **4.** What skills does a project manager need?

LO1 **5.** What are some aspects of the project manager's job that make it more demanding than the job of a manager working in a more routine organizational framework?

LO2 **6.** What does project planning involve?

LO2 **7.** List the steps in risk management planning.

LO2 **8.** What is a work breakdown structure, and how is it useful for project planning?

LO2 **9.** What are some of the reasons an activity/work package might take longer than expected?

L03 10. Compare a schedule Gantt chart and a precedence network.

L03 11. Identify the term used for each of the following:

L03   a. A sequence of activities in a project.

L03   b. The longest sequence of activities in a project.

L03   c. The technique used for probabilistic activity durations.

L05   d. The difference in length of time of any path and the critical path.

L04   e. The statistical distribution used to describe variability of an activity's duration.

L05   f. The statistical distribution used to describe variability of project duration.

L05   g. Shortening an activity by allocating additional resources.

L06 12. What are ES, EF, LF, and LS, and how are they calculated?

L04 13. What is a critical activity?

L04 14. Why might a probabilistic estimate of a project's completion time based solely on the variance of the *critical path* derived using the expected activity durations be misleading? Under what circumstances would it be acceptable?

L05 15. Define each of these terms used in the three-point estimation method, and indicate how each is determined.

  a. Expected activity duration.

  b. Variance of an activity's duration.

  c. Standard deviation of a path's duration.

L06 16. Describe the procedure for project crashing.

L07 17. Describe project execution.

L07 18. What is the critical chain method?

L07 19. What does project control involve?

L07 20. What is earned value analysis?

L08 21. How can Microsoft Project help to manage a project?

L01 22. What is involved in ExxonMobil's Capital Project Management System?

L01 23. What is the design–build method of construction delivery? Give an example.

L03 24. How does PCL ensure on-time completion of a project?

L07 25. Name two issues that can arise in project management.

Taking Stock

L06 1. What trade-offs are associated with duration and cost of an activity?

L01 2. Who needs to be involved in project management?

L08 3. State briefly how technology can assist in project management.

L01 4. What kind of ethical issues arise in project management?

Critical Thinking Exercise

L01 Project management techniques have been used successfully for a wide variety of projects, including the many NASA space missions, huge construction projects, implementation of major systems such as an ERP, production of movies, development of new goods and services, and much more. Why not use them for managing the operations function of any organization?

Experiential Learning Exercise

L01 Select a team project you are currently working on, or one that you have recently worked on.

  a. List the project objective.

  b. List the main activities.

  c. List the project milestones, such as required progress reports or the completion of major tasks.

  d. How important are (were) behavioural aspects of the project? For example, did the project team agree on the project's specific objective, individual work assignments, and so on?

  e. Were there any unforeseen problems? If so, how were they resolved?

Internet Exercises

 1. Visit https://www.pmi.org/business-solutions/case-studies, choose a case study, and summarize it.

 2. Read one of the following Deltek case studies, and summarize it.

a. https://www.deltek.com/~/media/customer%20testimonial%20pdf/ppm/cs_boeing.ashx?la=en.

b. https://www.deltek.com/~/media/customer%20testimonial%20pdf/acumen/bombardier%20case%20study.ashx?la=en

 3. Visit https://products.office.com/en-ca/project/project-customer-stories, choose a customer, and identify the types of projects for which the customer is using Microsoft Project.

4. Visit https://www.innotas.com/customers-success-stories, choose a customer, and briefly summarize the benefits of the project (portfolio) management software to the customer.

5. Visit http://www.wsp-pb.com/en/WSP-Canada/Careers/Join-Our-Team/Available-position/, find a project manager job ad, and summarize its duties.

6. Visit http://www.stantec.com/search.html?q=project+management&searchFilter=projects, choose a project, and summarize Stantec's project management role.

Problems

1. For each of the following precedence networks, determine the critical path and the project duration by determining the length of each path. The numbers above the nodes represent activity durations (in days).

a.

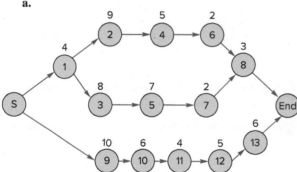

b.

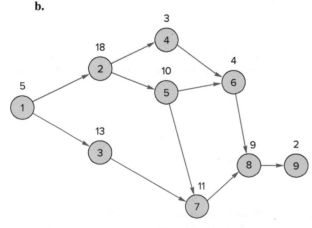

c.

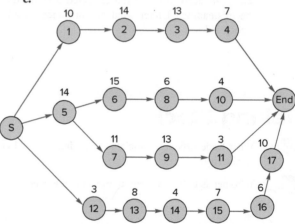

2. Claire received a new word-processing software program for her birthday. She also received a cheque with which she intends to purchase a new computer. Claire's university instructor assigned a paper due next week. Claire decided that she will prepare the paper on the new computer. She made a list of the activities and their estimated durations. Claire's friend has offered to shop for, select, and purchase a computer, and install the software.

a. Arrange the activities into two logical sequences.

b. Construct a precedence network.

c. Determine the critical path by determining the length of each path. What is the expected duration of the project?

d. What are some possible reasons for the project to take longer than expected?

Estimated Time (hours)	Activity (abbreviation)
0.8	Install software (Install)
0.4	Outline the paper (Outline)
0.2	Submit paper to instructor (Submit)
0.6	Choose a topic (Choose)

0.5	Use a grammar-checker and make corrections (Check)
3.0	Write the paper using the word-processing software (Write)
2.0	Shop for a new computer (Shop)
1.0	Select and purchase a computer (Select)
2.0	Library research on chosen topic (Library)

LO3 & 4

3. The following information pertains to a project that is about to commence. Which activities would you be concerned with in terms of timely project completion? Explain. (*Hint:* Determine the length of each path.)

Activity	Precedes	Estimated Duration (days)
A	B	15
B	C, D	12
C	E	6
D	End	5
E	End	3
F	G, H	8
G	I	8
H	J	9
I	End	7
J	K	14
K	End	6

LO3

4. Construct a precedence network for each of the following two projects.

(1) Activity	Precedes Activity	(2) Activity	Precedes Activity
A	D	J	L, N
B	E, F	K	R
C	G	L	M
D	K	M	End
E	K	N	P
F	H, I	P	End
G	I	Q	S, T
H	End	R	V
I	End	S	V
K	End	V	End
		T	V, W
		W	End

LO4

5. For each of the problems listed below, determine the following values for each activity: the earliest start time, earliest finish time, latest finish time, latest start time, and activity slack time. Identify the critical activities, and determine the duration of the project.
   a. Problem 1*a*.
   b. Problem 1*b*.
   c. Problem 3.

LO4

6. Reconsider the precedence network of Problem 1*a*. Suppose that after 12 days, activities 1, 9, and 2 have been finished; activity 3 is 75 percent finished; and activity 10 is half finished. How many days after the original start time would the project finish?

7. Three recent university graduates have formed a partnership and have opened an advertising firm. Their first project consists of activities listed in the following table.
   a. Draw the precedence network.
   b. What is the probability that the project can be completed in 24 days or less? In 21 days or less?
   c. Suppose that now is the end of the seventh day and that activities a and b have been completed while activity d is 50 percent completed. Three-point estimates for the remaining duration of activity d are now 5, 6, and 7 days. Activities c and h are ready to begin. Determine the probability of finishing the project by the end of (a) day 24 and (b) day 21.

		Duration in Days		
Activity	Precedes	Optimistic	Most Likely	Pessimistic
a	c	5	6	7
b	h	8	8	11
c	e	6	8	11
d	f	9	12	15
e	End	5	6	9
f	g	5	6	7
g	End	2	3	7
h	i	4	4	5
i	End	5	7	8

8. The new director of special events at a large university has decided to completely revamp the graduation ceremonies. To that end, a precedence network of the major activities has been developed. The network has five paths with expected durations and variances as shown in the following table. Graduation day is 16 full weeks from now. Assuming that the project begins now, what is the probability that the project will be completed before:
   a. Graduation day?
   b. The end of week 15?
   c. The end of week 13?

Path	Expected Duration (weeks)	Variance
A	10	1.21
B	8	2.00
C	12	1.00
D	15	2.89
E	14	1.44

9. Construct a precedence network for the information in the following table. What is the probability that a project will take more than 10 weeks to complete if the activity means and standard deviations (both in weeks) are as follows?

Activity	Precedes	Mean	Standard Deviation
a	b	5	1.3
b	End	4	1.0
c	End	8	1.6

10. The project described in the following table is scheduled to be completed in 11 weeks.
  a. Draw the precedence network.
  b. If you were the manager of this project, would you be concerned? Explain.
  c. If there is a penalty of $5,000 a week for each week the project is late, what is the probability of incurring a penalty of at least $5,000?

Activity	Precedes	Expected Duration (weeks)	Standard Deviation (weeks)
a	b	4	0.70
b	End	6	0.90
c	d	3	0.62
d	End	9	1.90

11. The following precedence network displays the three-point estimates for each activity of a project. Determine:
  a. The expected duration for each path and its variance.
  b. The probability that the project will require more than 49 weeks.
  c. The probability that the project can be completed in 46 weeks or less.

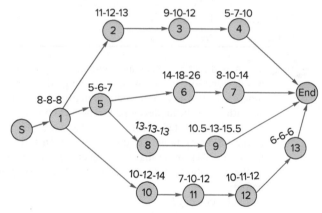

12. A project manager has compiled a list of major activities that will be required to install a computer information system in her company. The list includes three-point estimates of durations (optimistic, most likely, pessimistic) for activities and the precedence relationships.

Activity	Precedes	Three-Point Estimates (weeks)
a	d, f	2-4-6
d	e	6-8-10
e	h	7-9-12
h	End	2-3-5
f	g	3-4-8
g	End	5-7-9
b	i	2-2-3
i	j	2-3-6
j	k	3-4-5
k	End	4-5-8
c	m	5-8-12

m	n	1-1-1
n	o	6-7-11
o	End	8-9-13

If the project is finished within 26 weeks of its start, the project manager will receive a bonus of $1,000; and if the project is finished within 27 weeks of its start, the bonus will be $500. Find the probability of each bonus.

13. The project manager of the construction of a domed stadium had hoped to be able to complete the construction prior to the start of the next season. After a review of the activity duration estimates, it now appears that a certain amount of crashing will be needed to ensure project completion before the season opener. Given the following information, determine the minimum-cost crashing schedule that will shave five weeks off the project length.

Activity	Precedes	Normal Duration (weeks)	Crashing Costs First Week	Second Week
A	B	12	$15,000	$20,000
B	K	14	10,000	10,000
C	D, E, F	10	5,000	5,000
D	G	17	20,000	21,000
E	H	18	16,000	18,000
F	I	12	12,000	15,000
G	M	15	24,000	24,000
H	N, P	8	–	–
I	J	7	30,000	–
J	P	12	25,000	25,000
K	End	9	10,000	10,000
M	End	3	–	–
N	End	11	40,000	–
P	End	8	20,000	20,000

14. A construction project has indirect costs totalling $40,000 per week. Major activities in the project and their expected durations are shown in the following precedence network:

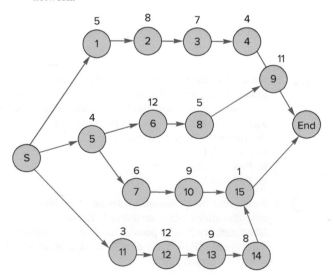

Crashing costs for each activity are:

	Crashing Costs ($000)		
Activity	**First Week**	**Second Week**	**Third Week**
1	$18	$22	$–
2	24	25	25
3	30	30	35
4	15	20	—
9	30	33	36
5	12	24	26
6	—	—	—
8	40	40	40
7	3	10	12
10	2	7	10
15	26	—	—
11	10	15	25
12	8	13	—
13	5	12	—
14	14	15	—

   a. Determine the minimum-cost crashing plan that will take off six weeks from the project duration.
   b. Plot the total cost curve against project duration. What is the optimum number of weeks to crash the project?

LO6 15. A company builds custom equipment. It has landed a contract with a major customer. Relevant data are shown below. The complication is that the delivery has been promised in 32 weeks and the company will have to pay a penalty of $375 for each week the equipment is late.

Activity	Precedes	Normal Duration (weeks)	Crashing Costs	
			1st Week	**2nd Week**
K	L, N	9	$410	$415
L	M	7	125	—
N	J	5	45	45
M	Q	4	300	350
J	Q	6	50	—
Q	P, Y	5	200	225
P	Z	8	—	—
Y	End	7	85	90
Z	End	6	90	—

Develop the minimum cost crashing schedule.

LO4 16. The following is the list of activities, their immediate predecessor(s), and their expected duration used by a component supplier to automobile manufacturers to plan for QS 9000 (the auto industry version of ISO 9000) certification (registration).[6]

The List of Activities in a QS-9000 Registration Project

Activity	Description	Immediate Predecessor(s)	Estimated Time (weeks)*
A	Appointment of QS-9000 taskforce	None	1
B	Preparation of a feasible plan	A	1
C	Delegation of responsibilities	B	1
D	Searching for a QS-9000 registrar	C	1
E	Preparation of three levels of documentation	C	12
F	QS-9000 awareness training	C	6
G	QS-9000 training of auditors and quality personnel	F	6
H	Preparing the plant for QS-9000 registrar	C	24
I	Conference with lead auditor	D	1
J	Examination of documentation	E, I	3
K	Internal audit of plant sections	G, H, J	12
L	Corrective actions of plant sections	K	12
M	Lead auditor and audit team audit plant	L	1
N	Audit conference and corrective action plan	M	2
O	Implementation of corrective action plans	N	12
P	Lead auditor re-audits corrective actions	O	2
Q	Lead auditor's recommendation	P	1

* These are estimates of time and may vary based upon situation, company, and registrar.

   a. Draw the precedence network.
   b. Determine the earliest and latest times, and identify the critical activities and the project duration.

LO5 17. Use the following activities and their three duration estimates (in days) to do the following:
   a. Determine the expected duration of the project.
   b. Calculate the probability that the project will take at least 18 days.

[6] J. K. Bandyopadhyay, "The CPM/PERT Project Scheduling Approach to QS-9000 Registration: A Case Study at a United States Auto Parts Company," *International Journal of Management* 19(3), September 2002, pp. 455–463.

Path	Activity	Durations t_o	t_m	t_p
	a	4	5	6
a-b-c	b	7	8	10
	c	3	5	9
	d	7	8	11
d-e-f	e	2	3	4
	f	1	4	6

LO4 **18.** Consider the construction of a research building for Eli Lilly & Co., a pharmaceutical company, a few years ago. This 550,000-sq.-ft, four-storey (in three wings), $135 million building was planned to be completed in five years. It required special ventilation for 162 labs, purified water, and special drainage. Consider the following list of major activities/bid packages (as seen by Eli Lilly), their expected duration, and their relationship to other activities/bid packages for the Eli Lilly building.

Activity/Work Packages	Duration (in months)	Immediate Predecessor
A. Project approval	3	–
B. Decide general requirements	6	A
C. Choose A/E firm	2	A
D. Preliminary design	3	B, C
E. Choose project management firm	2	B
F. Decide detailed requirements	6	D, E
G. Finalize design	6	F
H. Schedule, budget, manual	4	F
I. Start bid packages	2	G, H
J. Excavate, foundation, steel structure	10	I
K. Put up enclosures	7	J
L. HVAC, fire protection, plumbing	6	J
M. Electrical	5	J
N. Interior finishes	12	K, L, M
O. Close out project	2	N

a. Draw the precedence network.
b. Determine the ES, EF, LF, and LS times.
c. What is the project duration?
d. What are the critical activities?

LO6 *19. A project consists of the following activities, normal durations (days), immediate predecessors, cost per day to crash ($000/day), and available days to crash.[7]

Activity	Normal Duration (days)	Immediate Predecessor(s)	Cost per Day to Crash ($000/day)	Available Days to Crash
A	8	–	9	5
B	8	–	2	4
C	6	–	4	3
D	9	A	6	7
E	20	A	3	7
F	11	B, D	1	5
G	9	B, D	7	5
H	12	C, G	8	7

a. Draw the precedence network.
b. Calculate the project duration using normal activity durations.
c. Determine the minimum-cost crashing plan that will take 16 days off the project duration.

LO6 **20.** Here is a list of activity times for a project as well as crashing costs for its activities. Determine the minimum-cost crashing if the goal is to shorten the project by three weeks. First construct a precedence network.

Activity	Precedes	Normal Duration (weeks)	Crashing Costs ($000) 1st Week	2nd Week
A	B	5	$ 8	$10
B	C	6	7	9
C	End	3	14	15
D	E	3	9	11
E	C	7	8	9
F	G	5	10	15
G	H	5	11	13
H	End	5	12	14

LO4 **21.** The following is a list of activities/work packages and their precedence and duration, for a new-plant start-up project. Draw the precedence network, calculate earliest and latest times, and determine the project duration and critical activities.

Activity/ Work Packages	Description	Precedes	Duration (months)
A	Selection of plant manager	–	3
B	Site survey and soil test	–	1
C	Extension of road, water, utilities, sewer	–	6
D	Selection and purchase of equipment	A	2
E	Final plant design	B	3
F	Employee interviews and hiring	A	3
G	Equipment delivery	D	9
H	Construction of plant	E	11
I	Layout design	D, E	1
J	Setting up management system	A	4
K	Employee training	F, G, H	2
L	Equipment and system installation	G, H, I, J	1

LO4 **22.** At the top of the next page are the required activities of the fire protection bid package of the building project referred to in Problem 18, including their expected duration (in working days) and their immediate predecessor(s). Draw the precedence network. Calculate the earliest start, earliest finish, latest finish, and latest start times. What is the fire protection bid package duration? Name the critical activities.

[7] N. Siemens, "A Simple CPM Time–Cost Tradeoff Algorithm," *Management Science*, February 1971, 17(6), pp. B354–363.

Activity	Description	Precedes	Duration (days)
A	Invite bids	–	37
B	Award contract	A	22
C	Preliminary design and revision	B	110
D	Detailed drawing	B	60
E	Final owner review	C, D	15
F	Finalize design	E	25
G	Install pipe support	F	60
H	Procure pipes	F	35
I	Procure equipment	F	100
J	Install pipes	H	130
K	Install equipment	I	100
L	Test system	G, J, K	160

 MINI-CASE

Time, Please

"Smitty" Smith is a project manager for a large consumer electronics corporation. Although she has been with the company only four years, she has demonstrated an uncanny ability to bring projects in on time, meet technical specifications, and be close to budget.

Her latest assignment is a project that will involve merging two existing technologies. She and her team have almost finished developing the proposal that will be presented to a management committee for approval. All that remains to be done is to determine a duration estimate for the project. Smitty wants an estimated duration that will have a 95 percent probability of being met. The team has constructed a precedence network for the project. It has three paths. The expected durations and standard deviations for the paths are listed below.

Path	Expected Duration (weeks)	Standard Deviation (weeks)
A	10	4
B	14	2
C	13	2

Question

What project duration (in weeks) should Smitty include in the proposal?

 MINI-CASE

Fantasy Products

Company Background

The Fantasy Products Company (disguised name) is a manufacturer of high-quality small appliances intended for home use. The company's current product line includes irons, a small hand-held vacuum, and a number of kitchen appliances such as toasters, blenders, waffle irons, and coffeemakers. Fantasy Products has a strong R&D department that continually searches for ways to improve existing products as well as develops new ones.

Currently, the R&D department is working on the development of a new kitchen appliance that will chill foods quickly, much as a microwave oven heats them quickly, although the technology involved is quite different. Tentatively named The Big Chill, the product will initially carry a price tag of around $125, and the target market consists of upper-income consumers. At this price, it is expected to be a very profitable item. R&D engineers now have a working prototype and are satisfied that, with the cooperation from the production and marketing people, the product can be ready in time for the all-important Christmas buying season. A target date has been set for product introduction that is 24 weeks away.

Current Problem

Fantasy Products' marketing vice-president, Vera Sloan, has recently learned from reliable sources that a competitor is also in the process of developing a similar product, which it intends to bring out at almost the same time. In addition, her source indicated that the competitor plans to sell its product, which will be smaller than The Big Chill, for $99 in the hope of appealing to more customers. With the help of several of her key people who are to be involved in marketing The Big Chill, Vera has decided that in order to compete, the selling price for The Big Chill will have to be lowered to within $10 of the competitor's price. At this price level, it will still be profitable, although not nearly as profitable as originally anticipated.

However, Vera is wondering whether it would be possible to expedite the product introduction process in order to beat the competition to the market. If possible, she would like to get a six-week jump on the competition; this would put the product introduction date only 18 weeks away. During this initial period, Fantasy Products could sell The Big Chill for $125, reducing the selling price to $109 when the competitor's product actually enters the market. Since forecasts based on market research show that sales during the first six weeks will be about 400 units per week, there is an opportunity for $25 per unit profit if the early introduction can be accomplished. In addition, there is prestige involved in being first to the market. This should help enhance The Big Chill's image during the anticipated battle for market share.

Data Collection

Since Fantasy Products has been through the product-introduction process a number of times, Vera has developed a list of the tasks that must be accomplished and the order in which they must be completed. Although the duration and costs vary depending on the particular product, the basic process does not. The list of activities involved in product introduction and their precedence relationships are presented in Table 1. Duration and cost estimates for the introduction of The Big Chill are presented in Table 2. Note that some of the activities can be completed on a crash basis, with an associated increase in cost. For example, activity B can be crashed from eight weeks to six weeks at an additional cost of $3,000 (i.e., $12,000 − $9,000). Assume that if B is crashed to seven weeks, the additional cost will be $1,500 (i.e., $3,000/2).

Table 1   *List of activities involved in product introduction and precedence relationships.*

Activity	Description	Immediate Predecessor(s)
A	Select and order production equipment	–
B	Receive production equipment from supplier	A
C	Install and set up production equipment	B
D	Finalize bill of material	–
E	Order parts	D
F	Receive parts	E
G	First production run	C, F
H	Finalize marketing plan	–
I	Produce magazine ads	H
J	Script for TV ads	H
K	Produce TV ads	J
L	Begin ad campaign	I, K
M	Ship product to consumers	G, L

Table 2   *Duration and cost estimates for introduction of The Big Chill.*

Activity	Normal Duration (weeks)	Normal Cost	Crash Duration (weeks)	Normal and Crash Cost
A	3	$ 2,000	2	$ 4,400
B	8	9,000	6	12,000
C	4	2,000	2	7,000
D	2	1,000	1	2,000
E	2	2,000	1	3,000
F	5	0	5	0
G	6	12,000	3	24,000
H	4	3,500	2	8,000
I	4	5,000	3	8,000
J	3	8,000	2	15,000
K	4	50,000	3	70,000
L	6	10,000	6	10,000
M	1	5,000	1	5,000

Fantasy Products needs to decide whether to bring The Big Chill to market 18 weeks from now, as Vera Sloan is recommending. As the project management specialist in the R&D department, you have been asked to answer the following questions.

Questions

1. When would the project be completed using the normal durations?

2. Is it possible to complete the project in 18 weeks? What would be the associated additional cost? Which activities would need to be completed on a crash basis?

3. Is there some time frame shorter than the 18 weeks Vera has recommended that would make more sense in terms of profits?

Source: Adapted from an original case by R. J. Thieraus, M. Cunningham, and M. Blackwell, Xavier University, Cincinnati, Ohio.

Chapter 18
Waiting-Line Analysis

LEARNING OBJECTIVES

After completing this chapter, you should be able to:

LO1 Explain why waiting lines form, identify the goal of queueing (waiting-line) analysis, explore ways to deal with the perception of waiting, and discuss constraint management.

LO2 Describe the system characteristics and measures of performance used in queueing.

LO3 List and distinguish among the queueing models studied in this chapter and understand and use some basic queueing relationships.

LO4 Discuss and use the single server queueing models presented.

LO5 Discuss and use the multiple server queueing models presented.

LO6 Discuss and use the finite source queueing model presented.

Gunter Marx/Alamy Stock Photo

The Canadian Border Services Agency (CBSA) is charged with protecting the safety of all travellers and facilitating the smooth flow of goods into and out of the country. Approximately half of all traffic goes through the 21 land border crossings between Canada and the United States. Due to the sheer volume of people and goods moving across the border each day, excessive waiting times and long queues are a common occurrence. Since the terror attacks of September 11, 2001, Canadian and American border operations have seen increased cooperation with regards to improving public safety and efficiency.

Several new innovations have been implemented along the border to further these goals. One such innovation involves the use of sensors—known as loop detectors—and electronic displays. Border crossings are typically located at the end of highways, with potentially hilly terrain, and rear-end collisions are common whenever drivers have a limited view of what is in front of them. These automated electronic displays have been effective at reducing accidents by providing a visual warning whenever excessive lineups occur.

Another innovation involves shortening waiting lines by informing travellers of average waiting times. Based on the number of vehicles waiting at any given time, the average waiting time is estimated by multiplying the number of vehicles by the average service time per vehicle. The British Columbia and Washington State governments have collaborated to set up the Cascade Gateway[1] website (http://www.cascadegatewaydata.com) to help inform travellers about the best time to cross. The CBSA uses wait time information to schedule officers and determine the optimal number of booths to open.

---

[1] Sources: http://www.cascadegatewaydata.com/Crossing; http://theimtc.com/cascadegatewaydata/; http://www.sciencedirect.com/science/article/pii/S0965856416305080.

(L01) Introduction

Waiting lines occur when there is a temporary imbalance between supply (capacity) and demand. Waiting lines add to the cost of operation and they reflect negatively on customer service, so it is important to balance the cost of having customers wait with the cost of providing service capacity. Customer waiting lines occur when there is too little capacity to handle demand, but having more capacity than what is needed to handle demand means that there is idle (unproductive) capacity. From a managerial perspective, the key is to determine the balance that will provide an adequate level of service at a reasonable cost.

Waiting lines abound in all sorts of situations. For customers, having to wait for service can range from being acceptable (usually short waits), to being annoying (longer waits), to being a matter of life and death (e.g., in emergencies). For businesses, the costs of waiting come from lower productivity and competitive disadvantage. For society, the costs are wasted resources (e.g., fuel consumption of cars stuck in traffic) and reduced quality of life. Hence, it is important for system designers and managers of existing service systems to fully appreciate the impact of waiting lines.

Those waiting in line would all agree that the solution to the problem is obvious: simply add more servers or do something to speed up service. Although both ideas may be potential solutions, there are certain subtleties that must be dealt with. For one thing, most service systems have the capacity to process customers over the long run. Hence, the problem of customers waiting is a short-term phenomenon. And at certain times the servers are idle, waiting for customers. Thus, by increasing the service capacity, the server idle time would increase even more. Consequently, in designing service systems, the designer must weigh the cost of providing a given level of service capacity against the cost of having customers wait for service. This planning and analysis of service capacity frequently lends itself to **queueing theory**, which is a mathematical approach to the analysis of waiting lines.

queueing theory
Mathematical approach to the analysis of waiting lines.

Modern queueing theory is based on studies about automatic dialing equipment made in the early part of the last century by Danish telephone engineer A. K. Erlang. Prior to the Second World War, very few attempts were made to apply queueing theory to operations. Since then, queueing theory has been applied to a wide range of operations problems.

The mathematics of queueing theory can be complex; for that reason, the emphasis here will not be on the mathematics but on the use of formulas and tables for analysis.

Waiting lines are commonly found wherever customers arrive randomly for a service. Some examples of waiting lines we encounter in our daily lives include the line at the supermarket checkout, fast-food restaurant, hospital emergency department, college and university registration office, airport check-in counter, train station, movie theatre/concert venue, post office, call centre, government service office, and bank. In many situations, the "customers" are not people but orders waiting to be filled, trucks waiting to be unloaded, jobs waiting to be processed, equipment awaiting repairs, planes waiting to land or take off, and cars waiting at a traffic light or in a traffic jam.

Passengers wait to buy tickets at Termini train station in Rome. As one of the largest railway stations in Europe, Termini serves over 150 million passengers each year, connecting Rome to most of Italy and other European destinations.

Andreas Solaro/Getty

One reason that queueing analysis is important is that customers tend to associate waiting with poor service quality, especially if the wait is long. Similarly, for an organization, having employees wait (such as a truck driver waiting to unload) is a waste.

Why Is There Waiting?

In a queueing system, customers enter a waiting line of a service facility, receive service when their turn comes, and then leave the system. The number of customers in the system (awaiting service or being served) will vary randomly over time. Many people are surprised to learn that waiting lines tend to form even though a system is underloaded. For example, a fast-food restaurant may have the capacity to handle an average of 200 orders per hour and yet experience waiting lines even though the number of orders is only 150 per hour. In reality, customers arrive at random rather than at evenly spaced intervals and some orders take longer to fill than others. In other words, both arrival times and service durations exhibit a high degree of variability. As a result, the system at times becomes temporarily overloaded, giving rise to waiting lines; at other times, the system is idle because there are no customers. Thus, although a system may be *underloaded* from a *macro* standpoint, variabilities in arrival times and service durations imply that at times the system is *overloaded* from a *micro* standpoint. It follows that in systems where variability is minimal or non-existent (e.g., because arrivals can be scheduled and service durations are constant), waiting lines do not ordinarily form.

Goal of Waiting-Line Analysis

The goal of queueing analysis is to minimize total costs. There are two types of costs in a queueing situation: "cost" of customers waiting for service, and cost of provision of capacity (e.g., determining the number of cashiers at a supermarket or the number of repair people to handle equipment breakdowns). The cost of customers waiting, in addition to loss of goodwill, includes loss of business due to customers refusing to wait and going elsewhere. Also, if the "customers" are employees, the salaries paid to employees while they wait for service (e.g., mechanics waiting for tools, truck drivers waiting to unload) are part of the cost of customers waiting.

Figure 18-1 shows the two costs and the total cost as a function of service capacity. Note that as capacity increases, its capacity cost increases. For simplicity, the increase is shown as a linear relationship. On the other hand, as capacity increases, the number of customers waiting and the time they wait tend to decrease at a faster rate; also the dissatisfaction of a typical customer is a non-linear function of the waiting time (initially it is insignificant but increases at a faster rate as the wait time increases past a threshold); therefore, waiting cost decreases non-linearly. Total cost is a U-shaped curve, and the goal of queueing analysis is to identify that level of service capacity that

◀ FIGURE 18-1

The goal of queueing is to minimize the sum of two costs: customers waiting cost and service capacity cost.

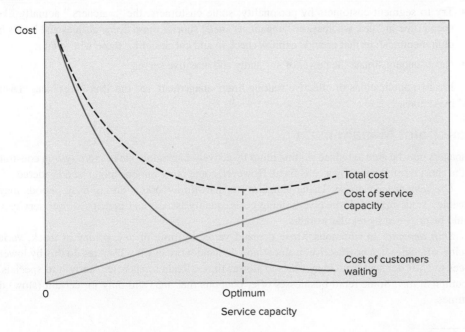

will minimize the total cost. (Unlike the situation in the EOQ model, the minimum point on the total cost curve is *not* necessarily where the two cost lines intersect.)

If pinning down the cost of customers waiting is difficult, another approach is to treat waiting times or line lengths as a policy variable: a manager simply specifies an acceptable level of waiting (e.g., average customer wait time of four minutes before service at a bank) and directs that enough capacity be established to achieve that level of waiting.

Psychology of Waiting

Despite management's best efforts, in some instances it is not feasible to shorten waiting times. Nevertheless, steps can be taken in certain situations that make the situation more acceptable to those waiting in line, particularly when the waiting line consists of people. The importance of doing so should not be underestimated.

Studies have shown a difference—sometimes a remarkable difference—between the actual time customers spend waiting and their perceived time. Several factors can influence the differences. One is the reason for being in line (e.g., waiting for police or fire personnel, waiting at the emergency room, having other appointments or a plane or train to catch). Aside from those situations, where the level of anxiety can make even short waits seem long, in many instances management can reduce their customers' perception of the waiting time. Some suggestions in this regard are:

- Determine the acceptable wait time for the operation.
- Try to keep the waiting time experienced by a customer consistent over time.
- Install distractions that entertain and involve customers. For example, provide magazines, TV, and mirrors outside elevators; ask the customer to fill out a form, and use the lounge before eating. Make the wait comfortable.
- Inform the customer of the cause of an abnormal wait and peak times.
- Keep the line moving continuously.
- Use first come, first served discipline (fairness is important).
- Allow customers to serve themselves.
- Prepare the customers for service before the actual service. For example, encourage customers to print their boarding pass at home the night before their flight.
- Make people conscious of time only if they overestimate the wait time.
- Keep staff who are not serving customers out of sight.
- Try to segment customers by personality; some customers, the "watchers," actually like to spend time in lines, whereas the "impatients" need shorter lines. Some airlines and hotels have club memberships that provide express check-in and check-out for those who want it.
- Never underestimate the power of a friendly and attentive server.[2]

For two applications of effective waiting line management, see the "Six Flags" and "Disney" OM in Actions.

Constraint Management

Managers may be able to reduce waiting times by actively managing one or more system constraints. In the short term, the facility size is fixed. However, some other options might be considered.

Use temporary workers. Using temporary or part-time workers during busy periods may be possible. Trade-offs might involve training costs, quality issues, and perhaps slower service than would be provided by regular workers.

Shift demand. In situations where demand varies by time of day, or day of week, variable pricing strategies can be effective in smoothing demand more evenly. Theatres do this by lowering prices to shift demand from busy times to slower times. Restaurants offer "early-bird specials" to accomplish this. Some retail businesses offer coupons that are valid only for certain (slow) days or times.

---

[2] K. L. Katz, B. M. Larson, and R. C. Larson, "Prescription for the Waiting-in-Line Blues: Entertain, Enlighten, and Engage," *Sloan Management Review,* Winter 1991, 32(2), pp. 44–53.

Standardize the service. The more the service can be standardized, the shorter the waiting line.

Look for a bottleneck. One part of a process may be largely responsible for a slow service rate; improving that part of the process might yield a disproportionate increase in the service rate. Employees often have insights that can be exploited.

 OM in Action   www.sixflags.com

Six Flags

Six Flags uses a ride reservation system called Flash Pass, which is similar to Disney's FastPass. The Flash Pass allows customers to reserve their place in line without actively waiting in line. This enables customers to have fun doing other activities such as visiting gift shops and sightseeing. Once the customer's turn comes up, the Flash Pass device provides an alert, and allows them to skip the waiting line and proceed directly to the Flash Pass entrance. This device benefits customers by significantly decreasing their waiting times.

Source: https://www.sixflags.com/greatadventure/store/flash-pass. Retrieved November 13, 2016

Photo source: http://www.wikihow.com/Use-a-Flash-Pass-at-Six-Flags.

 OM in Action

Disney

The mission of Walt Disney theme parks is to "make people happy," and the folks at Disney are masters at doing that. They realize that waiting in lines at attractions does not add to the enjoyment of their customers. They also realize that customers waiting in lines are not generating the revenue that they would if they visited restaurants and souvenir shops. Hence, they have several reasons for wanting to reduce waiting times.

Walt Disney theme parks are leaders in effectively managing waiting lines. Disney analysts are so good that they present seminars to other companies on managing waiting lines. Their success can serve as a benchmark and provide valuable insights for a wide range of services.

Helen Sessions/Alamy Stock Photo

Disney's methods are particularly relevant when circumstances make it impossible to quickly add capacity to alleviate waiting times. Here are some of the tactics Disney employs to achieve customer satisfaction:

- *Provide distractions.* Disney characters may entertain customers, videos provide safety information and build anticipation for the event, vendors move along some lines selling food and drinks, and other vendors sell souvenirs.

- *Provide alternatives to waiting in line.* Disney offers the "FastPass," which allows customers to reserve a time later in the day for a popular ride when they will be allowed to bypass the regular waiting line. This is a win–win solution: Customers are happier because they don't have to wait in line, and the park's potential for additional revenue is increased. Only one FastPass is issued to a person at any time. Another tactic is to sell passes that allow customers to enter the park earlier.

- *Keep customers informed.* Signs give approximate waiting times from that point on, allowing the customers to make a decision on whether or not to join the line.

- *Exceed expectations.* Wait times are usually shorter than the posted times, thereby exceeding customers' expectations.

- *Other tactics.* Disney maintains a comfortable waiting environment: Waiting lines are often inside, protected from weather. Lines are kept moving, giving the impression of making progress.

Sources: Based in part on "Queuing: Featuring Disney World," McGraw-Hill Irwin OM Video Series, and https://disneyworld.disney.go.com/plan/my-disney-experience/fastpass-plus/.

(L02) Queueing System Characteristics and Performance Measures

There are numerous queueing models from which an analyst can choose. Naturally, much of the success of the analysis will depend on choosing the appropriate model. Model choice is dependent on the characteristics of the waiting line system under investigation. The main characteristics are:

1. Potential number of customers.
2. Number of servers and structure of queueing system.
3. Arrival and service patterns.
4. Queue discipline (i.e., order of service).

Figure 18-2 depicts a simple queueing system.

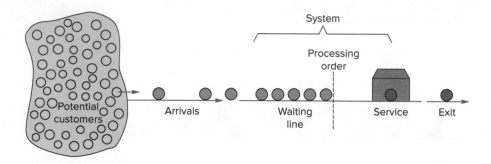

Potential Number of Customers

The approach to use in analyzing a queueing problem depends on whether the potential number of customers is limited or is very large. In an **infinite source** situation, the potential number of customers greatly exceeds system capacity. Examples are supermarkets, drugstores, banks, restaurants, theatres, amusement parks, and call centres. Theoretically, a large number of customers can request service at any given time. When the potential number of customers is limited, a **finite source** situation exists. An example is the repair technician responsible for a certain number of machines in a company. The potential number of machines that might need repairs at any one time cannot exceed the number of machines assigned to the repairer. Similarly, an operator may be responsible for loading and unloading a bank of four machines, a nurse may be responsible for answering patient calls for a 10-bed ward, a secretary may be responsible for taking dictation from three executives, and a company truck maintenance shop may perform repairs as needed on its 20 trucks.

infinite source The potential number of customers greatly exceeds system capacity.

finite source The number of potential customers is limited.

Number of Servers and Structure of Queueing System

The capacity of a queueing system is a function of the capacity of each server and the number of servers. Each server can handle one customer at a time. (*Note:* A table of four is considered one "customer.") A queueing system can have either *single* or *multiple servers*. (*Note:* A group of servers working together as a team such as a surgical team is treated as a "single" server.) Other examples of a single server system are small grocery stores with one cashier, some theatres, and single-bay car washes. Multiple server systems are commonly found in banks, at airline ticket counters, and at call centres.

Another distinctive characteristic is the number of steps or *phases* in a queueing system. For example, at most fast-food drive-throughs, cars first wait to order at the menu board, and then wait to pay at the pay window, and then wait to pick up the order at the pick-up window. Each stage constitutes a separate phase where queues can form.

Figure 18-3 illustrates some of the most common queueing systems. Because it would not be possible to cover all of these cases in sufficient detail in the limited amount of space available here, our discussion will focus on *single-phase* systems.

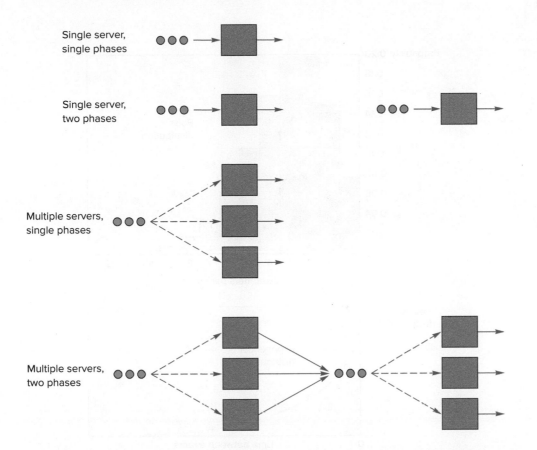

◀ FIGURE 18-3

Four common variations of queueing systems.

Single server, single phases

Single server, two phases

Multiple servers, single phases

Multiple servers, two phases

If customers are homogeneous (similar), then a single line feeding into multiple servers is usually preferred to multiple independent lines each feeding to its own server. The reasons for this are as follows: First, the average wait time will be less because if there is an idle server, the customer waiting at the top of the line will be directed to the idle server right away. This does not happen in multiple independent lines, especially if the other lines cannot be observed. Even if a customer can see and jump to a shorter queue, this process will consume some time and does not guarantee getting to the server first. Second, the customers will be served on a first-come, first-served basis, which is more equitable and preferred by most customers. The disadvantages of a joint line are that it might appear too long, it may take a large space, servers may not work as fast as if they were responsible for their own line, and customers cannot choose their favourite server.

However, if the customers are heterogeneous (different), then separate lines could be advantageous. For example, a line for 10 items or fewer in a grocery store moves faster, resulting in shorter wait times for customers who do not buy a lot. This reduces the total variability of service durations, resulting in a reduced average wait time for all customers. In some cases, the company can charge a higher price for providing a faster line; for example, the one-hour photo developing service is more expensive than the five-day economy service in The Real Canadian Superstore.

Arrival and Service Patterns

The most commonly used queueing models assume that the customer arrival *rate* (i.e., the number of arrivals per time unit) can be described by a Poisson distribution and that the service *duration* can be described by an exponential distribution. The **Poisson distribution** is a one-parameter discrete

Poisson distribution A one-parameter discrete probability distribution of the number of events occurring in an interval of time, provided that these events occur with a known average rate and independent of the time since the last event.

exponential distribution A one-parameter continuous probability distribution of the times between events that happen continuously and independently at a constant average rate.

probability distribution of the number of events occurring in an interval of time, provided that these events occur with a known average rate and independently of the time since the last event. The **exponential distribution** is a one-parameter continuous probability distribution of the times between events that happen continuously and independently at a constant average rate. Figure 18-4 illustrates these distributions.

FIGURE 18-4 ▶

Poisson and exponential distributions.

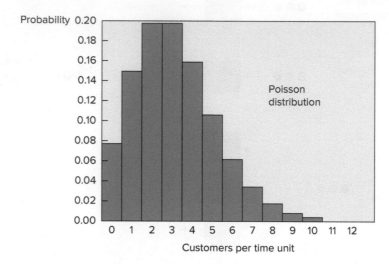

Customers per time unit

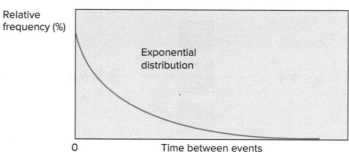

Time between events

Figure 18-5A illustrates how Poisson-distributed customer arrivals might occur during a three-day period. In some hours, there are three or four arrivals, in some other hours one or two arrivals, and in some other hours no arrivals.

Figure 18-5B illustrates how exponential service durations might appear for the same customers. Note that most service durations are very short but a few are relatively long.

Waiting lines are likely to occur when arrivals are bunched up and/or when service durations are particularly lengthy. For instance, note the long service duration of customer 7 on day 1 in Figure 18-5B. In Figure 18-5A, the seventh customer arrived just after 10 o'clock and the next two customers arrived shortly after that, making it very likely that a waiting line would form. A similar situation occurred on day 3 with the last three customers: the relatively long service duration for customer 13 (Figure 18-5B) and the short time before the next two arrivals (Figure 18-5A, day 3) would create (or increase the length of) a waiting line.

It is interesting to note that the Poisson and exponential distributions are alternative ways of presenting the same basic information. That is, if service durations are exponential, then the service rates (i.e., the number of services per time unit) are Poisson. Similarly, if the customer arrival rates are Poisson, then the interarrival durations (i.e., the times between two consecutive arrivals) are exponential. There is an inverse relationship between the means of these two distributions. For example, if a service facility can process 12 customers per hour, then average service duration is 1/12th of an hour or five minutes. And if the arrival rate is 10 per hour, then the average duration between two consecutive arrivals is six minutes.

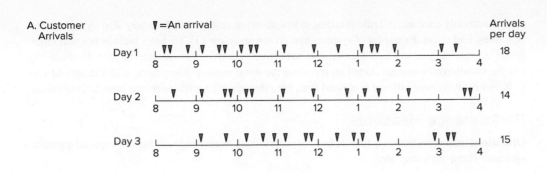

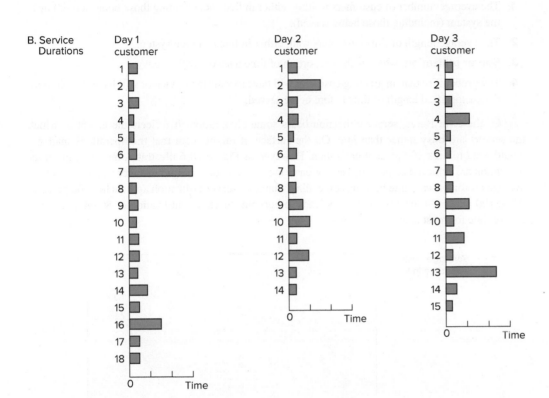

Examples of Poisson customer arrivals (A) and exponential service durations (B).

Most models described in this chapter require that arrival and service rates be approximately Poisson or, equivalently, that interarrival and service durations be approximately exponential. In practice, it is necessary to verify that these assumptions are met. Sometimes this is done by collecting data and plotting them, although the preferred approach is to use a chi-square goodness-of-fit test for that purpose. A discussion of the chi-square test is beyond the scope of this text, but it is covered in most statistics textbooks.

Research has shown that these assumptions are often appropriate for customer arrival rates but less likely to be appropriate for service durations. In situations where the assumptions are not reasonably satisfied, the alternatives would be to use (1) an approximate model or (2) a computer simulation. Each of these alternatives requires more effort or cost than the ones presented here.

The models in this chapter assume customers are patient and remain until they are served. Other possibilities are that (1) customers grow impatient and leave the line (reneging); (2) customers switch to another line (jockeying); or (3) upon arriving, customers decide the line is too long and, therefore, do not enter the line (balking).

Queue Discipline (Order of Service)

Queue discipline refers to the order in which customers are served. All but one of the models to be described assumes that service is provided on a *first-come, first-served* (FCFS) basis. This is the

queue discipline The order in which customers are served.

most commonly encountered rule at banks, stores, theatres, restaurants, four-way stop signs, registration lines, and so on. Examples of systems that do not serve on a FCFS basis include hospital emergency rooms, rush orders in a factory, and mainframe computer processing of jobs. In these and similar situations, customers do not all represent the same waiting costs; those with the highest cost (e.g., the most seriously ill) are processed first, even though other customers may have arrived earlier.

Performance Measures

Operations managers typically look at four measures when evaluating existing or proposed queueing systems. Those measures are:

1. The average number of customers waiting, either in line (not counting those being served) or in the system (including those being served).

2. The average length of time customers wait, either in line or in the system.

3. **Server utilization**, which is the proportion of time a server will be busy.

4. The probability that an arriving customer will have to wait for service or will have to wait more than a specified length of time before being served.

> **server utilization** The proportion of time a server will be busy.

Of these measures, server utilization bears some elaboration. It reflects the extent to which the servers are busy rather than idle. On the surface, it might seem that the operations manager would want to seek 100 percent utilization. However, as Figure 18-6 illustrates, increases in server utilization are achieved at the expense of greater increases in the average customer wait time. In fact, average customer wait time becomes exceedingly large as server utilization approaches 100 percent. Also, 100 percent utilization of servers leads to burnout. Instead, a utilization of 80–90 percent is appropriate for most queueing systems.

FIGURE 18-6 ▶

The average time customers wait in line increases non-linearly as the server utilization increases.

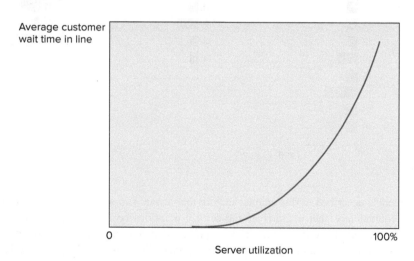

Healthcare in Canada is an example of a sector that operates at close to 100 percent utilization. See "Hospital Wait Times" and "Medical Tourism" OM in Actions for interesting Canadian examples.

⚙ OM in Action

Hospital Wait Times

The Wait Time Alliance (WTA) recently gave Canada a failing grade on meeting performance targets regarding patient wait times. The alliance is composed of several medical groups, including the Canadian Association of Emergency Physicians and the Association of General Surgeons, whose job is to address physicians' concerns over patient access to health care. Canadians have long indicated that wait times are one of the most significant barriers to accessing health care services. Many developed countries with universal health systems provide quicker access to care compared to Canada. For example, 27 percent of Canadians reported waiting times in excess of four hours, compared with 5 percent in the United Kingdom and only 1 percent in the Netherlands.

While there has been considerable effort in the past decade to address the issue of long wait times for Canadians, there has been virtually no improvement. The following steps have been recommended to ensure that all Canadians have more timely access to necessary medical care:

- Increase funding to health care providers to hire additional doctors and staff to clear up backlogs. With

fewer patients waiting for service, average wait times will be reduced.

- Establish maximum wait time guarantees for each procedure. When patient wait times exceed established thresholds, hospital administrators will be sanctioned and patients will be given the option to transfer to another health care provider.

- Reduce demand for specialty care by investing more heavily into primary care. Many procedures that can be performed by general practitioners are often referred to specialists, which increases waiting times and places further strain on the health care system.

Source: http://www.waittimealliance.ca/wp-content/uploads/2014/06/FINAL-EN-WTA-Report-Card.pdf

---

 OM in Action

Medical Tourism

In a recent report the Fraser Institute estimates that more than 45,000 Canadians travelled abroad in 2015 for the purpose of medical tourism. The British Columbia-based policy think tank suggests that increased patient wait times are one of the main reasons more and more Canadians are seeking medical attention outside the country. For instance, Canadian patients can now expect to wait an average of 9.8 weeks between a

referral from a family doctor to receipt of even a simple medical treatment, a figure which is nearly three weeks longer than what is considered clinically reasonable. Canada's universal health care system is a source of pride for many Canadians. However, the increasing lack of access to quality care in a timely manner has many citizens worried.

Source: https://www.fraserinstitute.org/sites/default/files/leaving-canada-for-medical-care-2016-post.pdf. Retrieved November 1, 2016.

Queueing Models: Infinite Source

Many infinite source queueing models are available for a manager or analyst to choose from. The discussion here includes eight of the most basic and widely used models. All models discussed (except Model 7) assume Poisson arrival rates. Moreover, they assume that the average arrival and service rates are constant. If they are not, then the operating hours should be divided into subperiods within which the rates are fairly constant. For example, each hour or half-hour may have a different average arrival rate. In addition, the results are for the steady state condition; the transient behaviour of the queueing system at the opening hour is ignored. The eight infinite source models described are:

1. Single server, exponential service durations.
2. Single server, exponential service durations, finite number in system.
3. Single server, constant service durations.
4. Single server, general service durations.
5. Multiple servers, exponential service durations.
6. Multiple servers, exponential service durations, finite number in system.
7. Multiple servers, general interarrival and service durations.
8. Multiple servers with priority, exponential service durations.

To facilitate your use of queueing models, Table 18-1 provides a list of the symbols used for the infinite source models.

TABLE 18-1 ▶

Symbols for infinite source queueing models.

Symbol	Represents
λ	Average arrival rate
μ	Average service rate
L_q	Average number of customers waiting in line for service
L_s	Average number of customers in the system (waiting and being served)
ρ	Server utilization
W_q	Average length of time customers wait in line
W_s	Average length of time customers spend in the system (waiting in line and being served)
$1/\mu$	Average service duration
P_o	Probability of zero customers in the system
P_n	Probability of n customers in the system
M	Number of servers
r	Average number of customers being served at any time

Basic Relationships

There are certain basic relationships that hold for all infinite source queueing models. Knowledge of these relationships can be very helpful in deriving the desired performance measures, given a few key values. Here are the basic relationships. Some are intuitive, others complex. For the latter, proof is omitted here.

Note: The average arrival and service rates, represented by λ and μ, respectively, must be in the same time units (e.g., per hour or per minute).

Server utilization, ρ (rho), is equal to the ratio of demand (as measured by the average arrival rate) to capacity (as measured by the product of the number of servers, M, and the average service rate, μ,):

$$\rho = \frac{\lambda}{M\mu} \tag{18-1}$$

The average number of customers being served (at any point in time), r, is equal to each server's utilization times the number of servers $= \rho M$, or:

$$r = \frac{\lambda}{\mu} \tag{18-2}$$

The average *number* of customers waiting in line for service, L_q: L_q [Model dependent. Obtain using a table or formula.] in the system (in line plus being served), L_s, is:

$$L_s = L_q + r \tag{18-3}$$

The average length of time customers wait in line, W_q, is:

$$W_q = \frac{L_q}{\lambda} \quad \text{[Little's Formula]} \tag{18-4}$$

The average length of time customers spend in the system, W_s, is:

$$W_s = W_q + \frac{1}{\mu} = \frac{L_s}{\lambda} \quad \text{[Little's Formula]} \tag{18-5}$$

All infinite source models require that server utilization be less than 1.0; the models apply only to underloaded systems.

The average number of customers waiting in line, L_q, is a key value because it determines the other measures of system performance. Hence, L_q will usually be one of the first values you will want to determine in problem solving. Figure 18-7 can help you relate the symbols to the basic relationships in a queueing system.

	Line	+	Service	=	System
Customers →	000	→	$\boxed{0}$	→	0000
Average number waiting:	L_q	+	$\dfrac{\lambda}{\mu}$	=	L_s
Average time waiting:	$W_q = \dfrac{L_q}{\lambda}$	+	$\dfrac{1}{\mu}$	=	W_s

◀ **FIGURE 18-7**

Basic relationships.

◀ **EXAMPLE 18-1**

Suppose that customers arrive at a bakery at an average rate of 18 per hour on weekday mornings. The arrival rate can be adequately described by a Poisson distribution. Suppose further that each server can serve a customer in an average of four minutes, where the service durations can be described by an exponential distribution.

a. What are the average arrival and service rates?

b. Calculate the average number of customers being served at any time (assume that at least two servers will be working to ensure that server utilization is less than 1.0).

c. Suppose that the average number of customers waiting in line is 3.6. Calculate the average number of customers in the system (i.e., waiting in line or being served), the average length of time customers wait in line, and the average length of time customers spend in the system.

d. Determine the server utilization if there are $M = 2, 3,$ or 4 servers.

SOLUTION

a. The average arrival rate is given in the problem: $\lambda = 18$ customers per hour. Change the average service duration to a comparable *hourly* service rate by first restating the duration in hours and then taking its reciprocal. Thus,

(4 minutes per customer)/(60 minutes per hour) = 1/15 hour per customer. Its reciprocal is $\mu = 15$ customers per hour, the average service rate.

b. $r = \dfrac{\lambda}{\mu} = \dfrac{18}{15} = 1.2$ customers

c. Given: $L_q = 3.6$ customers,

$L_s = L_q + r = 3.6 + 1.2 = 4.8$ customers

$W_q = \dfrac{L_q}{\lambda} = \dfrac{3.6}{18} = 0.20$ hour, or 12 minutes

$W_s = W_q + \dfrac{1}{\mu} = 0.20 + \dfrac{1}{15} = 0.267$ hour, or 16 minutes

d. Server utilization is $\rho = \dfrac{\lambda}{M\mu}$.

For $M = 2, \rho = \dfrac{18}{2(15)} = 0.60$

For $M = 3, \rho = \dfrac{18}{3(15)} = 0.40$

For $M = 4, \rho = \dfrac{18}{4(15)} = 0.30$

Hence, as the system capacity, measured by $M\mu$, increases, the server utilization (for a given arrival rate) decreases.

Single Server Models

LO4

Model 1: Single Server, Exponential Service Durations

The simplest model involves a system that has one server (or a single crew), the queue discipline is FCFS, and customer arrival rates can be approximated by a Poisson distribution and service durations by an exponential distribution. The length of queue is not a constraint.

Table 18-2 lists some formulas for Model 1, which should be used in conjunction with Formulas 18-1, 18-2, 18-3, 18-4, and 18-5.

TABLE 18-2 ▶

Formulas for Model 1: single server, exponential service durations.

Performance Measure	Equation	
Average number in line	$L_q = \dfrac{\lambda^2}{\mu(\mu - \lambda)}$	(18-6)
Probability of zero customers in the system	$P_0 = 1 - \left(\dfrac{\lambda}{\mu}\right)$	(18-7)
Probability of n customers in the system	$P_n = P_0 \left(\dfrac{\lambda}{\mu}\right)^n$	(18-8)
Probability of fewer than n customers in the system	$P_{<n} = 1 - \left(\dfrac{\lambda}{\mu}\right)^n$	(18-9)
Probability that a customer waits at least t time units in queue	$P_{W\,\text{in}\,Q\,>\,t} = \dfrac{\lambda}{\mu} e^{-(\mu - \lambda)t}$	(18-10)

EXAMPLE 18-2 ▶

A phone company is planning to open a kiosk in a new shopping mall, staffed by one sales agent. It is estimated that requests for phones, accessories, and information will average 15 per hour during the peak period, and number of requests will have a Poisson distribution. Service durations are assumed to be exponentially distributed. Previous experience with similar kiosks suggests that service duration should average about three minutes per request. Determine each of the following measures during the peak period:

 a. Server utilization.

 b. Percentage of time the sales agent will be idle.

 c. The expected number of customers waiting in line to be served.

 d. The average length of time customers will spend in the system.

 e. The probability of zero customers in the system and the probability of four customers in the system.

 f. The probability that a customer will have to wait.

 g. The probability that a customer will have to wait more than five minutes.

SOLUTION

$\lambda = 15$ per hour

$\mu = \dfrac{1}{\text{Average service duration}} = \dfrac{1\,\text{customer}}{3\,\text{minutes}} \times 60$ minutes per hour

$= 20$ customers per hour

 a. $\rho = \dfrac{\lambda}{M\mu} = \dfrac{15}{1(20)} = 0.75$

 b. Percentage idle time $= 1 - \rho = 1 - 0.75 = 0.25$, or 25 percent

 c. $L_q = \dfrac{\lambda^2}{\mu(\mu - \lambda)} = \dfrac{15^2}{20(20 - 15)} = 2.25$ customers

 d. $W_s = \dfrac{L_q}{\lambda} + \dfrac{1}{\mu} = \dfrac{2.25}{15} + \dfrac{1}{20} = 0.20$ hour, or 12 minutes

 e. $P_0 = 1 - \dfrac{\lambda}{\mu} = 1 - \dfrac{15}{20} = 0.25$ and

 $P_4 = P_0 \left(\dfrac{\lambda}{\mu}\right)^4 = 0.25 \left(\dfrac{15}{20}\right)^4 = 0.079$

 f. Probability that a customer will have to wait $= \rho = 0.75$

 g. $P_{W\,\text{in}\,Q\,>\,t} = \dfrac{\lambda}{\mu} e^{-(\mu - \lambda)t}$

 $= \dfrac{15}{20} e^{-(20 - 15)(5/60)}$

 $= 0.494$

Note that t should be in the same time unit as λ and μ.

Model 2: Single Server, Exponential Service Durations, Finite Number in System

In many cases, the number of customers or calls that can fit in the queuing system is limited. Let $K =$ Maximum number of customers (or calls) that can fit in the queuing system (in line and being served). If there are K customers already in the queuing system, the next customer will not be allowed to enter the system and has to balk (leave). In this case, P_0 and L_q can be calculated using the following two formulas. The probability of a customer balking is the same as probability of K customers in the system, P_k. The effective average arrival rate in this case is $\lambda(1 - P_k)$, and should be used to relate W_q to L_q.

$$P_0 = \left[1 + \frac{\left(\frac{\lambda}{\mu}\right)\left(1 - \left(\frac{\lambda}{\mu}\right)^K\right)}{\left(1 - \frac{\lambda}{\mu}\right)}\right]^{-1} \tag{18-11}$$

$$L_q = \frac{\left(\frac{\lambda}{\mu}\right)^2 P_0}{\left(1 - \frac{\lambda}{\mu}\right)^2}\left(1 - \left(\frac{\lambda}{\mu}\right)^K - K\left(1 - \frac{\lambda}{\mu}\right)\left(\frac{\lambda}{\mu}\right)^{K-1}\right) \tag{18-12}$$

$$P_K = \left(\frac{\lambda}{\mu}\right)^K P_0 \tag{18-13}$$

$$W_q = \frac{L_q}{\lambda(1 - P_K)} \tag{18-14}$$

EXAMPLE 18-3

Reconsider Example 18-2, but assume that if there are already four customers in the system (three in line and one being served), then no new customer will join the line. Calculate:

a. The average number in the line and compare it with Example 18-2.

b. The probability of balking.

c. The average time in the system and compare it with Example 18-2.

SOLUTION

a. Recall $\lambda = 15$ per hour and $\mu = 20$ per hour. $K = 4$.

$$P_0 = \left[1 + \frac{\left(\frac{15}{20}\right)\left(1 - \left(\frac{15}{20}\right)^4\right)}{\left(1 - \frac{15}{20}\right)}\right] = 0.327785$$

$$L_q = \frac{\left(\frac{15}{20}\right)^2 (0.327785)}{\left(1 - \frac{15}{20}\right)^2}\left(1 - \left(\frac{15}{20}\right)^4 - 4\left(1 - \frac{15}{20}\right)\left(\frac{15}{20}\right)^3\right) = 0.7721 \text{ customers} < 2.25$$

This is less than 2.25, the number of customers in Example 18-2.

b. $P_K = \left(\frac{15}{20}\right)^4\left(0.327785\right) = 0.1037$ or 10%.

c. $W_s = \frac{L_q}{\lambda(1 - P_k)} + \frac{1}{\mu} = \frac{0.7721}{15(1 - 0.1037)} + \frac{1}{20} = 0.10743$ hour or 6.4 minutes < 12 minutes

This is less than 12 minutes, the time in Example 18-2.

Model 3: Single Server, Constant Service Durations

As noted previously, waiting lines are a consequence of random arrival and service rates. If we can reduce or eliminate the variability of either or both arrivals and services, then we can shorten the waiting line. A case in point is a queueing system with constant service durations (and Poisson arrival rates). The effect of constant service durations is to cut the average number of customers waiting in line in half (relative to Model 1):

$$L_q = \frac{\lambda^2}{2\mu(\mu - \lambda)} \tag{18-15}$$

The average length of time customers wait in line, W_q, is also cut in half.

EXAMPLE 18-4

Consider a single bay automatic car wash that takes five minutes to wash a car. On a typical Saturday morning, cars arrive at a mean rate of eight per hour, according to Poisson distribution. Find:

a. The average number of cars in line.

b. The average length of time cars spend in line and service (i.e., system).

SOLUTION

$\lambda = 8$ cars per hour

$\mu = 1$ per 5 minutes, or 12 cars per hour

a. $L_q = \dfrac{\lambda^2}{2\mu(\mu - \lambda)} = \dfrac{8^2}{2(12)(12-8)} = 0.667$ car

b. $W_s = \dfrac{L_q}{\lambda} + \dfrac{1}{\mu} = \dfrac{0.667}{8} + \dfrac{1}{12} = 0.167$ hour, or 10 minutes

Model 4: Single Server, General Service Durations

For general service durations with standard deviation equal to σ_s, it can be shown that:

$$L_q = \frac{\lambda^2(\mu^2 \sigma_s^2 + 1)}{2\mu(\mu - \lambda)} \tag{18-16}$$

Note that when $\sigma_s = 0$, the above formula reduces to the L_q for constant service durations (Model 3), and when $\sigma_s = \frac{1}{\mu}$, it reduces to the L_q for exponential service durations (Model 1). Also, make sure that σ_s, λ and μ have the same time unit.

EXAMPLE 18-5

At a small post office with one server, during the peak lunch period customers arrive according to Poisson distribution with an average rate of 30 customers per hour. Customers have a service time that is the sum of a constant 30 seconds and an exponential service duration with average of 1 minute. Find:

a. The average number of customers in line during the lunch period.

b. The average customer waiting time in line.

SOLUTION

$\lambda = 30$ customers per hour

$1/\mu = 0.5 + 1 = 1.5$ minutes per customer or $\mu = 60/1.5 = 40$ customers per hour

$\sigma_s = 1$ minute or $1/60 = 0.0166667$ hour (because the constant 30 seconds time has zero variance and the standard deviation of an exponential distribution equals its mean). Note that service duration is *not* exponentially distributed.

a. $L_q = \dfrac{\lambda^2(\mu^2 \sigma_s^2 + 1)}{2\mu(\mu - \lambda)} = \dfrac{30^2(40^2(0.016667)^2 + 1)}{2(40)(40 - 30)}$

$= 1.625$ customers

b. $W_q = \dfrac{L_q}{\lambda} = \dfrac{1.625}{30} = 0.05417$ hour or 3.25 minutes.

(L05) Multiple Server Models

Model 5: Multiple Servers, Exponential Service Durations

A multiple server system exists whenever there are two or more servers working individually to provide service to customers. Use of the model involves the following assumptions:

1. Poisson arrival rates with average λ and exponential service durations with average $\frac{1}{\mu}$.

2. All M servers work at the same average rate.

3. Customers form a single waiting line.

Formulas for the multiple server, exponential service durations model are listed in Table 18-3. Obviously, the multiple server formulas are more complex than the single server formulas for L_q and P_0. Fortunately, you can also determine their values using Table 18-4, given values of λ/μ and M.

Performance Measure	Equation	
Average number of customers in line	$$L_q = \frac{\lambda\mu\left(\frac{\lambda}{\mu}\right)^M}{(M-1)!(M\mu-\lambda)^2}P_0$$	(18-17)
Probability of zero customers in the system	$$P_0 = \left[\sum_{n=0}^{M-1}\frac{\left(\frac{\lambda}{\mu}\right)^n}{n!} + \frac{\left(\frac{\lambda}{\mu}\right)^M}{M!\left(1-\frac{\lambda}{M\mu}\right)}\right]^{-1}$$	(18-18)
Probability of n customers in the system	$$P_n = \begin{cases} \frac{1}{n!}\left(\frac{\lambda}{\mu}\right)^n P_0 & \text{If } n \leq M \\ \frac{1}{M!M^{n-M}}\left(\frac{\lambda}{\mu}\right)^n P_0 & \text{If } n > M \end{cases}$$	(18-19)
Average waiting time (before being served) for an arrival who is not immediately served	$$W_a = \frac{1}{M\mu-\lambda}$$	(18-20)
Probability that an arrival will have to wait for service	$$P_W = \frac{W_q}{W_a}$$	(18-21)
Probability that a customer waits at least t time units in queue	$$P_{W \text{ in } Q > t} = \frac{\left(\frac{\lambda}{\mu}\right)^M P_0}{M!\left(1-\frac{\lambda}{M\mu}\right)}e^{-M\mu\left(1-\frac{\lambda}{M\mu}\right)t}$$	(18-22)

◀ TABLE 18-3

Formulas for the multiple server, exponential service durations model ($M = $ Number of servers).

λ/μ	M	L_q	P_0	λ/μ	M	L_q	P_0	λ/μ	M	L_q	P_0
0.15	1	0.026	0.850	0.65	1	1.207	0.350	1.0	2	0.333	0.333
	2	0.001	0.860		2	0.077	0.509		3	0.045	0.364
0.20	1	0.050	0.800		3	0.008	0.521		4	0.007	0.367
	2	0.002	0.818	0.70	1	1.633	0.300	1.1	2	0.477	0.290
0.25	1	0.083	0.750		2	0.098	0.481		3	0.066	0.327
	2	0.004	0.778		3	0.011	0.495		4	0.011	0.367
0.30	1	0.129	0.700	0.75	1	2.250	0.250	1.2	2	0.675	0.250
	2	0.007	0.739		2	0.123	0.455		3	0.094	0.294
0.35	1	0.188	0.650		3	0.015	0.471		4	0.016	0.300
	2	0.011	0.702	0.80	1	3.200	0.200		5	0.003	0.301
0.40	1	0.267	0.600		2	0.152	0.429	1.3	2	0.951	0.212
	2	0.017	0.667		3	0.019	0.447		3	0.130	0.264
0.45	1	0.368	0.550	0.85	1	4.817	0.150		4	0.023	0.271
	2	0.024	0.633		2	0.187	0.404		5	0.004	0.272
	3	0.002	0.637		3	0.024	0.425	1.4	2	1.345	0.176
0.50	1	0.500	0.500		4	0.003	0.427		3	0.177	0.236
	2	0.033	0.600	0.90	1	8.100	0.100		4	0.032	0.245
	3	0.003	0.606		2	0.229	0.379		5	0.006	0.246
0.55	1	0.672	0.450		3	0.030	0.403	1.5	2	1.929	0.143
	2	0.045	0.569		4	0.004	0.406		3	0.237	0.211
	3	0.004	0.576	0.95	1	18.050	0.050		4	0.045	0.221
0.60	1	0.900	0.400		2	0.277	0.356		5	0.009	0.223
	2	0.059	0.538		3	0.037	0.383				
	3	0.006	0.548		4	0.005	0.386				

◀ TABLE 18-4

Multiple server, exponential service durations model values for L_q and P_0, given values for λ/μ and M (number of servers).

TABLE 18-4 ▶

(continued)

λ/μ	M	L_q	P_0	λ/μ	M	L_q	P_0	λ/μ	M	L_q	P_0
1.6	2	2.844	0.111	2.6	3	4.933	0.035	3.5	4	5.165	0.015
	3	0.313	0.187		4	0.658	0.065		5	0.882	0.026
	4	0.060	0.199		5	0.161	0.072		6	0.248	0.029
	5	0.012	0.201		6	0.043	0.074		7	0.076	0.030
1.7	2	4.426	0.081		7	0.011	0.074		8	0.023	0.030
	3	0.409	0.166	2.7	3	7.354	0.025		9	0.007	0.030
	4	0.080	0.180		4	0.811	0.057	3.6	4	7.090	0.011
	5	0.017	0.182		5	0.198	0.065		5	1.055	0.023
1.8	2	7.674	0.053		6	0.053	0.067		6	0.295	0.026
	3	0.532	0.146		7	0.014	0.067		7	0.019	0.027
	4	0.105	0.162	2.8	3	12.273	0.016		8	0.028	0.027
	5	0.023	0.165		4	1.000	0.050		9	0.008	0.027
1.9	2	17.587	0.026		5	0.241	0.058	3.7	4	10.347	0.008
	3	0.688	0.128		6	0.066	0.060		5	1.265	0.020
	4	0.136	0.145		7	0.018	0.061		6	0.349	0.023
	5	0.030	0.149	2.9	3	27.193	0.008		7	0.109	0.024
	6	0.007	0.149		4	1.234	0.044		8	0.034	0.025
2.0	3	0.889	0.111		5	0.293	0.052		9	0.010	0.025
	4	0.174	0.130	3.0	4	1.528	0.038	3.8	4	16.937	0.005
	5	0.040	0.134		5	0.354	0.047		5	1.519	0.017
	6	0.009	0.135		6	0.099	0.049		6	0.412	0.021
2.1	3	1.149	0.096		7	0.028	0.050		7	0.129	0.022
	4	0.220	0.117		8	0.008	0.050		8	0.041	0.022
	5	0.052	0.121	3.1	4	1.902	0.032		9	0.013	0.022
	6	0.012	0.122		5	0.427	0.042	3.9	4	36.859	0.002
2.2	3	1.491	0.081		6	0.120	0.044		5	1.830	0.015
	4	0.277	0.105		7	0.035	0.045		6	0.485	0.019
	5	0.066	0.109		8	0.010	0.045		7	0.153	0.020
	6	0.016	0.111	3.2	4	2.386	0.027		8	0.050	0.020
2.3	3	1.951	0.068		5	0.513	0.037		9	0.016	0.020
	4	0.346	0.093		6	0.145	0.040	4.0	5	2.216	0.013
	5	0.084	0.099		7	0.043	0.040		6	0.570	0.017
	6	0.021	0.100		8	0.012	0.041		7	0.180	0.018
2.4	3	2.589	0.056	3.3	4	3.027	0.023		8	0.059	0.018
	4	0.431	0.083		5	0.615	0.033		9	0.019	0.018
	5	0.105	0.089		6	0.174	0.036	4.1	5	2.703	0.011
	6	0.027	0.090		7	0.052	0.037		6	0.668	0.015
	7	0.007	0.091		8	0.015	0.037		7	0.212	0.016
2.5	3	3.511	0.045	3.4	4	3.906	0.019		8	0.070	0.016
	4	0.533	0.074		5	0.737	0.029		9	0.023	0.017
	5	0.130	0.080		6	0.209	0.032				
	6	0.034	0.082		7	0.063	0.033				
	7	0.009	0.082		8	0.019	0.033				

λ/μ	M	L_q	P_0	λ/μ	M	L_q	P_0	λ/μ	M	L_q	P_0
4.2	5	3.327	0.009	4.9	5	46.566	0.001	5.5	6	8.590	0.002
	6	0.784	0.013		6	2.459	0.005		7	1.674	0.003
	7	0.248	0.014		7	0.702	0.007		8	0.553	0.004
	8	0.083	0.015		8	0.242	0.007		9	0.204	0.004
	9	0.027	0.015		9	0.087	0.007		10	0.077	0.004
	10	0.009	0.015		10	0.031	0.007		11	0.028	0.004
4.3	5	4.149	0.008		11	0.011	0.077		12	0.010	0.004
	6	0.919	0.012	5.0	6	2.938	0.005	5.6	6	11.519	0.001
	7	0.289	0.130		7	0.810	0.006		7	1.944	0.003
	8	0.097	0.013		8	0.279	0.006		8	0.631	0.003
	9	0.033	0.014		9	0.101	0.007		9	0.233	0.004
	10	0.011	0.014		10	0.036	0.007		10	0.088	0.004
4.4	5	5.268	0.006		11	0.013	0.007		11	0.033	0.004
	6	1.078	0.010	5.1	6	3.536	0.004		12	0.012	0.004
	7	0.337	0.012		7	0.936	0.005				
	8	0.114	0.012		8	0.321	0.006	5.7	6	16.446	0.001
	9	0.039	0.012		9	0.117	0.006		7	2.264	0.002
	10	0.013	0.012		10	0.042	0.006		8	0.721	0.003
4.5	5	6.862	0.005		11	0.015	0.006		9	0.266	0.003
	6	1.265	0.009	5.2	6	4.301	0.003		10	0.102	0.003
	7	0.391	0.010		7	1.081	0.005		11	0.038	0.003
	8	0.133	0.011		8	0.368	0.005		12	0.014	0.003
	9	0.046	0.011		9	0.135	0.005	5.8	6	26.373	0.001
	10	0.015	0.011		10	0.049	0.005		7	2.648	0.002
4.6	5	9.289	0.004		11	0.017	0.006		8	0.823	0.003
	6	1.487	0.008	5.3	6	5.303	0.003		9	0.303	0.003
	7	0.453	0.009		7	1.249	0.004		10	0.116	0.003
	8	0.156	0.010		8	0.422	0.005		11	0.044	0.003
	9	0.054	0.010		9	0.155	0.005		12	0.017	0.003
	10	0.018	0.010		10	0.057	0.005	5.9	6	56.300	0.000
4.7	5	13.382	0.003		11	0.021	0.005		7	3.113	0.002
	6	1.752	0.007		12	0.007	0.005		8	0.939	0.002
	7	0.525	0.008	5.4	6	6.661	0.002		9	0.345	0.003
	8	0.181	0.008		7	1.444	0.004		10	0.133	0.003
	9	0.064	0.009		8	0.483	0.004				
	10	0.022	0.009		9	0.178	0.004				
4.8	5	21.641	0.002		10	0.066	0.004				
	6	2.071	0.006		11	0.024	0.005				
	7	0.607	0.008		12	0.009	0.005				
	8	0.209	0.008								
	9	0.074	0.008								
	10	0.026	0.008								

To use Table 18-4, calculate the value of λ/μ and round it to two decimal places if $\lambda/\mu < 1$ and one decimal place if $\lambda/\mu \geq 1$. Then, simply read the values of L_q and P_0 for the appropriate number of servers, M. For instance, if $\lambda/\mu = 0.50$ and $M = 2$, the table provides a value of 0.033 for L_q and a value of 0.600 for P_0. These values can then be used to calculate other measures of system performance. Note that Table 18-4 can also be used for the single server, exponential service durations model (Model 1) (use $M = 1$ values).

Two new measures are given in Table 18-3: W_a and P_W. W_a is the average wait time for only those customers who have to wait. Note that $W_a > W_q$ because W_q also contains those customers who do not have to wait. P_W is the probability that a customer has to wait. These three terms are related through the following relationship:

$$W_q = \text{Average wait time if customer does not have to wait} \times \text{Probability of not waiting}$$
$$+ \text{Average wait time if customer has to wait} \times \text{Probability of waiting}$$

$$= 0(1 - P_W) + W_a P_W \text{ or, } P_W = \frac{W_q}{W_a}$$

EXAMPLE 18-6

A taxi company has seven cars stationed at an airport during late evening hours on weeknights. The company has determined that customers request taxis during these times at rates that follow Poisson distribution with a mean of 6.6 per hour. Service durations are exponential with a mean of 50 minutes (including the return time to the airport). Find each of the performance measures listed in Table 18-3, and each taxi's utilization. Use $t = 5$ minutes in Formula 18-22.

© Stephen Chernin/Getty Images

SOLUTION

$$\lambda = 6.6 \text{ per hour} \quad M = 7 \text{ taxis (servers)}$$

$$\mu = \frac{1}{50 \text{ minutes} \div 60 \text{ minutes per hour}}$$

$$= 1.2 \text{ per hour}$$

$\lambda/\mu = \frac{6.6}{1.2} = 5.5$. From Table 18-4, for $\frac{\lambda}{\mu} = 5.5$ and $M = 7$ we get $L_q = 1.674$ and $P_0 = 0.003$

$$P_1 = \frac{1}{1!}(5.5)^1(0.003) = 0.0165$$

$$P_2 = \frac{1}{2!}(5.5)^2(0.003) = 0.0454$$

$$\cdots$$

$$W_a = \frac{1}{M\mu - \lambda} = \frac{1}{7(1.2) - 6.6} = 0.556 \text{ hour, or } 33.36 \text{ minutes}$$

$$W_q = \frac{L_q}{\lambda} = \frac{1.674}{6.6} = 0.2536 \text{ hour, or } 15.22 \text{ minutes}$$

$$P_W = \frac{W_q}{W_a} = \frac{0.2536}{0.556} = 0.456$$

$$\rho = \frac{\lambda}{M\mu} = \frac{6.6}{7(1.2)} = 0.786$$

$$P_{W \text{ in } Q > \frac{5}{60}} = \frac{\left(\frac{6.6}{1.2}\right)^7 (0.003)}{7!\left(1 - \frac{6.6}{7(1.2)}\right)} e^{-7(1.2)\left(1 - \frac{6.6}{7(1.2)}\right)\left(\frac{5}{60}\right)} = \left(\frac{456.73}{1080}\right) e^{-.15} = 0.364$$

or 36.4%

The Excel template provided on *Connect2* can also be used to solve Example 18-6. After entering $\lambda = 6.6$ and $\mu = 1.2$ at the top of the template, the queuing statistics for seven servers are shown in the $M = 7$ column of the table in the template. Note that Excel is a little more accurate because it carries several decimal digits. The template also provides queuing statistics for eight through 12 servers, although these are not required for this example. In addition, the template can be used to increment λ and μ by a small amount, to perform sensitivity analysis.

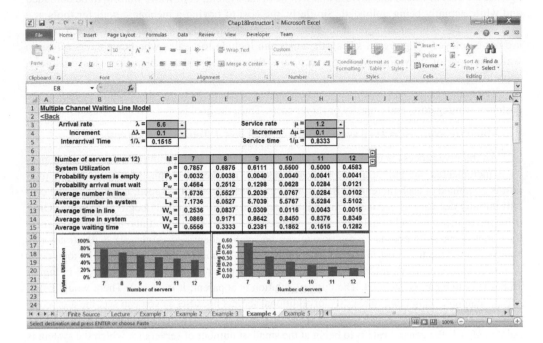

Determining the Number of Servers Using Wait Time Standards

So far we have determined the performance measures of Model 5 using λ, μ, and M. However, we can also do the reverse; that is, we can determine the number of servers M needed to achieve specified levels of various performance measures. This approach is illustrated in the following example.

The taxi company of Example 18-6 also plans to have taxis at a new railway station. The expected customer requests for taxis there during weekday mornings are 4.8 per hour, and the average service time (including the return time to the railway station) is expected to be 40 minutes. How many taxis will be needed to achieve an average customer wait time in line of close to but not exceeding 10 minutes during weekday mornings?

◄ **EXAMPLE 18-7**

SOLUTION

$\lambda = 4.8$ per hour

$\mu = \dfrac{1}{\left(\dfrac{40}{60}\right)} = 1.5$ per hour

$M = ?$

W_q (desired) $= 10$ minutes, or 0.167 hour

Using $L_q = \lambda W_q$, $L_q = (4.8/\text{hour})(0.167 \text{ hour}) = 0.8$. Thus, the average number waiting should be close to but not exceed 0.8. Referring to Table 18-4, with $\lambda/\mu = 4.8/1.5 = 3.2$, we obtain $L_q = 2.386$ for $M = 4$ and 0.513 for $M = 5$. Hence, five taxis will be needed during weekday mornings.

Determining the Number of Servers by Minimizing Total Cost

The design of a service system often reflects the desire of management to balance the cost of capacity with the expected cost of customers waiting in the system. (Note that customer waiting cost refers to the costs incurred by the organization due to customer waiting.) For example, in designing loading docks for a warehouse, the cost of docks plus loading crews must be balanced against the cost of trucks and drivers that will be in the system, both while waiting to be unloaded and while actually being unloaded. Similarly, the cost of having a mechanic wait for tools at a tool crib must be balanced against the cost of servers at the crib. In cases where the customers are not employees (e.g., retail sales), the costs can include lost sales when customers refuse to wait, the cost of providing waiting space, and the cost of added congestion (lost business, shoplifting).

The optimal capacity (usually in terms of number of channels) is one that minimizes the sum of customer waiting costs and capacity or server costs. Thus, the goal is:

Minimize total cost = Total average customer wait cost + Total server pay cost

An iterative process is used to identify the capacity size that will minimize total costs. Capacity is incremented one unit at a time (e.g., increase the number of channels by one) and the total cost is computed at each increment. Because the total cost curve is U-shaped, usually the total cost will initially decrease as capacity is increased, and then it will eventually begin to increase. Once it begins to increase, additional increases in capacity will cause it to continue to increase. Hence, once that occurs, the optimal capacity size can be readily identified. Figure 18.8 illustrates this approach. Find the total cost for $M = 1$, then $M = 2$, $M = 3$, and continue as long as the total costs continue to decline. However, as soon as the total cost begins to rise, as it does at $M = 3$ in Figure 18.8, the search can be stopped. The optimal solution is apparent; it is $M = 2$. There would be no need to continue computing total costs for additional servers because, as you can see, the total costs will continue to increase as more servers are added. *Note:* Although in many instances the starting point is $M = 1$, the general rule is to begin at the smallest number of servers for which the system is underloaded (i.e., the server utilization is less than 1.00).

FIGURE 18-8 ▶

As the number of servers is increased, the optimal number of servers becomes apparent when the total cost begins to increase

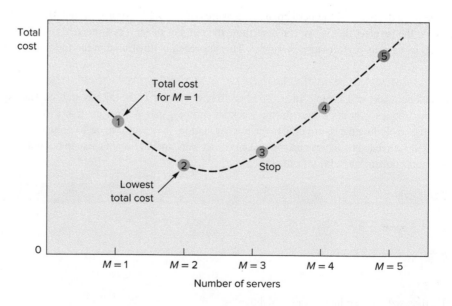

Total average customer wait time in the system during an hour is equal to the average number of customers arriving during the hour multiplied by the average wait time per customer in the system; that is, λW_s. But this equals L_s by Little's formula. To save on calculations, we will use the formula $L_s = L_q + \frac{\lambda}{\mu}$ to obtain the total average customer wait time in the system.

Trucks arrive at a warehouse at an average rate of 15 per hour during business hours. A crew of four work together to unload the trucks at an average rate of five per hour. (Both distributions are Poisson.) Both the trucks and the warehouse belong to the same company. Recent changes in wage rates and truck and driver costs have caused the warehouse manager to re-examine the question of how many crews to use. The new rates are the following: a crew (of four) costs $100 per hour; truck and driver cost $120 per hour. Assuming there are enough unloading docks, how many crews should the manager use?

◀ EXAMPLE 18-8

SOLUTION

L_q values are from Table 18-4 using $\frac{\lambda}{\mu} = \frac{15}{5} = 3.0$

Crew Size	Crew Cost	$\left[L_s = L_q + \frac{\lambda}{\mu}\right]$ Total Average Wait Time in System per Hour	$[L_s \times \$120]$ Total Average Driver/Truck Wait Cost per Hour	Total Cost
4	$400	1.528 + 3.0 = 4.528	$543.36	$ 943.36
5	500	0.354 + 3.0 = 3.354	402.48	902.48 (minimum)
6	600	0.099 + 3.0 = 3.099	371.88	971.88
7	700	0.028 + 3.0 = 3.028	363.36	1,063.36

Five crews will minimize the total cost. Because the total cost will continue to increase once the minimum is reached, it is not necessary to calculate the total cost for crew sizes larger than six.

One additional point should be made concerning the total cost approach. Because customer wait cost is often estimated, the apparent optimal solution may not represent the true optimum. If wait cost estimates can be obtained as *ranges* (e.g., between $40 and $50 per hour), total cost should be calculated using both ends of the range to see whether the optimal solution is different. If it is, management must decide whether to expend additional effort to obtain more precise cost estimates or to choose one of the two indicated optimal solutions.

Model 6: Multiple Servers, Exponential Service Durations, Finite Number in System

In many cases, the number of customers or calls that can fit in the queuing system is limited. Let K = Maximum number of customers (or calls) in the queuing system (in line and being served). Obviously, $K \geq M$, the number of servers. If there are K customers already in the queuing system, the next customer will not be allowed to enter the system and has to balk (leave). The probability of this is P_K. Because P_K proportion of customers are lost, the effective average arrival rate is $\lambda(1 - p_K)$. The formulas in this case are as follows:

$$P_0 = \left[\sum_{n=0}^{M-1} \frac{\left(\frac{\lambda}{\mu}\right)^n}{n!} + \frac{\left(\frac{\lambda}{\mu}\right)^M \left(1 - \left(\frac{\lambda}{M\mu}\right)^{K-M+1}\right)}{M!\left(1 - \frac{\lambda}{M\mu}\right)} \right]^{-1} \qquad (18\text{-}23)$$

$$L_q = \frac{\left(\frac{\lambda}{\mu}\right)^{M+1} P_0}{(M-1)!\left(M - \frac{\lambda}{\mu}\right)^2}\left(1 - \left(\frac{\lambda}{M\mu}\right)^{K-M+1} - (K - M + 1)\left(1 - \frac{\lambda}{M\mu}\right)\left(\frac{\lambda}{M\mu}\right)^{K-M}\right) \qquad (18\text{-}24)$$

$$P_K = \frac{\left(\frac{\lambda}{\mu}\right)^K P_0}{M^{K-M} M!} \tag{18-25}$$

$$W_q = \frac{L_q}{\lambda(1 - P_K)} \tag{18-26}$$

EXAMPLE 18-9 ▶

Reconsider Example 18-6, but assume that no more than 15 customers will wait for a taxi (the 16th customer will use the more expensive limousine service). Calculate:

a. The average number of customers waiting and compare it with Example 18-6.

b. The probability of balking.

c. The average time a customer is in the system, and compare it with Example 18-6.

SOLUTION

Recall that $\lambda = 6.6$ per hour, $\mu = 1.2$ per hour, and $M = 7$. Now, we also have $K = 15$.

a. $P_0 = \left[1 + \left(\frac{6.6}{1.2}\right) + \frac{\left(\frac{6.6}{1.2}\right)^2}{2} + \frac{\left(\frac{6.6}{1.2}\right)^3}{6} + \frac{\left(\frac{6.6}{1.2}\right)^4}{24} + \frac{\left(\frac{6.6}{1.2}\right)^5}{120} + \frac{\left(\frac{6.6}{1.2}\right)^6}{720} + \frac{\left(\frac{6.6}{1.2}\right)^7\left(1 - \left(\frac{6.6}{8.4}\right)^9\right)}{7!\left(1 - \frac{6.6}{8.4}\right)}\right]^{-1}$

$= [1 + 5.5 + 15.125 + 27.7292 + 38.1276 + 41.9404 + 38.4453 + 124.8784]^{-1} = 0.003416$

$L_q = \frac{\left(\frac{6.6}{1.2}\right)^8 0.003416}{6!\left(7 - \frac{6.6}{1.2}\right)^2}\left(1 - \left(\frac{6.6}{8.4}\right)^9 - 9\left(1 - \frac{6.6}{8.4}\right)\left(\frac{6.6}{8.4}\right)^8\right) = 1.070$ customers < 1.674 customers

in Example 18-6.

b. $P_{15} = \frac{\left(\frac{6.6}{1.2}\right)^{15} 0.003416}{7^8 7!} = 0.015$ or 1.5% probability of balking.

c. $W_q = \frac{L_q}{\lambda(1 - P_K)} = \frac{1.070}{6.6(1 - 0.015)} = 0.1646$ hour or 9.88 minutes < 15.22 minutes in Example 18-6.

For an application of Model 6, see the "L.L. Bean" OM in Action.

 OM in Action   www.llbean.com

L.L. Bean

L.L. Bean is a major catalogue phone-order outdoor-clothing company. The company has two large call centres in Maine that receive orders and answer questions. Like other call centres, capacity issues for these call centres range from long-term (i.e., number of phone lines, called trunks, to install) to medium-term (i.e., number of agents to employ) to short-term (i.e., staff scheduling). L.L. Bean determines the number of trunks to install (on a biweekly basis), the number of stations and agents to employ (on a weekly basis), and the maximum size of queue and the number of staff on duty (on a half-hour basis). These are determined hierarchically using a search procedure. L.L. Bean uses the finite line-length version of the multiple server model (Model 6) for two of these (see the following diagram): (a) for determining the number of trunks s_t, (the line length is assumed to be zero; the number of calls in the trunks system equals the number of trunks, s_t); and (b) for determining the number of agents on duty s_a and maximum queue size $K - s_a$ (after getting through but before talking to an agent). For each two-week period, a search procedure uses both the trunks model and agents queue model (for every half-hour within the two-week period) with various values of s_t, s_a, and K, $s_a \leq K \leq s_t$. For each set of values for s_t, s_a, and K, the probability of being blocked (getting

a busy signal) and average customer connect time are determined. The set of value (s_t, s_a, and K) over all half-hour periods of the two-week period that minimizes the total cost of lost orders (due to being blocked), connect time, and staff pay is the optimal solution. A small number of calls, about 1–2 percent, abandon the queue system because of excessive wait. These are ignored in the optimization. Before the above method, L.L. Bean used the following target service goal to determine the values for s_t, s_a, and K: the percentage of calls that wait more than 20 seconds is at most 15 percent.

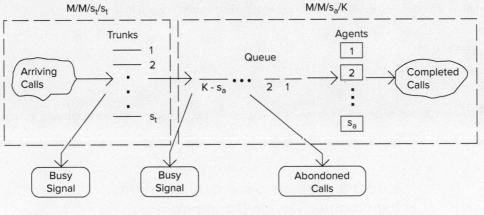

KEY:

s_t : number of trunks installed
s_a: number of agents on-duty
K : system capacity for calls waiting and in service

Source: P. Quinn et al., "Allocating Telecommunications Resources at L. L. Bean, Inc.," *Interfaces*, 21(1), January–February 1991, pp. 75–91.

Model 7: Multiple Servers, General Interarrival and Service Durations[3]

The solution to this model is difficult to obtain. Thus, we will provide an approximate solution.

Let σ_A = Standard deviation of interarrival durations (i.e., the difference between arrival times of consecutive arrivals), and σ_s = Standard deviation of service durations.

Then,

$$L_q \approx \frac{\rho^{\sqrt{2(M+1)}}}{1-\rho} \times \frac{\mu^2 \sigma_s^2 + \lambda^2 \sigma_A^2}{2} \qquad (18\text{-}27)[4]$$

---

[3] R.B. Chase et al., *Operations Management for Competitive Advantage*, 10th ed. (Boston: Irwin, 2004).

[4] We will evaluate the performance of this approximation by comparing it with the results of Examples 18-6 and 18-7. In Example 18-6, $\lambda = 6.6$, $\mu = 1.2$, $M = 7$, and $\rho = 0.786$. It is well known that the standard deviation of an exponential distribution equals its mean. Therefore, $\sigma_A = \frac{1}{\lambda}$ and $\sigma_s = \frac{1}{\mu}$ Substituting these in the L_q Formula 18-27 results in:

$$L_q = \frac{0.786^{\sqrt{2(7+1)}}}{1-0.786} \times \frac{1+1}{2} = 1.784,$$ which is very close to $L_q = 1.674$, the value obtained in Example 18-6.

In Example 18-7, $\lambda = 4.8$, $\mu = 1.5$, $\rho = \frac{4.8}{5(1.5)} = .64$. Substituting these in the L_q Formula 18-27 results in:

$$L_q = \frac{.64^{\sqrt{2(5+1)}}}{1-.64} \times \frac{1+1}{2} = .592,$$ which is very close to $L_q = 0.513$, the value obtained in Example 18-7 for $M = 5$.

EXAMPLE 18-10 ▶ An airport hotel receives groups of guests by airport shuttle vans. Each van may contain various numbers of guests arriving together. The average number of guests arriving per hour during work-day afternoons is forecast to be 30 and the standard deviation of interarrival time is estimated to be three minutes. The check-in process takes a constant time of one minute plus an exponential time with a mean of two minutes. According to hotel policy, the average waiting time in line should not exceed three minutes. Are two employees at the check-in counter adequate during workday afternoons?

SOLUTION

$\lambda = 30$ guests per hour, $\sigma_A = 3$ minutes $= 0.05$ hour

$\mu = 60/3 = 20$ guests per hour, $\sigma_S = 2$ minutes $= 0.0333$ hour. (*Note:* the constant part of service duration does not contribute to the standard deviation. The standard deviation of an exponential distribution is equal to its mean.)

$M = 2$

$\rho = \dfrac{\lambda}{M\mu} = \dfrac{30}{2(20)} = 0.75$

$L_q \approx \dfrac{0.75^{\sqrt{2(2+1)}}}{1 - 0.75} \times \dfrac{20^2 (0.0333)^2 + 30^2 (0.05)^2}{2} = 2.6627$

$W_q = \dfrac{L_q}{\lambda} = \dfrac{2.6627}{30} = 0.08876$ hour or 5.3 minutes > 3 minutes $\rightarrow$ No, 2 check-in counter employees are not adequate.

Model 8: Multiple Servers With Priority, Exponential Service Durations

In many queueing systems, processing occurs on a first-come, first-served (FCFS) basis. However, there are situations in which FCFS is inappropriate because the waiting cost or penalty incurred may not be the same for all the customers. For example, in a hospital emergency waiting room, a wide variety of injuries and illnesses need treatment. Some may be minor (e.g., sliver in finger) and others may be much more serious, even life threatening. It is more reasonable to treat the most serious cases first, letting the non-serious cases wait until all serious cases have been treated. Similarly, computer processing of jobs on large mainframe computers often follows rules other than FCFS (e.g., shortest job first). In such cases, a **multiple-server-with-priority model** is useful for describing the queueing system.

> **multiple-server-with-priority model** Customers (jobs) are processed not first come, first served, but according to some measure of importance.

This model incorporates all of the assumptions of the multiple server, exponential service durations model (Model 5) except that it uses a priority service rule instead of FCFS. Arrivals to the system are assigned a priority as they arrive (e.g., highest priority $= 1$, next priority class $= 2$, next priority class $= 3$, and so on). Let λ_k be the average arrival rate of priority class K. We have $\lambda = \sum \lambda_k$. An existing queue might look something like this:

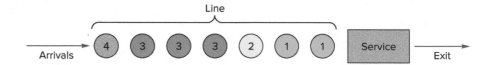

Within each class, waiting units are processed in the order they arrived (i.e., FCFS). Thus, in this sequence, the first 1 would be processed as soon as a server becomes available. The second 1 would be processed when that server or another one becomes available. We assume that each server can process any customer with any priority class and that the average service time is $\frac{1}{\mu}$ for any arrival. If, in the interim, another 1 arrived, it would be next in line *ahead of the first 2*. If there were no new arrivals, the only 2 would be processed by the next available server. At that point, if a new 1 or 2 arrived, it would be processed ahead of the 3s and the 4. We assume that any service already in progress would not be *pre-empted* or interrupted for another customer.

Obviously, a unit with a low priority could conceivably wait a rather long time for processing. In some cases, units that have waited more than a specified time are reassigned a higher priority.

Table 18-5 gives the appropriate formulas for the multiple-server-with-priority model.

Performance Measure	Formula	Formula Number
Server utilization	$\rho = \dfrac{\lambda}{M\mu}$	(18-28)
Intermediate values (L_q from Table 18-4)	$A = \dfrac{\lambda}{(1-\rho)L_q}$	(18-29)
	$B_k = 1 - \sum\limits_{c=1}^{k} \dfrac{\lambda_c}{M\mu}$ $(B_0 = 1)$	(18-30)
Average wait time in line for units in kth priority class	$W_k = \dfrac{1}{A \cdot B_{k-1} \cdot B_k}$	(18-31)
Average time in the system for units in the kth priority class	$W = W_k + \dfrac{1}{\mu}$	(18-32)
Average number of the kth priority class waiting in line	$L_k = \lambda_k \times W_k$	(18-33)

◀ **TABLE 18-5**

Multiple-server-with-priority model.

◀ **EXAMPLE 18-11**

A machine shop handles tool repairs in a large company. As each job arrives in the shop, it is assigned a priority based on urgency of the need for that tool: priority 1 is the highest and priority 3 is the lowest. Number of requests for repair per hour can be described by a Poisson distribution. Average arrival rates are $\lambda_1 = 2$ per hour, $\lambda_2 = 2$ per hour, and $\lambda_3 = 1$ per hour. The average service rate is one tool per hour for each mechanic, and the service rate has Poisson distribution. There are six mechanics in the shop. Determine the value of the following measures:

a. The server utilization.

b. The average time a tool in each of the priority classes will wait for repair.

c. The average time a tool spends in the system for each priority class.

d. The average number of tools waiting for repair in each class.

SOLUTION

$$\lambda = \sum \lambda_k = 2 + 2 + 1 = 5 \text{ per hour}$$

$$M = 6 \text{ servers}$$

$$\mu = 1 \text{ tool per hour}$$

a. $\rho = \dfrac{\lambda}{M\mu} = \dfrac{5}{6(1)} = 0.833$

b. Intermediate values. For $\lambda/\mu = 5/1 = 5$ and $M = 6$, from Table 18-4, $L_q = 2.938$

$$A = \frac{5}{(1-0.833)2.938} = 10.19$$

$$B_0 = 1$$

$$B_1 = 1 - \frac{2}{6(1)} = \frac{2}{3} = 0.667$$

$$B_2 = 1 - \frac{2+2}{6(1)} = \frac{1}{3} = 0.333$$

$$B_3 = 1 - \frac{2+2+1}{6(1)} = \frac{1}{6} = 0.167$$

$$W_1 = \frac{1}{A \cdot B_0 \cdot B_1} = \frac{1}{10.19(1)(0.667)} = 0.147 \text{ hour}$$

$$W_2 = \frac{1}{A \cdot B_1 \cdot B_2} = \frac{1}{10.19(0.667)(0.333)} = 0.442 \text{ hour}$$

$$W_3 = \frac{1}{A \cdot B_2 \cdot B_3} = \frac{1}{10.19(0.333)(0.167)} = 1.765 \text{ hours}$$

c. $W = W_k + 1/\mu$. In this case, $1/\mu = 1/1 = 1$. Thus:

Class	$w_k + 1 = W$ Hours
1	0.147 + 1 = 1.147
2	0.442 + 1 = 1.442
3	1.765 + 1 = 2.765

d. The average number of units waiting for repair in each class is $L_k = \lambda_k W_k$. Thus:

Class	$\lambda_k W_k = L_k$ Units
1	2(0.147) = 0.294
2	2(0.442) = 0.884
3	1(1.765) = 1.765

Using the Excel template on *Connect2*, the solution to Example 18-11 would appear as follows:

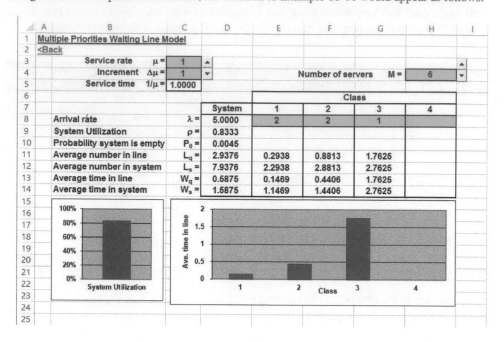

Note that the small differences between Excel and manual results are due to rounding.

Revising Priorities. If any of the wait times calculated in Example 18-11 are deemed too long by management (e.g., a wait time of 0.147 hour for tools in the first class might be too long), there are several options. One is to increase the number of servers. Another is to attempt to increase the service rate, say, by introducing new methods. If such options are not feasible, another approach is to re-examine the membership of each of the priority classes and relegate some jobs to lower priority classes. For example, if some repair requests in the first priority class can be reassigned to the second priority class, this will tend to decrease the average wait times for repair jobs in the highest priority class simply because the arrival rate of those items will be lower.

EXAMPLE 18-12 ▶

The manager of the repair shop in Example 18-11, after consulting with the managers of the departments that use the shop's services, has revised the list of tools that are given the highest priorities. The revised average arrival rates are now: $\lambda_1 = 1.5$, $\lambda_2 = 2.5$, and λ_3 remains unchanged at 1.0. Determine the value of the following measures:

a. The server utilization.

b. The average waiting time for units in each priority class.

SOLUTION

$\lambda = \Sigma\lambda_k = 1.5 + 2.5 + 1.0 = 5.0$

$M = 6$

$\mu = 1$

Note that these values are the same as in the previous example.

a. $\rho = \dfrac{\lambda}{M\mu} = 5.0/6\left(1\right) = 0.833$, the same as in the previous example.

b. The value of A, since it is a function of M, μ and λ, is the same as in the preceding example because these values are the same. Therefore, $A = 10.19$ and

$B_0 = 1 (\text{always})$

$B_1 = 1 - \dfrac{1.5}{6(1)} = 0.75$

$B_2 = 1 - \dfrac{1.5 + 2.5}{6(1)} = 0.333$, same

$B_3 = 1 - \dfrac{1.5 + 2.5 + 1.0}{6(1)} = 0.167$, same

Then

$W_1 = \dfrac{1}{10.19(1)(0.75)} = 0.131$ hour

$W_2 = \dfrac{1}{10.19(0.75)(0.333)} = 0.393$ hour

$W_3 = \dfrac{1}{10.19(0.333)(0.167)} = 1.765$ hour

Example 18-12 offers several interesting results. One is that through reduction of the average arrival rate of the highest priority class, the average wait time for units in that class has decreased. In other words, removing some members of the highest class and placing them into the next lower class reduced the average wait time for units that remained in the highest class. It is interesting that the average wait time for the second priority class also was reduced, even though units were added to that class. Although this may appear counterintuitive, the *total* average wait time (or total average number waiting) will remain unchanged. We can see this by noticing that the average *number* waiting (see Example 18-11, part *d*) is 0.294 + 0.884 + 1.765 = 2.943. In Example 18-12, using the average wait times just calculated, the average number waiting in all three classes in total is:

$$\sum_{k=1}^{3} \lambda_k W_k = 1.5(0.131) + 2.5(0.393) + 1.0(1.765) = 2.944.$$

Aside from a slight difference due to rounding, the totals are the same.

Another interesting observation is that the average wait time for customers in the third priority class did not change from the preceding example. The reason for this is that the *total* average arrival rates for the two higher-priority classes did not change and the average arrival rate for this class did not change.

Queueing Model: Finite Source

LO6

The finite source model is appropriate for cases in which the calling population is limited. For instance, in a queueing system for breakdowns of five machines, the size of the calling population is five.

As in the infinite source models, arrival rates are assumed to be Poisson and service durations exponential. A major difference between the finite and infinite source models is that the arrival rate of customers (machines) in a finite situation is *affected by* the length of the waiting line; the arrival rate decreases as the length of the line increases simply because there is a decreasing proportion of the population that is out and can generate calls for service. When *all* of the population is waiting in line, the arrival rate is zero because no additional units can arrive.

Because the mathematics of the finite source model can be complex, analysts often use a table (Table 18-6) in conjunction with simple formulas to analyze these systems. Table 18-7 contains a list of the key formulas and definitions. The inputs to the model are the average service duration *T*,

▼ TABLE 18-6

Finite source model table; values for D and F, given values for X and M.

X	M	D	F	X	M	D	F	X	M	D	F	X	M	D	F
	Population 5			.058	2	.019	.999	.080	2	.035	.998	.120	2	.076	.995
.012	1	.048	.999		1	.229	.984		1	.313	.969		1	.456	.927
.019	1	.076	.998	.060	2	.020	.999	.085	2	.040	.998	.125	2	.082	.994
.025	1	.100	.997		1	.237	.983		1	.332	.965		1	.473	.920
.030	1	.120	.996	.062	2	.022	.999	.090	2	.044	.998	.130	2	.089	.933
.034	1	.135	.995		1	.245	.982		1	.350	.960		1	.489	.914
.036	1	.143	.994	.064	2	.023	.999	.095	2	.049	.997	.135	2	.095	.933
.040	1	.159	.993		1	.253	.981		1	.368	.955		1	.505	.907
.042	1	.167	.992	.066	2	.024	.999	.100	2	.054	.997	.140	2	.102	.992
.044	1	.175	.991		1	.260	.979		1	.386	.950		1	.521	.900
.046	1	.183	.990	.068	2	.026	.999	.105	2	.059	.997	.145	3	.011	.999
.050	1	.198	.989		1	.268	.978		1	.404	.945		2	.109	.991
.052	1	.206	.988	.070	2	.027	.999	.110	2	.065	.996		1	.537	.892
.054	1	.214	.987		1	.275	.977		1	.421	.939	.150	3	.012	.999
.056	2	.018	.999	.075	2	.031	.999	.115	2	.017	.995		2	.115	.990
	1	.222	.985		1	.294	.973		1	.439	.933		1	.553	.885

TABLE 18-6 ▼

(continued)

X	M	D	F	X	M	D	F	X	M	D	F	X	M	D	F
.155	3	.013	.999	.270	3	.064	.994	.400	4	.026	.997	.600	4	.130	.981
	2	.123	.989		2	.323	.944		3	.186	.972		3	.497	.883
	1	.568	.877		1	.827	.677		2	.579	.845		2	.875	.652
.160	3	.015	.999	.280	3	.071	.993		1	.952	.493		1	.996	.333
	2	.130	.988		2	.342	.938	.420	4	.031	.997	.650	4	.179	.972
	1	.582	.869		1	.842	.661		3	.211	.966		3	.588	.850
.165	3	.016	.999	.290	4	.007	.999		2	.616	.826		2	.918	.608
	2	.137	.987		3	.079	.992		1	.961	.471		1	.998	.308
	1	.597	.861		2	.362	.932	.440	4	.037	.996	.700	4	.240	.960
.170	3	.017	.999		1	.856	.644		3	.238	.960		3	.678	.815
	2	.145	.985	.300	4	.008	.999		2	.652	.807		2	.950	.568
	1	.611	.853		3	.086	.990		1	.969	.451		1	.999	.286
.180	3	.021	.999		2	.382	.926	.460	4	.045	.995	.750	4	.316	.944
	2	.161	.983		1	.869	.628		3	.266	.953		3	.763	.777
	1	.683	.836	.310	4	.009	.999		2	.686	.787		2	.972	.532
.190	3	.024	.998		3	.094	.989		1	.975	.432	.800	4	.410	.924
	2	.117	.980		2	.402	.919	.480	4	.053	.994		3	.841	.739
	1	.665	.819		1	.881	.613		3	.296	.945		2	.987	.500
.200	3	.028	.998	.320	4	.010	.999		2	.719	.767	.850	4	.522	.900
	2	.194	.976		3	.103	.988		1	.980	.415		3	.907	.702
	1	.689	.801		2	.422	.912	.500	4	.063	.992		2	.995	.470
.210	3	.032	.998		1	.892	.597		3	.327	.936	.900	4	.656	.871
	2	.211	.973	.330	4	.012	.999		2	.750	.748		3	.957	.666
	1	.713	.783		3	.112	.986		1	.985	.399		2	.998	.444
.220	3	.036	.997		2	.442	.904	.520	4	.073	.991	.950	4	.815	.838
	2	.229	.969		1	.902	.583		3	.359	.927		3	.989	.631
	1	.735	.765	.340	4	.013	.999		2	.779	.728	Population 10			
.230	3	.041	.997		3	.121	.985		1	.988	.384	.016	1	.144	.997
	2	.247	.965		2	.462	.896	.540	4	.085	.989	.019	1	.170	.996
	1	.756	.747		1	.911	.569		3	.392	.917	.021	1	.188	.995
.240	3	.046	.996	.360	4	.017	.998		2	.806	.708	.023	1	.206	.994
	2	.265	.960		3	.141	.981		1	.991	.370	.025	1	.224	.993
	1	.775	.730		2	.501	.880	.560	4	.098	.986	.026	1	.232	.992
.250	3	.052	.995		1	.927	.542		3	.426	.906	.028	1	.250	.991
	2	.284	.955	.380	4	.021	.998		2	.831	.689	.030	1	.268	.990
	1	.794	.712		3	.163	.976		1	.993	.357	.032	2	.033	.999
.260	3	.058	.994		2	.540	.863	.580	4	.113	.984		1	.285	.988
	2	.303	.950		1	.941	.516		3	.461	.895	.034	2	.037	.999
	1	.811	.695						2	.854	.670		1	.301	.986
									1	.994	.345				

X	M	D	F	X	M	D	F	X	M	D	F	X	M	D	F
.036	2	.041	.999	.085	3	.037	.999	.150	4	.036	.998	.230	5	.037	.998
	1	.320	.984		2	.196	.988		3	.156	.989		4	.142	.988
.038	2	.046	.999		1	.692	.883		2	.483	.935		3	.400	.947
	1	.337	.982	.090	3	.043	.998		1	.939	.644		2	.791	.794
.040	2	.050	.999		2	.216	.986	.155	4	.040	.998		1	.995	.434
	1	.354	.980		1	.722	.867		3	.169	.987	.240	5	.044	.997
.042	2	.055	.999	.095	3	.049	.998		2	.505	.928		4	.162	.986
	1	.371	.978		2	.237	.984		1	.947	.627		3	.434	.938
.044	2	.060	.998		1	.750	.850	.160	4	.044	.998		2	.819	.774
	1	.388	.975	.100	3	.056	.998		3	.182	.986		1	.996	.416
.046	2	.065	.998		2	.258	.981		2	.528	.921	.250	6	.010	.999
	1	.404	.973		1	.776	.832		1	.954	.610		5	.052	.997
.048	2	.071	.998	.105	3	.064	.997	.165	4	.049	.997		4	.183	.983
	1	.421	.970		2	.279	.978		3	.195	.984		3	.469	.929
.050	2	.076	.998		1	.800	.814		2	.550	.914		2	.844	.753
	1	.437	.967	.110	3	.072	.997		1	.961	.594		1	.997	.400
.052	2	.082	.997		2	.301	.974	.170	4	.054	.997	.260	6	.013	.999
	1	.454	.963		1	.822	.795		3	.209	.982		5	.060	.996
.054	2	.088	.997	.115	3	.081	.996		2	.571	.906		4	.205	.980
	1	.470	.960		2	.324	.971		1	.966	.579		3	.503	.919
.056	2	.094	.997		1	.843	.776	.180	5	.013	.999		2	.866	.732
	1	.486	.956	.120	4	.016	.999		4	.066	.996		1	.998	.384
.058	2	.100	.996		3	.090	.995		3	.238	.978	.270	6	.015	.999
	1	.501	.953		2	.346	.967		2	.614	.890		5	.070	.995
.060	2	.106	.996		1	.861	.756		1	.975	.890		4	.228	.976
	1	.517	.949	.125	4	.019	.999	.190	5	.016	.999		3	.537	.908
.062	2	.113	.996		3	.100	.994		4	.078	.995		2	.886	.712
	1	.532	.945		2	.369	.962		3	.269	.973		1	.999	.370
.064	2	.119	.995		1	.878	.737		2	.654	.873	.280	6	.018	.999
	1	.547	.940	.130	4	.022	.999		1	.982	.522		5	.081	.994
.066	2	.126	.995		3	.110	.994	.200	5	.020	.999		4	.252	.972
	1	.562	.936		2	.392	.958		4	.092	.994		3	.571	.896
.068	3	.020	.999		1	.893	.718		3	.300	.968		2	.903	.692
	2	.133	.994	.135	4	.025	.999		2	.692	.854		1	.999	.357
	1	.577	.931		3	.121	.993		1	.987	.497	.290	6	.022	.999
.070	3	.022	.999		2	.415	.952	.210	5	.025	.999		5	.093	.993
	2	.140	.994		1	.907	.699		4	.108	.992		4	.278	.968
	1	.591	.926	.140	4	.028	.999		3	.333	.961		3	.603	.884
.075	3	.026	.999		3	.132	.991		2	.728	.835		2	.918	.672
	2	.158	.992		2	.437	.947		1	.990	.474		1	.999	.345
	1	.627	.913		1	.919	.680	.220	5	.030	.998	.300	6	.026	.998
.080	3	.031	.999	.145	4	.032	.999		4	.124	.990		5	.106	.991
	2	.177	.990		3	.144	.990		3	.366	.954		4	.304	.963
	1	.660	.899		2	.460	.941		2	.761	.815		3	.635	.872
					1	.929	.662		1	.993	.453		2	.932	.653
													1	.999	.333

TABLE 18-6 ▼

(continued)

X	M	D	F	X	M	D	F	X	M	D	F	X	M	D	F
.310	6	.031	.998	.420	7	.034	.993	.540	8	.034	.997	.750	9	.075	.994
	5	.120	.990		6	.130	.987		7	.141	.986		8	.307	.965
	4	.331	.957		5	.341	.954		6	.363	.949		7	.626	.897
	3	.666	.858		4	.646	.866		5	.658	.867		6	.870	.792
	2	.943	.635		3	.905	.700		4	.893	.729		5	.975	.666
.320	6	.036	.998		2	.994	.476		3	.986	.555		4	.998	.533
	5	.135	.988	.440	7	.045	.997	.560	8	.044	.996	.800	9	.134	.988
	4	.359	.952		6	.160	.984		7	.171	.982		8	.446	.944
	3	.695	.845		5	.392	.943		6	.413	.939		7	.763	.859
	2	.952	.617		4	.698	.845		5	.707	.848		6	.939	.747
.330	6	.042	.997		3	.928	.672		4	.917	.706		5	.991	.625
	5	.151	.986		2	.996	.454		3	.991	.535		4	.999	.500
	4	.387	.945	.460	8	.011	.999	.580	8	.057	.995	.850	9	.232	.979
	3	.723	.831		7	.058	.995		7	.204	.977		8	.611	.916
	2	.961	.600		6	.193	.979		6	.465	.927		7	.879	.818
.340	7	.010	.999		5	.445	.930		5	.753	.829		6	.978	.705
	6	.049	.997		4	.747	.822		4	.937	.684		5	.998	.588
	5	.168	.983		3	.947	.646		3	.994	.517	.900	9	.387	.963
	4	.416	.938		2	.998	.435	.600	9	.010	.999		8	.785	.881
	3	.750	.816	.480	8	.015	.999		8	.072	.994		7	.957	.777
	2	.968	.584		7	.074	.994		7	.242	.972		6	.995	.667
.360	7	.014	.999		6	.230	.973		6	.518	.915	.950	9	.630	.938
	6	.064	.995		5	.499	.916		5	.795	.809		8	.934	.841
	5	.205	.978		4	.791	.799		4	.953	.663		7	.994	.737
	4	.474	.923		3	.961	.621		3	.996	.500				
	3	.798	.787		2	.998	.417	.650	9	.021	.999				
	2	.978	.553	.500	8	.020	.999		8	.123	.988				
.380	7	.019	.999		7	.093	.992		7	.353	.954				
	6	.083	.993		6	.271	.966		6	.651	.878				
	5	.247	.971		5	.553	.901		5	.882	.759				
	4	.533	.906		4	.830	.775		4	.980	.614				
	3	.840	.758		3	.972	.598		3	.999	.461				
	2	.986	.525		2	.999	.400	.700	9	.040	.997				
.400	7	.026	.998	.520	8	.026	.998		8	.200	.979				
	6	.105	.991		7	.115	.989		7	.484	.929				
	5	.292	.963		6	.316	.958		6	.772	.836				
	4	.591	.887		5	.606	.884		5	.940	.711				
	3	.875	.728		4	.864	.752		4	.992	.571				
	2	.991	.499		3	.980	.575								
					2	.999	.385								

Source: L. G. Peck and R. N. Hazelwood, *Finite Queueing Tables* (New York: John Wiley & Sons, 1958). Reprinted by permission.

the average run duration U, the number of servers M, and total number of machines N. The desired quantities of interest are the average wait time (before service) W, average number running J, the average number in line L, and the average number in service H. You will find it helpful to study the diagram of a run-wait-service cycle that is presented in Table 18-7.

	Formulas		Notation
Service factor	$X = \dfrac{T}{T+U}$	(18-34)	D = Probability that a machine will have to wait in line before service
Average number waiting	$L = N(1 - F)$	(18-35)	F = Efficiency factor: proportion of machines being serviced or running
Average waiting time	$W = \dfrac{L(T+U)}{N-L} = \dfrac{T(1-F)}{XF}$	(18-36)	H = Average number of machines being serviced
Average number running	$J = NF(1-X)$	(18-37)	J = Average number of machines running
Average number being serviced	$H = FNX$	(18-38)	L = Average number of machines waiting for service
			M = Number of servers
Number in population	$N = J + L + H$	(18-39)	N = Number of machines
			T = Average service duration
			U = Average run duration
			W = Average wait duration
			X = Service factor; proportion of average service duration to sum of average service and average run durations

Cycle

| Running (J, U) | Waiting (L, W) | Being serviced (H, T) |

Average number: J L H
Average time: U W T

TABLE 18-7

Finite source model formulas and definitions.

L. G. Peck and R. N. Hazelwood, *Finite Queueing Tables* (New York: John Wiley & Sons, 1958). Reprinted with by permission.

Table 18-6 is an abbreviated finite source model table used to obtain values of D and F, given X and M. (Most of the formulas require a value for F.) In order to use this table, follow this procedure:

1. Identify the values for
   a. N, population size.
   b. M, number of servers.
   c. T, average service duration.
   d. U, average run duration.

2. Calculate the service factor, $X = T/(T + U)$.

3. Locate the section of the finite source model table for population size N. (Only values for $N = 5$ and 10 are shown here because of space limitation.)

4. Using the value of X as the point of entry, find the values of F and D that correspond to M.

5. Use the value of F to determine the values of the desired measures of system performance using the formulas in Table 18-7.

EXAMPLE 18-13 ▶

One operator loads and unloads a group of five machines. Service durations (i.e., one unloading and loading) are exponentially distributed with a mean of 10 minutes per machine. Machines run for an average of 70 minutes between loading and unloading, and this duration is also exponential. Find:

a. The average number of machines waiting for the operator.

b. The expected number of machines running.

c. Average duration of downtime.

d. The probability that a machine will not have to wait for service.

SOLUTION

$N = 5$

$T = 10$ minutes

$M = 1$

$U = 70$ minutes

$$\chi = \frac{T}{T + U} = \frac{10}{10 + 70} = 0.125$$

From Table 18-6, with $N = 5$, $M = 1$, and $X = 0.125$, we obtain $D = 0.473$ and $F = 0.920$.

a. Average number waiting, $L = N(1 - F) = 5(1 - 0.920) = 0.40$ machine.

b. Expected number running, $J = NF(1 - X) = 5(0.92)(1 - 0.125) = 4.025$ machines.

c. Downtime = Waiting time + Service time:

Average waiting time

$$W = \frac{L(T + U)}{N - L} = \frac{0.40(10 + 70)}{5 - 0.40} = 6.957 \text{ minutes}$$

Downtime = 6.957 minutes + 10 minutes = 16.957 minutes

d. Probability of not having to wait = 1 − Probability of having to wait
= $1 - D$
= $1 - 0.473 = 0.527$

Using the Excel template, the solution to Example 18-13 would appear as follows:

	A	B	C	D	E	F	G	H
1		Finite Source Waiting Line Model						
2		<Back						
3		Population Size	N =	5	5			
4		Number of servers	M =	1	2			
5		Average service time	T =	10	10			
6		Average time between service calls	U =	70	70			
7		P(wait) - from table	D =	0.4730	0.0820			
8		Efficiency factor - from table	F =	0.9200	0.9940			
9		Service factor	χ =	0.125	0.125			
10		Average number waiting	L =	0.4000	0.0300			
11		Average waiting time	W =	6.9565	0.4829			
12		Average number running	J =	4.0250	4.3488			
13		Average number being serviced	H =	0.5750	0.6213			
14								
15				Per Time				
16				Unit				
17		Service cost =	10	10	20			
18		Downtime cost =	16	15.6	10.42			
19		Total Cost =		25.6	30.42			
20								
21								
22		Note: You must enter D and F (based on N, χ, and M) from the table in the text.						
23								

Suppose that in Example 18-13, the operator is paid $10 per hour and machine downtime costs $16 per hour. Should the department add another operator if the goal is total cost minimization?

EXAMPLE 18-14

SOLUTION

Compare the total cost of the present system with the total cost of the proposed system:

M	Average Number Down, N − J	Average Down Cost (per hour), (N − J) × $16	Operator Cost (per hour)	Total Cost (per hour)
1	5 − 4.025 = 0.975	$15.60	$10	$25.60
2	0.651	10.42	20	30.42

where $N - J$ for $M = 2$ is obtained as follows: For $X = 0.125$ and $M = 2$, from Table 18-6 $F = 0.994$; therefore $J = NF(1 - X) = 5(0.994)(1 - 0.125) = 4.349$, and $N - J = 5 - 4.349 = 0.651$. Hence, the present system is superior because its total cost is less than the total cost of using two operators.

Summary

- Analysis of waiting lines can be an important aspect of the design of service systems.
- Waiting lines have a tendency to form even though, in a macro sense, the system is underloaded.
- The arrival of customers can be clumped together (lunch time) and service durations can be variable; combined, these events create temporary overloads. By the same token, at other times the servers are idle.
- The goal is to minimize total customer wait and server costs, but a standard on a performance measure such as "average wait time is less than three minutes" is also used to determine the number of servers.
- A major consideration in the analysis of queueing systems is whether the number of potential customers is limited (finite source) or unrestricted ("infinite" source).
- Nine queueing models are described, eight dealing with infinite source (four for single servers and four for multiple servers) and one dealing with finite source.
- Most models assume that customer arrival rates can be described by a Poisson distribution, that service durations can be described by an exponential distribution, and customers are served first come, first served (FCFS).
- Basic relationships are given so that starting from the average queue length, other measures such as average wait time in the line or in the system and probability of having to wait can be determined.

Key Terms

exponential distribution
finite source
infinite source

multiple-server-with-priority model
Poisson distribution
queue discipline

queueing theory
server utilization

Solved Problems

Problem 1

Infinite source, multiple servers, exponential service durations (Model 5). One of the features of a new machine shop will be a well-stocked tool crib. The manager of the shop must decide on the number of attendants needed to staff the crib. Attendants will receive $9 per hour in wages and fringe benefits.

Mechanics' time will be worth $30 per hour in wages and fringe benefits. Based on previous experience, the manager estimates that requests for tools will average 18 per hour with a service capacity of 20 requests per hour per attendant. How many attendants should be on duty in order to minimize total mechanics' wait cost and attendants' wages? Assume that the arrival rate is Poisson and service rates will be exponential. (Also assume that the number of mechanics is very large, in order for the infinite source model to be appropriate.)

Solution

$\lambda = 18$ per hour

$\mu = 20$ *per* hour

Number of Attendants, M	L_q*	$L_q + \frac{\lambda}{\mu} = L_s$	$9M$: Attendant Cost ($ per hour)	$30L_s$: Mechanic Cost ($ per hour)	Total Cost ($ per hour)
1	8.1	$8.1 + 0.9 = 9.0$	9	270	279
2	0.229	$0.229 + 0.9 = 1.129$	18	33.87	52†
3	0.03	$0.03 + 0.9 = 0.93$	27	27.9	55†

* L_q from Table 18-4, with $\lambda/\mu = 18/20 = 0.9$.
† Rounded.

Hence, two attendants will produce the lowest total cost.

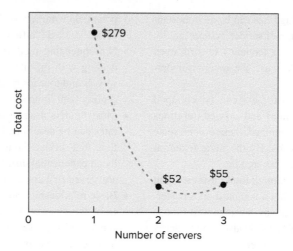

Problem 2

Infinite source. The following is a list of average service duration for three different operations:

Operation	Average Service Duration
A	8 minutes
B	1.2 hours
C	2 days

a. Determine the average service rate for each operation.

b. Would the calculated rates be different if these were interarrival durations rather than service durations?

Solution

a. The average service rate is the reciprocal of average service duration. Thus, the rates are:
A: 1/8 per minute = 0.125 per minute, or 7.5 per hour
B: 1/1.2 per hour = 0.833 per hour
C: 1/2 per day = 0.50 per day

b. No. In either case, the rate is simply the reciprocal of the duration.

Problem 3

Finite source. A group of 10 machines is loaded and unloaded by one of three servers. The machines run for an average of six minutes per cycle, and the average time to unload and reload is nine minutes. Run and service durations can be described by exponential distributions. While running, the machines could produce a total of 16 units per hour if they did not have to pause to wait for a server and be loaded and unloaded. What is the average hourly output of each machine when waiting and serving are taken into account?

Solution

$T = 9$ minutes

$U = 6$ minutes; $X = \dfrac{T}{T+U} = \dfrac{9}{9+6} = 0.60$

$N = 10$ machines

$M = 3$ servers; from Table 18-6 (Population 10), we obtain $F = 0.500$, $D = 0.996$

Calculate the average number of machines running:

$$J = NF(1 - X) = 10(0.500)(1 - 0.6) = 2$$

Determine the percentage of machines running, and multiply by output while running:

$$\frac{J}{N} \times (16 \text{ per hour}) = \frac{2}{10} \times (16 \text{ units per hour}) = 3.2 \text{ units per hour}$$

Discussion and Review Questions

Note: An asterisk indicates that a question or problem may be more challenging.

(LO1) 1. Give some examples of services where waiting lines are used.

(LO1) 2. Why do waiting lines form even though the system is underloaded?

(LO2) 3. What are the most common measures of system performance in queueing analysis?

(LO2) 4. What information is necessary to analyze a queueing system?

(LO2 & 4) 5. What effect would decreasing arrival and service variability have on the waiting line?

(LO2) 6. What approach do supermarkets use to reduce waiting times?

(LO2) 7. Contrast finite and "infinite" sources.

(LO2) 8. In a multiple server system, what is the rationale for having customers wait in a single joint line as is now done in many banks, rather than in multiple lines?

(LO2) 9. What happens to the average wait time if a manager attempts to achieve a high capacity utilization? What happens if $\lambda \geq \mu$?

(LO3) 10. Explain Little's formula: $L = \lambda W$.

(LO3) 11. What is the difference between W_q and W_s?

(LO4) 12. Will doubling the service rate of a single server system reduce the average waiting time in line by a factor of one-half? Explain briefly.

(LO4) 13. Can a service duration be more variable than an exponential distribution? Explain.

(LO5) 14. Is Model 1 a special case of Model 5? Explain.

(LO5) 15. Name two ways the number of servers can be determined.

(LO5) 16. How can Model 6 be used to determine the maximum length of the line (size of waiting room)?

(LO5) 17. Give an example where the distribution of interarrival times is not Poisson.

(LO5) 18. A traffic light and the cars waiting at the traffic light on one side of the street form a queueing system. If there are two lines on this side of the street, what queueing model best describes this situation?

(LO6) 19. Give an example of a situation where the finite source model can be used.

(LO1) 20. What are some psychological approaches to managing waiting lines, and why might a manger want to use them?

(LO1) 21. In what kinds of situations is queueing analysis most appropriate?

(LO5) 22. Under what circumstances would a multiple-servers-with-priority model be appropriate?

Taking Stock

 1. What general trade-offs need to be carefully considered when making waiting-line decisions?

 2. Who needs to be involved in assessing the waiting cost if customers (a) are from the general public and (b) are employees of the organization?

 3. How has technology (a) had an impact on analyzing waiting-line systems, and (b) improved waiting-line performance?

 4. Some airlines use priority seating when boarding passengers with first class customers boarding first. Is this ethical?

Critical Thinking Exercises

 1. The owner of a restaurant implemented an expanded menu early last year. The menu was a success, drawing many more customers than the previous menu. But good news soon became bad news as long waiting lines began to deter customers, and business dropped off. Describe how waiting-line analysis can help the restaurant.

 2. There are certain instances where pooling of operations can be desirable. For example, a large factory may have two or more locations where mechanics can obtain special tools or equipment they occasionally need. The separate locations mean less travel time for workers, but sometimes there will be a waiting line at one location while servers are idle at another location. What factors should an analysis of this sort of situation take into account in deciding on whether to keep separate locations or pool servers and equipment at one central location?

Experiential Learning Exercise

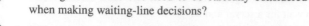 Contact a manager of a local business. Determine the average arrival rate and average service rate at one of these operations: a fast-food restaurant, supermarket, post office, or bank branch.

a. For the arrival rate, observe for 15 one-minute intervals. Count the number of arrivals in each minute. Construct a frequency distribution for arrivals. Does it resemble a Poisson distribution? Calculate its mean.

b. Now determine the service durations. To do this, observe the service time of 15 customers (e.g., how many minutes a teller at a bank spent with each customer). Make a frequency distribution. Does it look like exponential distribution? Calculate its mean.

Internet Exercise

 Visit http://www.qmatic.com/meet-qmatic/resource-library/, find a case study, and briefly describe how the Qmatic system helped the operation.

Problems

1. $\lambda = 3$ customers/hour
$\mu = 5$ customers/hour
$M = 1$

 a. What is the server utilization?

b. What is the average number of customers waiting for service?

c. What is the average time customers wait in line for service?

 2. Repair calls for Xerox copiers in a small city are handled by one repair person. Repair duration, including travel time, is exponentially distributed with a mean of two hours per call. Requests for copier repairs come in at a mean rate of three per eight-hour day (assume Poisson). Assume infinite source. Determine:

a. The average number of copiers waiting for repair.

b. Server utilization.

c. The amount of time during an eight-hour day that the repair person is not out on a call.

d. The probability of two or more copiers in the system (waiting to be or being repaired).

e. The probability that a copier waits more than four hours for repair to begin.

3. A vending machine dispenses hot chocolate or coffee. Service duration is 30 seconds per cup and is constant.

Customers arrive at a mean rate of 80 per hour (assume Poisson). Also assume that each customer buys only one cup. Determine:

a. The average number of customers waiting in line.

b. The average time customers spend in the system.

c. The average number of customers in the system.

 4. Many of a bank's customers use its automated banking machine (ABM). During the early evening hours in the summer months, customers arrive at the ABM at the rate of one every other minute (assume Poisson). Each customer spends an average of 90 seconds completing his or her transaction. Transaction times are exponentially distributed. Assume that the length of queue is not a constraint. Determine:

a. The average time customers spend at the machine, including waiting in line and completing transactions.

b. The probability that a customer will not have to wait upon arrival at the ABM.

c. Utilization of the ABM.

d. The probability that a customer waits four minutes or more in the line.

 5. A small town with one hospital has two ambulances. Requests for an ambulance during weekday mornings average 0.8 per hour and tend to be Poisson. Travel and loading/unloading time averages one hour per call and follows an exponential distribution. Find:

a. Server utilization.

b. The average number of patients waiting.

c. The average time patients wait for an ambulance.

d. The probability that both ambulances will be busy when a call comes in.

6. The following information pertains to telephone calls to a call centre on a typical workday. Assume Poisson arrivals and exponential service durations.

Period	Average Incoming Rate (calls per minute)	Average Service Rate (calls per minute per operator)	Number of Operators
Morning..............	1.8	1.5	2
Afternoon............	2.2	1.0	3
Evening..............	1.4	0.7	3

a. Determine the average time callers wait to have their calls answered for each period and the probability that a caller will have to wait during each period.

b. The call centre has seven leased phone lines (trunks). What is the probability that a phone call will receive a busy signal during each of the three periods?

 7. Trucks are required to check in at a weigh station (scale) so that they can be inspected for weight violations. Trucks arrive at the station at the rate of 40 an hour in the mornings

according to Poisson distribution. Currently two inspectors are on duty during those hours, each of whom can inspect 25 trucks an hour, according to Poisson distribution.

a. How many trucks would you expect to see at the weigh station, including those being inspected?

b. If a truck were just arriving at the station, how many minutes could the driver expect to wait before being inspected?

c. How many minutes, on average, would a truck that is not immediately inspected have to wait before being inspected?

d. What is the probability that both inspectors would be busy at the same time (i.e., the probability that an arrival will have to wait for service)?

e. What condition would exist if there were only one inspector?

f. If only 13 trucks fit in the system, what is the probability that a truck cannot enter the system?

 8. The manager of a new regional warehouse of a company must decide on the number of loading docks to request in order to minimize the sum of dock–crew and driver–truck costs. The manager has learned that each driver–truck combination represents a cost of $300 per day and that each dock plus crew represents a cost of $1,100 per day.

a. How many docks should she request if trucks will arrive at an average rate of four per day, each dock can handle an average of five trucks per day, and both rates are Poisson?

b. An employee has proposed adding new equipment that would speed up the service rate to 5.71 trucks per day. The equipment would cost $100 per day for each dock. Would this change the answer to part *a*? Should the manager invest in the new equipment?

 9. The parts department of a large automobile dealership has a counter used exclusively for its own service mechanics requesting parts. The length of time between requests can be modelled by an exponential distribution that has a mean of five minutes. A parts clerk can handle requests at an average rate of 15 per hour, and this can be modelled by a Poisson distribution. Suppose there are two parts clerks at the counter.

a. On average, how many mechanics would be at the counter, including those being served?

b. If a mechanic has to wait, how long would the average wait be?

c. What is the probability that a mechanic would have to wait for service?

d. What percentage of time is a clerk idle?

e. If clerks represent a cost of $20 per hour and mechanics represent a cost of $30 per hour, how many clerks would be optimal in terms of minimizing total cost?

 10. One field representative services five customers for a computer manufacturer. Customers request assistance at an average (Poisson-distributed) rate of once every four workdays. The field representative can handle an average (Poisson-distributed) of one call per day. Determine:

a. The expected number of customers waiting.

b. The average length of time customers must wait from the initial request for service until the service has been completed.

c. The percentage of time the service rep will be idle (i.e., the probability that a customer will not have to wait).

d. By how much would your answer to part *a* be reduced if a second field rep were added?

L06 **11.** Two operators handle adjustments for a group of 10 machines. Adjustment time is exponentially distributed and has a mean of 14 minutes per machine. The machines operate for an average of 86 minutes after an adjustment (exponentially distributed). While running, each machine can turn out 50 pieces per hour. Find:

a. The probability that a machine will have to wait for an adjustment.

b. The average number of machines waiting for adjustment.

c. The average number of machines being serviced.

d. The expected hourly output of each machine, taking adjustments into account.

e. Machine downtime represents a cost of $70 per hour; operator cost (including fringe benefits) is $15 per hour. What is the optimum number of operators?

L06 **12.** One operator services a group of five machines. Machine run time and service durations are both exponential. Machines run for an average of 90 minutes after a service, and service duration averages 35 minutes. The operator receives $20 per hour in wage and fringe benefits, and machine downtime costs $70 per hour per machine.

a. If each machine produces 60 pieces per hour while running, find the average hourly output of each machine when waiting and service times are taken into account.

b. Determine the optimum number of operators.

L06 **13.** A milling department has 10 machines. Each machine operates an average of eight hours before requiring adjustment, which takes an average of two hours. Both distributions are exponential. While running, each machine can produce 40 pieces an hour.

a. With one adjuster, what is the net average hourly output per machine?

b. If machine downtime cost is $80 per hour and adjuster cost is $20 per hour, how many adjusters would be optimal?

L04 **14.** Trucks arrive at the loading dock of a wholesale grocer at an average rate of 1.2 per hour in the mornings. A single crew consisting of two workers can load a truck in about 30 minutes. Crew members receive $10 per hour in wage and fringe benefits, and trucks and drivers reflect an hourly cost of $60. The manager is thinking of adding another member to the crew. The average service rate

would then be 2.4 trucks per hour. Assume both arrival and service rates are Poisson.

a. Would the third crew member be economical?

b. Would a fourth member be justifiable if the resulting average service capacity were 2.6 trucks per hour?

L05 **15.** Customers arriving at a service centre are assigned to one of three categories (1, 2, and 3); category 1 is the highest priority. Records indicate that an average of nine customers arrive per hour and that one-third are assigned to each category. There are two servers, and each can process customers at an average rate of five per hour. Arrival and service rates can be described by Poisson distributions.

a. What is the utilization of a server?

b. Determine the average wait time for customers in each class.

c. Find the average number of customers in each class that are waiting for service.

L05 **16.** A priority system is used to process customers, who are assigned to one of two classes when they enter the processing centre. The highest-priority class has an average arrival rate of four per hour; the other class has an average arrival rate of two per hour. Both can be described as Poisson distributed. There are two servers, and each can process customers in an average of six minutes (exponentially distributed).

a. What is the server utilization?

b. Determine the average wait time for each class.

c. Determine the average number of customers of each class that would be waiting for service.

d. If the manager could alter the assignment rules so that arrival rates of the two classes were equal, what would be the revised average wait time for each priority class?

L05 **17.** A priority waiting system assigns arriving customers one of four classes (class 1 has the highest priority). Arrival rates of the classes have Poisson distribution and their averages are:

Class	Average Arrivals per Hour
1	2
2	4
3	3
4	2

Five servers process the customers, and each can handle an average of three customers per hour. The service rate is Poisson.

a. What is the server utilization?

b. What is the average wait time for service by customers in the various classes? How many are waiting in each class on average?

c. If the average arrival rate of the second priority class could be reduced to three customers per hour by shifting some arrivals into the third priority class (which makes its average arrival rate four per hour), how would your answers to part *b* change?

  d. What observations can you make based on your answers to part *c?*

L05 **18.** Referring to Problem 17, suppose that each server could handle an average of four customers per hour. Answer the questions posed in Problem 17. Explain why the impact of reassigning customers in part *c* is much less in this case than in Problem 17.

L05 **19.** During the morning hours at a catalogue sales department, phone calls come in at an average rate of 40 per hour. Calls that cannot be answered immediately are put on hold. The system can handle eight callers on hold. If additional calls come in, they receive a busy signal. The three customer service representatives who answer the calls spend an average of three minutes with a customer. Both arrival and service rates are Poisson. What is the probability that a caller will get a busy signal?

L05 **20.** Since the terrorist attack of September 11, 2001, getting into the United States has been more difficult, and hence slower for Canadian cars and trucks at border crossings. This has resulted in long line-ups. One such case occurred on the Ambassador Bridge connecting Windsor to Detroit.[5] There were nine U.S. customs booths at the Detroit side of the bridge. Each truck took approximately two minutes to get cleared. During the busy hours, about 300 trucks (i.e., one every 12 seconds) arrived at the booths. Assuming that the standard deviation of getting cleared is 1 minute per truck and the standard deviation of interarrival durations is 6 seconds, how many more U.S. Customs booths were needed at the Ambassador Bridge to provide a reasonable average wait time (e.g., less than 10 minutes)?

L05 **21.** The number of customers coming to a bank between 1:00 p.m. and 1:30 p.m. of a "normal" day has a Poisson distribution with an average of 39 customers during the half hour. The length of time each customer spends with a teller is exponential with an average of 45.5 seconds. The average time a customer spends in the line waiting is desired to be three minutes. The manager is wondering how many tellers are required during this time period.

L05 ***22.** The Model 8300 Telemetry system used at Wesley Long Community Hospital, Greensboro, North Carolina, is a completely self-contained, wireless, one-patient cardiac monitor.[6] The system provides wireless transmission of a patient's heartbeat to a receiver either at a central station or at the bedside. A study was undertaken to analyze the service provided by the 18 currently held telemetry units and to investigate the cost/benefit of any additional units.

During a 38-day reviewing period, there were 156 requests for service (telemetry units are requested and used 24 hours a day). The average service duration was 93.6 hours per patient. Both interarrival and service durations had exponential distributions.

  a. What is the average arrival rate per day of patients needing telemetry?

  b. What is the average service rate per day of patients needing telemetry?

  c. If the average wait time before service is desired to be less than 5 hours, are 18 telemetry units enough? (*Hint:* For $\lambda/\mu = 16$ and $M = 18$, it can be shown that $L_q = 4.29$.)

L04 ***23.** The number of calls coming into a child abuse hotline during the 5:00 p.m. to 9:00 a.m. period on weekdays had a Poisson distribution with an average of 1.67 calls per hour. Call lengths had exponential distribution with an average of 5.4 minutes. It is considered important that a very high percentage of calls get through to the operator right away (as opposed to having to wait). If only one person is assigned to answer the phones, what is the probability that a call will have to wait because the operator is busy?

L06 ***24.** Becton-Dickinson manufactures medical supplies such as syringes.[7] In one plant it had 10 parallel syringe manufacturing lines. The problem was that syringes kept getting stuck in the lines, shutting the lines down. On average, a line got stuck again one minute after a blockage was removed (this time was distributed exponentially). One operator was assigned to five lines (i.e., a total of two operators). The average time it took the operator to walk to the blocked line and fix the problem was 10 seconds (this time was distributed exponentially). How long was a line expected to be down per hour? Assume that the two operators do not help each other.

L05 ***25.** Bendigo Health is a 672-bed hospital near Melbourne, Australia.[8] When the hospital administrators wanted to decide on the number of beds to set aside for a new program, transition care, some research staff suggested the use of queueing theory. Some hospital patients would qualify for the option of transition care before a group/nursing home is found for them. It is estimated that an average of $\lambda = 1.2$ patients per week would be eligible for and interested in transition care (Poisson distribution). The average stay in transition care is estimated to be $(1/\mu) = 9.5$ weeks. If a bed is not available in transition care, the patient leaves for another facility (i.e., there is no wait). The research staff suggested the following method: first assume that the number of beds in transition care is infinite. Then, determine the average occupancy (i.e., the average number of patients in the system) $= 1.2(9.5) = 11.4$. Finally, use the fact that the distribution of number

---

[5] D. Battagello, *Windsor Star Border Reporter,* November 9, 2004, http://web2.uwindsor.ca/math/hlynka /qreal.html.

[6] T. Scott and W.A. Hailey, "Queuing Model Aids Economic Analysis of Health Centre," *Industrial Engineering,* February 1981, pp. 56–61.

[7] M.A. Vogel, "Queueing Theory Applied to Machine Manning," *Interfaces,* 9(4), August 1979, pp. 1–7.

[8] A. Crombie, et al., "Planning the Transition Care," *Australian Health Review,* August 2008, 32(3), pp. 505–508.

of patients in the system is Poisson with a mean of 11.4 to determine the probability that a bed will not be used, given various maximum numbers of beds. For example, "If the hospital allocates nine beds to transition care, then in the long run there would be some empty beds on 19.84 percent of days, or about one day in five."

a. Use Excel to verify the 19.84 percent result. Note that the Poisson table at the end of the textbook goes up to only a mean of 9.5. *Hint:* Use =poisson(8,11.4,TRUE) in Excel, which gives the cumulative Poisson probability of observing up to $x = 8$, given the average of 11.4. Note that a nine-bed transition care will have some empty beds if $x \leq 8$.

b. An alternative method is to use the following (Erlang B) formula,[9] where p_n = Probability of n patients in the system and K = Maximum number of beds *(Note: this system is a special case of Model 6 where the finite size K equals the number of servers M, which is beds in this case):*

$$p_n = \frac{\frac{\left(\frac{\lambda}{\mu}\right)^n}{n!}}{\sum_{j=0}^{K}\left(\frac{\left(\frac{\lambda}{\mu}\right)^j}{j!}\right)}$$

Which method is more appropriate for this problem?

*26. Bay of Plenty Electricity (BOPE) is an electrical utility company in the Bay of Plenty, New Zealand.[10] BOPE has 21 company cars that the head-office employees share for company business. However, BOPE has to reduce its costs. Assuming that the average number of employees needing a car per work-hour is 4, the average time they need the car is 2.5 hours, and the average utilization of cars is desired to be 83 percent, how many cars does BOPE need?

*27. A Greek electrical appliance manufacturer has three trucks that its various departments—such as production, receiving, mould shop, and maintenance shop—use as needed.[11] The users have expressed that they wait an average of about nine minutes before a truck arrives (travel time is negligible). A study over 17 days (a day has 15 work hours) recorded 1,172 requests for truck service (randomly distributed over time, implying that the number of requests per hour was Poisson). The average

service time was 20.3 minutes with a standard deviation of 10.6 minutes.

a. Calculate the approximate average wait time in the queue for the truck users by using Model 7. *Note:* Variance of a Poisson distribution is equal to its mean.

b. Give some possible reasons for the actual wait time in the queue being so much larger than your answer to part *a.*

*28. The Department of Psychiatry in Cambridge Hospital (CH), Massachusetts, wanted to know the effect of the number of its beds on demand for beds in the local public mental health hospital (PH).[12] A study undertaken for one year found that the average number of in-state mental health patients arriving at CH was 1.44 per day, and the average number of out-of-state mental health patients arriving at CH was 0.54 per day (both Poisson). CH had 46 beds for mental patients. If there was no free bed in CH, the patient was directed to PH. The average stay in CH was 37.1 days (the length of stay had close-to-exponential distribution). Using the Erlang formula given in Problem 25b above, calculate the probability that a patient finds CH full (i.e., P_{46}).

29. A major New York bank commissioned a study to measure the service levels of its over 500 automatic teller machines (ATMs) in New York.[13] The ATMs were located in pairs inside vestibules attached to bank branches. The team used the finite queue version of the multiple server queueing model (i.e., Model 6) and suggested that the proportion of customers who balk (i.e., refuse to join the queue) should be used as the measure of service as opposed to the average wait time or average queue length. It was suggested that if the probability of balking during the busiest times is greater than 5 percent, then a vestibule should be expanded and an additional ATM installed in it. Consider a specific vestibule with two ATMs in it. There is space for 10 people in the vestibule (two being served, eight in line); average service time is 1.28 minutes per customer (approximately exponential), and average arrival rate is 86 customers per hour (approximately Poisson) during the busiest times of the week (noon–1:00 p.m. or 1:00 p.m.–2:00 p.m. weekdays). Determine the probability of balking at this vestibule. Should the vestibule be enlarged?

30. The Columbia University Hospital wanted to know if it needed to have more than one operating room (OR) crew present during the night shift (11:00 p.m. to 7:00 a.m.).[14] If the probability that one crew is busy is greater than 1

[9] S.C. Graves, et al., "A Simple Stochastic Model for Facility Planning in a Mental Health Care System," *Interfaces,* 13(5), October 1983, pp. 101–110

[10] J. Buchanan and J. Scott, "Vehicle Utilization at Bay of Plenty Electricity," *Interfaces,* 22(2), Mar–Apr 1992, pp. 28–35.

[11] G.P. Cosmetatos, "The Value of Queueing Theory—A Case Study," *Interfaces,* 9(3), May 1979, pp. 47–51.

[12] S.C. Graves, et al., "A Simple Stochastic Model for Facility Planning in a Mental Health Care System," *Interfaces,* 13(5), Oct 1983, pp. 101–110.

[13] P. Kolesar, "Stalking the Endangered CAT: A Queuing Analysis of Congestion at Automatic Teller Machines," *Interfaces,* 14(6), November–December 1984, pp. 16–26.

[14] J.B. Tucker, et al., "Using Queuing Theory to Determine Operating Room Staffing Needs," *Journal of Trauma,* 46(1), 1999, pp. 71–79.

percent, then a second OR crew would be required. During one year, 62 patients required emergency operations during the night shift. The average operation took 80.79 minutes. Does the hospital need a second OR crew during the night shift?

LO5 31. An average of 18 customers arrive at a service centre each hour according to a Poisson distribution. There are two servers on duty, and each server can process 12 customers per hour according to an exponential distribution.

   a. What is the server utilization?

   b. What is the average number of customers in the system?

   c. What is the average time customers wait for service?

   d. What is the average waiting time for customers who actually have to wait?

LO6 *32. With its cool alpine climate and majestic mountain ranges, featuring tremendous vertical drops and copious amounts of snow, Alberta is home to several world class ski resorts. At a small and highly exclusive resort located in the heart of Banff National Park, managers have been contending with customer complaints regarding excessive ski lift wait times during the winter peak season. An idea has been floated around to double the number of chairs on the lift and slow down its speed by half, which will still allow customers ample time to safely board and disembark. This means there will only be 100 feet between lift chairs, instead of 200 feet, and each trip to the top of the mountain will now take six minutes instead of three minutes. Management argues that customers will not mind having an additional three minutes to take in the breathtaking beauty of the Canadian Rockies. Using waiting line analysis, show that the proposed idea will help reduce the excessive waiting times. For simplicity, assume that there are currently four lift chairs, the average time to ski down is two minutes, and the same 10 skiers circulate continuously between waiting for the lift, being lifted, and skiing down the mountain.

Q MINI-CASE

Big Bank

The operations manager of a soon-to-open branch of a large bank in your city is in the process of configuring teller operations. Currently some branches have a separate teller line for customers who have a single transaction, while other branches do not have separate lines. A separate teller line can help reduce the number of complaints about long waits that have been received at some branches. Because the demographics differ from location to location, a system that works at one branch will not necessarily work at another. The manager has obtained data on processing times from the bank's home office, and is ready to explore different options for configuring operations.

   One time that will get special attention is the noon hour on Friday. The plan is to have five tellers available then. Under consideration are the following options:

a. Have one waiting line and have the first person in line go to the next available teller.

b. Have two waiting lines: one teller for customers who have a single transaction and four tellers who would handle customers who have multiple transactions.

   An average of 80 customers are served during the noon hour. The average service duration for customers with a single transaction is 90 seconds, while the average service duration for customers with multiple transactions is four minutes. Sixty percent of the customers are expected to have multiple transactions.

Question

If you were the manager, which option would you select? Why? Explain the disparity between the results for the two options. What assumptions did you make in your analysis?

Q MINI-CASE   www.lourdes.com

Lourdes Hospital

When doctors referred their patients to the Lourdes Hospital in Binghamton, New York, for various services such as X-rays, their office had a tough time getting through to the centralized appointment office of Lourdes. Most of the time, the line was busy. The installation of a call waiting system did not improve the situation, because callers were put on hold for indefinite lengths of time. The poor service had resulted in numerous complaints. One of the managers was put in charge of finding a solution, and a goal of answering at least 90 percent of calls without delay was set. The hospital was willing to employ more staff to receive calls. The manager studied this queueing problem by collecting data for 21 workdays during which additional staff was used to answer calls and no call received a busy signal or was put on hold. The number of calls per day ranged between 220 and

350, with no day-of-the-week seasonality. Most days, the number of calls was between 250 and 300. The average number of calls arriving during each 15-minute interval peaked at about 10 calls during the 9:00 a.m.–11:30 a.m. and 2:00 p.m.–3:45 p.m. periods. The 944 service durations during the data collection period had a distribution similar to exponential with a mean of 3.11 minutes. The manager also found out that previously the 6.5 full-time-equivalent employees usually spent half their time doing other tasks and turned off their phones while busy with other tasks. Using the multiple servers queueing model and a service goal of at least 90 percent probability of not having to wait, the manager determined the number of staff required during each 15-minute interval. When the original staffing levels were compared with the model-determined ones, it was discovered that

more staff were required earlier in the day and later in the afternoon, and fewer were needed around noon. The problem was solved by rearranging work shifts.

Question

During busy periods (9:00 a.m.–11:30 a.m. and 2:00 p.m.–3:45 p.m.), the central appointment office receives 40 calls per hour, on average. Each call takes an average of 3.11 minutes to serve. It is desired that at least 90 percent of calls are received without waiting. What is the minimum number of staff needed during these busy times?

Source: S. R. Agnihothri and P. F. Taylor, "Staffing a Centralized Appointment Scheduling Department in Lourdes Hospital," *Interfaces* 21(5), September–October 1991, pp. 1–11.

Q MINI-CASE

Peace Arch Border Crossing

The Peace Arch border crossing between Vancouver and Bellingham, Washington, has two distinct facilities: one controlled by U.S. Customs and Border Protections officers for drivers heading south into the state of Washington, and the other controlled by Canadian Border Services Agency officers for drivers heading north into British Columbia. Note that commercial trucks are not allowed to use the Peace Arch crossing (they should instead use the Pacific highway crossing). Consider the northbound vehicles. There are two types of cars that arrive at the crossing: Nexus holders and non-Nexus holders. Nexus

holders are assigned booths 1 or 2 (when busy) and their processing time is very fast, typically less than half a minute each. The non-Nexus holders are assigned to seven other booths, depending on how busy it is, and their processing time is approximately 1.1 minutes each. Non-Nexus cars arrive from two lanes off Highway I5 and then line up to go into these booths.

We will focus on the non-Nexus queuing system. The total number of daily northbound non-Nexus car arrivals at the border crossing varies by the day of the week (it is busier on Fridays, Saturdays, and Sundays). The numbers of arrivals (volume) for May 2017 are displayed below:

Sunday	Monday	Tuesday	Wednesday	Thursday	Friday	Saturday
30	1	2	3	4	5	6
	Volume 2631.0	Volume 2328.0	Volume 2207.0	Volume 2592.0	Volume 3236.0	Volume 3748.0
7	8	9	10	11	12	13
Volume 3394.0	Volume 2591.0	Volume 2245.0	Volume 2232.0	Volume 2487.0	Volume 3635.0	Volume 3744.0
14	15	16	17	18	19	20
Volume 2945.0	Volume 2639.0	Volume 2276.0	Volume 2383.0	Volume 2688.0	Volume 3130.0	Volume 3882.0
21	22	23	24	25	26	27
Volume 4136.0	Volume 5381.0	Volume 2998.0	Volume 2714.0	Volume 2404.0	Volume 3589.0	Volume 4414.0
28	29	30	31	1	2	3
Volume 3765.0	Volume 2854.0	Volume 2459.0	Volume 60.0			

The pattern of arrivals is slightly different from day to day. The numbers of arrivals (volume) during each five-minute interval on May 30, 2017, are given below:

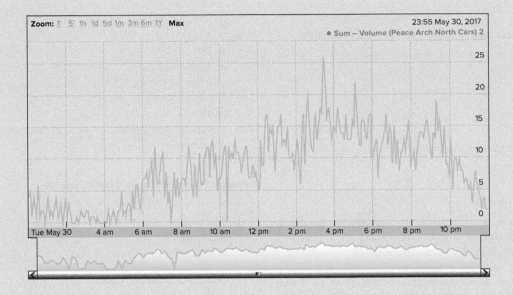

The number of arrivals during any hour of any day has a Poisson distribution and the average service time for non-Nexus cars varies only slightly based on the time of day (see http://www.sciencedirect.com/science/article/pii/S09658564 16305080). The CBSA opens booths based on the time of day, the day of the week, and the expected total volume. There is some flexibility as the officers can be shifted between the booths and the secondary screening, which is performed in a nearby building.

Consider the following problem. Suppose CBSA expects 3,500 non-Nexus cars on a specific day with the following percentage of this total during each hour:

Hour	1	2	3	4	5	6	7	8	9	10	11	12
Percentage	2.6	1.5	0.8	0.5	0.4	1.5	2.7	2.2	2.9	4.4	3.7	4.8

Hour	13	14	15	16	17	18	19	20	21	22	23	24
Percentage	6.5	5.6	5.7	6.4	7.2	7.4	5.2	5.4	6.0	5.9	7.7	3.0

Question

Assume service times are exponentially distributed with an average of 1.1 minutes. How many booths should CBSA open during each hour of the day to assure average wait times in the queues are less than 15 minutes?

To access "Simulation," the supplement to Chapter 18, please visit *Connect2*.

Appendix A   Answers to Selected Problems

Chapter 2: Competitiveness, Strategic Planning, and Productivity

2. A crew size of two has the highest productivity (250 m² per person per week installed).

3. Week 1: 5.62.
   Week 2: 5.45.
   Week 3: 5.20.
   Week 4: 5.01.
   Multifactor productivity is decreasing.

6. 4.3% increase.

Chapter 3: Demand Forecasting

1. a. blueberry has no trend or seasonality; cinnamon has an increasing trend; cupcakes has 5-workday seasonality.
   b. blueberry = 33, cinnamon = 35, cupcakes = 47.
   c. For blueberry, could use an averaging technique such as moving average or exponential smoothing; for cinnamon, could use simple regression for linear trend; for cupcakes, could use the seasonality technique.

4. a. 22.   b. 20.75.   c. 20.72.

7. a. $Y_t = 195.47 + 7.00t$.
      $Y_{16} = 307.47$.
   b. 311.16.

11. a. Fri. = 0.79, Sat. = 1.34, Sun. = 0.87.

14. a.

Day	Relative
1...	0.900
2...	0.833
3...	0.916
4...	1.031
5...	1.412
6...	1.482
7...	0.426

17. b.
   Jan 800
   Feb 810
   Mar 900
   Apr 809.6

25. b. −0.985. A strong negative relationship between sales and price.

32. a.

	MSE	MAD	MAPE
Forecast 1	9.4	2.8	0.36%
Forecast 2	38.2	3.6	0.46%

   Forecast 1 is superior.

Chapter 5: Strategic Capacity Planning

4. a. A: 8,000 units.
      B: 7,500 units.
   b. 10,000 units.
   c. A: $20,000.
      B: $18,000.
      A's profit would be higher.

6. a. A: $74.
      B: $50.
   c. A: 0 to 66 minutes.

7. Vendor best for $Q \leq 63{,}333$. For larger quantities, produce in-house with second process.

9. 3 machines.

12. a. one machine: BEP = 80.   two machines: BEP = 152.
    b. one machine.

Chapter 6: Process Design and Facility Layout

1. a. 8.
   b. 3.6 minutes.
   c. (i) 50 units.
      (ii) 30 units.

2. a.

Station	Tasks	Time
1	a	1.4
2	b, e	1.3
3	d, c, f	1.8
4	g, h	1.5

   b. 82%.

10.

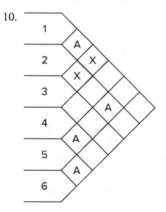

11.

4	3	1
5	8	6
7	2	

16. 3→A, 5→B, 1→C, 4→D, 6→E, 2→F.

Chapter 7: Work/Job Design

2. a. 1.2 minutes.
   b. 1.14 minutes.
   c. 1.27 minutes.

4.

Element	OT
1	4.10
2	1.50
3	3.25
4	2.77

7. 5.85 minutes.

8. 7.125 minutes.

11. 57 observations.

12. 37 work cycles.

13. a. 12%.   b. 254 observations.

Chapter 8: Location Planning and Analysis

2. a. A: 16,854; B: 17,416; C: 17,753.   b. C, profit = $14,670.

4. a. B: 0 to 33; C: 34 to 400; A: 400+.   b. C.

   c. Expansion leads to more control, whereas subcontracting leads to more flexibility.

9. A (Score = 87.02).

12. (5, 4).

Chapter 9: Management of Quality

2.

	Res.	Com.
Noisy	10	3
Failed	7	2
Odour	5	7
Warm	3	4

Residential customers   Commercial customers

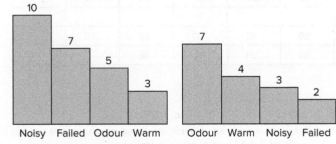

Chapter 10: Statistical Quality Control

1. a. 1.24%.   b. 24.4 kg and 24.6 kg.

2. a. LCL: 1.991 litres.

   UCL: 2.009 litres.

   b. Yes, process is in control.

3. a. Mean: LCL is 2.96; UCL is 3.24.

   Range: LCL is 0.099; UCL is 0.801.

   b. Yes.

6. a.

1	2	3	4
0.020	0.010	0.025	0.045

   b. 0.025.

   c. Mean = 0.025, standard deviation = 0.011.

   d. LCL = 0.001, UCL = 0.049.

   e. 0.0456.

   f. Yes.

   g. Mean = 0.02, standard deviation = 0.0099.

   h. LCL = 0.0002, UCL = 0.0398. No.

8. a. UCL = 16.266, LCL = 0, Yes.   b. No change.

11. 35 pieces.

16. b. 4.5, 0.192.

    c. 4.5, 0.086.

    d. 4.242 to 4.758. The risk is 0.0026.

    e. None.

21. a. 1.11.   b. Capable.

24. H: C_{pk} = 0.9375, incapable, K: C_{pk} = 1.0, capable, T: C_{pk} = 1.07, capable.

Chapter 11: Supply Chain Management

1. Use two-day freight ($29.38 saving).

Chapter 12: Inventory Management

3. a.

Item	Class
Z45	A
F95	A
K35	A
P05	B
F14	B
D45	B
K36	B
D57	B
K34	C
D52	C
M20	C
F99	C
N08	C
D48	C
M10	C

5. a. 228 packages.

   b. $228.04.

   c. Yes.

   d. Yes; TC = $310; save $81.96.

11. a. 1,633 bags.

    b. 490 bags.

    c. 3.27 days.

    d. 24.5 runs per year.

    e. $5,739.71.

15. a. 600 stones (total cost = $41,120).

    b. 150 stones.

19. 6,600 metres.

21. a. 91 kg.

    b. ROP = 691 kg.

30. a. EOQ = 126 cases.

    b. ROP = 81.6 cases.

33. K033: 581; K144: 458; L700: −16 (do not order).

36. 25 dozens, service level = 73%.

38. 78.86 kg.

Chapter 13: Aggregate Operations Planning and Master Scheduling

11. Produce 25 units per month during overtime in months 2–4, and 20 units per month using part-time workers in months 2–4 and 5 units in month 5 using part-time workers, at total cost of $13,170.

20. Total cost = $124,960.

23. Projected on-hand, wk1 = 31, wk2 = 71, wk3 = 41, wk4 = 11, wk5 = 41, wk6 = 71, wk7 = 31, wk8 = 61.

Chapter 14: Material Requirements Planning and Enterprise Resource Planning

1. a. $F = 2, G = 1, H = 1, J = 6, D = 10, L = 2, A = 4$
2. a. $E = 138$.
   b. Week 5.
11. Order 160 units in Week 2; projected on-hand wk4 = 15, wk5 = 35, wk6 = 5, . . .
14. b. Production schedule for golf carts.

Week number			1	2	3	4	5	6	7	8	9
Quantity								100		100	100

Item: Golf cart LT = 1 week											
Gross requirements								100		100	100
Scheduled receipts											
Projected on-hand											
Net requirements								100		100	100
Planned-order receipts								100		100	100
Planned-order releases							100		100	100	

Item: Bases LT = 1 week											
Gross requirements								100		100	100
Scheduled receipts											
Projected on-hand	20	20	20	20	50	100	50	100	50	0	
Net requirements											
Planned-order receipts				30	50	50	50	50	50		
Planned-order releases			30	50	50	50	50	50			

15. ERP = 79. Order 120 units in Month 2 and 60 units in Month 6.

Chapter 15: Just-in-Time and Lean Production

1. 4 or 5; fewer kanbans.
4. D-C-B-D-A-C-D-B-C-D.

Chapter 16: Job and Staff Scheduling

6. a. SPT = D-C-B-A,
      EDD = C-B-D-A.
   b.

	SPT	EDD
Avg. flow time	19.75	21
Avg. days late	6	6

   c. SPT.
9. B-A-G-E-F-D-C. Make-span = 11.7 hours.
21. B-A-G-E-F-D-C. Make-span = 11.7 hours.

Chapter 17: Project Management

1. a. S-9-10-11-12-13-End: 31 days.
   b. 1-2-5-7-8-9: 55 days.
   c. S-1-2-3-4-End: 44 days.

3. critical path activities F, H, J, K.
8. a. 0.6881.   b. 0.3978.   c. 0.0203.
14. a. wk1: act. 4, wk2: act. 1, wk3: act. 4 and 13, wk4: act. 9 and 12, wk5: act 9 and 11, wk6: act. 1, 5, and 13.

Chapter 18: Waiting-Line Analysis

6. a. Morning: 0.375 minute; 0.45.
      Afternoon: 0.678 minute; 0.54.
      Evening: 0.635 minute; 0.44.
   b. Morning: 0.01; Afternoon: 0.05; Evening: 0.03.
10. a. 0.995 customer.
    b. 2.24 days.
    c. 31.1 percent.
    d. 0.875 customer less.
16. a. 0.30
    b. W1 = 0.52 min.
       W2 = 0.74 min.
    c. L1 = 0.034.
       L2 = 0.025.
    d. W1 = 0.49 min.
       W2 = 0.69 min.

Appendix B Tables

A. Areas Under the Standardized Normal Curve, 0 to z
B. Areas Under the Standardized Normal Curve
   1. From $-\infty$ to $-z$, $z < 0$
   2. From $-\infty$ to $+z$
C. Cumulative Poisson Probabilities

TABLE A ▼

Areas Under the Standardized Normal Curve, 0 to z.

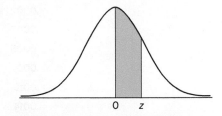

z	.00	.01	.02	.03	.04	.05	.06	.07	.08	.09
0.0.	.0000	.0040	.0080	.0120	.0160	.0199	.0239	.0279	.0319	.0359
0.1.	.0398	.0438	.0478	.0517	.0557	.0596	.0636	.0675	.0714	.0753
0.2.	.0793	.0832	.0871	.0910	.0948	.0987	.1026	.1064	.1103	.1141
0.3.	.1179	.1217	.1255	.1293	.1331	.1368	.1406	.1443	.1480	.1517
0.4.	.1554	.1591	.1628	.1664	.1700	.1736	.1772	.1808	.1844	.1879
0.5.	.1915	.1950	.1985	.2019	.2054	.2088	.2123	.2157	.2190	.2224
0.6.	.2257	.2291	.2324	.2357	.2389	.2422	.2454	.2486	.2517	.2549
0.7.	.2580	.2611	.2642	.2673	.2703	.2734	.2764	.2794	.2823	.2852
0.8.	.2881	.2910	.2939	.2967	.2995	.3023	.3051	.3078	.3106	.3133
0.9.	.3159	.3186	.3212	.3238	.3264	.3289	.3315	.3340	.3365	.3389
1.0.	.3413	.3438	.3461	.3485	.3508	.3531	.3554	.3577	.3599	.3621
1.1.	.3643	.3665	.3686	.3708	.3729	.3749	.3770	.3790	.3810	.3830
1.2.	.3849	.3869	.3888	.3907	.3925	.3944	.3962	.3980	.3997	.4015
1.3.	.4032	.4049	.4066	.4082	.4099	.4115	.4131	.4147	.4162	.4177
1.4.	.4192	.4207	.4222	.4236	.4251	.4265	.4279	.4292	.4306	.4319
1.5.	.4332	.4345	.4357	.4370	.4382	.4394	.4406	.4418	.4429	.4441
1.6.	.4452	.4463	.4474	.4484	.4495	.4505	.4515	.4525	.4535	.4545
1.7.	.4554	.4564	.4573	.4582	.4591	.4599	.4608	.4616	.4625	.4633
1.8.	.4641	.4649	.4656	.4664	.4671	.4678	.4686	.4693	.4699	.4706
1.9.	.4713	.4719	.4726	.4732	.4738	.4744	.4750	.4756	.4761	.4767
2.0.	.4772	.4778	.4783	.4788	.4793	.4798	.4803	.4808	.4812	.4817
2.1.	.4821	.4826	.4830	.4834	.4838	.4842	.4846	.4850	.4854	.4857
2.2.	.4861	.4864	.4868	.4871	.4875	.4878	.4881	.4884	.4887	.4890
2.3.	.4893	.4896	.4898	.4901	.4904	.4906	.4909	.4911	.4913	.4916
2.4.	.4918	.4920	.4922	.4925	.4927	.4929	.4931	.4932	.4934	.4936
2.5.	.4938	.4940	.4941	.4943	.4945	.4946	.4948	.4949	.4951	.4952
2.6.	.4953	.4955	.4956	.4957	.4959	.4960	.4961	.4962	.4963	.4964
2.7.	.4965	.4966	.4967	.4968	.4969	.4970	.4971	.4972	.4973	.4974
2.8.	.4974	.4975	.4976	.4977	.4977	.4978	.4979	.4979	.4980	.4981
2.9.	.4981	.4982	.4982	.4983	.4984	.4984	.4985	.4985	.4986	.4986
3.0.	.4987	.4987	.4987	.4988	.4988	.4989	.4989	.4989	.4990	.4990

TABLE B ▶

*1. Areas Under the
Standardized Normal
Curve, from −∞ to z.*

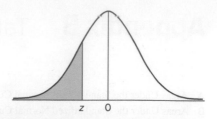

.09	.08	.07	.06	.05	.04	.03	.02	.01	.00	z
.0002	.0003	.0003	.0003	.0003	.0003	.0003	.0003	.0003	.0003	−3.4
.0003	.0004	.0004	.0004	.0004	.0004	.0004	.0005	.0005	.0005	−3.3
.0005	.0005	.0005	.0006	.0006	.0006	.0006	.0006	.0007	.0007	−3.2
.0007	.0007	.0008	.0008	.0008	.0008	.0009	.0009	.0009	.0010	−3.1
.0010	.0010	.0011	.0011	.0011	.0012	.0012	.0013	.0013	.0013	−3.0
.0014	.0014	.0015	.0015	.0016	.0016	.0017	.0018	.0018	.0019	−2.9
.0019	.0020	.0021	.0021	.0022	.0023	.0023	.0024	.0025	.0026	−2.8
.0026	.0027	.0028	.0029	.0030	.0031	.0032	.0033	.0034	.0035	−2.7
.0036	.0037	.0038	.0039	.0040	.0041	.0043	.0044	.0045	.0047	−2.6
.0048	.0049	.0051	.0052	.0054	.0055	.0057	.0059	.0060	.0062	−2.5
.0064	.0066	.0068	.0069	.0071	.0073	.0075	.0078	.0080	.0082	−2.4
.0084	.0087	.0089	.0091	.0094	.0096	.0099	.0102	.0104	.0107	−2.3
.0110	.0113	.0116	.0119	.0122	.0125	.0129	.0132	.0136	.0139	−2.2
.0143	.0146	.0150	.0154	.0158	.0162	.0166	.0170	.0174	.0179	−2.1
.0183	.0188	.0192	.0197	.0202	.0207	.0212	.0217	.0222	.0228	−2.0
.0233	.0239	.0244	.0250	.0256	.0262	.0268	.0274	.0281	.0287	−1.9
.0294	.0301	.0307	.0314	.0322	.0329	.0336	.0344	.0351	.0359	−1.8
.0367	.0375	.0384	.0392	.0401	.0409	.0418	.0427	.0436	.0446	−1.7
.0455	.0465	.0475	.0485	.0495	.0505	.0516	.0526	.0537	.0548	−1.6
.0559	.0571	.0582	.0594	.0606	.0618	.0630	.0643	.0655	.0668	−1.5
.0681	.0694	.0708	.0721	.0735	.0749	.0764	.0778	.0793	.0808	−1.4
.0823	.0838	.0853	.0869	.0885	.0901	.0918	.0934	.0951	.0968	−1.3
.0985	.1003	.1020	.1038	.1056	.1075	.1093	.1112	.1131	.1151	−1.2
.1170	.1190	.1210	.1230	.1251	.1271	.1292	.1314	.1335	.1357	−1.1
.1379	.1401	.1423	.1446	.1469	.1492	.1515	.1539	.1562	.1587	−1.0
.1611	.1635	.1660	.1685	.1711	.1736	.1762	.1788	.1814	.1841	−0.9
.1867	.1894	.1922	.1949	.1977	.2005	.2033	.2061	.2090	.2119	−0.8
.2148	.2177	.2206	.2236	.2266	.2296	.2327	.2358	.2389	.2420	−0.7
.2451	.2483	.2514	.2546	.2578	.2611	.2643	.2676	.2709	.2743	−0.6
.2776	.2810	.2843	.2877	.2912	.2946	.2981	.3015	.3050	.3085	−0.5
.3121	.3156	.3192	.3228	.3264	.3300	.3336	.3372	.3409	.3446	−0.4
.3483	.3520	.3557	.3594	.3632	.3669	.3707	.3745	.3783	.3821	−0.3
.3859	.3897	.3936	.3974	.4013	.4052	.4090	.4129	.4168	.4207	−0.2
.4247	.4286	.4325	.4364	.4404	.4443	.4483	.4522	.4562	.4602	−0.1
.4641	.4681	.4721	.4761	.4801	.4840	.4880	.4920	.4960	.5000	−0.0

(continued)

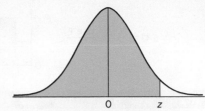

1. Areas Under the
Standardized Normal
Curve, from −∞ to z.

z	.00	.01	.02	.03	.04	.05	.06	.07	.08	.09
.0 . . .	.5000	.5040	.5080	.5120	.5160	.5199	.5239	.5279	.5319	.5359
.1 . . .	.5398	.5438	.5478	.5517	.5557	.5596	.5636	.5675	.5714	.5753
.2 . . .	.5793	.5832	.5871	.5910	.5948	.5987	.6026	.6064	.6103	.6141
.3 . . .	.6179	.6217	.6255	.6293	.6331	.6368	.6406	.6443	.6480	.6517
.4 . . .	.6554	.6591	.6628	.6664	.6700	.6736	.6772	.6808	.6844	.6879
.5 . . .	.6915	.6950	.6985	.7019	.7054	.7088	.7123	.7157	.7190	.7224
.6 . . .	.7257	.7291	.7324	.7357	.7389	.7422	.7454	.7486	.7517	.7549
.7 . . .	.7580	.7611	.7642	.7673	.7703	.7734	.7764	.7794	.7823	.7852
.8 . . .	.7881	.7910	.7939	.7967	.7995	.8023	.8051	.8078	.8106	.8133
.9 . . .	.8159	.8186	.8212	.8238	.8264	.8289	.8315	.8340	.8365	.8389
1.0 . . .	.8413	.8438	.8461	.8485	.8508	.8531	.8554	.8577	.8599	.8621
1.1 . . .	.8643	.8665	.8686	.8708	.8729	.8749	.8770	.8790	.8810	.8830
1.2 . . .	.8849	.8869	.8888	.8907	.8925	.8944	.8962	.8980	.8997	.9015
1.3 . . .	.9032	.9049	.9066	.9082	.9099	.9115	.9131	.9147	.9162	.9177
1.4 . . .	.9192	.9207	.9222	.9236	.9251	.9265	.9279	.9292	.9306	.9319
1.5 . . .	.9332	.9345	.9357	.9370	.9382	.9394	.9406	.9418	.9429	.9441
1.6 . . .	.9452	.9463	.9474	.9484	.9495	.9505	.9515	.9525	.9535	.9545
1.7 . . .	.9554	.9564	.9573	.9582	.9591	.9599	.9608	.9616	.9625	.9633
1.8 . . .	.9641	.9649	.9656	.9664	.9671	.9678	.9686	.9693	.9699	.9706
1.9 . . .	.9713	.9719	.9726	.9732	.9738	.9744	.9750	.9756	.9761	.9767
2.0 . . .	.9772	.9778	.9783	.9788	.9793	.9798	.9803	.9808	.9812	.9817
2.1 . . .	.9821	.9826	.9830	.9834	.9838	.9842	.9846	.9850	.9854	.9857
2.2 . . .	.9861	.9864	.9868	.9871	.9875	.9878	.9881	.9884	.9887	.9890
2.3 . . .	.9893	.9896	.9898	.9901	.9904	.9906	.9909	.9911	.9913	.9916
2.4 . . .	.9918	.9920	.9922	.9925	.9927	.9929	.9931	.9932	.9934	.9936
2.5 . . .	.9938	.9940	.9941	.9943	.9945	.9946	.9948	.9949	.9951	.9952
2.6 . . .	.9953	.9955	.9956	.9957	.9959	.9960	.9961	.9962	.9963	.9964
2.7 . . .	.9965	.9966	.9967	.9968	.9969	.9970	.9971	.9972	.9973	.9974
2.8 . . .	.9974	.9975	.9976	.9977	.9977	.9978	.9979	.9979	.9980	.9981
2.9 . . .	.9981	.9982	.9982	.9983	.9984	.9984	.9985	.9985	.9986	.9986
3.0 . . .	.9987	.9987	.9987	.9988	.9988	.9989	.9989	.9989	.9990	.9990
3.1 . . .	.9990	.9991	.9991	.9991	.9991	.9992	.9992	.9992	.9993	.9993
3.2 . . .	.9993	.9993	.9994	.9994	.9994	.9994	.9994	.9995	.9995	.9995
3.3 . . .	.9995	.9995	.9995	.9996	.9996	.9996	.9996	.9996	.9996	.9997
3.4 . . .	.9997	.9997	.9997	.9997	.9997	.9997	.9997	.9997	.9997	.9998

TABLE C ▶

Cumulative Poisson
Probabilities.

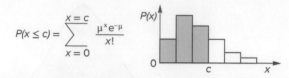

$$P(x \le c) = \sum_{x=0}^{x=c} \frac{\mu^x e^{-\mu}}{x!}$$

μ\x	0	1	2	3	4	5	6	7	8	9
0.05....	.951	.999	1.000							
0.10....	.905	.995	1.000							
0.15....	.861	.990	.999	1.000						
0.20....	.819	.982	.999	1.000						
0.25....	.779	.974	.998	1.000						
0.30....	.741	.963	.996	1.000						
0.35....	.705	.951	.994	1.000						
0.40....	.670	.938	.992	.999	1.000					
0.45....	.638	.925	.989	.999	1.000					
0.50....	.607	.910	.986	.998	1.000					
0.55....	.577	.894	.982	.998	1.000					
0.60....	.549	.878	.977	.997	1.000					
0.65....	.522	.861	.972	.996	.999	1.000				
0.70....	.497	.844	.966	.994	.999	1.000				
0.75....	.472	.827	.960	.993	.999	1.000				
0.80....	.449	.809	.953	.991	.999	1.000				
0.85....	.427	.791	.945	.989	.998	1.000				
0.90....	.407	.772	.937	.987	.998	1.000				
0.95....	.387	.754	.929	.984	.997	1.000				
1.0.....	.368	.736	.920	.981	.996	.999	1.000			
1.1.....	.333	.699	.900	.974	.995	.999	1.000			
1.2.....	.301	.663	.880	.966	.992	.998	1.000			
1.3.....	.273	.627	.857	.957	.989	.998	1.000			
1.4.....	.247	.592	.833	.946	.986	.997	.999	1.000		
1.5.....	.223	.558	.809	.934	.981	.996	.999	1.000		
1.6.....	.202	.525	.783	.921	.976	.994	.999	1.000		
1.7.....	.183	.493	.757	.907	.970	.992	.998	1.000		
1.8.....	.165	.463	.731	.891	.964	.990	.997	.999	1.000	
1.9.....	.150	.434	.704	.875	.956	.987	.997	.999	1.000	
2.0.....	.135	.406	.677	.857	.947	.983	.995	.999	1.000	
2.2.....	.111	.355	.623	.819	.928	.975	.993	.998	1.000	
2.4.....	.091	.308	.570	.779	.904	.964	.988	.997	.999	1.000
2.6.....	.074	.267	.518	.736	.877	.951	.983	.995	.999	1.000
2.8.....	.061	.231	.470	.692	.848	.935	.976	.992	.998	.999

(continued)

TABLE C ▼

(continued)

μ\x	0	1	2	3	4	5	6	7	8	9	10	11	12	13	14	15	16	17	18	19	20
3.0	.050	.199	.423	.647	.815	.916	.966	.988	.996	.999	1.000										
3.2	.041	.171	.380	.603	.781	.895	.955	.983	.994	.998	1.000										
3.4	.033	.147	.340	.558	.744	.871	.942	.977	.992	.997	.999	1.000									
3.6	.027	.126	.303	.515	.706	.844	.927	.969	.988	.996	.999	1.000									
3.8	.022	.107	.269	.474	.668	.816	.909	.960	.984	.994	.998	.999	1.000								
4.0	.018	.092	.238	.433	.629	.785	.889	.949	.979	.992	.997	.999	1.000								
4.2	.015	.078	.210	.395	.590	.753	.868	.936	.972	.989	.996	.999	1.000								
4.4	.012	.066	.185	.359	.551	.720	.844	.921	.964	.985	.994	.998	.999	1.000							
4.6	.010	.056	.163	.326	.513	.686	.818	.905	.955	.980	.992	.997	.999	1.000							
4.8	.008	.048	.143	.294	.476	.651	.791	.887	.944	.975	.990	.996	.999	1.000							
5.0	.007	.040	.125	.265	.441	.616	.762	.867	.932	.968	.986	.995	.998	.999	1.000						
5.2	.006	.034	.109	.238	.406	.581	.732	.845	.918	.960	.982	.993	.997	.999	1.000						
5.4	.005	.029	.095	.213	.373	.546	.702	.822	.903	.951	.978	.990	.996	.999	1.000						
5.6	.004	.024	.082	.191	.342	.512	.670	.797	.886	.941	.972	.988	.995	.998	.999	1.000					
5.8	.003	.021	.072	.170	.313	.478	.638	.771	.867	.929	.965	.984	.993	.997	.999	1.000					
6.0	.003	.017	.062	.151	.285	.446	.606	.744	.847	.916	.957	.980	.991	.996	.999	1.000	1.000				
6.2	.002	.015	.054	.134	.259	.414	.574	.716	.826	.902	.949	.975	.989	.995	.998	.999	1.000				
6.4	.002	.012	.046	.119	.235	.384	.542	.687	.803	.886	.939	.969	.986	.994	.997	.999	1.000				
6.6	.001	.010	.040	.105	.213	.355	.511	.658	.780	.869	.927	.963	.982	.992	.997	.999	.999	1.000			
6.8	.001	.009	.034	.093	.191	.326	.479	.627	.753	.848	.915	.955	.978	.990	.996	.998	.999	1.000			
7.0	.001	.007	.030	.082	.173	.301	.450	.599	.729	.830	.901	.947	.973	.987	.994	.998	.999	1.000			
7.2	.001	.006	.025	.072	.156	.276	.420	.569	.703	.810	.887	.937	.967	.984	.993	.997	.999	.999	1.000		
7.4	.001	.005	.022	.063	.140	.253	.392	.539	.676	.788	.871	.926	.961	.980	.989	.995	.998	.999	1.000		
7.6	.001	.004	.019	.055	.125	.231	.365	.510	.648	.765	.854	.915	.954	.976	.989	.995	.998	.999	1.000		
7.8	.000	.004	.016	.048	.112	.210	.338	.481	.620	.741	.835	.902	.945	.971	.986	.993	.997	.999	1.000		
8.0	.000	.003	.014	.042	.100	.191	.313	.453	.593	.717	.816	.888	.936	.966	.983	.992	.996	.998	.999	1.000	
8.2	.000	.003	.012	.037	.089	.174	.290	.425	.566	.692	.796	.873	.926	.960	.979	.990	.995	.998	.999	1.000	
8.4	.000	.002	.010	.032	.079	.157	.267	.400	.537	.666	.774	.857	.915	.952	.975	.987	.994	.997	.999	1.000	
8.6	.000	.002	.009	.030	.074	.150	.256	.386	.523	.653	.763	.849	.909	.949	.973	.986	.993	.997	.999	1.000	
8.8	.000	.002	.007	.024	.062	.128	.226	.348	.482	.614	.729	.822	.889	.935	.964	.981	.990	.995	.998	.999	1.000
9.0	.000	.001	.006	.021	.055	.116	.207	.324	.456	.587	.706	.803	.876	.926	.959	.978	.989	.995	.998	.999	1.000
9.5	.000	.001	.004	.015	.040	.089	.165	.269	.392	.522	.645	.752	.836	.898	.940	.967	.982	.991	.996	.998	.999

Appendix C Working With the Normal Distribution

The normal distribution is a theoretical distribution that approximates many real-life phenomena. It is widely used in many disciplines, including operations management. Consequently, having the ability to work with normal distributions is a skill that will serve you well.

The normal curve is symmetrical and bell-shaped, as illustrated in Figure C-1. Although the theoretical distribution extends in both directions, to plus or minus infinity, most of the distribution lies close to its mean, so values of a variable that is normally distributed will occur relatively close to the distribution mean.

▼ FIGURE C-1

The normal distribution.

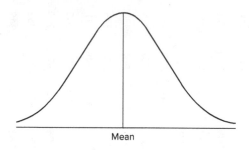

Mean

z Values

It is customary to refer to a value of a normally distributed random variable in terms of the number of standard deviations the value is from the mean of the distribution. This is known as its z value, or z score. In Figure C-2, you can see the normal distribution in terms of some selected z values. This particular distribution is referred to as the standard normal distribution. Notice that the z values to the left of (i.e., below) the mean are negative. Thus, a z value of −1.25 refers to a value that is 1.25 standard deviations below the distribution mean.

▼ FIGURE C-2

The standard normal distribution with selected values of z.

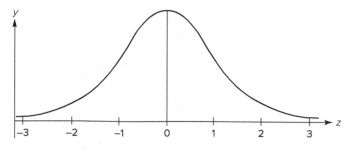

When working with a variable that is normally distributed, it is often necessary to convert an actual value of the variable to a z value. The z value can be computed using the following formula:

$$z = \frac{x - \mu}{\sigma}$$

where x = A specified value of a variable
μ = The distribution mean
σ = The distribution standard deviation

▼ EXAMPLE 1

A normal distribution has a mean of 20 and a standard deviation of 2. What is the z value of 17.5?

SOLUTION

$x = 17.5$
$\mu = 20$
$\sigma = 2$
Using the formula for z, we find:
$$z = \frac{x - \mu}{\sigma}$$
$$z = \frac{17.5 - 20}{2} = -1.25$$

z Values and Probabilities

Once the z value is known, it can be used to obtain various probabilities by referring to a table of the normal distribution, such as the probability that a value will occur by chance that is greater than, or less than, that value. Note that the probability of *exactly* that value is zero, because an infinite number of values could occur, so the probability of specifying in advance that any one particular value will occur is essentially equal to zero. z values can also be used to find the probability that a value will occur that is between ±z. Two such cases are shown in Figure C-3. Note that the total area underneath the curve represents 100 percent of the probability, so knowing that the probability is 0.9544 that a value will occur that is within the range of $z = \pm 2$, we can say that the probability that a value will occur that is outside of the range (e.g., either less than $z = -2$ or greater than $z = +2$) is equal to $1.0000 - 0.9544 = 0.0456$.

▼ FIGURE C-3

Areas under the normal curve between $z = \pm 2\sigma$ and $z = \pm 3\sigma$.

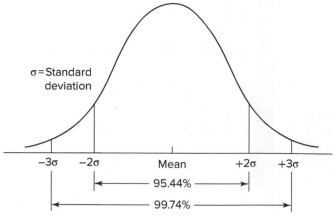

σ = Standard deviation

−3σ −2σ Mean +2σ +3σ

95.44%

99.74%

Tables of the Normal Distribution

Virtually all applications of the normal distribution involve working with a table of normal distribution probabilities. Tables make the process of obtaining probabilities and z values quite simple. This book has two slightly different normal distribution tables. Appendix B Table A has values for the right half of the distribution for the area under the curve (note the figure at the top of the table), which is the probability from the mean of the distribution

($z = 0$) to any other value of z, up to $z = +3.09$. Statistics books always have this version of the table, so you may already be familiar with it. A second table of normal probabilities is presented in Appendix B Tables B1 and B2. They show the area under the curve from negative infinity to any point z (see the figure at the top of the table), up to $z = +3.49$. In both tables, the values of z are shown in two parts. The integer and first decimal are shown along the side of the table, while the second decimal is shown across the top.

▼ EXAMPLE 2

Using Appendix B Table B.2, find the area under the curve to the left of $z = 1.12$.

SOLUTION

$z = 1.12$ becomes

$$\begin{array}{r} 1.1 \\ + 0.02 \\ \hline 1.12 \end{array}$$

Find the row where $z = 1.1$ down the left-hand side of the table. Find the .02 column across the top of the table. The probability is at the intersection of the 1.1 row and the .02 column.

z	.00	.01	.02	.03	.04	.05	.06	.07	.08	.09
.0	.5000	.5040	.5080	.5120	.5160	.5199	.5239	.5279	.5319	.5359
.1	.5398	.5438	.5478	.5517	.5557	.5596	.5636	.5675	.5714	.5753
.2	.5793	.5832	.5871	.5910	.5948	.5987	.6026	.6064	.6103	.6141
.3	.6179	.6217	.6255	.6293	.6331	.6368	.6406	.6443	.6480	.6517
.4	.6554	.6591	.6628	.6664	.6700	.6736	.6772	.6808	.6844	.6879
.5	.6915	.6950	.6985	.7019	.7054	.7088	.7123	.7157	.7190	.7224
.6	.7257	.7291	.7324	.7357	.7389	.7422	.7454	.7486	.7517	.7549
.7	.7580	.7611	.7642	.7673	.7703	.7734	.7764	.7794	.7823	.7852
.8	.7881	.7910	.7939	.7967	.7995	.8023	.8051	.8078	.8106	.8133
.9	.8159	.8186	.8212	.8238	.8264	.8289	.8315	.8340	.8365	.8389
1.0	.8413	.8438	.8461	.8485	.8508	.8531	.8554	.8577	.8599	.8621
1.1	.8643	.8665	.8686	.8708	.8729	.8749	.8770	.8790	.8810	.8830
1.2	.8849	.8869	.8888	.8907	.8925	.8944	.8962	.8980	.8997	.9015
1.3	.9032	.9049	.9066	.9082	.9099	.9115	.9131	.9147	.9162	.9177
1.4	.9192	.9207	.9222	.9236	.9251	.9265	.9279	.9292	.9306	.9319

Note: You will find versions of both tables at the very end of the book for easy reference. The above table repeats Appendix B Table B.2, the positive values of z. For problems that involve negative values of z, refer to the portion of Appendix B Table B.1 with negative values.

Finding the Probability of Observing a Value That Is Within ±z of the Mean or Outside of ±z

Use Appendix B Table A for this type of problem:

▼ EXAMPLE 3

Find the area under the curve that is *within* two standard deviations of the mean.

SOLUTION

What the problems is asking for:

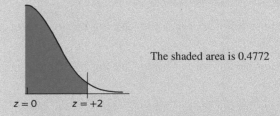

Appendix B Table A provides the right half of the area:

The shaded area is 0.4772

To find the total area between $\pm z = 2$, double the amount in the right half: $2(0.4772) = 0.9544$.

▼ EXAMPLE 4

Find the area under the curve that is *outside* of two standard deviations from the mean.

SOLUTION

What the problem is asking for:

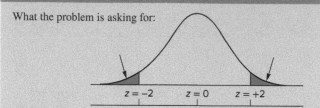

z = −2   z = 0   z = +2

Appendix B Table A provides the right half of the area between the mean and $z = +2$. To find the area in the right tail, subtract the amount between the mean and $z = +2$ from 0.5000:

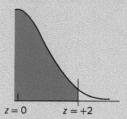

z = 0   z = +2

Area under the right side of the curve:	0.5000
Subtract the area from z = 0 to z = +2.00:	−0.4772
The area to the right of z = +2.00 is:	0.0228

The same amount will be in each tail, so the total area in both tails is $2(0.0228) = 0.0456$.

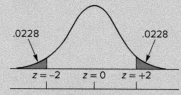

.0228   .0228

z = −2   z = 0   z = +2

Another way to arrive at the same answer is to note that the area *within* two standard deviations of the mean is 0.9544, as shown previously, so the area outside of that is $1.0000 - 0.9544 = 0.0456$.

Finding the Area (Probability) That Is to the Left or to the Right of *z*

Use Appendix B Table B.2 for this type of problem (e.g., "What is the probability that the time will not exceed 22 weeks?").

▼ EXAMPLE 5

A normal distribution has a mean of 20 and a standard deviation of 1.0. Find the probabilities:
a. A value that is 22 or less.
b. A value that is 22 or more.

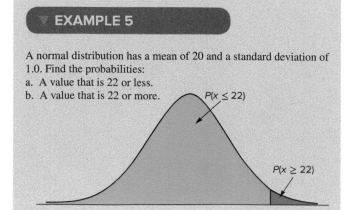

P(x ≤ 22)

P(x ≥ 22)

SOLUTION

First, determine the value of z for 22:

$$z = \frac{x - \mu}{\sigma} = \frac{22 - 20}{1} = +2.00$$

a. From Appendix B Table B, the area (probability) to the left of $z = +2.00$ is 0.9772.
b. Because the total area under the curve is 100 percent, or 1.0000, the area to the right of $z = +2.00$ is simply $1.0000 - 0.9772 = 0.0228$.

Points to Remember

1. The area under a normal curve represents probability.
2. The area under the curve is 100 percent, or 1.0000.
3. The area on either side of the mean is equal to half of the total, which is 50 percent, or 0.5000.
4. The curve extends to ± infinity, but 99.74 percent of the values will occur within ±3 standard deviations of the mean.
5. It is best to use Appendix B Table A for problems involving ±z (i.e., Chapters 7 and 10), and to use Appendix B Table B for problems involving one-sided probabilities such as the probability that *x* will be no more than a given (i.e., Chapters 4S, 13, and 17).
6. The probability of an exact value (e.g., 22 in Example 5) is zero. Therefore, $P(x \le 22) = P(x < 22)$.

Test Yourself

1. Suppose a normal distribution has a mean of 40 and a standard deviation of 5. Find the value of z for each of these values:
   a. 48   b. 30
   c. 34   d. 52.5
2. Using Appendix B Table A, find the area between ±z when z is:
   a. 1.00   b. 1.96
   c. 2.10   d. 2.50
3. Find the probability of observing a value that is beyond ±z when z is:
   a. 1.00   b. 1.80
   c. 1.88   d. 2.54
4. Use the appropriate Appendix B table to find the probability of a value that does not exceed a z value of:
   a. 0.40   b. 1.27
   c. −1.32   d. 2.75
5. Find the probability of observing a value that is more than a z value of:
   a. 0.77   b. 1.65
   c. −1.32   d. 2.75

Answers

1. a. +1.60   b. −2.00
   c. −1.20   d. +2.50
2. a. 0.6826   b. 0.9500
   c. 0.9642   d. 0.9876
3. a. 0.3174   b. 0.0718
   c. 0.0602   d. 0.0110
4. a. 0.6554   b. 0.8980
   c. 0.0934   d. 0.9970
5. a. 0.2206   b. 0.0495
   c. 0.9066   d. 0.0030

Index

Note: Boldface entries indicate key terms and the page numbers where they are defined. "n" after a page number indicates a footnote. In subheadings, CPFR refers to collaborative planning, forecasting, and replenishment; EOQ to economic order quantity; HACCP to Hazard Analysis Critical Control Point; JIT to just-in-time; MRP to material requirements planning; and PDSA to plan-do-study-act.